Anglo-Saxon Textual Illustration

This volume is produced in collaboration with
The Corpus of Insular and Anglo-Saxon Illuminated Manuscripts,
a research project housed at Purdue University
and directed by Dr. Thomas H. Ohlgren.

Anglo-Saxon Textual Illustration

Photographs of Sixteen Manuscripts with Descriptions and Index

Compiled and Edited by
Thomas H. Ohlgren

Medieval Institute Publications
WESTERN MICHIGAN UNIVERSITY
Kalamazoo, Michigan
1992

Printed in the United States of America

Cover design by Linda K. Judy

Library of Congress Cataloging-in-Publication data

Ohlgren, Thomas H., 1941–
Anglo-Saxon textual illustration : photographs of sixteen manuscripts with descriptions and index / compiled and edited by Thomas H. Ohlgren.
p. cm.
ISBN 1-879288-10-9 (hardbound)
1. Illumination of books and manuscripts. English--Themes, motives. 2. Illumination of books and manuscripts. English--Indexes. 3. Illumination of books and manuscripts. Anglo-Saxon--Themes, motives. 4 Illumination of books and manuscripts, Anglo-Saxon--Indexes. I. Title.
ND3128.044 1992
745.6'7'0942--dc20 92-4344
CIP

For my brother, David J. Ohlgren

Contents

Preface

Iconographic description functions as a well-intentioned surrogate when it attempts to verbalize and catalogue what at heart remains pictorial representation. This inadequacy becomes all the more severe when, in the absence of direct visual access for others to consider, only the iconographic description stands. Without that access, the verbal glosses impose serious restrictions upon scholars, who profit best when they can see for themselves. My awareness of this awkward circumstance was already acute when I assembled *Insular and Anglo-Saxon Illuminated Manuscripts: An Iconographic Catalogue* (New York and London: Garland Publishing, 1986). In that volume I had to negotiate as ably as I could the constraints of space and economics that eventually limited the number of published photographs to fifty. This quantity of direct evidence, while helpful, could hardly render full visual justice to the manuscripts. Determined to redress this imbalance, I originally conceived of the present volume as a photographic supplement to the Garland volume. But with the substantive additions and changes I have made to the existing codicological and iconographic information, coupled to the unprecedented reproduction of photographs, this new work bears only a slight resemblance to its precursor. Some 454 photographs of the illustrations and major decoration of sixteen Anglo-Saxon manuscripts, fully described and indexed, are reproduced here, many for the first time. Now researchers will be able to examine for themselves the full range of English illustration without having to rely necessarily upon the iconographic descriptions I have supplied.

History of the Project

In compiling the *Photo-bibliography* for the Garland volume, Carl T. Berkhout and I discovered that very few of the manuscripts in the Anglo-Saxon corpus had been published in modern facsimiles. While some of the miniatures in the corpus had been published dozens of times, many others only appeared in sources not readily available; still others have never been published at all. Even today huge gaps remain in the published record of Anglo-Saxon miniatures. To give but one notable example, the *Harley Psalter* (British Library, MS Harley 603), the earliest of three English copies of the Carolingian *Utrecht Psalter*, has not until now been published in its entirety. The repeated duplication of selected *masterpieces*, such as St. Dunstan prostrating himself at the feet of Christ in Bodleian Library, MS Auct F. 4. 32, has in some ways determined the tradition of Anglo-Saxon illumination.

Thanks to the efforts of Paul E. Szarmach, project director of the NEH-sponsored Symposium on the Sources of Anglo-Saxon Culture, held during the 1983–86 International Congresses on Medieval Studies at Western Michigan University, the need to remedy such deficiencies in the corpus of photographs became widely known. This need coincided with the plans of the J. Paul Getty Trust to expand the Photo Study Collection at the Getty Center for the History of Art and the Humanities in Santa Monica, California. In late 1986 I came to an agreement with the Getty Center to select, order, and catalogue over two thousand photographs of the miniatures and major decorated folios in some 230 manuscripts produced in the British Isles from A.D. 625 to 1100. As project director of the Corpus of Insular and Anglo-Saxon Illuminated Manuscripts, I was granted permission to publish a selection of the photographs before they were transferred to the Photo Study Collection and made available to the scholarly public.

The Getty project was undertaken during a period of three years, from 1 July 1987 to 30 June 1990. Using the first three volumes of *A Survey of Manuscripts Illuminated in the British Isles* [J. J. G. Alexander's *Insular Manuscripts*, Elżbieta Temple's *Anglo-Saxon Manuscripts*, and C. M. Kauffmann's *Romanesque Manuscripts* (London: Harvey Miller, 1978, 1976, 1975 respectively)] and my 1986 volume as guides, I placed scores of orders for the photographs. Some of the problems that directly affected the final selection of photos in this volume include:

(a) Many institutions were not prepared to handle in a timely manner the production of the large number of photographic prints that had been ordered; as a result, long delays were commonplace.

(b) Difficulties in communicating with foreign libraries, especially those in small cities, resulted in incorrect or incomplete orders.

(c) All photographs are black-and-white reproductions in order to spare the costs incurred by color reproduction.

(d) Some of the miniatures are reproduced in reduced scale of the original size of the folio in order to provide their textual context.

(e) The identification of the legal copyright holders of some of the photos was difficult in those situations where the actual owner differed from the institution supplying the prints. In several cases permission to publish photos had to be obtained from two different sources.

(f) A few of the photos are badly cropped, and some lack size indications because they were printed from old negative stock. This circumstance arose when, for conservation reasons, copyright holders prohibited new photography.

Scope of the Project

With over two thousand photographs of the manuscripts in my possession, I was next faced with the enviable but difficult task of selecting the manuscripts to be included in this volume. The selection I arrived at derives from the tenth and eleventh centuries because of the prodigious and sometimes precociously brilliant artistic invention of the period. This decision reduced the number of candidates to about 110 manuscripts. Next I eliminated those manuscripts that were already available in modern facsimiles, such as those in the series Early English Manuscripts in Facsimile. To aid me in my final selection and approach, I sought the advice of some twenty art historians and their graduate students in North America. In a questionnaire I outlined three possible approaches. I could focus on: (1) the miniatures and major decorated folios of manuscripts that have either not been published before or published in now remote, out-of-date sources; (2) the *masterpieces* of Anglo-Saxon illumination, conveniently assembling them into one volume; or (3) miniatures that exhibit a wide range of iconographic themes, arranging them alphabetically from Aaron to Zodiac Signs. Although my original inclination was to choose the third option—a volume of photos arranged by iconographic themes—my mind was quickly changed by the overwhelming recommendation by the art historical community to select the first option. Some of the compelling arguments are as follows:

> Because of the difficulty of finding adequate illustrations of any illuminated manuscript, I guess I would lean towards your first option of weighting your coverage towards unpublished, poorly published, or largely inaccessible sources—though ones with some significant features and a certain modicum of quality. (Robert G. Calkins, Cornell University)

> These [masterpieces] have indeed been published on many occasions, and although I agree that they represent the "tradition," it is primarily in my view the modern scholarly tradition, not the Anglo-Saxon tradition that they represent. To make readily available what are already viewed as the "important" works will tend further to enshrine them and previous scholarship with them. Why not provide a tool for those who might like to do something different, look at the material in a different way? (Lawrence Nees, University of Delaware)

> Although all three of the options you outline are attractive, I would be inclined to favor the first—to focus on previously unpublished or obscurely published miniatures and decorative features. Glaring gaps in the availability of basic material—B.L. Harley 603 is a superb example—constantly hamper even simple tasks of comparison from this side of the Atlantic. Consequently, we all keep treading the narrow path of your second option, the "masterpieces." I'm afraid that the fact of publication tends to overdetermine the "tradition," in a very limiting circular process. Your first option could help to open up that process and refresh the tradition. (Nell Gifford-Martin, University of North Carolina at Chapel Hill)

Format

This book consists of four main sections: *Descriptions of the Manuscripts*, *Descriptions of the Plates*, *Index to Iconographic Contents*, and *Photographic Plates*. Each manuscript has been assigned a number from one to sixteen; the number following the decimal point (e.g., 1.1) indicates the specific plate within the set. The assigned numbers are used consistently throughout the four sections.

(1) *Descriptions of the Manuscripts* consists of a heading and a narrative. The heading contains the following fields of information:

(a) a main entry number (1 to 16);

(b) title or type of manuscript;

(c) present location by city, library, and shelfmark;

(d) the place of origin followed by the place or places of provenance;

(e) the date of the manuscript, following Helmut Gneuss's system of notation (x in., x^1, x med., x^2, x ex., x/xi);

(f) dimensions in millimeters and number of folios; and

(g) cross-references to E. Temple's *Anglo-Saxon Manuscripts 900–1066* and T. Ohlgren's *Insular and Anglo-Saxon Illuminated Manuscripts*.

The second part of each entry is a brief narrative description of the manuscript and a short summary of scholarship. Since Temple's volume contains a bibliography up to about 1975 for each manuscript, I have not duplicated that material here; instead, I have noted significant scholarship since 1975 and some items, notably American doctoral dissertations, which Temple omits.

(2) *Descriptions of the Plates* consists of sixteen main entries, each of which is a folio-by-folio listing of iconographic contents and major decorative features. The descriptions are in two parts: a short title and a fuller narrative description. The short titles were adapted from the *Subject Headings* at the Index of Christian Art at Princeton University. Originally created for the professional staff at Princeton, the short titles provided a controlled thesaurus of iconographic descriptors. The short titles were also used as the index entries in the alphabetically-arranged *Index to Iconographic Contents*. Some of the fuller iconographic descriptions are based upon the master-file descriptions at Princeton, but in many cases I composed my own descriptions of a large number of illustrations. It is important to note that many of the descriptions are the result of a collaboration with contributors to the 1986 Garland volume. Although I have thoroughly revised this material, I am indebted to a number of individuals for their unselfish contributions; they are: Carl T. Berkhout, Mildred O. Budny, John J. Contreni, Helmut Gneuss, Robert M. Harris, John Higgitt, John B. Friedman, Louis Jordan, Lister Matheson, William M. Voelkle, and Charles Wright. Since the publication of the Garland volume, a number of scholars contributed information to the project: Robert Boenig, Mildred O. Budny, Robert Deshman, Richard Gameson, Helmut Gneuss, Carol Neuman de Vegvar, Jane E. Rosenthal, Kathleen Openshaw, and Elizabeth Teviotdale.

3) *Index to Iconographic Contents* is an alphabetically-arranged listing of the subjects that appear in the manuscript illustrations. As indicated, the index entries are based partially on the *Subject Headings* at the Princeton Index of Christian Art. While the form and style of the entries generally follow the Princeton system, I am totally responsible for the application of the system to this specific group of manuscripts. The index consists of a listing of subjects, focusing on the main *personage* represented in the miniature. Following the person's proper name is a short title indicating the precise

activity the person is conducting or associated with. I have also included a number of *see* and *see also* cross-references to guide users to the main entries and to suggest relevant associations. The numerical codes following each entry refer both to the *Descriptions of the Plates* and to the plates themselves.

4) *Photographic Plates* consists of 454 black and white photographs of the illustrated folios in sixteen manuscripts. Each plate is clearly numbered and captioned.

Acknowledgments

As a fundamental source of information about the manuscripts, Elżbieta Temple's *Anglo-Saxon Manuscripts 900–1066* has been indispensable. Each of the hundreds of times I have consulted her book, I have marvelled at the energy, knowledge, and vision that went into her pioneering work.

For more recent assessments of the dates and places of origin of the manuscripts, I have relied upon Helmut Gneuss's "A Preliminary List of Manuscripts Written or Owned in England up to 1100," published in *Anglo-Saxon England* 9 (1981), 1–60. I would like to thank Professor Gneuss for granting me permission to quote from his work.

For the form and style of the iconographic descriptions and the main titles in the *Index of Iconographic Subjects*, I am indebted to the Index of Christian Art at Princeton University. Director Brendan Cassidy graciously supplied me with a revised version of the *Subject Headings*.

For assistance with the iconographic descriptions in the 1986 volume I was indebted to a large group of colleagues here and abroad. To the extent that I relied upon these contributions in the *Descriptions of the Plates* in this volume, I am grateful. A large amount of that information, however, has been thoroughly revised and errors of commission and omission have been silently corrected. Any new errors are entirely my own, and I hope that attentive readers will bring them to my attention.

Without the active assistance of librarians, curators, and photoarchivists, this project would not have been possible. Those who have been particularly helpful are: Leonard Boyle, Vatican Library; Michael Evans, Warburg Institute; Constance Hill, Courtauld Institute; Kathleen Houghton, British Library; and William Voelkle, Pierpont Morgan Library.

For permission to reproduce photographs of manuscript material in their care, I thank the Biblioteca Apostolica Vaticana, Vatican City (3.1–3.49); Bibliothèque Municipale, Boulogne-sur-Mer (5.1–5.28); Bibliothèque Nationale, Paris (4.1–4.11); Bodleian Library, Oxford (1.18 and 16.1–16.51); British Library, London (2.4 and 10.1–10.15); Courtauld Institute of Art, London (1.1–1.17, 13.1–13.8, 14.1–14.15, and 15.1–15.53); Kestner-Museum, Hannover (8.1–8.21); Master and Fellows of Pembroke College, Cambridge (9.1–9.23 and 14.1–14.15); Master and Fellows of Trinity College, Cambridge (7.1–7.24); Pierpont Morgan Library, New York (6.1–6.17, 11.1–11.19, 12.1–12.9) and the Warburg Institute of Art, London (2.1–2.3 and 2.5–2.102).

Jeanne Marty, Fran Terpak, and Karen Campbell, all of the Getty Center for the History of Art and the Humanities, have been instrumental in facilitating the project that has made this volume possible.

My gratitude extends to friends and colleagues—Carl Berkhout, Paul Szarmach, Thomas E. Kelly, Shaun Hughes, Ann Astell, and James Cruise—whose interest and support sustained me.

Thanks are due, finally, to Thomas H. Seiler, Managing Editor of Medieval Institute Publications, whose good counsel, perspicacity, and meticulousness considerably improved this volume; Juleen Audrey Eichinger, who prepared the final text with care and patience; and Linda K. Judy, who tastefully designed the cover, title page, and photo layout.

Descriptions of the Manuscripts

1. **ATHELSTAN PSALTER (PLATES 1.1 TO 1.18)**
London, British Library Cotton MS Galba A. XVIII and Oxford, Bodleian Library MS Rawl. B. 484, f. 85.
Liège region; Winchester, Old Minster
ix, English additions x^1
128 x 88 mm., fols. 200
Temple no. 5; Ohlgren no. 83

King Athelstan (924–39), grandson of Alfred the Great, was an avid collector of manuscripts, many of which, like the psalter that bears his name, were acquired on the continent and donated to religious houses throughout England. According to Temple, the Anglo-Saxon additions to the ninth-century psalter from the Liège region included a metrical calendar, computus, prayers and a litany in Greek, and four miniatures on fols. 2^v, 21^r, 120^v, and a detached leaf (fol. 85^r) in Oxford.[1] Temple, in addition, suggests that the Instruments of the Passion on fol. 2^v may connect the manuscript with "the gift of a priceless relic, Longinus' lance, to Athelstan from Hugh, Duke of the Franks in 926." Simon Keynes, however, questions the traditional association between the manuscript and the king: "One can only conclude that while there is nothing in the manuscript which is incompatible with the notion that it may have belonged to Athelstan, equally there is nothing which proves that it did."[2]

The iconographic sources of the four Anglo-Saxon miniatures have been thoroughly analyzed by Robert Deshman.[3] In brief, for the depictions of Christ with choirs of angels on fols. 2^v and 21^r, Deshman (pp. 176–83) points to the influence of a scene of the Last Judgment, possibly monumental in nature and Insular in origin. For the Ascension (fol. 120^v) and the Oxford Nativity (fol. 85^r), Deshman (pp. 183–92) examines a number of Carolingian and Byzantine sources, and concludes that the Anglo-Saxons may have had direct knowledge of Middle Byzantine artistic models. For an argument that the miniatures represent an early Christological cycle in a psalter, see Elizabeth Parker McLachlan, "The Athelstan Psalter and the Gallican Connection," *Transactions of the Third Canadian Conference of Medieval Art Historians*, ed. William Dale (London, Canada, 1985), pp. 21–27.

2. **HARLEY PSALTER (PLATES 2.1 TO 2.102)**
London, British Library MS Harley 603
Canterbury, Christ Church
xi^1, drawings xi^1 (Group 1), xi^2 (Group 2), xii^1 (Group 3)
380 x 309 mm., fols. 73
Temple no. 64; Ohlgren no. 169

The *Harley Psalter* was produced at Christ Church, Canterbury in the second quarter of the eleventh century with later additions. This profusely illustrated manuscript is the earliest of three English copies of the *Utrecht Psalter*, which was made at the abbey of Hautvillers near Reims in the early ninth century. It is not known how or when the Carolingian manuscript reached England, but it was housed for a period of time at Christ Church, where it, or a lost recension, was copied at least three times. It is not known when or why the manuscript was removed, if it actually was, before the cycle of colored-ink drawings in Harley 603 was completed. According to Francis Wormald, "the drawings can be divided into three groups corresponding roughly to the first half of the 11th century, the second half of the 11th century, and the first half of the 12th century"[4]:

Group I	Hand A, fols. 1^{v}–11^{v}, 16^{r}, 16^{v}
	Hand B, fols. 12^{r}, 15^{r}, 17^{r}, 18^{r}–27^{v}
	Hand C, fols. 13^{r}, 13^{v}, 14^{r}, 14^{v}
	Hand D, fols. 50^{r}–57^{v}
	Hand E, fols. 1^{r}, 15^{r}, 15^{v}, 53^{r}, 58^{v}, 61^{r}, 61^{v}, 62^{v}, 67^{r}, 70^{r}, 70^{v}, 72^{v}
	Hand F, fols. 58^{r}–73^{v}
Group II	fols. 17^{v}, 28^{r}, 28^{v}
Group III	fols. 29^{r}–35^{r}.

The two artists, called Hands E and F, who worked in the early years of the second quarter of the eleventh century, did not follow the *Utrecht Psalter* as a model. Because two later artists revived the Utrecht iconography, it has been assumed that the manuscript was removed from Christ Church for a period of time, possibly as a loan to another scriptorium. As a result, due to the absence of the model, artists E and F were forced to improvise.

In her excellent dissertation, Judith E. Duffey, examines the thirty-five drawings of Hand F on fols. 58^{r}–73^{v}.[5] Of these some twenty-three images from sixteen of the drawings are what Duffey calls "unusual" or "inventive" in deviating from the iconography of the *Utrecht Psalter* (p. 107). Because these images contain visual references to royal, political, and monastic life, they should be of great interest to cultural historians and literary scholars. Duffey, finally, disagrees "with the argument that has assumed that the inventive nature of the Harley group was due to the temporary absence of the original model." She goes on to say, "I believe that the departure was deliberate and conscious, rather than necessary, that this was for very specific reasons, and that the *Utrecht Psalter* remained available to the artist to draw upon, as he drew on other sources when it was deemed necessary or appropriate" (p. 105).

3. **BURY PSALTER (PLATES 3.1 TO 3.49)**
   Vatican City, Biblioteca Apostolica, Vaticana MS Reg. lat. 12
   Canterbury, Christ Church?; Bury St. Edmunds
   xi^{1}
   326 x 244 mm., fols. 182
   Temple no. 84; Ohlgren no. 189

The *Bury Psalter* was written for Bury St. Edmunds Abbey in Suffolk. Because of stylistic and iconographic similarities to MS Harley 603, it is believed that the manuscript was not created at Bury St. Edmunds but at the Canterbury scriptorium that produced the Harley volume (Temple, p. 100). Temple suggests that "it may have been one of a number of important illuminated manuscripts probably produced at Canterbury to be sent elsewhere" (p. 101).

The manuscript contains two full-folio, framed miniatures on fols. 21^r and 62^r and forty-seven folios with numerous marginal drawings in colored inks, mainly in brown, red, and green. The unframed drawings appear mainly in the inner and outer margins, and occasionally in the upper and lower margins. An unusual feature is the way in which some of the compositions extend over a double opening; for instance, a demon armed with a bow in the lower right corner of fol. 24^v shoots an arrow at a woman seated in the upper right corner of fol. 25^r.

The drawings illustrate a variety of Old and New Testament themes, a full analysis of which is contained in a superb dissertation by Robert Mark Harris.[6] Harris places the drawings not only in the tradition of "literal" psalter illustration but in Anglo-Saxon art and culture of the eleventh century. Like the inventive drawings of MS Harley 603, the marginal illustrations of the Vatican manuscript display a remarkable amount of originality, due to, as Harris fully demonstrates, the influence of liturgical usage, royal and ceremonial ritual, and Old English literature.

4. **PARIS PSALTER (PLATES 4.1 TO 4.11)**
Paris, Bibliothèque Nationale MS lat. 8824
Canterbury?
xi med.
526 x 186 mm., fols. 182
Temple no. 83; Ohlgren no. 188

The *Paris Psalter* contains the only surviving translation of the Psalms into Old English. Each folio is composed of a double column with the Roman version of the Latin text on the left and the Old English translation on the right. Psalms 1–50 are rendered in Old English prose, while Psalms 51–150 are in an Old English metrical translation.[7]

The manuscript originally had a frontispiece with David harping, decorated pages before Psalms 26, 38, 51, 68, 80, 97, and 109, and a decorated page before the canticles (Temple, p. 99). The surviving illustration consists of thirteen small, unframed pen drawings, which literally depict specific verses of the Psalms. According to Robert Mark Harris, the pen-drawings, which end abruptly after Psalm 7, are placed with one exception (fol. 4^r) immediately after the Latin verses they illustrate (p. 30). The precise alignment of text and image as well as the lack of elaborate landscape features lead Harris to conclude cautiously that, although seven of the thirteen drawings in the manuscript agree in iconography with the *Utrecht Psalter*, the Paris images appear to have been derived from an Early Christian archetype common to both manuscripts (p. 42). The artist of the *Paris*

Psalter, then, must have had access to an illustrated psalter other than the Carolingian one.

Of the thirteen drawings only one was not inspired by the Latin text of the Psalm it illustrates. Instead, as Harris has clearly proved, the textual source of the drawing on fol. 6^r is the parallel Old English translation of and commentary on the Latin text of Psalm 7:12–14. The significance of Harris's discovery is two-fold: Anglo-Saxon artists were capable of inventing new iconography; and, the sources of the artistic invention include vernacular Old English texts.[8]

5. **BOULOGNE GOSPELS (PLATES 5.1 TO 5.28)**
Boulogne-sur-Mer, Bibliothèque Municipale MS. 11
(St. Bertin)
x ex.
330 x 260 mm., fols. 130
Temple no. 44; Ohlgren no. 149

The manuscript was illuminated in Flanders by an Anglo-Saxon artist working at the Abbaye de Saint Bertin in St. Omer. Like the abbeys of St. Bavo and St. Peter in Ghent and St. Benoît sur Loire at Fleury, St. Bertin was reformed according to strict Benedictine monasticism in the second quarter of the tenth century.[9] It was to Flanders that St. Dunstan, the Anglo-Saxon reformer, went in exile in 955. Inspired by the reforms, he returned to England in 957 when he was appointed archbishop of Canterbury by King Edgar.[10]

The manuscript, according to Temple, is the "most copiously illuminated of the surviving Anglo-Saxon Gospel Books" (p. 66). It consists of sixteen Canon Tables decorated with a profusion of angels, musicians, hunters, buildings, peacocks and other birds, an Agnus Dei, and a Christ in Majesty. In addition there are four Evangelist portraits (fols. 10^v, 55^v, 61^v, 107^r) and depictions of Christ in Majesty (fol. 10^r), the Ancestors of Christ (fols. 11^r–11^v), the Visitation (fol. 11^v), the Annunciation to the Shepherds (fol. 12^r), the Nativity of Christ (fol. 12^r), Isaiah's Prophecy (fol. 56^r), the Annunciation to Zacharias (fol. 62^r), and the Christ in Majesty (fol. 107^v).

6. **ARENBERG GOSPELS (PLATES 6.1 TO 6.17)**
New York, Pierpont Morgan Library M. 869
Canterbury, Christ Church
x ex.
302 x 191 mm. fols. 167
Temple no. 56; Ohlgren no. 161

Because of its stylistic and iconographic affinities with British Library MS Harley 603, its script, and its use of colored ink outline, the *Arenberg Gospels* has been assigned to Christ Church, Canterbury by Temple (p. 75) and others. The manuscript had been in the private collection of the Dukes of Arenberg until 1954, when it was purchased by the Pierpont Morgan Library.

The illumination consists of a full-folio Crucifixion of Christ (fol. 9^{v}), eight Canon Tables with an elaborate sequence of drawings (fols. 10^{r}–13^{v}), four Evangelist portraits (fols. 17^{v}, 57^{v}, 83^{v}, 126^{v}), and four initial pages (fols. 18^{r}, 58^{r}, 84^{r}, 127^{r}). The Crucifixion and eight historiated Canon Tables have been fully analyzed by Jane E. Rosenthal.[11] The main theme of the sequence of drawings is Christ as *Salvator mundi* (p. 84). The cycle was designed to elucidate "in symbolic form, the meaning of the Savior's advent in the flesh and His redemptive death" (p. 81). As Rosenthal convincingly demonstrates, the eight drawings above the canon frames which follow the image of the Crucifixion are "divided into four pairs of scenes, each pair representing one of the four periods in the history of salvation" (p. 279). Rosenthal has also analyzed the four Evangelist portraits in a 1985 article.[12] In brief, she offers an ingenious interpretation of the complex architectural structures enclosing the Evangelists as representations of *Ecclesia* and explains the different forms of gable housing the beasts in terms of the symbolism associated with the four animals in Jerome's prologue, "the only one of four traditional prefatory texts to the gospels to be included in the Arenberg manuscript" (p. 150).

7. **TRINITY GOSPELS (PLATES 7.1 TO 7.24)**
Cambridge, Trinity College MS B. 10. 4 (215)
Canterbury, Christ Church ?
xi^{1}
328 x 235 mm., fols. 174
Temple no. 65; Ohlgren no. 170

According to Temple, the manuscript was probably made at Christ Church Cathedral Priory in the first quarter of the eleventh century (pp. 83-84).[13] The illumination consists of fifteen lavishly decorated Canon Tables, a full-page miniature of Christ in Majesty, four Evangelist portraits, and four framed initial pages. The Canon Tables are constructed of a wide variety of round, triangular, and trefoil arches supported on columns with acanthus capitals and bases. The tympana contain a profusion of vegetation, animals (peacocks, dragons, eagles, lions, Evangelist symbols), and human forms (angels, apostles, saints, the Virgin Mary, and Christ). A notable feature is early examples of "clambering" initials (fols. 60^{r}, 133^{r}); the shaft of the letter is inhabited by climbing and biting animals.[14]

8. **EADUI CODEX (PLATES 8.1 TO 8.21)**
Hannover, Kestner-Museum WM XXI^{a}, 36
Canterbury, Christ Church
xi^{1}
224 x 164 mm., fols. 194
Temple no. 67; Ohlgren no. 172

On fol. 183^{v} is the colophon: "Liber istum monachus scripsit Eaduis cognomento Basan." Eadius Basan was not only the scribe but possibly the illuminator as well. Living at Christ Church Cathedral Priory, he worked on a number of other important manuscripts, including a section (fols. 28^{r}–49^{v}) of MS Harley 603 (Temple, pp. 85–86).

The illumination consists of fourteen Canon Tables, four Evangelist portraits, and three initial pages (the one to Matthew is missing). The tympana of the Canon Tables contain a variety of subjects, including the Hand of God with compass and scales (fol. 9^{v}), Christ with cross as nimbus (fol. 10^{r}), numerous Evangelist symbols, dogs biting roosters, and vegetation. The portrait of John (fol. 147^{v}) is unique in showing the Evangelist, seated on a cushioned bench, trample the head of Arius the Heretic.[15]

9. **Gospel Book (Plates 9.1 to 9.23)**
Cambridge, Pembroke College MS. 301
Peterborough?
xi in.
292 x 215 mm., fols. 134
Temple no. 73; Ohlgren no. 178

According to Temple, the manuscript is of uncertain origin but displays some stylistic affinities with Canterbury books (p. 92). Helmut Gneuss, however, attributes it to Peterborough, presumably because it was written by the same scribe responsible for Bodleian Library, MS Bodley 163, which has a known Peterborough origin.[16]

The illumination consists of fifteen pages of decorated Canon Tables (fols. 1^{v}–8^{v}), four Evangelist portraits (fols. 10^{v}, 44^{v}, 70^{v}, 108^{v}), and four facing-page initial pages (fols. 11^{r}, 45^{r}, 71^{r}, 109^{r}). The Canon Tables contain a large variety of figures: the Agnus Dei (fol. 1^{v}), Christ blessing (fol. 2^{r}), the Virgin Mary (fol. 2^{v}), St. Michael (fol. 3^{r}), apostles, saints, Evangelist symbols, buildings, and vegetation. Three of the Evangelist portraits are in various stages of completion.

10. **Bury Gospels (Plates 10.1 to 10.15)**
London, British Library MS Harley 76
Canterbury, Christ Church ?; Bury
xi
265 x 200 mm., fols. 141
Temple no. 75; Ohlgren no. 180

In spite of its name, the manuscript was not made at Bury St. Edmunds, but, like a number of other books, it was probably produced at Christ Church, Canterbury for use elsewhere. Late eleventh-century additions to the manuscript indicate that it was housed at Bury, which was not reformed until about 1020.[17]

According to Temple, the manuscript originally contained Evangelist portraits and initial pages (p. 93). All that survives are fourteen Canon Tables and one initial page. The Canons are richly decorated with figures and foliage: Christ blessing (fol. 6^{r}), St. Peter (fol. 7^{v}), St. Paul (fol. 8^{r}), Christ flanked by angels (fol. 8^{v}), the Virgin Mary with female saints (fol. 9^{r}), angels, lions, dragons, and beast heads.

11. **Judith of Flanders Gospels (Plates 11.1 to 11.10)**
New York, Pierpont Morgan Library M. 709

Origin uncertain
xi med.
293 x 191 mm., fols. 154
Temple no. 93; Ohlgren no. 198

Three Anglo-Saxon Gospel Books (nos. 11, 12, 13 in this volume) are closely associated with a remarkable woman, Judith of Flanders (c. 1032–94). Daughter of Baldwin IV, Count of Flanders, she married Tostig, one of three sons of Godwine, the powerful Earl of Wessex. After Godwine's exile in Flanders ended in 1051, Judith accompanied her husband to England, where, as prominent nobility, they gave generously to churches and monastic foundations. C. R. Dodwell records that they donated a crucifix with figures clothed in gold and silver to the religious establishment at Durham.[18] They also commissioned the production of, or were given as gifts, a number of lavishly decorated and illuminated manuscripts, including Morgan 709 and 708. Meta Harrsen speculates that the manuscripts were produced at "the monastery of Thorney in Cambridgeshire, a foundation of the See of Winchester, to whose endowment Tostig had been a contributor."[19] According to C. J. Godfrey, the fenland monastery at Thorney, which had been devastated by the Danes, was re-established and reformed according to Benedictine monasticism by Bishop Æthelwold in the 970s.[20] Several other locations have been proposed, including Canterbury and Winchester (Temple, p. 110). The manuscripts may even have been produced by a group of itinerant scribes and scholars in Judith's retinue, such as the scribe, noted by Harrsen and T. A. M. Bishop, who worked on the Gospel Books owned by Judith.[21] Because Tostig was exiled again in 1064, he and Judith returned to Flanders. He was subsequently killed at the battle of Stamford Bridge in 1066. Judith next married Duke Welf IV of Bavaria and donated her manuscripts to the Abbey of Weingarten.

Both Morgan 709 and 708 (see next entry) are bound in contemporary or near-contemporary gold and silver gilt covers. According to Temple, the cover of M. 709, with a gold repoussé plaque depicting Christ in Majesty, dates to the end of the eleventh century and is probably Flemish in origin (p. 110). The origin of the cover of M. 708, showing a Christ in Majesty and a Crucifixion, is more uncertain. Temple (p. 110) dates it to the third quarter of the eleventh century and assigns it to English workmanship. For an argument that the cover is from the north-east France / Belgium area, see C. R. Dodwell, *Anglo-Saxon Art*, p. 311.

The illumination of M. 709 consists of a prefatory Crucifixion (fol. 1^v), four Evangelist portraits (fols. 2^v, 48^v, 77^v, 122^v), and four facing-page *incipit* pages (fols. 3^r, 49^r, 78^r, 123^r). Calling it "one of the most moving renderings of that subject in English illumination," Temple (pp. 108–09) describes how the Virgin Mary in the Crucifixion miniature "lovingly raises the edge of her headcloth to wipe the wound in Christ's side, the impulsiveness of her tender gesture, unparalleled in this context, anticipating the highly emotional portrayals of the Crucifixion in the following centuries." The woman kneeling and clutching the foot of the cross has been variously identified as Judith herself, as Mary Magdalene, and most recently as Judith in the guise of Mary Magdalene.[22]

12. **JUDITH OF FLANDERS GOSPELS (PLATES 12.1 TO 12.9)**
New York, Pierpont Morgan Library M. 708
Origin uncertain
xi med.
296 x 197 mm., fols. 86
Temple no. 94; Ohlgren no. 199

The second of three Anglo-Saxon Gospel Books owned by Judith of Flanders, M. 708 has been dated to the period 1051–64, when Judith lived in England with her husband Tostig, Earl of Northumbria. For a discussion of the manuscript and its binding, see entry no. 11. The illumination consists of four Evangelist portraits (fols. 2^{v}, 26^{v}, 42^{v}, 66^{v}) and four facing-page *incipit* pages (fols. 3^{r}, 27^{r}, 43^{r}, 67^{r}).

13. **GOSPEL BOOK (PLATES 13.1 TO 13.8)**
Monte Cassino, Archivio della Badia MS BB. 437, 439
Origin uncertain
xi med.
216 x 155 mm., pp. 240
Temple no. 95; Ohlgren no. 200

According to Temple (p. 112) this Gospel Book, like Pierpont Morgan M. 708 and M. 709, belonged to Judith of Flanders, who lived in England from 1051 to 1064. The Anglo-Saxon scriptorium in which the manuscript was produced is unknown, but several scholars have assigned it to the same workshop responsible for Morgan M. 709, possibly Crowland or Thorney (Temple, p. 110). See the discussion in entry 11.

The illustration consists of four Evangelist portraits and facing-page *incipit* pages. The *incipits* are enclosed by round and mitred arches supported on columns with acanthus-leaf capitals. Within the tympana are Evangelist symbols, two of which (Mark and Luke) are anthropomorphic types. The capital letters of the *incipits* are composed of a variety of animals: birds, dragons, and beast heads. A noteworthy feature is the interaction between the four Evangelists, all located on the verso, and their symbols on the facing-page rectos. Instead of looking at the books in which they are writing, the Evangelists are gazing at their inspiring symbols on the facing pages; similarly, the heads of the symbols are turned to the left in the direction of the Evangelists.

14. **HEREFORD GOSPELS (PLATES 14.1 TO 14.15)**
Cambridge, Pembroke College MS. 302
Canterbury ?; Hereford
xi med.
197 x 102 mm., fols. 117
Temple no. 96; Ohlgren no. 201

According to Temple (p. 113) fol. 8^{r} contains a description in Old English of the boundaries of the see of Hereford drawn up by Athelstan, bishop of Hereford from 1012 to 1056. The text begins: "Ðus ligð þæt bisceoprice into hereforda."[23] The inscription indicates that the manuscript was at Hereford in the eleventh century and that it may have been produced there.

The illustration consists of twelve Canon Tables (fols. 1^{r}–7^{r}), four Evangelist portraits (fols. 9^{r}, 38^{r}, 60^{v}, 88^{v}), and four unframed *incipit* pages (fols. 9^{v}, 38^{v}, 61^{r}, 89^{r}). The Canon Tables are decorated with acanthus-leaf foliage, flowers, birds, and three human figures. The activities of the two male figures, wearing cowls or hoods, on fols. 5^{v}–6^{r} are puzzling. John Higgitt has suggested that the figure on fol. 5^{v} is apparently shaking a finger at the figure on fol. 6^{r}.[24] The position of the hands and fingers of both figures, however, suggests that the two clerics are engaged in digital sign language and/or finger calculus. The drawings may in fact reflect contemporary Anglo-Saxon observances concerning the Benedictine rule of silence.[25] The style of the four Evangelist portraits, according to C. M. Kauffmann, points to the Romanesque style of the twelfth century: the "firm outlines, solid figures, rhythmically parallel drapery folds, stylized curling beards and hair, symmetrical compositions and heavy coloring" are elements derived from late Ottonian art.[26]

15. **Psychomachia of Prudentius (Plates 15.1 to 15.53)**
London, British Library MS Cotton Cleopatra C. VIII
Canterbury, Christ Church
x/ xi
215 x 135 mm., fols. 4–37
Temple no. 49; Ohlgren no. 154

The *Psychomachia* by Prudentius (Aurelius Prudentius Clemens, b. A.D. 348) was one of the most popular Latin poems of the early Middle Ages. Some twenty illustrated manuscripts survive, three of which, in addition to MS Cotton Cleopatra C. VIII, are from Anglo-Saxon England [Cambridge, Corpus Christi College MS. 23; London, British Library MS Additional 24199; and a fragment, Munich, Bayerische Staatsbibliothek CLM. 29031b].

The Cotton manuscript dates to the late tenth or early eleventh century and has been assigned to Christ Church, Canterbury (Gneuss, p. 22). The eighty-three (not eighty-two as Temple states) drawings are accompanied by titles and glosses in Latin and Old English, the latter having been added at a slightly later date.[27] The manuscript has been re-foliated in modern times; as a result, the folio numbers appearing in the plates are three behind those now in use.

After a preface describing Abraham's rescue of Lot from his captors (based on Gen. 14), the poem, in brief, recounts battles between seven pairs of virtues and vices, personified as warrior maidens:

> Fides (Faith) and Veterum Cultura Deorum (Worship-of-Old-Gods);
> Pudicitia (Chastity) and Sodomita Libido (Lust the Sodomite);
> Patientia (Patience) and Ira (Anger);
> Mens Humilis (Humility) and Superbia (Pride);
> Sobrietas (Soberness) and Luxuria (Indulgence);
> Operatio (Good Works) and Avaritia (Avarice);
> Concordia (Concord) and Discordia (Discord).

The 915-line poem ends with a description of the construction of Sapientia's temple and with a prayer of thanksgiving.[28]

For a treatment of the influences, direct and indirect, of the *Psychomachia* on Old English literature, see John P. Hermann, *Allegories of War: Language and Violence in Old English Poetry* (Ann Arbor, MI, 1989).

16. **JUNIUS MANUSCRIPT (PLATES 16.1 TO 16.51)**
Oxford, Bodleian Library MS Junius 11
Canterbury, Christ Church ?
x/ xi (c. 1000)
318 x 195 mm., fols. 115
Temple no. 58; Ohlgren no. 163

Scholarly interest in MS Junius 11 has been enormous. Because the manuscript contains not only four poems in Old English—*Genesis*, *Exodus*, *Daniel*, and *Christ and Satan*—but a sequence of forty-eight textual illustrations to *Genesis*, the codex has attracted the attention of both literary scholars and art historians.[29]

A wide variety of scholarly opinions exists about the date of the extant manuscript, the dates of the individual literary texts, and the dates and iconographic sources of the drawings.[30] Although it is beyond the scope of this brief introduction to enter these murky waters, we can say in brief that the manuscript has been assigned to scriptoria at Christ Church, Canterbury, Winchester, Malmesbury, and Glastonbury. Estimates of the date of the manuscript range from the late tenth century to the second quarter of the eleventh century. The date *circa* 1000 thus seems to be a reasonable compromise. This date, by the way, would place the codex in the reign of King Æthelred (978–1016). Given the emphasis placed in the poems *Genesis* and *Christ and Satan* on the rebellion of a prince (Lucifer) against his king or lord (God) and the exile of the prince with his loyal retainers (fall of the angels into Hell), it is plausible to speculate that these episodes, recounted three times in *Genesis* alone, may refer to the tumultuous events leading up to the death of Æthelred and the elevation of Cnut to the throne in 1016.

The illustrations reproduced in this volume are: (a) all of the full and half-page drawings, many of which contain multiple iconographic units; and (b) three metal stylus sketches inserted at an unknown date into the blank spaces on pages 12 and 70. Photographed under ultra-violet light, these preliminary sketches are barely legible. Additional metal stylus sketches, not reproduced here, are on pages 54, 55, and 99. The manuscript also contains twenty-two zoomorphic initials, of which only those on pages 1, 58, 63, and 73 are reproduced here. Also not reproduced here are thirty-three large plain initials. Finally, two designs exhibiting Scandinavian "taste" on pages 225 and 229 are not reproduced. The manuscript contains eighty-nine blank spaces for drawings that were never executed; the illustrated portion of the text extends to line 2095 in George Krapp's edition or page 96 of the manuscript. Thus, the final 841 lines of *Genesis* are unillustrated.

Notes

1. For a description of the manuscript and a bibliography to 1976, see Elżbieta Temple, *Anglo-Saxon Manuscripts 900–1066*, A Survey of Manuscripts Illuminated in the British Isles 2 (London, 1976), pp. 36–37. All subsequent citations will be parenthetical.

2. Simon Keynes, "King Athelstan's Books," in *Learning and Literature in Anglo-Saxon England: Studies Presented to Peter Clemoes on the Occasion of His Sixty-fifth Birthday*, ed. Michael Lapidge and Helmut Gneuss (Cambridge, 1985), p. 196. In a personal communication, Robert Deshman called my attention to the article, "English Square Minuscule Script: The Background and Earliest Phases" (*Anglo-Saxon England* 16 [1987], 147–79), in which David N. Dumville convincingly dates the Anglo-Saxon additions, including the miniatures, to the first quarter of the tenth century. Professor Deshman is also dubious about the connection of Athelstan's lance relic with the manuscript, as Jennifer O'Reilly has argued in "Early Medieval Text and Image: The Wounded and Exalted Christ," *Peritia* 6–7 (1987–88), 73–118.

3. Robert Deshman, "Anglo-Saxon Art after Alfred," *Art Bulletin* 56/2 (1974), 176–200.

4. Francis Wormald, *English Drawings of the Tenth and Eleventh Centuries* (London, 1952), pp. 69–70. For more recent discussions of the artistic hands, see Janet Backhouse, "The Making of the Harley Psalter," *British Library Journal* 10 (1984), 79–113, and Richard Gameson, "The Anglo-Saxon Artists of the Harley 603 Psalter," *Journal of the British Archaeological Association* 143 (1990), 29–48. Gameson observes (p. 33) that several of the later artists added elements to earlier drawings; for instance, Hand E completed the picture on folio 15^r and Wormald's Group II artist added details to at least ten drawings.

5. Judith E. Duffey, "The Inventive Group of Illustrations in the Harley Psalter," Ph.D. diss., University of California at Berkeley, 1977.

6. Robert Mark Harris, "The Marginal Drawings of the Bury St. Edmunds Psalter," Ph.D. diss., Princeton University, 1960. Professor Harris was one of the original contributors to the Corpus of Insular and Anglo-Saxon Illuminated Manuscripts. I regret to announce that he died on March 19, 1986.

7. The manuscript has been published in facsimile by John Bromwich, et al., *The Paris Psalter*, Early English Manuscripts in Facsimile 8 (London, 1958). The Old English prose translation is available in James W. Bright and Robert L. Ramsay, eds., *Liber Psalmorum: The West-Saxon Psalms* (Boston, 1907). For the Roman version of the Psalms, see Robert Weber, ed., *Le Psautier Romain et les autres Anciens Psautiers Latins*, Collectanea Biblica Latina X (Vatican City, 1953).

8. For a revised version of Harris's interpretation of fol. 6^r, see his "An Illustration in an Anglo-Saxon Psalter in Paris," *Journal of the Warburg and Courtauld Institutes* 26 (1963), 255–63.

9. See C. J. Godfrey, *The Church in Anglo-Saxon England* (Cambridge, 1962), pp. 300–01.

10. See J. Armitage Robinson, *The Times of Saint Dunstan* (Oxford, 1969), pp. 86–87.

11. Jane E. Rosenthal, "The Historiated Canon Tables of the Arenberg Gospels," Ph.D. diss., Columbia University, 1974. In a personal communication Professor Rosenthal kindly vetted my descriptions of the manuscript and the miniatures and offered many helpful suggestions.

12. Jane E. Rosenthal, "The Unique Architectural Settings of the Arenberg Evangelists," *Studien*

zur mittelalterlichen Kunst 800–1250: Festschrift für Florentine Mütherich zum 70. Geburtstag (Munich, 1985), 145–56.

13. For a recent description of the manuscript, see Simon Keynes, *Anglo-Saxon Manuscripts in the Library of Trinity College, Cambridge, Old English Newsletter, Subsidia* 18 (1992), 32–33.

14. For discussions of the "clambering" type initial, see E. Temple, *Anglo-Saxon Manuscripts 900–1066*, p. 83, and C. M. Kauffmann, *Romanesque Manuscripts 1066–1190*, A Survey of Manuscripts Illuminated in the British Isles 3 (London, 1975), p. 19.

15. The only other depiction of Arius in Anglo-Saxon illustration is on fol. 75ᵛ of British Library, MS Titus D. XXVII (Ohlgren, *Catalogue*, p. 198).

16. See Helmut Gneuss, "A Preliminary List of Manuscripts Written or Owned in England up to 1100," *Anglo-Saxon England* 9 (1981), p. 12.

17. See Janet Backhouse, D. H. Turner, and Leslie Webster, eds., *The Golden Age of Anglo-Saxon Art* (London, 1984), p. 74.

18. See C. R. Dodwell, *Anglo-Saxon Art: A New Perspective* (Ithaca, 1982), p. 119.

19. See Meta Harrsen, "The Countess Judith of Flanders and the Library of Weingarten Abbey," *Papers of the Bibliographical Society of America* 24 (1930), 1–13. Jane E. Rosenthal, however, questions the Thorney connection, noting that there is no evidence to support the existence of a scriptorium there (persoal communication).

20. See C. J. Godfrey, *The Church in Anglo-Saxon England*, p. 303.

21. T. A. M. Bishop, *English Caroline Minuscule* (Oxford, 1971), pp. xvi–xvii.

22. See Barbara C. Raw, *Anglo-Saxon Crucifixion Iconography and the Art of the Monastic Revival*, Cambridge Studies in Anglo-Saxon England 1 (Cambridge, 1990), pp. 24, 158–61. The miniature has also been analyzed by Thomas H. Ohlgren in *Anglo-Saxon Art: Texts and Contexts, Old English Newsletter, Subsidia* 17 (1991), 23–24.

23. See N. R. Ker, *Catalogue of Manuscripts Containing Anglo-Saxon* (Oxford, 1957), pp. 125–26.

24. John Higgitt was one of the contributors to the description of manuscripts in Thomas H. Ohlgren, *Insular and Anglo-Saxon Manuscripts: An Iconographic Catalogue*, p. 262.

25. The miniatures are treated in Thomas H. Ohlgren, "The Grumbling Monk in the Hereford Gospels," *Old English Newsletter* 24/3 (1991), 22–24.

26. C. M. Kauffmann, *Romanesque Manuscripts*, pp. 18–19.

27. The glosses listed in the Descriptions of the Plates are taken from Julius Zupitza, "Englisches aus Prudentius-handschriften," *Zeitschrift für deutsches Altertum* 20 (1876), 36–44. See also N. R. Ker, *Catalogue of Manuscripts*, p. 185.

28. For the text of the poem cited in this work, see H. J. Thomson, ed., *Prudentius*, Loeb Classical Library (Cambridge, MA, 1948; rpt. 1969), pp. 274–343.

29. For a facsimile of the manuscript, see Israel Gollancz, *The Cædmon Manuscript of Anglo-Saxon Biblical Poetry* (Oxford, 1927). This *de luxe* volume had a limited printing of 250 copies; the photographic plates, in addition, were reproduced using the collotype or photogelatin process. For an older edition with a series of engravings, see Benjamin Thorpe, *Cædmon's Metrical Paraphrase of Parts of the Holy Scriptures in Anglo-Saxon* (London, 1832). The literary texts have also been edited by George P. Krapp, *The Junius Manuscript* (New York, 1931; rpt. 1964); all line citations are to this edition. For separate editions of *Genesis*, see B. J. Timmer, *The Later Genesis* (Oxford, 1948) and A. N. Doane, *Genesis A: A New Edition* (Madison, 1978).

30. For a bibliography up to 1974, see Temple, *Anglo-Saxon Manuscripts 900–1066*, pp. 77–78. The following items were published since 1975: George Henderson, "The Programme of Illustrations in Bodleian MS Junius 11," in *Essays in Honour of David Talbot Rice* (Edinburgh, 1975), pp. 113–45; Milton McC. Gatch, "Noah's Raven in Genesis A and the Illustrated Old English Hexateuch," *Gesta* 14 (1975), 3–16; Thomas H. Ohlgren, "Some New Light on the Old English Cædmonian Genesis," *Studies in Iconography* 1 (1975), 38–73; P. Blum, "The Cryptic Creation Cycle in MS Junius XI," *Gesta* 15 (1976), 211–26; Barbara Raw, "The Probable Derivation of Most of the Illustrations in Junius 11 from an Illustrated Old Saxon Genesis," *Anglo-Saxon England* 5 (1976), 133–48; Herbert R. Broderick, "The Iconographic and Compositional Sources of the Drawings in Oxford, Bodleian Library, MS Junius 11," Ph.D. diss., Columbia University, 1978; the latter contains a convenient summary of scholarship on the date and origin of the manuscript on pages 39–52; and, finally, Herbert R. Broderick, "Some Attitudes toward the Frame in Anglo-Saxon Manuscripts of the Tenth and Eleventh Centuries," *Artibus et Historiae* 5 (1982), 31–42.

Descriptions of the Plates

Unless otherwise noted the biblical citations and quotations used in the descriptions are taken from the *Biblia Sacra Iuxta Vulgatam Clementinam*, ed. Alberto Colunga and Laurentio Turrado (Madrid: Biblioteca De Autores Cristianos, 1965). Attentive readers will notice slight differences, mainly in punctuation, spelling, and word separation, between the source text and the various manuscript texts that are visible in the plates. Thus, it is *not* my intention to include transcriptions of the Latin texts as they appear in the photographs.

1. Athelstan Psalter (London: British Library, MS Cotton Galba A. XVIII and Oxford, Bodleian Library MS Rawl. B. 484, fol. 85)

Plates 1.1 to 1.18

PLATE/FOLIO

1.1 fol. 2v Christ enthroned with choirs of angels, patriarchs, prophets, and apostles. In the upper register, Christ, beardless, nimbed, right hand outstretched to show wound, closed book in left hand, seated on draped bench with footstool, flanked by Instruments of Passion (lance, cross, sponge) within mandorla flanked and surrounded by choir of nimbed angels (inscribed "omnis chorus angelorum"). In the second register, a choir of Patriarchs with Cain and Abel making their offerings; two small buildings, probably symbolizing, according to Robert Deshman ("Anglo-Saxon Art After Alfred," *Art Bulletin* 56/2 [1974], 182), the Heavenly Jerusalem and Bethlehem. The inscription "omnis chorus prophetarum" must refer to the third register, which contains a row of Prophets. In the fourth register, the Apostles, including Peter and Paul, and a thirteenth figure, possibly the Virgin Mary. At the corners of the frame, four lions bite the frame while holding it in their paws. Deshman (p. 179) interprets the miniature as a pictorial translation of the litany of the saints, or prayers for intercession, that was recited as part of the Divine Office. The inscriptions on the miniature were derived directly from textual formulas used in the litanies. For a discussion of the inhabited frame, see Herbert R. Broderick, "Some Attitudes toward the Frame in Anglo-Saxon Manuscripts of the Tenth and Eleventh Centuries," *Artibus et Historiae* 5 (1982), 31–32.

fol. 3r Capricorn in a medallion; KL monogram.

1.2	fol. 3^{v}	Within a decorated rectangular frame, a standing male saint, nimbed and wearing a tonsure, raises hand in benediction.
	fol. 4^{r}	Within a circular medallion, Aquarius personified as a male figure pouring water from an urn into a vat; KL monogram marks beginning of calendar passage.
1.3	fol. 4^{v}	Within a decorated rectangular frame, a standing male saint, nimbed, holds book.
	fol. 5^{r}	Within a circular medallion, Pisces personified as two fish linked by the mouths; KL monogram with interlaced ribbon terminating in beast-heads and human head.
1.4	fol. 5^{v}	Within a rectangular frame, a standing male saint, nimbed, holds book.
	fol. 6^{r}	Within a circular medallion, Aries personified as a Ram; KL monogram terminating in beast-heads.
1.5	fol. 6^{v}	Within a rectangular frame, a standing male saint, nimbed, holds open book.
	fol. 7^{r}	Within a circular medallion, Taurus personified as a Bull; KL monogram.
1.6	fol. 7^{v}	Within a circular medallion, bust portrait of nimbed male saint holds closed book.
	fol. 8^{r}	Within a decorated circular medallion, Gemini personified as two standing male figures holding staffs; KL monogram terminating in beast-head.
1.7	fol. 8^{v}	Within a plain circular medallion, bust portrait of nimbed saint holds roll.
	fol. 9^{r}	Within a circular medallion, Cancer personified as Crab; KL monogram with serpent forming ascender of letter.
1.8	fol. 9^{v}	Within a rectangular frame decorated with foliage, a male saint, nimbed, stands in orant position.
	fol. 10^{r}	Within a circular medallion, Leo personified as Lion; KL monogram terminating in beast-heads.
1.9	fol. 10^{v}	Within a rectangular frame with biting beast-heads, a standing male saint, nimbed, holds a closed book and raises hand in benediction.

	fol. 11^r	Within circular medallion, Virgo personified as a standing female holding floreate staff and branch; KL monogram with serpent forming ascender of letter.
1.10	fol. 11^v	Within a rectangular frame with beasts at the top corners, a standing male saint, nimbed, holds closed book.
	fol. 12^r	Libra personified as standing female holding scales; KL monogram terminating in beast-head with foliate tongue.
1.11	fol. 12^v	Within a rectangular frame, a standing male saint, nimbed, holds staff and closed book; column on the lower right.
	fol. 13^r	Within a circular medallion, Scorpio personified as a standing male holding a double-headed serpent; KL monogram with beast-head.
1.12	fol. 13^v	Within a rectangular frame, a standing male saint, nimbed, raises hand in benediction.
	fol. 14^r	Within a circular medallion, Sagittarius personified as a standing male figure holding bow and arrow; a column is on the left. KL monogram with beast-head.
1.13	fol. 14^v	Within a rectangular frame, a standing male saint, nimbed, holds a closed book and raises hand in benediction.
	fol. 15^r	Text page.
1.14	fol. 20^v	Text page.
	fol. 21^r	Christ enthroned with choirs of martyrs, confessors, and virgins. Christ, beardless, cross-nimbed, flanked by Alpha and Omega, right side uncovered and right arm raised to reveal wound, holding cross in left hand, seated on architectural bench, building at feet, within decorated mandorla enclosed in larger mandorla (inscribed "omnis chorus martyrum" and "omnis chorus virginum") divided into sections in which are busts of martyrs, confessors, and virgins. Within each corner of frame, half figures of angels, one nimbed and two holding books. At the upper corners of the decorated rectangular frame, two pairs of human heads; inscription outside frame: "omnis chorus confessorum." As seen on fol. 2^v the inscriptions in the miniature are derived from the litany of the saints. According to Robert Deshman, this miniature is "placed before a series of prayers invoking respectively the Holy Cross, Michael, Raphael, Mary, John, the martyrs, the confessors, and the virgins" ("Anglo-Saxon Art After Alfred," p. 179).
1.15	fol. 34^v	Text page in display letters.

	fol. 35r	Initial page *B* / *Beatus vir* (beginning of Psalm 1).
1.16	fol. 79v	Text page.
	fol. 80r	Initial page *Q* / *Quid gloriaris* (beginning of Psalm 51) with lion forming the tail of the letter.
1.17	fol. 120v	Christ: Ascension. Christ, beardless, cross-nimbed, left hand holding closed book, seated on bench with footstool, within mandorla supported by two nimbed angels. Virgin Mary, name inscribed "Maria," nimbed, orant, flanked by two flowering plants, and half figures of nimbed angels above clouds addresses two groups of men, probably Apostles and others, inscribed "Viri galilei." Upper section of plain rectangular frame inscribed with "ascensio d(o)mi(ni)." According to Robert Deshman ("Anglo-Saxon Art After Alfred," pp. 186–87) the iconographic elements were derived directly from Middle Byzantine art, not a Carolingian intermediary.
	fol. 121r	Initial page *D* / *Domine* (beginning of Psalm 101).
1.18	fol. 85r	Christ: Nativity. In an architectural setting, Joseph, name inscribed, seated on stool, left hand on chin; ox and ass above Christ Child, cross-nimbed, in architectural crib, inscribed; Virgin Mary reclines on mattress, her head supported by pillow. Below, two midwives, one pouring water from pitcher, bathe the Christ Child, cross-nimbed, sitting in a basin. According to Deshman ("Anglo-Saxon Art After Alfred," pp. 183–86), the miniature is an amalgam of Byzantine and Carolingian motifs; he speculates that the Winchester artist added the Byzantine elements to a Carolingian composition, which strongly suggests that near-contemporary Eastern models had reached England.

2. Harley Psalter (London: British Library MS Harley 603)

Plates 2.1 to 2.102

2.1	fol. 1r	Trinity: four angels surround and support a mandorla that encloses the Holy Dove on roll held by God, who is cross-nimbed, seated on cushioned bench, with feet on footstool, and who supports and embraces the Christ Child, whose right hand is raised and who holds a large globe in his draped left hand.
2.2	fol. 1v	Psalm 1. On the upper left, the Just Man, seated in *sancta ecclesia* and inspired by an angel, meditates on an open book (the Law). Above are personifications of the sun, moon, and stars. In the middle, two figures discuss and point to the two buildings on either side. On the right, the Ungodly One, inspired by a demon, sits in the Chair of

Pestilence surrounded by hostile-looking soldiers with spears (vv. 1–2). On the lower left is a river god with urn and a tree bearing fruit (v. 3). In the center, a wind personification blows at the ungodly (v. 4). On the lower right, the impious are tormented by two demons with hook and tridents, one of whom falls into a pit in which a personification of Hades clasps lost souls to his bosom (v. 6).

2.3 fol. 2r Initial *B* / *Beatus vir*. Christ, cross-nimbed and bearded, stands within a mandorla holding an open book while an archbishop lies prostrate at his feet. Psalm 2. On the left, God directs five angels, some with exposed genitals, to destroy the raging and vain people below with arrows, spears, and battle-axes (vv. 1–5). In the center, God, standing on Mount Sion (v. 6), holds an iron rod (v. 9) with which he breaks a potter's vessel. Below, a group of people with spears huddles in fear. On the right, a group of kings with spears and shields stands in fear under the Hand of God (v. 10).

2.4 fol. 2v Psalm 3 (upper miniature). On the left, the Psalmist is threatened by a group of impious with spears (v. 2). In the center, the Psalmist, lying in bed, cries out to God, cross-nimbed, who is seated above. An angel at the foot of the bed grasps the left hand of the rising Psalmist and with his right hand breaks the teeth (v. 8) of one of the impious with a spear. On the far right is a group of people holding palm fronds (v. 9).

Psalm 4 (lower miniature). On the far right, the Psalmist, standing in his coffin, raises his right hand to heaven where God stands (v. 1). At the end of the coffin are the sons of men, who are shown in another grouping doing vain things, i.e., hunting with two horses and dogs (v. 2–4). A priest stands behind a fiery altar in front of a temple to which people bring offerings (v. 6). In the lower center are jugs and casks for the multiplied corn and wine (v. 8).

2.5 fol. 3r Psalm 5. On the left, the Psalmist enters a temple with an altar within (v. 8). In the lower center, a winged demon with flaming hair flees the temple (v. 6). In the center right is a group of impious people whose "throat is an open sepulchre"; an open coffin is in the lower center (v. 11). To the far right, three demons prod the impious in a pit of fire (v. 11). In the upper left, the Hand of God and an angel extend wreaths to a group of the righteous holding palm fronds (vv. 12–13).

2.6 fol. 3v Psalm 6. In the upper left, the Psalmist in bed complains to God, above with a spear and closed book (v. 7). In another bed is the Psalmist's soul (vv. 4–5). In the lower left, four demons, two with exposed genitals, torment with spears the damned in hell, who are surrounded by curled serpents (v. 6). In the lower right, a group of sinners is turned back (v. 9).

2.7 fol. 4r

Psalm 7. On the left, the Psalmist, threatened by four men with bow and arrow, spears, and battle-axe, prays to God above who holds a sword and a bow and arrows (v. 2); a congregation of people holding spears stands below (v. 8). On the lower left, a lion stands over a nude man (v. 3). On the right, a demon runs towards the Psalmist (v. 6). On the lower right, a female demon nurses triplets (v. 15). A man falls into a pit (v. 16).

2.8 fol. 4v

Psalm 8. Above, God, enthroned in a mandorla supported by four angels, is flanked by six angels with cross-staffs (v. 2). Below, the Psalmist, standing with outstretched hands, is surrounded by a group of people (the infants and sucklings of v. 3?). To the right, an angel pushes three demons into a pit (v. 3). In the upper right are the moon and the stars (v. 4). In the lower left are sheep and oxen (v. 8), and in the lower right, birds and fish (v. 9).

2.9 fol. 5r

Psalm 9 (Hebrew 9 and 10). The left side of the miniature, which illustrates vv. 1–21, depicts God, seated within a mandorla and flanked by six angels, holding a pair of scales (vv. 5, 8–9). On the lower left, the Psalmist stands on a tower above the gate of a city, in which a group of five people stand; before the gate, three soldiers kill four men with a sword and spears (v. 13). In the center foreground, an angel, holding a cross-staff, forces six impious men into a fiery furnace with a lion's head (v. 18). In the center, two cities are destroyed (v. 7). In the center left, the lawgiver stands on a hill and points up to God (v. 21). The right side of the miniature, which illustrates vv. 22–39, depicts three scenes. In the upper right, two groups of people, talking and gesturing (v. 28?), watch a horseman, holding a spear, trample underfoot three people (the innocent and the poor, v. 30). In the lower portion, another group of men, talking and gesturing, sits within and without a roofed enclosure (v. 29?). On the far lower right, a group of men watches a man (the "sinner") fall from a pedestal (v. 36?). The beginning of the text is marked by an initial *C / Confitebor* with beast-heads.

2.10 fol. 6r

Psalm 10 (11). On the left of center, the Psalmist, holding a pair of scales, points to a flying bird (his soul, v. 2). Below are two impious men with bow and arrows and quiver (v. 3). In the lower right, four impious men destroy a building with spears and axe (v. 4). In the upper left, God, nimbed, sitting in the portal of a temple (v. 5), looks down upon the sons of men (v. 5) and causes fire and brimstone to fall upon the impious (vv. 6–7).

2.11 fol. 6v

Psalm 11 (12). In the upper level, four angels watch as God, cross-nimbed, steps out of his mandorla and hands a spear to another angel, who, in the lower right, smites the deceitful lips of a group of proud men holding spears and shields (v. 4). In the lower left are the crippled with canes and a trestle and the poor (v. 6). In the lower foreground, the impious walk around a table while another group walks around a turnstile (v. 9). In the upper right, the Psalmist holds an open roll, and two blacksmiths stand at a forge; one smith holds a hammer and tongs (v. 7).

2.12 fol. 7r Psalm 12 (13). The Psalmist, sitting under a tree, receives the rays of a fiery torch held by God, cross-nimbed, in the upper left (v. 4). On the lower left, the enemy appears with a bow, arrows, spears, and shields (v. 3). In the center foreground is an open coffin (v. 4).

2.13 fol. 7v Psalm 13 (14). God, cross-nimbed, enthroned in a decorated mandorla and flanked by six angels with bannered staffs, looks down upon the children of men (v. 2). On the left, a king with drawn sword sits on a cushioned bench under a domed canopy with snakes entwined around the columns; two men with swords present him with severed human heads (v. 3). An open coffin lies outside (v. 3). Two men are about to saw a woman in half. Two men are killed with sword and spear. In the center, three horsemen, holding bannered spears, ride towards a group of women and children, who are appealing to a soldier with a shield who stands on a hill (v. 7). Left of the center the Psalmist, standing with outstretched arms, looks up to God.

2.14 fol. 8r Upper miniature: Psalm 14 (15). On the upper right, the Psalmist, standing under a tree, addresses his questions to the Hand of God, which blesses a kneeling figure reading the Law from an open book (v. 1). On the lower left, two figures stand outside a temple (v. 1). In the center, a man gives a bag of money to the poor and the crippled (v. 5).

Lower miniature: Psalm 15 (16). On the upper right, God, cross-nimbed and holding a roll, stands surrounded by six angels; below are the saints who are in the land (v. 3). In the lower right corner are three men in their beds (v. 4). On the upper left, the Psalmist stands holding a cup and a rope (v. 6) in one hand and touches his lips with the other (v. 4). In the lower left, the Harrowing of Hell: Christ, treading a small demon, releases Adam and Eve from a pit (v. 10). In the center foreground are the Holy Women at the Sepulchre (v. 10).

2.15 fol. 8v Psalm 16 (17). The Psalmist, standing on a fiery furnace (v. 3) and holding two pairs of scales (v. 2), looks up to God, cross-nimbed. An angel, holding a sword, protects the Psalmist from two groups of enemies, holding spears and shields (vv. 8–9). In the foreground are two lions (v. 12), and on either side, two groups of nude children feast at two tables (v. 14).

2.16 fol. 9r Psalm 17 (18). In the center foreground, the Psalmist, holding a spear, shield, and unstrung bow (v. 33), tramples an enemy (v. 39).

On either side is a lighted lamp on a standard (v. 29) and the fountains of water as three spilled pots (v. 16). On the left, the enemies turn their backs on the Psalmist (v. 41). Beyond them is a city with people, a hanging lamp and altar within (v. 7). Above, God, cross-nimbed, flanked by seraphim, leans out of his mandorla holding a fiery torch (vv. 9–10). Two angels hold drapery (v. 11). Four other angels with spears attack the enemy that threatens the Psalmist (v. 15). On the lower right are hell with burning souls and a large head of Hades (vv. 5–6). In the upper right, a deer herd (v. 34).

2.17 fol. 10r Text page with blank space for drawing.

2.18 fol. 10v Psalm 18 (19). In the upper left, two sets of sun and moon personifications (v. 3) and a group of figures with rolls and books who gesture and talk (v. 5). On the upper right, God, cross-nimbed, flanked by two angels, departs from a temple in the sun (v. 6). A bust figure of sun personification, holding a torch, is on the right. Below, on the left, is a giant with spear and shield (v. 6). In the center foreground, a man holds an open book and a platter with crown, pitcher, and bowl of food (the testimony and the law, v. 8); the little ones are on either side. In the lower right, the Psalmist, as a king, wears a crown and holds a cross-staff and globe; a group of God's servants is on the far right (v. 14).

2.19 fol. 11r Psalm 19 (20). On the left, the Psalmist, dressed as a warrior with helmet, spear, and shield, stands on a mountain prospect and appeals to God above, nimbed, who holds a closed book and hands him a bow (vv. 2–3). In the center, the Psalmist, now dressed as a crowned king, makes an offering in draped hands to a priest standing in front of a temple (v. 4). On the right is a group of fallen men, horses, and chariot (v. 8).

2.20 fol. 11v Psalm 20 (21). Above, God, cross-nimbed and holding a decorated, closed book, sits in a mandorla flanked by six angels (vv. 2–3). On the left, a king, attended by soldiers holding spears and shields, is handed a roll and crowned by an angel (vv. 2–4). On the right, the Psalmist, standing on a hill, points to a group of soldiers who are wielding shields and spears and forcing a group of enemies into a fiery furnace surmounted by a cross (v. 10). Above, the Hand of God grasps a bundle of spears (v. 9).

2.21 fol. 12r Psalm 21 (22). In the right foreground, the Psalmist, standing in a coffin (v. 16) and holding two vessels (v. 15), complains to God (v. 2), who, flanked by six angels holding bannered staffs and a personification of the sun, moon, and stars (v. 3), blesses the congregation (v. 23) standing on the steps of a temple on the far left. Surrounding the coffin are bulls, dogs, lions, and unicorn (vv. 13–14, 21–22). Two men dig at the base of the coffin with mattocks (v. 17). In the center foreground are a candlestick with burning candle (v. 15), an empty cross with Passion Instruments (vv. 17–18), and a machine for casting lots with two men dividing a garment (v. 19). To the lower right, a woman with bared breasts (v. 10) sits on a throne and, behind her, a group of the enemy with spears (vv. 7–8). On the left is a group of women with infants (vv. 24–25), and above, another group eats at a round table (v. 27).

2.22 fol. 13ʳ Psalm 22 (23). The Psalmist, sitting in a pasture by a stream (v. 2), is handed a staff (v. 4) by an angel, who anoints his head with a horn of oil (v. 5). In front of the Psalmist is a table covered with bread and bowls (v. 5), and in the lower right are his enemies with spears and a bow and arrow. On the left is a temple with altar and hanging lamp (v. 6); herds of animals in mountain prospect. Above is the Hand of God.

2.23 fol. 13ᵛ Psalm 23 (24). In the upper left, the Hand of God, flanked by five angels, blesses the King of Glory (v. 5), cross-nimbed and carrying a bannered spear, who stands with a group of soldiers, wearing helmets and bearing spears and shields, before the gate of a walled city (vv. 7–8). Three men, one with a drawn sword, welcome the King of Glory; other men holding books and rolls are within. A temple with altar and hanging lamp stands on the mountain of the Lord (v. 3). In the lower foreground is a river with ships, fish, and serpents (vv. 2–3).

2.24 fol. 14ʳ Psalm 24 (25). In the center, the Psalmist, standing with outstretched hands, is shown the roll of the law held by God, cross-nimbed, flanked by six angels (vv. 4–5). On the left is a group of enemies armed with spears and shields; two archers with bows aimed at the Psalmist reach back for arrows held by a servant (v. 3). In the upper right is a group of the mild and meek (vv. 8–9). In the lower right, a woman comforts children while a man distributes food to the poor and crippled (v. 12).

2.25 fol. 14ᵛ Psalm 25 (26). On the left, the Psalmist stands with outstretched arms upon a fiery furnace in front of a temple (vv. 1–2). Above, God, cross-nimbed, is flanked by six angels. In the center, an aqueduct carries water to a lion-headed fountain filling a basin in which a group of people washes their hands (v. 6). On the lower right are three groups of sinners: two men beat a victim with switches; another man beats a victim with a whip; two men offer bribes (vessels) to a group of seated men, some of whom are inspired by winged demons (vv. 5, 9–10). In the lower right is a fiery pit with Hades head. In the upper right are two temples surmounted by crosses, an altar, and two groups of people (v. 12).

2.26 fol. 15ʳ Psalm 26 (27). Standing in the portal of an elaborate building (v. 4),

God, holding a torch (v. 1), grasps the Psalmist's hand. The Psalmist stands next to an altar with sacrificial sheep (v. 6). In the foreground, an army of enemies—military tents, falling horsemen, archers, soldiers with spears and shields—is defeated as it attacks the Psalmist (vv. 2–3). In the upper right, a mother and father turn away from their child (v. 10).

2.27 fol. 15v Psalm 27 (28). In the upper left, God, cross-nimbed and holding a spear, is accompanied by three angels. Below, the Psalmist, wearing a crown, stands with outstretched arms before a temple with hanging lamp (v. 2). An angel holds an umbrella over the Psalmist's head. In the foreground are two groups of sinners, armed with spears and shields, some of whom are being tormented by angels with tridents in a fiery pit (vv. 2–5). In the upper right, the Psalmist stands with raised arms (v. 6).

2.28 fol. 16r Psalm 28 (29). On the right, a procession of people brings sheep for sacrifice to a domed temple within an elaborate walled enclosure; within, a priest stands at an altar. In the upper left, God, cross-nimbed and holding a book, sits within a mandorla flanked by six angels. Three sets of winds are released by personifications on the waters, on the cedars of Lebanon, and upon the stags, unicorn, and bullock (vv. 5–10). In the center, the Psalmist stands with outstretched arms. The beginning of the text is marked by an initial *A* / *Afferte* with a beast-head.

2.29 fol. 16v Psalm 29 (30). In the center, God, cross-nimbed and holding a bannered cross-staff, pulls the Psalmist out of an open coffin, as two demons attempt to pull him with hooks into a fiery pit in which burning souls are tormented by devils with staffs (vv. 2–4). On the upper right, the Psalmist, sitting in a mountain prospect under the moon and stars, weeps (vv. 6–8). In the lower right, a group of saints sings praise to God (v. 5). On the upper left, the Psalmist stands with raised arms under a personification of the sun (v. 6). Above, the Hand of God issues from the clouds.

2.30 fol. 17r Psalm 30 (31). In the upper right, God, nimbed, standing on the ramparts of a fortress (v. 3), bends down towards an angel, who is extending a hand to the Psalmist standing by a pit covered with a net; a demon in the pit tries to hook the Psalmist's leg (v. 5). In the lower right, a large crowd of people watches two musicians and a dancing bear (v. 7). In the upper left and right are two groups of enemies (v. 12). In the center, a broken vessel lies at the feet of an angel and there is an open coffin with a corpse inside (v. 13). In the lower left, a demon with flaming hair drags the enemy into a fiery pit (v. 18).

2.31 fol. 17v This added drawing by Hand E repeats some of the iconographic components of the previous drawing. The Psalmist struggles with outstretched arms to grasp the hands of an angel who bends down to reach him from a hill. Beneath, a demon with flaming hair tries to spear the Psalmist with a trident. A jar spilling its contents recalls v. 13.

2.32 fol. 18^r Psalm 31 (32). God, cross-nimbed and standing in a mandorla, is flanked by six angels. On either side are the sun (personification), moon, and stars. In the center, three angels raise two large draperies over two groups of the blessed (v. 1). On a hill the Psalmist sits among the thorns (v. 4). In the foreground is a river with fish (v. 6). Two armies with spears and shields threaten the Psalmist (v. 7). In the lower foreground, a horseman subdues a horse with a whip; two other demons beat a mule with whips (v. 9).

2.33 fol. 18^v Psalm 32 (33). In the center, the Psalmist, holding a harp, stands on a hill accompanied by a group of musicians (vv. 1–3) and looks up to God, standing in front of a temple with drawn curtain; three angels are on the left (v. 14). In the center, a sea personification sits on the back of a sea-monster and empties a jar of water (v. 7). In the upper right, five angels with spears and bow and arrow attack a group of soldiers (v. 10). In the lower right, a giant is killed with an arrow (v. 16), and riders fall with their horses (v. 17). In the lower left, an angel offers a table filled with food to two groups of women and children (v. 19).

2.34 fol. 19^r Psalm 33 (34). In the center, the Psalmist, with a hand to his mouth (v. 2), instructs a group of the meek to praise God, who stands in a mandorla flanked by six angels. Another angel flies up to heaven to receive a sword from God (v. 5). On the lower right, five angels attack the evil ones with spears and force them into a fiery pit (v. 17). In the foreground, three angels wait to receive the souls in draped hands of three martyred saints (vv. 7–8): St. Lawrence is roasted on a grate; St. Paul is beheaded; and St. Peter is crucified upside down. In the upper left, the Psalmist addresses a group of children (v. 12).

2.35 fol. 19^v Psalm 34 (35). In the center, the Psalmist, surrounded by warring groups with spears, shields, and whips, appeals to God, cross-nimbed and wielding a spear and shield, to help him (vv. 1–2). Two lions are at the Psalmist's feet (v. 17). In the foreground, three angels with sword and spears force the enemy with spears and shields into its own nets (vv. 7–8). At the right, the Psalmist sits on the ground (v. 13). In the upper left, six people stand before a temple with drawn curtains (v. 18).

2.36 fol. 20^v Psalm 35 (36). In the center, the Psalmist stands looking up to God, cross-nimbed, in a mandorla flanked by six angels (v. 6). On either side are mountains on which sit two groups of the righteous, and below is the great deep with horses and bulls (v. 7). In the center is a covered portico with an angel spreading his wings over the children of men (v. 8). Within the portico are two quatrefoil fountains from which two birds spout water into goblets held by two groups of people (vv. 9–10). In the lower corners are the workers of iniquity: those on the left are cast into a fiery pit; those on the right whisper together (v. 12). The beginning of the text is marked by an initial *D / Dixit* with a beast-head and body.

2.37 fol. 21ʳ Psalm 36 (37). In the center, the Psalmist sits at a lectern with an open book and a pair of scales (v. 6). Above are a sun personification and God, cross-nimbed, flanked by six angels (v. 6). In the foreground are agricultural scenes: reaping with a scythe; sharpening a scythe with a stone; plowing with oxen; sowing; and gathering (vv. 3, 11, 19, 22, 26, 29, 34). On the lower left, the sinners draw their swords, hold spears, and wield a bow (vv. 14–15). On the upper left are two men in trees, one of whom falls down with his sword (vv. 35–36). In the upper right, four men at a table are served by a servant holding a jug and a vessel (v. 19); an angel catches a falling man (v. 24). In the center right, a man distributes food to the poor, who hold sacks (v. 26).

2.38 fol. 22ʳ Psalm 37 (38). The Psalmist with arrows sticking in his arms and legs (v. 3), and with leperous wounds (v. 4), bows (v. 7), points to his eye (v. 11), and begs God, cross-nimbed, standing in a mandorla, and flanked by six angels holding bannered staffs, not to forsake him (v. 22). On the left, a group of friends and neighbors stands far off (v. 12) and, on the right stands a large group of enemies with scourges, spears, and shields (v. 20).

2.39 fol. 22ᵛ Psalm 38 (39). In the upper center, the Psalmist, pointing to his mouth (vv. 2–3) and holding a pot of fire (v. 4), prays to God above, cross-nimbed, standing in a mandorla flanked by three angels, to deliver him from his iniquities (v. 9). Before the Psalmist are three demons: one holds a measuring tape; one counts with his fingers; and one holds a pair of scales and a trident; an open coffin is on the left (vv. 5–6). On the far left, a man, sitting in the porch of a building, holds a pair of scales, while another man holds a sack. Below, a group of horsemen transports a large chest. On the lower right, a crowned king, enthroned, supervises the gathering, counting, and storing of his vast riches (vv. 6–7).

2.40 fol. 23ʳ Psalm 39 (40). In the center, the Psalmist, standing on a rock (v. 3) and putting his hand to his mouth (v. 4), addresses God above, cross-nimbed and holding a book, flanked by six angels. An angel, holding an open book, supports the Psalmist. Three winged demons threaten the Psalmist with spears and tridents (v. 13). On the left, the enemy is pushed into a pit by two demons with spears (v. 15). In the center right, two men lead two rams away from an empty altar in front of a temple (v. 7). On the lower right, a king and queen, both crowned, stand conversing while their retainers prepare for the hunt; horsemen prepare to mount; a man holds a falcon(?) on his wrist; and another man holds two hunting dogs on leashes (v. 5).

2.41 fol. 24r Psalm 40 (41). In the upper center, the Psalmist, standing next to a table with bread and a bowl (v. 10), looks up to the Hand of God. On the far right, the Psalmist, sitting on a throne with footstool, instructs a servant to feed the needy from a table (v. 2). At the bottom of a hill is an overturned bed (v. 4). At the left, the Psalmist stands before his enemies, armed with spears (v. 8). At his feet is an open coffin (v. 6). In the lower left are a temple with domed cupola (the Holy Sepulchre) and a standing figure (Christ?), who speaks to two kneeling women (two of the Marys?) (v. 9). In the upper left, a rooster stands on a column.

2.42 fol. 24v Psalm 41 (42). On the lower right, a pair of hunting dogs chases a hart from a grove of trees up a hill to a stream (v. 2). In the center, the Psalmist is pushed into the stream by his enemies, armed with spears and shields (v. 8); he points to a table with bread and wine and to sun and moon personifications above (v. 4). In the upper right is a cross-surmounted tent with people within and, in the lower left, a feast scene with dancers and musicians (two shawms? being fingered, v. 5). In the upper center, Misericordia stands holding a palm frond (v. 9).

2.43 fol. 25r Upper miniature: Psalm 42 (43). The Psalmist, holding a lute (v. 5), is led by a woman with a palm frond (personification of Truth) to the holy hill where there is a temple with draped altar, hanging lamp, and open curtains (vv. 3–4); the Hand of God appears above. On the right are two tents and four men. On the left is a group of enemies with spears and shields (v. 1).

Lower miniature: Psalm 43 (44). In the center of a walled city, the Psalmist, holding a shield and spear, and an armed host stand before a pile of weapons (sword, quiver, and war-horn, v. 7). At the right rear of the enclosure, two groups of men stand with rolls and open books ("our fathers," v. 2). At the left, a group of men humble themselves before a temple (v. 25). Before the city walls, an elaborate battle scene: two groups of mounted soldiers with spears, bows and arrows, and shields attack a group of enemies (v. 11). In the foreground, a herd of sheep grazes and is slaughtered (v. 12). Above, in heaven, God, flanked by angels, is asleep in bed (v. 23).

2.44 fol. 26r Psalm 44 (45). In the left center, the Psalmist, standing with arms outstretched, addresses the King of God's kingdom while a scribe writes down his words in a roll (v. 2). In the upper register, the King, girt with a sword (v. 4) and treading a demon underfoot, stands in the portico of his palace. On the right wing of the building are female personifications of Truth, Meekness, and Justice (v. 5). On the left wing of the palace, the Queen and her daughters bring a box to the King (v. 10). At the corner of the building, an archer shoots arrows and subdues a group of enemies in the lower left corner (v. 6). On the center right, a group of women (the daughters of Tyre) bears gifts of food and crowns (v. 13) and, below, four princes offer crowns (v. 17).

2.45 fol. 26ᵛ Psalm 45 (46). On the upper left, the Psalmist, standing by an altar in front of a temple, observes the City of God (v. 5), in which God, cross-nimbed and standing in a mandorla, is flanked by the faithful (v. 6). Four angels blowing horns represent "the voice" (v. 7). Beneath God, a group of the faithful sits near the streams of a river (v. 5). On the right, three men destroy a pile of weapons (v. 10). Outside the city walls are two armed groups, and, in the foreground, a group of cowering figures is seated on hills; two sea personifications(?) on either side blow horns (vv. 3–4).

2.46 fol. 27ʳ Psalm 46 (47). Within the City of God, the Psalmist, standing with outstretched arms, and two groups of musicians sing praises (v. 2). Above, God, cross-nimbed, sits in a mandorla supported by horn-blowing angels; on either side are three angels (v. 3). In front of the city gate are two groups of cowering figures (v. 4). On either side of the city walls, two groups of crowned princes hold palm fronds (v. 10).

2.47 fol. 27ᵛ Psalm 47 (48). In the upper left, the Psalmist sings praises to God in the City of God on the right (vv. 2–4). Outside the gates, crowned kings approach with gifts (v. 5). On the far right, a group of people marvels at the City of God (v. 6). On the left is a woman in labor with midwife (v. 7). In the lower left, two ships of Tharsis are blown by wind personifications (v. 8). Within the city, the daughters of Judah dance with joy (v. 12).

2.48 fol. 28ʳ Psalm 48 (49). In the upper center, the Psalmist, holding his heel with his right hand (v. 6), reaches out with his left hand towards the Hand of God and proclaims His wisdom (v. 4). On the right, three figures with rod, psaltery, and bannered staff (v. 5) urge a group on the far right to give ear (v. 1). In the center foreground is a three-tiered sepulchre with a group of people preparing a corpse for burial; two open coffins are nearby. A woman tears her hair (vv. 11–12). On the left are three horses (v. 13). On the far lower left, sheep lie in a fiery pit (v. 15). On the lower right, a king, holding a spear and scales, oversees the counting of his wealth. In the upper left is a Sol personification (v. 15).

2.49 fol. 28ᵛ Psalm 49 (50). On each side of the upper level are Sol and Luna personifications (v. 1). In the upper center, God, cross-nimbed and holding a book, flanked by six angels holding staffs on either side, stands in a mandorla. Wind personifications blow fire on the earth (v. 3). In the middle register on the left, the Psalmist, standing on a rock, and an angel, holding a palm frond, gather together a group of God's saints (v. 5) In the lower left, three men, emerging from a temple, drive a ram and two bullocks toward an altar (vv. 8–10). In the center foreground, a crowned woman (Terra) sits on an architectural throne holding two long staffs (v. 12). Goat and bull herds are on the upper right (v. 13). In the lower right, a nimbed angel, holding a drapery and an open roll, addresses a group of people (vv. 16–17).

2.50 fol. 29r Upper miniature: in a blank space next to the text of Psalm 51 (52), a twelfth-century artist (Wormald Hand 8) has added a drawing that has no apparent relation to the text it accompanies (unless it forms the letter Q of "Qui potens" in the text). Christ, cross-nimbed and holding an open book, sits on an arc within a circular medallion supported by an angel and winged wind personification.

Lower miniature: Psalm 52 (53). This twelfth-century addition reproduces the iconography of fol. 7v. God, cross-nimbed and holding a cross-scepter, sits in a mandorla flanked by angels, two of whom hold spears; he looks down on scenes of iniquity (v. 3). On the left, a crowned king, holding a sword, sits under a domed enclosure with drawn curtain while a winged demon whispers to him. Two soldiers with drawn swords present him with severed human heads; two bodies lie at their feet. Below, two men attack a third man with stones; two men fight with swords; and two men with trident and spear trample a third man. On the right, women and children, captured by three horsemen with bannered spears, appeal to a soldier with shield and bannered spear.

2.51 fol. 29v Psalm 53 (54). In the upper left, the Psalmist, holding a shield and banner-spear, offers a bull as a sacrifice at a fiery altar (v. 8). To the right, a priest stands before a temple with drawn curtains, altar, and hanging lamp. On the lower left are two horsemen, with double-bladed axe and spear (v. 5). In the foreground, a group of the enemy falls from their horses (vv. 7, 9). Above, Hand of God issues from clouds.

2.52 fol. 30r Psalm 54 (55). In the upper left, the Psalmist, standing under the moon and stars (v. 6) is threatened by a group of enemies with spears and shields (vv. 2–4). In the center is a city with scenes of violence and iniquity (vv. 10–12): a group of falling men; four men attack the city gate; usury as a man holding scales (v. 12). In the upper right is a Sol personification (v. 11?). A man ("the guide," v. 14?) stands next to a table with food and a knife (v. 15). In the lower right is the enemy in the fiery pit of hell (vv. 16, 24).

2.53 fol. 30ᵛ Psalm 55 (56). In the center of the foreground, the Psalmist stands with his left hand to his eyes (v. 9) and his right heel raised (v. 7). On the left are the enemies armed with axe, spears, and rocks (v. 3). In the upper right, the Hand of God; God, wielding a bannered cross-spear, turns back a group of the enemy (v. 10). In the lower right is a large Hades head in the fiery pit of hell (v. 13).

2.54 fol. 31ʳ Psalm 56 (57). In the center foreground, the Psalmist, standing by his bed (v. 5), is rescued from the pit (v. 7) by an angel with outspread wings (v. 2). On either side are attacking lions (v. 5) and two workmen with mattock and spade (v. 7). In the upper left and lower right is the enemy (the "sons of men," v. 5). In the upper center, two groups of people (the "nations," v. 10) stand beneath God, cross-nimbed and holding a closed book, in a mandorla supported by two angels (v. 6).

2.55 fol. 31ᵛ Psalm 57 (58). On the left, five judges sit within a gabled building (v. 2). Outside are a serpent and asp (vv. 5–6). In the center is a group of the impious (v. 4). The Psalmist stands with outstretched arms. On the right a lion is stabbed in the teeth (v. 7). Below are a river god personification (v. 8) and a candlestick with lighted candle (v. 9). Above and lower right, four angels, armed with spears, bow and arrows, and axes, attack the sinners (v. 11).

2.56 fol. 32ʳ Psalm 58 (59). In the center, the Psalmist, being attacked by three men with swords, runs toward God, standing cross-nimbed on the left (vv. 2–5). In the lower left is a pack of dogs within and without a walled enclosure (v. 7). On the upper right, four angels with spears and a bow and arrow attack the enemy below (v. 12). In the center foreground, a group of the impious stands at an empty table (vv. 15–16).

2.57 fol. 32ᵛ Psalm 59 (60). In the upper level, God, nimbed, sits on an arc in a fiery mandorla; flanked by six angels, he is handed a pair of shoes by another angel (v. 10). On the right, an angel, holding a staff, points towards a city (v. 11). In the center foreground, the City of Edom is attacked: two men hurl stones from the walls; others wield spears and shields (vv. 10–11). On the left, soldiers with spears and swords defeat the enemy (vv. 12–14).

2.58 fol. 33ʳ Upper miniature: Psalm 60 (61). On the right, the Psalmist sits in front of a tent on a rock (v. 3). In the center, an angel, standing on a tower, bends over and gives the Psalmist, standing with outstretched arms by the sea, a drapery (vv. 4–5). On the left, a crowned king stands in the portico of his palace; seven men with spears and shields are behind him (v. 7). Above, God, nimbed, holds a sun symbol and a fiery torch (v. 7).

Lower miniature: Psalm 61 (62). In the center, the Psalmist appeals to God, standing above holding a banner-spear and shield and flanked by six angels (vv. 2–3). In the right center, a wall falls (v. 4). On either side, the sons of men kill each other with spears and swords (v. 10). In the center of the foreground, the sons of men, one with a pair of scales, stand around a table (v. 10). On the left, a congregation of people hides in a cave (v. 9). In the lower right, two sinners are bitten by a serpent in a fiery pit (v. 13).

2.59 fol. 33^{v} Psalm 62 (63). In the lower left, the Psalmist rising from his bed (v. 7) and touching his lips (v. 2) looks up to the Hand of God, an angel with outspread wings (v. 8), and the sun (v. 2). On the left is a temple with open curtains, altar, and hanging lamp (v. 3). To the right are a sheep and ox (v. 6). A crowned king and his followers raise their hands (v. 12). In the lower right corner, a group of sinners is pushed into a fiery pit (v.10), and two foxes trample a sinner (v. 11).

2.60 fol. 34^{r} Psalm 65 (66). Above, God, nimbed, flanked by six angels, holds a shield ("thy strength," v. 3). In the center, the Psalmist, pointing to his mouth (v. 14), drives a flock of sacrificial animals to an altar before a temple with hanging lamp (vv. 13, 15). Standing on the lower right is a group of four gesticulating men whom the Psalmist urges to praise God (v. 8). In the foreground are depicted various trials; four men with scourges and rocks, four men in a fiery furnace, and two men passing through the water (vv. 10–12).

2.61 fol. 34^{v} Psalm 66 (67). An unfinished faint sketch of the second quarter of the twelfth century. In the center, the Psalmist, standing on a rock, addresses God, who leans from heaven holding a pair of scales (v. 5). On the left is a group of people, representing the "nations upon earth" (v. 5). On the right, the earth yields its fruit—trees and vines (v. 7).

2.62 fol. 35^{r} Psalm 67 (68). An unfinished drawing, barely visible in the original ms., of the twelfth century. In the center, the Psalmist stands with one hand raised toward heaven and with the other hand points to various scenes. Above, God, flanked by angels, rides in a chariot (v. 18). On the center right, widows and orphans hold out their hands (v. 6). On the upper left are two open coffins with corpses inside (v. 7). In the far upper left, sheep and bulls graze on the Mountain of God (v. 16). In the lower left, an angel treads on the enemy before the City of Jerusalem (v. 22). Three princes approach the city with gifts (v. 28). In the foreground is a herd of wild beasts (v. 31).

There are twenty-five blank spaces for drawings on folios 36^{r}, 37^{r} (two spaces), 38^{r}, 38^{v}, 39^{r}, 40^{r} (two spaces), 40^{v}, 41^{r}, 41^{v}, 43^{r}, 43^{v}, 44^{r}, 44^{v}, 45^{r}, 45^{v}, 46^{r}, 46^{v}, 47^{r}, 47^{v}, 48^{r}, 48^{v}, 49^{r}, and 49^{v}.

2.63 fol. 50r Psalm 101 (102). God, cross-nimbed and holding a closed book, sits on a globe-mandorla flanked by six angels. Below, in the center, the Psalmist, standing next to a table with pitcher, goblet, and plate, holds a goblet (v. 10) and points to a fiery altar on the left. Also on the left are a pelican, raven, and sparrow (vv. 7–8). On the right, angels with hammers and chisels build the City of Sion (v. 17). In the lower right, a reclining nude woman holding a cornucopia (personification of Terra) is accompanied by a group of children (v. 19). On the lower right, three figures genuflect and pray (v. 18). In the lower left are two crowned kings and their retainers (v. 23).

2.64 fol. 51r Psalm 102 (103). On the left, the Psalmist, standing by a tree with an eagle within (v. 5), receives a wreath from an angel with a cross-staff (v. 4). On the lower right, Moses stands before the Children of Israel (v. 7). On the lower left are the pit of hell with a large Hades head, two demons tormenting the sinners with tridents, and a coiled serpent (v. 10). In the center of the foreground, a group of children stands with their hands raised (v. 13). The landscape sprouts small plants (v. 15). In the upper level, God, cross-nimbed and holding a closed book, sits on a globe-mandorla flanked by nine angels, six holding cross-banner staffs (vv. 19–20). On either side are personifications of the sun and moon (v. 12).

2.65 fol. 51v Psalm 103 (104). In the right of center, the Psalmist praises the creation of God. Above, God, cross-nimbed and holding a closed book, is supported by four wind personifications (vv. 2–3) and flanked by four angels and the moon, stars, and a sun personification (v. 19). In the middleground are the works of creation: birds nesting in rocks and trees (v. 12); herds of bulls, sheep, and horses (v. 20); a man plowing with two oxen (v. 23); three men feasting at a table, one of which is served a drink and anointed with a horn (v. 15); and in the far right, a hart nibbling a tree and an animal hiding in the rocks (v. 18). In the lower right, two lions devour their prey (v. 21). In the foreground are the sea with ships, the Leviathan, birds, and creeping things (vv. 25–26).

2.66 fol. 52v Psalm 104 (105). In the center, the Psalmist, standing on a rock and surrounded by a large crowd of people (Abraham's seed and Jacob's sons, v. 6), praises God. Above, God, cross-nimbed and holding an open roll, sits in a globe-mandorla (vv. 7–8) flanked by two angels with cross-staffs. In the upper right, Abraham, Isaac, and Jacob all hold rolls (vv. 9–10).

2.67 fol. 53r In a blank space at the end of Psalm 104, the artist (Hand E) added a drawing of two prophets(?) looking left and, below, an angel spearing a demon.

2.68 fol. 53v Psalm 105 (106). In the upper level, the Psalmist directs an angel's attention to a temple with murmuring people within and without (vv. 24–25). In the lower center, Moses with Aaron places a rod over the Red Sea in which the Egyptians drown (v. 11; see Ex. 14:27). On the left, Moses is plotted against by men in a walled city (v. 16). In the lower right, a group of enemies holds spears and shields. Above, Hand of God issues from clouds.

2.69 fol. 54ᵛ Psalm 106 (107). In the upper center, the Psalmist looks up to God, cross-nimbed and flanked by three angels and personifications of the sun and moon (v. 3). Beneath the Psalmist is the sea with two ships manned by three men, one of whom is rowing with an oar (v. 23). On either side of the Psalmist are empty thrones and groups of people standing before walled cities (v. 32). The city on the left is being built by workers with tools; one man carries a sack and an axe; another man lifts up a sack to another man on the wall; and a man cuts or shapes a stone block with a hammer and chisel. In the lower center, a man plows with oxen and two men cut vines (v. 37). In the lower left are four women with infants (v. 38). In the lower right is a group of prisoners; one sits in stocks, and two are chained to columns (v. 10).

2.70 fol. 55ᵛ Psalm 107 (108). In the upper left, the Psalmist, holding a harp, lute, and measuring rod (vv. 3, 8), stands before a temple with altar, open curtains, hanging lamp, and globe-cross. Above, God, cross-nimbed and flanked by angels, stands in a mandorla supported by four other angels (vv. 5–6). On the upper left, a sun personification issues rays on the Psalmist (v. 3). In the center is the City of Edom as a walled enclosure with towers and gate. Within the left side of the wall, David, crowned, holds a pair of shoes in his extended left arm (v. 10). Within the right side of the wall, a standing male, Moab, holds a cup in his left hand (v. 10). Gilead, Manasseh, and Ephraim sit in the center of the city (v. 9). Outside the walls, a man measures the ground with a rod (v. 8). In the lower left is an army with spears and shields (v. 12).

2.71 fol. 56ʳ Psalm 108 (109). On the right side of a hill, the Psalmist, supported by an angel, cries out to God, cross-nimbed, holding a cross-inscribed, closed book, sitting on a globe-mandorla, and flanked by six angels (vv. 21–24). At the Psalmist's feet, a horn of spilled oil (v. 24). On the upper left and right, two groups of enemies cower (v. 3). On the left of the hill, a winged demon drags away one of the sinners (v. 6). In the lower left, a soldier, holding a spear, kicks a nude child (v. 10), and two men plunder a chest (v. 11). In the center foreground, a partially clad woman, kneeling on a hill next to a tree, pulls her hair and holds her garment (vv. 18–19). On the branches of the tree hang a girdle, garment, and horn spilling its oil (vv. 18–19). At the base of the tree, another vessel spills water.

2.72 fol. 56ᵛ Psalm 109 (110). Within a circular mandorla, God and Christ, seated on a bench, rest their feet on two nude enemies; on either side are three angels (v. 1). On the left, a group of saints holding torches receives rays from the morning star (v. 3). On the right, an angel throws spears and defeats an army led by a crowned king (vv. 5–6). On the lower right, a soldier with helmet, spear, and shield stands on the body of an enemy and takes water from a stream with a bowl (v. 7).

2.73 fol. 57r Psalm 110 (111). On the right, the Psalmist, standing before a table filled with vessels (v. 5), looks up to God. Above, God, cross-nimbed, supported by wind personifications, holds an open roll (v. 9) and a pair of scales (vv. 7–8); three angels hold a cross-staff and banner staffs. An angel flies down from heaven with a dish of food (v. 5). In the lower left, a group of people, holding open rolls, stands before a temple with altar and hanging lamp (v. 9).

2.74 fol. 57v Psalm 111 (112). In the portico of an elaborate house and temple, a king or rich man, seated on a throne, and his wife, distribute food to two groups of the poor and crippled (v. 5). The roof of the house is surmounted by a stag's head while that of the temple has a globe-cross (v. 3). On the left side of the building are two nude figures and a group of soldiers with spears and shields (v. 2). In the center foreground, two men distribute money or food from jars to the poor and crippled (v. 9); a cripple crawls on his hands supported by trestles. On the lower left, a winged demon with trident pushes the sinners, armed with spears and shields, into a fiery pit (v. 10). Above is the Hand of God.

2.75 fol. 58r Upper miniature: Psalm 112 (113). On the lower left and center, three groups of the faithful, led by the Psalmist(?), praise God above, seated on a globe-mandorla and flanked by an angel (v. 1), a Sol personification (crowned and holding a torch), and the moon and stars (v. 3). In the center, another angel lifts a nude man from the ground (v. 7). In the upper right, four princes, crowned, sit on a cushioned bench (v. 8); three of the princes hold swords and turn toward the second figure on the left ("ritual subjection of kings to a king of higher rank"(?); see Judith Duffey, "The Inventive Group of Illustrations in the Harley Psalter," diss. University of California at Berkeley, 1977, p. 109). In the lower right, the barren mother, sitting in front of a building, enfolds a group of nude children with her cloak (a gesture of protection; see Duffey, p. 110).

Lower miniature: Psalm 113 (114–15). Moses, at the head of a large group of people, stretches his rod toward the River Jordan (vv. 3, 7–8). A ram is in the rocks (v, 4). Above, the Hand of God (v. 7).

2.76 fol. 58v An added drawing. The Psalmist(?) extends a cup to God, cross-nimbed and holding an open roll. On the left, the Israelites praise God. On the right, an angel holds a bannered cross-staff.

2.77 fol. 59^r^ Upper miniature: Psalm 114 (115). The Psalmist, being attacked by two demons with tridents, reaches up to God, cross-nimbed, who leans out of his mandorla and grasps the Psalmist and presses his cheek with his own (v. 2). In the Psalmist's outstretched left hand, a small figure (representing his soul) reaches up to touch God's nimbus (v. 7). On the left, God, cross-nimbed and holding a bannered cross-staff, stands before a group of children (v. 6). On the right, the Psalmist raises his hand to God, cross-nimbed and holding a staff, who blesses him (v. 9?).

Lower miniature: Psalm 115 (116). In the upper right, God, sitting in a globe-mandorla, holds a torch issuing rays towards the Psalmist, who raises his hand to his mouth (v. 11). On the right, the Psalmist, standing before a building (the house of the Lord, v. 19), raises a cup in his left hand (v. 13). In the center, saints are martyred by decapitation; a man, holding a sword, grasps the hair of another man whose hands are bound; four human heads are on the ground. Two angels fly down with draped hands to receive their souls (v. 15).

2.78 fol. 59^v^ Upper miniature: Psalm 115 (116) continued. Between two hills, a walled enclosure contains a triple-arched domed building (v. 19). Standing on a hill, God, cross-nimbed and holding a staff, leans over and blesses the Psalmist who, climbing the hill, lifts a cup (*calicem salutaris*) with draped hands (v. 13). At the foot of the hill are two groups of men holding spears and watching (v. 18). Judith Duffey observes that "one of the figures on the left raises a hand to his head in a conspicuous but unidentifiable gesture, as if scratching his head, but no text accounts for this" (p. 42).

Lower miniature: Psalm 116 (117). In a single-level composition, a large group of people, including veiled women and men holding spears, looks upwards to God, cross-nimbed and holding a closed book, standing in a mandorla flanked by three half-length angels (vv. 1-2). At the front of the group is a small cluster of unarmed men wearing cowls; Judith Duffey speculates that they represent monks (p. 43). In the lower left, two small figures, one cowled, hold an object between them; Duffey states that the drawing is a later addition, perhaps depicting the plucking of a goose (p. 43).

2.79 fol. 60^r^ Psalm 117 (118). In the center of the foreground, the Psalmist, standing between two angels spearing two groups of the enemy, cries out to God (vv. 5–11). Above, God, holding an open roll and closed book, stands in a mandorla, which physically touches the roof of a building (v. 22?). In the upper right is a series of dots, which probably represent the bees mentioned in v. 12. In the center and upper left are the temple of the just and a group of the righteous (v. 15). At the door of the building, a standing male points the end of a long, bannered staff (vv. 19–20). At the top of the folio, the text of Psalm 116 begins with an initial *L* / *Laudate* terminating in a beast-head. For the identification of Christ with the corner-stone of a temple, see Judith Duffey (pp. 122–23).

2.80 fol. 60v Psalm 117 (118) continued. In the lower right, the Psalmist, holding an open book and pointing to a large group of people, declares "the works of the Lord" (v. 17). On the upper level, five angels praise God who stands, holding an open book, in a mandorla supported by two angels.

2.81 fol. 61r In a small space at the end of Psalm 118 (119), the Psalmist, holding an open book, speaks to a group of kneeling figures (v. 13?).

2.82 fol. 62v In a small space at the end of v. 96 of Psalm 118, two animals nibble foliage (the sheep of v. 176?).

2.83 fol. 64r Psalm 119 (120). In the center, the Psalmist receives a spear and shield from God, cross-nimbed, who leans out of his globe-mandorla (vv. 1–3). In the lower right, a dark-bearded angel, wearing a quiver with arrows, shoots three "arrows of the mighty with coals that lay waste"; a pile of coals is in the center (v. 4). The archer is inscribed "agelmund." On the far left is a walled enclosure (the City of Cedar) with inhabitants looking out (v. 5); on the wall is a worker with hammer and chisel.

2.84 fol. 64v Upper miniature: Psalm 120 (121). On the left, the Psalmist, pointing to his eyes, stands looking up to God above, who, holding a spear, leans out of his mandorla and gestures with his right hand (a faint drawing) (vv. 1–2). A sun personification and the moon and stars issue rays downwards on the Psalmist (v. 6). In the center, an angel, bearing a cross-staff, steps forward on his right foot (v. 3?). Another figure, a man dressed in a loin-cloth and holding a basket, walks away from a group of people on the right (v. 8). At the far right, God(?) (or the Psalmist), sitting in bed and attended by an angel, blesses the group of people (v. 4).

Lower miniature: Psalm 121 (122). Within the portico of an elaborate city (Jerusalem), the Psalmist and another figure observe the Hand of God issuing from the roof of the building (vv. 1–3). On the left, the tribes of the Lord enter the city through a gate (v. 4).

2.85 fol. 65r Psalm 122 (123). In the center, the Psalmist receives a long spear from God, cross-nimbed, who, flanked by two angels, leans over to hand it to him (v. 1). A winged demon seizes the Psalmist with a hook (v. 3?). A group of people watches on the lower right. On the left, within the portico of a domed building, a seated woman (the "mistress") holds another woman's face (the "handmaid") in her hands (v. 2). In a side porch, a seated, bearded male (the "master") touches a sword to the shoulder of a standing male (the "servant," v. 2). According to Judith Duffey (pp. 129–30) this scene may represent the ceremony of "dubbing" to knighthood with a sword.

2.86 fol. 65v Upper miniature: Psalm 123 (124). In the center, the Psalmist and another figure, seated on rocks, praise God, cross-nimbed and holding a spear, seated in a globe-mandorla supported by two angels (vv. 2, 6, 8). On the left, the faithful are threatened by three men with spears and shields (vv. 2–3).

Lower miniature: Psalm 124 (125). God, cross-nimbed, bearded, and flanked by two angels, stands within a walled enclosure filled with rocky landscape (vv. 1–2). Within the enclosure is a group of people who trust in the Lord (v. 1). On the lower left, outside the city walls, an angel with a spear thrusts two sinners into a fiery pit (vv. 3, 5).

2.87 fol. 66r Psalm 125 (126). On the left, God, cross-nimbed and enthroned in a fiery globe-mandorla, directs (or casts down?) three winged figures who hold double-bladed axes (v. 1). In the center, the Psalmist, pointing to his forehead, and another figure, holding an open book, stand on a small hill and look left toward God (v. 3?). On the upper right, three workers carry on their shoulders sheaves of grain (v. 7). Below, a man sows seeds and another man plows with oxen (v. 6).

2.88 fol. 66v Upper miniature: Psalm 126 (127). Within a walled city with buildings and two cross-surmounted towers, five workers with a variety of tools (hammer, chisel, and axes) build the city (v. 1). On the upper right, God, cross-nimbed and flanked by an angel, sits in his globe-mandorla and observes the scene.

Lower miniature: Psalm 127 (128). In the upper right, a king and a queen, both crowned and sitting at a round table within a building, are served by three servants holding vessels; vine plants grow on either side (vv. 1–3). On the left, within a domed building surmounted by a cross, is a footwashing ceremony: a kneeling cowled figure washes in a basin the feet of a seated, cowled man while two other cowled figures watch (v. 1). In the center foreground, a crowned king distributes money to the poor, one of whom wears a satchel around his neck. For a discussion of these scenes, see Judith Duffey, pp. 130–35.

2.89 fol. 67r Upper miniature: Psalm 128 (129). In the center, two impious men, holding a hammer and tongs with a red-hot piece of metal (plowshare; see Duffey, p. 137), attack a bent-over, bearded man (personification of Israel, v. 1). The man with the tongs is burning the victim's back (v. 3). Directed by the Hand of God, an angel, wielding a sword, is about to decapitate one of the sinners, who holds a hammer; three decapitated bodies lie on a hill covered with grass and a vine plant (vv. 4–6). On the left, three workers weave a wattle enclosure (v. 6 of the Roman version). According to Duffey (pp. 135–38), the artist drew upon three textual versions of the Psalms (Gallican, Roman, and Iuxta Hebraeos) in order to illustrate the scenes.

Lower miniature: an added drawing. The Psalmist stands in the center with his arms raised; on either side, groups of men hold symbols of the sun (Psalm 129, v. 6?).

2.90 fol. 67v Upper miniature: Psalm 129 (130). On the left, the Psalmist, standing on a hill, cries out to God above flanked by six angels (vv. 1–2). In the center, a group of people (Israel) looks toward heaven (v. 6). On the right is the resurrection of the dead; a nude figure rises from one of four open coffins (v. 5 or 7).

Lower miniature: Psalm 130 (131). On the left, the Psalmist holds out his hands to receive (or reject?) rays issuing from the Hand of God above (v. 1). In the center, four bearded figures (Israel) sit holding their hands to their faces (v. 3). At the right, a female, seated under a domed arcade, gives with one hand a large round ring to a male, holding a staff, and with the other hand touches his forehead (v. 2). According to Duffey (pp. 138–44), the latter scene might be interpreted as a mother giving her son the gift of a ring and her benediction before his departure from her household.

2.91 fol. 68r Psalm 131 (132). In the right foreground, David, crowned and holding a harp, sits upon a bed (v. 3); he is flanked by a standing woman (v. 11?) and two soldiers with spears and shields. On the left is the temple of God, with God, cross-nimbed and winged, standing before the entrance (vv. 5–7). In the center, six bearded figures kneel on a hill (v. 12) before God standing in a tent surmounted by a globe and cross (v. 13).

2.92 fol. 68v Upper miniature: Psalm 132 (133). On the right, seven figures sit together under a gable surmounted by an acanthus-leaf ornament; the third figure from the right holds a cup or chalice, and to his left is a woman wearing a headdress. According to Duffey (pp. 150–51) the woman represents either a contemporary abbess or some important secular female, possibly Anglo-Saxon royalty. In the center, Aaron is anointed by an angel with a horn of ointment (v. 2). On the left, dew falls on Mount Sion (v. 3).

Lower miniature: Psalm 133 (134). Within a gabled building, eight servants of the Lord stand and bless God above, seated in a globe-mandorla (vv. 1–3). Dark lines around the mandorla indicate that it is night (v. 2).

2.93 fol. 69r Psalm 134 (135). In the upper left, God, cross-nimbed, sitting in a fiery globe-mandorla, releases three personifications of the winds (v. 7), and directs three angels, armed with spears and double-bladed axes, to destroy the enemy below (v. 10); a group of soldiers, some falling from their horses, is attacked both from above and on the right by three horsemen, who represent the victorious (v. 19). Judith Duffey (p. 152) notes that the horseman on the far right carries no weapon, is tonsured, and wears a cowled robe; she speculates that "this must be taken as some contemporary reference, perhaps in a rather general way, to the role of the ecclesiastic who, while prohibited from direct participation in warfare or the carrying of weapons, could support and encourage, even direct, battle on behalf of his heavenly Superior." By contrast, Thomas H. Ohlgren has argued that there are four horsemen attacking from the right, two of whom are monastic warriors actively participating in the battle ("Anglo-Saxon Art: Texts and Contexts," *Old English Newsletter, Subsidia* 17 [1991], pp. 11–12).

2.94 fol. 69v Psalm 135 (136). In the center, a monumental God, bearded, cross-nimbed, and standing in a mandorla, holds a cross-staff and observes the works of creation below (vv. 1–5). On the left, four angels stand with banner-staffs. In the upper right, a sun personification issues flames (v. 8), and the moon and the stars (v. 9). In the lower left, a river flows from the mandorla (v. 13, the Red Sea?), and herds of animals graze (v. 25). On the far right, a man holds his chin in his hand (v. 22?) and, below, an abbot(?), holding a long cross-staff, humbles himself before God (vv. 26–27).

2.95 fol. 70r Psalm 136 (137). On the lower right is the River of Babylon with seven figures sitting beneath three trees (v. 1). Musical instruments, including a harp, hang in the trees (v. 2). On the left is a walled city surmounted by a cross and a mountain within (v. 1, Sion?). Upon a tower of the city, a crowned man, bearing a spear, tugs at the garment of one of the seated figures (v. 3). In the upper right is the blessing Hand of God (v. 7). In the lower right corner of the folio there is a faint drawing of God, cross-nimbed and holding an open book, flanked by two sun symbols.

2.96 fol. 70v Upper miniature: Psalm 137 (138). On the left, nine kings in Phrygian hats praise God, cross-nimbed, seated above in a globe-mandorla (vv. 4–5). Before the kings, the Psalmist(?) raises his hands toward God (v. 1). On the right, the Psalmist bows before a temple with open curtains and an altar (v. 2).

Lower miniature: an added drawing to Psalm 138. On the right, the Psalmist, holding his hand to his face (v. 4?), sits within a gabled building surmounted by a bird (v. 2). Holding a hanging lamp, the Hand of God emerges from behind one of the curtains (vv. 11–12). In the center, a seated man holds a bowl and, on the left, two souls rise from open coffins (v. 2, "my rising up").

2.97 fol. 71r Psalm 138 (139). On the lower left, a small winged man sits on an island in a sea and looks up to the Hand of God (vv. 9–10). Dark shadings indicate that it is night (vv. 11–12). In the center is depicted the Harrowing of Hell: while Christ raises two nude souls from a hell-mouth, an angel flies down to receive the souls in a garment (v. 8). On the right are the three women at the Sepulchre guarded by an angel, who points across his body to the empty, domed sepulchre (v. 18). Above, God, cross-nimbed and holding a closed book, stands in a mandorla flanked by two angels.

2.98 fol. 71v Psalm 139 (140). The Psalmist, being attacked by three enemies with ropes (v. 6) and serpents issuing from their mouths (v. 4), prays to God above, who, cross-nimbed and leaning out of his mandorla, pours the contents of a fiery torch on the Psalmist (v. 8). Burning coals fall on the enemies (v. 11). On the right, another enemy is tormented in a pit by an angel with a pole (v. 11).

2.99 fol. 72r Psalm 140 (141). On the left, the Psalmist points a horn of burning incense (v. 2) toward God, cross-nimbed and seated in a globe-mandorla flanked by two angels. On the upper left are the moon and the stars (v. 2). In the left of center, an angel (the "just man," v. 5), wielding a whip, reproves the bowed-over Psalmist. In the center is a group of nude people with their feet cut off (v. 7). On the far right, a demon with a trident torments one of the sinners who has fallen into a pit with a net (v. 10).

2.100 fol. 72v Upper miniature: Psalm 141 (142). On the left, the Psalmist, pointing to the Hand of God above, is threatened by four persecutors holding swords (v. 7). In the center, the Psalmist's soul (a nude man wearing a loincloth) is rescued from the abyss by an angel (v. 8). In the upper right, a group of the righteous "wait[s] for me" (v. 8). On the lower right, the Psalmist, seated with his hand to his face, cries out to God (vv. 1, 8).

Lower miniature: an added drawing with no apparent relation to the text. Two men, holding staffs, stand back to back before horned animals.

2.101 fol. 73r Psalm 142 (143). On the left, an angel spears a demon (v. 12) who has cast the Psalmist into a pit (v. 3). Above are the moon and stars (v. 3). In the center, the Psalmist, holding his chin, looks up to God, seated in a globe-mandorla and holding a book (open?), flanked by three angels (v. 1). On the lower right, an angel lifts the nude soul of the Psalmist from one of two coffins (vv. 10–11).

2.102 fol. 73^{v} Psalm 143 (144). In the center, the Psalmist, wearing a crown and playing the harp, stands on the backs of six enemies (vv. 2, 9). On the left, God, cross-nimbed and walking down a mountain, bears an unstrung bow and arrows (vv. 5–6). On the upper right, David, holding a sling, fights Goliath, wearing a pointed helmet and carrying a spear. Below, David prepares to behead Goliath, lying on the ground, with a sword (v. 10; see I Sam. 17:48–51).

3. Bury Psalter (Biblioteca Apostolica Vaticana, MS Reg. lat. 12)

Plates 3.1 to 3.49

3.1 fol. 21^{r} Psalm 1. Initial page *B / Beatus vir*. The initial is composed of animal-headed interlace knotwork at both ends of the shaft of the letter; the bows are filled with large-leaved scrolls ending in griffins' heads. In the middle of the shaft is a roundel with a cowled monk, sitting in a draped chair and writing with a pen. The Winchester-style frame is composed of acanthus friezes, rosettes on the four corners, and two lozenges with single birds (Temple, p. 100).

3.2 fol. 22^{r} Psalm 2:6: *Ego autem constitutus sum rex ab eo / Super Sion, montem sanctum eius, / Praedicans praeceptum eius.*

A king (David or Christ as King of Sion?), crowned, bearded, and holding a foliated scepter and long, open roll (inscribed with Ps. 2:6), stands on a mountain inscribed "Mons Syon."

3.3 fol. 22^{v} Psalm 3:6: *Ego dormivi, et soporatus sum; / Et exsurrexi, quia Dominus suscepit me.*

The Hand of God grasps the upraised hands of Christ or the Psalmist, bearded and wearing a fillet, who rises from a mattress in his draped bed.

3.4 fol. 24^{v} Psalm 7:13–14: (13) *Nisi conversi fueritis, gladium suum vibrabit; / Arcum suum tetendit, et paravit illum.* (14) *Et in eo paravit vasa mortis, / Sagittas suas ardentibus effecit.*

In the lower right corner of the folio, a demon with flaming hair and shaggy body draws an arrow in a bow; he wears a quiver with three arrows. See description of next folio.

3.5 fol. 25^{r} Psalm 7:13–14 continued. In the upper outer margin, an arrow from the bow of the demon archer on fol. 24^{v} pierces the right arm of a seated female with flaming hair, her right hand covering her face; with her left hand she holds a fiery vessel, inscribed "vas mortis," on her knee. In her bosom are eight human heads, possibly representing personifications of the vices Iniquity, Mischief, Deceit, and others.

Lower miniature: Psalm 8:5–6: (5) *Quid est homo, quod memor es eius? / Aut filius hominis, quoniam visitas eum?* (6) *Minuisti eum paulo minus ab angelis; / Gloria et honore coronasti eum.*

In the lower right margin, God, cross-nimbed, bearded, and wearing a fillet, places a crown on the head of a beardless man, possibly David.

3.6 fol. 27v Psalm 10:2–3: (2) *In Domino confido; quomodo dicitis animae meae: / Transmigra in montem sicut passer?* (3) *Quoniam ecce peccatores intenderunt arcum; / Paraverunt sagittas suas in pharetra, / Ut sagittent in obscuro rectos corde.*

In the outer margin, the standing Psalmist, with out-stretched hands, looks up to the Hand of God. In the inner margin, a bestial demon, with flaming hair and body and clawed feet, draws arrows from a quiver.

3.7 fol. 28r Psalm 12:4–5: (4) *Illumina oculos meos, ne unquam obdormiam in morte;* (5) *Nequando dicat inimicus meus: Praevalui adversus eum.*

God, painted cross-nimbed, beardless, holding a gold cross-shaft and a painted fiery torch, stands on the shoulders of the Psalmist or David, bearded, who sits with arms extended holding an open roll inscribed with Ps. 12:4–5.

3.8 fol. 29r Psalm 14:1–2: *Domine, quis habitabit in tabernaculo tuo? / Aut quis requiescet in monte sancto tuo?* (2) *Qui ingreditur sine macula, / Et operatur iustitiam.*

In the outer margin, the standing Psalmist, bearded, looks above to the Hand of God which appears over a tent, in blue outline, inscribed "SCI S." On the lower right is a mound, inscribed "Mons scs dni."

3.9 fol. 30r Psalm 16:3: *Probasti cor meum, et visitasti nocte; / Igne me examinasti, et non est inventa in me iniquitas.*

The Psalmist, nimbed and beardless, half immersed in a cauldron, with two round rings attached at the rim, over a fiery grate, receives an open roll from the Hand of God.

3.10 fol. 30v Psalm 16:15: *Ego autem in iustitia apparebo conspectui tuo; / Satiabor cum apparuerit gloria tua.*

The Psalmist, bearded and wearing a fillet, stands on a mound and raises a pair of scales to the Hand of God, pointing downward.

3.11 fol. 32r Psalm 17:33: *Deus qui praecinxit me virtute, / Et posuit immaculatam viam meam.*

God, bearded and wearing a golden cross-nimbus, ties a golden sword around the waist of Christ, bearded and wearing a golden cross-nimbus and fillet.

3.12 fol. 35r Psalm 21:2: *Deus, Deus meus, respice in me, quare me dereliquisti?*

Christ: Crucifixion. Hand of God holds scepter above Christ, bearded, golden cross-nimbed, wearing circlet or fillet and long, blue loincloth; nailed to plain, rectangular cross with four nails; blank titulus; golden suppedaneum; and coiled serpent and chalice on lower stem of cross.

3.13 fol. 36r Psalm 21:22: *Salva me ex ore leonis, / Et a cornibus unicornium humilitatem meam.*

The bearded Psalmist, reaching upwards with outstretched arms, receives a shield and spear from God, unnimbed and beardless, who leans out of the frame of the mandorla. A lion and unicorn are in the lower margin.

3.14 fol. 37v On the left, a drawing corresponding to Psalm 23:8: *Quis est iste rex gloriae? / Dominus fortis et potens, / Dominus potens in praelio.*

Christ, bearded and wearing a crown, stands holding in his right hand a cross-inscribed banner-staff and in his left a shield with central boss.

On the right is a drawing that corresponds to Psalm 24:1: *Ad te, Domine, levavi animam meam.* A genuflecting monk, beardless, tonsured, and wearing a cowl, holds an open book (inscribed "Ad te Dme levavi an") in extended arms.

3.15 fol. 40r Psalm 27:2: *Exaudi, Domine, vocem deprecationis meae, dum oro ad te, / Dum extollo manus meas ad templum sanctum tuum.*

The drawing is unfinished. The Psalmist, bearded and wearing a fillet, prays to a Hand of God above a building with tiled roof, tower, and doorway.

3.16 fol. 54r Psalm 41:2–3: (2) *Quemadmodum desiderat cervus ad fontes aquarum, / Ita desiderat anima mea ad te, Deus.* (3) *Sitivit anima mea ad Deum fortem, vivum; / Quando veniam, et apparebo ante faciem Dei?*

In the inner margin, the beardless Psalmist drinks from a chalice offered by the Hand of God. In the outer margin, a horned stag drinks from a stream.

3.17 fol. 62r Initial page *Q* / *Quid gloriaris in malitia.* (Psalm 51:3)

The letter Q is historiated with a crowned, veiled female figure, possibly representing the Virgin Mary or a personification of the Church; she holds a green branch in her right hand and a golden scepter in her left; she is seated on a cushioned bench and flanked by curtains. Above the letter is the inscription: "OLIVA FRUCTIFERA" (see Ps. 51:10). The tail of the letter is formed by a dragon biting itself. The Winchester-style frame is composed of panels of acanthus leaves, rosettes on the four corners, and two medallions enclosing half figures of two veiled women, each with closed, cross-inscribed book.

3.18 fol. 62v Psalm 51:3 ff: *Quid gloriaris in malitia, / Qui potens es in iniquitate?*

In the outer margin, two bestial devils with horns, beards, and shaggy coats hold an open roll and a nude personification of the Psalmist's soul; below, the Psalmist, holding a long, open roll, looks up.

3.19 fol. 63v Psalm 53:8: *Voluntarie sacrificabo tibi, / Et confitebor nomini tuo, Domine, quoniam bonum est.*

In the inner margin, the standing Psalmist, beardless, holds a sacrificial animal (a lamb) in his draped hands.

3.20 fol. 66v Psalm 57:7: *Deus conteret dentes eorum in ore ipsorum; / Molas leonum confringet Dominus.*

David, bearded and wearing a fillet, left leg around lion, rends its jaws.

3.21 fol. 68v Psalm 60:7–8: (7) *Dies super dies regis adiicies; / Annos eius usque in diem generationis et generationis.* (8) *Permanet in aeternum in conspectu Dei. / Misericordiam et veritatem eius quis requiret?*

A crowned king, right arm raised, genuflects beneath a diagrammatic representation of God the Creator, cross-nimbed, bearded, from whose lips extend two fiery horns and whose hand holds a pair of scales.

3.22 fol. 69v Psalm 62:5: *Sic benedicam te in vita mea; / Et in nomine tuo levabo manus meas.*

In the outer margin, the Psalmist, standing with arms raised, looks up to a monumental standing God who is bearded and holds a closed book.

3.23 fol. 70v Psalm 64:2–3: (2) *Te decet hymnus, Deus, in Sion, / Et tibi reddetur votum in Ierusalem.* (3) *Exaudi orationem meam; / Ad te omnis caro veniet.*

The Psalmist, holding two sacrificial doves in extended draped hands, looks up to the City of Jerusalem with a cross on one of its two towers; inscribed "hierlm."

3.24 fol. 71ᵛ Psalm 65:10–11: (10) *Quoniam probasti nos, Deus; / Igne nos examinasti, sicut examinatur argentum.* (11) *Induxisti nos in laqueum; / Posuisti tribulationes in dorso nostro.*

In the lower margin are four nude figures: one emerging from red flames; one swimming in water; the third with a vessel inscribed "opa justie" (opera justitiae); and the fourth with extended arms grasped by God(?), beardless and unnimbed.

3.25 fol. 72ʳ Psalm 65:12: *Imposuisti homines super capita nostra. / Transivimus per ignem et aquam, / Et eduxisti nos in refrigerium.*

Within a quatrefoil mandorla, Abraham, bearded and nimbed, sits on the arc of heaven, feet on footstool, a group of souls clutched to bosom with left arm, extending right hand to a nimbed angel carrying soul in draped hands. Within mandorla is an inscription: "loc refrigerii qui est sin abrache."

3.26 fol. 73ᵛ Psalm 67:19: *Ascendisti in altum, cepisti captivitatem, / Accepisti dona in hominibus; / Etenim non credentes inhabitare Dominum Deum.*

Christ: Ascension: Disappearing type. Christ, standing in a mandorla, disappears into clouds; only his feet and hem of robe are visible. On either side of the upper margins, a nimbed angel holds an open roll. In the outer margin, one of the Apostles and the Virgin Mary, who holds the other end of the open roll; both look upwards. Below, two pairs of Apostles look upwards. In the inner margin, seven Apostles, some holding closed books, look upwards.

3.27 fol. 74ʳ Psalm 67:28: *Ibi Beniamin adolescentulus, in mentis excessu; / Principes Iuda, duces eorum; / Principes Zabulon, principes Nephthali.*

Benjamin, represented by the Apostle Paul, drypoint nimbus, with arms extended, holds an open roll. Above is the inscription: "paulu adholescente hic dicit eo quod esset de tribu beniamin."

3.28 fol. 78ᵛ Psalm 71:10: *Reges Tharsis et insulae munera offerent; / Reges Arabum et Saba dona adducent.*

Adoration of the Magi. A curtain draping an arch of a building encloses the Virgin Mary, veiled, seated, holding unnimbed Christ Child who extends his arms toward crowned, bearded Magus behind two Magi, one bearded and crowned and kissing the foot of the Christ Child, the other wearing Phrygian hat and holding vessel in draped hands (see Matt. 2:11).

3.29 fol. 80r

Psalm 72:24: *Tenuisti manum dexteram meam, / Et in voluntate tua deduxisti me, / Et cum gloria suscepisti me.*

God, bearded and unnimbed, bends down to grasp the extended wrist of the Psalmist, who holds a closed book and looks up.

3.30 fol. 81r

Psalm 73:13, 14, 16: (13) *Tu confirmasti in virtute tua mare; / Contribulasti capita draconum in aquis.* (14) *Tu confregisti capita draconis; / Dedisti eum escam populis Aethiopum.* (16) *Tuus est dies, et tua est nox; / Tu fabricatus es auroram et solem.*

God, bearded and unnimbed, treading on a coiled, interlaced serpent, holds two orbs (inscribed "dies" and "nox"?) representing day and night. Below, a figure with extended hands witnesses the event.

3.31 fol. 83v

Psalm 77:1: *Attendite, popule meus, legem meam; / Inclinate aurem vestram in verba oris mei.*

In the outer margin, Moses, bearded, with fiery emanations around his head, holds the Tables of the Law in his draped left hand. In the inner margin, Aaron, bearded, holding a closed book in his right hand, bears a shaggy serpent with extended tongue in his left hand (Exodus 34:29).

3.32 fol. 87v

Psalm 78:1–3: (1) *Deus, venerunt gentes in haereditatem tuam; / Polluerunt templum sanctum tuum; / Posuerunt Ierusalem in pomorum custodiam.* (2) *Posuerunt morticina servorum tuorum escas volatilibus caeli, / Carnes sanctorum tuorum bestiis terrae.* (3) *Effuderunt sanguinem eorum tanquam aquam in circuitu Ierusalem.*

Massacre of the Innocents. In the middle of the outer margin, King Herod, bearded and wearing a Phrygian hat, standing within a walled city with towers and barred gate, commands his soldiers to kill the male children of Bethlehem. In the upper left, a soldier aims a spear at a nude child upheld by the foot; another man tears a child apart. In the upper margin, an eagle flies with a human head in its beak and a severed hand in its claws; a sitting dog eats human legs. In the upper right, a soldier, with upraised sword in his right hand, grasps a nude child by the head, who is being held by a seated woman with flaming hair; name inscribed "Rachel" (Matthew 2:18). In the lower right, Saul, name inscribed "Saulus adolescens," sits on a bench with footstool, upraised sword in left hand, right hand indicating kneeling youth extending garments (Acts 7:57). Stoning of Stephen Protomartyr: in the lower left margin, a group of four Jews, inscribed "Sinagoga judeorum," one with stones in the skirt of his tunic, hurls stones across the folio to the genuflecting figure of St. Stephen wearing a tonsure; inscribed "Lapidatio Stephani" (Acts 7:58).

3.33 fol. 88r Psalm 78:10–11: (10) *Ne forte dicant in gentibus: Ubi est Deus eorum? / Et innotescat in nationibus coram oculis nostris, / Ultio sanguinis servorum tuorum qui effusus est.* (11) *Introeat in conspectu tuo gemitus compeditorum; / Secundum magnitudinem brachii tui posside filios mortificatorum.*

In the upper margin, the Trinity. An arc encloses a half figure of Christ, nimbed and beardless, with an upraised sword in his right hand and a shield with a boss in his left; in the center is a half figure of God, bearded and nimbed, with his right hand raised and his left hand raised above an open book; on the right is the nimbed Holy Dove; each figure is within a mandorla. In the left margin, the Hand of God emerges from a cloud above an upward flying bird, possibly representing the soul of Stephen Protomartyr (see fol. 87v).

3.34 fol. 88v Psalm 79:14: *Exterminavit eam aper de silva, / Et singularis ferus depastus est eam.*

In the lower outer margin, a wild boar with tusks appears within acanthus-like vines. Above is the inscription: "vineam tytum significat depredantem judaeam."

3.35 fol. 90v Psalm 82:14: *Deus meus, pone illos ut rotam, / Et sicut stipulam ante faciem venti.*

In the lower outer margin, a man topples backwards off a wheel with spokes, rim, and axel; a small circular schema in red is above.

3.36 fol. 92r Psalm 84:11: *Misericordia et veritas obviaverunt sibi; / Iustitia et pax osculatae sunt.*

Two veiled women, possibly the Virgin Mary and Elizabeth (Visitation) or personifications of Mercy and Truth or of Justice and Peace, cheeks touching, join hands.

3.37 fol. 93r Psalm 86:5: *Numquid Sion dicet: Homo et homo natus est in ea, / Et ipse fundavit eam Altissimus?*

Nativity of Christ: architectural setting (two towers, arch, and windows) encloses Joseph, left hand to face, extending right hand toward Christ Child who, lying in manger, raises right hand toward Virgin Mary, veiled, hands extended, beside ass and ox (Matt. 1:25; Luke 2:6–7).

3.38 fol. 95ʳ Psalm 88:21: *Inveni David, servum meum, / Oleo sancto meo unxi eum.*

David anointed: God, bearded and nimbed, or Samuel, pours oil from a horn over the head of David, half kneeling. The cloak embraces or surrounds David (I Kings 16:13).

3.39 fol. 98ʳ Psalm 90:13: *Super aspidem et basiliscum ambulabis, / Et conculcabis leonem et draconem.*

Christ treading on the beasts. Christ, nimbed and beardless, holds open book in left hand, transfixes dragon with lance with circular head or nimbus, held in right hand, and treads dragon and lion.

3.40 fol. 103ʳ Psalm 98:6–7: (6) *Moyses et Aaron in sacerdotibus eius, / Et Samuel inter eos qui invocant nomen eius; / Invocabant Dominum, et ipse exaudiebat eos;* (7) *In columna nubis loquebatur ad eos. / Custodiebant testimonia eius.*

God, bearded, nimbed, and half immersed in clouds, holds an inscribed open roll, which descends to Moses, Aaron, and Samuel who stand below. The inscription reads: "Ego sum ds Abraeham ds Isaac ds jacob. custodite legem meam et inimicus ero inimicis tuis."

3.41 fol. 107ᵛ Psalm 103:15, 18, 21, 23: (15) *Et vinum laetificet cor hominis; / Ut exhilaret faciem in oleo, / Et panis cor hominis confirmet.* (18) *Montes excelsi cervis, / Petra refugium herinaciis.* (21) *Catuli leonum rugientes ut rapiant, / Et quaerant a Deo escam sibi.* (23) *Exibit homo ad opus suum, / Et ad operationem suam usque ad vesperum.*

In the upper inner margin, a youth extends a knife toward a bearded man, holding to his lips a drinking horn decorated with an animal head, knife in left hand, behind draped table with claw feet, on which are loaf and vessel (v. 15). In the center, a horned stag attacks a coiled and interlaced serpent (v. 18). Below, two lions symmetrically posed look above (v. 21). In the lower corner, a man digs at the base of a plant with a spade (v. 23).

3.42 fol. 108ʳ Psalm 103:25–26. (25) *Hoc mare magnum et spatiosum manibus: / Illic reptilia quorum non est numerus, / Animalia pusilla cum magnis.* (26) *Illic naves pertransibunt; / Draco iste quem formasti ad illudendum ei.*

In the upper outer margin, three men, one holding an oar, are in a ship decorated with an animal head; in the water, a large fish (v. 25). Below are a horned dragon with wings and coiled tail, a rabbit, and an elephant with trunk, tusks, and clawed feet (v. 26).

3.43 fol. 109r Psalm 104:6, 37: (6) *Semen Abraham, servi eius; / Filii Iacob, electi eius. (37) Et eduxit eos cum argento et auro, / Et non erat in tribubus eorum infirmus.*

The Twelve Tribes of Israel are depicted, each labeled with name and attribute (see also fol. 109v). In the upper outer margin, Reuben, bearded and veiled, holds a mandrake in his right hand and an upraised sword in his left hand; Simeon holds a shield in his right hand and a spear in his left. In the middle, Levi, bearded, head draped, holds horned sacrificial animal behind Ark of the Covenant; Judah, bearded, foliate scepter in right hand, raises left to crown on head, behind lion. In the lower margin, Issachar, bearded, raises right hand behind ass; Zabulon, bearded, rows boat on water. All names inscribed.

3.44 fol. 109v Psalm 104:6, 37 continued.

The Twelve Tribes of Israel are depicted, each labeled with name and attribute (see also fol. 109r). In the upper outer margin, Naphtali, axe in left hand, grasps horn of stag with right hand; Gad, son of Jacob, armed with shield, stands behind lioness. In center, Joseph, armed with bow, stands behind a bull; Benjamin stands behind a wolf. Below, Dan stands behind a coiled serpent; Asher holds a vessel; all figures bearded; all names inscribed.

3.45 fol. 117r Initial *D / Dixit* (cut out of leaf) introduces Psalm 109.

3.46 fol. 118r Psalm 111:9: *Dispersit, dedit pauperibus. / Iustitia eius manet in saeculum saeculi. / Cornu eius exaltabitur in gloria.*

A king, seated, wearing conical hat or crown, extends loaf to bearded kneeling man, arms extended, sack hung over shoulder.

3.47 fol. 120v Psalm 115:13: *Calicem salutaris accipiam, / Et nomen Domini invocabo.*

Hand of God issues from cloud toward cup in draped hands of standing Psalmist.

3.48 fol. 168v *Oratio ad Patrem.* Christ, crossed pearled nimbus, beardless, right hand raised, closed book in draped left hand, seated, feet on footstool, in mandorla; inscribed "Maiestas Di Patris."

Oratio ad Filium. Agnus Dei: Lamb of God, crossed pearl nimbus, holds cross-staff and closed book, in medallion; inscribed "Agn Di omip."

3.49 fol. 169r *Oratio ad Spiritum Sanctum.* Within roundel is the Dove of the Holy Ghost, crossed pearled nimbus, inscribed "sps scs."

4. Paris Psalter (Paris: Bibliothèque Nationale MS lat. 8824)

Plates 4.1 to 4.11

4.1 fol. 1r

Psalm 1:3: *et erit tamquam lignum quod plantatum est secus decursus aquarum quod fructum suum dabit in tempore suo et folium eius decidet et omnia quaecumque fecerit prosperabuntur* (Roman version). Parallel Old English prose translation: "Him byð swa þam treowe þe byð aplantod neah wætera rynum."

A river personification holds a vase from which a stream flows before a tree with blossoms and fruit on its branches.

4.2 fol. 1v

Psalm 2:4: *qui habitat in caelis inridebit eos et Dominus subsannabit eos* (Roman version). Parallel English prose translation: "Hwæt forstent heora spræc, cwæð se witega, þeah hi swa cweðen? For þam se God þe on heofonum ys hig gehyspð, and Drihten hyg gescent."

Half figure of God, bearded and with cross as nimbus, holds cross-inscribed bannered lance emerging from clouds above heads of group of men in pit.

4.3 fol. 2r

Psalm 2:9: *reges eos in uirga ferrea et tamquam uas figuli confringes eos* (Roman version). Parallel Old English prose translation: "And ic gedo þæt þu heora wylst mid isernre gyrde, and hi miht swa eaðe abrecan swa se croccwyrhta mæg ænne croccan."

Beside two small trees, God, bearded and wearing cross as nimbus, closed book in draped left hand, breaks a potter's vessel with a long rod.

4.4 fol. 2v

Psalm 3:4: *tu autem Domine susceptor meus es gloria mea et exaltans caput meum* (Roman version). Parallel Old English prose translation: "Þa ongan ic slapan and slep, and eft aras; for ðam þe Drihten me awehte, and me upp arærde."

Bearded man kneels with extended hands, chin grasped by Hand of God issuing from clouds.

4.5 fol. 3r

Upper drawing. Psalm 4:2: *cum inuocarem te exaudisti me Deus iustitiae meae in tribulatione dilatasti me. miserere mihi Domine et exaudi orationem meam* (Roman version). Parallel Old English prose translation: "þonne ic cleopode to þe, þonne gehyrdest þu me, Drihten; for ðam þu eart se ðe me gerihtwisast, and on minum earfoðum and nearonessum ðu me gerymdest. Gemiltsa me, Drihten, and gehyr min gebed."

A man, walking with outstretched arms, looks up to the Hand of God.

4.6 fol. 3r Center drawing. Psalm 4:6: *sacrificate sacrificium iustitiae et sperate in Domino. multi dicunt quis ostendit nobis bona* (Roman version). Parallel Old English prose translation: "Offriað ge mid rihtwisnesse, and bringað þa Gode to lacum, and hopiað to Drihtne."

A man approaches a draped altar with a cup and a ram.

4.7 fol. 3r Lower drawing. Psalm 4:8: *a tempore frumenti uini et olei sui multiplicati sunt* (Roman version). Parallel Old English prose translation: "Þæt ys þæt þu sealdest blisse minre heortan, and þin folc gemicladest, and him sealdest geniht hwætes and wines and eles and ealra goda, þeah hi his ðe ne ðancien."

Two men, one with a draped head, carry a sack and a vessel.

4.8 fol. 3v Upper drawing. Psalm 5:5: *mane adstabo tibi et uidebo quoniam non uolens deus iniquitatem tu es* (Roman version). Parallel Old English prose translation: "Ic stande on ærmergen beforan ðe at gebede, and seo þe; þæt is þæt ic ongite þinne willan butan tweon, and eac þone wyrce; for ðam þu eart se ylca God þe nan unriht nelt."

Standing between two plants, the Psalmist, with hands extended, looks up to the Hand of God issuing from a cloud and holding a compass.

Lower drawing. Psalm 5:7: *odisti Domine omnes qui operantur iniquitatem perdes eos qui loquuntur mendacium* (Roman version). Parallel Old English prose translation: "Þu hatast ealle þa þe unriht wyrcað, and þæt ne forlætað, ne his ne hreowsiað; and þu fordest þa þe symle leasinga specað."

A fiery hell-mouth is filled with six human heads.

4.9 fol. 4r Psalm 5:7: *uirum sanguinum et dolosum abominabitur Dominus* (Roman version). Parallel Old English prose translation: "And þa manslagan and þa swicolan þu forsyhst."

Two men fighting. One man grasps the hair of his opponent and thrusts his spear; the other man, holding a shield, stabs his attacker in the thigh with a sword. This is the only case where the drawing appears in the Old English column.

4.10 fol. 5r Upper drawing. Psalm 7:3: *nequando rapiat ut leo animam meam dum non est qui redimat neque qui saluum faciat* (Roman version). Parallel Old English prose translation: "Þæt næfre mine fynd ne gripen mine sawlẹ swa swa leo; for þam ic nat ealles hwa me ahredde and gehæle, butan þu wylle."

A lion stands over a nude figure lying on the ground.

Lower drawing. Psalm 7:4: *Domine Deus meus si feci istud si est iniquitas in manibus meis* (Roman version). Parallel Old English prose translation: "Drihten, min God, gif ic to þisum þe me nu swencað þæs geearnod hæbbe þæt hi nu doð, oððe ænig unriht wið hi gedon hæbbe."

The bearded Psalmist, with extended hands, prays to the Hand of God issuing from a cloud.

4.11 fol. 6r Psalm 7:13–14: (13) *nisi conuertamini gladium suum uibrauit arcum suum tetendit et parauit illum.* (14) *et in ipso parauit uasa mortis sagittas suas ardentibus effecit* (Roman version).

Within a building, a man and a veiled woman are seated and embracing; from above a nude man with flaming hair emerges from the clouds shooting arrows from a bow at the couple.

According to Robert M. Harris ("The Marginal Drawings of the Bury St. Edmunds Pslater," diss. Princeton University, 1960, pp. 60–62), the drawing does not correspond to the sense of the Latin verses; instead, the artist used the parallel Old English prose translation as his inspiration. The Old English text is as follows: "And he bende his bogan, se is nu gearo to sceotanne; he teohað þæt he scyle sceotan þæt deaðes fæt, þæt synt þa unrihtwisan; he gedeð his flan fyrena þæt he mæge mid sceotan, and bærnan þa þe her byrnað on wrænnesse and on unðeawum." The text is from James W. Bright and Robert L. Ramsay, eds., *Liber Psalmorum: The West-Saxon Psalms* (Boston: D.C. Heath, 1907), p. 12. An expanded version of Harris's interpretation was published as "An Illustration in an Anglo-Saxon Psalter in Paris," *Journal of the Warburg and Courtauld Institutes* 26 (1963), 255–63.

5. Boulogne Gospels (Boulogne-sur-Mer: Bibliothèque Municipale MS. 11)

Plates 5.1 to 5.28

5.1 fol. 2 Canon Table: beneath a row of rectangular lintels supported on columns, four nimbed angels hold (from left to right) an open roll; a closed book; a pen and a closed book; a pen and a closed book.

5.2 fol. 2v Canon Table: within an arcade of four small arches supported on columns are four Evangelist symbols (winged man with fillet, winged lion, winged ox, winged eagle), each with six wings, a nimbus, and a book.

5.3 fol. 3^r Canon Table: beneath a lintel supported on columns, four bearded men with nimbi and wings (Evangelists?) hold an open roll and pen; two books (one open, one closed); an open book; and an open book and a pen.

5.4 fol. 3^v Canon Table: in the spaces above three round arches supported on four columns, three angels, all nimbed, hold an open roll; two closed books; and an open roll.

5.5 fol. 4^r Canon Table: within an arcade of two pointed and one round arch are three Evangelist symbols (winged and nimbed man with open roll, winged and nimbed lion with open roll, winged and nimbed ox with book). Perching on the capitals of the arcades are a peacock and a phoenix(?). At the foot of the right column, a man shoots an arrow with a bow at the phoenix. At the foot of the left column is a plant.

5.6 fol. 4^v Canon Table: A large round arch is supported by an arcade of three smaller arches (two pointed and one round). At the upper right spandrel, a beardless male plays a harp; on the upper left spandrel, a male plays a bowed lyre. At the foot of the left column, a man, looking upwards, blows a trumpet; at the base of the right column, a lion runs upwards.

5.7 fol. 5^r Canon Table: Two large intersecting round arches crown two smaller round and one pointed arch, all supported on four columns with capitals and bases. Above is a cluster of buildings with tiled roofs, round and square windows, arched doorway; one building is surmounted by a cross.

5.8 fol. 5^v Canon Table: Within three round arches supported on a lintel, three angels hold two closed books; a closed book and pen; and a closed book; at the spandrels are two towers with tiled roofs and windows.

5.9 fol. 6^r Canon Table: At the spandrels of the intersecting round arches, two beardless men in long robes blow trumpets; wavy lines indicate clouds or sky. Within the four main columns are foliated medallions.

5.10 fol. 6^v Canon Table: Above a series of three intersecting round arches, supported on five columns, four angels hold an open roll; a closed book; a closed book; and an open roll. At the spandrels are two buildings with tiled roofs and windows.

5.11 fol. 7^r Canon Table: Within an arcade of four round arches, Christ, bearded and nimbed, hands raised, lower legs concealed by clouds, sits on arc in mandorla, flanked by four nimbed, beardless Evangelists, two holding open rolls, two holding closed books.

5.12 fol. 7^v Canon Table: Within the tympanum of a large round arch, two men in short tunics shoot arrows with bows at a lion and a stag with antlers in the spandrels; the stag is wounded in the side by one of the arrows.

5.13 fol. 8r Canon Table: Acanthus foliage is between the intersections of two round arches and plant forms (fronds) in the spandrels.

5.14 fol. 8v Canon Table: In the tympanum of a round arch flanked by two intersecting pointed arches is the Hand of God(?) with outstretched fingers and, in the spandrels, two long-legged, long-necked birds preening their wings with long beaks.

5.15 fol. 9r Canon Table: Two round and one pointed arch supported on five columns with central foliage and plant forms in the spandrels.

5.16 fol. 9v Canon Table: A trefoil arch, with large leafy forms, supported on two outer columns, crowns an arcade comprised of two pointed and two round arches on five columns. Within the tympanum, the Agnus Dei (Lamb of God), with cross nimbus, holds a decorated, closed book with its forefeet.

5.17 fol. 10r Christ in Mandorla. Christ, bearded, cross-nimbed, crowned, open book in left hand inscribed "Liber Vitae," feet on globe inscribed "Terra (autem) scabellum pe(dum meorum)" (see Isaiah 66:1), sits on arc and globe within mandorla (inscribed with Greek letters Alpha and Omega) enclosed in circle with sun, moon, and stars, inscribed "(Numquid non) caelum et terram ego impleo?" (see Jeremiah 23:24), representing the cosmos.

5.18 fol. 10v St. Matthew the Evangelist. Matthew, bearded, nimbed, holding pen and knife, sits on bench before draped lectern, writing in open book; architectural setting and inscription. In the upper right are the Ancestors of Christ. David, bearded, name inscribed, crowned, scepter in right hand, sits on bench beside Abraham, bearded, name inscribed, nimbed, holding palm frond. In the lower right are Isaac, name inscribed, and Jacob, name inscribed, both nimbed and bearded, and holding palm fronds and seated on cushioned bench (Matthew 1:1–2). The Winchester-style frame is composed of a double gold band filled with foliage and four foliated corner bosses.

5.19 fol. 11r Ancestors of Christ: Half figures of twenty-four ancestors, some wearing crowns, some holding scepters, palm fronds, and closed books; all bearded; all names inscribed. The rectangular frame is composed of two plain bands.

5.20 fol. 11v Above, Ancestors of Christ. Twelve ancestors are in two rows under arcades: one wears crown and holds scepter; some hold palm fronds; names inscribed. On the lower left is the Annunciation to the Virgin Mary. Within an architectural setting, Gabriel, nimbed and winged, holding scepter, addresses the Virgin Mary, nimbed and veiled, seated on cushioned bench beside draped lectern with open book under draped curtains (see Luke 1:26–38). To the right is the Visitation: the Virgin Mary and Elizabeth, both nimbed and veiled, stand in close embrace; architectural setting; scene inscriptions (see Luke 1:40–56). The rectangular frame is composed of two plain bands.

5.21 fol. 12r In the upper left is the Annunciation to the Shepherds: two shepherds holding staffs are addressed by a nimbed and winged angel holding scepter; inscribed. In the middle and lower left is the Nativity of Christ: the Virgin Mary, nimbed and veiled, lies on bed against pillow arranged by midwife; Joseph, bearded and nimbed, feet on footstool, sits on cushioned bench. In the lower left, Joseph, bearded and nimbed, sits looking at Christ Child, cross-nimbed, in swaddling clothes, lying in crib before ox and ass in architectural setting. In the upper right are half figures of five nimbed angels, three wearing fillets, in arc of heaven above initial *L* / *Liber generationis* (beginning text of Matthew) (Matt. 1:25; Luke 2:6–7). The rectangular frame is composed of two plain bands.

5.22 fol. 55v St. Mark the Evangelist with symbol. Mark, bearded and nimbed, biting fingers of left hand, sits on cushioned, architectural bench, writing in open book on draped lectern. On the upper right, the lion, winged and nimbed, holds open book; building with curtained archway; scene inscription. The Winchester-style frame is composed of plain panelled enclosures with four square corner bosses with foliage.

5.23 fol. 56r Initial page *I* / *Initium* with Isaiah's Prophecy. Within the lunette of the architectural frame flanked by two birds, Christ, bearded and cross-nimbed, open book in left hand, right hand raised, sits on arc within mandorla supported by two nimbed angels. In the middle and lower left, Mark, bearded and nimbed, sits on cushioned, architectural bench, pen in right hand, open roll inscribed with Mark 1:3 draped over shoulder and across lap, raised left hand holding end of open roll inscribed with Isa. 40:3 held by Isaiah, bearded and nimbed, seated on cushioned bench, feet on footstool, writing on roll and pointing toward Christ. Initial *I* ends in two beast-heads.

5.24 fol. 61v Within an architectural setting, St. Luke the Evangelist, bearded and nimbed, sits on cushioned, architectural bench between draped curtains, holding open book in left hand, dipping pen in inkwell with the right; a draped altar is within an open archway. The frame is composed of plain panels with four triangular rosettes on the corners.

5.25 fol. 62r Initial page *Q* / *Quo* with the Annunciation to Zacharias. Standing in front of a building next to a draped altar, Zacharias, bearded, is addressed by a standing angel, nimbed, holding a scepter (Luke 1:11). The frame is composed of two bands filled with foliage.

5.26 fol. 104v Initial *B* composed of standing male, bearded and wearing Phrygian hat, holding double-headed, winged serpent by the tail.

5.27 fol. 107r St. John the Evangelist with symbol. Holy Dove on the shoulder of John, who is bearded and nimbed, seated on cushioned bench between draped curtains, left hand raised to face, writing with a pen in an open book on draped lectern; nimbed eagle holds open book inscribed with John 1:1; architectural setting with curtains. The frame is composed of three plain bands.

5.28 fol. 107v Initial page *In / In Principio* with Christ, bearded and nimbed, left hand holding closed book, right hand raised, seated on arc, flanked by two adoring angels, nimbed, with raised hands; Alpha and Omega; scene inscription. The frame is composed of two plain bands.

6. Arenberg Gospels (New York: Pierpont Morgan Library M. 869)

Plates 6.1 to 6.17

6.1 fol. 9v Crucifixion of Christ. Christ, bearded and cross-nimbed, head inclined, wears long loincloth, four nails, blood from wounds in feet issuing into chalice on mound on bottom pedestal of the Cross. Two nimbed angels, wearing fillets, with draped hands flank the Hand of God issuing from the cloudy arc of heaven on the upper arm of the Cross. On the lower left, the Virgin Mary, nimbed and veiled, stands holding a fold of her mantle in her right hand and points to Christ with her left hand. On the lower right, Evangelist John, beardless and nimbed, stands holding a closed book in his left hand and points to Christ with his right. According to Jane E. Rosenthal ("The Historiated Canon Tables of the Arenberg Gospels," diss. Columbia University, 1974, pp. 88–94) the tortured and twisted body of Christ, the presence of Mary and Evangelist John as witnesses, the hovering angels, the chalice on the raised mound of Golgotha, and the cross with its broad arms and architectonic terminals all support an interpretation of the cross as the *ara crucis* or cross as altar.

6.2 fol. 10r Canon Table: Archangel (Michael?), nimbed, wearing fillet, holds crossed sticks over his head; on either side, two nimbed angels, wearing fillets, hold open rolls and palm fronds, one in each hand. According to Rosenthal (pp. 169–71) the angelic triad is proclaiming the future triumph of the cross; the central figure, the archangel Michael, holds two branches crossed over his head in a triumphal gesture. The branches, drawn in brown ink, are a prefiguration of the cross.

6.3 fol. 10v Canon Table: Archangel (Gabriel?), nimbed, wearing fillet, holds in draped right hand a wafer or sphere with inscribed cross and three dots; on either side is a nimbed angel, wearing fillet: the one on the left holds a closed book, the other a palm frond. According to Rosenthal (pp. 173–78) the central figure represents the archangel Gabriel prophesying Christ's sovereignty over the world; the inscribed disk symbolizes the earth and its tetradic structure.

6.4 fol. 11^r Canon Table: Virgin Mary and Child adored by archangels. Virgin Mary, nimbed and veiled, standing and holding palm frond, holds on left arm the Christ Child, sitting in profile, facing left, a small cross behind his head. Frame enclosing Virgin is in the shape of an Alpha. On either side appears an adoring Archangel (Michael and Gabriel?), each nimbed, wearing fillet, and extending draped hands. Rosenthal (pp. 200–18) interprets the scene as an innovative depiction of the Incarnation of Christ. Novel elements include the Alpha frame, the Virgin bearing the Child's palm of victory, the absence of the Child's nimbus, his strict profile pose, and the small cross behind his head.

6.5 fol. 11^v Canon Table: Christ in Mandorla. Christ, beardless and cross-nimbed, wearing fillet, holds both a cross-inscribed disk or sphere and an open book. On the left, the Virgin Mary, nimbed and veiled, holding a closed book, stands with the Holy Dove perched on her head. On the right is a reclining horned ram. On either side is a nimbed angel, wearing fillet: one holds a closed book, the other a palm frond. The mandorla is in the shape of an Omega. Unusual elements, according to Rosenthal, are: the mandorla in the shape of an Omega (p. 207); Christ as the resurrected Lord enthroned holding a symbol of his earthly dominion (p. 234); the frontal bird sitting on the Virgin's head (p. 240); and the adult horned ram, instead of the lamb, as a symbol of the humanity of the crucified Christ (p. 244).

6.6 fol. 12^r Canon Table: Christ flanked by Peter and Paul. Christ, beardless and cross-nimbed, holds a closed book decorated with four dots and a cross-surmounted staff. On the left, Peter, nimbed and tonsured, stands holding a closed book with hand raised. On the right, Paul, bearded and nimbed, stands holding a closed book. The drawing, according to Rosenthal, symbolizes the apostolic foundation of the Church under Christ (p. 247). Christ, holding a book (the New Law) and cross-scepter (source of his power and authority), appears in the celestial realm to Peter and Paul, the leaders of the earthly Church.

6.7 fol. 12^v Canon Table: Christ flanked by two saints. Christ, beardless and cross-nimbed, holds an open book in right hand while left hand holds paten with Agnus Dei holding closed book, is flanked by two nimbed saints, possibly Apostles or wingless angels, one with open roll, the other with a closed book. According to Rosenthal (p. 252) the drawing symbolizes the institution of the Church, specifically the ritual of the mass with Christ officiating as High Priest. Christ is offering his own sacrifice symbolized by the horned ram (Christ's historical body) on a paten (pp. 260–61).

6.8 fol. 13^r Canon Table: Christ flanked by seraphs. Christ, beardless and cross-nimbed, three-quarter standing figure turning to left, holds cross-staff and open book, flanked by either nimbed seraphim or cherubim, wearing fillets, with eyes in wings. Rosenthal (p. 163) identifies the scene as the Second Coming of Christ. Christ is depicted "as both the triumphant ruler of the universe and the victorious Redeemer, who comes from His heavenly throne, bearing the book of the law by which all shall be judged, to perform the final act in the drama of salvation" (p. 268).

6.9 fol. 13ᵛ Canon Table: Christ treading on beasts. Christ, beardless and cross-nimbed, open book in right hand, with cross-lance in left hand piercing the basilisk, treads on both the lion and basilisk. He is flanked by two nimbed angels, wearing fillets, one with hands raised, the other holding open roll. According to Rosenthal (pp. 268–69) the drawing is a symbolic representation of the Last Judgment. To render Christ's final victory over evil, the artist drew the treading on the beasts from Psalm 90:13. In an interpretative *tour de force*, Rosenthal (p. 277) convincingly argues that the entire grouping of figures is arranged to form the Greek letter Omega (ω), which symbolizes the last things or judgment.

6.10 fol. 17ᵛ St. Matthew the Evangelist with symbol. Within the trapezoidal roof gable of a complex two-story building, a winged man, nimbed, wearing fillet, holds an open roll; on either side is a slender tower with windows. Below, within the enframing architecture—composed of two columns with foliate capitals and two buildings with tiled roofs and two portals, one draped and the other with a staircase leading up to an open window—Matthew, beardless and nimbed, pen in right hand, left hand on open book on draped lectern, sits on a cushioned bench with feet on draped footstool. Inscription in Latin from Caelius Sedulius, *Carmen Paschale*, Bk. I, line 355: "Hoc Matthaeus agens, hominem generaliter implet" (PL 19, col. 195). Jane E. Rosenthal asserts that the architecture represents Ecclesia or the Church, symbolizing the acceptance of Matthew's gospel within the Church; see her "The Unique Architectural Settings of the Arenberg Evangelists," *Studien zur mittelalterlichen Kunst 800–1250. Festschrift für Florentine Mütherich zum 70 Geburtstag* (Munich, 1985), pp. 145–56.

6.11 fol. 18ʳ Initial page *L* / *Liber generationis* (beginning of Matthew).

6.12 fol. 57ᵛ St. Mark the Evangelist with symbol. Within the trefoil arch of a complex, multi-storied structure, a winged lion, nimbed, holds a closed book in its forepaws. Sitting within a space crowned by a round arch and enframed by two slender columns on stepped bases, Mark, beardless, nimbed, sitting on a cushioned and draped faldstool, feet on a draped footrest, holds a book open on a draped lectern and writes in it with a pen. The outer borders consist of two multi-storied towers with tiled roofs and windows; the structure on the lower left has a draped portal and open door with iron hinges. Inscription in Latin from Caelius Sedulius, *Carmen Paschale*, Bk. I, line 356: "Marcus ut alta fremit vox per deserta leonis" (PL 19, col. 195).

6.13 fol. 58ʳ Initial page *I* / *Initium* (beginning of Mark).

6.14 fol. 83ᵛ St. Luke the Evangelist with symbol. Within the triangular gable supported on short columns, a winged, horned ox holds in its jaws and forepaw one end of an open roll while the other end descends to the picture space below. Within the enframing architecture, composed of multi-storied buildings with tiled roofs, square and round towers, stepped bases, and a draped doorway, Luke, beardless and nimbed, sits on a cushioned bench with his feet on an architectural footstool, pen in raised right hand, left hand on open book on draped lectern. Inscription in Latin from Caelius Sedulius, *Carmen Paschale*, Bk. I, line 357: "Jura sacerdotis Lucas tenet ore juvenci" (PL 19, col. 195).

6.15 fol. 84ʳ Initial page *Q* / *Q(uonia)m quidem multi* (beginning of Luke).

6.16 fol. 126ᵛ St. John the Evangelist with symbol. Within a medallion framed in leaves and surmounted by a building, a winged eagle, nimbed, holds a closed roll in its claws. Below, the Hand of God issues from clouds above John, bearded, nimbed, seated (but with no chair visible), feet on draped footstool, pen in right hand, left hand holding book open on draped lectern, turning and looking upwards to the Hand of God. The spandrels of the three-sided arch, supported on thick columns with foliate capitals and stepped bases, contain towers, tiled roofs, cupolas, and partially-open doors. Inscription in Latin from Caelius Sedulius, *Carmen Paschale*, Bk. I, line 358: "More volans aquilae, verbo petit astra Joannes" (PL 19, col. 195). According to Jane E. Rosenthal, "the medallion encircling the eagle, which is framed in leaves bound at the top like a wreath, transforms the beast of John into a symbol of Christ's victorious ascension" ("The Unique Architectural Settings," p. 152).

6.17 fol. 127ʳ Initial page *In* / *In principio* (beginning of John).

7. Trinity Gospels (Cambridge: Trinity College MS B. 10. 4)

Plates 7.1 to 7.24

7.1 fol. 9ʳ Canon Table: within the tympana of three round arches supported on five columns with acanthus bases and capitals are dragons and acanthus foliage; in the spandrels, two peacocks.

7.2 fol. 9ᵛ Canon Table: within the tympana of two round and one pointed arches supported on five columns with acanthus bases and capitals are two winged griffins and acanthus foliage; in the spandrels, two dragons and foliage.

7.3 fol. 10^r Canon Table: within the tympana of two round and one pointed arches supported on five columns with acanthus bases and capitals are two winged griffins and acanthus foliage; in the spandrels two dragons nibble foliage.

7.4 fol. 10^v Canon Table: within the tympanum of a triangular arch supported on four columns with acanthus bases and capitals, an angel, nimbed, wearing fillet, holds a scepter and open roll; on the left of the angel is a small building with tiled roof, tower, and side aisles (Ecclesia?). In the spandrels are two square towers with tiled roofs, windows, and foliate crosses. At the apex of the triangular arch, a mask-head sprouts foliage.

7.5 fol. 11^r Canon Table: within the tympanum of a triangular arch supported on four columns with acanthus bases and capitals, an angel, nimbed, wearing fillet, holds a scepter and disk (orb?); on the right of the angel is a small building with tiled roof, windows, and side aisles (Ecclesia?). In the spandrels are two buildings with tiled roofs, windows, and crosses, and projecting foliage. At the apex of the triangular arch, a mask-head sprouts foliage.

7.6 fol. 11^v Canon Table: within the tympanum of a round arch supported on four columns with acanthus bases and capitals, male figure (Evangelist Mark?), nimbed, beardless, and tonsured, wears a chasuble and holds an open roll; on either side is a building with tiled roof, towers, and windows. In the spandrels are two lions (symbols of Mark?) and projecting foliage.

7.7 fol. 12^r Canon Table: within the tympanum of a round arch supported on four columns with acanthus bases and capitals, male figure (Evangelist Mark?), nimbed, beardless, and tonsured, wears a chasuble and holds a closed book; on either side is a building with tiled roof, towers, and windows. In the spandrels are two lions (symbols of Mark?) and projecting foliage.

7.8 fol. 12^v Canon Table: within the tympana of two round intersecting arches supported on four columns with acanthus bases and capitals, three female figures, nimbed and veiled, hold gold books (one closed, two open) and blue flowers; perhaps Virgin Mary and two virgin saints. In the spandrels are two eagles (symbols of John?) and projecting foliage.

7.9 fol. 13^r Canon Table: within the tympana of two round intersecting arches supported on four columns with acanthus bases and capitals, Christ, bearded and cross-nimbed, holding closed book and blessing, flanked by two angels, nimbed, wearing fillets, holding scepters and disks (orbs?). The Greek letters Alpha and Omega flank Christ. On either side is an eagle (symbol of John?) and projecting foliage.

7.10 fol. 13^{v} Canon Table: within the tympana of four round arches supported on five columns with acanthus bases and capitals, two birds (eagles?) and two lions. In the spandrels, acanthus foliage.

7.11 fol. 14^{r} Canon Table: within the tympana of four round arches supported on five columns with acanthus bases and capitals, two birds (eagles?) and two lions. In the spandrels, acanthus foliage.

7.12 fol. 14^{v} Canon Table: within the tympanum of a trefoil arch supported on triangular and round arches are two lions. In the corner foliage are a bird (eagle?) and a griffin. An unusual feature is the addition of two horizontal bars to the three columns on the lower right; the composition forms the cross of the Crucifixion. This is confirmed by the listing of "Lucas xxiii" in the column under the left arm of the cross.

7.13 fol. 15^{r} Canon Table: within the tympanum of a trefoil arch supported on triangular and round arches are two lions. In the corner foliage are a griffin(?) and a bird.

7.14 fol. 15^{v} Canon Table: within the tympana of two round arches supported on five columns are Matthew and Mark symbols. On the left, a winged man, nimbed, holds a gold, closed, cross-inscribed book with draped hands. On the right, a winged lion, nimbed, holds a closed, cross-inscribed book in forepaws. In the spandrels, animals nibble acanthus foliage.

7.15 fol. 16^{r} Canon Table: within the tympana of two round arches supported on five columns are Luke and John symbols. On the left, a winged ox, nimbed, holds a closed, cross-inscribed book in its forefeet. On the right, a winged eagle, nimbed, holds a closed gold book in its feet. In the spandrels, animals nibble acanthus foliage.

7.16 fol. 16^{v} Christ in Mandorla. Within a columned arcade decorated with plant rolls and acanthus foliage, Christ, bearded, nimbed, and crowned, cross-inscribed closed book in left hand, right hand blessing, feet on footstool, sits on cushion in mandorla.

7.17 fol. 17^{v} St. Matthew the Evangelist with symbol. Four roundels are in frame, each with bust of nimbed Apostle, three bearded and holding closed books; at top Peter, tonsured, with key and closed book. Within frame is a half figure of winged man, nimbed, wearing fillet, holding open roll. Below, Matthew, beardless, nimbed, wearing fillet, dips pen into inkwell and holds open book, feet on footstool. The Winchester-style frame is composed of two bands filled with foliage and four corner rosettes.

7.18 fol. 18r Initial page *L / Liber generationis* (beginning of Matthew). The Winchester-style frame, composed of two bands filled with foliage and four corner rosettes, has four inset roundels containing bust figures of saints and Apostles; at the top, a woman, nimbed and veiled, holds a flower and a closed book; at the sides and bottom, three nimbed and bearded men hold closed books and rolls. The letter L is a Franco-Saxon type with animal-headed interlace terminals, acanthus panels, and a round boss.

7.19 fol. 59v St. Mark the Evangelist with symbol. Frame is Winchester style with four quatrefoils, containing standing figures of nimbed saints, two with pearled nimbi, three holding closed books, one with flower, one with palm frond. Within the frame is half-figure of lion-headed symbol with human body, pearled nimbus, holding open roll in human hands. Below, Mark, beardless, pearled nimbus, sits on high-backed architectural chair, right hand dipping pen into inkwell on cushion, left hand on open book on draped lectern.

7.20 fol. 60r Initial page *I / Initium Evangelii* (beginning of Mark). The shaft of the initial is inhabited by two lions, a dragon, and a bird (eagle?), who bite the frame of the letter. In the Winchester-style frame are four quatrefoils, each with a half figure of a nimbed saint, three holding rolls, one with a closed book.

7.21 fol. 89v St. Luke the Evangelist with symbol. Within the Winchester-style frame, the half figure of a winged and nimbed ox with a human body holds an open roll with human hands. Below, Luke, beardless and nimbed, sits on a cushioned chair, writing with a pen in an inscribed open book on a draped lectern.

7.22 fol. 90r Initial page *Q / Quoniam quidem multi conati* (beginning of Luke). The letter is composed of beast-filled panels, a mask head, and a large dragon forming the tail. The Winchester-style frame is composed of two bands filled with foliage.

7.23 fol. 132v St. John the Evangelist with symbol (unfinished). Within the Winchester-style frame, the half figure of an eagle-headed symbol with human body holds an open roll. Below, John, nimbed, fillet on head, holds a pen and open book inscribed with John 1:1. Lozenges in frame contain half figures of angels with closed books, some with scepters.

7.24 fol. 133r Initial page *In / In principio* (beginning of John). The shaft of the initial is inhabited by birds, lions, and dragons. The Winchester-style frame has four lozenges, containing standing figures of nimbed angels. The decoration is unfinished.

8. Eadui Codex (Hannover: Kestner-Museum WM XXIa, 36)

Plates 8.1 to 8.21

8.1	fol. 9^v	Canon Table: in the tympanum of the arch supported by columns, the Hand of God, issuing from a cloudy arc, holds a compass and scales; large leafy ornaments in the spandrels.
8.2	fol. 10^r	Canon Table: in the tympanum of the arch supported by columns, Christ, bearded, wearing fillet, nails(?) beside head or cross as nimbus; large leafy ornaments in the spandrels.
8.3	fol. 10^v	Canon Table: in the tympana of three intersecting round arches, large leafy foliage.
8.4	fol. 11^r	Canon Table: in the tympana of three intersecting round arches, three Evangelist symbols: Matthew (man), Luke (ox), and Mark (lion); large leafy ornaments in the spandrels.
8.5	fol. 11^v	Canon Table: in the tympana of three decorated round arches, three Evangelist symbols: Mark (lion), Luke (ox), and Matthew (man); large leafy ornaments in the spandrels.
8.6	fol. 12^r	Canon Table: in the tympana of three round arches, three Evangelist symbols: Mark (lion), Luke (ox), and Matthew (man); in the spandrels, dog heads spitting foliage.
8.7	fol. 12^v	Canon Table: in the tympana of two round and one pointed arches, three Evangelist symbols: Matthew (man), Mark (lion), and Luke (ox); in the spandrels, two dog heads.
8.8	fol. 13^r	Canon Table: in the tympana of two round and one pointed arches, three Evangelist symbols: Matthew (man), Mark (lion), and Luke (ox); in the spandrels, two dog heads.
8.9	fol. 13^v	Canon Table: in the tympana of two round arches, two Evangelist symbols: Luke (ox) and Matthew (man); in the spandrels, two dog heads biting roosters.
8.10	fol. 14^r	Canon Table: in the tympana of two arches, two Evangelist symbols: Luke (ox) and Matthew (man); in the spandrels, two eagle heads (symbols of John?) biting interlace knotwork.
8.11	fol. 14^v	Canon Table: in the tympana of two pointed arches and one round arch, three Evangelist symbols: Matthew (man), John (eagle), and Luke (ox); in the spandrels, leafy ornaments.
8.12	fol. 15^r	Canon Table: in the tympana of two pointed arches and one round arch, three Evangelist symbols: John (eagle), Matthew (man), and a

second human head (Matthew?); in the spandrels, leafy ornaments.

8.13 fol. 15v Canon Table: in the tympana of two round arches, leafy ornament or clouds(?); in the spandrels, acanthus foliage.

8.14 fol. 16r Canon Table: in the tympana of two round arches, leafy ornament or clouds(?); in the spandrels, acanthus foliage.

8.15 fol. 17v St. Matthew the Evangelist. Matthew, nimbed, bearded, holding pen above inkwell in right hand, and knife beside open book in left hand, is seated frontally on cushioned chair with footstool; Winchester frame is composed of leaf ornaments in the four corners, acanthus foliage projecting from the sides, and intersecting bands. The *incipit* page for Matthew is missing.

8.16 fol. 65v St. Mark the Evangelist. Mark, nimbed, bearded, sits on a high-backed, cushioned chair with footstool, holding knife in right hand, pen in left hand over an open book on a draped lectern with claw-foot; frame is composed of intersecting bands, acanthus foliage projecting from the sides, and plain corners.

8.17 fol. 66r Initial page *I* / *Initium* (beginning of Mark).

8.18 fol. 96v St. Luke the Evangelist. Luke, nimbed, bearded, sits in three-quarter view on cushioned chair with footstool, writing with a pen in an open book; frame is composed of intersecting bands, acanthus foliage projecting from the sides, four circular rosettes, and four pairs of dog heads biting foliage on the corners.

8.19 fol. 97r Initial page *Q* / *Quoniam* (beginning of Luke).

8.20 fol. 147v St. John the Evangelist. John, nimbed, bearded, sits on a cushioned bench with footstool, inkwell above left shoulder, holding pen, knife, and long roll inscribed with John 1:1 "In principio erat verbum et verbum erat apud D(eu)m. Et D(eu)s erat verbu(m). h(oc) erat in p(ri)ncipio." He tramples the head of Arius the Heretic, name inscribed "Arrius," holding roll inscribed "Erat tempus quando nonerat." Frame is composed of intersecting bands, acanthus foliage projecting from the sides, and four corner foliated rosettes.

8.21 fol. 148r Initial page *In* / *In principio* (beginning of John).

9. Gospel Book (Cambridge: Pembroke College MS 301)

Plates 9.1 to 9.23

9.1 fol. 1v Canon Table: within the tympana of the intersecting round and pointed arches supported by five columns, the Agnus Dei, nimbed with a cross-staff, and the four Evangelist symbols (ox, angel, eagle, lion), all nimbed and holding closed books. At either side of the spandrels, leafy acanthus foliage.

9.2 fol. 2r Canon Table: within the uppermost tympanum of three round arches supported by five columns, Christ, bearded, cross-nimbed, wearing fillet, standing within a mandorla, holds a closed book in his left hand and blesses with his right. Below are half figures of two angels, nimbed and wearing fillets. The frame contains four corner rosettes with foliage and two roundels with interlace.

9.3 fol. 2v Canon Table: within the uppermost tympanum of three round arches supported by five columns, the Virgin Mary, nimbed and veiled, standing in a mandorla, holds a closed book and a scepter. Below are half figures of two female saints, nimbed and veiled, one holding a closed book, the other a small cross. The frame contains four corner rosettes and two roundels with interlace.

9.4 fol. 3r Canon Table: within the triangular pediment supported by a triple arcade on columns, the half figure of St. Michael, nimbed and beardless, holds a rod or scepter and a pair of scales. On either side is a building with tiled roof, tower, and windows. In the spandrels, leafy acanthus ornament.

9.5 fol. 3v Canon Table: within the triangular pediment supported by a triple arcade on columns, a nimbed angel holds a scepter or rod and blows a long horn. On either side is a building with tiled roof, tower, and windows. In the spandrels, leafy acanthus ornament.

9.6 fol. 4r Canon Table: at the intersection of two overlapping triangular arches supported on four columns, a bust figure of the Apostle Peter, beardless, nimbed, and tonsured, holds a large key and blesses. On either side, a standing Apostle, nimbed, beardless, and barefoot, holds an open roll and a rod or scepter. The columns contain four roundels filled with cruciform designs. On the lower corners two mask-heads bite foliage.

9.7 fol. 4v Canon Table: at the intersection of two overlapping triangular arches supported on four columns, a bust figure of the Apostle Paul, bearded and nimbed, holds and points to a closed book. On either side is an Apostle, beardless, nimbed, and barefoot: the one on the left holds a closed book and blesses; the one on the right holds in draped hands a gold disk with two blue circles. The columns contain five roundels filled with cruciform designs; the bases of two columns have Alphas(?). On the lower corners two mask-heads bite foliage.

9.8 fol. 5r Canon Table: within the openings of three round arches supported on four columns with acanthus bases, three Apostles. On the left, a bearded Apostle holds a large blue cross and closed book; in center, a beardless Apostle holds a palm frond or trefoil-headed scepter and a closed book; on the right, a bearded Apostle holds a closed book; all are barefoot and nimbed. The columns contain four roundels filled with cruciform designs, rosettes, and interlace.

9.9 fol. 5ᵛ Canon Table: within the openings of three round arches supported on four columns with acanthus bases, three Apostles. On the left, a beardless Apostle holds a hand-cross and closed book; in center, a bearded Apostle holds in draped hand a closed book; on the right, a beardless Apostle holds a closed book and trefoil-headed scepter; all are barefoot and nimbed. The columns contain four roundels filled with cruciform designs and interlace.

9.10 fol. 6ʳ Canon Table: within the tympana of three intersecting round arches supported on five columns are two dragons with protruding tongues and two male saints, nimbed, beardless, and holding closed books. On the lower corners are two mask-heads.

9.11 fol. 6ᵛ Canon Table: within the tympana of three intersecting round arches supported on five columns are two lions and two beardless, nimbed saints holding rods. On the lower corners are two mask-heads.

9.12 fol. 7ʳ Canon Table: within the tympanum of a round arch with two large rosettes, a beardless, nimbed saint points to a closed book. At the bases of three columns are three pairs of adorsed lions with protruding tongues.

9.13 fol. 7ᵛ Canon Table: within the tympanum of a round arch with two large rosettes, a beardless, nimbed saint holds a closed book. At the bases of three columns are three pairs of adorsed lions with protruding tongues.

9.14 fol. 8ʳ Canon Table: within the tympana of two round arches supported on five columns are two angels, one holding open roll, the other a closed book. Mask-heads form the capitals of three columns.

9.15 fol. 8ᵛ Canon Table: within the tympana of two arches supported on five columns are two angels, one holding a bowl with five circular objects, the other standing with hands raised. Mask-heads form the capitals of three columns.

9.16 fol. 10ᵛ St. Matthew the Evangelist with symbol. Matthew, bearded, with pearled nimbus and wearing fillet, pen in right hand, holds open book on lectern supported in mouth of bird perched in foliage, and sits between draped curtains on cushioned throne, feet on decorated footstool. Above is a medallion enclosing symbol (winged man), pearled nimbus, flying down, holding open roll. In sides of frame are two lozenges, each enclosing half figure of nimbed saint holding closed book, one also holds cross-staff. Frame has panels with acanthus friezes and corner medallions with acanthus rosettes.

9.17 fol. 11r Initial page *L* / *Liber*: Franco-Saxon type surrounded by late Winchester border with two lozenges enclosing two nimbed saints holding closed books. Frame has panels with acanthus friezes and corner medallions with acanthus rosettes.

9.18 fol. 44v St. Mark the Evangelist with symbol. Mark, nimbed, beardless, right hand raised, open book in left hand on draped lectern, sits on throne with high back, feet on footstool resting on hilly ground, flanked by curtains suspended on rod, within arcade decorated with foliate ornament at capitals, bases, squares in pillars, roundel at head of arch. Above, nimbed symbol (lion) blows trumpet and holds cross-inscribed closed book.

9.19 fol. 45r Initial page *I* / *Initium*: Initial is composed of gold-bordered, blue-filled panels with interlace, animal heads, and foliage terminals.

9.20 fol. 70v St. Luke the Evangelist. Luke, nimbed, beardless, seated in three-quarter view and holding a pen, turns toward a draped lectern with open book; an inspiring angel, nimbed, holding scepter, stands on the left; draped curtains. Frame is composed of gold border and panels of various colors with roundels containing rosettes of interlace and corner squares containing rosettes.

9.21 fol. 71r Initial page *Q* / *Quoniam*. Frame is composed of gold borders and panels of various colors with roundels containing interlace or rosettes and corner squares containing rosettes.

9.22 fol. 108v St. John the Evangelist. John, nimbed and bearded, sits beside a draped lectern with open book. He is addressed by a nimbed angel holding a scepter. Frame is composed of gold borders and panels of various colors with foliage at the corners.

9.23 fol. 109r Initial page *In* / *In principio*. Initial has foliate terminal and blue panels. Frame is composed of gold borders and panels of various colors with foliage at the corners.

10. Bury Gospels (London: British Library MS Harley 76)

Plates 10.1 to 10.15

10.1 fol. 6r Canon Table: within the tympanum of a round arch supported on three columns with acanthus bases and capitals, Christ, beardless, cross-nimbed, and wearing fillet, holding gold closed book and blessing, stands in oval mandorla.

10.2 fol. 6^v Canon Table: standing on the tops of intersecting round and pointed arches supported on five columns with acanthus bases and capitals, two lions bite acanthus foliage. A mask-head is in the capital of the central column.

10.3 fol. 7^r Canon Table: standing on the tops of intersecting round and pointed arches supported on five columns with acanthus bases and capitals, two dragons bite foliage.

10.4 fol. 7^v Canon Table: within the tympanum of a round arch supported on four columns, St. Peter, gold nimbus, tonsured, beardless, holds key and closed book, seated within quatrefoil. Some of the capitals and bases contain mask-heads.

10.5 fol. 8^r Canon Table: within the tympanum of a round arch supported on four columns, St. Paul, gold nimbus, bearded, holds closed book, seated within quatrefoil. Some of the capitals and bases contain mask-heads.

10.6 fol. 8^v Canon Table: within the tympanum of a round arch supported by two intersecting round arches on four columns, Christ, cross-nimbed, beardless, holds closed book and blesses; he is flanked by two nimbed angels holding a long open roll. Two of the capitals are beast-heads.

10.7 fol. 9^r Canon Table: within the tympanum of a round arch supported by two intersecting round arches on four columns, the Virgin Mary, veiled, holds a palm frond; she is flanked by two veiled female saints (or Holy Women?). Two of the bases contain mask-heads.

10.8 fol. 9^v Canon Table: within the pediment of a pointed arch supported on four columns, an angel, nimbed and wearing a fillet, holds a scepter and long, open roll; on either side are elaborate gabled buildings.

10.9 fol. 10^r Canon Table: within the pediment of a pointed arch supported on four columns, an angel, nimbed and wearing a fillet, holds a scepter and long, open roll; on either side are elaborate gabled buildings.

10.10 fol. 10^v Canon Table: interlaced among the bands of two pairs of intersecting arches supported on five columns is elaborate acanthus foliage.

10.11 fol. 11^r Canon Table: interlaced among the bands of two pairs of intersecting arches supported on five columns is elaborate acanthus foliage.

10.12 fol. 11^v Canon Table: in the center of a large round arch supported on two smaller round arches and a pointed arch is a roundel filled with foliage in the shape of a cross. The base of the right-hand column contains a mask-head.

10.13 fol. 12ʳ — Canon Table: in the center of a large round arch supported by two smaller round arches and a pointed arch is a roundel filled with foliage in the shape of a cross. The base of the right-hand column contains a mask-head.

10.14 fol. 12ᵛ — Canon Table: three round arches supported on five columns with acanthus bases and capitals; two of the capitals contain beast-masks.

10.15 fol. 45ʳ — Initial page *I / Initium*. According to E. Temple (p. 93) the initial is "made up of two heavy yellow and green panels framed in gold, a foliage terminal with a long-eared dragon's head at the bottom, and animal-headed interlace knotwork on the top"; the frame is constructed of "two heavy gold bands enclosing pink and blue leaf patterns, interlaced on the corners, and ornamented round the outer edge with animal and bird heads nibbling at fruit on fine hair-like stalks."

11. Judith of Flanders Gospels (New York: Pierpont Morgan Library M. 709)

Plates 11.1 to 11.10

11.1 — Jeweled binding, third quarter of the eleventh century, English(?). Christ, bearded(?), cruciform nimbus, blesses with right hand, holds closed book in left hand, and stands on a cloud in a mandorla. Alpha and Omega flank his head. In the four corners are four winged, nimbed Evangelist symbols: eagle with roll (upper left), man with closed book (upper right), lion (lower left), and ox (lower right) with closed books.

11.2 fol. 1ᵛ — Crucifixion of Christ. Christ, decorated cross-nimbus, bearded, head inclined, eyes closed, four nails, hangs on tree-trunk cross with blank titulus. On the left, the Virgin Mary, decorated nimbus, with closed book in right hand, raises the edge of her headcloth to wipe the wound in Christ's right side. On the right, Evangelist John, decorated nimbus, beardless, writes with a pen in an open book; his left foot rests on an elevated mound. Below, a woman kneels and clutches the foot of the cross; the woman represents either the patron, Judith of Flanders, or Mary Magdalene, or both figures in one. See Barbara C. Raw, *Anglo-Saxon Crucifixion Iconography* (Cambridge, 1990), pp. 159–61. Above are personifications of the Sun and the Moon, each veiling face; in the center, the Hand of God emerges from a dark, cloudy sky.

11.3 fol. 2ᵛ — St. Matthew the Evangelist with symbol. Matthew, nimbed, beardless, dipping pen into gold inkwell, holds open book inscribed with Matt. 1:1 ["Liber generationis JHU"] on draped lectern. Above, winged symbol (man), nimbed, holding open roll, issues from cloudy arc of heaven. The frame has four quatrefoils on the corners, two quatrefoils containing angels in orant positions on the sides, and roundels containing birds—one possibly the dove of the Holy Ghost—on the top and bottom.

11.4	fol. 3r	Initial page *L / Liber*. The letter L is composed of gold bands enclosing leaves, beast-headed interlace, and a foliated quatrefoil. The frame has four quatrefoils on the corners, two quatrefoils containing angels in orant positions on the sides, and roundels containing birds on the top and bottom.
11.5	fol. 48v	St. Mark the Evangelist with symbol. Mark, nimbed, beardless, dipping pen into gold inkwell, seated on high-backed throne with footstool, receives a long, open roll from a nimbed, winged ox (instead of the lion). The frame is composed of leaf-filled panels, two bosses, and four corner rosettes.
11.6	fol. 49r	Initial page *I / Initium*. The letter I is composed of "two gold-edged panels and topped by a quatrefoil with griffin's head and a fleuron" (Temple, p. 109). The frame is composed of leaf-filled panels, two bosses, and four corner rosettes.
11.7	fol. 77v	St. Luke the Evangelist with symbol. Luke, nimbed, beardless, dipping pen into inkwell on side of frame, left hand scraping error in open book on draped lectern, sits on cushioned bench with footstool. Above, the winged, nimbed symbol (lion, instead of ox) holds an open roll in its forefeet above the head of Luke. The frame is composed of leaf-filled panels, two bosses, four rosettes on corners, and a quatrefoil on each side.
11.8	fol. 78r	Initial page *Q / Quoniam*. The letter Q is composed of leaf-filled panels, a mask-head, and a dragon forming the tail. The frame is composed of leaf-filled panels, two bosses, four rosettes on corners, and a quatrefoil on each side.
11.9	fol. 122v	St. John the Evangelist with symbol. John, nimbed, bearded, sits on cushioned bench with footstool, holding a knife or scraper in left hand and pen in right, writing John 1:1: "In principio erat verbu[m] &" in open book on draped lectern. Above, nimbed symbol (eagle) holds long, open roll above the head of John. Frame is composed of leaf-filled panels, two medallions enclosing half figures of two men gesturing with their hands, and four corner rosettes.
11.10	fol. 123r	Initial page *In / In principio*. The letter I has a beast-headed terminal and a round boss on its shaft. The frame is composed of leaf-filled panels, two medallions enclosing half figures of two men, and four corner rosettes.

12. Judith of Flanders Gospels (New York: Pierpont Morgan Library M. 708)

Plates 12.1 to 12.9

12.1 Jeweled binding, second half of the eleventh century, English or Continental(?). Above, Christ in Mandorla. Christ, bearded, wearing cross-decorated crown and long robe, blessing with right hand, holding closed book in left, sits within mandorla, flanked by two orant seraphs. In the center is a damaged enamel inscription: "IESVS NAZA...IVDEORVM." Below is portrayed the Crucifixion of Christ. Christ, bearded with moustache, head inclined, four nails, hangs on tree-trunk cross. A serpent is coiled at the foot of the cross. On the left is the Virgin Mary with left hand supporting her head. On the right is John the Evangelist with moustache, right hand raised to his chin, left holds closed book.

12.2 fol. 2v St. Matthew the Evangelist with symbol. Matthew, nimbed, beardless, left hand raised to face, right hand writing with pen in open book on draped lectern, sits on cushioned bench with feet on footstool. On the right, nimbed and winged symbol (Man) holds long, open roll. On the left is a curtain suspended from the frame composed of plain gold bands.

12.3 fol. 3r Initial page *L* / *Liber* in large capitals followed by "generationis IHV XPI filii David filii Abraham."

12.4 fol. 26v St. Mark the Evangelist with symbol. Mark, decorated nimbus, bearded, seated on cushioned, architectural bench with feet on footstool, is flanked by open book on draped lectern, and dips pen into inkwell. A long, open roll in his left hand is grasped by winged symbol (nimbed lion) descending. A curtain is suspended from arch supported on slender columns; acanthus-leaf ornament in the capitals and projecting upwards from the spandrels.

12.5 fol. 27r Initial page *I* / *Initium* in large capitals followed by "Evangelli IHV XPI Filii Dei." Frame is composed of leaf-filled panels in arch supported by slender columns with acanthus-leaf capitals and projecting foliage.

12.6 fol. 42v St. Luke the Evangelist with symbol. Luke, decorated nimbus, beardless, left hand holding a knife, right hand writing with pen in a golden open book supported on a draped lectern, sits on a wide, high-backed, cushioned throne. Above, winged and nimbed symbol (ox) holds long, open roll. On the left, a curtain is suspended from the frame.

12.7 fol. 43r Initial page *Q* / *Quoniam* in large capitals followed by "quide(m) multi conati sunt ordinare narratione(m)."

12.8 fol. 66^{v} St. John the Evangelist with symbol. John, decorated nimbus, bearded, wearing fillet, writing with pen in golden open book on draped lectern, sits on cushioned, architectural bench, feet on footstool. Above a winged symbol (eagle) descends toward John's ear. On either side, curtains are suspended from trefoil arch supported by columns.

12.9 fol. 67^{r} Initial page *I* / *In principio* in large capitals followed by "erat verbu(m); Et verbum erat apud Deum: Et Deus erat Verbum."

13. Gospel Book (Monte Cassino: Archivio della Badia MS BB. 437, 439)

Plates 13.1 to 13.8

13.1 p. 2^{v} St. Matthew the Evangelist. Matthew, decorated nimbus, beardless, left hand holding knife, right hand writing with pen in open book resting on draped lectern, sits on wide, high-backed, cushioned throne, feet on footstool. The raised head and eyes indicate that the Evangelist is looking at his inspiring symbol with open roll on the recto of the facing page. Curtains are suspended from arch supported by columns. Acanthus foliage projects from the spandrels.

13.2 p. 3^{r} Initial page *L* / *Liber*. The letter L is composed of a bird biting foliage and a dragon. The text reads: "Liber generationis IHV XPI filii David filii Abraham." In the tympanum of the arch supported by columns are a roundel enclosing a bird (Eagle or Holy Dove?) and the Evangelist symbol for Matthew: a half-length Man, winged and nimbed, holding an open roll against a cloudy background. At the spandrels of the arch, two male figures, wearing short tunics, grasp the acanthus foliage. The two male figures may represent the generation of Christ.

13.3 p. 102^{v} St. Mark the Evangelist. Mark, decorated nimbus, beardless, sits on draped, cushioned bench, feet on footstool, right hand writing with pen in open book on draped lectern. The raised head and eyes of the Evangelist indicate that he is looking at his inspiring symbol on the recto of the facing page. Curtains suspended from the arch are looped around a gold bar. Acanthus foliage projects from the spandrels.

13.4 p. 103^{r} Initial page *I* / *Initium*. The letter I is composed of a leaf-filled shaft, a large leafy boss, and a beast-headed terminal. The text in capitals reads: "Initium Evangelii IHV XPI Filii Dei. Sicut scriptu(m) est in Isaia p(ro)pheta." In the tympanum of the arch supported by columns is the symbol of Mark: an anthropomorphic figure of a lion, nimbed and winged, holding a closed book in human hands against a background of clouds. Foliage projects from the spandrels.

13.5 p. 126^{v} St. Luke the Evangelist with symbols(?). Luke, nimbed, beardless, seated frontally on a cushioned bench, feet on footstool, wearing shoes, turns toward an open book on a draped lectern and writes with a pen in his left hand and a pen or brush in his right hand. The pupils of the Evangelist's eyes are raised towards his inspiring symbol on the recto of the facing page. A curtain is suspended from the mitred arch supported by columns. At the top of the arch are a lion and eagle (Evangelist symbols?), and foliage projects from the spandrels.

13.6 p. 127r Initial page *Q / Quoniam*. The letter Q has a mask-head spitting leaves, and a dragon, whose neck is wrapped around the letter frame, forms the tail. The text in capitals reads: "Quoniam quidem multi conati sunt." In the tympanum of the mitred arch supported by columns is the symbol of Luke: an anthropomorphic figure of an ox, nimbed and winged, holding a closed book against a cloudy background. At the top of the arch are two rampant lions (Evangelist symbols?), and foliage projects from the spandrels.

13.7 p. 166v St. John the Evangelist with symbol. The symbol (eagle) is perched on the head of John, who is nimbed, bearded, wearing fillet, seated on cushioned, draped bench, writing with pen in open book on lectern. As in the previous portraits, the Evangelist's eyes are raised towards his inspiring symbol on the recto of the facing page. The round arch, supported on columns, has two confronted lions (Evangelist symbols?) and foliage projecting from the spandrels.

13.8 p. 167r Initial page *I / In principio*. The letter I is composed of a vertical dragon with foliated tail. The text in capitals reads: "In principio erat verbum: Et verbu(m) erat apud D(eu)m. Et D(eu)s erat verbum." In the tympanum of a round arch supported by columns is the symbol of John: a full-length, winged eagle, holding an open roll against a cloudy background; at the spandrels is projecting acanthus foliage.

14. Hereford Gospels (Cambridge: Pembroke College MS 302)

Plates 14.1 to 14.15

14.1 fol. 1r Canon Table: twin arches, decorated with foliage, are supported by slender columns with spiral bands; the capitals and bases are decorated with acanthus foliage.

14.2 fols. 1v–2r Canon Tables: two birds (eagles?) are perched in the spandrels of the arches on fol. 1v; the spandrels of fol. 2r have large leafy ornaments.

14.3 fols. 2v–3r Canon Tables: on both folios triple arches, decorated with acanthus foliage, are supported by slender columns, some of which have spiral bands; the capitals and bases are decorated with acanthus leaves.

14.4 fols. 3^{v}–4^{r} Canon Tables: on both folios triple arches, decorated with acanthus foliage, are supported by slender columns, some of which have spiral bands; the capitals and bases are decorated with acanthus leaves.

14.5 fols. 4^{v}–5^{r} Canon Tables: two birds (eagles?) are perched in the spandrels of the arches on fol. 4^{v}; acanthus leaves are in spandrels of fol. 5^{r}. On both folios a tulip-shaped flower is in the middle of two arches.

14.6 fols. 5^{v}–6^{r} Canon Tables: in the tympana of the round arches, a cowled figure, on fol. 5^{v}, holds an open book and shakes his finger(?) at the figure on fol. 6^{r}, who wears a cowled garment and holds his right hand to his unshaven face. The left figure probably represents a master monk admonishing the monk on the right. The open codex in the master's left hand possibly represents the *Regula Sancti Benedicti*. The raised right hand either indicates the *Regula* or is a hand sign for "listen," the opening word of the *Prologus* to the *Regula*. The monk on the right is indicating his closed mouth with his right hand [see Psalm 38(39), vv. 2–3] and counting the measure of his days on the fingers of his left hand [see Psalm 38(39), vv. 5–6]. The monk represents the Psalmist as an Old Testament type of the grumbling disciple of God. See Thomas H. Ohlgren, "The Grumbling Monk in the Hereford Gospels," *Old English Newsletter* 24/3 (Spring, 1991), 22-24.

14.7 fol. 6^{v} Canon Table: in the space between two pointed arches, a tonsured male with unshaven chin holds an open book; in the spandrels, two roosters hold gold objects in their beaks. John Higgitt has identified the scene as the Apostle Peter denying Christ (Ohlgren, *Catalogue*, p. 262). The scene is explained by Matthew 26:34 ("Jesus said to him: Amen I say to thee that in this night before the cock crow thou wilt deny me thrice").

14.8 fol. 9^{r} St. Matthew the Evangelist. Matthew, pearled nimbus, beardless, right hand dipping pen into inkwell, left hand holding knife and open book, sits on high-backed, cushioned throne and rests feet on a decorated footstool with roundel and quatrefoils. Curtains are suspended from rod and draped around frame.

14.9 fol. 9^{v} Initial page *L / Liber*. The letter L is composed of panels, interlace, and foliate and animal-headed terminals. The text in capitals reads: "Liber generationis IHV XPI fili David filii Abraham."

14.10 fol. 38^{r} St. Mark the Evangelist. Mark, pearled nimbus, bearded, turning backwards to the right, sharpening pen with knife, sits on high-backed, architectural throne before draped lectern with open book and inkwell. Above are an open window and curtain suspended from a rod. In the upper right corner is the sun(?). According to Temple, "The abrupt movement of his torso is echoed by the drapery end flying beyond the frame-bar, by the chair placed diagonally in perspective, by the emphatic twist of the curtain with its rings set aslant on the bar, and by his garment flaring widely out at the bottom. It is a crowded composition, conceived in terms of movement and counter-movement heralding the oncoming Romanesque style" (p. 113).

14.11 fol. 38v Initial page *I / Initium*. The letter is composed of decorated panels, foliate terminal at the bottom, and two griffins' heads chewing foliage at the top. The text reads: "Initiu(m) Evangelii IHV XPI Filii D(e)i. Sicut scriptum est in Isaia p(ro)pheta; Ecce (ego) mitto ang(e)l(u)m meu(m) ante faciem tua(m), q(u)i pr(a)eparabit via(m) tua(m); Vox clamantis in deserto: Parate via(m) D(omin)i rectas facite semitas eius; Fuit Ioannes in deserto" (Mark 1:1–4).

14.12 fol. 60v St. Luke the Evangelist. Luke, pearled nimbus, bearded, pen placed behind ear, sits sideways on cushioned, architectural bench, holding knife and open book on draped lectern with inkwell; an elaborate curtain is suspended from a rod.

14.13 fol. 61r Initial page *Q / Quoniam*. The letter Q is composed of panels, a large tulip-like flower in the bowl, and a dragon fighting a basilisk in the tail. The text reads: "Q(uonia)m quidem multi conati sunt ordinare narratione(m) qu(a)e in nobis complet(a)e sunt rerum; sicut tradiderunt nobis qui ab initio ipsi viderunt et ministi fuerunt sermonis. visum est & mihi adsecuto a principio omnibus diligenter ex ordine tibi scribere: obtime theophile ut cognoscas" (Luke 1:1–5).

14.14 fol. 88v St. John the Evangelist. John, pearled nimbus, beardless, wearing fillet, sits sideways on cushioned bench with footstool; part of mantle extends through the frame; left hand holds knife; right hand writes with pen in open book on draped lectern; above, two curtains wrapped around the inner frame.

14.15 fol. 89r Initial page *In / In principio*. The letter I is composed of panels and interlaced knotwork terminating in animal heads above and bird heads biting fruit below. Part of the text reads: "In principio erat Verbum. Et Verbum erat apud Deum" (John 1:1).

15. Psychomachia of Prudentius (London: British Library, MS Cotton Cleopatra C. VIII)

Plates 15.1 to 15.53

15.1 fol. 4r Latin gloss: *Abraham exemplum fideliter credentium fuit*. Old English gloss: "Her Abraham bysene onstealde geleaffullum. Þa he wolde his agen bearn acwellan, swa him seo stefen bead of heofonum."

Abraham's sacrifice of Isaac. In the left corner, a ram is caught in a thicket. Abraham, bearded, wearing a long robe and holding a raised sword, looks over his shoulder to the Hand of God. Isaac, his hands ties behind his back, bends his head over a fiery altar. *Praefatio*, vv. 1–14 (Gen. 22:9–10).

15.2 fol. 4v Upper drawing. Latin gloss: *Ubi quinque reges predati sunt Loth.* Old English gloss: "Her þa fif cyningas mit huðe læddan Loth gebundenne."

Lot taken prisoner by Kings. Lot, hands bound in front, accompanied by his veiled wife, is being driven on a line by one of five kings mounted on horseback; one holds a shield, and all bear spears and helmets. *Praefatio*, vv. 15–18 (Gen. 14:12). The horses are outfitted with bridles and reins, saddles with bellybands, and harnesses (a martingale in the front and breeching straps around the haunches). *Praefatio*, vv. 15–18 (Gen. 14:12).

Lower drawing. Latin gloss: *Abram post praedones.* Old English gloss: "Her Abram after þære."

Abraham pursues Lot's captors. Abraham, bearded, wearing helmet and carrying spear, rides on a horse outfitted with bridle and reins, saddle with stirrup and bellyband, and harnesses (martingale and breeching straps). Five soldiers, one on horseback, carry spears and shields, and all wear helmets. On the right, another rider with a spear turns back and looks at the group. *Praefatio*, vv. 19–31 (Gen. 14:14–16).

15.3 fol. 5r Latin gloss: *Abram devictis hostibus recepto Loth cum victoria revertitur.* Old English gloss: "Her Abram oferwunnenum feondum onfeng Loth ⁊ mid sige gehwearf."

Abraham returns after freeing Lot. Abraham, bearded and wearing a helmet, Lot, bearded and carrying a spear, and Lot's wife, veiled, and five soldiers, wearing helmets and carrying spears, all ride on horseback. Abraham's horse is outfitted with bridle and reins, saddle with stirrup and bellyband, and harnesses (martingale and breeching straps). *Praefatio*, vv. 32–37 (Gen. 14:16).

15.4 fol. 5v Upper drawing. Latin gloss: *Ubi Abram decimas offert et Melchisedech Habrahae panem et vinum: Melchisedech rex et sacerdos dei summi.* Old English gloss: "Her Abram his teoþan sceattas offrede ⁊ Melchisedec offrede Habrahe hlaf ⁊ win: Melchisedec was cyninge ⁊ massepreost þas hean godes."

Abraham and Melchisedec sacrifice at an altar. Abraham, bearded, offers a sacrificial lamb in draped hands; on the right, Melchisedec, holding a loaf of ceremonial bread in draped hand and a cup, stands beside an altar on a stepped base. *Praefatio*, vv. 38–44 (Gen. 14:18).

Lower drawing. Latin gloss: *Ubi tres angeli aparent Abrahe in convalle Mambre.* Old English gloss: "Her ateowdon ðry englas Abrahame on ða(m) dene, ðe Mambre was haten" (from Corpus Christi College MS. 23).

Abraham greets the three Angels. On the left, Sarah, veiled, holding her hand to her face, sits on a bench in a tent. Standing under an acanthus-leaf tree, Abraham, bearded, greets the three Angels, standing on a rocky prospect; one is nimbed, two hold closed books, one a scepter. *Praefatio*, vv. 45–49 (Gen. 18:2).

15.5 fol. 6v Latin gloss: *Prudentius orat.* Old English gloss: "Her seo gleawnes heo gebit."

Prudentius, tonsured, genuflects before an altar with an architectural pyx (vv. 1–11).

15.6 fol. 7r Upper drawing. Latin gloss: *Fides idolatriam repugnat prima.* Old English gloss: "Her se goda geleafa ærest ongean þ(at) deofolgyld wind." Fides (Faith) attacked by Veterum Cultura Deorum (Worshipper of the Old Gods).

On the right, Veterum Cultura Deorum, a woman with flaming hair, standing beside an altar with a sacrificial bullock, attacks with a spear Fides, veiled, standing, and holding a closed book in her draped hand (vv. 21–29).

Lower drawing. Latin gloss: *Fides conculcat idolatriam.* Old English gloss: "Her se geleafa ofertret þ(at) deofolgyld."

Fides, veiled, holding a cross-inscribed, closed book, defeats Veterum Cultura Deorum, who falls with her altar and sacrificial animal to the earth (vv. 30–35).

15.7 fol. 7v Upper drawing. Latin gloss: *Fides post victoriam virtutes coronat.* Old English gloss: "Her se geleafa after þam sige cynehelmode þa magnu."

Fides crowns the Virtues. On the left, Fides, veiled, places a crown on the head of one of the Virtues; three Virtues, all veiled, with hands raised watch (vv. 36–39).

Lower drawing. Latin gloss: *Pudicitia contra libidinem armis pugnat.* Old English gloss: "Her seo clænnes mid wæpnum wind ongean þa fulnesse."

Libidio (Lust), with long, flaming hair, attacks with a torch Pudicitia (Chastity), who is armed with a helmet, shield, and spear (vv. 40–45).

15.8 fol. 8r — Upper drawing. Latin gloss: *Pudicitia libidinem cum saxo percutit.* Old English gloss: "Her seo clænnes þa fulnesse mid flinte torfað."

Pudicitia, with helmet and shield, is about to cast a stone at the kneeling Libidio, who has long, flaming hair. (vv. 46–48).

Lower drawing. Latin gloss: *Pudicitia libidinem transfigit gladio.* Old English gloss: "Her se clænnys ðurhðyð þa galnysse mid swurde" (from Corpus Christi College MS. 23).

Pudicitia, wearing a helmet and holding a shield, strikes Libidio in the neck with a sword (vv. 49–52).

15.9 fol. 8v — Latin gloss: *Pudicitia libidinem extinctam increpat.* Old English gloss: "Her seo clænnes þa fulnesse ofercumene þreað."

Pudicitia, veiled, holding a cross-inscribed closed book, stands in victory over Libidio, who lies on her back on the ground (vv. 53–57).

15.10 fol. 9v — Latin gloss: *Sancta pudicitia gladium purificat.* Old English gloss: "Seo halige clænnes þat sweord feormað."

Pudicitia, wearing a robe with veil and flying flap, dips her sword in the River Jordan; on the right, a River god personification, with long hair and a beard, holds an inverted urn spilling its contents and two V-shaped sticks(?) (vv. 98–104).

15.11 fol. 10r — Upper drawing. Latin gloss: *Pudicitia gladium suum sub altare in templo recondit.* Old English gloss: "Seo clænnes hyre sweord under þam weofode on þa(m) temple hyt."

Pudicitia, veiled, kneels with her sword before the Temple, a gabled building with windows, towers, and tiled roof (vv. 104–08).

Lower drawing. Latin gloss: *Ubi patientia inter acies vitiorum intrepida stat.* Old English gloss: "Her þ(at) geðyld stent unforht betweonan ðara leahtra truman" (from Corpus Christi College MS. 23).

Patientia (Patience), veiled, standing in orant position, is flanked by two groups of soldiers, two of whom threaten her with torches (vv. 109–12).

15.12 fol. 10v — Upper drawing. Latin gloss: *Ira patientiam conto percutit.* Old English gloss: "Her þ(at) yrre þ(at) geþyld mid þam sceafte slihð."

Patientia, wearing a long robe with a veil, stands in orant position, while Ira (Wrath), with flaming hair, holds a spear (vv. 113–15).

Lower drawing. *Ira patientiam increpat.* Old English gloss: "Her þ(at) yrre þ(at) geþyld stent: þread."

Patientia, veiled, holding a closed book in her raised left hand, is threatened by Ira with a spear (vv. 116–20).

15.13 fol. 11ʳ Upper drawing. Latin gloss: *Ira lanceam suam iacit contra patientiam.* Old English gloss: "Her þ(at) yrre hys spere scotað ongean þ(at) geðyld."

Ira, with flaming hair, holds two spears in her left hand and prepares to throw a spear at Patientia, veiled, standing and holding an open roll (vv. 121–22).

Lower drawing. Latin gloss: *Arma fracta, quae miserat ira contra patientiam.* Old English gloss: "Her þa wæp :: weorda : to ::: cene, þe þ(at) yrre sende ongean þ(at) geðyld."

Patientia, veiled, holding a book (open?), deflects Ira's spears and sword, which lie broken on the ground (vv. 122–37).

15.14 fol. 11ᵛ Latin gloss: *Ira patientiam gladio percutit.* Old English gloss: "þ(at) yrre þ(at) geðyld mid sweorde sloh."

Ira, holding a shield, strikes with a sword at Patientia, veiled, standing in orant position (vv. 138–39).

15.15 fol. 12ʳ Upper drawing. Latin gloss: *Gladius ire frangitur in capite patientiae.* Old English gloss: "Sweord þas yrres tobrocen weard on heafde þas geðyldes."

Ira, holding a shield, strikes Patientia, standing in orant position, but her sword breaks into two pieces (vv. 145–48).

Lower drawing. Latin gloss: *Ira se sagitta interficit.* Old English gloss: "Her þ(at) yrre hit sylf mid flane ofstang."

Ira commits suicide by falling on her spear; Patientia, veiled, stands on the right (vv. 149–54).

15.16 fol. 12ᵛ Upper drawing. Latin gloss: *Patientia victrix iram mortuam increpat.* Old English gloss: "þ(at) geðyld oferswiðende þ(at) yrre dead hit þreade."

Patientia, veiled, stands victorious over Ira, who has fallen backwards on the earth (vv. 154–61).

Lower drawing. Latin gloss: *Patientia cum Iob medias acies transit.*

Old English gloss: "Þ(at) geðyld mid Iobe on middeweardum werode for."

Patientia, veiled, and Job, bearded, walk unharmed through the warring host; six soldiers, wearing helmets, carry spears and shields (vv. 162–68).

15.17 fol. 13r Upper drawing. Latin gloss: *Patientia cum Iob loquitur.* Old English gloss: "Þ(at) geðyld wið Iob sprac."

Patientia, veiled, standing on the left, points towards Job, bearded and holding a sword, and promises him peace (vv. 169–71).

Lower drawing. Latin gloss: *Patientia devictis vitiis ad virtutes loquitur.* Old English gloss: "Þ(at) geðyld ofercumenum leahtrum to þam magnum sprac."

Patientia, veiled, holding a closed book, returns to the host of Virtues, one of whom carries an open roll (vv. 174–77).

15.18 fol. 13v Latin gloss: *Superbia in turmas effreni volitat aequo.* Old English gloss: "Seo ofermodnes on heape ungemidledum horse fleah."

Superbia (Pride), with her mantle flying over her head, rides an unbridled horse with a lion's skin on its back through the host; five men in short tunics stand on the right (vv. 178–82).

15.19 fol. 14r Upper drawing. Latin gloss: *Superbia acquitat.* Old English gloss: "Her seo ofermodnes rad."

Superbia, wearing a flying mantle, rides back and forth on her horse with a bridle and lion's skin on its back (vv. 183–97).

Lower drawing. Latin gloss: *Superbia in equo minatur turbis. humilitas et spes intrepidae stant.* Old English gloss: "Seo ofermodnes on horse þywde þ(at) folc. seo eaðmodnes ⁊ s: hopa unfor:::."

Superbia, with flying mantle, rides her horse with bridle and reins toward Humilitas (Humility) and Spes (Hope); two other Virtues stand on the left (vv. 197–205).

15.20 fol. 15v Upper drawing. Latin gloss: *Superbia inruere vult super humilitatem et spem.* Old English gloss: "Seo ofermodnes stellan wile ofer eaðmodnesse ⁊ þone hopan."

Superbia, riding her bridled horse, attempts to trample Humilitas and Spes, both veiled and one holding a closed book (vv. 253–56).

Lower drawing. Latin gloss: *Superbia cadit in fovem.* Old English gloss: "Her seo ofermodnes feol, þ(at) heo on þone fulan seað lag."

Superbia falls from her horse into a dark pit (vv. 257–73).

15.21 fol. 16r Latin gloss: *Humilitas deridet superbiam iacentem.* Old English gloss: "Seo eaðmodnes hloh þære ofermodignesse fylles."

Humilitas, veiled, in orant position, stands over the fallen Superbia and her horse (vv. 274–77).

15.22 fol. 16v Upper drawing. Latin gloss: *Spes offert gladium humilitati.* Old English gloss: "Se hopa aræhte sweord þære eadmodnesse."

Spes, veiled, offers the sword of vengeance to Humilitas, veiled, who holds a closed book (vv. 278–79).

Lower drawing. Latin gloss: *Humilitas amputet caput superbiae.* Old English gloss: "Seo eaðmodnes of acearf heafod þære ofermodignesse."

Humilitas, accompanied by Spes, both veiled, decapitates Superbia with a sword (vv. 280–83).

15.23 fol. 17r Upper drawing. Latin gloss: *Humilitas caput superbiae offert spei.* Old English gloss: "Seo eaðmodnes heafod þære ofermodignesse aræhte þam hopan."

Humilitas, veiled, holds Superbia's severed head by the hair; Spes, veiled, standing on the left, upbraids the dead Vice (v. 284).

Lower drawing. Latin gloss: *Extinctam superbiam spes increpat.* Old English gloss: "Oferwunnenre þære ofermodignesse se hopa heo þreade."

Spes, veiled, holding a closed book, stands victorious over the headless corpse of Superbia (vv. 285–304).

15.24 fol. 17v Latin gloss: *Humilitas ascendit in caelum. virtutes mirantur eam.* Old English gloss: "Seo eaðmodnes astah on heofon, ⁊ þa magnu wundredon hyre." The glossator is in error. As the text clearly shows, it is Spes, not Humilitas, who is speaking; a scribe even identifies the speaker with a marginal note, *Spes loquit*, on line 12 of the text on fol. 17v.

Ascension of Spes to heaven. Spes, winged, with arms outstretched, flies unassisted upwards; the Virtues, holding closed books, watch (vv. 305–08).

15.25 fol. 18r Latin gloss: *Luxuria in caena sedit*. Old English gloss: "Seo galnes at hyre æfengereordum sitt."

Luxuria at feast. Three figures, one female and two male, sit by a round, draped table with knife, bowl, and other objects. Superbia and one of the males hold drinking cups, while the third figure is handed a cup by a standing servant (vv. 310–16).

15.26 fol. 18v Upper drawing. Latin gloss: *Luxuria auditis tubis ad bellum currit*. Old English gloss: "Seo galnes gehyrendu(m) byman to þam gefeohte arn."

Luxuria prepares for battle. On the left, a veiled virtue and a soldier who blows a war-horn; on the right, two soldiers, wearing short tunics, with helmets and shields, brandish swords (vv. 317–18).

Lower drawing. Latin gloss: *Luxuriam mirantur viri in curru*. Old English gloss: "Þære galnesse wundredon weras on þam crate."

Luxuria, veiled, holding a whip, rides her chariot (a two-wheeled cart pulled by two bridled horses) into battle; two figures stand on the far right (vv. 321–22).

15.27 fol. 19r Upper drawing. Latin gloss: *Luxuria blandimentis virtutes decipit*. Old English gloss: "Seo galnes swæsum wordum þa magnu beswac."

Luxuria, wearing a crown and riding in her chariot, enchants two of the Virtues. The two-wheeled cart is pulled by two bridled horses (vv. 323–31).

Lower drawing. Latin gloss: *Viri deiectis armis sequuntur luxuriam*. Old English gloss: "Her weras aworpenum wæpnum fylgedon þære galnesse."

The Virtues, on the left, discard their weapons; two spears lie on the ground; on the right, Luxuria, with flying mantle and a whip, drives her chariot, a two-wheeled cart pulled by two bridled horses (vv. 332–39).

15.28 fol. 19v Upper drawing. Latin gloss: *Cuncta acies versis signis ad deditionem transit*. Old English gloss: "Eal werod gehwyrfedum tacnum to þære biswicenesse foron."

While two musicians play a lyre, cymbals, and a wind instrument, Luxuria dances; on the right, the Virtues surrender (vv. 340–43).

Lower drawing. Latin gloss: *Sobrietas increpat acies dicens, ne sequantur luxuriam*. Old English gloss: "Her seo syfernes þreade þ(at) werod cweðende, þ(at) hit ne fyligde þære galnesse."

Sobrietas (Sobriety), wearing a veil and holding a closed book, chastises the dissenting Virtues, four of whom stand on the left (vv. 344–406).

15.29 fol. 21ʳ Latin gloss: *Sobrietas cruce(m) d(omi)ni offert currui luxuriae*. Old English gloss: "Seo syfernes drihtnes rode brohte ongean þære galnesse crate."

Sobrietas, standing with a cross-staff and closed book, confronts Luxuria, veiled, in her chariot, a two-wheeled cart pulled by two bridled horses (vv. 407–12).

15.30 fol. 21ᵛ Latin gloss: *Sobrietas lapidem iacit et percutit os luxuriae*. Old English gloss: "Seo syfernes mid stane wearp þa galnesse on þone muð, þ(at) heo fleah, þ(at) heo lag."

Luxuria's horses panic at the sight of the cross, turning over the chariot, and Luxuria is thrown on to the ground; on the right, Sobrietas, holding a long cross-staff, casts a great stone at the fallen Luxuria (vv. 412–26).

15.31 fol. 22ʳ Upper drawing. Latin gloss: *Sobrietas increpat luxuriam extinctam*. Old English gloss: "Seo syfernes þreade þa galnesse ofercumene."

Sobrietas, holding a closed book, delivers a victory speech over the body of Luxuria, lying on the ground (vv. 427–31).

Lower drawing. Latin gloss: *Iocus cymbala proiciens fugit*. Old English gloss: "Her þara cymbala stow aworpen was."

Jocus (Jest), upon hearing of the death of Luxuria, casts aways his cymbals (vv. 432–35).

15.32 fol. 22ᵛ Upper drawing. Latin gloss: *Amor, qui et cupido, faretram, arcu(m) et sagittas dimittens fugit*. Old English gloss: "Seo lufu þære grædignesse cocor ⁊ bogan ⁊ flan forlet fleonde."

Amor, a winged nude male, turns his back in flight, abandoning his bow, arrows, and quiver (vv. 436–38).

Lower drawing. Latin gloss: *Pompa ornamenta sua proiciens fugit*. Old English gloss: "Se woruldwela his fratewunga aweorpende fleah."

Pompa (Ostentation) is dressed in her vain flowing robe (vv. 439–40).

15.33 fol. 23ʳ Upper drawing. Latin gloss: *Voluptas laceratis pedibus p[er] spinas fugit*. Old English gloss: "Seo gelustfullung gewundedum fotum þurh þa þornas fleah."

Voluptas (Pleasure), holding up the hem of her robe, runs through the thorns (vv. 443–46).

Lower drawing. Latin gloss: *Sobrietas et alie virtutes abstinent se a spoliis*. Old English gloss: "Seo syfernes ⁊ oðre magnu forhafdon heo fram herereafe."

Sobrietas and the Virtues, all veiled, trample on Luxuria's treasure (a pitcher, two bowls, a drinking horn, and a crown) (vv. 447–53).

15.34 fol. 23ᵛ Upper drawing. Latin gloss: *Avaritia aurum inter arenas legit*. Old English gloss: "Her seo gytsung hyre gold betweoh þa wateraedran raet."

Avaritia (Avarice), sitting by a stream, picks up the broken pieces of gold left behind by Luxuria (vv. 454–58).

Lower drawing. Latin gloss: *Avaritia spolia in sinistro latere protegit*. Old English gloss: "Seo gytsung hyre reaf on þære wynstran sidan scylt."

Avaritia with her booty (a pitcher and a mantle filled with coins) (vv. 458–63).

15.35 fol. 24ʳ Latin gloss: *Multitudinem vitiorum avaritia nigro lacte nutrit*. Old English gloss: "Micel leahtra menigeo seo gytsung sweartre meolce fet."

Avaritia, sitting on a rocky mound, nurses the Vices Cura, Famis, Metus, Anxietas, Periuria, Pallor, Corruptela, Dolus, Commenta, Insomnia, and Sordes (vv. 464–69).

15.36 fol. 24ᵛ Latin gloss: *Avaritia multos sternit, alios cecos errare sinit*. Old English gloss: "Her seo gytsung manega ofertret ⁊ oðre blinde dwelian let."

Avaritia as the cause of crimes. On the left, Avaritia forces a smaller male figure to the ground with her left arm (vv. 480–82) and points with her right hand to a standing man on the right; the man, with slits for eyes, has been blinded by Avaritia (vv. 482–85). On the right is a group of four men, one of whom reaches out with open arms. (vv. 486–89).

15.37 fol. 25ʳ Upper drawing. Latin gloss: *Avaritia, du[m] aliquid boni ostendit, iaculo percutere vult*. Old English gloss: "Her seo gytsung, þon(ne) heo ænigne godne ongif, mid stræle heo þonne stician wile."

Avaritia, holding a spear, lures a man to his death by offering him treasure (round object) (vv. 486–89).

Lower drawing. Latin gloss: *Avaritia multos precipitat in ignem.* Old English gloss: "Her seo gytsung manega bescyfð on fyr."

Avaritia drives five men into a fiery pit (vv. 490–96).

15.38 fol. 26v Latin gloss: *Avaritia transformatur in habitum honestum.* Old English gloss: "Her seo gytsung gehiwod was weordlice on gegyrelan."

In order to deceive her victims, Avaritia disguises herself as the virtue Frugi (Frugality) represented as a woman, standing in orant position, with arms raised (vv. 551–63).

15.39 fol. 27r Upper drawing. Latin gloss: *Avaritia fallit.* Old English gloss: "Her seo gytsung leas spel sagde þam folce."

Avaritia, disguised as the virtue Frugi, deceives a group of four people, standing on the right (vv. 564–65).

Lower drawing. Latin gloss: *Avaritia hos, quos fallit, ligat.* Old English gloss: "Her seo gytsung wrað þa, þe heo ær leas spel sagde."

Avaritia, disguised as the virtue Frugi, binding a man's hands (vv. 565–67).

15.40 fol. 27v Upper drawing. Latin gloss: *Virtutes dubitant avaritiam non plene cognoscentes.* Old English gloss: "Her þa magnu tweonedon be þære gytsunge, þ(at) hio fullice hio ne oncnewon."

Avaritia, disguised as the virtue Frugi, confuses the Virtues, standing on the right (vv. 568–72).

Lower drawing. Latin gloss: *Largitas pugnat contra avaritiam et spolia eius pauperibus erogat.* Old English gloss: "Her seo rumgifolnes wind ongean þa gytsunge ⁊ hyre reaf hio þearfum behet."

On the left, Operatio (Good Works), wielding a single-bladed axe and holding a shield, fights Avaritia, wearing a helmet, mail-shirt, and scabbard, and holding a spear (vv. 574–98). On the right, Operatio distributes Avaritia's money to the poor and the crippled (vv. 598–603).

15.41 fol. 28r Latin gloss: *Avaritia stupefacta fatescit.* Old English gloss: "Her seo gytsung wundrede hyre geteorodnesse."

Upon seeing Operatio, Avaritia stands speechless with shock (vv. 584–88).

15.42 fol. 28v Upper drawing. Latin gloss: *Largitas avaritiam ligat.* Old English gloss: "Her seo rumgyfolnes þa gytsunge wrað."

Operatio presses Avaritia's arms (vv. 589–93).

Lower drawing. Latin gloss: *Largitas avaritiam genibus et calcibus perfodit*. Old English gloss: "Her seo rumgyfolnes þa gytsunge mid cneowum ⁊ mid fotum hio ofertrað."

Operatio kills Avaritia (vv. 593–97).

15.43 fol. 29r Upper drawing. Latin gloss: *Largitas spolia avaritiae pauperibus dat*. Old English gloss: "Her seo rumgyfolnes reaf þære gytsunge þearfum dælde."

Operatio distributes Avaritia's treasure to the poor and crippled; on the left, the poor and a crippled person with trestles receive a crown, bowl, drinking horn, robe, and other objects (vv. 598–603).

Lower drawing. Latin gloss: *Largitas cu[m] gaudio turbas alloquitur*. Old English gloss: "Seo rumgyfolnes mid gefean to þa(m) folce spac."

Operatio, holding a long, open roll, addresses the troops, a group of five figures standing on the right (vv. 604–28).

15.44 fol. 30r Upper drawing. Latin gloss: *Pax venit, et fugiunt metus et labor et vis*. Old English gloss: "Her seo gesibsumnes com, ⁊ fleah se ege ⁊ þ(at) geswinc ⁊ seo strengð."

Pax (Peace) drives away Metus, Labor, and Vis. Metus (Fear) wears a helmet and carries a spear and shield; Labor (Suffering) carries a large circular object; Vis (Violence) turns away with raised hands (vv. 629–31).

Lower drawing. Latin gloss: *Tubae silent, gladii reconduntur in vaginas*. Old English gloss: "Her þa byman swigedon ⁊ þa sweord on hiora sceaðum behydde wæron."

The Virtues disarm and the war-horns are silenced; one Virtue puts her sword in a scabbard; another lowers her sword; and two Virtues lower their war-horns (vv. 631–39).

15.45 fol. 30v Upper drawing. Latin gloss: *Virtutum legio gaudet victo certamine*. Old English gloss: "Her þa magnu þære æwfastnesse blissiað þas gewunnenan siges."

Six standing veiled Virtues, two with hands raised to heaven, one (on far right) in orant position, rejoice in their victory (vv. 640–43).

Lower drawing. Latin gloss: *Concordia iubet reducere vexilla in castris*. Old English gloss: "Her seo geþwærnes het beran þa guðfanan in on ða ceastre."

Concordia, on the left, gives the signal to return to camp; three Virtues, holding spears, turn toward a walled enclosure with towers (vv. 644–45).

15.46 fol. 31r — Latin gloss: *Turba psallentium equitum ac pedestrium.* Old English gloss: "Þis is þ(at) hleoðrigende folc ridende ⁊ eac fotum gangende."

The Army of the Virtues, one mounted on horseback, two bearing staffs, returns to camp. The horse is outfitted with bridle, reins, and harnesses (vv. 646–65).

15.47 fol. 31v — Upper drawing. Latin gloss: *Virtutes urbem ingrediuntur.* Old English gloss: "Her þa magnu in on þa burh gangað."

The Virtues, all veiled, arrive at the gate of the camp, a walled enclosure with windowed towers, crenelated walls, and gateway (vv. 665–66).

Lower drawing. Latin gloss: *Discordia occultae vulnerat concordiam.* Old English gloss: "Her seo ungeðwærnes dygollice wundode þa geðwærnesse."

Discordia, standing within an arch, attacks Concordia, veiled, with a spear (vv. 667–93).

15.48 fol. 32r — Latin gloss: *Discordia virtutibus insidiatur et capitur.* Old English gloss: "Her seo ungeðwærnes þa magnu syrwde ⁊ gehafte."

Discordia, disguised as a Virtue, is captured by a group of five Virtues, all veiled, who seize her wrists, head, and shoulder (vv. 694–714).

15.49 fol. 34r — Latin gloss: *Fides virtutum turmas alloquitur.* Old English gloss: "Her se geleafa þara magna wið þ(at) werod specð."

Fides (Faith), veiled, standing on the left, addresses a group of three Virtues (vv. 799–822).

15.50 fol. 34v — Latin gloss: *Fides et caritas metiuntur locum, ubi templum domini aedificetur.* Old English gloss: "Se geleafa ⁊ seo lufu mæton þone stede, hwær hio drihtnes tempel ræran woldan."

Fides, veiled, and Concordia lay out the foundations of the temple with a measuring rod (vv. 823–29).

15.51 fol. 35r — Latin gloss: *Hic templum domini.* Old English gloss: "Her is drihtnes templ."

The Temple of the Lord: a gabled building with windows, tiled roof, and doorway (vv. 830–74).

15.52 fol. 36ʳ Latin gloss: *Domus interior, ubi sapientia sedet.* Old English gloss: "Þis is þ(at) hus, þær se wisdom on innan sit."

Sapientia (Wisdom), veiled, seated upon a cushioned, architectural throne and holding a long staff, is within the portal of the temple with seven columns; curtains, suspended from the roof, are looped around two of the columns (vv. 875–87).

15.53 fol. 36ᵛ Latin gloss: *Prudentius gratias deo agit.* Old English gloss: "Her seo gleawnes deð gode þanc."

Prudentius, standing in orant position, prays before the temple thanking God (vv. 888–915).

16. Junius Manuscript (Oxford: Bodleian Library, MS Junius 11)

Plates 16.1 to 16.51

16.1 Frontispiece: God enthroned above Chaos. God, bearded and cross-nimbed, holding tubular scepter or roll, seated on a cushioned throne, is flanked by two seraphim with eyes in their wings; two wind personifications support the throne. Wavy lines surrounding the throne suggest the cloudy arc of heaven (lines 1–16). At the top is the Latin inscription: *Genesis in anglico* (Gen. 1:1–2).

p. 1 Beginning of the Old English poetic text. The first line has a capital letter U formed by two winged dragons followed by the capitals "(U)S IS RIHT MICEL ĐÆT."

16.2 p. 2 God confronting Lucifer. God, bearded and cross-nimbed, holding tubular scepter or roll, seated on a cushioned throne and flanked by two seraphim, addresses a small, nimbed angel (Lucifer), who has announced his rebellion in heaven. On the upper left, another angel, archangel Michael (St. Michael), stands with raised hands (lines 20–46). In the left margin is the inscription: "hælendes hehseld." In the lower margin is a medallion portrait of a beardless man in profile, inscribed "alfwine."

16.3 p. 3 In the first register, Lucifer, crowned and holding a scepter, standing on a pedestal or dais, points to a two-storied palace containing a throne. He is surrounded by three groups of adoring angels, some wearing fillets; the group on the lower right offers him crowns. In the upper margin is the inscription (partially cut off): "Hu se engyl ongon ofermod wesan."

In the second register, Lucifer, wearing a decorated fillet (wreath?), receives palm fronds from angels on either side. In the right margin is the inscription: "Her se hælend gesce(op) helle heom to wite." Jane Rosenthal, by contrast, identifies the scene as an angel handing fronds to the good angels in celebration of the victory of the spear-bearing Lord below ("Historiated Canon Tables," diss. Columbia University, 1974, pp. 190–91).

In the third register, God, bearded and cross-nimbed, with tubular scepter or roll, holds three spears in raised right arm; he is attended by five angels, some wearing fillets and holding palm fronds.

In the fourth register, the fall of the rebel angels into a hell-mouth. Lucifer, his angelic allies, and the broken remains of his throne are shown falling downwards into hell. At the bottom, Lucifer, now Satan, with flaming hair and clawed hands and feet, lies bound in the jaws of hell (lines 49–69).

16.4 p. 6 Creation: First and Second Days. God, cross-nimbed and beardless, sits upon the arc of the firmanent, his feet resting on a scabellum. Above God is an angel holding an inverted bowl issuing light rays (the creation of light?). Below is another angel covering its face with a drapery on the surface of the water (Gen. 1:2?; *super faciem abyssi*). In the left margin is the inscription: "Her he gesyndrode wæter and eorðan" (lines 103-34; Gen. 1:3–8).

16.5 p. 7 Creation: the Third, Fifth and Sixth Days. In the upper circle, God, cross-nimbed, bearded, and holding a closed book, stands in a mandorla (inscribed "Salvator") above the creation of vegetation, birds, and animals in the second circle. The small cross in the acanthus-tree is probably a typological reference to the *lignum vitae* legend. The bird (a pelican?; see Psalm 101:7) and the stag (see Psalm 41:2) may also be symbolic. Wavy lines seem to represent water. In the third circle, the work of the Fourth Day. God, cross-nimbed, beardless, and holding a closed book, stands over the creation of the stars in the lower circle. Above God is an angel holding an inverted bowl issuing rays (lines 154–68). In the right margin is the inscription: "Her he todalde dæg wið nihte" (Gen. 1:9–25).

16.6 p. 9 Eve: Creation. At lower right, God, cross-nimbed and bearded, removes a rib from the sleeping, nude Adam; the scene is inscribed "Her drihten gewearp sclep on adam and genam him an rib of þa sidan and gescop his wif of þam ribbe." Above, on left, God, cross-nimbed and beardless, raises and blesses the nude figure of Eve, name inscribed "EVA." The scene is inscribed "Her drihten gescop adames wif euam." An angel climbs a ladder reaching from Eden to heaven. In the open door (with hinges) of heaven, archangel

Michael stands under an arch; name inscribed "Michael." Another angel, wearing fillet, holds a double-warded key in one hand and the door of heaven in the other; other angels hold a stringed instrument, a closed book, and a palm frond. In the upper frame is the inscription: "Her godes englas astigan of heouenan into paradisum" (lines 169–85; Gen. 2:21–22).

16.7 p. 10 Adam and Eve: Within an architectural frame, blessing by God and/or Prohibition. On the left, Adam and Eve, both nude, stand with arms raised and look upwards; on the right, God, cross-nimbed, bearded, and holding a closed book, raises his hand in benediction. Eve treads the hind leg of a small animal or beast (see Genesis 3:15; *Et tu insidiaberis calcaneo eius*). On the lower right, a basilisk (lines 192–205; Gen. 2:16–17).

16.8 p. 11 Creation: God resting. Within a walled enclosure with towers, God, beardless, wearing fillet, and holding a closed book, stands on a dais and raises his hand in benediction. Below, Adam and Eve, both nude, stand in the midst of three acanthus-trees, each holding a branch and looking upwards. Beneath their feet is a group of animals, including birds, a peacock, stags, and two lions (lines 206–10; Gen. 2:2–3).

16.9 p. 12 St. Michael fights the dragon: an unfinished dry stylus sketch of uncertain date. Ultra-violet light illumination of the blank space reveals the existence of the outline of a standing male with a round shield in his left hand and the fragment of a lance in his upraised right hand (Rev. 20:1–3). See Thomas H. Ohlgren, "Five New Drawings in the MS Junius 11: Their Iconography and Thematic Significance," *Speculum* 47/2 (1972), 227–33.

16.10 p. 13 Adam and Eve: in Garden of Eden. Within an architectural frame, Adam and Eve, both nude, point to the Tree of Life ("lifes beam," line 468) and the Tree of Death ("deaðes beam," line 478). Above is a bust figure of God in a mandorla issuing rays. Below is a group of animals, birds, and fish: a dog-like animal nibbles foliage; a winged stag or horse; a fantastic creature with curled tail; fish swim in water [inscribed "q(u)odda(m) mare"] (lines 237–45).

16.11 p. 16 Fall of the Angels. Above, God, cross-nimbed, beardless, and holding a closed book, accompanied by three angels, turns and gestures toward three angels on the left, one of whom (Lucifer?) holds a palm frond and wears a fillet or crown. The semi-circular arc of heaven contains six stars. In the middle register, eight rebel angels, one with male genitals, fall downwards into hell, which is composed of a structure with crenelated walls and towers enclosing a hell-mouth (a beast-head with gaping jaws). In the lower portion, Satan, with flaming hair, clawed feet, and tail, is tied hand and foot to stakes; standing on a tower issuing flames, a demon with a tail harasses Satan with a flail (lines 292–320; Rev. 20:3).

16.12 p. 17 Fall of the Angels. Above, God, beardless, holding open book, right hand blessing, sits on cushioned bench, feet on footstool, within decorated mandorla, flanked by two seraphim wearing fillets. Below, within a walled structure with two towers, Satan, bearded and wearing a crown, sits on the ground, bound hand and foot by chains; he is surrounded by the fallen angels, who bear flails and hooks. The demon in the upper center has male genitals (lines 320–29; Rev. 20:3).

16.13 p. 20 Adam and Eve: fall of man, Devil sent. Below, Satan, a nude, winged human figure with flaming hair, fettered over flames in hell, sends an emissary devil to Eden to tempt Adam and Eve. Satan and the emissary devil, a small, nude figure, touch hands, which signifies their covenant. Four other devils also appear, two with hooks. The emissary ascends through the gate of hell and, above, assumes the shape of the serpent in the Tree of Death, next to which Eve stands restraining her arm. On the upper right, Adam and Eve point to a tree (lines 356–466; Gen. 3:1). For a recent discussion, see Thomas H. Ohlgren, "Anglo-Saxon Art: Texts and Contexts," *Old English Newsletter, Subsidia* 17 (1991), pp. 15–16.

16.14 p. 24 Eve: tempted by Devil disguised as angel. Standing between two trees (Trees of Life and Death?), Eve accepts the fruit from the disguised devil, winged, wearing red robes and a crown. This drawing has been prematurely placed in the sequence as the poetic account is on p. 27 in lines 547–625.

16.15 p. 28 Adam and Eve: tempted by Devil disguised as angel. In the center stands the disguised emissary devil, winged, wearing fillet, and outlined in red ink. On either side are Adam and Eve. The tempter, holding the forbidden fruit in each hand, appears to be offering them to Adam and Eve at the same time. The devil's head is turned toward Adam, which may indicate that he is being tempted first (his extended right hand may be a gesture of refusal), but the scene is ambiguous because Eve is shown eating her piece of fruit. The artist's conflation of the two temptations may have been intended to resolve the textual deviation from the traditional sequence of the temptation (lines 495–546). The thornlike projections in the frame above the tempter's head may symbolize, as Herbert R. Broderick suggests, the treachery and daemonic nature of the disguised figure; the projections resemble Satan's toes in the drawings on pages 2, 16, 17, and 20. For Broderick's discussion of this and other framing devices in MS. Junius 11, see "Some Attitudes toward the Frame in Anglo-Saxon Manuscripts of the Tenth and Eleventh Centuries," *Artibus et Historiae* 5 (1982), 31–42.

16.16 p. 31 Adam and Eve: Devil inspires Eve to tempt Adam. Above, the disguised emissary devil seduces Eve into tempting Adam with a piece of fruit; Adam, standing next to a tree (the Tree of Death?), accepts the fruit with his right hand (lines 684–93). Below, Adam and Eve's remorse. Adam and Eve, still nude, bow down on the ground; a tree is between them. On the right, the emissary devil, flaming hair, winged, blowing wind?, wearing an animal-skin loincloth with tail as belt, sheds his disguise (lines 723–83). In the lower margin is an outline drawing of a lion (of uncertain date).

16.17 p. 34 Adam and Eve: knowing nakedness. Above, Adam and Eve cover their nakedness with one hand and raise the other hand to their cheeks (a gesture of shame; lines 783–84). Below, Adam and Eve, hiding among trees, cover their nakedness with acanthus leaves and hold their hands to their faces (lines 836–46; Gen. 3:7).

16.18 p. 36 Adam and Eve: knowing nakedness. Emissary devil returns to hell. Adam and Eve, holding their hands to their faces, cover their nakedness with acanthus leaves. The emissary devil, winged and wearing an animal-skin loincloth, leans over to re-enter the gate of hell and, below, he, now totally nude, reports the success of his mission to Satan, bearded and bound hand and foot by shackles; four smaller devils surround him (lines 760–65). The lines in Old English at the top of the page read: "sceolde he þa bradan ligas / secan helle gehliðo, þær his hearra læg" (Gen. 3:7).

16.19 p. 39 Adam and Eve: remorse. Above, Adam and Eve, covering their nakedness with acanthus leaves, separate in the woods. Below, Adam and Eve, covering their nakedness, sit apart in the woods with their hands to their faces (lines 838–46; Gen. 3:8).

16.20 p. 41 Serpent: cursed by God. Above, within an irregular frame, composed of an unadorned column on the right and an interlaced column surmounted by a mask-head on the left, God, cross-nimbed, beardless, and holding a closed book, judges the serpent, which is shown standing erect and then lying on its belly (lines 903–17). Below, Adam and Eve: called by God. God, cross-nimbed, beardless, and holding a tubular scepter or roll, calls to Adam and Eve, who are hiding among the trees and covering their nakedness. Eve holds acanthus leaves over her breasts and genitals (lines 852–71; Gen. 3:14–15). For a discussion of the frame, see Herbert R. Broderick, "Some Attitudes toward the Frame," p. 38.

16.21 p. 44 Adam and Eve: judged by God. God, cross-nimbed, bearded, holding a closed book, and standing on a central hill, is represented twice. On the left, he, holding a decorated book, judges Eve, who stands, looking up and covering her nakedness. On the right, God, holding a closed book, points his left arm, around which a piece of his robe is looped, toward Adam, who looks up and covers his nakedness. A large tree is in the foreground (lines 918–38; Gen. 3:16–19).

16.22 p. 45 Adam and Eve: Expulsion from Eden. Within a frame composed of two columns supporting an angular arch with windows, God, cross-nimbed, bearded, and holding a closed book, pronounces the banishment of Adam and Eve, now fully dressed and standing on the left with gesturing arms. In the lower right, Adam, with a metal-tipped spade and bag of seeds, and Eve, with spindle and veil, are about to leave Eden (lines 941–44; Gen. 3:23–24).

16.23 p. 46 Adam and Eve: Expulsion from Eden. While an angel, wearing a fillet and holding a sword, guards the paradisaical doorway, composed of an architectural archway supported by columns, four steps, and an open door with elaborate hinges, Adam, holding a metal-tipped spade and a bag of seeds, turns and looks backwards toward the open doorway; Eve, wearing a veil, faces forwards. There are indications of sky, land, and vegetation (lines 945–64; Gen. 3:24).

16.24 p. 47 Abel: birth. Within an arcade with windows, Eve, on the left, lying in bed, holds the infant Abel. In the center opening is another infant, probably Cain. Adam, bearded, sits on a cushioned throne with hand extended (lines 965–69; Gen. 4:2).

16.25 p. 49 Adam: at labor. In the upper left, Adam and Cain (or Eve?) dig in the earth with metal-tipped spades. In the upper right, Cain and Abel make offerings at an altar with the Hand of God issuing from clouds above; Cain holds a bowl with three stalks(?) and Abel holds a horned animal (Gen. 4:3–4). In the left center, Abel, holding a rough-hewn staff, tends a flock of goats. In the lower right, Cain, holding a wooden club over his head, kills Abel, whose blood issues from his head (Gen. 4:8). In the lower left, Abel's blood cries out to God, cross-nimbed and bearded (lines 969–1001; Gen. 4:10).

16.26 p. 51 Cain: cursed by God. The upper level depicts Cain receiving God's judgment; on the left, Cain, bearded, stands with arms extended; on the right, God, bearded, cross-nimbed, and holding a closed book, stands with left arm extended. The zigzag line dividing the two figures refers to Gen. 4:14 and lines 1034–35 of the poem: "Ic awyrged sceal, / þeoden, of gesyhðe þinre hweorfan." In the second register, Cain, carrying a spear, is a wanderer in the land of Nod; a building with windows, a tower, and tiled roof is on the right (lines 1047–53; Gen. 4:16). In the lower level are Enoch and his wife with Irad (Jared in the poem) in the City of Enoch (Gen. 4:18). On the upper corners of the frame are two beast-heads. For a discussion of the frame, see Herbert R. Broderick, "Some Attitudes toward the Frame," pp. 39–40.

16.27 p. 53 — In the upper left, Irad, bearded, sits on a cushioned bench. In the upper right, Irad's wife, lies in bed, attended by a midwife. In the second level, Maviael's wife, seated on a cushioned bench, holds the infant Mathusael (OE Mathusal) and, on the right, Maviael (OE Malalehel) stands with raised arms. In the lower level, Lamech is flanked by his wives Adah and Zillah (lines 1063–77; Gen. 4:18–19). For a discussion of the names in the lines of Cain and Seth, see A. N. Doane, *Genesis A: A New Edition* (Madison, University of Wisconsin Press, 1978), pp. 249–52.

16.28 p. 54 — In the upper left, Jubal, bearded, plays a lyre. In the upper right, Tubal-Cain, bearded, is a blacksmith at forge with hammer, tongs, and anvil. In the second level, Tubal-Cain, bearded, holding an axe, drives a two-wheeled plow pulled by yoked oxen (Gen. 4:21–22). In the lower level, Adam, bearded, stands on the left with his arms raised; on the left, Eve, veiled, sits on a cushioned bench and holds the infant Seth on her lap (lines 1077–89; Gen. 4:25).

16.29 p. 56 — Within an elaborate architectural frame, composed of columns supporting a tent-like arch with a Ringerike-style ornament in the center, Seth, bearded, stands holding a long spear; on the right, his wife, veiled, holding his infant son Enos, raises her hand. At the bottom of the frame are a series of decorated building tiles(?) and a closed door with hinges. Above the figure of Seth is the inscription "Seth wæs sæli" (re. line 1138; lines 1128–42; Gen. 4:26).

16.30 p. 57 — Cainan: son of Enos. Cainan, bearded, crowned, and holding a sword, seated with legs crossed on an elaborate faldstool, gives instructions to his people, some of whom bear swords and a shield. On the right, his wife, seated on a chair, holds the infant Malaleel (OE Malalehel). The frame is composed of columns with Ringerike capitals supporting an arch with three towers; a curtain is wrapped around a slender column (lines 1155–66; Gen. 5:12).

16.31 p. 58 — Within an arch supported by columns, Malaleel, bearded, stands with arms raised before a draped altar with steps (lines 1160–77; Gen. 5:15). Initial *H* / *HIM* (line 1167) is composed of two interlaced birds spitting foliage.

16.32 p. 59 — Malaleel: death and burial. The dead body of Malaleel, nude to the waist, is laid out on a coffin or sarcophagus; one of his sons, Jared(?), stands by the coffin holding the corpse's head and left arm. To the right are six standing males (his other sons?), one of whom holds a censer from the index finger of his left hand. On the upper left are three females (his daughters?), two of whom veil their faces. On the far left is a building with a tower and tiled roof (lines 1177–80; Gen. 5:16–17).

16.33 p. 60 Enoch: son of Jared. Enoch, nimbed, bearded, and holding an open book, treads underfoot a beast or dragon, while an angel, on the upper right, issues from a cloud and addresses him (lines 1187–1202; Gen. 5:22–24). According to Israel Gollancz, the nimbus is intended to differentiate him from Enoch the son of Cain; the book, which contains indications of writing, reflects the Hebrew legend that Enoch was the inventor of writing; and finally, the dragon symbolizes the great dragon in Rev. 12; see *The Cædmon Manuscript of Anglo-Saxon Biblical Poetry* (Oxford, 1927), p. xliv.

16.34 p. 61 Translation of Enoch. Below, Enoch, bearded and wearing a Phrygian hat, standing on a raised rock, is flanked by two angels grasping his arms; on the sides, twelve kinsmen look upwards. Above, Enoch's upper body has disappeared into the clouds; two angels hold his waist (lines 1202–17). The rock upon which Enoch stands, the twelve kinsmen, and the two angels are mentioned neither in the poetic text nor in the Bible (Gen. 5:24). The ultimate source for this illustration, according to Meyer Schapiro, is a new type of the Ascension of Christ (Acts 1:9), which was conceived by Anglo-Saxon artists about the year 1000; see "The Image of the Disappearing Christ: The Ascension in English Art Around The Year 1000," in *Gazette des Beaux Arts* Series 6 (March, 1943), 135–52; rpt. in *Late Antique, Early Christian and Medieval Art: Selected Papers* (New York, 1979), pp. 267–87.

16.35 p. 62 Lamech: birth. On the left, Mathusael (OE Mathusal), bearded, sits on cushioned bench, feet on footstool, hands raised; behind are four men who represent his tribe. On the right, Mathusael's wife lies in bed, attended by two midwives, one of whom holds the infant Lamech. On the left is a column with a winged mask-head and biting serpent (intended for the letter L of Lamech in line 1225?) (Gen. 5:25).

16.36 p. 63 Noah: birth. Within the first of three arches, Noah's mother lies in bed; a midwife adjusts the checkered pillow behind her head. An unfinished figure (the infant Noah?) is above. In the second arch, Noah, crowned and standing in front of a cushioned bench, touches hands(?) with the foremost member of his tribe. In the third arch, Noah, crowned, bearded, and holding a staff, sits on a cushioned bench in front of his three sons (lines 1237–47; Gen. 5:28–29). Below is a large initial *O* / *Oðæt* (line 1248), composed of biting birds.

16.37 p. 65 Above, Noah: commanded to build Ark. God, bearded and crowned but lacking a nimbus, holds a closed book and raises his right hand towards Noah, bearded, who stands on the right with raised right arm. Below, Noah: building Ark. Noah, bearded, holds an axe or adz in his upraised arms; the unfinished Ark has a double-prow, planking, and a doorway in the hull (lines 1285–1355; Gen. 6: 13–16).

16.38 p. 66 — Noah: in Ark. The completed Ark, whose three-level superstructure contains doors, arches, and roofed tower, consists of a hull with an elaborate dragon's head on the bow and a curving tail-like stern section. The first level has three scenes: on the left, Noah, bearded, holding the rudder, addresses one of two sons standing in an arch; in the center, God, bearded and cross-nimbed, holds the edge of an open door, while within the doorway are two veiled women; on the right, the third son, standing on a ladder, turns towards a veiled woman standing on the ground (Noah's reluctant wife?). Behind God are birds, stags, and sheep. On the second level, birds, stags, and vegetation are in the arches. Two roosters stand on two towers. On the upper level, a man releases a bird from his hands and, on the right, a bird grasps a branch in its beak. Hovering over the Ark, which is on the water, are two seraphim with fillets (lines 1356–71; Gen. 7:1–8:12).

16.39 p. 68 — Above, Noah's Ark upon the Waters. The Ark's superstructure has two-levels, closed doors, twin towers with windows, and a central tent-like roof. The hull has a dragon's head at the prow and a curved tail at the stern (Gen. 7:17–20). Below, God, beardless and cross-nimbed, standing on dry ground, is about to open the closed and locked door of the Ark, which is similar to the one above (lines 1371–1492; Gen. 8:15–16).

16.40 p. 70 — Ultra-violet illumination of this largely "blank" folio has revealed the presence of two metal stylus sketches, which were presumably intended as preliminary under-drawings to be inked-in and completed at a later stage. In the upper level is a strange lemon-shaped structure with a central open door; on the lower right is a bird with a large pointed beak. The presence of the bird suggests two related interpretations: the scene represents either the disembarkation of the animals from the Ark (Gen. 8:17) or, as Herbert R. Broderick argues ("The Iconographic and Compositional Sources of the Drawings in Oxford, Bodleian Library, MS Junius 11," diss. Columbia University, 1978, pp. 424–25), the episode of the raven and the dove (Gen. 8:6–12). In the lower level is a large ship, which extends from the edge of the vellum into the binding; the hull of the Viking-style ship resembles those on pages 66 and 68. One would expect a disembarkation scene at this point in the pictorial narrative, but the outline of a fish seems to indicate that the ship is still afloat. For a fuller discussion, see Thomas H. Ohlgren, "Five New Drawings in the MS. Junius 11," pp. 231–32.

16.41 p. 73 — Noah: Disembarkation from the Ark. God, beardless, decorated nimbus, holds open the door of the Ark, which is rendered as a curious lemon-shaped structure with decorated square panels. Exiting the door are four disembodied veiled female heads (Noah's wife and daughters-in-law); on the left, Noah, bearded, and his three sons walk on dry land. For a discussion, see George Henderson, "Late-Antique Influences in Some Illustrations of Genesis," *Journal of the Warburg and Courtauld Institutes*, 25 (1962), 183–90. Above is the large initial letter *þ/þa* (line 1483). The initial is composed of a complete winged dragon with gaping jaw gripping the bow and a tail of acanthus.

16.42 p. 74 Noah: offering sacrifice. On the left, God, beardless and lacking a nimbus, holds a tubular scepter or roll with four bands in his left hand and extends his right hand in blessing toward Noah, bearded, and his three sons. In draped hands Noah extends a sacrificial bird toward the Deity; beneath Noah's arms is a horned animal with cloven hooves and wings. The drawing is unframed (lines 1503–10; Gen. 8:20).

16.43 p. 76 Noah: Covenant with God. Noah, bearded, kneels and extends his hands toward (and touches?) the right hand of God, beardless and lacking a nimbus, who holds a tubular scepter or roll with bands and dots (lines 1510–42; Gen. 9:1).

16.44 p. 77 Noah: as husbandman. On the left of the unframed full-page drawing a tall structure is supported by two arches. Within the first arch are two standing male figures, one bearded (Noah's two sons). In the second arch is a veiled female figure (Noah's wife?). On the right, Noah, bearded and holding a stick in his upraised right hand, drives a plow pulled by two oxen. On the far right, a man (the third son) holds a long staff (lines 1555–61; Gen. 9:20).

16.45 p. 78 Noah: nakedness. The drawing consists of three consecutive scenes with repeated characters. In the upper portion, Noah, bearded, head on checkered pillow, lies asleep (inebriated) in an elaborate bed supported on columns and decorated with acanthus-leaf plants (representing grape vines); except for a spread that covers his lower legs, he is naked with his genitals exposed. On the left, Ham, with his arms raised, witnesses his father's nakedness. Beneath the bed, Ham, on the left, tells his two brothers, Japheth and Shem, about their father's drunkenness. On the lower left, Japheth and Shem, hiding their faces with draperies, cover their father, who lies asleep, head on checkered pillow, in bed; acanthus-leaf plants grow at either end (lines 1562–1601; Gen. 9:21–23).

16.46 p. 81 Nimrod: Planning to Build the Tower of Babel. Above, within an elaborate structure with towers, crenelated walls, and a locked gate, Nimrod, bearded and wearing a crown, stands with hands raised among his princes, who are holding building implements (axes) in order to enlarge his territories (lines 1628–36; Gen. 10:8). Below, Nimrod, bearded, crowned, and bearing a large spear, leads a large group of men wearing swords and holding spears; a herd of animals moves to the right. Gollancz identifies the scene as Nimrod as the mighty hunter before the Lord (p. xlvi), but Gen. 10:9 is not mentioned in the Old English text. Herbert Broderick, "The Iconographic and Compositional Sources of the Drawings," p. 348, is correct when he cites lines 1649–50 as the textual source for the drawing: "Gewiton him þa eastan æhta lædan, / feoh and feorme."

16.47 p. 82 Tower of Babel: visited by God. On the upper left, God, cross-nimbed, beardless, and holding a tubular scepter or roll with rings or bands, rebukes a group of four workmen holding axes; on the right, two men, wielding axes, are at work on the Tower of Babel, a four-tiered structure supported by an arcade. In the middle register, two groups of Babylonians, some holding spears, separate and turn in different directions (lines 1661–1701; Gen. 11:5–9). In the lower level, Terah, Abraham, Sarah, Haran, and Lot approach the land of Haran, which is represented by a building (lines 1730–38; Gen. 11:31).

16.48 p. 84 Abraham: communicating with God. In the upper left, God, cross-nimbed, beardless, and holding a tubular scepter or roll, raises his right hand in blessing toward Abraham, bearded, who stands with his arms raised; God is commanding Abraham to leave Haran (Gen. 12:1–3). In the upper right, Sarah, veiled, and Lot sit within an arch of a building (Abraham's house). In the middle level, Abraham, bearded and holding a spear, leads Sarah and Lot out of Haran into the land of Canaan, which is represented by the building on the right (Gen. 12:5). In the lower level, God, cross-nimbed and beardless, tells Abraham that "To thy seed will I give this land" (lines 1784–90; Gen. 12:7).

16.49 p. 87 Abraham: builds altar. Above, Abraham, bearded, holding an axe, stands between two buildings, representing Bether and Hai (called "Bethlem," line 1799 in the poetic text); he is presumably building the altar. In the lower right, Abraham, bearded, makes an offering of a pot of incense in front of a building; the drawing corresponds more closely to the poetic text than to the Genesis account (Gen. 13:4): "Abraham þa oðere siðe / wibed worhte. He þæar wordum god / torhtum cigde, tiber onsægde / his liffrean, (him þæs lean ageaf / nalles hneawlice þurh his hand metend)" (lines 1805–09). In the lower left, God, cross-nimbed and beardless, again appears before Abraham. This scene, as Herbert Broderick points out ("The Iconographic and Compositional Sources of the Drawings," pp. 360–61), does not occur in the Genesis account; the figure of God pointing his finger at Abraham's hands appears to reinforce line 1809 of the poem.

16.50 p. 88 Abraham: approaching Egypt. Abraham, bearded and carrying a spear, leads his tribe, including Sarah, veiled, holding a spindle, toward Egypt, represented as a walled enclosure with towers, windows, and a gate; four people are within (lines 1811–19; Gen. 12:10).

16.51 p. 96 Abraham and the messenger (late addition of uncertain date) (lines 2018–23; Gen. 14:14).

Index to Iconographic Contents

The index consists of an alphabetical listing of subjects, focusing on the main **personage** represented in the miniature. Following the persons's name is a short title indicating the precise **activity** with which the person is associated. I have, in addition, included numerous *see* and *see also* cross-references to lead users to the main entries and to suggest relevant associations. The numerical codes following each entry refer both to the *Descriptions of the Plates* and to the photographic plates themselves.

Plates

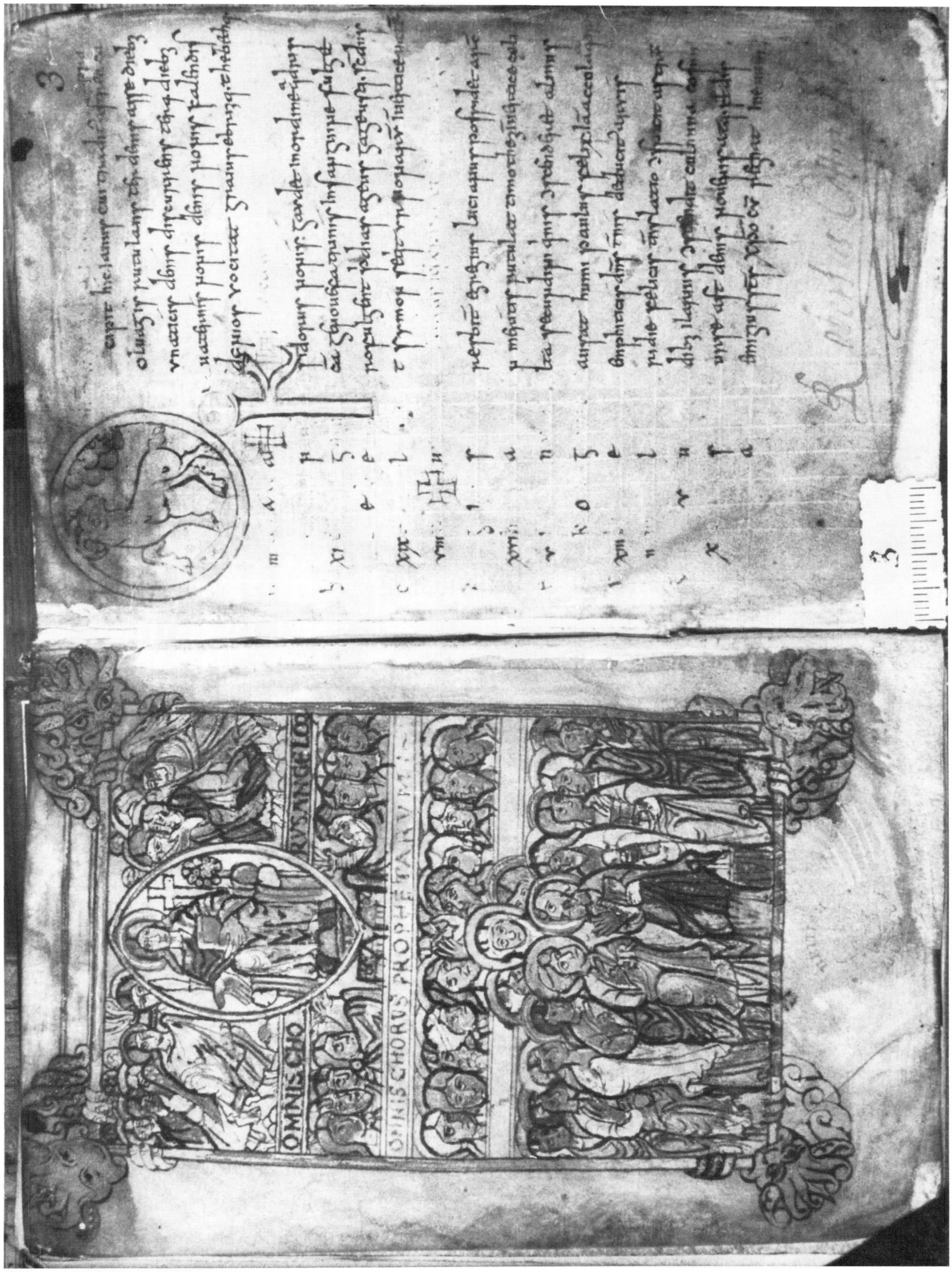

1.1 London, B.L., Cotton Galba A. XVIII, ff. 2^v–3^r

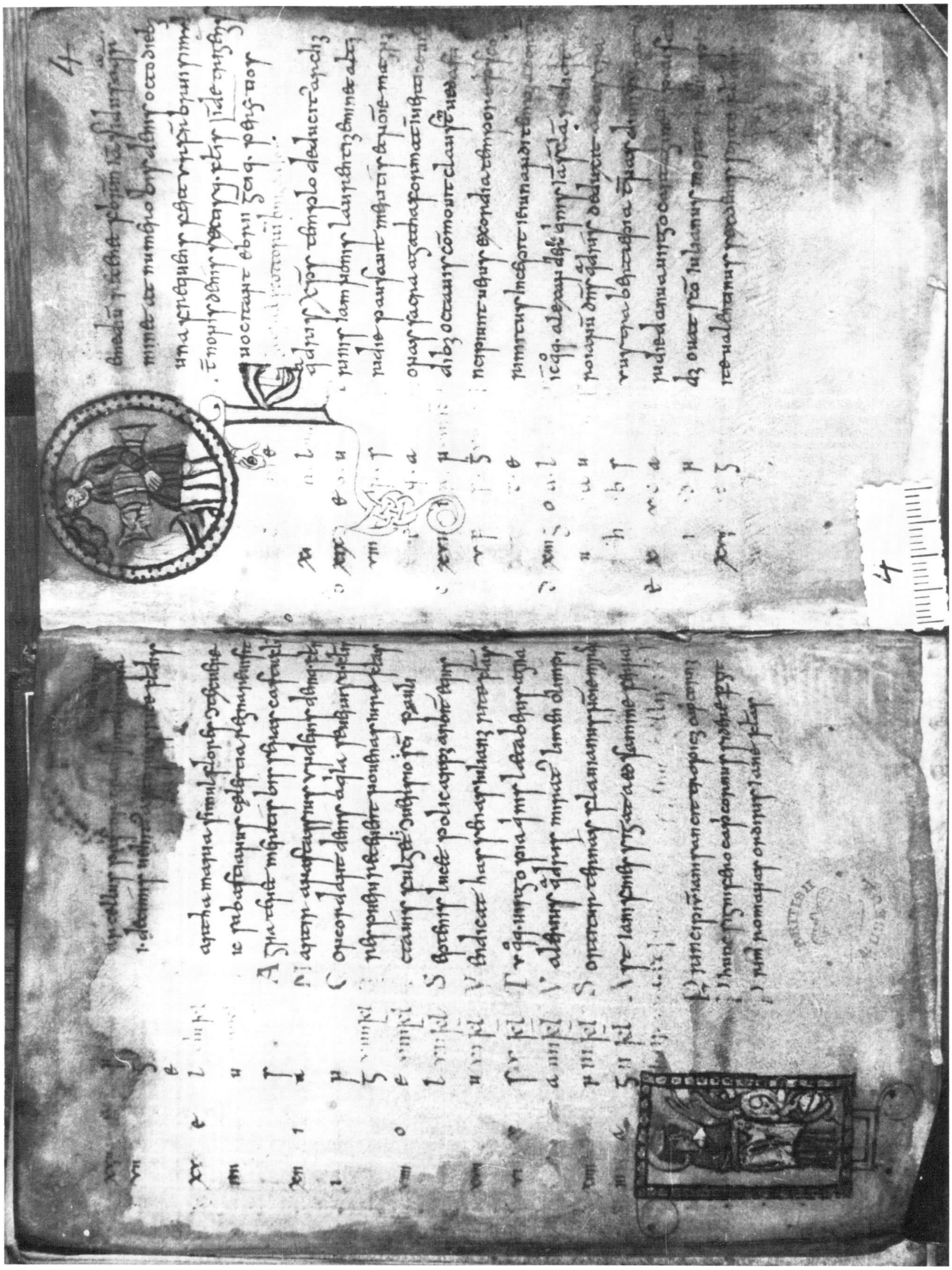

1.2 London, B.L., Cotton Galba A. XVIII, ff. 3^v–4^r

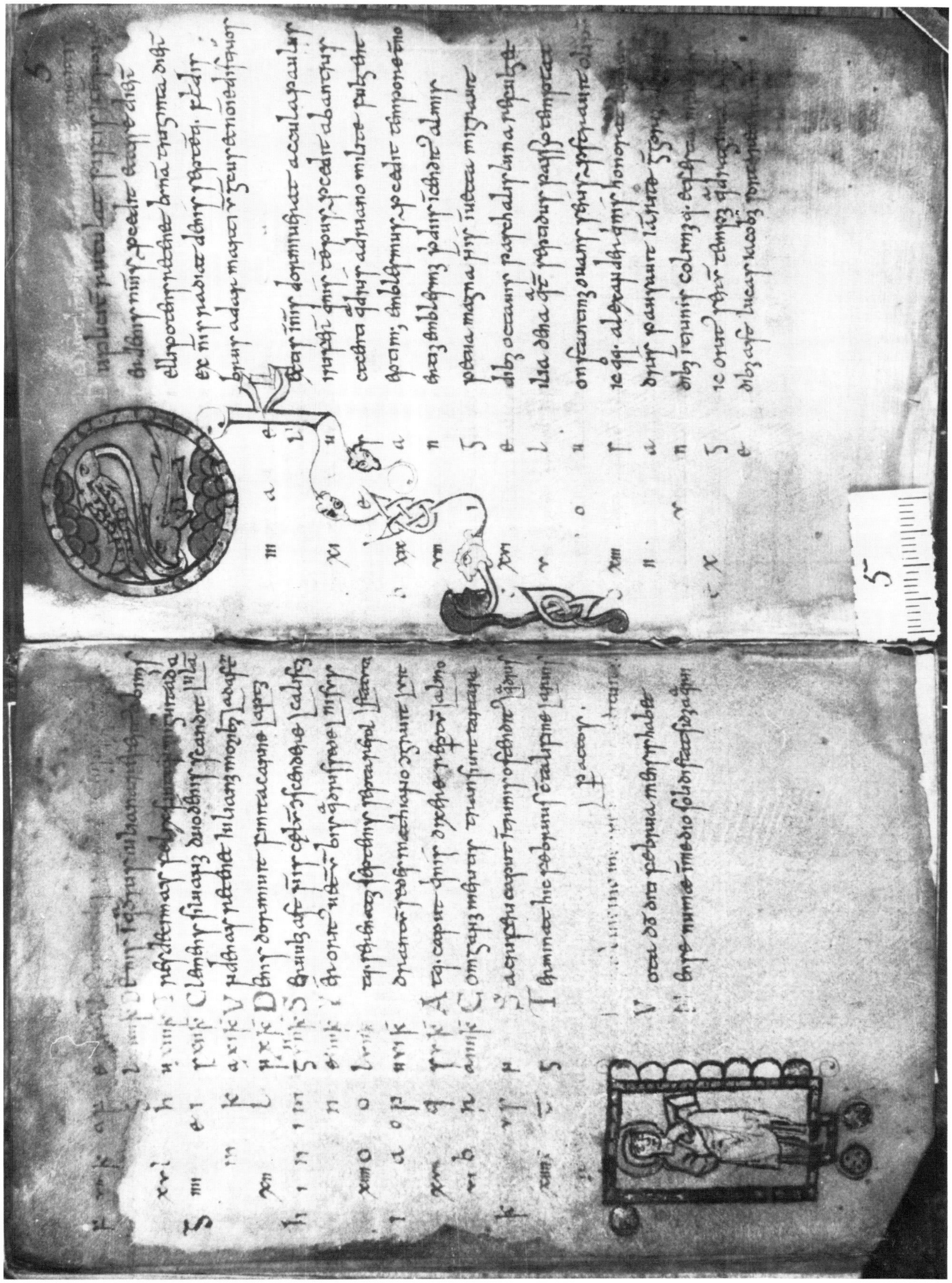

1.3 London, B.L., Cotton Galba A. XVIII, ff. 4^{v}–5^{r}

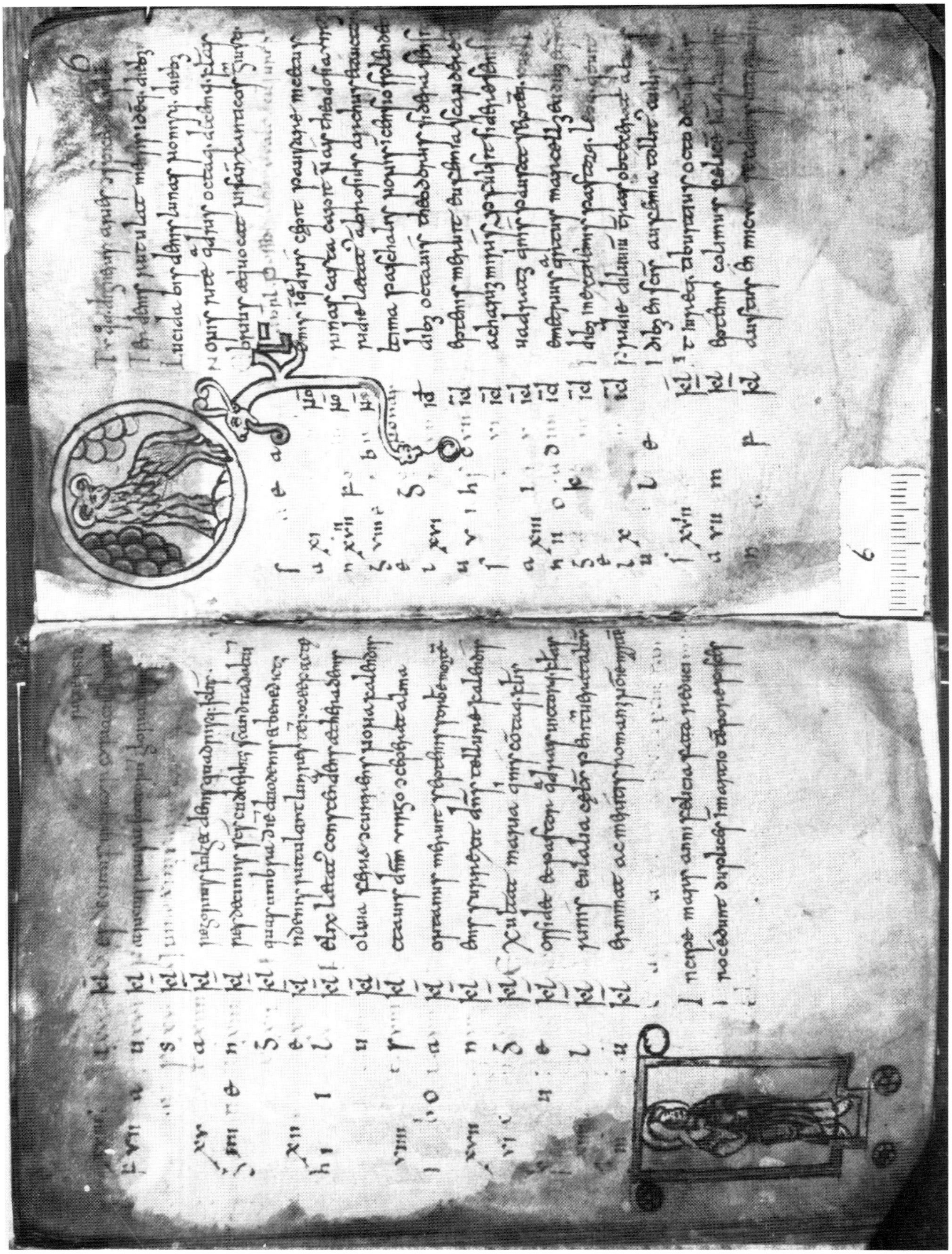

1.4 London, B.L., Cotton Galba A. XVIII, ff. 5ᵛ–6ʳ

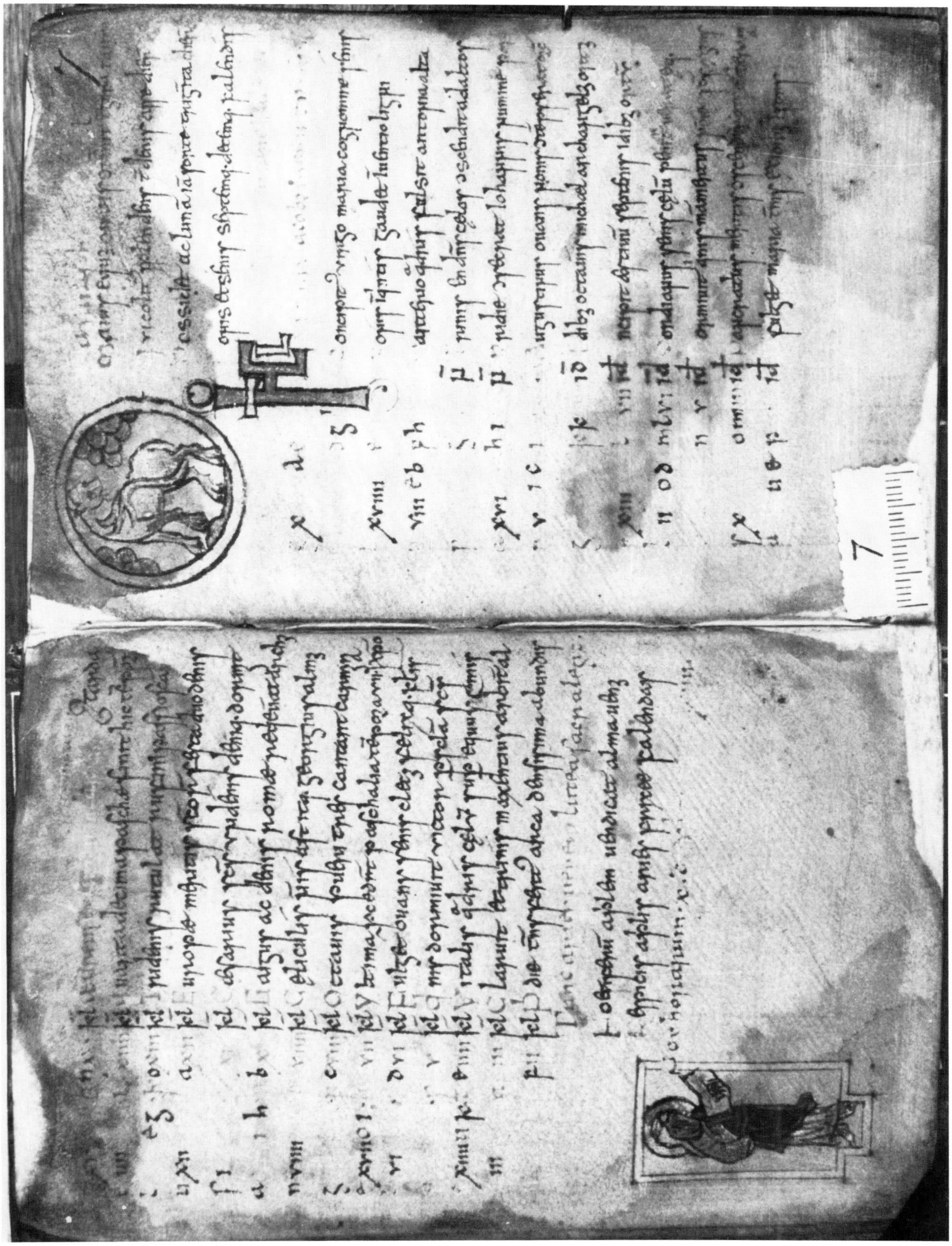

1.5 London, B.L., Cotton Galba A. XVIII, ff. 6v–7r

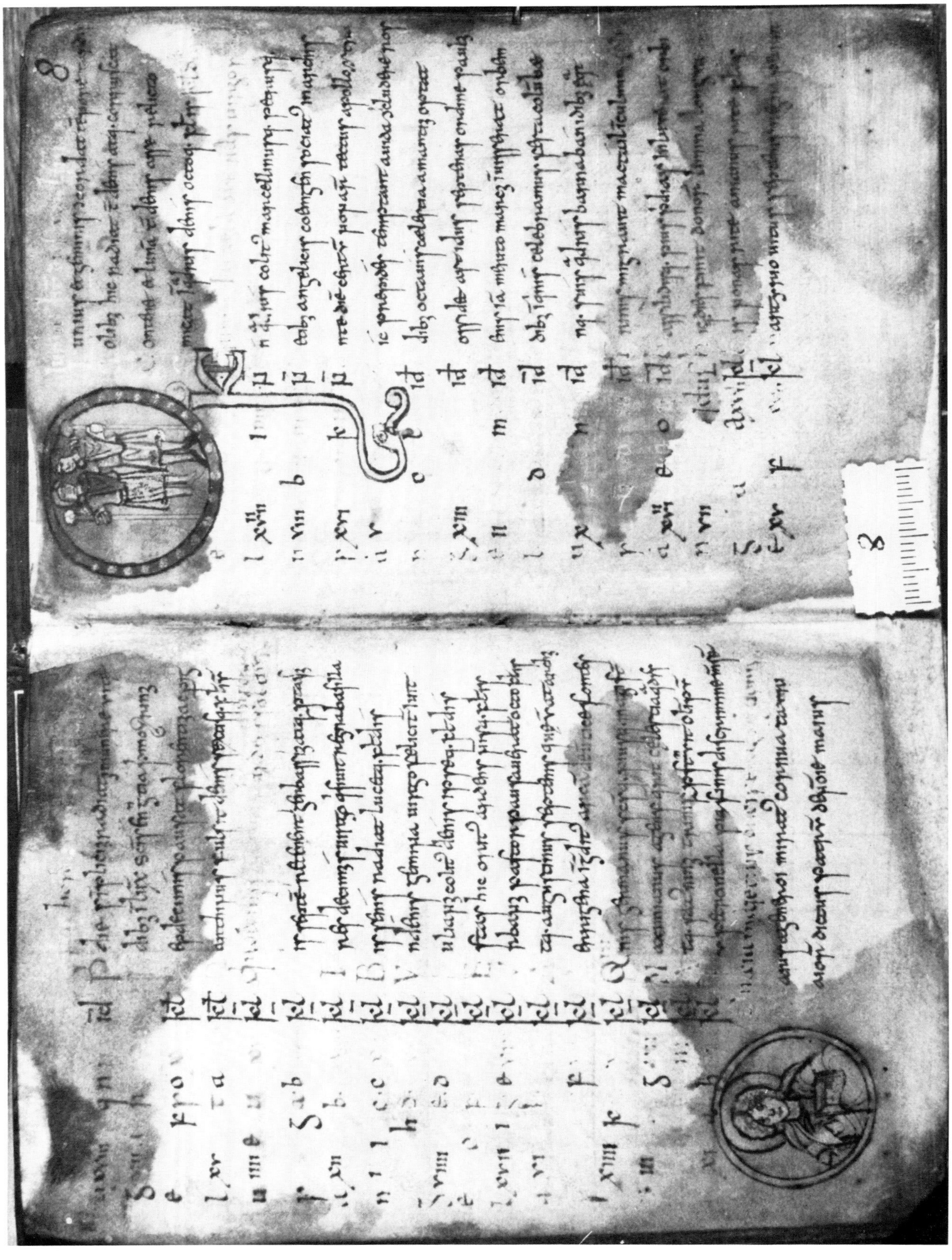

1.6 London, B.L., Cotton Galba A. XVIII, ff. 7v–8r

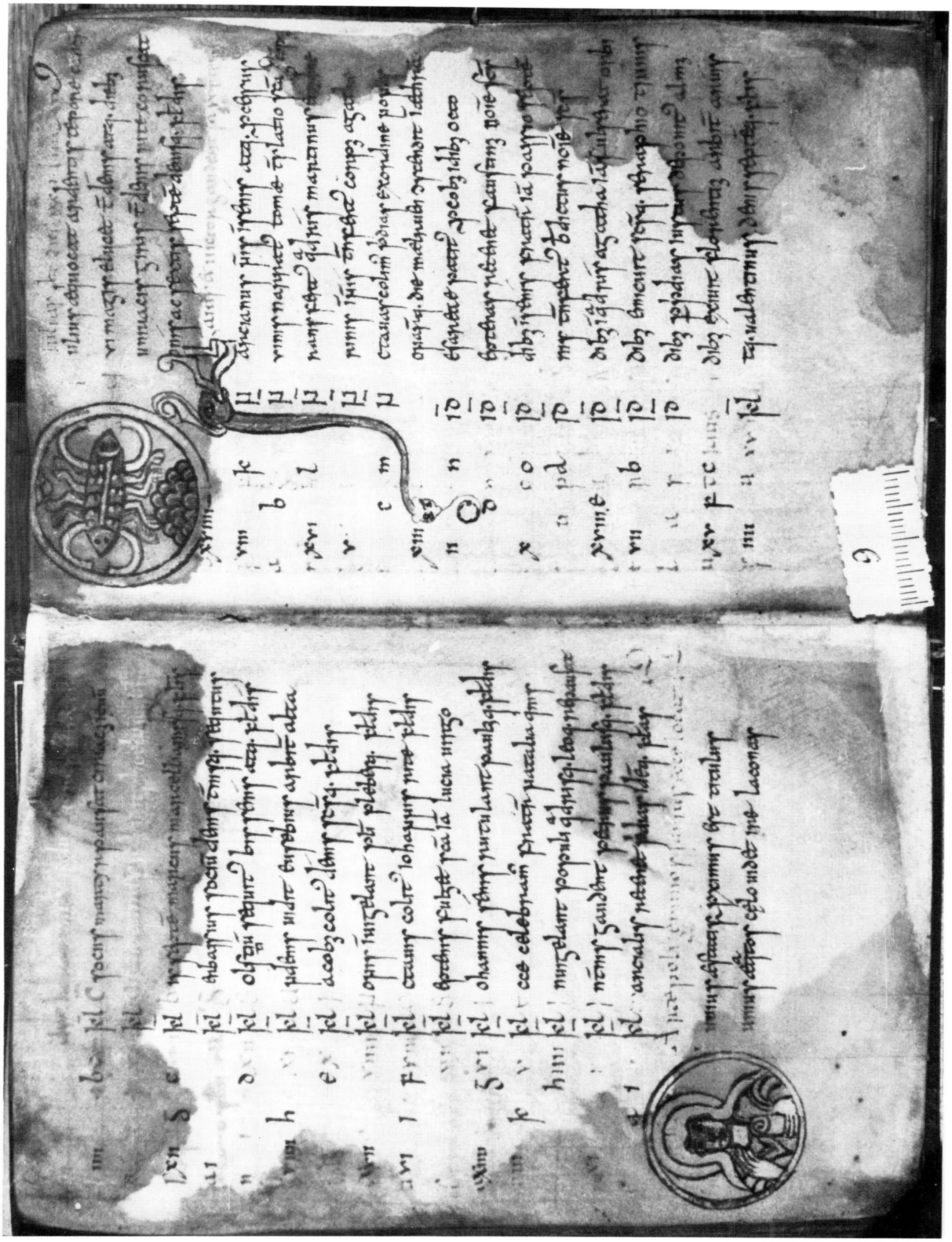

1.7 London, B.L., Cotton Galba A. XVIII, ff. 8v–9r

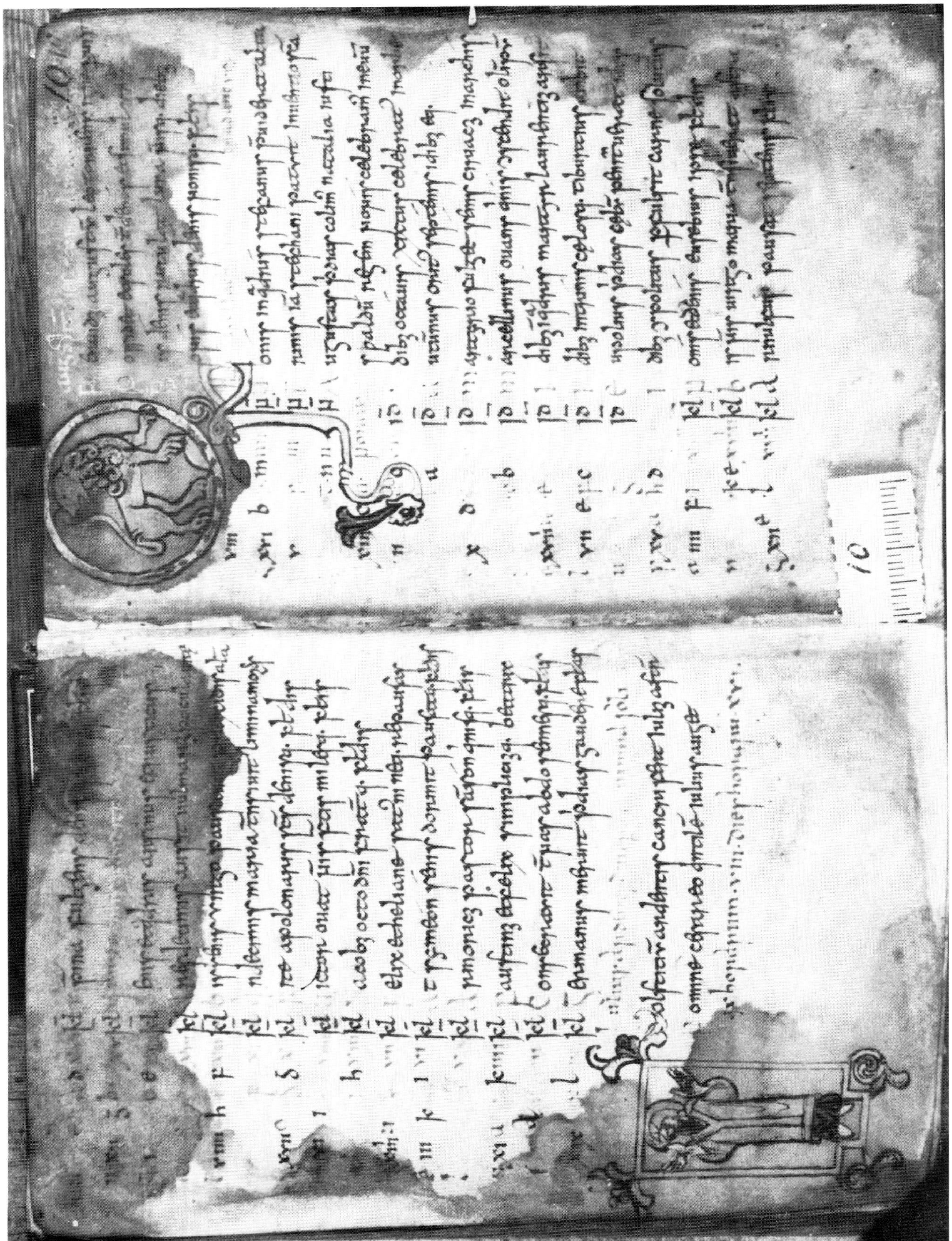

1.8 London, B.L., Cotton Galba A. XVIII, ff. 9v–10r

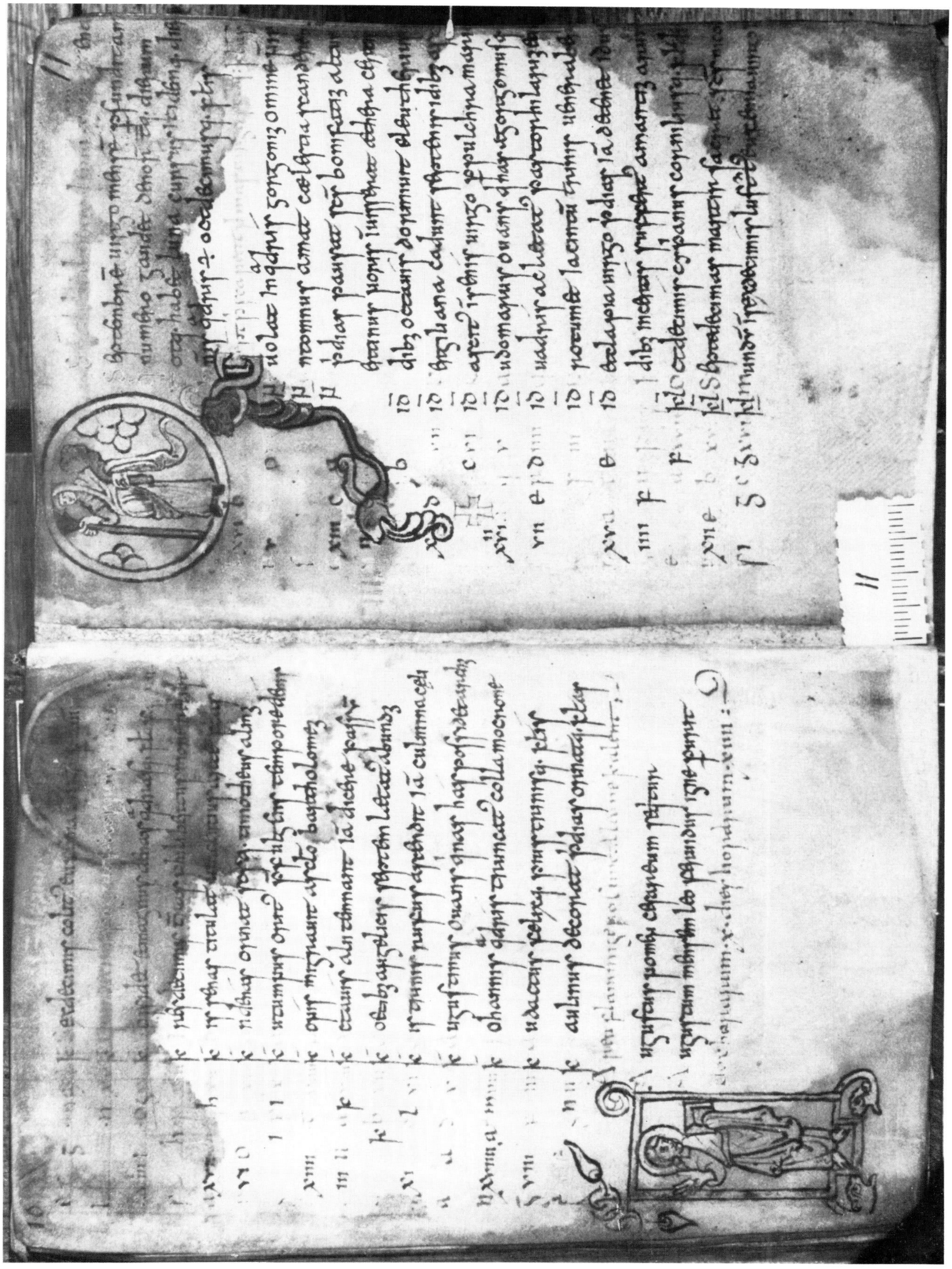

1.9 London, B.L., Cotton Galba A. XVIII, ff. 10^{v}–11^{r}

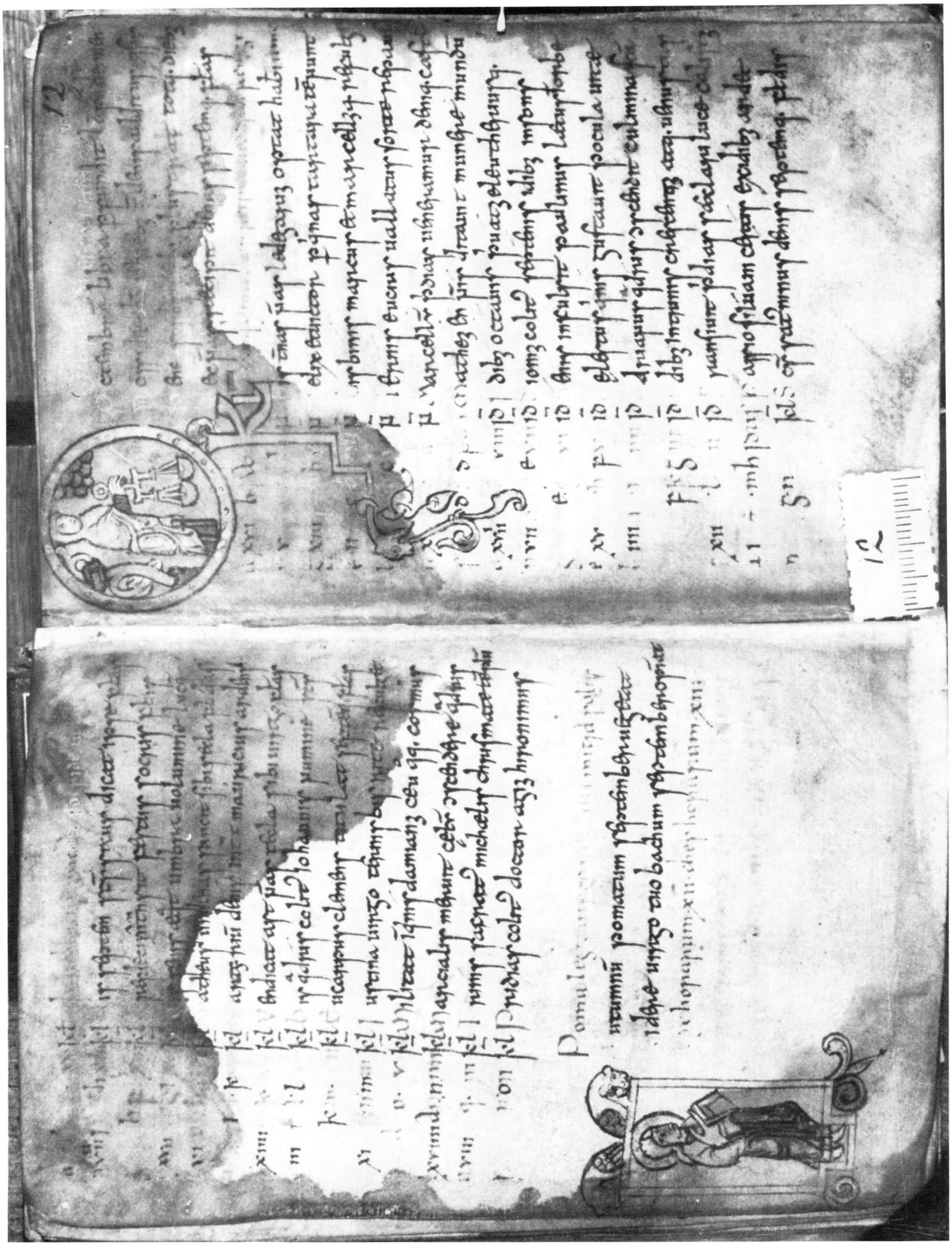

1.10 London, B.L., Cotton Galba A. XVIII, ff. 11v–12r

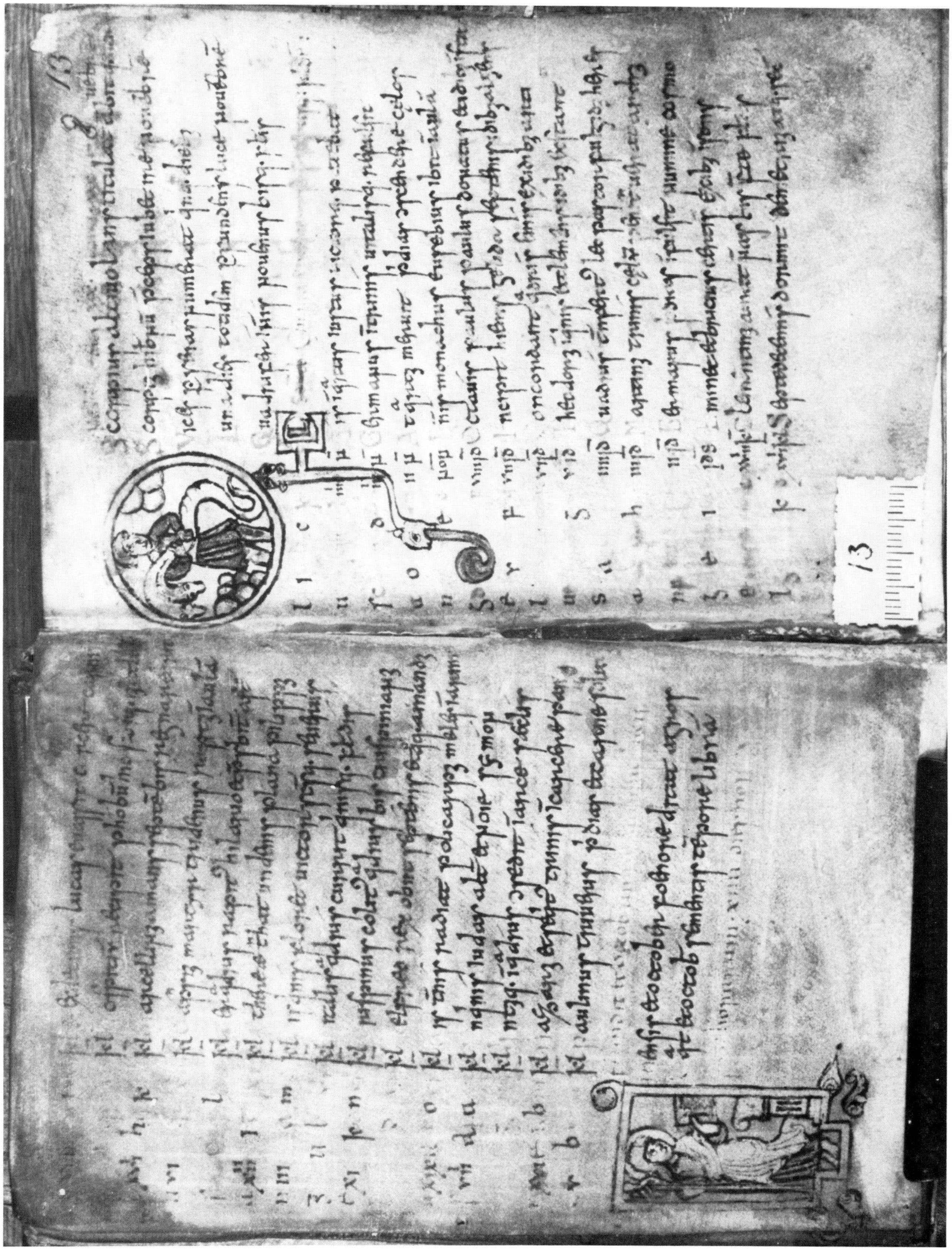

1.11 London, B.L., Cotton Galba A. XVIII, ff. 12^{v}–13^{r}

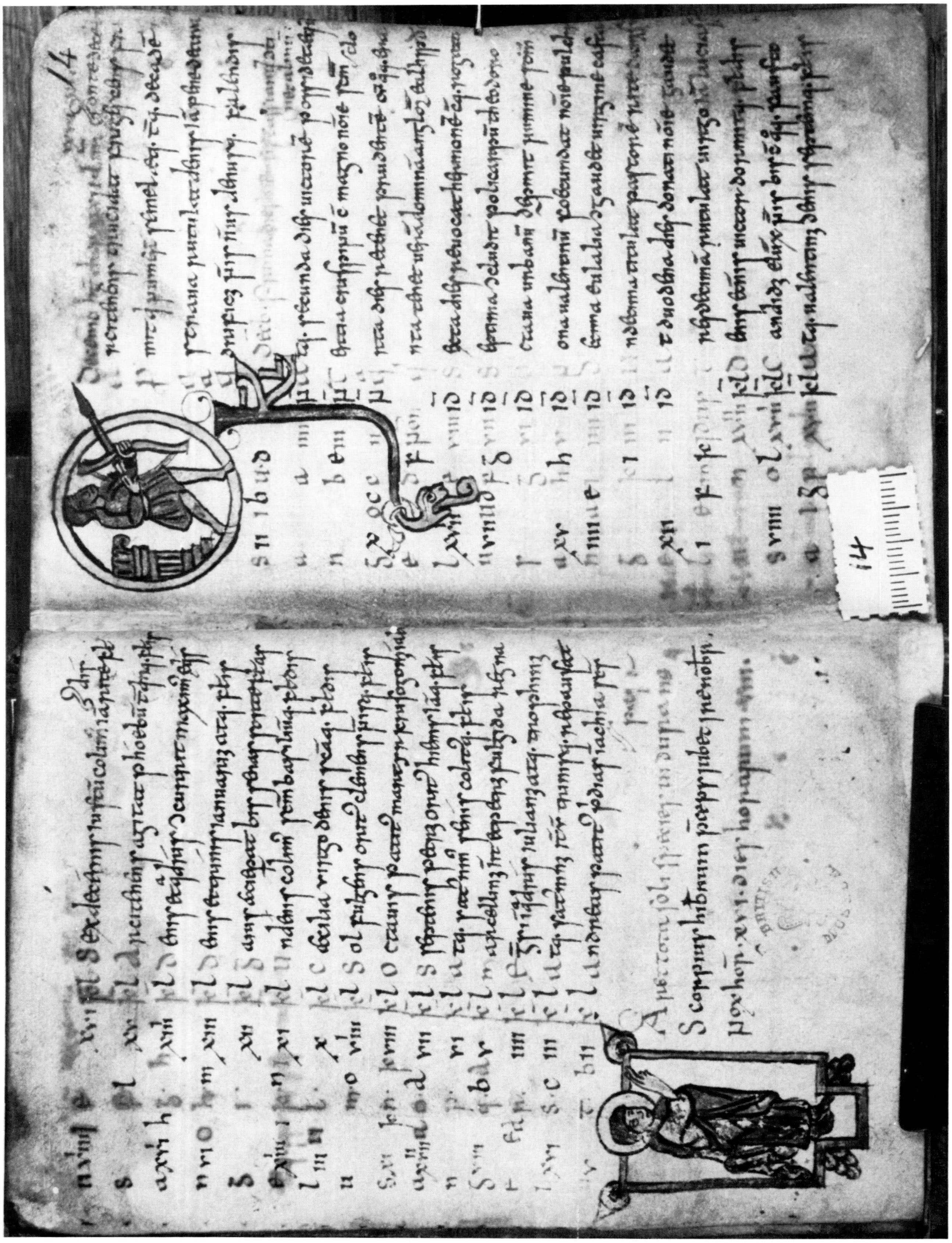

1.12 London, B.L., Cotton Galba A. XVIII, ff. 13v–14r

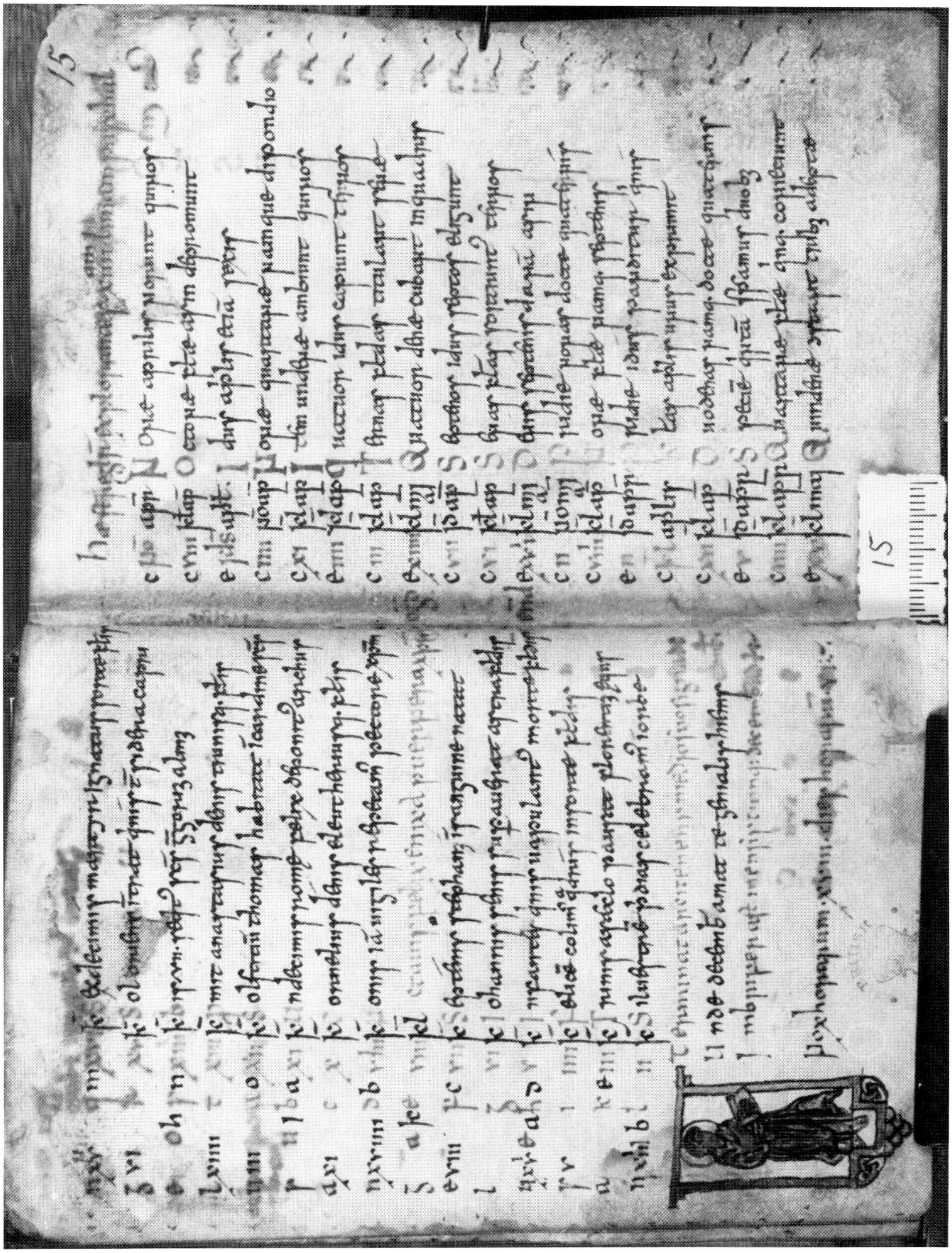

1.13 London, B.L., Cotton Galba A. XVIII, ff. 14v–15r

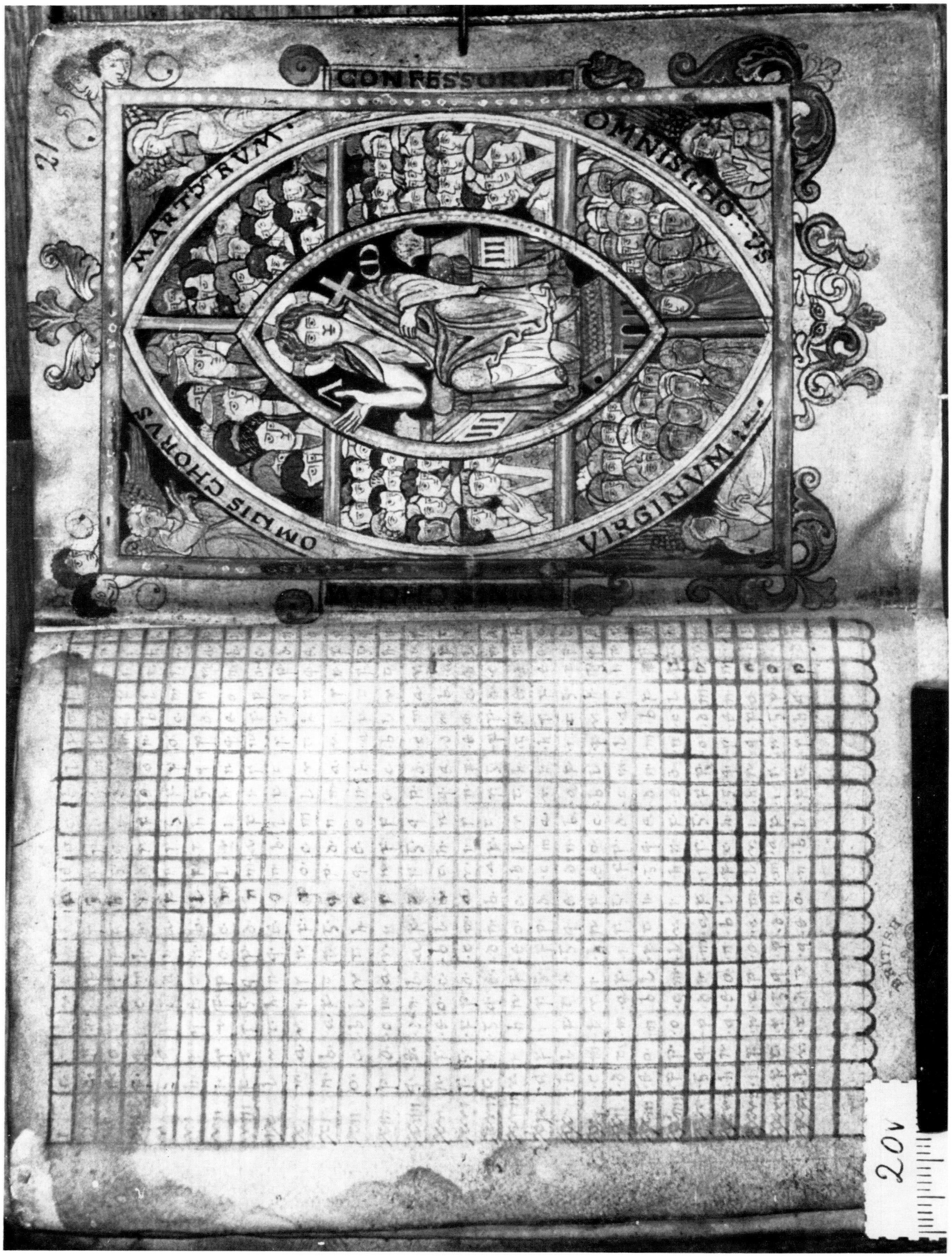

1.14 London, B.L., Cotton Galba A. XVIII, ff. 20^v–21^r

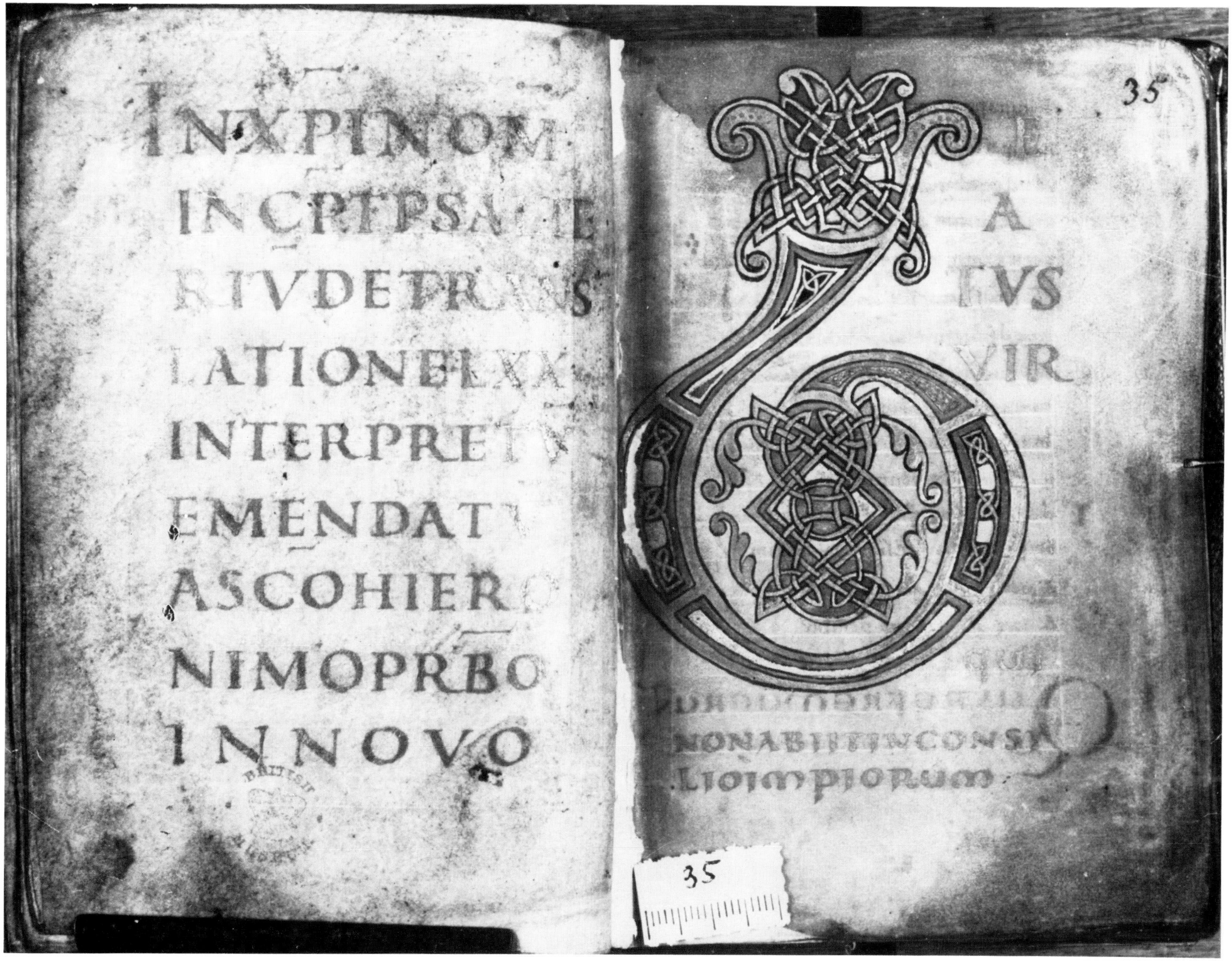

1.15 London, B.L., Cotton Galba A. XVIII, ff. 34^{v}–35^{r}

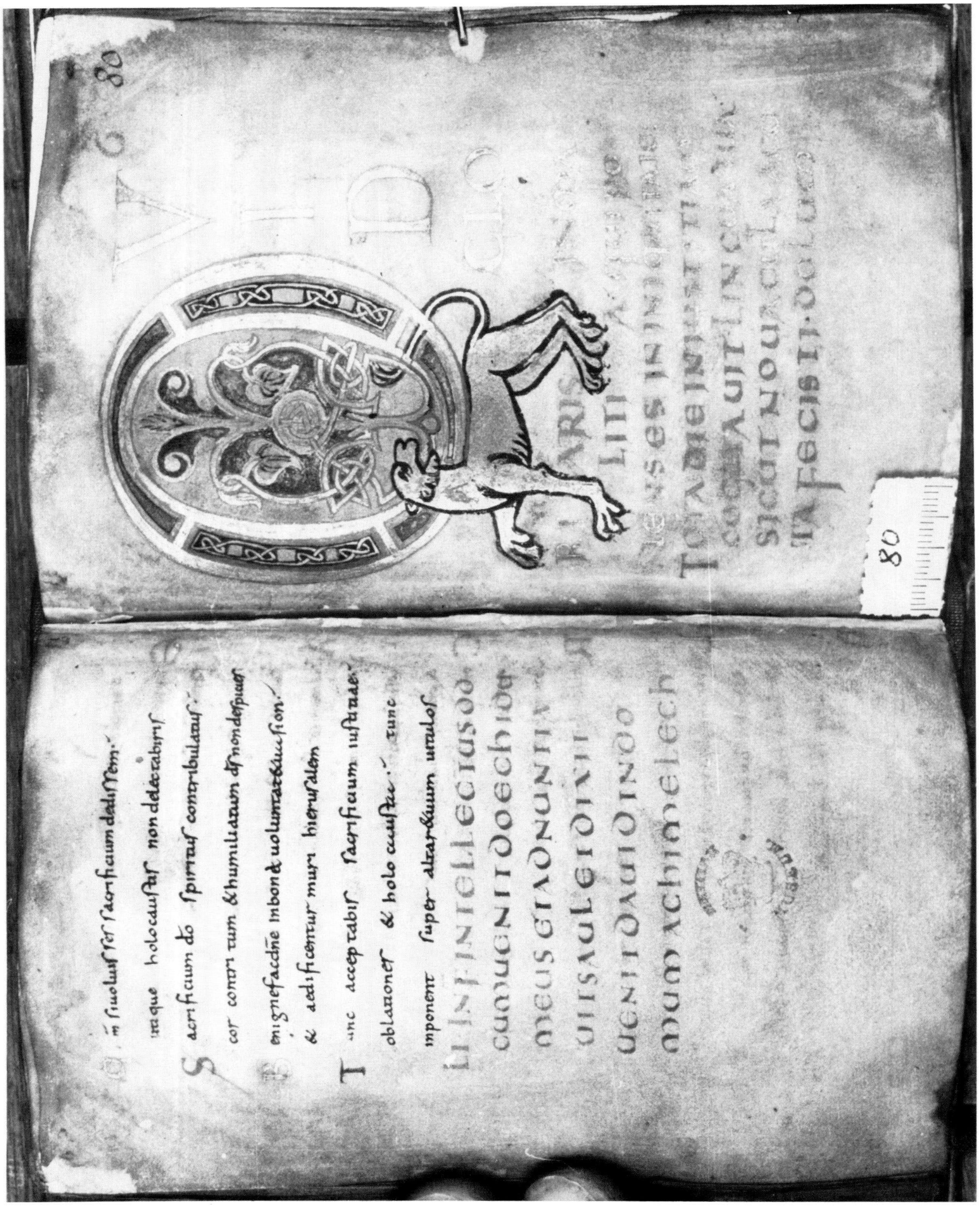

1.16 London, B.L., Cotton Galba A. XVIII, ff. 79ᵛ–80ʳ

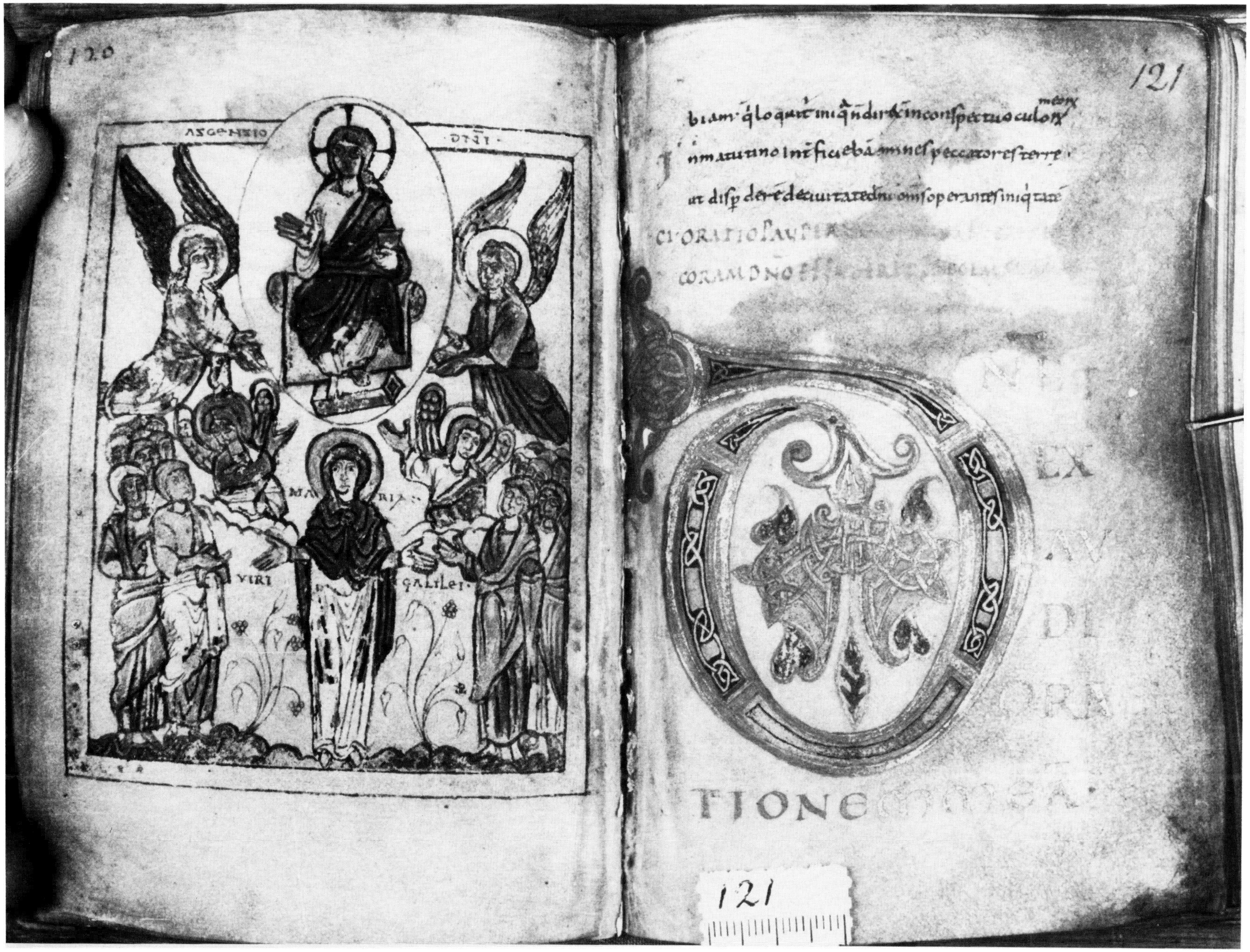

1.17 London, B.L., Cotton Galba A. XVIII, ff. 120^{v}–121^{r}

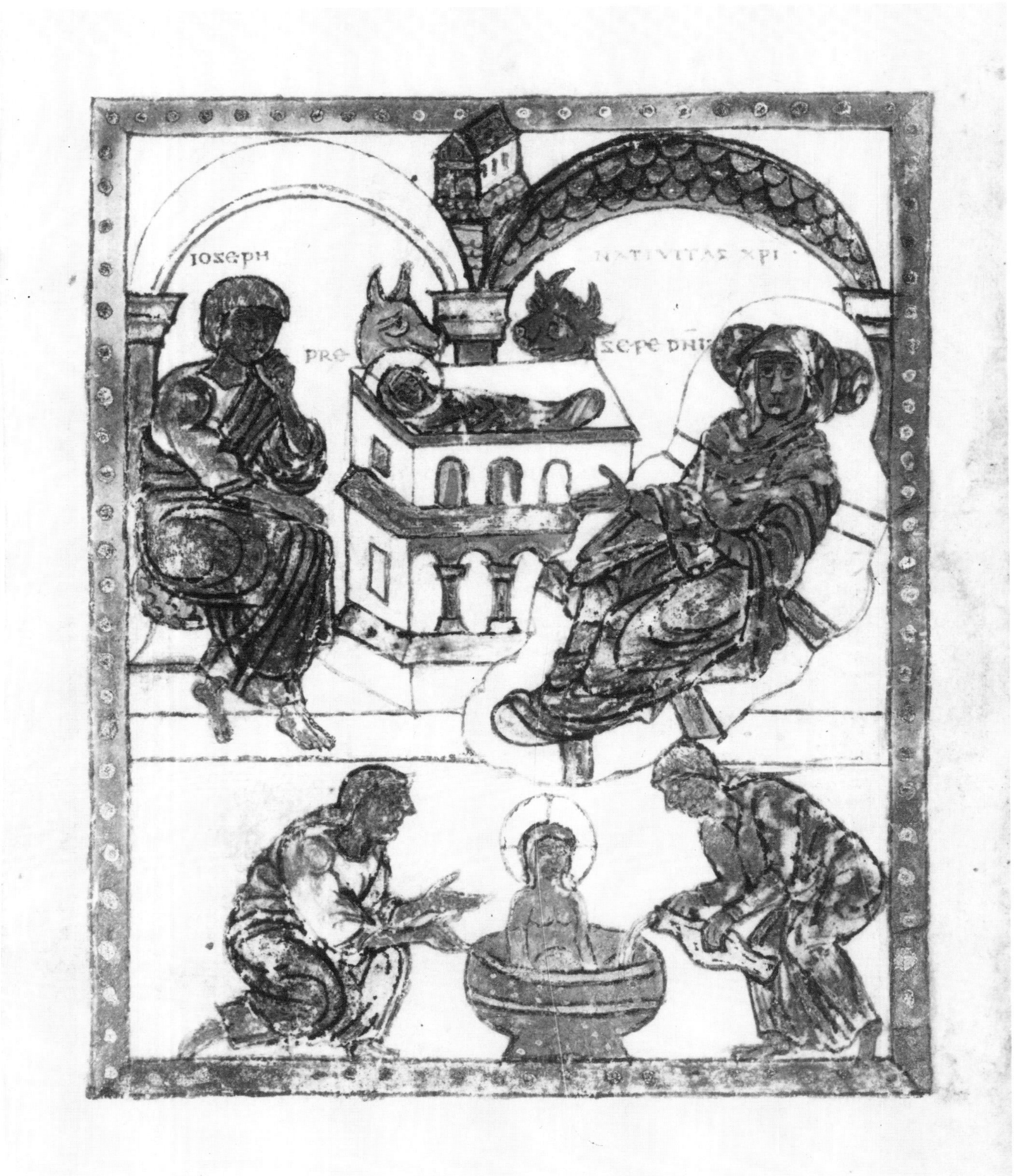

1.18 Oxford, Bodleian Library, Rawl. B. 484, f. 85r

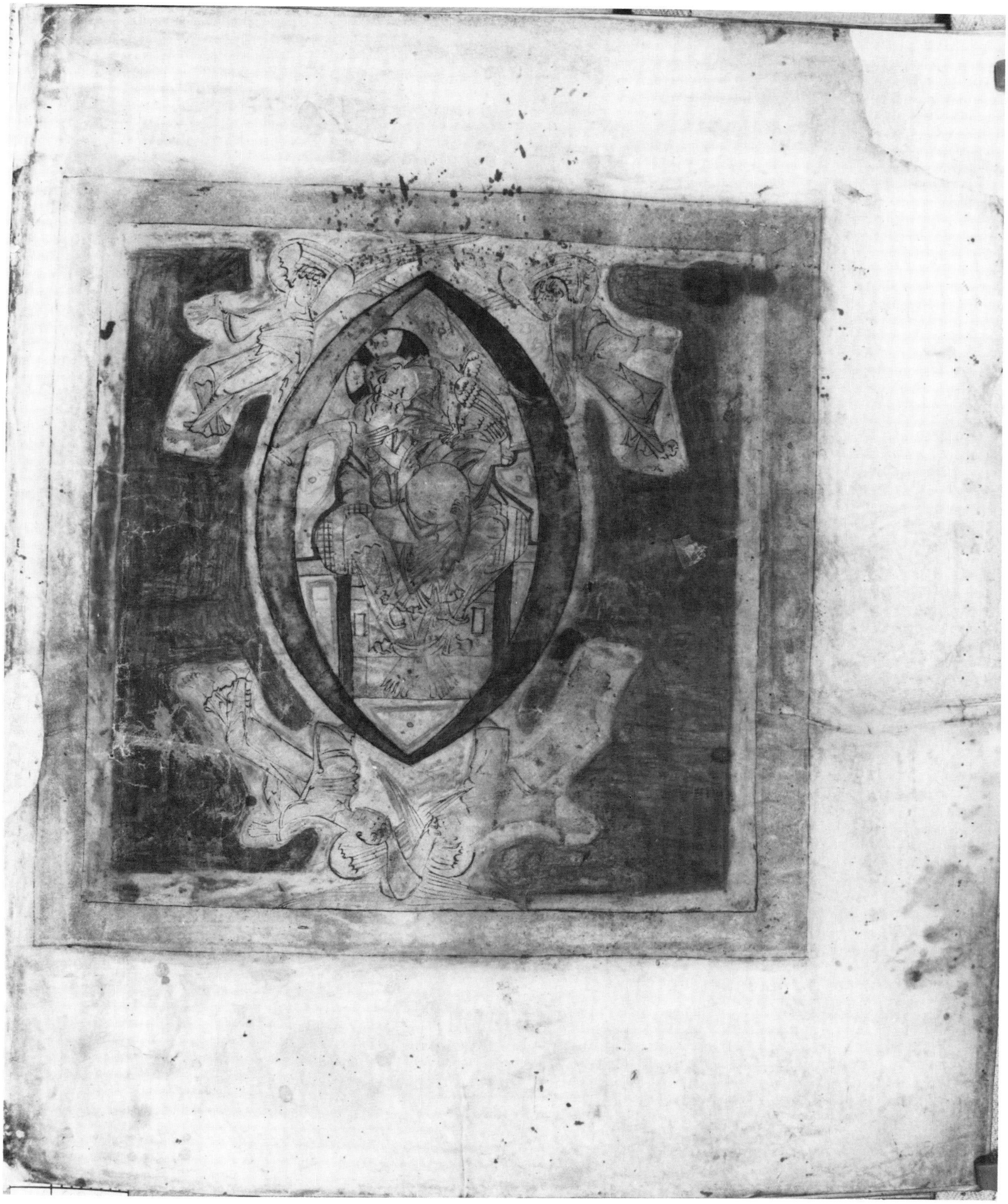

2.1 London, B.L., Harley 603, f. 1r

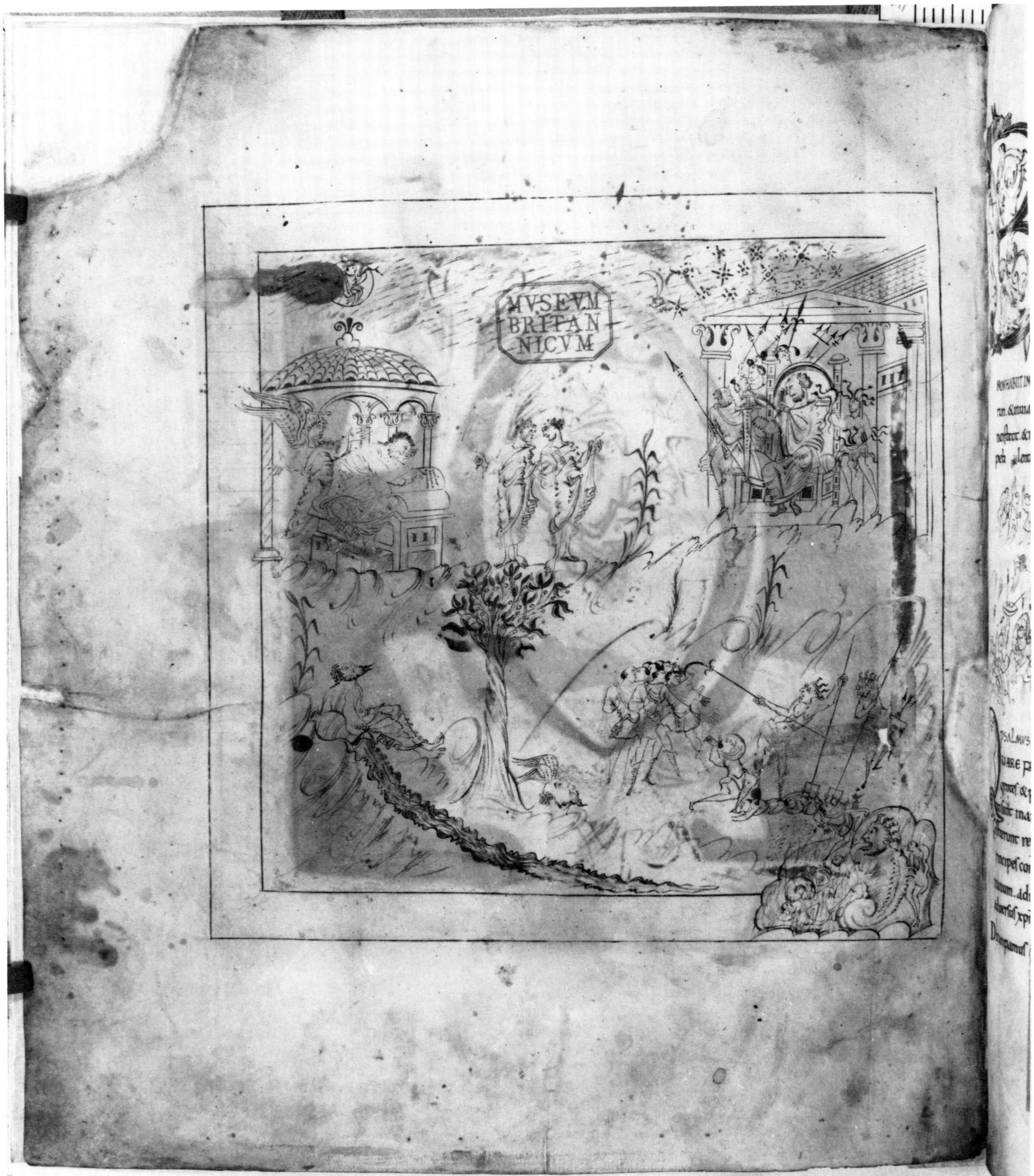

2.2 London, B.L., Harley 603, f. 1[v]

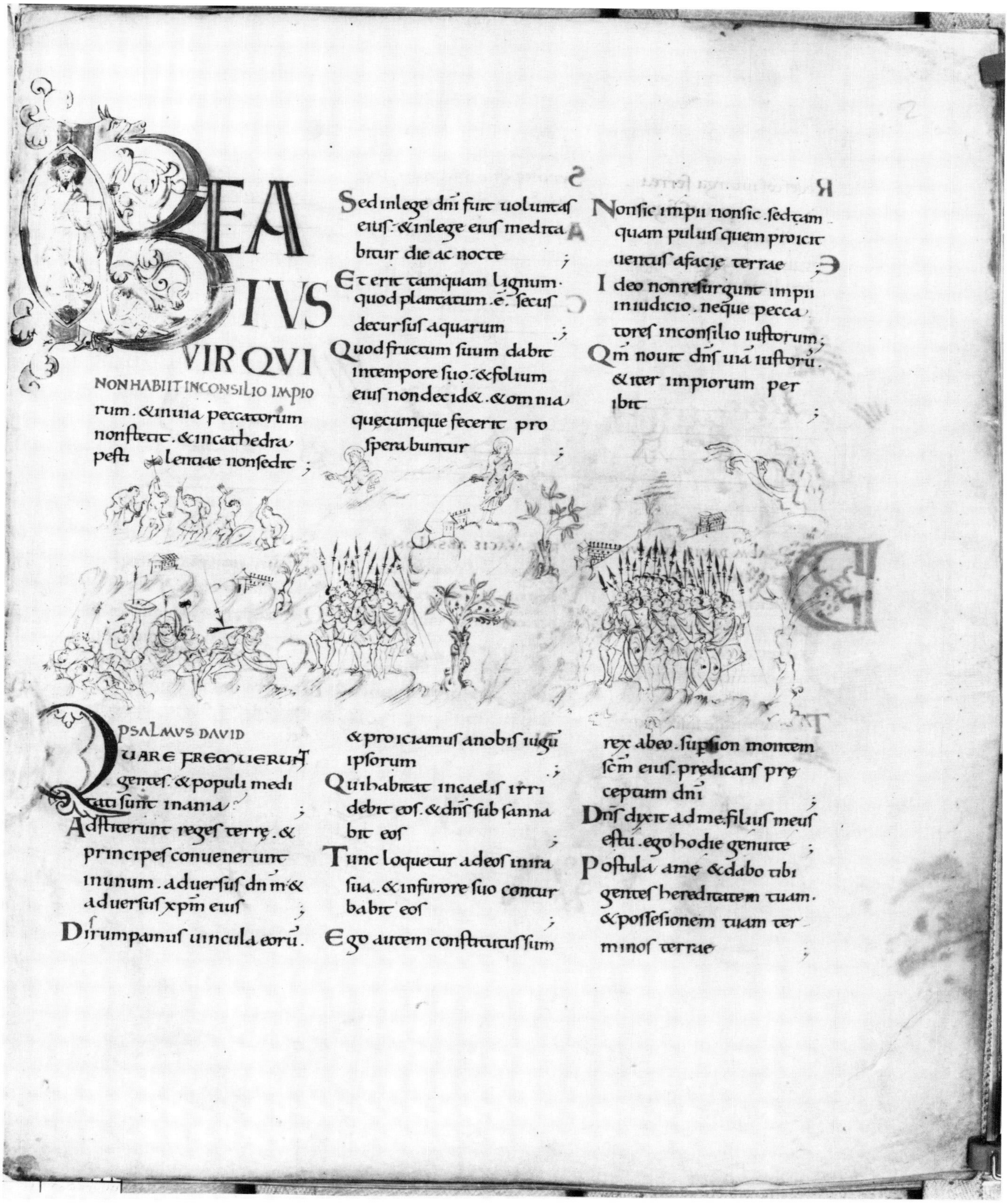

BEATUS VIR QUI NON HABIIT IN CONSILIO IMPIOrum. & in uia peccatorum non stetit. & in cathedra pestilentiae non sedit ;

Sed in lege dni fuit uoluntas eius: & in lege eius meditabitur die ac nocte ;

Et erit tamquam lignum quod plantatum .e. secus decursus aquarum ;

Quod fructum suum dabit in tempore suo: & folium eius non decid&. & omnia quecumque fecerit prosperabuntur ;

Non sic impii non sic. sed tamquam puluis quem proicit uentus a facie terrae ;

Ideo non resurgunt impii in iudicio. neque peccatores in consilio iustorum ;

Qm nouit dns uia iustorũ. & iter impiorum peribit ;

PSALMUS DAVID

QUARE FREMUERUNT gentes. & populi meditati sunt inania ;

Adstiterunt reges terrę. & principes conuenerunt in unum. aduersus dnm & aduersus xpm eius ;

Dirumpamus uincula eorũ. & proiciamus a nobis iugũ ipsorum ;

Qui habitat in caelis irridebit eos. & dns subsannabit eos ;

Tunc loquetur ad eos in ira sua. & in furore suo conturbabit eos ;

Ego autem constitutus sum rex ab eo. sup sion montem scm eius. predicans preceptum dni ;

Dns dixit ad me. filius meus es tu. ego hodie genui te ;

Postula a me & dabo tibi gentes hereditatem tuam. & possessionem tuam terminos terrae ;

2.3 London, B.L., Harley 603, f. 2r

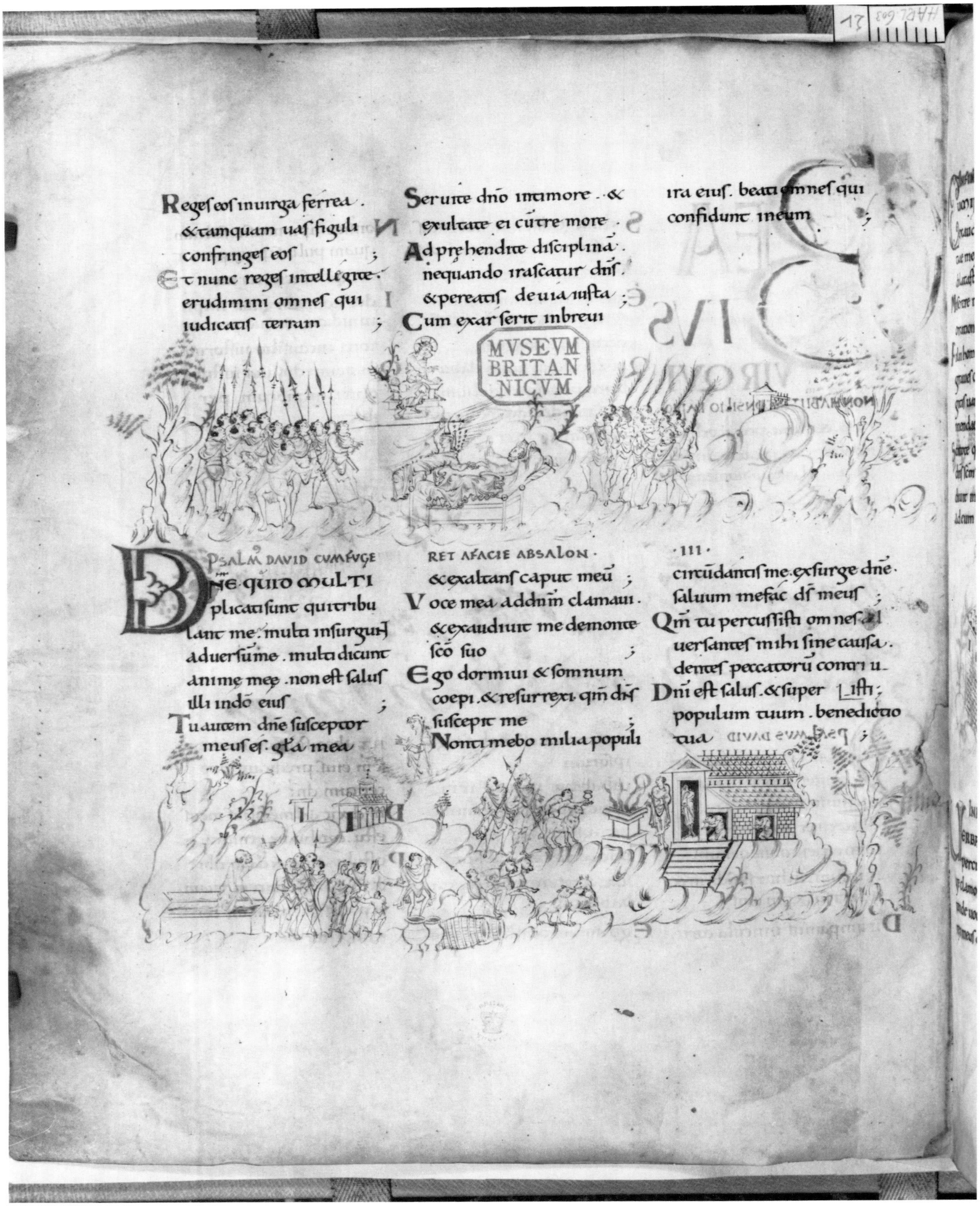

Reges eos in uirga ferrea . & tamquam uas figuli confringes eos ;
Et nunc reges intellegite . erudimini omnes qui iudicatis terram ;
Seruite dno in timore . & exultate ei cu tre more .
Adprehendite disciplina . nequando irascatur dns . & pereatis de uia iusta ;
Cum exarserit in breui ira eius . beati omnes qui confidunt in eum ;

MVSEVM BRITANNICVM

PSALM DAVID CUM FUGERET A FACIE ABSALON . III .

Dne quid multi plicati sunt qui tribulant me . multi insurgunt aduersum me . multi dicunt animę meę . non est salus illi in do eius ;
Tu autem dne susceptor meus es . gl'a mea & exaltans caput meu ;
Voce mea ad dnm clamaui . & exaudiuit me de monte sco suo ;
Ego dormiui & somnum coepi . & resurrexi . qm dns suscepit me ;
Non timebo milia populi circumdantis me . exsurge dne . saluum me fac ds meus ;
Qm tu percussisti omnes aduersantes mihi sine causa . dentes peccatoru contriuisti .
Dni est salus . & super populum tuum . benedictio tua ;

2.4 London, B.L., Harley 603, f. 2v

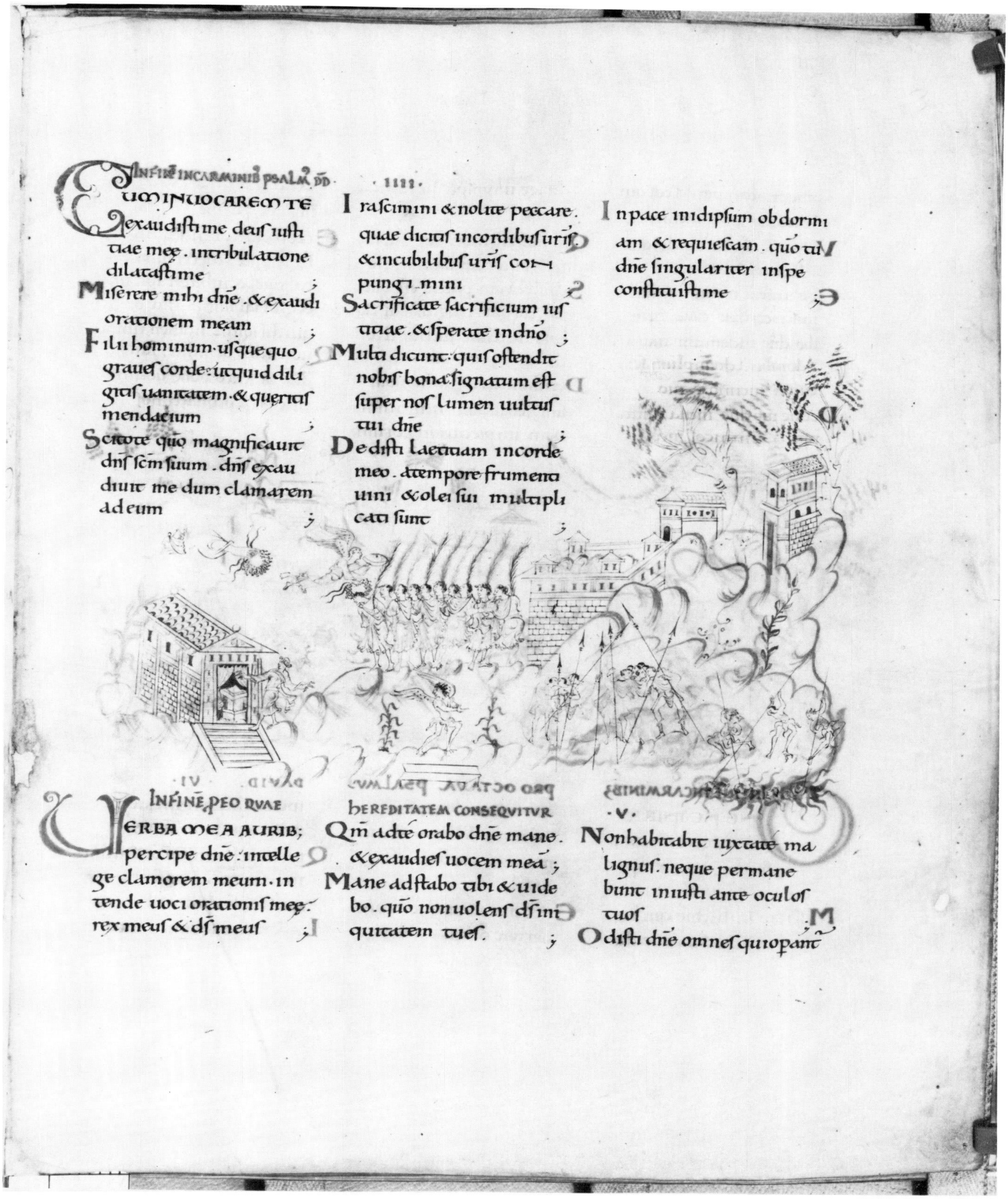

IN FINE IN CARMINIS PSALM DD IIII.

CUM INUOCAREM TE exaudisti me deus iusti
tiae meę. in tribulatione
dilatasti me
Miserere mihi dne. & exaudi
orationem meam
Filii hominum usque quo
graues corde: ut quid dili
gitis uanitatem. & queritis
mendacium
Scitote quo magnificauit
dns scm suum. dns exau
diuit me dum clamarem
ad eum

Irascimini & nolite peccare.
quae dicitis in cordibus uris
& in cubilibus uris con
pungimini
Sacrificate sacrificium ius
titiae. & sperate in dno
Multi dicunt: quis ostendit
nobis bona. signatum est
super nos lumen uultus
tui dne
Dedisti laetitiam in corde
meo. a tempore frumenti
uini & olei sui multipli
cati sunt

In pace in idipsum obdormi
am & requiescam. quo tu
dne singulariter in spe
constituisti me

IN FINE PRO EA QUAE HEREDITATEM CONSEQUITUR DAVID. VI

VERBA MEA AURIB; percipe dne: intelle
ge clamorem meum. in
tende uoci orationis meę.
rex meus & ds meus
Qm ad te orabo dne mane.
& exaudies uocem meā
Mane adstabo tibi & uide
bo. quo non uolens ds ini
quitatem tu es.

PRO OCTAVA PSALMUS ... IN CARMINIS .V.

Non habitabit iuxta te ma
lignus. neque permane
bunt iniusti ante oculos
tuos
Odisti dne omnes qui operant

2.5 London, B.L., Harley 603, f. 3r

iniquitatem . perdes eos qui
locuntur mendacium ;
Virum sanguinū & dolosum
abominabitur dns ;
Ego autem in multitudine
misericordiae tuae intro
ibo dne in domum tuam
adorabo ad templum scm
tuum in timore tuo ;
Deduc me dne in tua iustitia
ppt inimicos meos
dirige in conspectu tuo uiā
meam
Qm non est in ore eorū ueri
tas . cor eorum uanum est ;
Sepulchrum patens est gut
tur eorum . linguis suis do
lose agebant . iudica illos
ds
Decidant a cogitationibus
suis . secundum multitudi
nem impietatum eorum
expelle eos . quo exacerba
uerunt te dne ;
Et letentur omnes qui spe
rant in te in eternum exul
tabunt & inhabitabis in eis .
& gloriabuntur in te omnes
qui diligunt nomen tuum ;
Quo tu dne benedices iusto
dne ut scuto bone uolunta
tis tuae coronasti nos ;

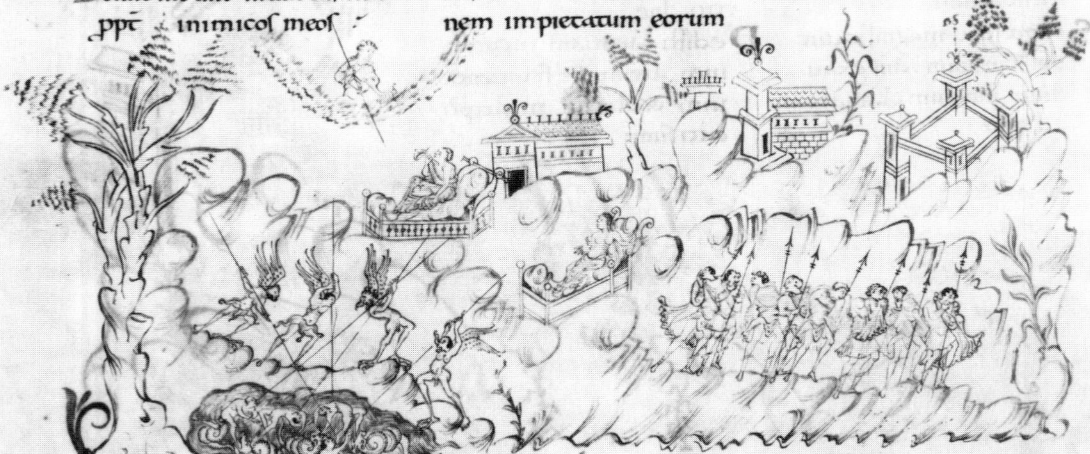

IN FINĒ IN CARMINIB; PRO OCTAVA PSALMUS DAVID . VI .
DNE NE IN IRA
tua arguas me . neq;
in furore tuo corripias
me
Miserere mihi dne qm in
firmus sum . sana me dne
quo conturbata sunt
omnia ossa mea . & ani
ma mea turbata est
ualde
Et tu dne usquequo . con
uertere & eripe animam
meam saluum me fac ppt
misericordiam tuam ;
Quo non est in morte qui me
mor sit tui . in inferno autē
quis confitebitur tibi
Laboraui in gemitu meo

2.6 London, B.L., Harley 603, f. 3v

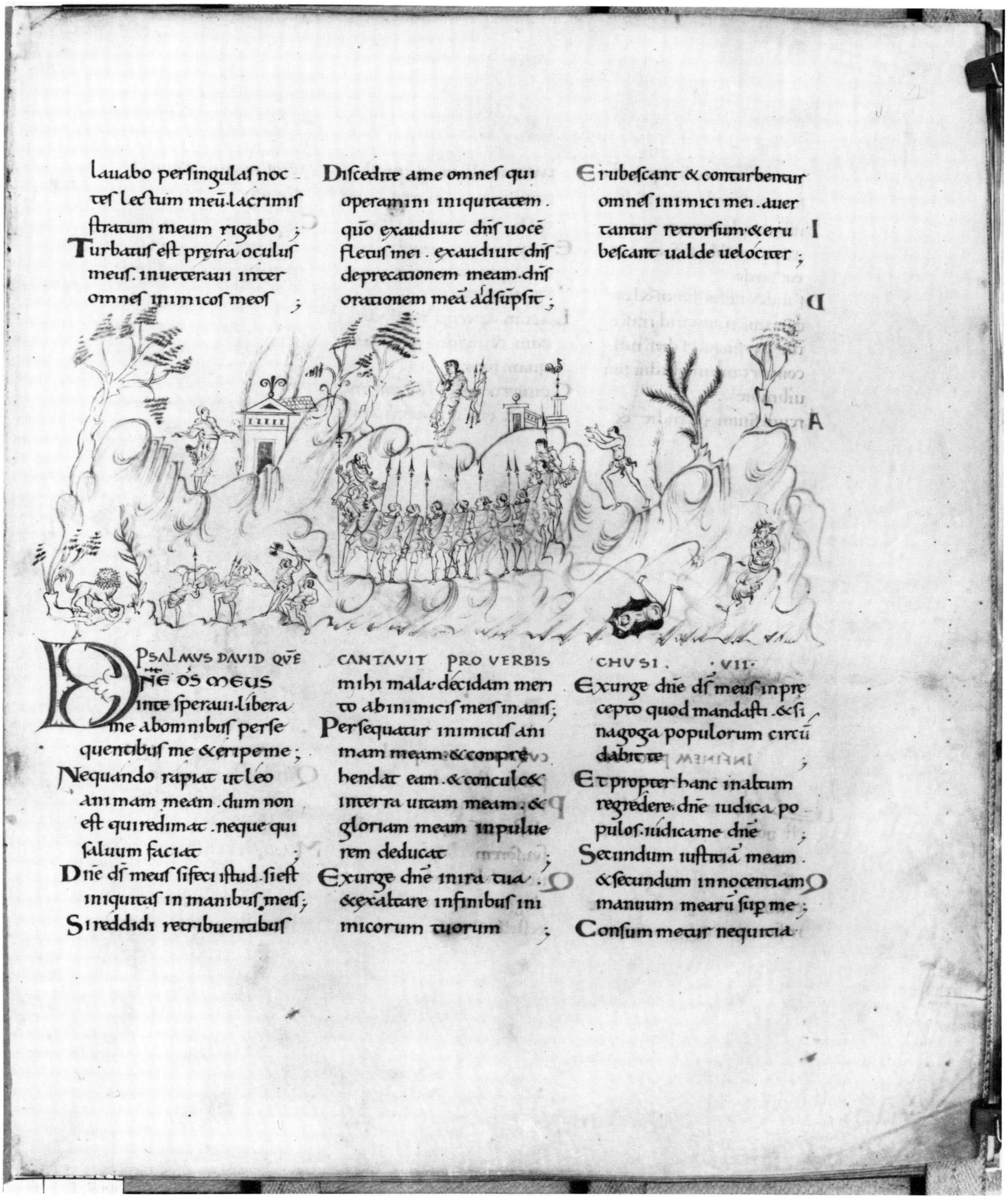
lauabo per singulas noc-
tes lectum meū. lacrimis
stratum meum rigabo ;
Turbatus est prae ira oculus
meus. inueteraui inter
omnes inimicos meos ;
Discedite ame omnes qui
operamini iniquitatem.
quō exaudiuit dns uocē
fletus mei. exaudiuit dns
deprecationem meam. dns
orationem meā adsumpsit ;
Erubescant & conturbentur
omnes inimici mei. auer
tantur retrorsum & eru
bescant ualde uelociter ;

PSALMUS DAVID QUĒ CANTAVIT PRO VERBIS CHUSI. VII.
DNE DS MEUS
in te speraui. libera
me ab omnibus perse
quentibus me & eripe me ;
Nequando rapiat ut leo
animam meam. dum non
est qui redimat. neque qui
saluum faciat
Dne ds meus si feci istud. si est
iniquitas in manibus meis ;
Si reddidi retribuentibus
mihi mala. decidam meri
to ab inimicis meis inanis ;
Persequatur inimicus ani
mam meam. & conprē
hendat eam. & conculcet
in terra uitam meam. &
gloriam meam in puluē
rem deducat ;
Exurge dne in ira tua.
& exaltare in finibus ini
micorum tuorum ;
Exurge dne ds meus in prē
cepto quod mandasti. & si
nagoga populorum circū
dabit te ;
Et propter hanc in altum
regredere. dne iudica po
pulos. iudica me dne ;
Secundum iustitiā meam.
& secundum innocentiam
manuum mearū sup me ;
Consummetur nequitia

2.7 London, B.L., Harley 603, f. 4r

peccatorum. & dirige iustū.
scrutans corda & renes ds ;
Iustum adiutorium meum
a dño. qui saluos facit rec
tos corde ;
Ds iudex iustus fortis & lon
ganimis. numquid irasce
tur per singulos dies? nisi
conuertamini gladiū suū
uibrabit ;
Arcum suum tetendit &

parauit illum. & in ipso
parauit uasa mortis. sagit
tas suas ardentibus effecit ;
Ecce parturit iniustitiam.
concepit dolorem. & pepe
rit iniquitatem ;
Lacum aperuit & effodit
eum. & incidit in foueam
quam fecit ;
Conuertetur dolor eius in
caput eius. & in uerticem

eius iniquitas eius de
scendet ;
Confitebor dño secundum
iustitiam eius. & psallam
nomini dñi altissimi ;

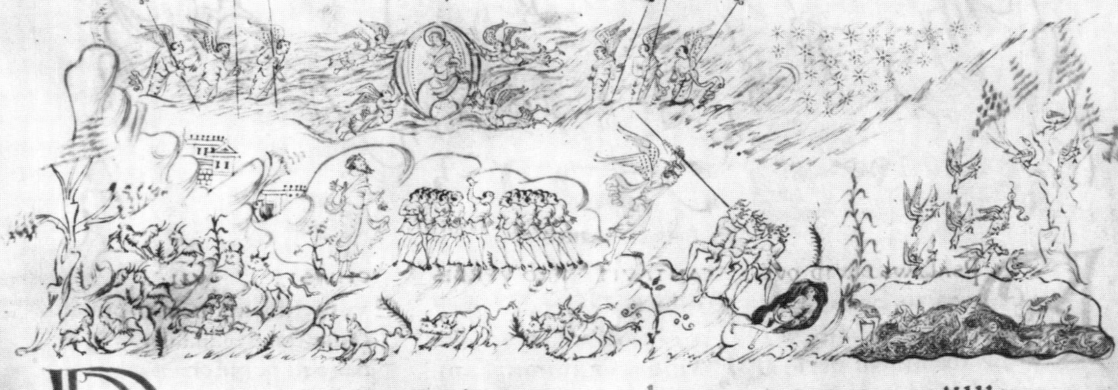

INFINEM PRO TOR CULARIBUS PSALMUS DAVID. VIII.

Dñe dns noster : quam admirabile
est nomen tuū in uniuersa
terra ;
Quō eleuata est magnifi
centia tua sup caelos. ex ore
infantium & lactantium

perfecisti laudem ;
Propter inimicos tuos. ut
destruas inimicū & de
fensorem ;
Quō uidebo caelos opera
digitorum tuorū. lunā
& stellas quas tu fundasti ;

Quid est homo quod memor
es eius. aut filius hominis
quō uisitas eum ;
Minuisti eum paulominus
ab angelis. gloria & ho
nore coronasti eum : & con
stituisti eum sup opera

2.8 London, B.L., Harley 603, f. 4v

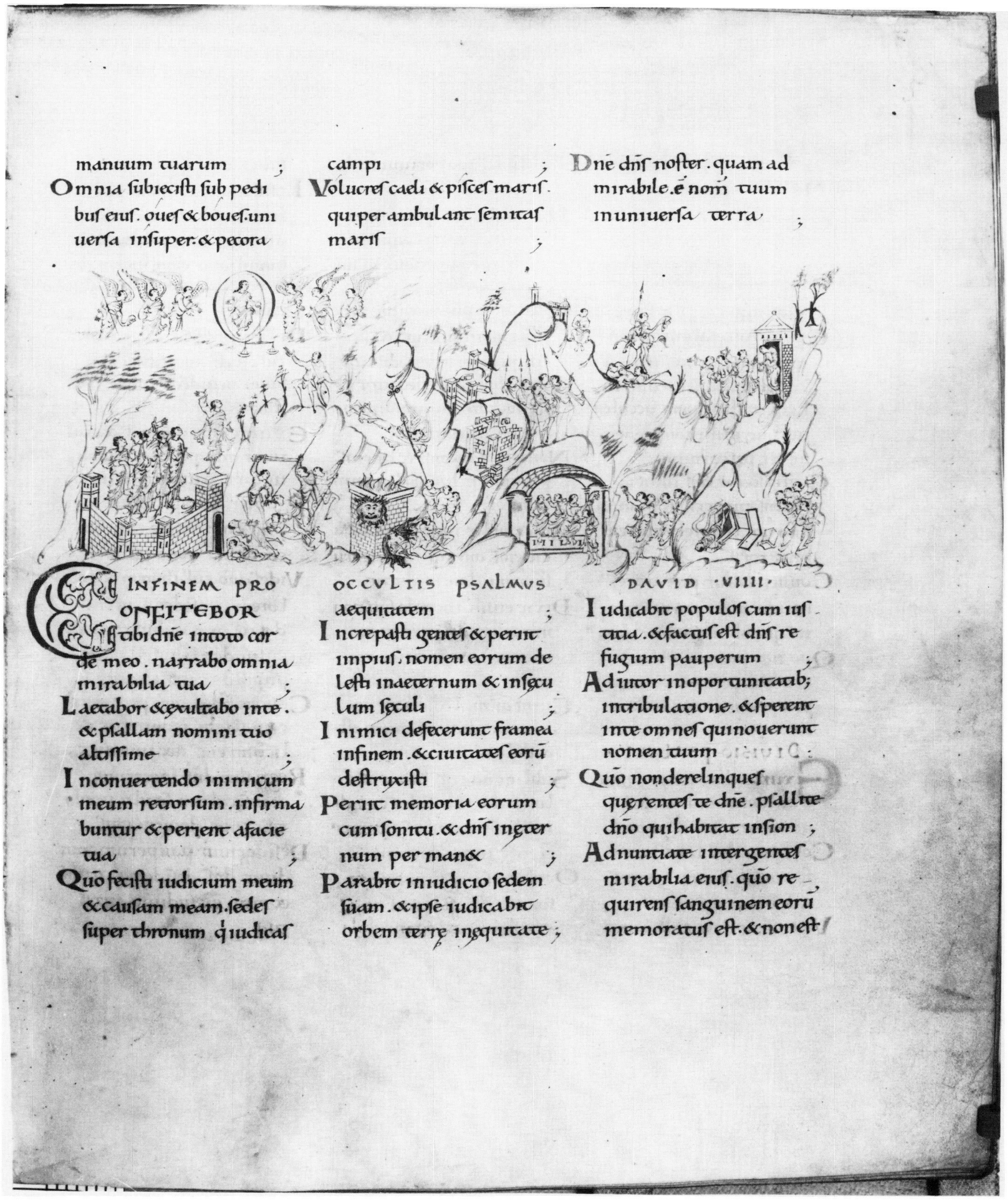

manuum tuarum ;
Omnia subiecisti sub pedi
bus eius. oues & boues uni
uersa insuper. & pecora
campi ;
Volucres caeli & pisces maris.
qui perambulant semitas
maris ;
Dne dns noster. quam ad
mirabile. ē nom̄ tuum
in uniuersa terra ;

IN FINEM PRO OCCULTIS PSALMUS DAVID VIIII.

CONFITEBOR
tibi dne in toto cor
de meo. narrabo omnia
mirabilia tua ;
Laetabor & exultabo in te.
& psallam nomini tuo
altissime ;
In conuertendo inimicum
meum retrorsum. infirma
buntur & peribunt a facie
tua ;
Quō fecisti iudicium meum
& causam meam. sedes
super thronum q iudicas
aequitatem ;
Increpasti gentes & periit
impius. nomen eorum de
lesti in aeternum & in secu
lum seculi ;
Inimici defecerunt framea
in finem. & ciuitates eorū
destruxisti ;
Periit memoria eorum
cum sonitu. & dns in eter
num permanet ;
Parabit in iudicio sedem
suam. & ipse iudicabit
orbem terre in equitate ;
Iudicabit populos cum ius
titia. & factus est dns re
fugium pauperum ;
Adiutor in oportunitatib;
in tribulatione. & sperent
in te omnes qui nouerunt
nomen tuum ;
Quō non derelinques
querentes te dne. psallite
dno qui habitat in sion ;
Adnuntiate inter gentes
mirabilia eius. quō re
quirens sanguinem eorū
memoratus est. & non est

2.9 London, B.L., Harley 603, f. 5r

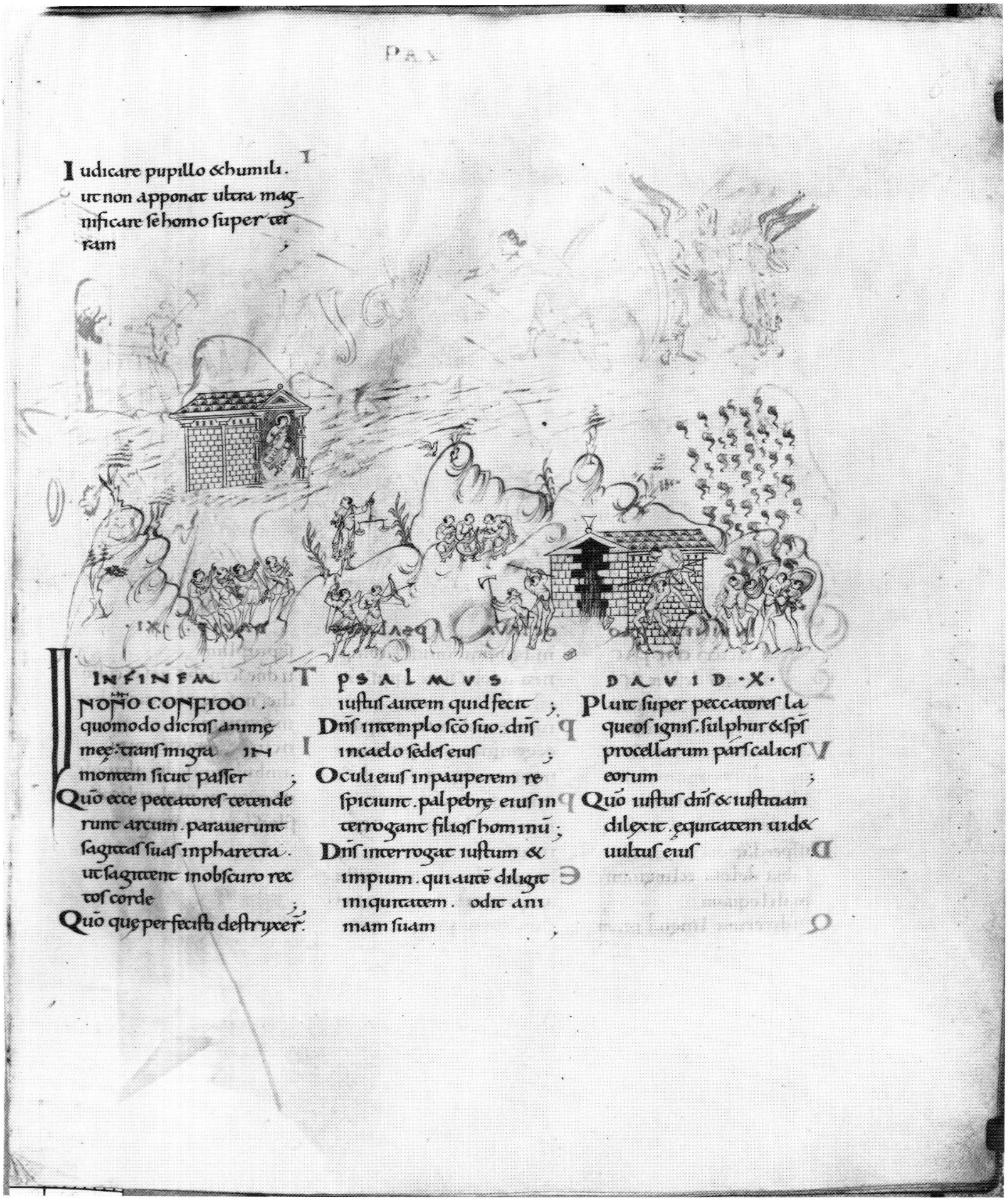
Iudicare pupillo & humili.
ut non apponat ultra mag-
nificare se homo super ter
ram

IN FINEM PSALMUS DAVID X.

IN DOMINO CONFIDO. quomodo dicitis animae
meae transmigra in
montem sicut passer
Quoniam ecce peccatores tetende
runt arcum. parauerunt
sagittas suas in pharetra.
ut sagittent in obscuro rec
tos corde
Quoniam quae perfecisti destruxer.
iustus autem quid fecit
Dominus in templo sancto suo. dominus
in caelo sedes eius
Oculi eius in pauperem re
spiciunt. palpebrae eius in
terrogant filios hominum
Dominus interrogat iustum &
impium. qui autem diligit
iniquitatem. odit ani
mam suam
Pluit super peccatores la
queos ignis. sulphur & spiritus
procellarum pars calicis
eorum
Quoniam iustus dominus & iustitiam
dilexit. aequitatem uidit
uultus eius

2.10 London, B.L., Harley 603, f. 6r

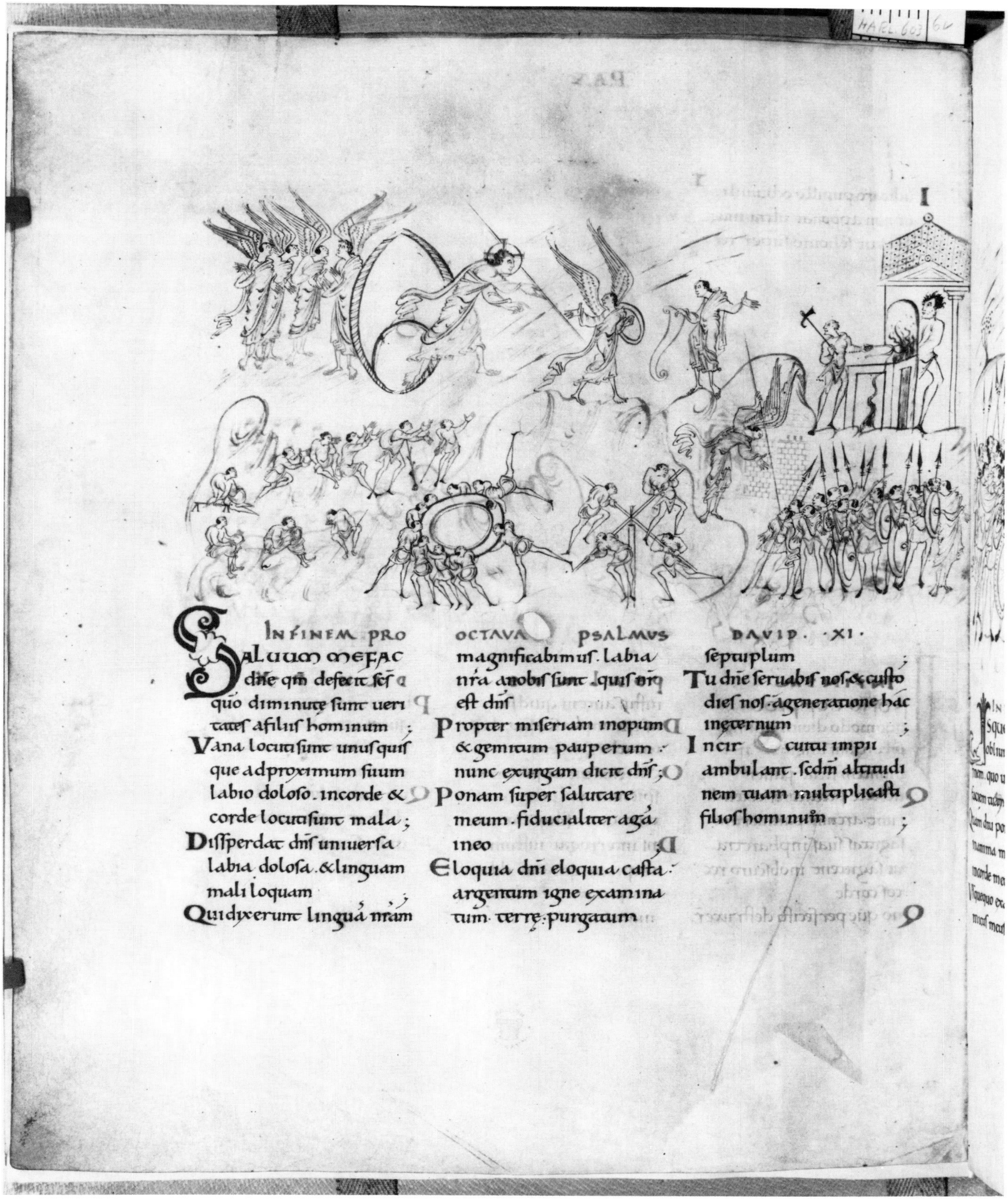

2.11 London, B.L., Harley 603, f. 6v

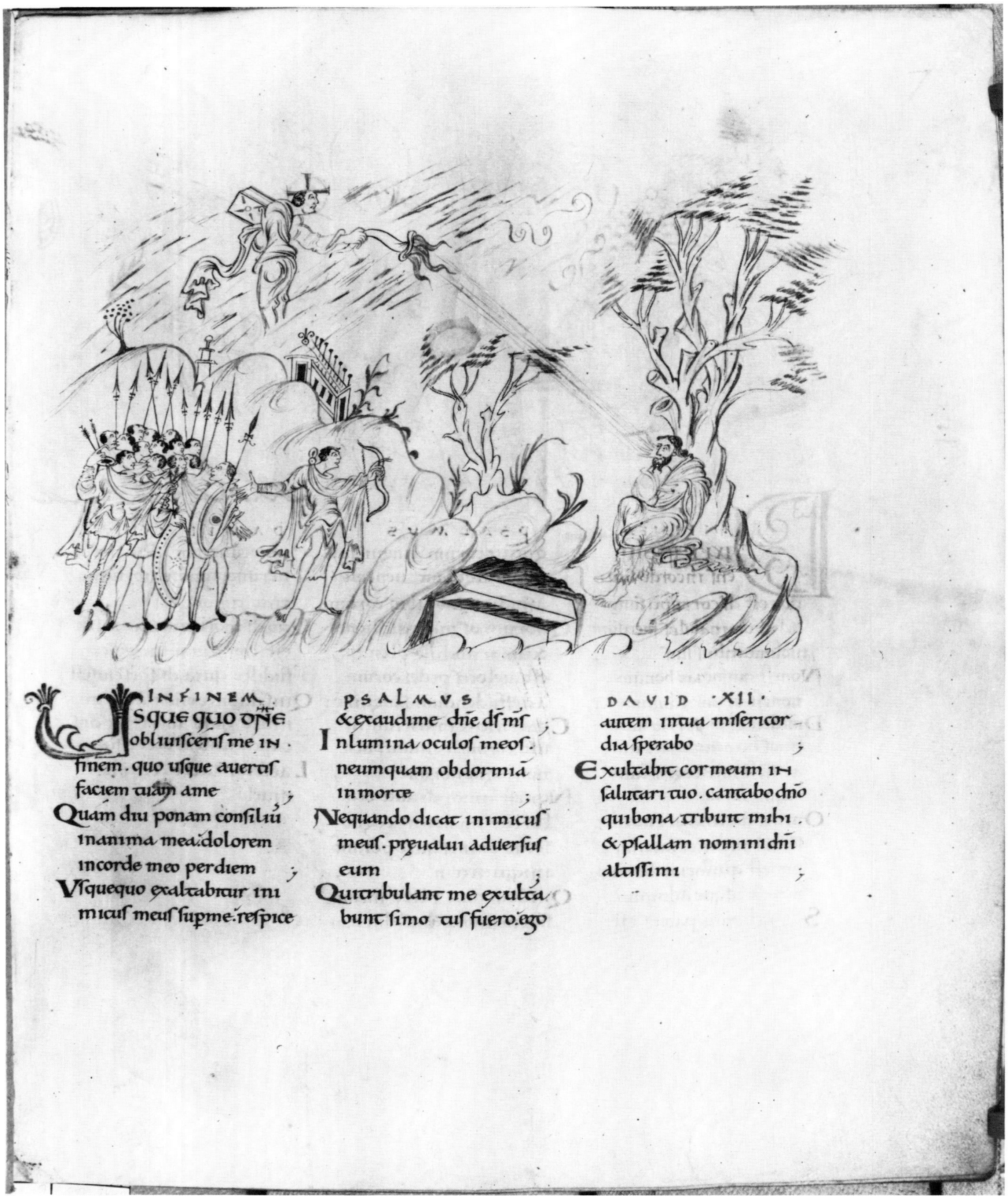

IN FINEM
USQUE QUO DÑE
oblivisceris me in
finem. quo usque avertis
faciem tuam a me
Quam diu ponam consiliũ
in anima mea. dolorem
in corde meo per diem
Usquequo exaltabitur ini
micus meus sup me. respice

PSALMUS
& exaudi me dñe ds ms
Inlumina oculos meos.
ne umquam obdormiã
in morte
Nequando dicat inimicus
meus. praevalui adversus
eum
Qui tribulant me exulta
bunt si mo tus fuero. ego

DAVID XII
autem in tua misericor
dia sperabo
Exultabit cor meum in
salutari tuo. cantabo dño
qui bona tribuit mihi.
& psallam nomini dñi
altissimi

2.12 London, B.L., Harley 603, f. 7r

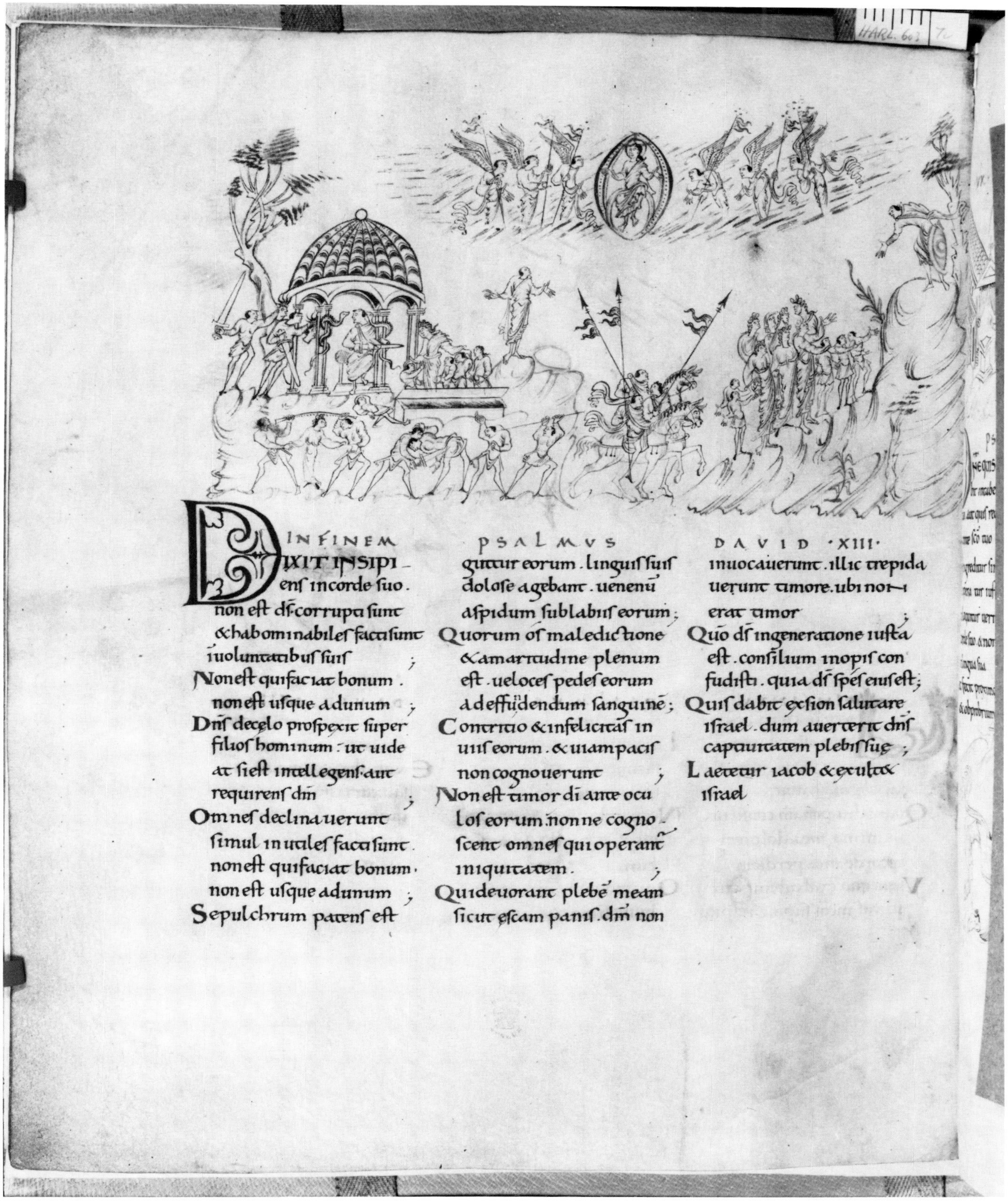

IN FINEM PSALMUS DAVID XIII

DIXIT INSIPI-
ens in corde suo.
non est ds. corrupti sunt
& abominabiles facti sunt
in uoluntatibus suis ;
Non est qui faciat bonum.
non est usque ad unum ;
Dns de celo prospexit super
filios hominum : ut uide
at si est intellegens aut
requirens dm ;
Omnes declinauerunt
simul inutiles facti sunt.
non est qui faciat bonum.
non est usque ad unum ;
Sepulchrum patens est
guttur eorum. linguis suis
dolose agebant. uenenu
aspidum sub labiis eorum ;
Quorum os maledictione
& amaritudine plenum
est. ueloces pedes eorum
ad effundendum sanguine ;
Contritio & infelicitas in
uiis eorum. & uiam pacis
non cognouerunt ;
Non est timor di ante ocu
los eorum. nonne cogno-
scent omnes qui operant
iniquitatem ;
Qui deuorant plebe meam
sicut escam panis. dm non
inuocauerunt. illic trepida
uerunt timore. ubi non
erat timor ;
Quo ds in generatione iusta
est. consilium inopis con
fudisti. quia ds spes eius est ;
Quis dabit ex sion salutare
israel. dum auerterit dns
captiuitatem plebis suę ;
Laetetur iacob & exultet
israel

2.13 London, B.L., Harley 603, f. 7v

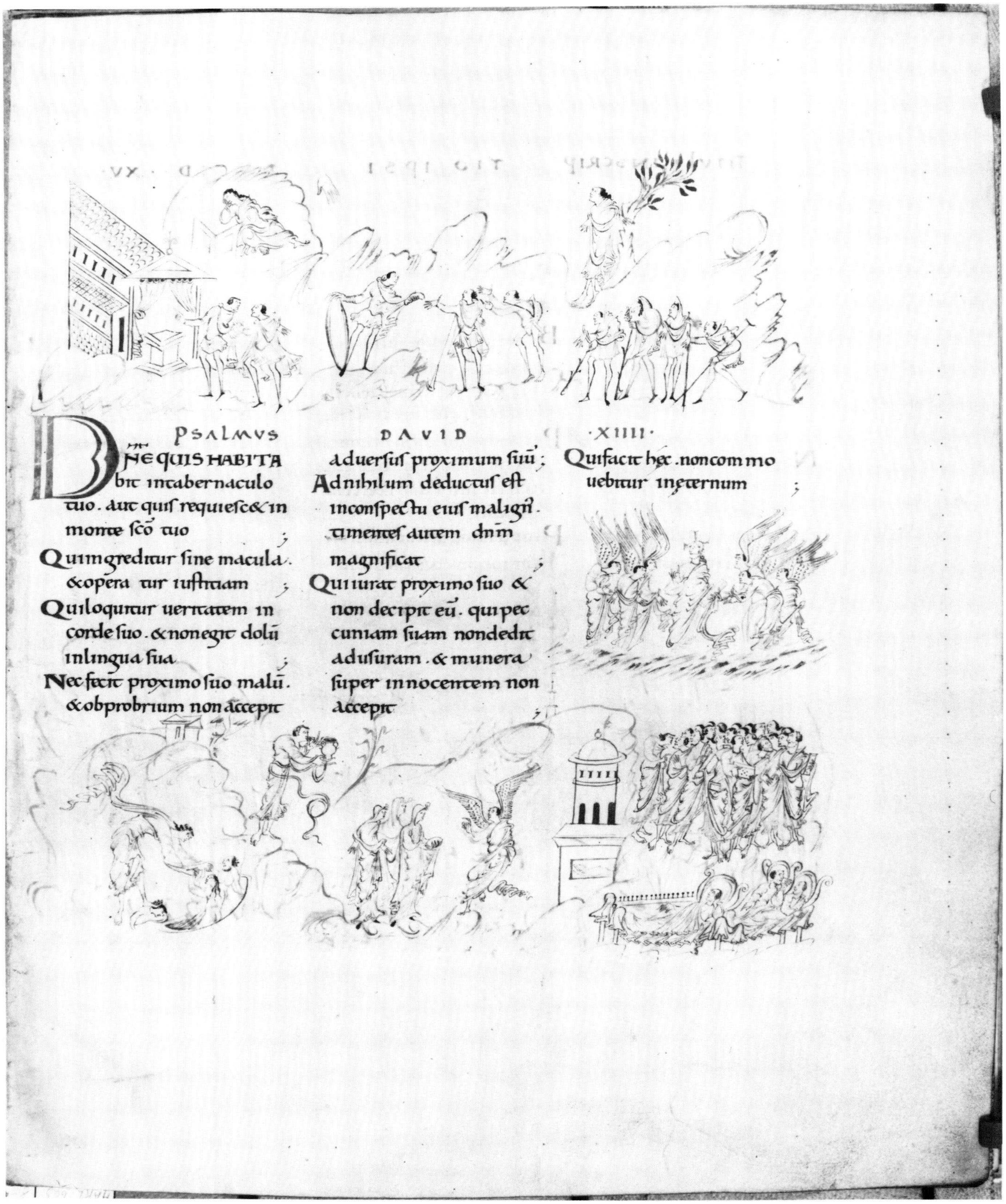

2.14 London, B.L., Harley 603, f. 8r

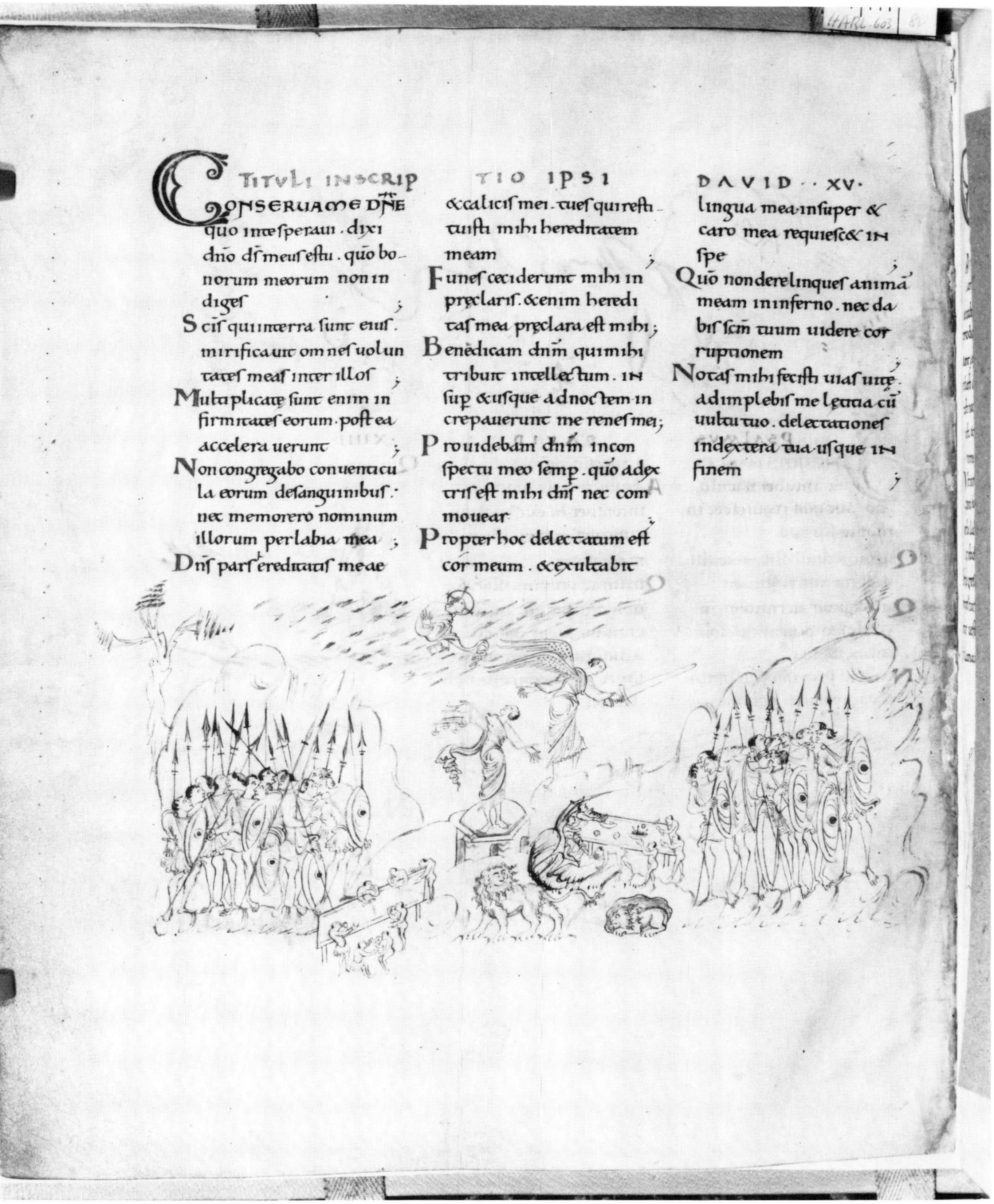

TITULI INSCRIPTIO IPSI DAVID .. XV.

Conserua me dne
quo in te speraui . dixi
dno ds meus es tu . quo bo
norum meorum non in
diges ;
Scis qui in terra sunt eius .
mirificauit omnes uolun
tates meas inter illos ;
Multiplicatae sunt enim in
firmitates eorum . post ea
accelera uerunt ;
Non congregabo conuenticu
la eorum de sanguinibus .
nec memor ero nominum
illorum per labia mea ;
Dns pars hereditatis meae
& calicis mei . tu es qui resti
tuisti mihi hereditatem
meam ;
Funes ceciderunt mihi in
preclaris . & enim heredi
tas mea preclara est mihi ;
Benedicam dnm qui mihi
tribuit intellectum . in
sup & usque ad noctem in
crepauerunt me renes mei ;
Prouidebam dnm in con
spectu meo semp . quo a dex
tris est mihi dns nec com
mouear
Propter hoc delectatum est
cor meum . & exultabit
lingua mea . insuper &
caro mea requiescet in
spe ;
Quo non derelinques anima
meam in inferno . nec da
bis scm tuum uidere cor
ruptionem ;
Notas mihi fecisti uias uitae .
adimplebis me laetitia cu
uultu tuo . delectationes
in dextera tua usque in
finem ;

2.15 London, B.L., Harley 603, f. 8v

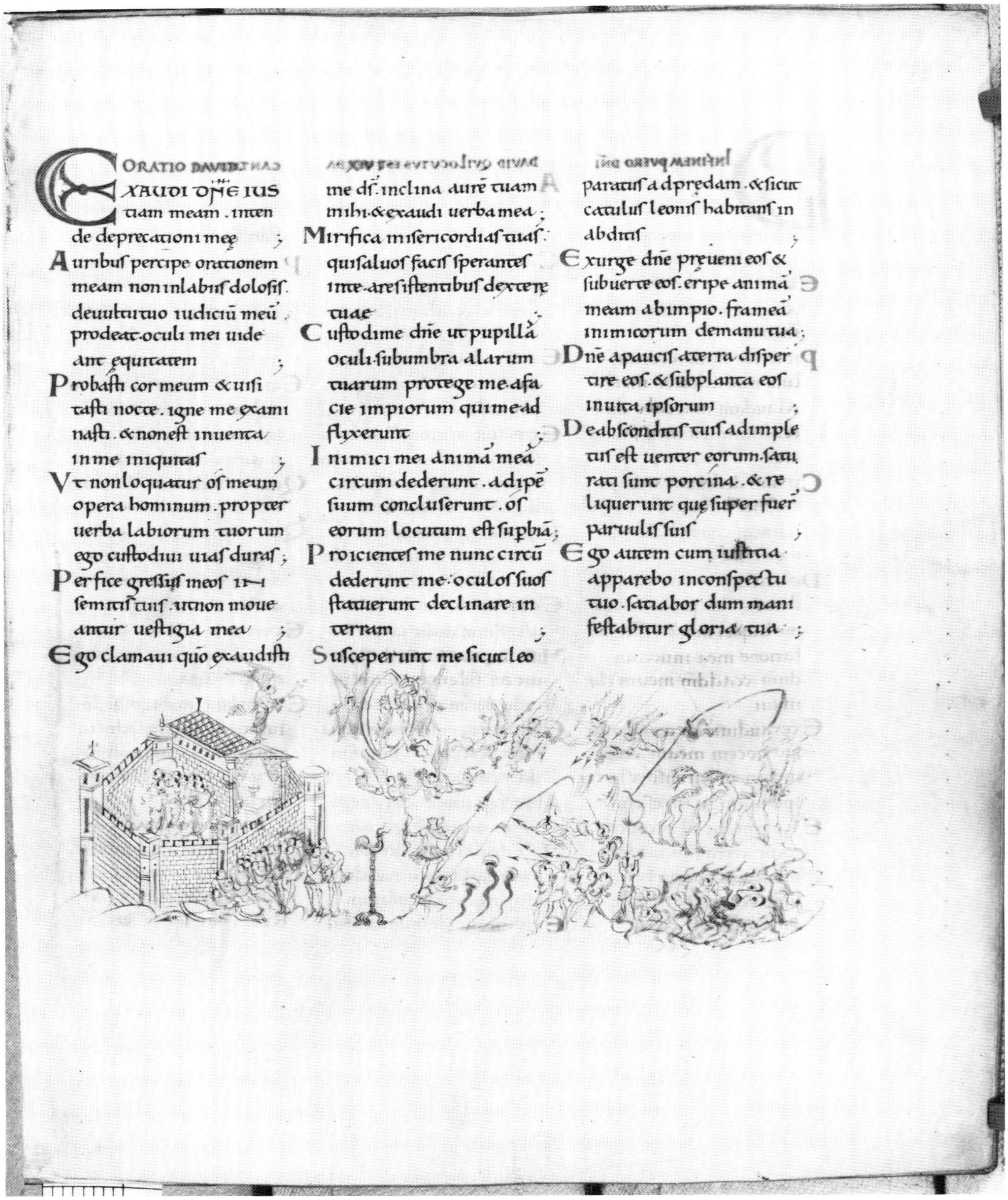

ORATIO DAVID . CAN[illegible]
Exaudi dne ius
tiam meam . inten
de deprecationi meę ;
Auribus percipe orationem
meam non in labiis dolosis.
de uultu tuo iudiciū meū ,
prodeat . oculi mei uide
ant equitatem ;
Probasti cor meum & uisi
tasti nocte . igne me exami
nasti . & non est inuenta
in me iniquitas ;
Ut non loquatur os meum
opera hominum . propter
uerba labiorum tuorum
ego custodiui uias duras ;
Perfice gressus meos in
semitis tuis . ut non moue
antur uestigia mea ;
Ego clamaui quō exaudisti
me ds . inclina aurē tuam
mihi . & exaudi uerba mea ;
Mirifica misericordias tuas .
qui saluos facis sperantes
in te . a resistentibus dexterę
tuae ;
Custodi me dne ut pupillā
oculi . sub umbra alarum
tuarum protege me . a fa
cie impiorum qui me ad
flixerunt ;
Inimici mei animā meā
circum dederunt . adipē
suum concluserunt . os
eorum locutum est supbiā ;
Proicientes me nunc circū
dederunt me . oculos suos
statuerunt declinare in
terram ;
Susceperunt me sicut leo
paratus ad prędam . & sicut
catulus leonis habitans in
abditis ;
Exurge dne pręueni eos &
subuerte eos . eripe animā
meam ab impio . frameā
inimicorum de manu tua ;
Dne a paucis a terra disper
tire eos . & subplanta eos
in uita ipsorum ;
De absconditis tuis adimple
tus est uenter eorum . satu
rati sunt porcina . & re
liquerunt quę super fuer
paruulis suis ;
Ego autem cum iustitia
apparebo in conspectu
tuo . satiabor dum mani
festabitur gloria tua ;

2.16 London, B.L., Harley 603, f. 9r

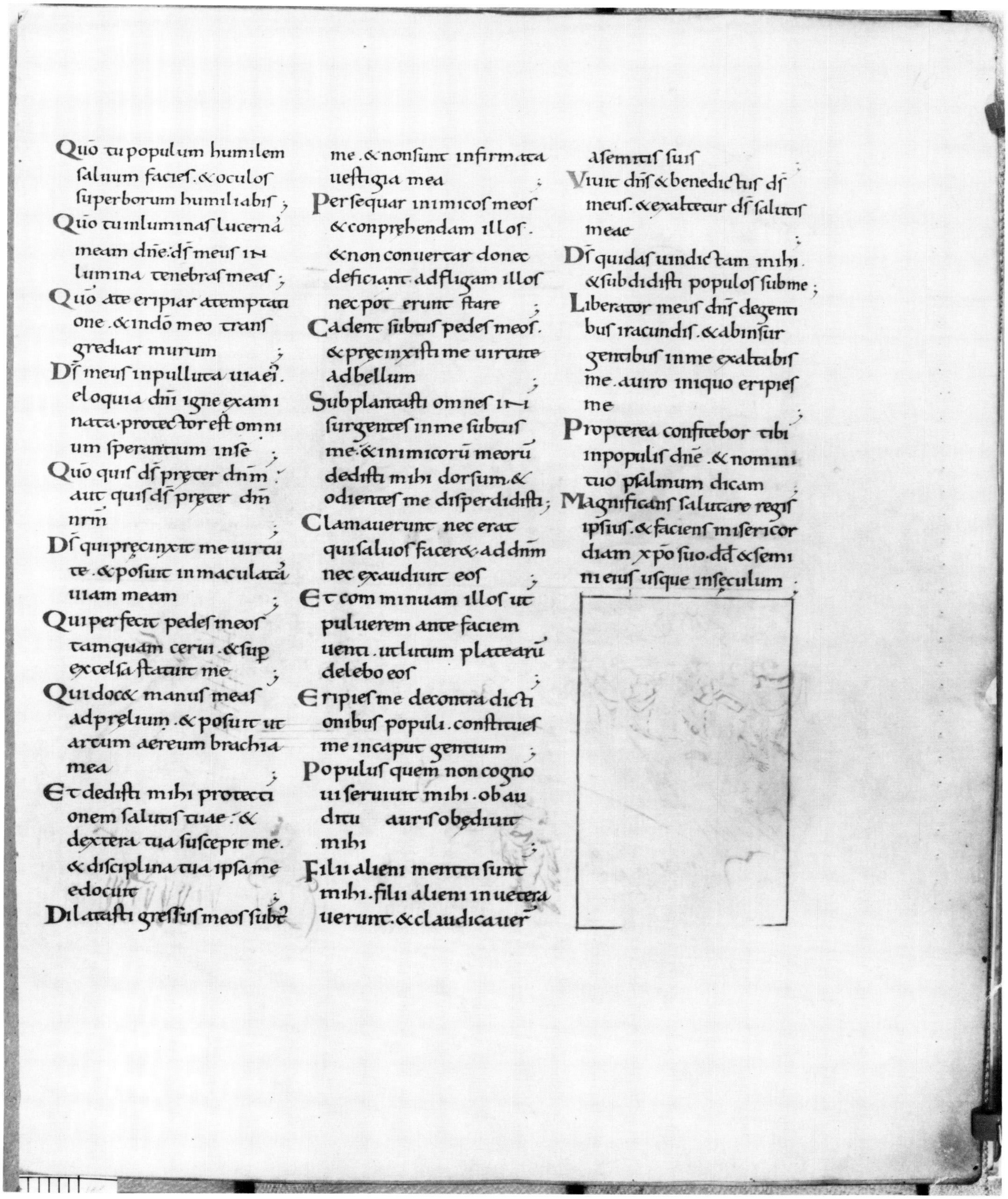

Quo tu populum humilem
saluum facies. & oculos
superborum humiliabis ;
Quo tu inluminas lucernā
meam dn͞e. ds͞ meus in-
lumina tenebras meas ;
Quo a te eripiar a temptati
one . & in do meo trans
grediar murum ;
Ds͞ meus inpolluta uia eī.
eloquia dn͞i igne exami
nata. protector est omni
um sperantium in se ;
Quo quis ds͞ preter dn͞m ;
aut quis ds͞ preter dn͞m
nr͞m ;
Ds͞ qui precinxit me uirtu
te . & posuit inmaculatā
uiam meam ;
Qui perfecit pedes meos
tamquam ceruī . & sup
excelsa statuit me ;
Qui docet manus meas
ad prelium . & posuit ut
arcum aereum brachia
mea ;
Et dedisti mihi protecti
onem salutis tuae . &
dextera tua suscepit me.
& disciplina tua ipsa me
edocuit ;
Dilatasti gressus meos subt͞
me . & non sunt infirmata
uestigia mea ;
Persequar inimicos meos
& conprehendam illos .
& non conuertar donec
deficiant. ad flugam illos
nec pot erunt stare ;
Cadent subtus pedes meos.
& precinxisti me uirtute
ad bellum ;
Subplantasti omnes in-
surgentes in me subtus
me. & inimicorū meorū
dedisti mihi dorsum. &
odientes me disperdidisti ;
Clamauerunt nec erat
qui saluos faceret. ad dn͞m
nec exaudiuit eos ;
Et comminuam illos ut
puluerem ante faciem
uenti . ut lutum platearū
delebo eos ;
Eripies me de contra dicti
onibus populi . constitues
me in caput gentium ;
Populus quem non cogno
ui seruiuit mihi . ob au
ditu auris obediuit
mihi ;
Filii alieni mentiti sunt
mihi. filii alieni inuetera
uerunt. & claudicauer
a semitis suis ;
Viuit dn͞s & benedictus ds͞
meus. & exaltetur ds͞ salutis
meae ;
Ds͞ qui das uindictam mihi.
& subdidisti populos sub me ;
Liberator meus dn͞s de genti
bus iracundis. & ab insur
gentibus in me exaltabis
me. a uiro iniquo eripies
me ;
Propterea confitebor tibi
in populis dn͞e . & nomini
tuo psalmum dicam ;
Magnificans salutare regis
ipsius. & faciens misericor
diam xp͞o suo. dd͞ & semi
ni eius usque in seculum ;

2.17 London, B.L., Harley 603, f. 10r

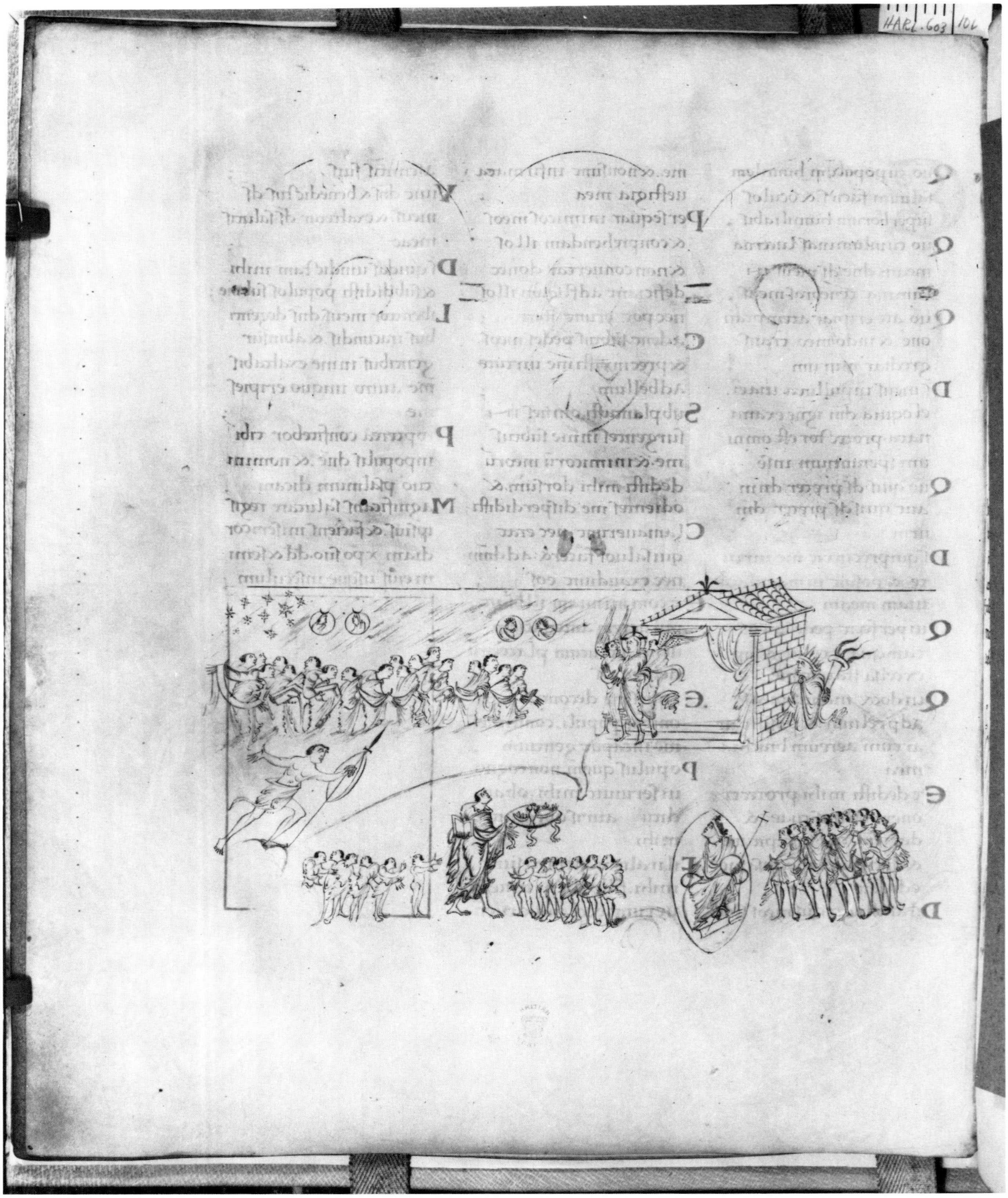

2.18 London, B.L., Harley 603, f. 10^{v}

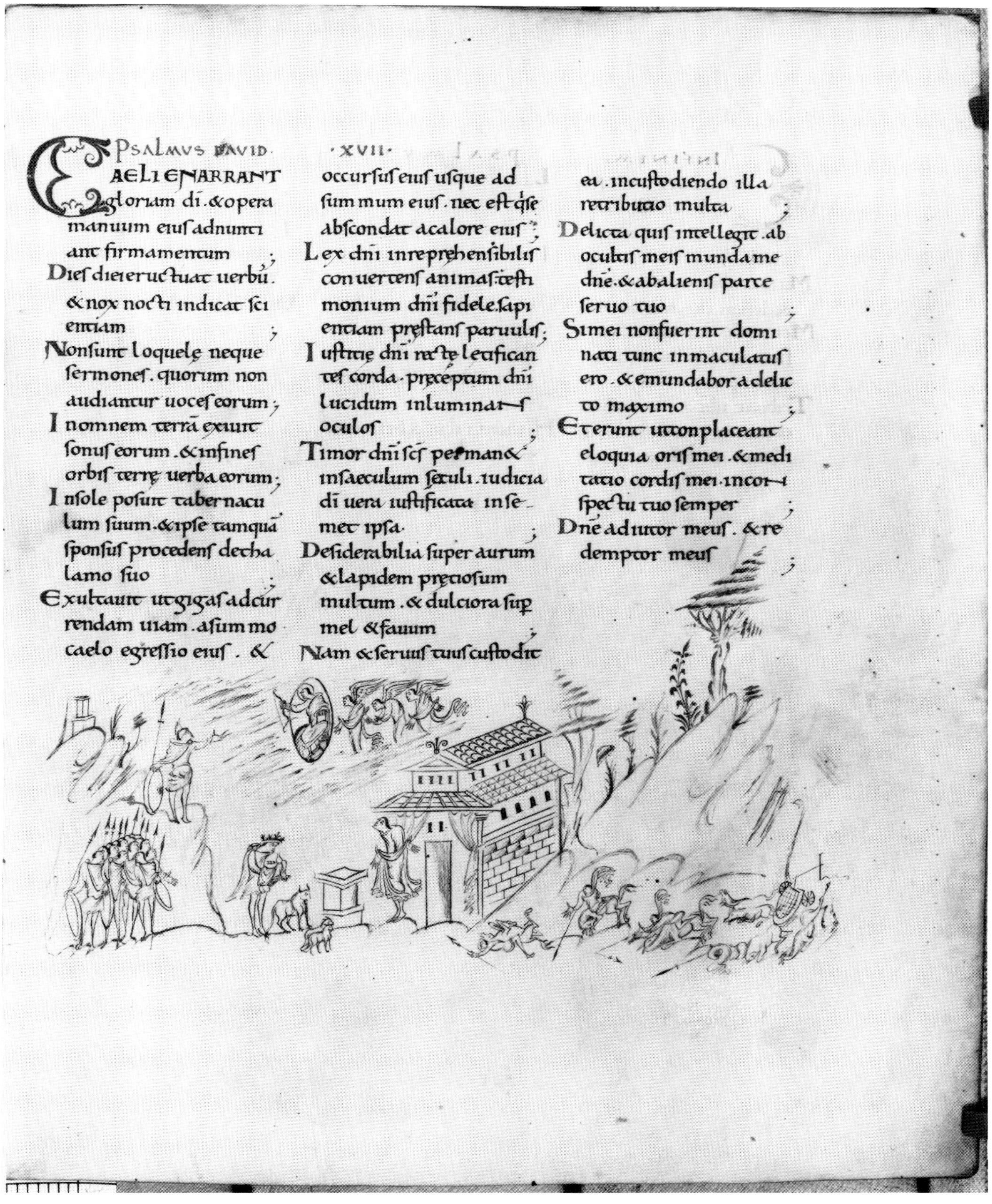
PSALMUS DAVID. ·XVII·
CAELI ENARRANT
gloriam dī. & opera
manuum eius adnunti
ant firmamentum ;
Dies diei eructuat uerbū.
& nox nocti indicat sci
entiam ;
Non sunt loquelę neque
sermones. quorum non
audiantur uoces eorum ;
In omnem terrā exiuit
sonus eorum. & in fines
orbis terrę uerba eorum ;
In sole posuit tabernacu
lum suum. & ipse tamquā
sponsus procedens de tha
lamo suo ;
Exultauit ut gigas ad cur
rendam uiam. a summo
caelo egressio eius. &
occursus eius usque ad
summum eius. nec est qui se
abscondat a calore eius ;
Lex dni inreprehensibilis
conuertens animas. testi
monium dni fidele. sapi
entiam prestans paruulis ;
Iustitię dni rectę letifican
tes corda. preceptum dni
lucidum inluminat
oculos ;
Timor dni scs permanet
in saeculum seculi. iudicia
dī uera iustificata in se
met ipsa ;
Desiderabilia super aurum
& lapidem pretiosum
multum. & dulciora sup
mel & fauum ;
Nam & seruus tuus custodit
ea. in custodiendo illa
retributio multa ;
Delicta quis intellegit. ab
occultis meis munda me
dne. & ab alienis parce
seruo tuo ;
Si mei non fuerint domi
nati tunc inmaculatus
ero. & emundabor a delic
to maximo ;
Et erunt ut conplaceant
eloquia oris mei. & medi
tatio cordis mei in con
spectu tuo semper ;
Dne adiutor meus. & re
demptor meus ;

2.19 London, B.L., Harley 603, f. 11r

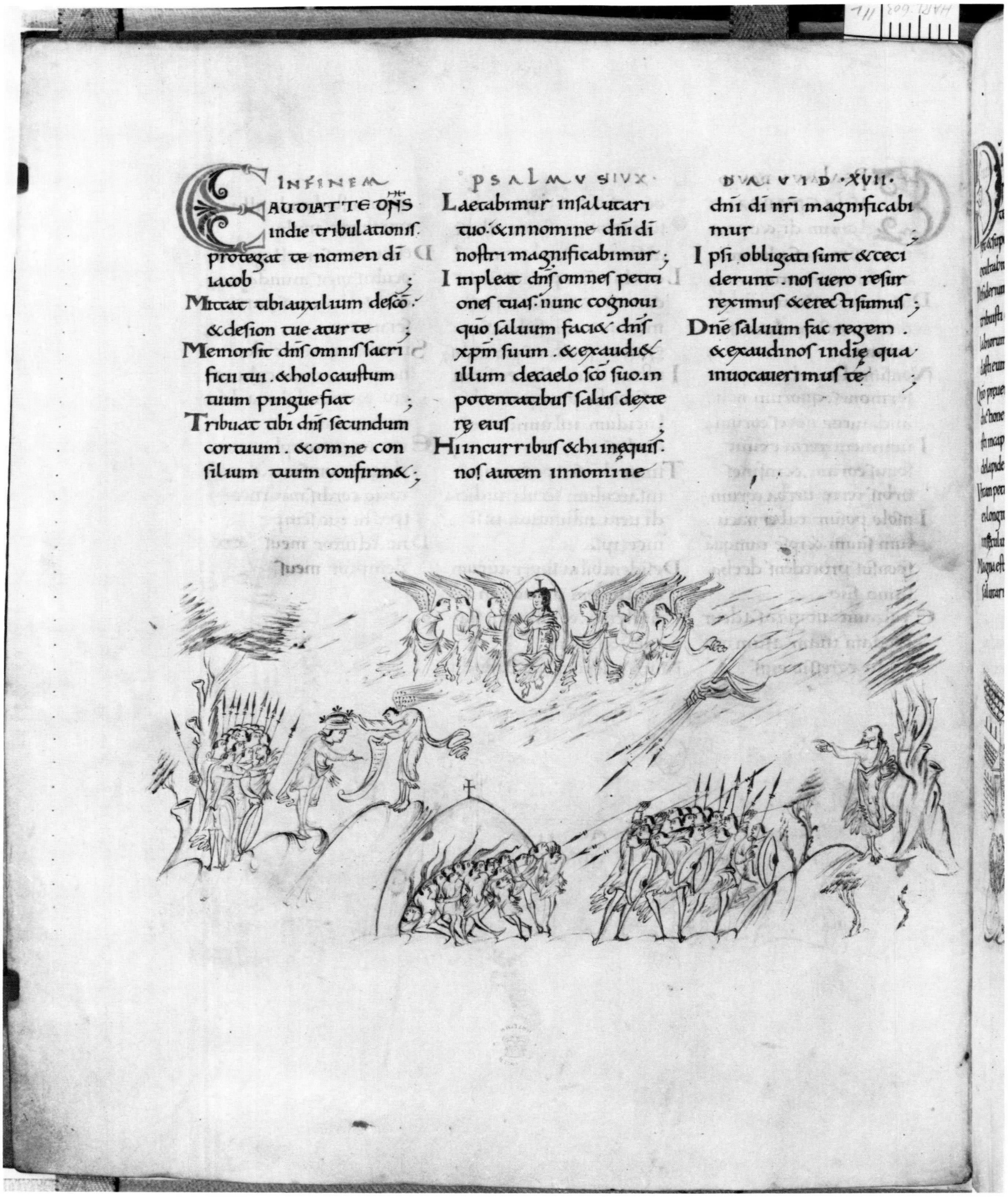

IN FINEM · PSALMUS SIUX · DAUID · XVII ·

EXAUDIAT TE DNS in die tribulationis. protegat te nomen di iacob; Mittat tibi auxilium de sco & de sion tueatur te; Memor sit dns omnis sacrificii tui. & holocaustum tuum pingue fiat; Tribuat tibi dns secundum cor tuum. & omne consilium tuum confirmet;

Laetabimur in salutari tuo. & in nomine dni di nostri magnificabimur; Impleat dns omnes petitiones tuas. nunc cognoui quo saluum facit dns xpm suum. & exaudiet illum de caelo sco suo. in potentatibus salus dextere eius Hi in curribus & hi in equis. nos autem in nomine dni di nri magnificabimur; Ipsi obligati sunt & ceciderunt. nos uero resurreximus & erecti sumus; Dne saluum fac regem. & exaudi nos in die qua inuocauerimus te;

2.20 London, B.L., Harley 603, f. 11v

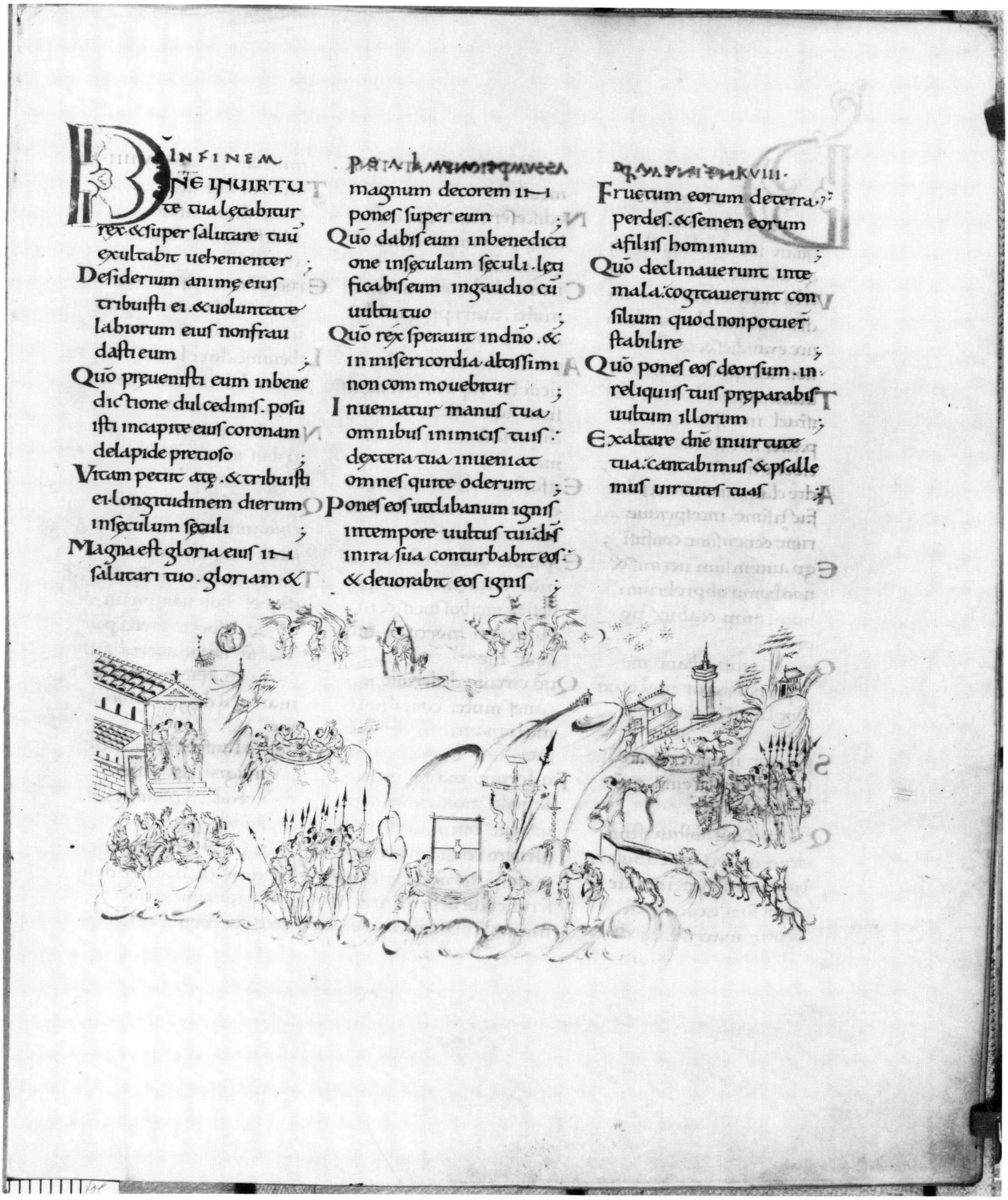

IN FINEM

DNE IN UIRTU
TE TUA LETABITUR
rex & super salutare tuu
exultabit uehementer
Desiderium anime eius
tribuisti ei. & uoluntate
labiorum eius non frau
dasti eum
Quo preuenisti eum in bene
dictione dulcedinis. posu
isti in capite eius coronam
de lapide pretioso
Vitam petiit a te. & tribuisti
ei longitudinem dierum
in seculum seculi
Magna est gloria eius in
salutari tuo. gloriam &

[illegible]
magnum decorem in
pones super eum
Quo dabis eum in benedicti
one in seculum seculi. leti
ficabis eum in gaudio cu
uultu tuo
Quo rex sperauit in dno. &
in misericordia altissimi
non commouebitur
Inueniatur manus tua
omnibus inimicis tuis.
dextera tua inueniat
omnes qui te oderunt
Pones eos ut clibanum ignis
in tempore uultus tui. dns
in ira sua conturbabit eos.
& deuorabit eos ignis

[illegible]
Fructum eorum de terra
perdes. & semen eorum
a filiis hominum
Quo declinauerunt in te
mala. cogitauerunt con
silium quod non potuer
stabilire
Quo pones eos deorsum. in
reliquiis tuis preparabis
uultum illorum
Exaltare dne in uirtute
tua. cantabimus & psalle
mus uirtutes tuas

2.21 London, B.L., Harley 603, f. 12r

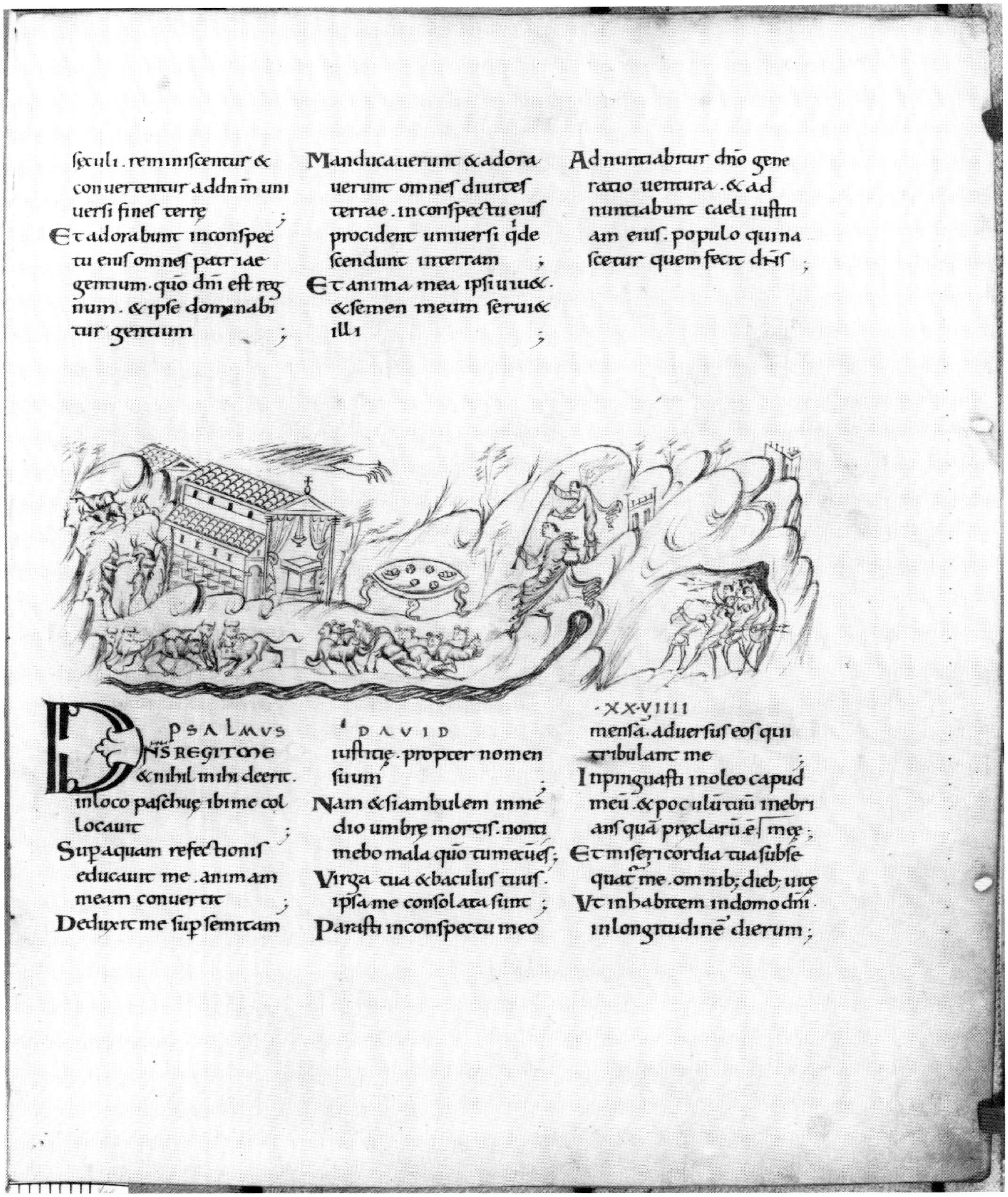

sęculi. reminiscentur &
conuertentur ad dn̄m uni
uersi fines terrę ;
Et adorabunt inconspec
tu eius omnes patriae
gentium. quō dn̄i est reg
num. & ipse dominabi
tur gentium ;

Manducauerunt & adora
uerunt omnes diuites
terrae. in conspectu eius
procident uniuersi q̄ de
scendunt interram ;
Et anima mea ipsi uiuet.
& semen meum seruiet
illi ;

Adnuntiabitur dn̄o gene
ratio uentura. & ad
nuntiabunt caeli iustiti
am eius. populo qui na
scetur quem fecit dn̄s ;

PSALMUS DAVID

·XX·VIIII

Dn̄s regit me
& nihil mihi deerit.
in loco pascuę ibi me col
locauit ;
Sup aquam refectionis
educauit me. animam
meam conuertit ;
Deduxit me sup semitam
iustitię. propter nomen
suum ;
Nam & si ambulem in me
dio umbrę mortis. non ti
mebo mala quō tu mecū es ;
Virga tua & baculus tuus.
ipsa me consolata sunt ;
Parasti in conspectu meo
mensa. aduersus eos qui
tribulant me ;
Inpinguasti in oleo capud
meū. & poculū tuū inebri
ans quā pręclarū ē mer ;
Et misericordia tua subse
quat me. omnib; dieb; uitę
Vt inhabitem indomo dn̄i.
in longitudinē dierum ;

2.22 London, B.L., Harley 603, f. 13r

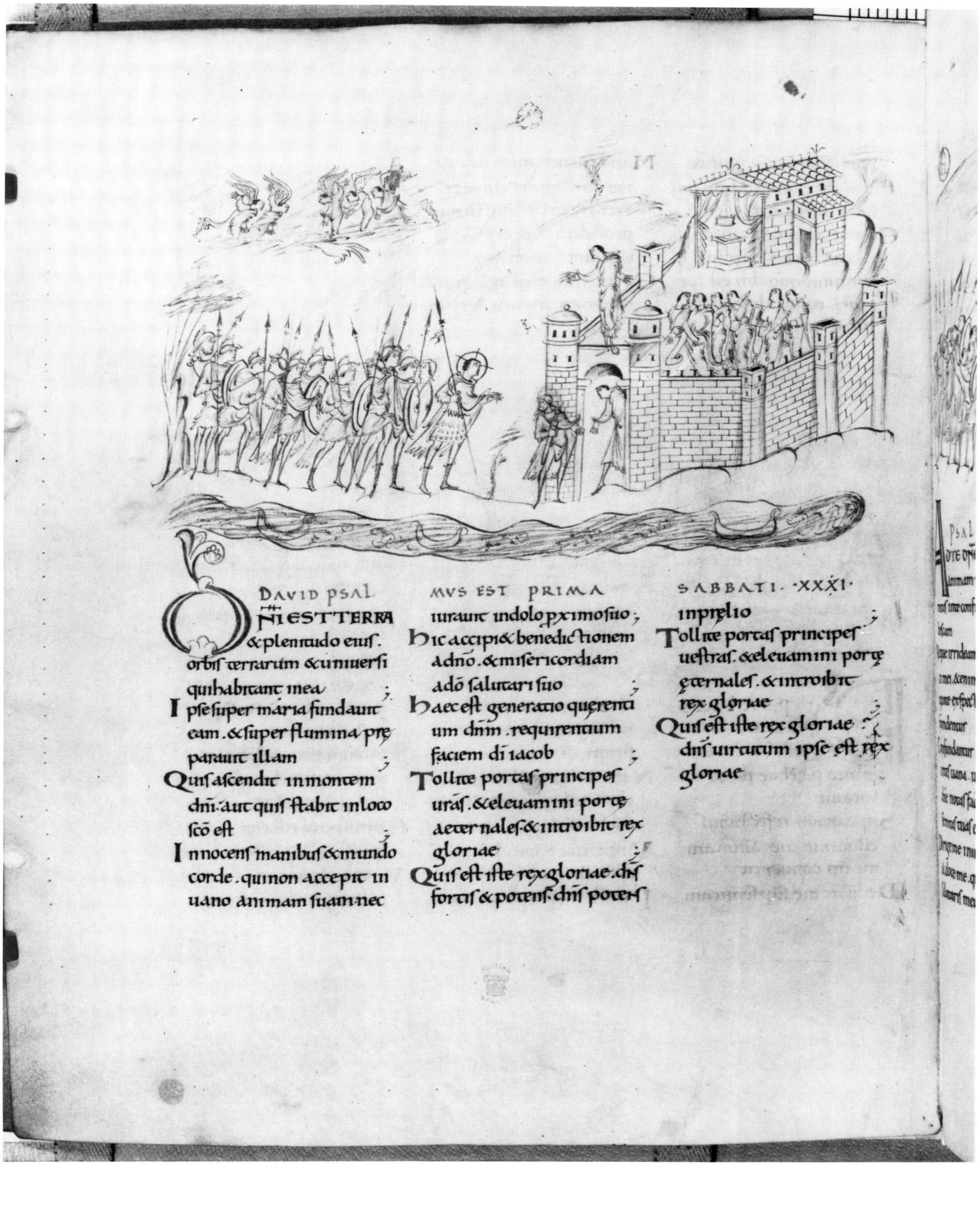
DAVID PSALMUS EST PRIMA SABBATI ·XXXI·

DNI EST TERRA
& plenitudo eius.
orbis terrarum & universi
qui habitant in ea
Ipse super maria fundavit
eam. & super flumina prę
paravit illam
Quis ascendit in montem
dni. aut quis stabit in loco
sco eius
Innocens manibus & mundo
corde. qui non accepit in
vano animam suam nec
iuravit in dolo pximo suo
Hic accipi& benedictionem
a dno. & misericordiam
a do salutari suo
Haec est generatio quaerenti
um dnm. requirentium
faciem di iacob
Tollite portas principes
uras. & elevamini portę
aeternales. & introibit rex
gloriae
Quis est iste rex gloriae. dns
fortis & potens. dns potens
in prelio
Tollite portas principes
vestras. & elevamini portę
ęternales. & introibit
rex gloriae
Quis est iste rex gloriae
dns virtutum ipse est rex
gloriae

2.23 London, B.L., Harley 603, f. 13v

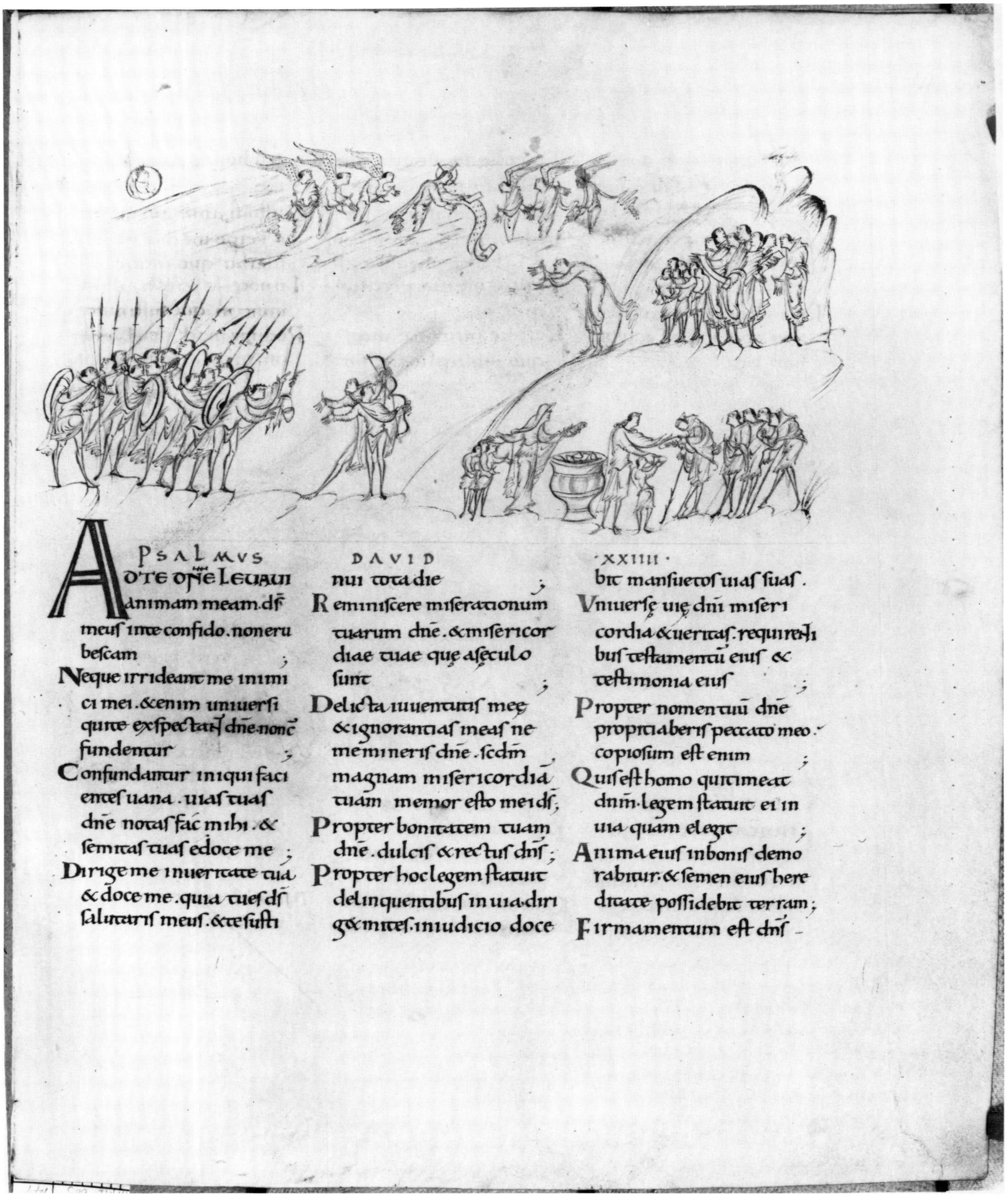

PSALMUS DAVID ·XXIIII·

AD TE DNE LEVAVI
animam meam. ds
meus in te confido. non eru
bescam ;
Neque irrideant me inimi
ci mei. & enim universi
qui te exspectant dne non c
fundentur ;
Confundantur iniqui faci
entes vana. vias tuas
dne notas fac mihi. &
semitas tuas edoce me ;
Dirige me in veritate tua
& doce me. quia tu es ds
salutaris meus. & te susti
nui tota die ;
Reminiscere miserationum
tuarum dne. & misericor
diae tuae que a seculo
sunt ;
Delicta iuventutis mee
& ignorantias meas ne
memineris dne. secdm
magnam misericordia
tuam memor esto mei ds;
Propter bonitatem tuam
dne. dulcis & rectus dns;
Propter hoc legem statuit
delinquentibus in via. diri
get mites in iudicio doce
bit mansuetos vias suas.
Universe vie dni miseri
cordia & veritas. requirenti
bus testamentu eius &
testimonia eius ;
Propter nomen tuu dne
propitiaberis peccato meo.
copiosum est enim ;
Quis est homo qui timeat
dnm. legem statuit ei in
via quam elegit ;
Anima eius in bonis demo
rabitur. & semen eius here
ditate possidebit terram;
Firmamentum est dns

2.24 London, B.L., Harley 603, f. 14r

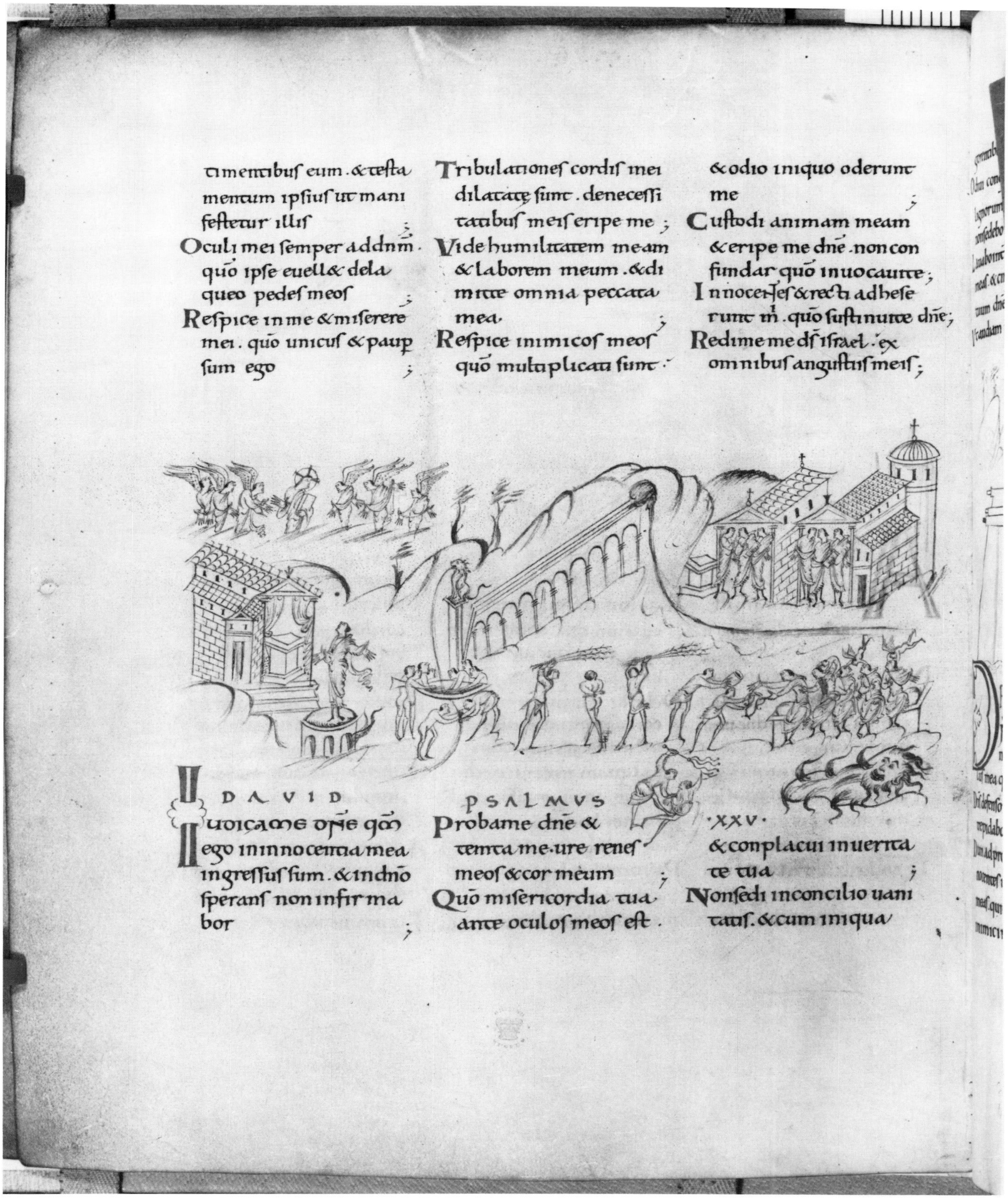

timentibus eum. & testa
mentum ipsius ut mani
festetur illis ;
Oculi mei semper ad dnm.
quo ipse euell& de la
queo pedes meos ;
Respice in me & miserere
mei. quo unicus & paup
sum ego ;

Tribulationes cordis mei
dilatatae sunt. de necessi
tatibus meis eripe me ;
Vide humilitatem meam
& laborem meum. & di
mitte omnia peccata
mea ;
Respice inimicos meos
quo multiplicati sunt.

& odio iniquo oderunt
me ;
Custodi animam meam
& eripe me dne. non con
fundar quo inuocaui te ;
Innocentes & recti adhese
runt mi. quo sustinui te dne ;
Redime me ds israel. ex
omnibus angustiis meis ;

DAVID PSALMUS .XXV.

Iudica me dne quo
ego in innocentia mea
ingressus sum. & in dno
sperans non infirma
bor ;

Proba me dne &
tempta me. ure renes
meos & cor meum ;
Quo misericordia tua
ante oculos meos est.

& conplacui in uerita
te tua ;
Non sedi in concilio uani
tatis. & cum iniqua

2.25 London, B.L., Harley 603, f. 14v

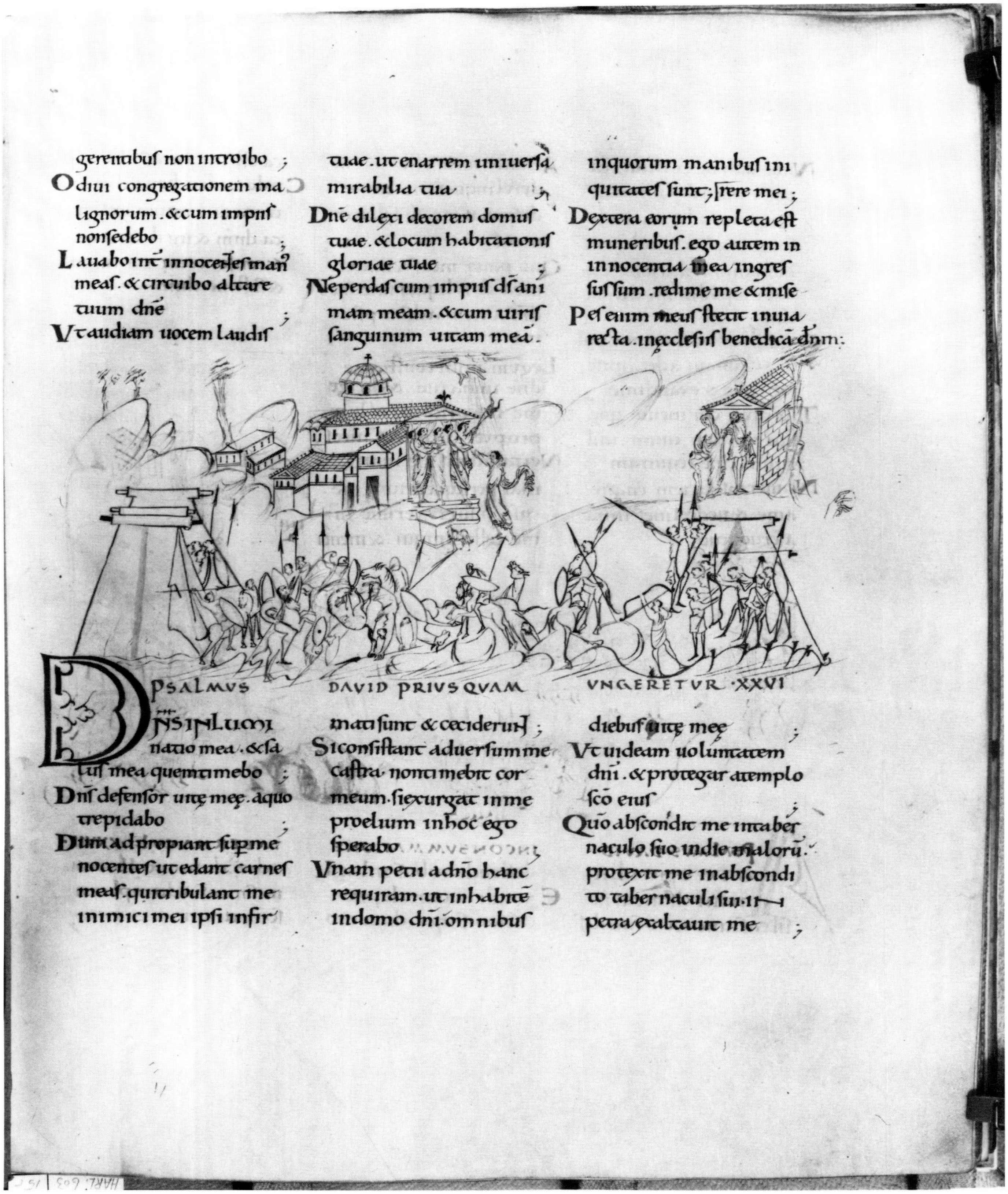

gerentibus non introibo ;
Odiui congregationem ma
lignorum . & cum impiis
non sedebo
Lauabo inter innocentes manus
meas . & circuibo altare
tuum domine ;
Ut audiam uocem laudis

tuae . ut enarrem uniuersa
mirabilia tua ;
Domine dilexi decorem domus
tuae . & locum habitationis
gloriae tuae ;
Ne perdas cum impiis deus ani
mam meam . & cum uiris
sanguinum uitam meam .

in quorum manibus ini
quitates sunt ; rere mei ;
Dextera eorum repleta est
muneribus . ego autem in
innocentia mea ingres
sus sum . redime me & mise
Pes enim meus stetit in uia
recta . in ecclesiis benedicam dominum ;

Domini psalmus David prius quam ungeretur XXVI

Dominus inlumi
natio mea . & sa
lus mea quem timebo ;
Dominus defensor uitae meae . a quo
trepidabo ;
Dum adpropiant super me
nocentes ut edant carnes
meas . qui tribulant me
inimici mei ipsi infir

mati sunt & ceciderunt ;
Si consistant aduersum me
castra . non timebit cor
meum . si exurgat in me
proelium in hoc ego
sperabo ;
Unam petii a domino hanc
requiram . ut inhabitem
in domo domini omnibus

diebus uitae meae ;
Ut uideam uoluntatem
domini . & protegar a templo
sancto eius ;
Quoniam abscondit me in taber
naculo suo in die malorum .
protexit me in abscondi
to tabernaculi sui . in
petra exaltauit me ;

2.26 London, B.L., Harley 603, f. 15r

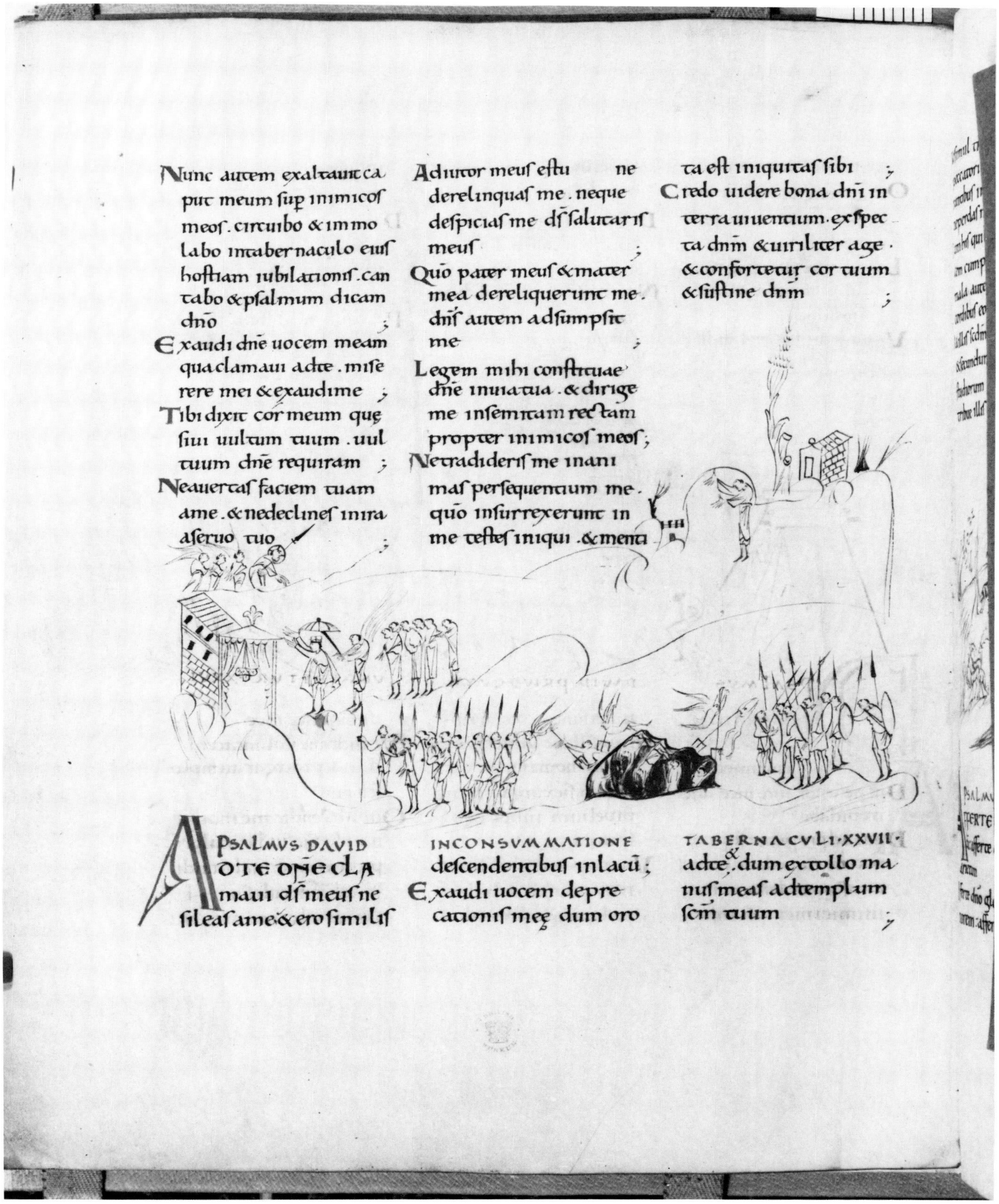

Nunc autem exaltauit ca
put meum sup inimicos
meos. circuibo & immo
labo intabernaculo eius
hostiam iubilationis. can
tabo & psalmum dicam
dno ;
Exaudi dne uocem meam
qua clamaui adte. mise
rere mei & exaudi me ;
Tibi dixit cor meum que
siui uultum tuum. uul
tuum dne requiram ;
Ne auertas faciem tuam
ame. & ne declines inira
aseruo tuo ;

Adiutor meus esto ne
derelinquas me. neque
despicias me ds salutaris
meus ;
Quo pater meus & mater
mea dereliquerunt me.
dns autem adsumpsit
me ;
Legem mihi constitue
dne in uia tua. & dirige
me in semitam rectam
propter inimicos meos ;
Ne tradideris me inani
mas persequentium me.
quo insurrexerunt in
me testes iniqui. & menti

ta est iniquitas sibi ;
Credo uidere bona dni in
terra uiuentium. exspec
ta dnm & uiriliter age.
& confortetur cor tuum
& sustine dnm ;

PSALMUS DAVID
AD TE DNE CLA
MAUI DS MEUS NE
SILEAS AME & ERO SIMILIS

INCONSUMMATIONE
descendentibus in lacu ;
Exaudi uocem depre
cationis meę dum oro

TABERNACULI. XXVII.
& adte. dum extollo ma
nus meas ad templum
scm tuum ;

2.27 London, B.L., Harley 603, f. 15^v

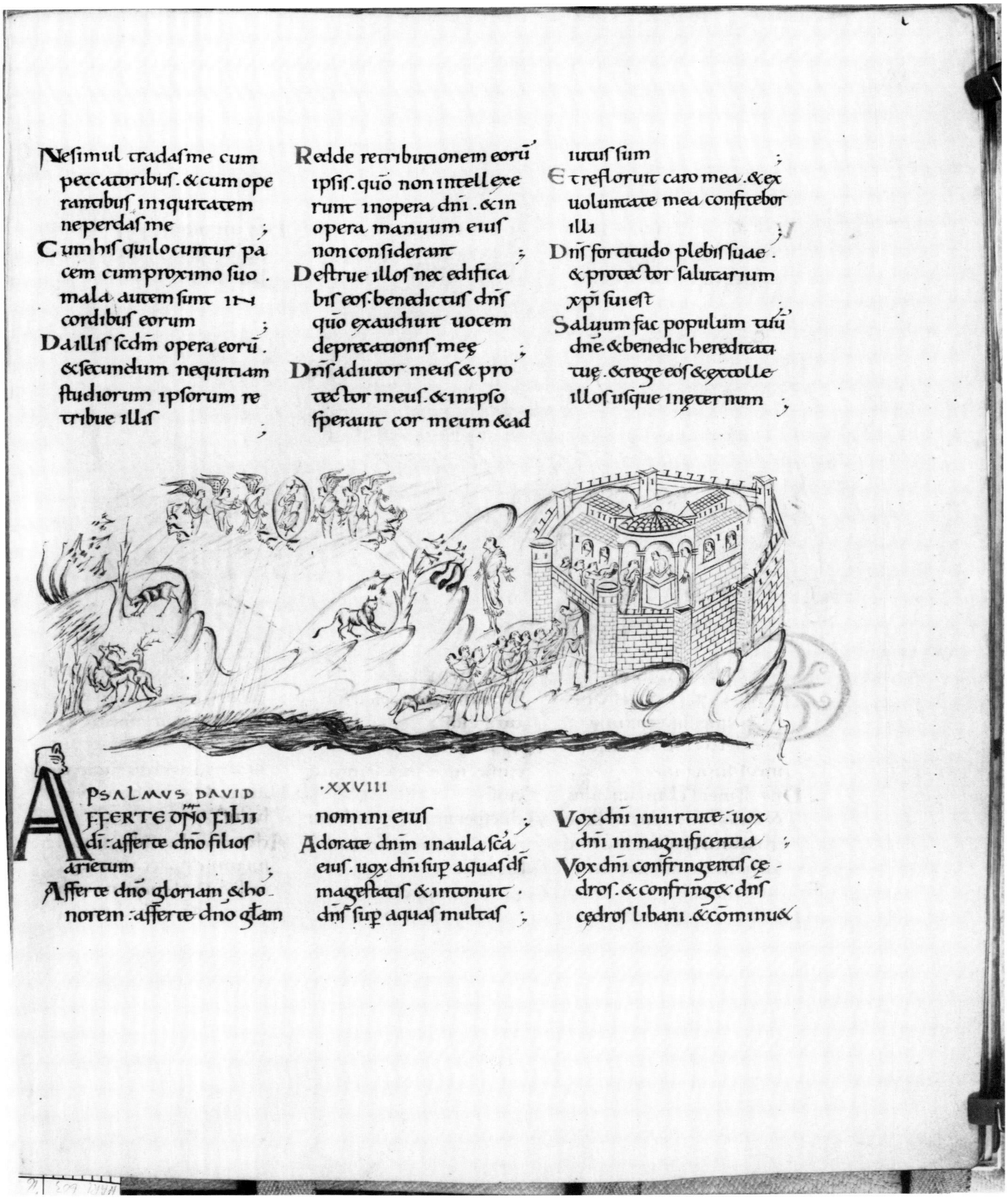

Ne simul tradas me cum
peccatoribus. & cum ope
rantibus iniquitatem
ne perdas me ;
Cum his qui locuntur pa
cem cum proximo suo.
mala autem sunt in
cordibus eorum ;
Da illis sc̄dm opera eorū.
& secundum nequitiam
studiorum ipsorum re
tribue illis ;

Redde retributionem eorū
ipsis. quō non intellexe
runt in opera dn̄i. & in
opera manuum eius
non considerant ;
Destrue illos nec edifica
bis eos. benedictus dn̄s
quō exaudiuit uocem
deprecationis meę ;
Dn̄s adiutor meus & pro
tector meus. & in ipso
sperauit cor meum & ad

iutus sum ;
Et refloruit caro mea. & ex
uoluntate mea confitebor
illi ;
Dn̄s fortitudo plebis suae.
& protector salutarium
xp̄i sui est ;
Saluum fac populum tuū
dn̄e. & benedic hereditati
tuę. & rege eos & extolle
illos usque in eternum ;

PSALMUS DAVID ·XXVIIII
AFFERTE DN̄O FILII
dī: afferte dn̄o filios
arietum ;
Afferte dn̄o gloriam & ho
norem: afferte dn̄o glām
nomini eius ;
Adorate dn̄m in aula scā
eius. uox dn̄i sup aquas ds
magestatis & intonuit.
dn̄s sup aquas multas ;
Vox dn̄i in uirtute: uox
dn̄i in magnificentia ;
Vox dn̄i confringentis ce
dros. & confringet dn̄s
cedros libani. & comminuet

2.28 London, B.L., Harley 603, f. 16r

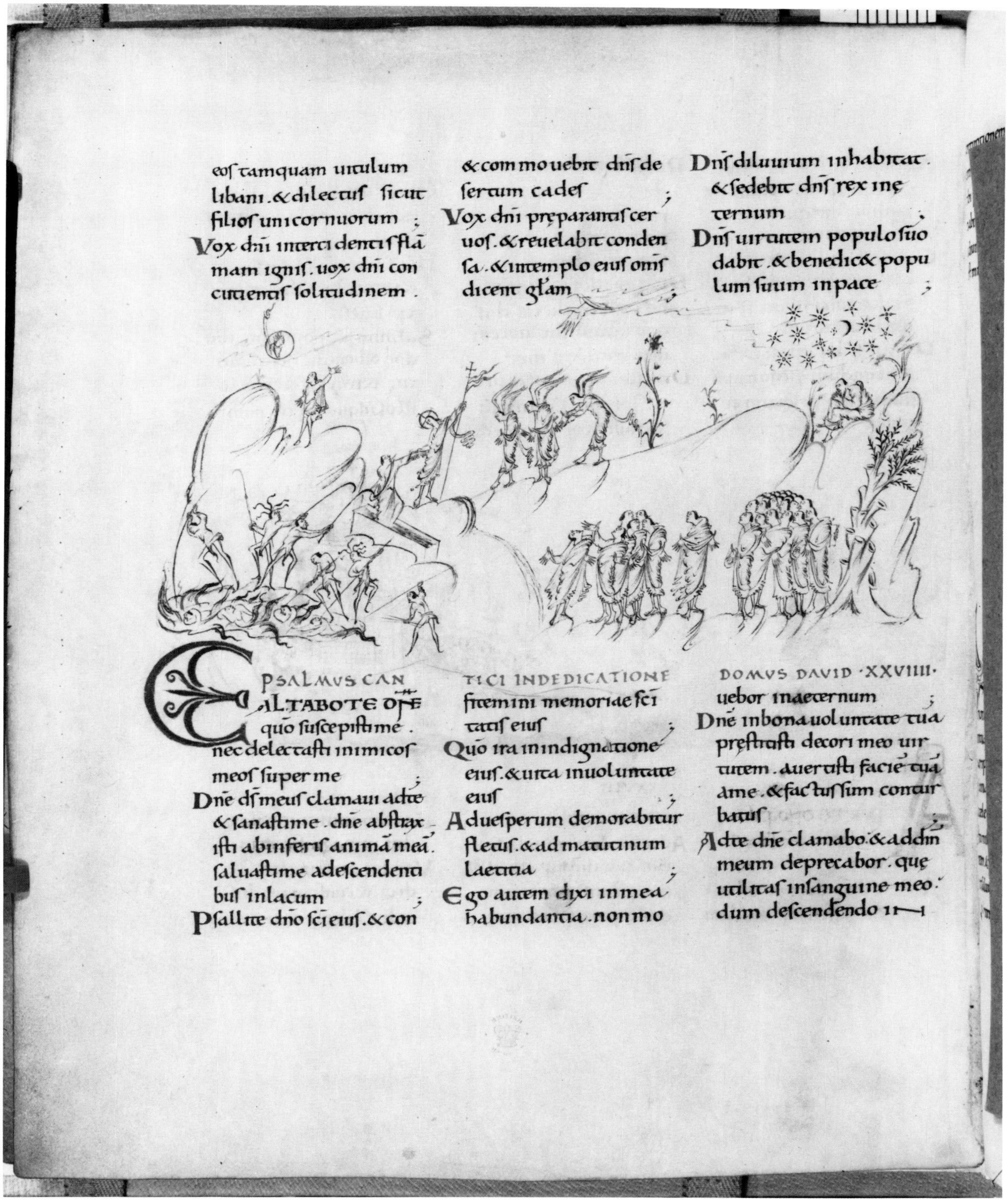

eos tamquam uitulum
libani. & dilectus sicut
filios unicornuorum ;
Vox dni intercidentis flã
mam ignis. uox dni con
cutientis solitudinem .
& commouebit dns de
sertum cades ;
Vox dni praeparantis cer
uos. & reuelabit conden
sa. & in templo eius omis
dicent glam
Dns diluuium inhabitat.
& sedebit dns rex in ę
ternum ;
Dns uirtutem populo suo
dabit. & benedic& popu
lum suum in pace ;

E PSALMUS CANTICI IN DEDICATIONE DOMUS DAVID ·XXVIIII·
XALTABO TE DNE
quo suscepisti me.
nec delectasti inimicos
meos super me ;
Dne ds meus clamaui ad te
& sanasti me. dne abstrax
isti ab inferis animã meã.
saluasti me a descendenti
bus in lacum
Psallite dno sci eius. & con
fitemini memoriae sci
tatis eius ;
Quo ira in indignatione
eius. & uita in uoluntate
eius ;
Ad uesperum demorabitur
fletus. & ad matutinum
laetitia ;
Ego autem dixi in mea
habundantia. non mo
uebor in aeternum ;
Dne in bona uoluntate tua
praestitisti decori meo uir
tutem. auertisti faciẽ tua
a me. & factus sum contur
batus ;
Ad te dne clamabo. & ad dm
meum deprecabor. quę
utilitas in sanguine meo.
dum descendendo in

2.29 London, B.L., Harley 603, f. 16v

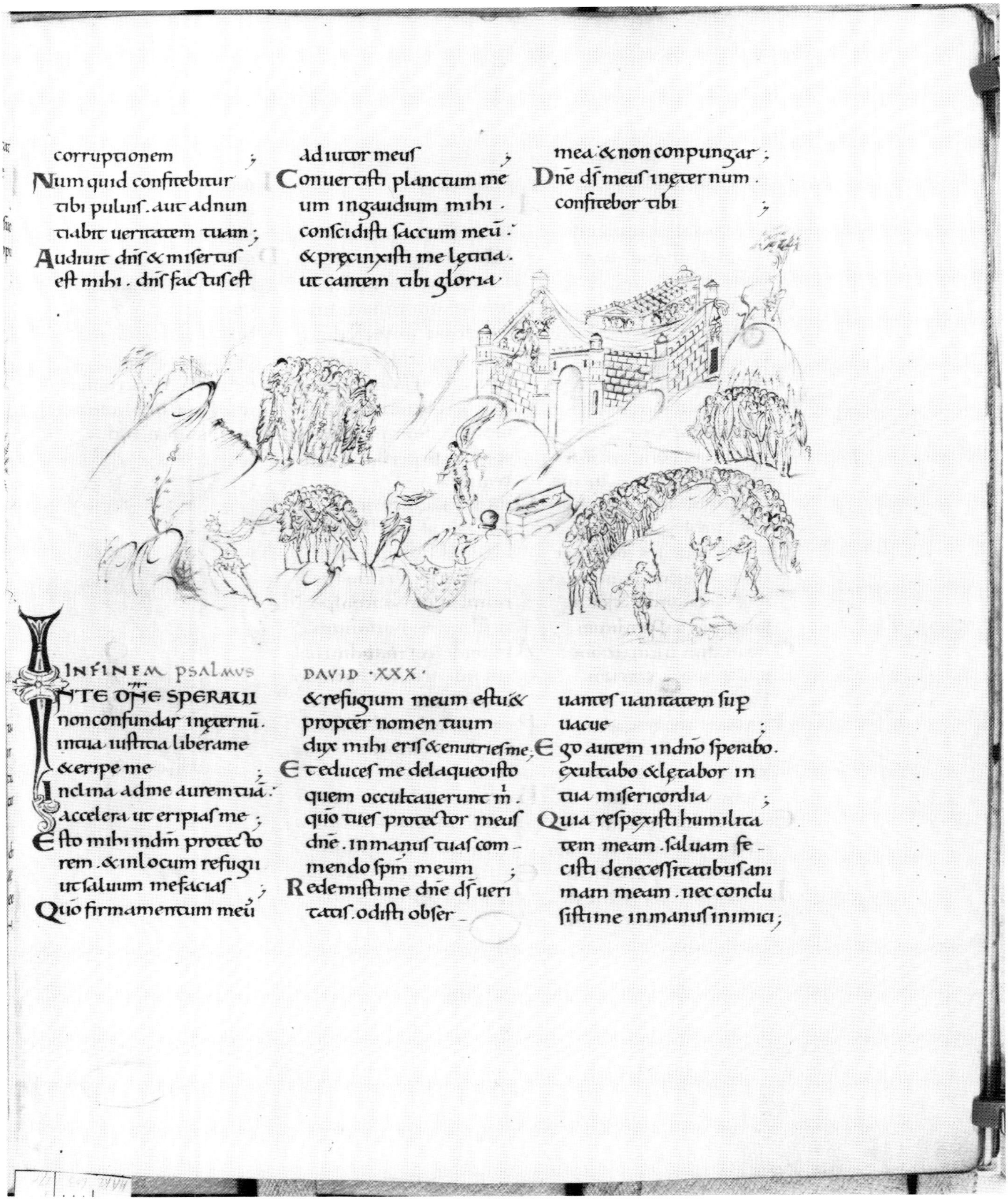

corruptionem ;
Numquid confitebitur
tibi puluis. aut adnun
tiabit ueritatem tuam ;
Audiuit dns & misertus
est mihi. dns factus est
adiutor meus ;
Conuertisti planctum me
um ingaudium mihi .
conscidisti saccum meū .
& precinxisti me letitia .
ut cantem tibi gloria
mea & non conpungar ;
Dne ds meus ineternum .
confitebor tibi ;

IN FINEM PSALMUS DAVID · XXX ·
IN TE DNE SPERAUI
nonconfundar ineternū .
intua iustitia liberame
& eripe me ;
Inclina adme aurem tuā .
accelera ut eripias me ;
Esto mihi indm protecto
rem . & inlocum refugii
ut saluum mefacias ;
Quo firmamentum meū
& refugium meum es tu &
propter nomen tuum
dux mihi eris & enutries me ;
Et educes me delaqueo isto
quem occultauerunt m .
quo tu es protector meus
dne . inmanus tuas com-
mendo spm meum ;
Redemisti me dne ds ueri
tatis . odisti obser-
uantes uanitatem sup
uacue ;
Ego autem indno sperabo .
exultabo & letabor in
tua misericordia ;
Quia respexisti humilita
tem meam . saluam fe-
cisti denecessitatibus ani
mam meam . nec conclu
sisti me inmanus inimici ;

2.30 London, B.L., Harley 603, f. 17r

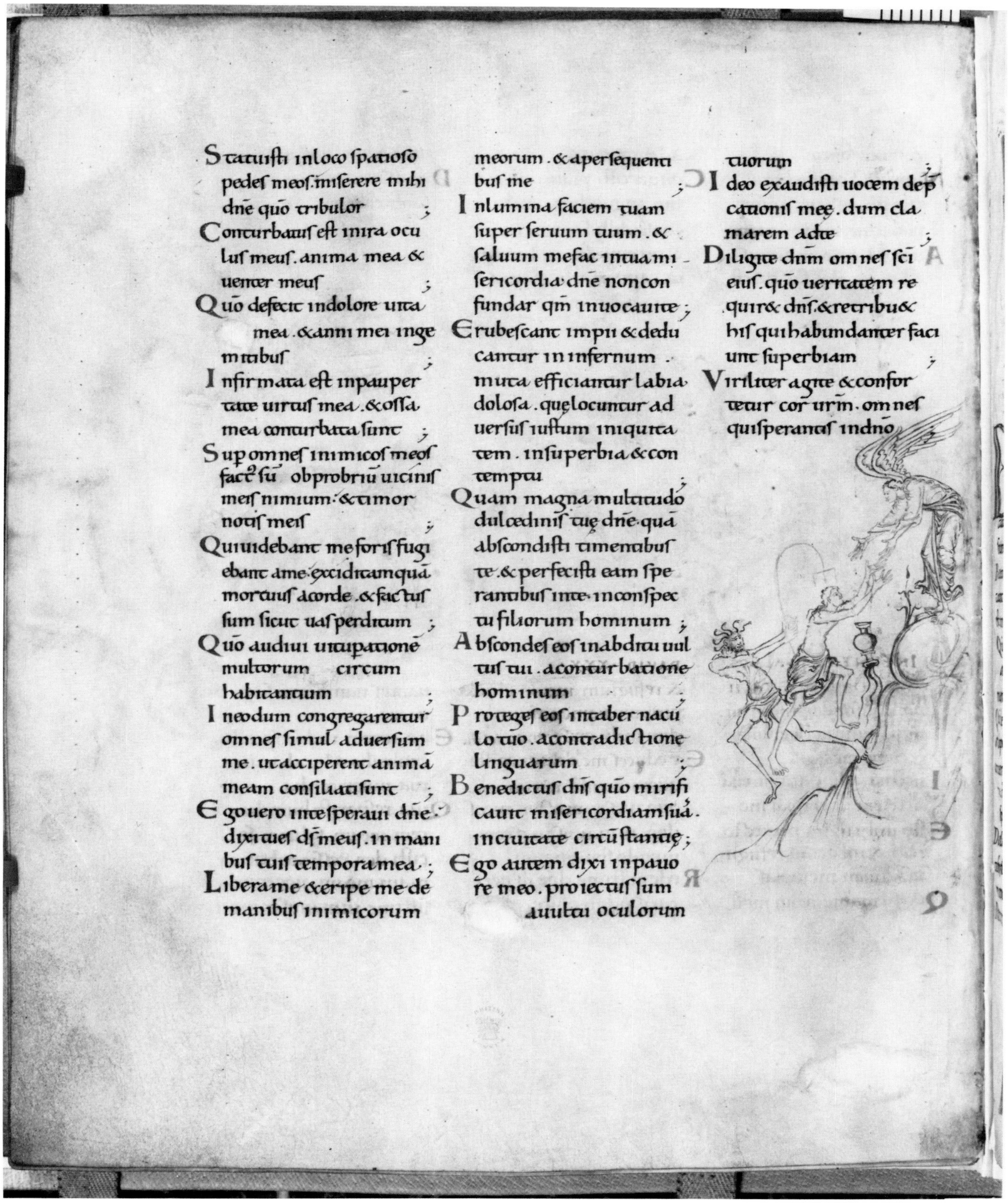

Statuisti in loco spatioso
pedes meos. miserere mihi
dne quo tribulor ;
Conturbatus est in ira ocu
lus meus. anima mea &
uenter meus ;
Quo defecit in dolore uita
mea. & anni mei in ge
mitibus ;
Infirmata est in pauper
tate uirtus mea. & ossa
mea conturbata sunt ;
Sup omnes inimicos meos
fact su obprobriu uicinis
meis nimium. & timor
notis meis ;
Qui uidebant me foris fugi
ebant a me. excidi tamquā
mortuus a corde. & factus
sum sicut uas perditum ;
Quo audiui uituperatione
multorum circum
habitantium
In eo dum congregarentur
omnes simul aduersum
me. ut acciperent animā
meam consiliati sunt ;
Ego uero in te speraui dne.
dixi tu es ds meus. in mani
bus tuis tempora mea ;
Libera me & eripe me de
manibus inimicorum
meorum. & a persequenti
bus me ;
Inlumina faciem tuam
super seruum tuum. &
saluum me fac in tua mi
sericordia dne non con
fundar qm inuocaui te ;
Erubescant impii & dedu
cantur in infernum.
muta efficiantur labia
dolosa. quę locuntur ad
uersus iustum iniquita
tem. in superbia & con
temptu ;
Quam magna multitudo
dulcedinis tuę dne. quā
abscondisti timentibus
te. & perfecisti eam spe
rantibus in te. in conspec
tu filiorum hominum ;
Abscondes eos in abdito uul
tus tui. a conturbatione
hominum ;
Proteges eos in tabernacu
lo tuo. a contradictione
linguarum ;
Benedictus dns quo mirifi
cauit misericordiam suā.
in ciuitate circūstantię ;
Ego autem dixi in pauo
re meo. proiectus sum
a uultu oculorum
tuorum ;
Ideo exaudisti uocem dep
cationis meę. dum cla
marem ad te ;
Diligite dnm omnes sci
eius. quo ueritatem re
quiret dns. & retribuet
his qui habundanter faci
unt superbiam ;
Viriliter agite & confor
tetur cor urm. omnes
qui speratis in dno

2.31 London, B.L., Harley 603, f. 17v

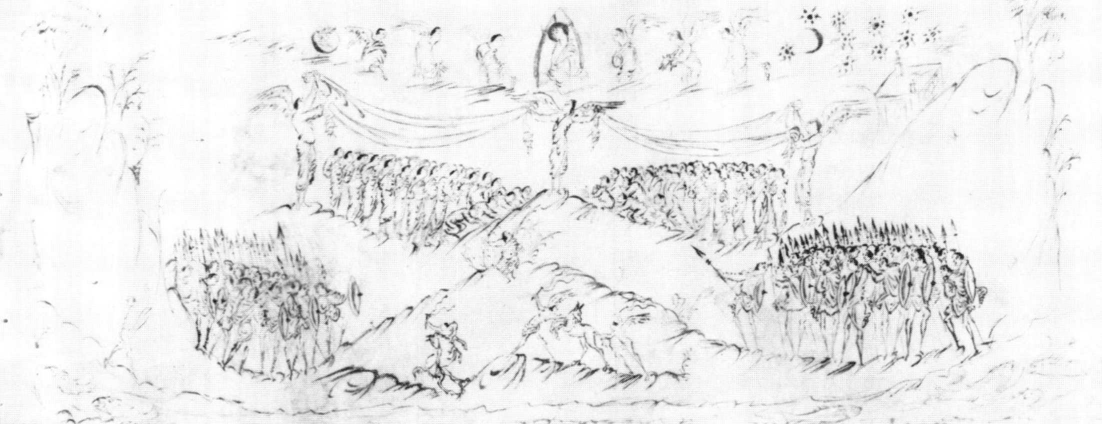

HUIC DAVID INTELLECTUS · XXXI ·

BEATI QUORUM
remisse sunt iniqui
tates & quorum tecta
sunt peccata
Beatus uir cui non inpu
tauit dns peccatum nec
est in ore eius dolus
Quo tacui inueterauerunt
omnia ossa mea dum cla
marem tota die
Quo die ac nocte grauata
est super me manus tua
conuersus sum in erumna
mea dum confringitur
spina
Delictum meum cognitu
tibi feci & iniustitias meas
non operui
Dixi pronuntiabo aduersu
me iniustitias meas dno
& tu remisisti impieta
tem cordis mei
Pro hac orabit ad te omnis
scs in tempore oportuno
uerum tamen in diluuio
aquarum multarum ad
eum non adproximabunt
Tu es mihi refugium a pres
sura que circumdedit me
exultatio mea redime me
a circumdantibus me
Intellectum dabo tibi &
instruam te in uia hac
qua ingredieris firmabo
super te oculos meos
Nolite fieri sicut equus
& mulus in quibus non est
intellectus
In freno & camo maxillas
eorum constringe qui
non adproximabunt
ad te
Multa flagella peccatoru
sperantes autem in dno
misericordia circumdabit
Laetamini in dno & exul
tate iusti & gloriamini
omnes recti corde

2.32 London, B.L., Harley 603, f. 18r

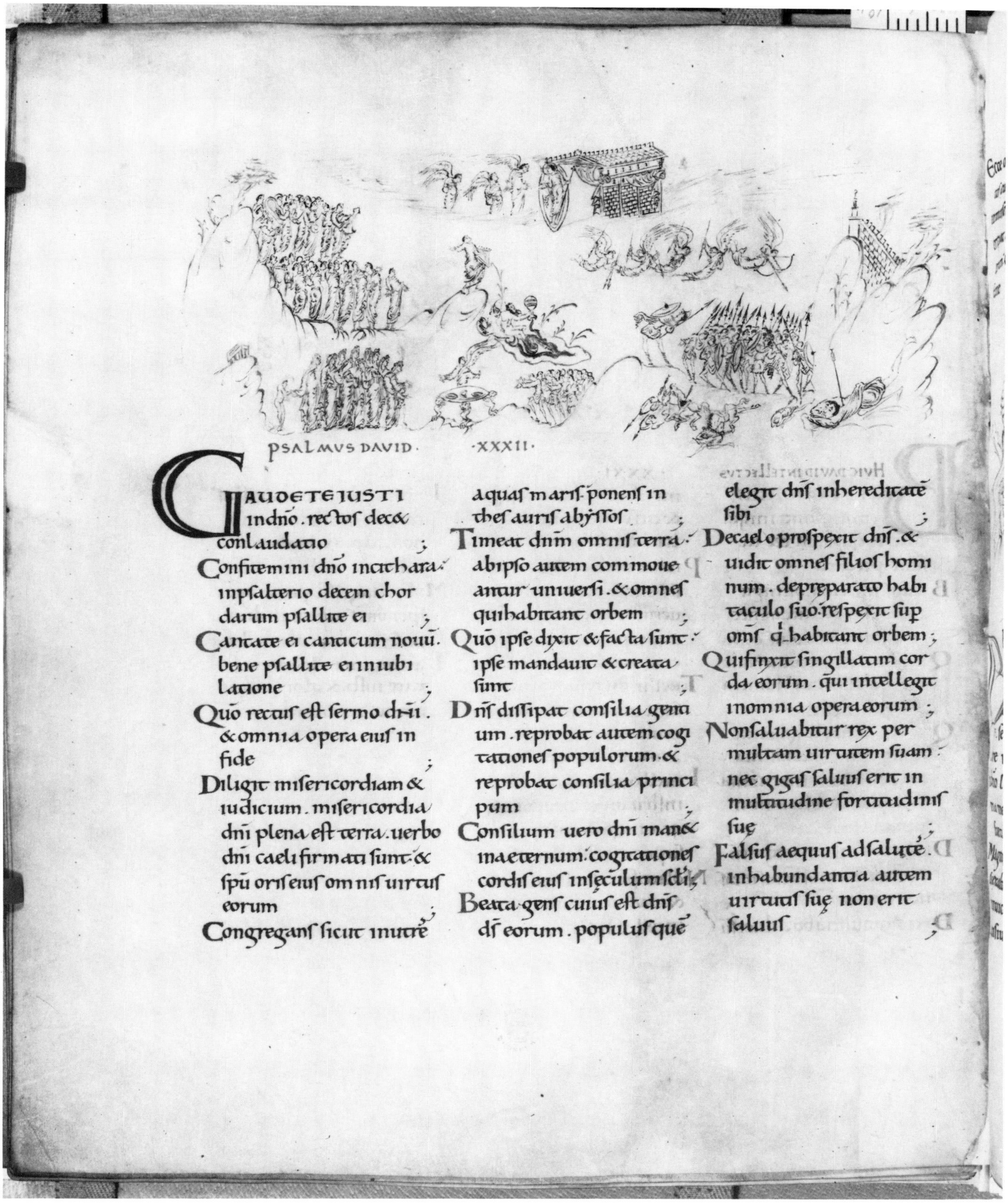
PSALMUS DAVID. XXXII.

GAUDETE IUSTI
in dno. rectos dec&
conlaudatio ;
Confitemini dno in cithara
in psalterio decem chor
darum psallite ei ;
Cantate ei canticum nouu.
bene psallite ei in iubi
latione ;
Quo rectus est sermo dni.
& omnia opera eius in
fide ;
Diligit misericordiam &
iudicium. misericordia
dni plena est terra. uerbo
dni caeli firmati sunt &
spu oris eius omnis uirtus
eorum ;
Congregans sicut in utre
aquas maris. ponens in
thesauris abyssos ;
Timeat dnm omnis terra.
ab ipso autem commoue
antur uniuersi. & omnes
qui habitant orbem ;
Quo ipse dixit & facta sunt.
ipse mandauit & creata
sunt ;
Dns dissipat consilia genti
um. reprobat autem cogi
tationes populorum. &
reprobat consilia princi
pum ;
Consilium uero dni manet
in aeternum. cogitationes
cordis eius in seculum sctli ;
Beata gens cuius est dns
ds eorum. populus que
elegit dns in hereditate
sibi ;
De caelo prospexit dns. &
uidit omnes filios homi
num. de preparato habi
taculo suo. respexit sup
omis q habitant orbem ;
Qui finxit singillatim cor
da eorum. qui intellegit
in omnia opera eorum ;
Non saluabitur rex per
multam uirtutem suam.
nec gigas saluus erit in
multitudine fortitudinis
suae ;
Falsus aequus ad salute.
in habundantia autem
uirtutis suae non erit
saluus ;

2.33 London, B.L., Harley 603, f. 18v

Ecce oculi dn̄i super timen
tes eum. sperantes autē
in misericordia eius. ut
eripiat a morte animas
eorum: & alat eos in
fame ;

Anima autem nostra
sustinet dn̄m: quo adiu
tor & protector noster
est. & in ipso laetabitur
cor nostrum. & in no
mine sc̄o eius sperabim̄ ;

Fiat dn̄e misericordia
tua super nos. quem
admodum sperauim̄
in te ;

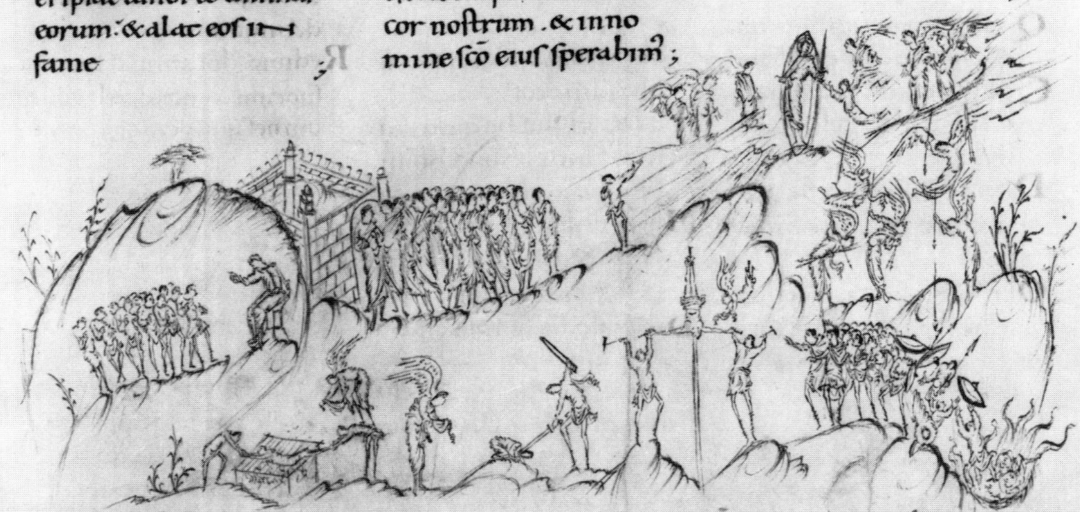

PSALMUS DD CUM MUTAVIT FACIEM SUAM CORAM ABIMELEH. XXXIII.

BENEDICAM
dn̄m in omni tem
pore. semper laus eius
in ore meo ;
In dn̄o laudabitur ani
ma mea. audiant man
sueti & laetentur ;
Magnificate dn̄m mecum.
& exaltemus nomen eius
in inuicem ;
Inquisiui dn̄m & exau

diuit me. & ex omnibus
tribulationibus meis
eripuit me ;
Accedite ad eum & in
luminamini. & uultus
ur̄i non erubescent ;
Iste pauper clamauit.
& dn̄s exaudiuit eum.
& ex omnibus tribulati
onibus eius liberauit
eum ;

Inmittet angelum dn̄s
in circuitu timentium
eum: & eripiet eos ;
Gustate & uidete quo suauis
est dn̄s. beatus uir qui
sperat in eum ;
Timete dn̄m omnes sc̄i
eius. quo nihil deest
timentibus eum ;
Diuites eguerunt & esuri
erunt. inquirentes autē

2.34 London, B.L., Harley 603, f. 19r

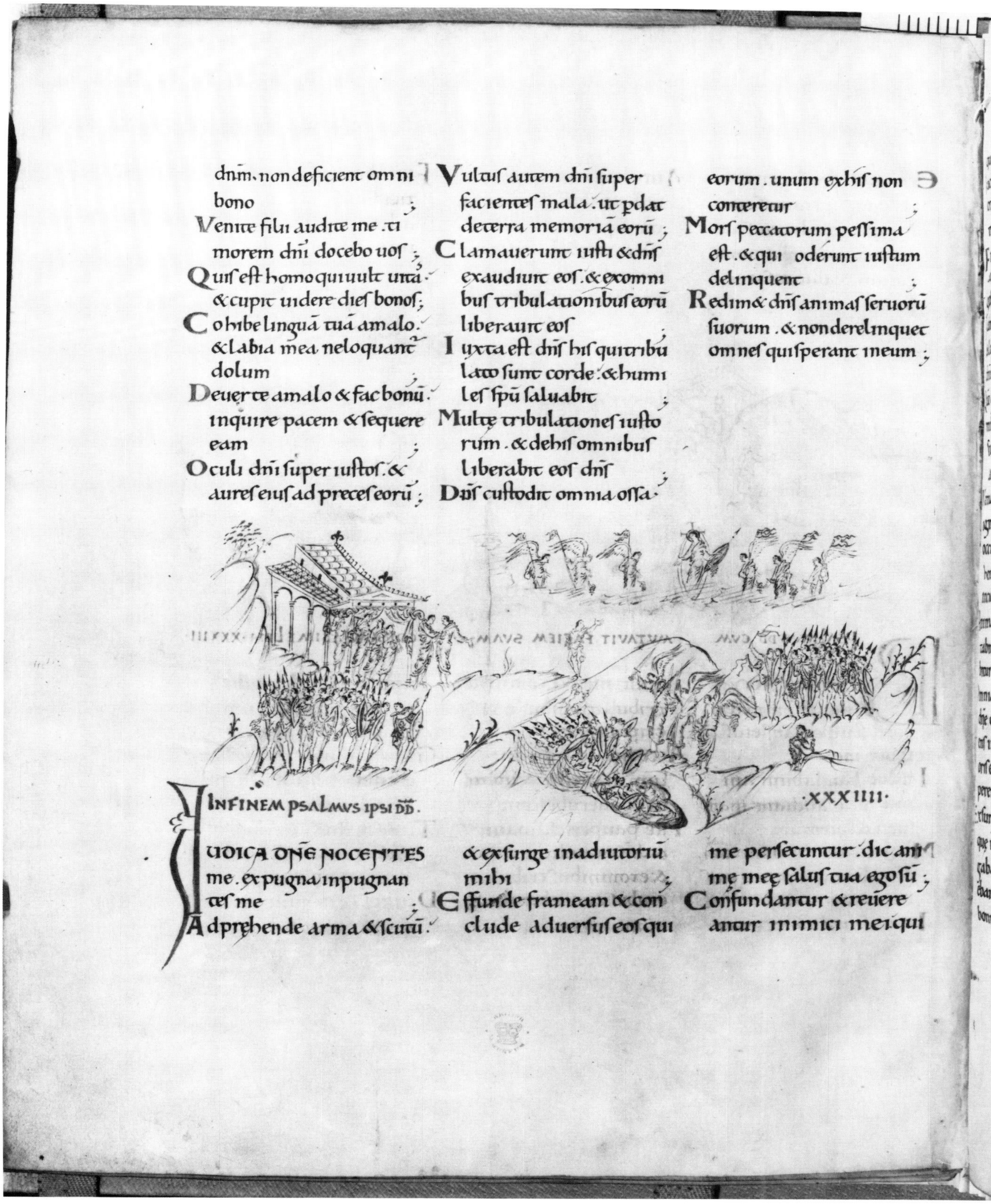

dnm. non deficient omni bono;
Venite filii audite me. timorem dni docebo uos;
Quis est homo qui uult uitã & cupit uidere dies bonos;
Cohibe linguã tuã a malo. & labia mea ne loquant dolum;
Deuerte a malo & fac bonũ. inquire pacem & sequere eam;
Oculi dni super iustos. & aures eius ad preces eorũ;
Vultus autem dni super facientes mala. ut pdat de terra memoriã eorũ;
Clamauerunt iusti & dns exaudiuit eos. & ex omnibus tribulationibus eorũ liberauit eos;
Iuxta est dns his qui tribulato sunt corde. & humiles spũ saluabit;
Multe tribulationes iustorum. & de his omnibus liberabit eos dns;
Dns custodit omnia ossa eorum. unum ex his non conteretur;
Mors peccatorum pessima est. & qui oderunt iustum delinquent;
Redimet dns animas seruorũ suorum. & non derelinquet omnes qui sperant in eum;

IN FINEM PSALMUS IPSI DD. XXXIIII.

IUDICA DNE NOCENTES me. expugna inpugnantes me
Adprehende arma & scutũ. & exsurge in adiutoriũ mihi
Effunde frameam & conclude aduersus eos qui me persecuntur. dic anime mee salus tua ego sũ;
Confundantur & reuereantur inimici mei qui

2.35 London, B.L., Harley 603, f. 19v

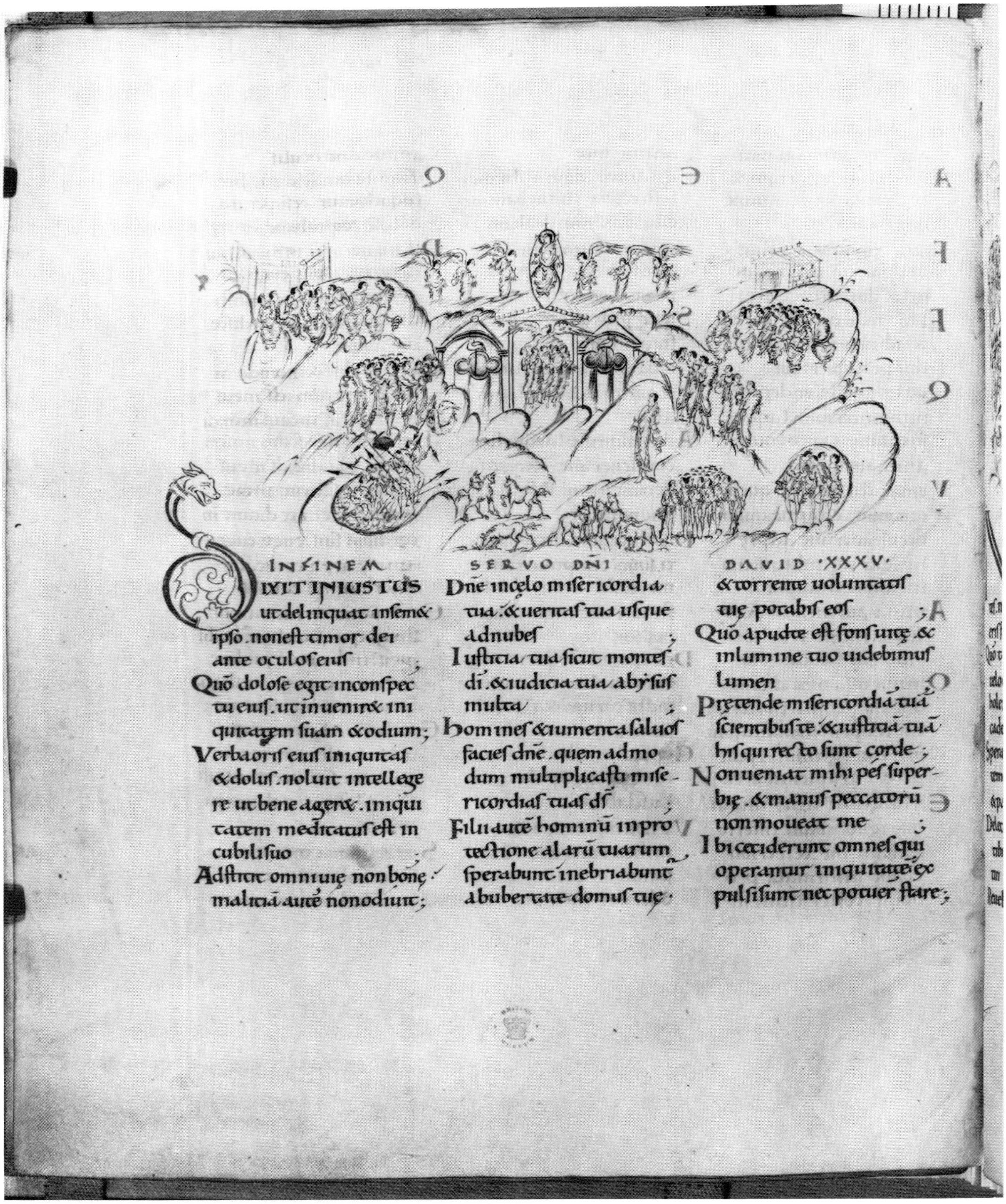

IN FINEM SERVO DNI DAVID XXXV.

DIXIT INIUSTUS ut delinquat in se met ipso. non est timor dei ante oculos eius;
Quoniam dolose egit in conspectu eius. ut inueniret iniquitatem suam et odium;
Verba oris eius iniquitas et dolus. noluit intellegere ut bene ageret. iniquitatem meditatus est in cubili suo
Adstitit omni uiae non bonae. malitiam autem non odiuit;
Dne in caelo misericordia tua. et ueritas tua usque ad nubes
Iusticia tua sicut montes di. et iudicia tua abyssus multa;
homines et iumenta saluos facies dne. quemadmodum multiplicasti misericordias tuas ds;
Filii autem hominum in protectione alarum tuarum sperabunt. inebriabunt ab ubertate domus tuae.
et torrente uoluntatis tuae potabis eos;
Quoniam apud te est fons uitae. et in lumine tuo uidebimus lumen
Praetende misericordiam tuam scientibus te. et iustitiam tuam his qui recto sunt corde;
Non ueniat mihi pes superbiae. et manus peccatorum non moueat me;
Ibi ceciderunt omnes qui operantur iniquitatem. expulsi sunt nec potuerunt stare;

2.36 London, B.L., Harley 603, f. 20v

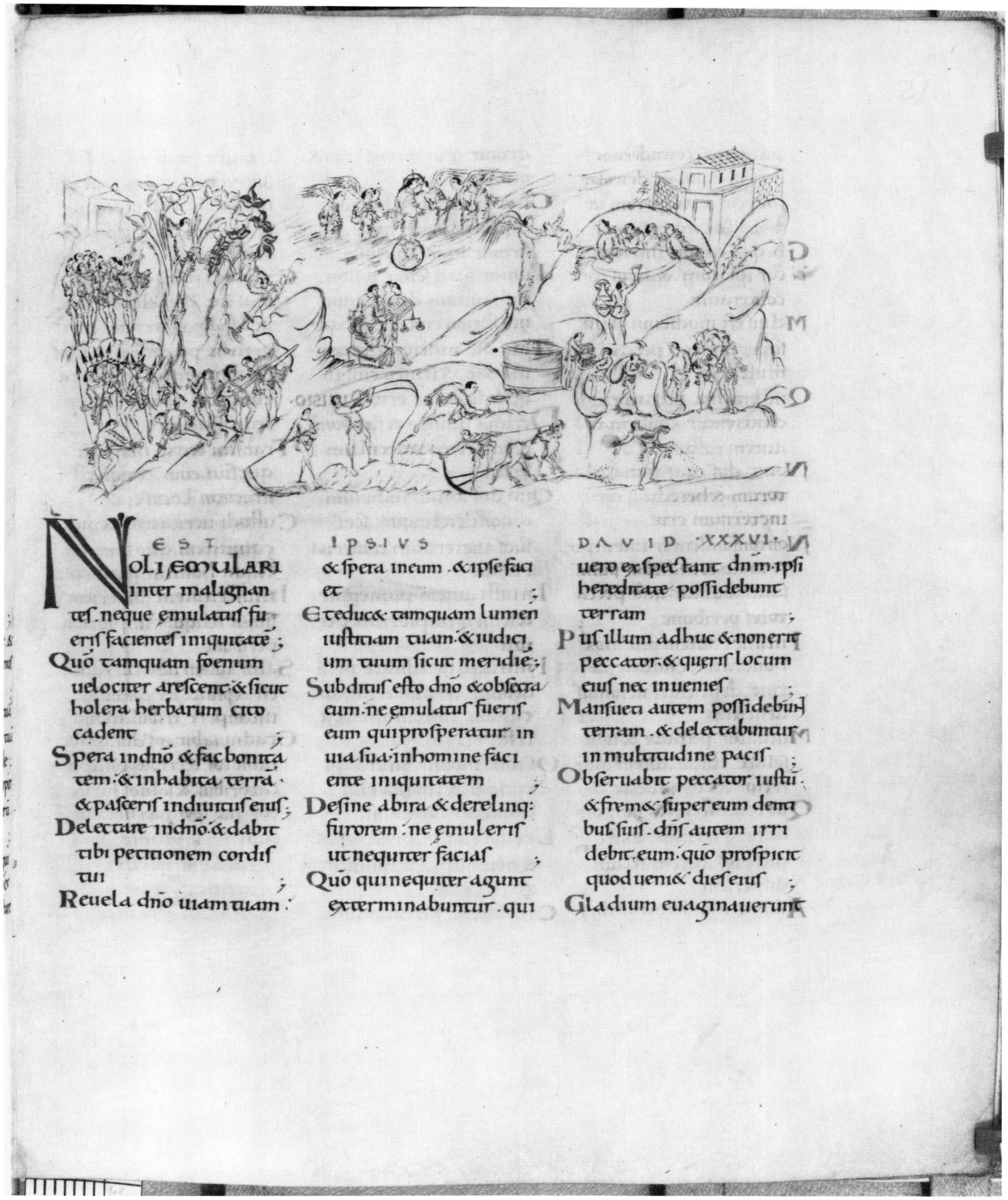

E S T I P S I U S D A V I D XXXVI.

Noli emulari
inter malignan
tes. neque emulatus fu
eris facientes iniquitate ;
Quo tamquam foenum
uelociter arescent & sicut
holera herbarum cito
cadent ;
Spera indno & fac bonita
tem & inhabita terra
& pasceris in diuitiis eius ;
Delectare indno & dabit
tibi petitionem cordis
tui ;
Reuela dno uiam tuam
& spera ineum . & ipse faci
et ;
Et educet tamquam lumen
iustitiam tuam & iudici
um tuum sicut meridie ;
Subditus esto dno & obsecra
eum . ne emulatus fueris
eum qui prosperatur in
uia sua in homine faci
ente iniquitatem ;
Desine abira & derelinq
furorem . ne emuleris
ut nequiter facias ;
Quo qui nequiter agunt
exterminabuntur . qui
uero expectant dnm ipsi
hereditate possidebunt
terram ;
Pus illum adhuc & non erit
peccator & queris locum
eius nec inuenies ;
Mansueti autem possidebunt
terram . & delectabuntur
in multitudine pacis ;
Obseruabit peccator iustu
& fremet super eum denti
bus suis . dns autem irri
debit eum quo prospicit
quod ueniet dies eius
Gladium euaginauerunt

2.37 London, B.L., Harley 603, f. 21r

22

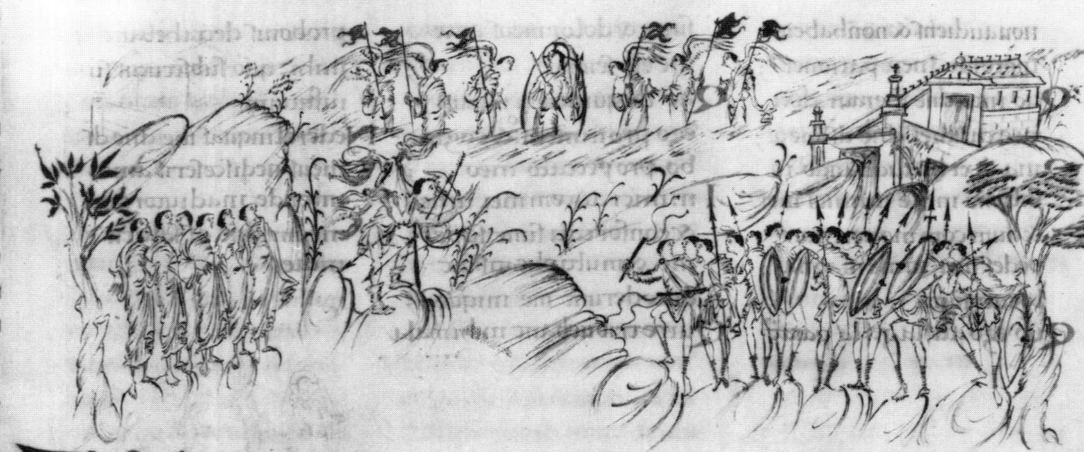

PSALMUS DAVID
DNE NE IN IRA TUA
arguas me: neque
in furore tuo corripias
me
Quo sagitte tue infixe sunt
mihi. & confirmasti sup
me manum tuam
Nec est sanitas in carne mea
a uultu ire tue. & non est
pax ossibus meis a facie
peccatorum meorum
Quo iniquitates mee sup
posuerunt caput meum:
sicut onus graue gra
uate sunt super me
Conputruerunt & deteri
orauerunt cicatrices
mee a facie insipientie

IN REMEMORATIONEM
mee
Miserias adflictus sum &
turbatus sum usque in
finem: tota die contrista
tus ingrediebar
Quo anima mea completa
est inlusionibus. & non est
sanitas in carne mea
Incuruatus sum & humili
atus sum usquequaque:
rugiebam a gemitu cor
dis mei. & ante te est omne
desiderium meum. & ge
mitus meus a te non est
absconditus
Cor meum conturbatum
est in me. & deseruit me
fortitudo mea: & lumen

EST DE SABBATO XXXVII
oculorum meorum non
est mecum
Amici mei & proximi mei
aduersum me adpropia
uerunt & steterunt: &
proximi mei a longe
steterunt
Et uim faciebant qui que
rebant animam meam:
& qui inquirebant mala
mihi locuti sunt uanita
tem: & dolos tota die
meditabantur
Ego autem uelut surdus
non audiebam: & sicut
mutus qui non aperuit
os suum
Et factus sum ut homo

2.38 London, B.L., Harley 603, f. 22r

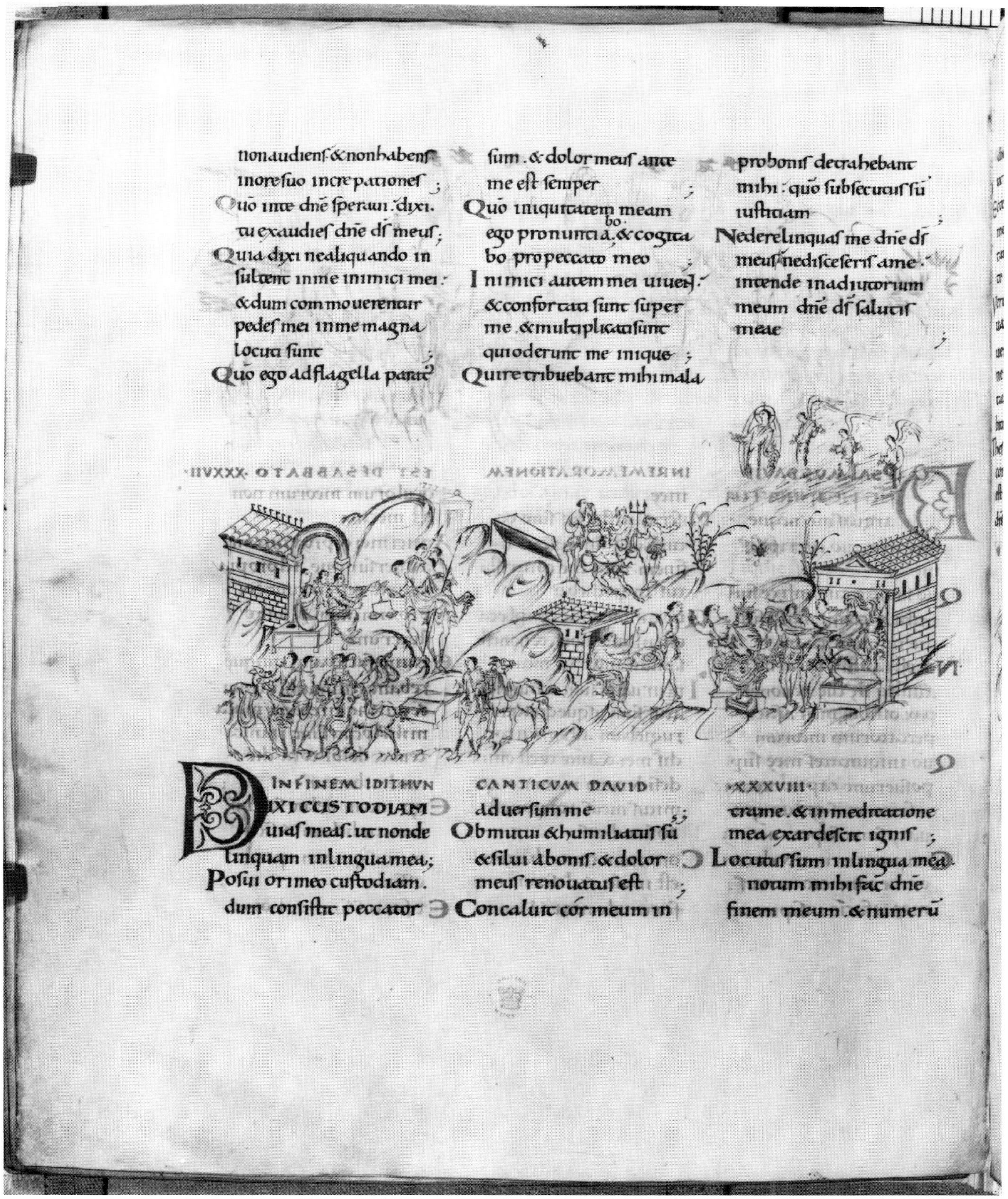

nonaudiens&nonhabens
inoresuo increpationes ;
Quõ inte dñe speraui: dixi.
tu exaudies dñe ds meus;
Quia dixi nealiquando in
sultent inme inimici mei:
&dum commouerentur
pedes mei inme magna
locuti sunt ;
Quõ ego adflagella parat
sum. & dolor meus ante
me est semper ;
Quõ iniquitatem meam
ego pronuntia(bo). & cogita
bo propeccato meo ;
Inimici autem mei uiuent
&confortati sunt super
me. &multiplicati sunt
quioderunt me inique ;
Quiretribuebant mihi mala
probonis detrahebant
mihi: quõ subsecutus sũ
iustitiam ;
Nederelinquas me dñe ds
meus nediscesseris ame.
intende inadiutorium
meum dñe ds salutis
meae

IN FINEM IDITHUN CANTICUM DAVID
DIXI CUSTODIAM
uias meas. ut nonde
linquam inlingua mea;
Posui ori meo custodiam.
dum consistit peccator
aduersum me ;
Obmutui &humiliatus sũ
&silui abonis. &dolor
meus renouatus est ;
Concaluit cor meum in
trame. &inmeditatione
mea exardescit ignis ;
Locutus sum inlingua mea.
notum mihi fac dñe
finem meum. &numerũ

2.39 London, B.L., Harley 603, f. 22v

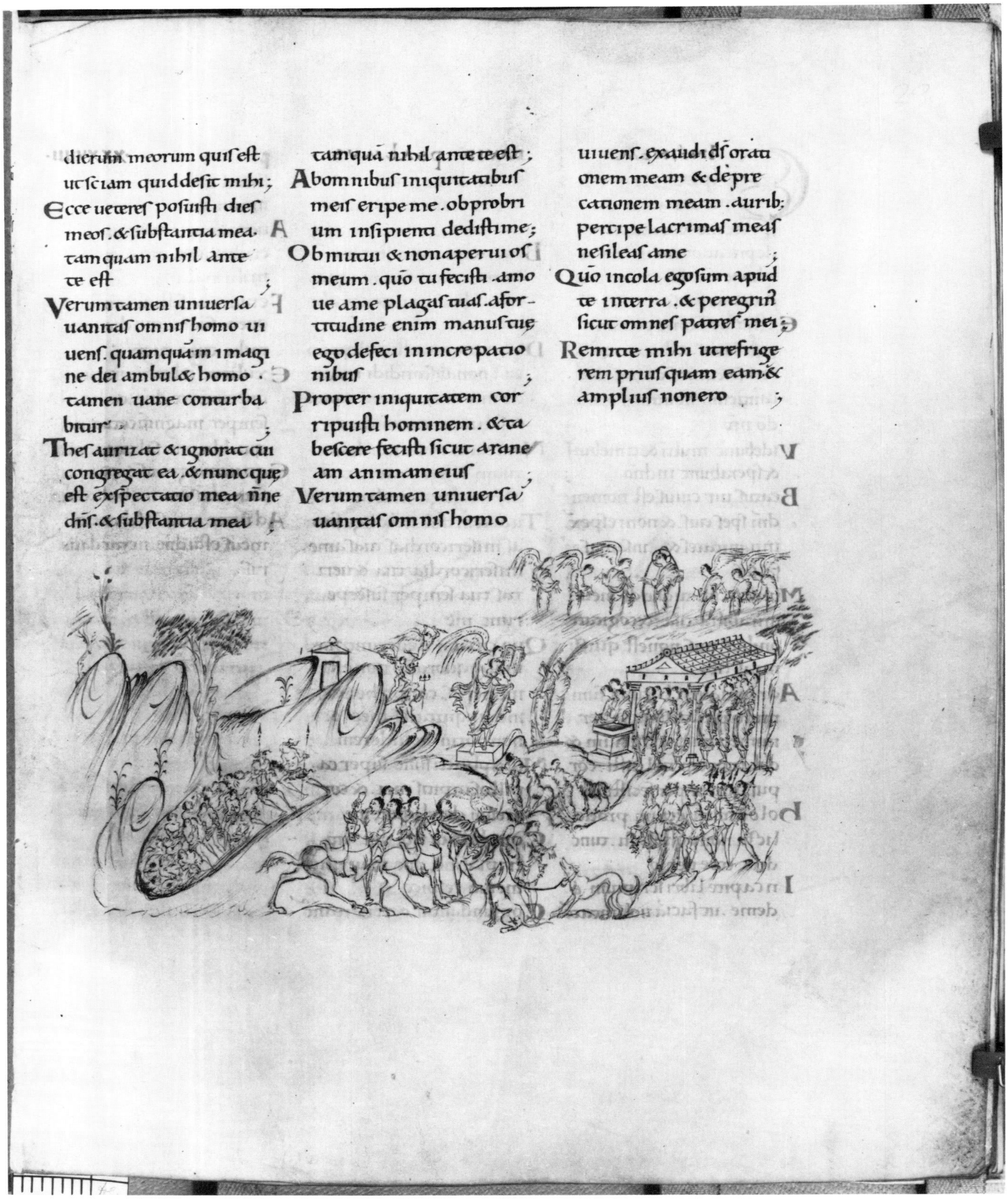

dierum meorum quis est
ut sciam quid desit mihi;
Ecce ueteres posuisti dies
meos. & substantia mea
tamquam nihil ante
te est;
Verumtamen uniuersa
uanitas omnis homo ui
uens. quamquam in imagi
ne dei ambul& homo.
tamen uane conturba
bitur;
Thesaurizat & ignorat cui
congregat ea. & nunc quę
est exspectatio mea nonne
dns. & substantia mea
tamquā nihil ante te est;
Ab omnibus iniquitatibus
meis eripe me. obprobri
um insipienti dedisti me;
Obmutui & non aperui os
meum. quō tu fecisti. amo
ue a me plagas tuas. a for
titudine enim manus tuę
ego defeci in increpatio
nibus;
Propter iniquitatem cor
ripuisti hominem. & ta
bescere fecisti sicut arane
am animam eius;
Verumtamen uniuersa
uanitas omnis homo
uiuens. exaudi ds orati
onem meam & depre
cationem meam. aurib;
percipe lacrimas meas
ne sileas a me;
Quō incola ego sum apud
te in terra. & peregrinus
sicut omnes patres mei;
Remitte mihi ut refrige
rem priusquam eam &
amplius non ero

2.40 London, B.L., Harley 603, f. 23r

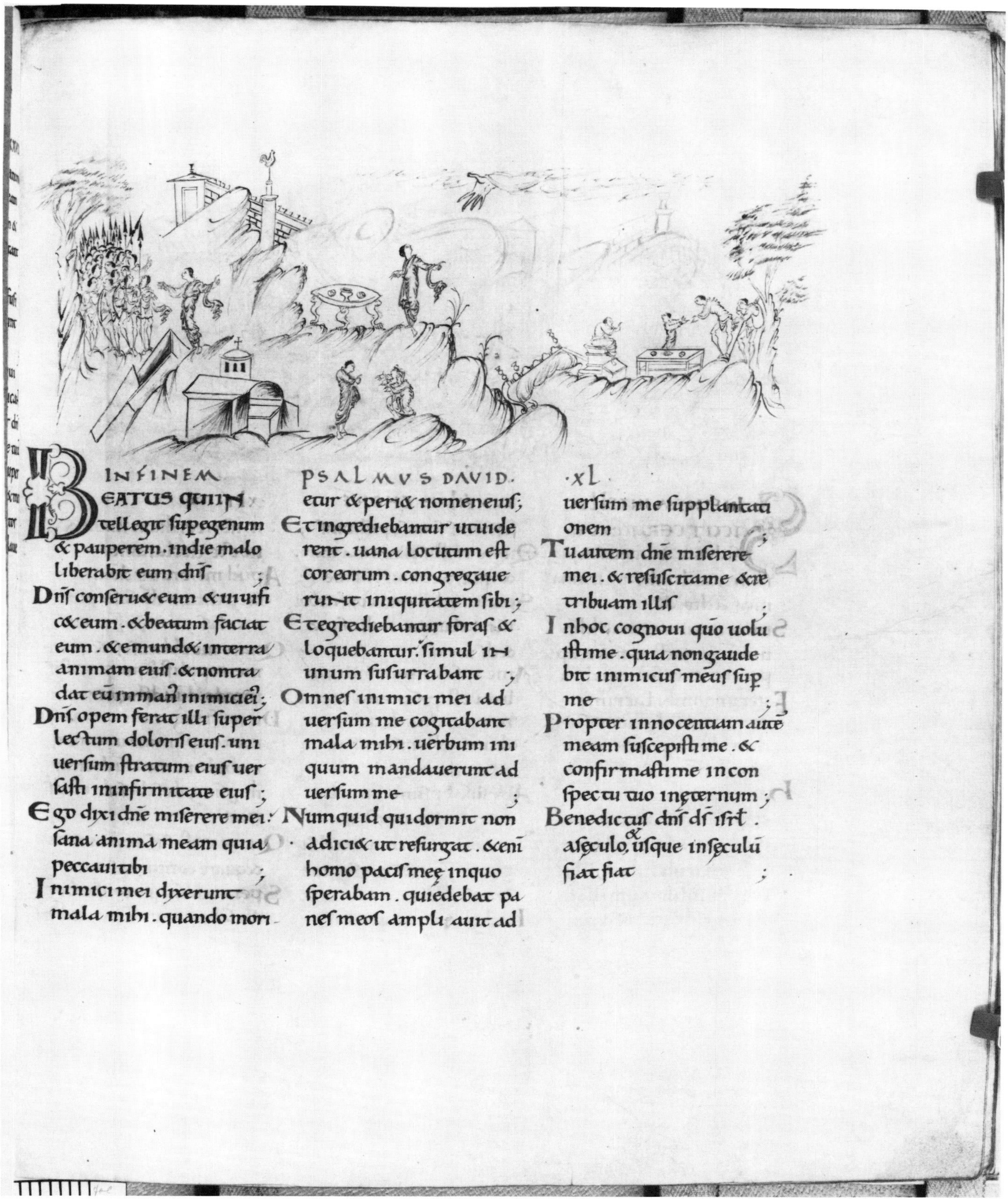

2.41 London, B.L., Harley 603, f. 24r

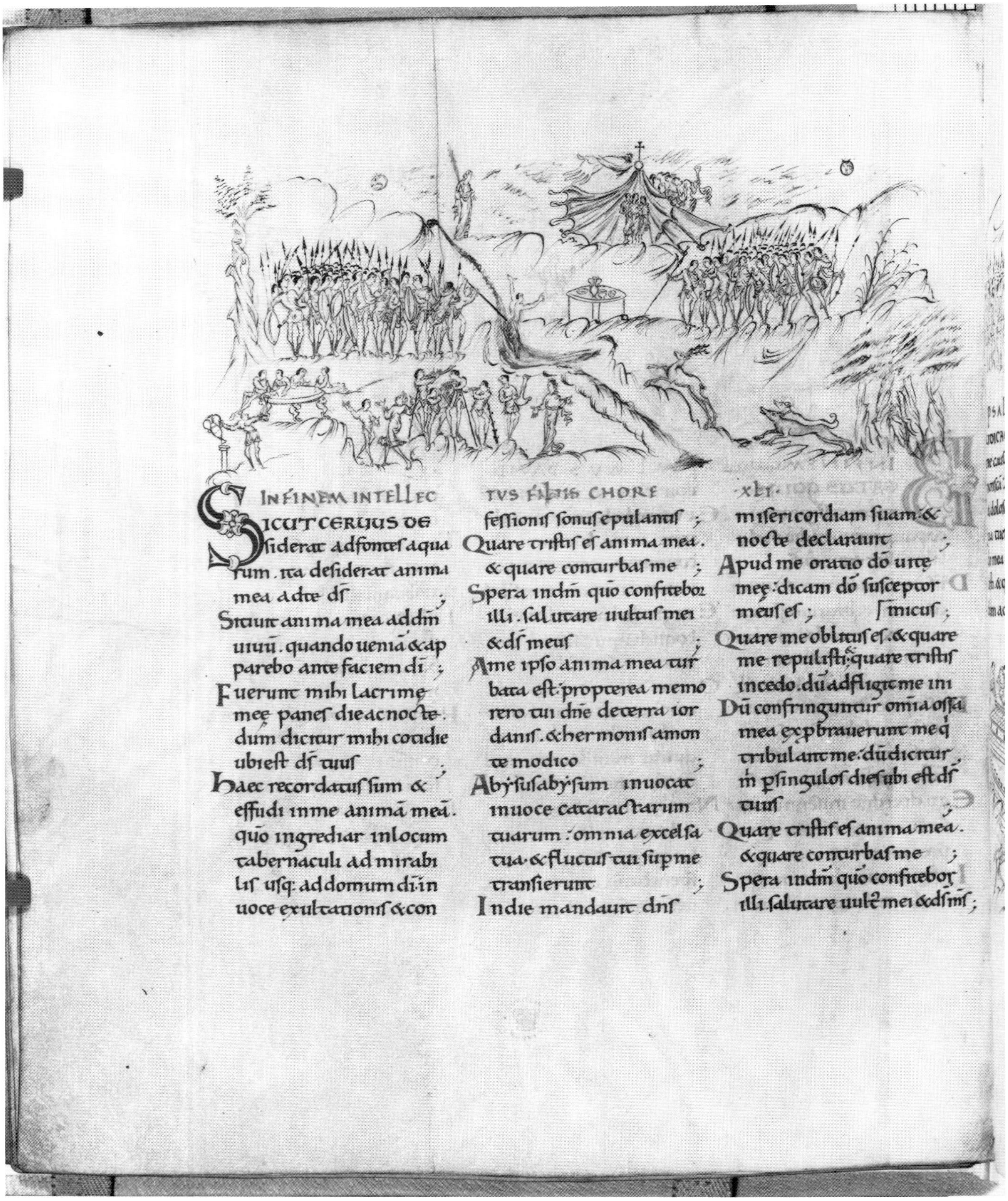

2.42 London, B.L., Harley 603, f. 24^{v}

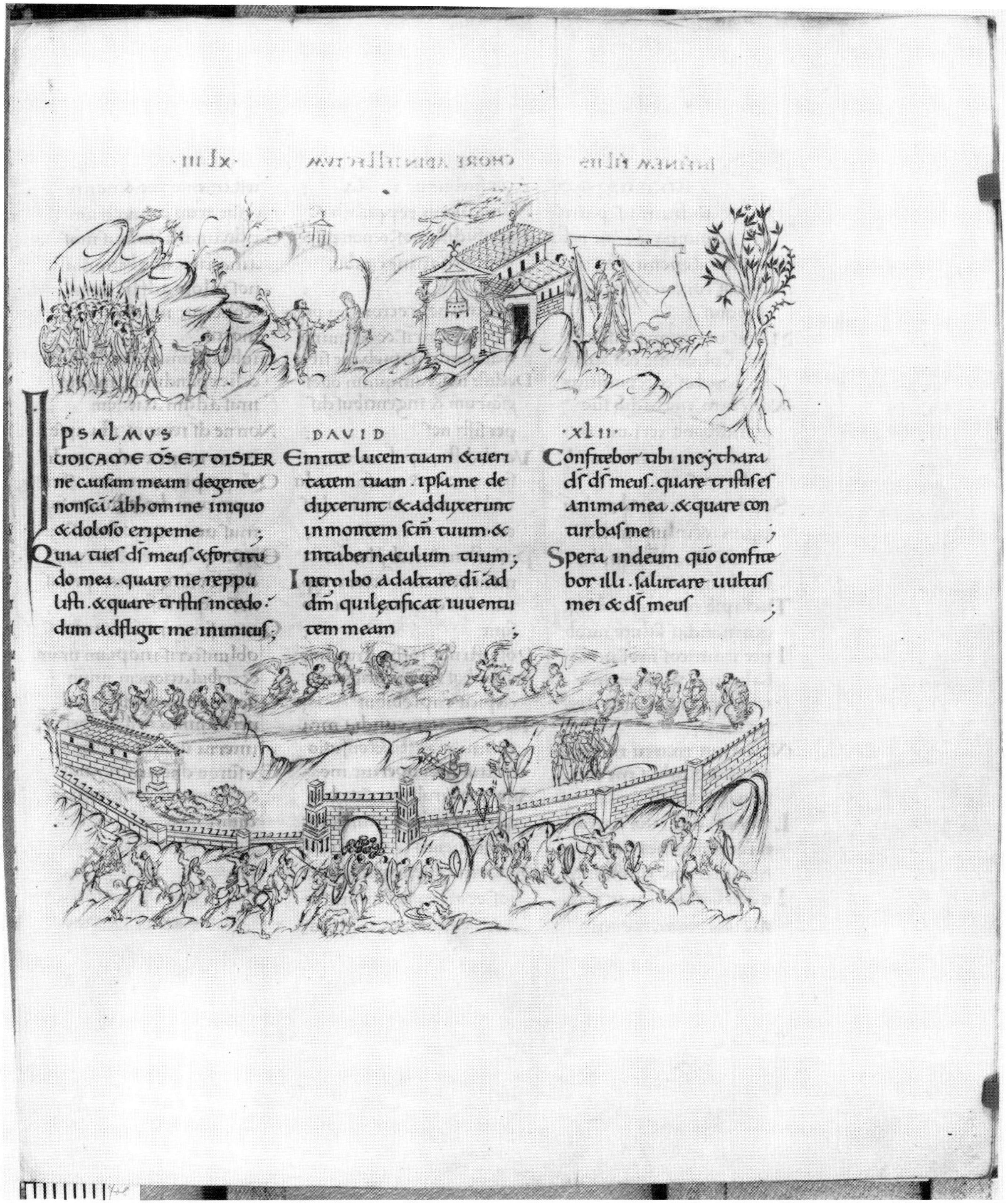

PSALMUS DAVID XLIII

IUDICA ME DS ET DISCER
ne causam meam degente
nonscã abhomine iniquo
& doloso eripe me;
Quia tu es ds meus & fortitu
do mea. quare me reppu
listi. & quare tristis incedo.
dum adfligit me inimicus;

Emitte lucem tuam & veri
tatem tuam. ipsa me de
duxerunt & adduxerunt
in montem scm tuum &
in tabernaculum tuum;
Introibo ad altare dī ad
dm̄ qui letificat iuventu
tem meam

Confitebor tibi in cythara
ds ds meus. quare tristis es
anima mea. & quare con
turbas me;
Spera in deum quõ confite
bor illi. salutare vultus
mei & ds meus;

2.43 London, B.L., Harley 603, f. 25r

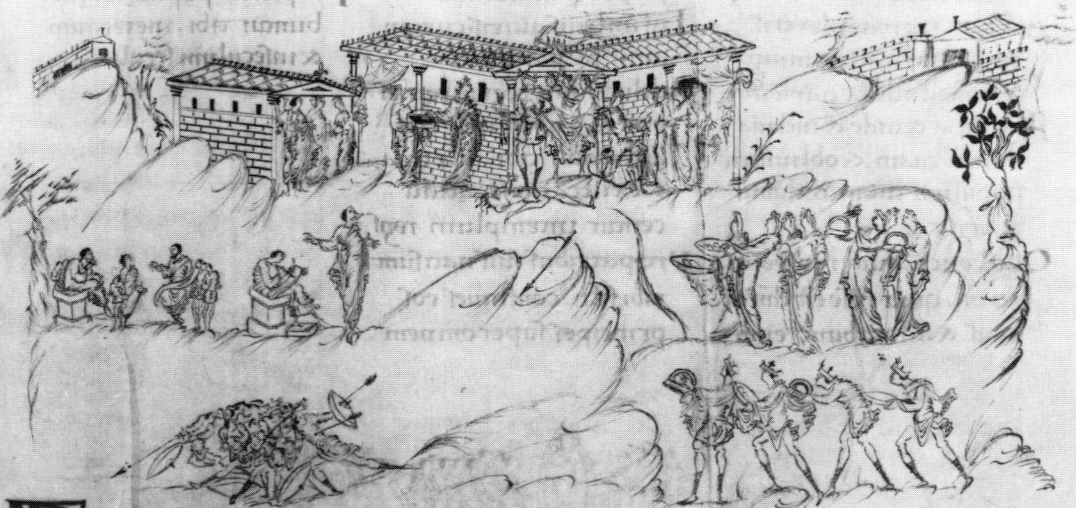

E IN FINEM PRO HIS QVI COMITABVNTVR FILIIS CHORE AD INTELLECTVM CANTICI PRO DILECTO . XLIIII .

Eructauit cor meum uerbum bonu(m) dico ego opera mea regi ;
Lingua mea calamus scribe uelociter scribentis ;
Speciosus forma pre filiis hominum : difusa est gratia in labiis tuis ;
Propterea benedixit te ds in eternum . accingere gladio tuo circa femur potentissime ;
Specie tua & pulchritudine tua . intende prospere procede & regna ;
Propter ueritatem & mansuetudinem & iustitiam . & deducet te mirabiliter dextera tua ;
Sagitte tue acute potentissime . populi sub te cadent . in corde inimicorum regis ;
Sedes tua ds in seculum seculi . uirga recta est uirga regni tui ;
Dilexisti iustitiam & odisti iniquitatem . propterea unxit te ds ds tuus oleo letitie pre consortib; tuis ;

2.44 London, B.L., Harley 603, f. 26r

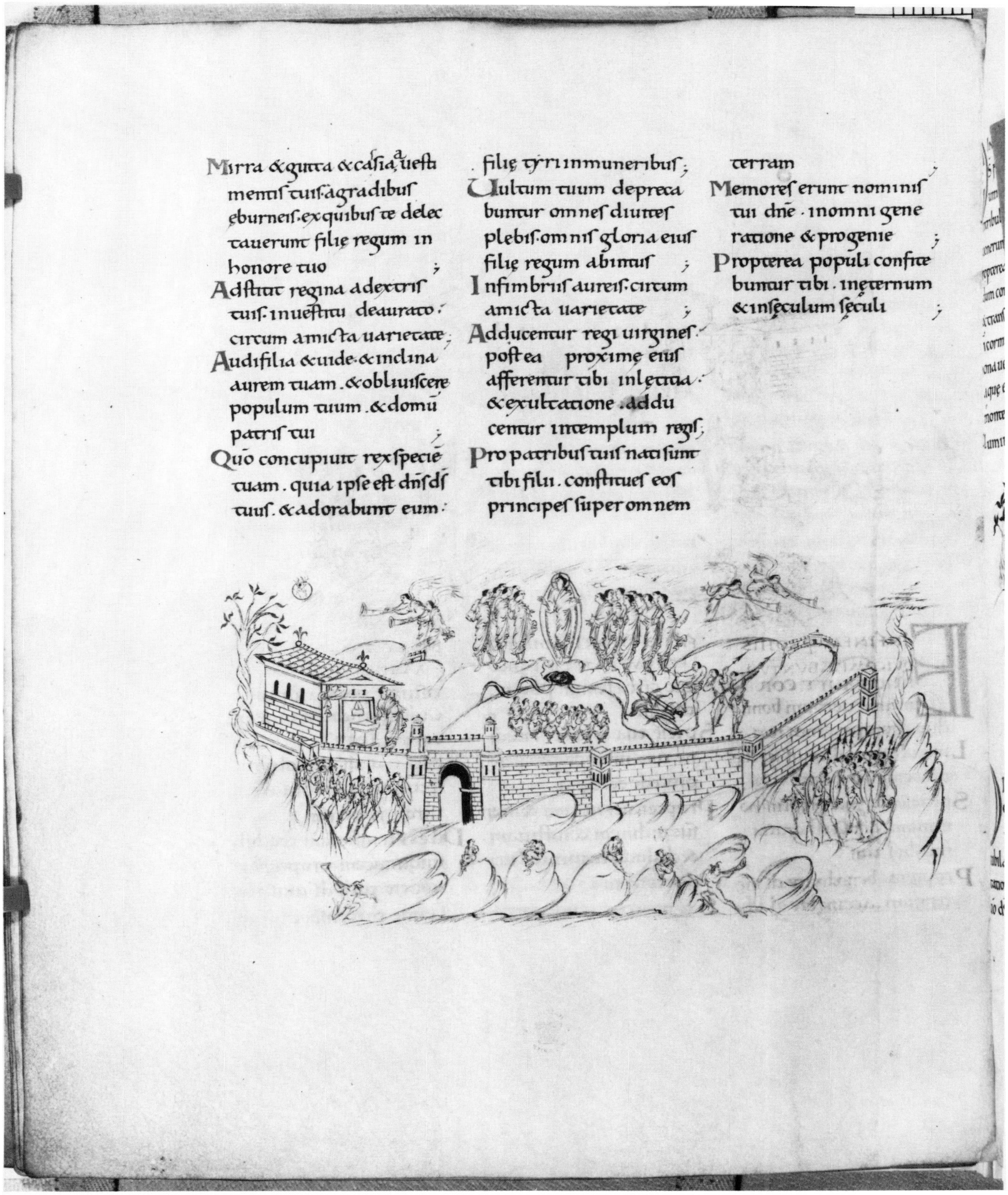

2.45 London, B.L., Harley 603, f. 26v

D IN FINEM FILIIS
DS NOSTER REFUGI
um & uirtus. adiutor
in tribulationibus quę in
uenerunt nos nimis ;
Propterea non timebimus
dum conturbabitur terra.
& transferentur montes
i cor maris ;
Sonauerunt & turbatę sunt
aquę eius. conturbati sunt
montes in fortitudine eius ;
Fluminis impetus lętificat

CHORE PRO ARCHANIS.
ciuitatem di. scificauit
tabernaculum suū altis
simus. ds in medio eius non
commouebitur ;
Adiuuabit eam ds uultu suo.
conturbatę sunt gentes.
& inclinata sunt regna.
dedit uocem suam altissi
mus. & mota est terra ;
Dns uirtutum nobiscum. su
sceptor noster ds iacob ;
Venite & uidete opera dni.

. XLV.
quę posuit prodigia sup
terram ;
Auferens bella usque ad
fines terrę. arcum conte
ret & confringet arma &
scuta comburet igni ;
Vacate & uidete quō ego
sum ds. exaltabor in genti
bus. & exaltabor in terra ;
Dns uirtutum nobiscum.
susceptor noster ds iacob ;

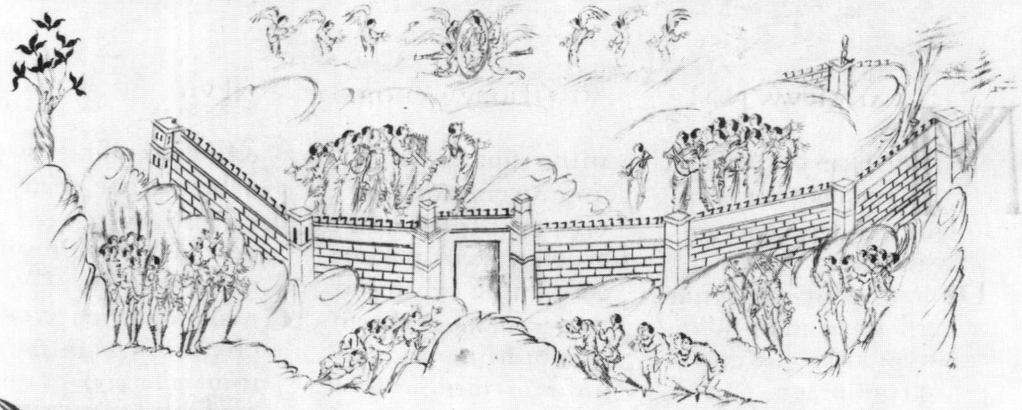

O IN FINEM PRO FILIIS
OMNES GENTES
plaudite manibus.
iubilate dō in uoce exul
tationis ;
Quō ds summus terribilis.

CHORE PSALMUS
& rex magnus super omnes
deos ;
Subiecit populos nobis. &
gentes sub pedibus nrīs ;
Elegit nos in hereditatem

. XLVI.
sibi. speciem iacob quam
dilexit ;
Ascendit ds in iubilatione.
& dns in uoce tubę ;
Psallite dō nrō psallite.

2.46 London, B.L., Harley 603, f. 27r

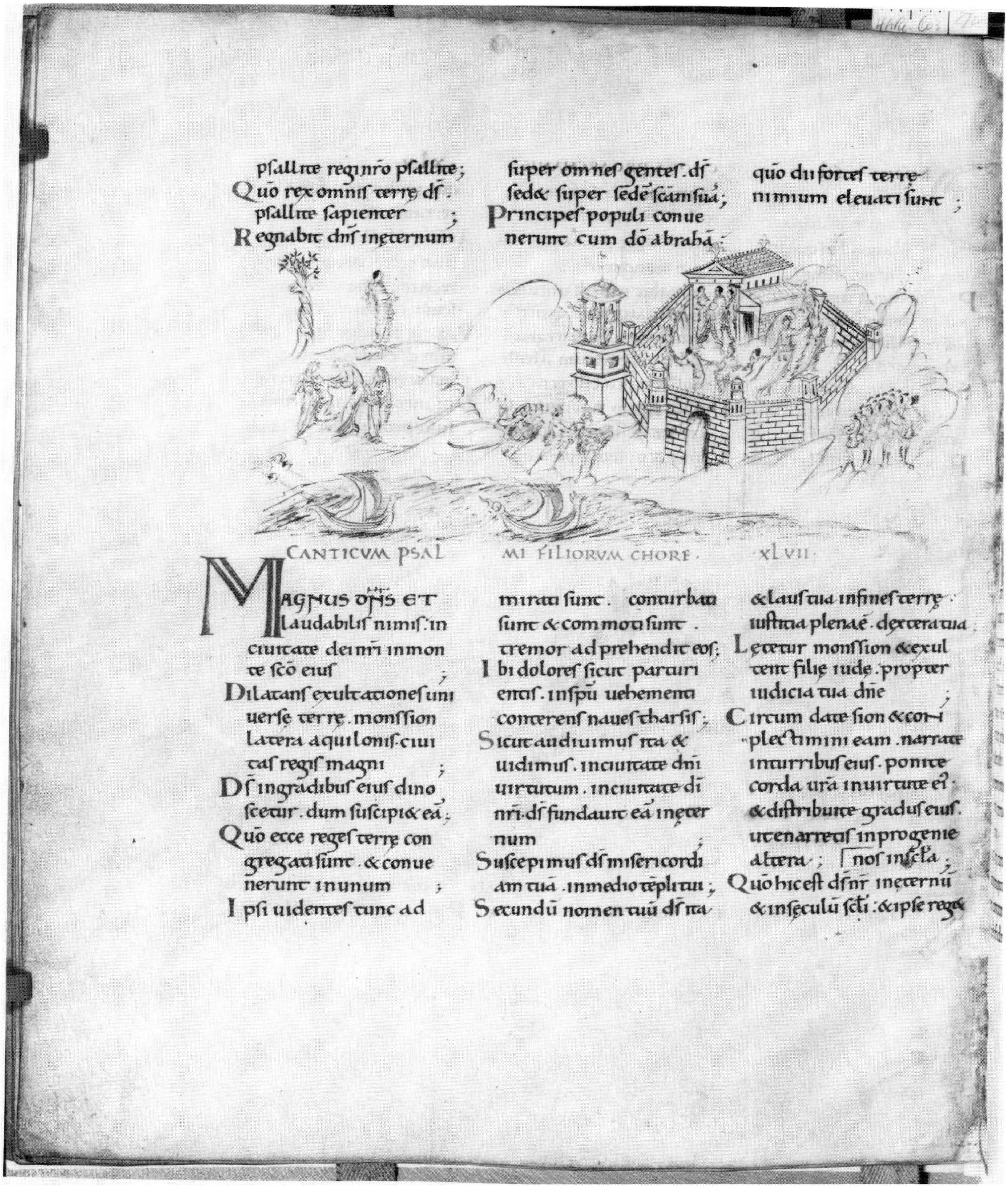

psallite regi nr̄o psallite;
Quō rex omnis terrę ds̄.
psallite sapienter;
Regnabit dn̄s in eternum
super omnes gentes. ds̄
sedet super sedē scām suā;
Principes populi conue
nerunt cum dō abrahā.
quō dii fortes terrę
nimium eleuati sunt;

CANTICUM PSALMI FILIORUM CHORE. XLVII.

MAGNUS DN̄S ET
laudabilis nimis. in
ciuitate dei nr̄i in mon
te scō eius;
Dilatans exultationes uni
uersę terrę. mons sion
latera aquilonis. ciui
tas regis magni;
Ds̄ in gradibus eius dino
scetur. dum suscipiet eā;
Quō ecce reges terrę con
gregati sunt. et conue
nerunt in unum;
Ipsi uidentes tunc ad
mirati sunt. conturbati
sunt et commoti sunt.
tremor adprehendit eos;
Ibi dolores sicut parturi
entis. in spū uehementi
conterens naues tharsis;
Sicut audiuimus ita et
uidimus. in ciuitate dn̄i
uirtutum. in ciuitate di
nr̄i. ds̄ fundauit eā in eter
num;
Suscepimus ds̄ misericordi
am tuā. in medio templi tui;
Secundū nomen tuū ds̄ ita
et laus tua in fines terrę.
iustitia plena ē. dextera tua;
Letetur mons sion et exul
tent filię iudę. propter
iudicia tua dn̄e;
Circumdate sion et com
plectimini eam. narrate
in turribus eius. ponite
corda urā in uirtute eī;
et distribuite gradus eius.
ut enarretis in progenie
altera; nos in scla;
Quō hic est ds̄ nr̄ in eternū
et in seculū scli. et ipse reget

2.47 London, B.L., Harley 603, f. 27v

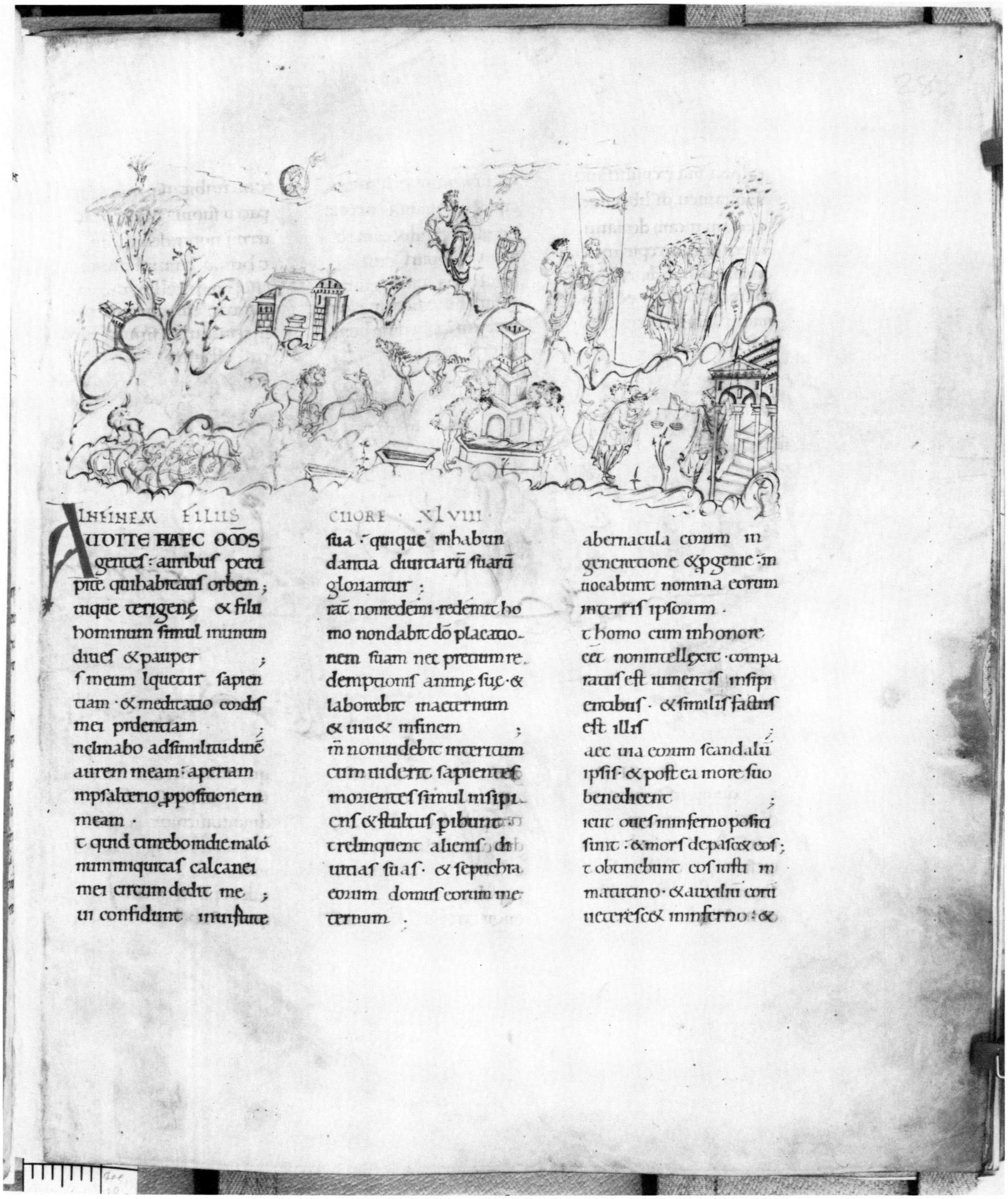

2.48 London, B.L., Harley 603, f. 28r

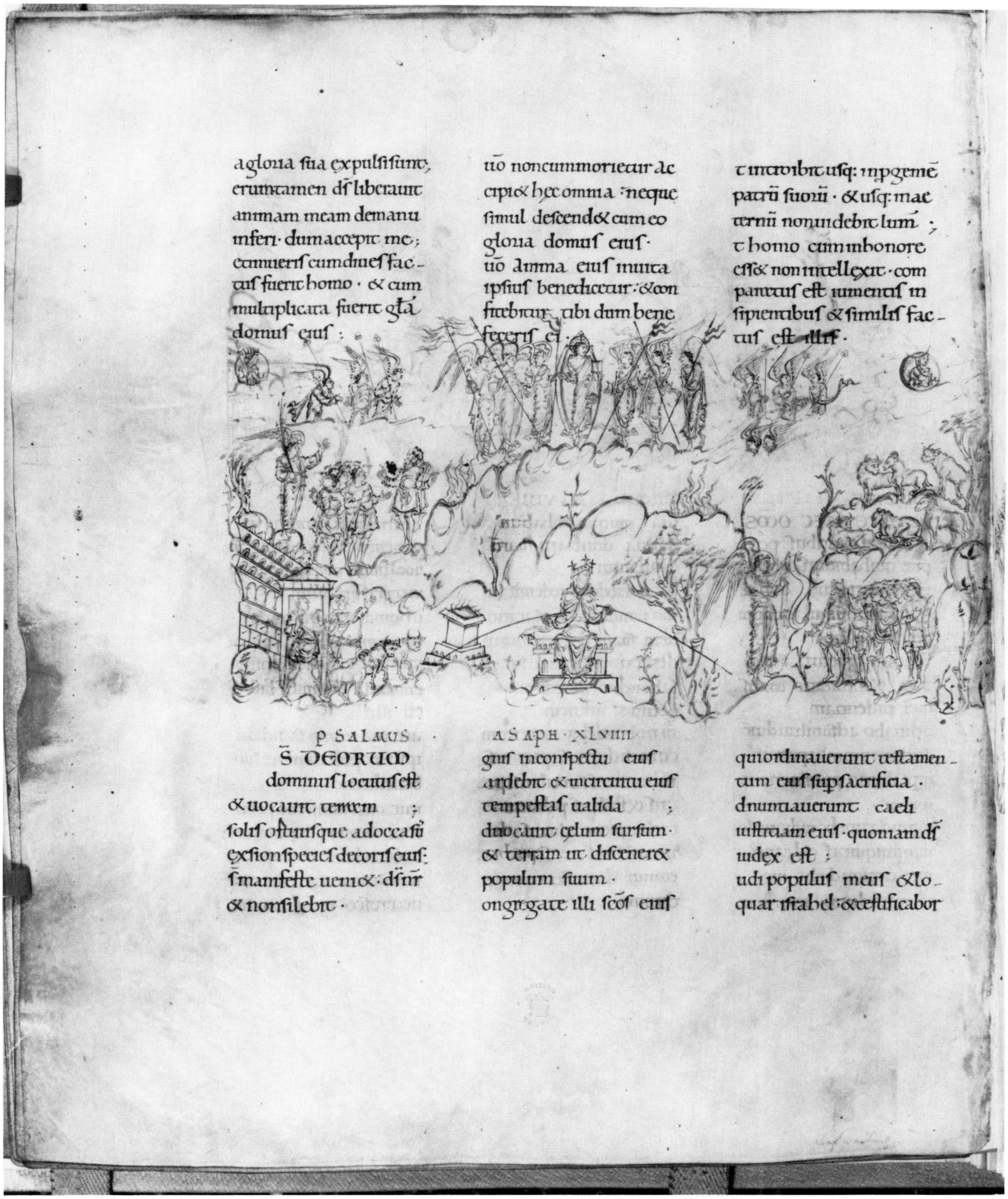

2.49 London, B.L., Harley 603, f. 28v

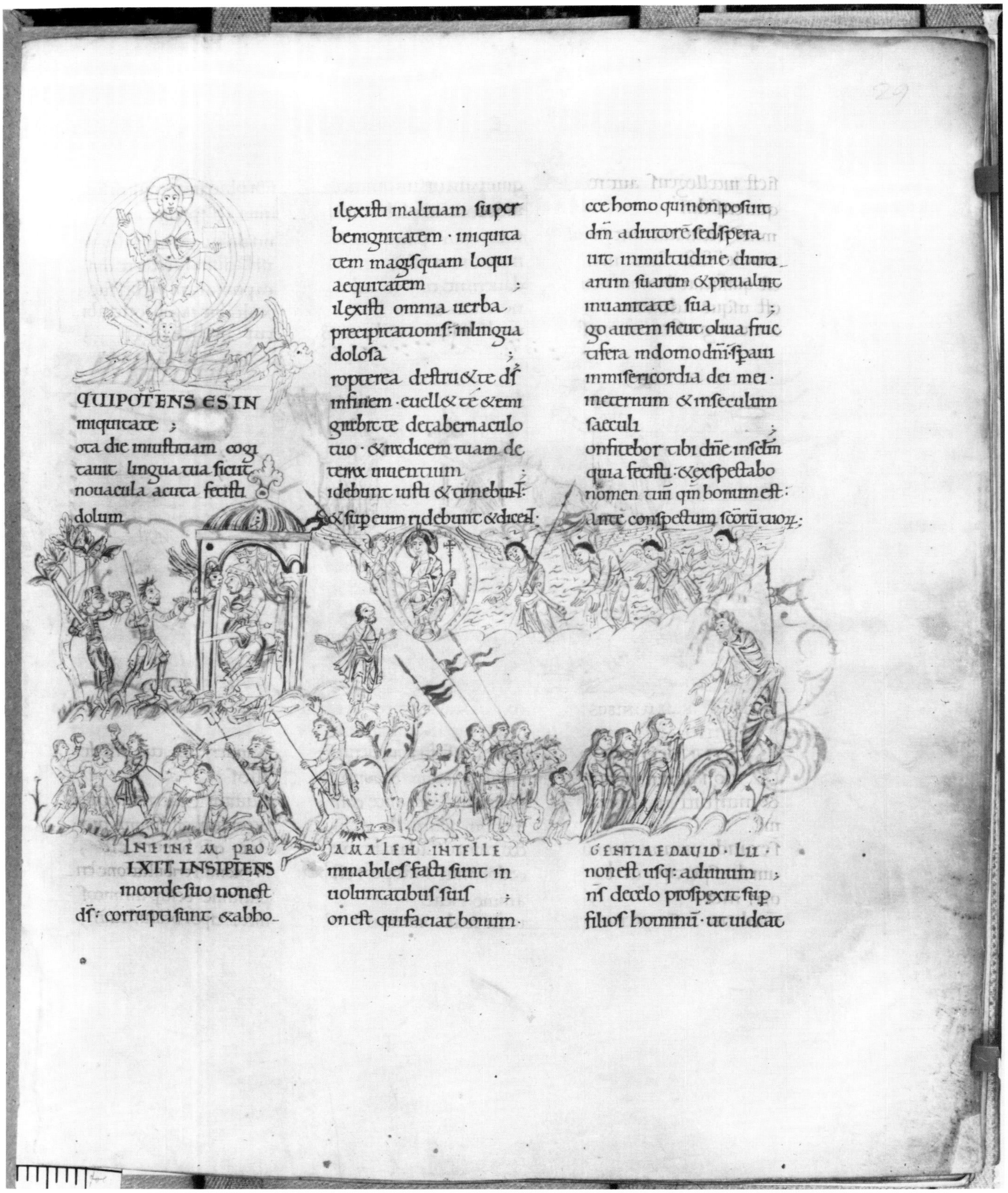

2.50 London, B.L., Harley 603, f. 29[r]

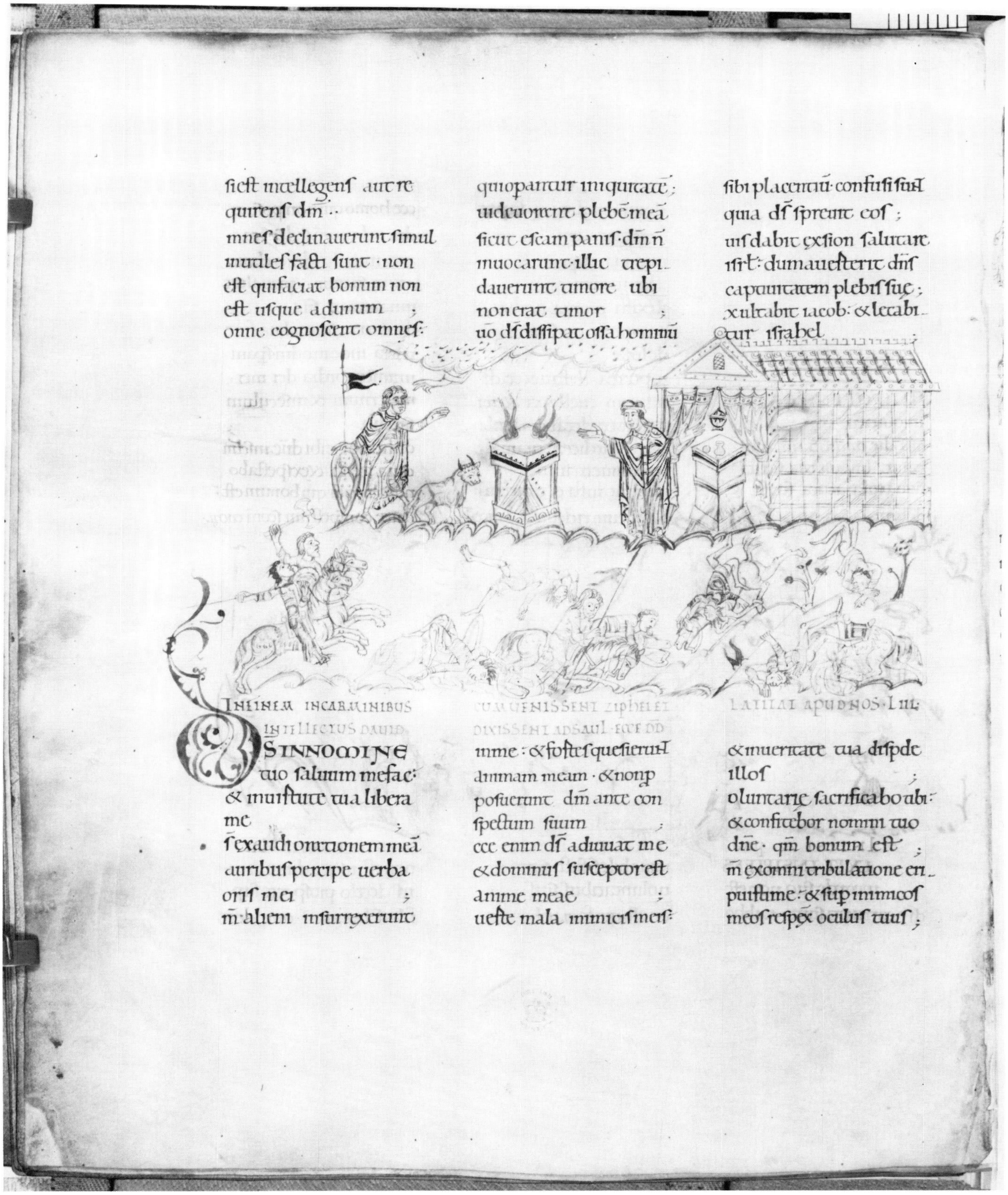

2.51 London, B.L., Harley 603, f. 29v

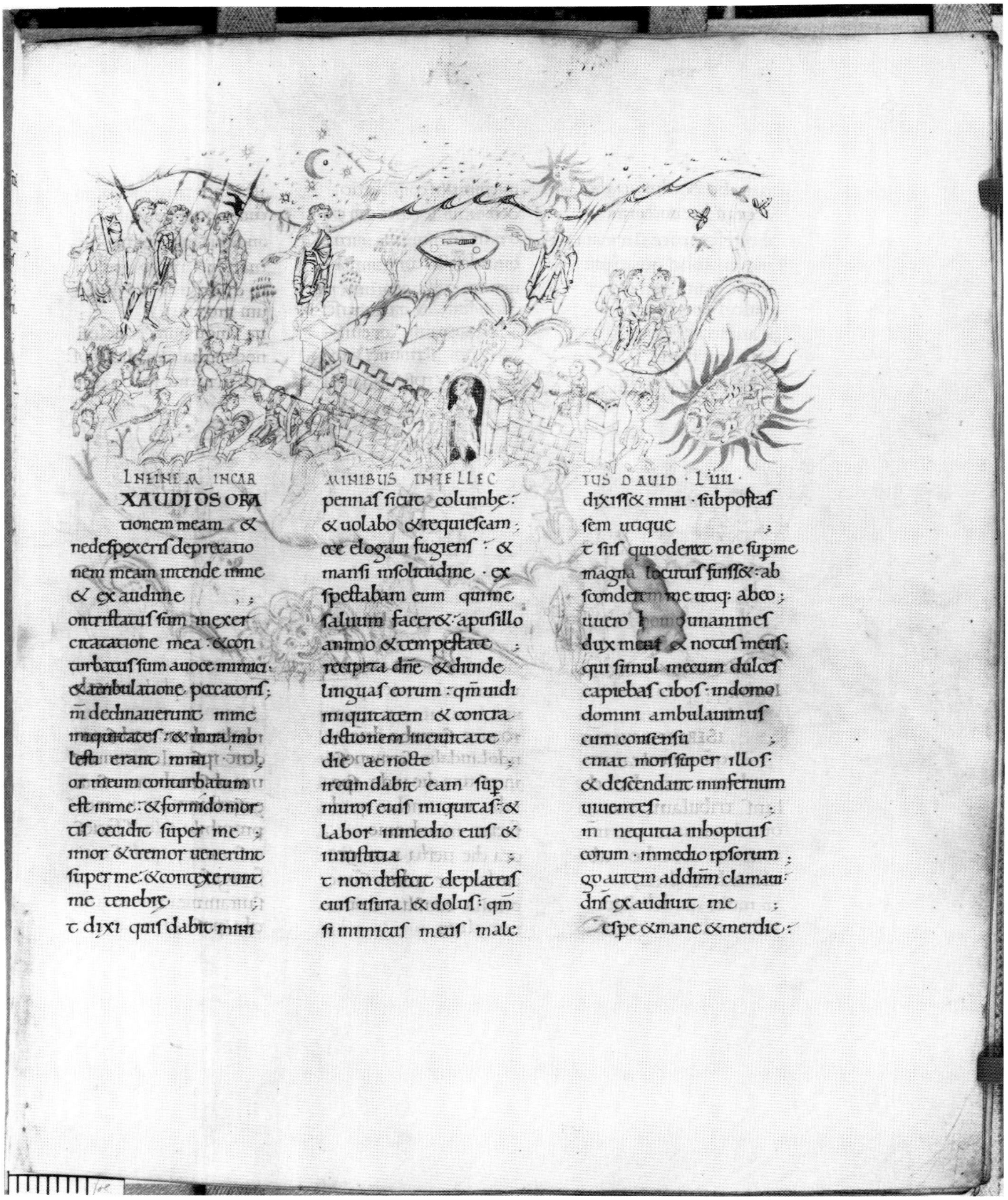

2.52 London, B.L., Harley 603, f. 30r

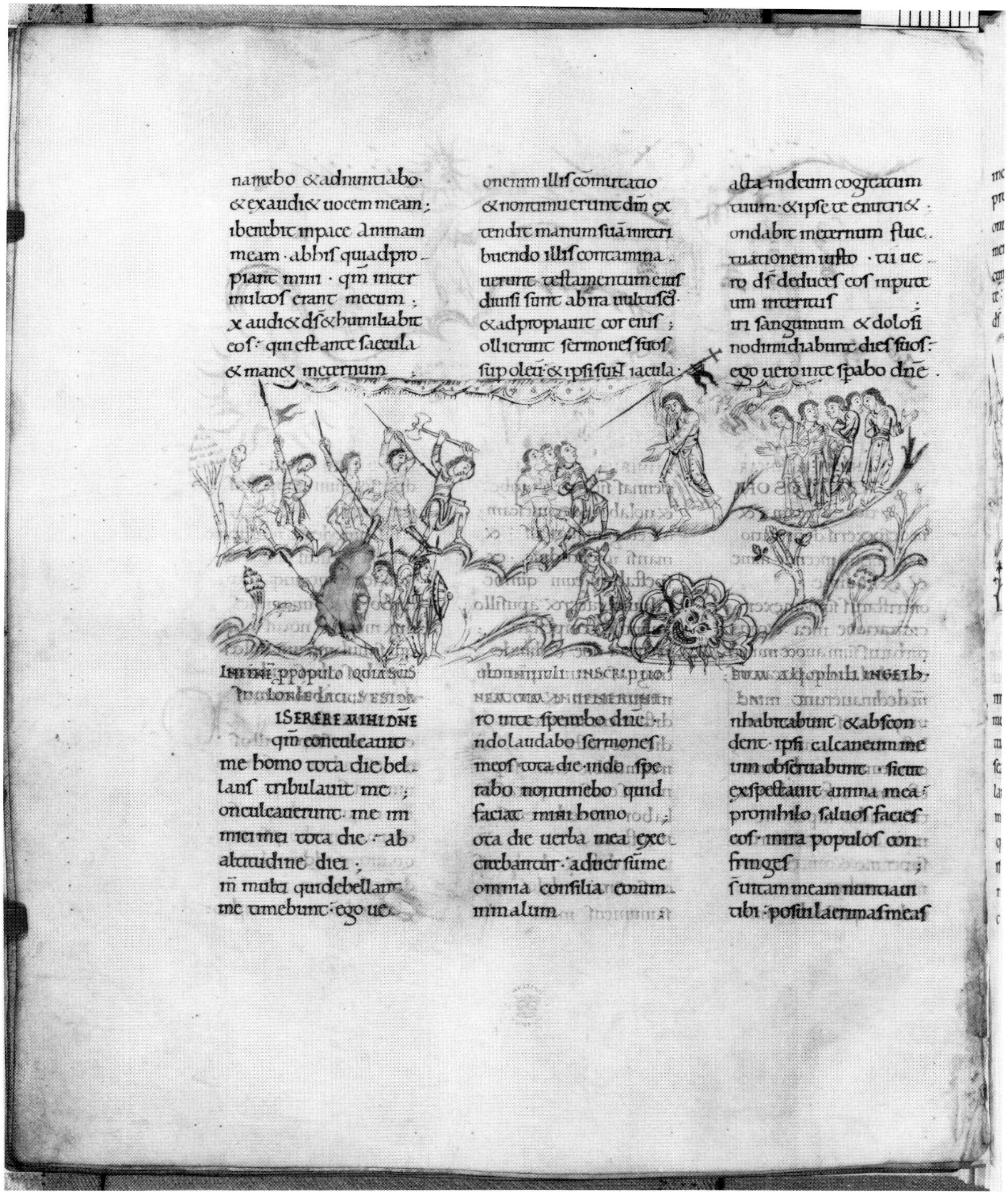

2.53 London, B.L., Harley 603, f. 30v

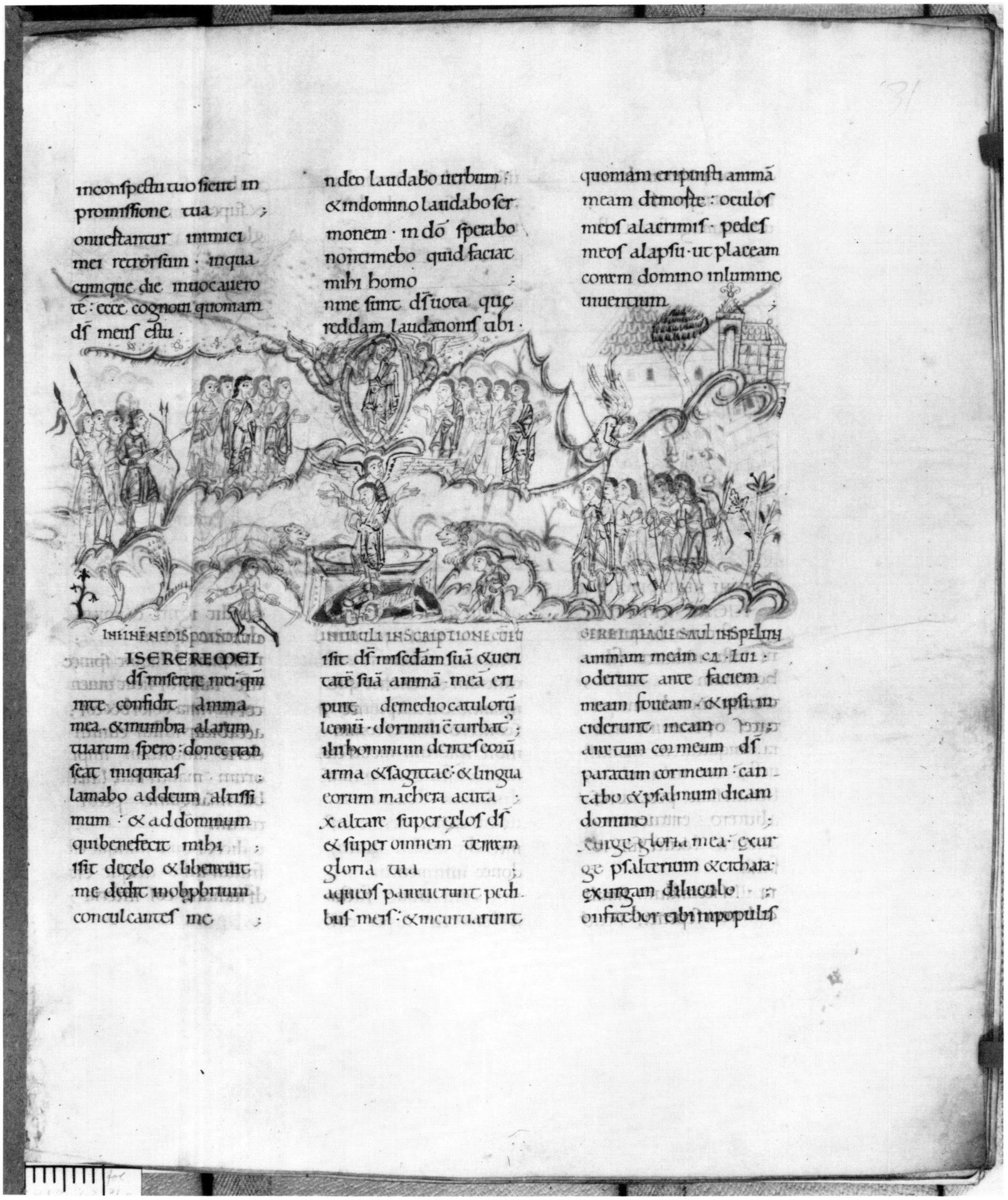
inconspectu tuo sicut in
promissione tua ;
onuertantur inimici
mei retrorsum · inqua
cumque die inuocauero
te : ecce cognoui quoniam
ds meus es tu ·

n deo laudabo uerbum ;
& indomino laudabo ser
monem · in dō sperabo
non timebo quid faciat
mihi homo ;
in me sunt ds uota que
reddam laudationis tibi ·

quoniam eripuisti animā
meam de morte : oculos
meos a lacrimis · pedes
meos a lapsu · ut placeam
coram domino in lumine
uiuentium ;

IN FINE̅ NE DISPERDAS
ISERERE MEI
ds miserere mei · qm̄
in te confidit anima
mea · & in umbra alarum
tuarum spero : donec tran
seat iniquitas ;
lamabo ad deum altissi
mum · & ad dominum
qui benefecit mihi ;
isit de celo & liberauit
me dedit in obprobrium
conculcantes me ;

IN TITULI INSCRIPTIONE CUM
isit ds misericordiam suā & ueri
tatē suā animā meā eri
puit de medio catulorū
leonū · dormiui c̄ turbat' ;
ilii hominum dentes eorū
arma & sagittae · & lingua
eorum machera acuta ;
xaltare super celos ds
& super omnem terram
gloria tua ;
aqueos parauerunt pedi
bus meis · & incuruauerunt

GERET A FACIE SAUL IN SPELUNCA
animam meam ... ;
oderunt ante faciem
meam foueam · & ipsi in
ciderunt in eam ;
aratum cor meum ds
paratum cor meum : can
tabo & psalmum dicam
domino ;
xurge gloria mea · exur
ge psalterium & cithara :
exurgam diluculo ·
onfitebor tibi in populis

2.54 London, B.L., Harley 603, f. 31r

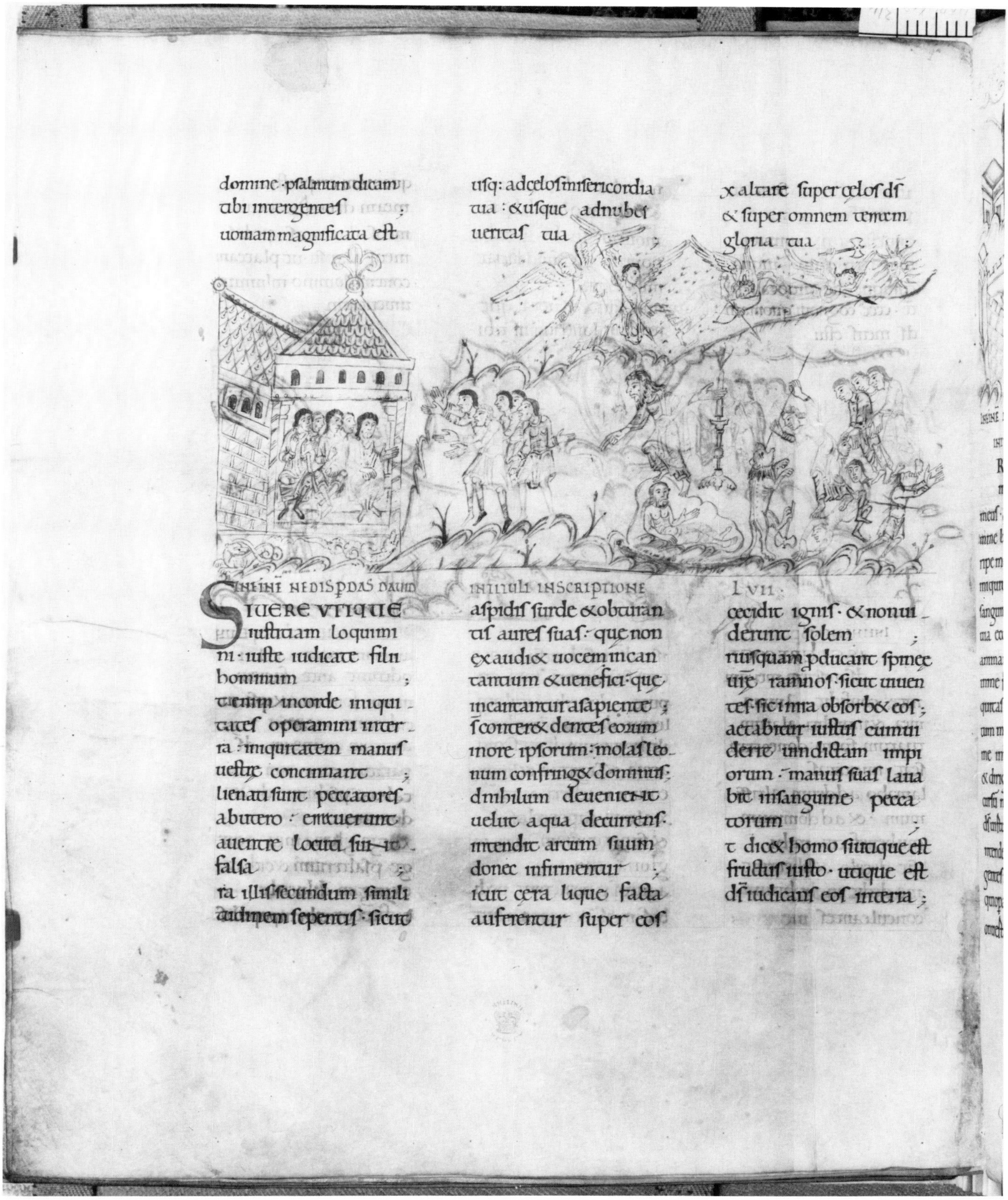

domine · psalmum dicam
tibi inter gentes ;
uoniam magnificata est

usq: ad celos misericordia
tua : & usque ad nubes
ueritas tua

x altare super celos ds
& super omnem terram
gloria tua

IN FINE NE DISPDAS DAUID
SIUERE UTIQUE
iustitiam loquimi
ni · iuste iudicate filii
hominum ;
tenim in corde iniqui
tates operamini in ter
ra : iniquitatem manus
uestre concinnant ;
lienati sunt peccatores
ab utero : errauerunt
a uentre locuti sunt · fal
sa
ra illis secundum simili
tudinem serpentis · sicut

TITULI INSCRIPTIONE
aspidis surde & obturan
tis aures suas : que non
exaudiet uocem incan
tantium & uenefici : que
incantantur a sapiente ;
s conteret dentes eorum
in ore ipsorum : molas leo
num confringet dominus ;
d nihilum deuenient · ta
uelut aqua decurrens :
intendit arcum suum
donec infirmentur ;
icut cera liquefacta
auferentur super eos

LVII
cecidit ignis · & non ui
derunt solem ;
riusquam intellegerent spine
uestras ramnos · sicut uiuen
tes sic in ira obsorbet eos ;
aetabitur iustus cum ui
derit uindictam impi
orum · manus suas laua
bit in sanguine pecca
torum
t dicet homo si utique est
fructus iusto · utique est
ds iudicans eos in terra ;

2.55 London, B.L., Harley 603, f. 31v

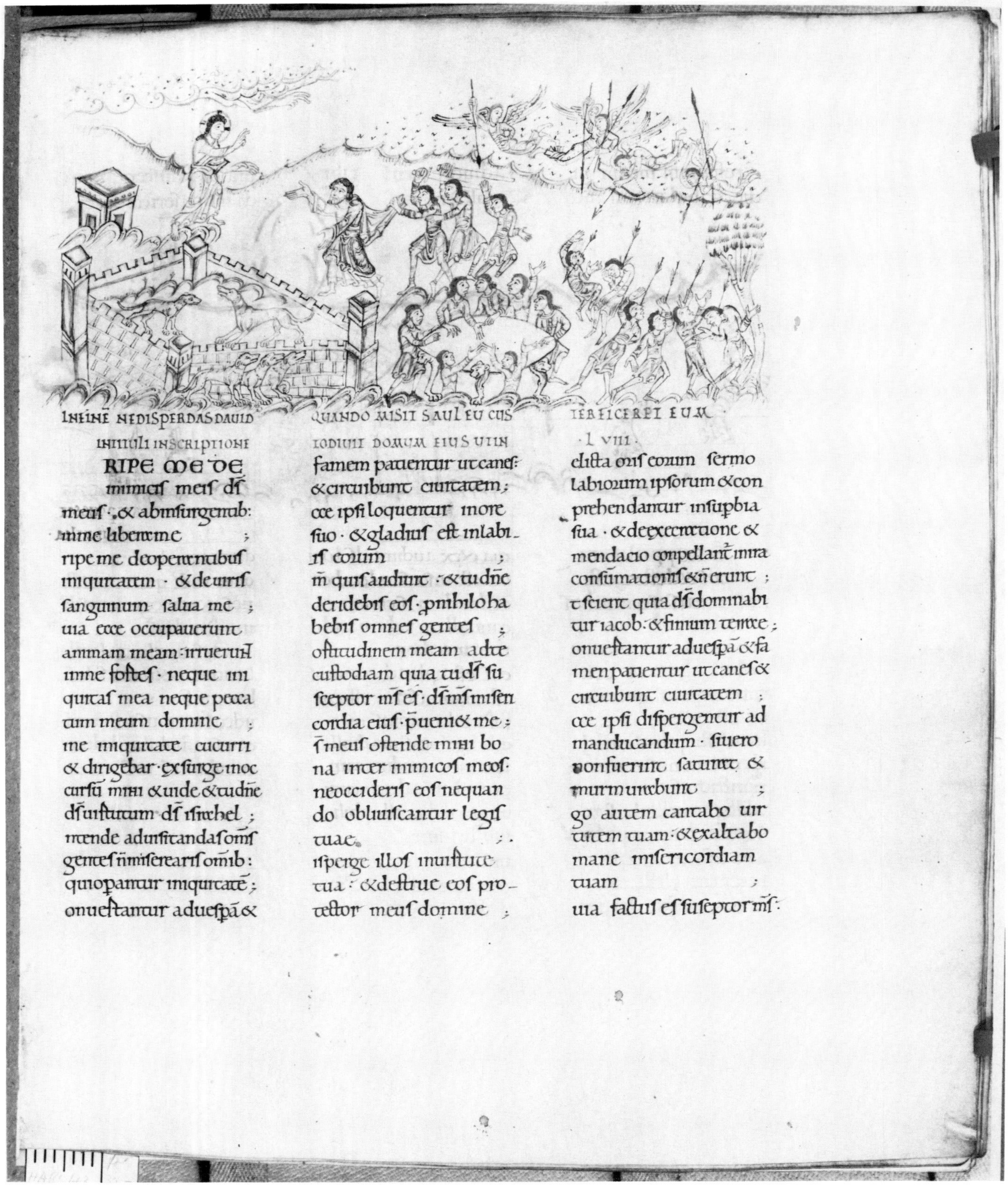

INFINE NE DISPERDAS DAVID
IN TITULI INSCRIPTIONE
RIPE ME DE
inimicis meis ds
meus · & ab insurgentib:
in me libera me ;
ripe me de operantibus
iniquitatem · & de uiris
sanguinum salua me ;
uia ecce occupauerunt
animam meam · irruerunt
in me fortes · neque ini
quitas mea neque pecca
tum meum domine ;
ine iniquitate cucurri
& dirigebar · exsurge in oc
cursu mihi & uide & tu dne
ds uirtutum ds isrrhel ;
intende ad uisitandas omis
gentes · n miserearis omib:
qui operantur iniquitate ;
onuertantur ad uespa &

QUANDO MISIT SAUL ET CUS
TODIUIT DOMUM EIUS UT IN
famem patientur ut canes:
& circuibunt ciuitatem ;
cce ipsi loquentur in ore
suo · & gladius est in labi
is eorum ;
m quis audiuit · & tu dne
deridebis eos · p nihilo ha
bebis omnes gentes ;
ortitudinem meam ad te
custodiam quia tu ds su
sceptor ms es · ds ms miseri
cordia eius · pueniet me ;
s meus ostende mihi bo
na inter inimicos meos ·
ne occideris eos nequan
do obliuiscantur legis
tuae ;
isperge illos in uirtute
tua · & destrue eos pro
tector meus domine ;

TERFICERET EUM
· L VIII ·
elicta oris eorum sermo
labiorum ipsorum & con
prehendantur in supbia
sua · & de execratione &
mendacio conpellant in ira
consumationis & n erunt ;
t scient quia ds dominabi
tur iacob · & finium terrae ;
onuertantur ad uespa & fa
men patientur ut canes &
circuibunt ciuitatem ;
cce ipsi dispergentur ad
manducandum · si uero
non fuerint saturati &
murmurabunt ;
go autem cantabo uir
tutem tuam · & exaltabo
mane misericordiam
tuam ;
uia factus es susceptor ms ·

2.56 London, B.L., Harley 603, f. 32r

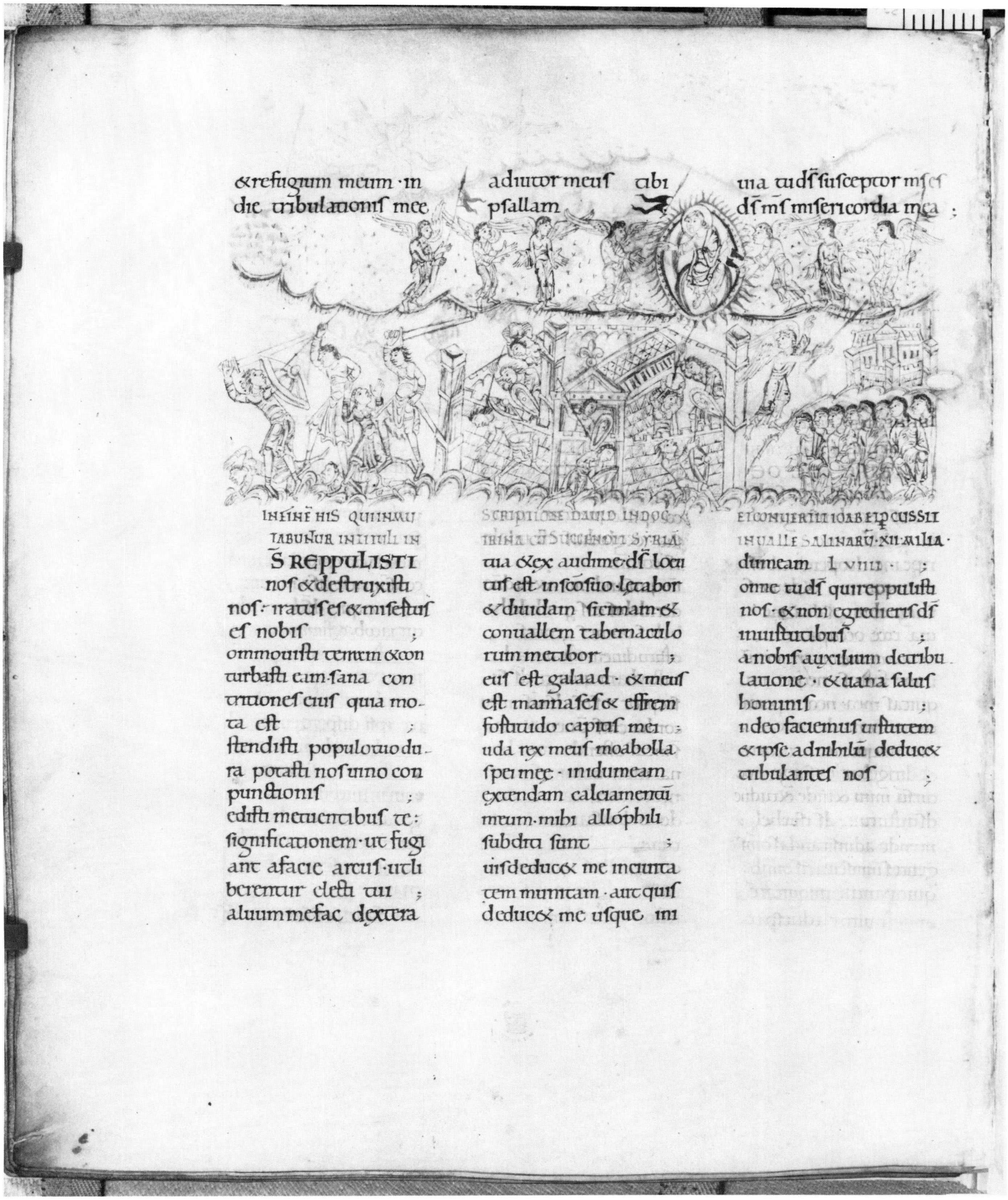

2.57 London, B.L., Harley 603, f. 32v

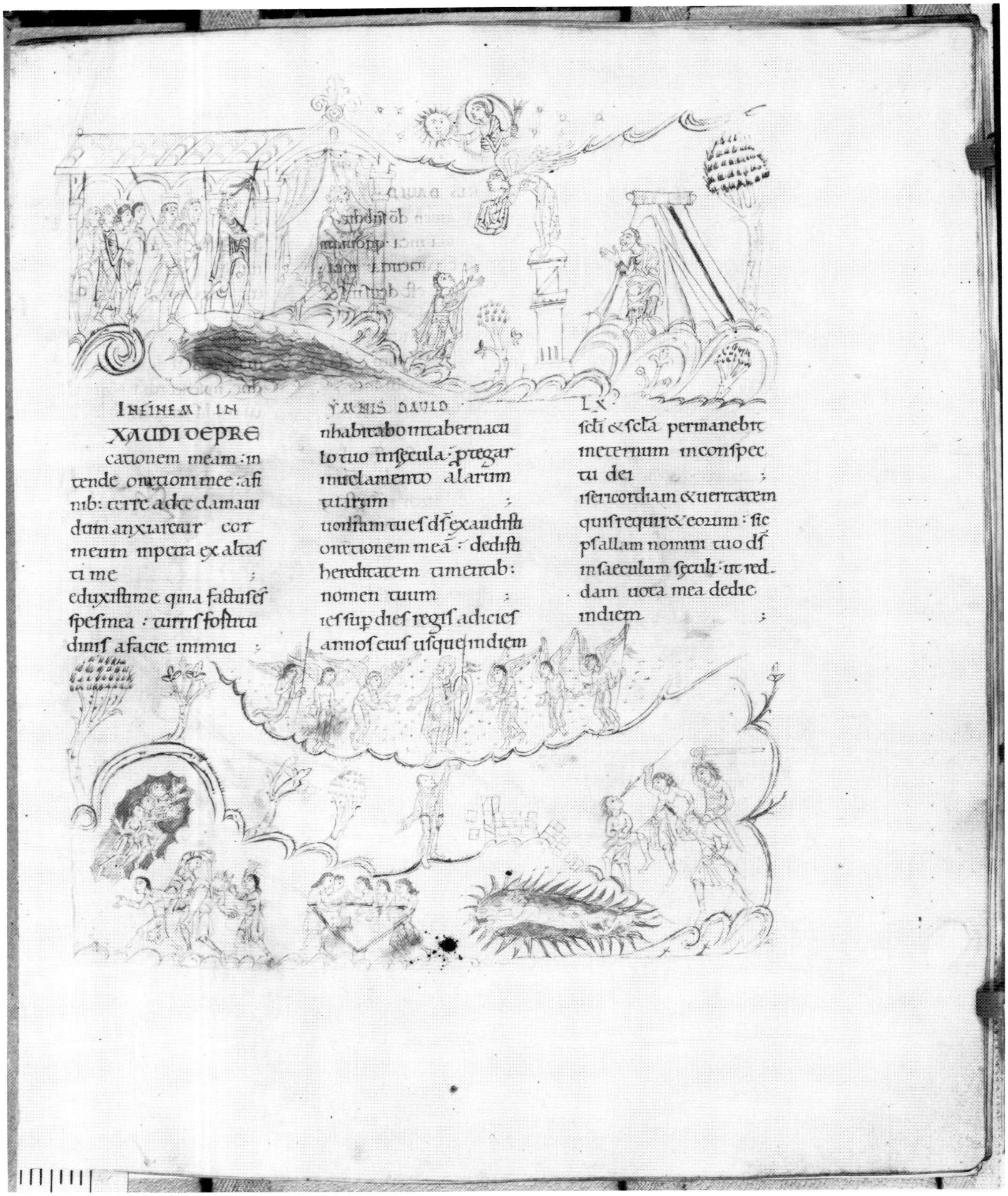

INFINEM IN
XAUDI DEPRE
cationem meam: in
tende orationi meae: afi
nib: terre ad te clamaui
dum anxiaretur cor
meum in petra exaltas
ti me ;
eduxisti me quia factus es
spes mea : turris forti
dinis a facie inimici ;

YMNIS DAUID
nhabitabo in tabernacu
lo tuo in secula: protegar
in uelamento alarum
tuarum ;
uoniam tu es ds exaudisti
orationem meā: dedisti
hereditatem timentib:
nomen tuum ;
ies sup dies regis adicies
annos eius usque in diem

LX
sclī & sclā permanebit
in eternum in conspec
tu dei ;
isericordiam & ueritatem
quis requiret eorum: sic
psallam nomini tuo ds
in saeculum seculi: ut red
dam uota mea de die
in diem ;

2.58 London, B.L., Harley 603, f. 33r

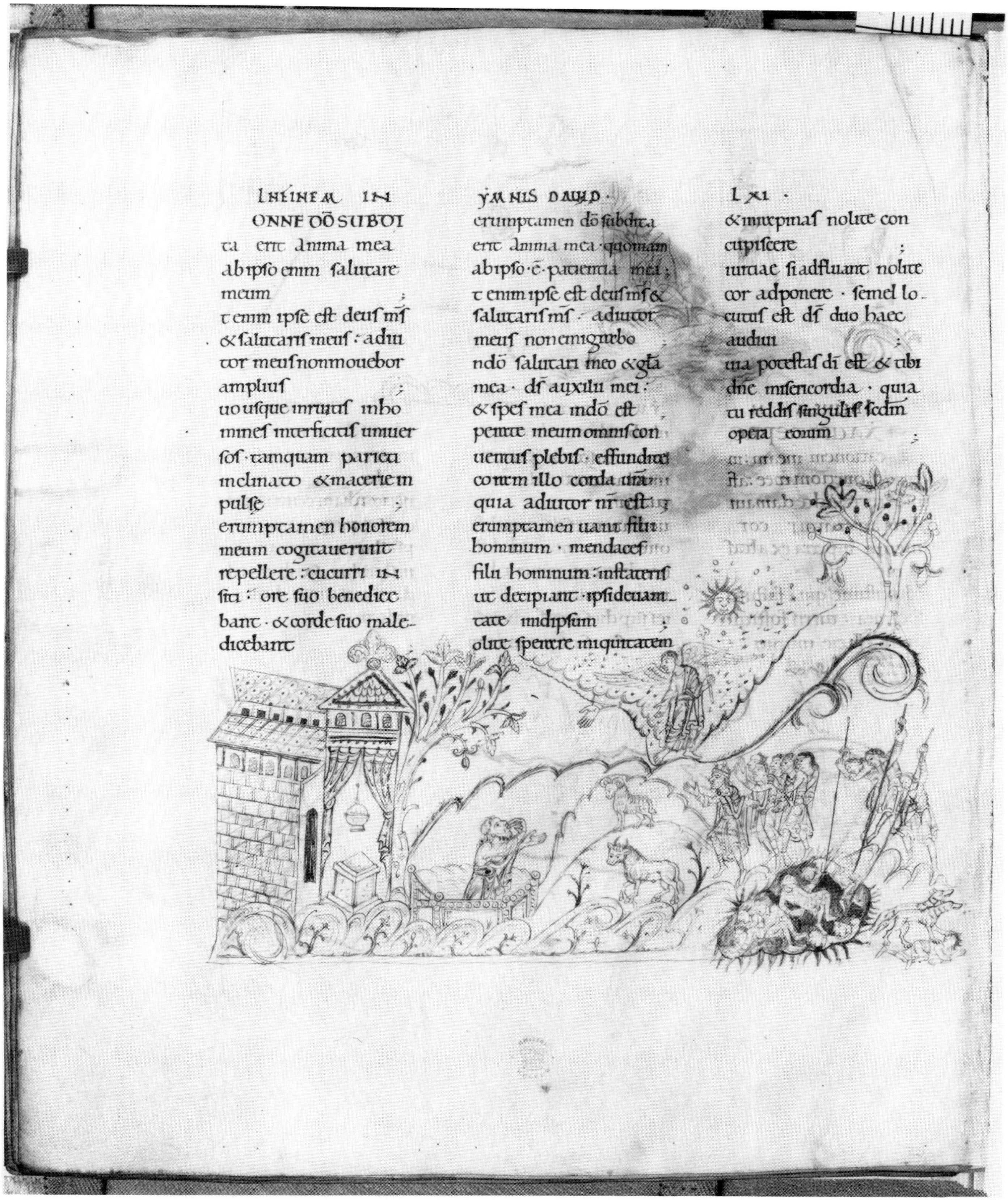

INFINEM IN
ONNE DO SUBDI
ta erit anima mea
ab ipso enim salutare
meum ;
t enim ipse est deus ms
& salutaris meus : adiu
tor meus non mouebor
amplius ;
uo usque inruitis in ho
mines interficitis uniuer
sos · tamquam parieti
inclinato & maceriae in
pulse ;
erumptamen honorem
meum cogitauerunt
repellere : cucurri in
siti : ore suo benedice
bant · & corde suo male
dicebant

YMNIS DAVID ·
erumptamen do subdita
erit anima mea · quoniam
ab ipso e · patientia mea ;
t enim ipse est deus ms &
salutaris ms · adiutor
meus non emigrabo
in do salutari meo & gla
mea · ds auxilii mei ·
& spes mea in do est ;
perate in eum omnis con
uentus plebis · effundite
coram illo corda ura
quia adiutor nr est ;
erumptamen uani filii
hominum · mendaces
filii hominum in stateris
ut decipiant · ipsi de uani
tate in idipsum ;
olite sperare in iniquitatem

LXI ·
& in rapinas nolite con
cupiscere ;
iuitiae si adfluant nolite
cor adponere · semel lo
cutus est ds duo haec
audiui ;
uia potestas di est & tibi
dne misericordia · quia
tu reddis singulis secdm
opera eorum ;

2.59 London, B.L., Harley 603, f. 33v

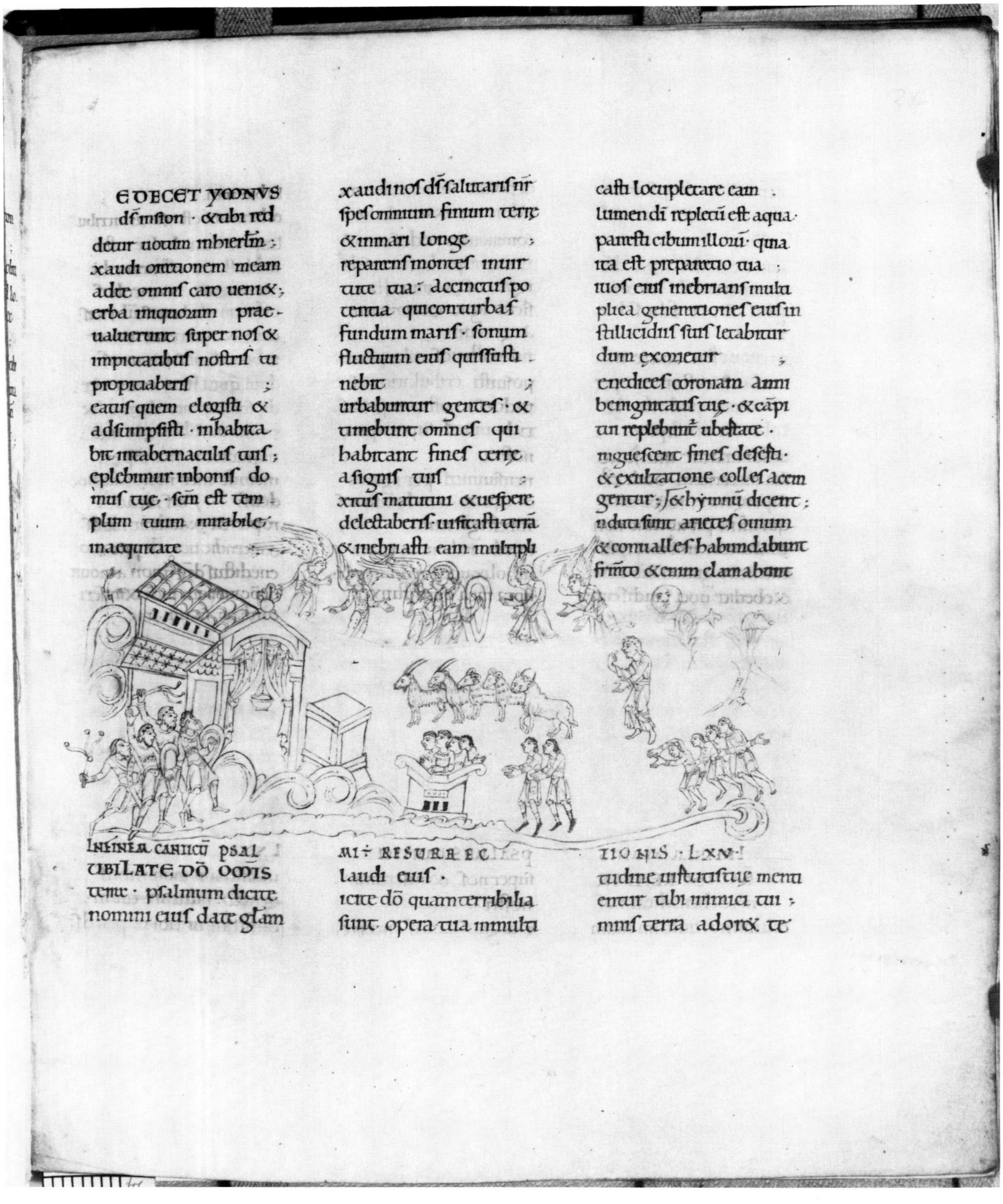

2.60 London, B.L., Harley 603, f. 34r

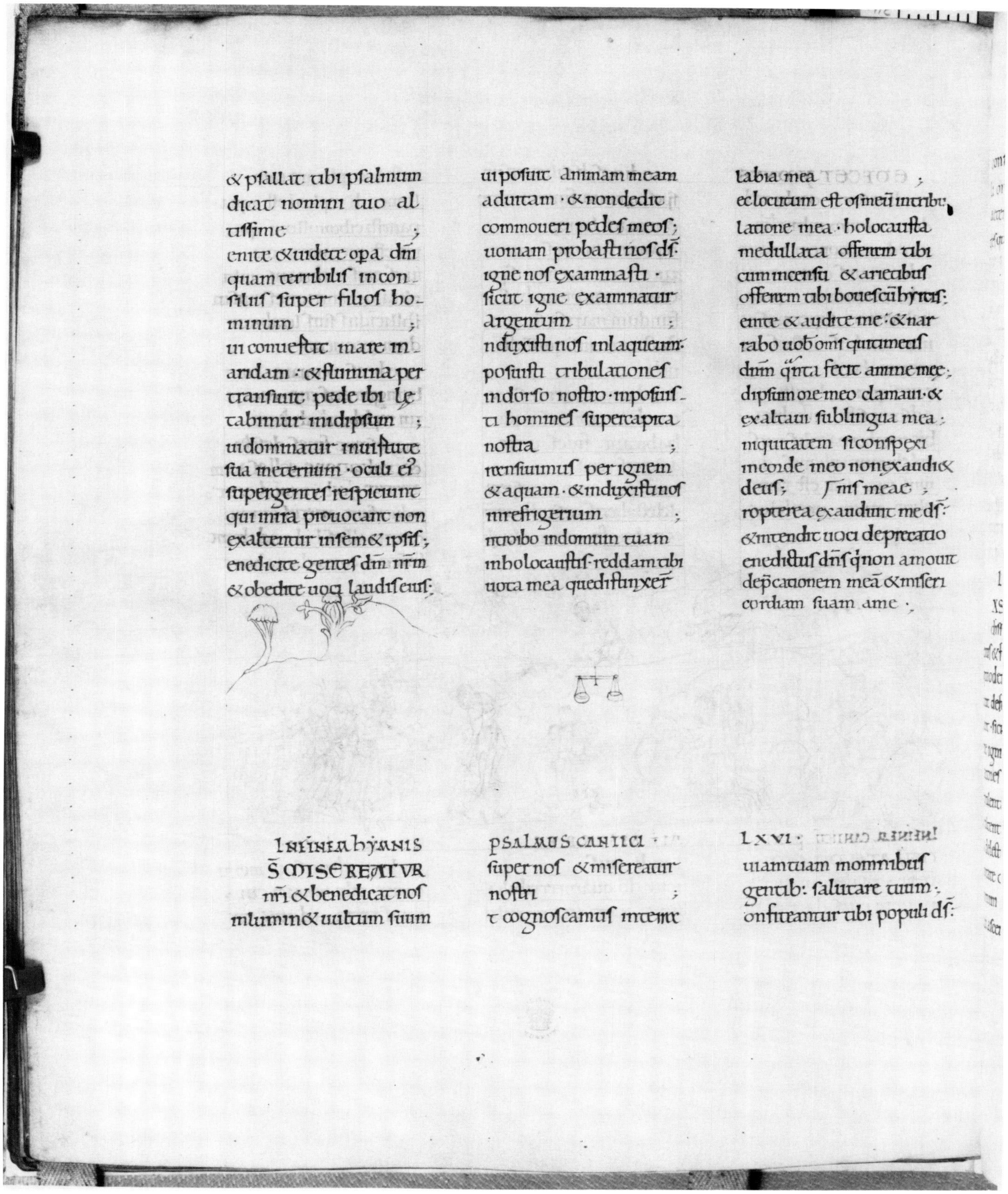

& psallat tibi psalmum
dicat nomini tuo al
tissime ;
enite & uidete opa dni
quam terribilis in con
siliis super filios ho-
minum ;
ui conuertit mare in
aridam : & flumina per
transiunt pede ibi le
tabimur in ipsum ;
ui dominatur in uirtute
sua in aeternum · oculi ei
super gentes respiciunt
qui inrita prouocant non
exaltentur in semet ipsis ;
enedicite gentes dnm nrm
& obaudite uoci laudis eius ;

ui posuit animam meam
ad uitam · & non dedit
commoueri pedes meos ;
uoniam probasti nos ds ·
igne nos examinasti ·
sicut igne examinatur
argentum ;
nduxisti nos in laqueum ·
posuisti tribulationes
in dorso nostro · inposuis-
ti homines super capita
nostra ;
ransiuimus per ignem
& aquam · & induxisti nos
in refrigerium ;
ntroibo in domum tuam
in holocaustis · reddam tibi
uota mea quae distinxer

labia mea ;
et locutum est os meum in tribu
latione mea · holocausta
medullata offeram tibi
cum incensu & arietibus
offeram tibi boues cum hyrcis ;
enite & audite me · & nar
rabo uobis omnes qui timetis
dnm quanta fecit animae meae ;
d ipsum ore meo clamaui · &
exaltaui sub lingua mea ;
niquitatem si conspexi
in corde meo non exaudiet
deus ; [illegible] meae ;
ropterea exaudiuit me ds ·
& intendit uoci deprecatio
enedictus dns qui non amouit
deprecationem meam & miseri
cordiam suam a me ·

In finem in hymnis
s misereatur
nri & benedicat nos
inluminet uultum suum

psalmus cantici
super nos & misereatur
nostri ;
t cognoscamus in terra

LXVI
uiam tuam in omnibus
gentib: salutare tuum ;
onfiteantur tibi populi ds ·

2.61 London, B.L., Harley 603, f. 34v

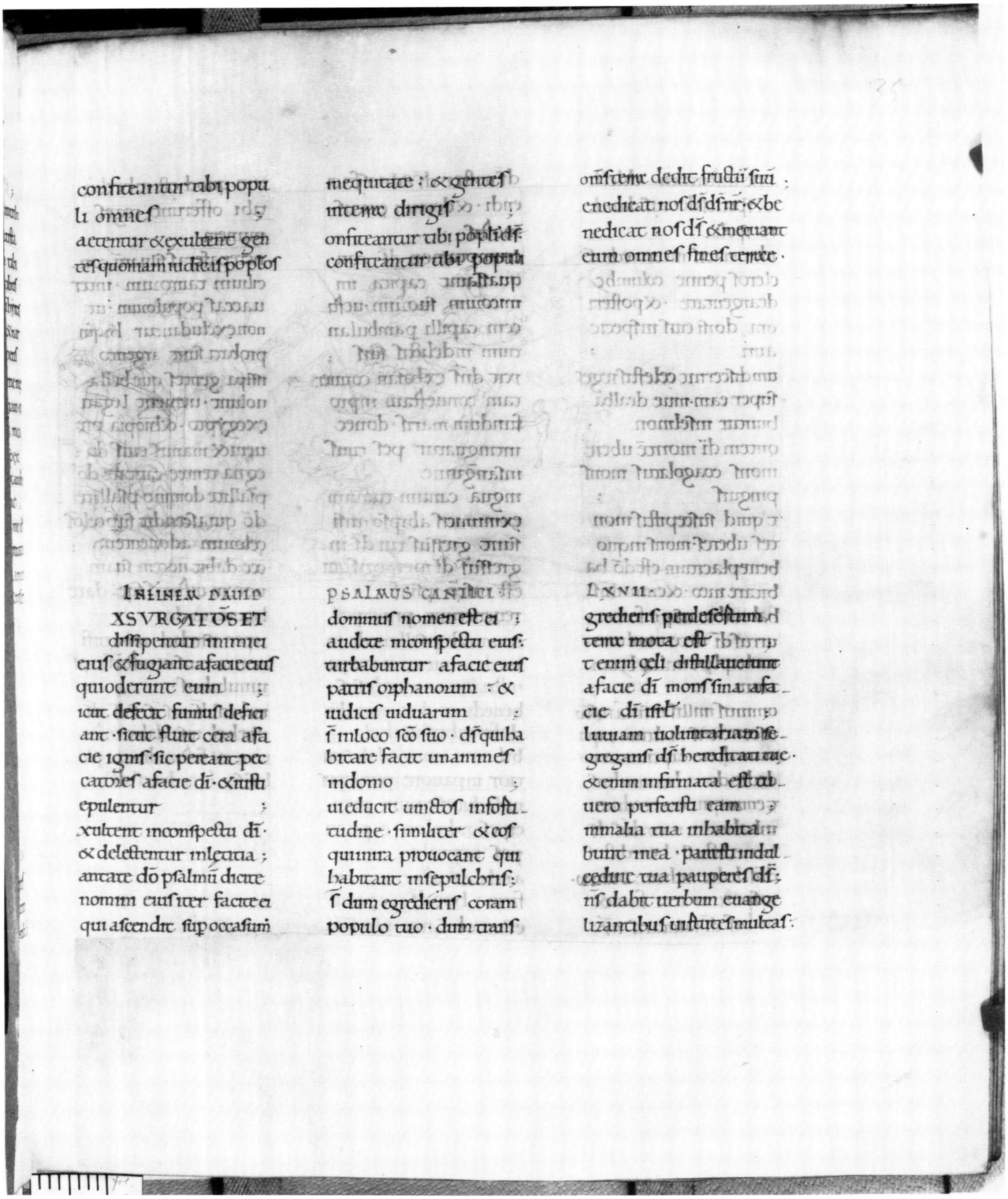
confiteantur tibi popu
li omnes ;
aetentur & exultent gen
tes quoniam iudicas popl'os

INFINEM DAUID
XSURGAT DS ET
dissipentur inimici
eius & fugiant a facie eius
qui oderunt eum ;
icut deficit fumus defici
ant · sicut fluit cera a fa
cie ignis · sic pereant pec
catores a facie di · & iusti
epulentur ;
xultent in conspectu di ·
& delectentur in laetitia ;
antate dō psalmū dicite
nomini eius iter facite ei
qui ascendit sup occasum

in equitate : & gentes
in terra dirigis ;
onfiteantur tibi popl'i ds ·
confiteantur tibi populi

PSALMUS CANTICI
dominus nomen est ei ;
audete in conspectu eius ·
turbabuntur a facie eius
patris orphanorum : &
iudicis uiduarum ;
s in loco sco suo · ds qui ha
bitare facit unanimes
in domo ;
ui educit uinctos in forti
tudine · similiter & eos
qui inritant prouocant qui
habitant in sepulchris ;
s dum egredieris coram
populo tuo · dum trans

om's terra dedit fructū suū ;
enedicat nos ds ds nr · & be
nedicat nos ds & metuant
eum omnes fines terrae ·

LXVII
gredieris per desertum ;
terra mota est ·
t enim caeli distillauerunt
a facie di mons sina a fa
cie di isrl ;
luuiam uoluntariam se
gregans ds hereditati tuae ·
& enim infirmata est tu
uero perfecisti eam ;
nimalia tua inhabita
bunt in ea · parasti in dul
cedine tua pauperes ds ;
ns dabit uerbum euange
lizantibus uirtute multa ;

2.62 London, B.L., Harley 603, f. 35r

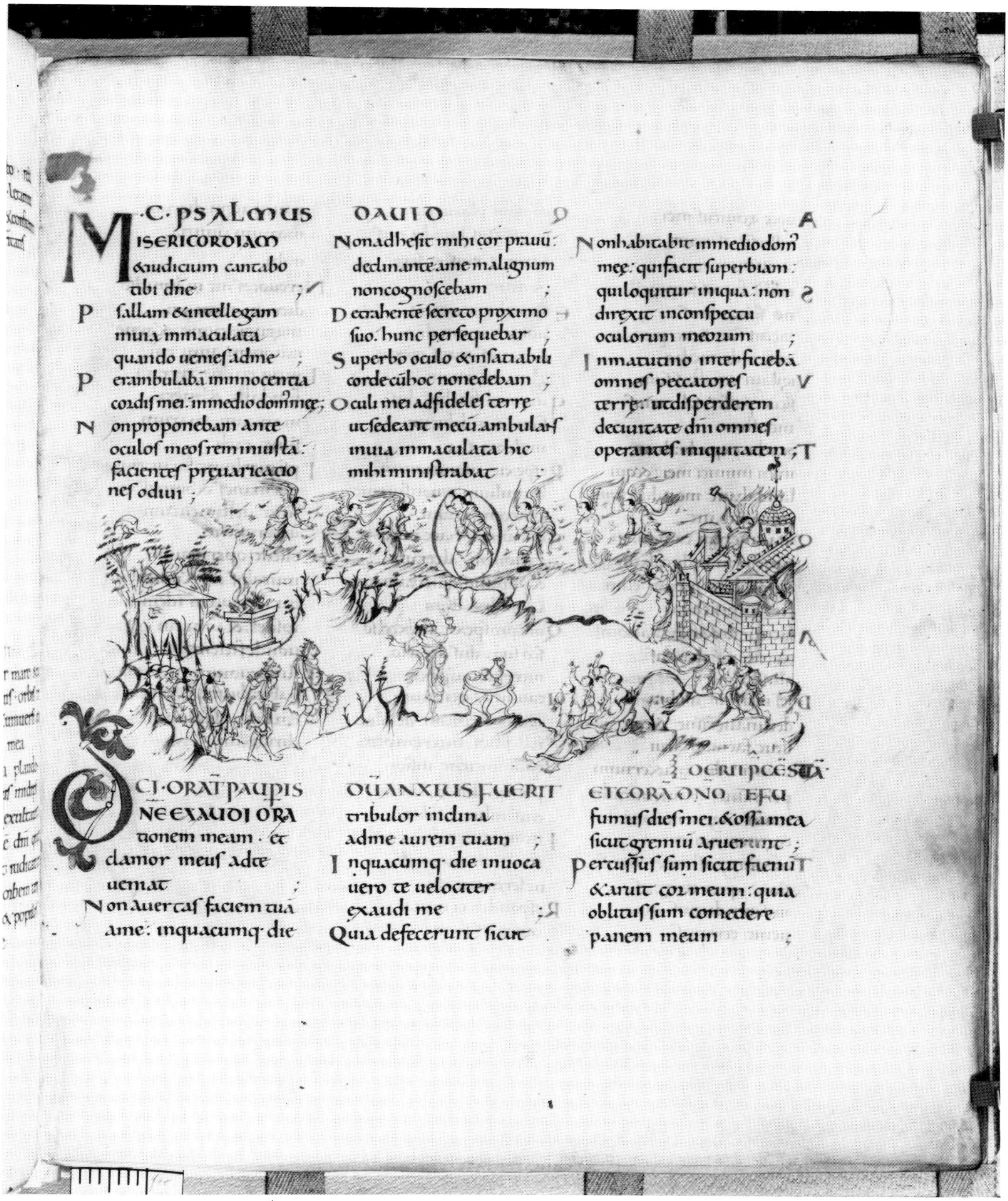

C. PSALMUS DAVID

MISERICORDIAM et iudicium cantabo tibi domine ;
Psallam et intellegam in uia inmaculata quando uenies ad me ;
Perambulabam in innocentia cordis mei in medio domus meae ;
Non proponebam ante oculos meos rem iniustam facientes preuaricationes odiui ;
Non adhesit mihi cor prauum declinantem a me malignum non cognoscebam ;
Detrahentem secreto proximo suo hunc persequebar ;
Superbo oculo et insatiabili corde cum hoc non edebam ;
Oculi mei ad fideles terrae ut sedeant mecum ambulans in uia inmaculata hic mihi ministrabat
Non habitabit in medio domus meae qui facit superbiam : qui loquitur iniqua non direxit in conspectu oculorum meorum ;
In matutino interficiebam omnes peccatores terrae ut disperderem de ciuitate domini omnes operantes iniquitatem ;

CI. ORAT PAUPIS CU ANXIUS FUERIT ET CORA DNO EFFU DERIT PCES SUA

DOMINE EXAUDI ORAtionem meam . et clamor meus ad te ueniat ;
Non auertas faciem tuam a me : in quacumque die tribulor inclina ad me aurem tuam ;
In quacumque die inuocauero te uelociter exaudi me
Quia defecerunt sicut fumus dies mei et ossa mea sicut gremium aruerunt ;
Percussus sum sicut faenum et aruit cor meum : quia oblitus sum comedere panem meum ;

2.63 London, B.L., Harley 603, f. 50[r]

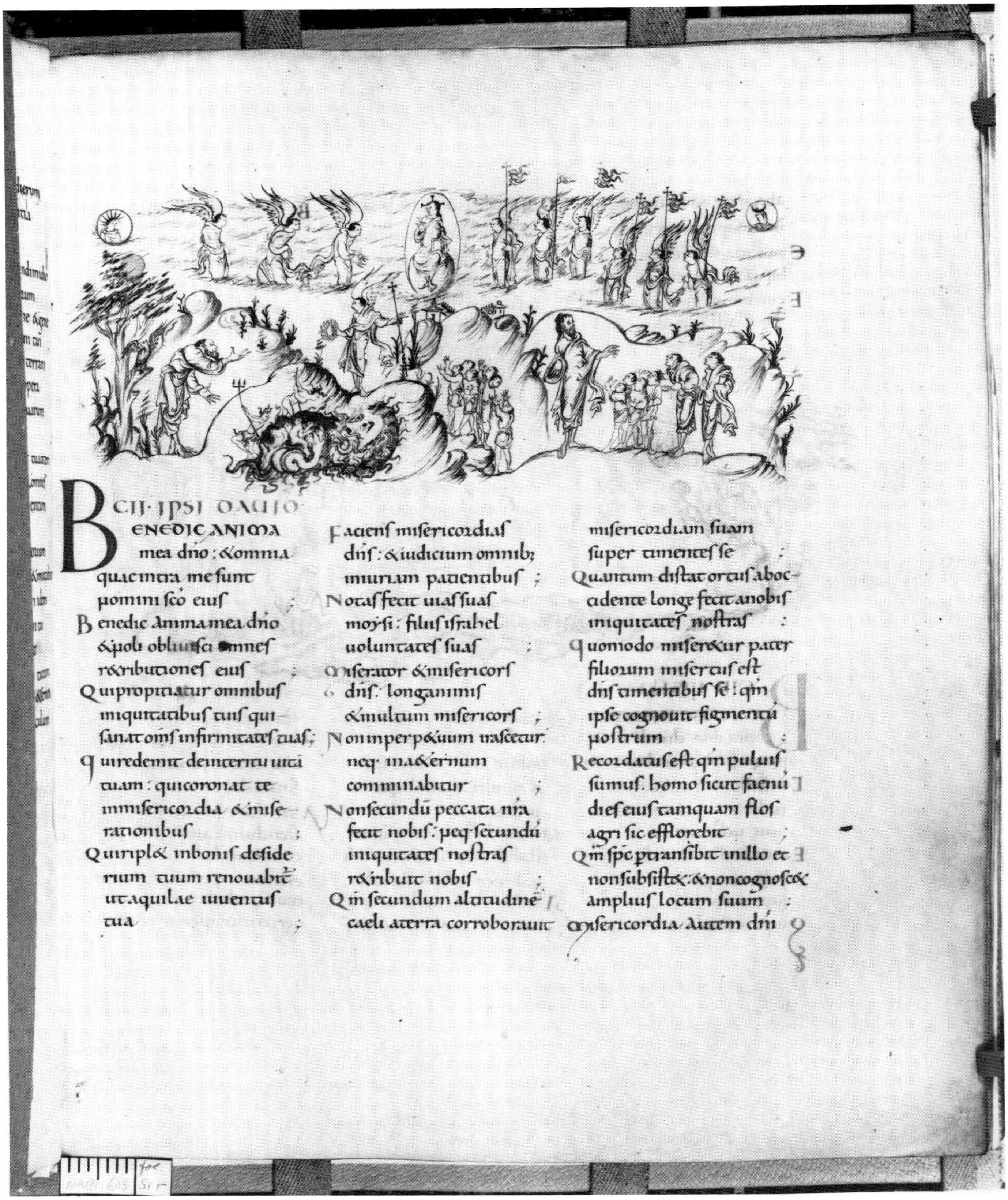

CII. IPSI DAVID
BENEDIC ANIMA
mea dno: & omnia
quae intra me sunt
nomini sco eius ;
Benedic anima mea dno
& noli oblivisci omnes
retributiones eius ;
Qui propitiatur omnibus
iniquitatibus tuis qui
sanat omns infirmitates tuas ;
Qui redemit de interitu vita
tuam: qui coronat te
in misericordia & mise-
rationibus ;
Qui replet in bonis deside
rium tuum renovabitur
ut aquilae iuventus
tua ;

Faciens misericordias
dns: & iudicium omnib;
iniuriam patientibus ;
Notas fecit vias suas
moysi: filiis israhel
voluntates suas ;
Miserator & misericors
dns: longanimis
& multum misericors ;
Non in perpetuum irascetur:
neq; in aeternum
comminabitur ;
Non secundu peccata nra
fecit nobis: neq; secundu
iniquitates nostras
retribuit nobis ;
Qm secundum altitudine
caeli a terra corroboravit

misericordiam suam
super timentes se ;
Quantum distat ortus aboc-
cidente longe fecit a nobis
iniquitates nostras ;
Quomodo miseretur pater
filiorum misertus est
dns timentibus se: qm
ipse cognovit figmentu
nostrum ;
Recordatus est qm pulvis
sumus. homo sicut faenu
dies eius tamquam flos
agri sic efflorebit ;
Qm sps pertransibit in illo et
non subsistet: & non cognoscet
amplius locum suum ;
Misericordia autem dni

2.64 London, B.L., Harley 603, f. 51r

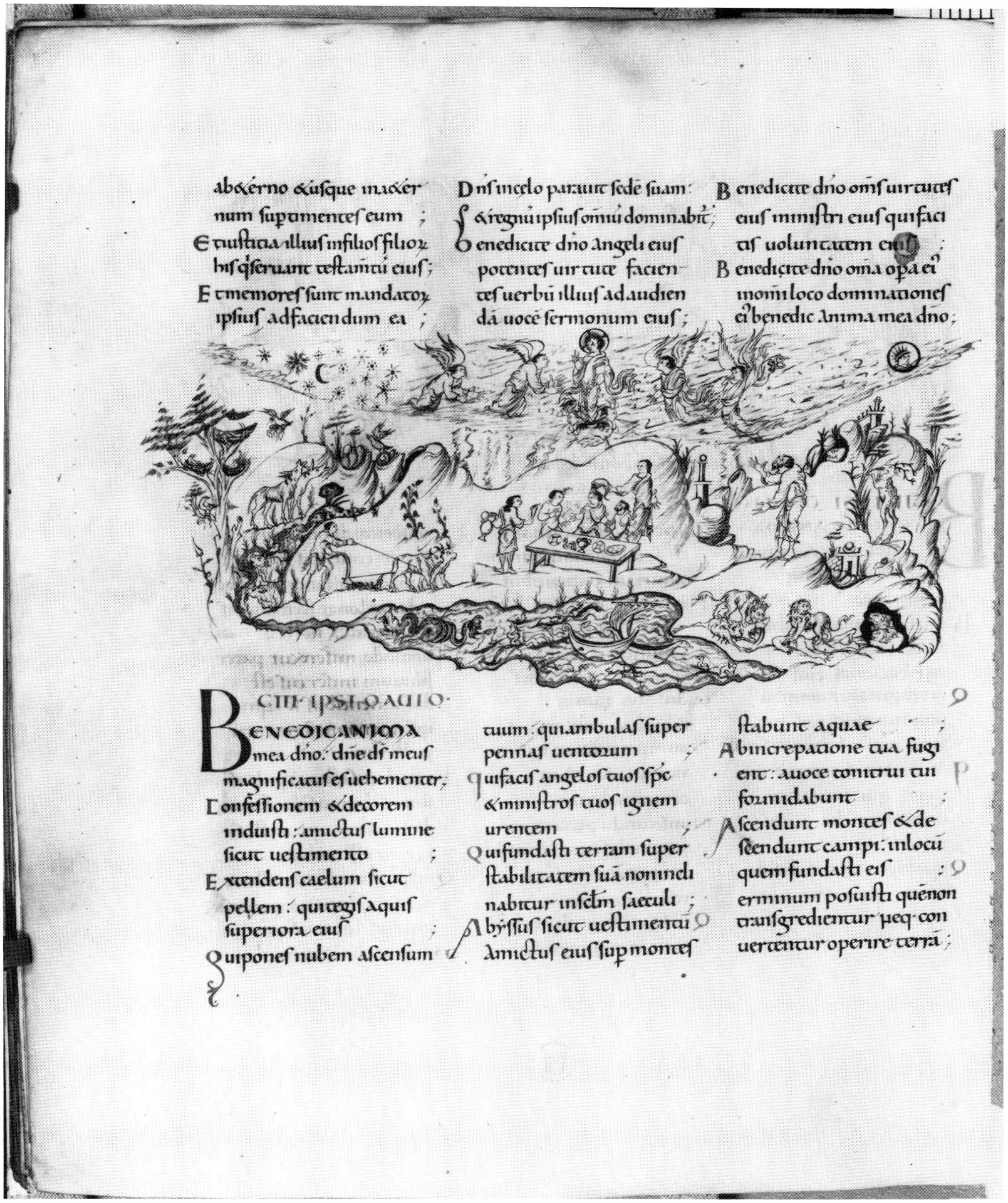
ab æterno & usque in æter-
num sup timentes eum ;
Et iustitia illius in filios filiorum
his qui seruant testamentum eius ;
Et memores sunt mandatorum
ipsius ad faciendum ea ;
Dns in celo parauit sedē suam :
& regnū ipsius omnibus dominabitur ;
Benedicite dño angeli eius
potentes uirtute facien-
tes uerbū illius ad audien-
dā uocē sermonum eius ;
Benedicite dño omnes uirtutes
eius ministri eius qui faci
tis uoluntatem eius ;
Benedicite dño omnia opera ei
in omni loco dominationes
ei benedic anima mea dño ;

CIII. IPSI DAUID.
BENEDIC ANIMA
mea dño : dne ds meus
magnificatus es uehementer ;
Confessionem & decorem
induisti : amictus lumine
sicut uestimento ;
Extendens caelum sicut
pellem : qui tegis aquis
superiora eius ;
Qui pones nubem ascensum
tuum : qui ambulas super
pennas uentorum ;
Qui facis angelos tuos spc
& ministros tuos ignem
urentem ;
Qui fundasti terram super
stabilitatem suā non incli
nabitur in sclm saeculi ;
Abyssus sicut uestimentu
amictus eius sup montes
stabunt aquae ;
Ab increpatione tua fugi
ent : a uoce tonitrui tui
formidabunt ;
Ascendunt montes & de
scendunt campi : in locū
quem fundasti eis ;
Terminum posuisti quē non
transgredientur neq con
uertentur operire terrā ;

2.65 London, B.L., Harley 603, f. 51v

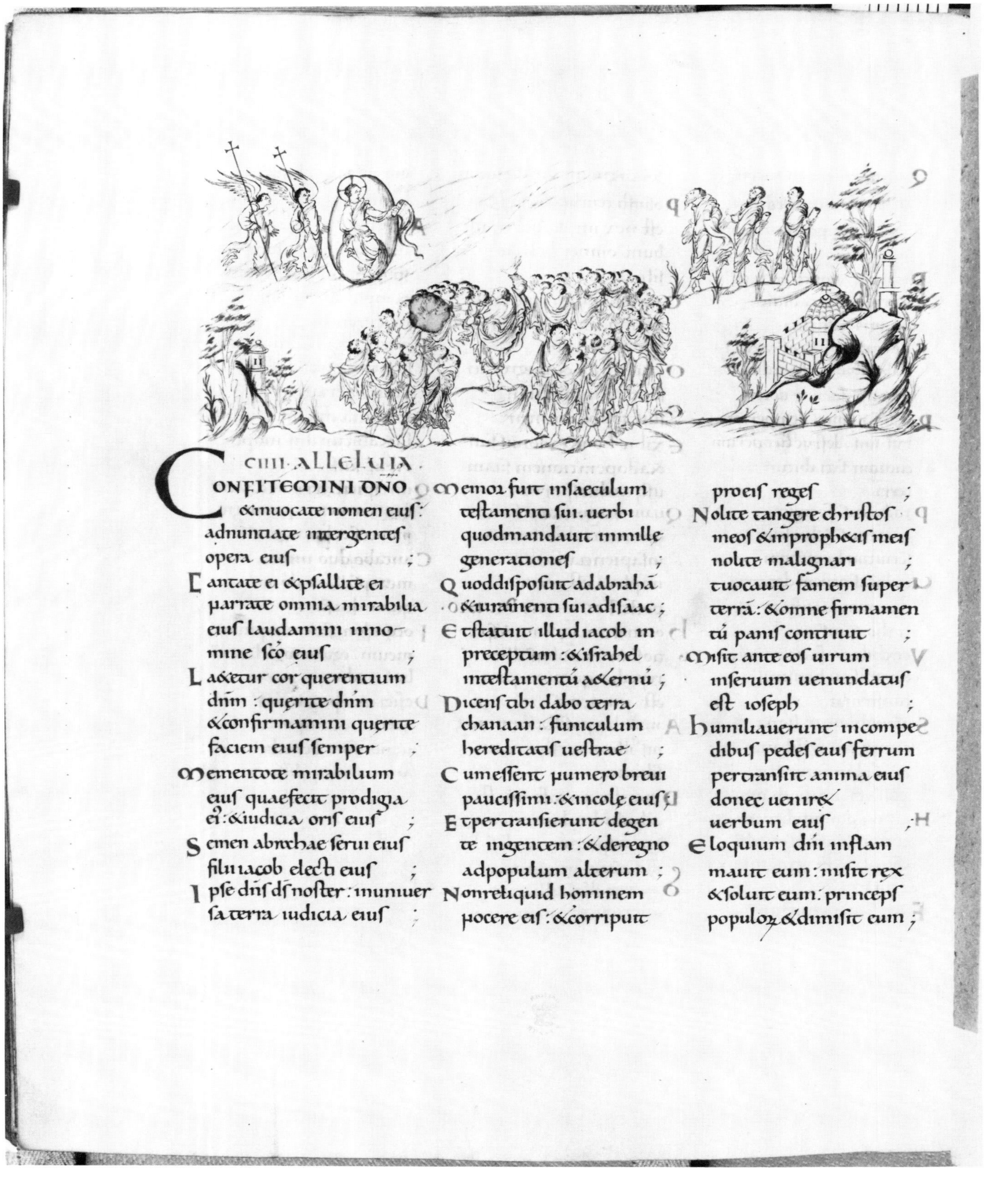

CIIII ALLELUIA
CONFITEMINI DNO
& inuocate nomen eius :
adnuntiate inter gentes
opera eius ;
Cantate ei & psallite ei
narrate omnia mirabilia
eius laudamini in no-
mine sco eius
Laetetur cor querentium
dnm : querite dnm
& confirmamini querite
faciem eius semper ;
Mementote mirabilium
eius quae fecit prodigia
ei : & iudicia oris eius ;
Semen abrahae serui eius
filii iacob electi eius ;
Ipse dns ds noster : in uniuer
sa terra iudicia eius ;

Memor fuit in saeculum
testamenti sui . uerbi
quod mandauit in mille
generationes ;
Quod disposuit ad abrahā
& iuramenti sui ad isaac ;
Et statuit illud iacob in
preceptum : & israhel
in testamentū aeternū ;
Dicens tibi dabo terra
chanaan : funiculum
hereditatis uestrae ;
Cum essent numero breui
paucissimi : & incole eius ;
Et pertransierunt de gen
te in gentem : & de regno
ad populum alterum ;
Non reliquid hominem
nocere eis : & corripuit

pro eis reges ;
Nolite tangere christos
meos & in prophetis meis
nolite malignari ;
Et uocauit famem super
terrā : & omne firmamen
tū panis contriuit ;
Misit ante eos uirum
in seruum uenundatus
est ioseph ;
Humiliauerunt in compe
dibus pedes eius ferrum
pertransiit anima eius
donec ueniret
uerbum eius ;
Eloquium dni inflam
mauit eum : misit rex
& soluit eum : princeps
populorum & dimisit eum ;

2.66 London, B.L., Harley 603, f. 52v

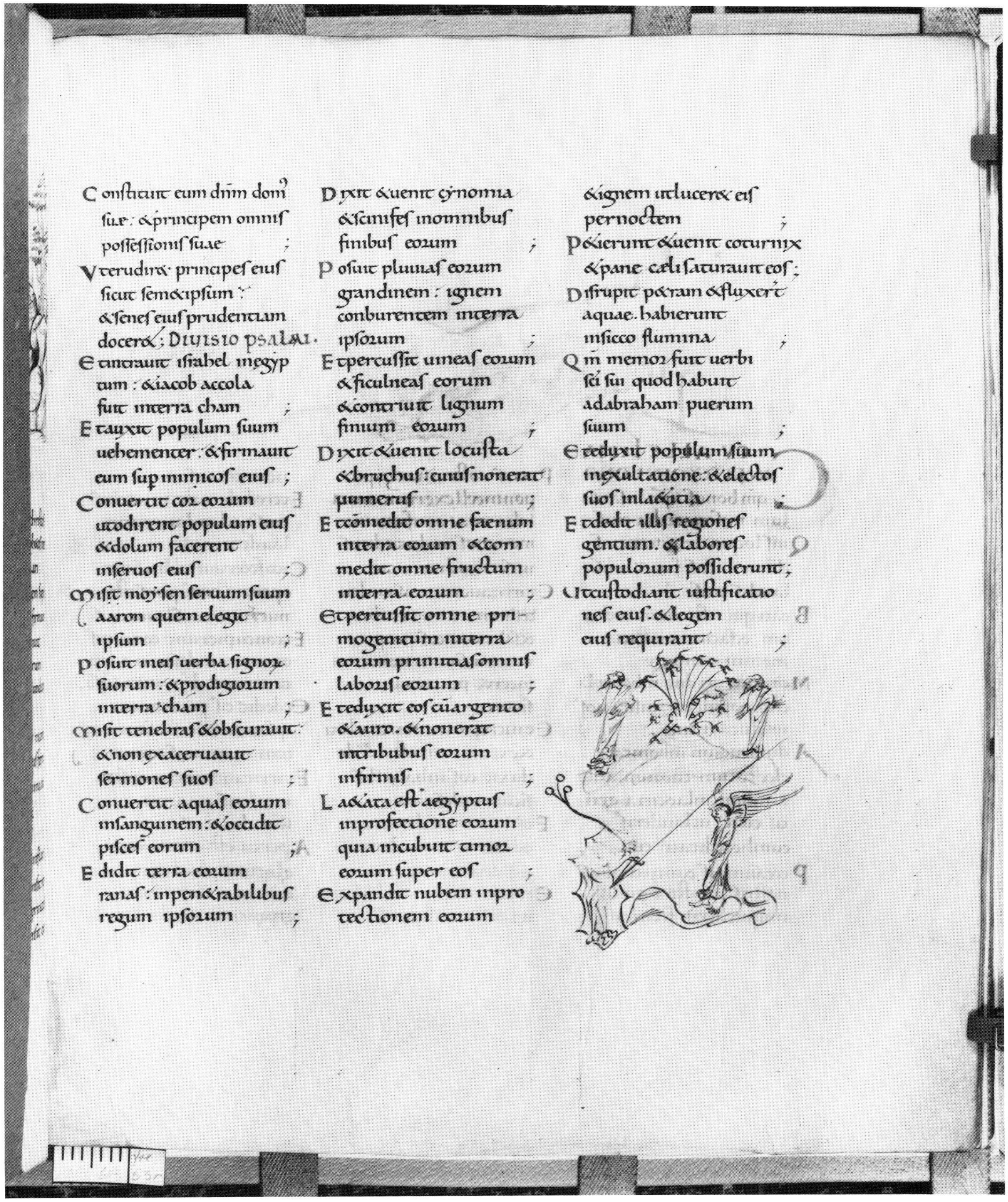

Constituit eum dnm domꝰ
sui : & principem omnis
possessionis suae ;
Vt erudiret principes eius
sicut semet ipsum :
& senes eius prudentiam
doceret ; DIVISIO PSALMI.
Et intrauit israhel in egyp
tum : & iacob accola
fuit in terra cham ;
Et auxit populum suum
uehementer : & firmauit
eum sup inimicos eius ;
Conuertit cor eorum
ut odirent populum eius
& dolum facerent
in seruos eius ;
Misit moysen seruum suum
aaron quem elegit
ipsum
Posuit in eis uerba signorum
suorum : & prodigiorum
in terra cham ;
Misit tenebras & obscurauit :
& non exacerbauit
sermones suos ;
Conuertit aquas eorum
in sanguinem : & occidit
pisces eorum ;
Edidit terra eorum
ranas : in penetrabilibus
regum ipsorum ;

Dixit & uenit cynomia
& sciniphes in omnibus
finibus eorum ;
Posuit pluuias eorum
grandinem : ignem
conburentem in terra
ipsorum ;
Et percussit uineas eorum
& ficulneas eorum
& contriuit lignum
finium eorum ;
Dixit & uenit locusta
& bruchus : cuius non erat
numerus ;
Et comedit omne faenum
in terra eorum & com
medit omne fructum
in terra eorum ;
Et percussit omne pri
mogenitum in terra
eorum primitias omnis
laboris eorum ;
Et eduxit eos cum argento
& auro : & non erat
in tribubus eorum
infirmus ;
Laetata est aegyptus
in profectione eorum
quia incubuit timor
eorum super eos ;
Expandit nubem in pro
tectionem eorum

& ignem ut luceret eis
per noctem ;
Petierunt & uenit coturnix
& pane caeli saturauit eos ;
Disrupit petram & fluxerunt
aquae : abierunt
in sicco flumina ;
Quoniam memor fuit uerbi
sci sui quod habuit
ad abraham puerum
suum ;
Et eduxit populum suum
in exultatione : & electos
suos in laetitia ;
Et dedit illis regiones
gentium : & labores
populorum possiderunt ;
Vt custodiant iustificatio
nes eius : & legem
eius requirant ;

2.67 London, B.L., Harley 603, f. 53r

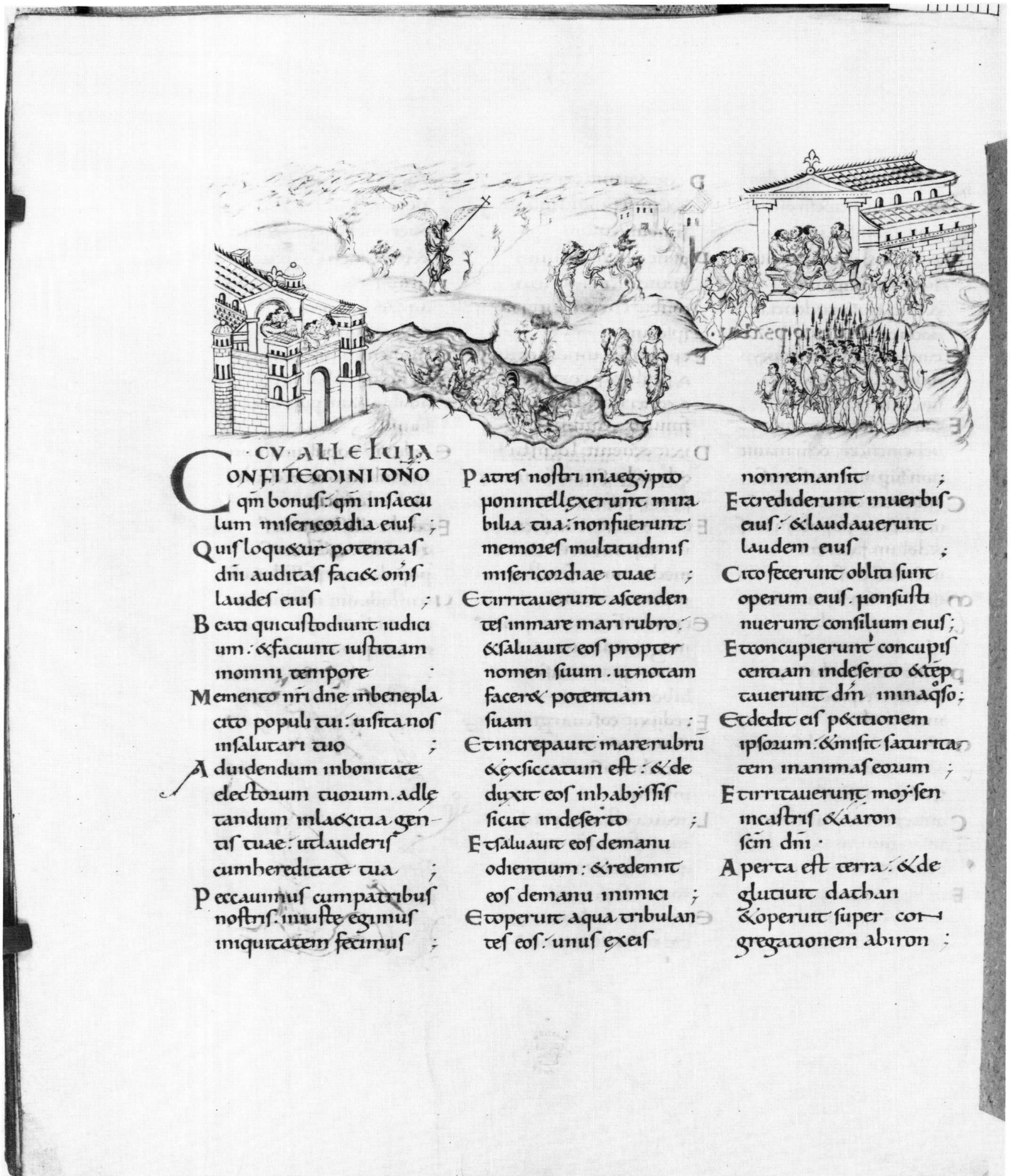

CU ALLELUIA
CONFITEMINI DNO
qm bonus: qm in saecu
lum misericordia eius;
Quis loquetur potentias
dni auditas faciet omnes
laudes eius;
Beati qui custodiunt iudici
um: & faciunt iustitiam
in omni tempore;
Memento nri dne in benepla
cito populi tui: uisita nos
in salutari tuo;
Ad uidendum in bonitate
electorum tuorum. adlae
tandum in laetitia gen
tis tuae: ut lauderis
cum hereditate tua;
Peccauimus cum patribus
nostris: iniuste egimus
iniquitatem fecimus;

Patres nostri in aegypto
non intellexerunt mira
bilia tua: non fuerunt
memores multitudinis
misericordiae tuae;
Et inritauerunt ascenden
tes in mare mari rubro;
& saluauit eos propter
nomen suum. ut notam
faceret potentiam
suam;
Et increpauit mare rubru
& exsiccatum est: & de
duxit eos in abyssis
sicut in deserto;
Et saluauit eos de manu
odientium: & redemit
eos de manu inimici;
Et operuit aqua tribulan
tes eos: unus ex eis

non remansit;
Et crediderunt in uerbis
eius: & laudauerunt
laudem eius;
Cito fecerunt obliti sunt
operum eius. non susti
nuerunt consilium eius;
Et concupierunt concupis
centiam in deserto & temp
tauerunt dm in inaquoso;
Et dedit eis petitionem
ipsorum: & misit saturita
tem in animas eorum;
Et irritauerunt moysen
in castris & aaron
scm dni;
Aperta est terra: & de
glutiuit dathan
& operuit super con
gregationem abiron;

2.68 London, B.L., Harley 603, f. 53v

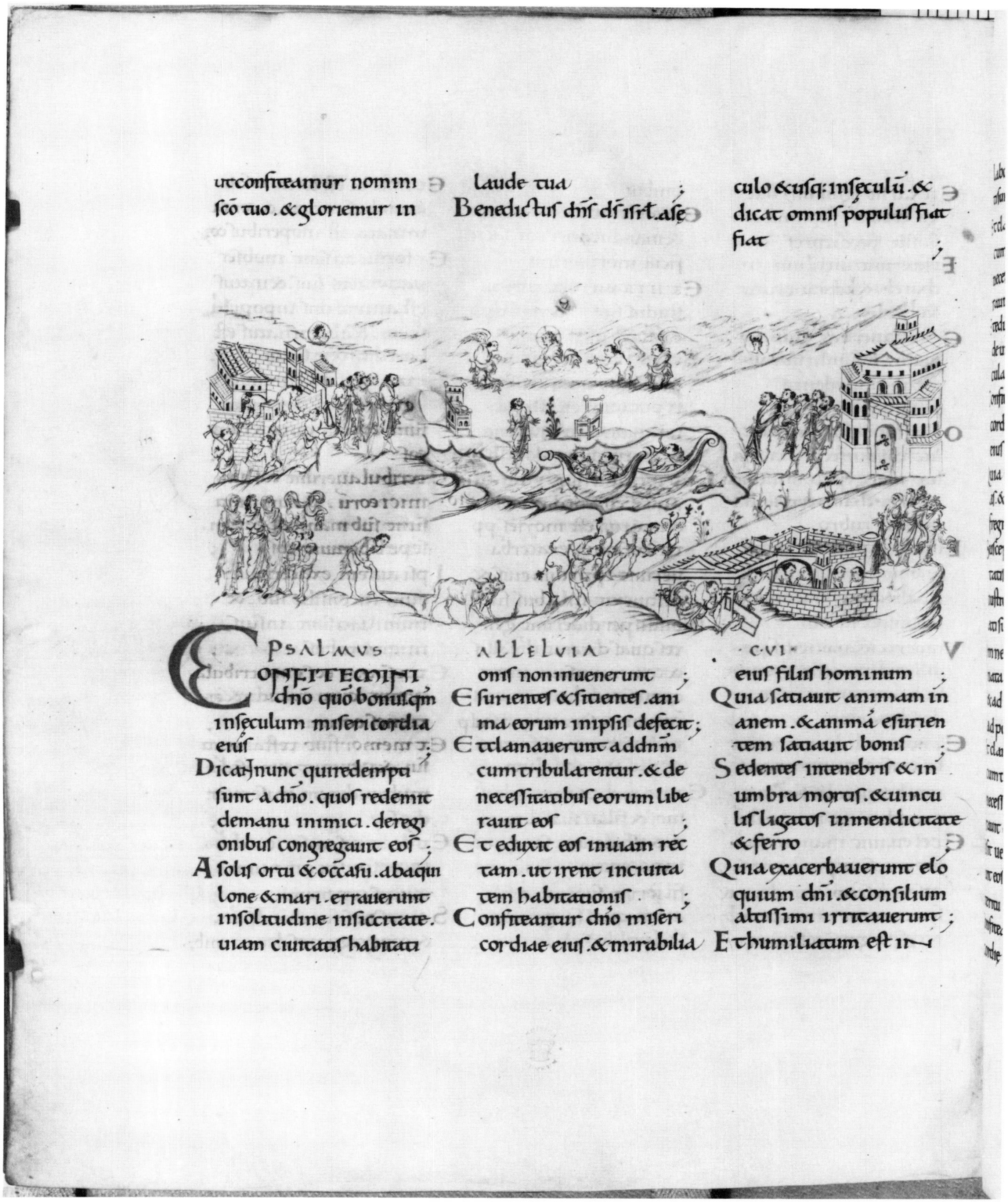

ut confiteamur nomini
sancto tuo. & gloriemur in
laude tua
Benedictus dominus deus israel. a se-
culo & usque in seculum. &
dicat omnis populus fiat
fiat

PSALMUS ALLELUIA .CVI.
CONFITEMINI
domino quoniam bonus quoniam
in seculum misericordia
eius
Dicant nunc qui redempti
sunt a domino. quos redemit
de manu inimici. de regi-
onibus congregauit eos
A solis ortu & occasu. ab aqui-
lone & mari. errauerunt
in solitudine in siccitate.
uiam ciuitatis habitati-
onis non inuenerunt
Esurientes & sitientes. ani-
ma eorum in ipsis defecit
Et clamauerunt ad dominum
cum tribularentur. & de
necessitatibus eorum libe-
rauit eos
Et eduxit eos in uiam rec-
tam. ut irent in ciuita-
tem habitationis
Confiteantur domino miseri-
cordiae eius. & mirabilia
eius filiis hominum
Quia satiauit animam in-
anem. & animam esurien-
tem satiauit bonis
Sedentes in tenebris & in
umbra mortis. & uincu-
lis ligatos in mendicitate
& ferro
Quia exacerbauerunt elo-
quium domini. & consilium
altissimi irritauerunt
Et humiliatum est in

2.69 London, B.L., Harley 603, f. 54v

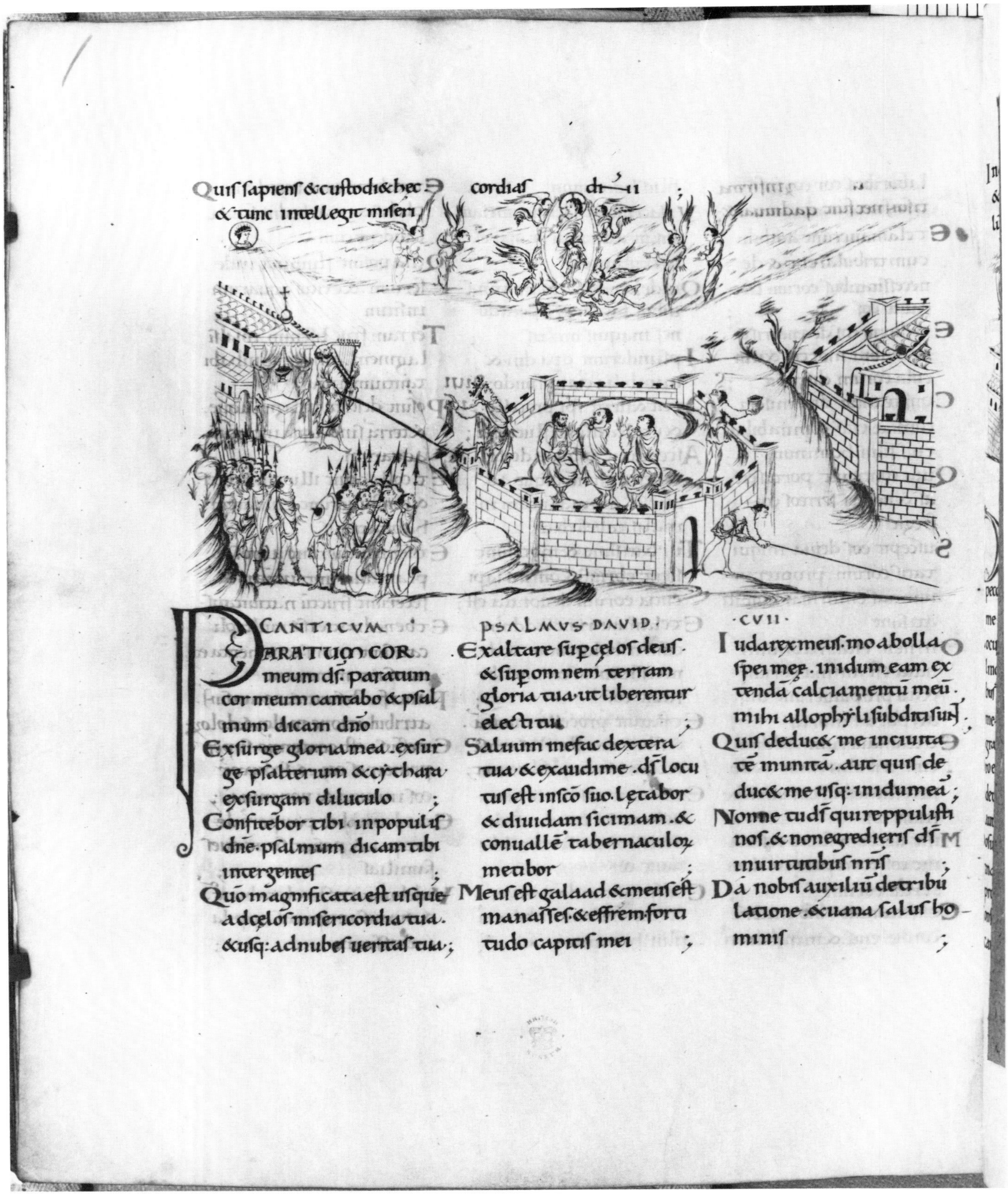

Quis sapiens & custodi& hec : & tunc intellegit misericordias dni ;

CANTICUM PSALMUS DAVID CVII.

Paratum cor meum ds. paratum cor meum cantabo & psalmum dicam dno

Exsurge gloria mea. exsurge psalterium & cythara exsurgam diluculo ;

Confitebor tibi in populis dne. psalmum dicam tibi in gentes ;

Quo magnificata est usque ad celos misericordia tua. & usq: ad nubes ueritas tua ;

Exaltare sup celos deus. & sup omnem terram gloria tua ut liberentur electi tui ;

Saluum me fac dextera tua & exaudi me. ds locutus est in sco suo. letabor & diuidam sicimam. & conualle tabernaculoru metibor ;

Meus est galaad & meus est manasses. & effrem fortitudo capitis mei ;

Iuda rex meus. moab olla spei mee. in idumeam extendam calciamentu meu. mihi allophyli subditi sunt ;

Quis deduc& me in ciuitate munita. aut quis deduc& me usq: in idumea ;

Nonne tu ds qui repulisti nos. & non egredieris ds in uirtutibus nris ;

Da nobis auxiliu de tribulatione. & uana salus hominis ;

2.70 London, B.L., Harley 603, f. 55v

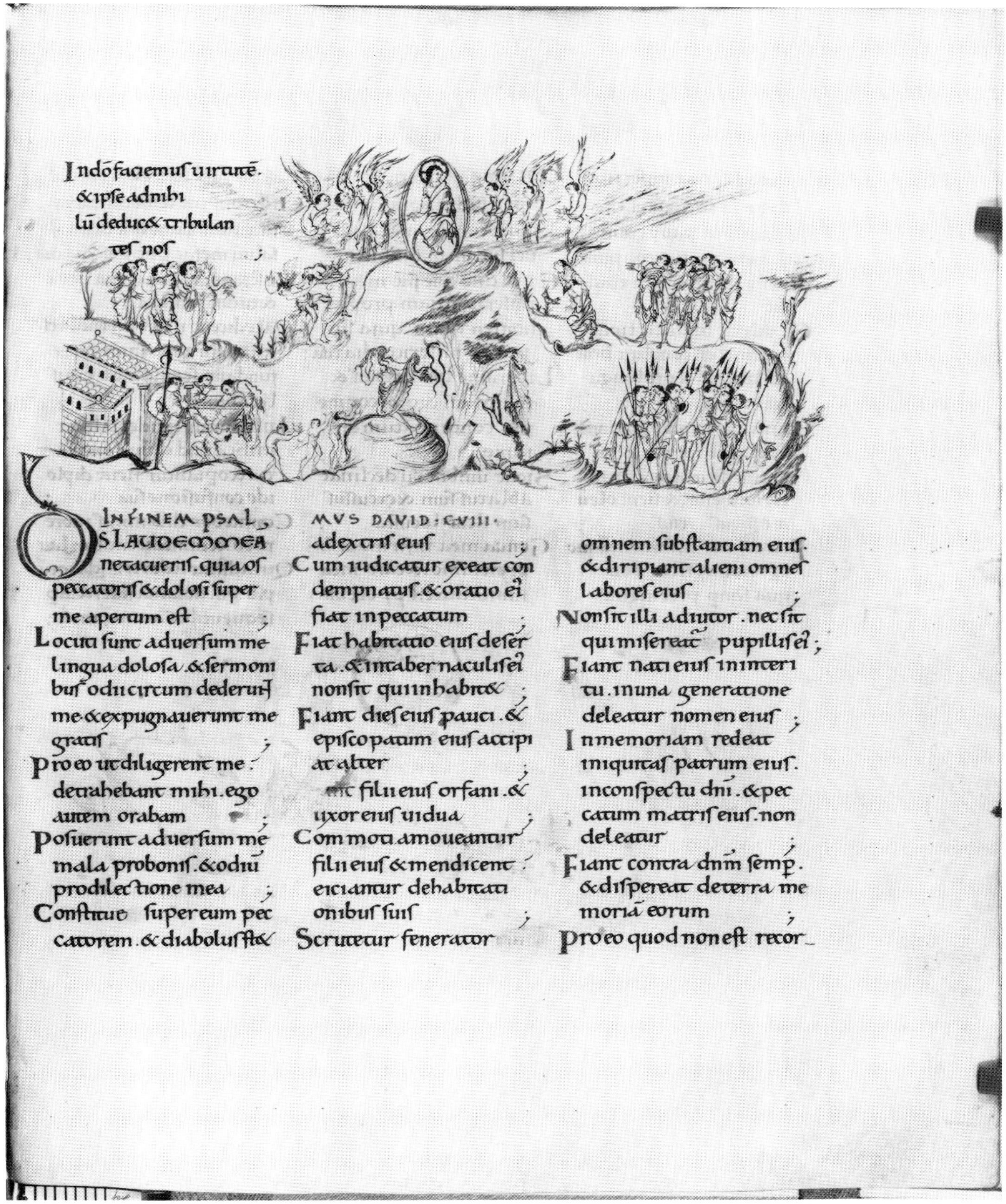
In dō faciemus uirtutē. & ipse ad nihi lū deducet tribulantes nos ;

IN FINEM PSAL
DS LAUDEM MEA
ne tacueris. quia os
peccatoris & dolosi super
me apertum est ;
Locuti sunt aduersum me
lingua dolosa. & sermoni
bus odii circum dederunt
me & expugnauerunt me
gratis ;
Pro eo ut diligerent me.
detrahebant mihi. ego
autem orabam ;
Posuerunt aduersum me
mala pro bonis. & odiū
pro dilectione mea ;
Constitue super eum pec
catorem. & diabolus stet

MUS DAVID. CVIII.
a dextris eius ;
Cum iudicatur exeat con
dempnatus. & oratio eī
fiat in peccatum ;
Fiat habitatio eius deser
ta. & in tabernaculis eī
non sit qui inhabitet ;
Fiant dies eius pauci. &
episcopatum eius accipi
at alter ;
Fiant filii eius orfani. &
uxor eius uidua ;
Com moti amoueantur
filii eius & mendicent.
eiciantur de habitati
onibus suis ;
Scrutetur fenerator

omnem substantiam eius.
& diripiant alieni omnes
labores eius ;
Non sit illi adiutor. nec sit
qui misereatur pupillis eī ;
Fiant nati eius in interi
tu. in una generatione
deleatur nomen eius ;
In memoriam redeat
iniquitas patrum eius.
in conspectu dn̄i. & pec
catum matris eius. non
deleatur ;
Fiant contra dn̄m semp̄.
& dispereat de terra me
moria eorum ;
Pro eo quod non est recor–

2.71 London, B.L., Harley 603, f. 56r

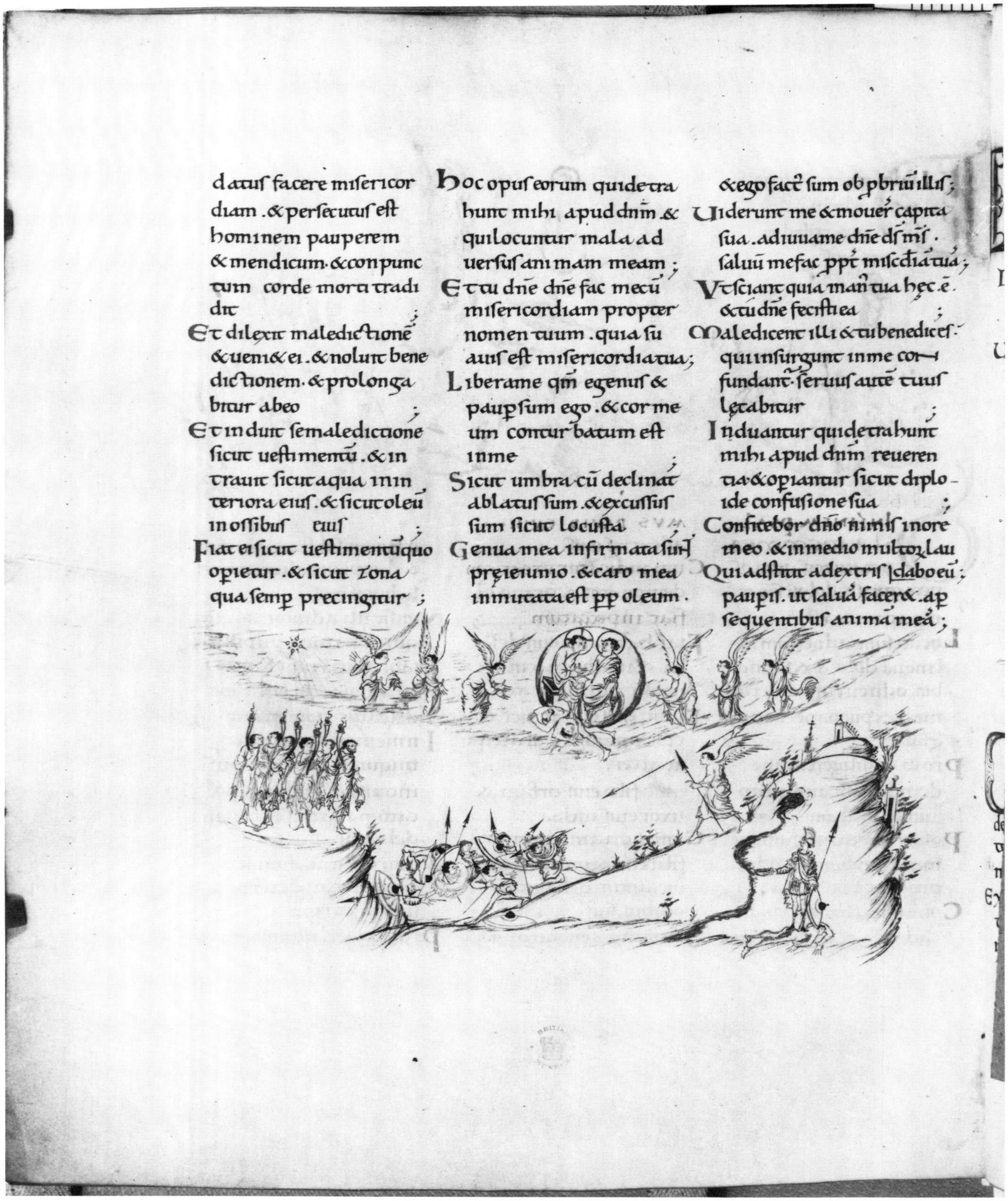

datus facere misericor
diam. & persecutus est
hominem pauperem
& mendicum. & conpunc
tum corde morti tradi
dit;
Et dilexit maledictionē
& ueniet ei. & noluit bene
dictionem. & prolonga
bitur abeo;
Et induit se maledictione
sicut uestimentū. & in
trauit sicut aqua in in
teriora eius. & sicut oleū
in ossibus eius;
Fiat ei sicut uestimentū quo
operitur. & sicut zona
qua semp precingitur;

Hoc opus eorum qui detra
hunt mihi apud dnm̄ &
qui locuntur mala ad
uersus animam meam;
Et tu dn̄e dn̄e fac mecū
misericordiam propter
nomen tuum. quia su
auis est misericordia tua;
Liberame qm̄ egenus &
paup sum ego. & cor me
um conturbatum est
in me;
Sicut umbra cū declinat
ablatus sum. & excussus
sum sicut locusta;
Genua mea infirmata sunt
prę ieiunio. & caro mea
inmutata est pp oleum.

& ego fact sum obpbriū illis;
Uiderunt me & mouer capita
sua. adiuua me dn̄e ds̄ mš.
saluū me fac ppt misc̄dia tua;
Ut sciant quia man tua hęc ē.
& tu dn̄e fecisti ea;
Maledicent illi & tu benedices.
qui insurgunt in me con
fundant. seruus autē tuus
lętabitur;
Induantur qui detrahunt
mihi apud dnm̄ reueren
tia & opiantur sicut diplo
ide confusione sua;
Confitebor dn̄o nimis in ore
meo. & in medio multoꝝ lau
Qui adstitit adextris dabo eū;
paupis. ut saluā faceret ab p
sequentibus animā meā;

2.72 London, B.L., Harley 603, f. 56ᵛ

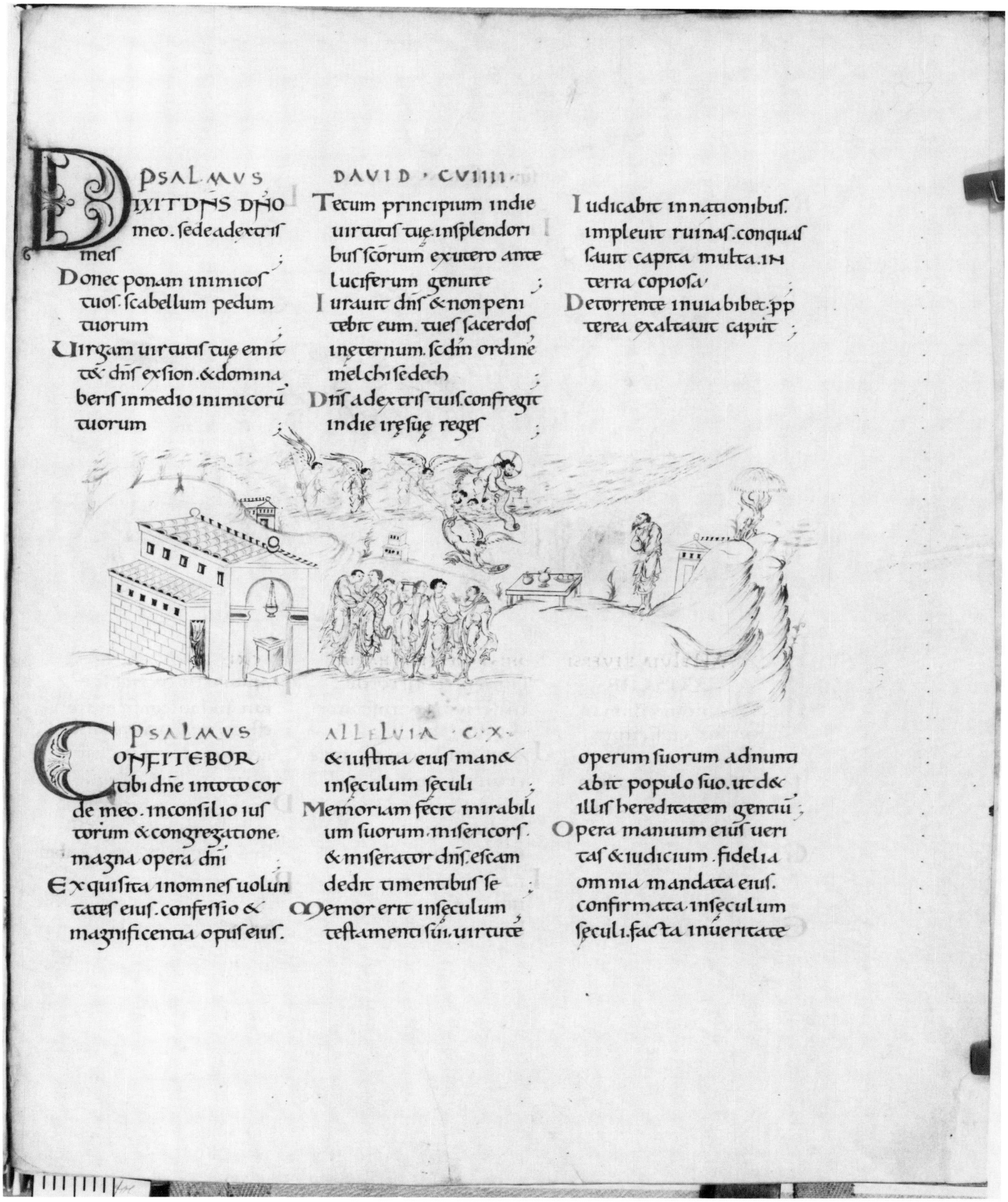

D PSALMUS DAVID · CVIIII ·

DIXIT DNS DNO meo. sede a dextris meis ;

Donec ponam inimicos tuos. scabellum pedum tuorum ;

Uirgam uirtutis tuę emittet dns ex sion. & dominaberis in medio inimicorū tuorum ;

Tecum principium in die uirtutis tuę. in splendoribus scorum ex utero ante luciferum genui te ;

Iurauit dns & non penitebit eum. tu es sacerdos in eternum. scdm ordinē melchisedech ;

Dns a dextris tuis. confregit in die irę suę reges ;

Iudicabit in nationibus. impleuit ruinas. conquassauit capita multa. in terra copiosa ;

De torrente in uia bibet. pp terea exaltauit caput ;

C PSALMUS ALLELUIA · C · X ·

CONFITEBOR tibi dne in toto corde meo. in consilio iustorum & congregatione. magna opera dni ;

Exquisita in omnes uoluntates eius. confessio & magnificentia opus eius. & iustitia eius manet in seculum seculi ;

Memoriam fecit mirabilium suorum. misericors & miserator dns. escam dedit timentibus se.

Memor erit in seculum testamenti sui. uirtutē operum suorum adnuntiabit populo suo. ut det illis hereditatem gentiū ;

Opera manuum eius ueritas & iudicium. fidelia omnia mandata eius. confirmata in seculum seculi. facta in ueritate

2.73 London, B.L., Harley 603, f. 57r

& equitate ;
Redemptionem misit po
pulo suo. mandauit in e
ternum. testamentum

suum. scm & terribile
nomen eius ;
Initium sapientie timor
dni. intellectus bonus

omnibus facientibus eu :
Laudatio eius manet in
seculum seculi ;

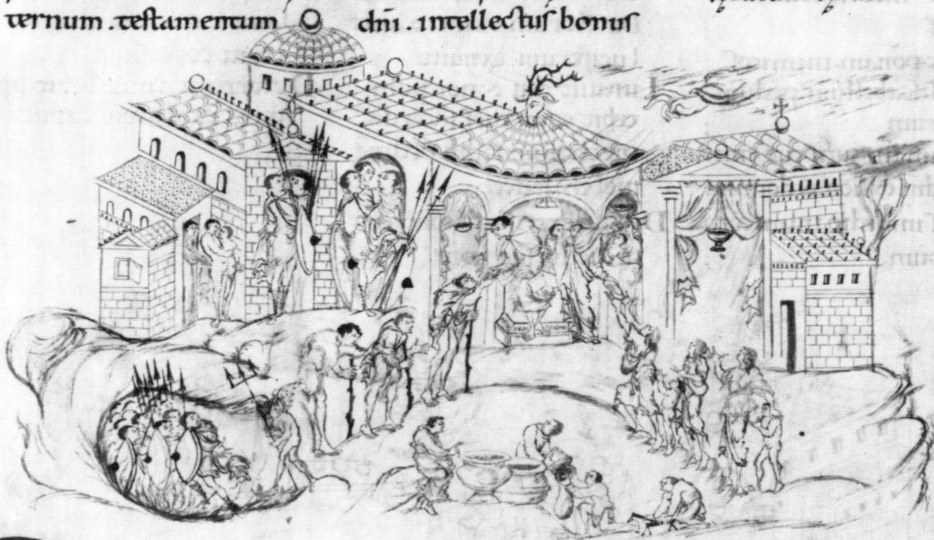

ALLELUIA REVERSIONIS AGGEI ET ZACHARIAE. CXI.

BEATUS UIR
qui timet dnm. in
mandatis eius cupit
nimis ;
Potens in terra erit sem
eius. generatio rectoru
bene dicetur
Gloria & diuitie in domo
eius. & iustitia eius ma
net in seculum seculi ;
Exortum est in tenebris

lumen rectis corde :
misericors & miserator
& iustus dns ;
Iocundus homo qui mise
retur & commodat dis
ponet sermones suos in
iudicio. quia in eternu
non commouebitur ;
In memoria eterna erit
iustus. ab auditione ma
la non timebit ;

Paratum est cor eius spe
rare in dno. confirmatu
est cor eius non commo
uebitur. donec uideat
inimicos suos ; in gla ;
Dispersit dedit pauperibus.
iustitia eius manet in sclm
seculi. cornu eius exaltabit
Peccator uidebit & irascet.
dentibus suis fremebit & ta
bescet. desideriu peccator p
ibit ;

2.74 London, B.L., Harley 603, f. 57v

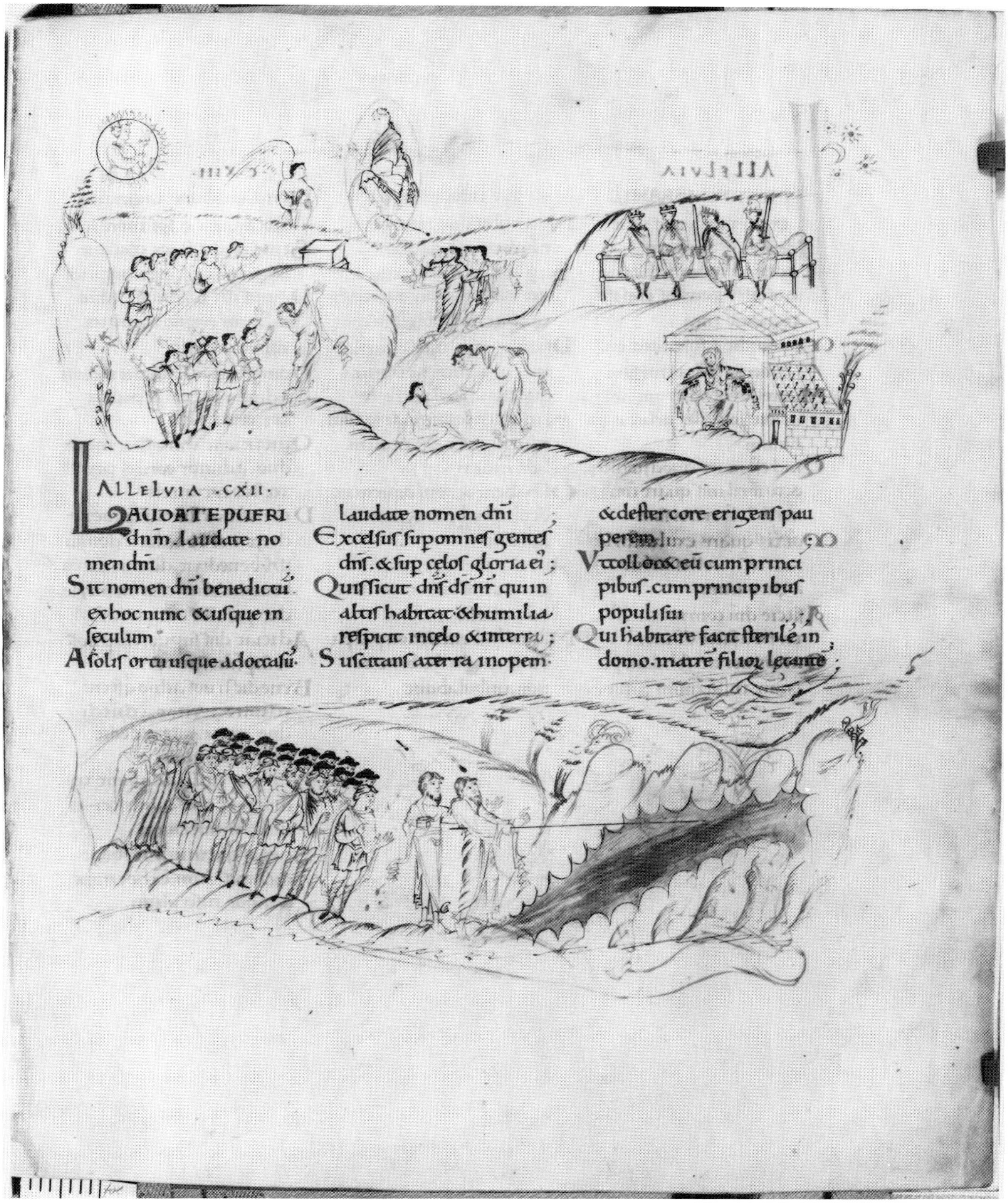
ALLELVIA ·CXII·
LAUDATE PUERI dnm laudate nomen dni
Sit nomen dni benedictu ex hoc nunc & usque in seculum
A solis ortu usque ad occasu laudate nomen dni
Excelsus sup omnes gentes dns. & sup celos gloria ei;
Quis sicut dns ds nr qui in altis habitat & humilia respicit in celo & in terra;
Suscitans a terra inopem & de stercore erigens pauperem;
Ut colloc& eu cum principibus. cum principibus populi sui
Qui habitare facit sterile in domo. matre filioz letante;

2.75 London, B.L., Harley 603, f. 58r

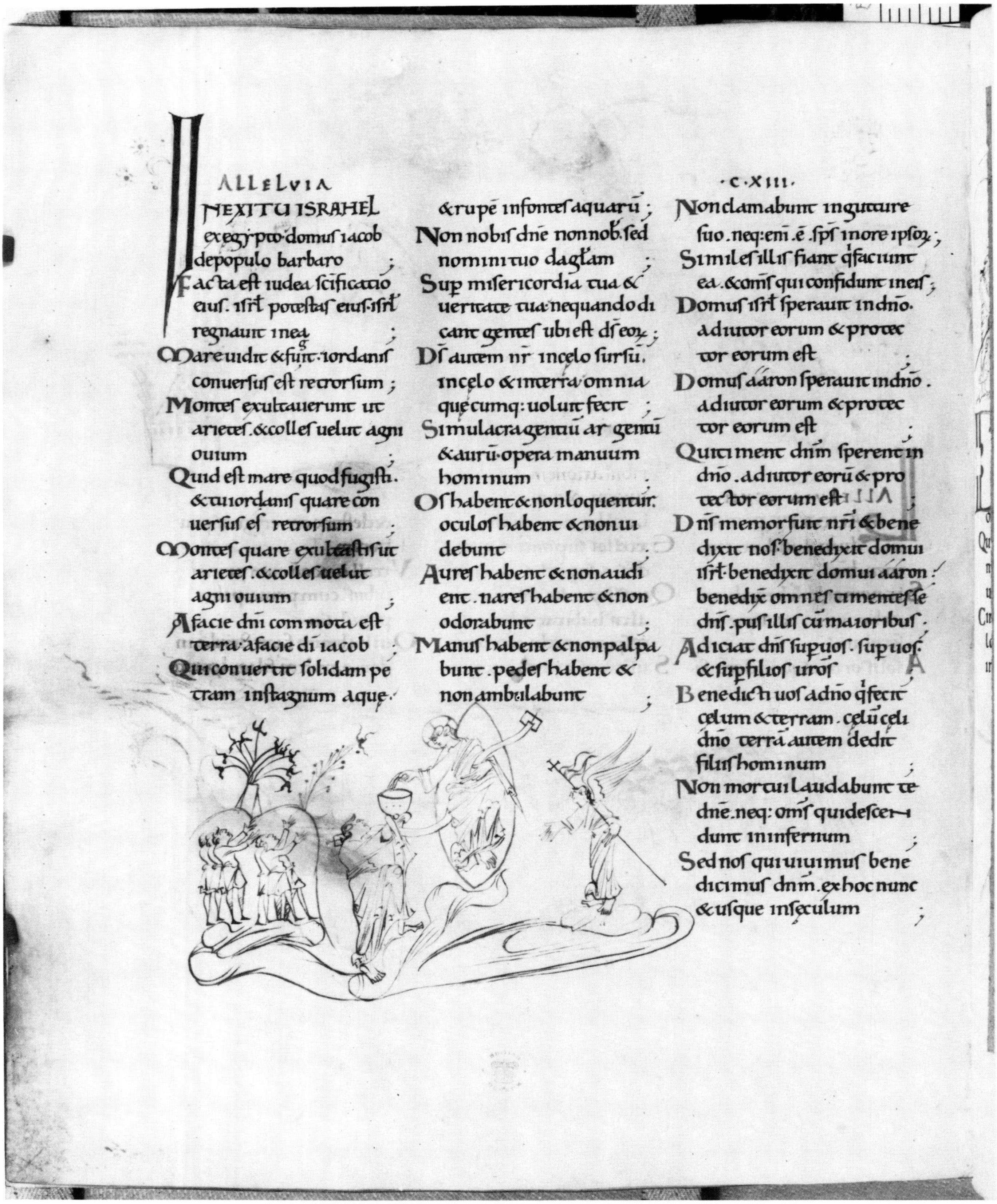

ALLELUIA
IN EXITU ISRAHEL
ex egypto domus iacob
de populo barbaro ;
Facta est iudea scificatio
eius. isrl potestas eius. isrl
regnauit in ea ;
Mare uidit & fugit. iordanis
conuersus est retrorsum ;
Montes exultauerunt ut
arietes. & colles uelut agni
ouium ;
Quid est mare quod fugisti.
& tu iordanis quare con
uersus es retrorsum ;
Montes quare exultastis ut
arietes. & colles uelut
agni ouium ;
A facie dni commota est
terra a facie di iacob ;
Qui conuertit solidam pe
tram in stagnum aque.
& rupē in fontes aquarū ;
Non nobis dne non nob. sed
nomini tuo da glam ;
Sup misericordia tua &
ueritate tua nequando di
cant gentes ubi est ds eoz ;
Ds autem nr in celo sursū.
in celo & in terra omnia
quecumq: uoluit fecit ;
Simulacra gentiū argentū
& aurū. opera manuum
hominum ;
Os habent & non loquentur.
oculos habent & non ui
debunt ;
Aures habent & non audi
ent. nares habent & non
odorabunt ;
Manus habent & non palpa
bunt. pedes habent &
non ambulabunt ;
.C.XIII.
Non clamabunt in gutture
suo. neq: enī ē sps in ore ipsoz ;
Similes illis fiant qui faciunt
ea. & omns qui confidunt in eis ;
Domus isrl sperauit in dno.
adiutor eorum & protec
tor eorum est ;
Domus aaron sperauit in dno.
adiutor eorum & protec
tor eorum est ;
Qui timent dnm sperent in
dno. adiutor eorū & pro
tector eorum est ;
Dns memor fuit nri & bene
dixit nos. benedixit domui
isrl. benedixit domui aaron.
benedix omnes timentes se
dns. pusillis cū maioribus.
Adiciat dns sup uos. sup uos
& sup filios uros ;
Benedicti uos a dno q fecit
celum & terram. celū celi
dno terra autem dedit
filiis hominum ;
Non mortui laudabunt te
dne. neq: omns qui descen
dunt in infernum ;
Sed nos qui uiuimus bene
dicimus dnm. ex hoc nunc
& usque in seculum ;

2.76 London, B.L., Harley 603, f. 58v

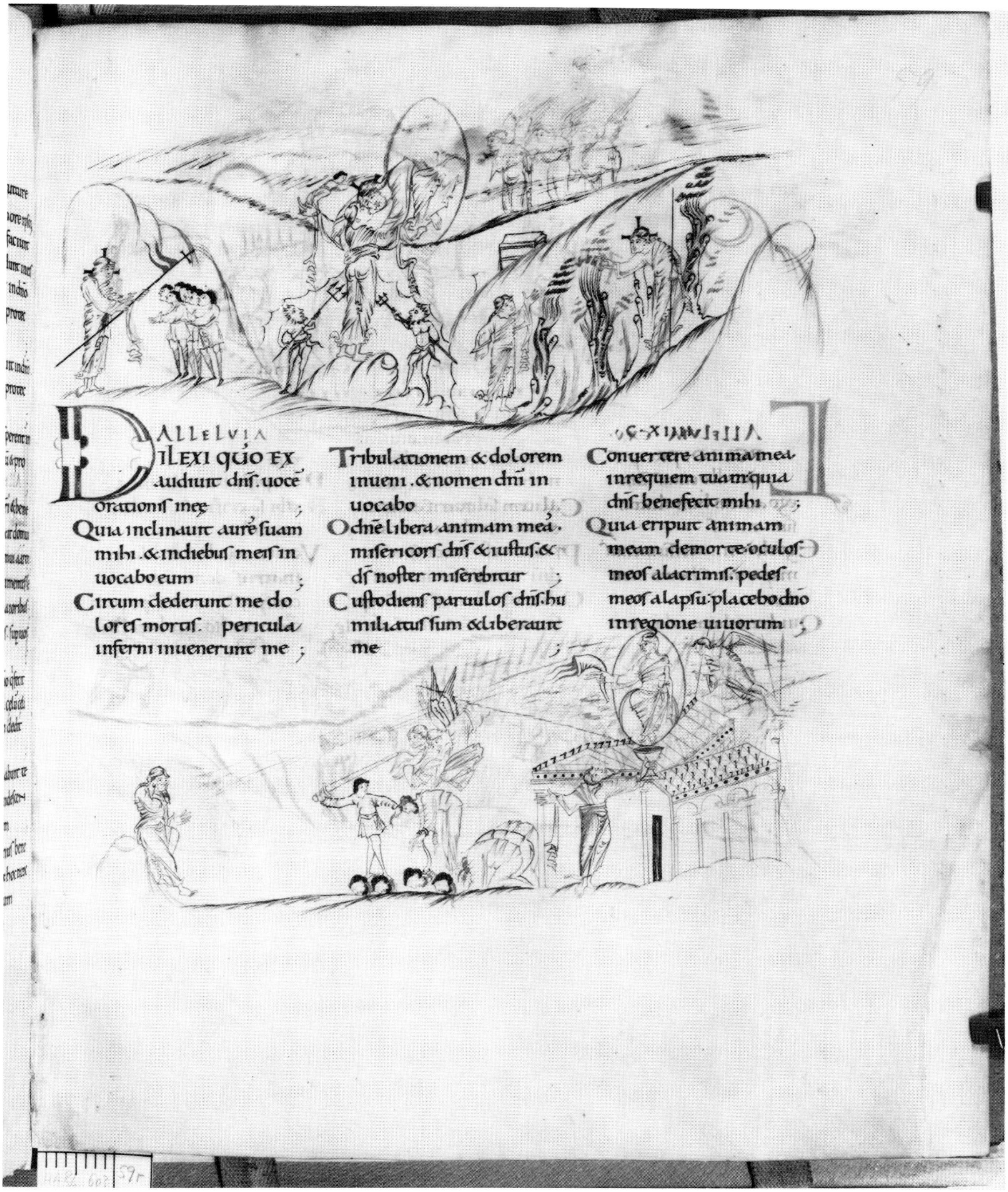

2.77 London, B.L., Harley 603, f. 59r

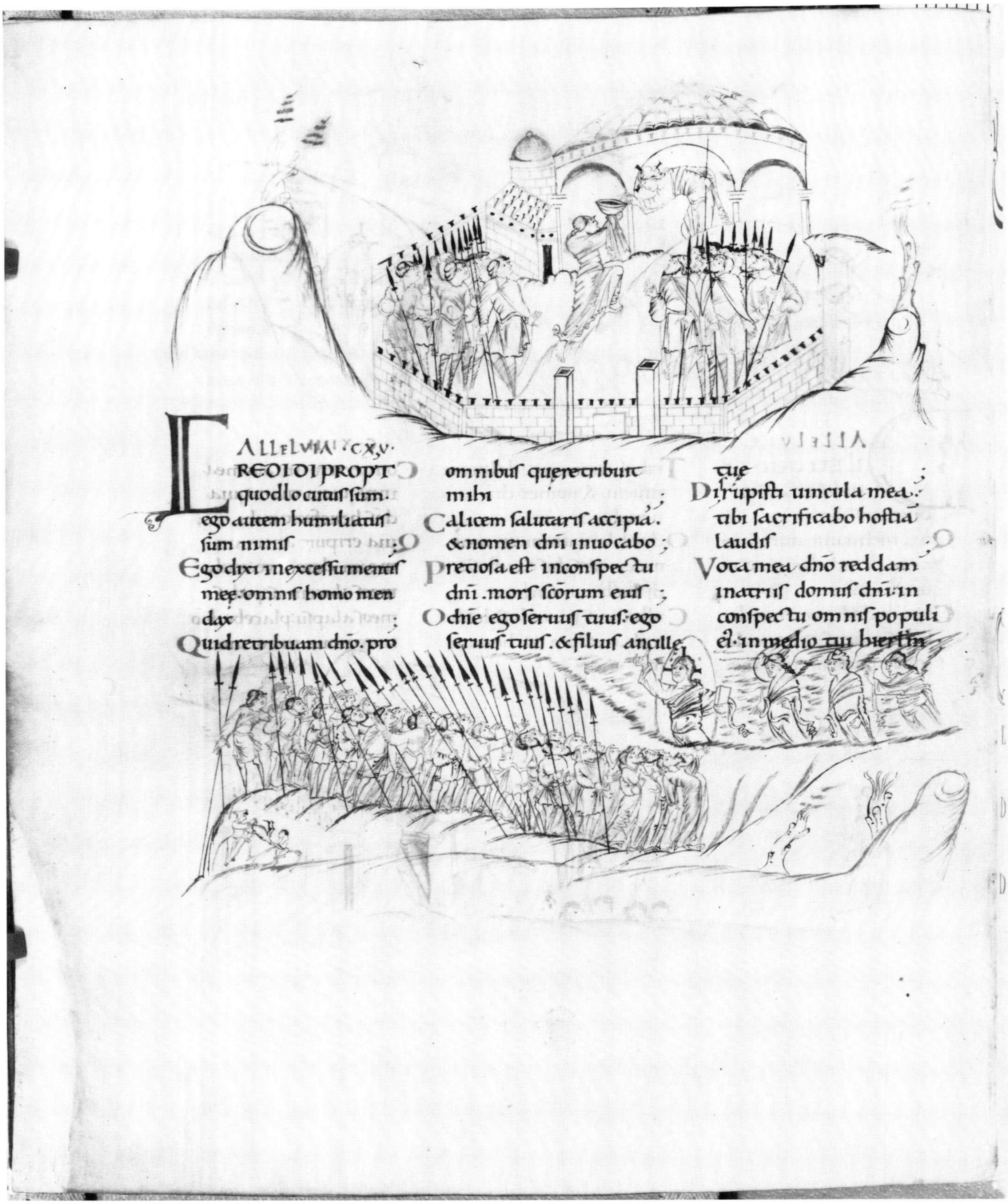

2.78 London, B.L., Harley 603, f. 59v

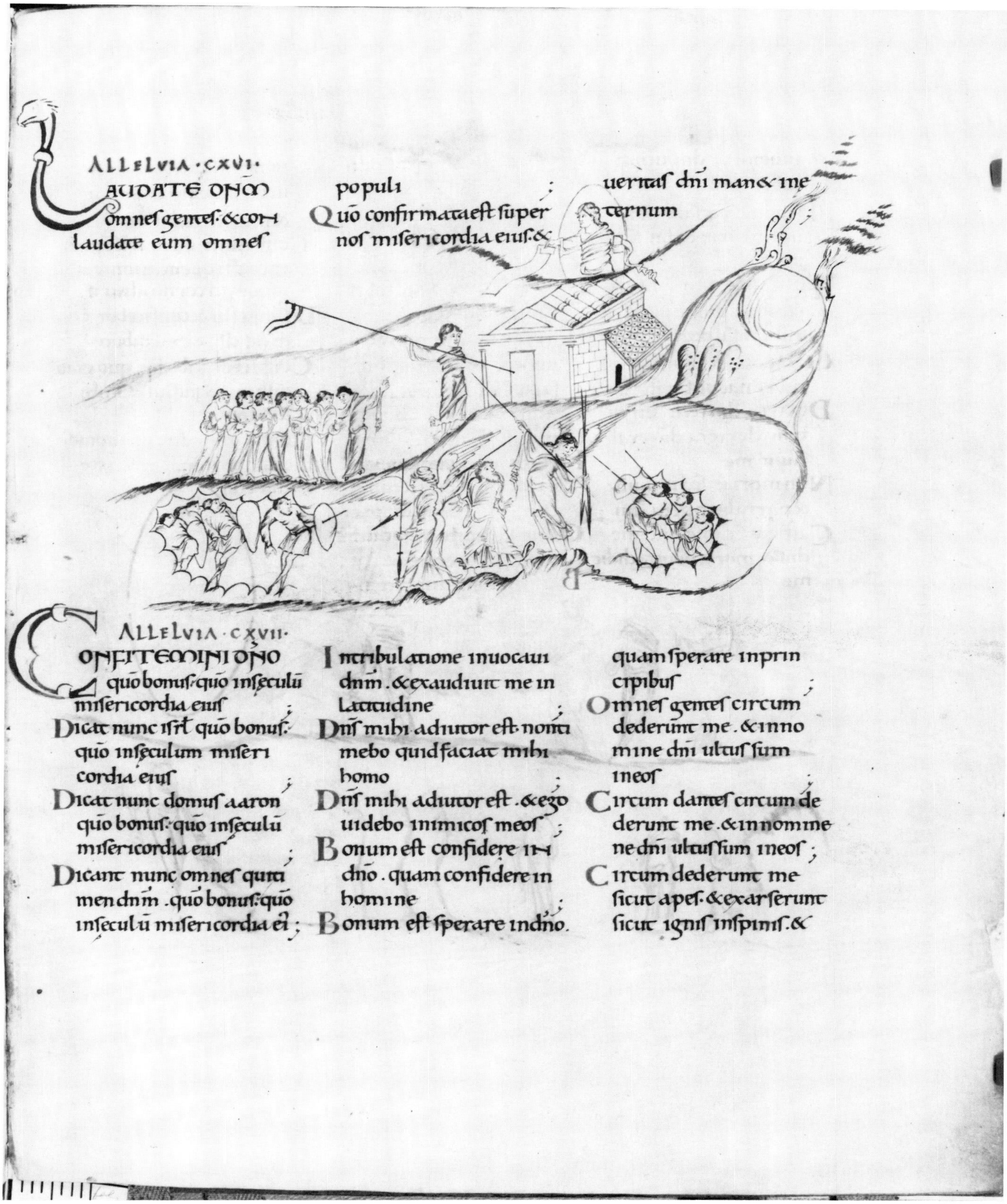

ALLELUIA · CXVI ·
LAUDATE DNM
omnes gentes & con
laudate eum omnes
populi ;
Quo confirmata est super
nos misericordia eius &
ueritas dni manet in e
ternum

ALLELUIA · CXVII ·
CONFITEMINI DNO
quo bonus quo inseculū
misericordia eius ;
Dicat nunc isrl quo bonus
quo inseculum miseri
cordia eius ;
Dicat nunc domus aaron
quo bonus quo inseculū
misericordia eius ;
Dicant nunc omnes qui ti
ment dnm . quo bonus quo
inseculū misericordia ei ;
In tribulatione inuocaui
dnm . & exaudiuit me in
latitudine ;
Dns mihi adiutor est non ti
mebo quid faciat mihi
homo ;
Dns mihi adiutor est . & ego
uidebo inimicos meos ;
Bonum est confidere in
dno . quam confidere in
homine ;
Bonum est sperare in dno .
quam sperare in prin
cipibus ;
Omnes gentes circum
dederunt me . & in no
mine dni ultus sum
in eos ;
Circum dantes circum de
derunt me . & in nomine
ne dni ultus sum in eos ;
Circum dederunt me
sicut apes . & exarserunt
sicut ignis in spinis . &

2.79 London, B.L., Harley 603, f. 60r

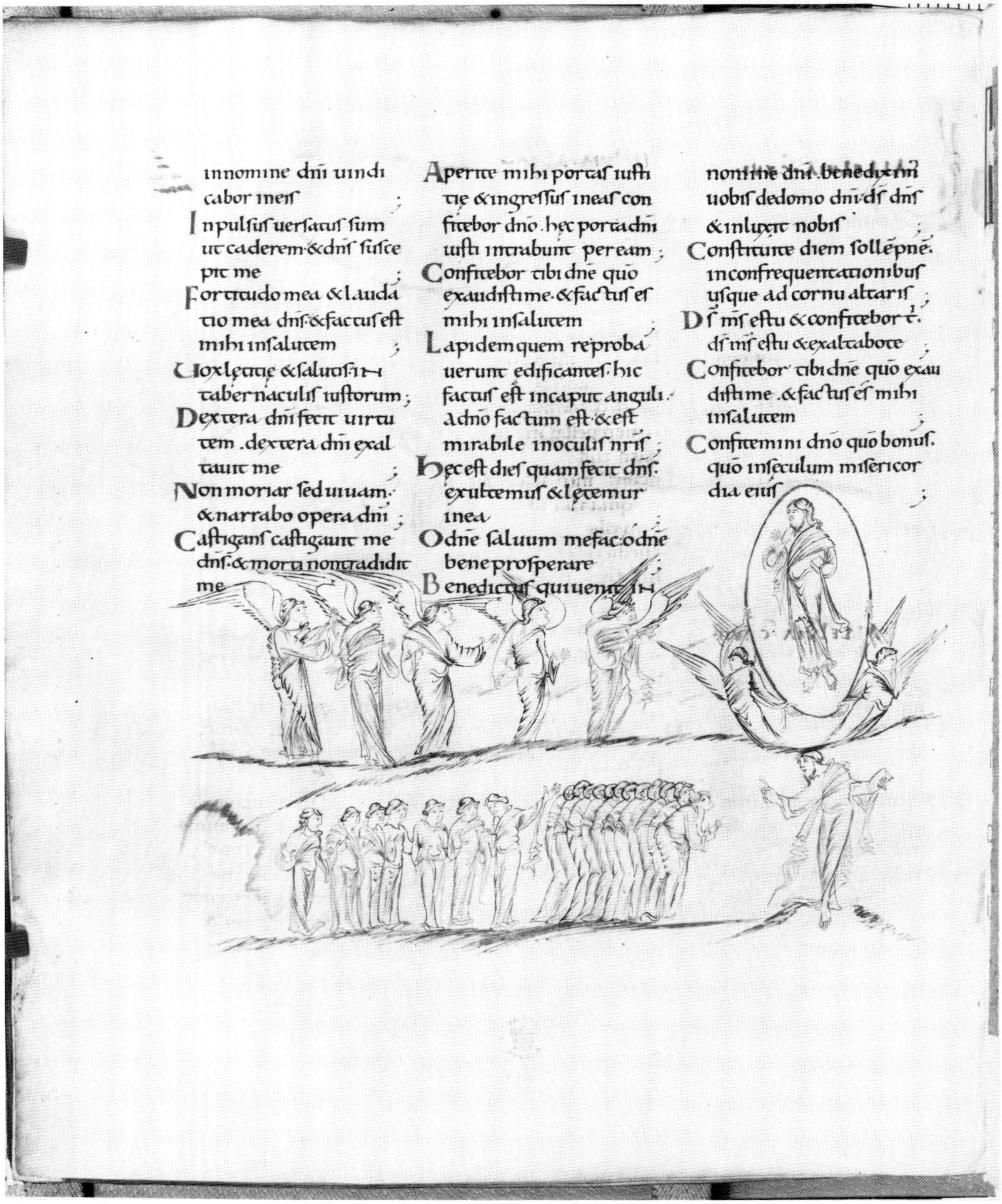

innomine dni uindi
cabor ineos ;
Inpulsus uersatus sum
ut caderem & dns susce
pit me ;
Fortitudo mea & lauda
tio mea dns & factus est
mihi insalutem ;
Uox letitie & salutis in
tabernaculis iustorum ;
Dextera dni fecit uirtu
tem . dextera dni exal
tauit me ;
Non moriar sed uiuam
& narrabo opera dni ;
Castigans castigauit me
dns & morti non tradidit
me

Aperite mihi portas iusti
tie & ingressus in eas con
fitebor dno . hec porta dni
iusti intrabunt per eam ;
Confitebor tibi dne quo
exaudisti me . & factus es
mihi insalutem ;
Lapidem quem reproba
uerunt edificantes hic
factus est incaput anguli .
a dno factum est & est
mirabile inoculis nris ;
Hec est dies quam fecit dns
exultemus & letemur
in ea ;
O dne saluum me fac o dne
bene prosperare ;
Benedictus qui uenit in

nomine dni . benediximus
uobis de domo dni . ds dns
& inluxit nobis ;
Constituite diem sollempne
in confrequentationibus
usque ad cornu altaris ;
Ds ms es tu & confitebor tibi .
ds ms es tu & exaltabo te ;
Confitebor tibi dne quo exau
disti me . & factus es mihi
insalutem
Confitemini dno quo bonus .
quo inseculum misericor
dia eius ;

2.80 London, B.L., Harley 603, f. 60v

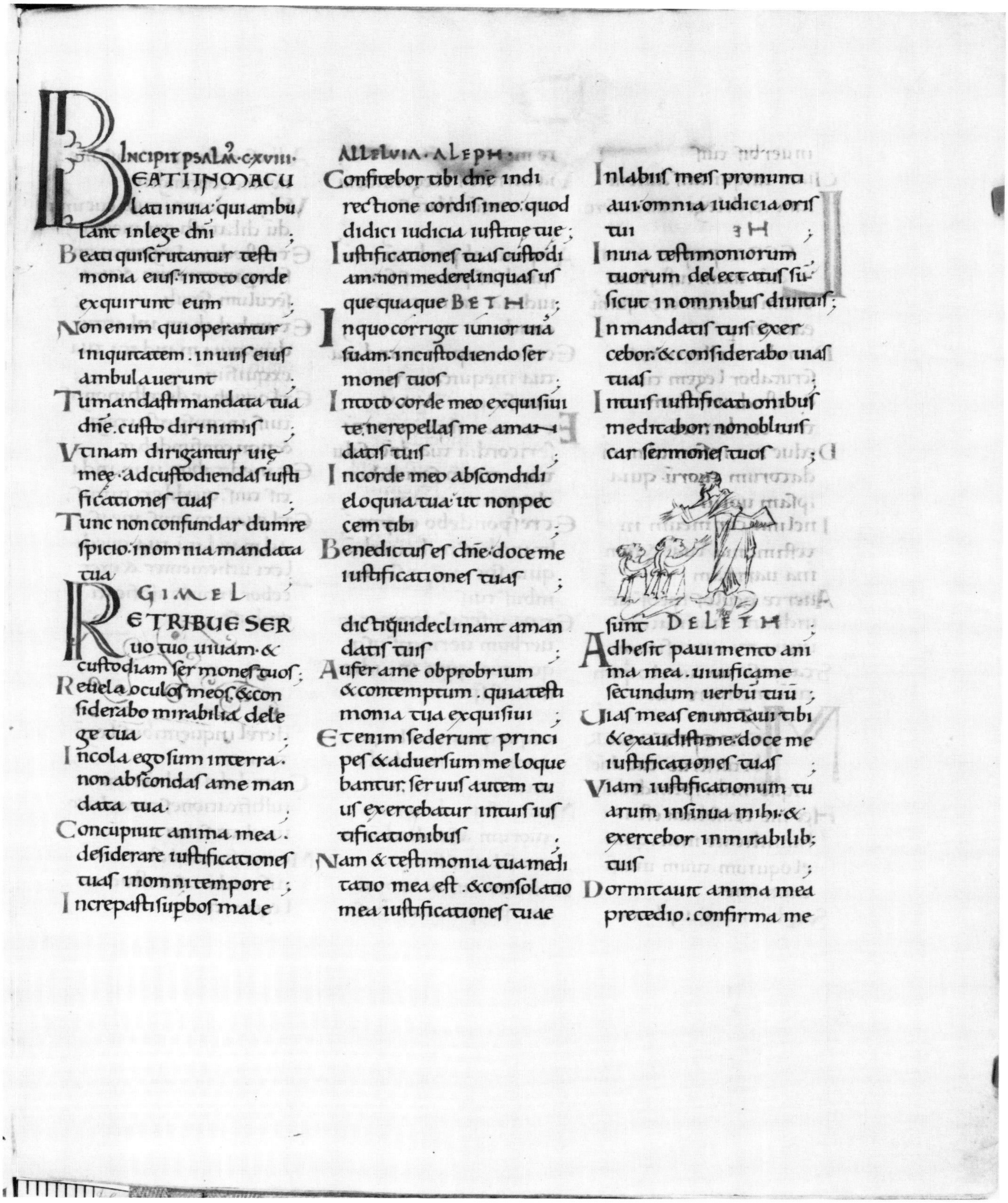

INCIPIT PSALM̄. CXVIII.
BEATI INMACU
LATI IN UIA. QUI AMBU
LANT IN LEGE DNI
Beati qui scrutantur testi
monia eius. in toto corde
exquirunt eum
Non enim qui operantur
iniquitatem. in uiis eius
ambulauerunt
Tu mandasti mandata tua
dne. custodiri nimis
Utinam dirigantur uię
meę ad custodiendas iusti
ficationes tuas
Tunc non confundar dum re
spicio in omnia mandata
tua
GIMEL
RETRIBUE SER
UO TUO. UIUAM. &
custodiam sermones tuos
Reuela oculos meos. & con
siderabo mirabilia de le
ge tua
Incola ego sum in terra.
non abscondas a me man
data tua
Concupiuit anima mea.
desiderare iustificationes
tuas in omni tempore
Increpasti superbos male

ALLELUIA. ALEPH.
Confitebor tibi dne in di
rectione cordis mei. quod
didici iudicia iustitię tuę
Iustificationes tuas custodi
am. non me derelinquas us
que quaque BETH
In quo corrigit iunior uia
suam. in custodiendo ser
mones tuos
In toto corde meo exquisiui
te. ne repellas me a man
datis tuis
In corde meo abscondidi
eloquia tua. ut non pec
cem tibi
Benedictus es dne. doce me
iustificationes tuas
dicti qui declinant a man
datis tuis
Aufer a me obprobrium
& contemptum. quia testi
monia tua exquisiui
Etenim sederunt princi
pes & aduersum me loque
bantur. seruus autem tu
us exercebatur in iustis ius
tificationibus
Nam & testimonia tua medi
tatio mea est. & consolatio
mea iustificationes tuae

In labiis meis pronunti
aui omnia iudicia oris
tui ZH
In uia testimoniorum
tuorum delectatus su
sicut in omnibus diuitiis
In mandatis tuis exer
cebor. & considerabo uias
tuas
In tuis iustificationibus
meditabor. non obliuis
car sermones tuos
sunt DELETH
Adhesit pauimento ani
ma mea. uiuifica me
secundum uerbū tuū
Uias meas enuntiaui tibi
& exaudisti me. doce me
iustificationes tuas
Viam iustificationum tu
arum insinua mihi. &
exercebor in mirabilib;
tuis
Dormitauit anima mea
pretedio. confirma me

2.81 London, B.L., Harley 603, f. 61r

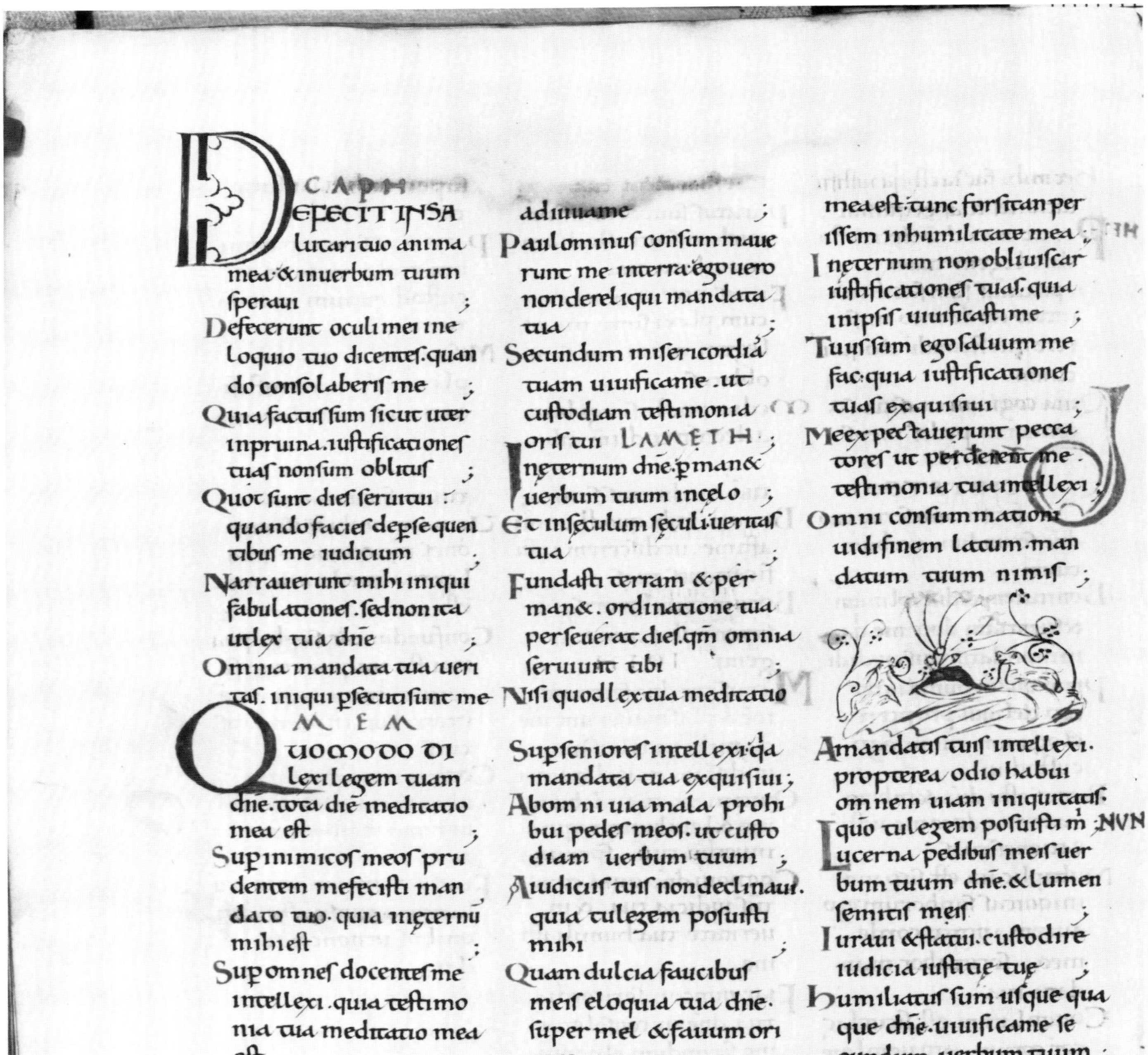

CAPH
DEFECIT IN SA
lutari tuo anima
mea & in uerbum tuum
speraui ;
Defecerunt oculi mei in e
loquio tuo dicentes. quan
do consolaberis me ;
Quia factus sum sicut uter
in pruina. iustificationes
tuas non sum oblitus ;
Quot sunt dies serui tui :
quando facies de persequen
tibus me iudicium
Narrauerunt mihi iniqui
fabulationes. sed non ita
ut lex tua dne ;
Omnia mandata tua ueri
tas. iniqui psecuti sunt me
adiuua me ;
Paulominus consummaue
runt me in terra. ego uero
non dereliqui mandata
tua ;
Secundum misericordiā
tuam uiuifica me. ut
custodiam testimonia
oris tui ; LAMETH
In aeternum dne. p manet
uerbum tuum in celo ;
Et in seculum seculi ueritas
tua
Fundasti terram & per
manet. ordinatione tua
perseuerat dies. qm omnia
seruiunt tibi
Nisi quod lex tua meditatio
mea est. tunc forsitan per
issem in humilitate mea ;
In aeternum non obliuiscar
iustificationes tuas. quia
in ipsis uiuificasti me ;
Tuus sum ego saluum me
fac. quia iustificationes
tuas exquisiui ;
Me exspectauerunt pecca
tores ut perderent me.
testimonia tua intellexi ;
Omni consummationi
uidi finem latum. man
datum tuum nimis ;
MEM
QUOMODO DI
lexi legem tuam
dne. tota die meditatio
mea est ;
Sup inimicos meos pru
dentem me fecisti man
dato tuo. quia in aeternu
mihi est ;
Sup omnes docentes me
intellexi. quia testimo
nia tua meditatio mea
est ;
Sup seniores intellexi. qa
mandata tua exquisiui ;
Ab omni uia mala prohi
bui pedes meos. ut custo
diam uerbum tuum ;
A iudiciis tuis non declinaui.
quia tu legem posuisti
mihi
Quam dulcia faucibus
meis eloquia tua dne.
super mel & fauum ori
meo ;
A mandatis tuis intellexi.
propterea odio habui
omnem uiam iniquitatis.
quo tu legem posuisti m̄ ; NUN
Lucerna pedibus meis uer
bum tuum dne. & lumen
semitis meis
Iuraui & statui. custodire
iudicia iustitiae tuae ;
Humiliatus sum usque qua
que dne. uiuifica me se
cundum uerbum tuum ;

2.82 London, B.L., Harley 603, f. 62v

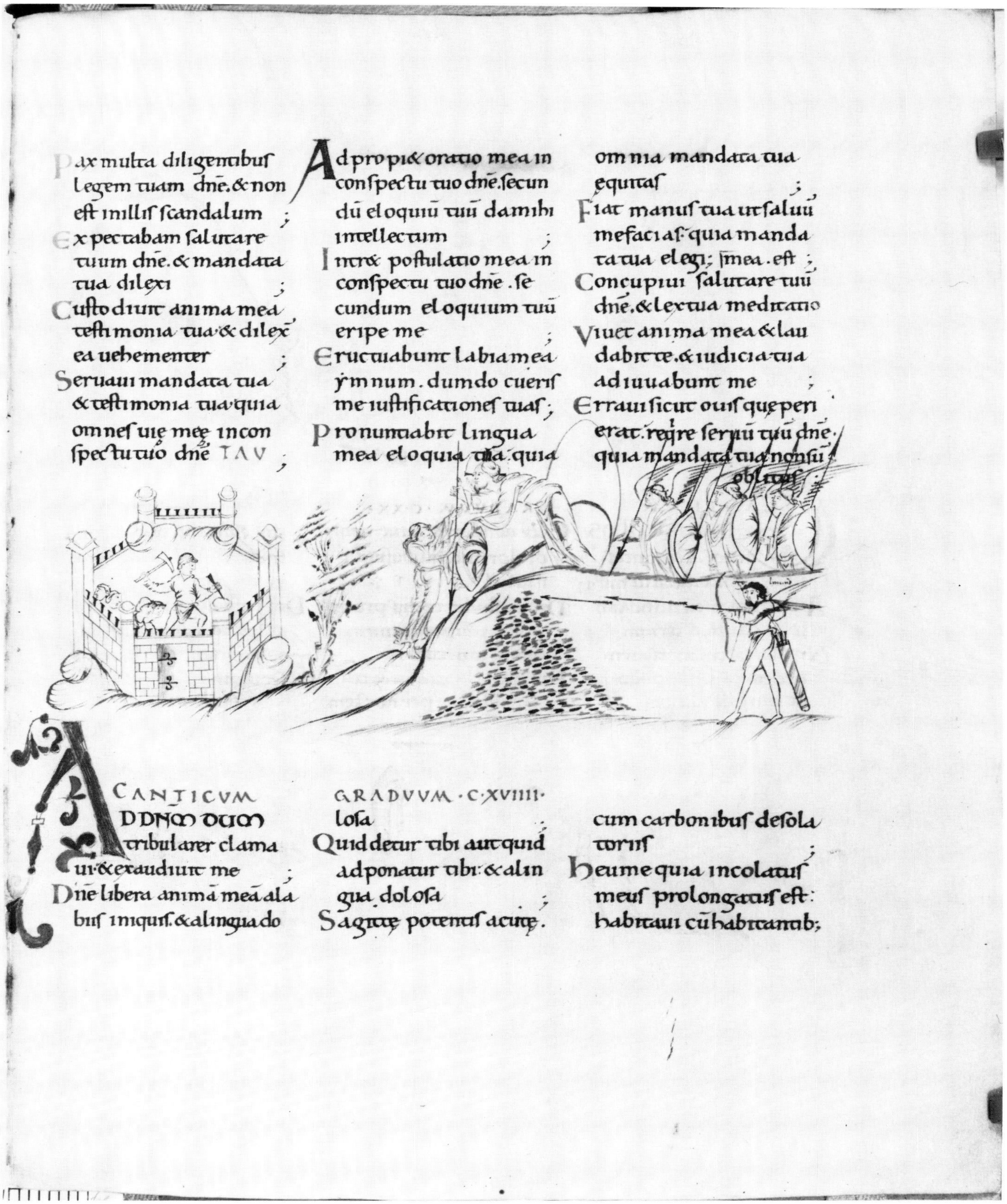

2.83 London, B.L., Harley 603, f. 64r

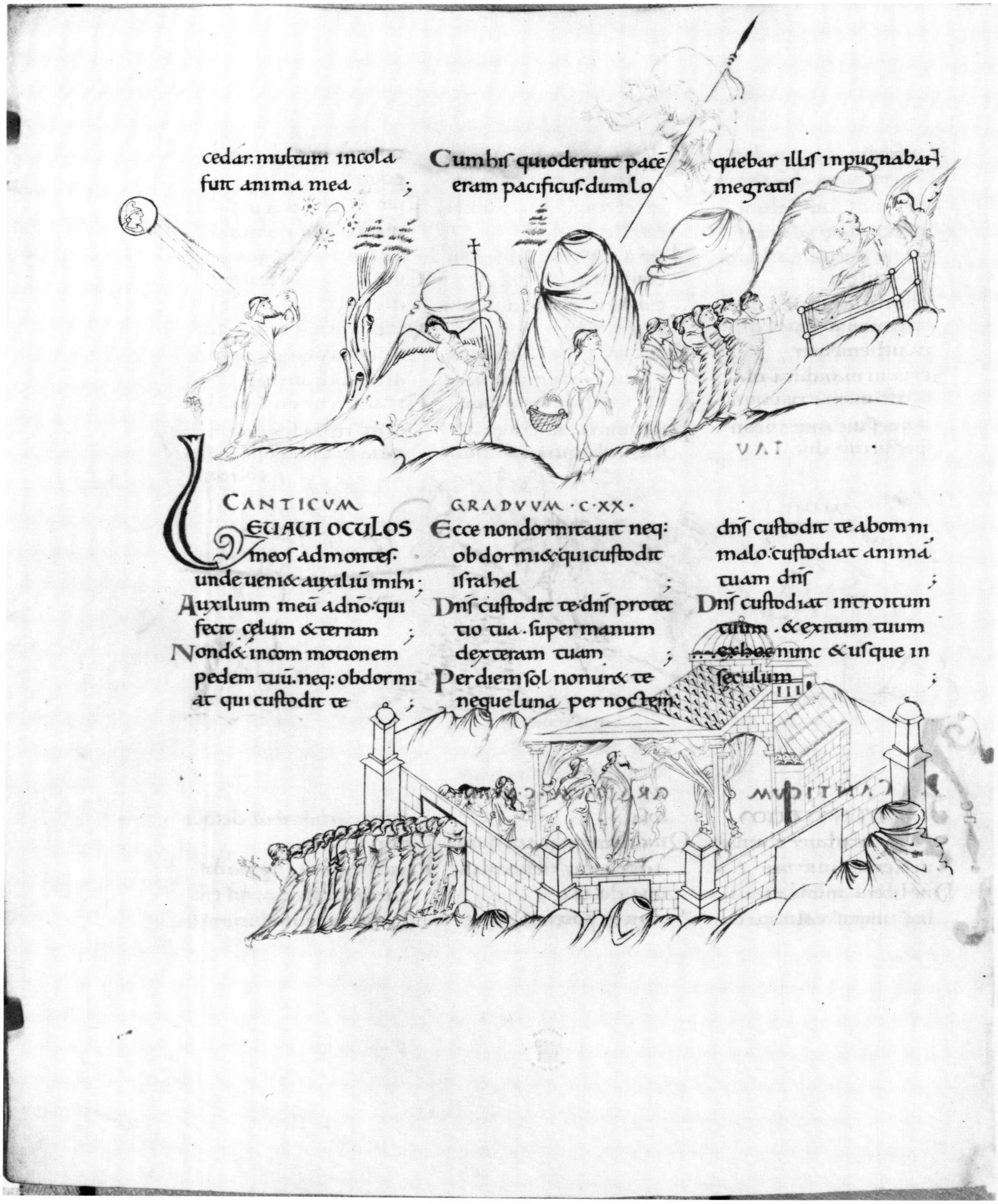

2.84 London, B.L., Harley 603, f. 64ᵛ

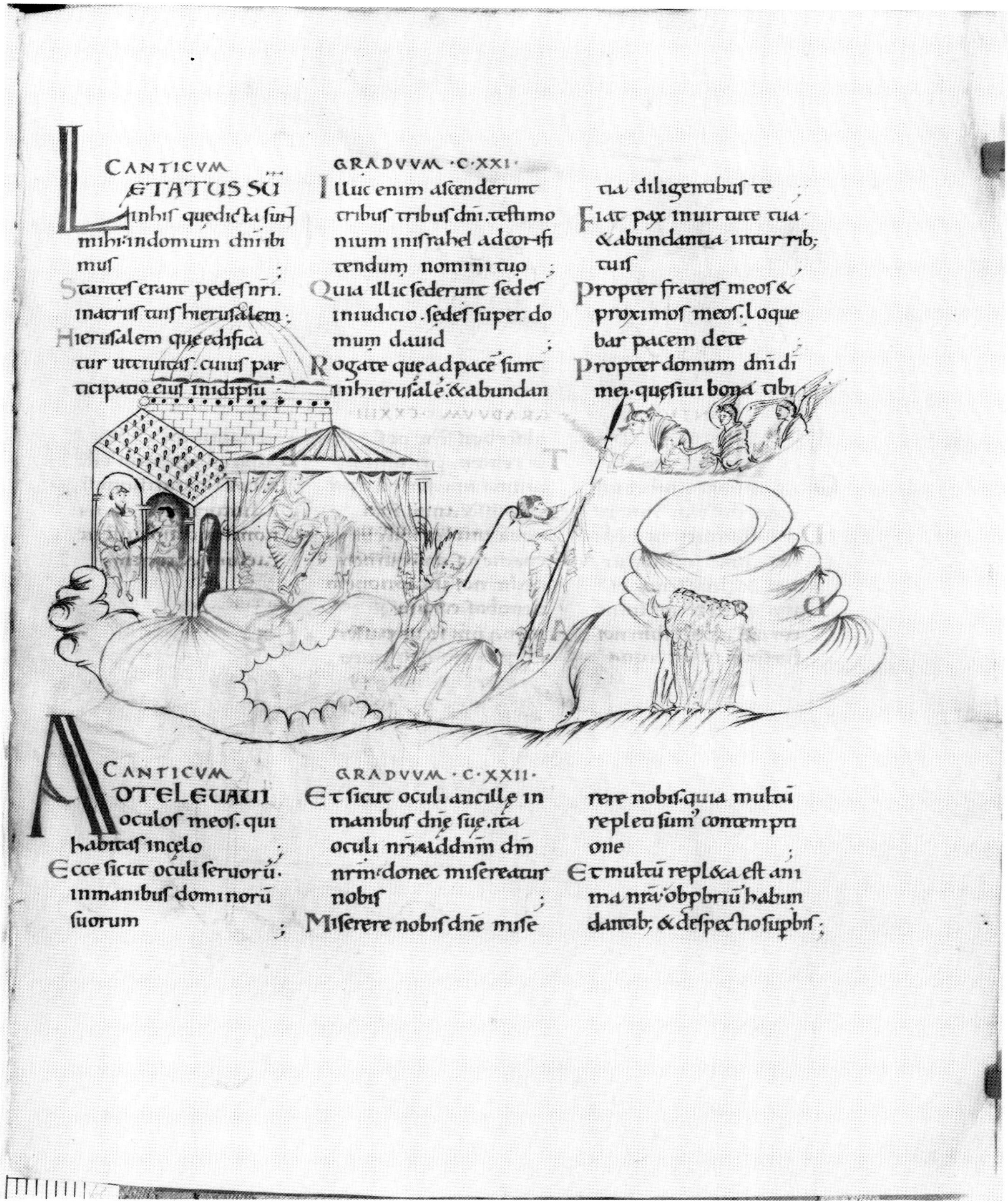

2.85 London, B.L., Harley 603, f. 65r

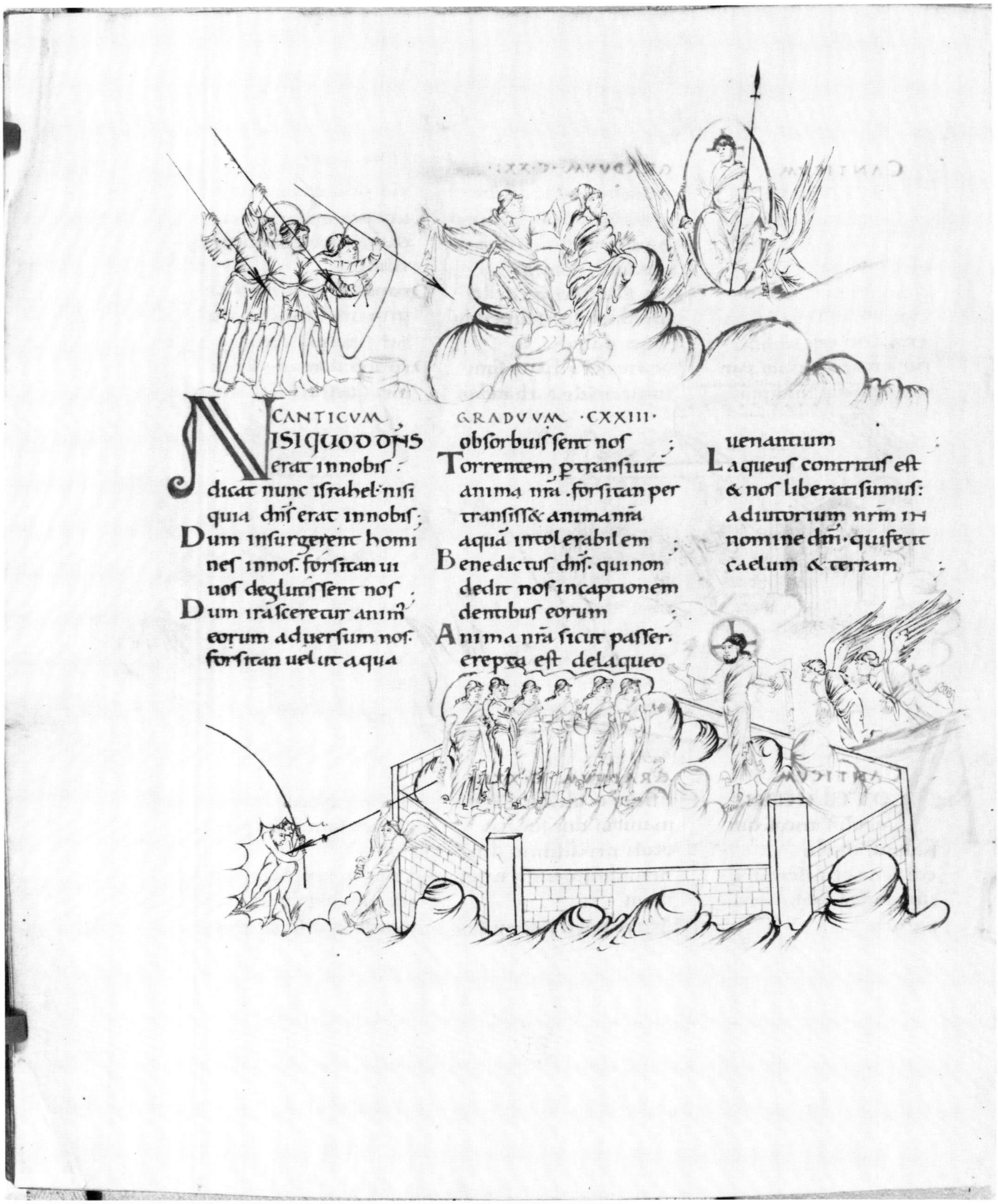

N CANTICUM GRADUUM ·CXXIII·
NISI QUOD DNS
erat in nobis:
dicat nunc israhel· nisi
quia dns erat in nobis;
Dum insurgerent homi
nes in nos. forsitan ui
uos deglutissent nos
Dum irasceretur anim
eorum aduersum nos.
forsitan uel ut aqua
obsorbuissent nos;
Torrentem ptransiuit
anima nra. forsitan per
transisset anima nra
aqua intolerabilem;
Benedictus dns. qui non
dedit nos in captionem
dentibus eorum;
Anima nra sicut passer.
erepta est de laqueo
uenantium;
Laqueus contritus est
& nos liberati sumus:
adiutorium nrm in
nomine dni· qui fecit
caelum & terram;

2.86 London, B.L., Harley 603, f. 65v

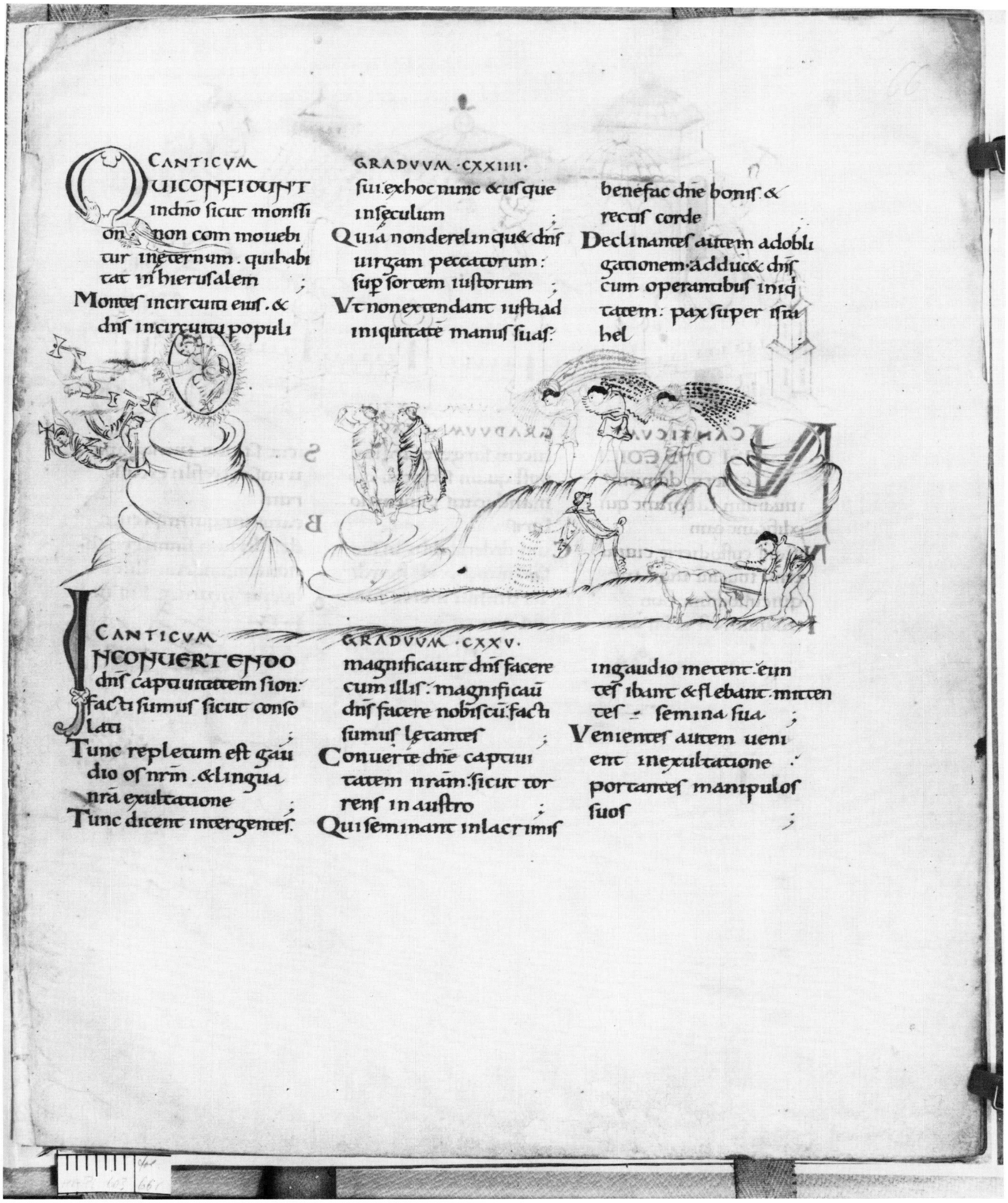

CANTICUM GRADUUM ·CXXIIII·

QUICONFIDUNT indno sicut monsti
on non com mouebi
tur ineternum . quihabi
tat in hierusalem ;
Montes incircuitu eius . &
dns incircuitu populi
sui : exhoc nunc & usque
inseculum ;
Quia nonderelinquet dns
uirgam peccatorum :
sup sortem iustorum ;
Ut nonextendant iusti ad
iniquitate manus suas :
benefac dne bonis &
rectis corde ;
Declinantes autem adobli
gationem adducet dns
cum operantibus iniq
tatem : pax super isra
hel

CANTICUM GRADUUM ·CXXV·

INCONUERTENDO
dns captiuitatem sion :
facti sumus sicut conso
lati ;
Tunc repletum est gau
dio os nrm . & lingua
nra exultatione ;
Tunc dicent intergentes :
magnificauit dns facere
cum illis : magnificauit
dns facere nobiscu : facti
sumus letantes ;
Conuerte dne captiui
tatem nram : sicut tor
rens in austro ;
Qui seminant inlacrimis
ingaudio metent : eun
tes ibant & flebant mitten
tes semina sua ;
Uenientes autem ueni
ent inexultatione ;
portantes manipulos
suos ;

2.87 London, B.L., Harley 603, f. 66r

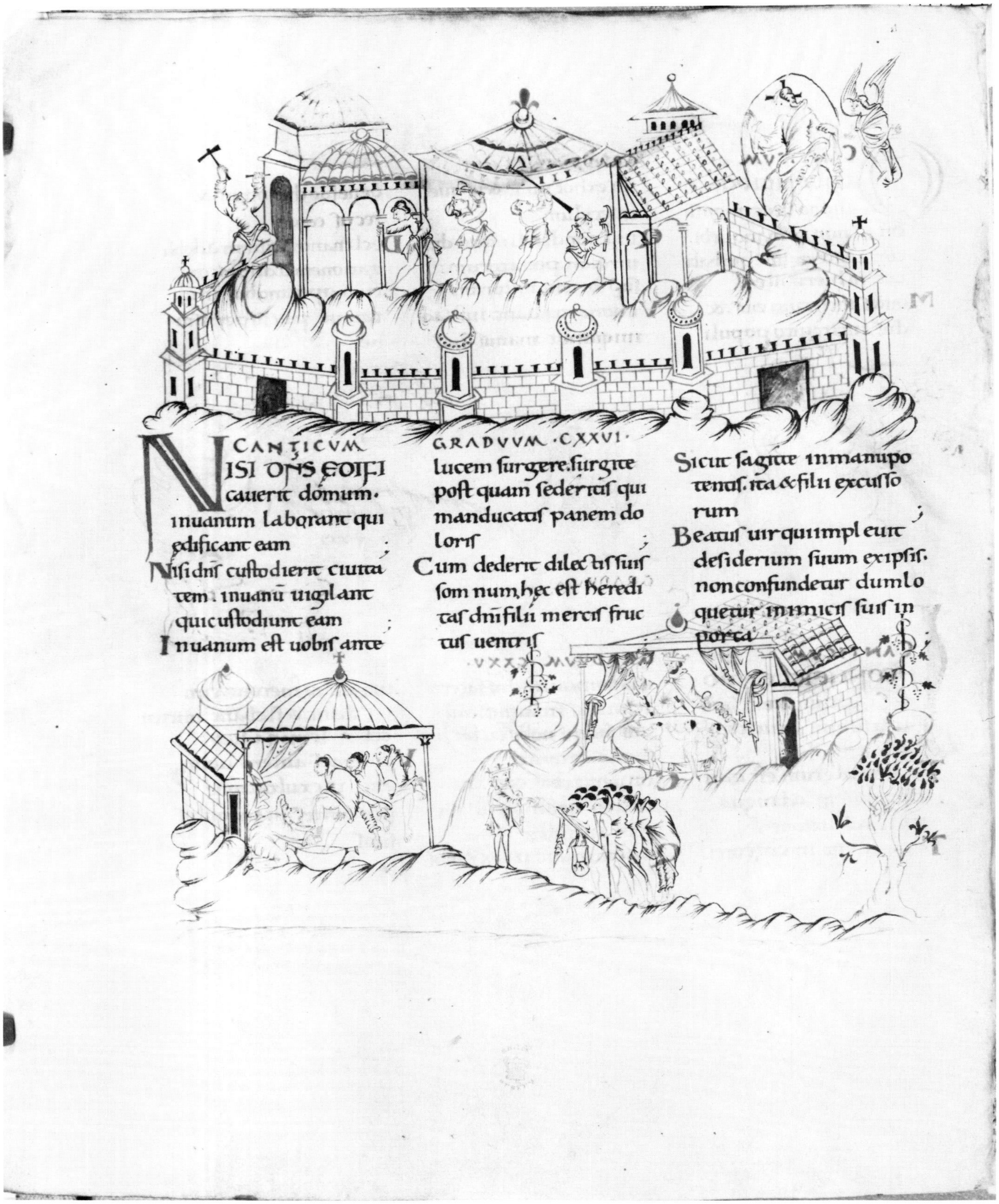

2.88 London, B.L., Harley 603, f. 66v

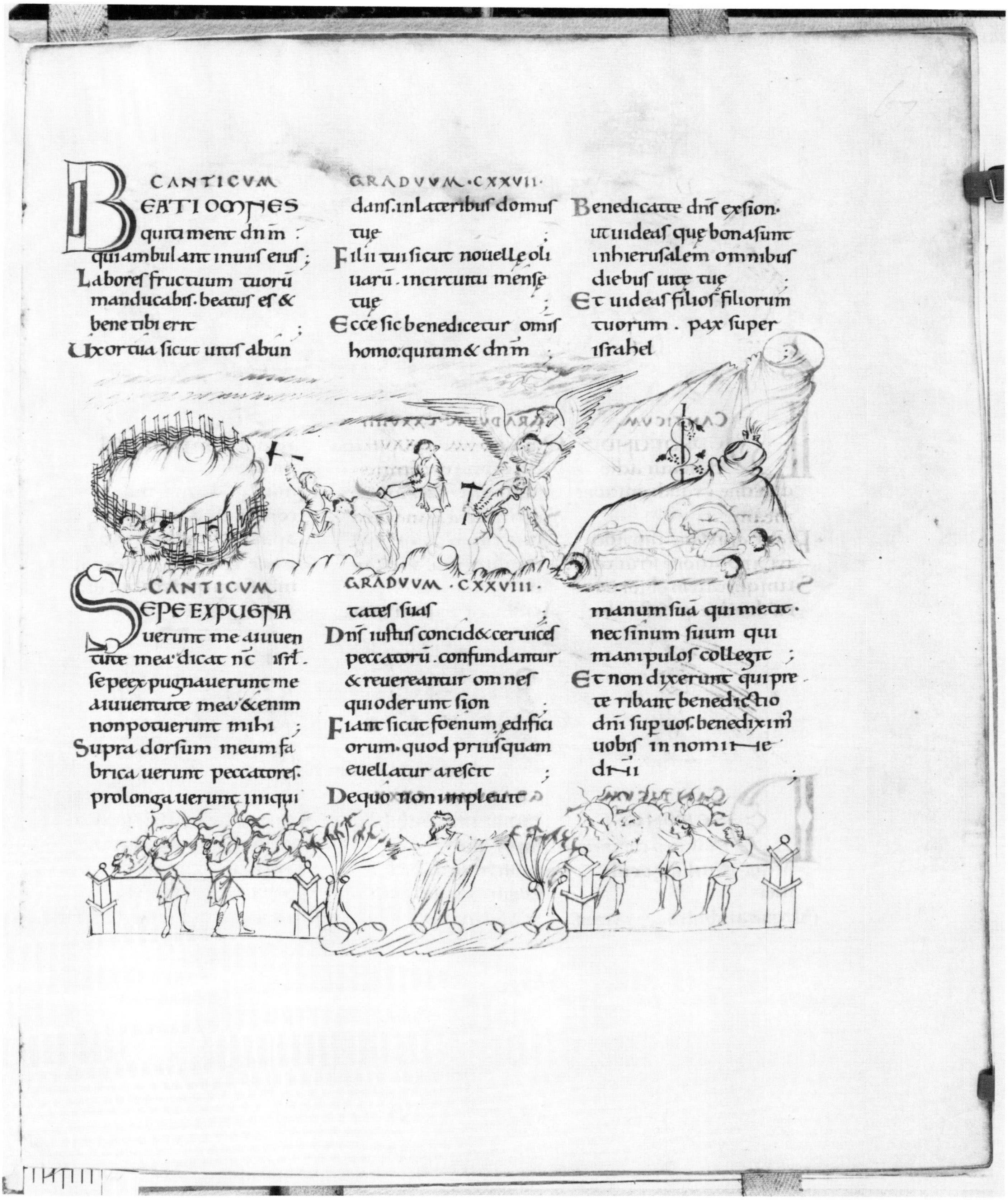

2.89 London, B.L., Harley 603, f. 67r

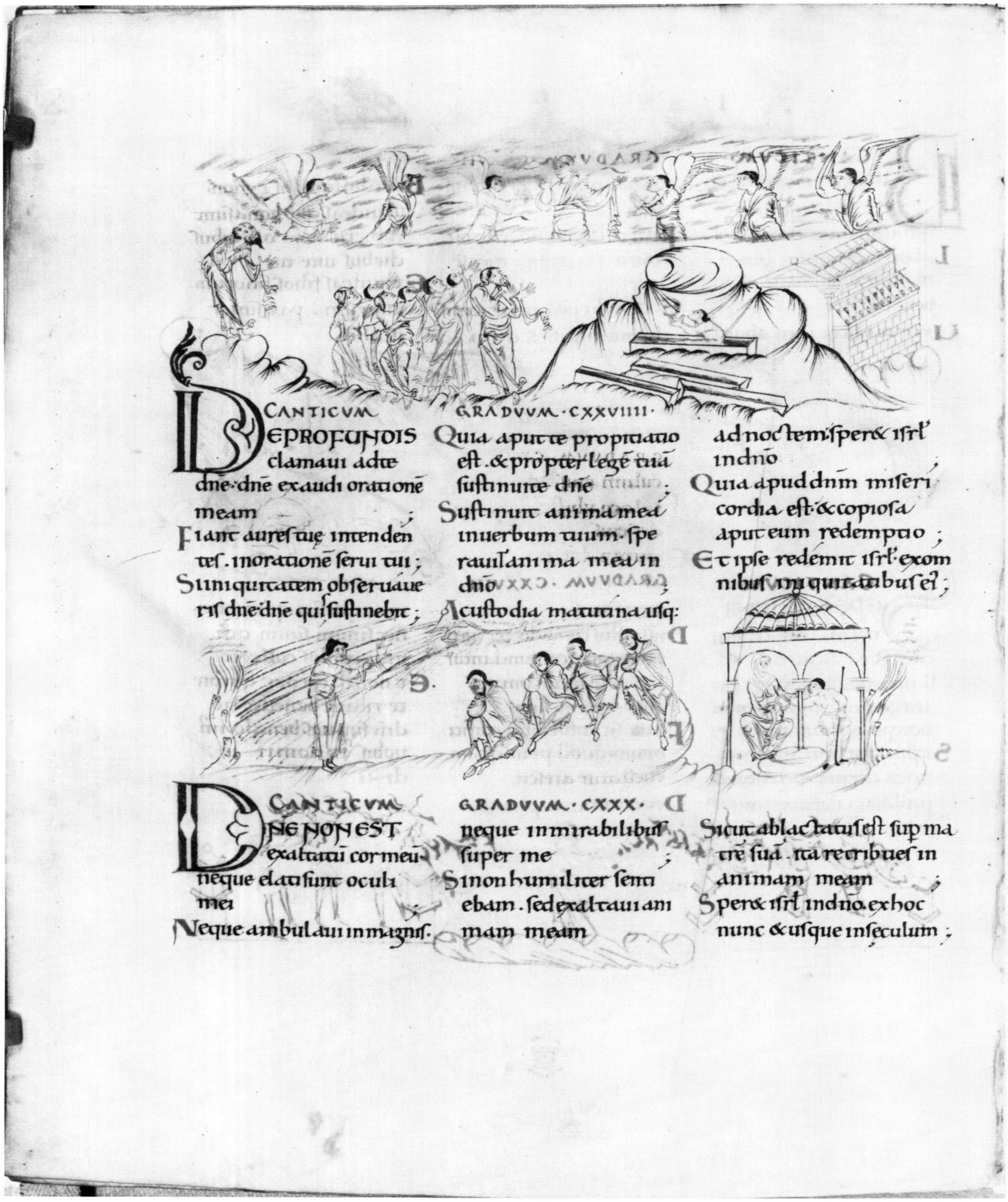
CANTICUM GRADUUM · CXXVIIII ·
DE PROFUNDIS clamaui ad te
dne dne exaudi orationē
meam ;
Fiant aures tuę intenden
tes . in orationē serui tui ;
Si iniquitatem obseruaue
ris dne dne quis sustinebit ;
Quia apud te propitiatio
est . & propter legē tuā
sustinui te dne ;
Sustinuit anima mea
in uerbum tuum . spe
rauit anima mea in
dno .
A custodia matutina usq:
ad noctem speret isrl
in dno ;
Quia apud dnm miseri
cordia est . & copiosa
apud eum redemptio ;
Et ipse redemit isrl ex om
nibus iniquitatibus eī ;
CANTICUM GRADUUM · CXXX ·
DNE NON EST exaltatū cor meū
neque elati sunt oculi
mei
Neque ambulaui in magnis .
neque in mirabilibus
super me ;
Si non humiliter senti
ebam . sed exaltaui ani
mam meam
Sicut ablactatus est sup ma
trē suā . ita retribues in
animam meam ;
Speret isrl in dno ex hoc
nunc & usque in seculum ;

2.90 London, B.L., Harley 603, f. 67v

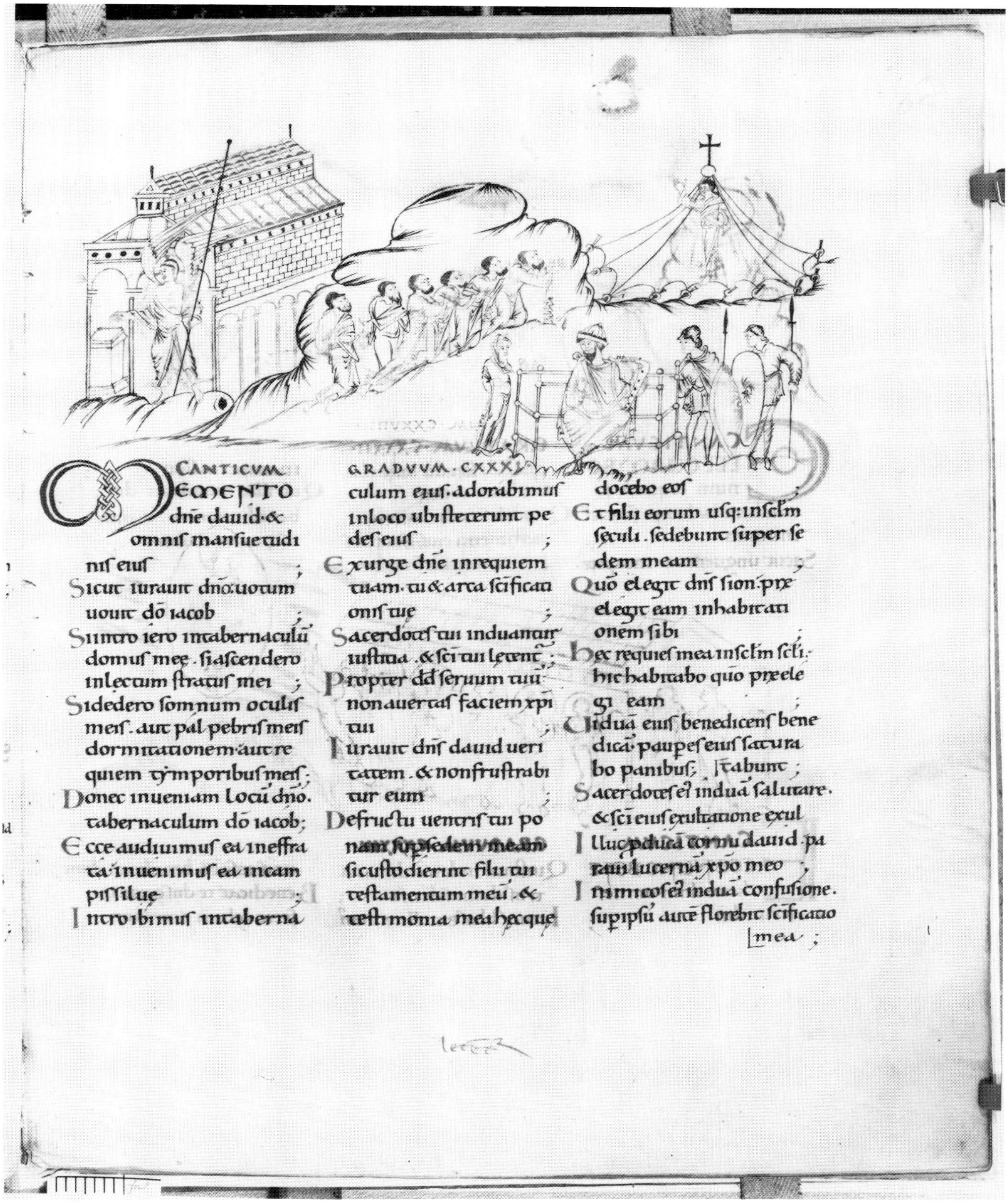

2.91 London, B.L., Harley 603, f. 68[r]

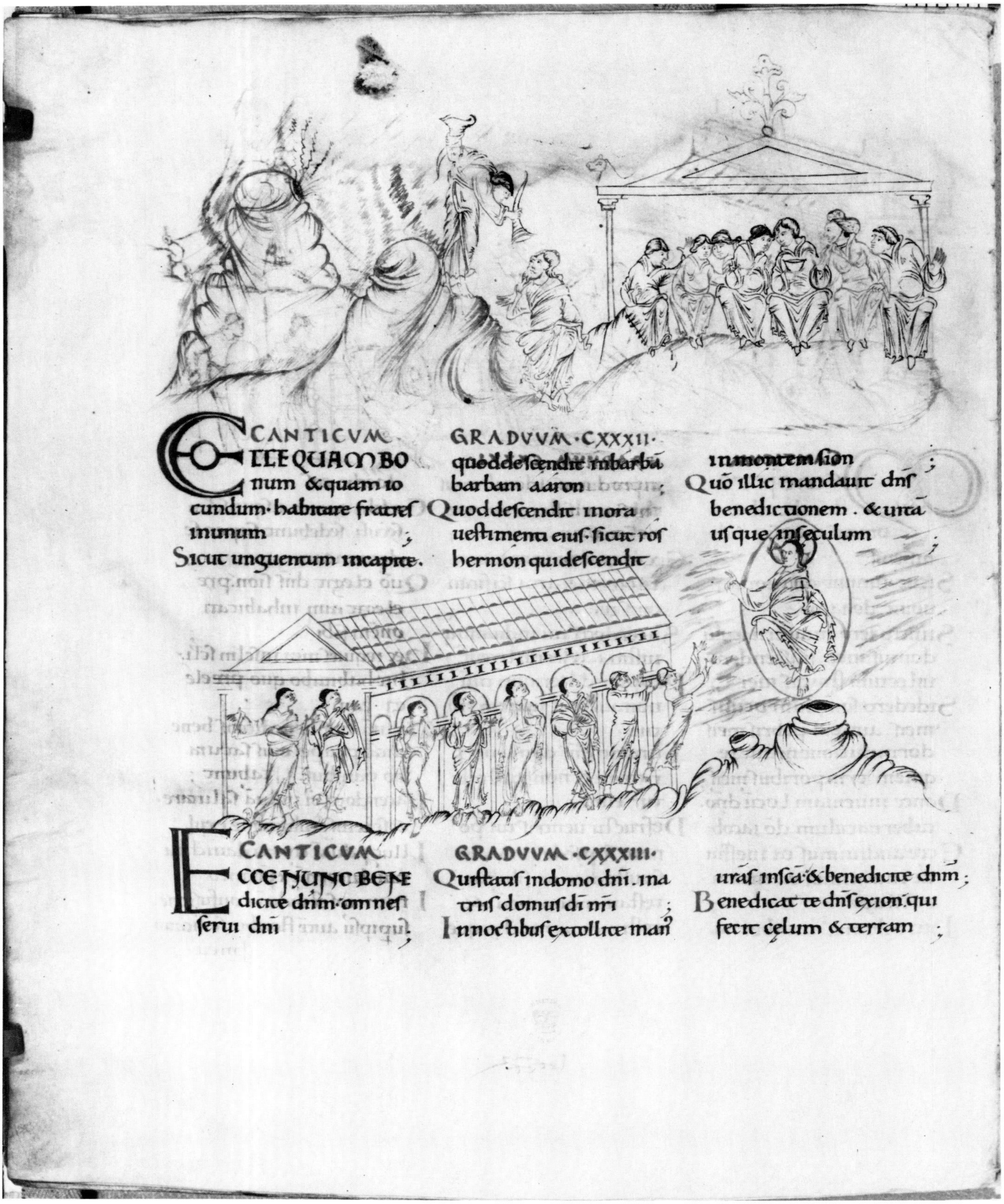

2.92 London, B.L., Harley 603, f. 68v

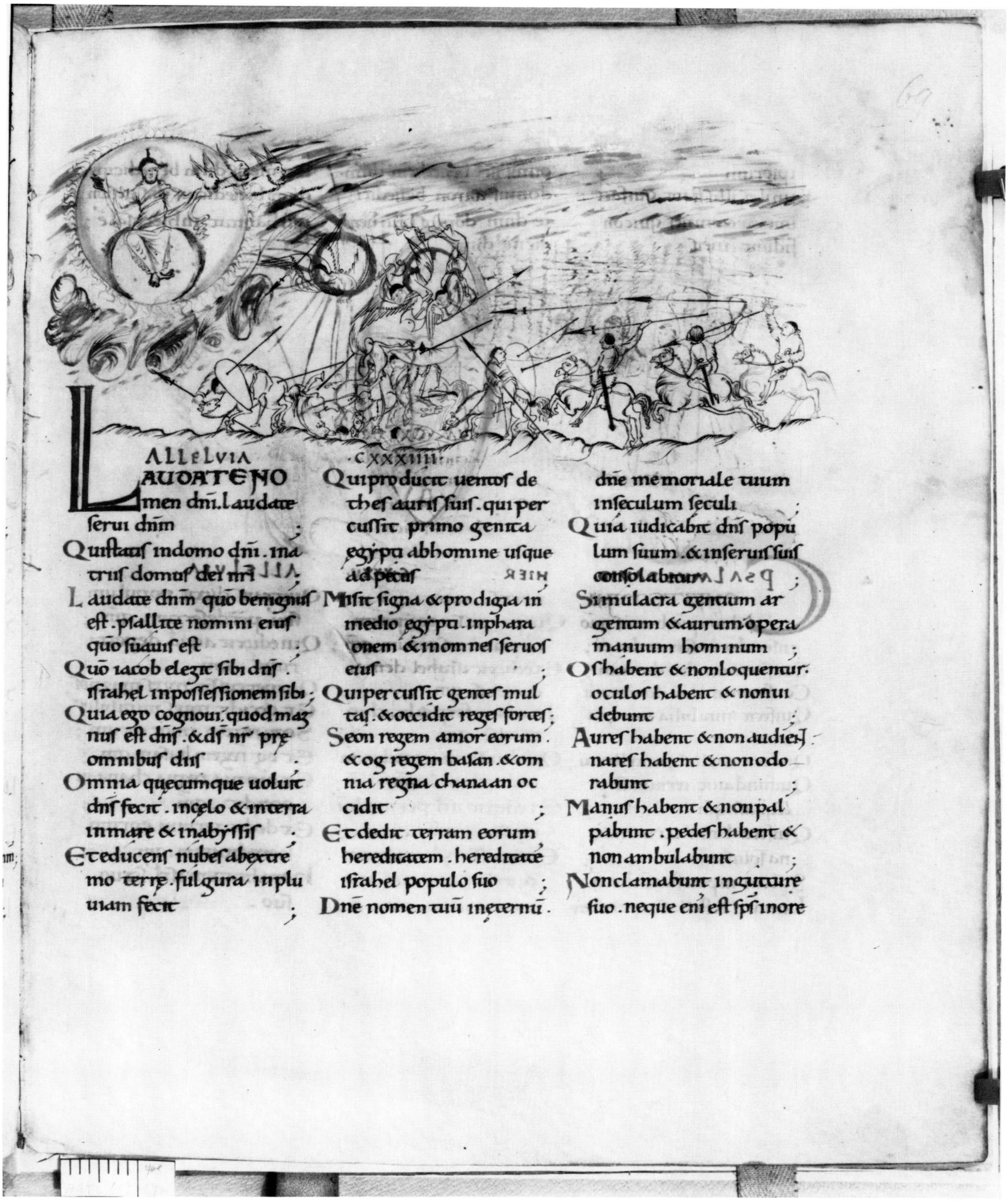

ALLELUIA
LAUDATE NO
men dni. laudate
serui dnm ;
Qui statis indomo dni. ina
triis domus dei nri ;
Laudate dnm quo benignus
est. psallite nomini eius
quo suauis est
Quo iacob elegit sibi dns.
israhel inpossessionem sibi ;
Quia ego cognoui. quod mag
nus est dns. & ds nr pre
omnibus dis
Omnia quecumque uoluit
dns fecit. incelo & interra
inmare & inabyssis
Et educens nubes abextre
mo terre. fulgura inplu
uiam fecit ;

.CXXXIIII.
Qui producit uentos de
thesauris suis. qui per
cussit primo genita
egypti abhomine usque
ad pecus
Misit signa & prodigia in
medio egypti. inphara
onem & inomnes seruos
eius
Qui percussit gentes mul
tas. & occidit reges fortes ;
Seon regem amorreorum.
& og regem basan. & om
nia regna chanaan oc
cidit ;
Et dedit terram eorum
hereditatem. hereditate
israhel populo suo ;
Dne nomen tuu ineternu.

dne memoriale tuum
inseculum seculi ;
Quia iudicabit dns popu
lum suum. & inseruis suis
consolabitur ;
Simulacra gentium ar
gentum & aurum opera
manuum hominum ;
Os habent & non loquentur.
oculos habent & non ui
debunt
Aures habent & non audient.
nares habent & non odo
rabunt
Manus habent & non pal
pabunt. pedes habent &
non ambulabunt
Non clamabunt inguture
suo. neque enim est sps inore

2.93 London, B.L., Harley 603, f. 69r

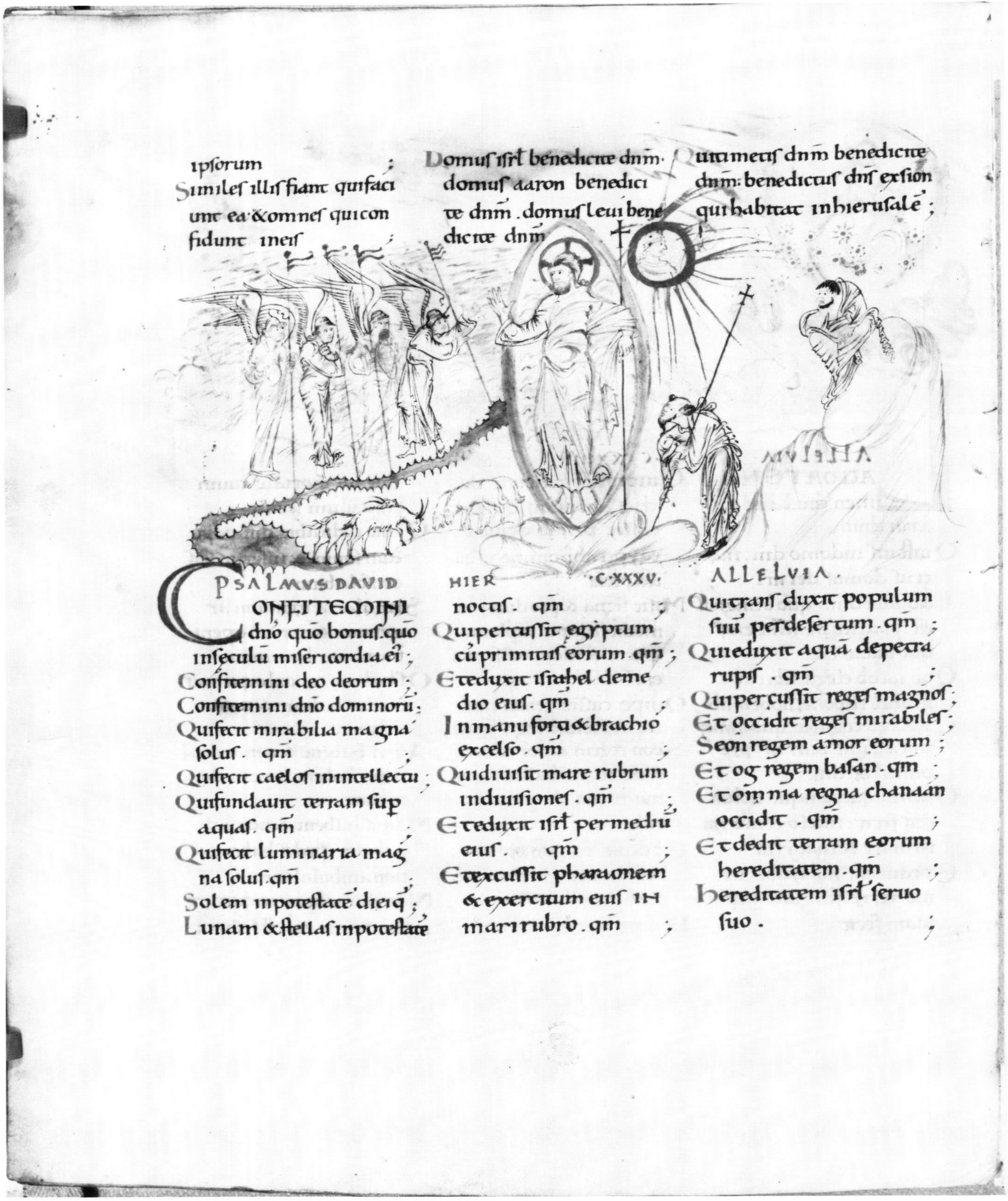

2.94 London, B.L., Harley 603, f. 69^{v}

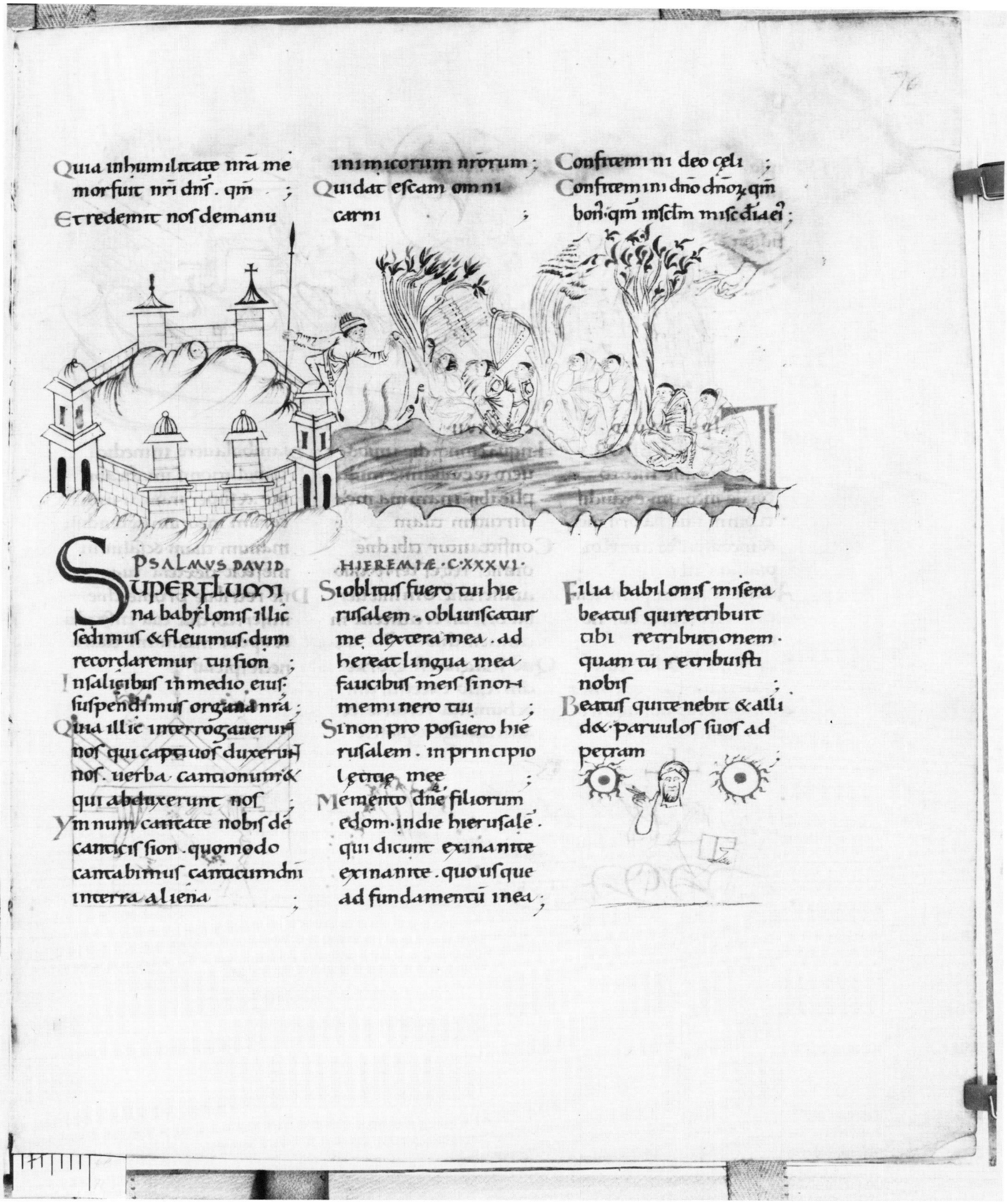

2.95 London, B.L., Harley 603, f. 70r

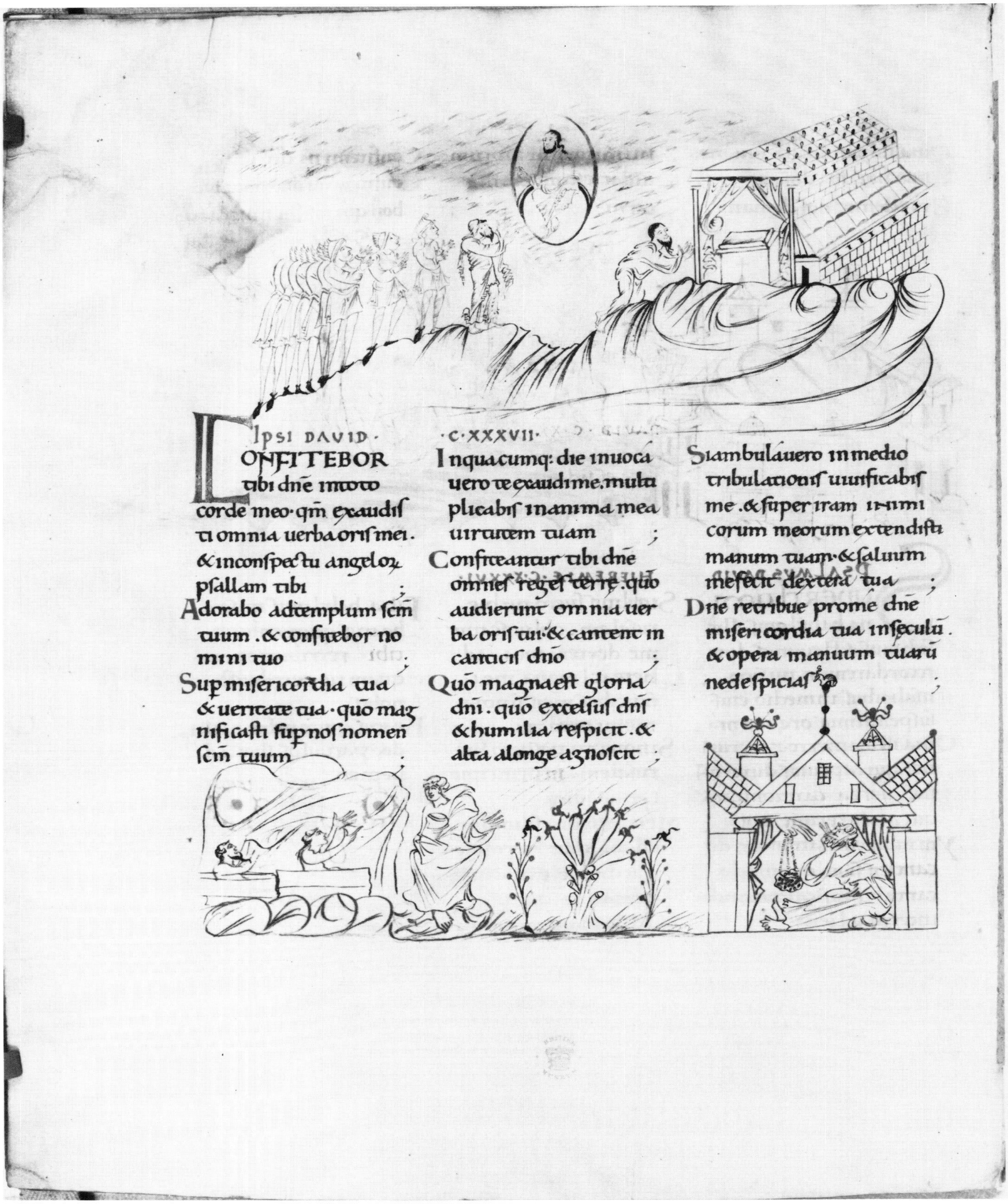

Ipsi david ·
CONFITEBOR tibi dne in toto corde meo · qm exaudis ti omnia uerba oris mei . & in conspectu angelorum psallam tibi ;
Adorabo ad templum scm tuum . & confitebor no mini tuo ;
Sup misericordia tua & ueritate tua · quo mag nificasti sup nos nomen scm tuum

·C·XXXVII·
In quacumq: die inuoca uero te exaudi me . multi plicabis in anima mea uirtutem tuam ;
Confiteantur tibi dne omnes reges terre . quo audierunt omnia uer ba oris tui · & cantent in canticis dno ;
Quo magna est gloria dni . quo excelsus dns & humilia respicit . & alta alonge agnoscit ;

Si ambulauero in medio tribulationis uiuificabis me . & super iram inimi corum meorum extendisti manum tuam · & saluum me fecit dextera tua ;
Dne retribue pro me dne misericordia tua in seculu . & opera manuum tuaru ne despicias ;

2.96 London, B.L., Harley 603, f. 70v

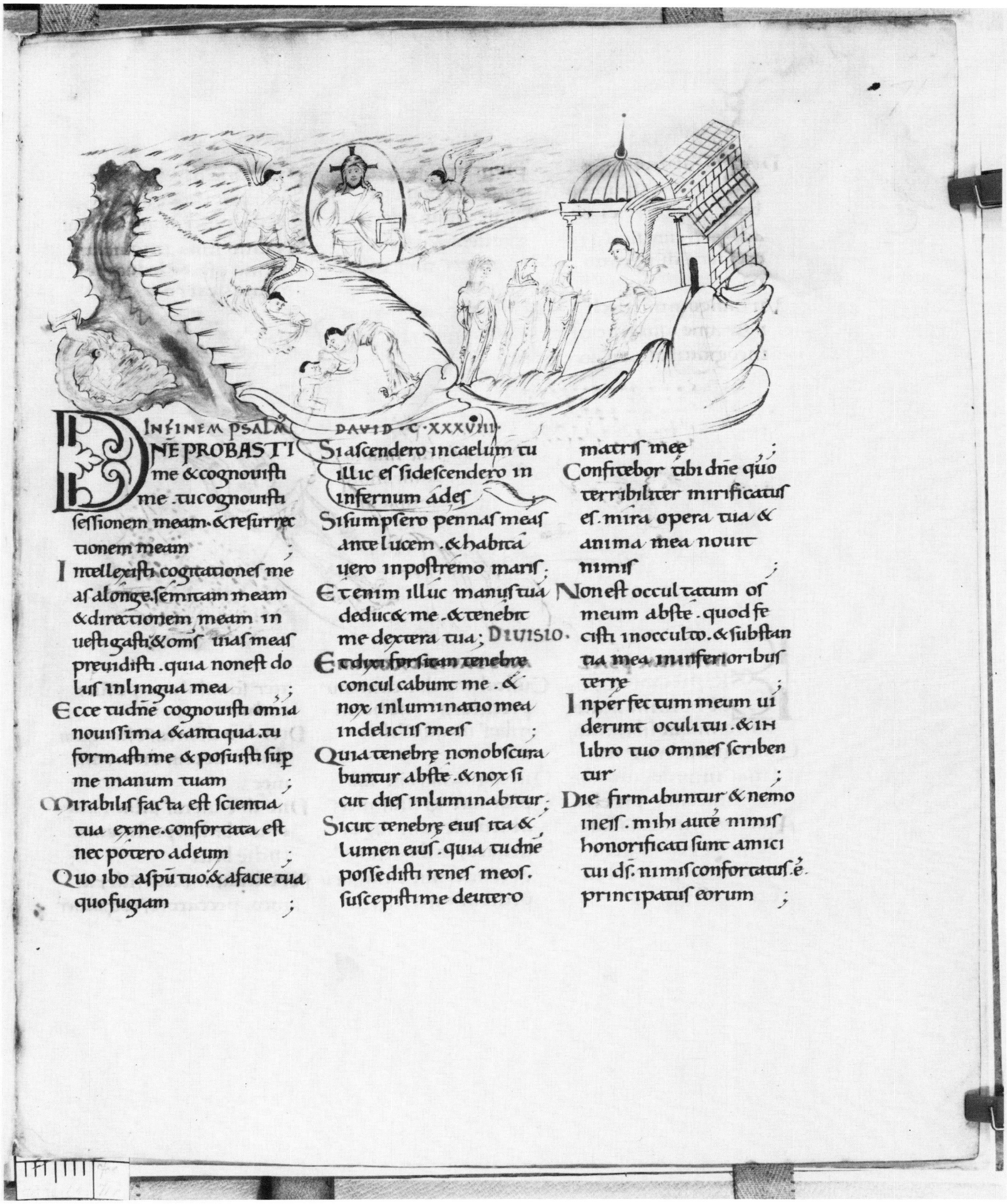

2.97 London, B.L., Harley 603, f. 71r

Di numerabo eos & sup
arenam multiplica
buntur. resurrexi &
adhuc tecum sum. si
occideris ds peccato
res;
Viri sanguinum decli
nate a me. quia dicitis
in cogitatibus uris. acci

pient in uanitate
ciuitates suas;
Non ne qui te oderunt
ds oderam illos. & sup
inimicos tuos tabe
scebam;
Perfecto odio oderam
illos. inimici facti sunt
mihi

Proba me ds & scito cor
meum. interroga me
& cognosce semitas meas;
Et uide si uia iniquitatis
in me est. & deduc me
in uia eterna;

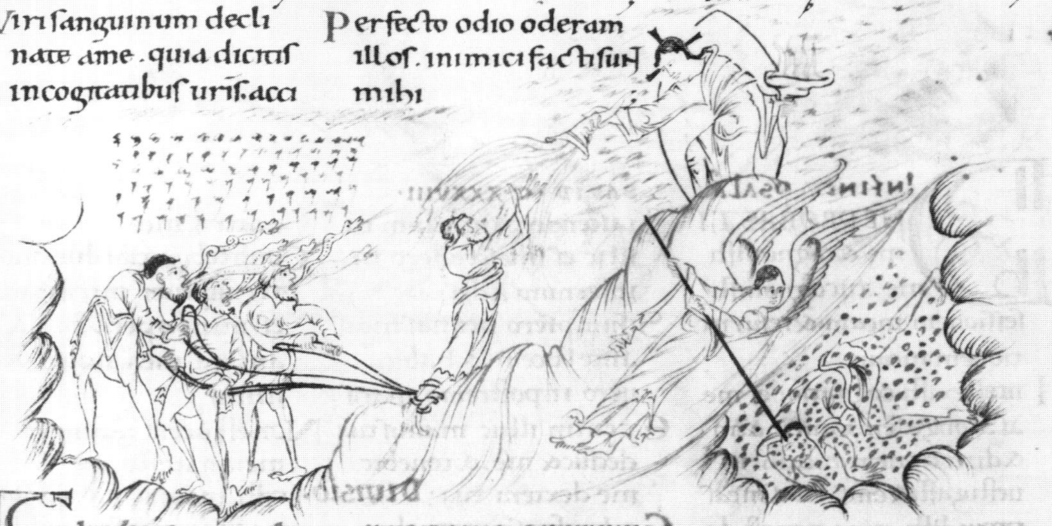

IN FINEM PSAL
ERIPE ME DNE
ab homine malo.
a uiro iniquo libera me;
Qui cogitauerunt ma
litias in corde. tota die
constituebant proelia;
Acuerunt linguas suas
sicut serpentes. uene
num aspidum sub la
biis eorum;

MUS DAVID. CXXXVIIII
Custodi me dne de manu
peccatoris. ab homi
nibus iniquis libera
me;
Qui cogitauerunt sub
plantare gressus meos.
absconderunt superbi
laqueos mihi. & funes
extenderunt in laqueũ
pedibus meis. iuxta

iter scandalum posuer
mihi;
Dixi dno ds meus es tu. exau
di dne uocem orationis
mee;
Dne dne uirtus salutis mee.
obumbra capud meum
in die belli;
Ne tradas me a desiderio
meo. peccatores cogitauer

2.98 London, B.L., Harley 603, f. 71v

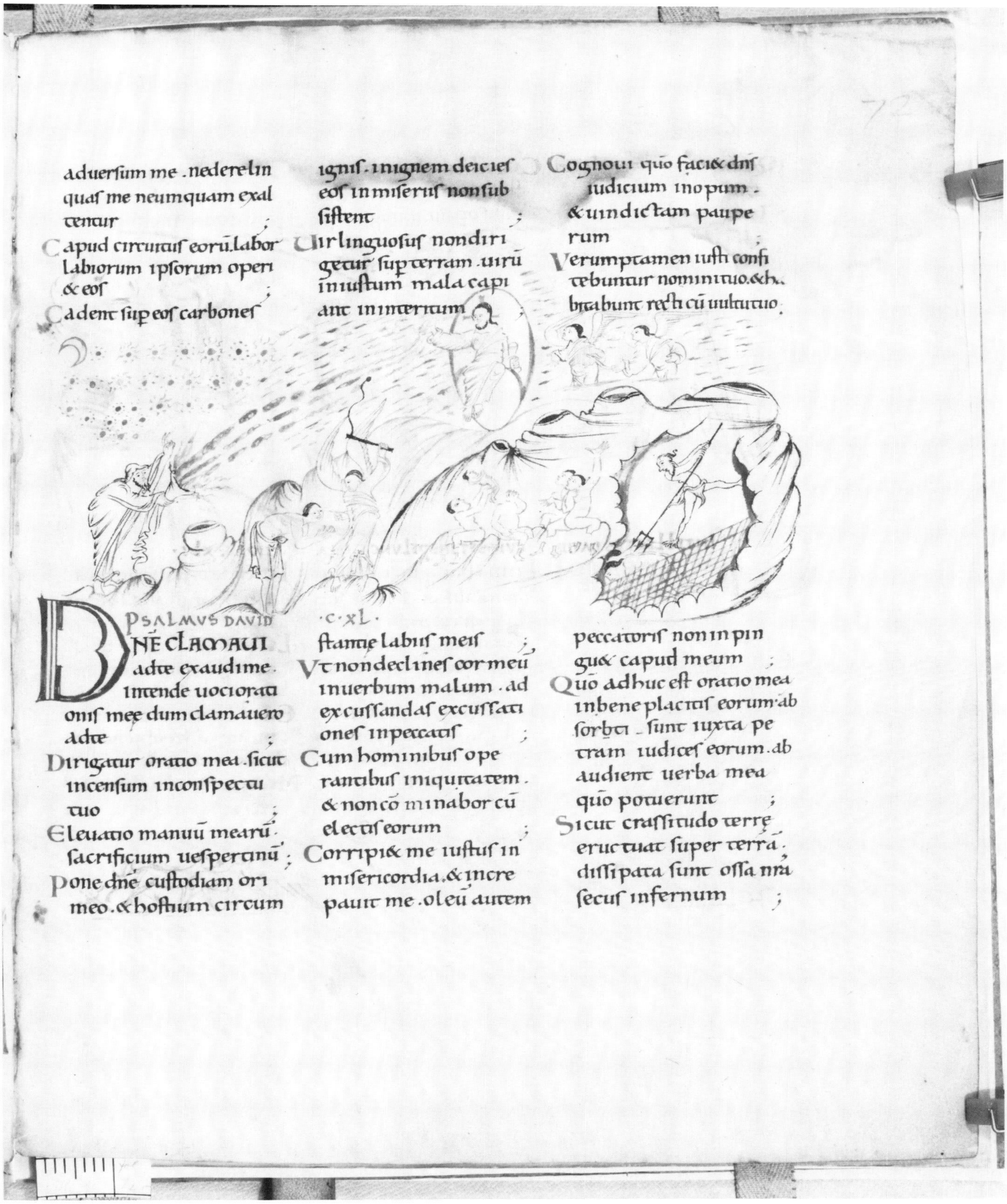

aduersum me . nedereLin
quas me neumquam exal
tentur ;
Capud circuitus eoru̅ . labor
labiorum ipsorum operi
& eos ;
Cadent sup eos carbones
ignis . in ignem deicies
eos in miseriis non sub
sistent ;
Uir linguosus non diri
getur sup terram . uiru̅
iniustum mala capi
ant in interitum
Cognoui quo faci& dns
iudicium inopum .
& uindictam paupe
rum ;
Verumptamen iusti confi
tebuntur nomini tuo . & ha
bitabunt recti cu̅ uultu tuo ;

PSALMUS DAVID .c.xl.
DNE CLAMAUI
adte exaudi me .
intende uoci orati
onis meę dum clamauero
adte ;
Dirigatur oratio mea . sicut
incensum inconspectu
tuo ;
Eleuatio manuu̅ mearu̅ .
sacrificium uespertinu̅ ;
Pone dne custodiam ori
meo . & hostium circum
stantię labiis meis ;
Ut non declines cor meu̅
in uerbum malum . ad
excussandas excussati
ones in peccatis ;
Cum hominibus ope
rantibus iniquitatem .
& non co̅ minabor cu̅
electis eorum ;
Corripi& me iustus in
misericordia . & incre
pauit me . oleu̅ autem
peccatoris non inpin
gu& capud meum ;
Quo adhuc est oratio mea
in bene placitis eorum . ab
sorbti sunt iuxta pe
tram iudices eorum . ab
audient uerba mea
quo potuerunt ;
Sicut crassitudo terrę
eructuat super terra̅ .
dissipata sunt ossa nra
secus infernum ;

2.99 London, B.L., Harley 603, f. 72r

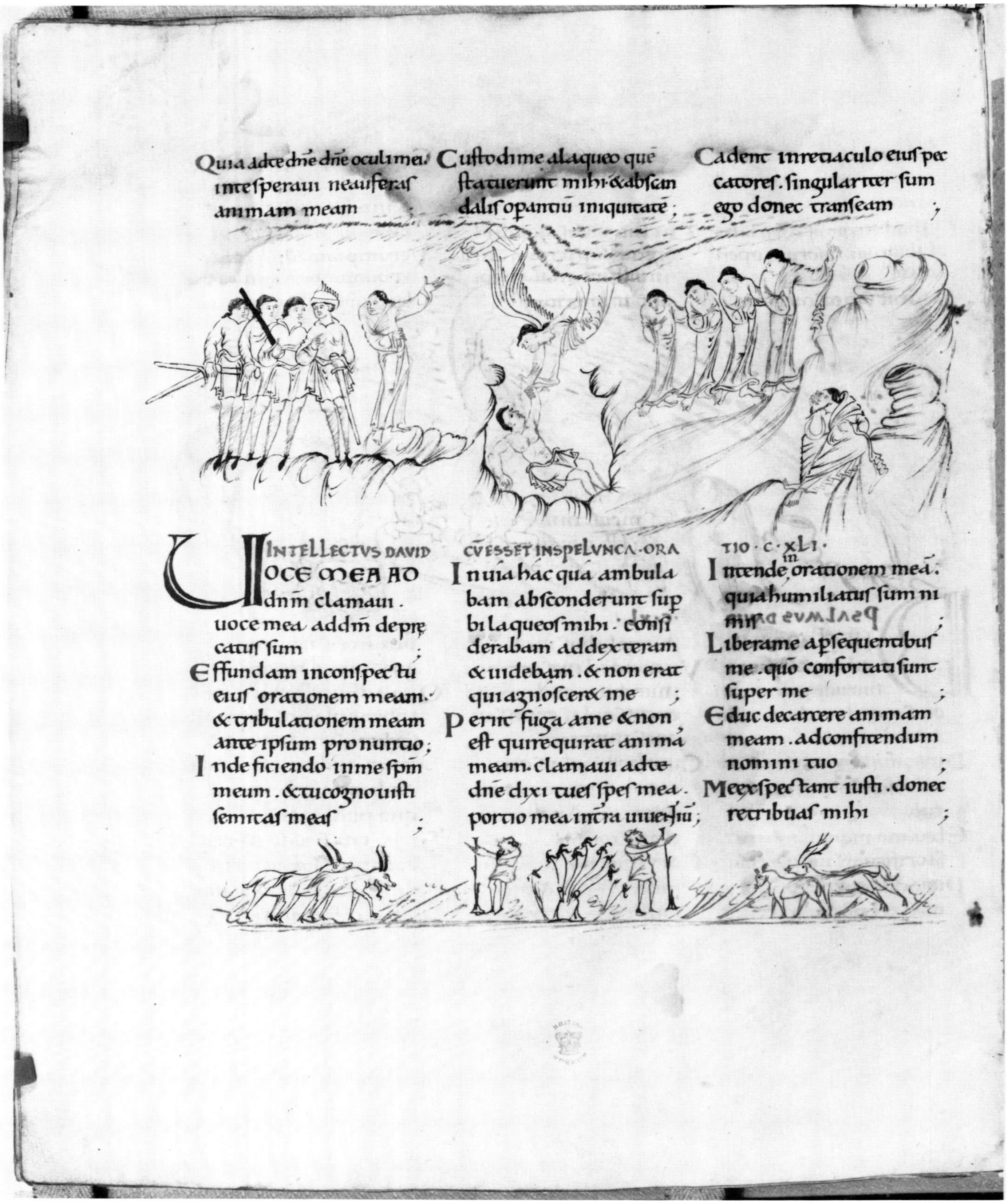

Quia ad te dñe dñe oculi mei: in te speraui ne auferas animam meam

Custodi me a laqueo quē statuerunt mihi & ab scandalis opantiū iniquitatē;

Cadent in retiaculo eius peccatores. singulariter sum ego donec transeam;

INTELLECTVS DAVID CVESSET IN SPELVNCA · ORATIO · C · XLI ·

UOCE MEA AD dnm clamaui. uoce mea ad dm̄ depręcatus sum;
Effundam in conspectu eius orationem meam. & tribulationem meam ante ipsum pronuntio;
Inde ficiendo in me spm̄ meum. & tu cognouisti semitas meas;
In uia hac qua ambulabam absconderunt superbi laqueos mihi. Considerabam ad dexteram & uidebam. & non erat qui agnosceret me;
Periit fuga a me & non est qui requirat animā meam. clamaui ad te dñe dixi tu es spes mea. portio mea in terra uiuentiū;
Intende in orationem meā: quia humiliatus sum nimis;
Libera me a persequentibus me. quō confortati sunt super me;
Educ de carcere animam meam. ad confitendum nomini tuo;
Me expectant iusti. donec retribuas mihi;

2.100 London, B.L., Harley 603, f. 72v

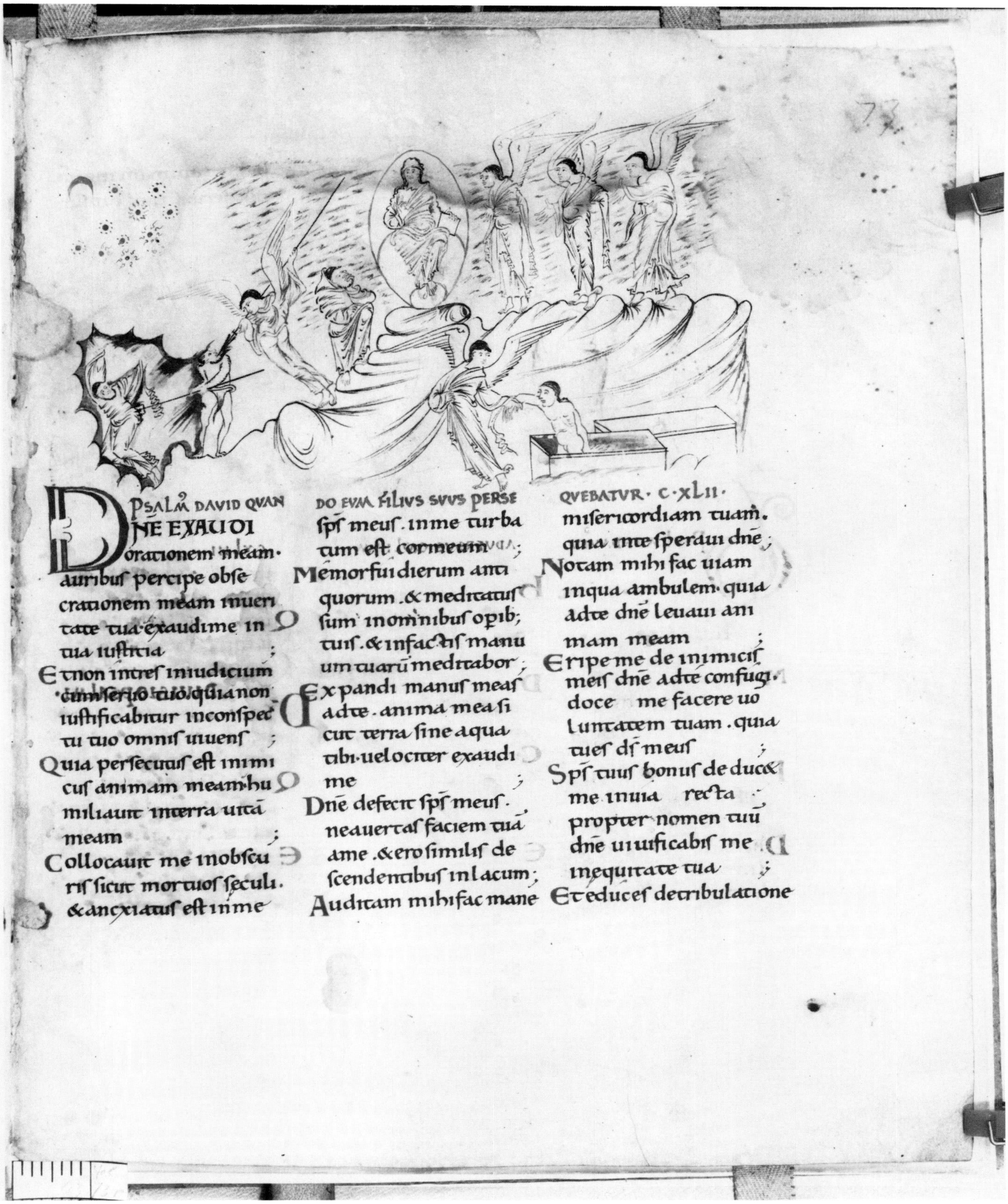

PSALM̄ DAVID QUANDO EUM FILIUS SUUS PERSEQUEBATUR· C·XLII·
DN̄E EXAUDI
orationem meam·
auribus percipe obse
crationem meam in ueri
tate tua exaudi me in
tua iustitia ;
Et non intres in iudicium
cum seruo tuo quia non
iustificabitur in conspec
tu tuo omnis uiuens ;
Quia persecutus est inimi
cus animam meam hu
miliauit in terra uitā
meam ;
Collocauit me in obscu
ris sicut mortuos seculi·
& anxiatus est in me
sp̄s meus· in me turba
tum est cor meum ;
Memor fui dierum anti
quorum & meditatus
sum in omnibus opib;
tuis· & in factis manu
um tuarū meditabor ;
Expandi manus meas
ad te· anima mea si
cut terra sine aqua
tibi· uelociter exaudi
me ;
Dn̄e defecit sp̄s meus·
ne auertas faciem tuā
a me· & ero similis de
scendentibus in lacum ;
Auditam mihi fac mane
misericordiam tuam·
quia in te speraui dn̄e ;
Notam mihi fac uiam
in qua ambulem· quia
ad te dn̄e leuaui ani
mam meam ;
Eripe me de inimicis
meis dn̄e ad te confugi·
doce me facere uo
luntatem tuam· quia
tu es d̄s meus ;
Sp̄s tuus bonus deducet
me in uia recta ;
propter nomen tuū
dn̄e uiuificabis me
in equitate tua ;
Et educes de tribulatione

2.101 London, B.L., Harley 603, f. 73[r]

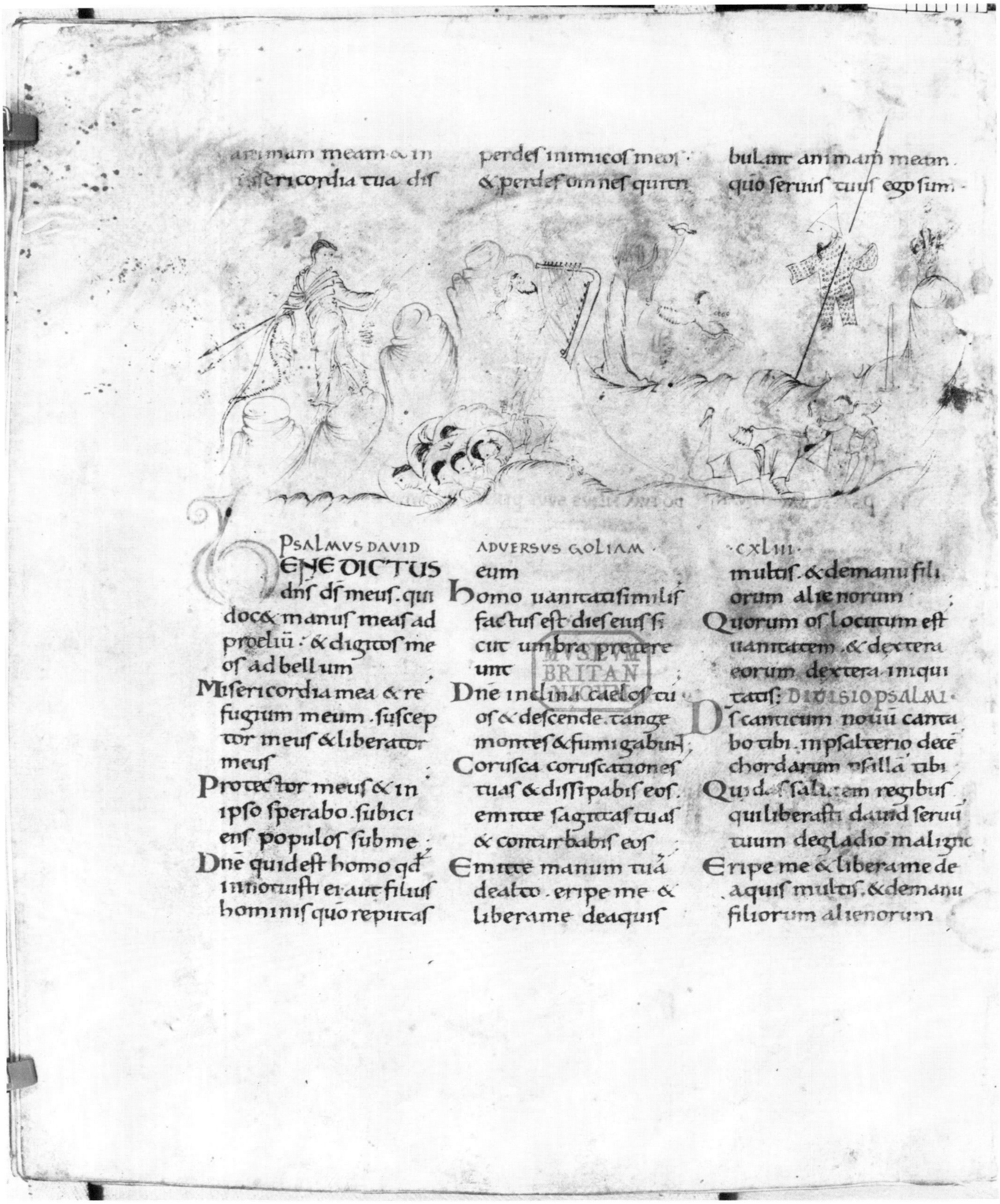
animam meam & in [mi]sericordia tua dis perdes inimicos meos & perdes omnes qui tribulant animam meam quo seruus tuus ego sum.

PSALMUS DAVID ADVERSUS GOLIAM · CXLIII ·

Benedictus dns ds meus. qui doce& manus meas ad proeliu : & digitos meos ad bellum
Misericordia mea & refugium meum. susceptor meus & liberator meus
Protector meus & in ipso sperabo. subiciens populos sub me
Dne quid est homo qd innotuisti ei aut filius hominis quo reputas eum
Homo uanitati similis factus est dies eius sicut umbra praetereunt
Dne inclina caelos tuos & descende. tange montes & fumigabunt
Corusca coruscationes tuas & dissipabis eos. emitte sagittas tuas & conturbabis eos
Emitte manum tuã de alto. eripe me & libera me de aquis multis. & de manu filiorum alienorum
Quorum os locutum est uanitatem. & dextera eorum dextera iniquitatis: DIVISIO PSALMI ·
Ds canticum nouũ cantabo tibi. in psalterio decẽ chordarum psallã tibi
Qui das salutem regibus qui liberasti dauid seruũ tuum de gladio maligno
Eripe me & libera me de aquis multis. & de manu filiorum alienorum

2.102 London, B.L., Harley 603, f. 73ᵛ

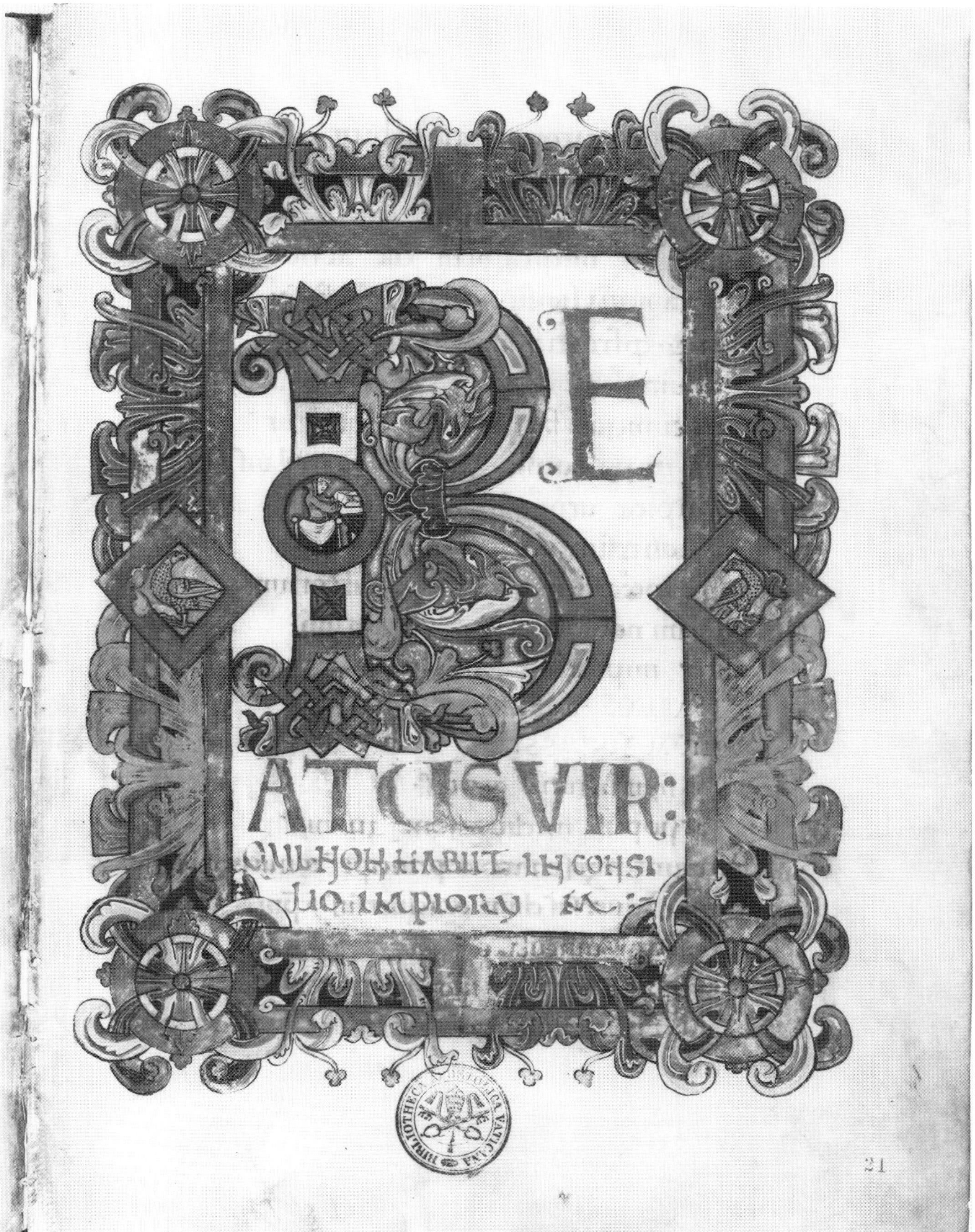

3.1 Vatican, Biblioteca Apostolica, Reg. lat. 12, f. 21r

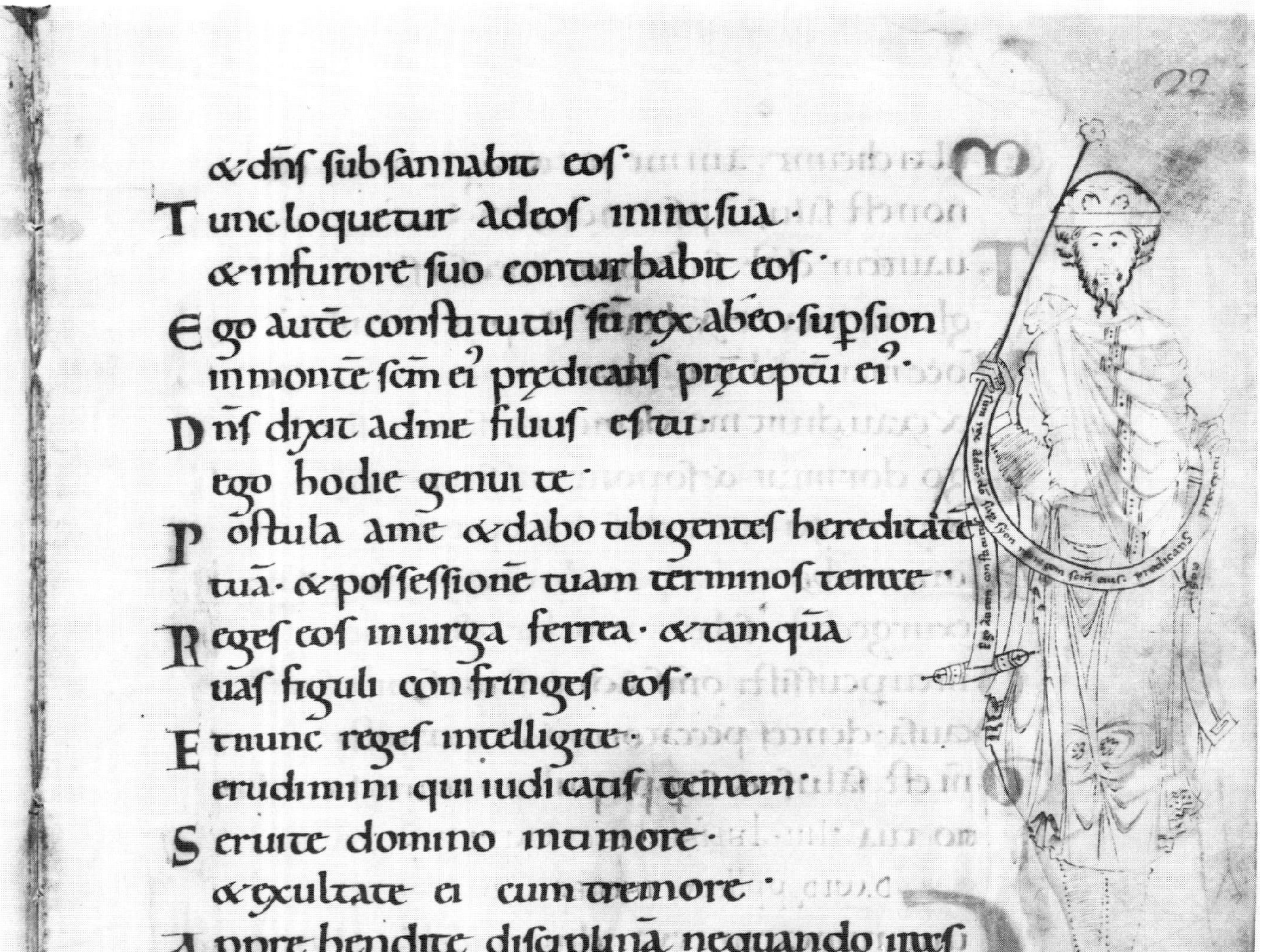
& dns subsannabit eos·
Tunc loquetur ad eos in ira sua·
& in furore suo conturbabit eos·
Ego autē constitutus sū rex ab eo· sup sion
in montē scm ei9 predicans preceptū ei9·
Dns dixit ad me filius es tu·
ego hodie genui te·
Postula a me & dabo tibi gentes hereditatē
tuā· & possessionē tuam terminos terrę·
Reges eos in uirga ferrea· & tamquā
uas figuli confringes eos·
Et nunc reges intelligite·
erudimini qui iudicatis terram·
Seruite domino in timore·
& exultate ei cum tremore·
Apprehendite disciplinā nequando iras
catur dns· & pereatis de uia iusta·
Cum exarserit in breui ira eius·
beati omnes qui confidunt in eo· III·
PSALM DAUID· CUM FUGERET A FACIE ABSOLON FILII
SUI· UOX XPI AD PATREM DE FIDE IUDAEIS DICIT·
Dne quid multiplicati sunt qui tribulant
me· multi insurgunt aduersum me·

3.2 Vatican, Biblioteca Apostolica, Reg. lat. 12, f. 22r

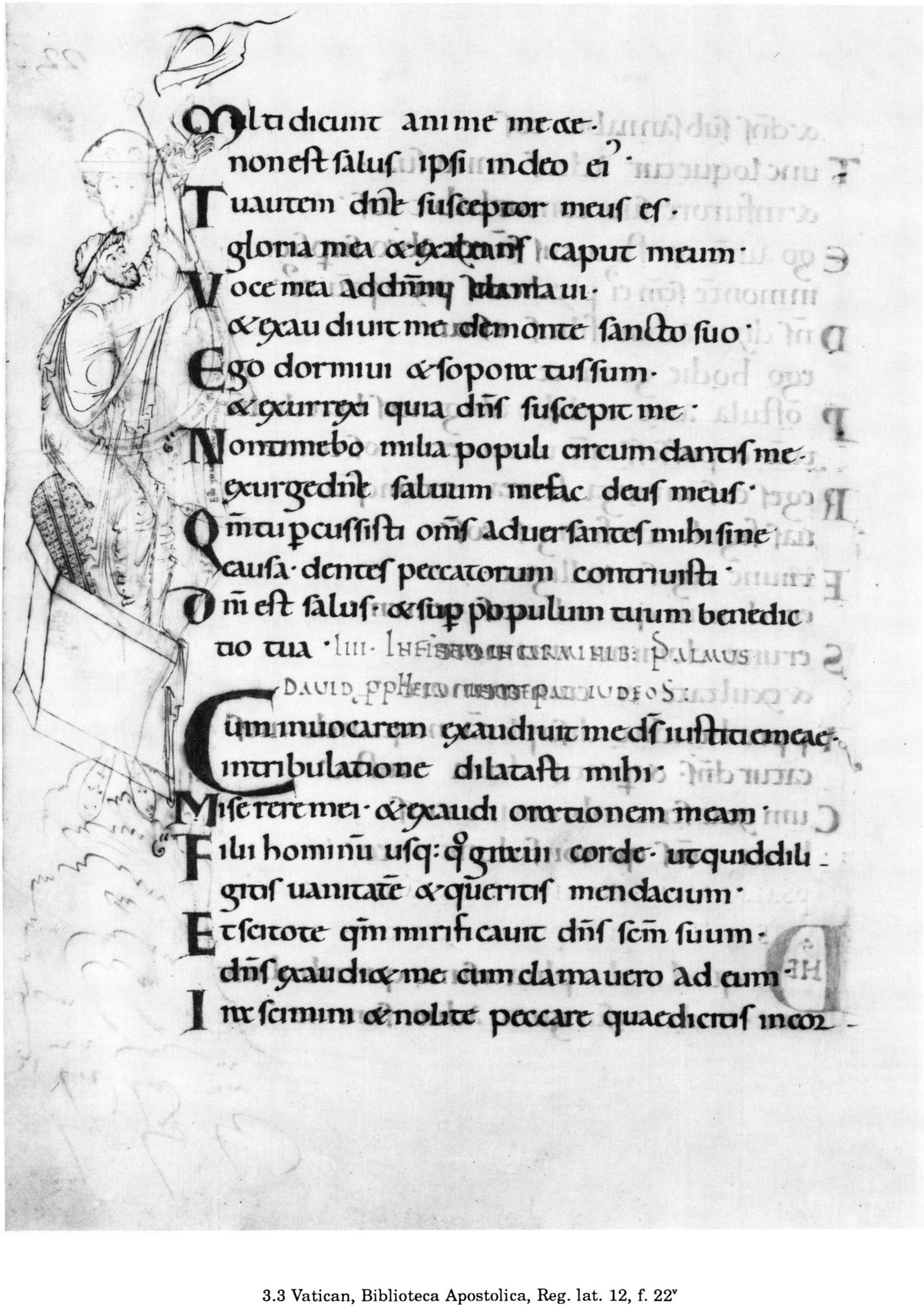

Multi dicunt animę meę ·
non est salus ipsi in deo eius ·
Tu autem dn̄e susceptor meus es ·
gloria mea et exaltans caput meum ·
Voce mea ad dn̄m clamaui ·
et exaudiuit me de monte sancto suo ·
Ego dormiui et soporatus sum ·
et exurrexi quia dn̄s suscepit me ·
Non timebo milia populi circumdantis me ·
exurge dn̄e saluum me fac deus meus ·
Qm̄ tu pcussisti om̄s aduersantes mihi sine
causa · dentes peccatorum contriuisti ·
Dn̄i est salus · et sup populum tuum benedic
tio tua · IIII · In finem in carminibus · Psalmus
DAVID ...
Cum inuocarem exaudiuit me ds̄ iustitię meę ·
in tribulatione dilatasti mihi ·
Miserere mei · et exaudi orationem meam ·
Filii hominum usq: quo graui corde · ut quid dili
gitis uanitatem et queritis mendacium ·
Et scitote qm̄ mirificauit dn̄s scm̄ suum ·
dn̄s exaudiet me cum clamauero ad eum ·
Irascimini et nolite peccare quae dicitis in cor

3.3 Vatican, Biblioteca Apostolica, Reg. lat. 12, f. 22v

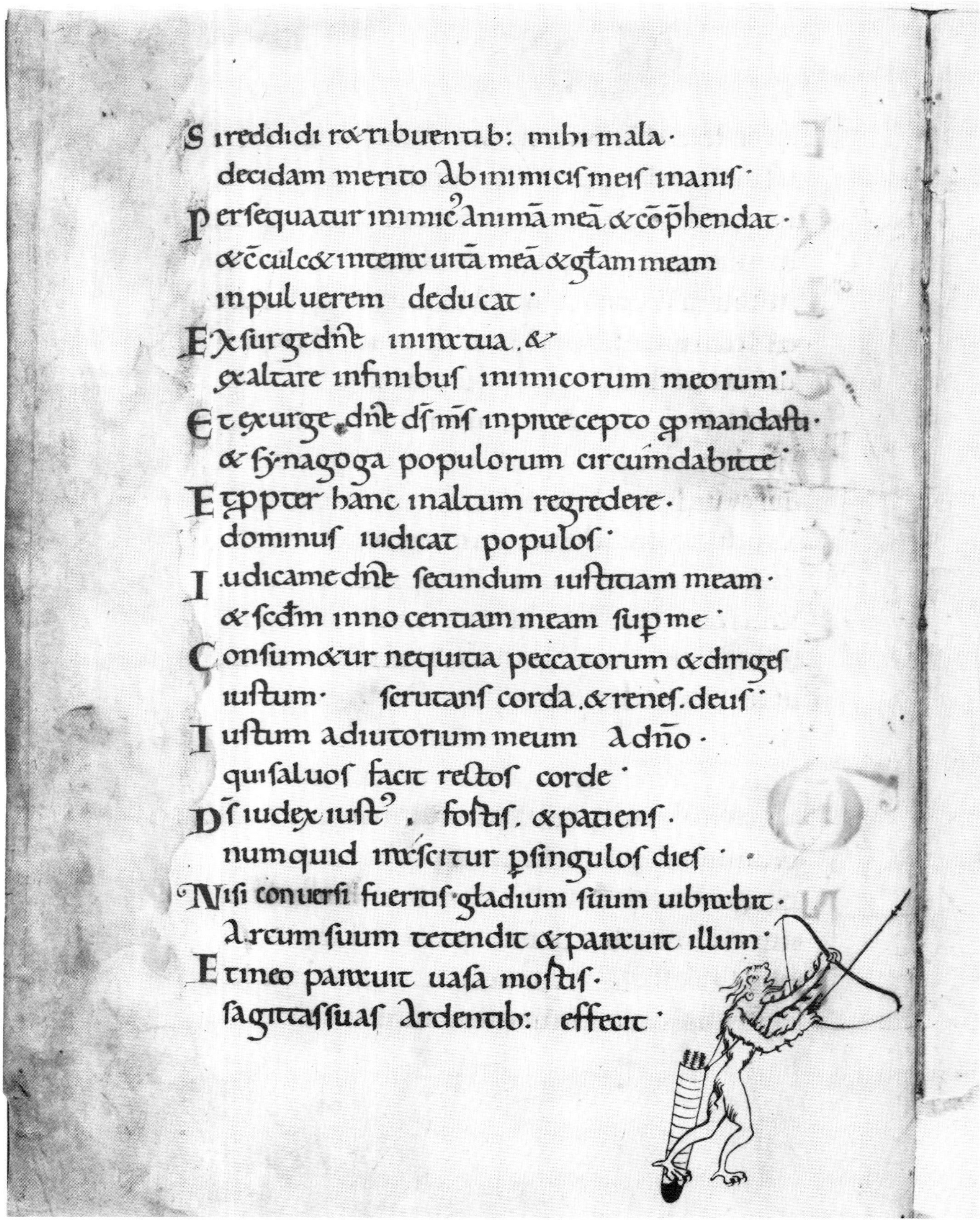
S i reddidi retribuentib: mihi mala ·
decidam merito ab inimicis meis inanis ·
P ersequatur inimicꝰ animā meā & cōphendat ·
& c̄culcet interra uitā meā & gl̄am meam
in puluerem deducat ·
E xsurge dn̄e in ira tua . &
exaltare in finibus inimicorum meorum ·
E t exurge dn̄e ds̄ m̄s in precepto q̄d mandasti ·
& synagoga populorum circumdabit te ·
E t ppter hanc in altum regredere ·
dominus iudicat populos ·
I udica me dn̄e secundum iustitiam meam ·
& scd̄m innocentiam meam sup me ·
C onsumetur nequitia peccatorum & diriges
iustum · scrutans corda . & renes . deus ·
I ustum adiutorium meum a dn̄o ·
qui saluos facit rectos corde ·
D s iudex iustꝰ , fortis . & patiens ·
numquid irascitur p singulos dies ·
N isi conuersi fueritis gladium suum uibrabit ·
A rcum suum tetendit & parauit illum ·
E t in eo parauit uasa mortis ·
sagittas suas ardentib: effecit ·

3.4 Vatican, Biblioteca Apostolica, Reg. lat. 12, f. 24v

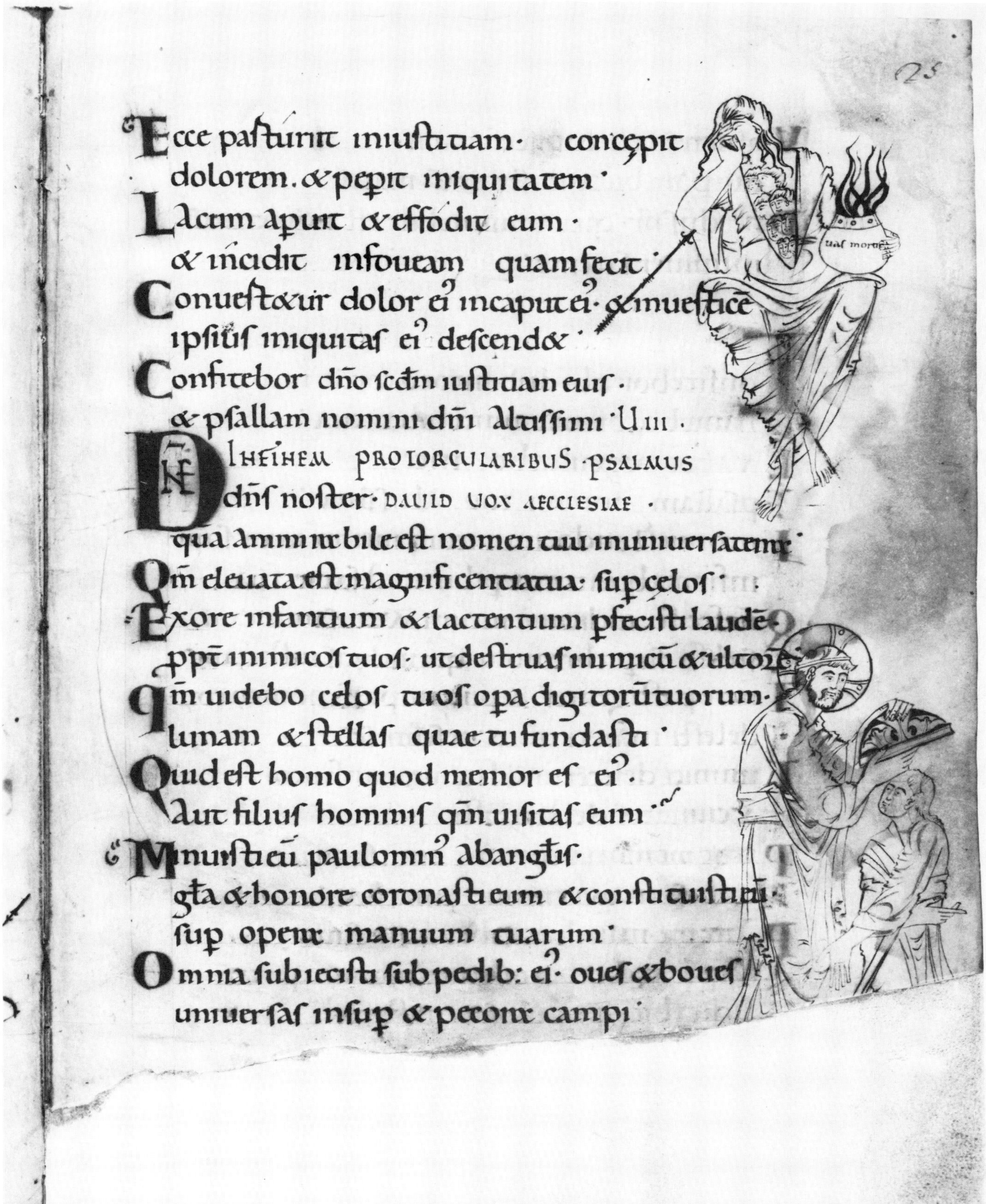

25

Ecce parturiit iniustitiam · concepit
dolorem . & peperit iniquitatem ·
Lacum aperuit & effodit eum ·
& incidit in foueam quam fecit ·
Conuertetur dolor eius in caput eius · & in uerticem
ipsius iniquitas eius descendet ·
Confitebor dno scdm iustitiam eius ·
& psallam nomini dni altissimi · VIII ·
IN FINEM PRO TORCULARIBUS PSALMUS
Dne dns noster · DAVID VOX AECCLESIAE ·
quam ammirabile est nomen tuum in uniuersa terra ·
Qm eleuata est magnificentia tua super celos ·
Ex ore infantium & lactentium perfecisti laudem ·
propter inimicos tuos · ut destruas inimicum & ultorem ·
Qm uidebo celos tuos opera digitorum tuorum ·
lunam & stellas quae tu fundasti ·
Quid est homo quod memor es eius ·
aut filius hominis qm uisitas eum ·
Minuisti eum paulominus ab angelis ·
gloria & honore coronasti eum & constituisti eum
super opera manuum tuarum ·
Omnia subiecisti sub pedibus eius · oues & boues
uniuersas insuper & pecora campi

3.5 Vatican, Biblioteca Apostolica, Reg. lat. 12, f. 25r

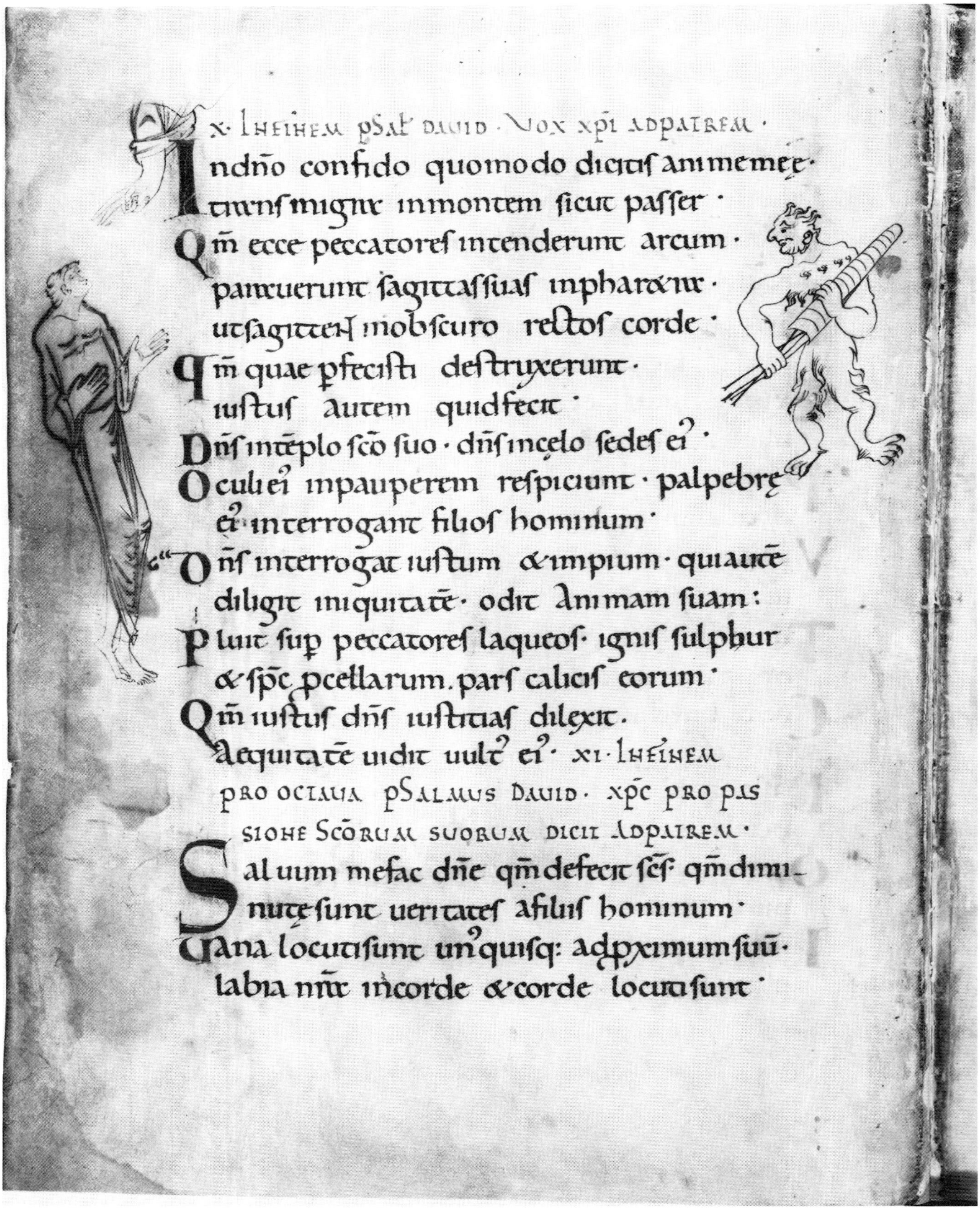

3.6 Vatican, Biblioteca Apostolica, Reg. lat. 12, f. 27v

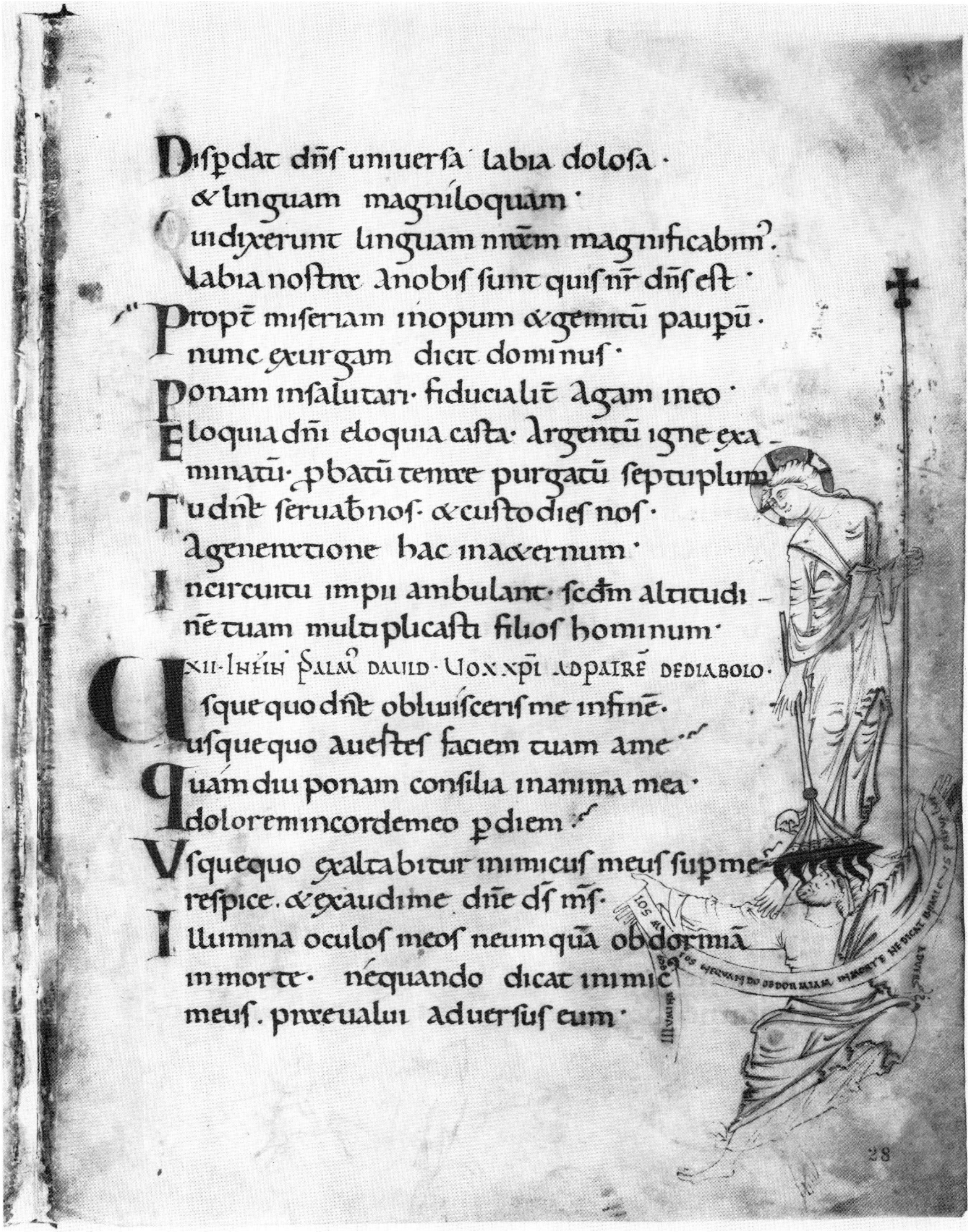

3.7 Vatican, Biblioteca Apostolica, Reg. lat. 12, f. 28r

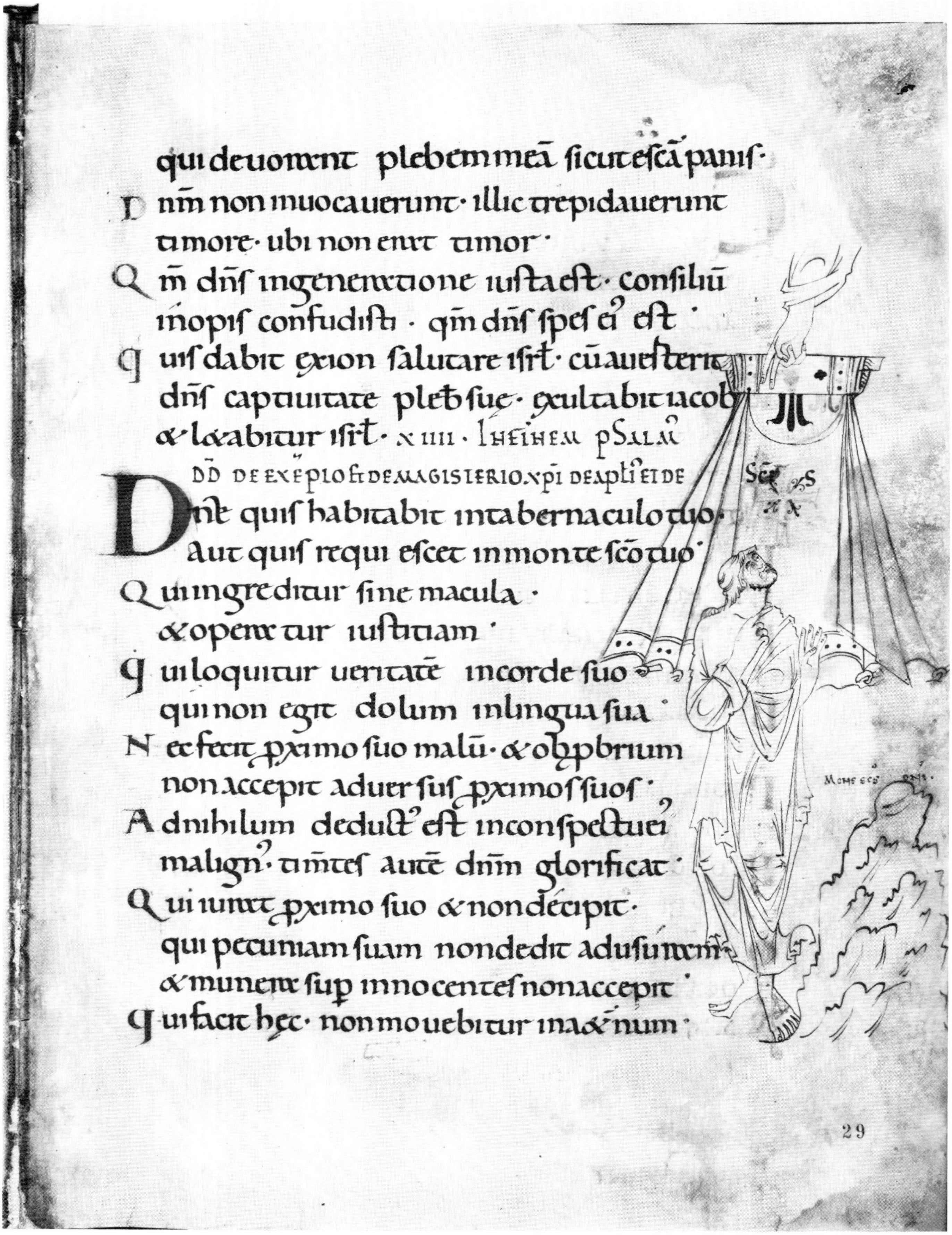
qui deuorant plebem meā sicut escā panis·
D nm̄ non inuocauerunt· illic trepidauerunt
timore· ubi non erat timor·
Q m̄ dn̄s in generatione iusta est· consiliū
inopis confudisti· qm̄ dn̄s spes ei est·
Q uis dabit ex sion salutare isrl· cū auerterit
dn̄s captiuitate plebis sue· exultabit iacob
& laetabitur isrl· XIIII· IN FINEM PSALM
DD DE EXEPLO FIDE MAGISTERIO XPI DE APLIS ET DE
D ne quis habitabit in tabernaculo tuo·
aut quis requiescet in monte sc̄o tuo·
Q ui ingreditur sine macula·
& operatur iustitiam·
Q ui loquitur ueritatē in corde suo
qui non egit dolum in lingua sua·
N ec fecit pximo suo malū· & obpbrium
non accepit aduersus pximos suos·
A d nihilum deductus est in conspectu ei
malign· timentes autē dn̄m glorificat·
Q ui iurat pximo suo & non decipit·
qui pecuniam suam non dedit ad usuram·
& munera sup innocentes non accepit·
Q ui facit hec· non mouebitur in aeternum·
29

3.8 Vatican, Biblioteca Apostolica, Reg. lat. 12, f. 29r

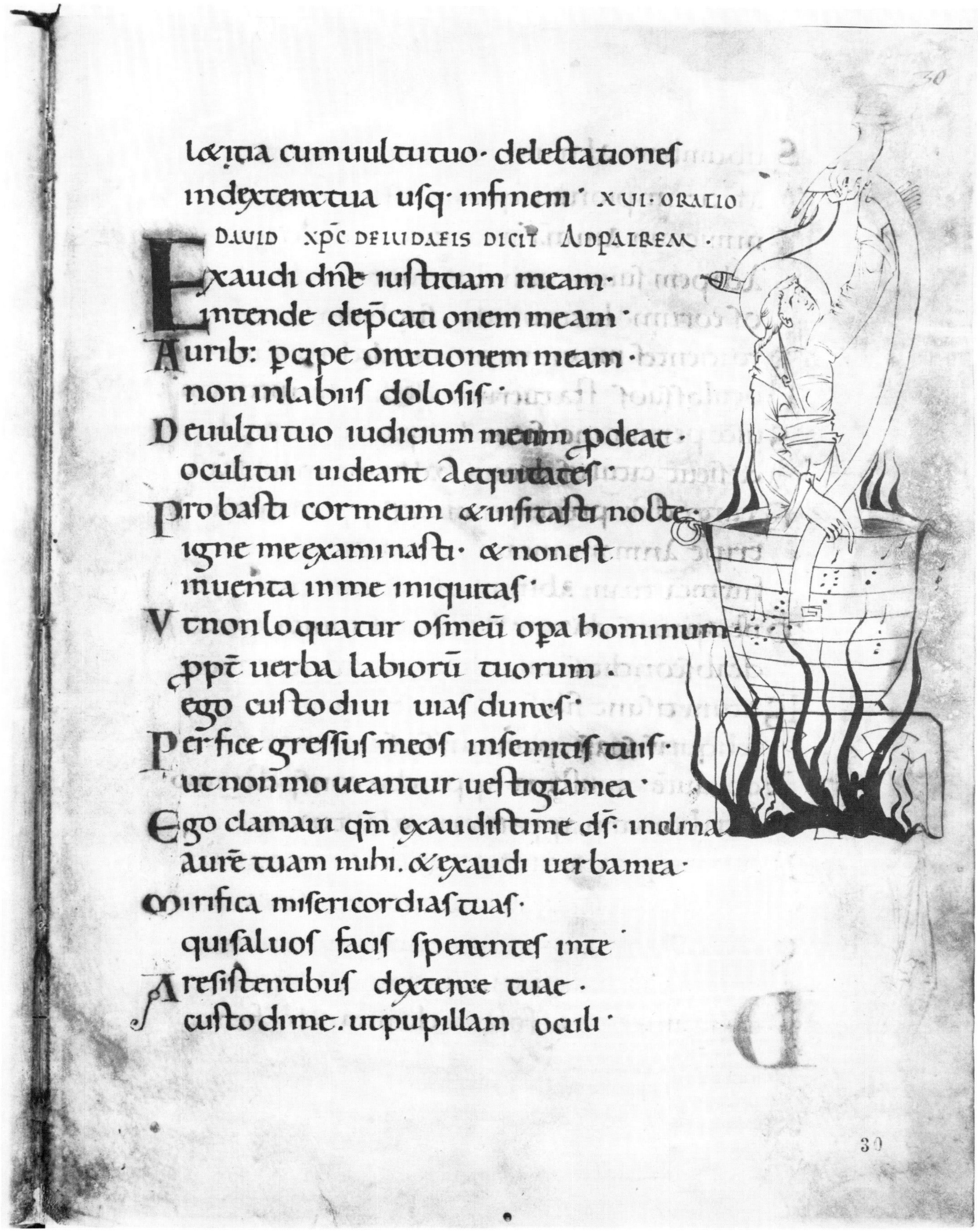
laetitia cum uultu tuo · delectationes
in dexteram tua usq in finem · XVI · ORATIO
DAVID XPC DE IUDAEIS DICIT AD PATREM ·
Exaudi dne iustitiam meam ·
intende depcati onem meam ·
Aurib: pcipe orationem meam ·
non in labiis dolosis ·
De uultu tuo iudicium meum pdeat ·
oculi tui uideant aequitates ·
Probasti cor meum et uisitasti nocte ·
igne me examinasti · et non est
inuenta in me iniquitas ·
Ut non loquatur os meum opa hominum
ppt uerba labiorum tuorum ·
ego custodiui uias duras ·
Perfice gressus meos in semitis tuis ·
ut non moueantur uestigia mea ·
Ego clamaui qm exaudisti me ds · inclina
aure tuam mihi · et exaudi uerba mea ·
Mirifica misericordias tuas ·
qui saluos facis sperantes in te
A resistentibus dexterae tuae ·
custodi me · ut pupillam oculi ·

3.9 Vatican, Biblioteca Apostolica, Reg. lat. 12, f. 30r

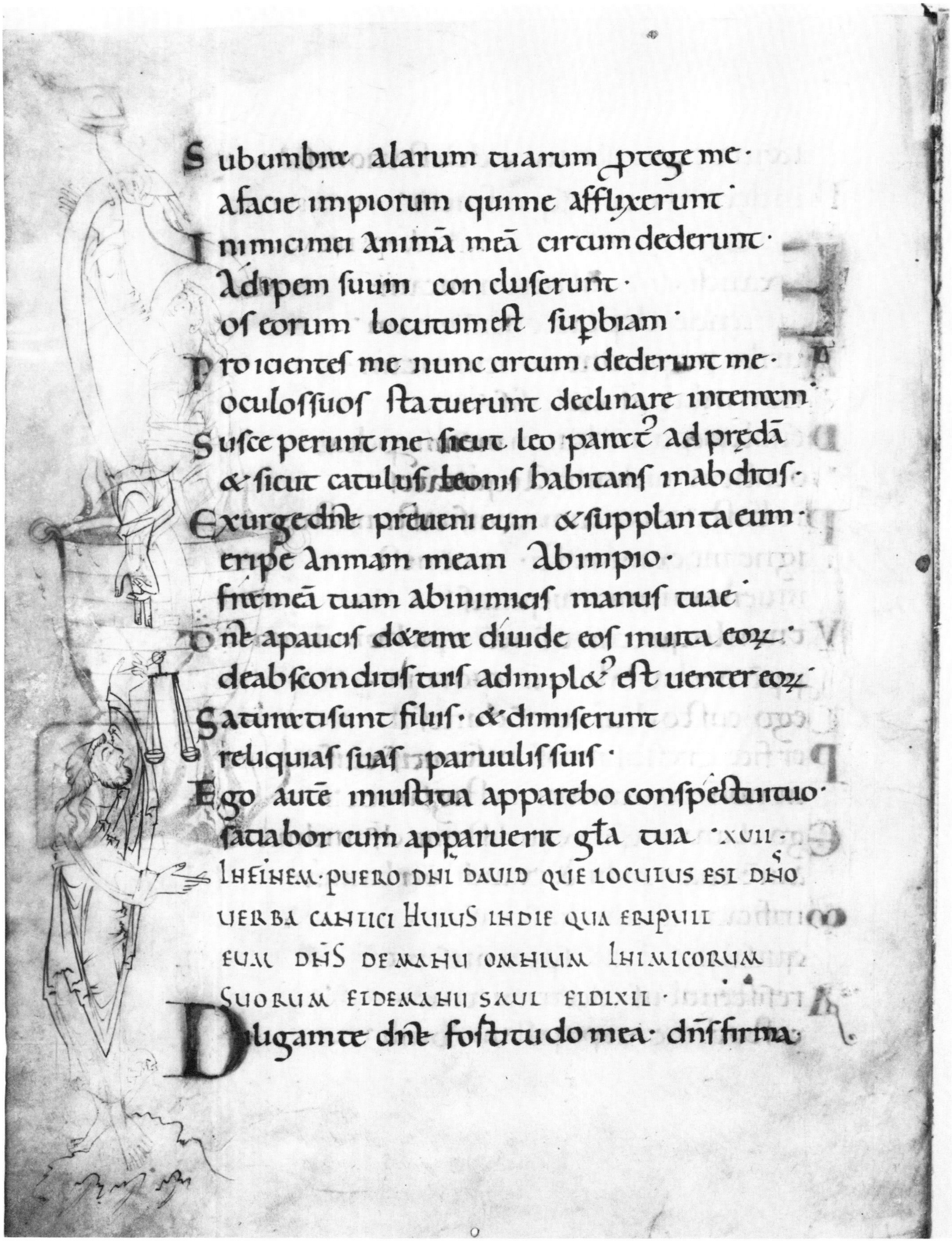
Sub umbra alarum tuarum protege me.
a facie impiorum qui me afflixerunt.
Inimici mei animam meam circumdederunt.
Adipem suum concluserunt.
os eorum locutum est superbiam.
Proicientes me nunc circumdederunt me.
oculos suos statuerunt declinare in terram.
Susceperunt me sicut leo paratus ad predam.
et sicut catulus leonis habitans in abditis.
Exurge domine preveni eum et supplanta eum.
eripe animam meam ab impio.
frameam tuam ab inimicis manus tuae.
Domine a paucis de terra divide eos in vita eorum.
de absconditis tuis adimpletus est venter eorum.
Saturati sunt filiis. et dimiserunt
reliquias suas parvulis suis.
Ego autem in iustitia apparebo conspectui tuo.
satiabor cum apparuerit gloria tua. XVII.
IN FINEM. PUERO DOMINI DAVID QUI LOCUTUS EST DOMINO
VERBA CANTICI HUIUS IN DIE QUA ERIPUIT
EUM DOMINUS DE MANU OMNIUM INIMICORUM
SUORUM ET DE MANU SAUL ET DIXIT.
Diligam te domine fortitudo mea. dominus firma-

3.10 Vatican, Biblioteca Apostolica, Reg. lat. 12, f. 30v

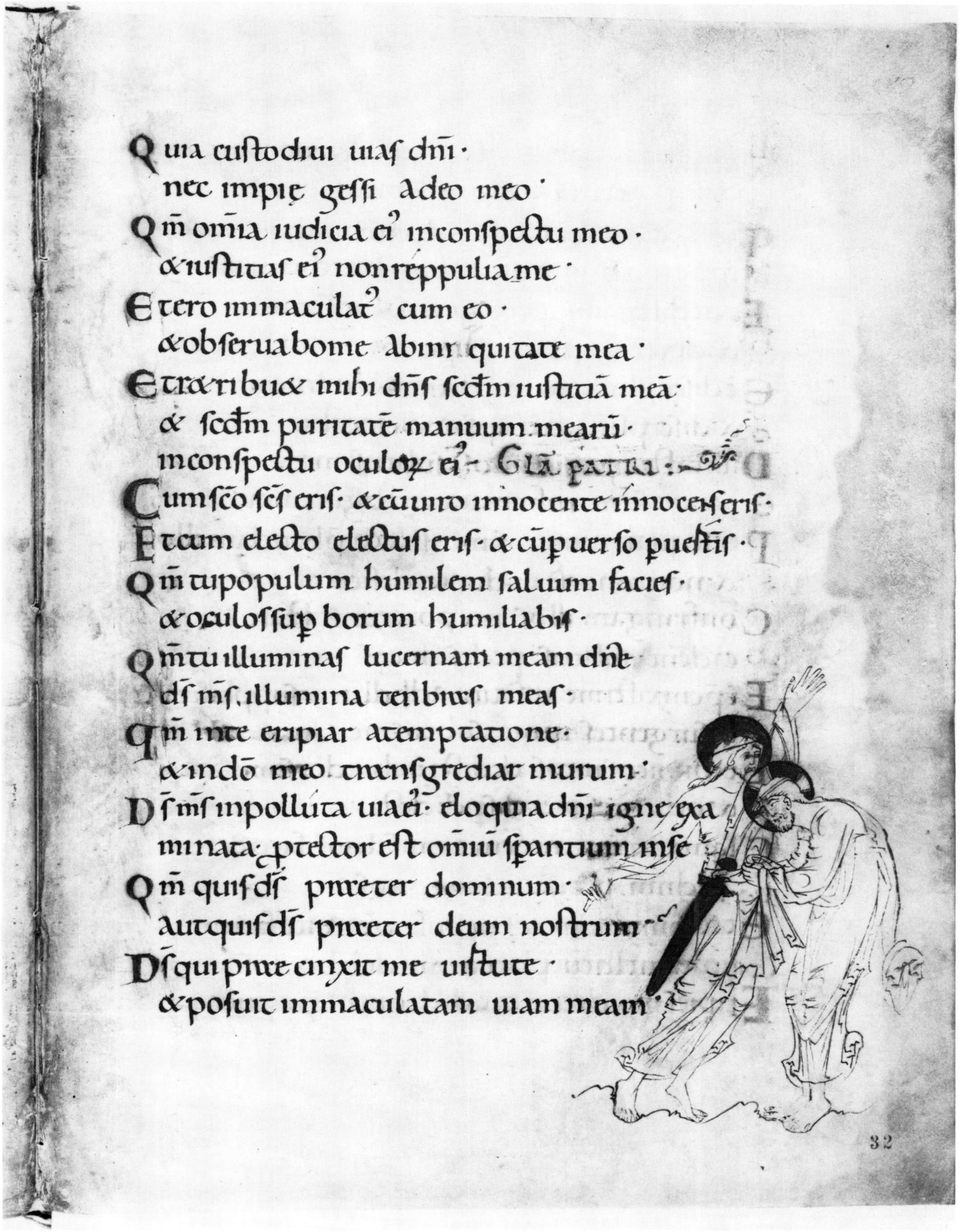

Quia custodiui uias dn̄i ·
nec impie gessi a deo meo ·
Qm̄ omnia iudicia ei⁹ in conspectu meo ·
& iustitias ei⁹ non reppuli a me ·
Et ero immaculat⁹ cum eo ·
& obseruabo me ab iniquitate mea ·
Et retribuet mihi dn̄s secd̄m iustitiā meā ·
& secd̄m puritatē manuum mearū ·
in conspectu oculoꝝ ei⁹ - Glā patri :
Cum sc̄o sc̄s eris · & cū uiro innocente innocens eris ·
Et cum electo electus eris · & cū puerso puerteris ·
Qm̄ tu populum humilem saluum facies ·
& oculos sup̄ borum humiliabis ·
Qm̄ tu illuminas lucernam meam dn̄e ·
ds̄ m̄s illumina tenebras meas ·
Qm̄ in te eripiar a temptatione ·
& in do̅ meo transgrediar murum ·
Ds̄ m̄s inpolluta uia ei · eloquia dn̄i igne exa
minata · ptector est omniū sperantium in se ·
Qm̄ quis ds̄ preter dominum ·
aut quis ds̄ preter deum nostrum ·
Ds̄ qui precinxit me uirtute ·
& posuit immaculatam uiam meam ·

32

3.11 Vatican, Biblioteca Apostolica, Reg. lat. 12, f. 32r

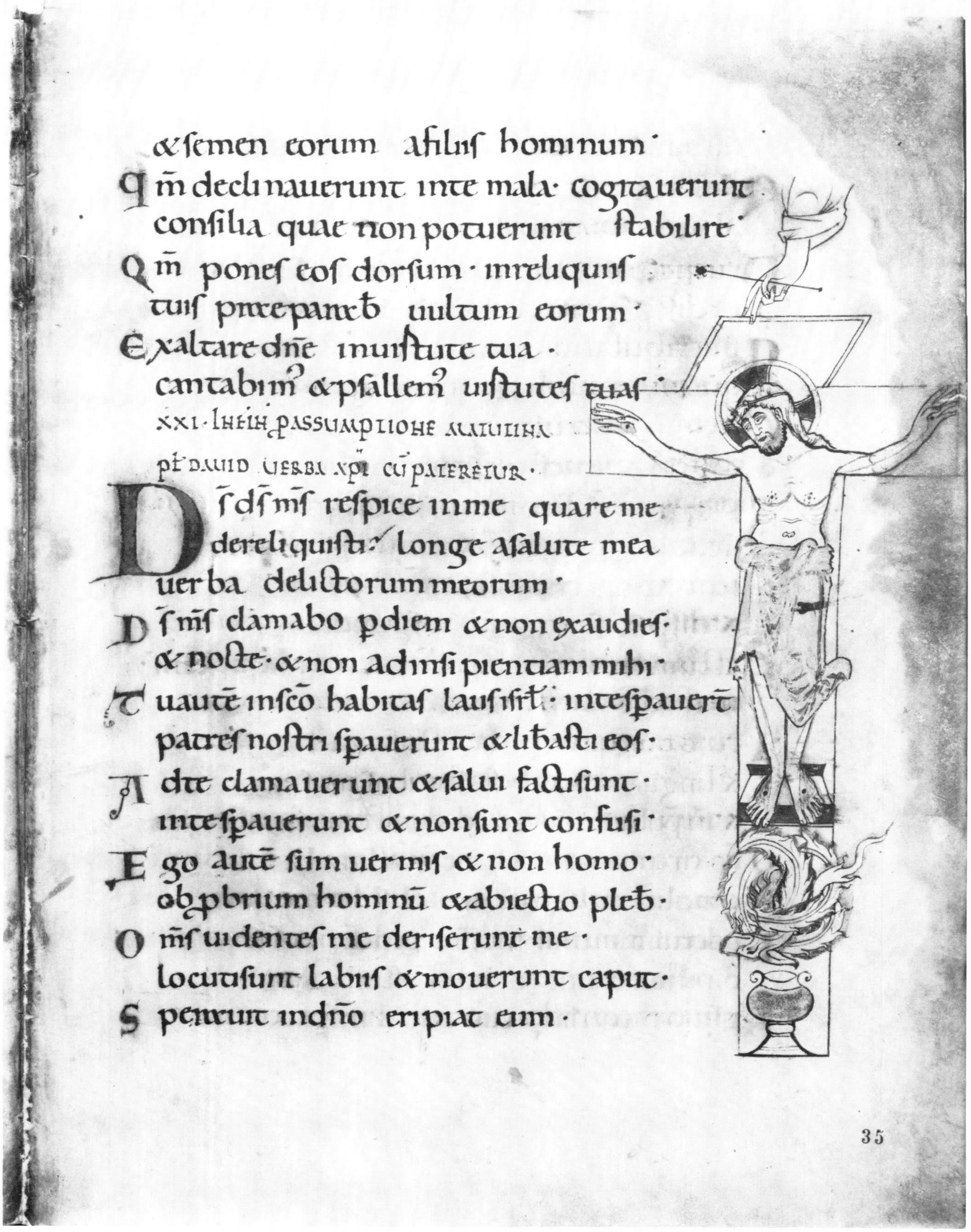
& semen eorum a filiis hominum ·
Q m̄ declinauerunt in te mala · cogitauerunt
consilia quae non potuerunt stabilire ·
Q m̄ pones eos dorsum · in reliquiis
tuis praeparabis uultum eorum ·
E xaltare dn̄e in uirtute tua ·
cantabimus & psallemus uirtutes tuas ·
XXI · IN FIN PRO ASSUMPTIONE MATUTINA
PS DAVID VERBA XPI CUM PATERETUR ·
D s ds m̄s respice in me quare me
dereliquisti? longe a salute mea
uerba delictorum meorum ·
D s m̄s clamabo per diem & non exaudies ·
& nocte · & non ad insipientiam mihi ·
T u autē in scō habitas laus isrl̄ · in te sperauerunt
patres nostri sperauerunt & liberasti eos ·
A d te clamauerunt & salui facti sunt ·
in te sperauerunt & non sunt confusi ·
E go autē sum uermis & non homo ·
obprobrium hominū & abiectio plebis ·
O m̄s uidentes me deriserunt me ·
locuti sunt labiis & mouerunt caput ·
S perauit in dn̄o eripiat eum ·
35

3.12 Vatican, Biblioteca Apostolica, Reg. lat. 12, f. 35r

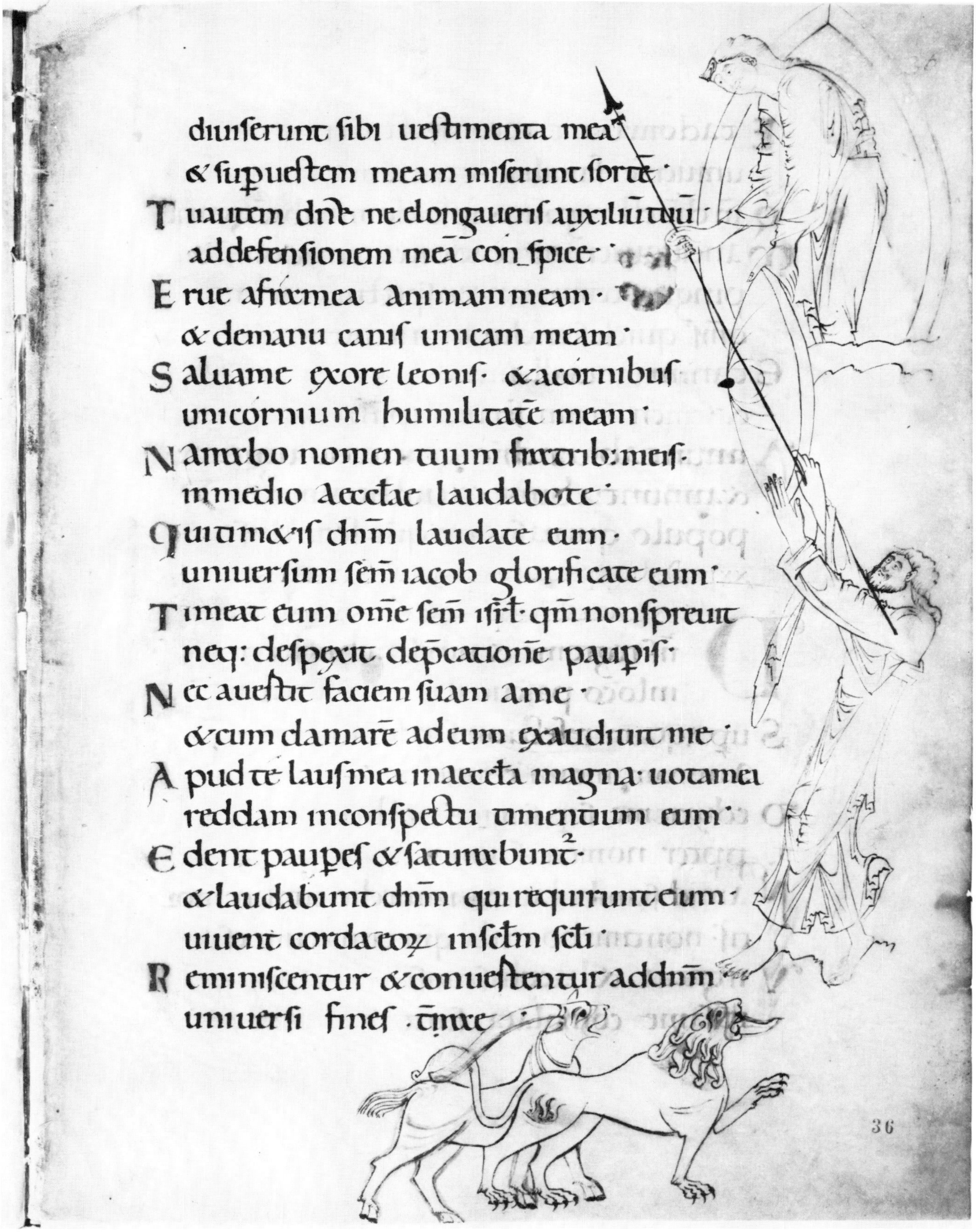

diuiserunt sibi uestimenta mea
& sup uestem meam miserunt sortē·
T u autem dnē ne elongaueris auxiliū tuū·
ad defensionem meā con spice·
E rue a framea animam meam·
& de manu canis unicam meam·
S alua me ex ore leonis· & a cornibus
unicornium humilitatē meam·
N arrabo nomen tuum fratrib: meis·
in medio aecclae laudabo te·
Q ui timetis dnm̄ laudate eum·
uniuersum sem̄ iacob glorificate eum·
T imeat eum om̄e sem̄ isrl· qm̄ non spreuit
neq: despexit dep̄cationē paupis·
N ec auertit faciem suam a me·
& cum clamarē ad eum exaudiuit me·
A pud te laus mea in aeccta magna: uota mea
reddam in conspectu timentium eum·
E dent paupes & saturabunt·
& laudabunt dnm̄ qui requirunt eum·
uiuent corda eorum in sclm scli·
R eminiscentur & conuertentur ad dnm̄
uniuersi fines terrae·

36

3.13 Vatican, Biblioteca Apostolica, Reg. lat. 12, f. 36r

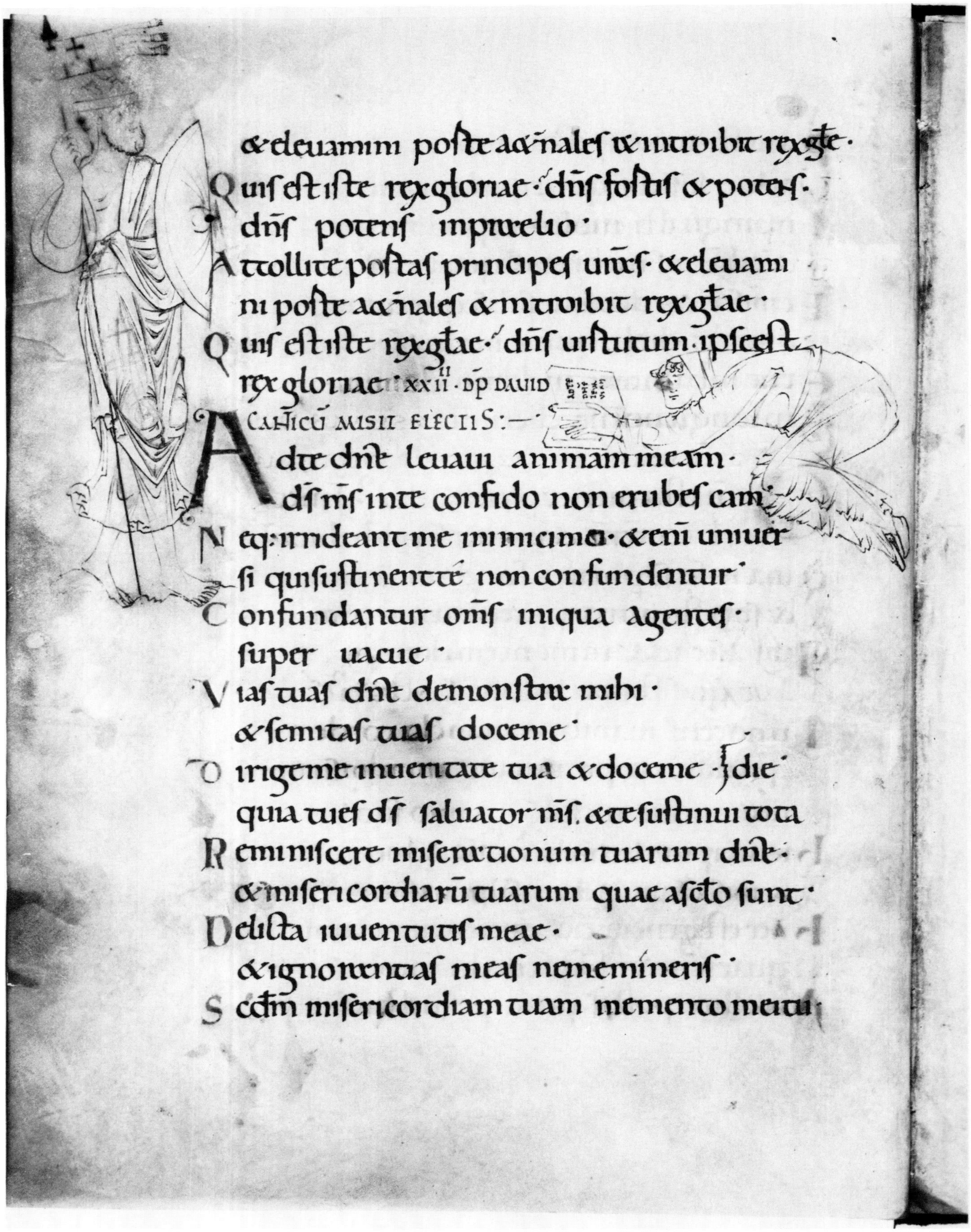
& eleuamini poste ae(ter)nales & introibit rex gl(ori)e ·
Quis est iste rex gloriae · dns fortis & potens ·
dns potens in proelio ·
Attollite portas principes uestras · & eleuami
ni poste ae(ter)nales & introibit rex gl(ori)ae ·
Quis est iste rex gl(ori)ae · dns uirtutum ipse est
rex gloriae · XXIII · DP DAUID
CANTICU MISIT ELECTIS :—
Ad te dne leuaui animam meam ·
ds ms in te confido non erubescam ·
Neque irrideant me inimici mei · & enim uniuer
si qui sustinent te non confundentur ·
Confundantur omnes iniqua agentes ·
super uacue ·
Vias tuas dne demonstra mihi ·
& semitas tuas doce me ·
Dirige me in ueritate tua & doce me · die
quia tu es ds saluator ms. & te sustinui tota
Reminiscere miserationum tuarum dne ·
& misericordiarum tuarum quae a s(ae)c(u)lo sunt ·
Delicta iuuentutis meae ·
& ignorantias meas ne memineris ·
Secundum misericordiam tuam memento mei tu

3.14 Vatican, Biblioteca Apostolica, Reg. lat. 12, f. 37v

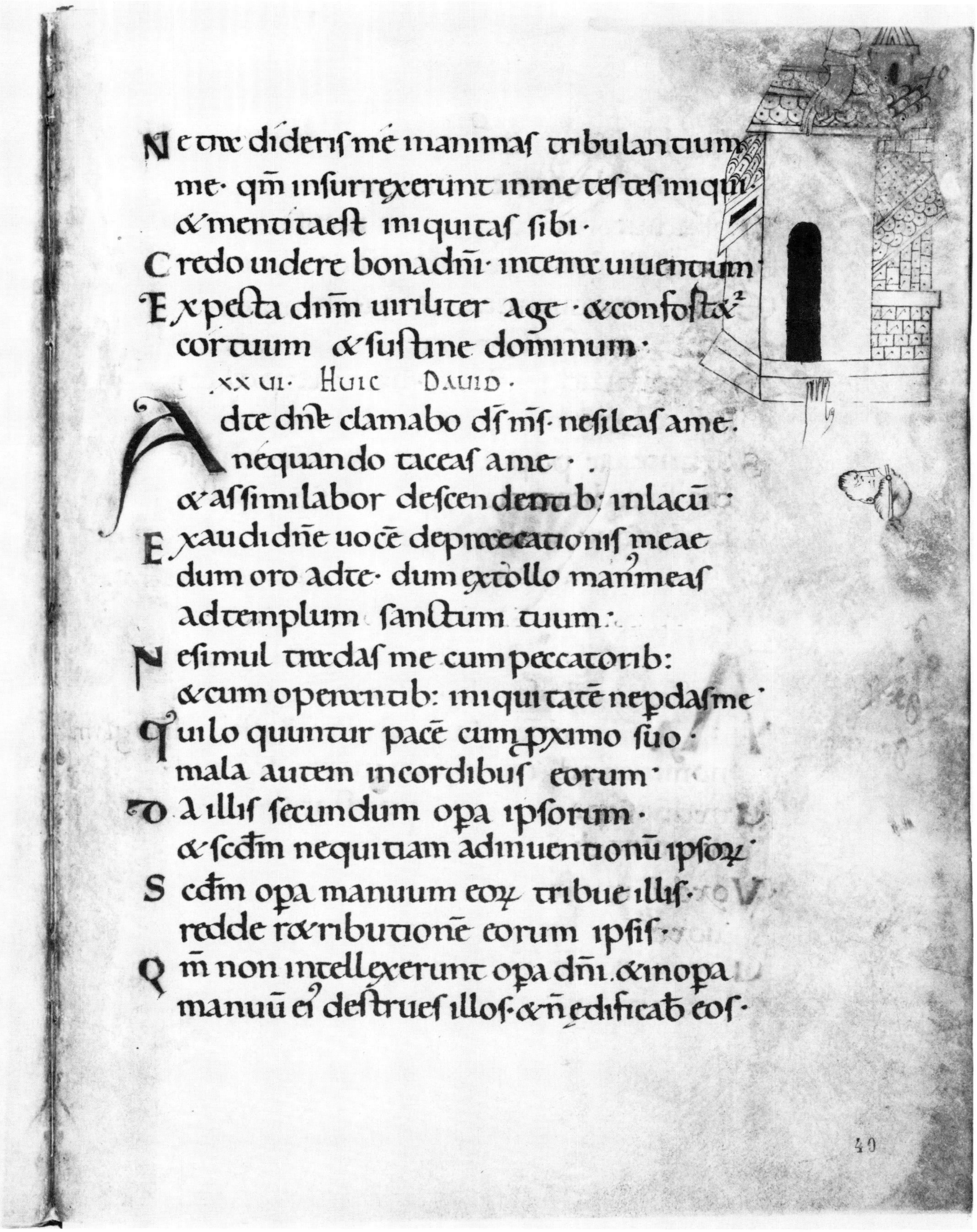

Ne tradideris me in animas tribulantium
me · qm̄ insurrexerunt in me testes iniqui
& mentita est iniquitas sibi ·
Credo uidere bona dn̄i · in terra uiuentium
Expecta dn̄m uiriliter age · & confortetur
cor tuum & sustine dominum ·
XXVI · HUIC DAVID ·
Ad te dn̄e clamabo ds̄ ms̄ · ne sileas a me.
ne quando taceas a me · .
& assimilabor descendentib; in lacū ·
Exaudi dn̄e uocē deprecationis meae
dum oro ad te · dum extollo manus meas
ad templum sanctum tuum ·
Ne simul tradas me cum peccatorib;
& cum operantib; iniquitatē ne pdas me ·
Qui loquuntur pacē cum pximo suo ·
mala autem in cordibus eorum ·
Da illis secundum opa ipsorum ·
& scdm̄ nequitiam adinuentionū ipsorum ·
Scdm̄ opa manuum eorum tribue illis ·
redde retributionē eorum ipsis ·
Qm̄ non intellexerunt opa dn̄i. & in opa
manuū ei destrues illos · & n̄ edificab eos ·

3.15 Vatican, Biblioteca Apostolica, Reg. lat. 12, f. 40r

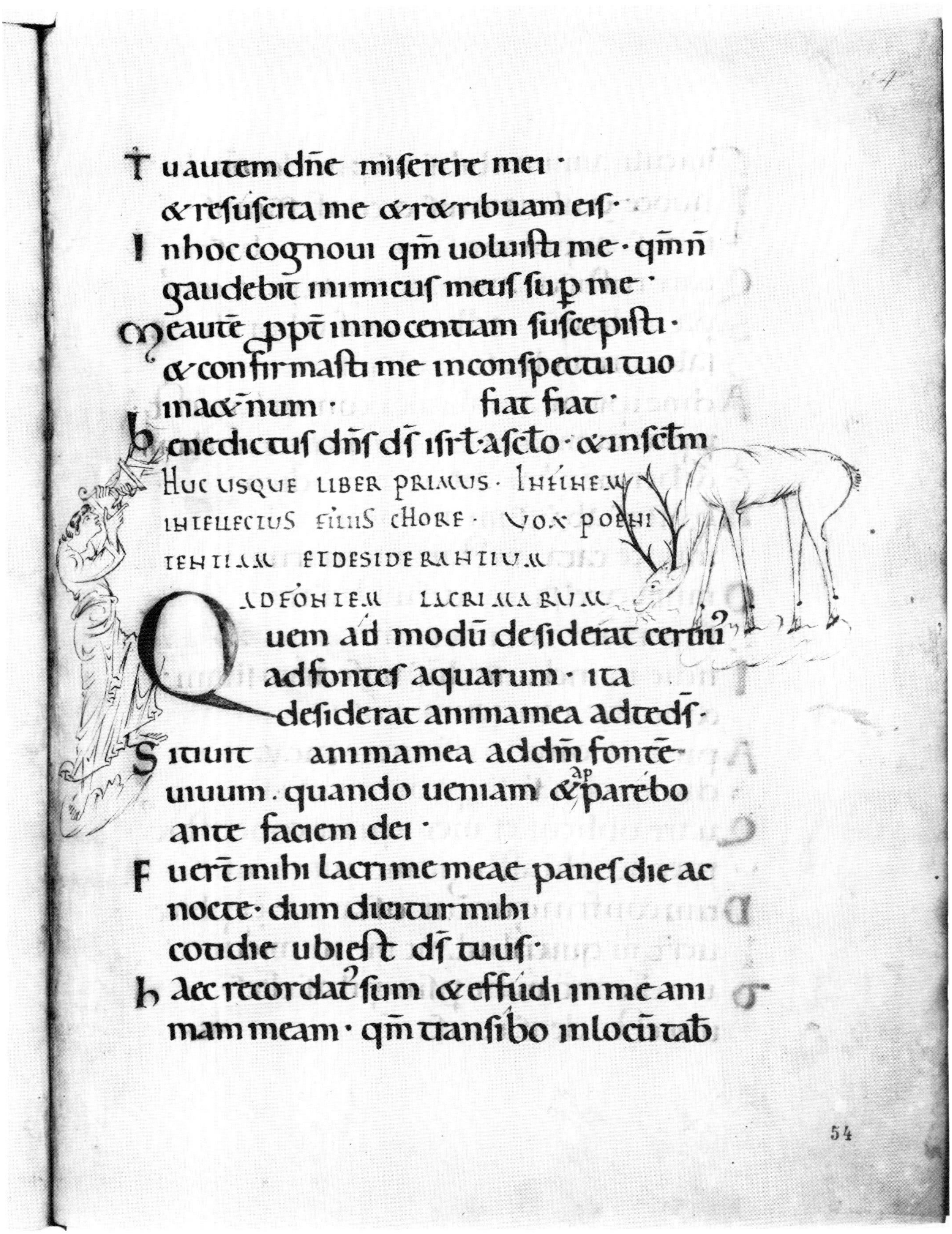
Tu autem dne miserere mei ·
& resuscita me & retribuam eis ·
In hoc cognoui qm uoluisti me · qm n
gaudebit inimicus meus sup me ·
Me autē ppt innocentiam suscepisti ·
& confirmasti me in conspectu tuo
in aet'num · fiat fiat ·
Benedictus dns ds isrl · a sclo · & in sclm
HUCUSQUE LIBER PRIMUS · IN FINEM
INTELLECTUS FILIIS CHORE · VOX POENI
TENTIAM ET DESIDERANTIUM
AD FONTEM LACRIMARUM
Quem ad modū desiderat ceruus
ad fontes aquarum · ita
desiderat anima mea ad te ds ·
Sitiuit anima mea ad dm fontē
uiuum. quando ueniam & apparebo
ante faciem dei ·
Fuerūt mihi lacrimae meae panes die ac
nocte · dum dicitur mihi
cotidie ubi est ds tuus ·
Haec recordatus sum & effudi in me ani
mam meam · qm transibo in locū tab
54

3.16 Vatican, Biblioteca Apostolica, Reg. lat. 12, f. 54r

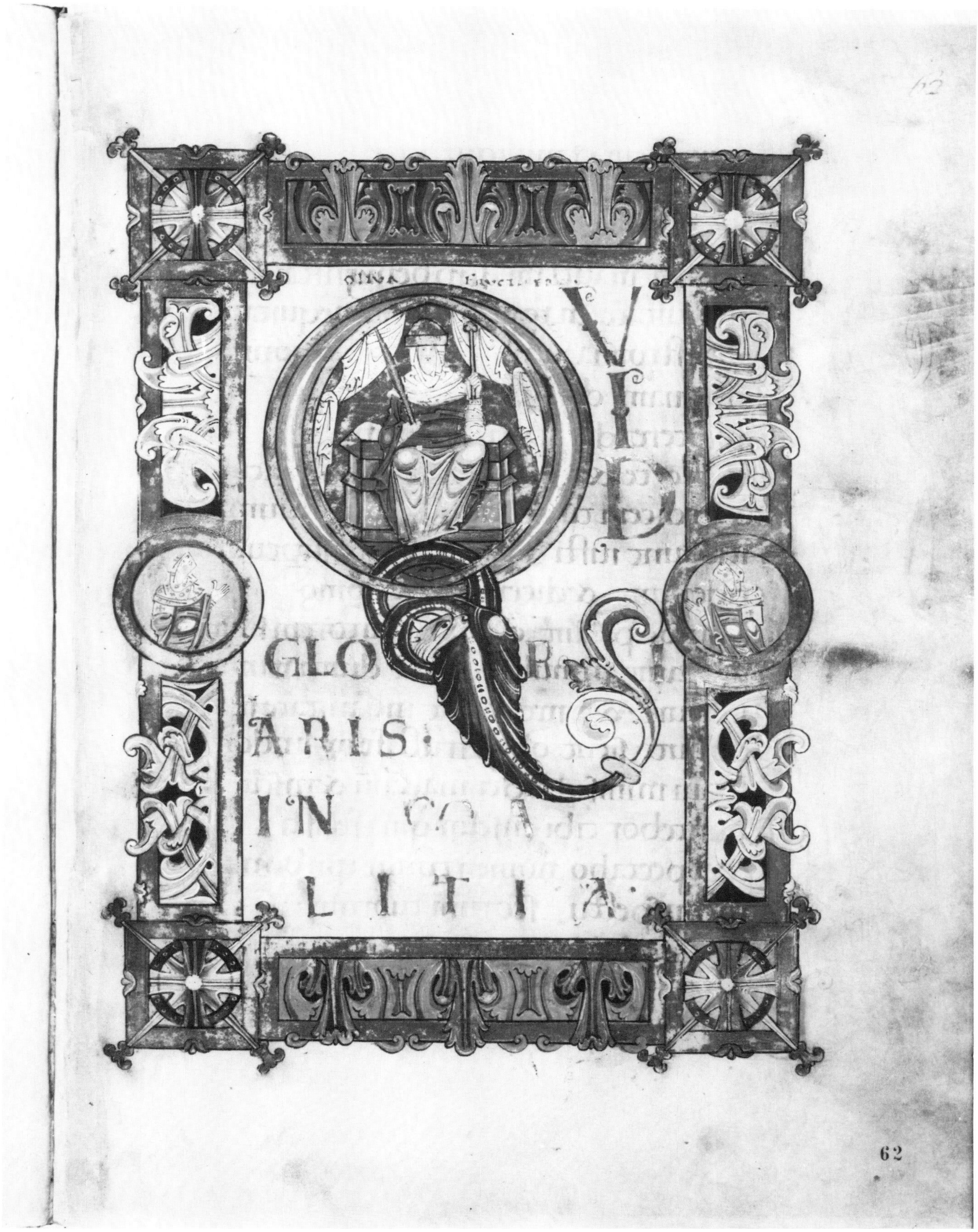

3.17 Vatican, Biblioteca Apostolica, Reg. lat. 12, f. 62[r]

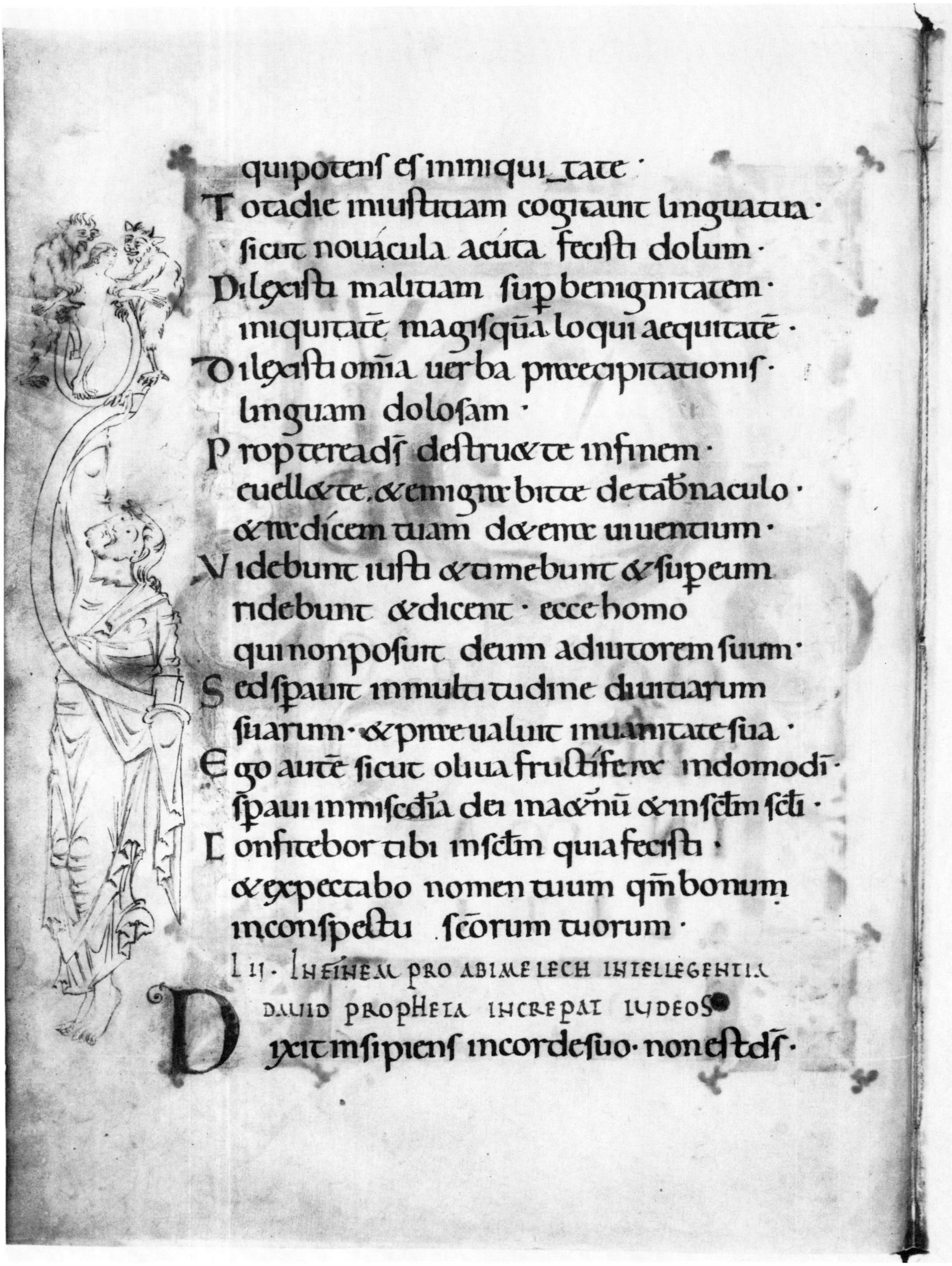
quipotens es in iniquitate ·
Tota die iniustitiam cogitauit lingua tua ·
sicut nouacula acuta fecisti dolum ·
Dilexisti malitiam sup benignitatem ·
iniquitatē magis quā loqui aequitatē ·
Dilexisti omīa uerba praecipitationis ·
linguam dolosam ·
Propterea ds destruet te in finem ·
euellet te. & emigrabit te de tabnaculo ·
& radicem tuam de terra uiuentium ·
Videbunt iusti & timebunt & sup eum
ridebunt & dicent · ecce homo
qui non posuit deum adiutorem suum ·
Sed sperauit in multitudine diuitiarum
suarum · & praeualuit in uanitate sua ·
Ego autē sicut oliua fructifera in domo dī ·
speraui in misericordia dei in aeternū & in saeclm saecli ·
Confitebor tibi in saeclm quia fecisti ·
& expectabo nomen tuum qm bonum
in conspectu scorum tuorum ·
LII · IN FINEM PRO ABIMELECH INTELLEGENTIA
DAUID PROPHETA INCREPAT IUDEOS
Dixit insipiens in corde suo · non est ds ·

3.18 Vatican, Biblioteca Apostolica, Reg. lat. 12, f. 62v

aurib: pcipe uerba oris mei ·
Q m̄ alieni insurrexerunt aduersum me ·
& fortes quaesierunt animam meam ·
n̄ pposuerunt dm̄ ante conspectū suum ·
E cce enim ds̄ adiuuat me ·
dn̄s susceptor ÷ animae meae ·
A uerte mala inimicis meis ·
in ueritate tua disp̄de illos ·
V oluntarię sacrificabo tibi ·
confitebor nomini tuo qm̄ bonū est
Q m̄ ex omni tribulatione eripuisti me ·
& sup inimicos meos despexit
oculus m̄s · LIIJ · IN FINEM IN CARMI
NIBUS · INTELLECTUS DAVID · VOX XP̄I
ADVERSUS MAGNOTOS IUDAEORUM ·
E xaudi ds̄ orationem meam ·
& ne despexeris dep̄cationem meam
intende mihi & exaudi me ·
C ontristatus sum in exercitatione mea ·
& conturbatus sum a uoce inimici ·
& a tribulatione peccatoris ·
Q m̄ declinauerunt in me iniquitates ·
& in ira molesti erant mihi ·

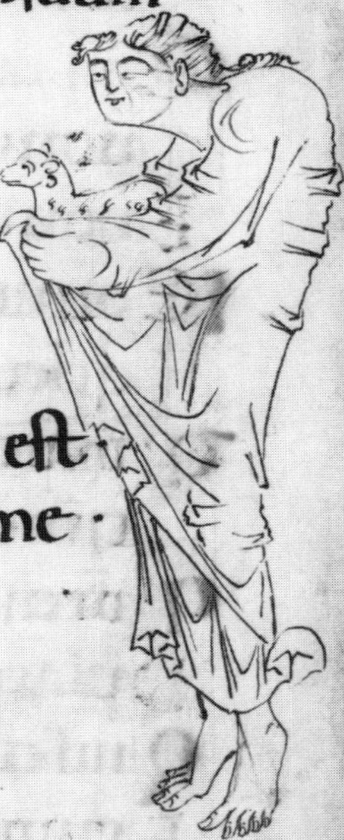

3.19 Vatican, Biblioteca Apostolica, Reg. lat. 12, f. 63v

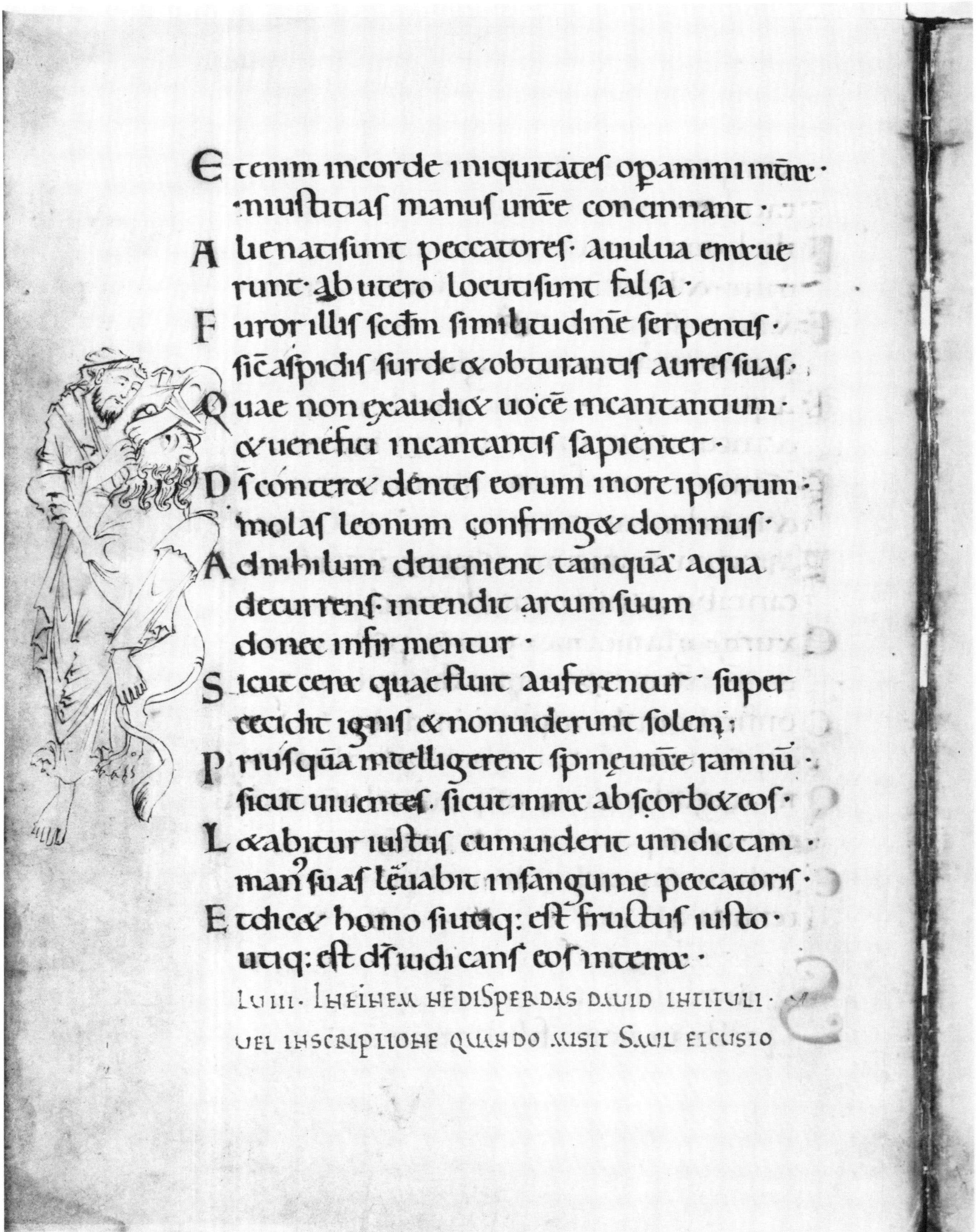
Etenim in corde iniquitates operamini in terra
iniustitias manus uestrae concinnant
Alienati sunt peccatores a uulua errauerunt ab utero locuti sunt falsa
Furor illis secundum similitudinem serpentis
sicut aspidis surdae et obturantis aures suas
Quae non exaudiet uocem incantantium
et uenefici incantantis sapienter
Deus conteret dentes eorum in ore ipsorum
molas leonum confringet dominus
Ad nihilum deuenient tamquam aqua
decurrens intendit arcum suum
donec infirmentur
Sicut cera quae fluit auferentur super
cecidit ignis et non uiderunt solem
Priusquam intellegerent spinae uestrae ramnum
sicut uiuentes sicut in ira absorbet eos
Laetabitur iustus cum uiderit uindictam
manus suas lauabit in sanguine peccatoris
Et dicet homo si utique est fructus iusto
utique est deus iudicans eos in terra
LVIII. IN FINEM NE DISPERDAS DAVID IN TITULI
UEL INSCRIPTIONE QUANDO MISIT SAUL ET CUSTO

3.20 Vatican, Biblioteca Apostolica, Reg. lat. 12, f. 66v

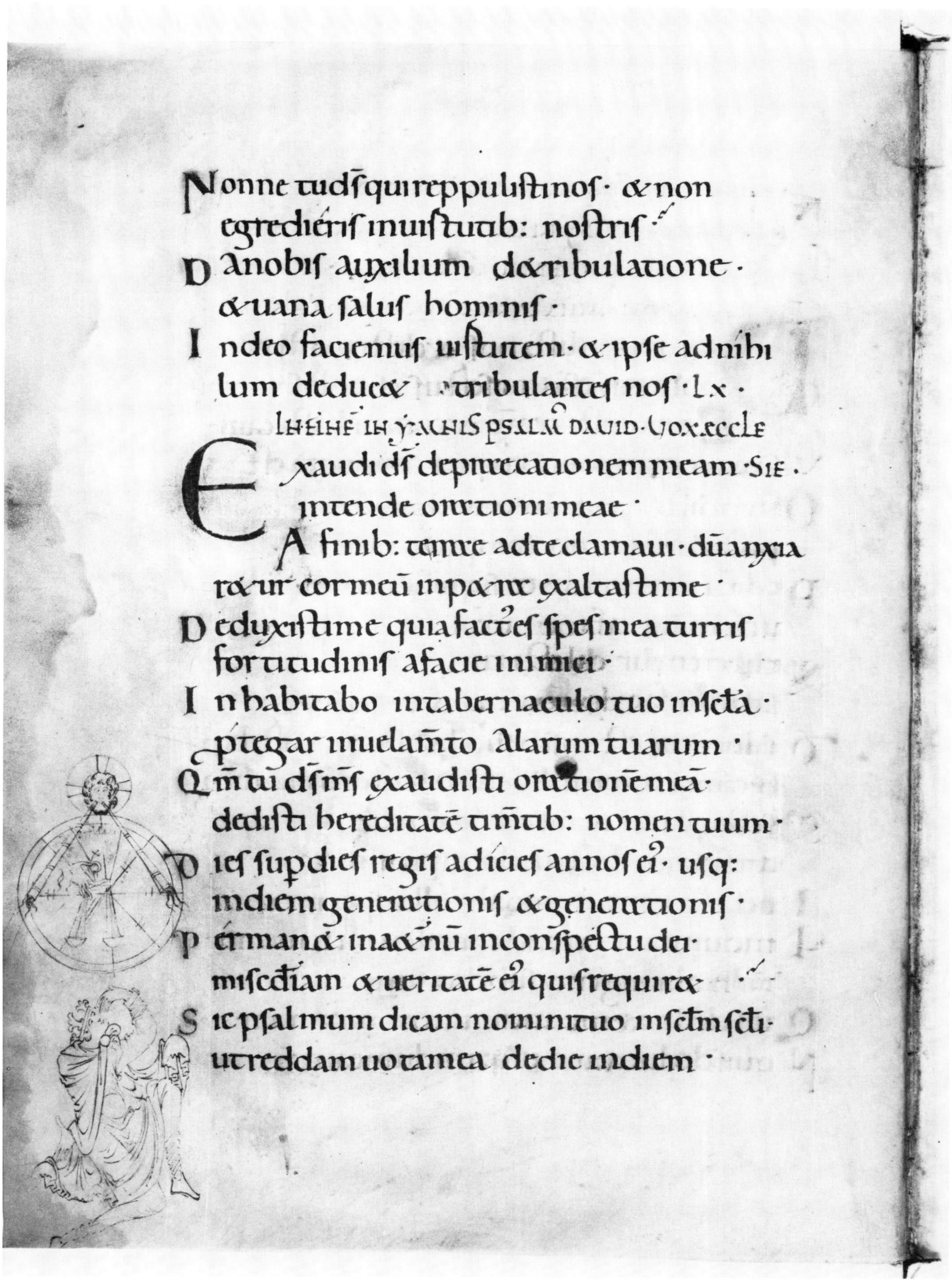
Nonne tu ds qui reppulisti nos · & non egrederis in uirtutib: nostris ·
Da nobis auxilium de tribulatione · & uana salus hominis ·
In deo faciemus uirtutem · & ipse ad nihilum deducet tribulantes nos · LX ·
IN FINE IN YMNIS PSALM DAVID · VOX ECCLE
Exaudi ds deprecationem meam · SIE · intende orationi meae ·
A finib: terrae ad te clamaui · dũ anxiaretur cor meũ in petra exaltasti me ·
Deduxisti me quia factus es spes mea turris fortitudinis a facie inimici ·
Inhabitabo in tabernaculo tuo in sectã · ptegar in uelamto alarum tuarum ·
Qm tu ds ms exaudisti orationẽ meã · dedisti hereditatẽ timtib: nomen tuum ·
Dies sup dies regis adicies annos eĩ · usq: in diem generationis & generationis ·
Permanet in aeternũ in conspectu dei · miscdiam & ueritatẽ eĩ quis requiret ·
Sic psalmum dicam nomini tuo in sectm secti · ut reddam uota mea de die in diem ·

3.21 Vatican, Biblioteca Apostolica, Reg. lat. 12, f. 68v

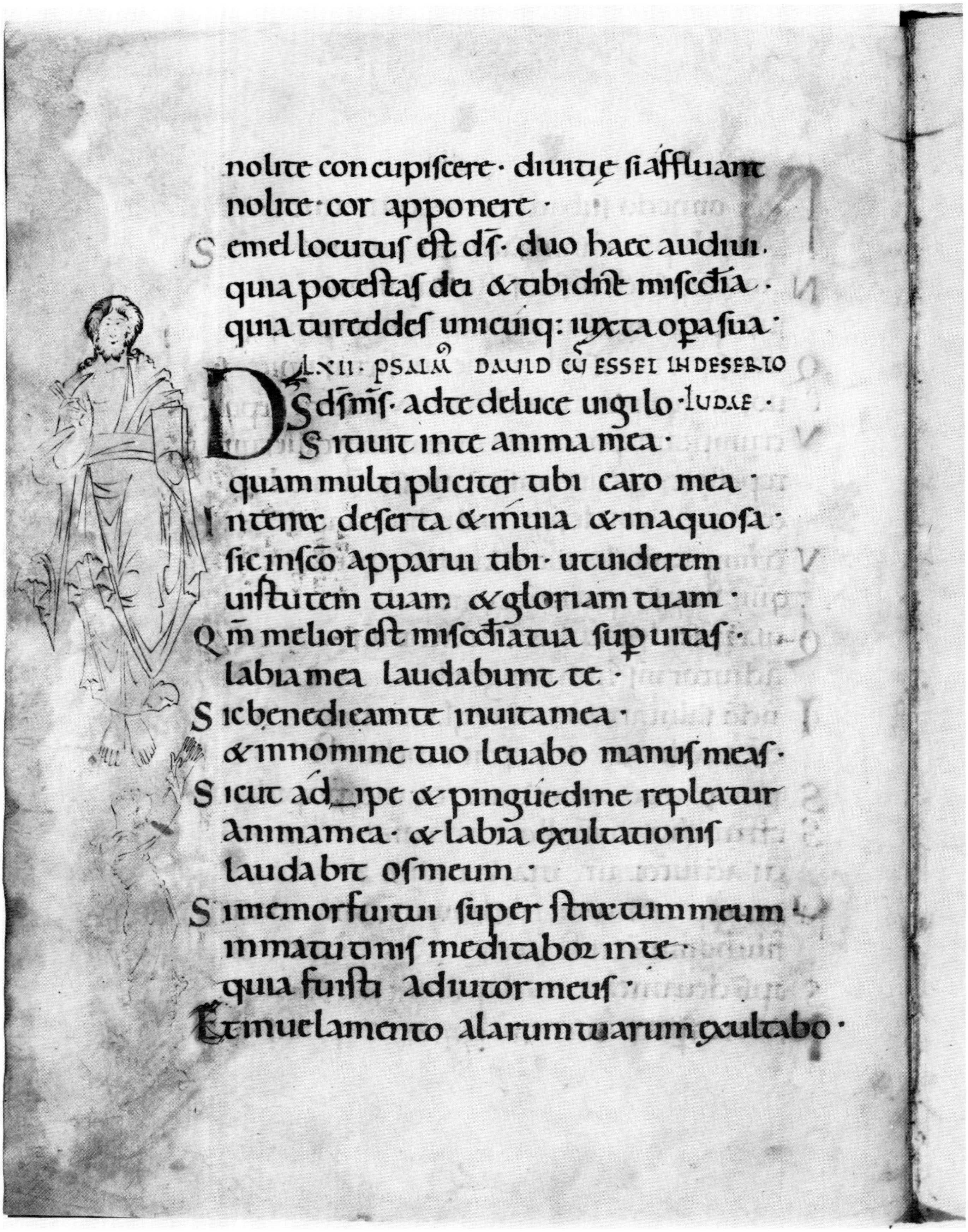
nolite concupiscere · diuitię si affluant
nolite · cor apponere ·
Semel locutus est ds · duo haec audiui.
quia potestas dei & tibi dne misecdia ·
quia tu reddes unicuiq: iuxta opa sua ·
LXII · PSALM DAUID CU ESSET IN DESERTO
Ds ds ms · ad te de luce uigilo · IUDAE ·
Sitiuit in te anima mea ·
quam multipliciter tibi caro mea ·
In terra deserta & inuia & inaquosa ·
sic in sco apparui tibi · ut uiderem
uirtutem tuam & gloriam tuam ·
Qm melior est misecdia tua sup uitas ·
labia mea laudabunt te ·
Sic benedicam te in uita mea ·
& in nomine tuo leuabo manus meas ·
Sicut ad_ipe & pinguedine repleatur
anima mea · & labia exultationis
laudabit os meum ·
Si memor fui tui super stratum meum
in matutinis meditabor in te ·
quia fuisti adiutor meus ·
Et in uelamento alarum tuarum exultabo ·

3.22 Vatican, Biblioteca Apostolica, Reg. lat. 12, f. 69v

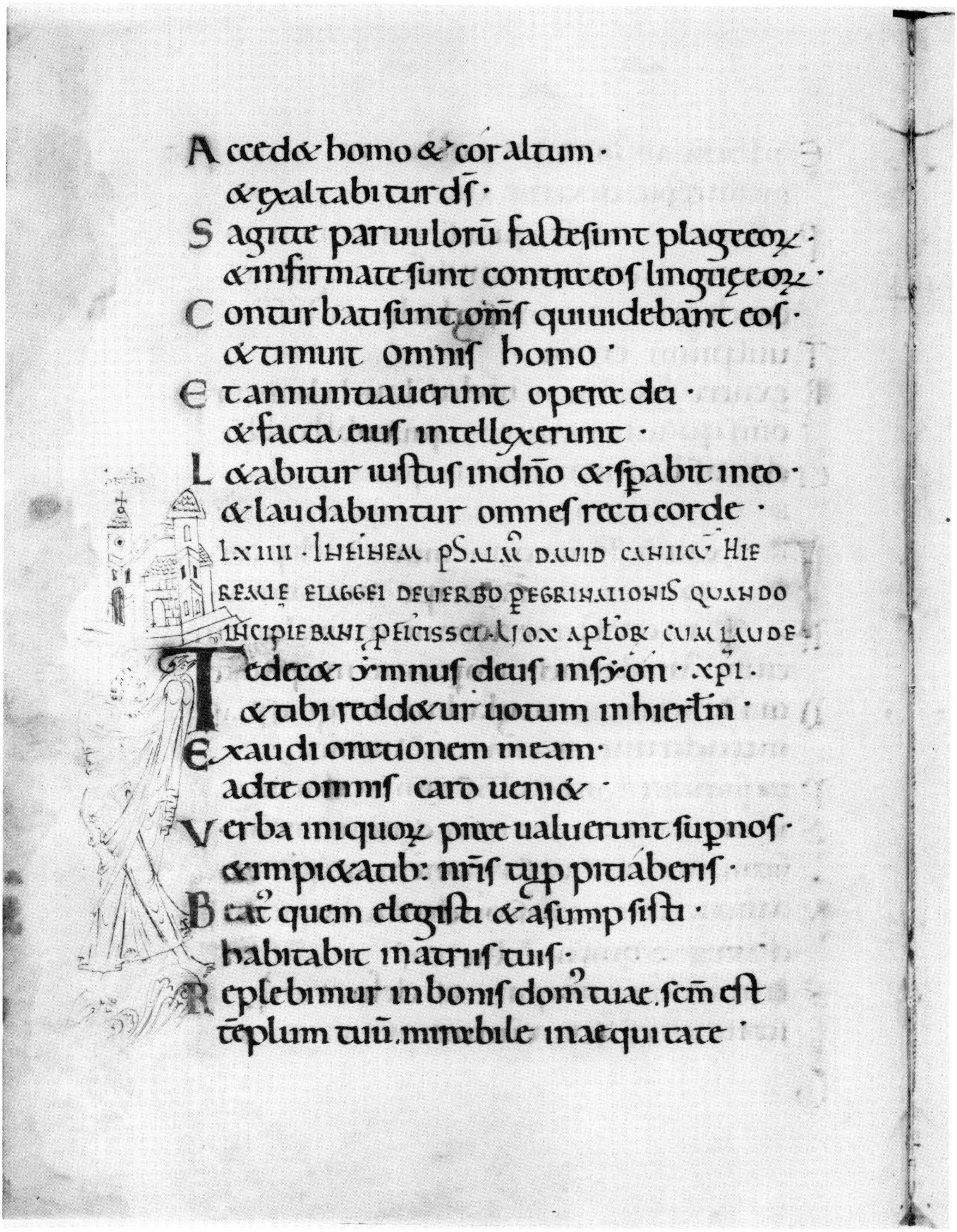
Accedet homo & cor altum ·
& exaltabitur ds̄ ·
Sagitte paruulorū facte sunt plage eorum ·
& infirmate sunt contra eos lingue eorum ·
Conturbati sunt omn̄s qui uidebant eos ·
& timuit omnis homo ·
Et annuntiauerunt opera dei ·
& facta eius intellexerunt ·
Letabitur iustus in dn̄o & sperabit in eo ·
& laudabuntur omnes recti corde ·
LXIIII · IN FINEM PSALMUS DAVID CANTICUM HIE
REMIE ET AGGEI DE UERBO PEREGRINATIONIS QUANDO
INCIPIEBANT PROFICISCI · ... CUM LAUDE
Te decet ymnus deus in syon · xpi ·
& tibi reddetur uotum in hierlm̄ ·
Exaudi orationem meam ·
ad te omnis caro ueniet ·
Verba iniquorum preualuerunt super nos ·
& impietatibus nr̄is tu propitiaberis ·
Beatus quem elegisti & asumpsisti ·
habitabit in atriis tuis ·
Replebimur in bonis domus tuae. scm̄ est
templum tuū. mirabile in aequitate ·

3.23 Vatican, Biblioteca Apostolica, Reg. lat. 12, f. 70v

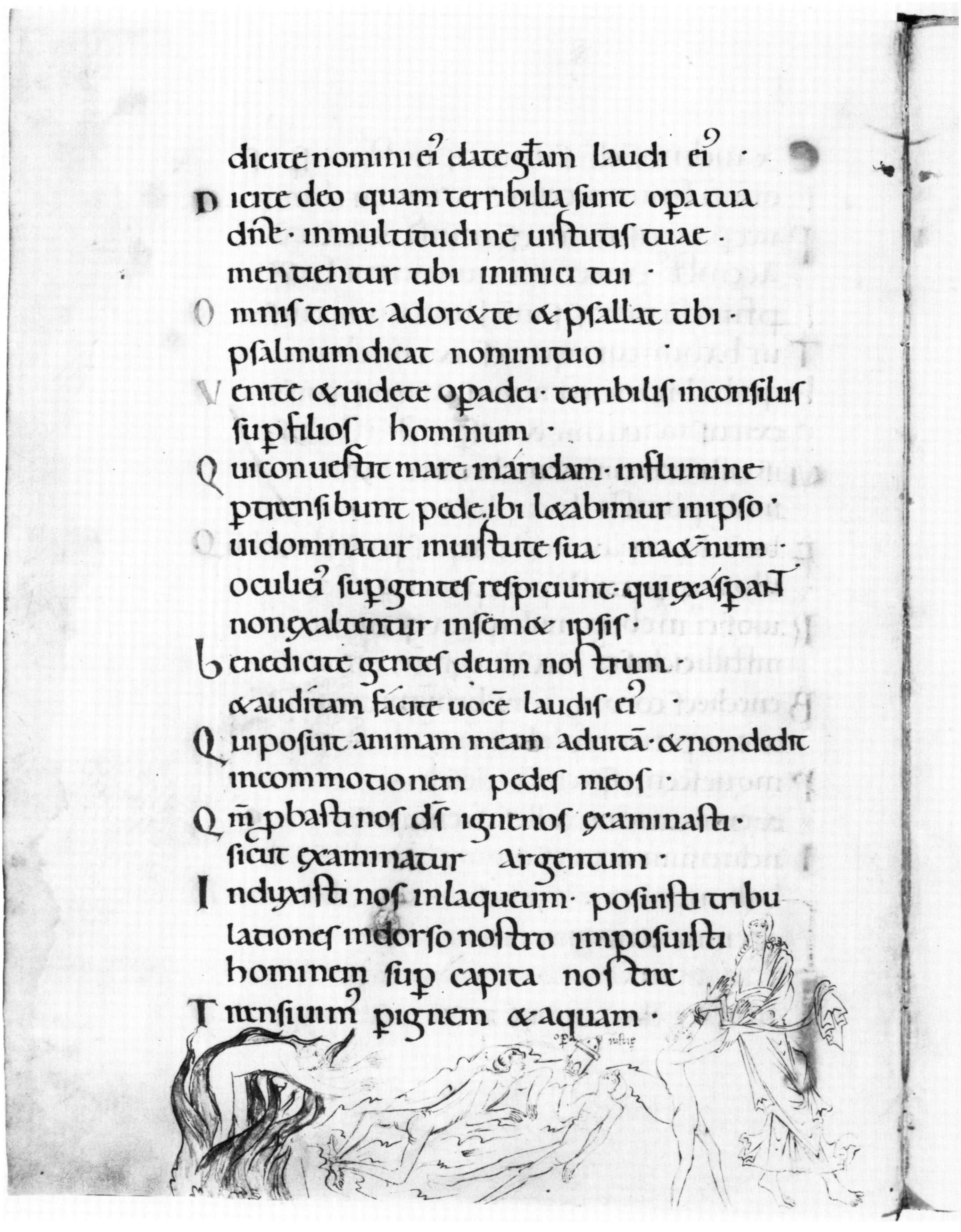
dicite nomini eius date gloriam laudi eius ·
D icite deo quam terribilia sunt opera tua
domine · in multitudine uirtutis tuae ·
mentientur tibi inimici tui ·
O mnis terra adoret te et psallat tibi ·
psalmum dicat nomini tuo ·
V enite et uidete opera dei · terribilis in consiliis
super filios hominum ·
Q ui conuertit mare in aridam · in flumine
pertransibunt pede · ibi laetabimur in ipso ·
Q ui dominatur in uirtute sua in aeternum ·
oculi eius super gentes respiciunt · qui exasperant
non exaltentur in semet ipsis ·
B enedicite gentes deum nostrum ·
et auditam facite uocem laudis eius ·
Q ui posuit animam meam ad uitam · et non dedit
in commotionem pedes meos ·
Q uoniam probasti nos deus igne nos examinasti ·
sicut examinatur argentum ·
I nduxisti nos in laqueum · posuisti tribu
lationes in dorso nostro · imposuisti
homines super capita nostra
T ransiuimus per ignem et aquam ·

3.24 Vatican, Biblioteca Apostolica, Reg. lat. 12, f. 71v

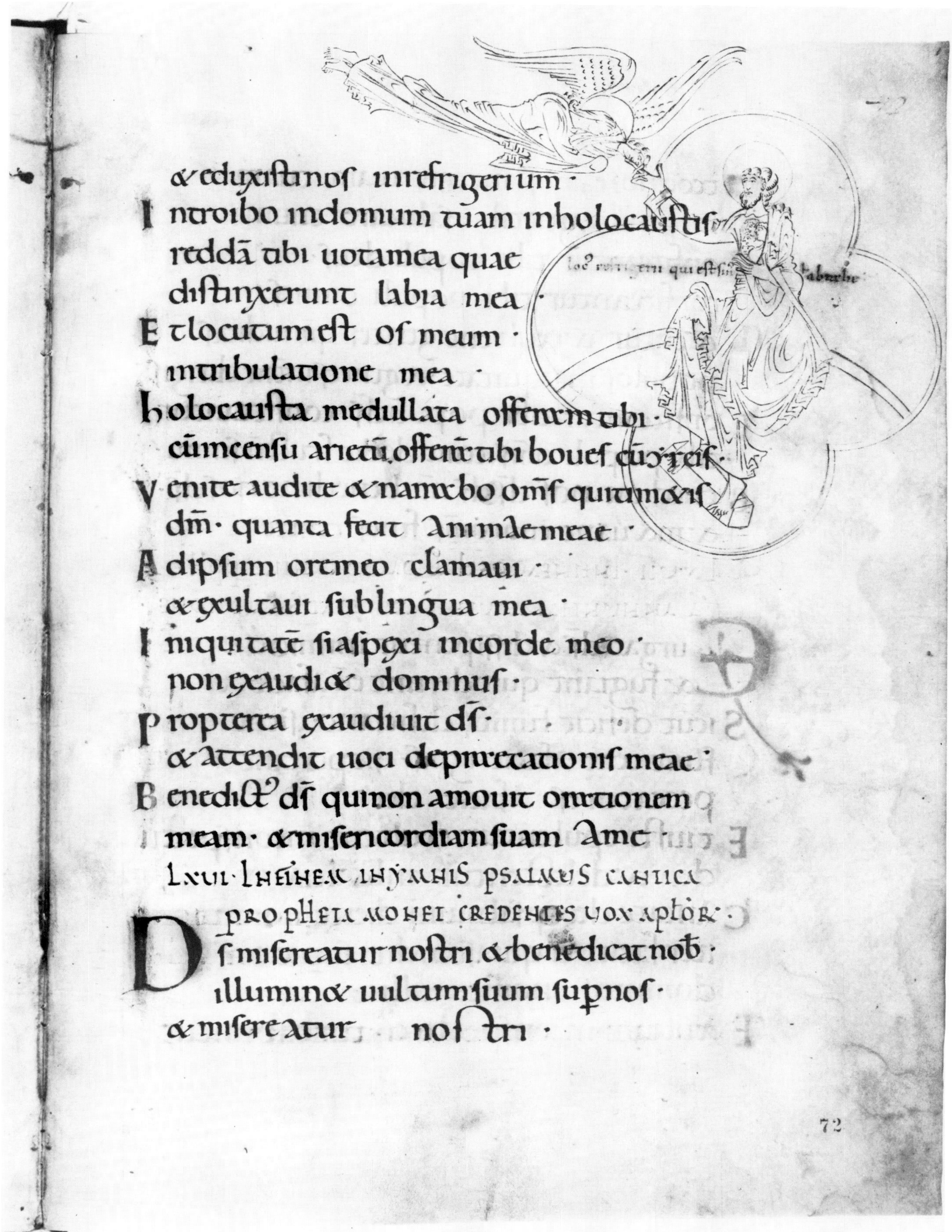

& eduxisti nos in refrigerium ·
I ntroibo in domum tuam in holocaustis
reddā tibi uota mea quae
distinxerunt labia mea ·
E t locutum est os meum ·
in tribulatione mea ·
h olocausta medullata offeram tibi ·
cū incensu arietū · offerā tibi boues cū hircis ·
V enite audite & narrabo om̄s qui timetis
dm̄ · quanta fecit animae meae ·
A d ipsum ore meo clamaui ·
& exultaui sub lingua mea ·
I niquitatē si aspexi in corde meo ·
non exaudiet dominus ·
P ropterea exaudiuit ds̄ ·
& attendit uoci deprecationis meae ·
B enedictus ds̄ qui non amouit orationem
meam · & misericordiam suam a me ·
LXVI · IN FINEM IN HYMNIS PSALMUS CANTICI
PROPHETIA MOYSI CREDENTES UOX APLOR ·
D s misereatur nostri & benedicat nob ·
illuminet uultum suum sup nos ·
& misereatur nostri ·

72

3.25 Vatican, Biblioteca Apostolica, Reg. lat. 12, f. 72r

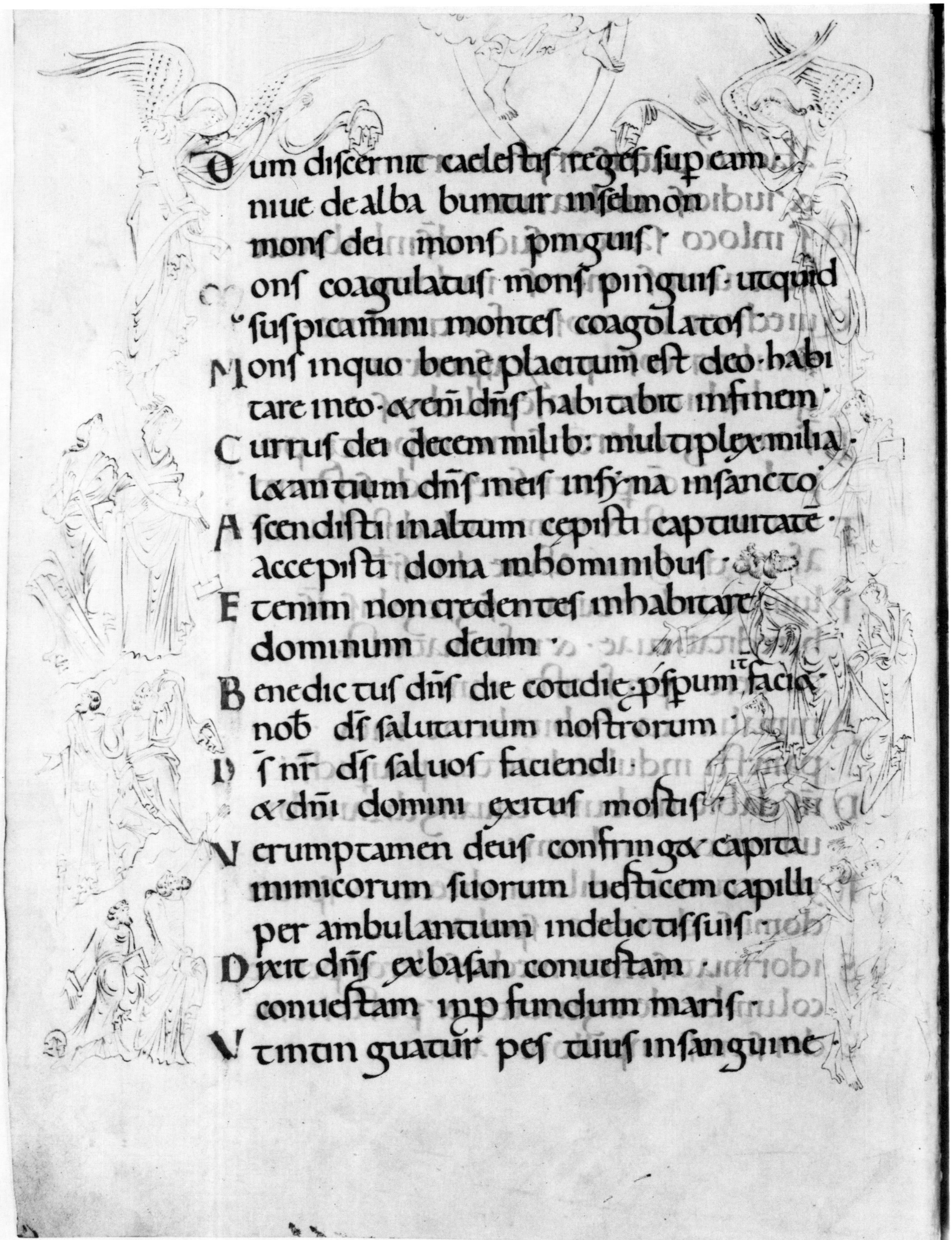

Dum discernit caelestis reges sup eam ·
niue dealbabuntur in selmon
mons dei mons pinguis ·
Mons coagulatus mons pinguis · ut quid
suspicamini montes coagolatos ·
Mons in quo bene placitum est deo habi
tare in eo · et enim dñs habitabit in finem ·
Currus dei decem milib: multiplex milia
laetantium dñs in eis in syna in sancto ·
Ascendisti in altum cepisti captiuitatē ·
accepisti dona in hominibus ·
Etenim non credentes inhabitare
dominum deum ·
Benedictus dñs die cotidie · psperum iter faciet
nob ds salutarium nostrorum ·
Ds nr ds saluos faciendi ·
et dñi domini exitus mortis ·
Uerumptamen deus confringet capita
inimicorum suorum uerticem capilli
perambulantium in delictis suis ·
Dixit dñs ex basan conuertam ·
conuertam in pfundum maris ·
Ut intinguatur pes tuus in sanguine ·

3.26 Vatican, Biblioteca Apostolica, Reg. lat. 12, f. 73v

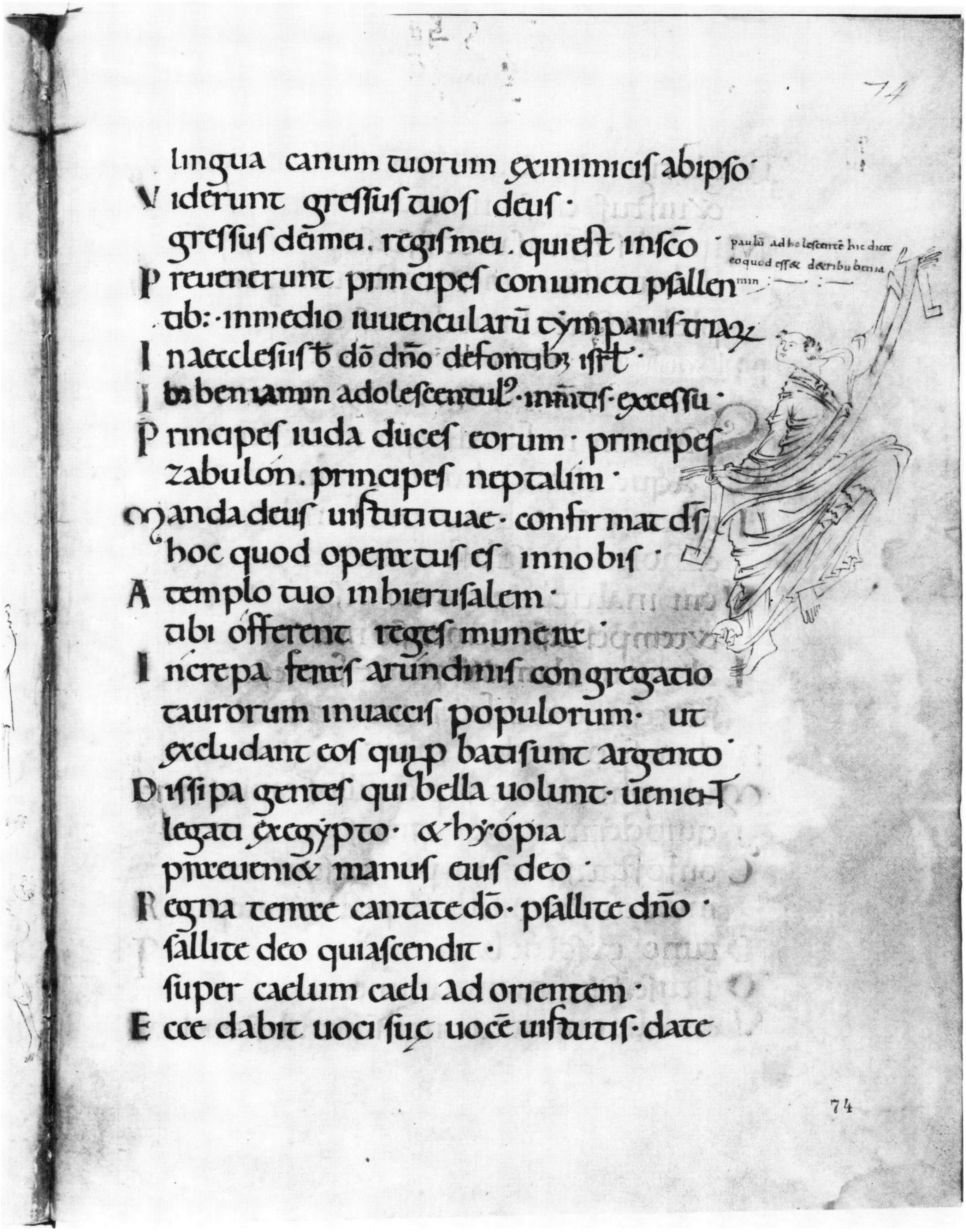
lingua canum tuorum ex inimicis ab ipso.
Viderunt gressus tuos deus.
gressus dei mei. regis mei. qui est in sco
Preuenerunt principes coniuncti psallen
tib: in medio iuuenculaȓ tympanistriaȝ
In ecclesiis b dō dño de fontib; isrt.
Ibi beniamin adolescentulus in mentis excessu.
Principes iuda duces eorum. principes
zabulon. principes neptalim.
Manda deus uirtuti tuae. confirma ds
hoc quod operatus es in nobis.
A templo tuo in hierusalem.
tibi offerent reges munera.
Increpa feras arundinis congregatio
taurorum in uaccis populorum. ut
excludant eos qui p batisunt argento.
Dissipa gentes qui bella uolunt. uenient
legati ex egypto. & ethyopia
preueniet manus eius deo.
Regna terrae cantate dō. psallite dño.
psallite deo qui ascendit.
super caelum caeli ad orientem.
Ecce dabit uoci suae uocē uirtutis. date

3.27 Vatican, Biblioteca Apostolica, Reg. lat. 12, f. 74r

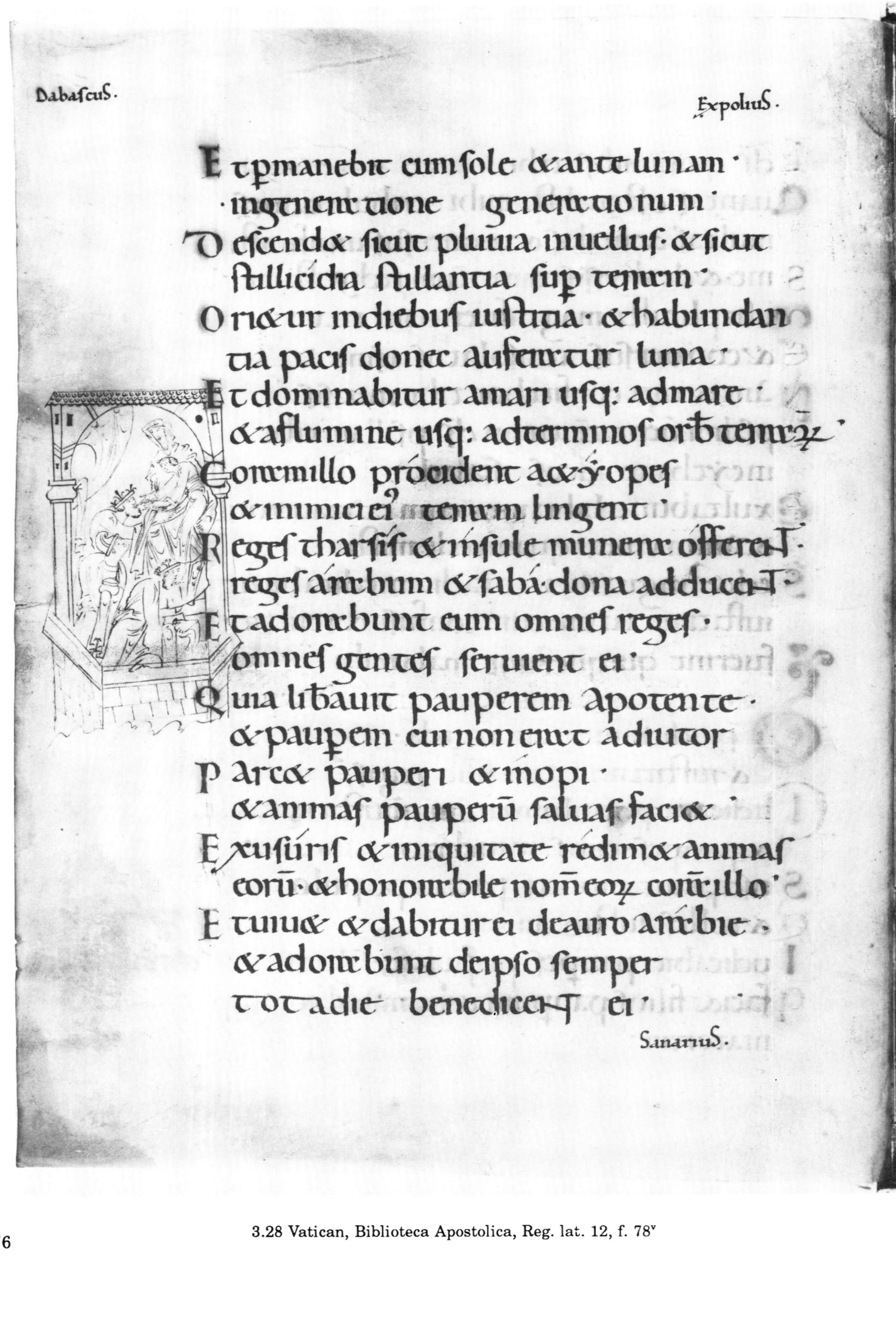
Dabascus.

Expolius.

Et permanebit cum sole & ante lunam ·
· in generatione generationum ·
Descendet sicut pluuia in uellus · & sicut
stillicidia stillantia super terram ·
Orietur in diebus iustitia · & habundan
tia pacis donec auferatur luna ·
Et dominabitur a mari usq: ad mare ·
& a flumine usq: ad terminos orbis terrarum ·
Coram illo procident aethiopes
& inimici eius terram lingent ·
Reges tharsis & insule munera offerent ·
reges arabum & saba dona adducent ·
Et adorabunt eum omnes reges ·
omnes gentes seruient ei ·
Quia liberauit pauperem a potente ·
& pauperem cui non erat adiutor
Parcet pauperi & inopi ·
& animas pauperum saluas faciet ·
Ex usuris & iniquitate redimet animas
eorum · & honorabile nomen eorum coram illo ·
Et uiuet & dabitur ei de auro arabie ·
& adorabunt de ipso semper
tota die benedicent ei ·

Sanarius.

3.28 Vatican, Biblioteca Apostolica, Reg. lat. 12, f. 78v

E t existimabam ut cognoscerem ·
hoc labor est ante te ·
D onec intrem in sanctuarium dei · &
intelligam in nouissimis eorum ·
V erumtamen ppter dolos posuisti eis ·
deiecisti eos dum alleuarentur ·
Q uomodo facti sunt in desolatione ·
subito defecerunt · perierunt
propter iniquitatem suam ·
V elut somnium surgentium · dñe in ciuita
te tua imaginē ipsorum ad nihilū rediges ·
Q uia inflammatū est cor meum ·
& renes mei commutati sunt ·
& ego ad nihilum redactus sū & nesciui
V t iumentum factus sum aput te ·
& ego semper tecum ·
T enuisti manum dexteram meam · &
in uoluntate tua deduxisti me
& cum gloria suscepisti me ·
Q uid enim mihi est in cęlo & a te
quid uolui sūp terram ·
D efecit caro mea & cor meum dš cordis
mei · & pars mea deus in aeternum ·

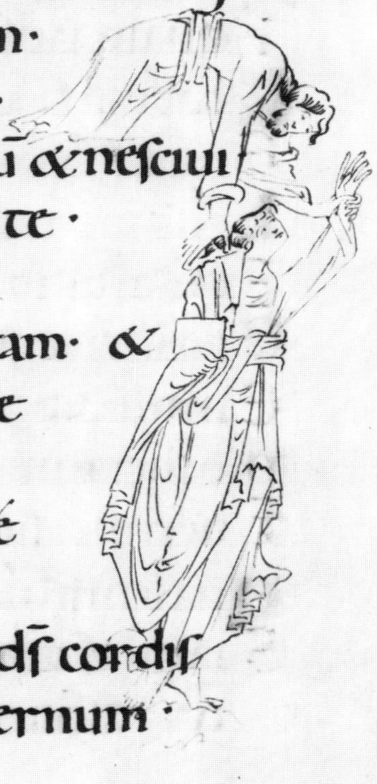

80

3.29 Vatican, Biblioteca Apostolica, Reg. lat. 12, f. 80r

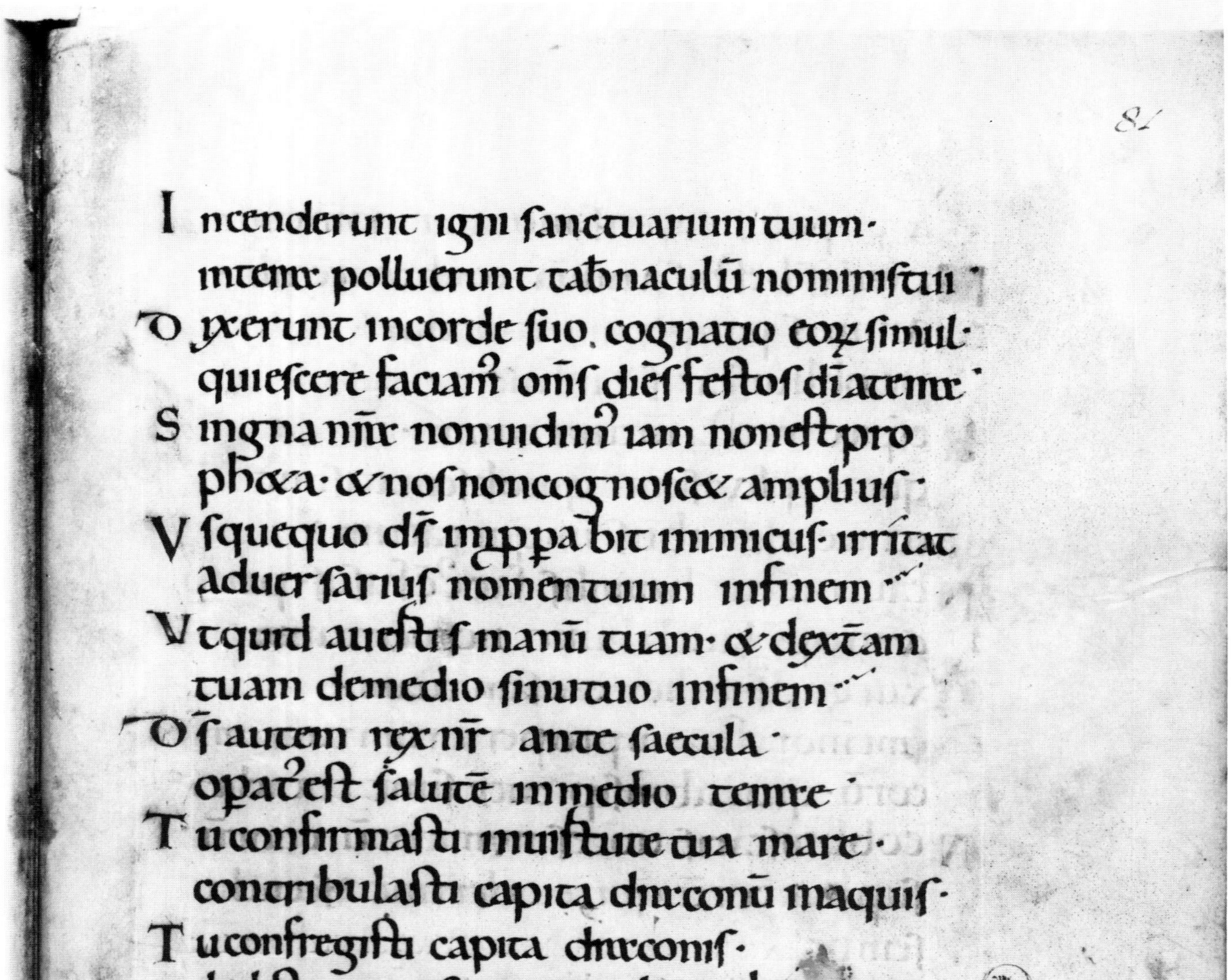

Incenderunt igni sanctuarium tuum ·
in terra polluerunt tabernaculum nominis tui ·
Dixerunt in corde suo, cognatio eorum simul ·
quiescere faciamus omnes dies festos dei a terra ·
Signa nostra non vidimus iam non est pro
pheta · et nos non cognoscet amplius ·
Usquequo deus improperabit inimicus · irritat
adversarius nomen tuum in finem ·
Ut quid avertis manum tuam · et dexteram
tuam de medio sinu tuo in finem ·
Deus autem rex noster ante saecula ·
operatus est salutem in medio terrae ·
Tu confirmasti in virtute tua mare ·
contribulasti capita draconum in aquis ·
Tu confregisti capita draconis ·
dedisti eum escam populis aethiopum ·
Tu disrupisti fontes et torrentes ·
tu siccasti fluvios aetham ·
Tuus est dies et tua est nox ·
tu fabricatus es auroram et solem ·
Tu fecisti omnes terminos terrae ·
aestatem et ver tu plasmasti ea ·
Memor esto huius inimicus improperabit domino ·

3.30 Vatican, Biblioteca Apostolica, Reg. lat. 12, f. 81r

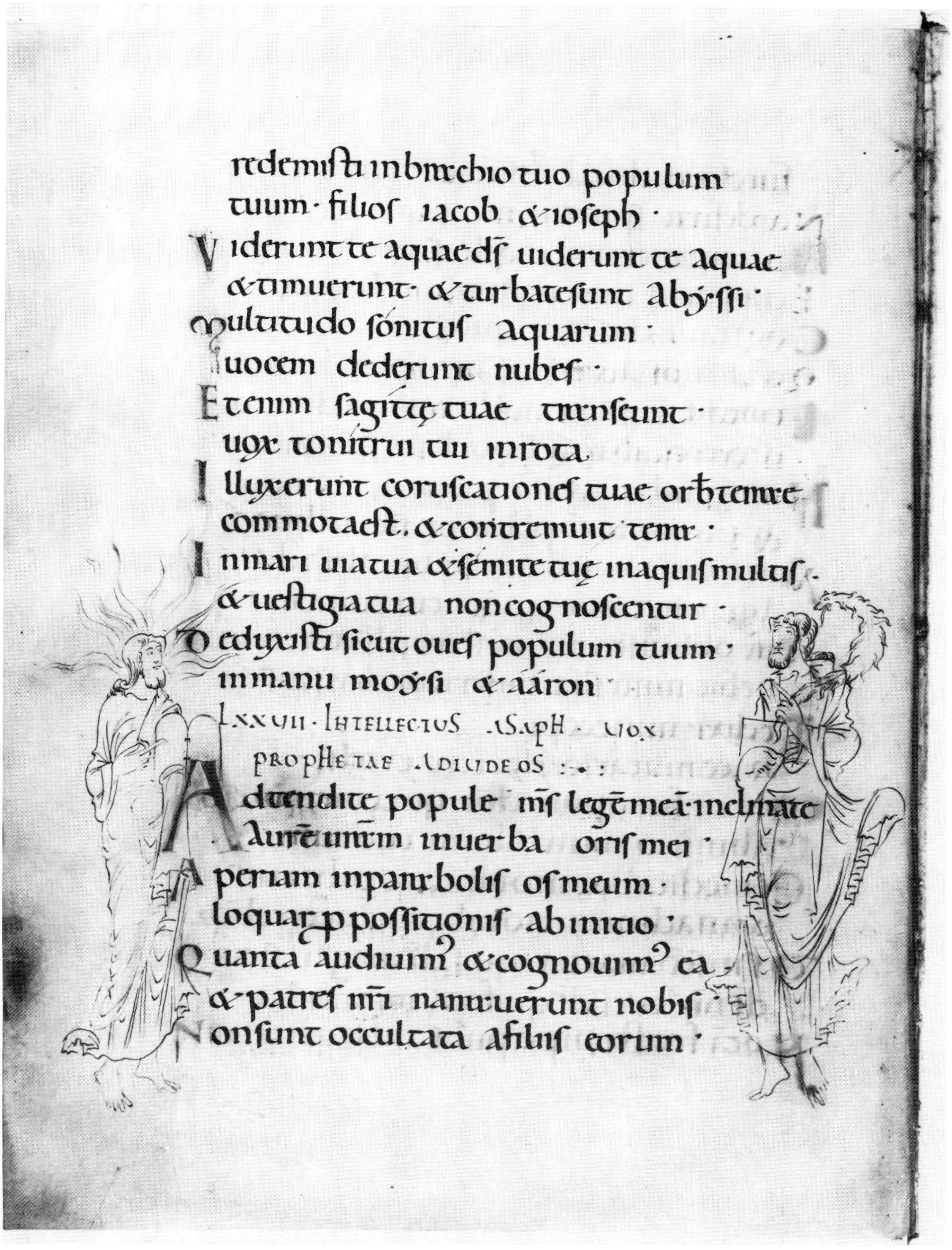
redemisti in brachio tuo populum
tuum· filios iacob & ioseph·
Viderunt te aquae ds̄ uiderunt te aquae
& timuerunt· & turbate sunt abyssi·
Multitudo sonitus aquarum·
uocem dederunt nubes·
Etenim sagittę tuae transeunt·
uox tonitrui tui in rota.
Illuxerunt coruscationes tuae orbi terrae
commota est. & contremuit terra·
In mari uia tua & semitę tuę in aquis multis·
& uestigia tua non cognoscentur·
Deduxisti sicut oues populum tuum·
in manu moysi & aaron·
LXXVII· INTELLECTUS ASAPH· UOX
PROPHETAE AD IUDEOS :·:
Adtendite popule ms̄ legē meā· inclinate
aurē uestrā in uerba oris mei·
Aperiam in parabolis os meum·
loquar ꝑ possitiones ab initio·
Quanta audiuim⁹ & cognouim⁹ ea·
& patres nr̄i narrauerunt nobis·
Non sunt occultata a filiis eorum·

3.31 Vatican, Biblioteca Apostolica, Reg. lat. 12, f. 83v

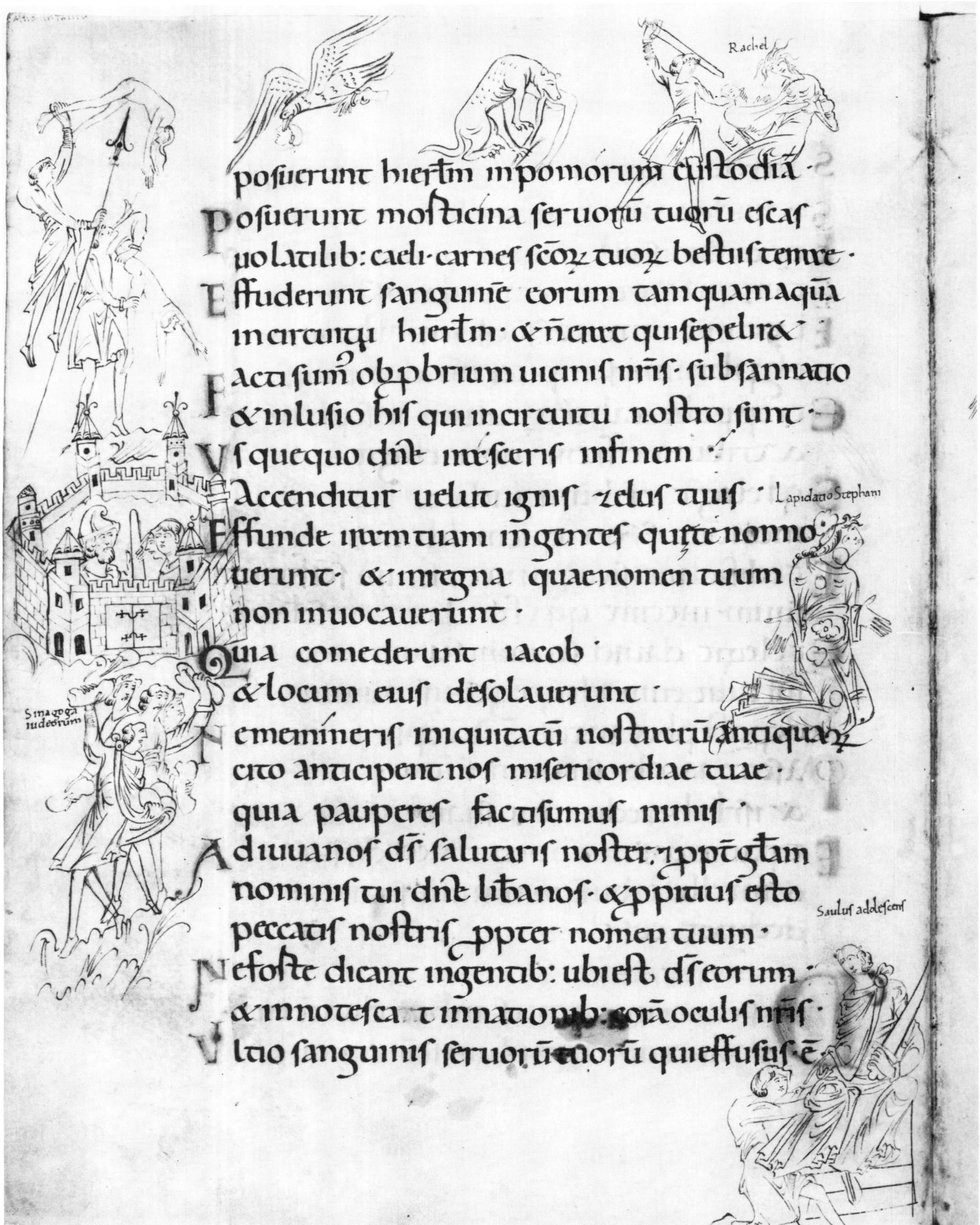

3.32 Vatican, Biblioteca Apostolica, Reg. lat. 12, f. 87v

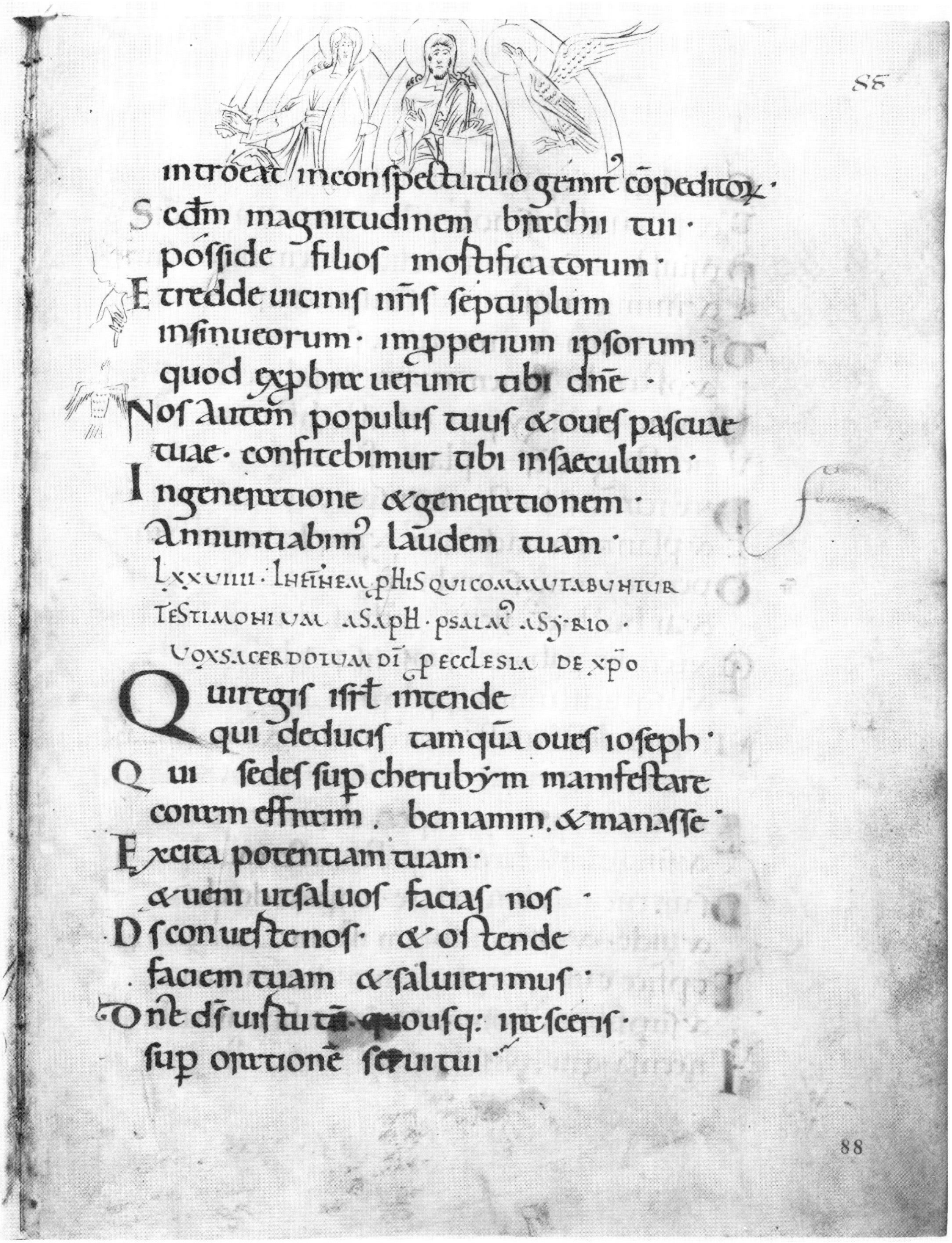

88

introeat in conspectu tuo gemitus compeditorum ·
Secundum magnitudinem brachii tui ·
possidE filios mortificatorum ·
Et redde uicinis nostris septuplum
in sinu eorum · impperium ipsorum
quod exprobrauerunt tibi domine ·
Nos autem populus tuus et oues pascuae
tuae · confitebimur tibi in saeculum ·
In generatione et generationem ·
adnuntiabimus laudem tuam ·
LXXVIIII · IN FINEM PRO HIS QUI COMMUTABUNTUR
TESTIMONIUM ASAPH · PSALMUS ASYRIO ·
VOX SACERDOTUM DEI PRO ECCLESIA DE XPO
Qui regis israhel intende
qui deducis tamquam oues ioseph ·
Qui sedes super cherubym manifestare
coram effraim . beniamin . et manasse ·
Excita potentiam tuam ·
et ueni ut saluos facias nos ·
Deus conuerte nos · et ostende
faciem tuam et salui erimus ·
Domine deus uirtutum quousque irasceris ·
super orationem serui tui

88

3.33 Vatican, Biblioteca Apostolica, Reg. lat. 12, f. 88r

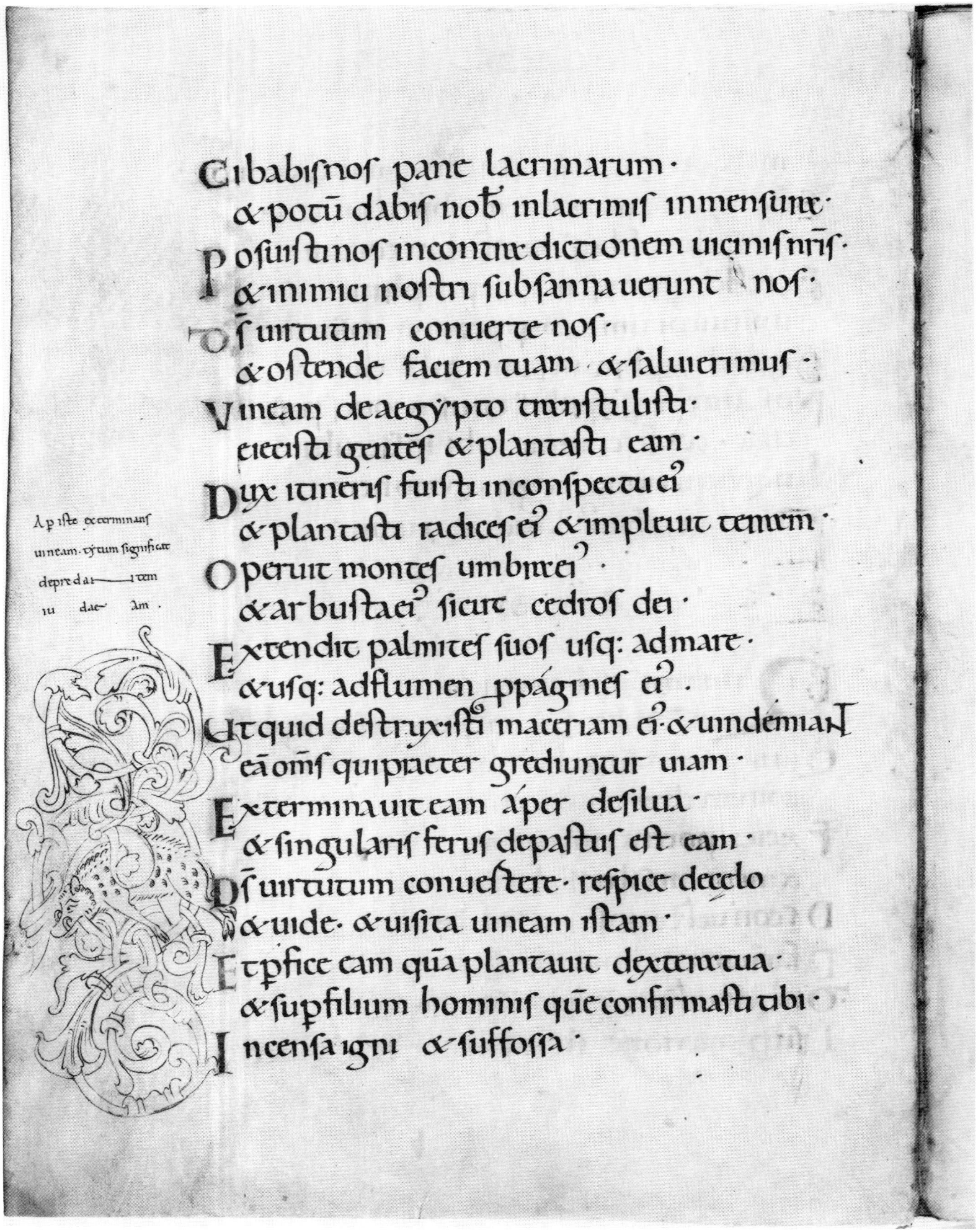
Cibabis nos pane lacrimarum ·
& potū dabis nob in lacrimis in mensura ·
Posuisti nos in contradictionem uicinis nr̄is ·
& inimici nostri subsannauerunt nos ·
Dš uirtutum conuerte nos ·
& ostende faciem tuam · & salui erimus ·
Vineam de aegypto transtulisti ·
eiecisti gentes & plantasti eam ·
Dux itineris fuisti in conspectu eiꝰ
& plantasti radices eiꝰ & impleuit terram ·
Operuit montes umbra eiꝰ ·
& arbusta eiꝰ sicut cedros dei ·
Extendit palmites suos usq: ad mare ·
& usq: ad flumen ꝓpagines eiꝰ ·
Ut quid destruxisti maceriam eiꝰ · & uindemiant
eā om̄s qui praetergrediuntur uiam ·
Exterminauit eam aper de silua ·
& singularis ferus depastus est eam ·
Dš uirtutum conuertere · respice de celo
& uide · & uisita uineam istam ·
Et ꝑfice eam quā plantauit dextera tua ·
& sup filium hominis quē confirmasti tibi ·
Incensa igni & suffossa ·

3.34 Vatican, Biblioteca Apostolica, Reg. lat. 12, f. 88v

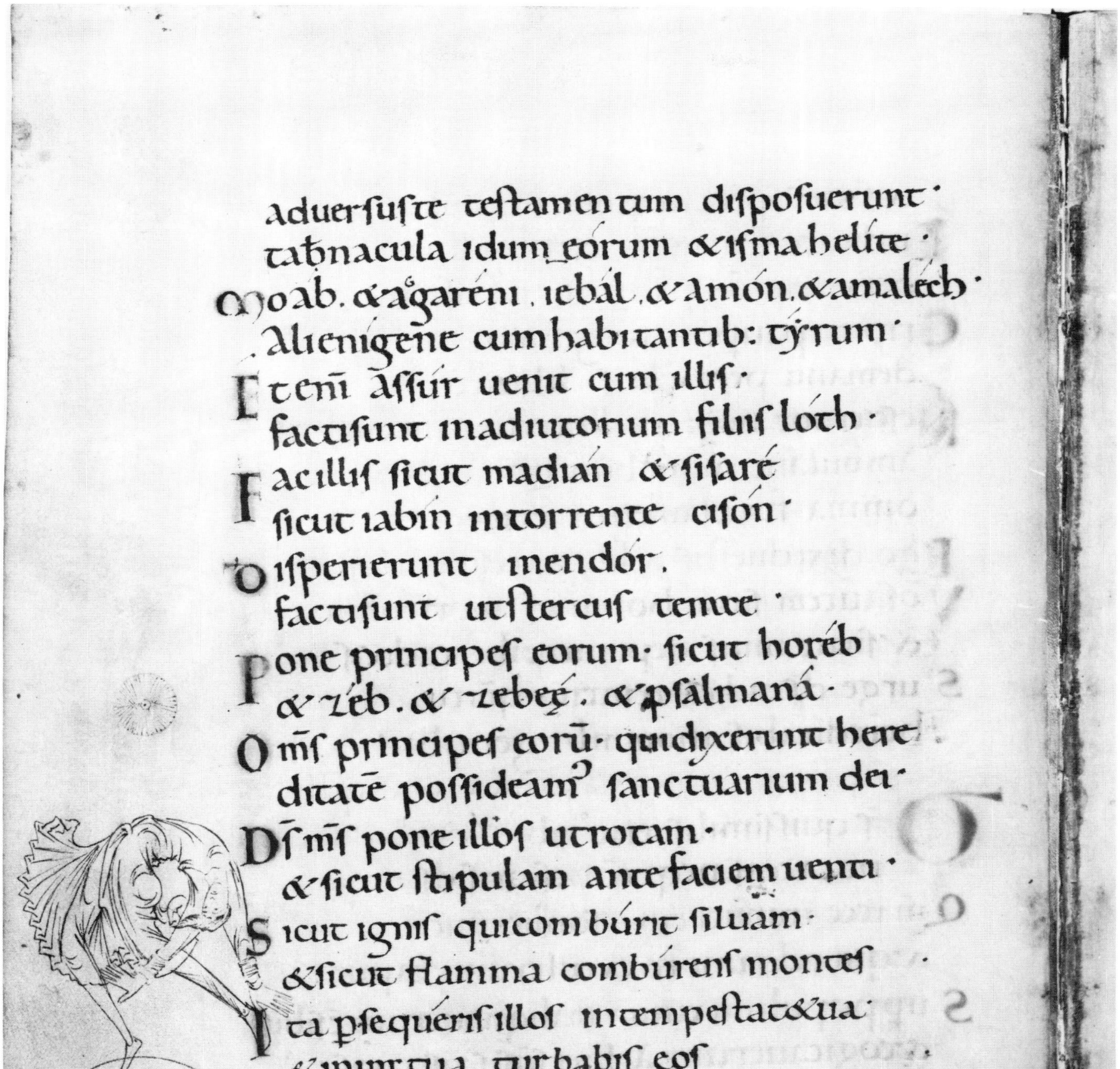
aduersus te testamentum disposuerunt ·
tabernacula idumeorum et ismahelite ·
Moab. et agareni. gebal. et amon. et amalech ·
Alienigene cum habitantibus tyrum ·
Etenim assur uenit cum illis ·
facti sunt in adiutorium filiis loth ·
Fac illis sicut madian et sisare ·
sicut iabin in torrente cison ·
Disperierunt in endor ·
facti sunt ut stercus terre ·
Pone principes eorum · sicut horeb
et zeb. et zebee. et salmana ·
Omnes principes eorum · qui dixerunt here·
ditate possideamus sanctuarium dei ·
Deus meus pone illos ut rotam ·
et sicut stipulam ante faciem uenti ·
Sicut ignis qui comburit siluam ·
et sicut flamma comburens montes ·
Ita persequeris illos in tempestate tua ·
et in ira tua turbabis eos ·
Imple facies eorum ignominia ·
et querent nomen tuum domine ·
Erubescant et conturbentur in seculum seculi ·

3.35 Vatican, Biblioteca Apostolica, Reg. lat. 12, f. 90v

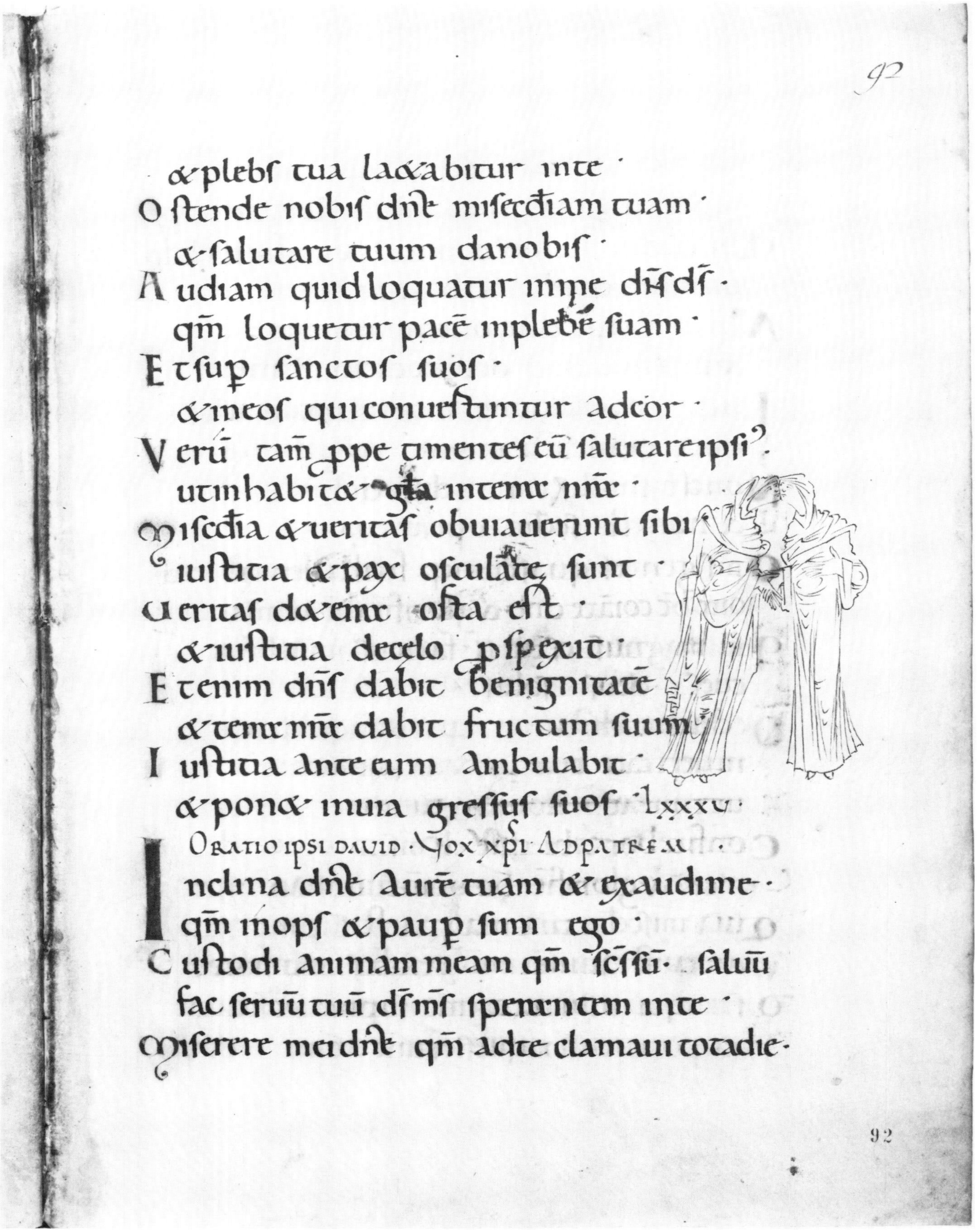

92

& plebs tua laetabitur in te.
Ostende nobis domine misericordiam tuam.
& salutare tuum da nobis.
Audiam quid loquatur in me dominus deus.
quoniam loquetur pacem in plebem suam.
Et super sanctos suos.
& in eos qui convertuntur ad cor.
Verum tamen prope timentes eum salutare ipsius.
ut inhabitet gloria in terra nostra.
Misericordia & veritas obviaverunt sibi
iustitia & pax osculatae sunt.
Veritas de terra orta est.
& iustitia de caelo prospexit.
Etenim dominus dabit benignitatem.
& terra nostra dabit fructum suum.
Iustitia ante eum ambulabit.
& ponet in via gressus suos. LXXXV.
ORATIO IPSI DAVID. VOX XPI AD PATREM.
Inclina domine aurem tuam & exaudi me.
quoniam inops & pauper sum ego.
Custodi animam meam quoniam sanctus sum. salvum
fac servum tuum deus meus sperantem in te.
Miserere mei domine quoniam ad te clamavi tota die.

92

3.36 Vatican, Biblioteca Apostolica, Reg. lat. 12, f. 92r

93

& non ꝓposuerunt te in conspectu suo ·
Et tu dne ds miserator & misericors ·
patiens & multe misericordiae & uerax ·
Respice in me & miserere mei · da imperium tuum
puero tuo & saluum fac filium ancillę tuae ·
Fac mecum signum in bono ut uideant
qui oderunt me & confundantur ·
qm tu dne adiuuasti me & consolatus es me ·
LXXXVI · IN FINEM FILIIS CHORE PSALMUS
CANTICI · UOX APOSTOLICA DE ECCLESIA ·
Fundamenta eius in montibus scis · diligit
dns portas syon super omnia tabernacula iacob ·
Gloriosa dicta sunt de te · ciuitas dei
Memor ero raab & babylonis
scientium me ·
Ecce alienigene & tyrus & populus
aethyopum · hi fuerunt illic ·
Numquid syon dicet homo · & homo natus
in ea · & ipse fundauit eam altissimus ·
Dns narrabit in scripturis populorum ·
& principum horum qui fuerunt in ea ·
Sicut letantium omnium habitatio in te ·
LXXXVII CANTICUM FILIIS CHORE · IN FINEM

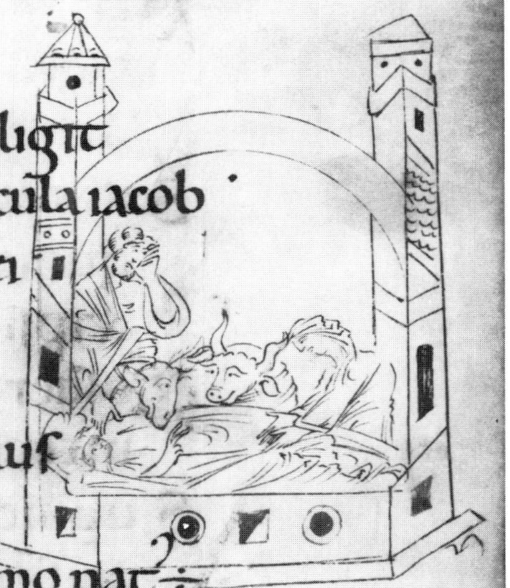

93

3.37 Vatican, Biblioteca Apostolica, Reg. lat. 12, f. 93r

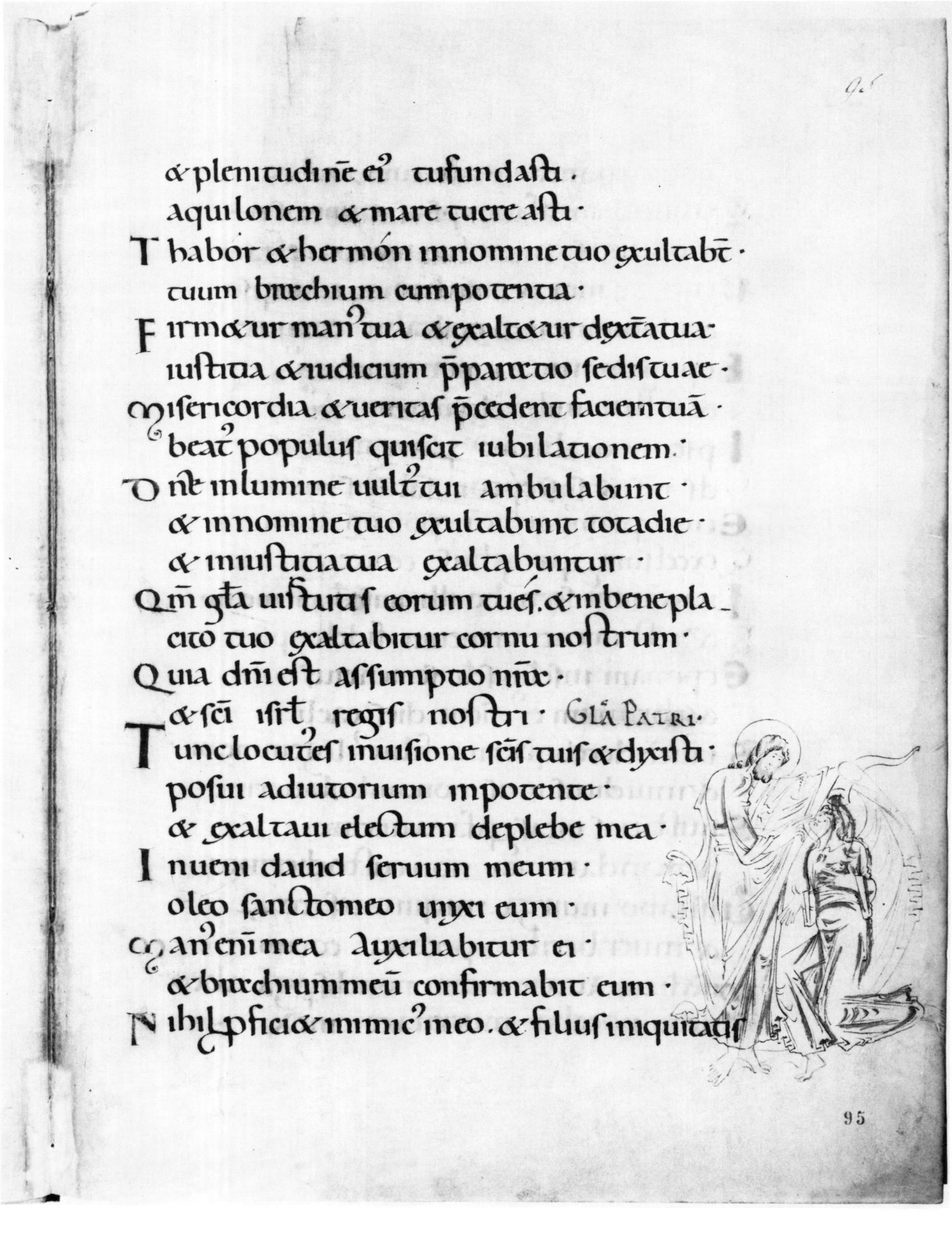
& plenitudinē eiꝰ tu fundasti.
aquilonem & mare tu creasti.
Thabor & hermon in nomine tuo exultab̄t.
tuum brachium cum potentia.
Firmetur manꝰ tua & exaltetur dextera tua.
iustitia & iudicium p̄paratio sedis tuae.
Misericordia & ueritas p̄cedent faciem tuā.
beatꝰ populus qui scit iubilationem.
Dn̄e in lumine uultꝰ tui ambulabunt.
& in nomine tuo exultabunt tota die.
& in iustitia tua exaltabuntur.
Qm̄ glā uirtutis eorum tu es. & in beneplacito tuo exaltabitur cornu nostrum.
Quia dn̄i est assumptio nr̄a.
& sc̄i isrt regis nostri. Glā Patri.
Tunc locutus es in uisione sc̄is tuis & dixisti.
posui adiutorium in potente.
& exaltaui electum de plebe mea.
Inueni dauid seruum meum.
oleo sancto meo unxi eum.
Manꝰ enī mea auxiliabitur ei.
& brachium meū confirmabit eum.
Nihil p̄ficiet inimicꝰ in eo. & filius iniquitatis

95

3.38 Vatican, Biblioteca Apostolica, Reg. lat. 12, f. 95r

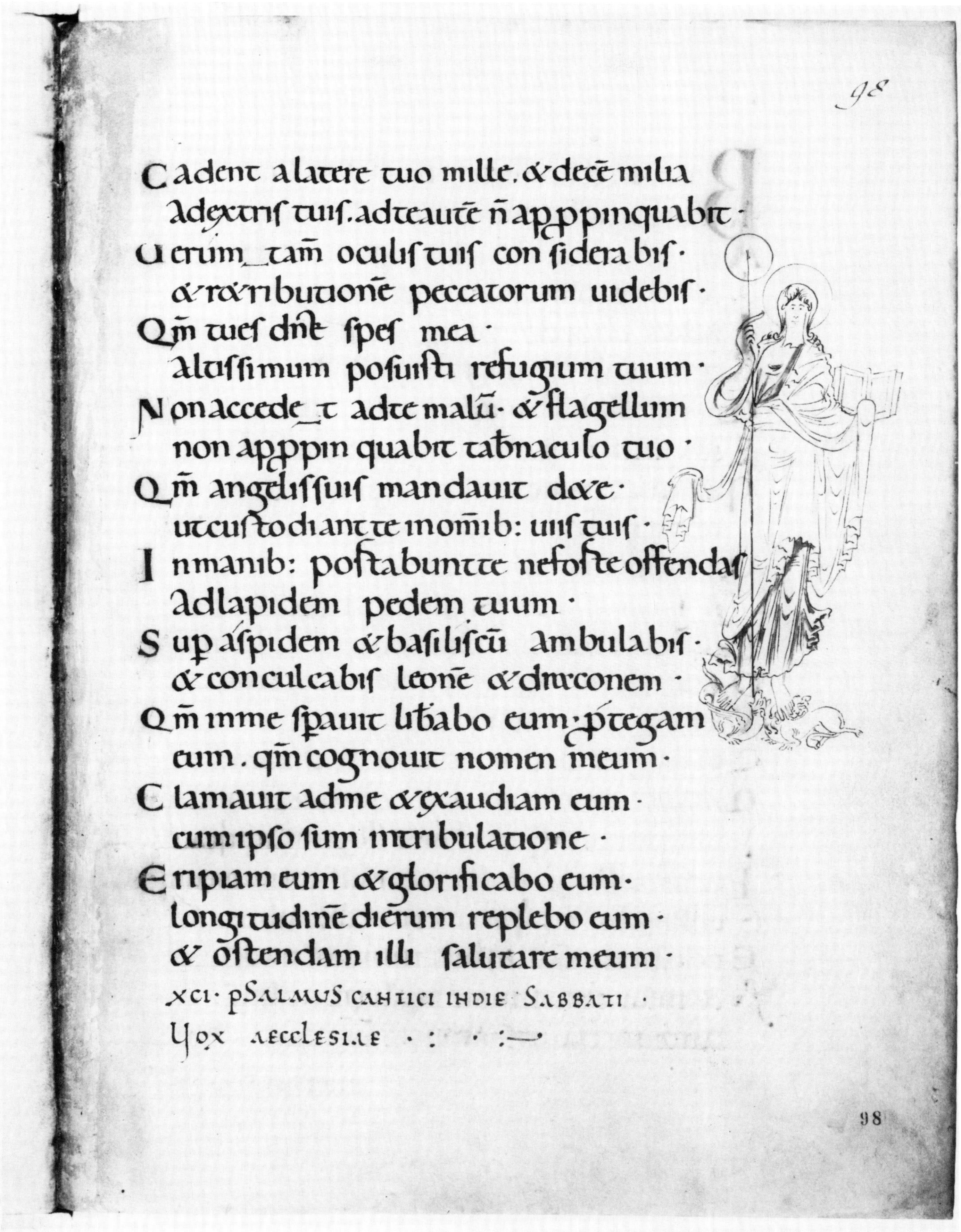

98

Cadent alatere tuo mille. & dece(m) milia
adextris tuis. adte aute(m) n(on) appropinquabit·
Uerum tam(en) oculis tuis considerabis·
& retributione(m) peccatorum uidebis·
Q(uonia)m tu es d(omi)ne spes mea·
altissimum posuisti refugium tuum·
Non accedet adte malu(m)· & flagellum
non appropinquabit tab(er)naculo tuo·
Q(uonia)m angelis suis mandauit dete·
utcustodiant te inom(n)ib(us) uiis tuis·
In manib(us) portabunt te nefortte offendas
adlapidem pedem tuum·
Sup(er) aspidem & basiliscu(m) ambulabis·
& conculcabis leone(m) & draconem·
Q(uonia)m inme sp(er)auit lib(er)abo eum· p(ro)tegam
eum. q(uonia)m cognouit nomen meum·
Clamauit adme & exaudiam eum·
cum ipso sum intribulatione·
Eripiam eum & glorificabo eum·
longitudine(m) dierum replebo eum·
& ostendam illi salutare meum·
XCI· PSALMUS CANTICI INDIE SABBATI·
UOX AECCLESIAE ·:·:—

98

3.39 Vatican, Biblioteca Apostolica, Reg. lat. 12, f. 98r

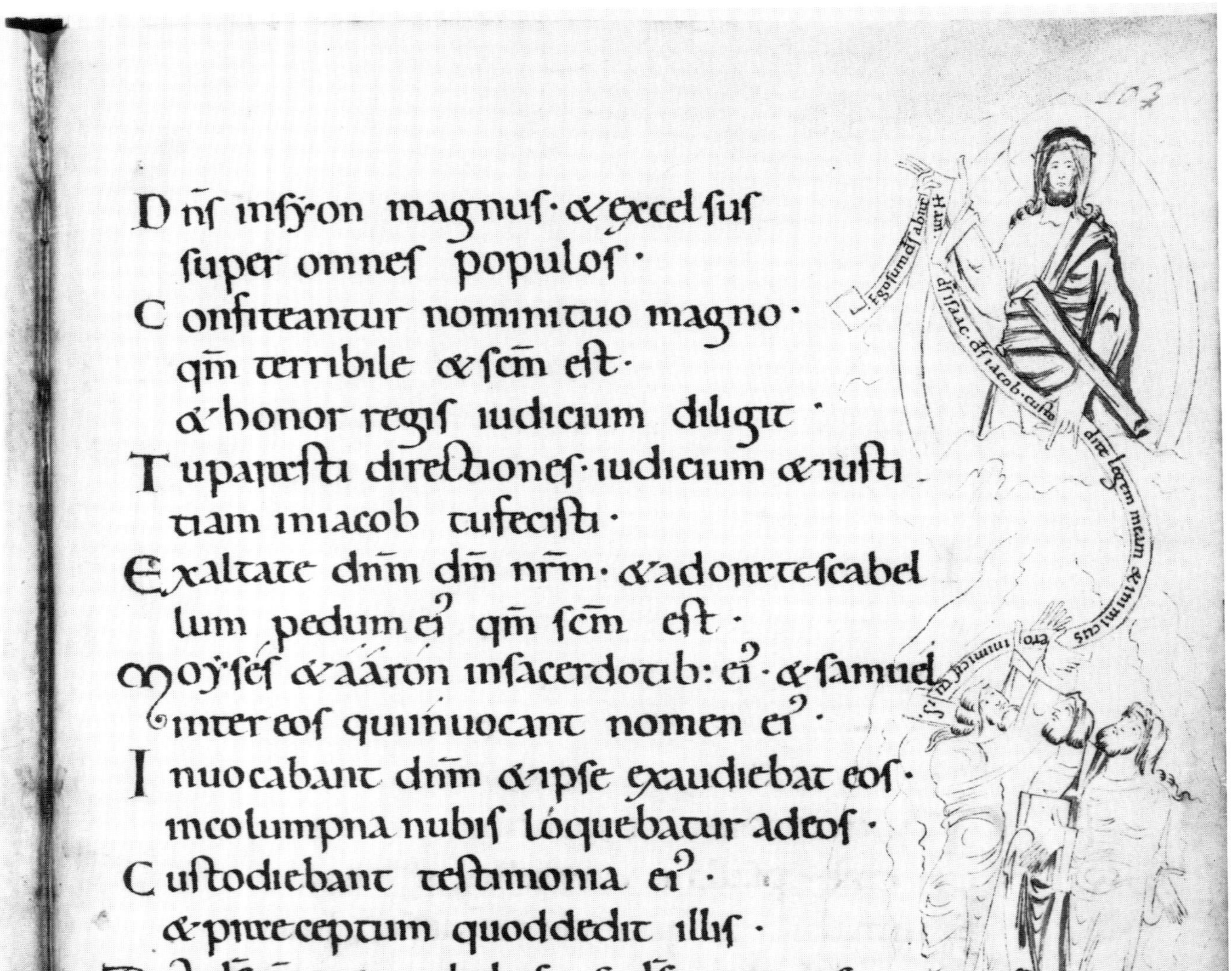

Dns in syon magnus & excelsus
super omnes populos.
Confiteantur nomini tuo magno.
qm terribile & scm est.
& honor regis iudicium diligit.
Tu parasti directiones. iudicium & iusti
tiam in iacob tu fecisti.
Exaltate dnm dm nrm. & adorate scabel
lum pedum ei qm scm est.
Moyses & aaron in sacerdotib: ei. & samuel
inter eos qui inuocant nomen ei.
Inuocabant dnm & ipse exaudiebat eos.
in columpna nubis loquebatur ad eos.
Custodiebant testimonia ei.
& praeceptum quod dedit illis.
Dne ds nr tu exaudiebas eos. ds tu ppitius
fuisti eis. & ulciscens in omnes
adinuentiones eorum.
Exaltate dnm dm nrm. & adorate
in monte sco ei. qm scs dns ds noster.
XCVIIII. PSALM DAVID IN CONFESSIONE. VOX
APTORUM AD POPULUM.
Iubilate dno omnis terra.

103

3.40 Vatican, Biblioteca Apostolica, Reg. lat. 12, f. 103r

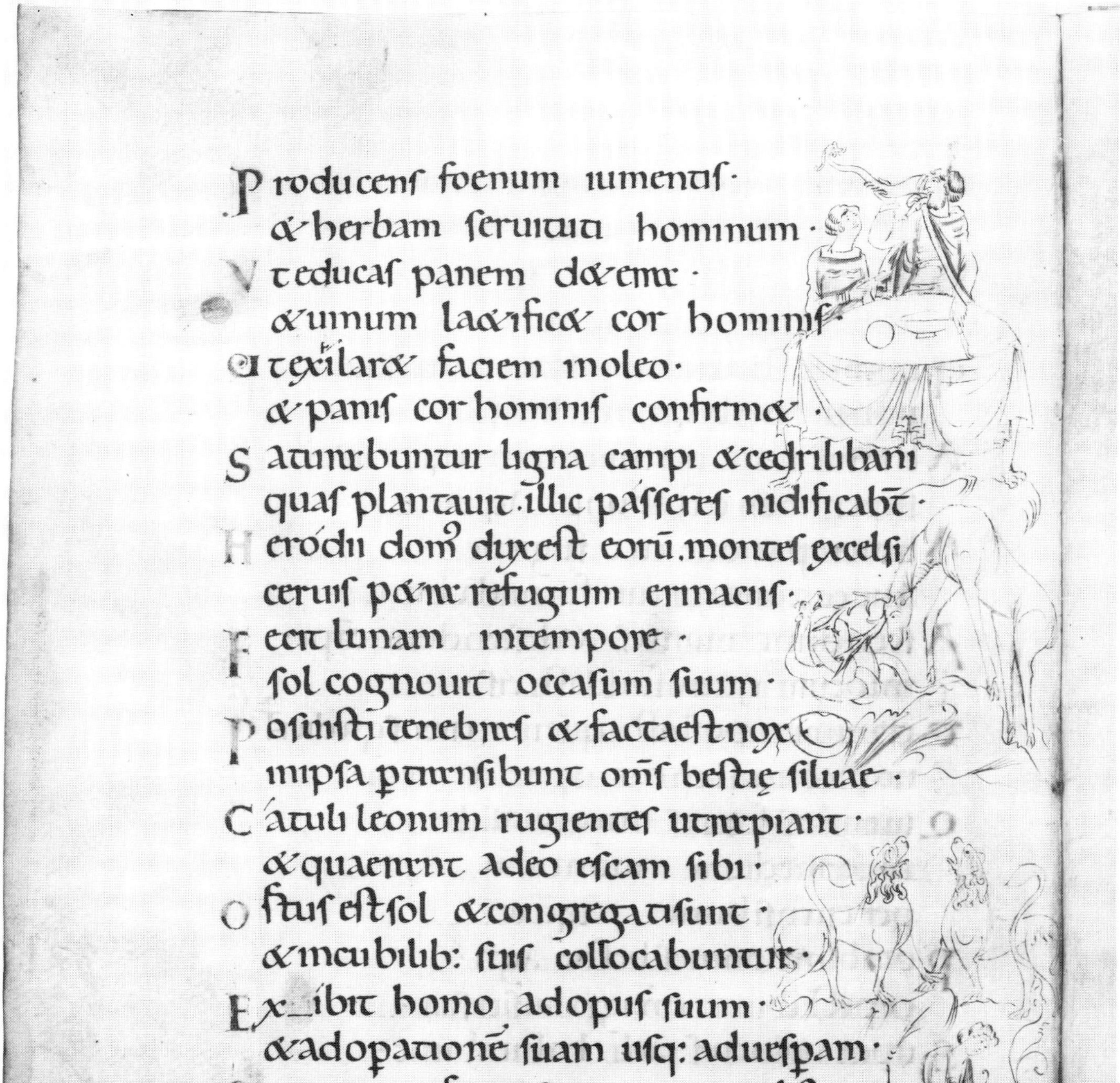
Producens foenum iumentis ·
et herbam servituti hominum ·
Ut educas panem de terra ·
et vinum laetificet cor hominis ·
Ut exhilaret faciem in oleo ·
et panis cor hominis confirmet ·
Saturabuntur ligna campi et cedri libani
quas plantavit . illic passeres nidificabunt ·
Herodii domus dux est eorum . montes excelsi
cervis petra refugium erinaciis ·
Fecit lunam in tempore ·
sol cognovit occasum suum ·
Posuisti tenebras et facta est nox ·
in ipsa pertransibunt omnes bestiae silvae ·
Catuli leonum rugientes ut rapiant ·
et quaerant a deo escam sibi ·
Ortus est sol et congregati sunt ·
et in cubilibus suis collocabuntur ·
Exibit homo ad opus suum ·
et ad operationem suam usque ad vesperam ·
Quam magnificata sunt opera tua domine ·
omnia in sapientia fecisti . impleta est
terra possessione tua · Gloria patri ·

3.41 Vatican, Biblioteca Apostolica, Reg. lat. 12, f. 107v

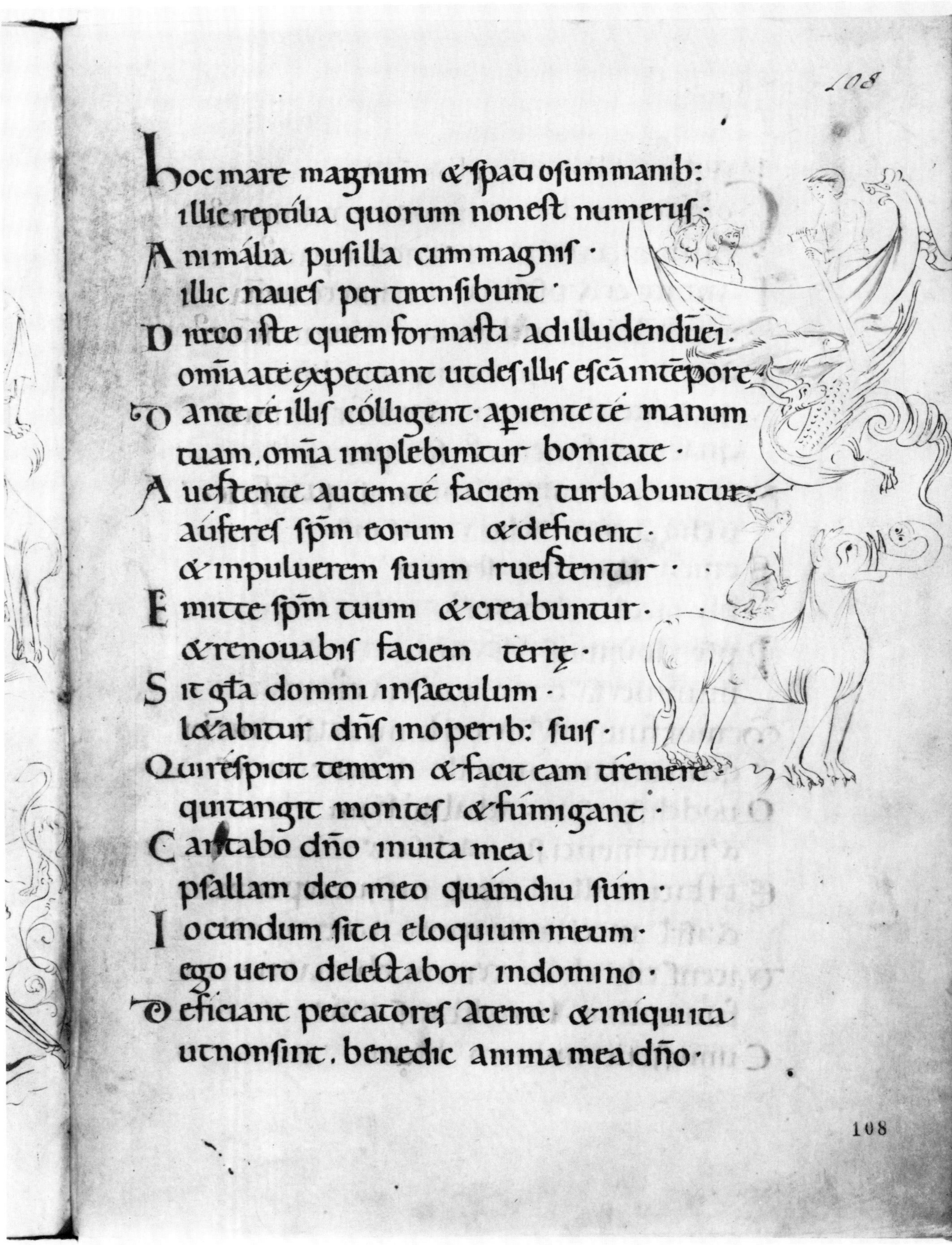

108

Hoc mare magnum et spatiosum manib:
illic reptilia quorum non est numerus.
Animalia pusilla cum magnis.
illic naues pertransibunt.
Draco iste quem formasti ad illudendum ei.
omnia a te expectant ut des illis escam in tempore
Dante te illis colligent. aperiente te manum
tuam, omnia implebuntur bonitate.
Auertente autem te faciem turbabuntur.
auferes spm eorum et deficient.
et in puluerem suum reuertentur.
Emitte spm tuum et creabuntur.
et renouabis faciem terre.
Sit gla domini in saeculum.
laetabitur dns in operib: suis.
Qui respicit terram et facit eam tremere.
qui tangit montes et fumigant.
Cantabo dno in uita mea.
psallam deo meo quamdiu sum.
Iocundum sit ei eloquium meum.
ego uero delectabor in domino.
Deficiant peccatores a terra et iniqui ita
ut non sint. benedic anima mea dno.

108

3.42 Vatican, Biblioteca Apostolica, Reg. lat. 12, f. 108r

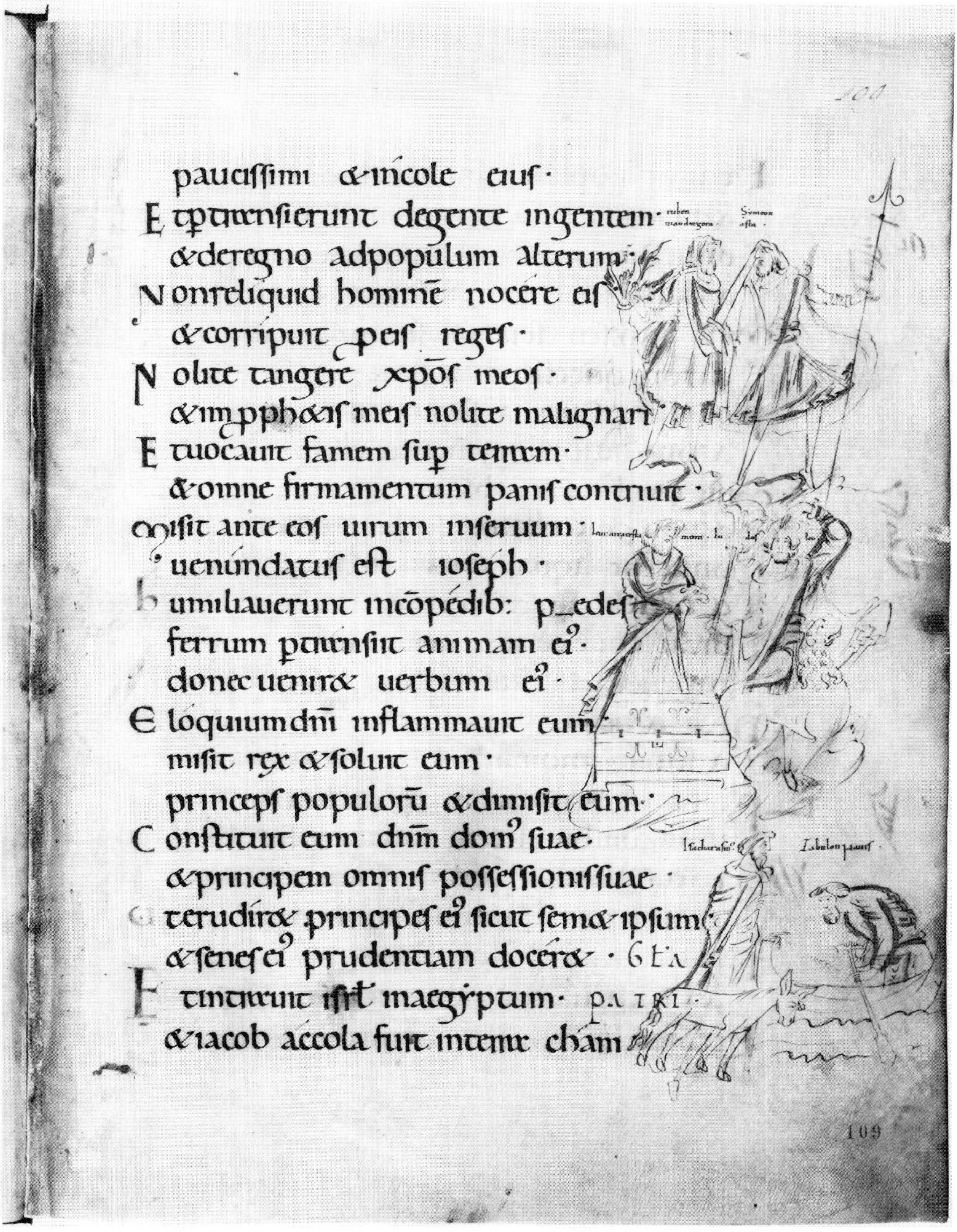
paucissimi et incole eius.
Et ptransierunt de gente in gentem.
et de regno ad populum alterum.
Non reliquid hominē nocēre eis
et corripuit p eis reges.
Nolite tangere xpōs meos.
et in pphetis meis nolite malignari.
Et uocauit famem sup terram.
et omne firmamentum panis contriuit.
Misit ante eos uirum in seruum
uenundatus est ioseph.
humiliauerunt in cōpedib: pedes
ferrum ptransiit animam ei.
donec ueniret uerbum ei.
Eloquium dni inflammauit eum
misit rex et soluit eum.
princeps populorū et dimisit eum.
Constituit eum dnm dom suae.
et principem omnis possessionis suae.
ut erudiret principes ei sicut semet ipsum.
et senes ei prudentiam doceret.
Et intrauit isrl in aegyptum.
et iacob accola fuit in terra cham.

3.43 Vatican, Biblioteca Apostolica, Reg. lat. 12, f. 109r

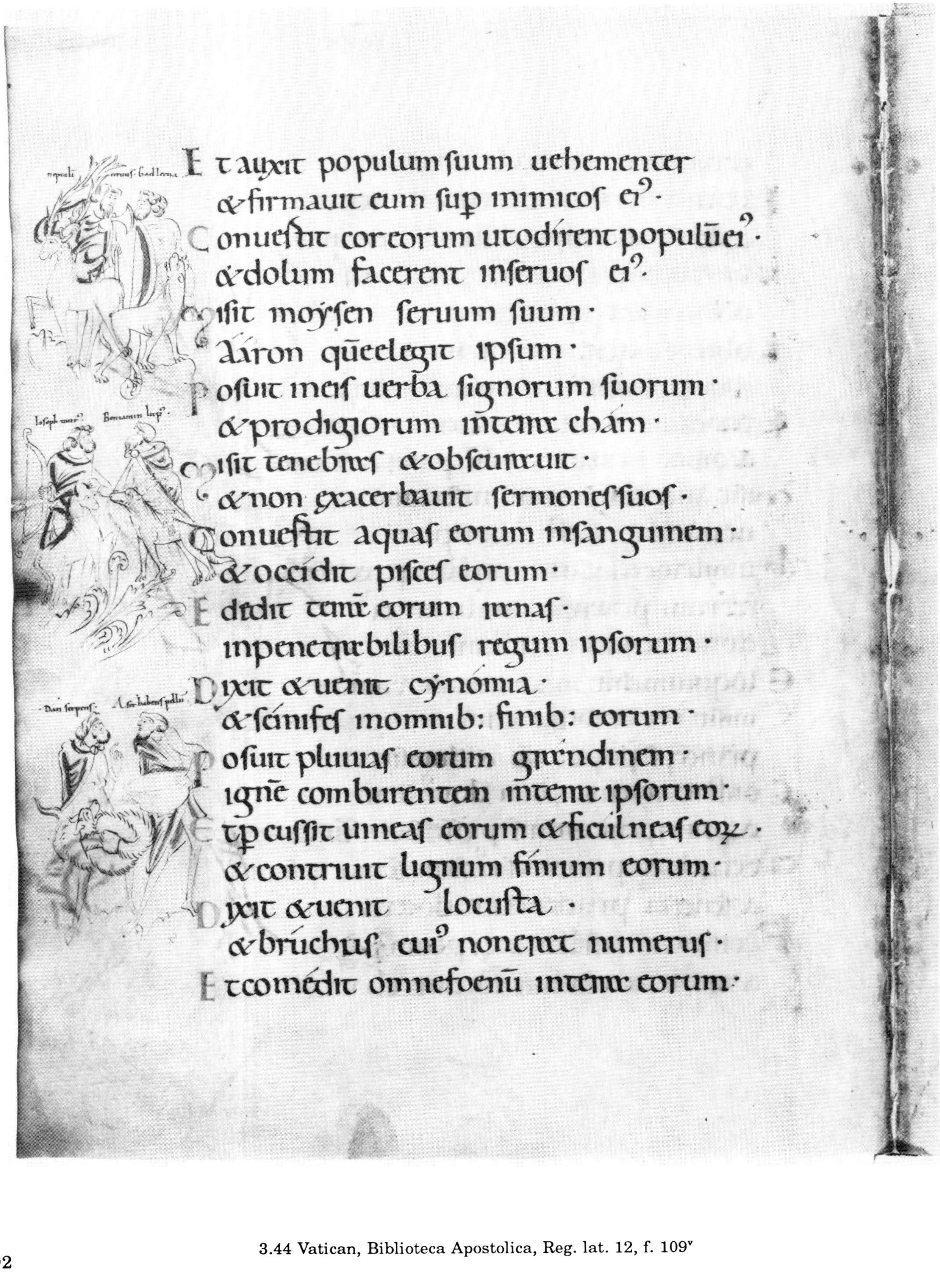

Et auxit populum suum uehementer
& firmauit eum sup inimicos ei9 ·
Conuestit cor eorum ut odirent populu͞ ei9 ·
& dolum facerent in seruos ei9 ·
Misit moysen seruum suum ·
Aaron que͞ elegit ipsum ·
Posuit in eis uerba signorum suorum ·
& prodigiorum in terra cham ·
Misit tenebras & obscurauit ·
& non exacerbauit sermones suos ·
Conuestit aquas eorum in sanguinem ·
& occidit pisces eorum ·
Edidit terra eorum ranas ·
in penetrabilibus regum ipsorum ·
Dixit & uenit cynomia ·
& scinifes in omnib: finib: eorum ·
Posuit pluuias eorum grandinem ·
igne͞ comburentem in terra ipsorum ·
Et pcussit uineas eorum & ficulneas eoꝝ ·
& contriuit lignum finium eorum ·
Dixit & uenit locusta ·
& bruchus cui9 non erat numerus ·
Et comedit omne foenu͞ in terra eorum ·

3.44 Vatican, Biblioteca Apostolica, Reg. lat. 12, f. 109v

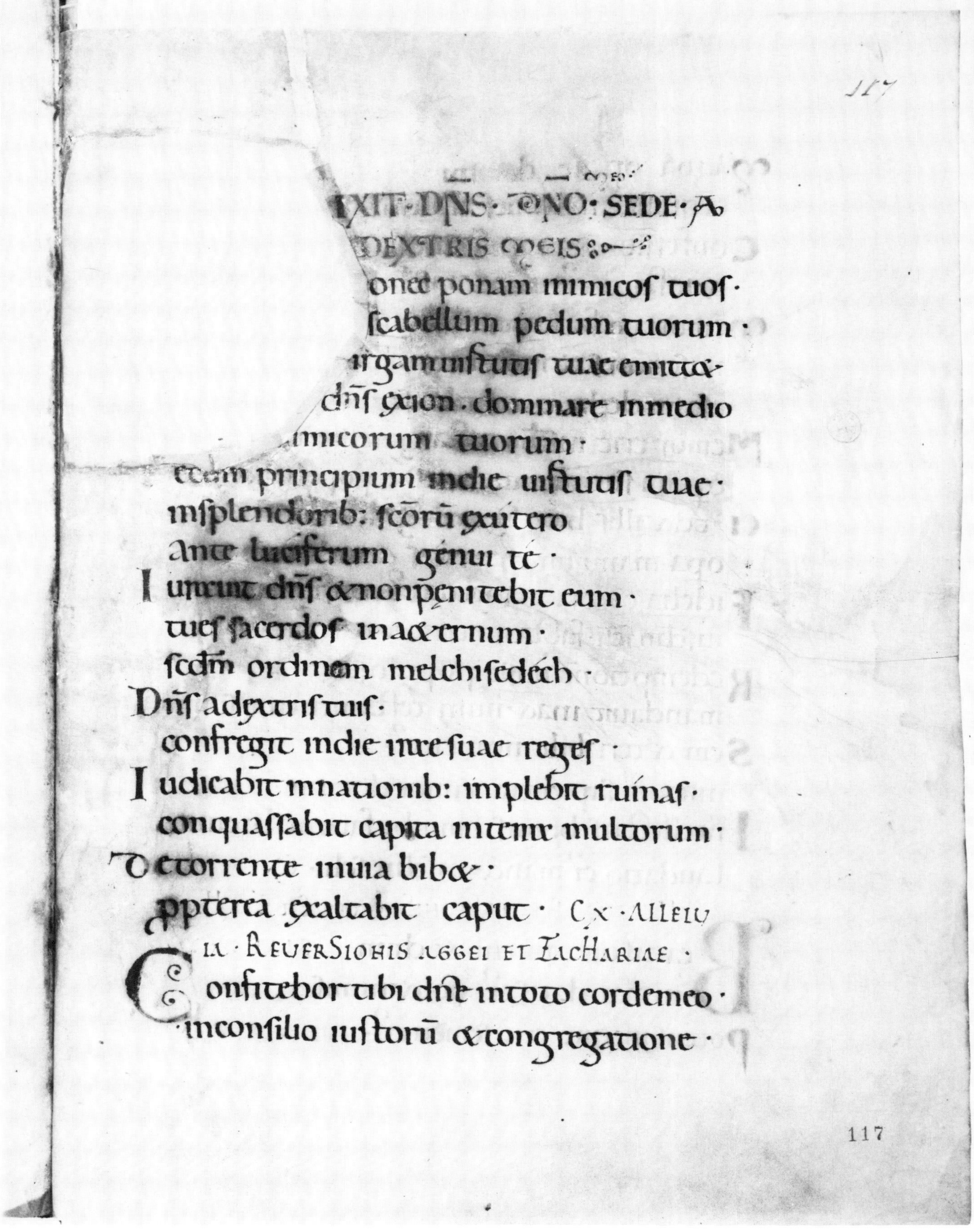
117

DIXIT DNS DNO SEDE A
DEXTRIS MEIS
onec ponam inimicos tuos
scabellum pedum tuorum
irgam uirtutis tuae emittet
dns ex sion. dominare in medio
inimicorum tuorum
ecum principium in die uirtutis tuae
in splendorib: scorum ex utero
ante luciferum genui te
Iurauit dns et non penitebit eum
tu es sacerdos in aeternum
secdm ordinem melchisedech
Dns a dextris tuis
confregit in die irae suae reges
Iudicabit in nationib: implebit ruinas
conquassabit capita in terra multorum
De torrente in uia bibet
ppterea exaltabit caput. CX. ALLELU
IA. REUERSIONIS AGGEI ET ZACHARIAE
Confitebor tibi dne in toto corde meo
in consilio iustoru et congregatione
117

3.45 Vatican, Biblioteca Apostolica, Reg. lat. 12, f. 117^{r}

118

generatio rectorum benedicetur ·
Gloria et diuitię indomo eius ·
et iustitia ei manet insclm scli ·
Exortum est intenebris lumen rectis ·
misericors et miserator et iustus ·
Iocundus homo qui miseretur et cōmodat ·
disponet sermones suos iniudicio ·
quia inaeternum noncommouebitur ·
Inmemoria aeterna erit iustus ·
Abauditione mala nontimebit ·
Paratū cor ei sperare indn̄o ·
confirmatum est. cor ei' noncōmouebitur.
donec despiciat inimicos suos ·
Dispsit dedit paupib: iustitia ei manet
insclm scli · cornu ei' exaltabitur ingla ·
Peccator uidebit et irascetur. dentib: suis
fremet et tabescet. desideriū peccatorū
peribit · CXII · Uox aecclesiae
Laudate pueri dn̄m ·
laudate nomen dn̄i ·
Sit nomen dn̄i benedictum ·
exhocnunc et usq: insclm ·
A solis ortu usq: ad occasum ·

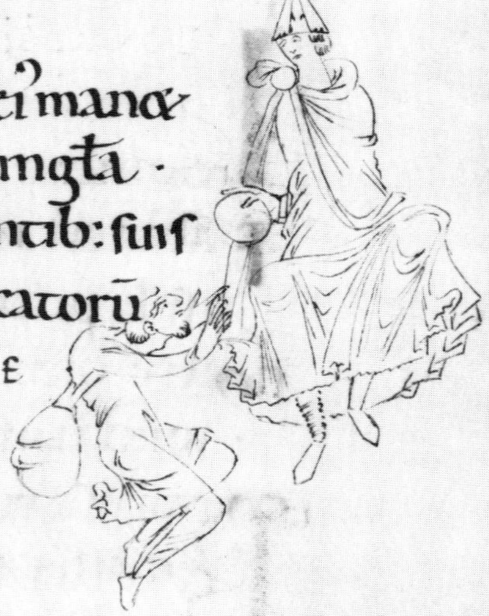

118

3.46 Vatican, Biblioteca Apostolica, Reg. lat. 12, f. 118r

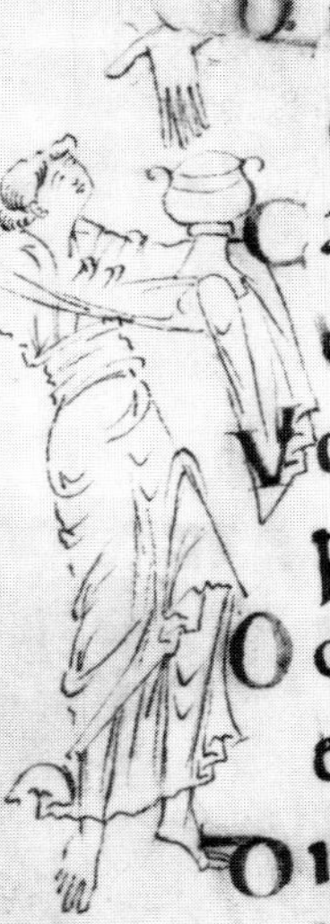

Quid retribuam dno pro omnib: ·
quae retribuit mihi ·
Calicem salutaris accipiam ·
& nomen dni inuocabo ·
Vota mea dno reddam coram omni populo ei9 ·
pretiosa in conspectu dni mors sanctorum ei9 ·
O dne quia ego seruus tuus ·
ego seruus tuus · & filius ancillae tuae ·
Dirupisti uincula mea · tibi sacrificabo
hostiam laudis · & nomen dni inuocabo ·
Vota mea dno reddam in conspectu omnis
populi ei9 in atriis domus dni
in medio tui hierusalem · CXVI · ALLELUIA
HOC AD FINE SUPIORIS PERTINET PSALMI ·
UOX APOSTOLORUM AD GENTES ·
Laudate dnm omnes gentes ·
laudate eum omnes populi ·
Qm confirmata est sup nos misericordia ei9 ·
& ueritas dni manet in aeternum ·
CXVII · ALLELUIA HOC AD PRINCIPIUM · CXVII
PTINENT PSALMI · UT OSTENDATUR HOMINIBUS
UIA ID EST XPC P QUAM INGREDITUR AD PORTAM
QUAM INGRESSUS CLAUDI NON POSSIT ·

3.47 Vatican, Biblioteca Apostolica, Reg. lat. 12, f. 120v

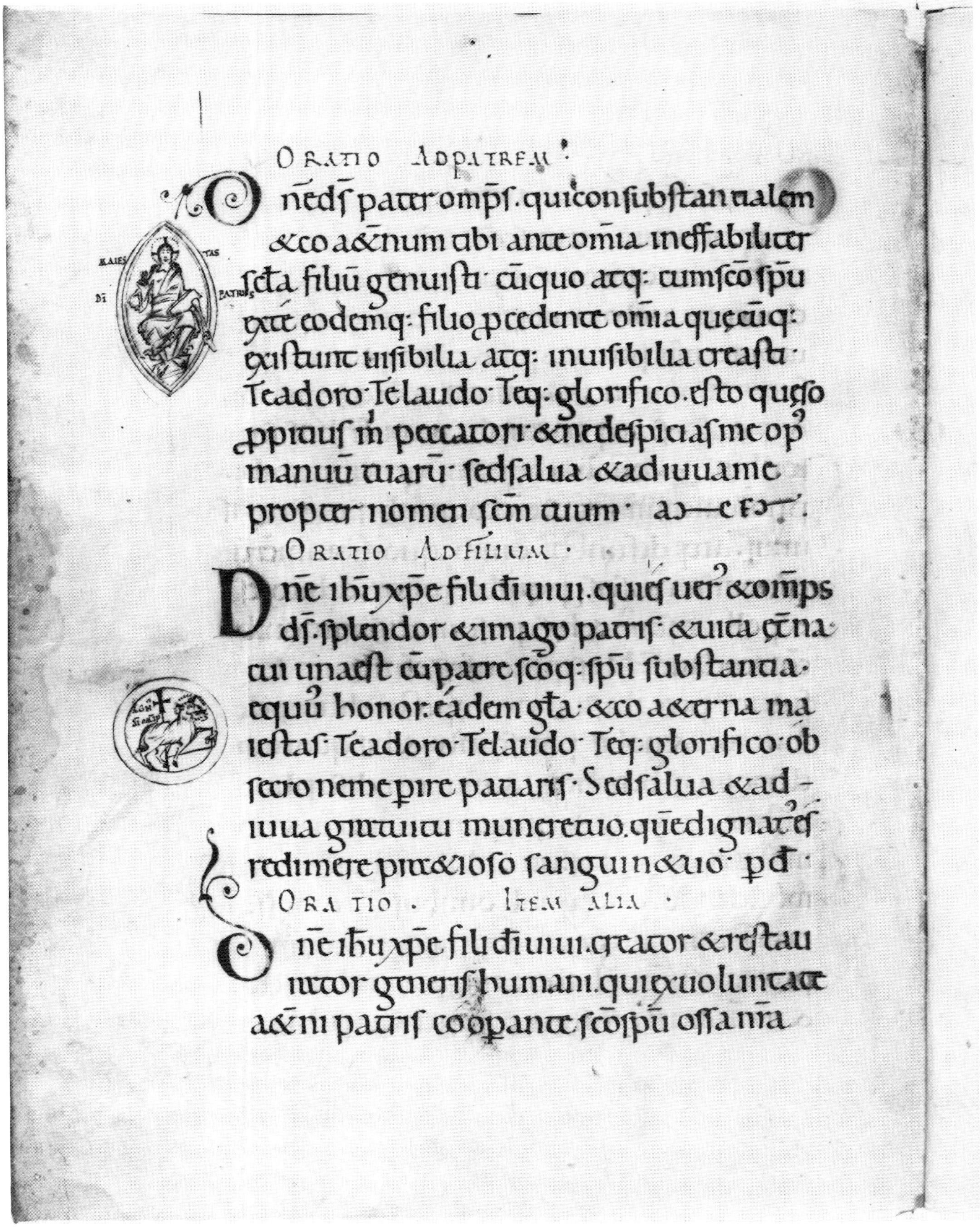

ORATIO AD PATREM.
Dne ds pater omps. qui consubstantialem
& coaeternum tibi ante omia ineffabiliter
scta filiu genuisti cu quo atq; cum sco spu
ex te eodemq; filio pcedente omia quecuq;
existunt uisibilia atq; inuisibilia creasti.
Te adoro Te laudo Teq; glorifico. esto queso
ppitius m peccatori & ne despicias me op
manuu tuaru sed salua & adiuua me
propter nomen scm tuum. amen.
ORATIO AD FILIUM.
Dne ihu xpe fili di uiui. qui es uerus & omps
ds. splendor & imago patris & uita aeterna
cui una est cu patre scoq; spu substantia.
equu honor. eadem gla. & coaeterna ma
iestas. Te adoro Te laudo Teq; glorifico ob
secro ne me perire patiaris. Sed salua & ad-
iuua gratuito munere tuo. que dignatus es
redimere pretioso sanguine tuo. p d.
ORATIO. ITEM ALIA.
Dne ihu xpe fili di uiui. creator & restau
rator generis humani. qui ex uoluntate
aeterni patris cooperante sco spu ossa nra

3.48 Vatican, Biblioteca Apostolica, Reg. lat. 12, f. 168v

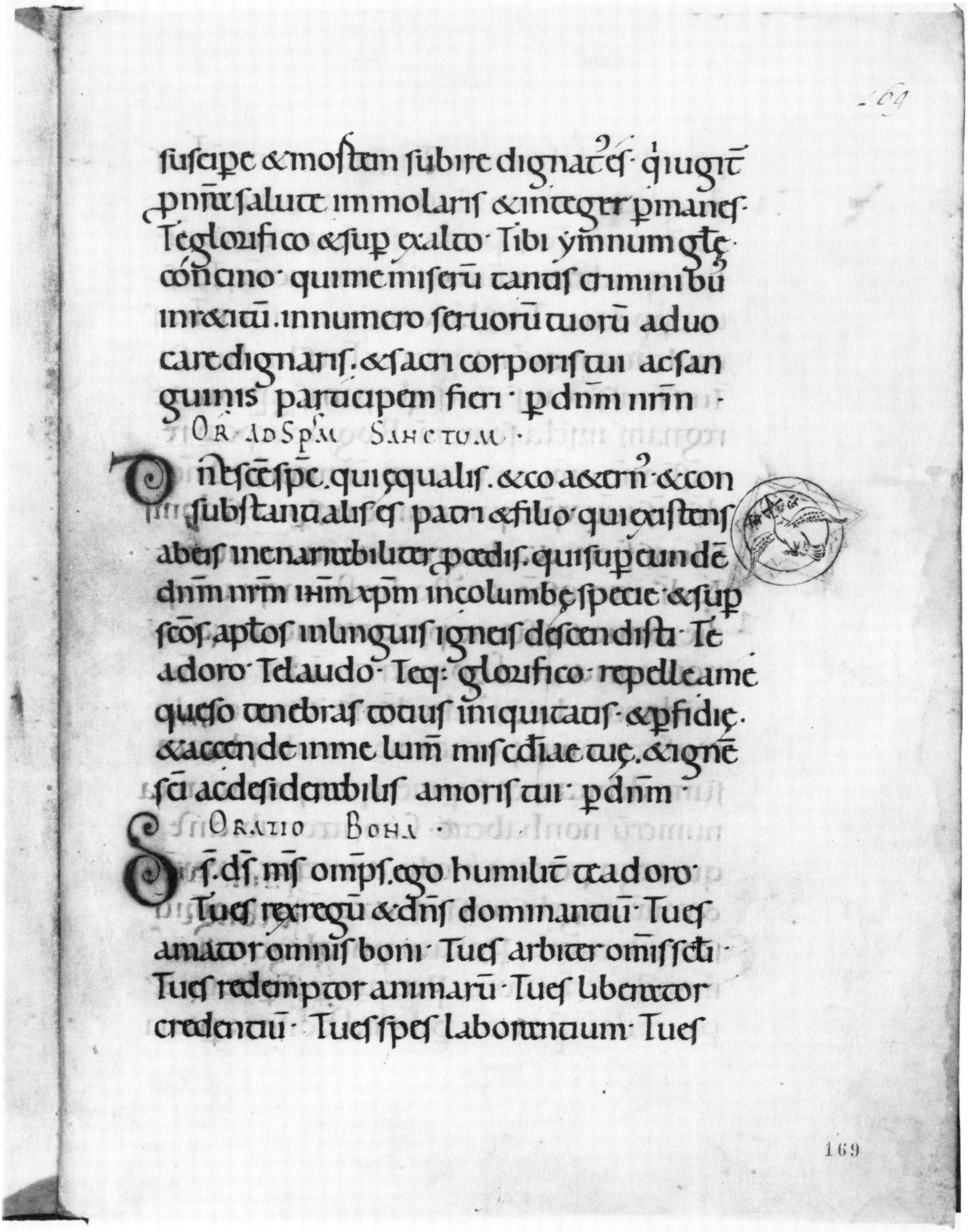

169

suscipe & mortem subire dignatus es· qui iugiter
pro nostra salute immolaris & integer permanes·
Te glorifico & super exalto· Tibi hymnum gloriae·
concino· qui me miserum tantis criminibus
irretitum. in numero seruorum tuorum aduo
care dignaris. & sacri corporis tui ac san
guinis participem fieri· per dominum nostrum·

OR AD SPM SANCTUM·

Domine sancte spiritus. qui coaequalis. & coaeternus & con
substantialis es patri & filio qui ex istens
ab eis inenarrabiliter procedis. qui super eundem
dominum nostrum ihesum christum in columbae specie & super
sanctos apostolos in linguis igneis descendisti· Te
adoro· Te laudo· Teque glorifico· repelle a me
queso tenebras totius iniquitatis· & perfidiae·
& accende in me lumen misericordiae tuae. & ignem
sancti ac desiderabilis amoris tui· per dominum·

ORATIO BONA·

Domine deus meus omnipotens. ego humiliter te adoro·
Tu es rex regum & dominus dominantium· Tu es
amator omnis boni· Tu es arbiter omnis saeculi·
Tu es redemptor animarum· Tu es liberator
credentium· Tu es spes laborantium· Tu es

169

3.49 Vatican, Biblioteca Apostolica, Reg. lat. 12, f. 169r

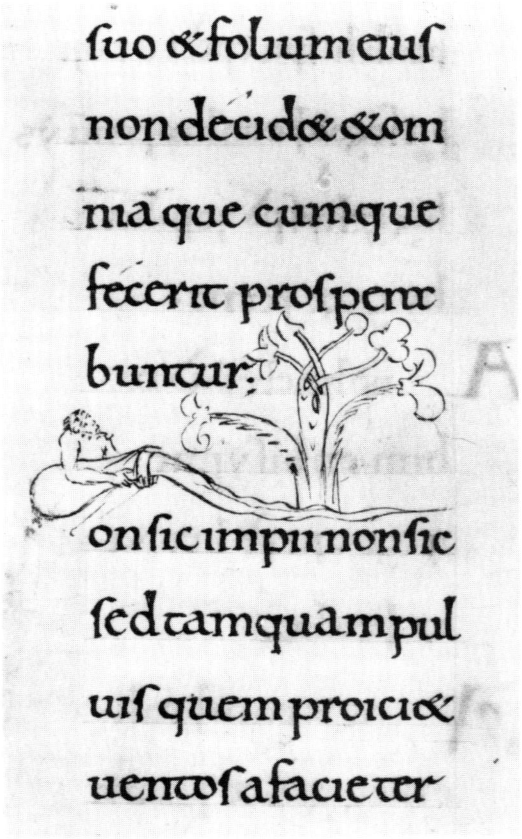
suo & folium eius
non decid& & om
nia que cumque
fecerit prosper&
buntur;
on sic impii non sic
sed tamquam pul
uis quem proici&
uentos a facie ter

4.1 Paris, Bibl. Nat., lat. 8824, f 1[r]

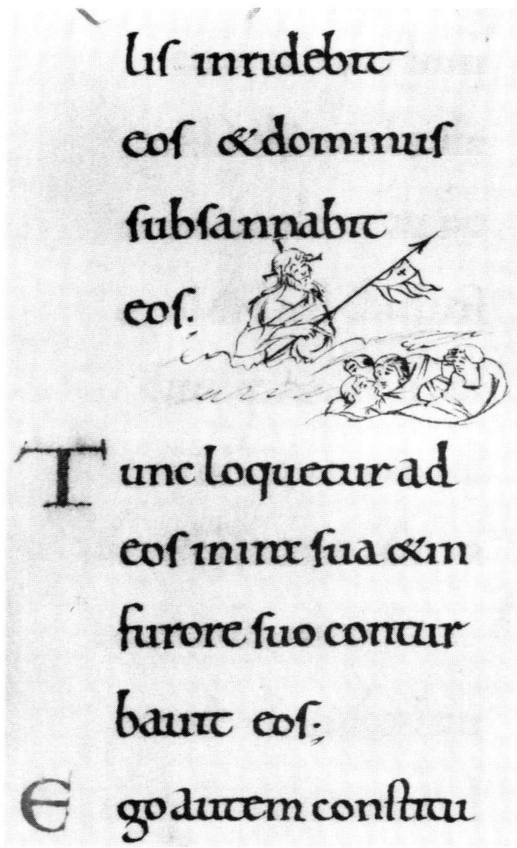
lis inridebit
eos & dominus
subsannabit
eos.
Tunc loquetur ad
eos in ira sua & in
furore suo contur
babit eos;
Ego ducem constitu

4.2 Paris, Bibl. Nat., lat. 8824, f 1[v]

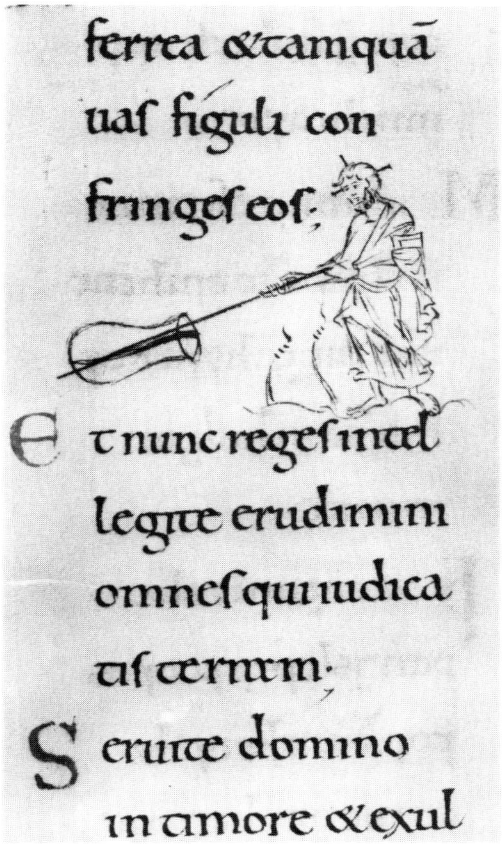

4.3 Paris, Bibl. Nat., lat. 8824, f 2r

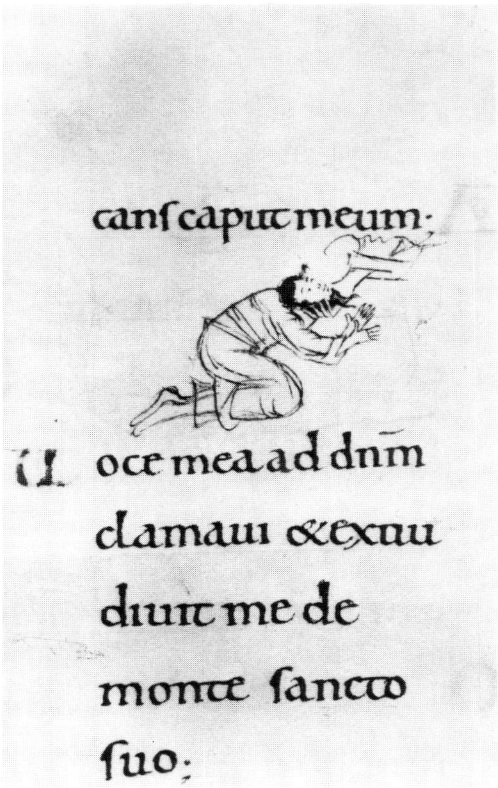

4.4 Paris, Bibl. Nat., lat. 8824, f 2v

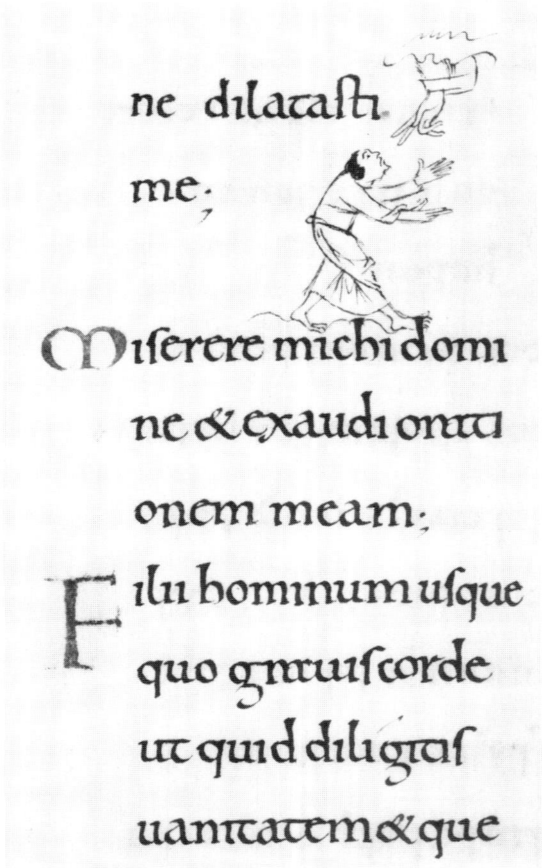
ne dilatasti
me;
Miserere michi domi
ne & exaudi orati
onem meam;
Filii hominum usque
quo graves corde
ut quid diligitis
uanitatem & que

4.5

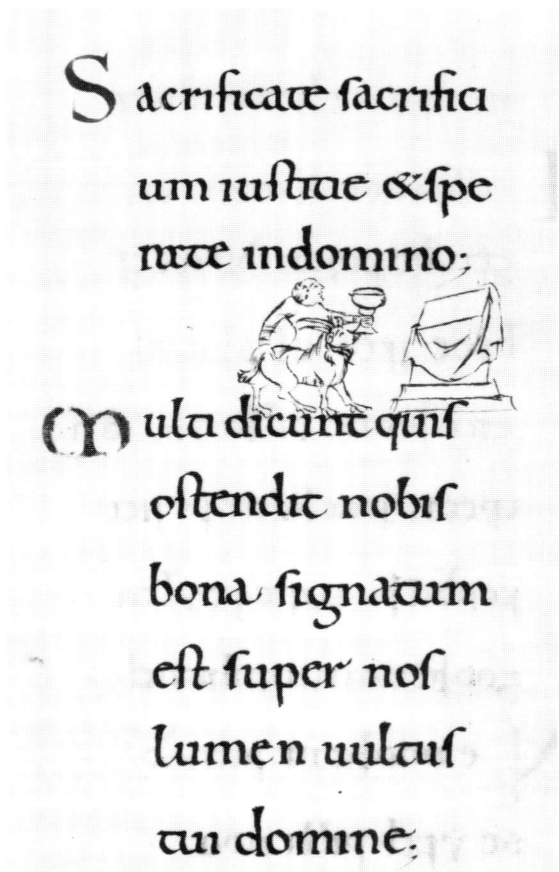
Sacrificate sacrifici
um iustitiae & spe
rate indomino;
Multa dicunt quis
ostendit nobis
bona signatum
est super nos
lumen uultus
tui domine;

4.6

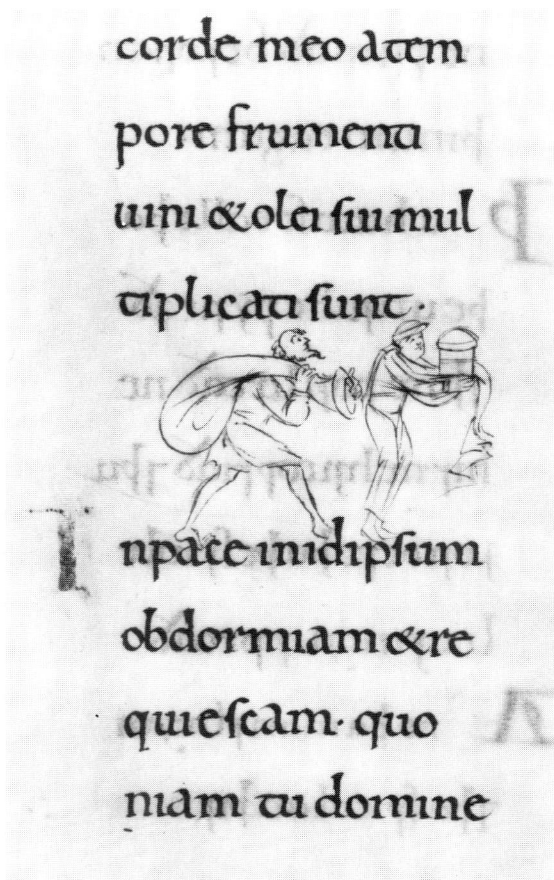
corde meo a tem
pore frumenti
uini & olei sui mul
tiplicati sunt.
In pace inidipsum
obdormiam & re
quiescam. quo
niam tu domine

4.7

4.5 Paris, Bibl. Nat., lat. 8824, f 3r
(upper drawing)

4.6 Paris, Bibl. Nat., lat. 8824, f 3r
(lower drawing)

4.7 Paris, Bibl. Nat., lat. 8824, f 3r
(center drawing)

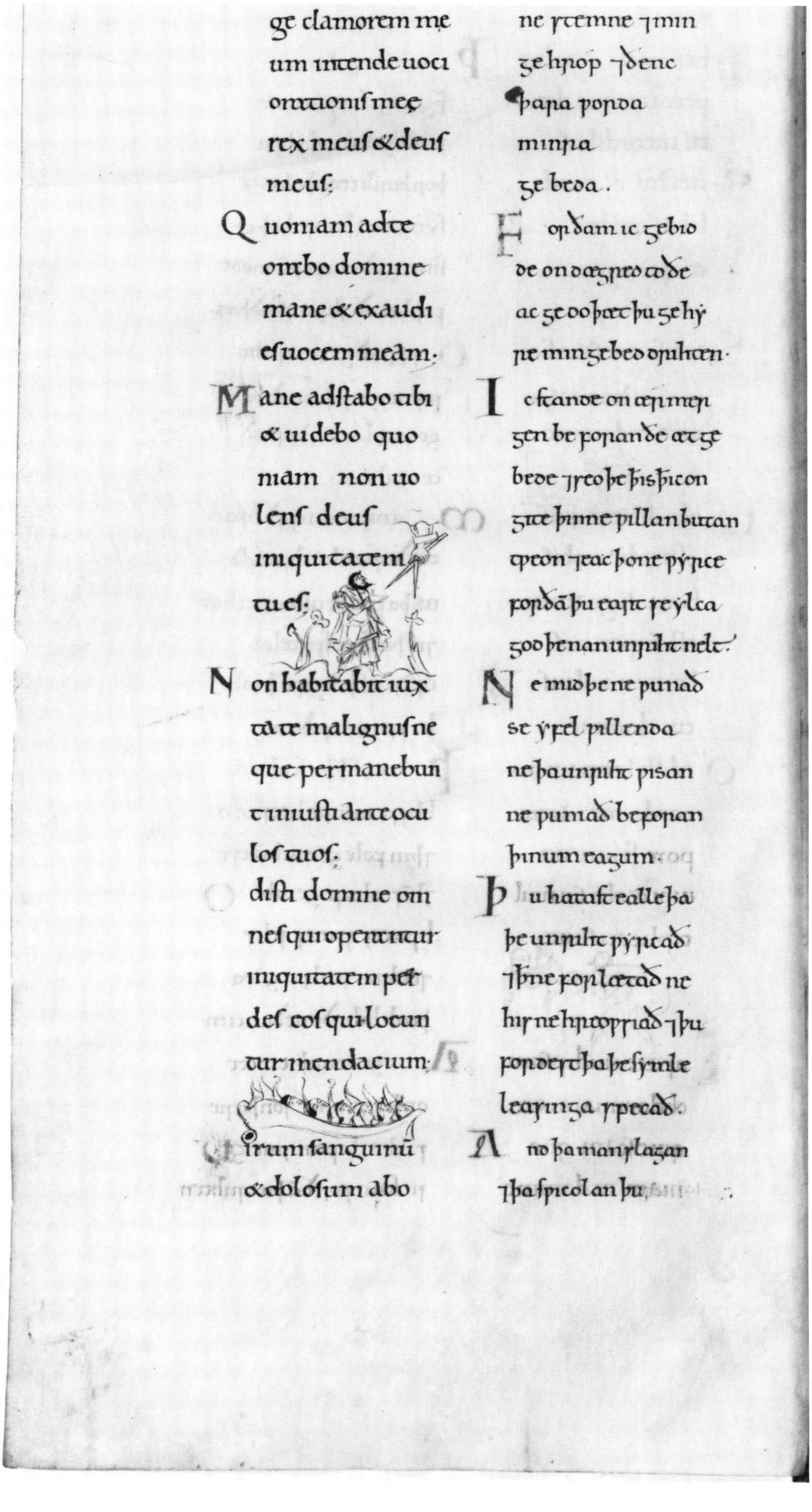

4.8 Paris, Bibl. Nat., lat. 8824, f 3v

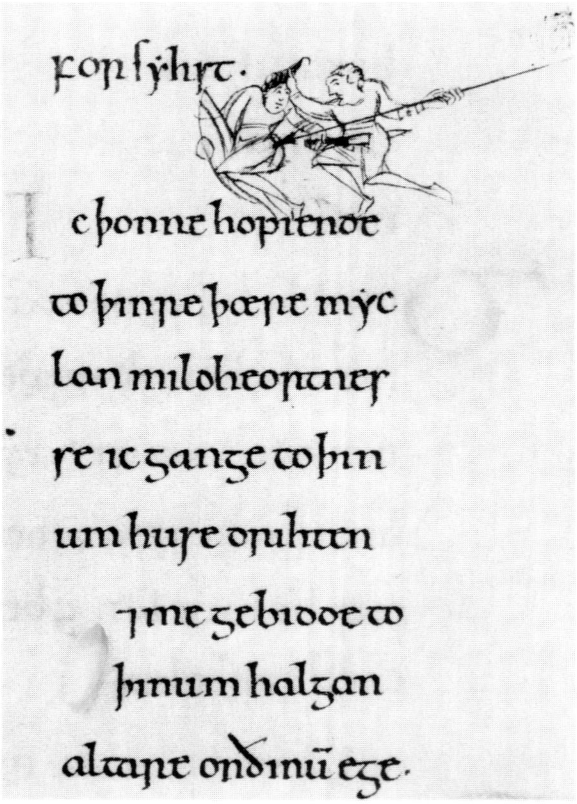

4.9

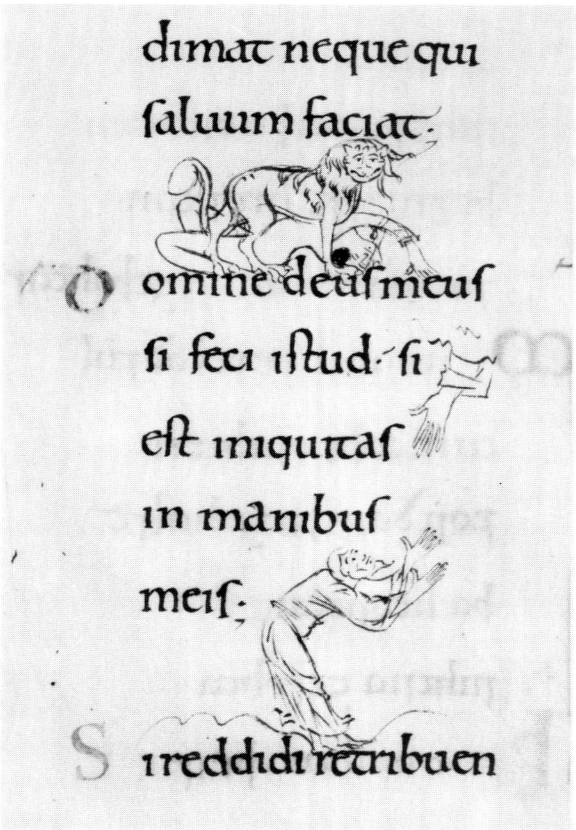

4.10

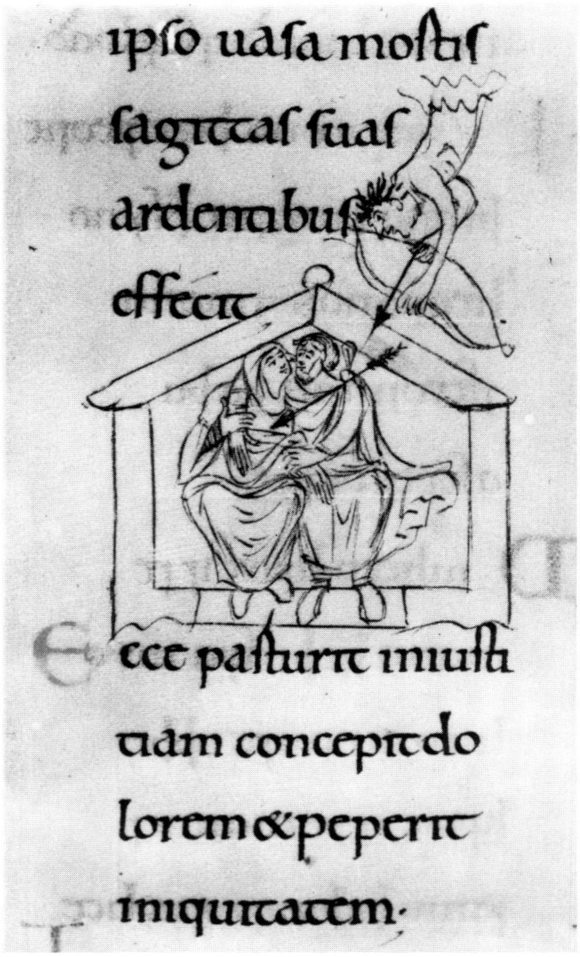

4.11

4.9 Paris, Bibl. Nat., lat. 8824, f 4r

4.10 Paris, Bibl. Nat., lat. 8824, f 5r

4.11 Paris, Bibl. Nat., lat. 8824, f 6r

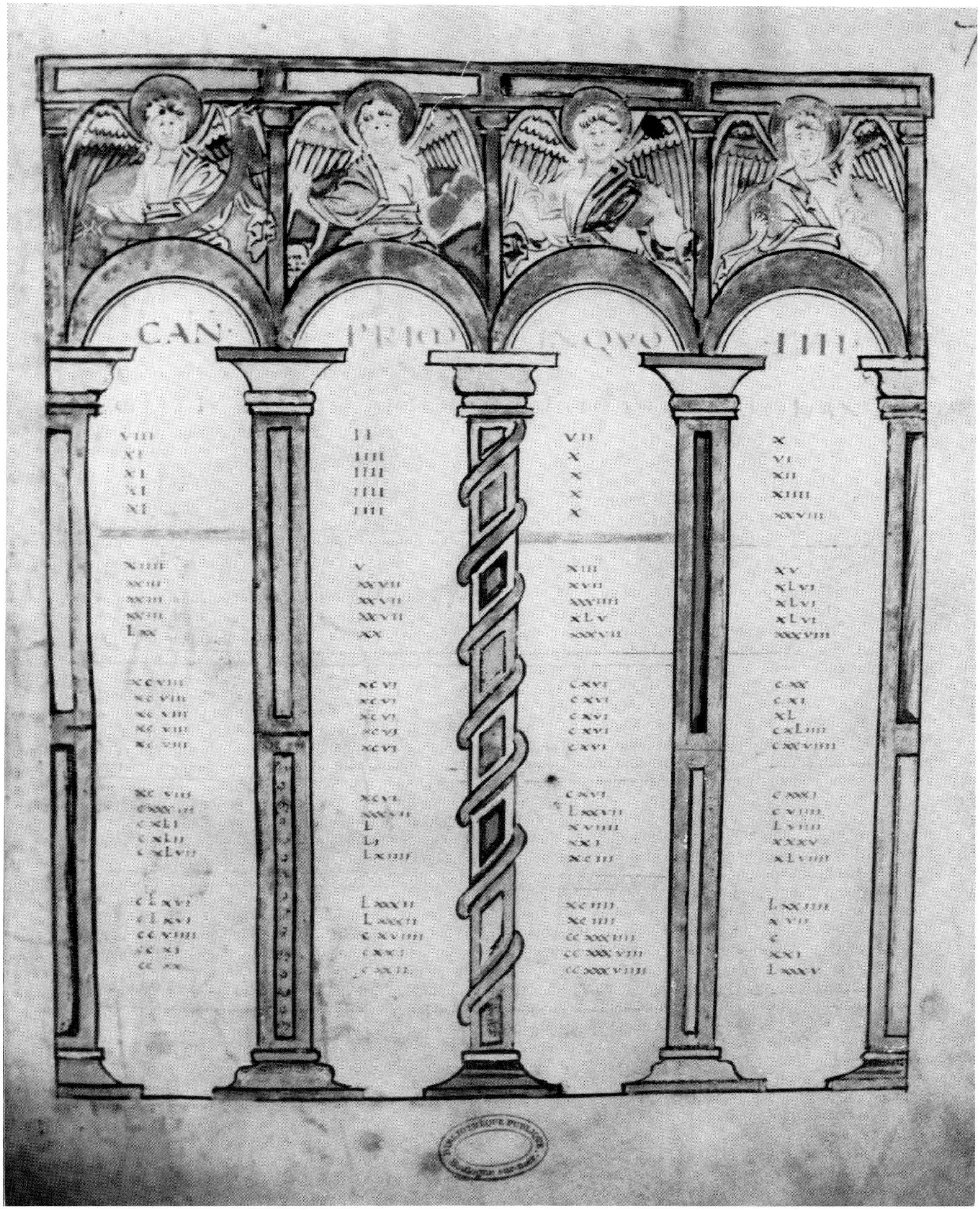

5.1 Boulogne, Bibl. Mun., 11 f. 2r

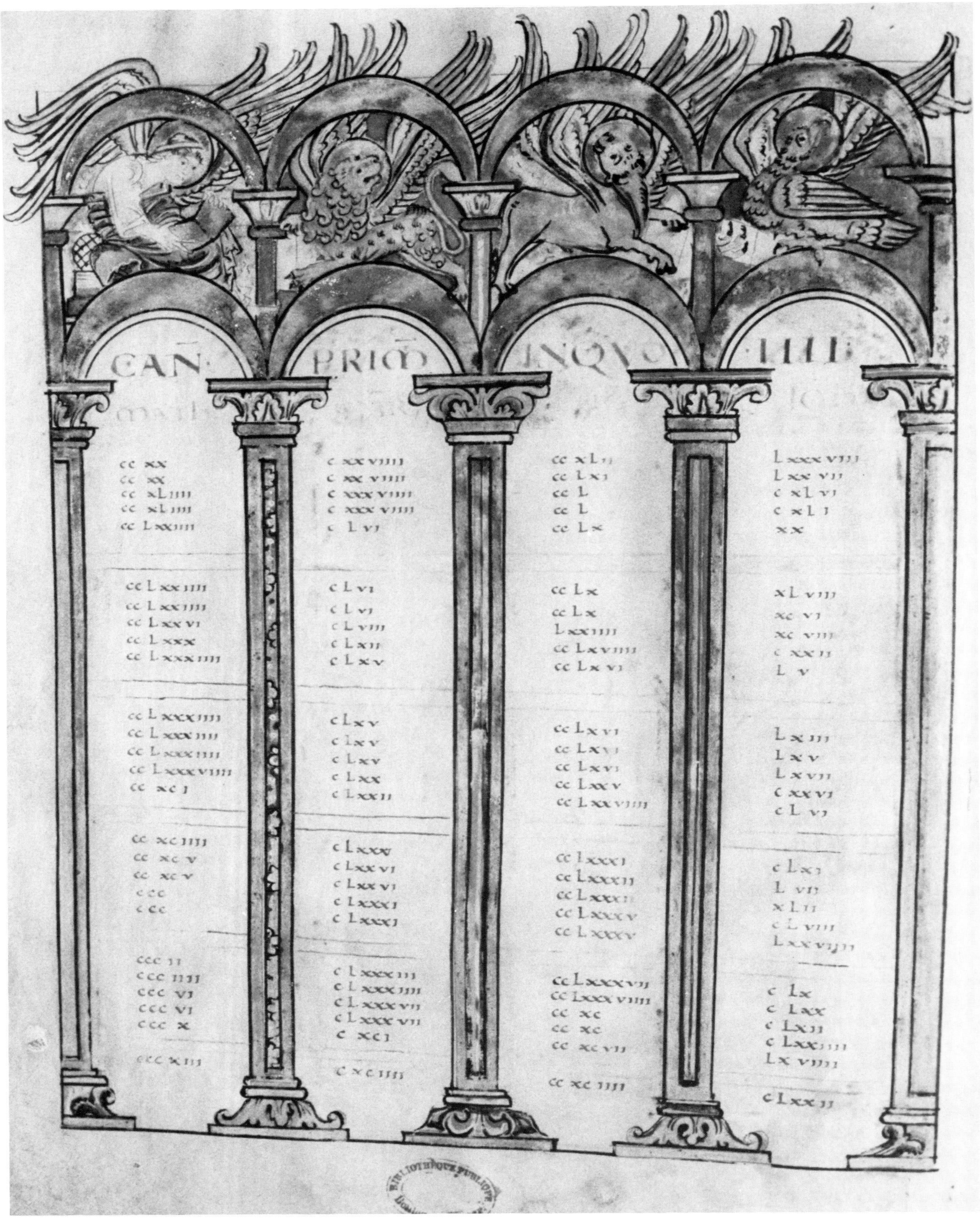

5.2 Boulogne, Bibl. Mun., 11 f. 2v

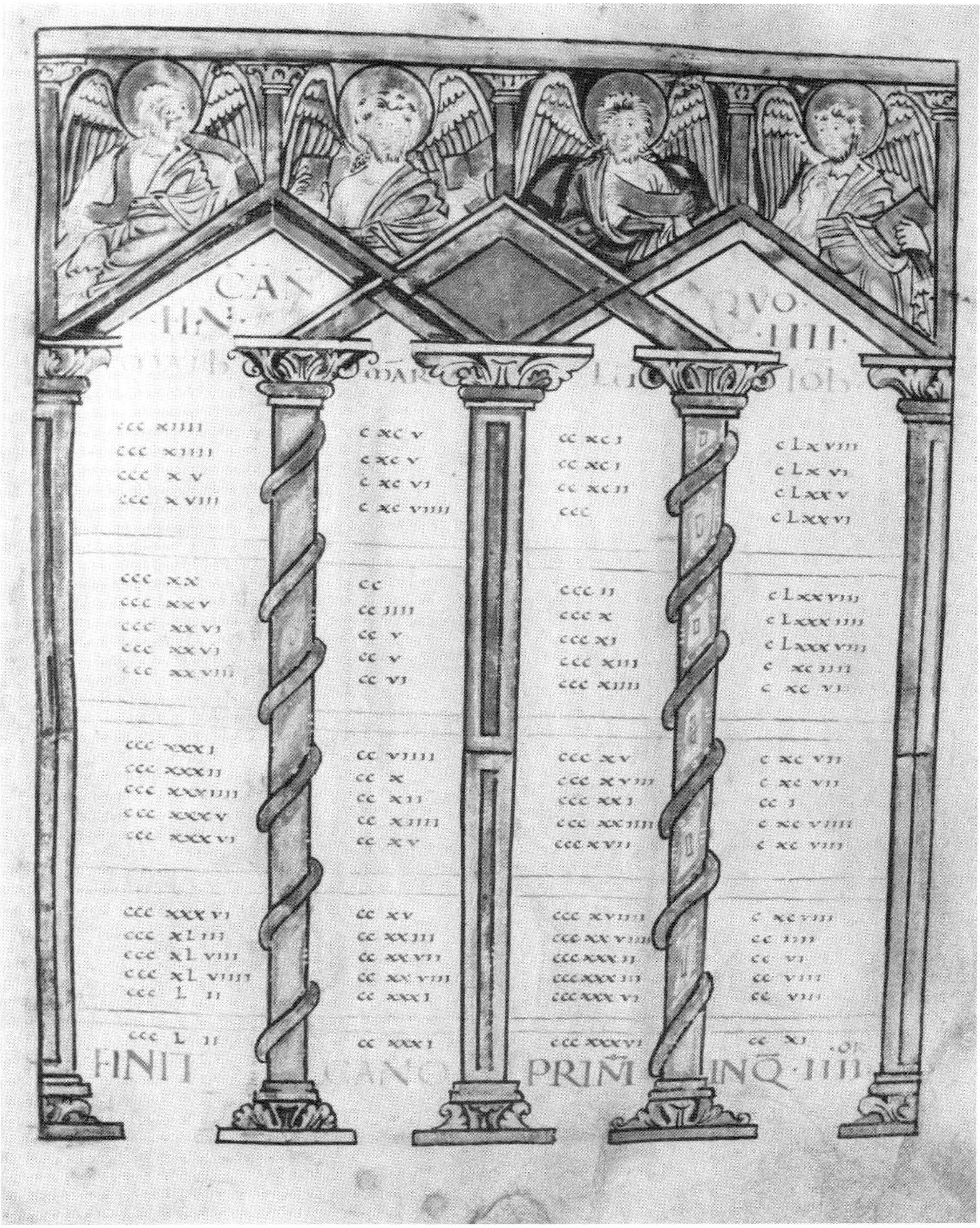

5.3 Boulogne, Bibl. Mun., 11 f. 3r

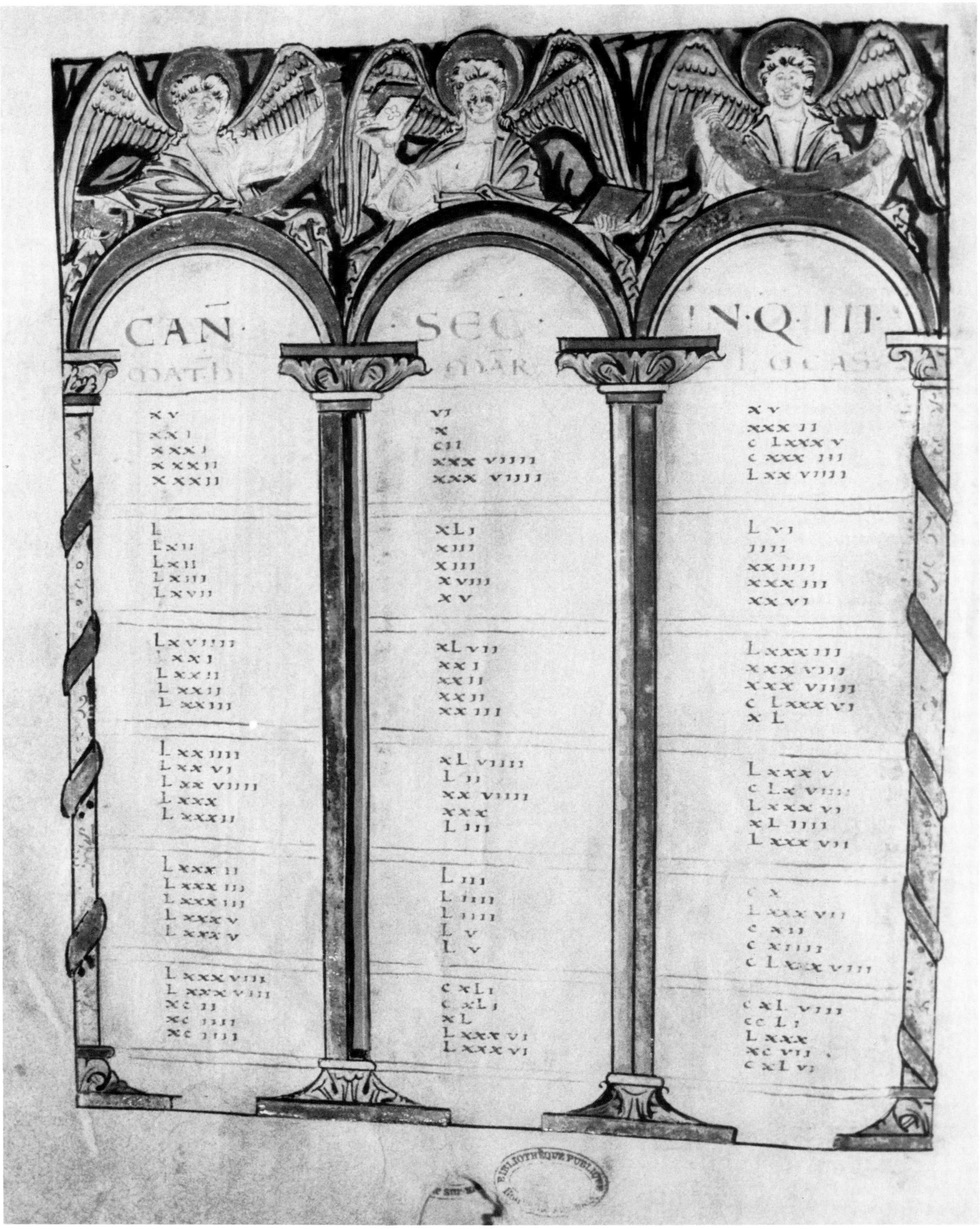

5.4 Boulogne, Bibl. Mun., 11 f. 3v

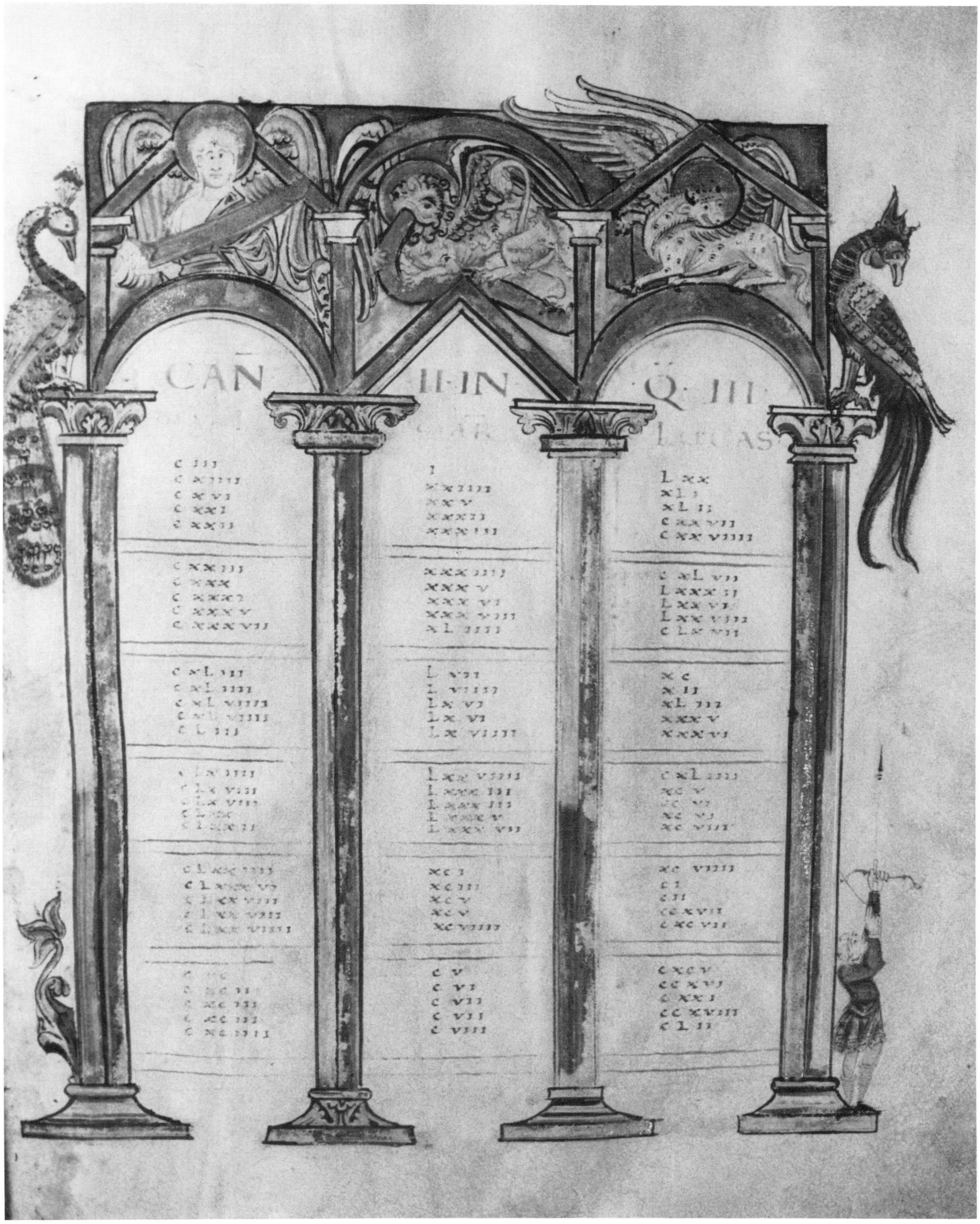

5.5 Boulogne, Bibl. Mun., 11 f. 4r

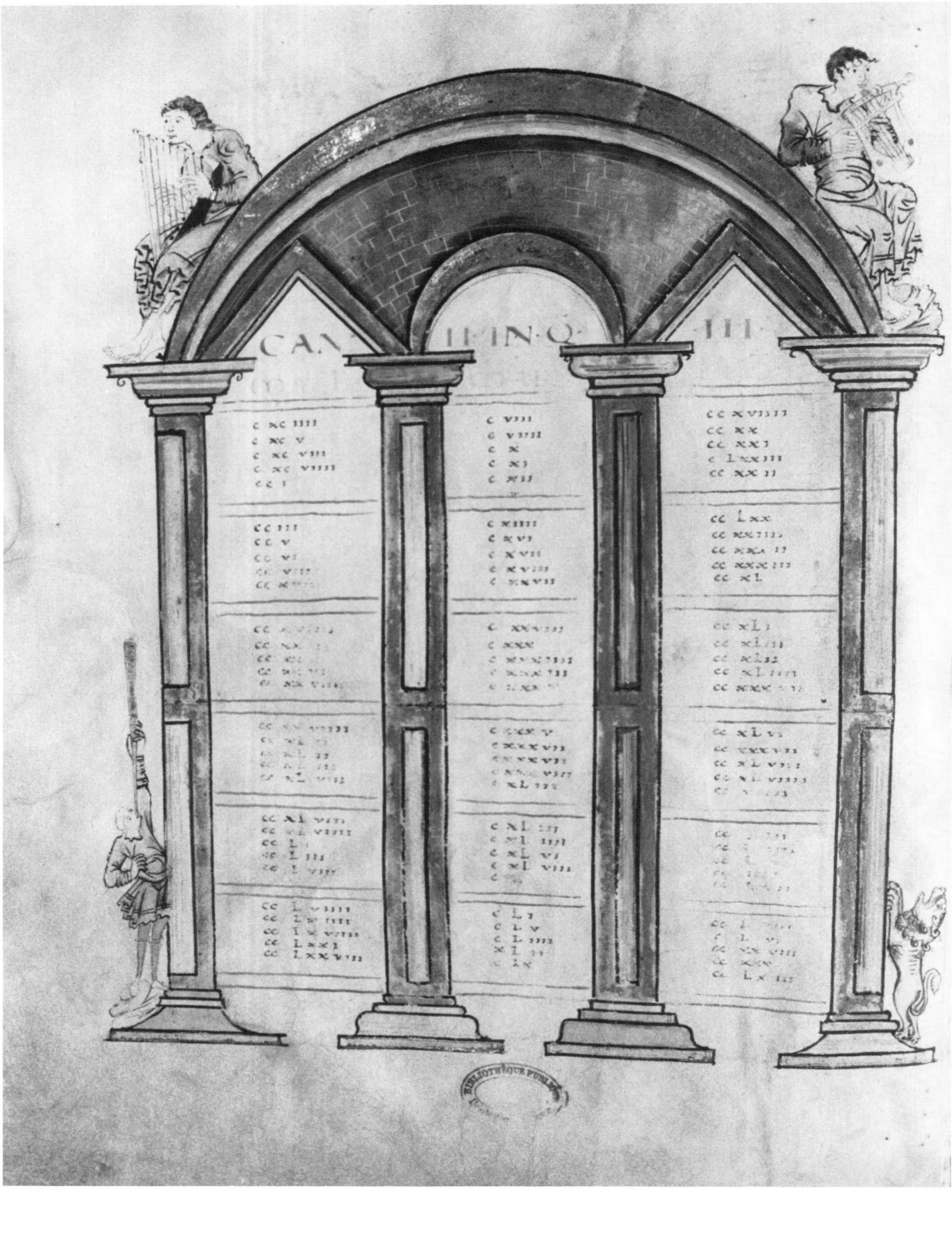

5.6 Boulogne, Bibl. Mun., 11 f. 4v

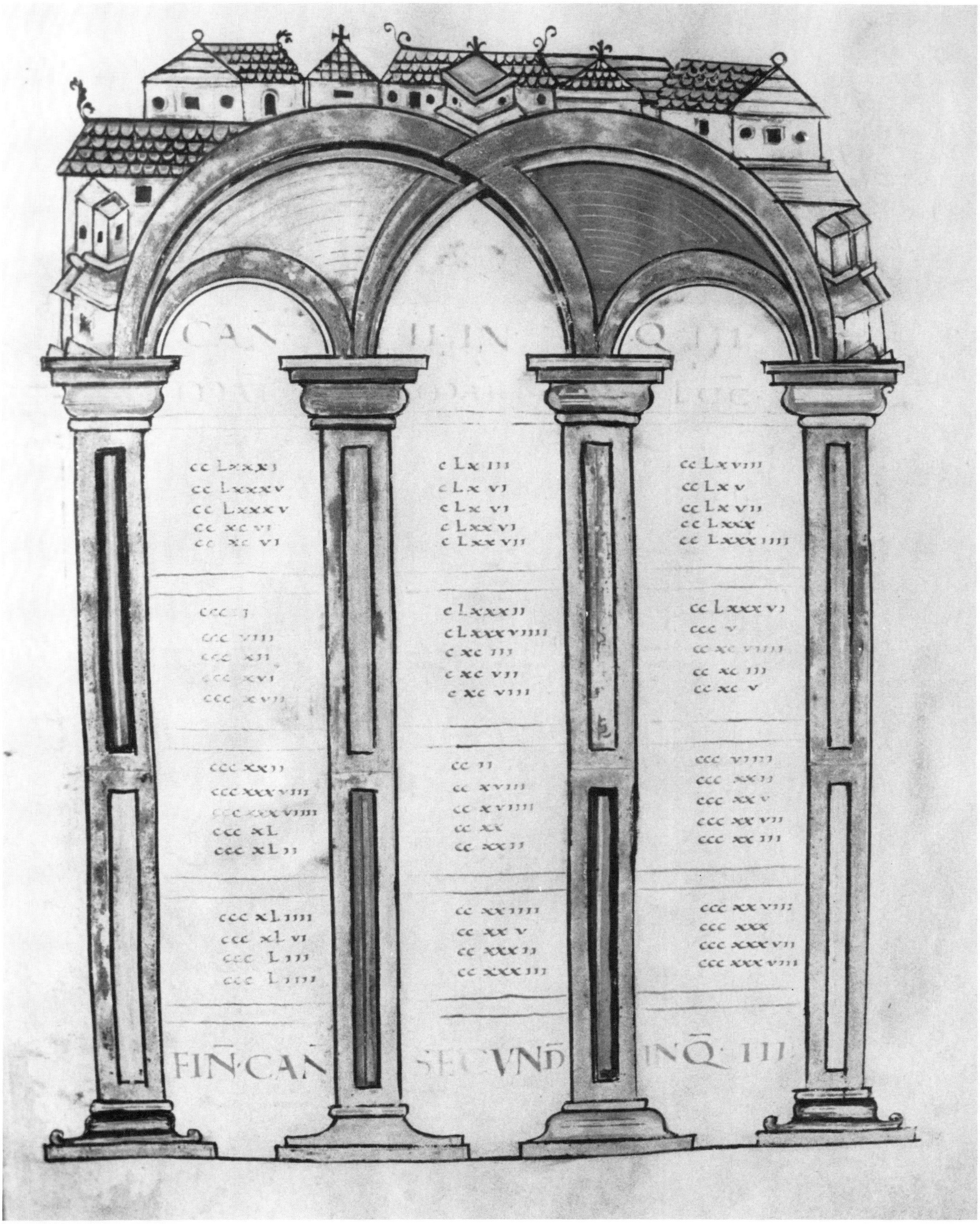

5.7 Boulogne, Bibl. Mun., 11 f. 5r

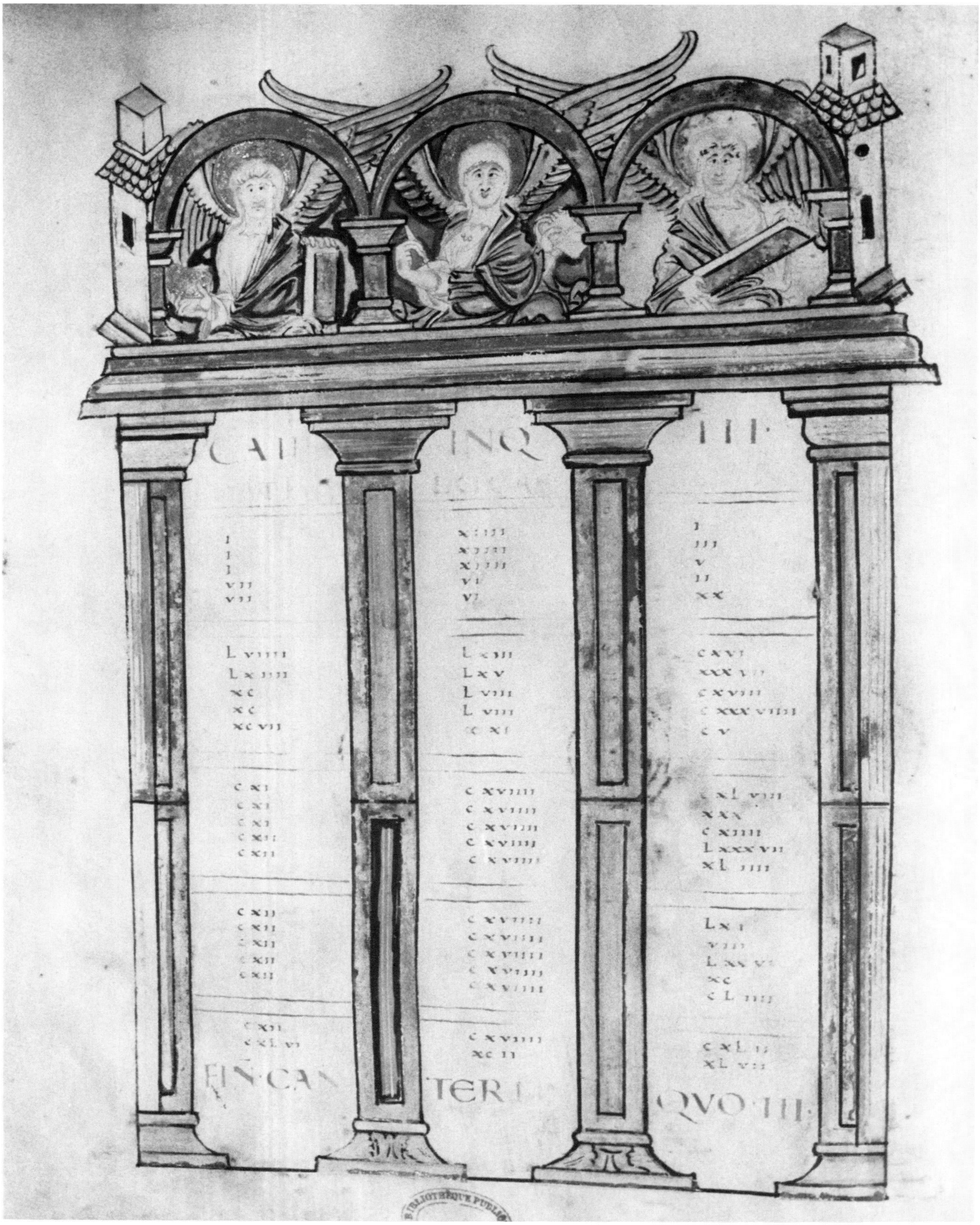

5.8 Boulogne, Bibl. Mun., 11 f. 5^{v}

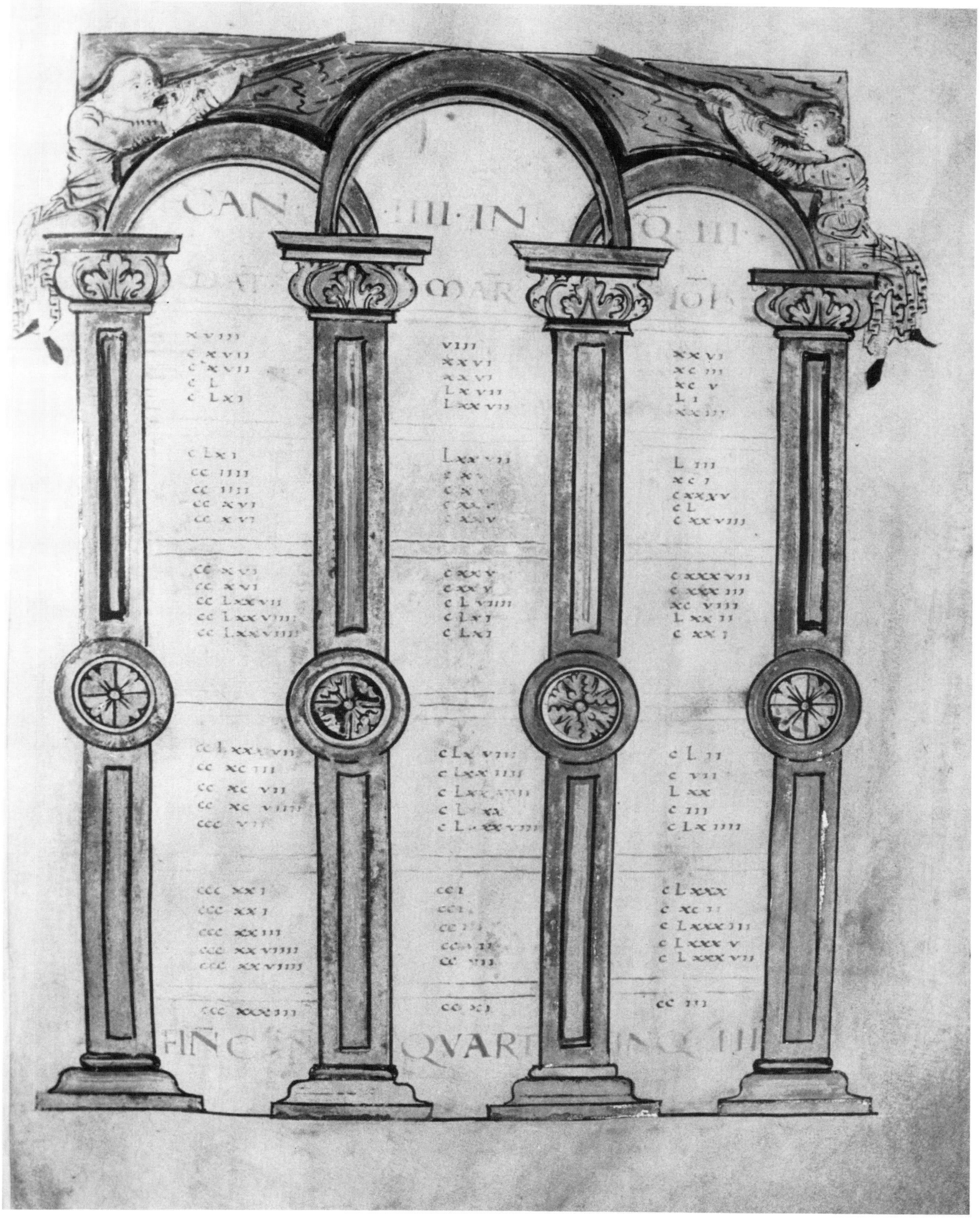

5.9 Boulogne, Bibl. Mun., 11 f. 6ʳ

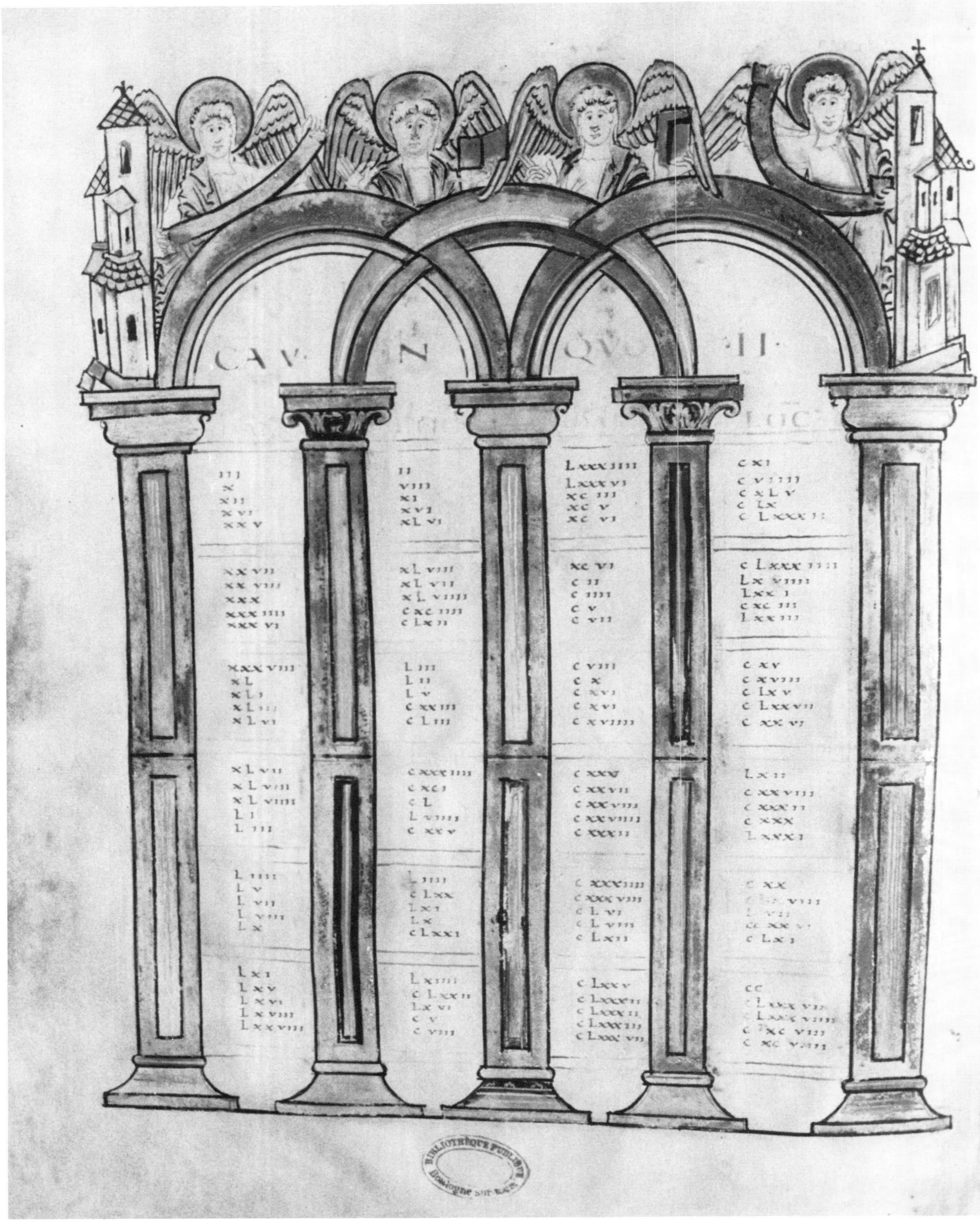

5.10 Boulogne, Bibl. Mun., 11 f. 6v

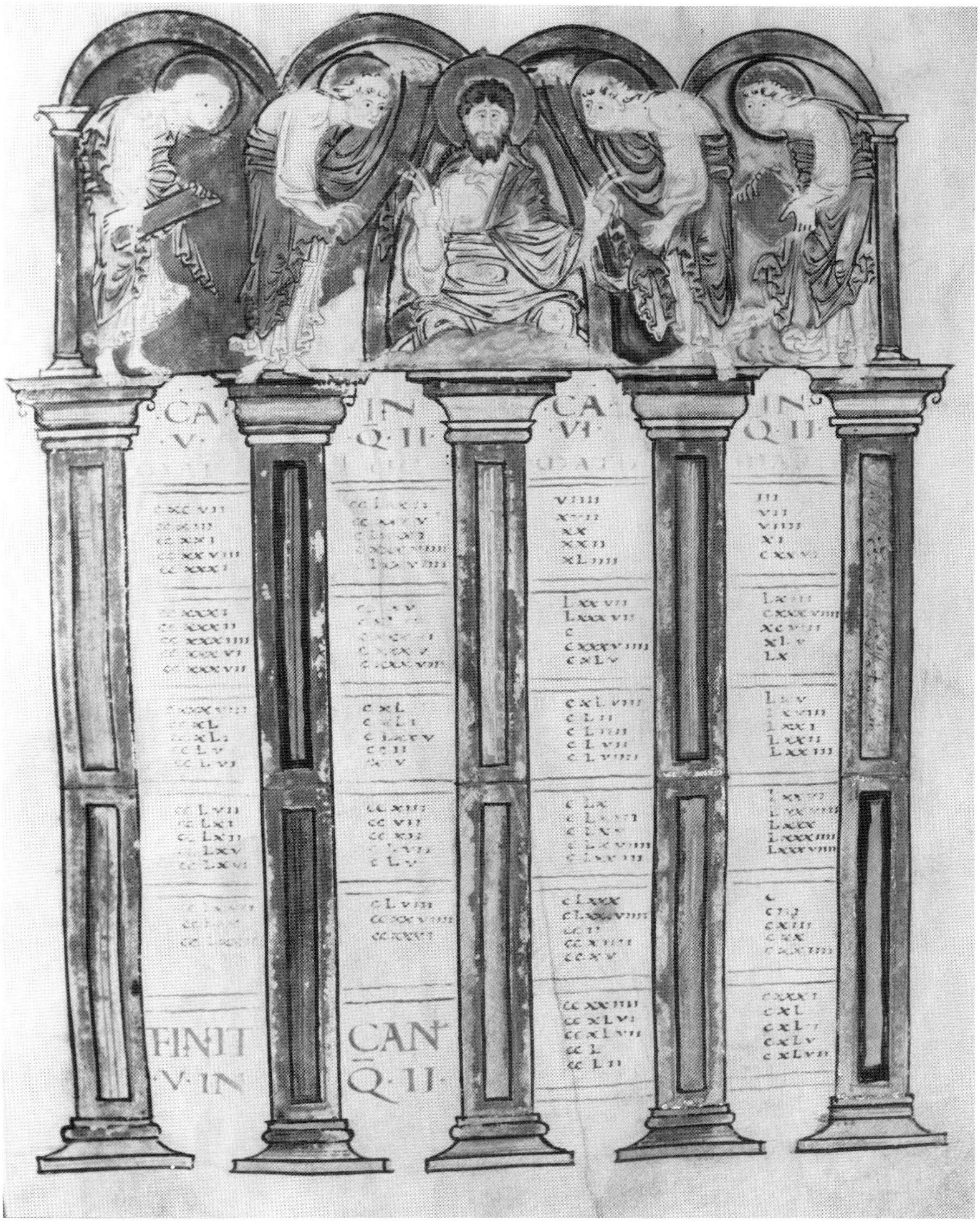

5.11 Boulogne, Bibl. Mun., 11 f. 7r

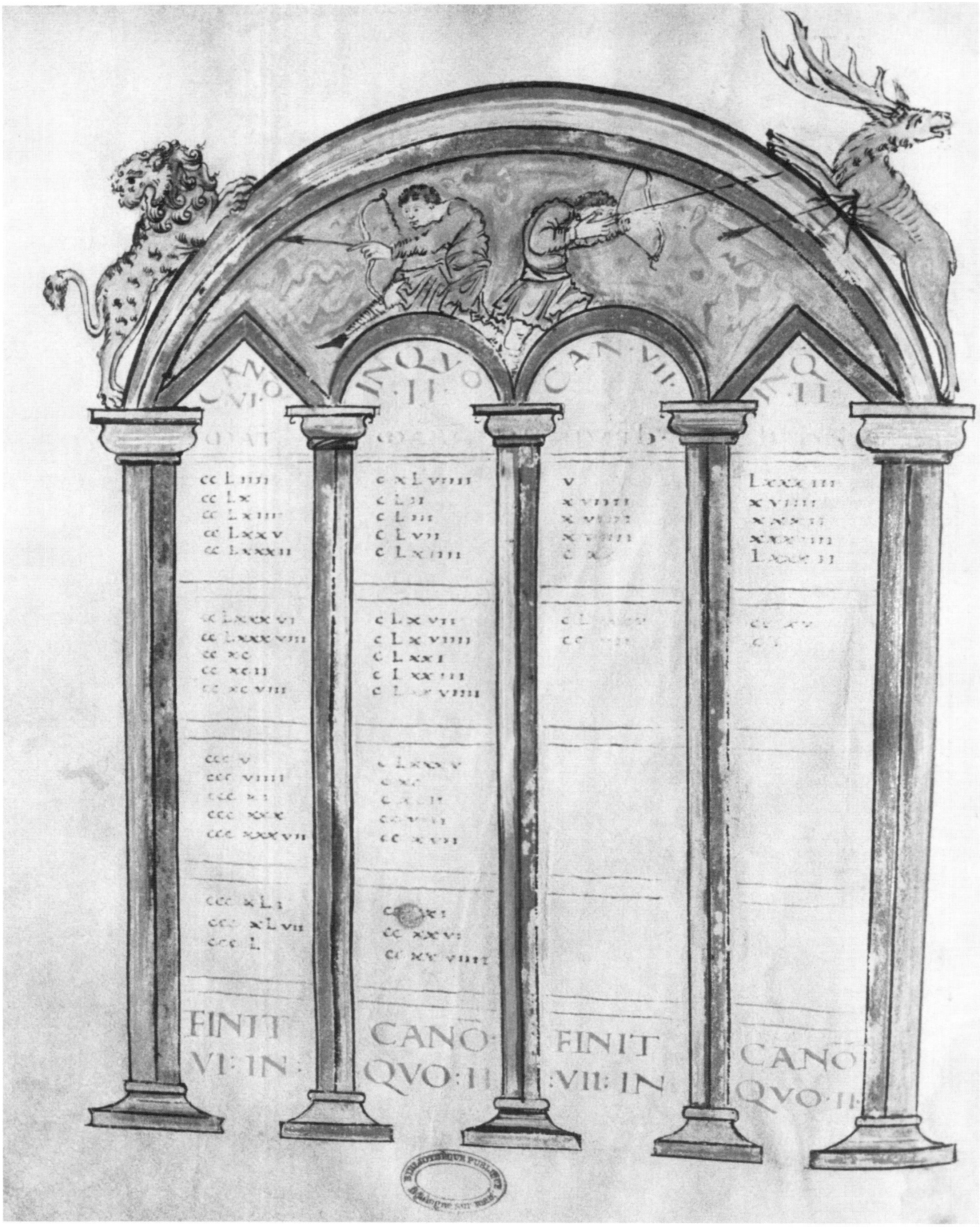

 5.12 Boulogne, Bibl. Mun., 11 f. 7v

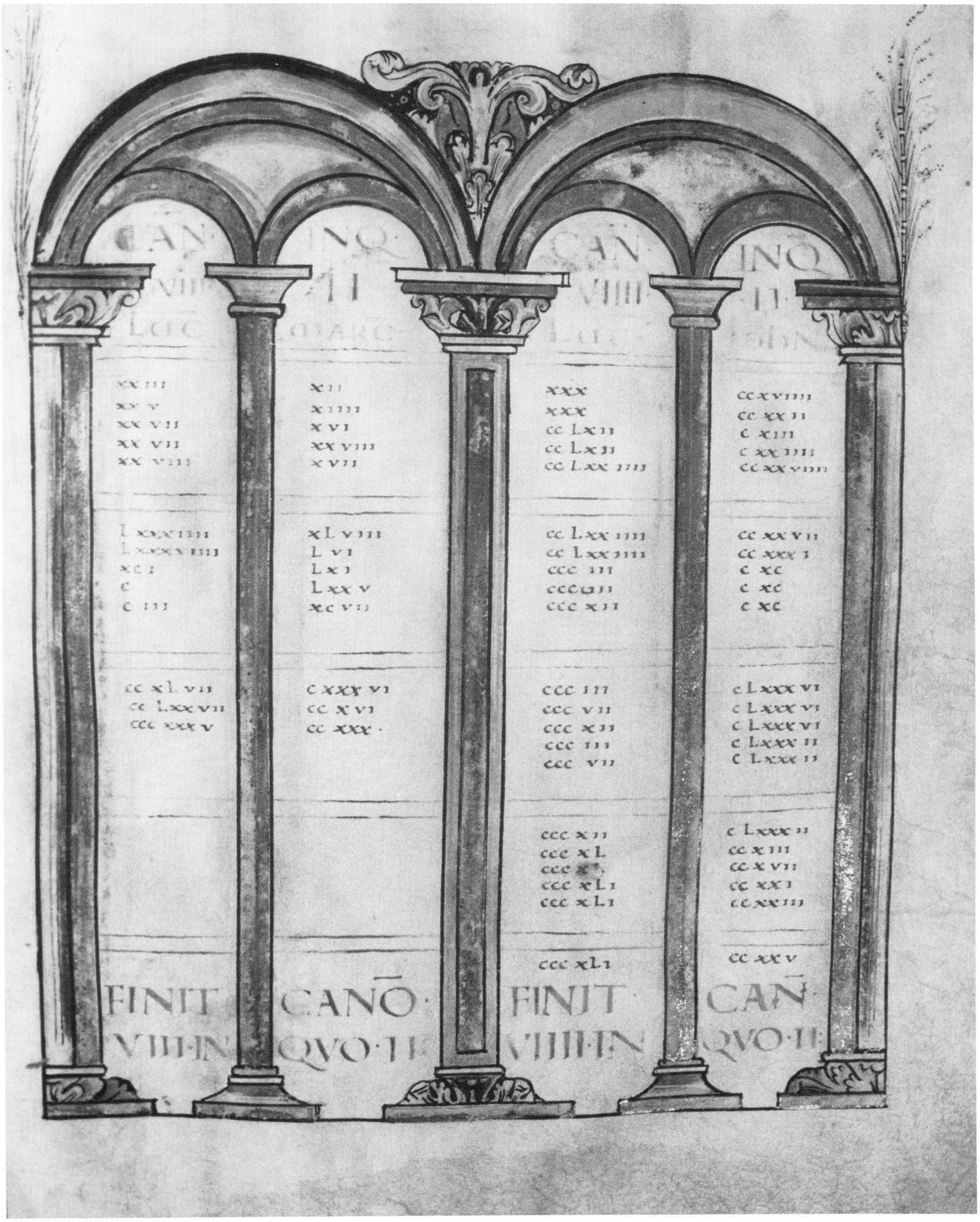

5.13 Boulogne, Bibl. Mun., 11 f. 8r

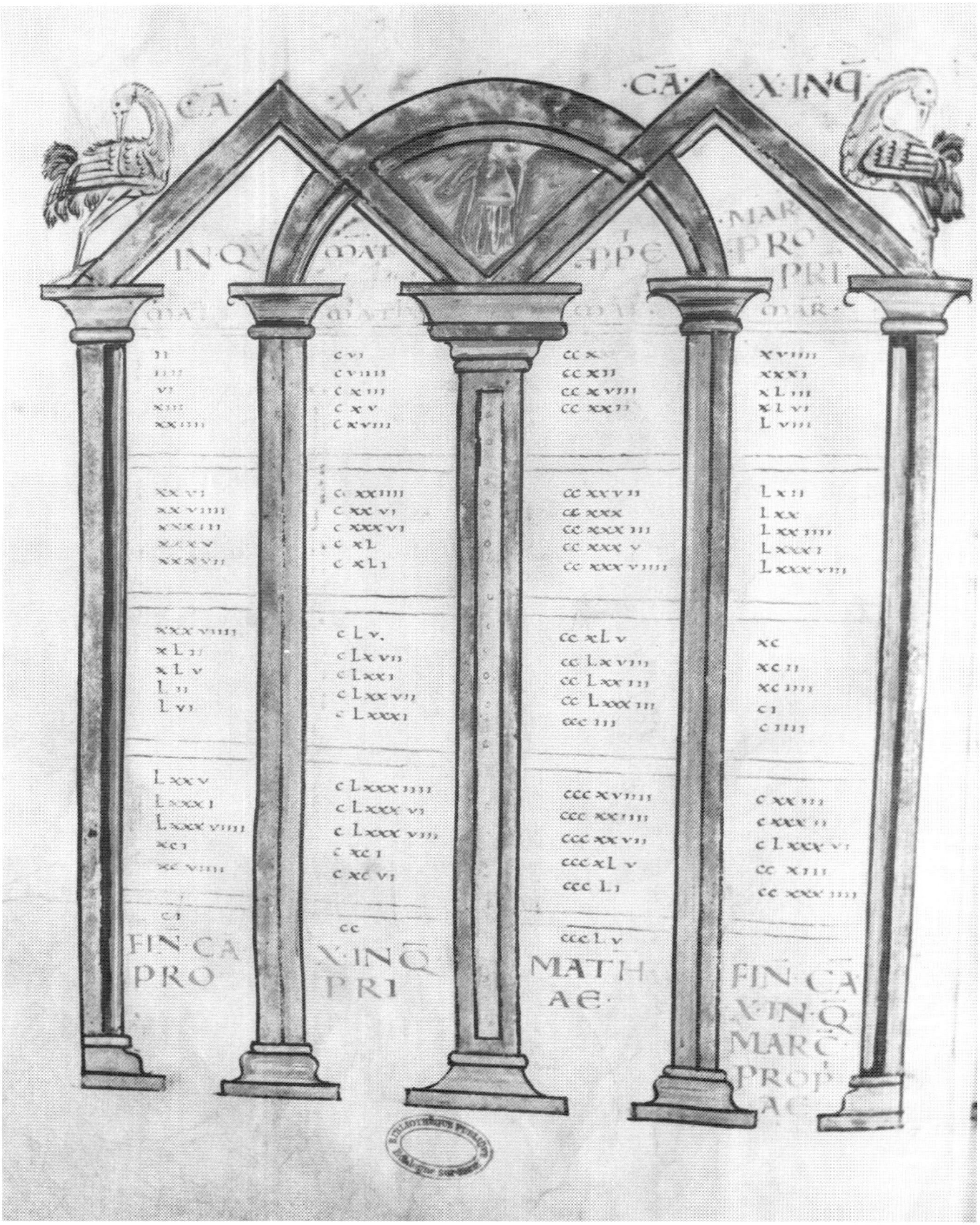

5.14 Boulogne, Bibl. Mun., 11 f. 8v

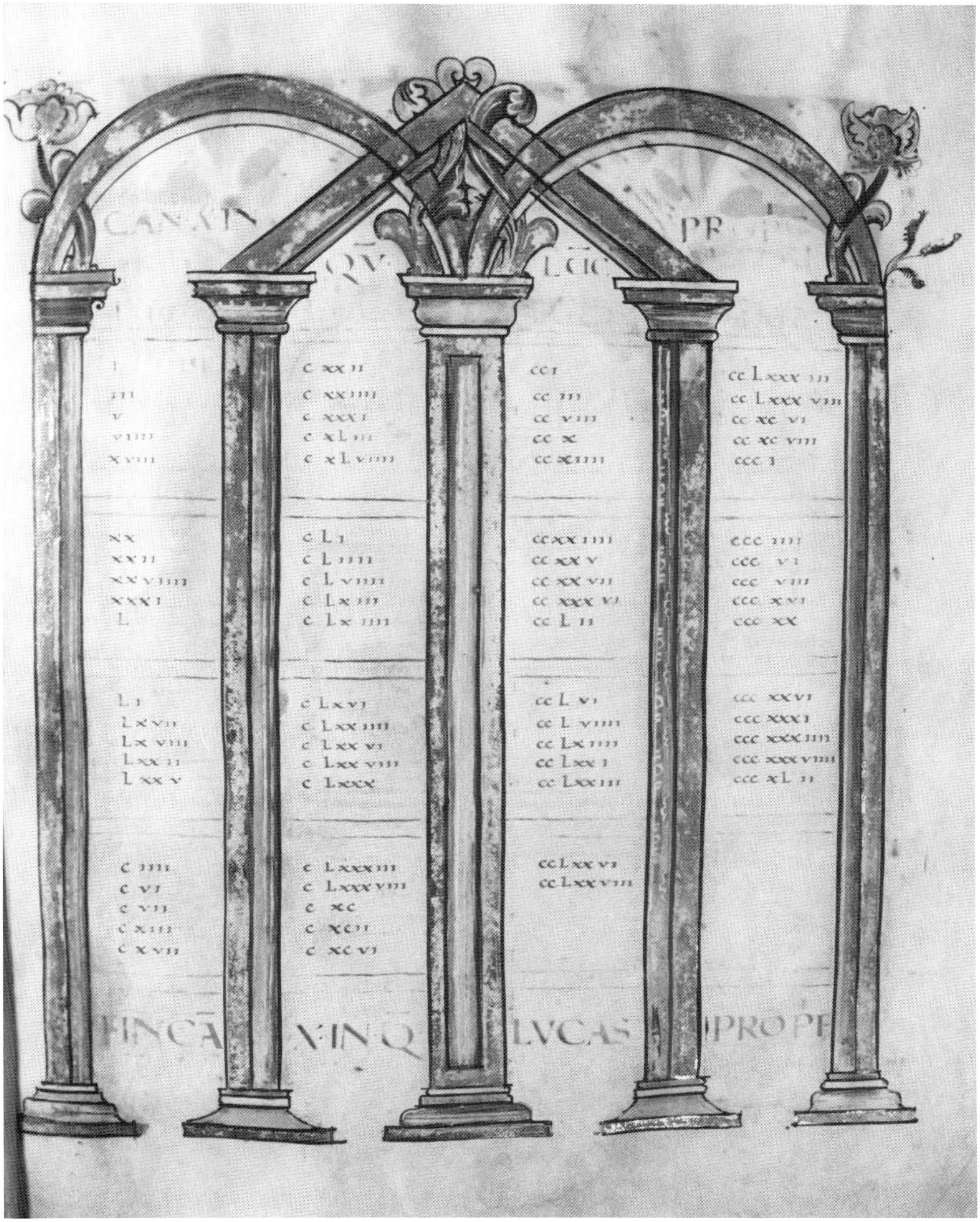

5.15 Boulogne, Bibl. Mun., 11 f. 9r

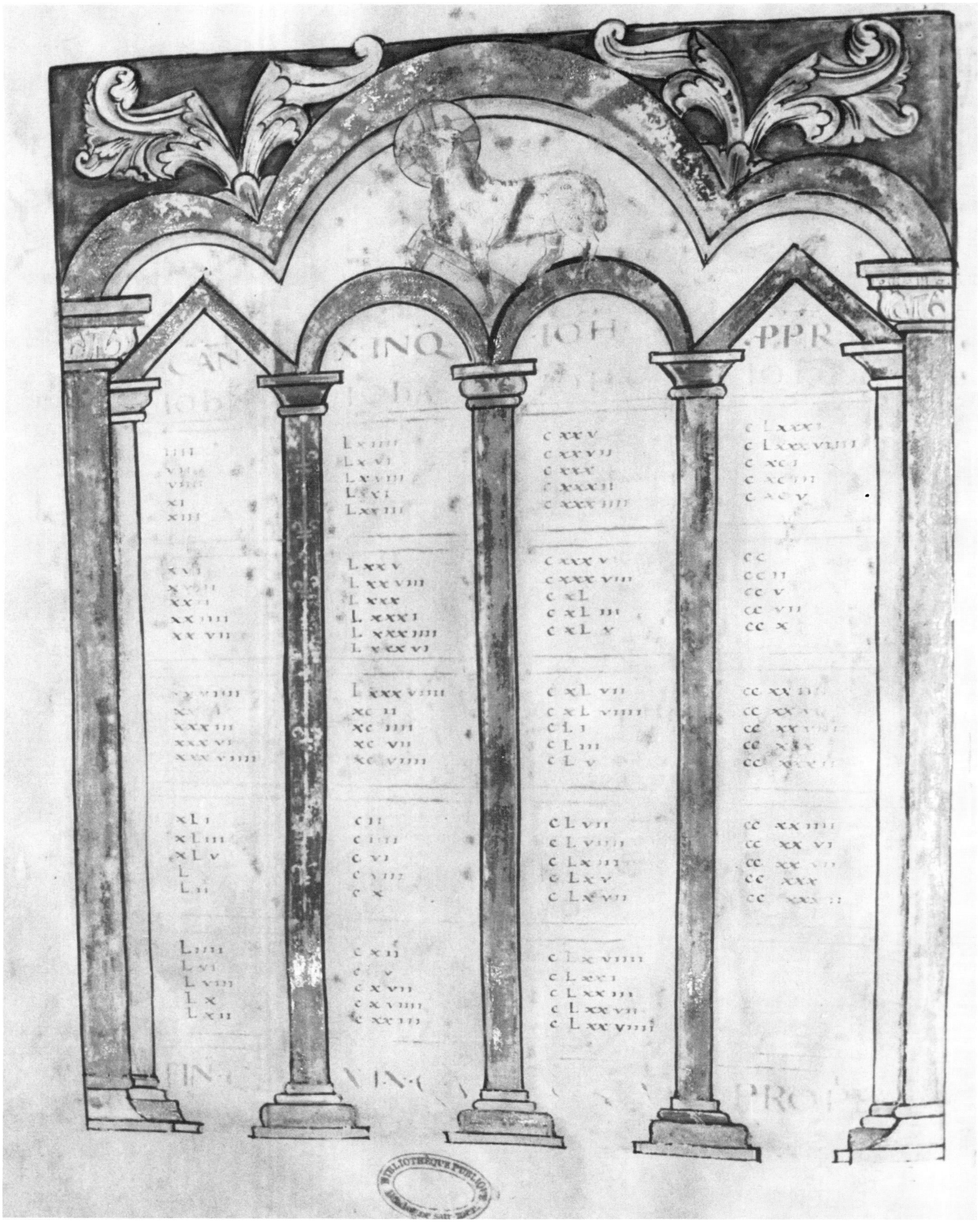

5.16 Boulogne, Bibl. Mun., 11 f. 9v

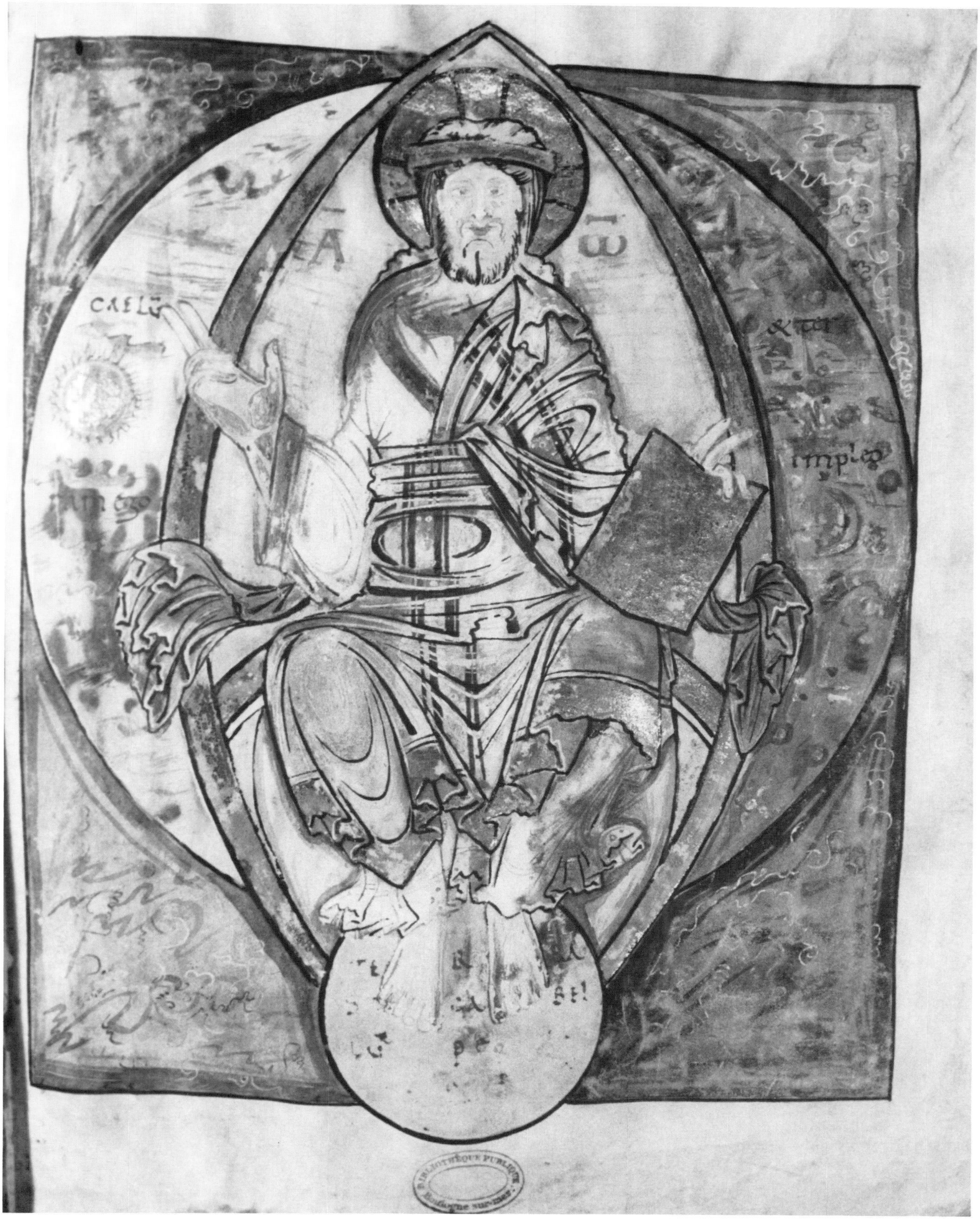

5.17 Boulogne, Bibl. Mun., 11 f. 10ʳ

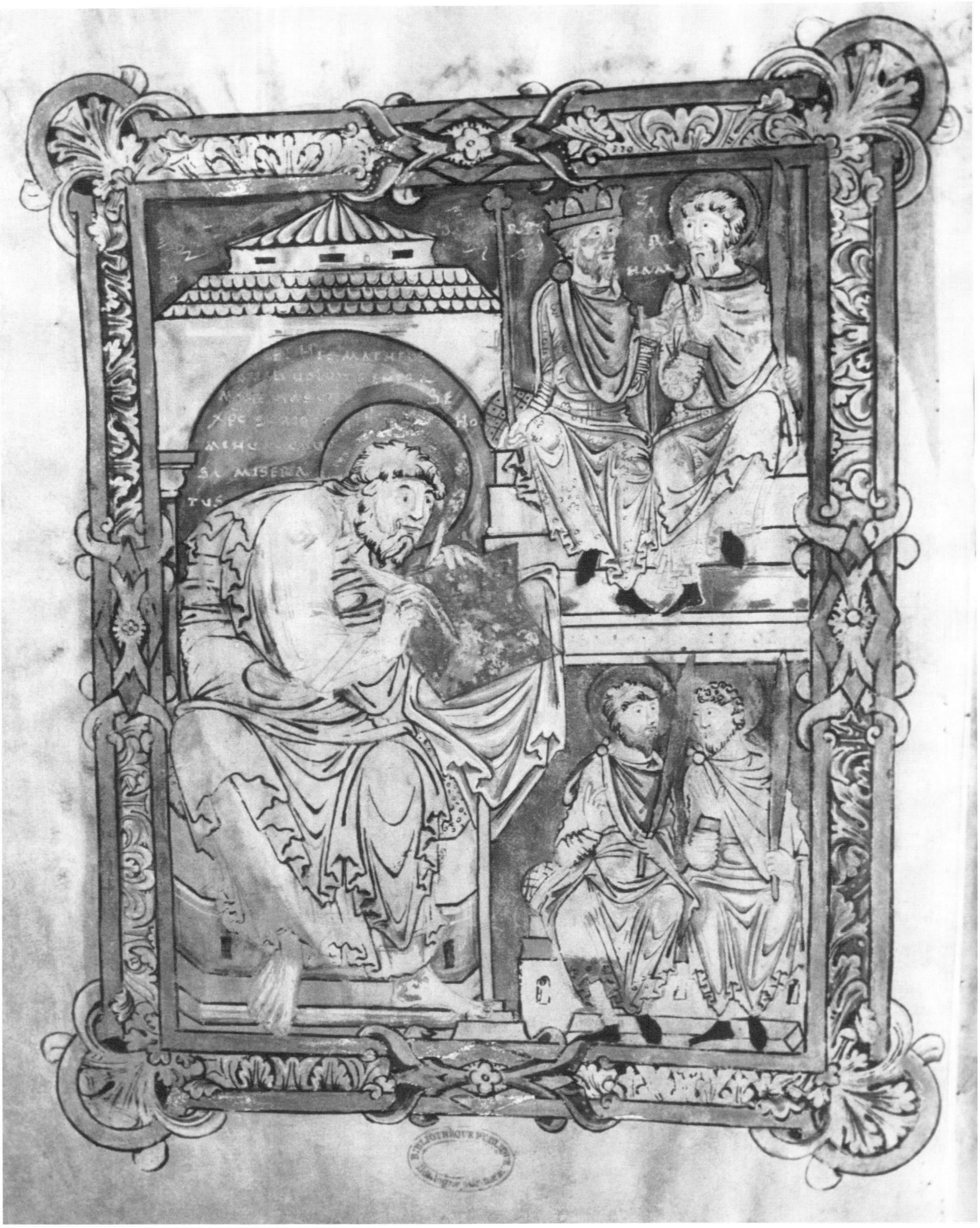

5.18 Boulogne, Bibl. Mun., 11 f. 10^{v}

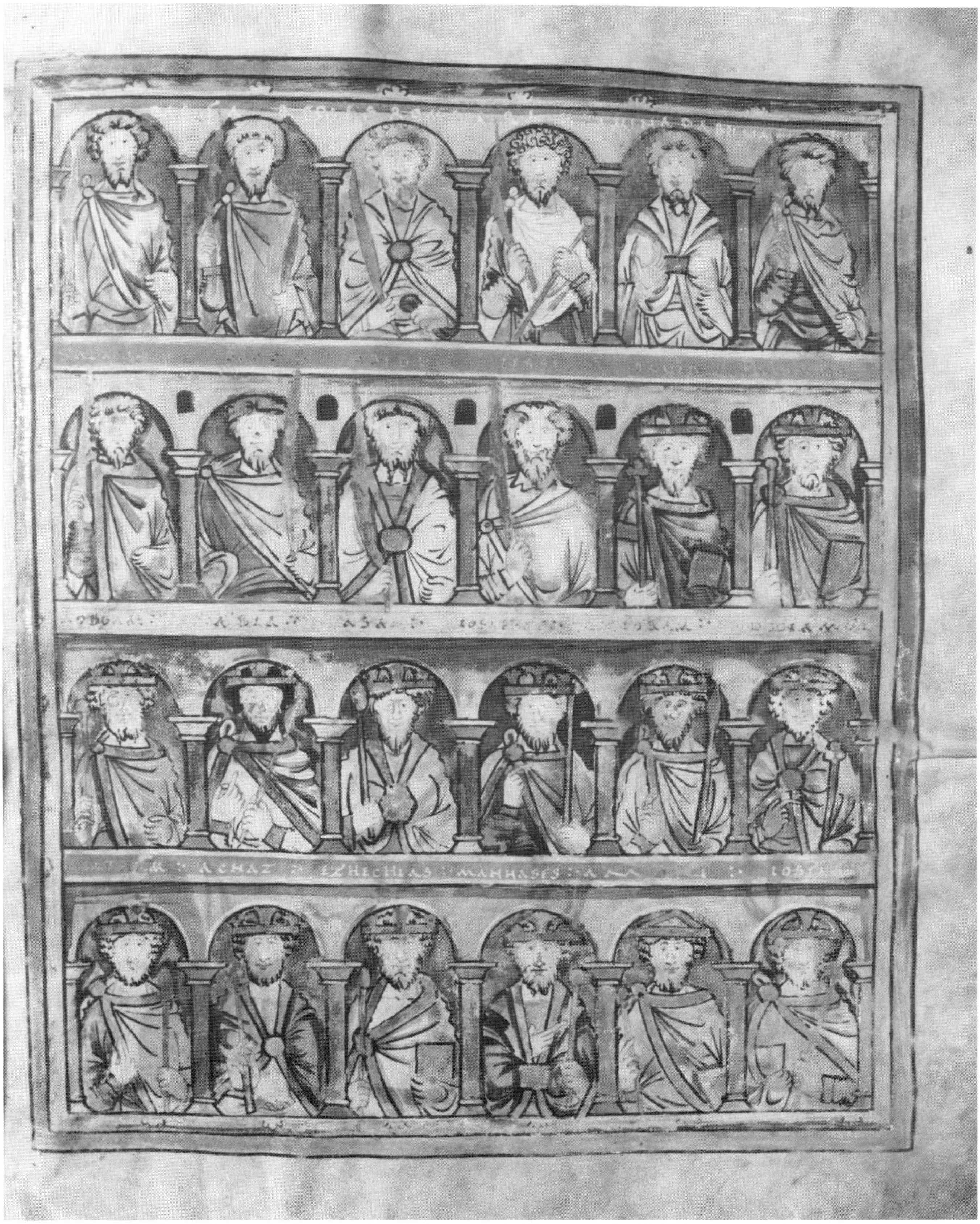

5.19 Boulogne, Bibl. Mun., 11 f. 11^{r}

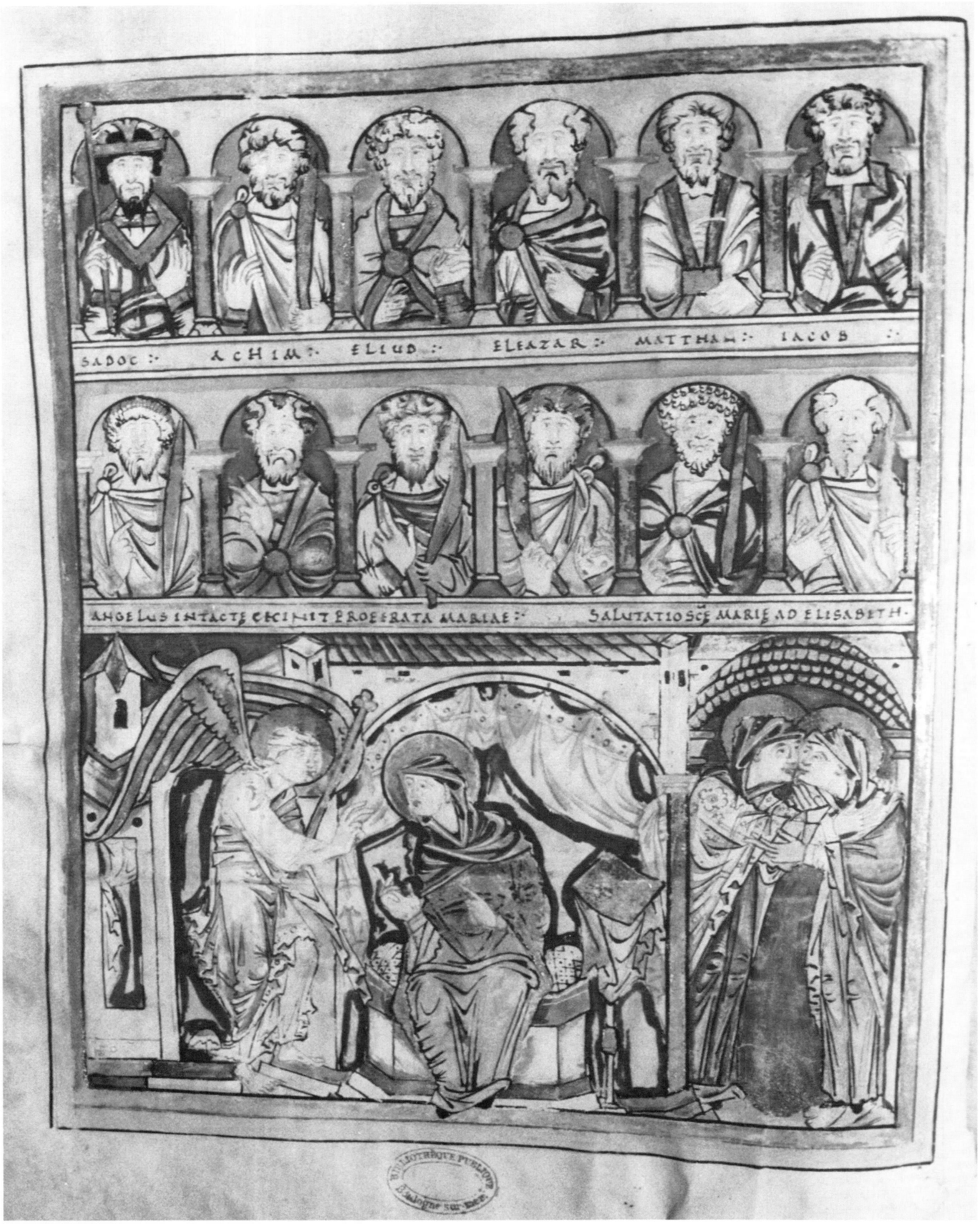

5.20 Boulogne, Bibl. Mun., 11 f. 11v

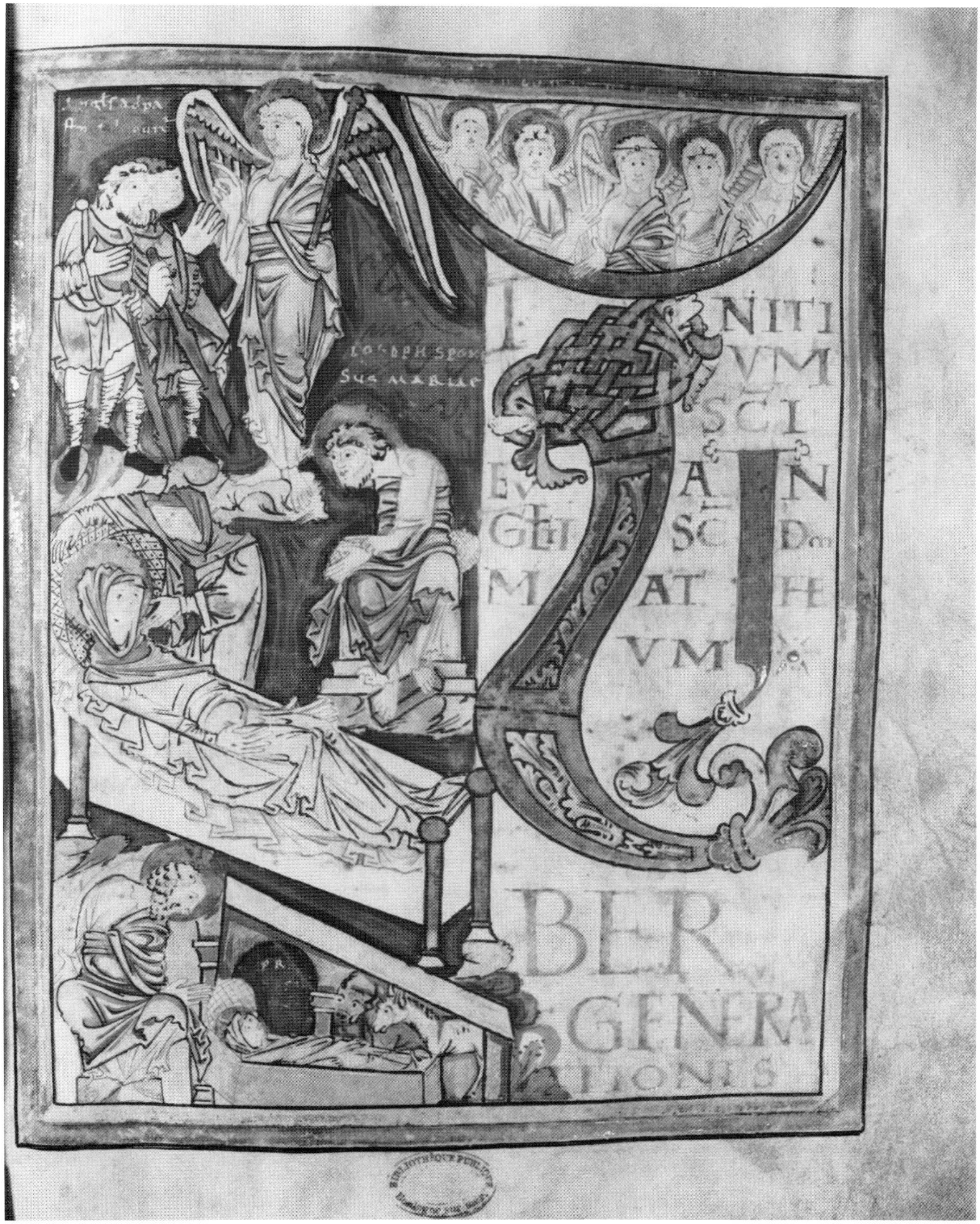

5.21 Boulogne, Bibl. Mun., 11 f. 12r

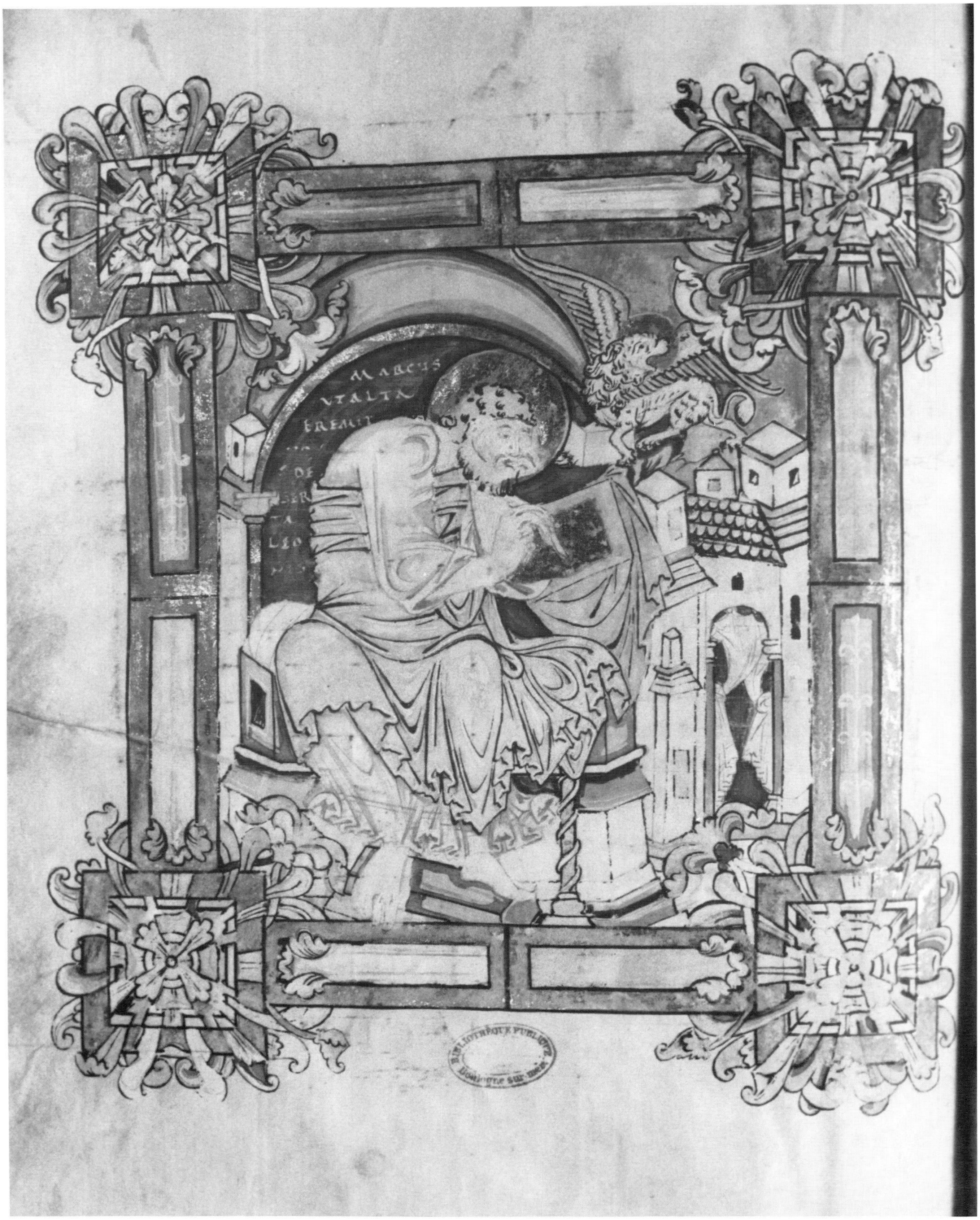

5.22 Boulogne, Bibl. Mun., 11 f. 55v

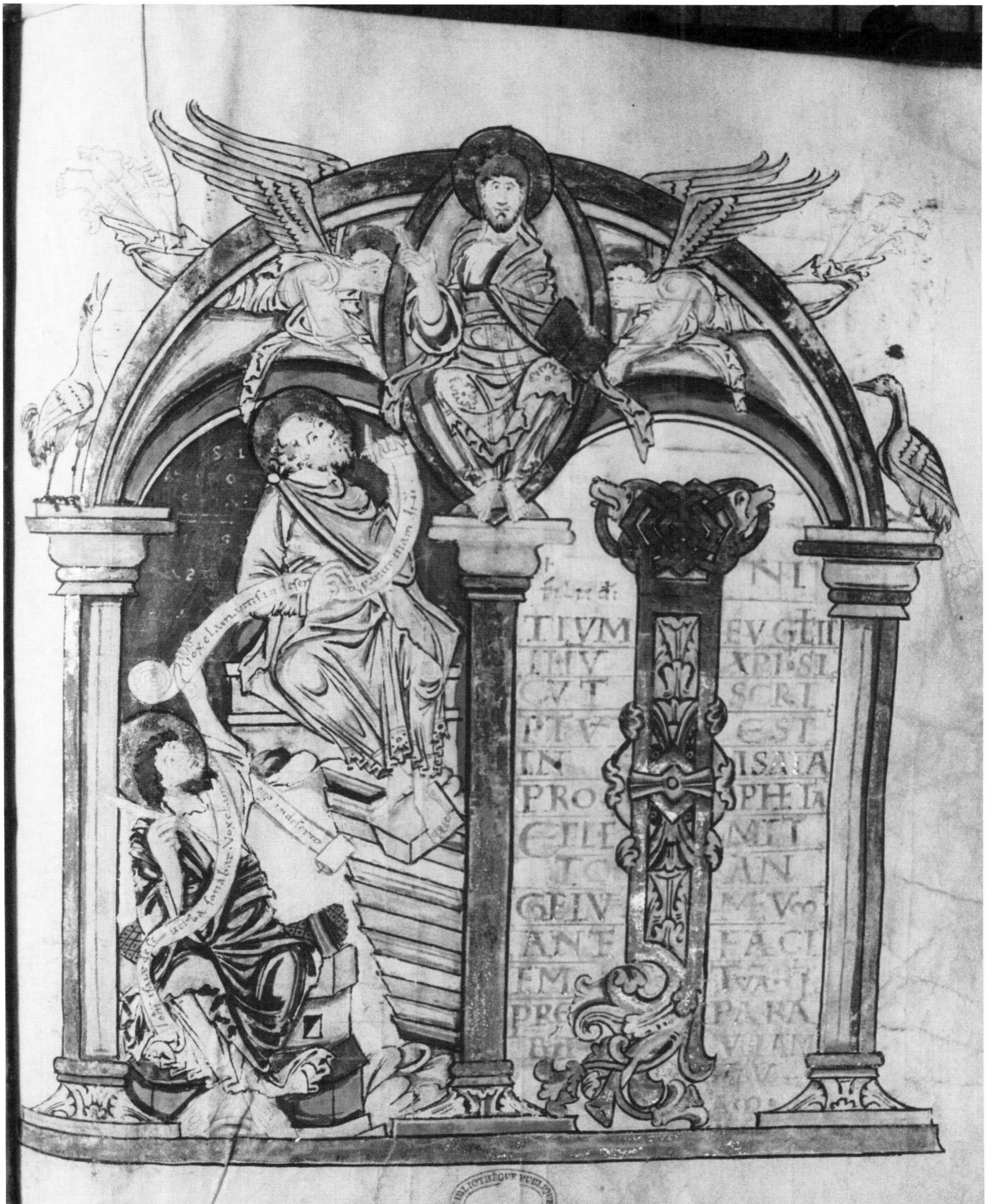

5.23 Boulogne, Bibl. Mun., 11 f. 56r

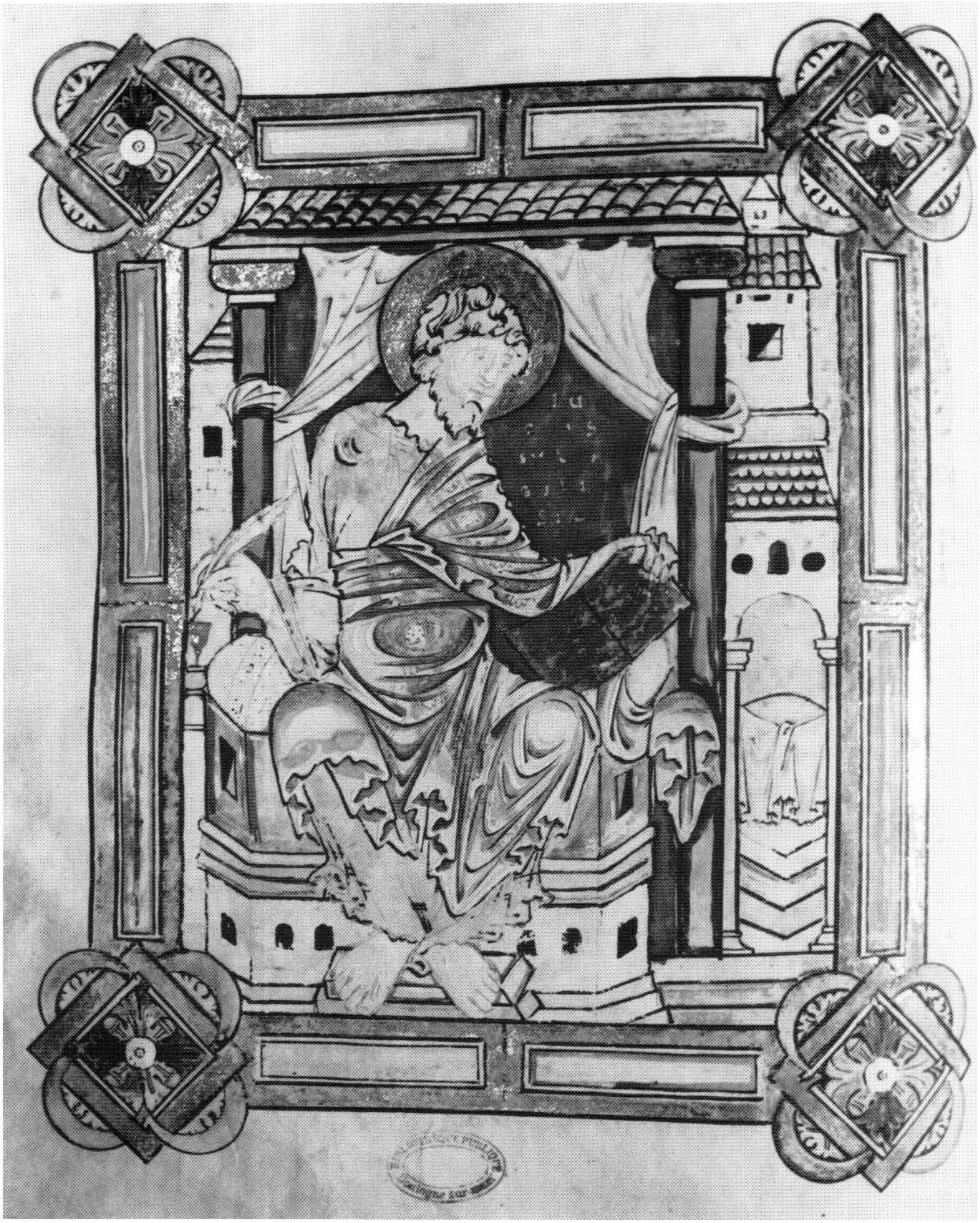

5.24 Boulogne, Bibl. Mun., 11 f. 61v

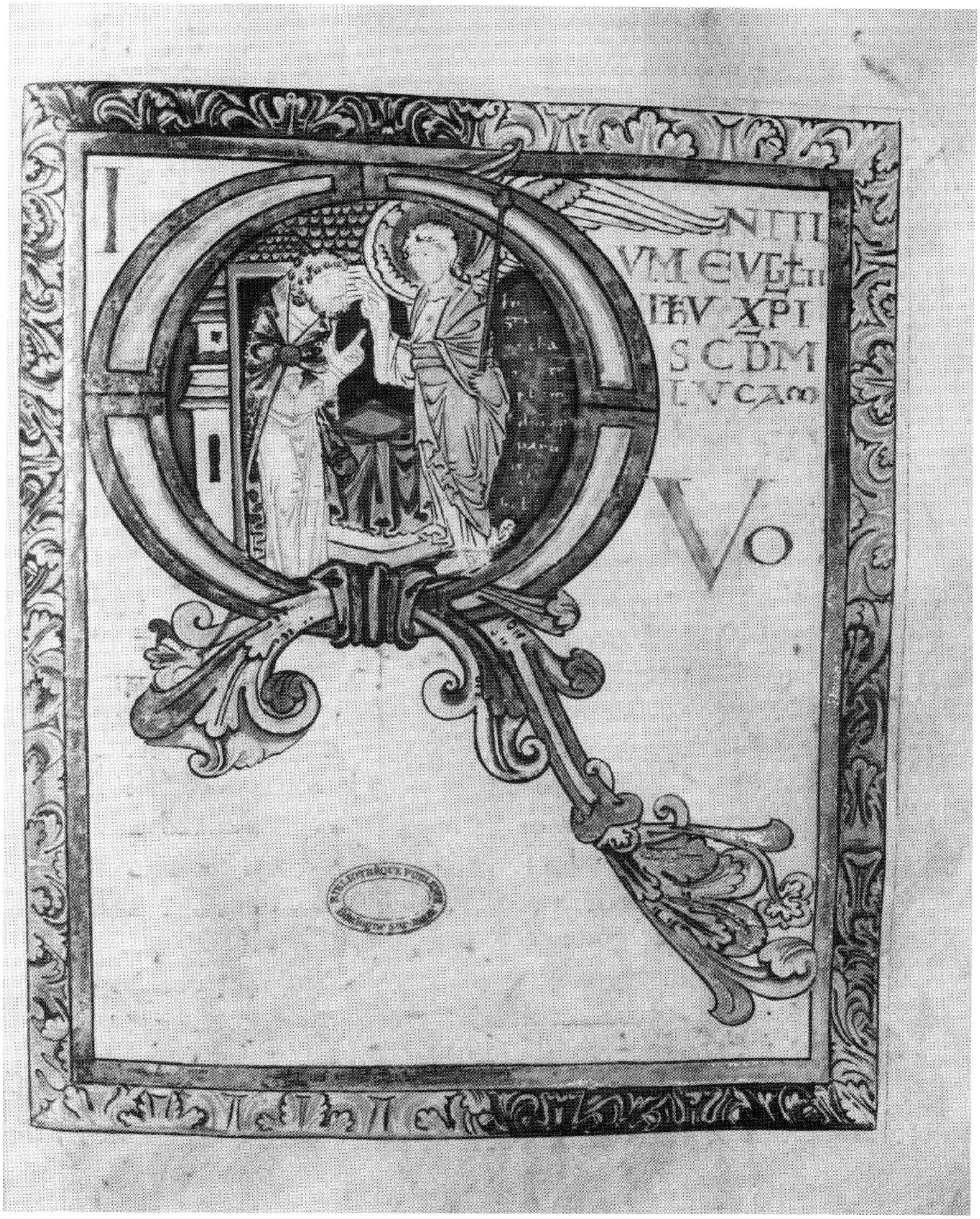

5.25 Boulogne, Bibl. Mun., 11 f. 62r

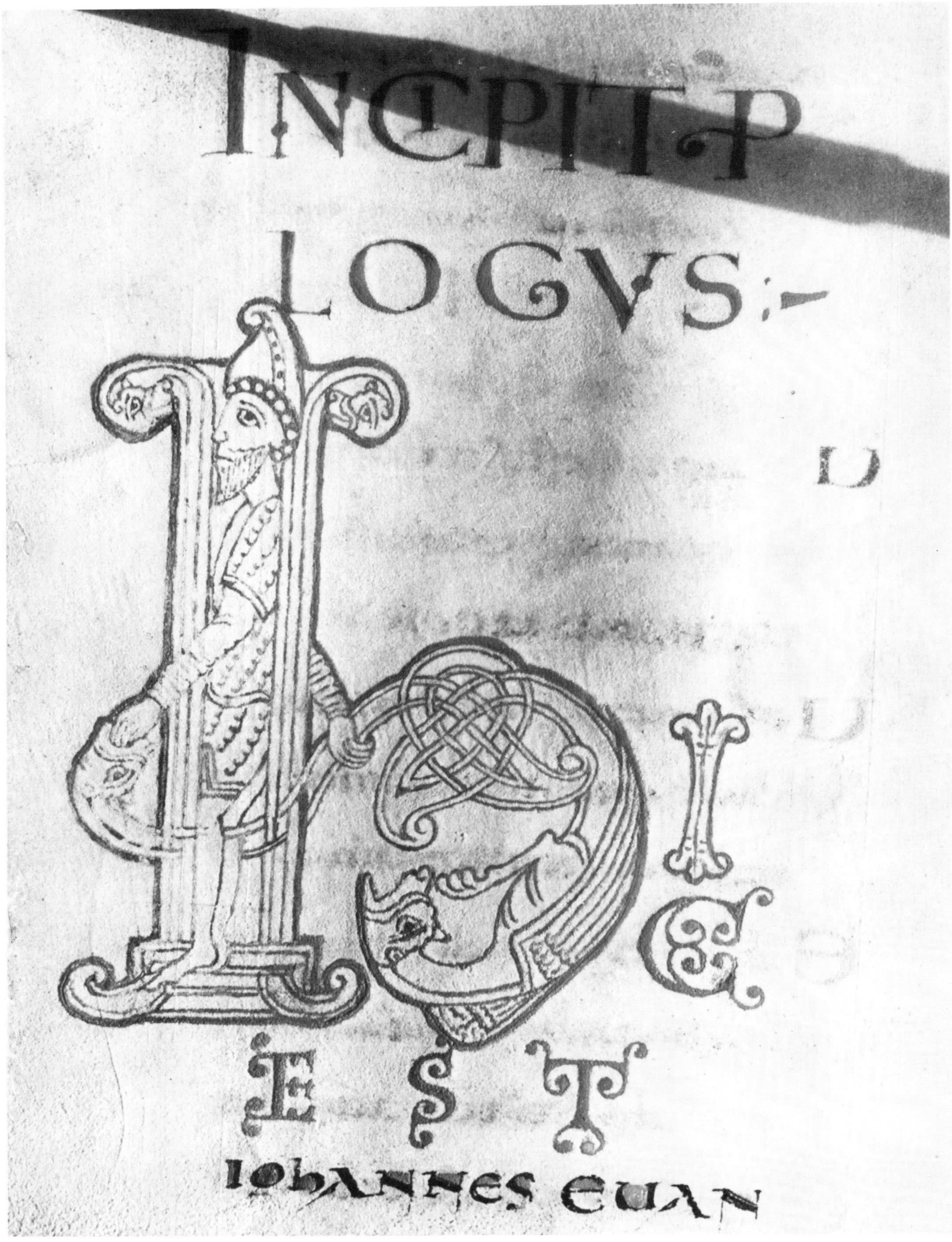

5.26 Boulogne, Bibl. Mun., 11 f. 104v

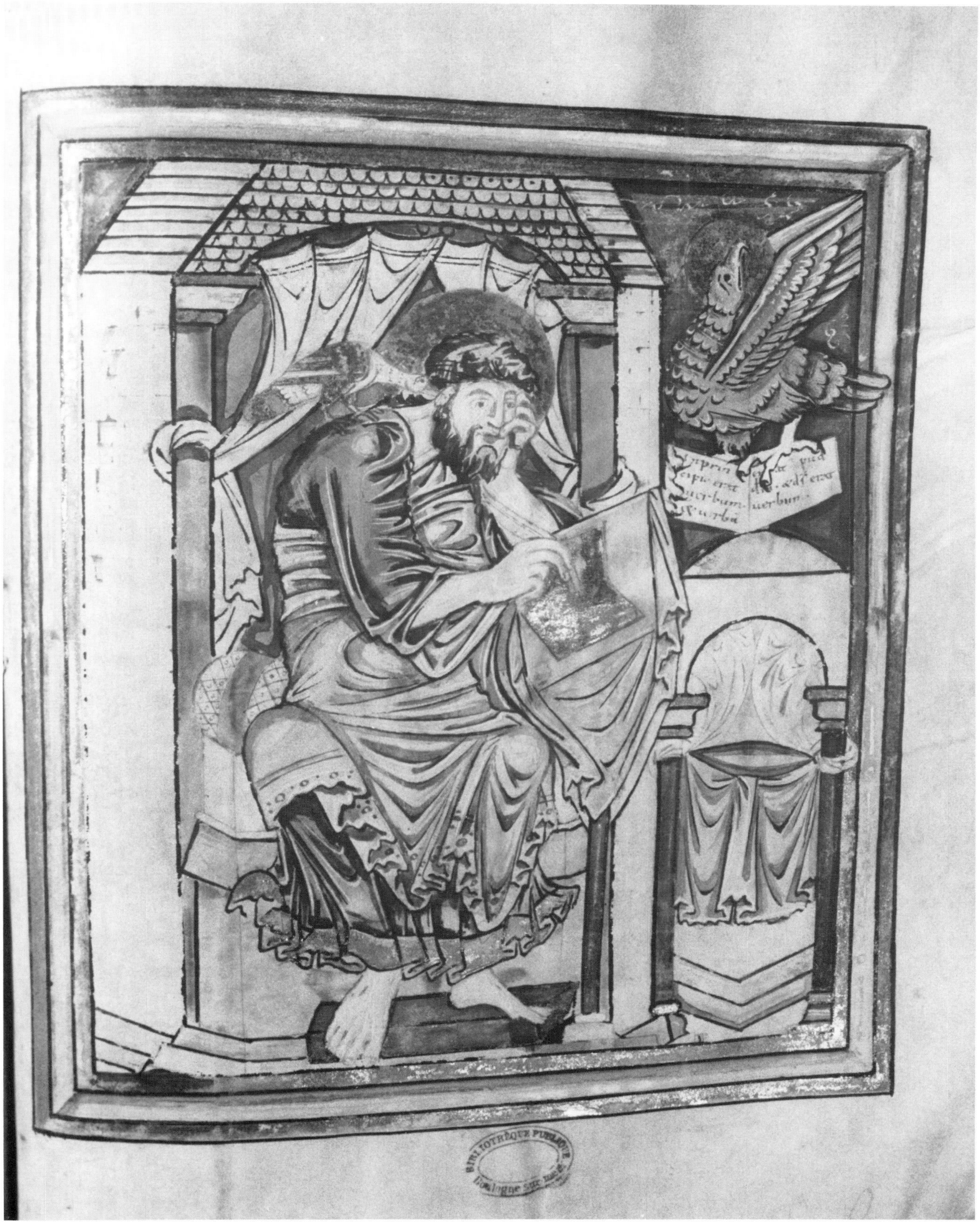

5.27 Boulogne, Bibl. Mun., 11 f. 107r

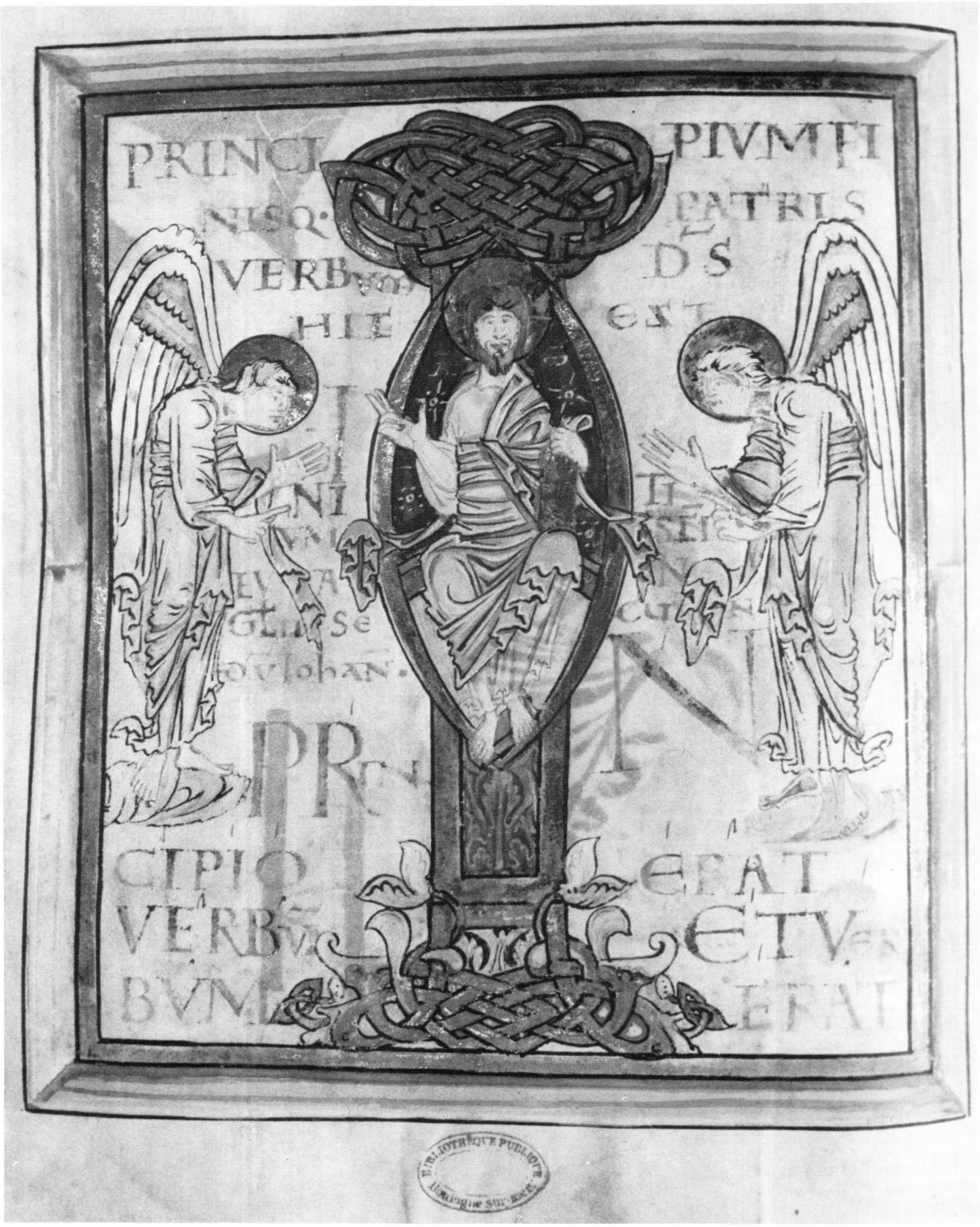

5.28 Boulogne, Bibl. Mun., 11 f. 107v

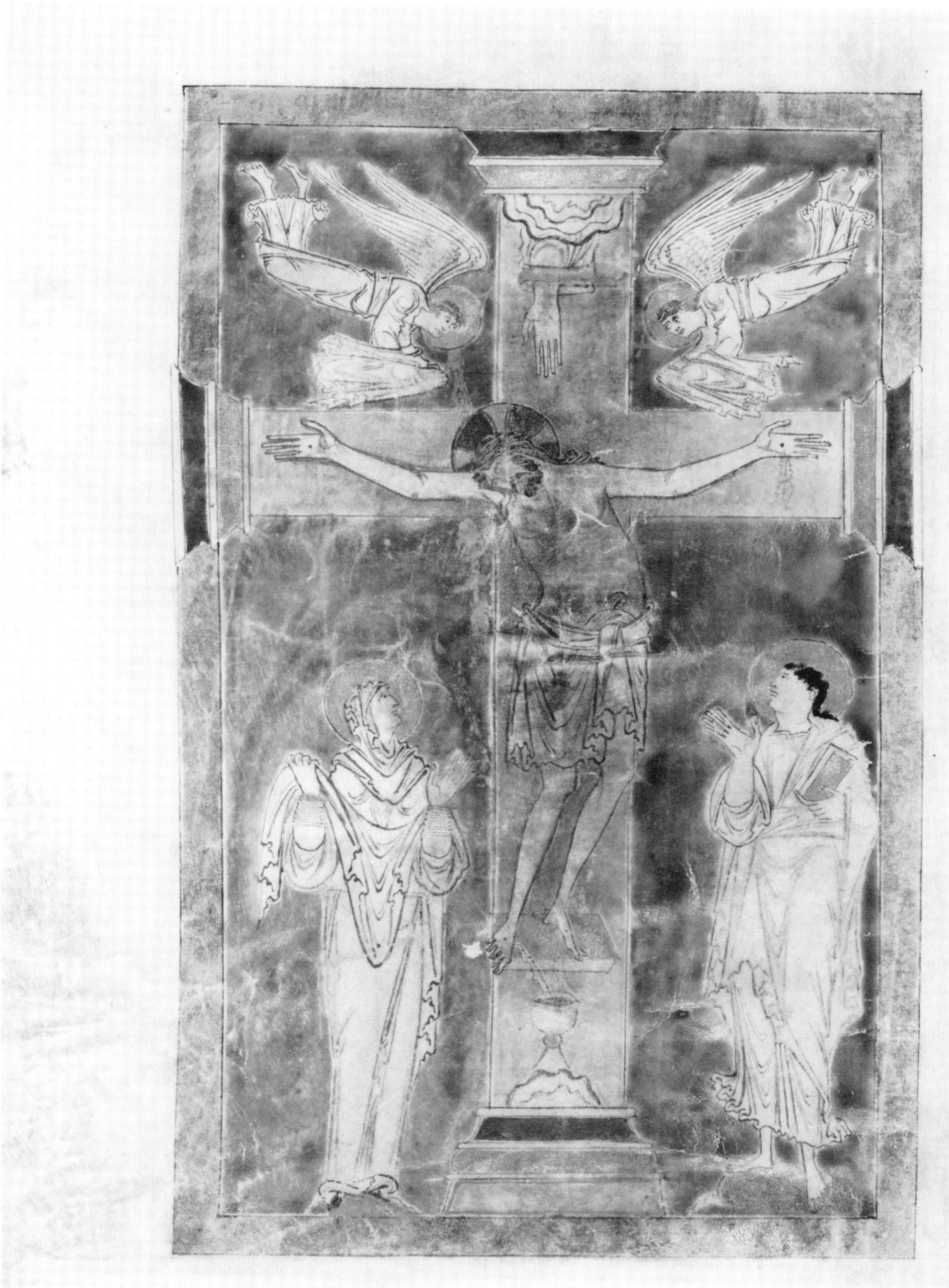

6.1 New York, Pierpont Morgan, M. 869, f 9v

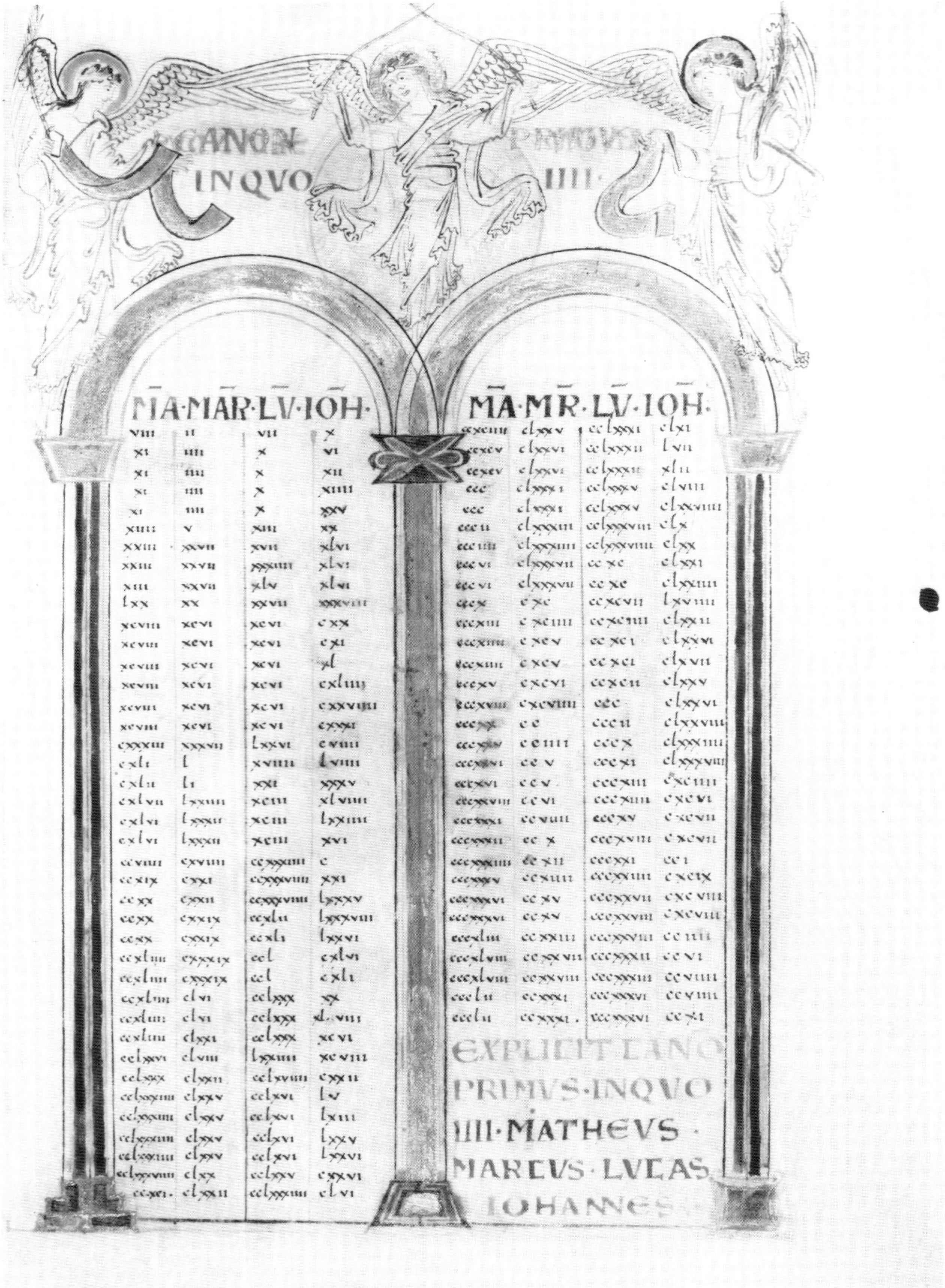

6.2 New York, Pierpont Morgan, M. 869, f 10r

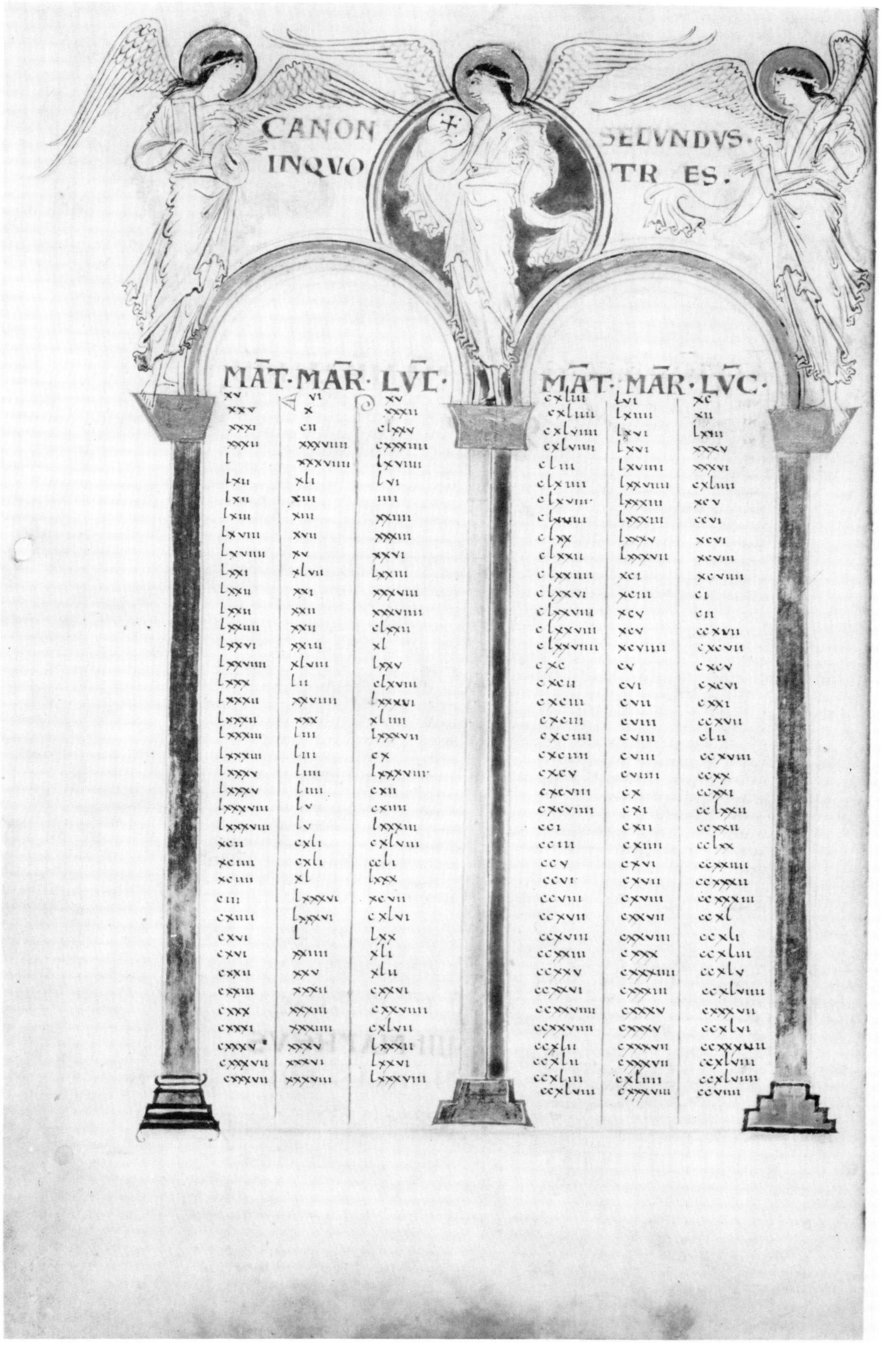

6.3 New York, Pierpont Morgan, M. 869, f 10[v]

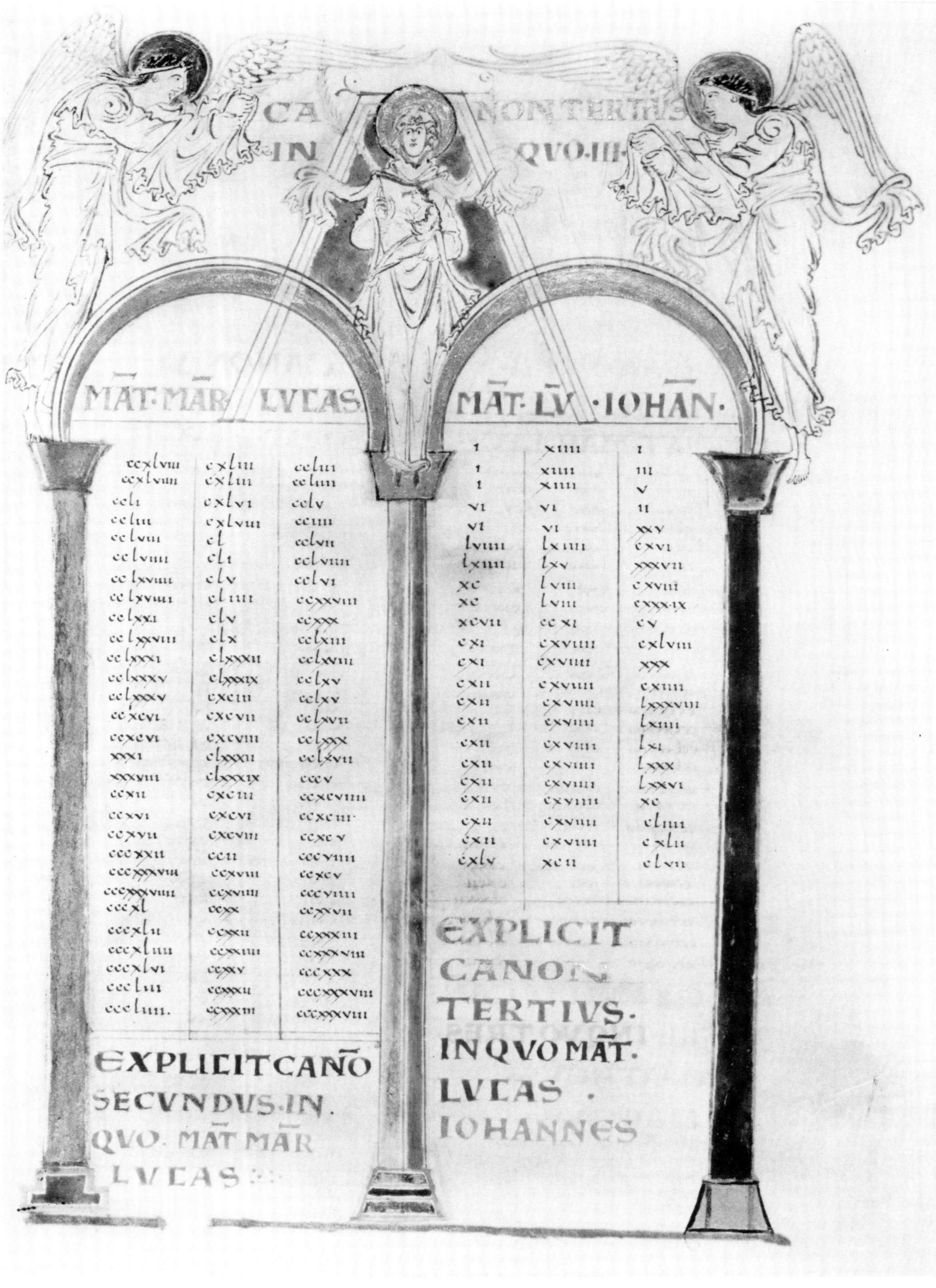

6.4 New York, Pierpont Morgan, M. 869, f 11r

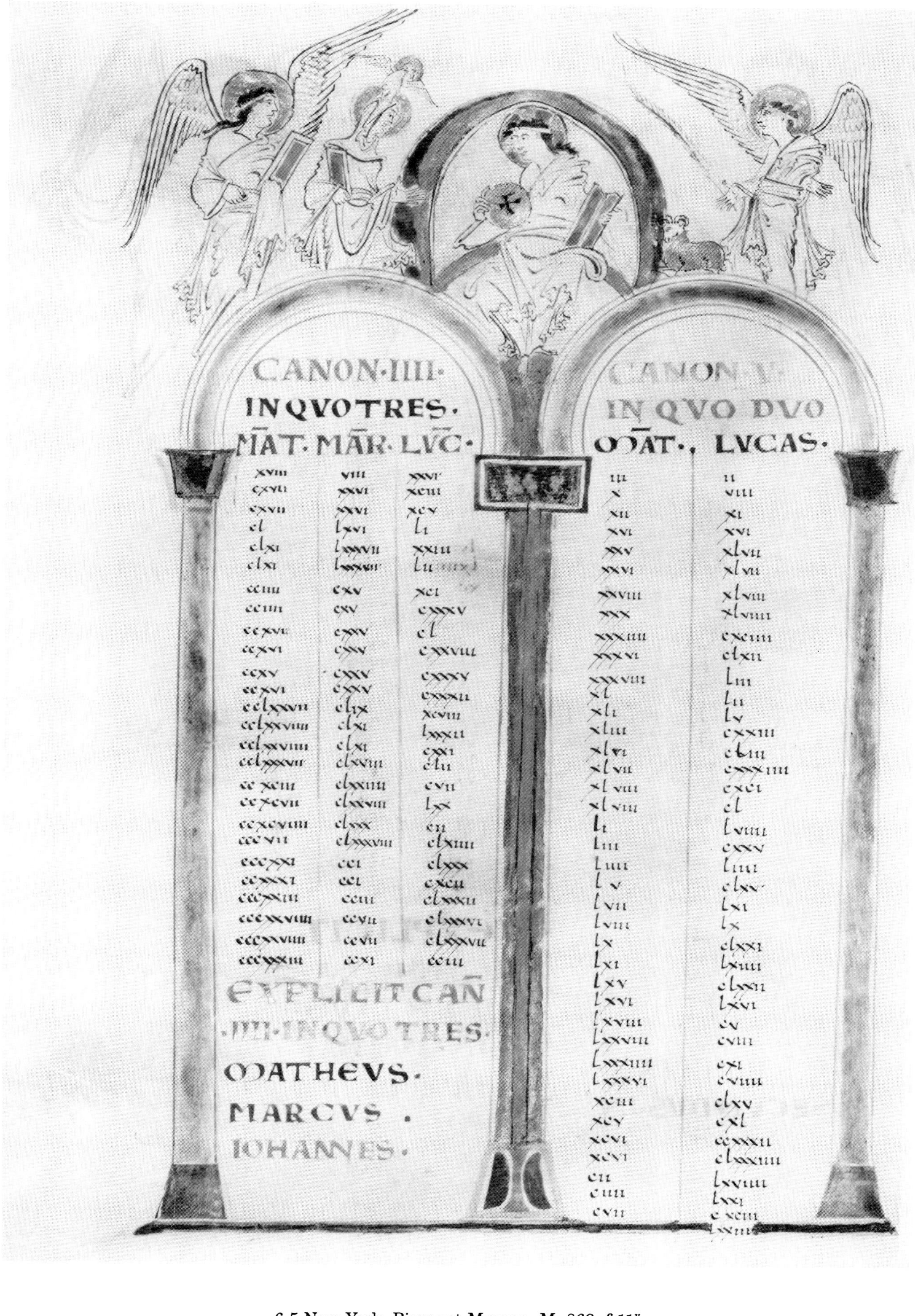

6.5 New York, Pierpont Morgan, M. 869, f 11v

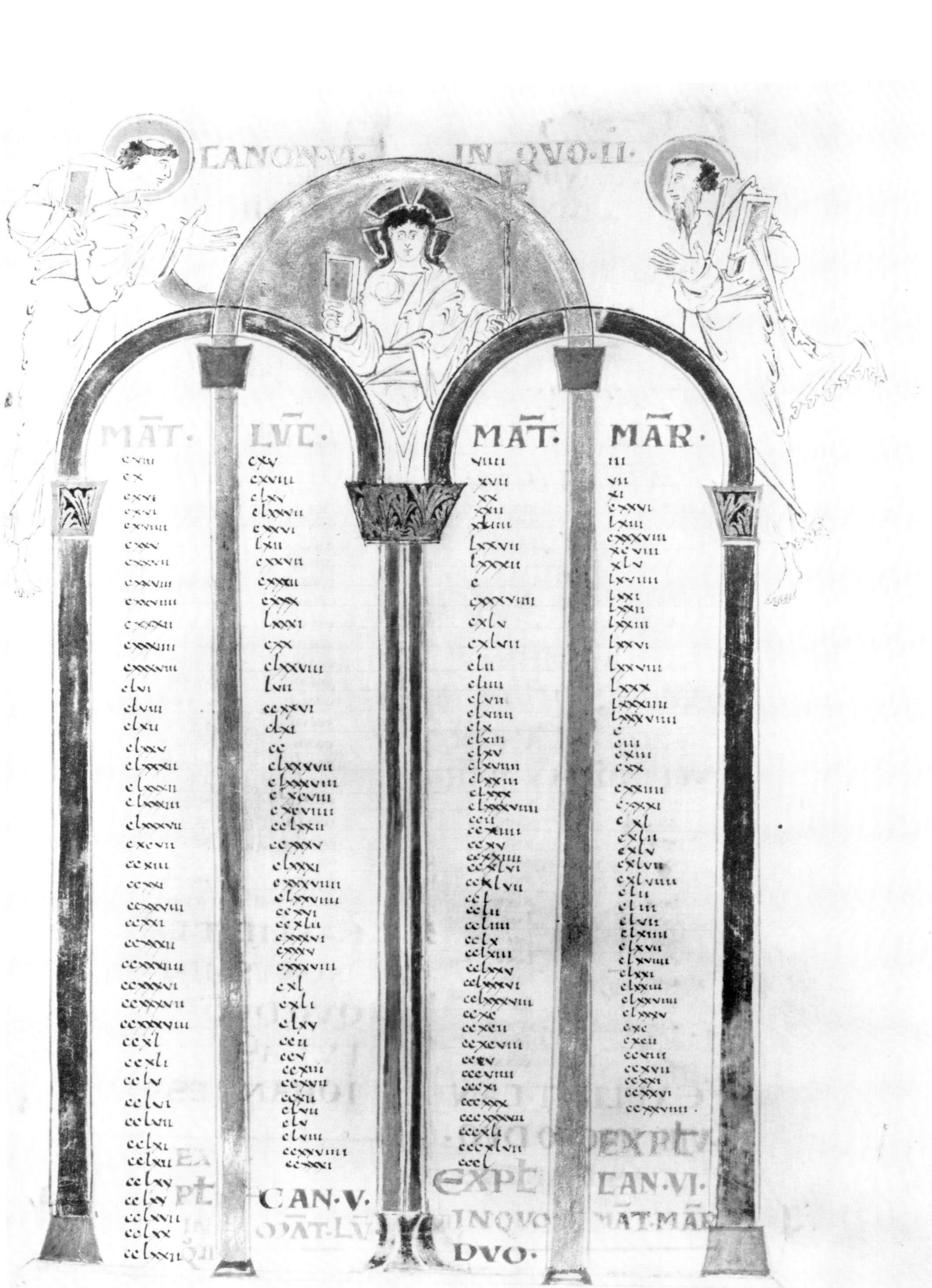

6.6 New York, Pierpont Morgan, M. 869, f 12r

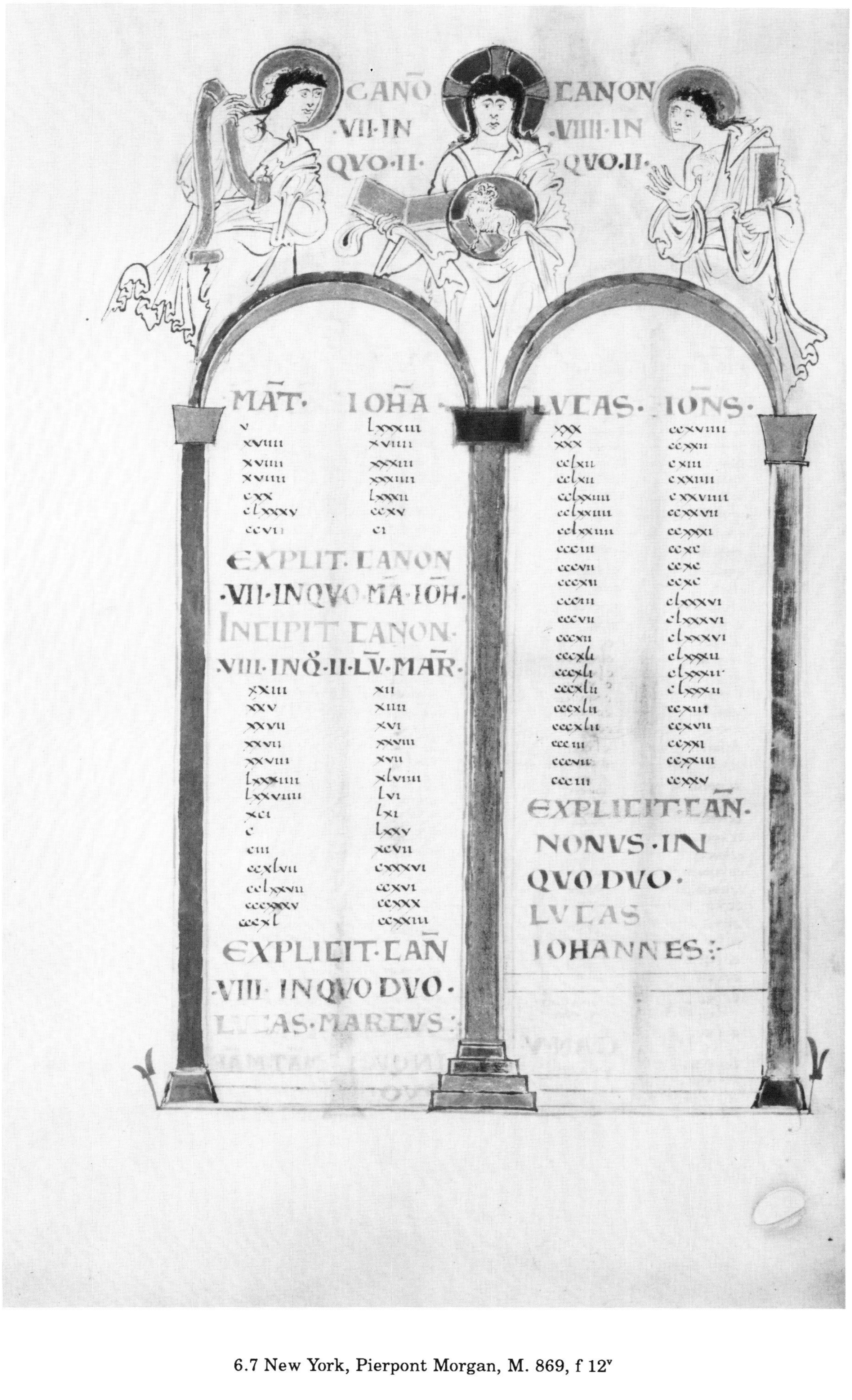

6.7 New York, Pierpont Morgan, M. 869, f 12v

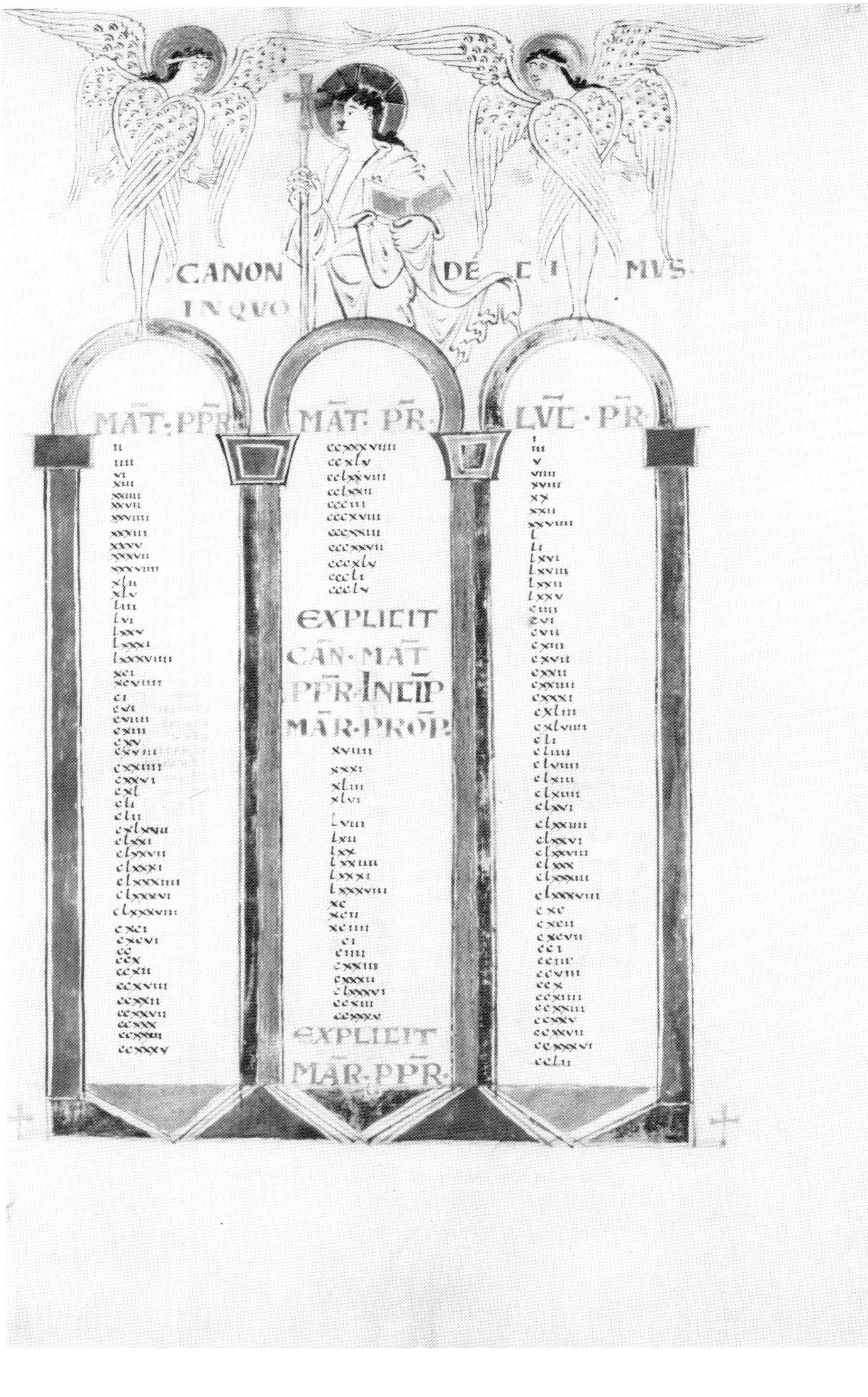

6.8 New York, Pierpont Morgan, M. 869, f 13r

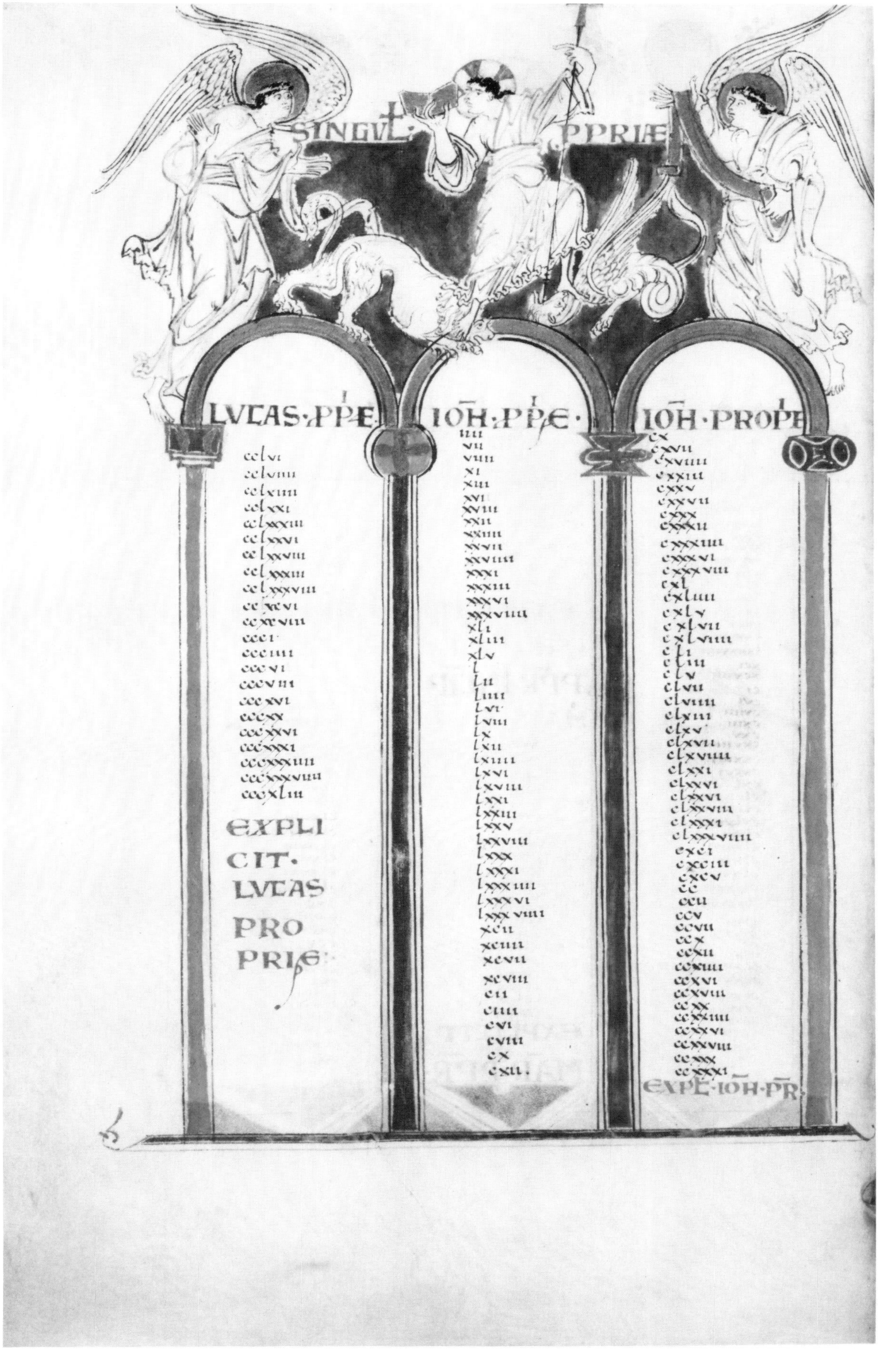

6.9 New York, Pierpont Morgan, M. 869, f 13v

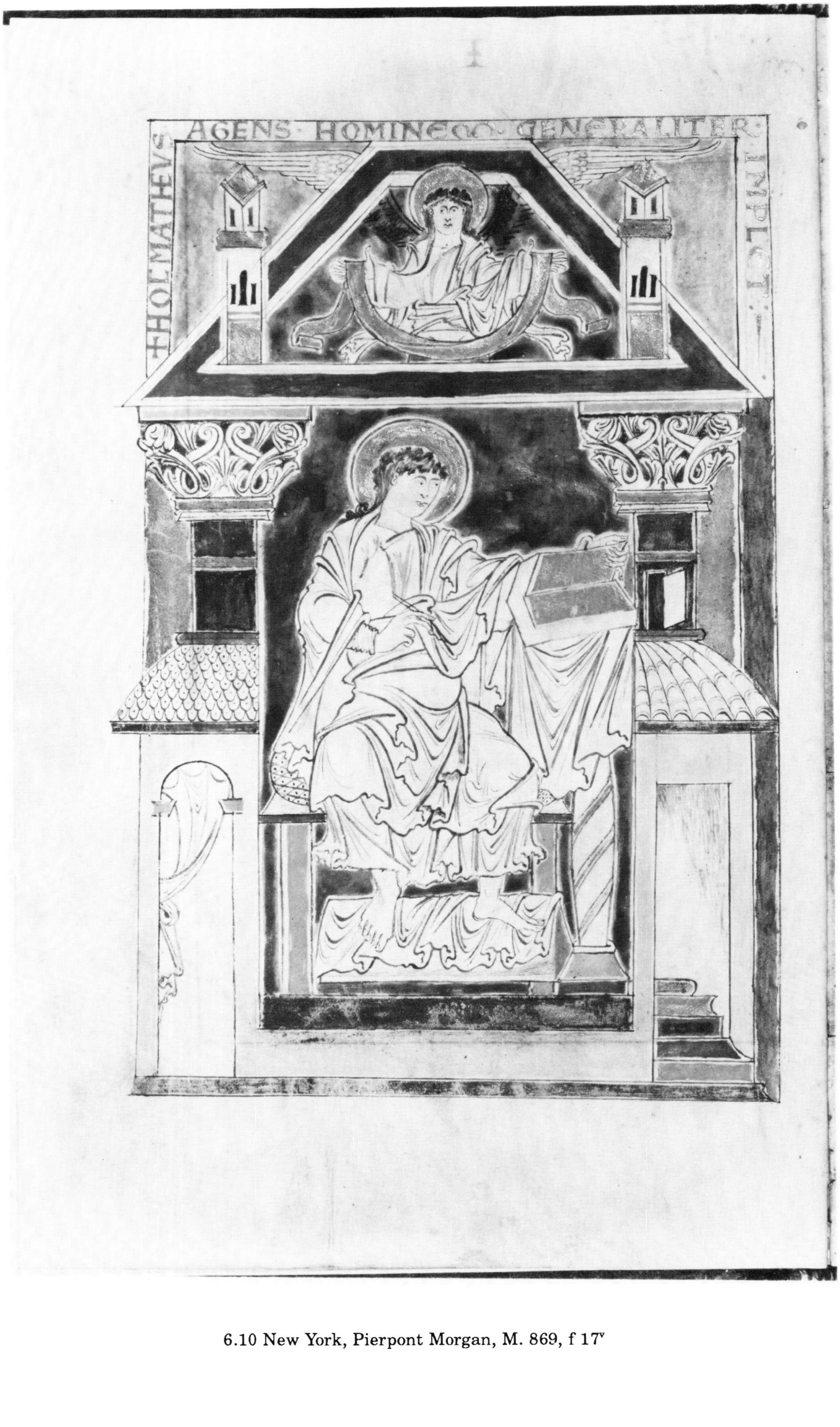

6.10 New York, Pierpont Morgan, M. 869, f 17v

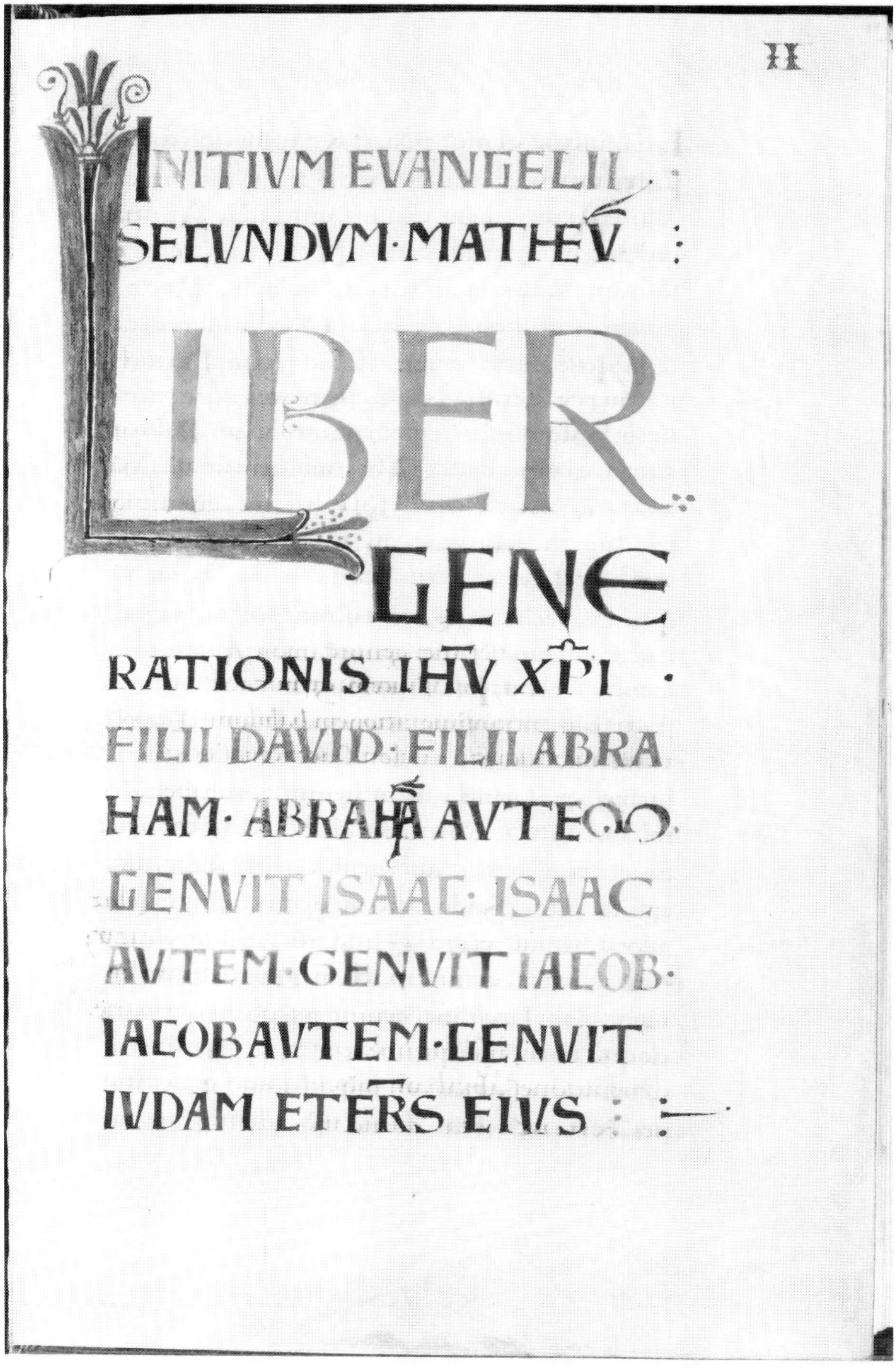

II

INITIUM EVANGELII :
SECUNDUM · MATHEU :
LIBER
· GENE
RATIONIS IHU XPI ·
FILII DAVID · FILII ABRA
HAM · ABRAHA AUTEM
GENUIT ISAAC · ISAAC
AUTEM · GENUIT IACOB ·
IACOB AUTEM · GENUIT
IUDAM ET FRS EIUS :

6.11 New York, Pierpont Morgan, M. 869, f 18r

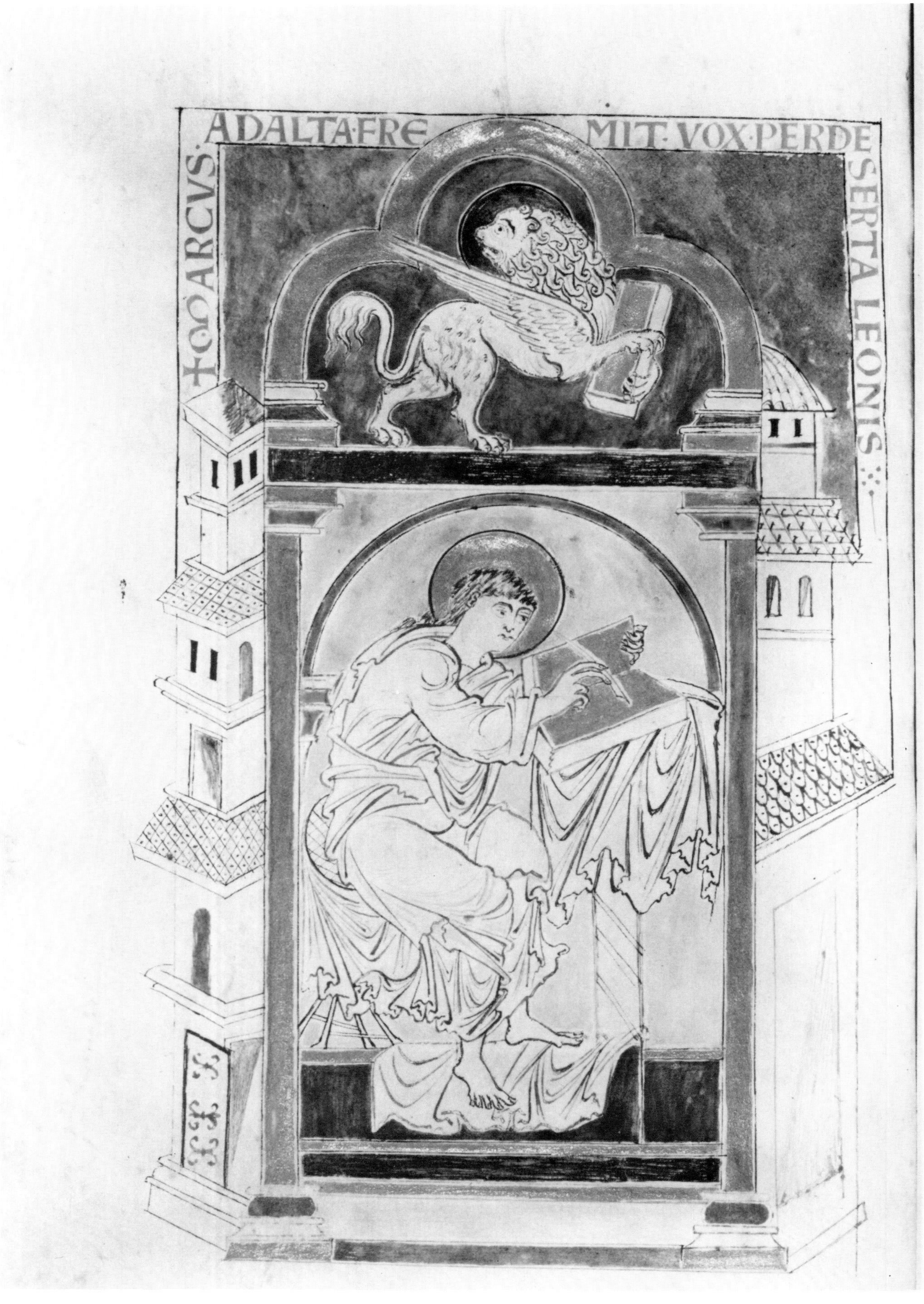

6.12 New York, Pierpont Morgan, M. 869, f 57v

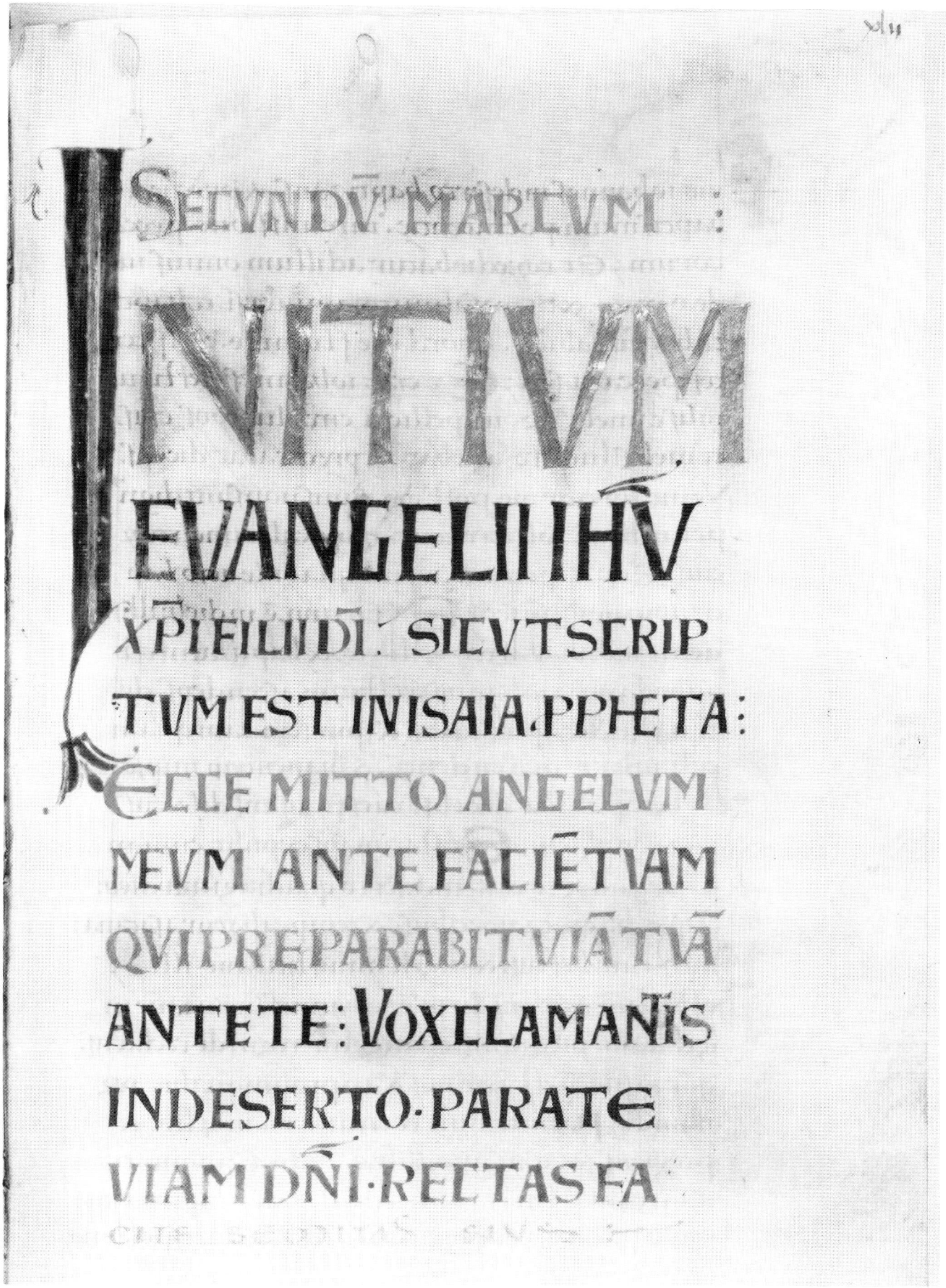

SECVNDV MARCVM :

INITIVM

EVANGELII IHV

XPI FILII DI : SICVT SCRIP

TVM EST IN ISAIA PPHETA :

ECCE MITTO ANGELVM

MEVM ANTE FACIĒ TVAM

QVI PREPARABIT VIĀ TVĀ

ANTE TE : VOX CLAMANTIS

IN DESERTO · PARATE

VIAM DNI · RECTAS FA

6.13 New York, Pierpont Morgan, M. 869, f 58r

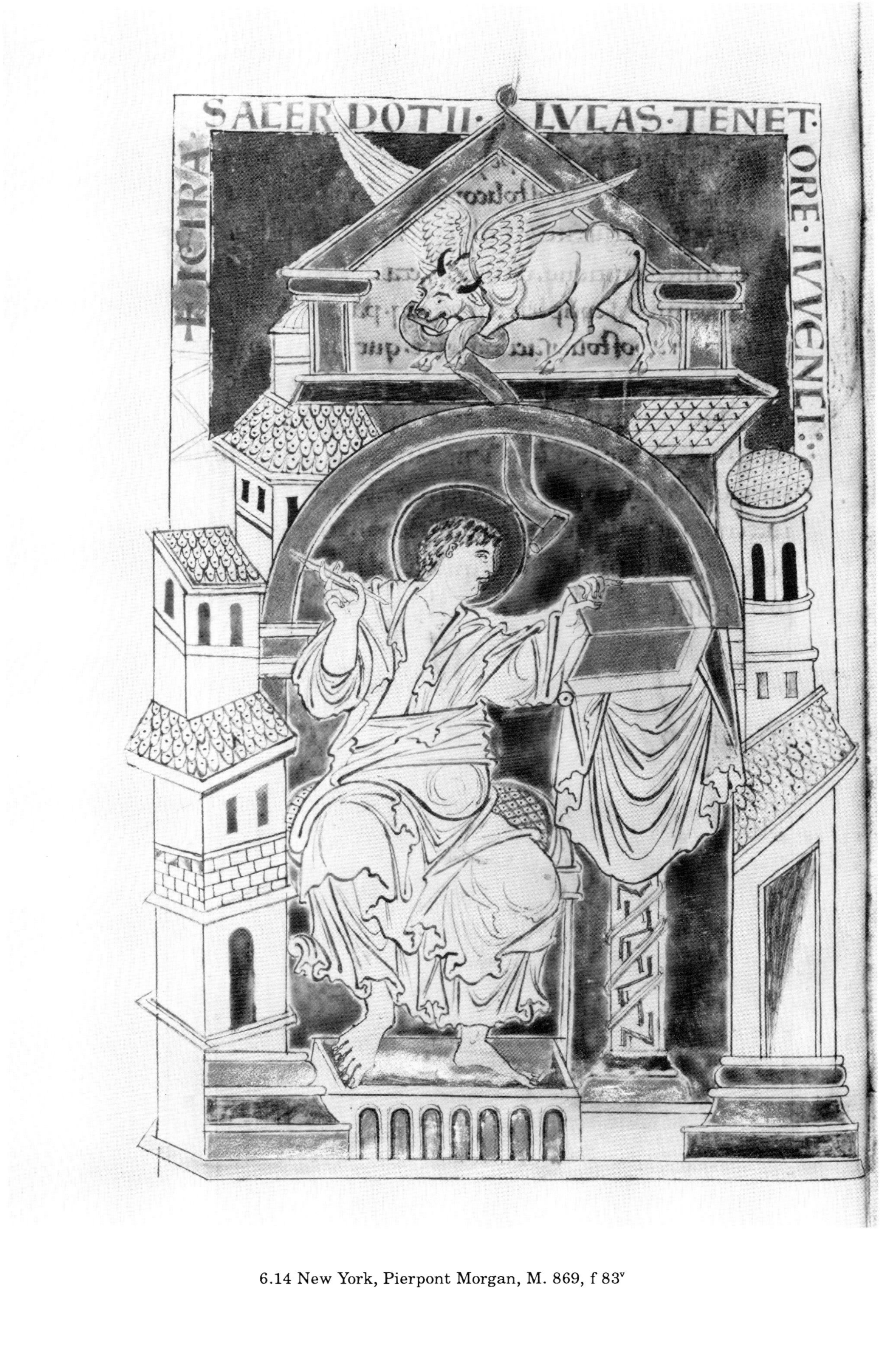

6.14 New York, Pierpont Morgan, M. 869, f 83ᵛ

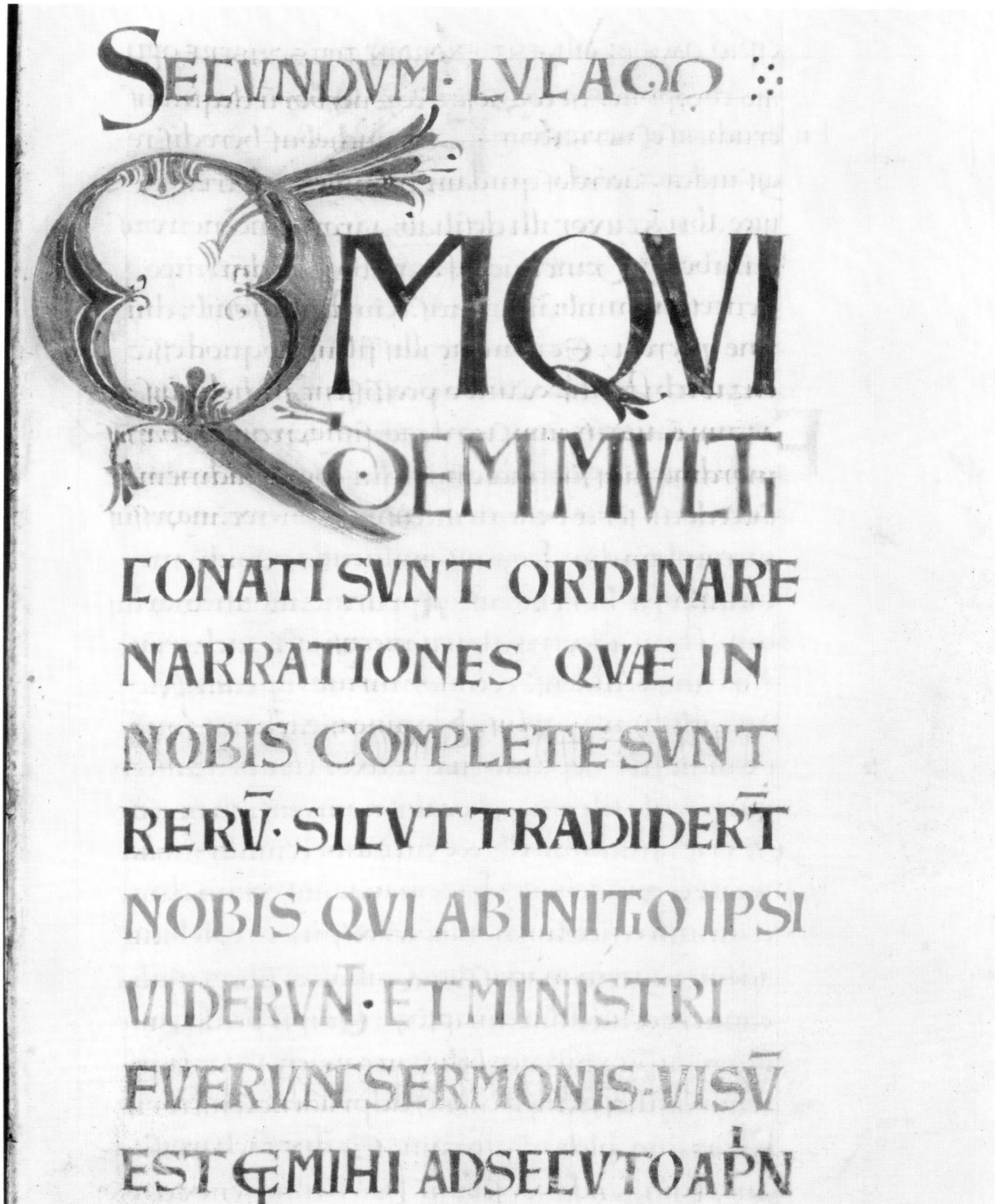

SECUNDUM· LUCAM ::
QM QUI
QDEM MULTI
CONATI SUNT ORDINARE
NARRATIONES QUÆ IN
NOBIS COMPLETE SUNT
RERŪ· SICUT TRADIDERT̄
NOBIS QUI AB INITIO IPSI
VIDERUN· ET MINISTRI
FUERUN SERMONIS· VISŪ
EST ET MIHI ADSECUTO APN

6.15 New York, Pierpont Morgan, M. 869, f 84r

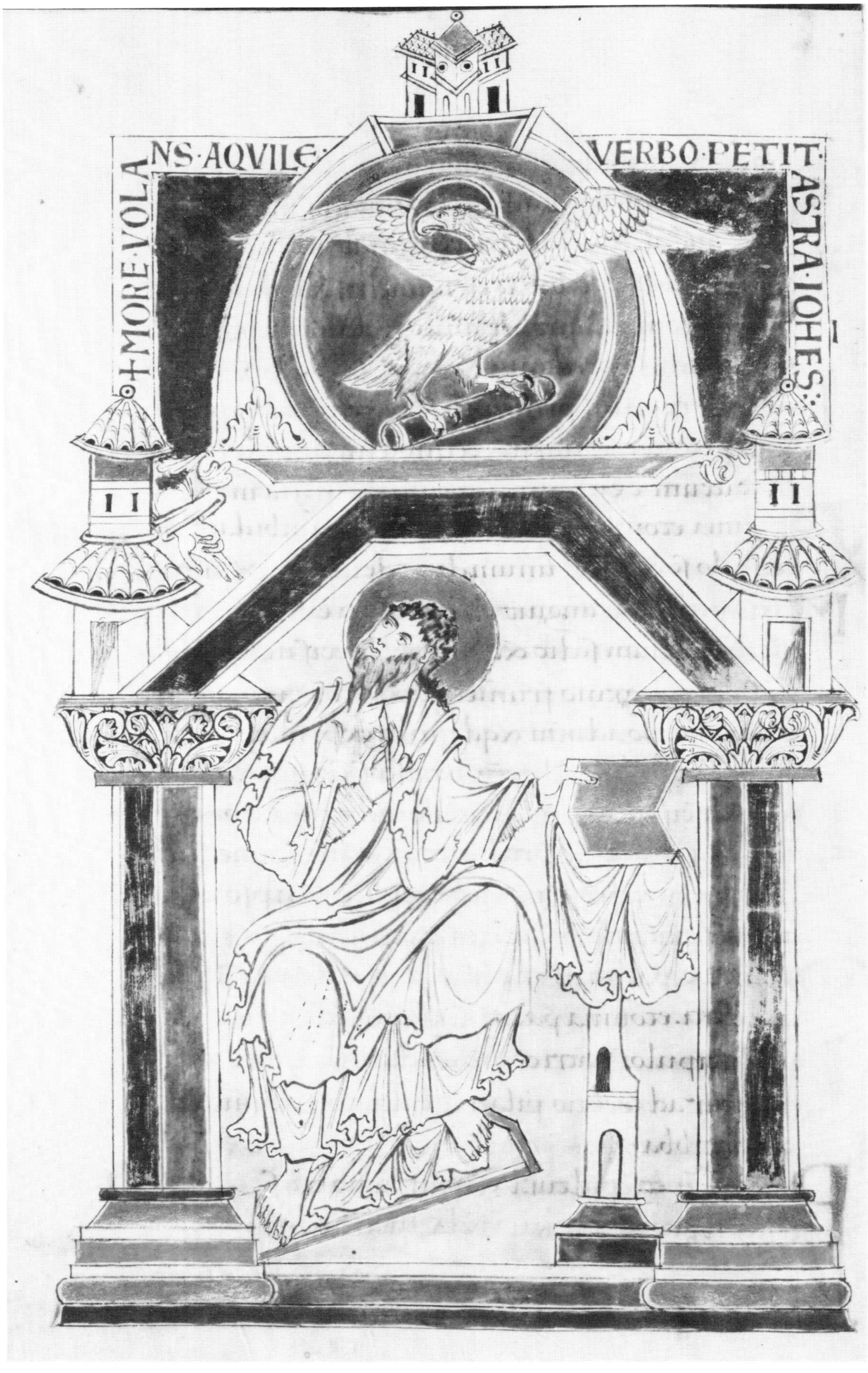

6.16 New York, Pierpont Morgan, M. 869, f 126v

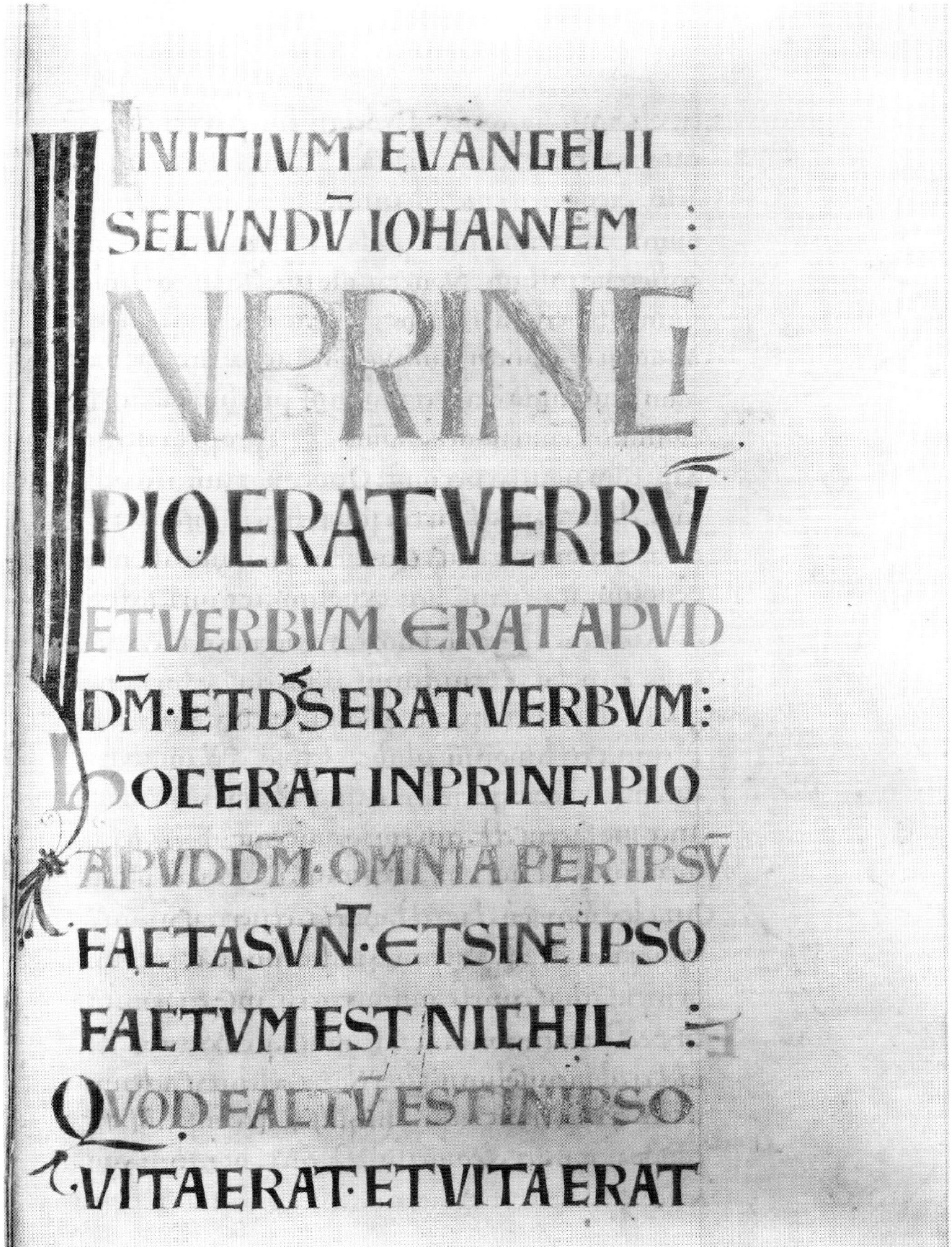
INITIVM EVANGELII
SECVNDV IOHANNEM :
INPRINCI
PIO ERAT VERBV
ET VERBVM ERAT APVD
DM· ET DS ERAT VERBVM :
HOC ERAT INPRINCIPIO
APVD DM· OMNIA PER IPSV
FACTA SVNT· ET SINE IPSO
FACTVM EST NICHIL :
QVOD FACTV EST IN IPSO
VITA ERAT· ET VITA ERAT

6.17 New York, Pierpont Morgan, M. 869, f 127r

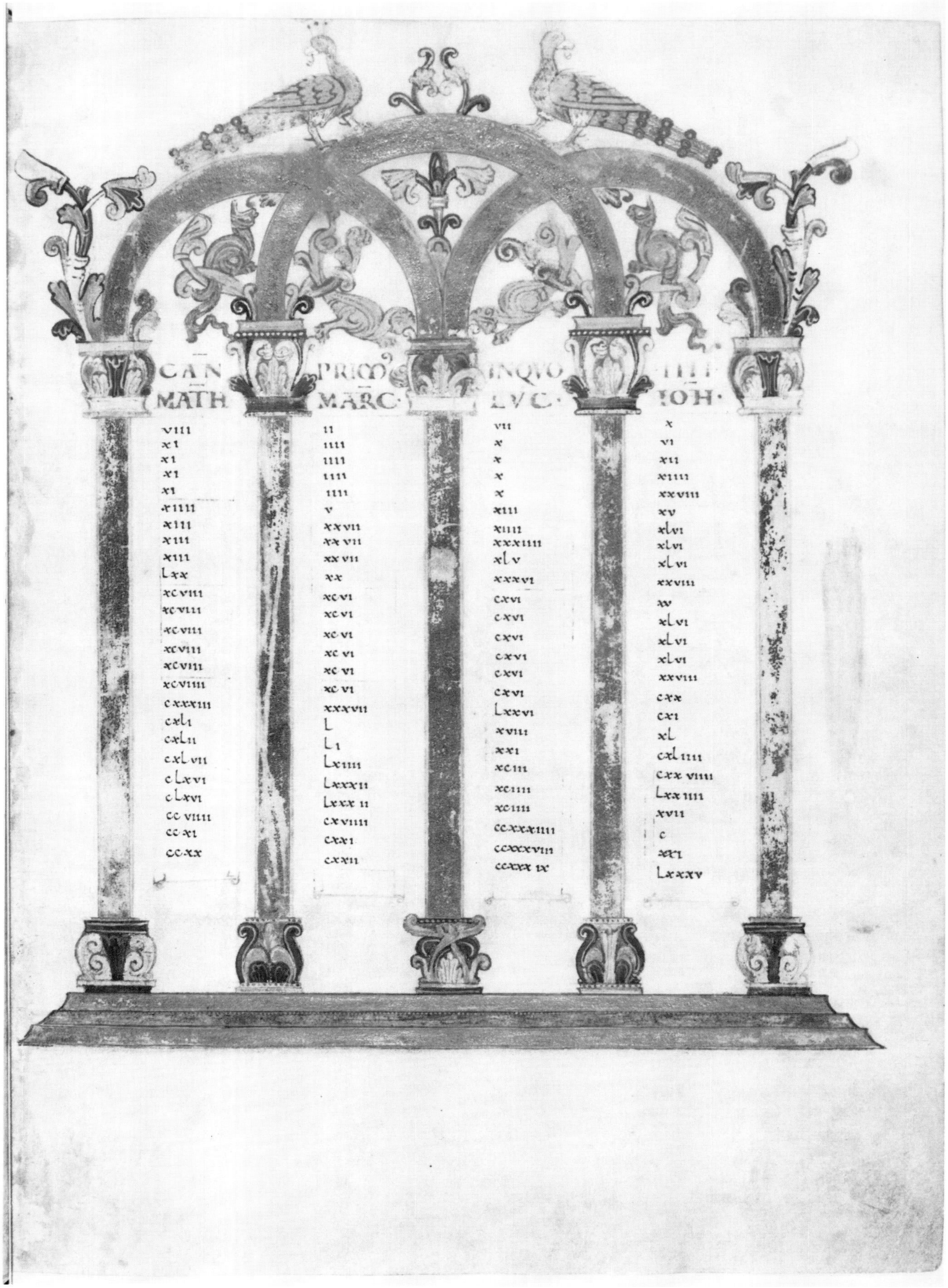

7.1 Cambridge, Trinity College, B. 10. 4, f. 9r

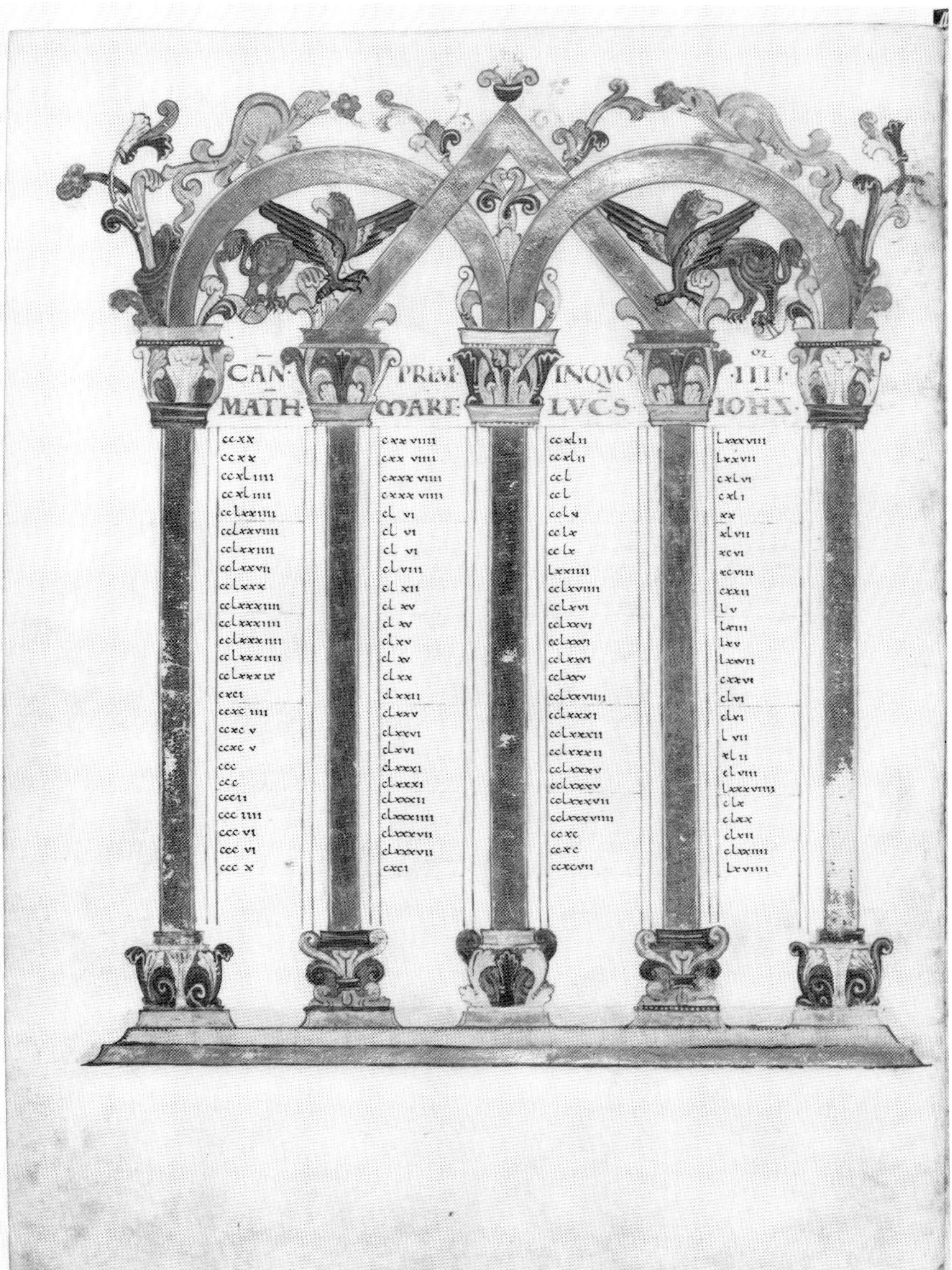

7.2 Cambridge, Trinity College, B. 10. 4, f. 9ᵛ

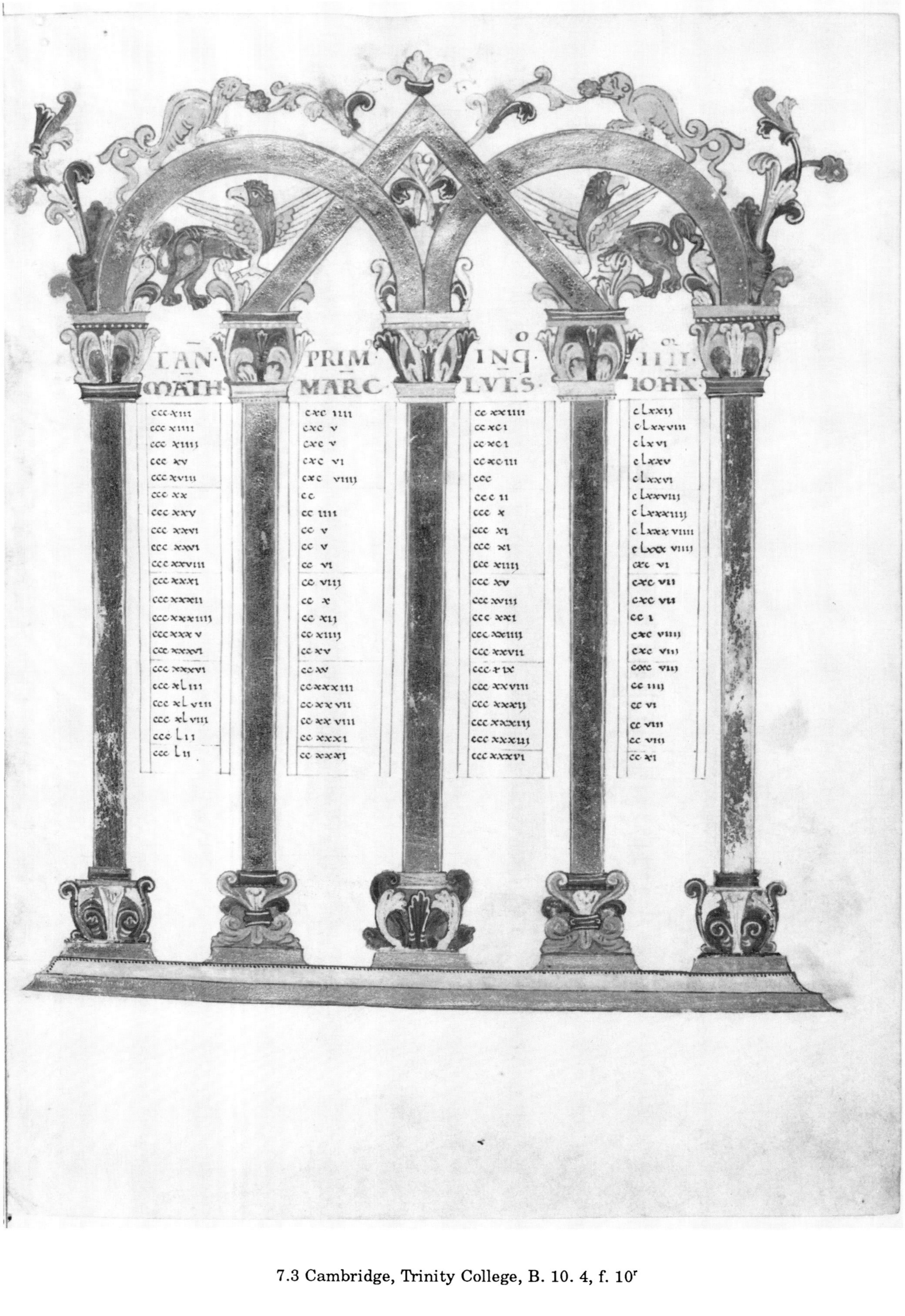

7.3 Cambridge, Trinity College, B. 10. 4, f. 10r

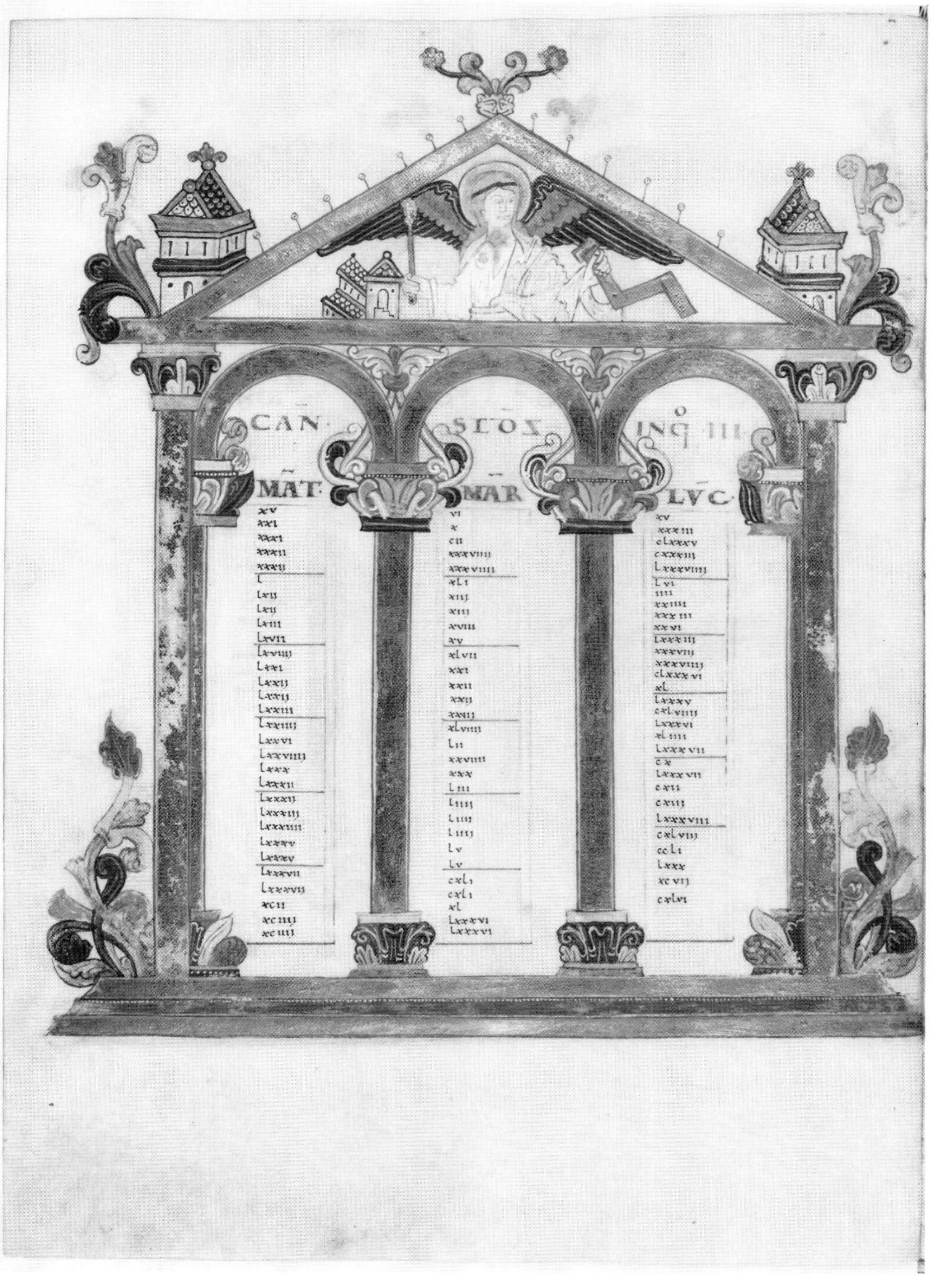

7.4 Cambridge, Trinity College, B. 10. 4, f. 10v

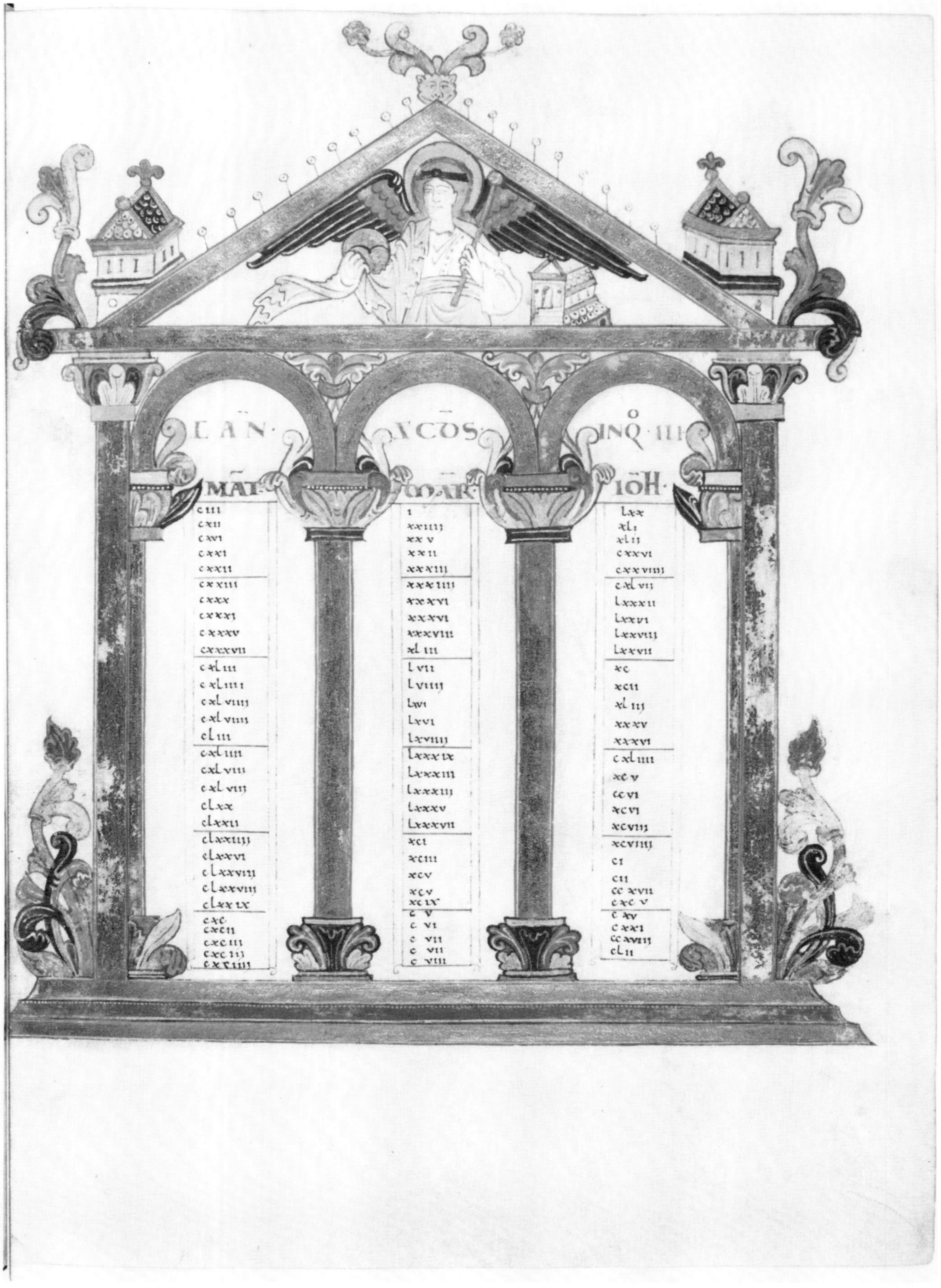

7.5 Cambridge, Trinity College, B. 10. 4, f. 11r

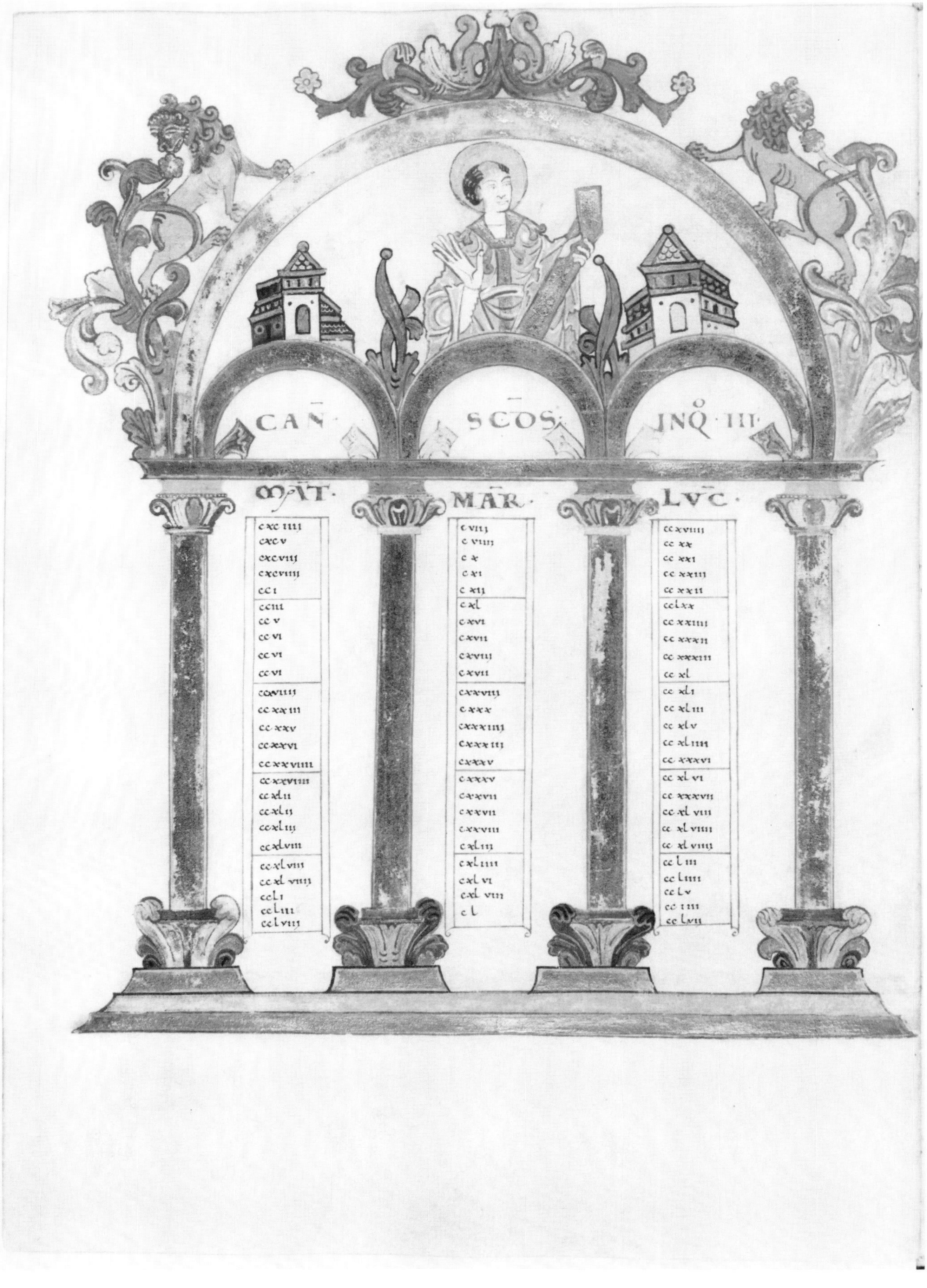

7.6 Cambridge, Trinity College, B. 10. 4, f. 11ᵛ

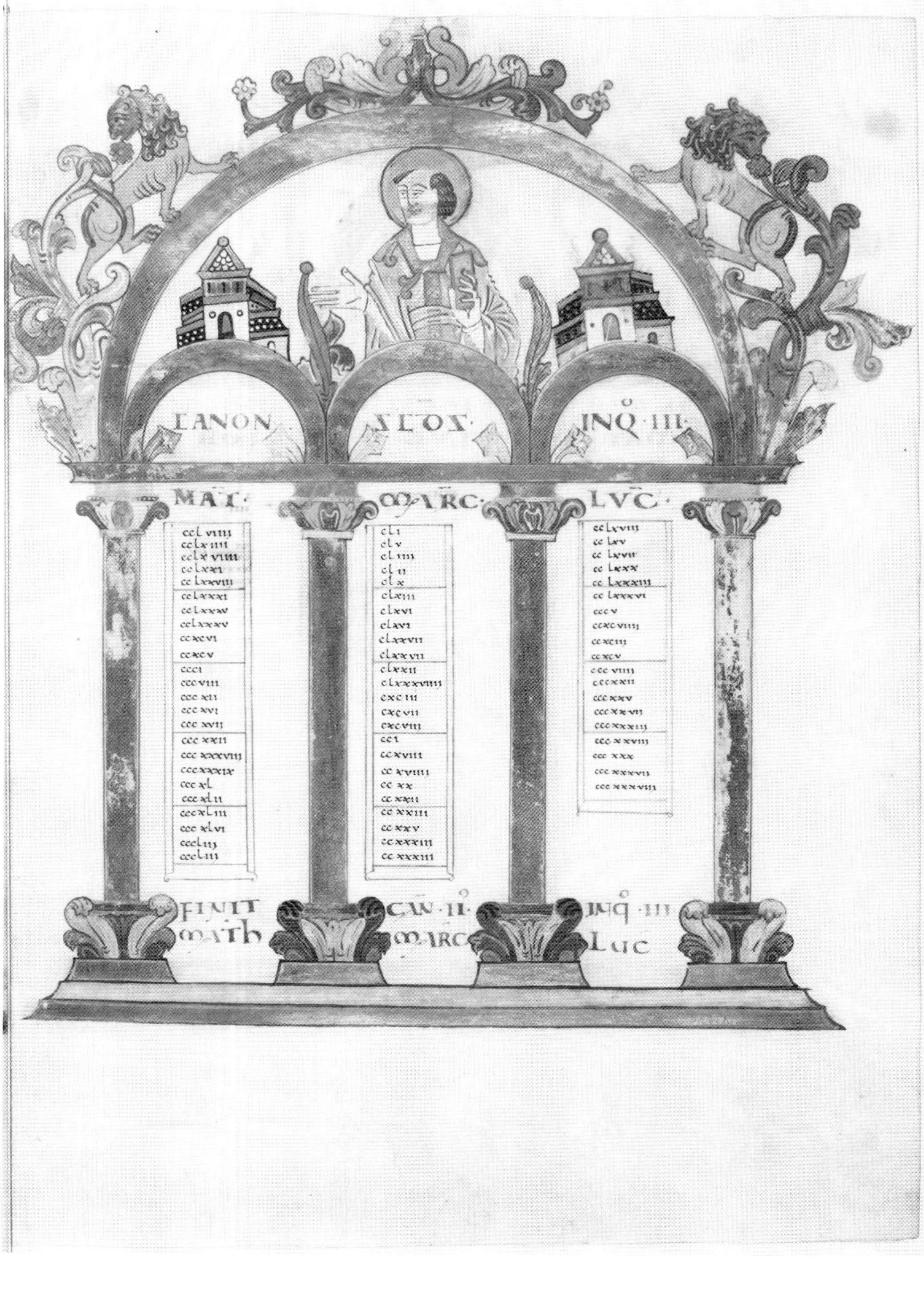

7.7 Cambridge, Trinity College, B. 10. 4, f. 12r

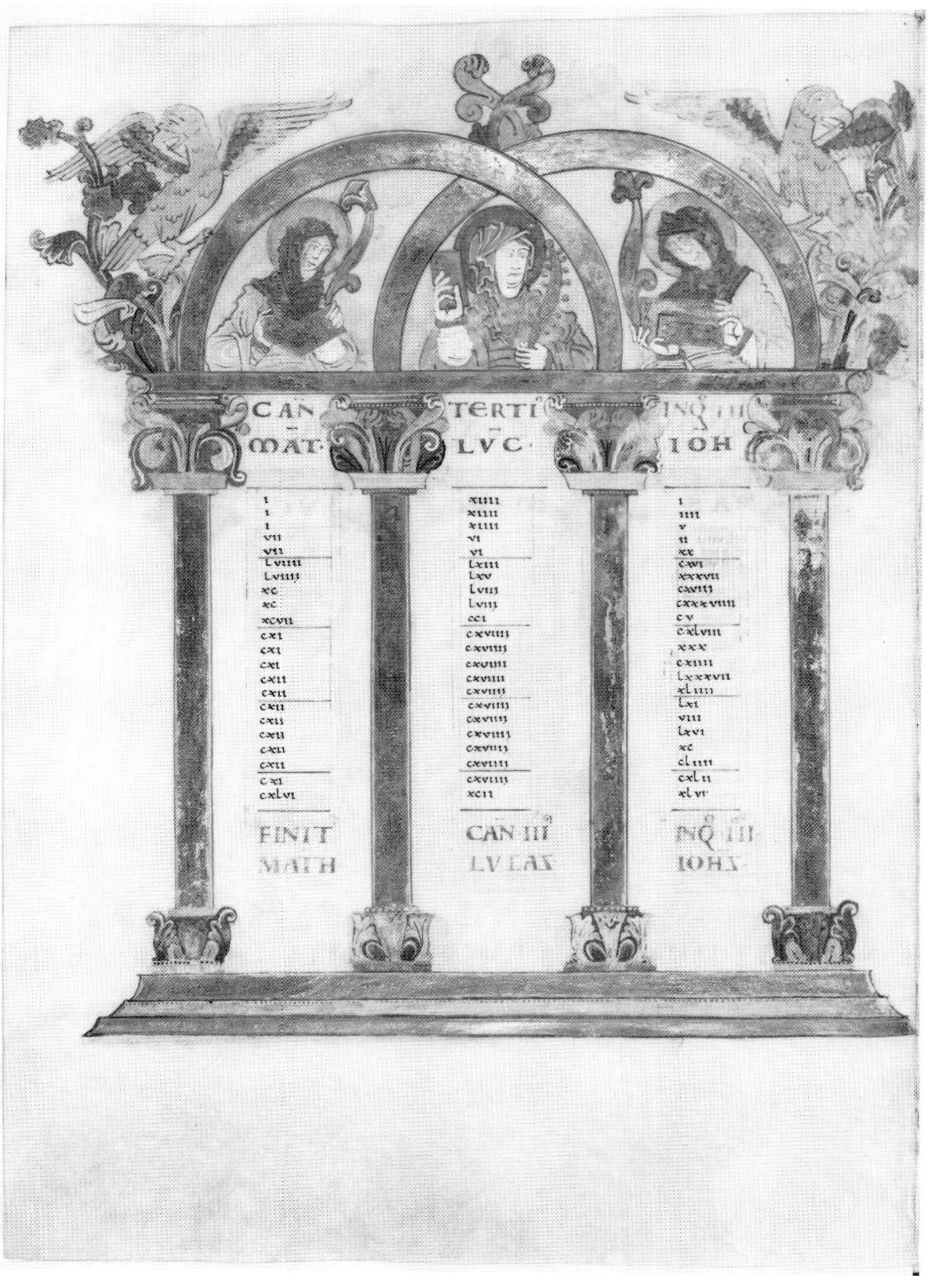

7.8 Cambridge, Trinity College, B. 10. 4, f. 12v

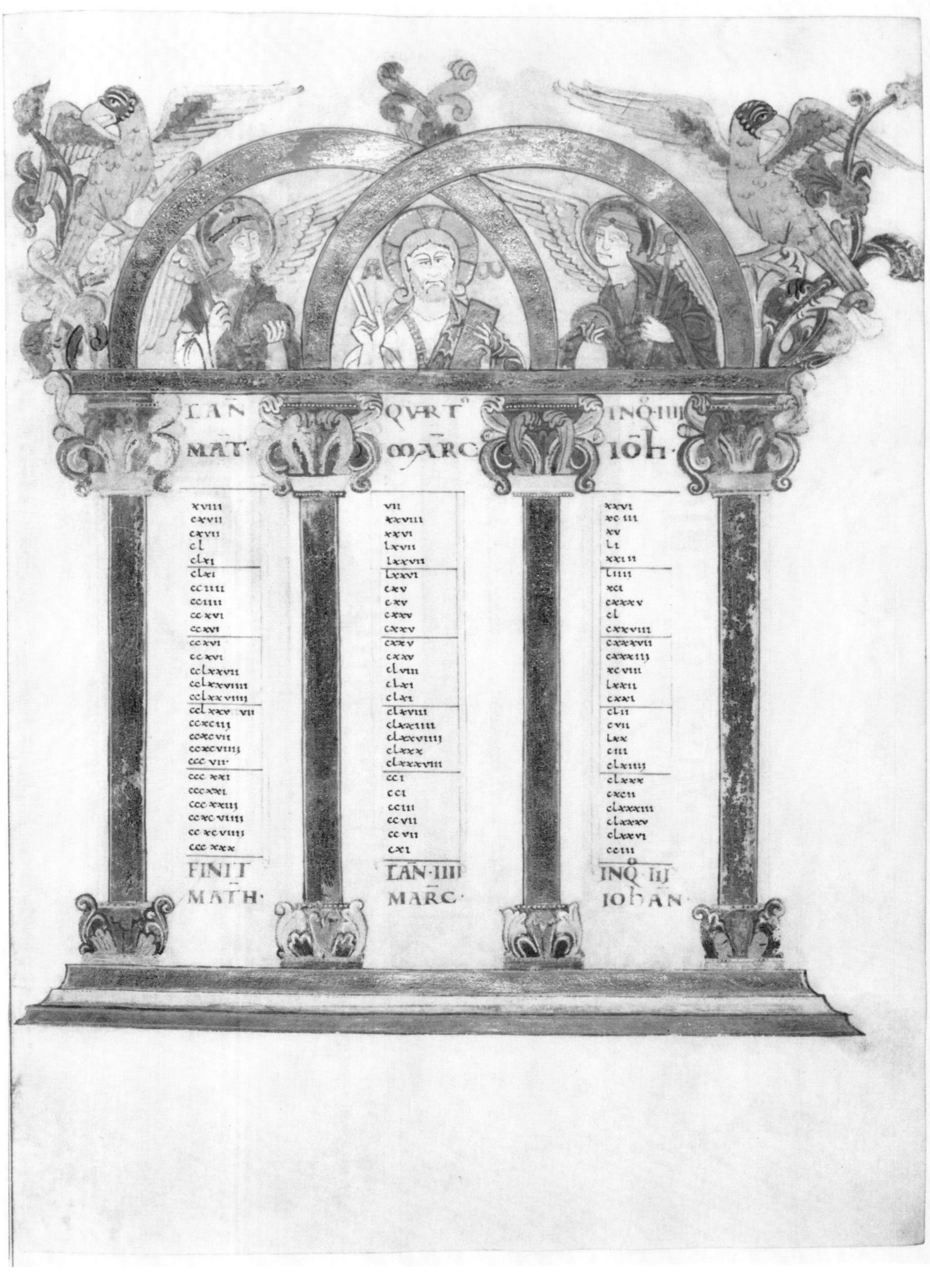

7.9 Cambridge, Trinity College, B. 10. 4, f. 13r

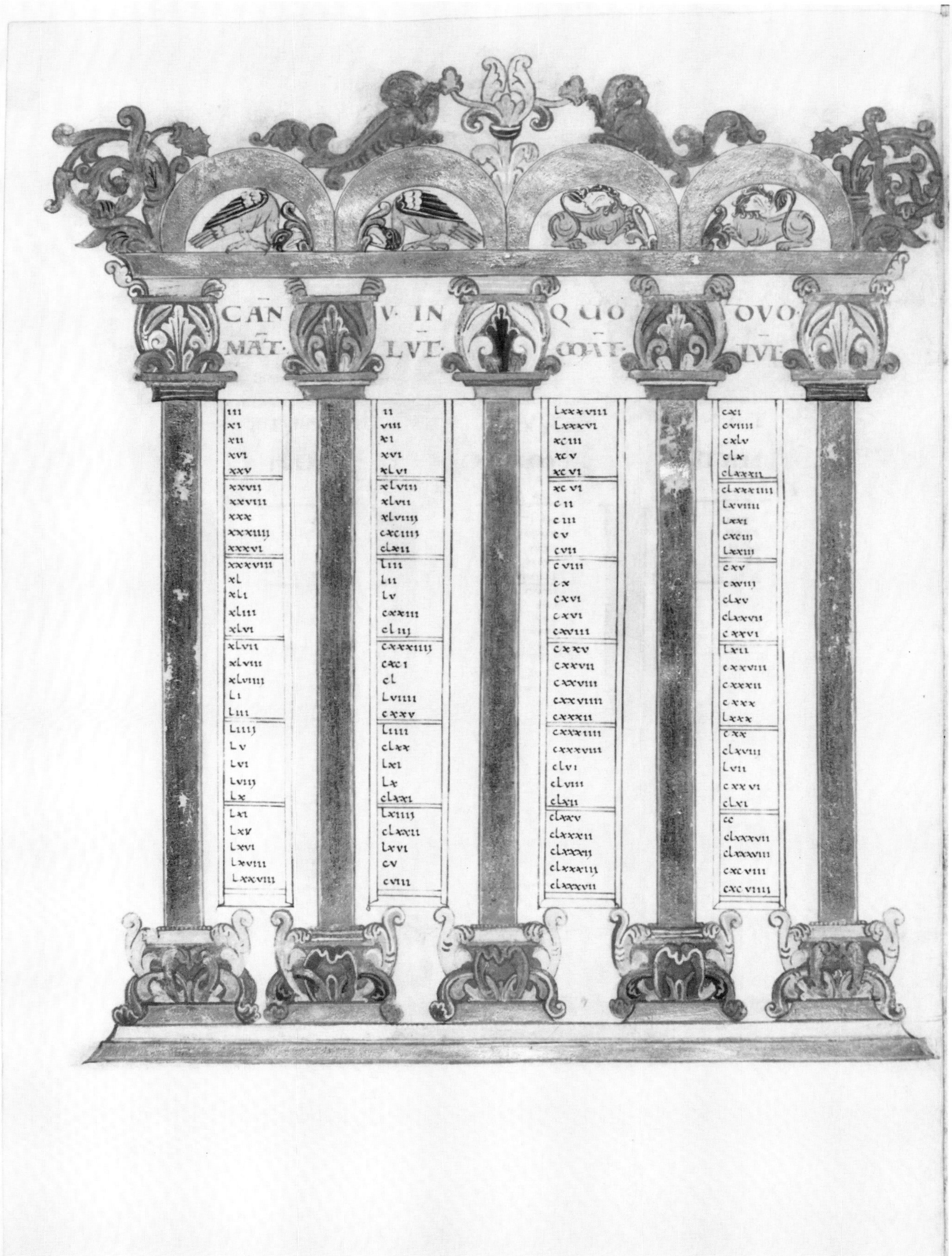

7.10 Cambridge, Trinity College, B. 10. 4, f. 13v

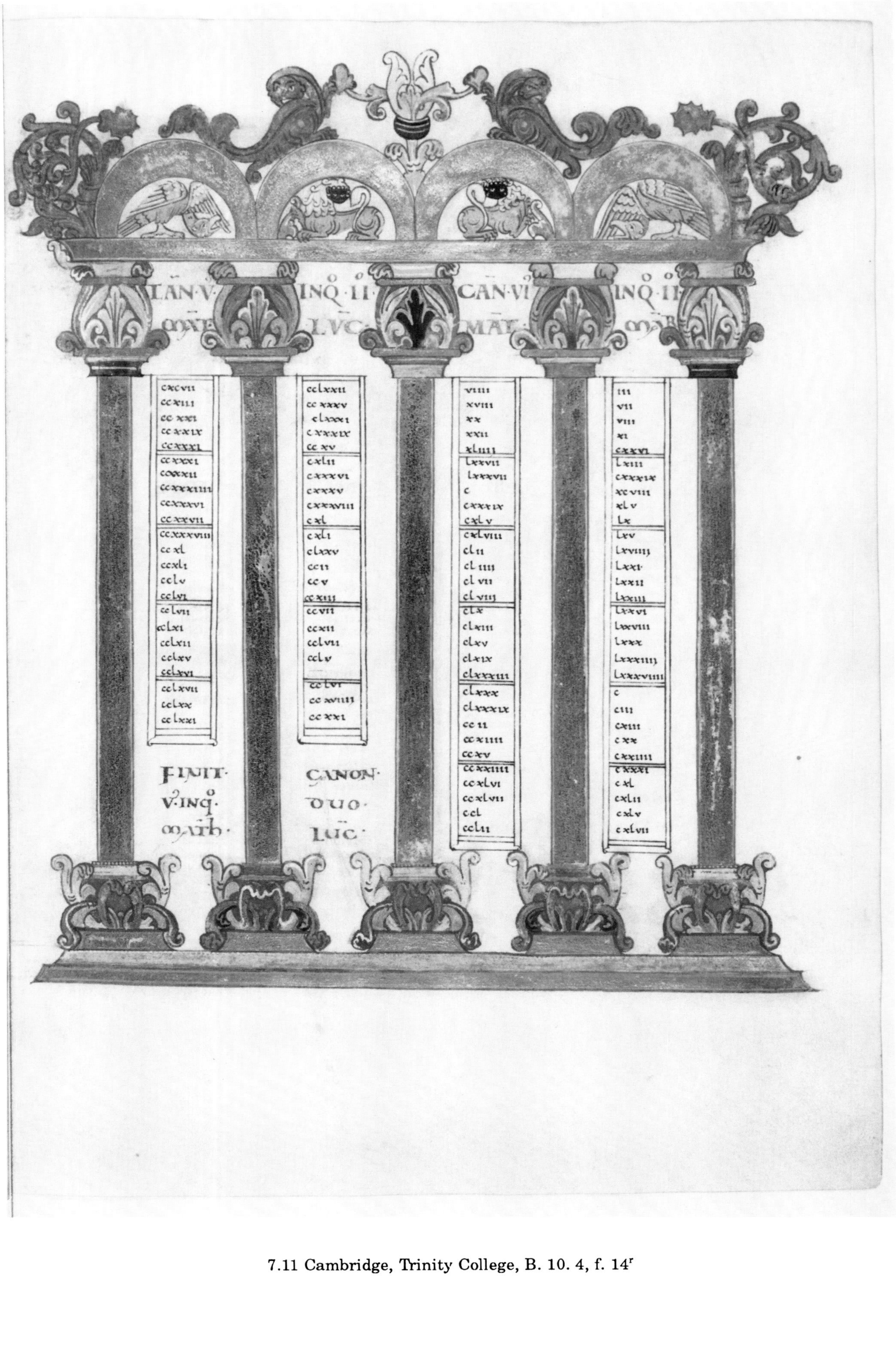

7.11 Cambridge, Trinity College, B. 10. 4, f. 14r

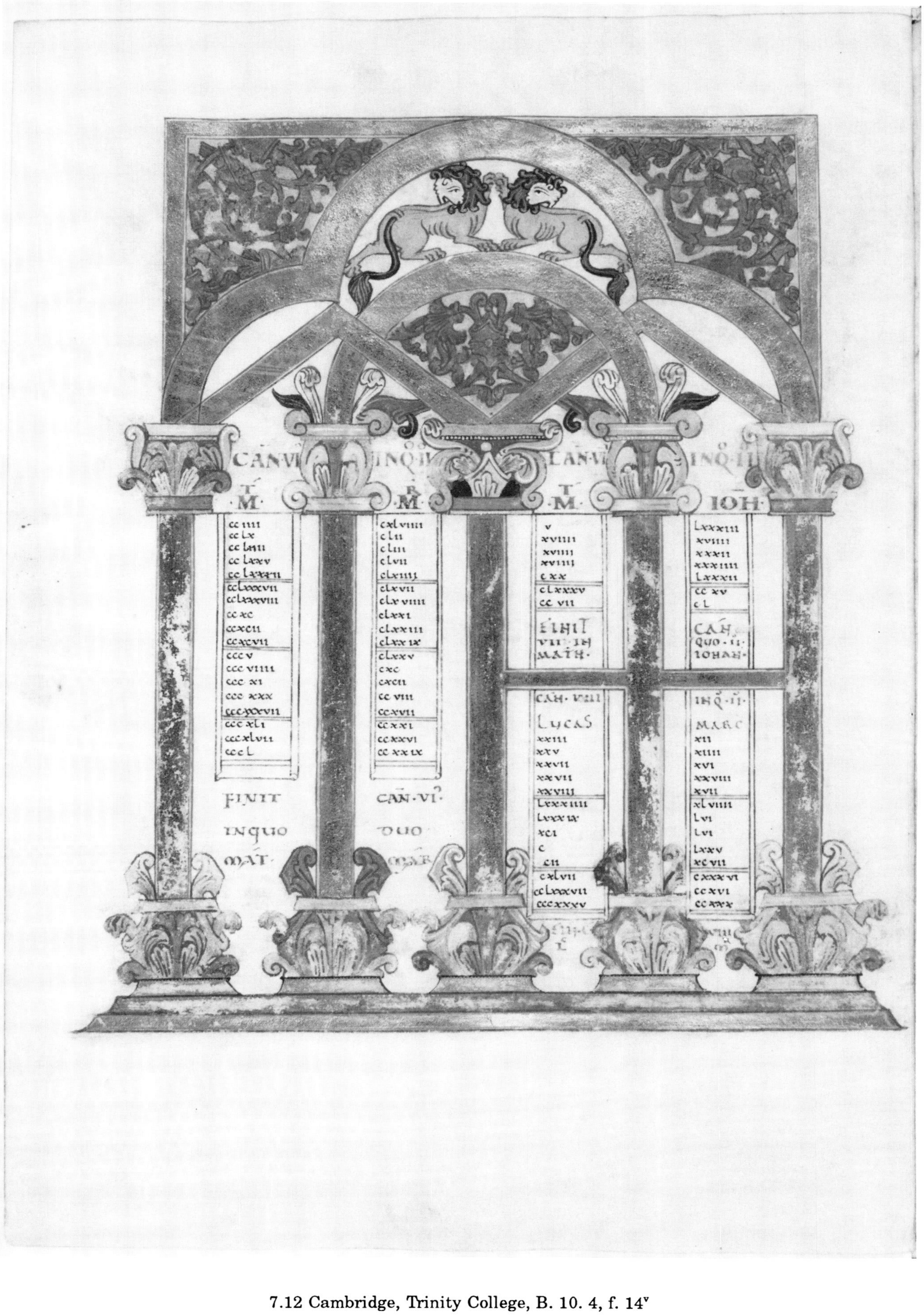

7.12 Cambridge, Trinity College, B. 10. 4, f. 14v

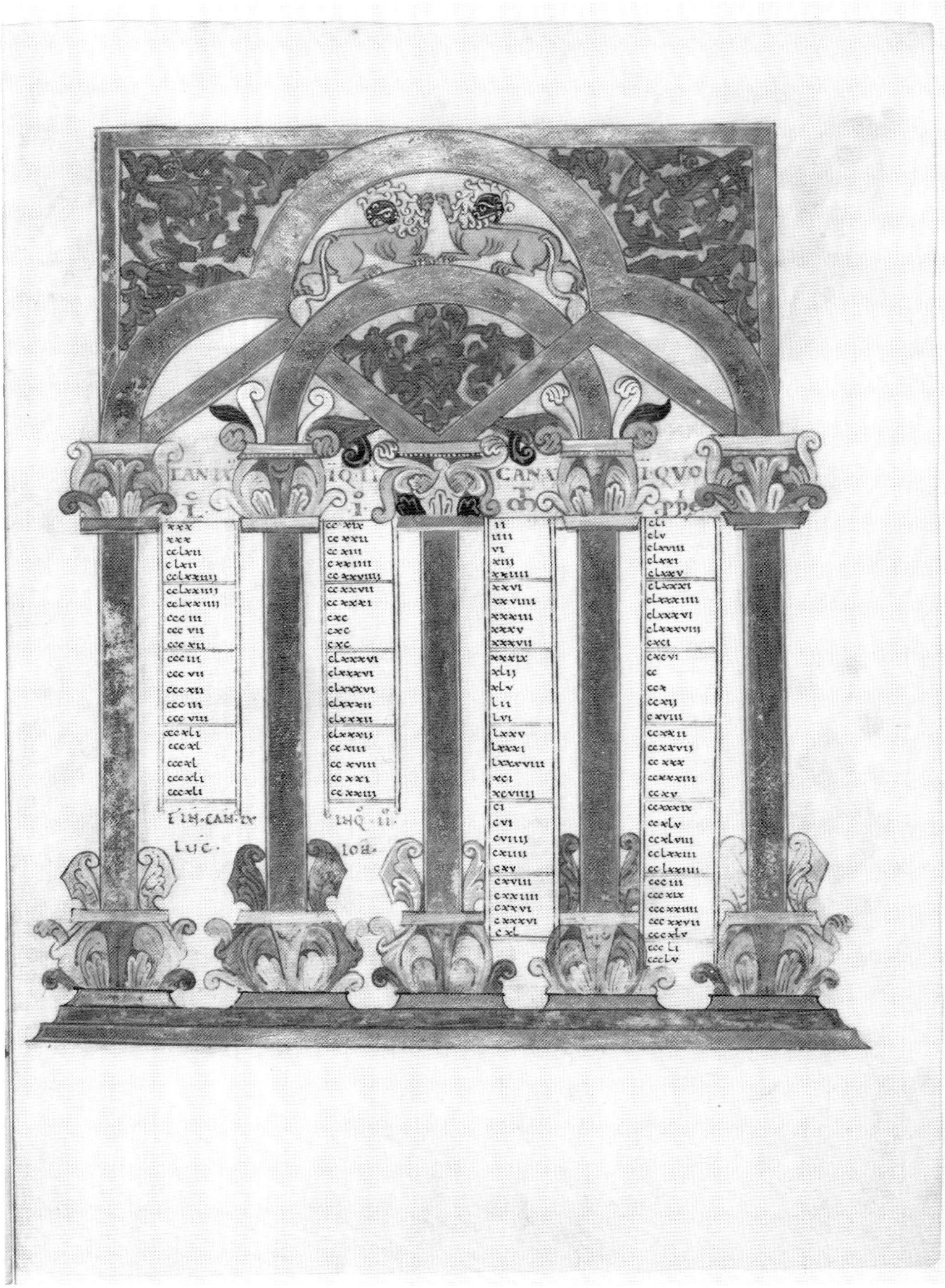

7.13 Cambridge, Trinity College, B. 10. 4, f. 15r

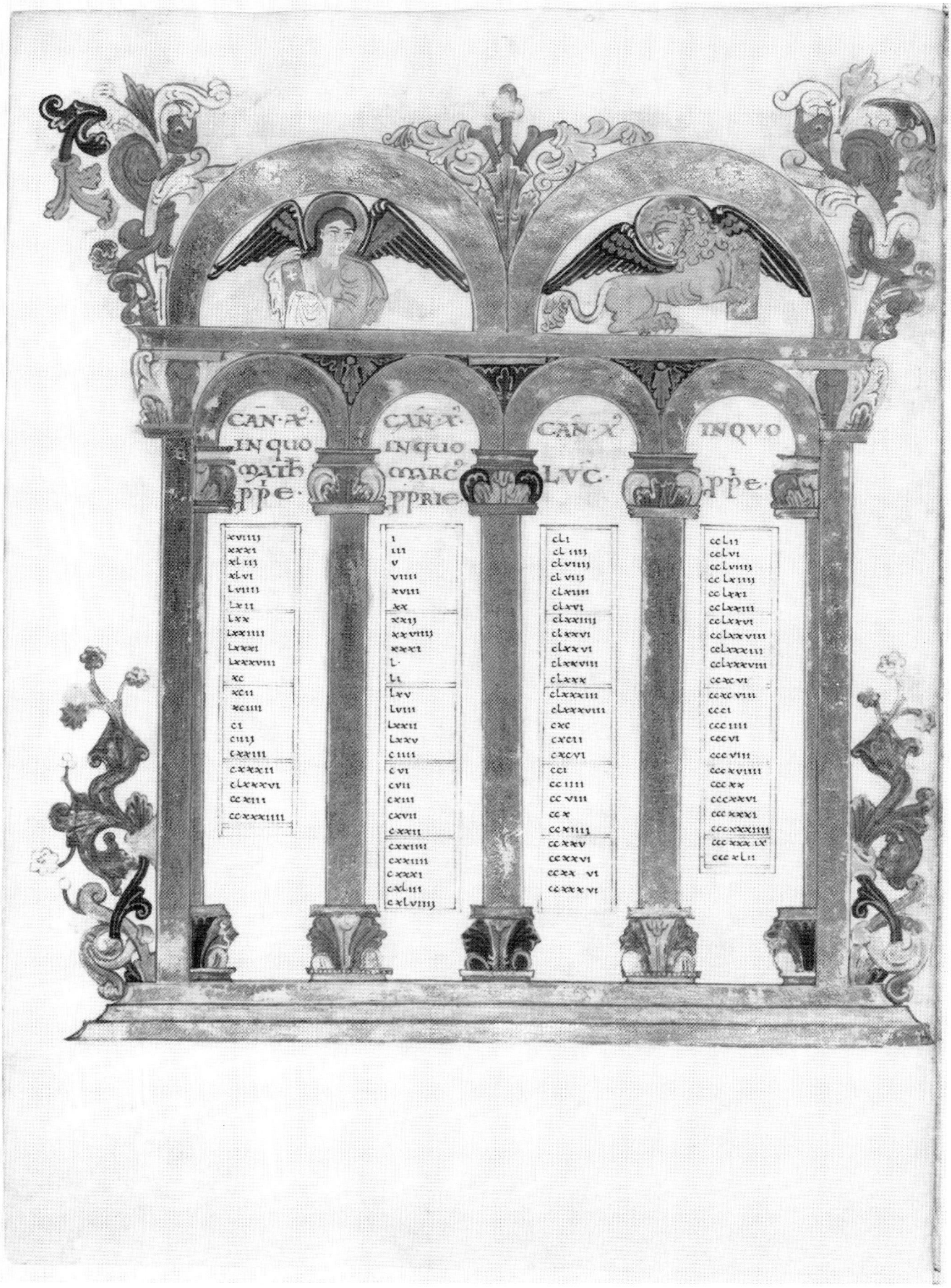

7.14 Cambridge, Trinity College, B. 10. 4, f. 15v

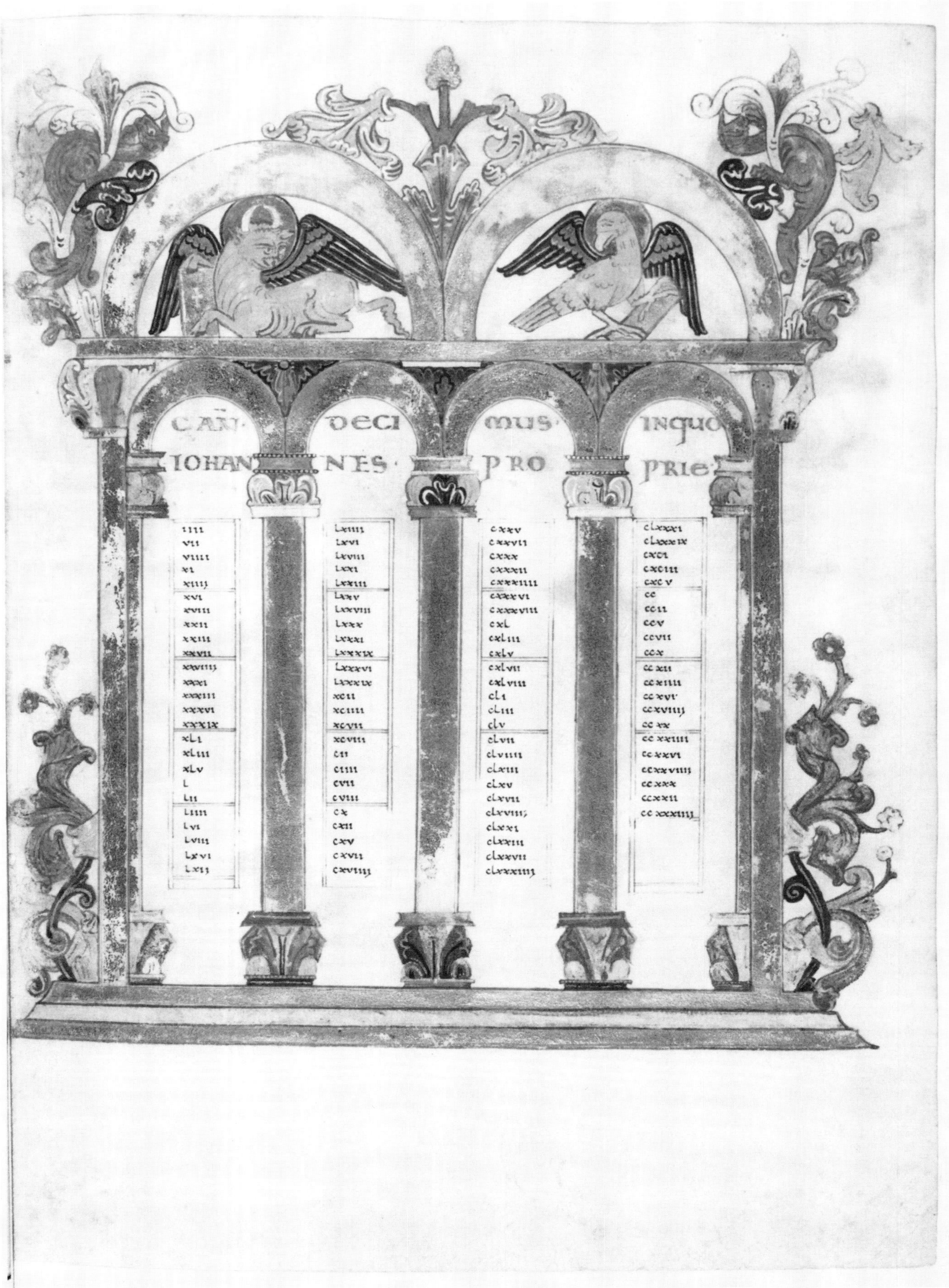

7.15 Cambridge, Trinity College, B. 10. 4, f. 16r

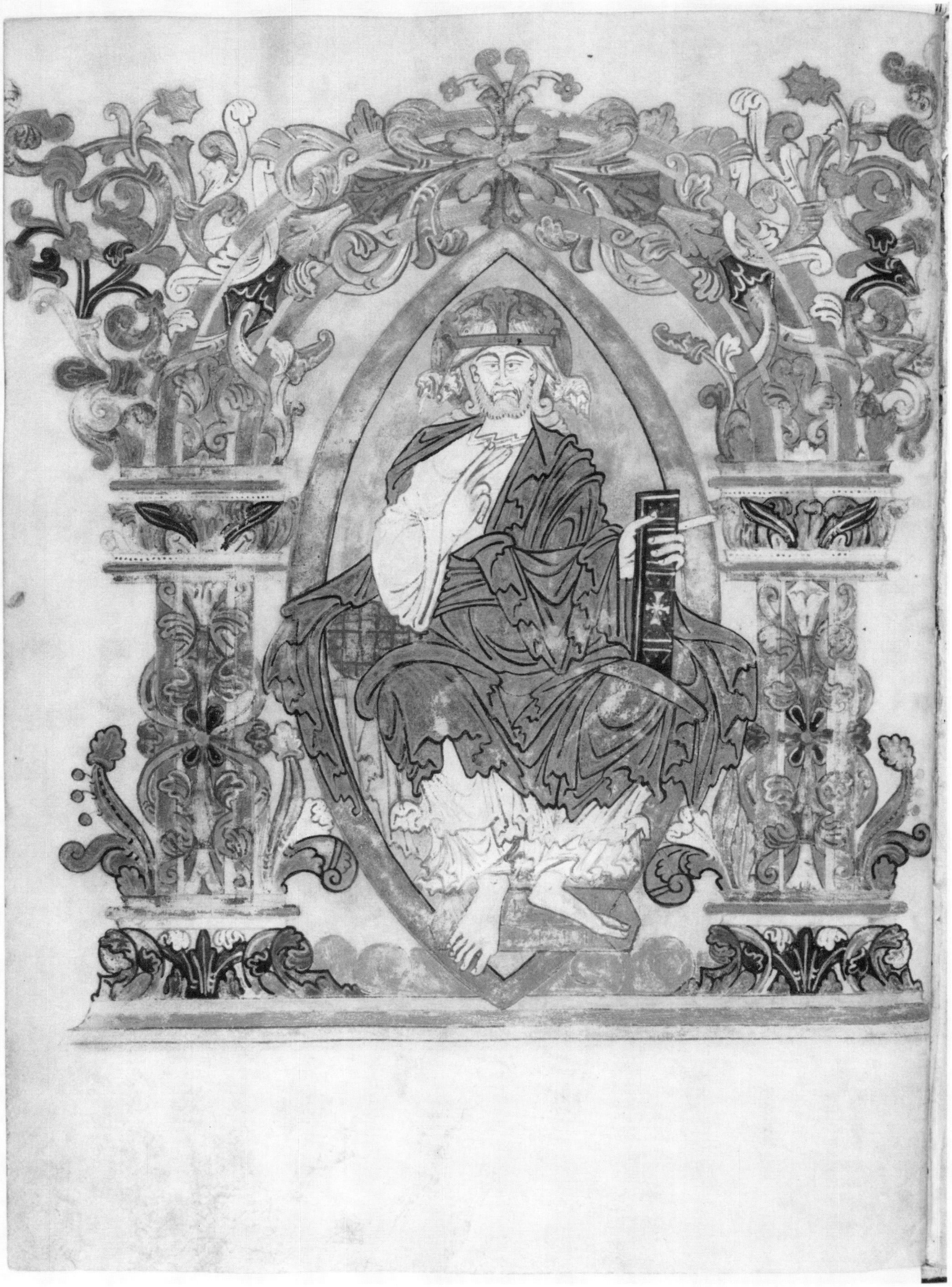

7.16 Cambridge, Trinity College, B. 10. 4, f. 16v

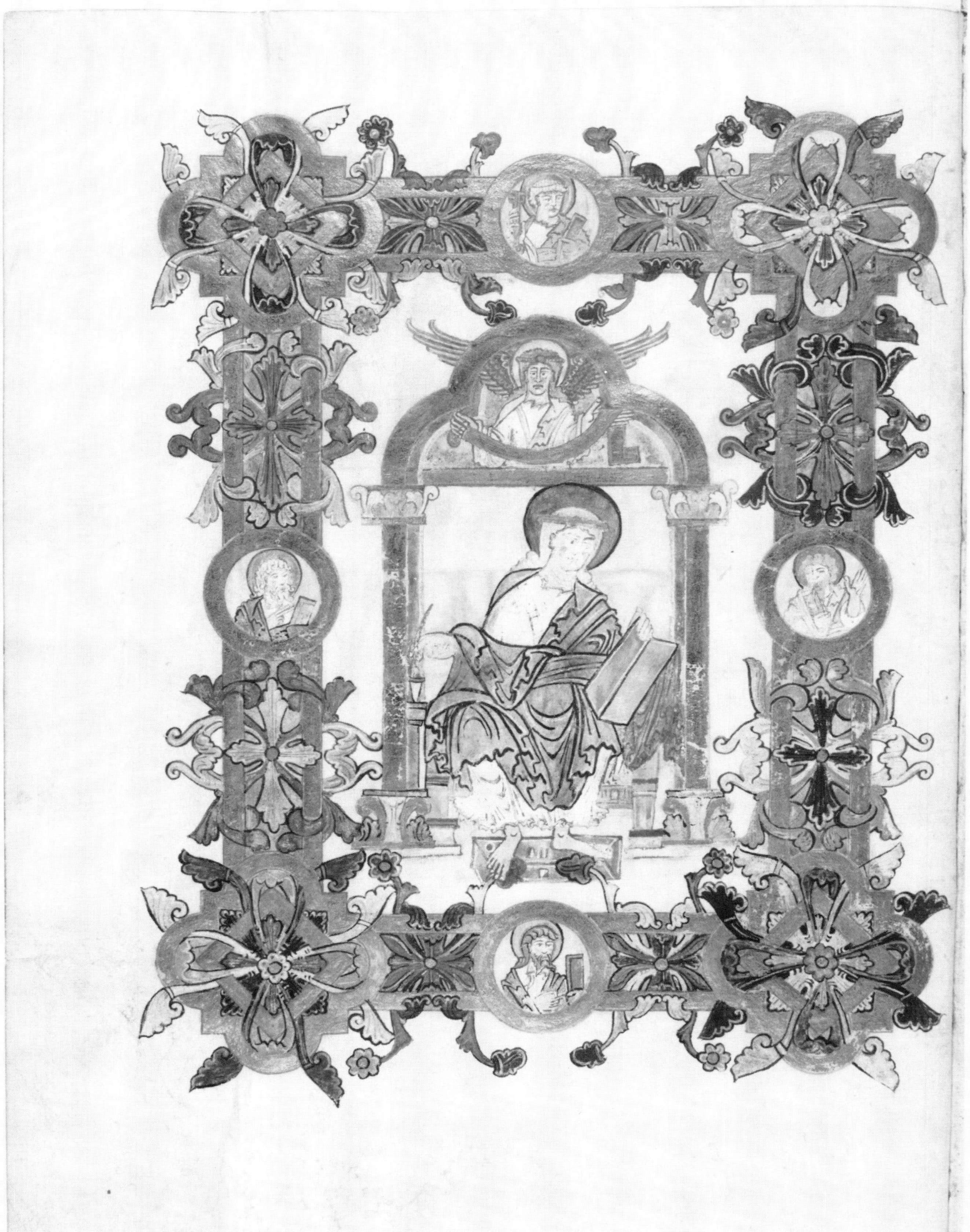

7.17 Cambridge, Trinity College, B. 10. 4, f. 17v

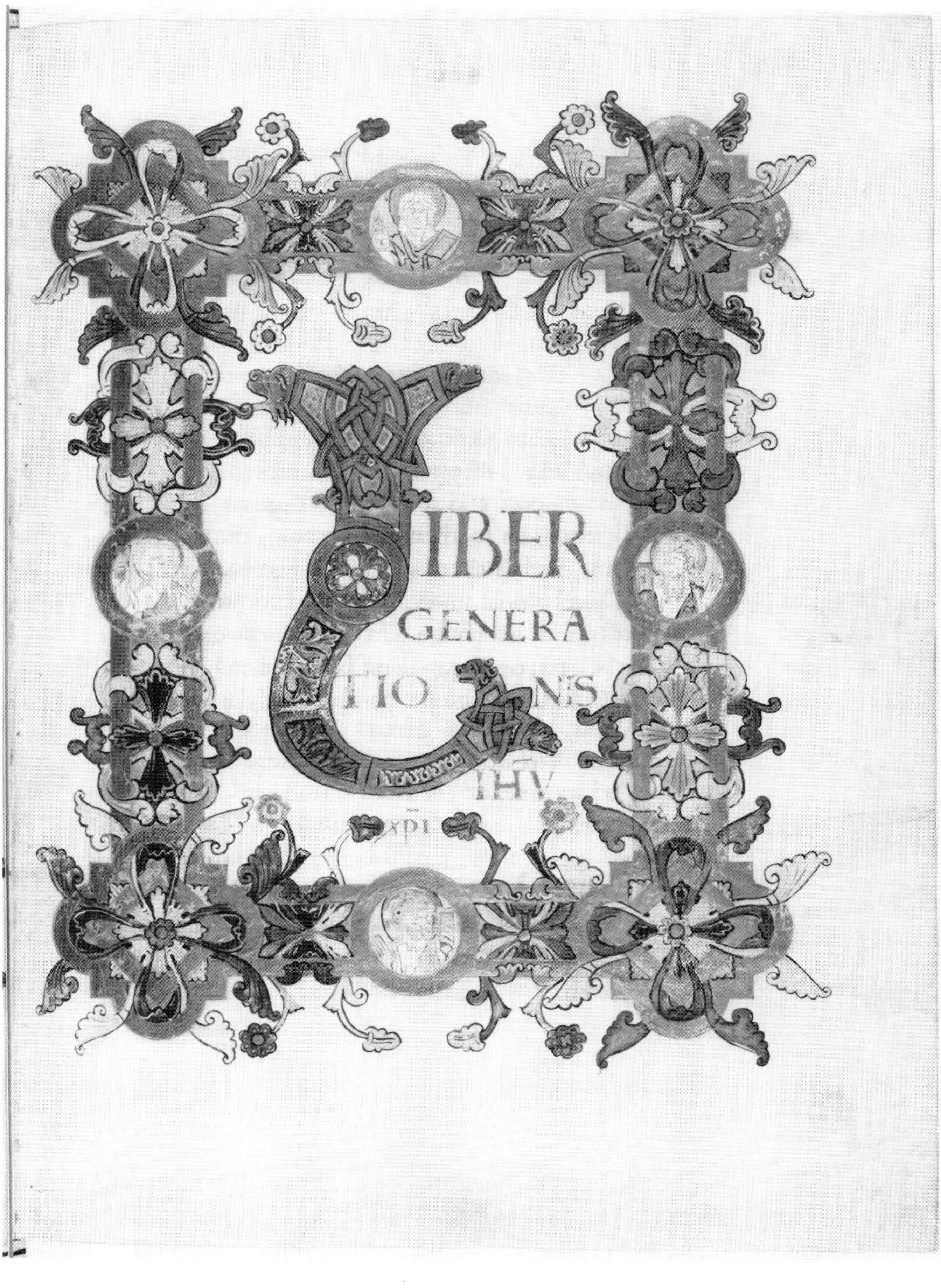

7.18 Cambridge, Trinity College, B. 10. 4, f. 18r

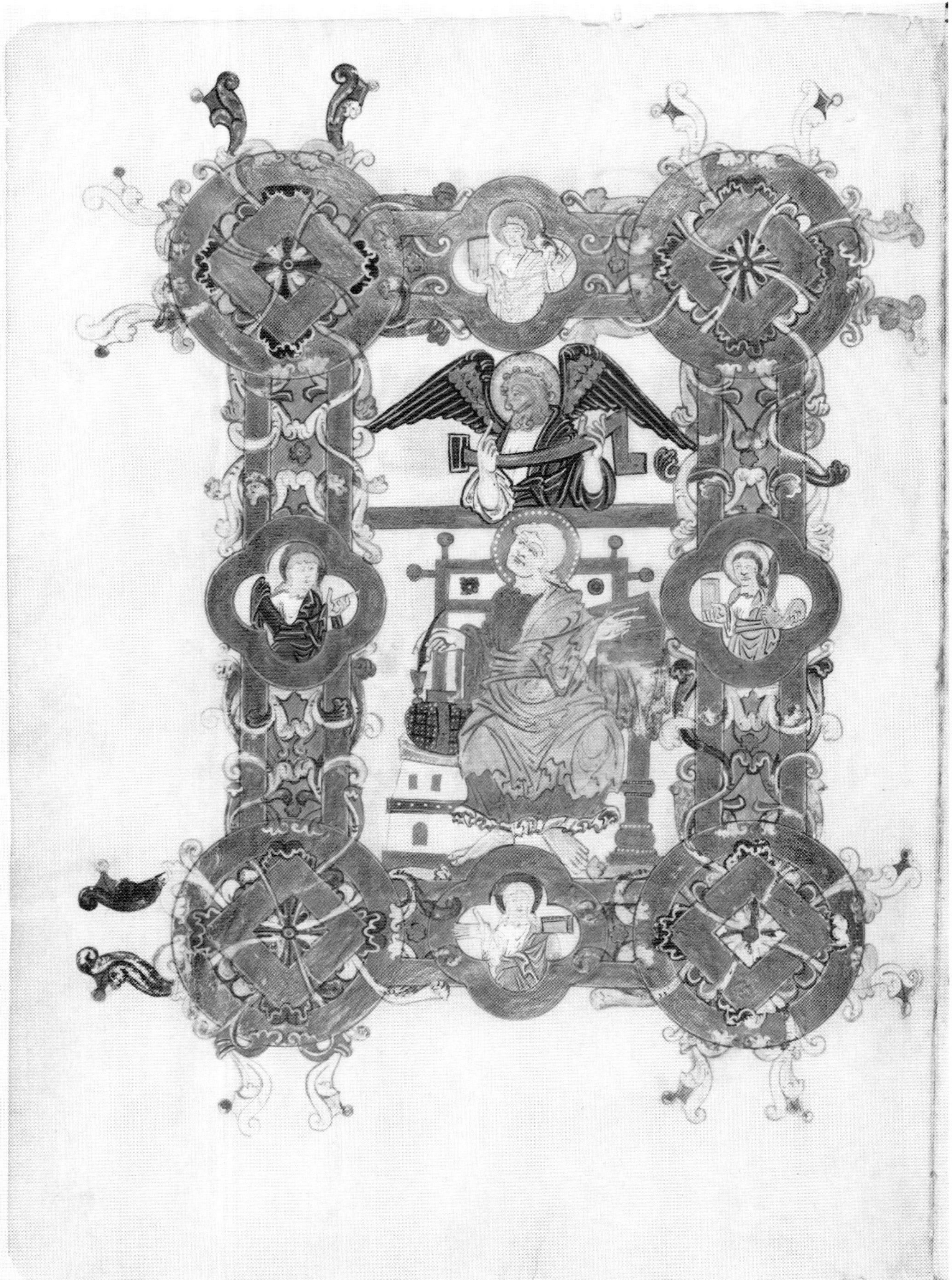

7.19 Cambridge, Trinity College, B. 10. 4, f. 59v

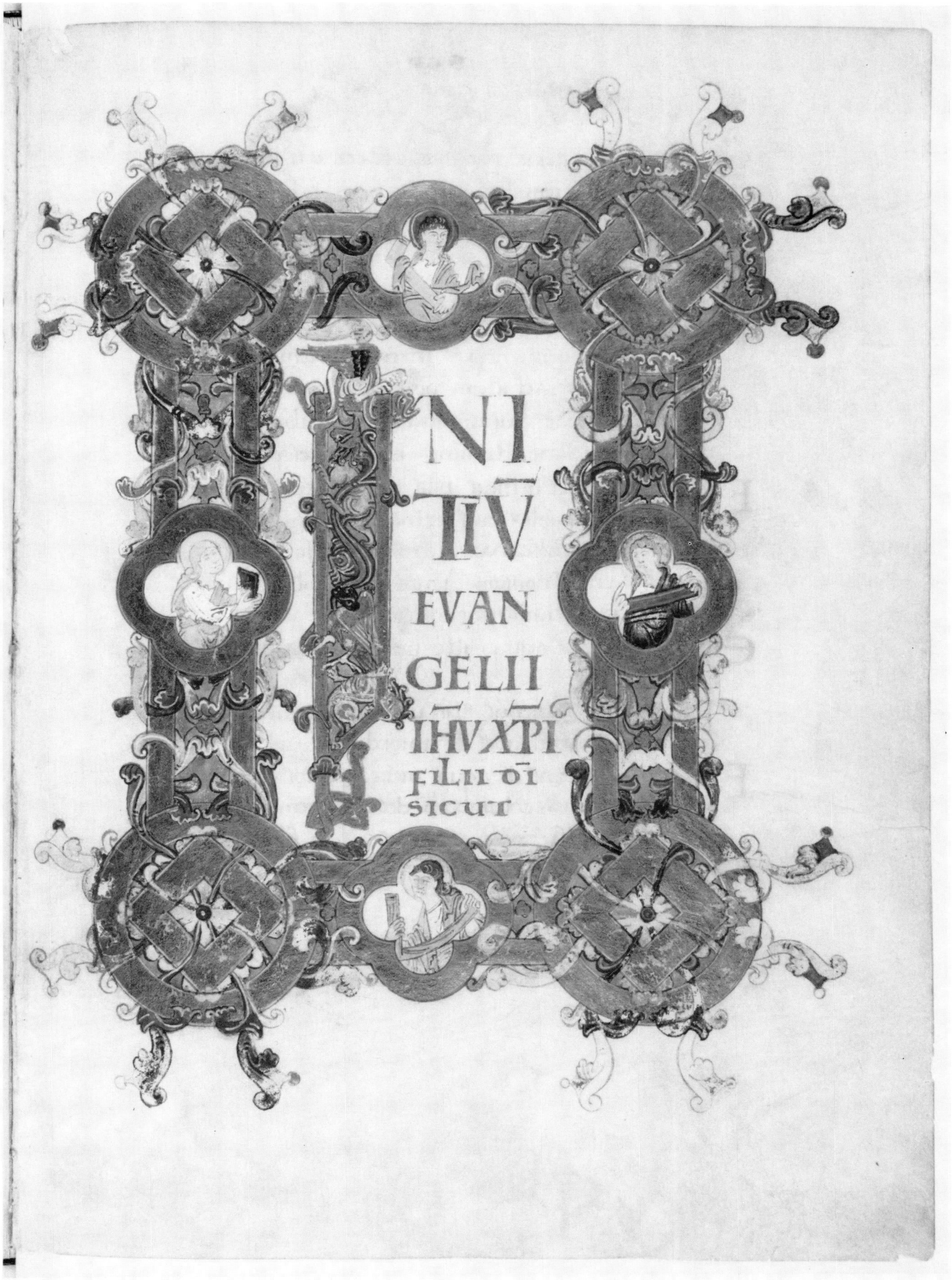

7.20 Cambridge, Trinity College, B. 10. 4, f. 60r

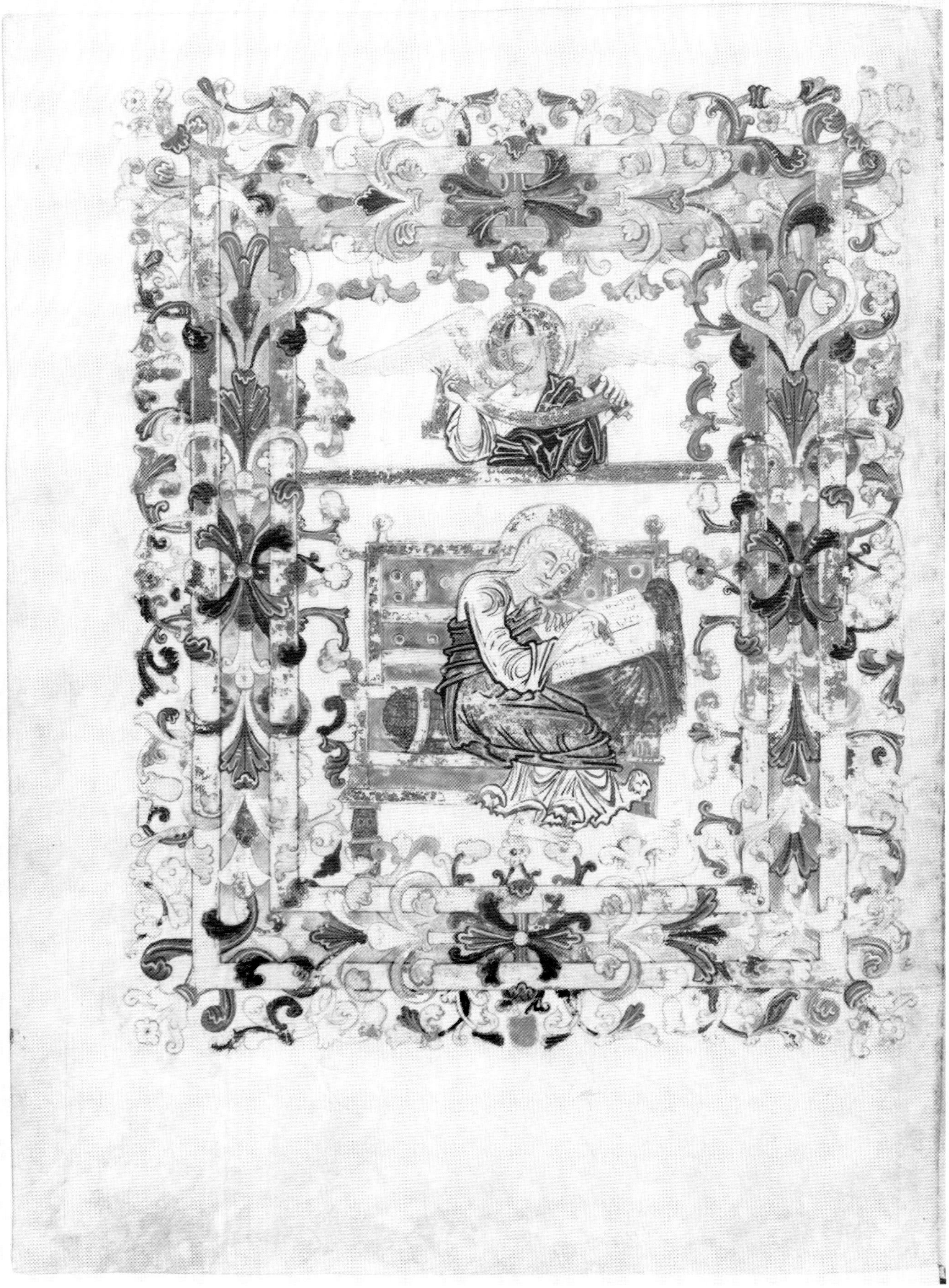

7.21 Cambridge, Trinity College, B. 10. 4, f. 89v

7.22 Cambridge, Trinity College, B. 10. 4, f. 90r

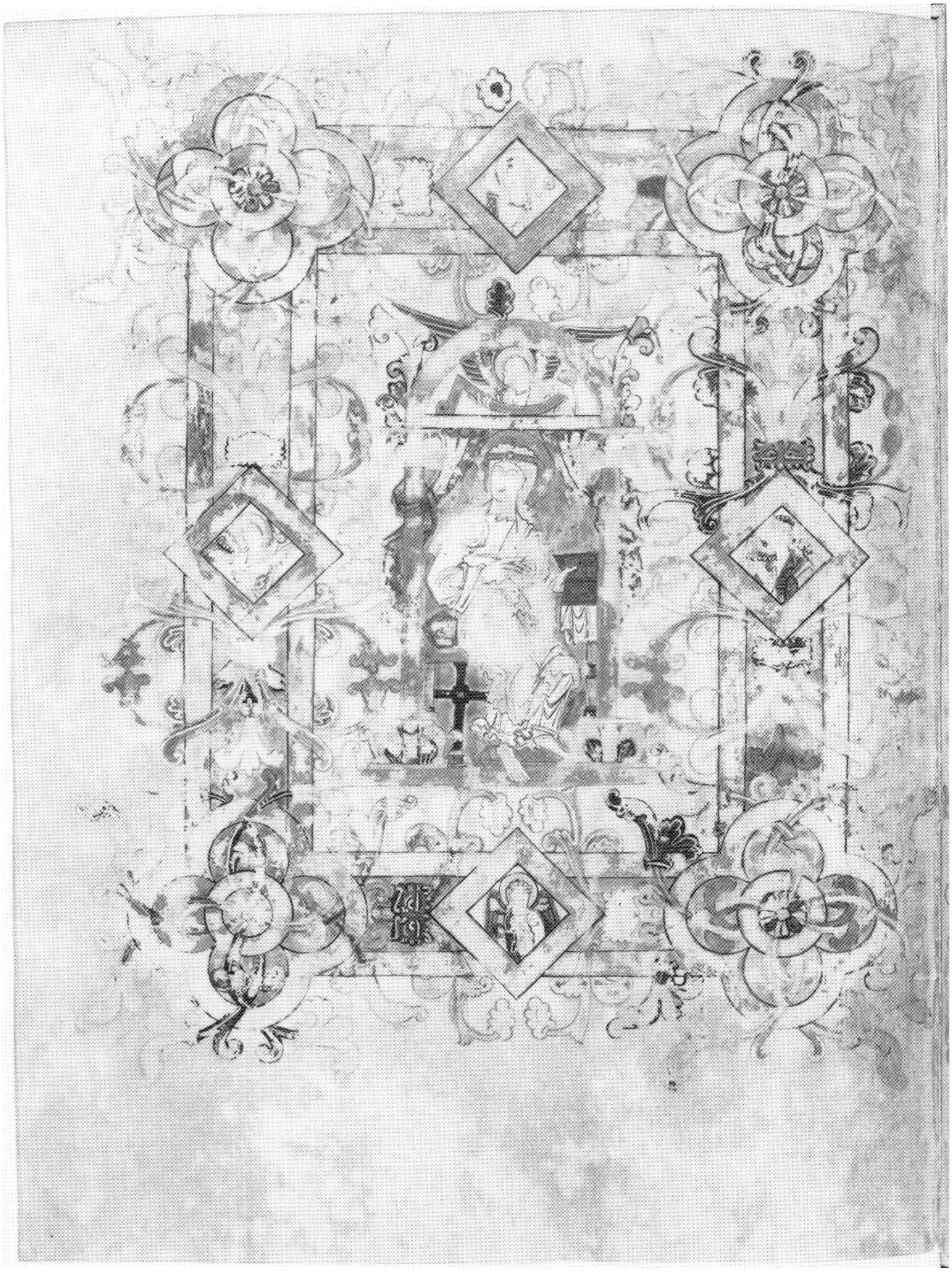

7.23 Cambridge, Trinity College, B. 10. 4, f. 132ᵛ

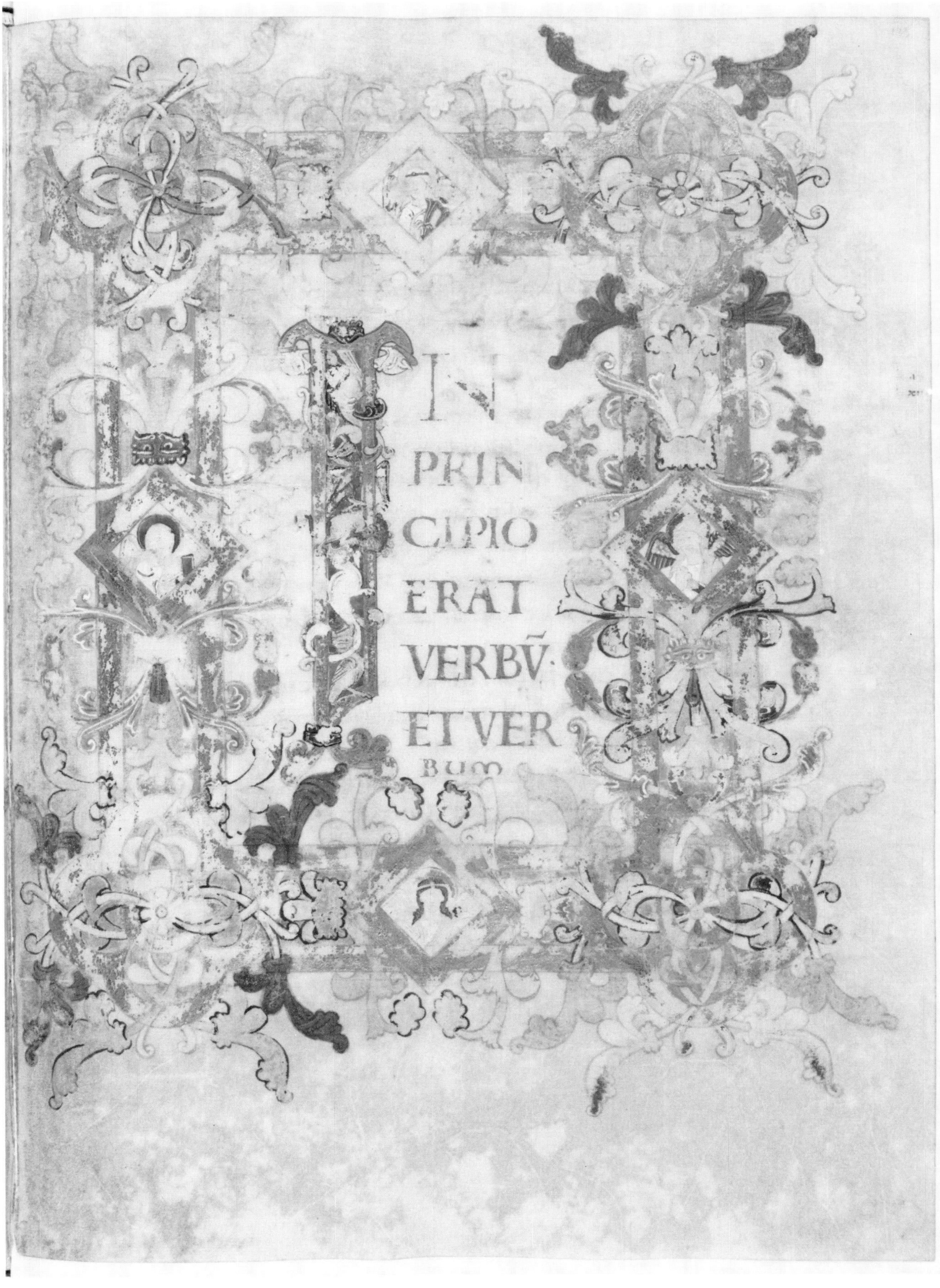

7.24 Cambridge, Trinity College, B. 10. 4, f. 133r

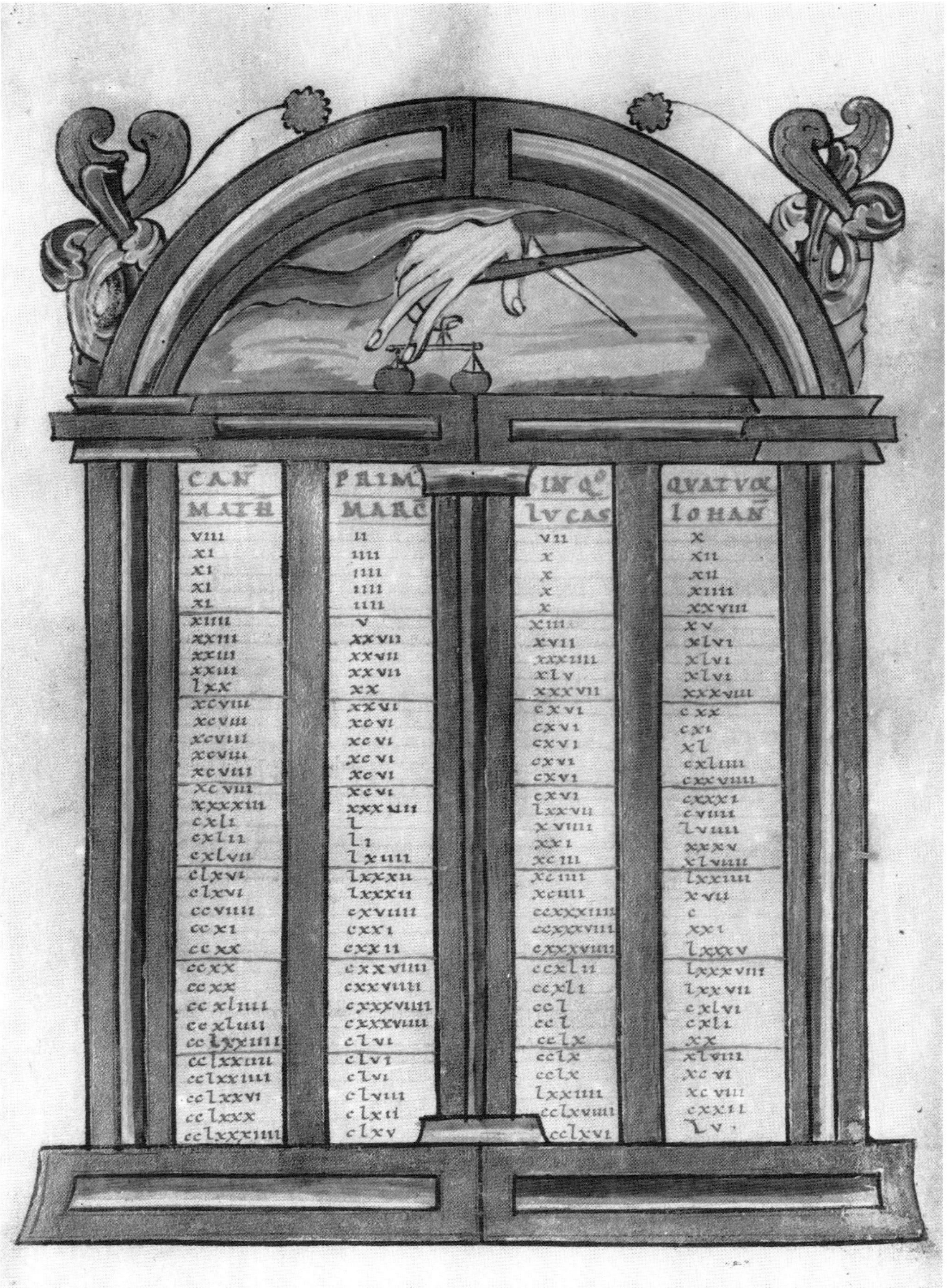

8.1 Hannover, Kestner-Museum WM XXI[a], 36, f. 9[v]

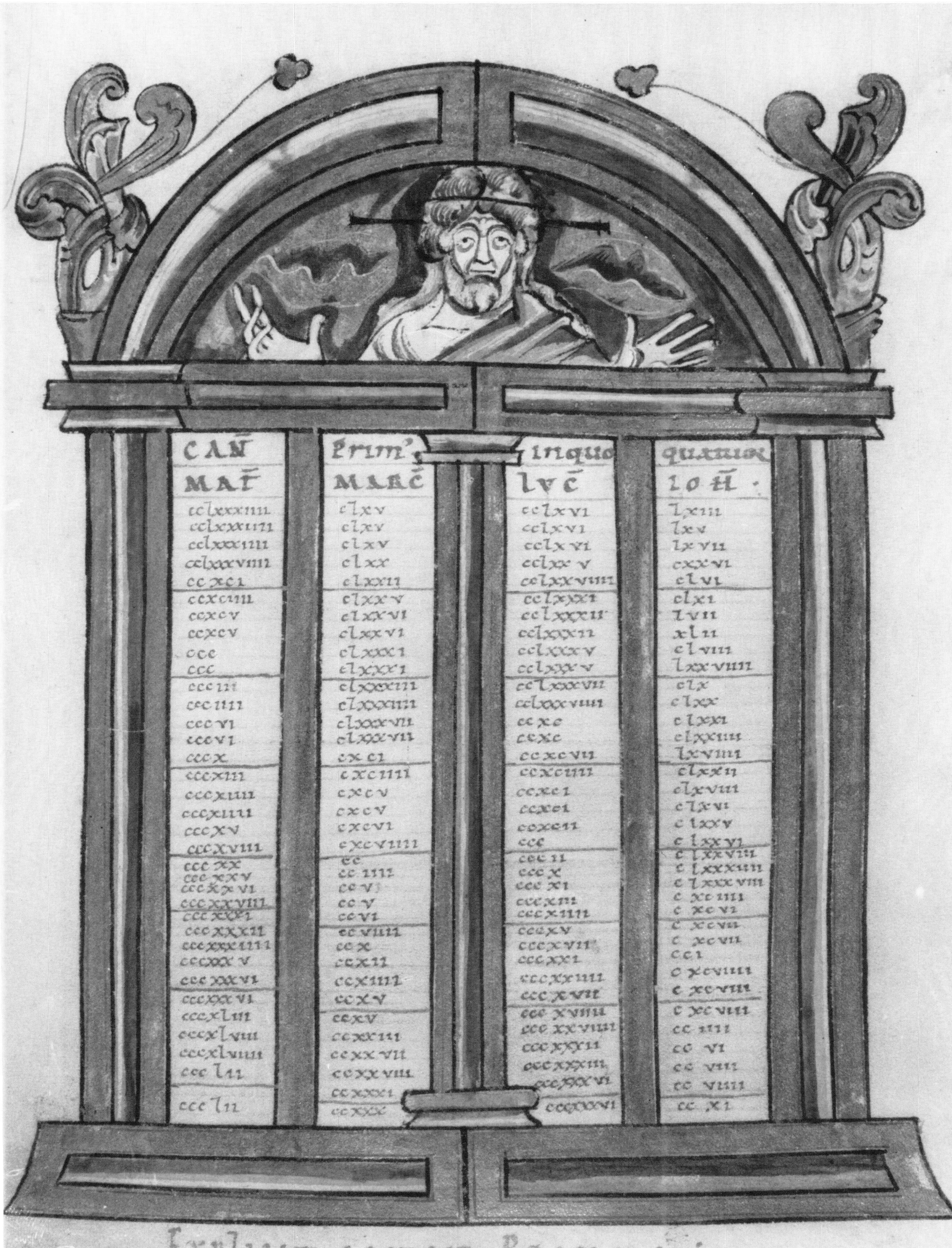

8.2 Hannover, Kestner-Museum WM XXI^{a}, 36, f. 10^{r}

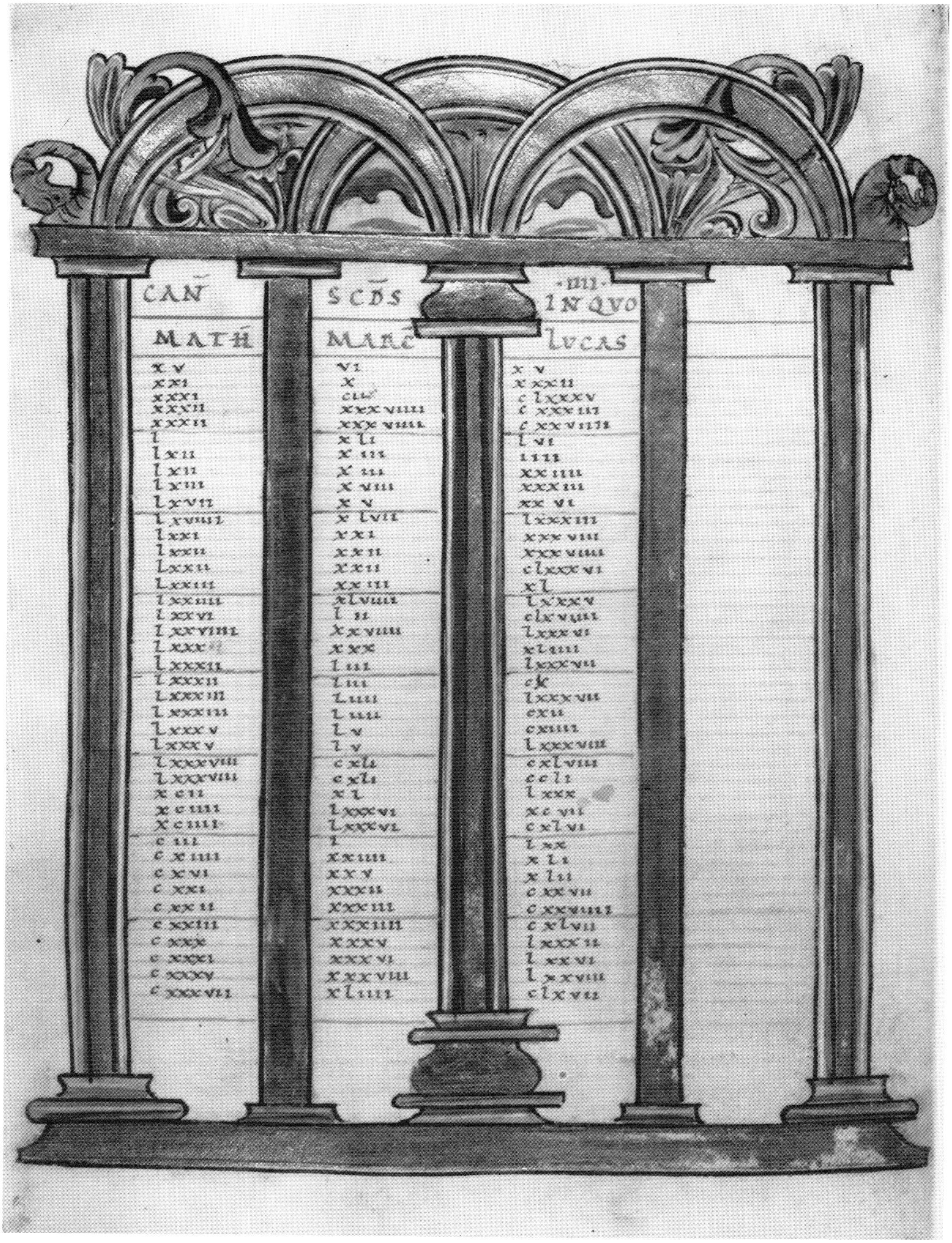

8.3 Hannover, Kestner-Museum WM XXI[a], 36, f. 10[v]

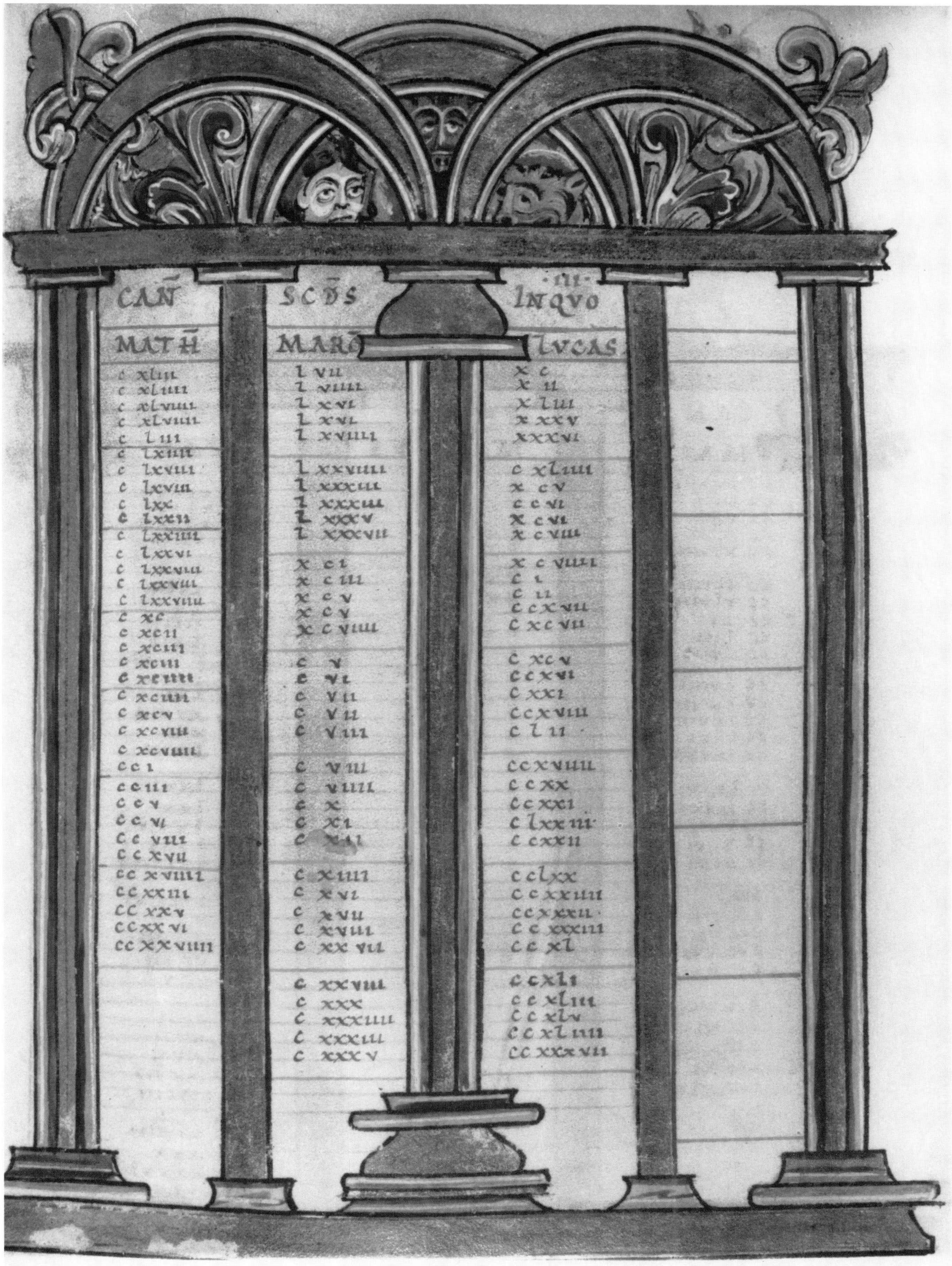

8.4 Hannover, Kestner-Museum WM XXI[a], 36, f. 11[r]

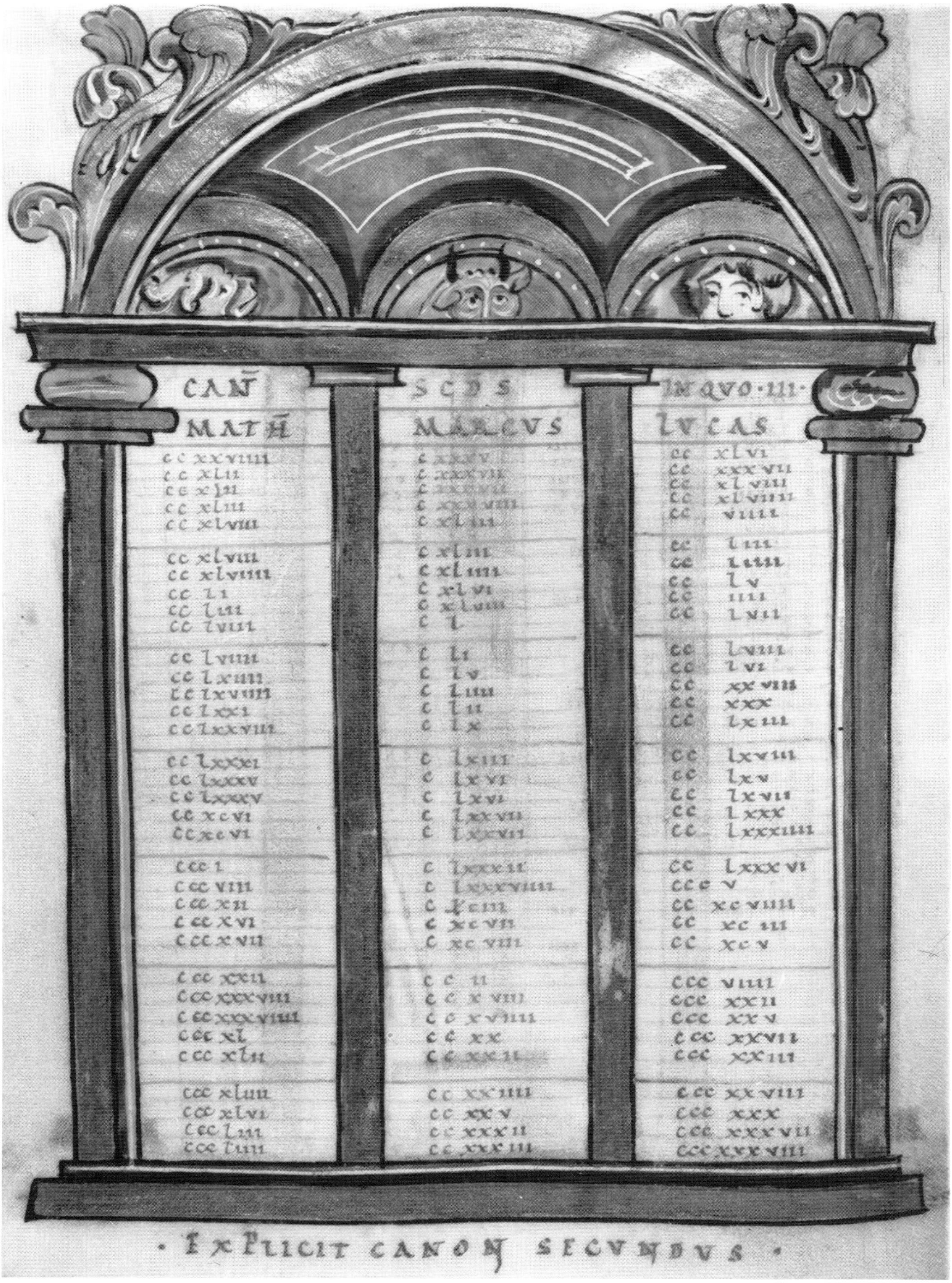

8.5 Hannover, Kestner-Museum WM XXI[a], 36, f. 11[v]

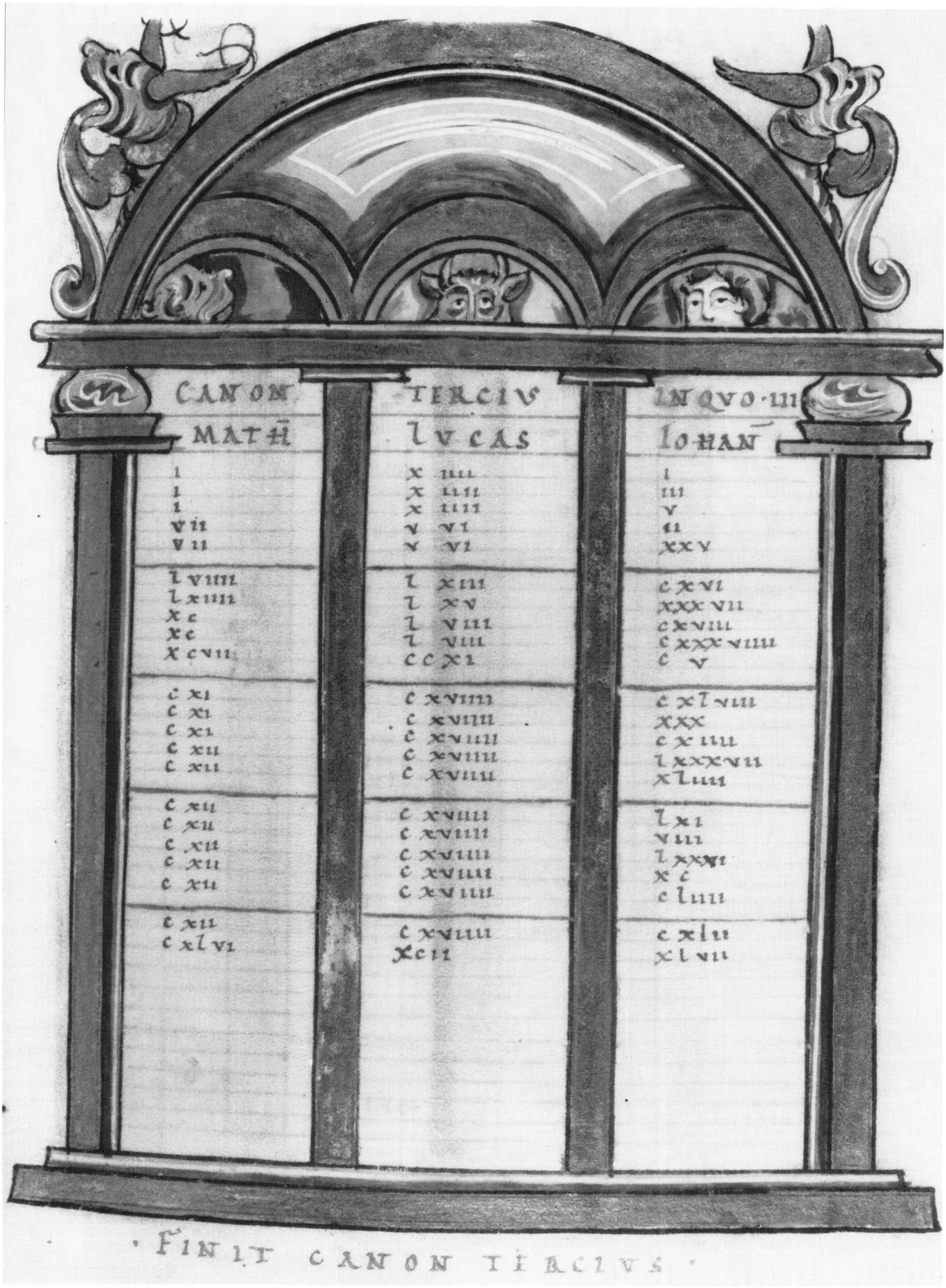

8.6 Hannover, Kestner-Museum WM XXI[a], 36, f. 12[r]

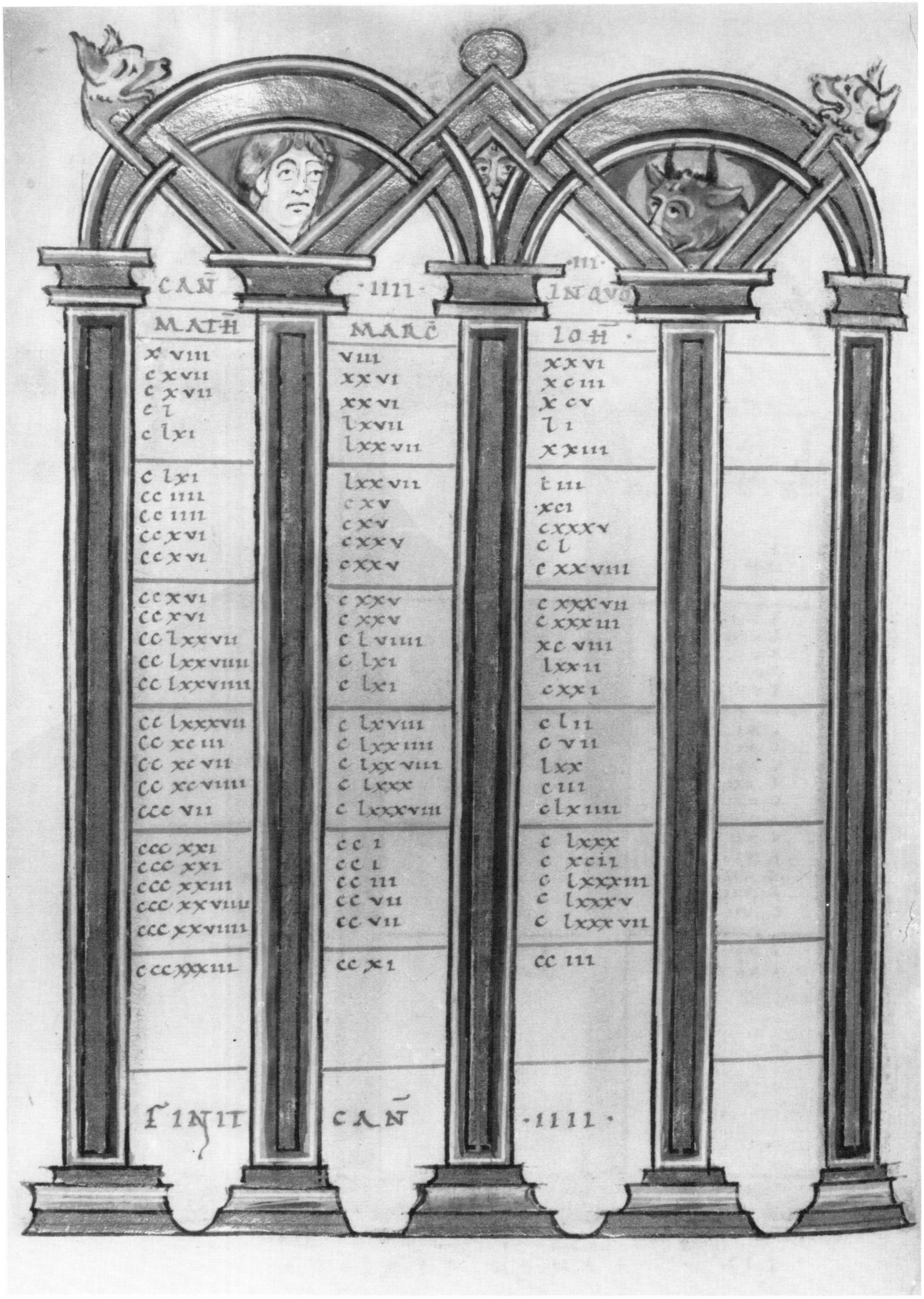

8.7 Hannover, Kestner-Museum WM XXI[a], 36, f. 12[v]

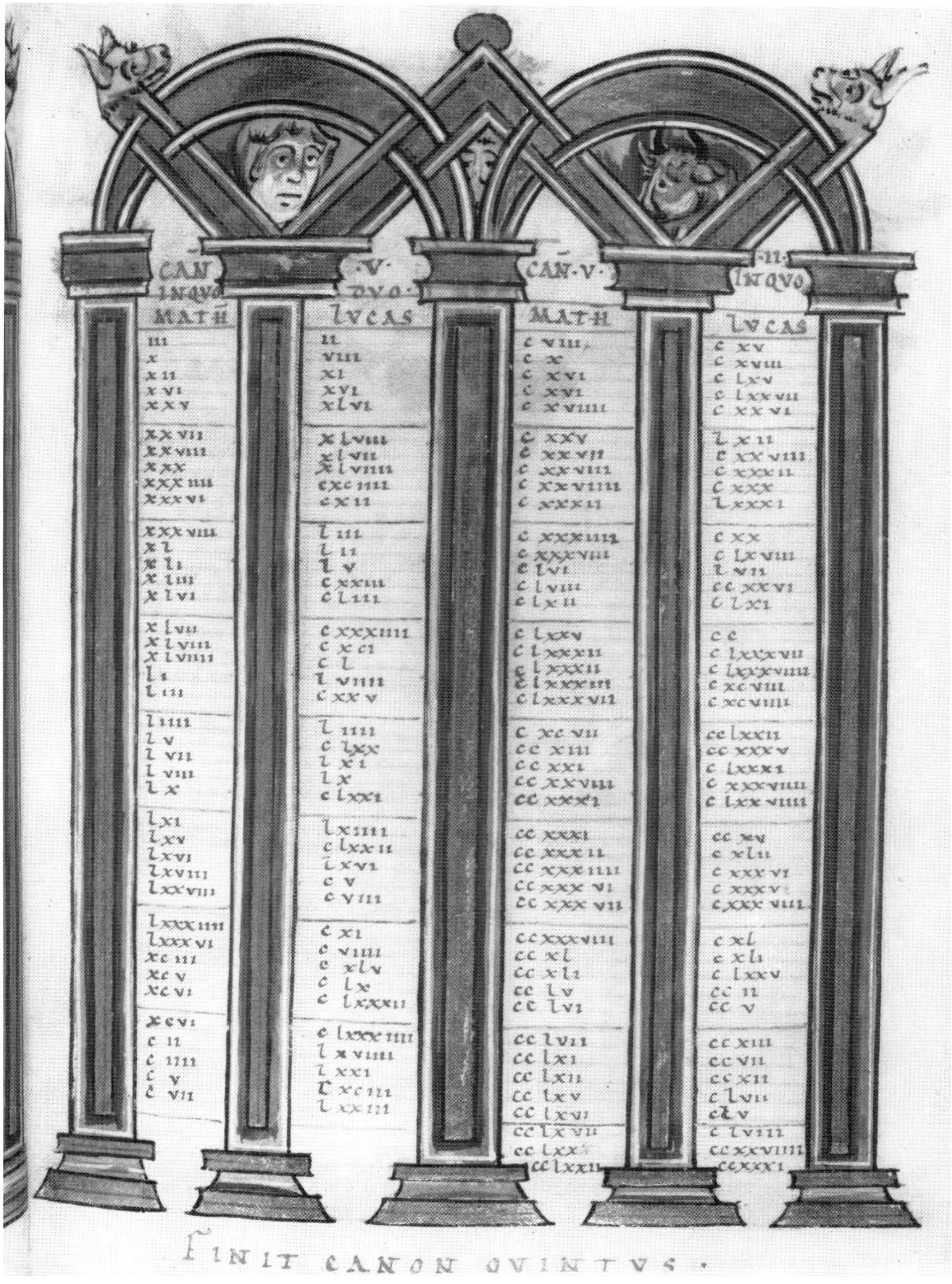

8.8 Hannover, Kestner-Museum WM XXI[a], 36, f. 13[r]

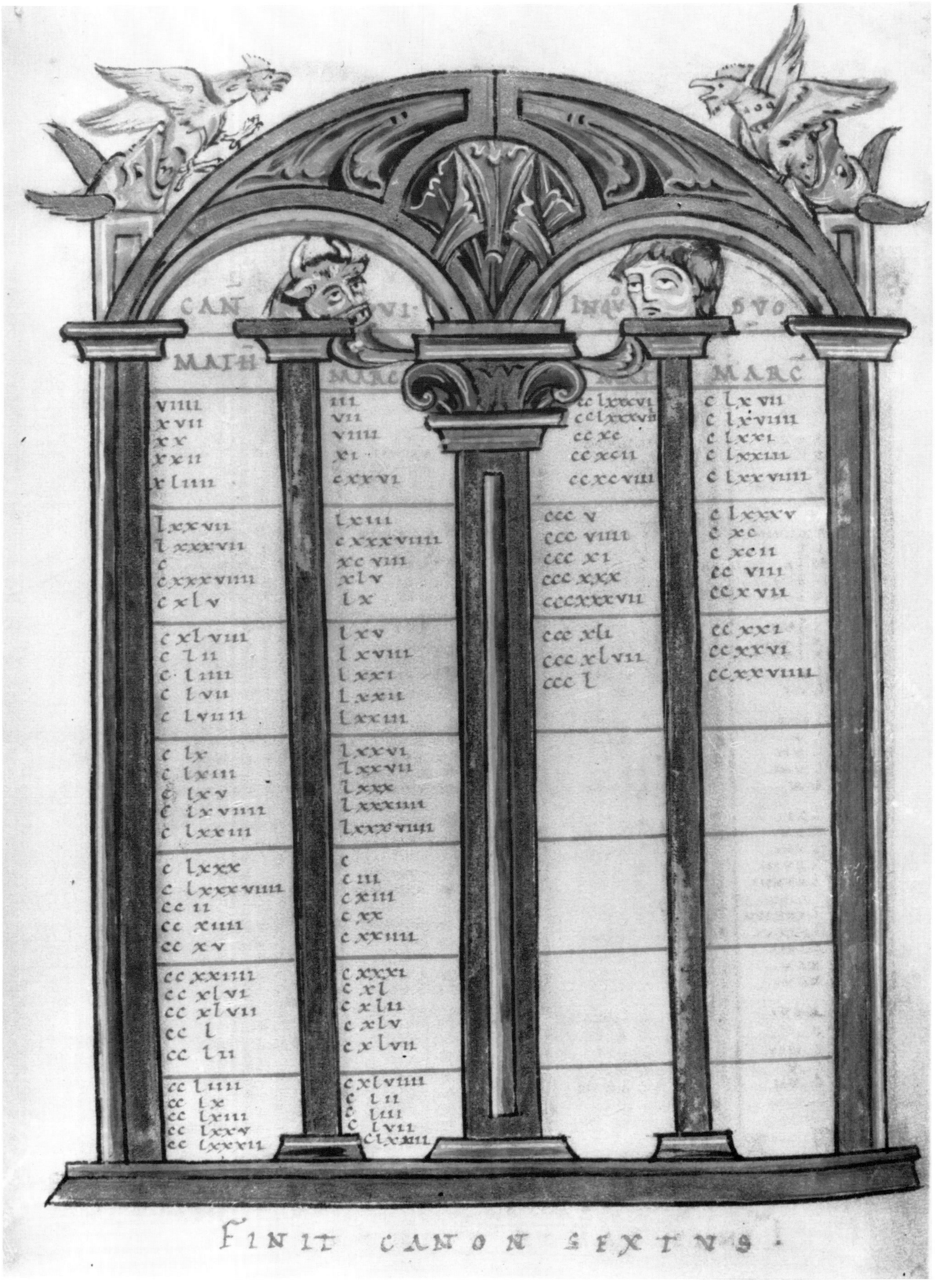

8.9 Hannover, Kestner-Museum WM XXI[a], 36, f. 13[v]

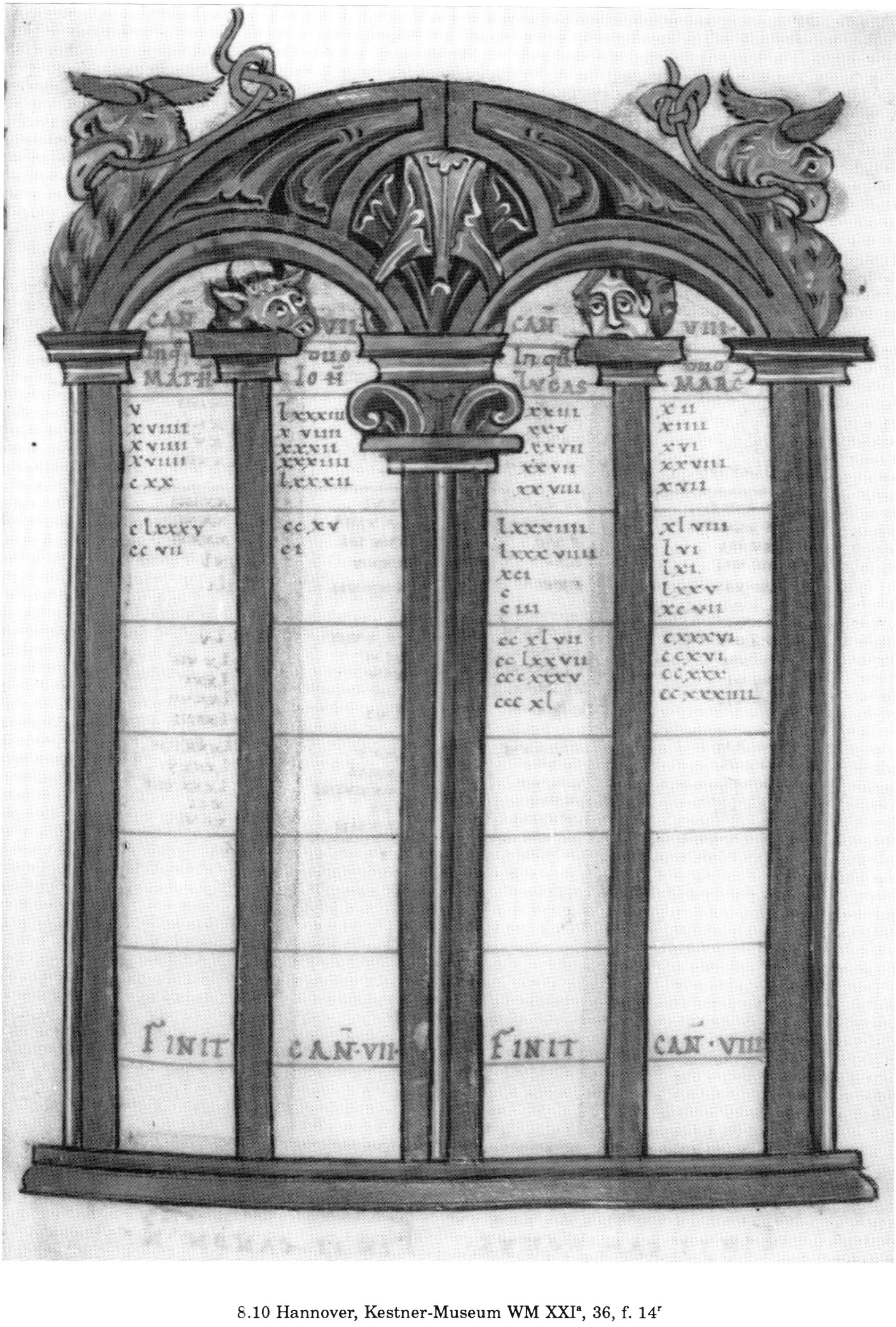

8.10 Hannover, Kestner-Museum WM XXI[a], 36, f. 14[r]

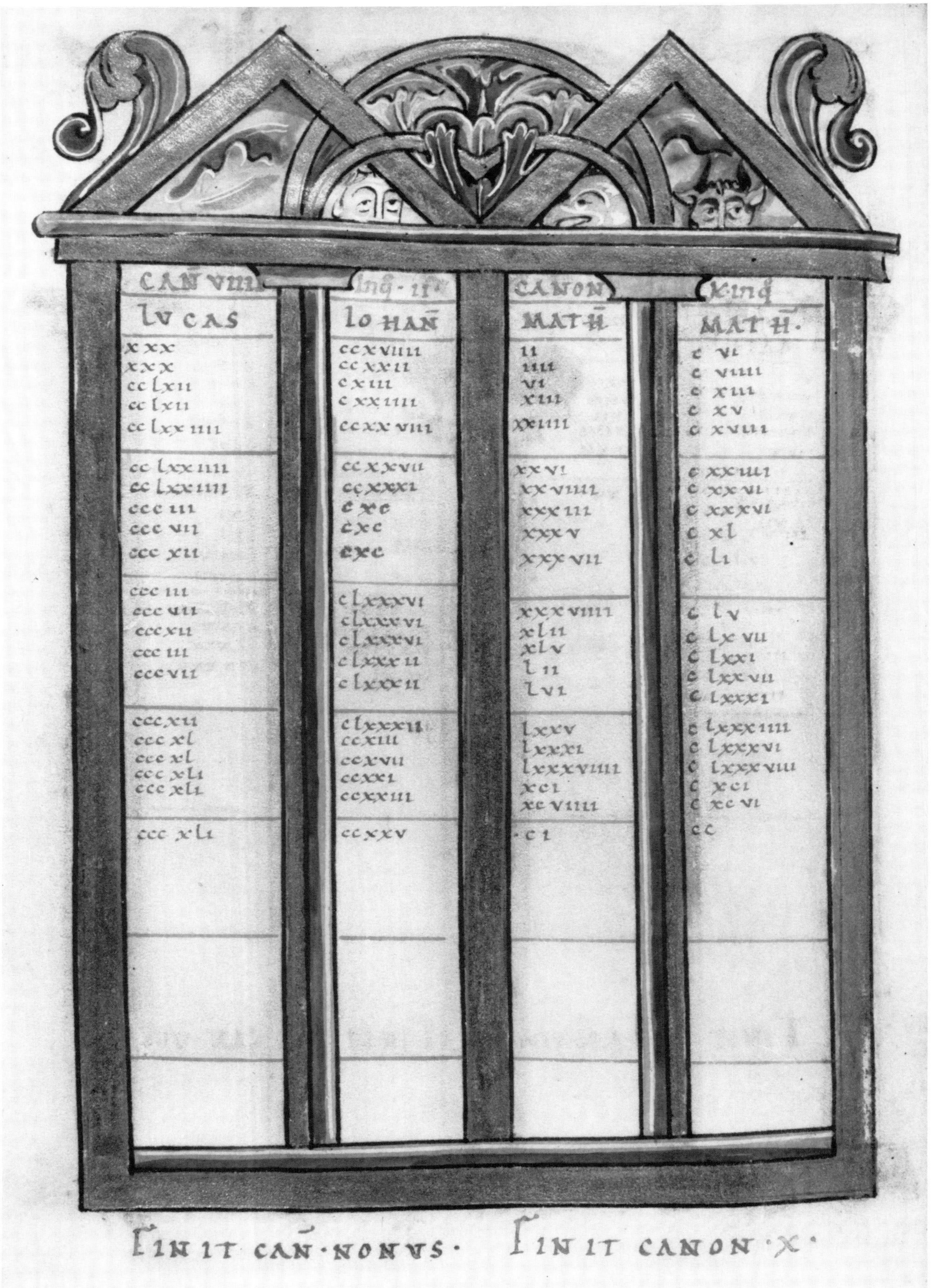

8.11 Hannover, Kestner-Museum WM XXI[a], 36, f. 14[v]

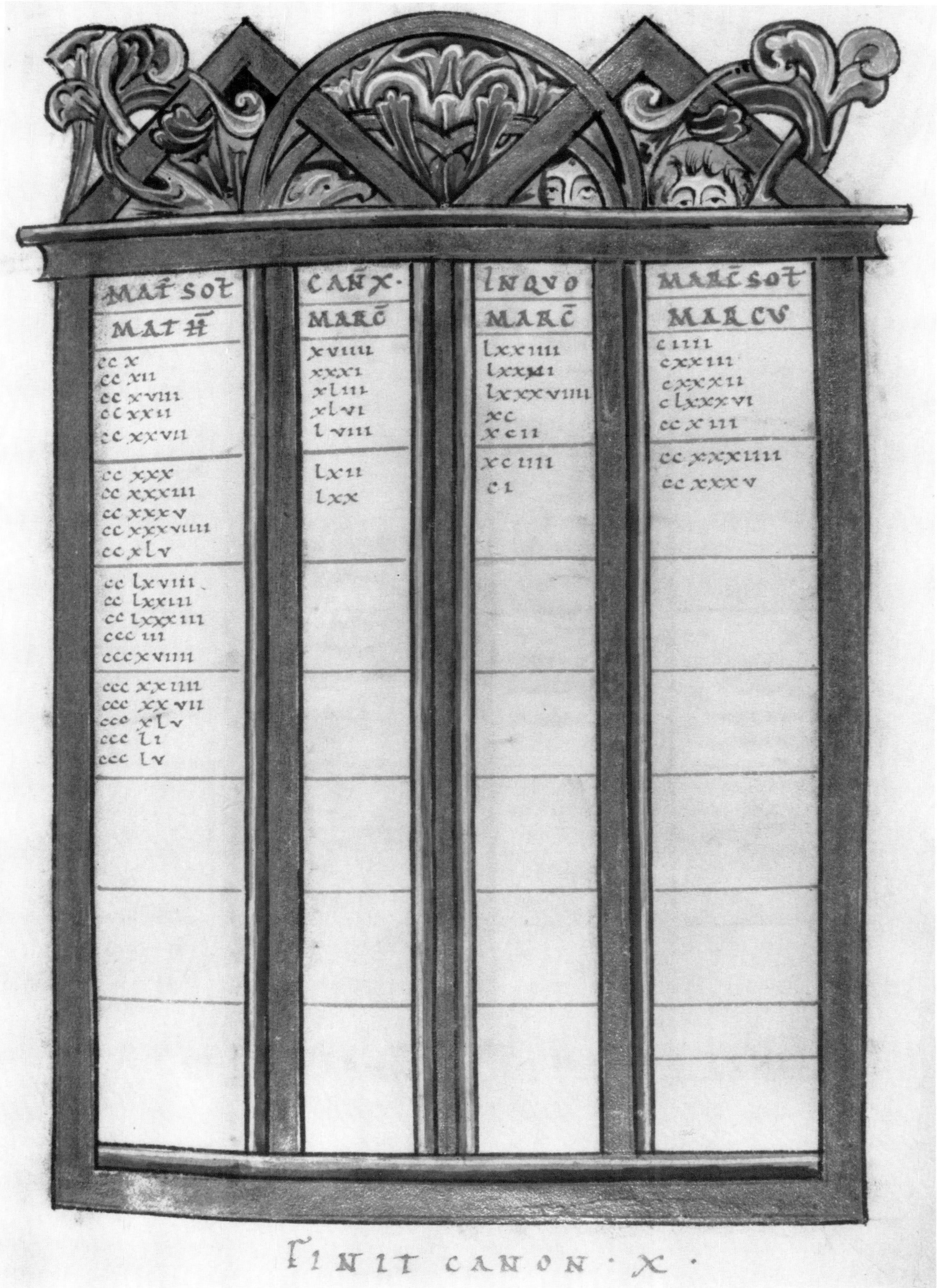

MAT SOT	CAN X.	IN QVO	MARC SOT
MATH	MARC	MARC	MARCVS
cc x	xviiii	lxxiiii	ciiii
cc xii	xxxi	lxxvi	cxxiii
cc xviii	xliii	lxxxviiii	cxxxii
cc xxii	xlvi	xc	clxxxvi
cc xxvii	l viii	xcii	cc xiii
cc xxx	lxii	xc iiii	cc xxxiiii
cc xxxiii	lxx	ci	cc xxxv
cc xxxv			
cc xxxviiii			
cc xlv			
cc lxviii			
cc lxxiii			
cc lxxxiii			
ccc iii			
ccc xviiii			
ccc xxiiii			
ccc xxvii			
ccc xlv			
ccc li			
ccc lv			

FINIT CANON · X ·

8.12 Hannover, Kestner-Museum WM XXI[a], 36, f. 15[r]

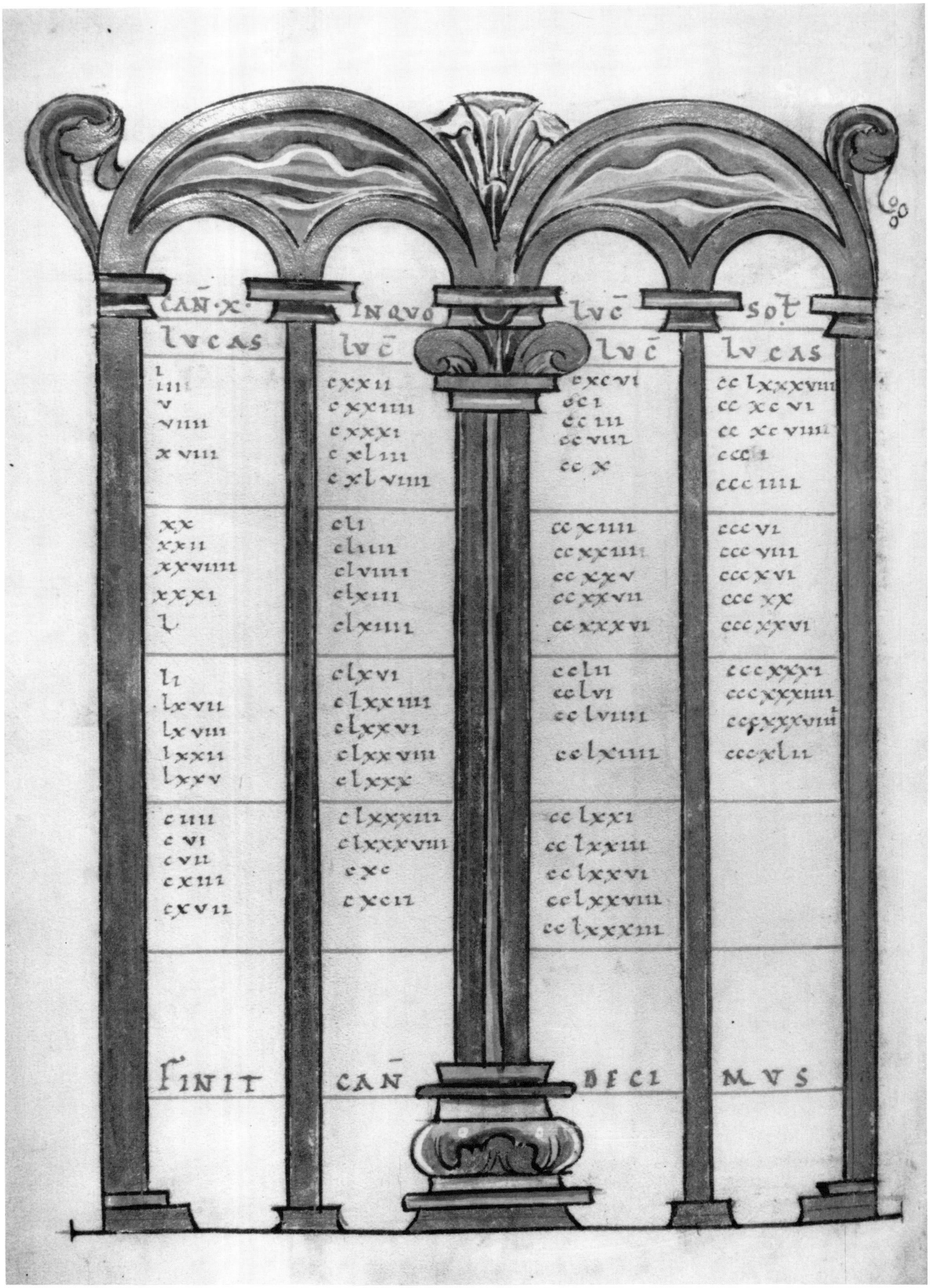

8.13 Hannover, Kestner-Museum WM XXI[a], 36, f. 15[v]

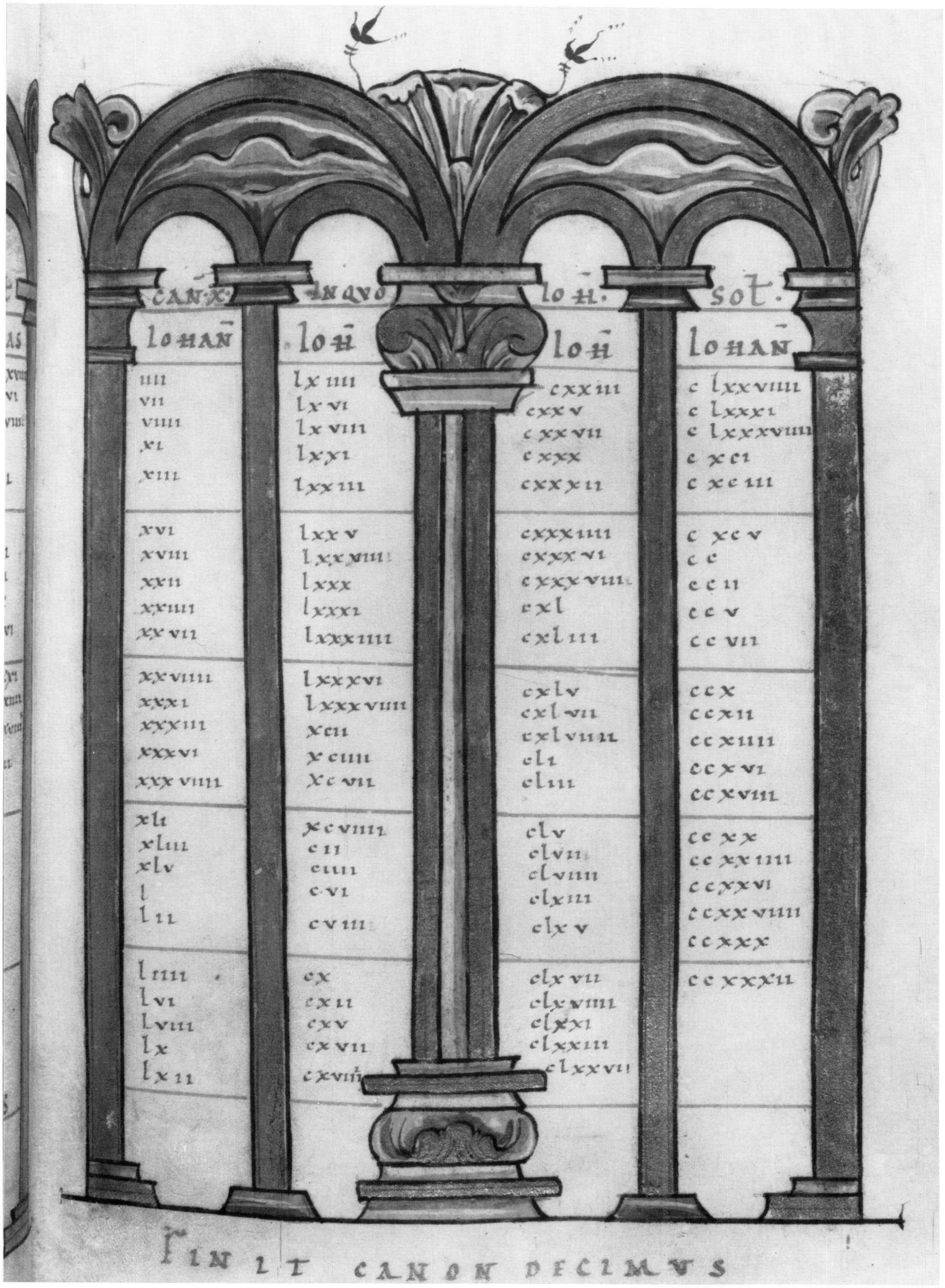

8.14 Hannover, Kestner-Museum WM XXI[a], 36, f. 16[r]

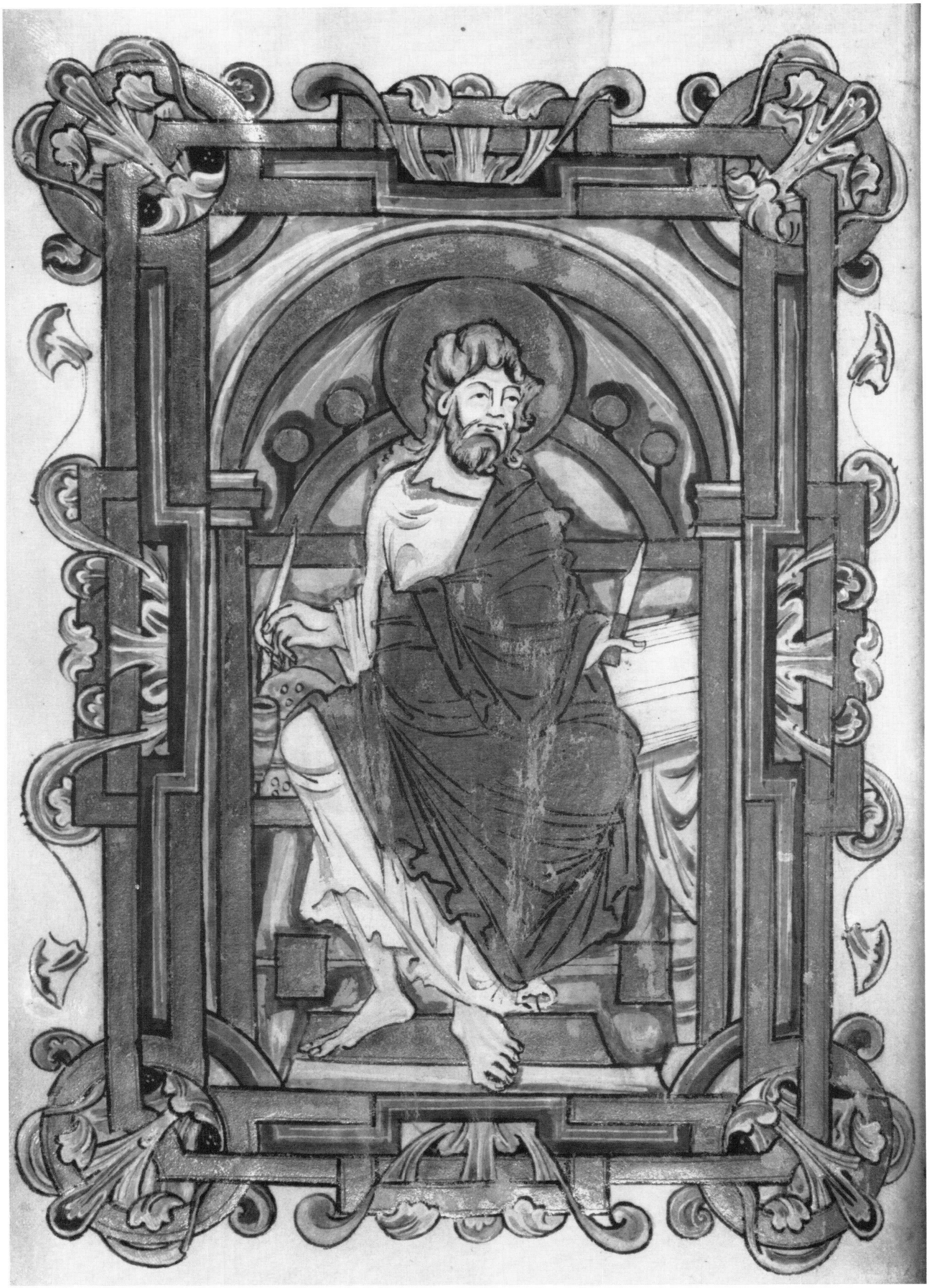

8.15 Hannover, Kestner-Museum WM XXI[a], 36, f. 17[v]

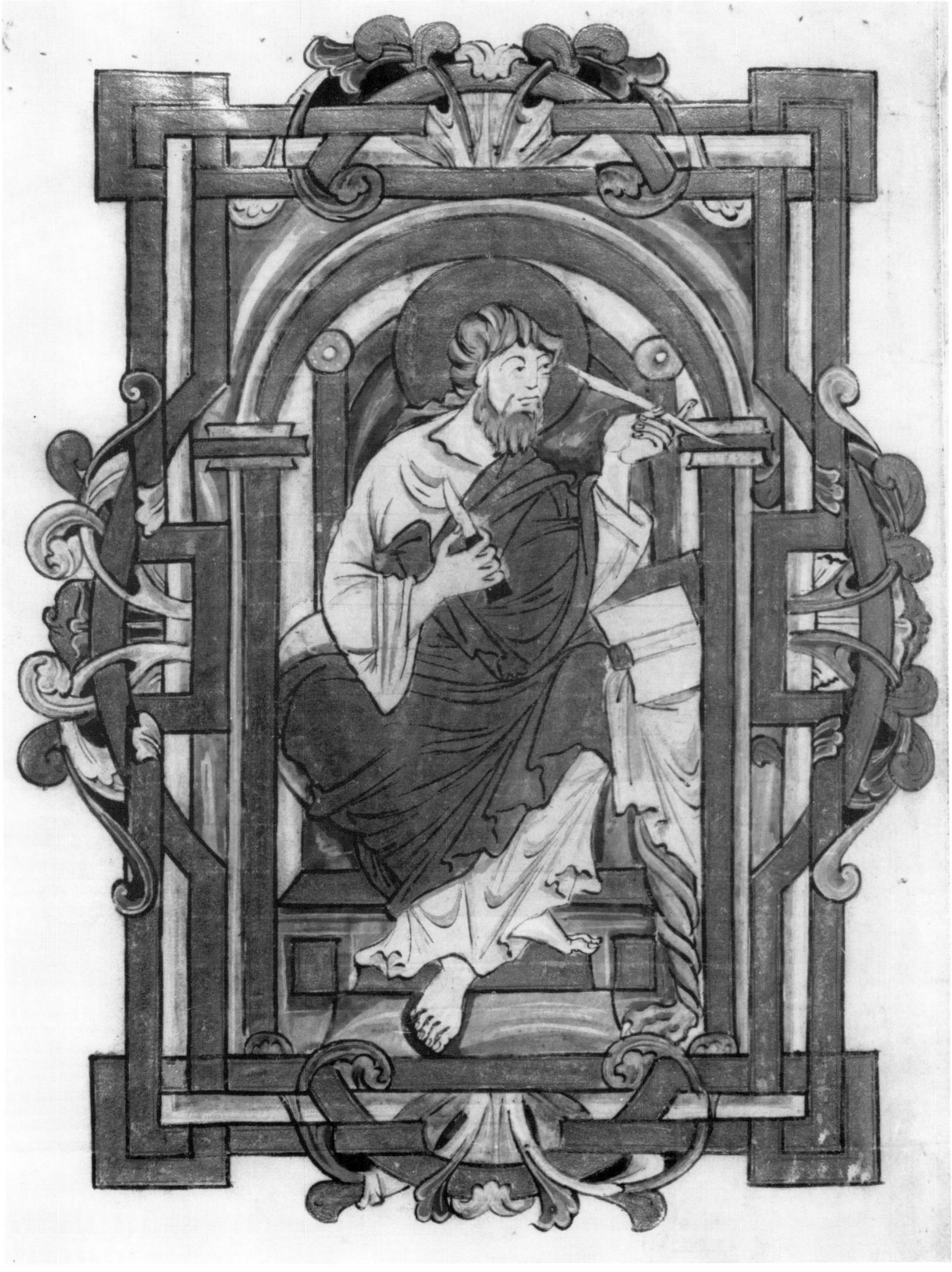

8.16 Hannover, Kestner-Museum WM XXI[a], 36, f. 65[v]

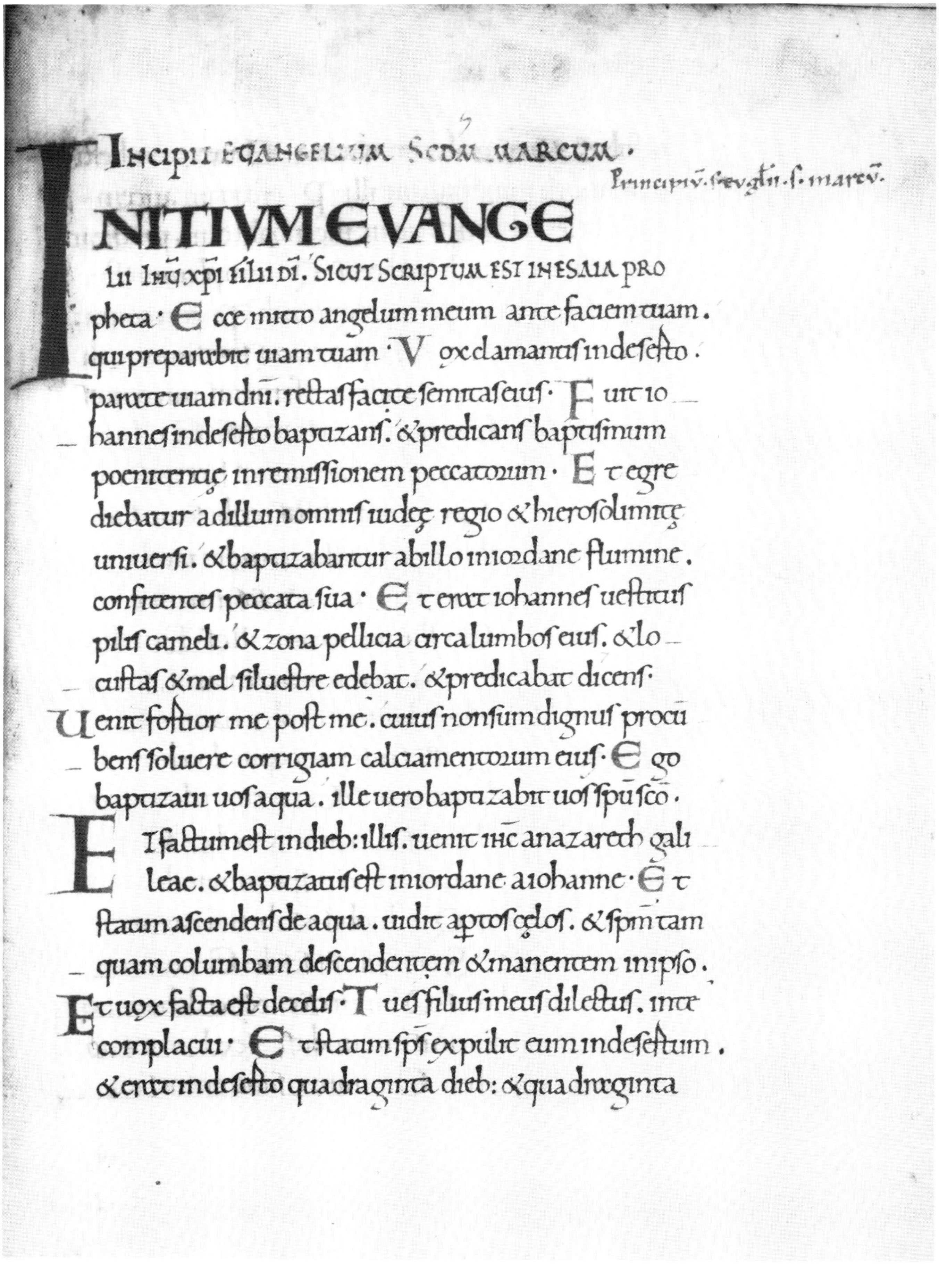

INCIPIT EVANGELIUM SCDM MARCUM.
INITIUM EVANGE
LII IHU XPI FILII DI. SICUT SCRIPTUM EST IN ESAIA PRO
pheta. Ecce mitto angelum meum ante faciem tuam.
qui preparabit uiam tuam. Vox clamantis in deserto.
parate uiam dni. rectas facite semitas eius. Fuit io
hannes in deserto baptizans. & predicans baptismum
poenitentiae in remissionem peccatorum. Et egre
diebatur ad illum omnis iudeae regio & hierosolimitae
uniuersi. & baptizabantur ab illo in iordane flumine.
confitentes peccata sua. Et erat iohannes uestitus
pilis cameli. & zona pellicia circa lumbos eius. & lo
custas & mel siluestre edebat. & predicabat dicens.
Venit fortior me post me. cuius non sum dignus procu
bens soluere corrigiam calciamentorum eius. Ego
baptizaui uos aqua. ille uero baptizabit uos spu sco.
Et factum est in dieb: illis. uenit ihc a nazareth gali
leae. & baptizatus est in iordane a iohanne. Et
statim ascendens de aqua. uidit apertos caelos. & spm tam
quam columbam descendentem & manentem in ipso.
Et uox facta est de caelis. Tu es filius meus dilectus. in te
complacui. Et statim sps expulit eum in desertum.
& erat in deserto quadraginta dieb: & quadraginta

8.17 Hannover, Kestner-Museum WM XXI[a], 36, f. 66[r]

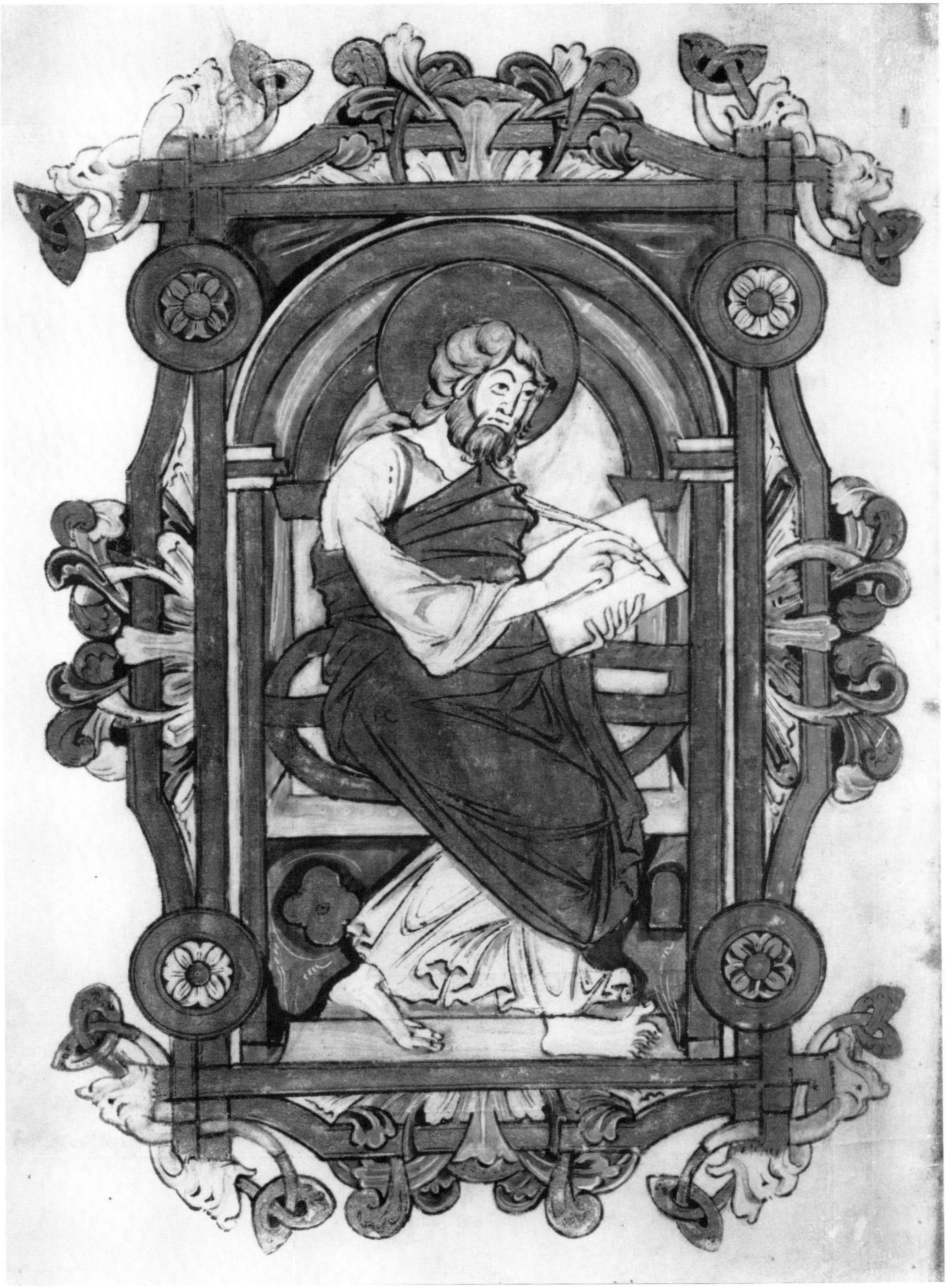

8.18 Hannover, Kestner-Museum WM XXI[a], 36, f. 96[v]

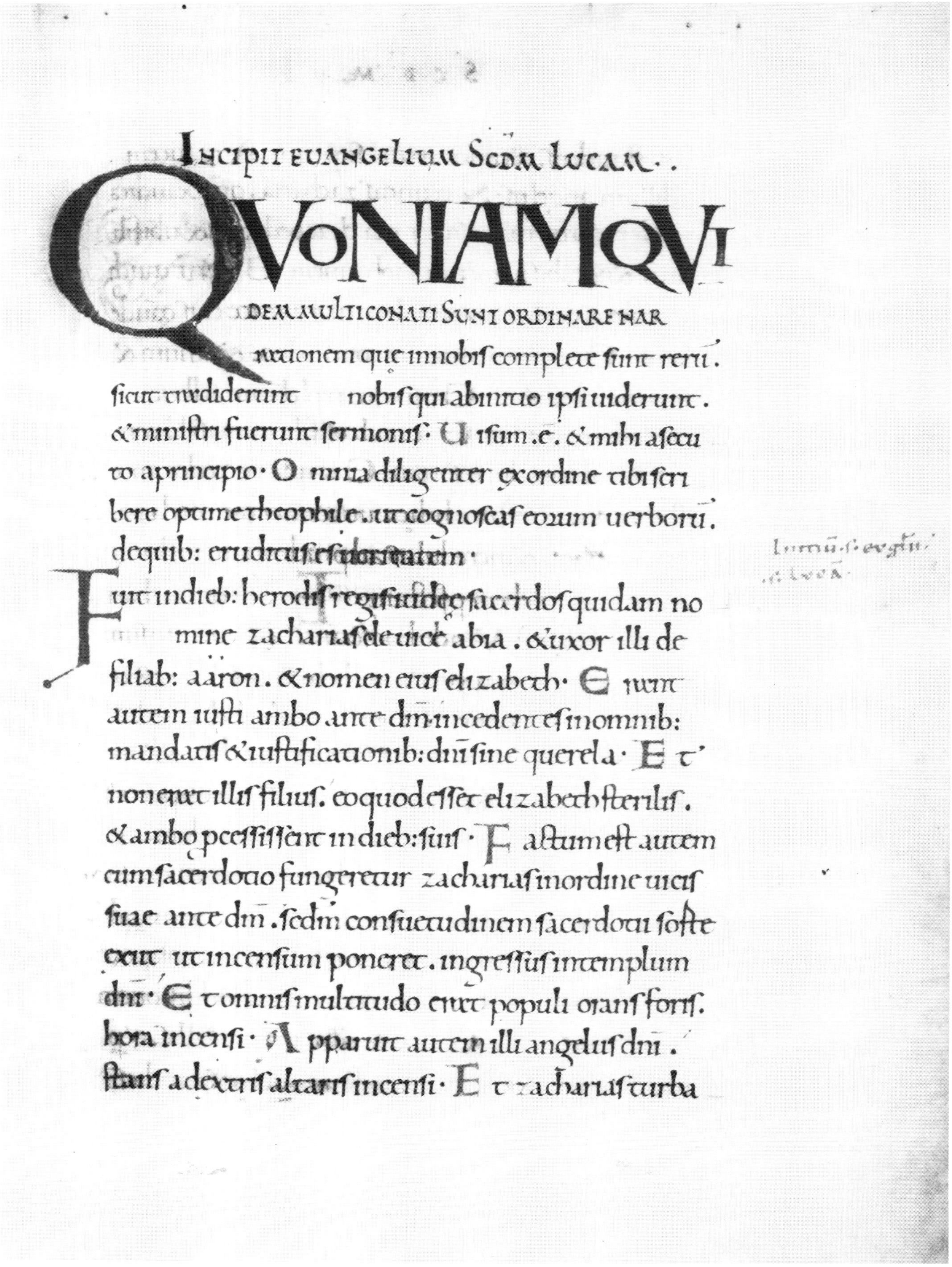

INCIPIT EUANGELIUM SCDM LUCAM..

QUONIAM QUI
DEM MULTI CONATI SUNT ORDINARE NAR
rationem quę in nobis complete sunt rerum.
sicut tradiderunt nobis qui ab initio ipsi uiderunt.
& ministri fuerunt sermonis. Uisum .e. & mihi assecu
to a principio. Omnia diligenter ex ordine tibi scri
bere optime theophile. ut cognoscas eorum uerborum.
de quib: eruditus es ueritatem.
Fuit in dieb: herodis regis iudeę sacerdos quidam no
mine zacharias de uice abia. & uxor illi de
filiab: aaron. & nomen eius elizabeth. Erant
autem iusti ambo ante dm incedentes in omnib:
mandatis & iustificationib: dni sine querela. Et
non erat illis filius. eo quod esset elizabeth sterilis.
& ambo pcessissent in dieb: suis. Factum est autem
cum sacerdotio fungeretur zacharias in ordine uicis
suae ante dm. secdm consuetudinem sacerdotii sorte
exiit ut incensum poneret. ingressus in templum
dni. Et omnis multitudo erat populi orans foris.
hora incensi. Apparuit autem illi angelus dni.
stans a dextris altaris incensi. Et zacharias turba

8.19 Hannover, Kestner-Museum WM XXI[a], 36, f. 97[r]

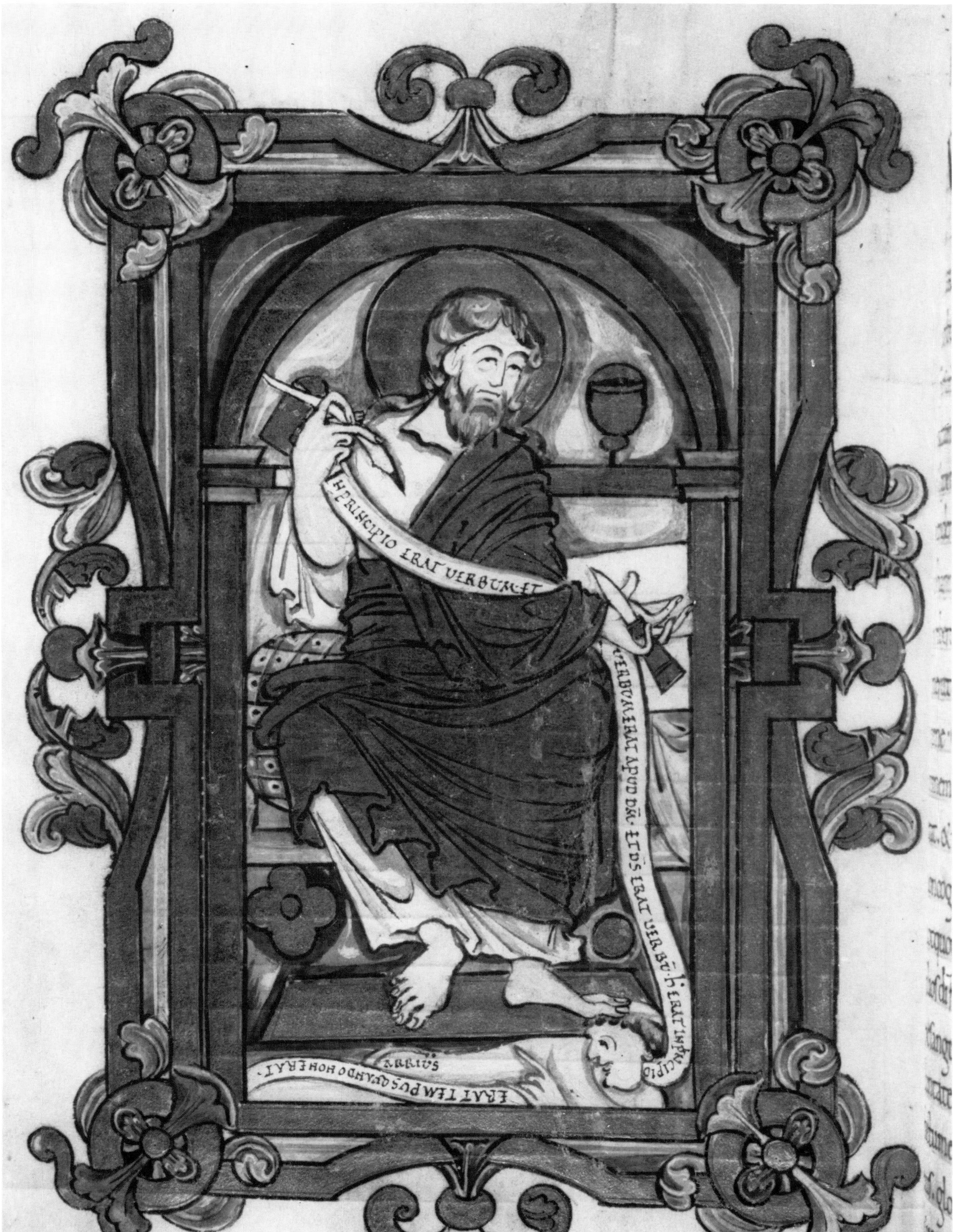

8.20 Hannover, Kestner-Museum WM XXI[a], 36, f. 147[v]

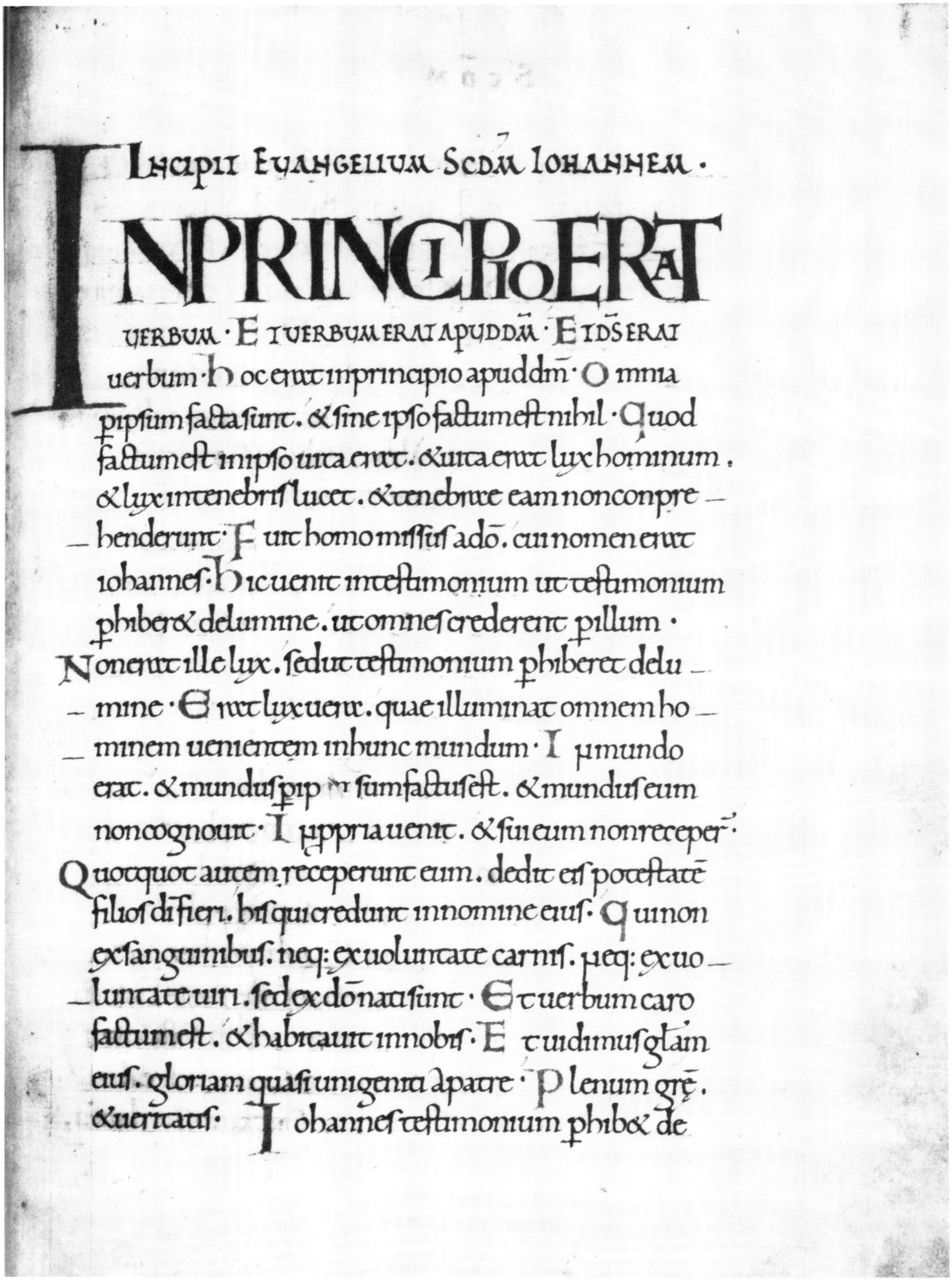

INCIPIT EUANGELIUM SCDM IOHANNEM ·

IN PRINCIPIO ERAT
UERBUM · ET UERBUM ERAT APUD DM · ET DS ERAT
uerbum · hoc erat in principio apud dm · Omnia
p ipsum facta sunt . & sine ipso factum est nihil · Quod
factum est in ipso uita erat . & uita erat lux hominum .
& lux in tenebris lucet . & tenebrae eam non conpre-
-henderunt · Fuit homo missus a do . cui nomen erat
iohannes · Hic uenit in testimonium ut testimonium
phiberet de lumine . ut omnes crederent p illum ·
Non erat ille lux . sed ut testimonium phiberet delu-
-mine · Erat lux uera . quae illuminat omnem ho-
-minem uenientem in hunc mundum · In mundo
erat . & mundus p ip sum factus est . & mundus eum
non cognouit · In ppria uenit . & sui eum non receper ·
Quotquot autem receperunt eum . dedit eis potestate
filios di fieri . his qui credunt in nomine eius · Qui non
ex sanguinibus . neq; ex uoluntate carnis . neq; ex uo-
-luntate uiri . sed ex do nati sunt · Et uerbum caro
factum est . & habitauit in nobis · Et uidimus glam
eius . gloriam quasi unigeniti a patre · Plenum grę .
& ueritatis · Iohannes testimonium phib& de

8.21 Hannover, Kestner-Museum WM XXI[a], 36, f. 148[r]

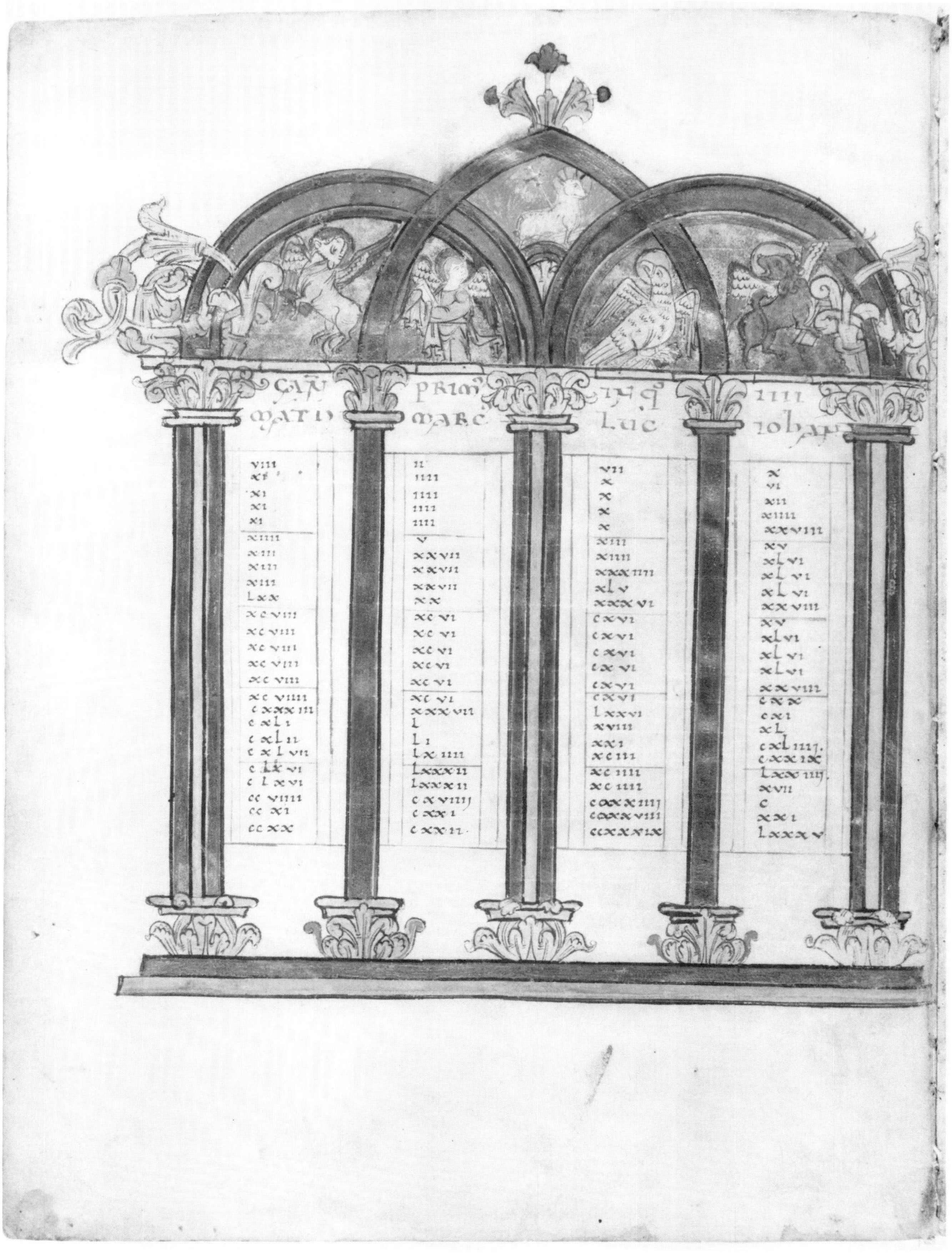

9.1 Cambridge, Pembroke College 301, f. 1v

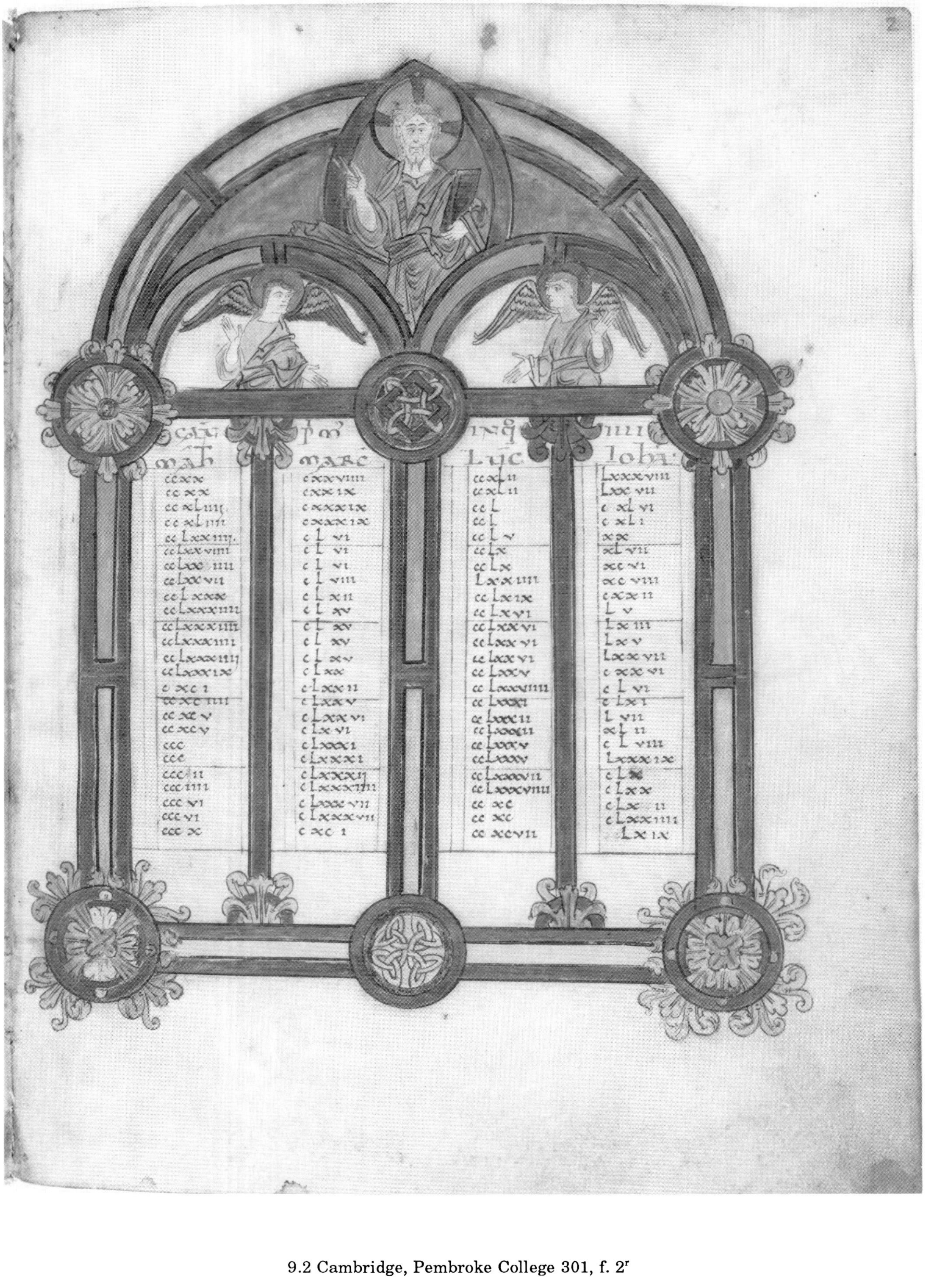

9.2 Cambridge, Pembroke College 301, f. 2r

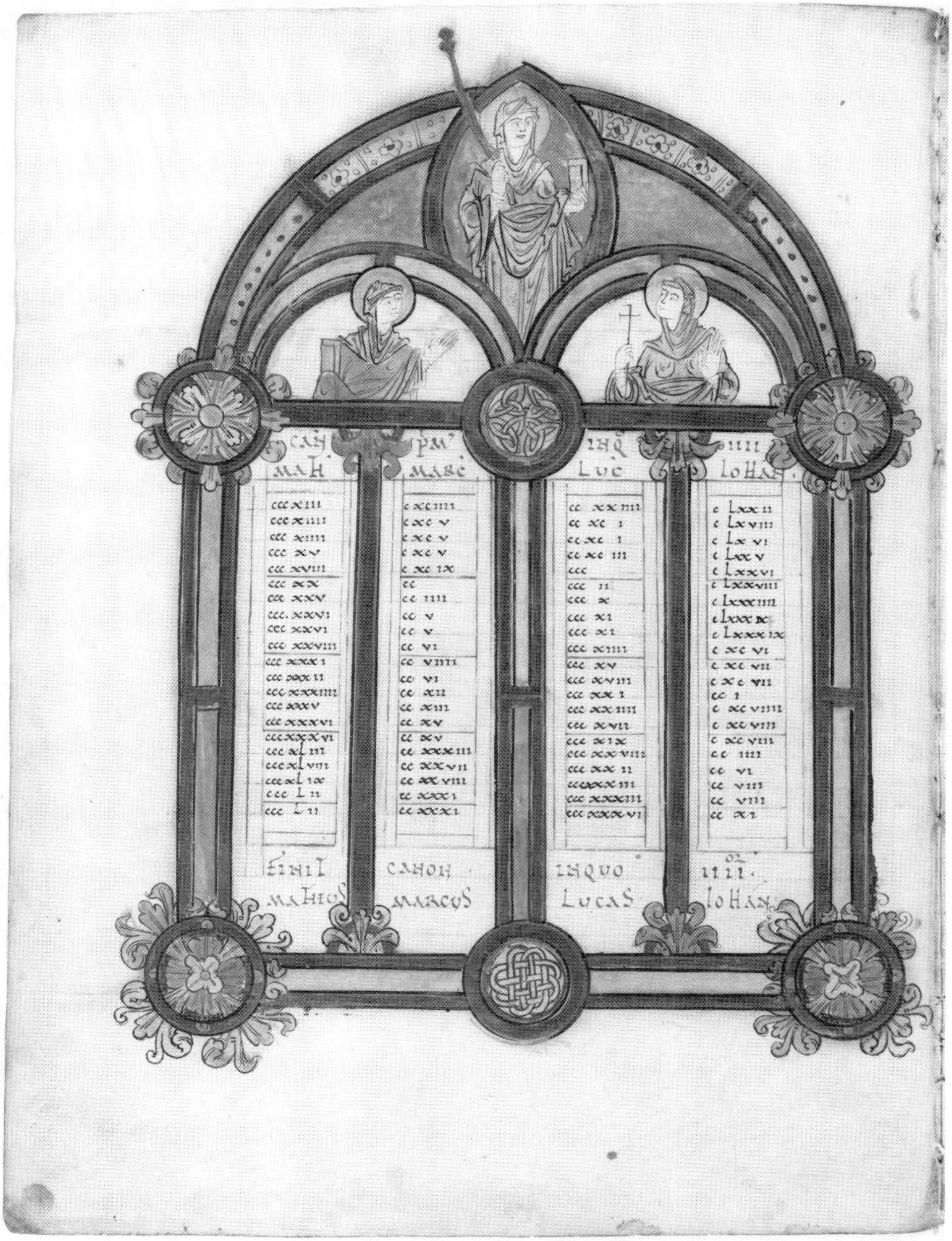

9.3 Cambridge, Pembroke College 301, f. 2ᵛ

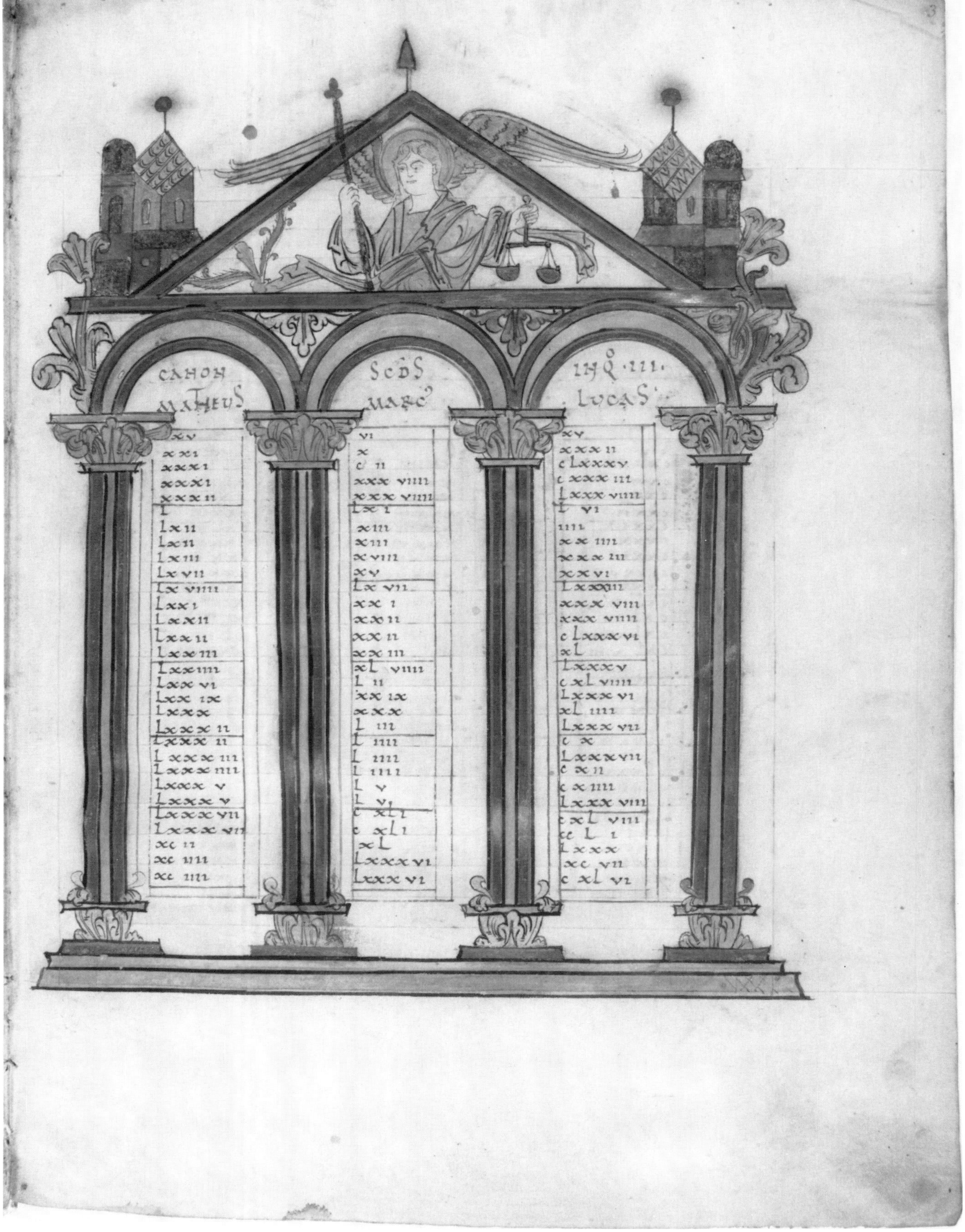

9.4 Cambridge, Pembroke College 301, f. 3r

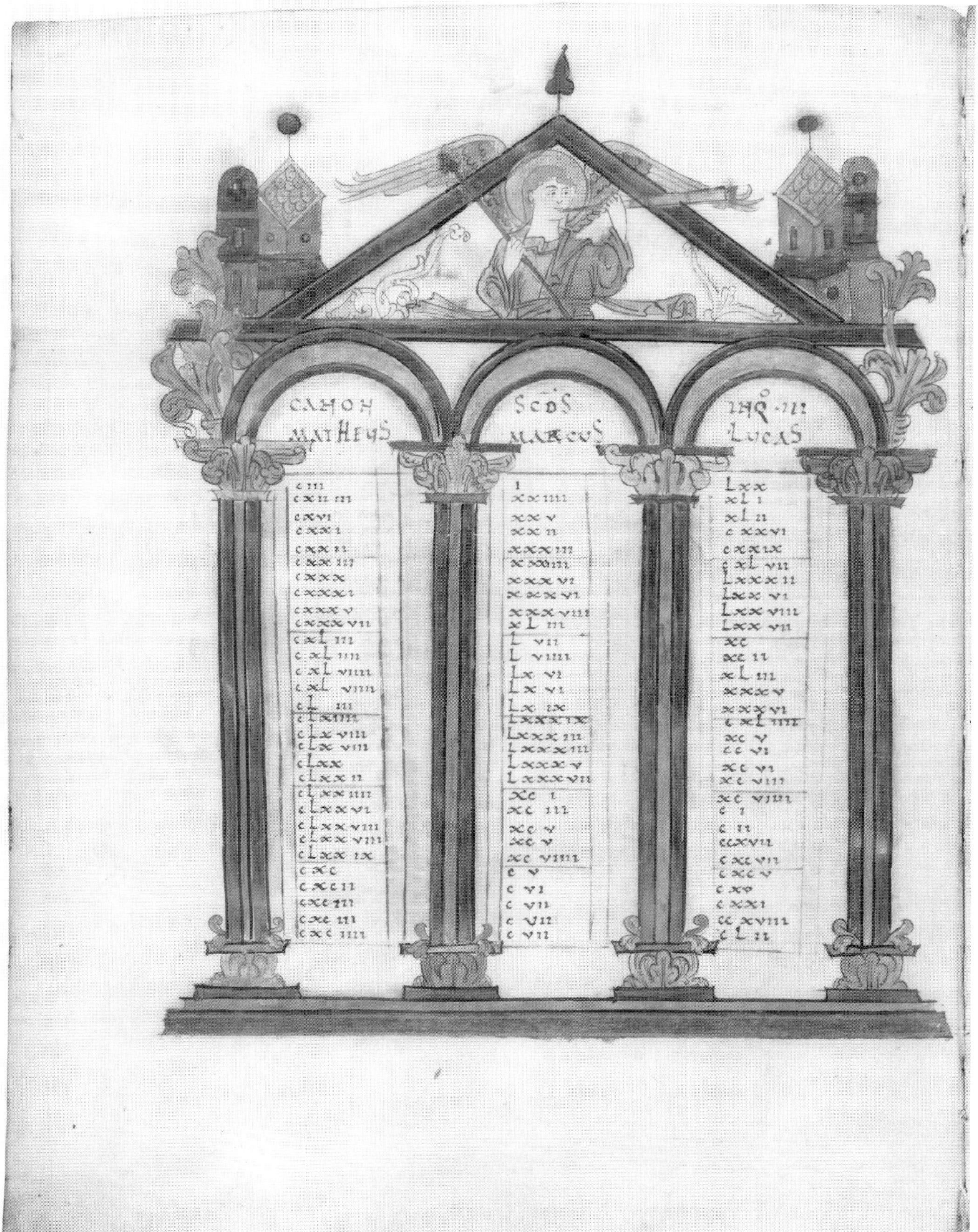

9.5 Cambridge, Pembroke College 301, f. 3v

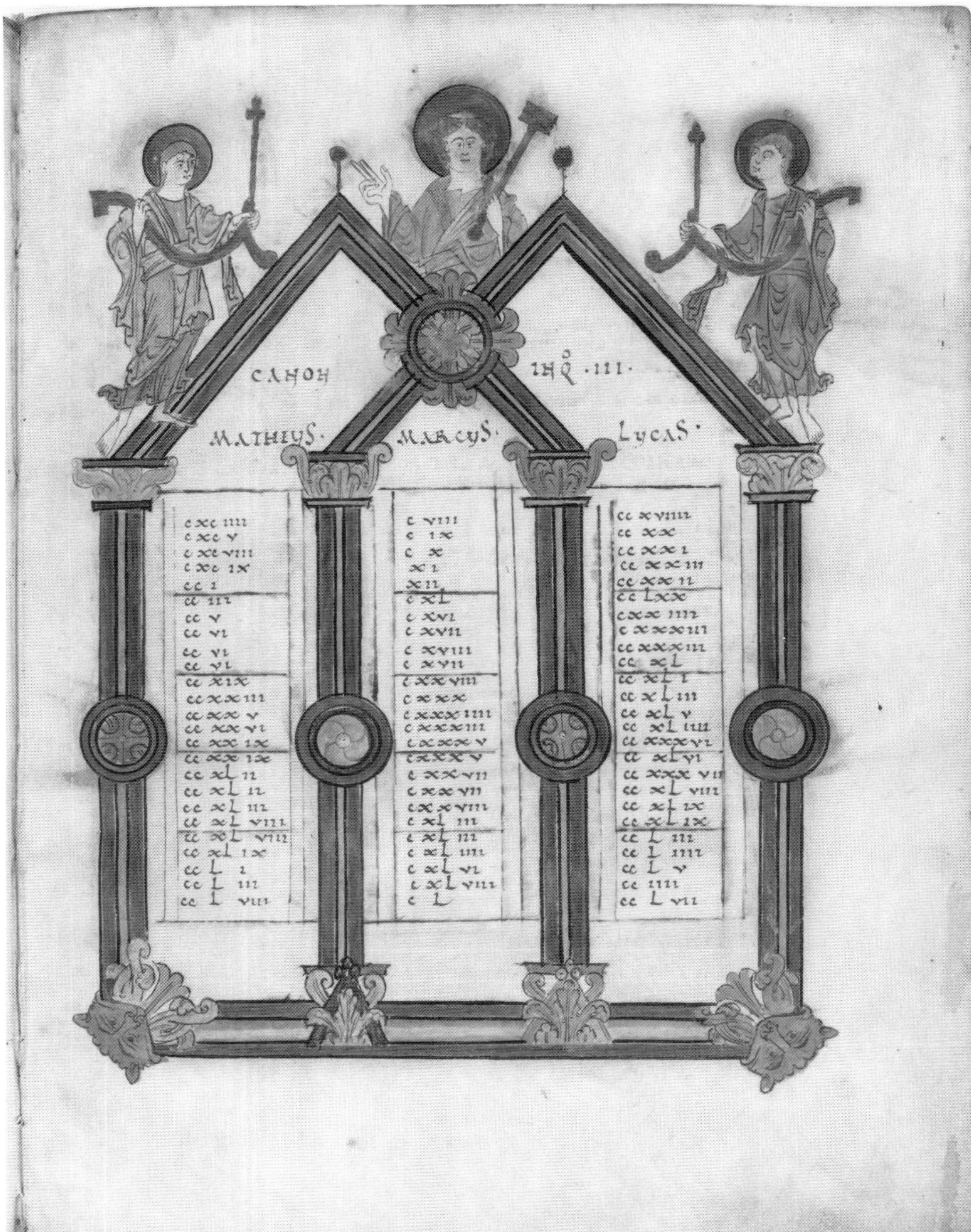

9.6 Cambridge, Pembroke College 301, f. 4r

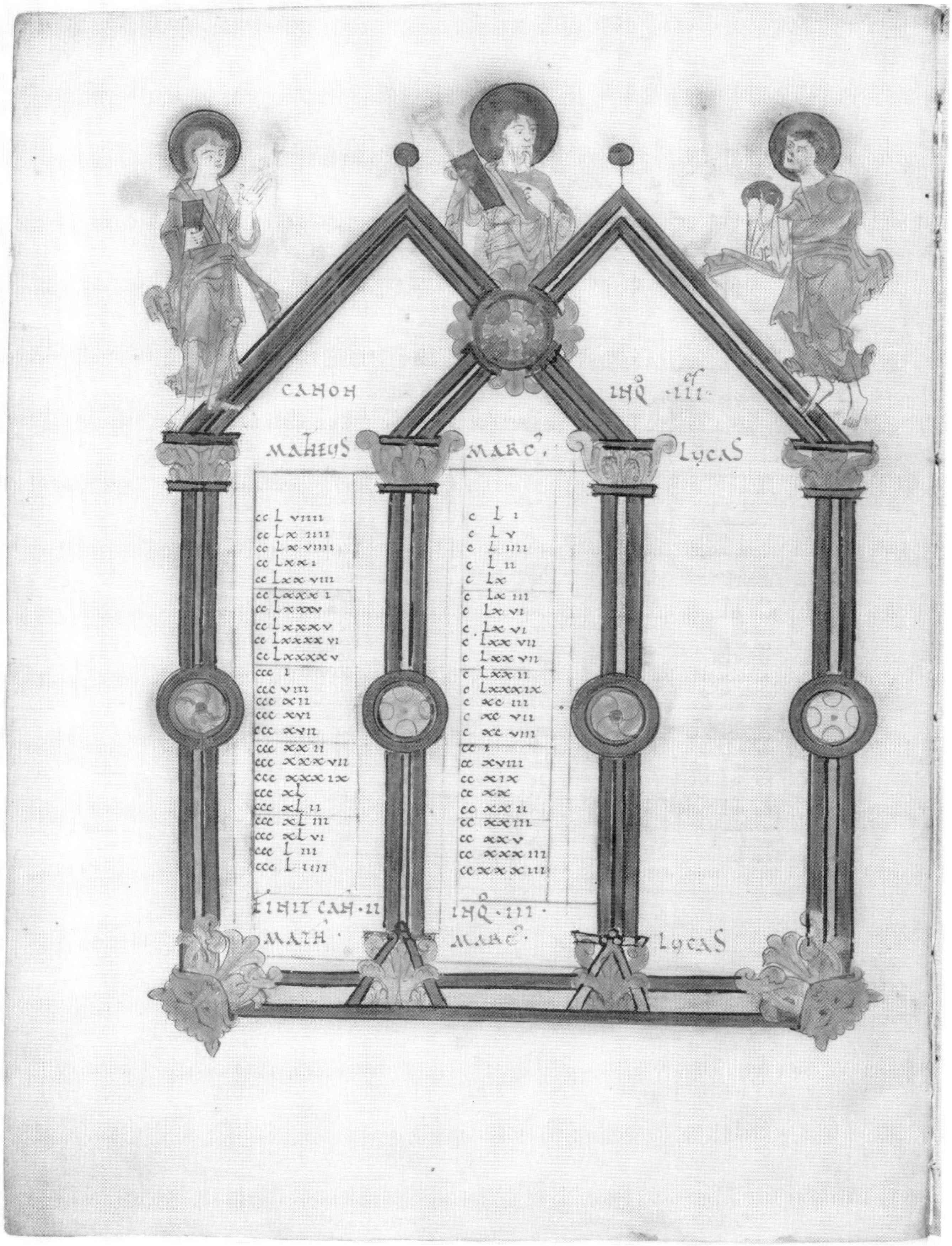

9.7 Cambridge, Pembroke College 301, f. 4v

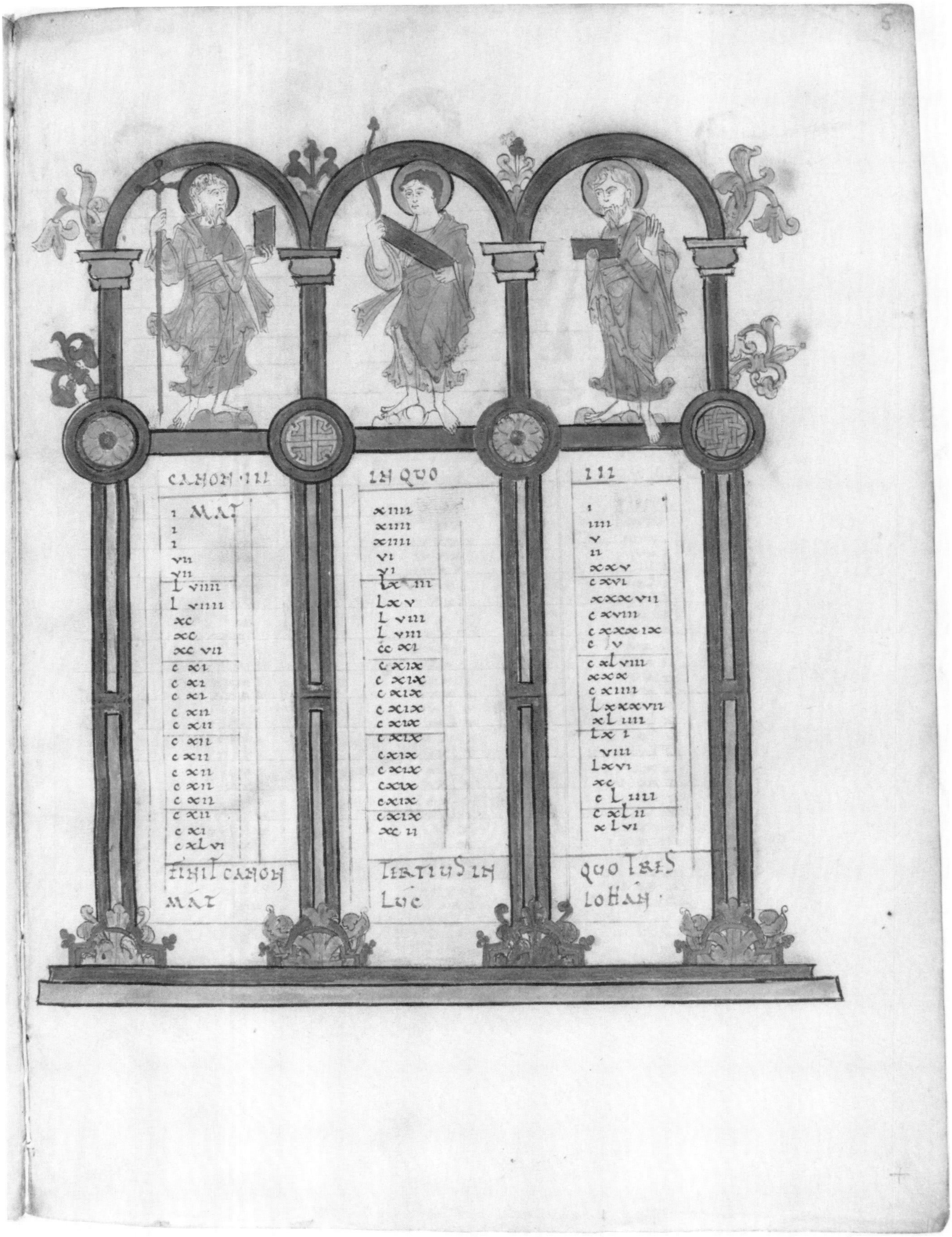

9.8 Cambridge, Pembroke College 301, f. 5r

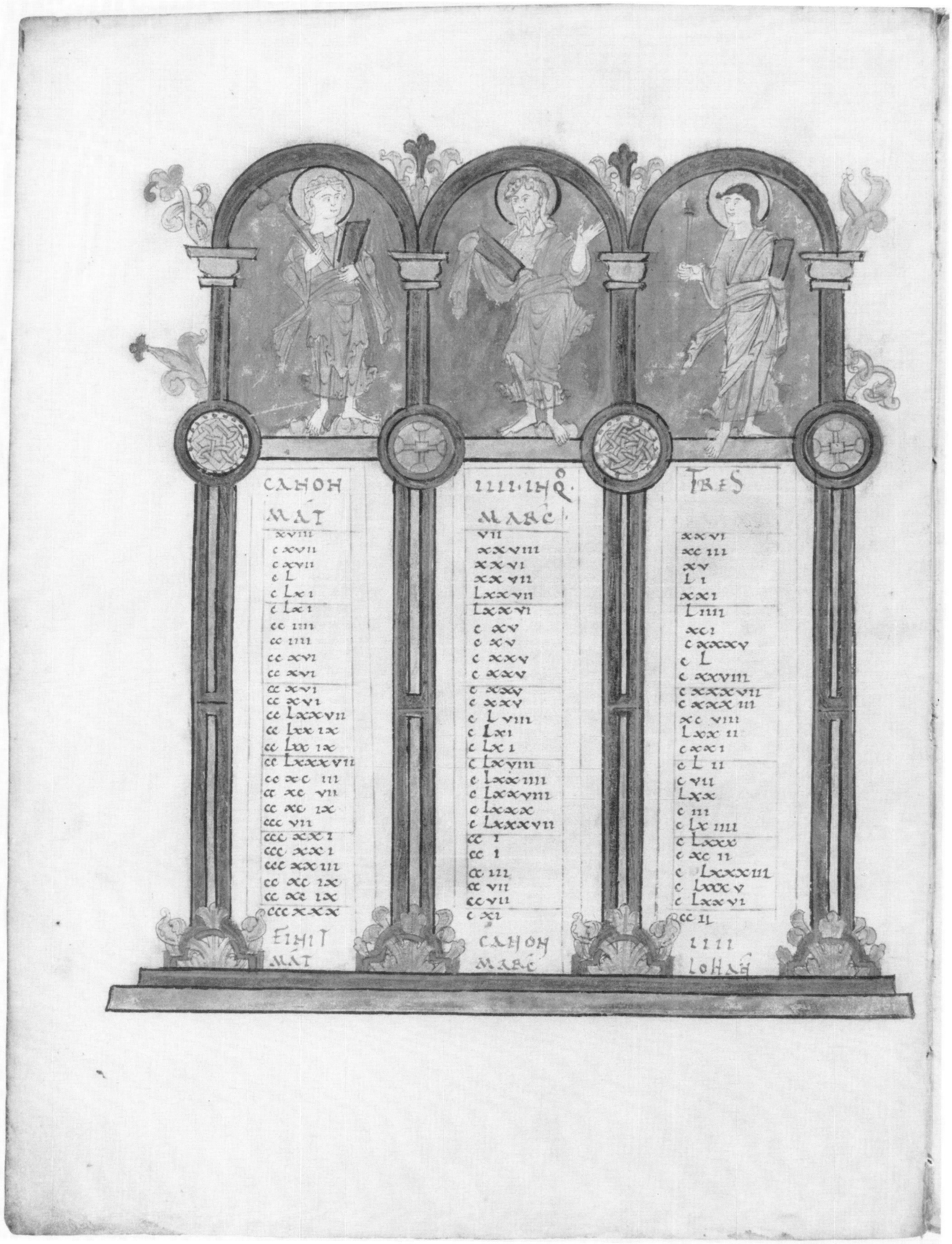

9.9 Cambridge, Pembroke College 301, f. 5v

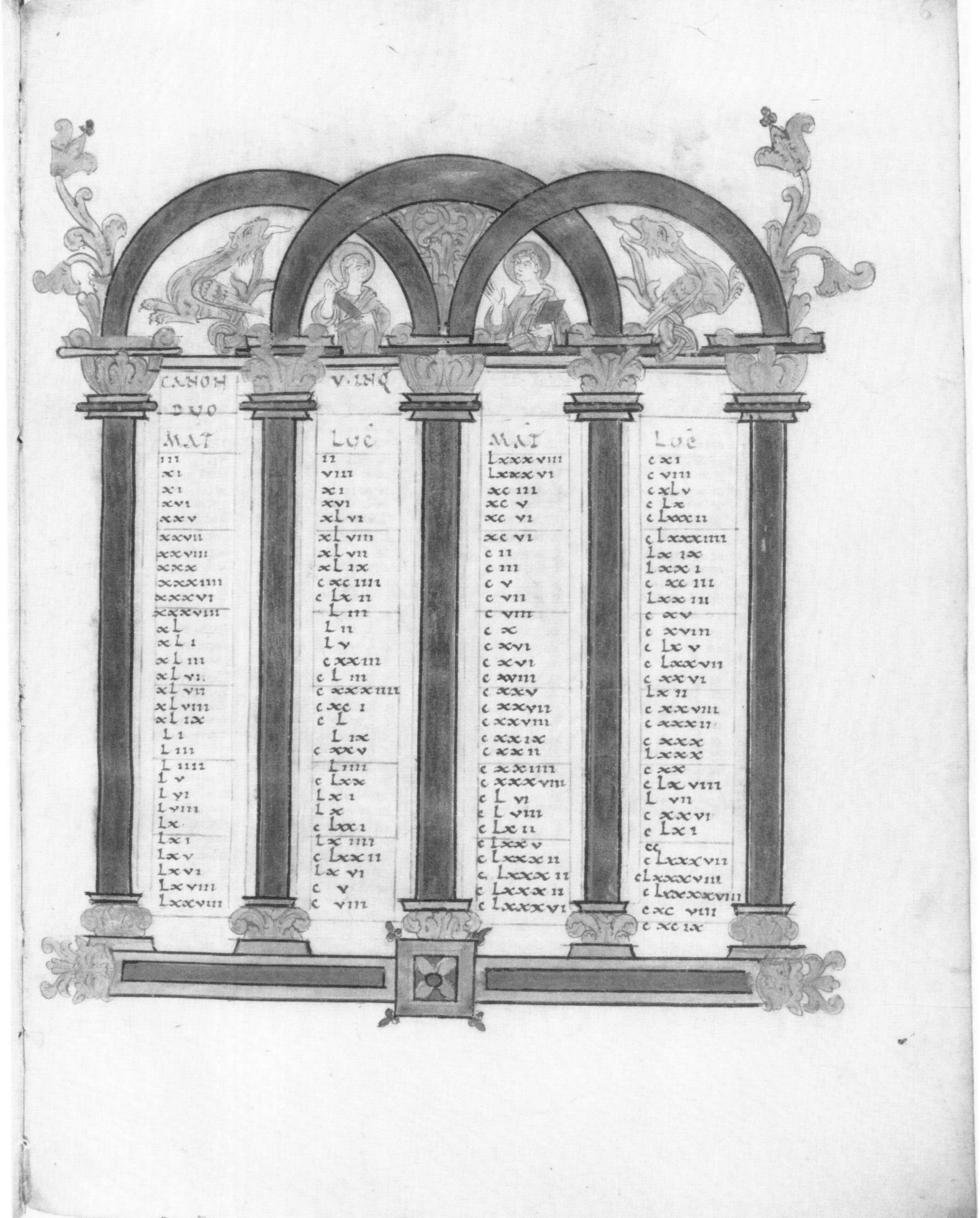

9.10 Cambridge, Pembroke College 301, f. 6r

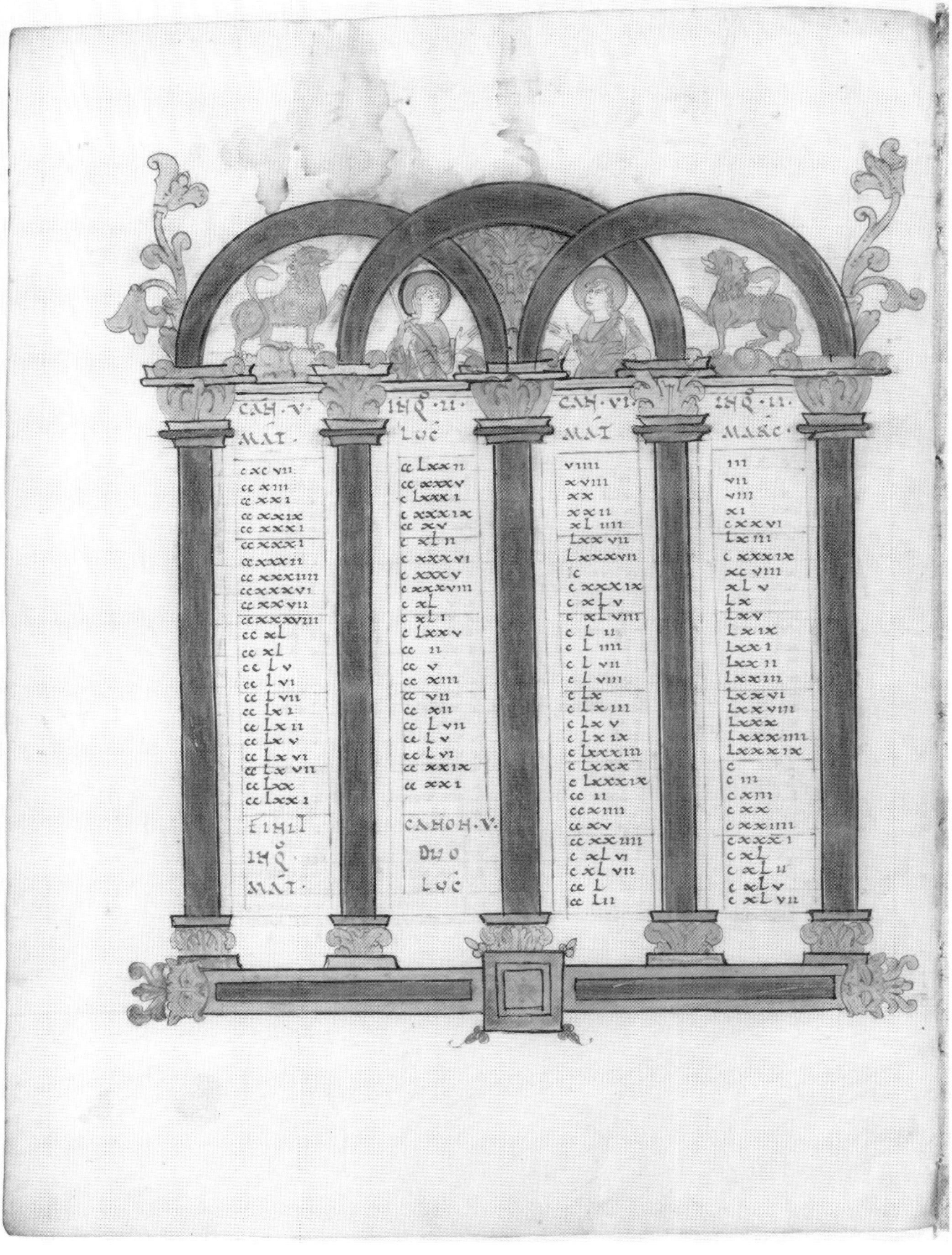

9.11 Cambridge, Pembroke College 301, f. 6v

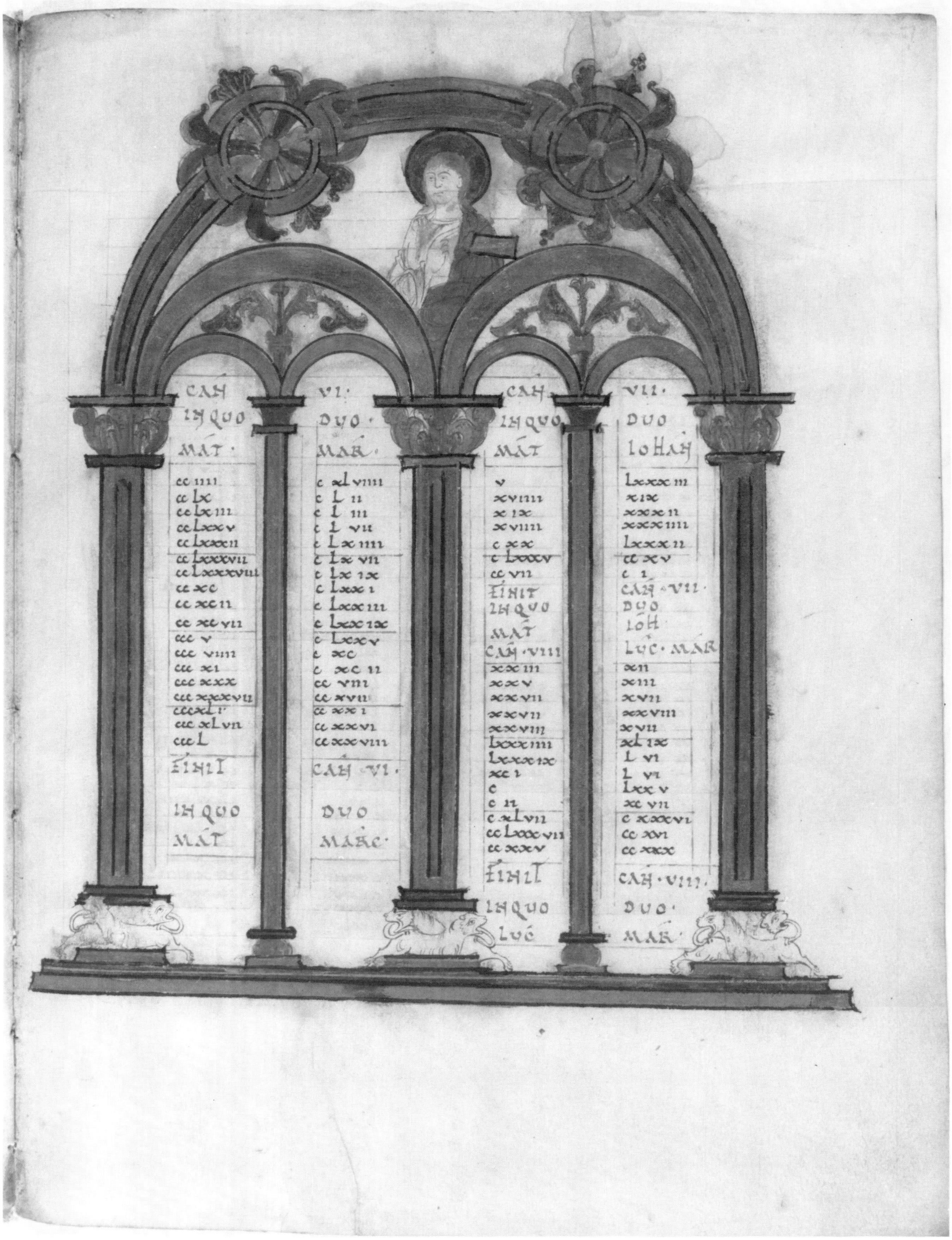

9.12 Cambridge, Pembroke College 301, f. 7r

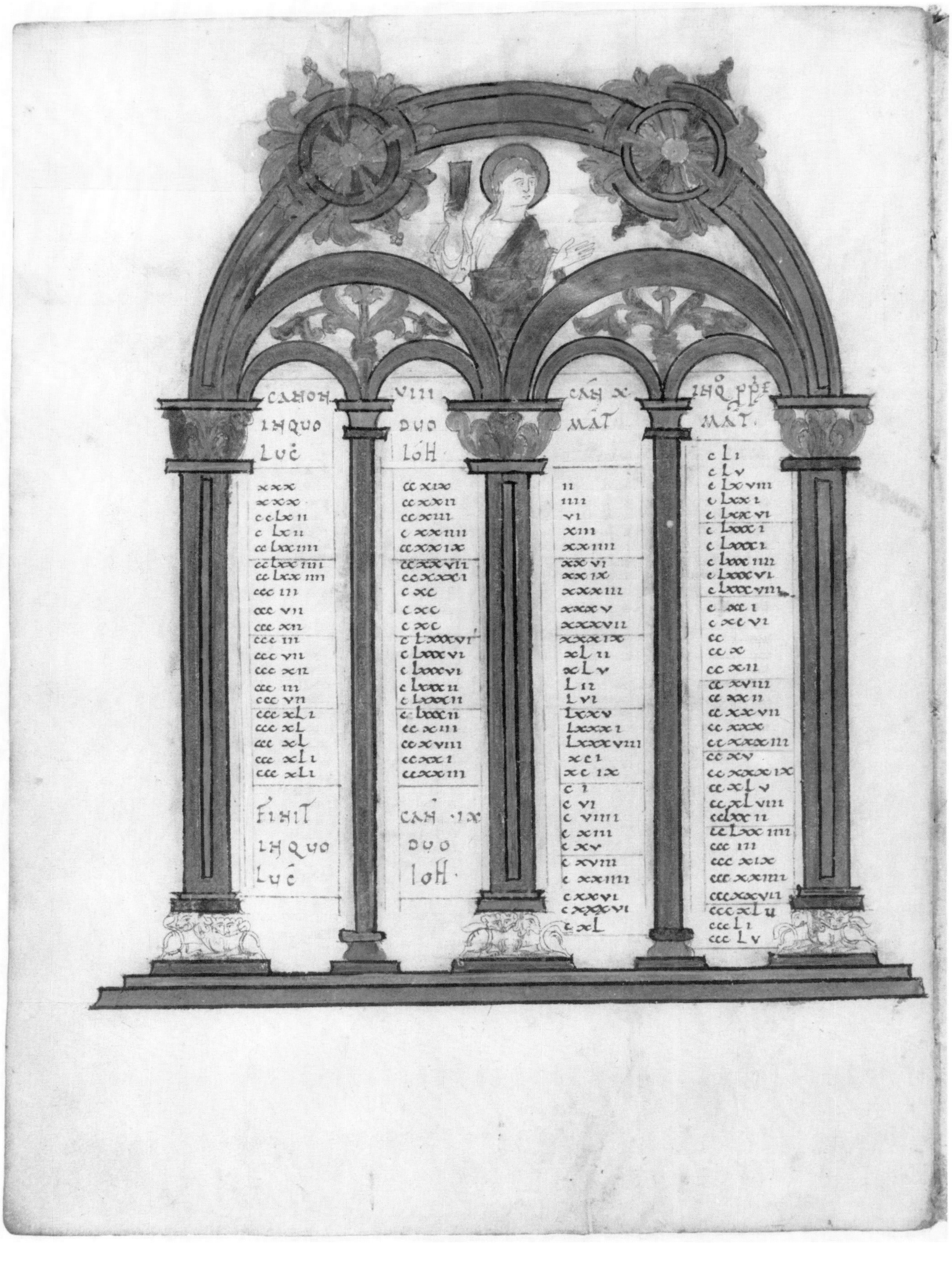

9.13 Cambridge, Pembroke College 301, f. 7v

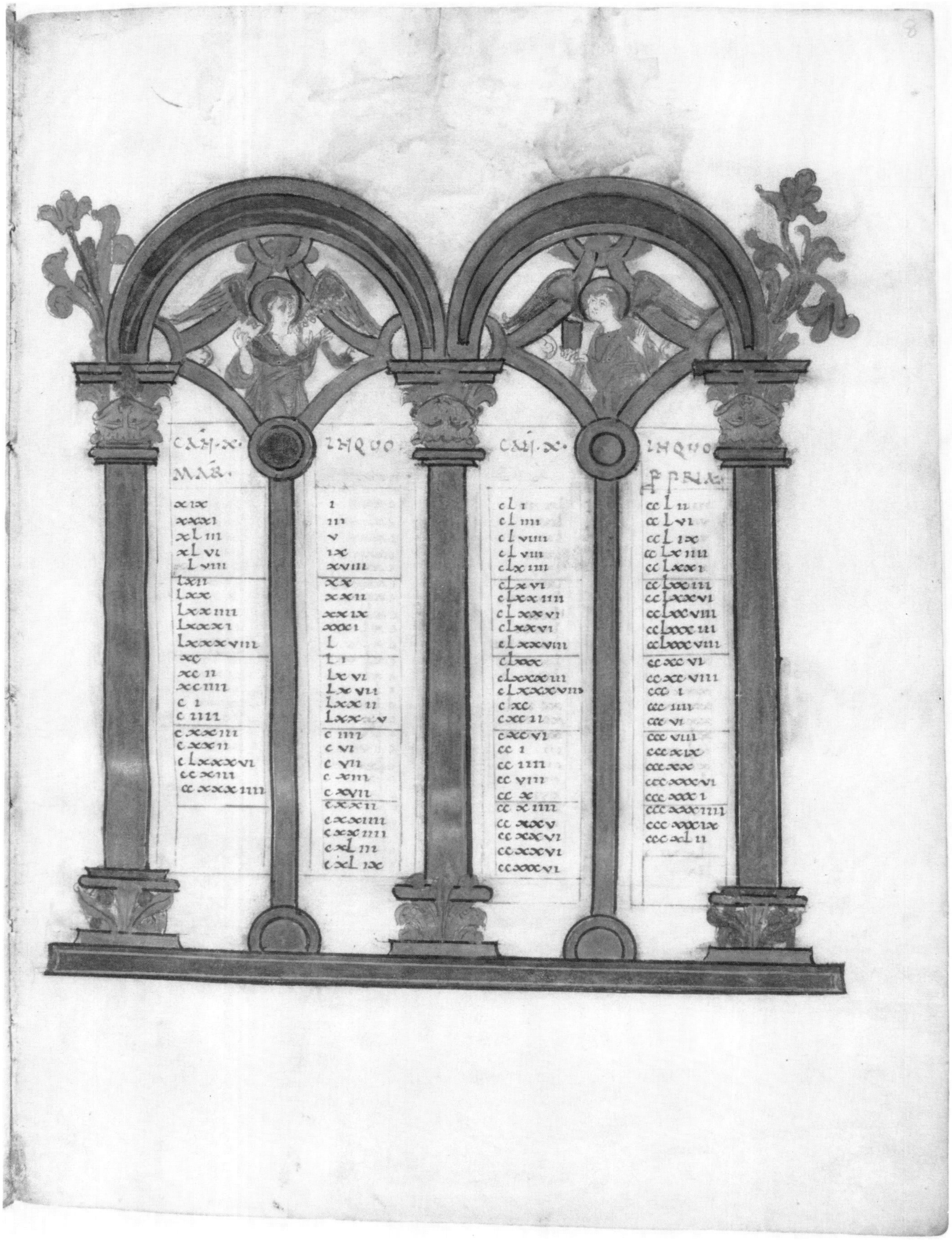

9.14 Cambridge, Pembroke College 301, f. 8r

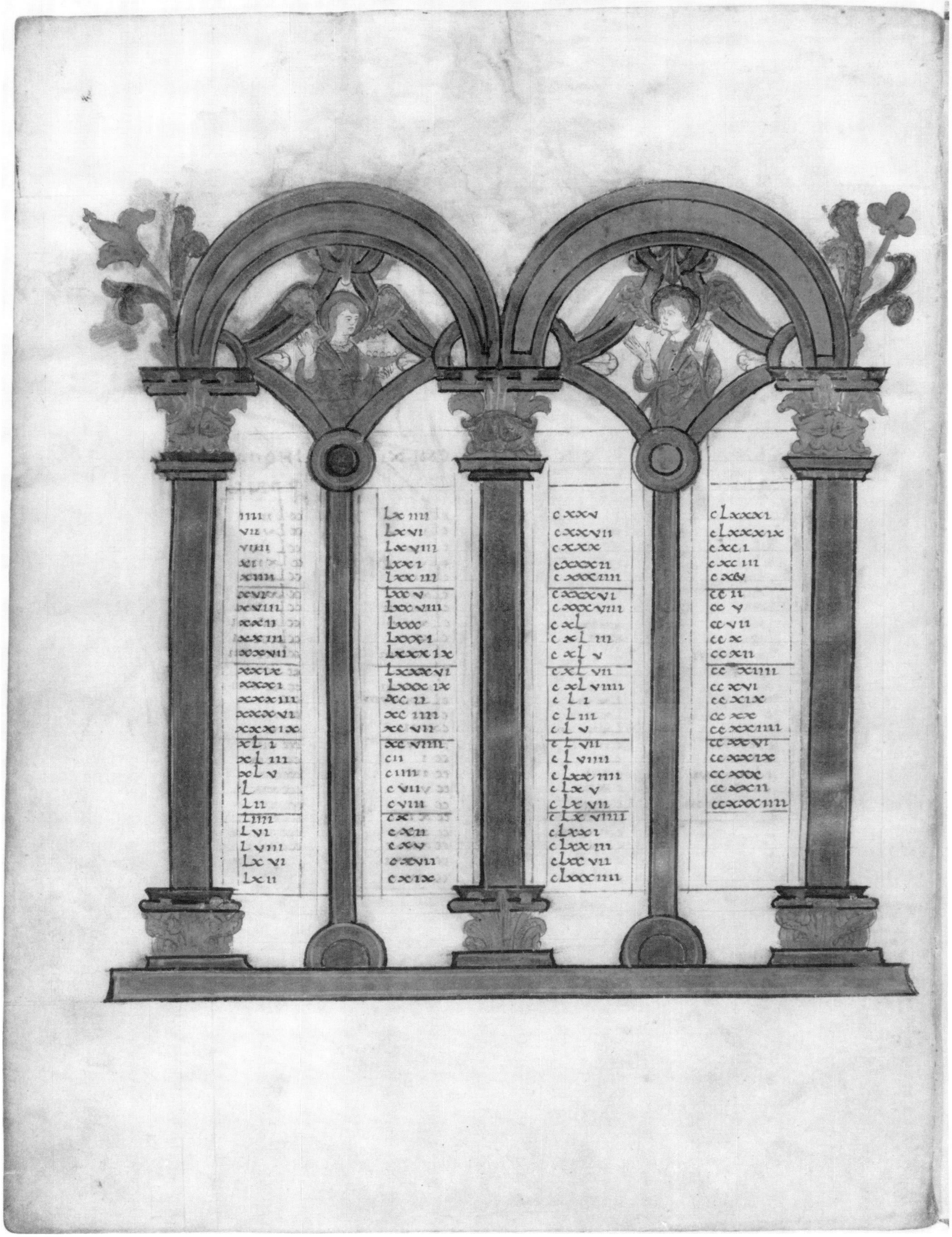

9.15 Cambridge, Pembroke College 301, f. 8ᵛ

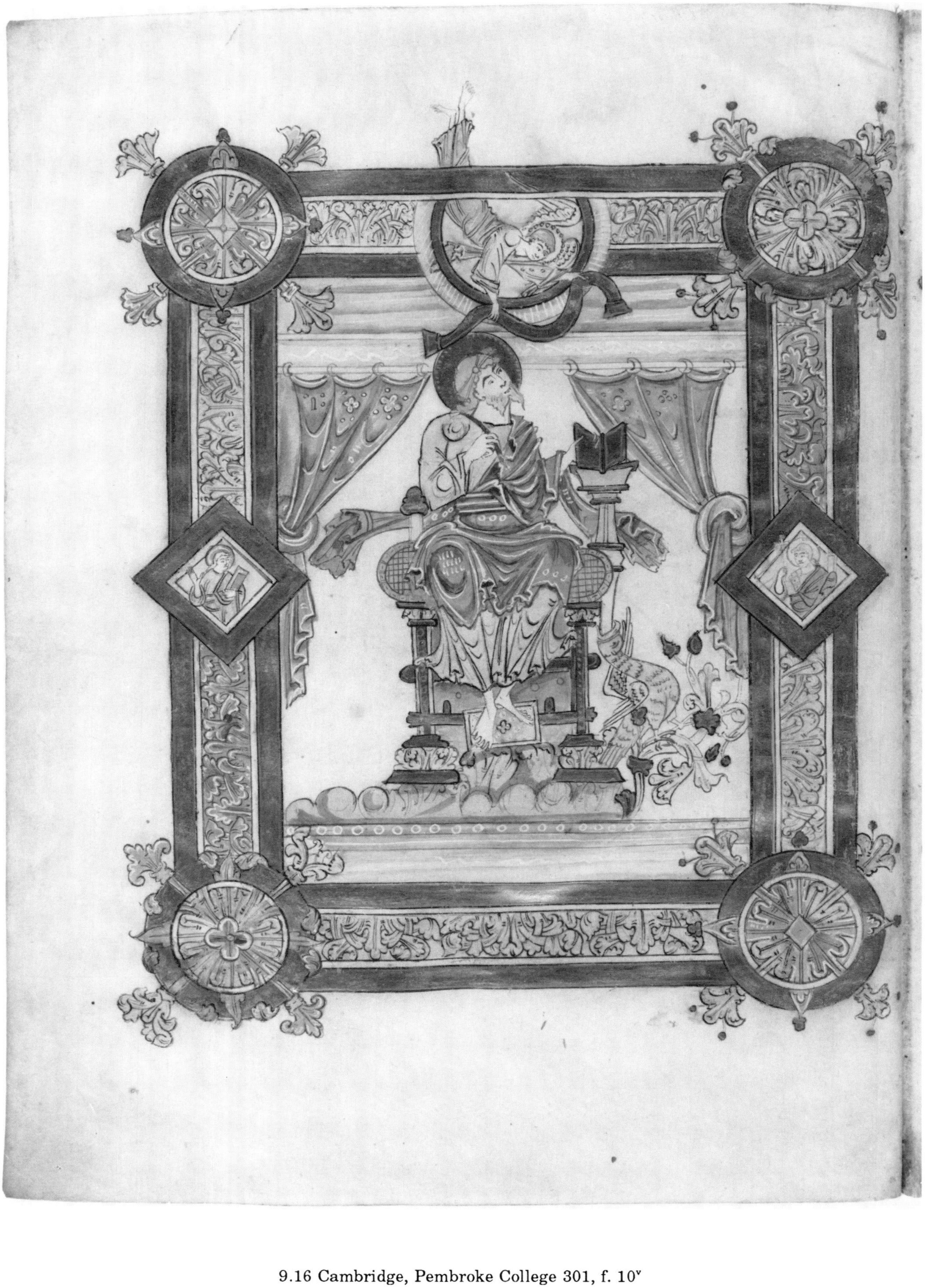

9.16 Cambridge, Pembroke College 301, f. 10v

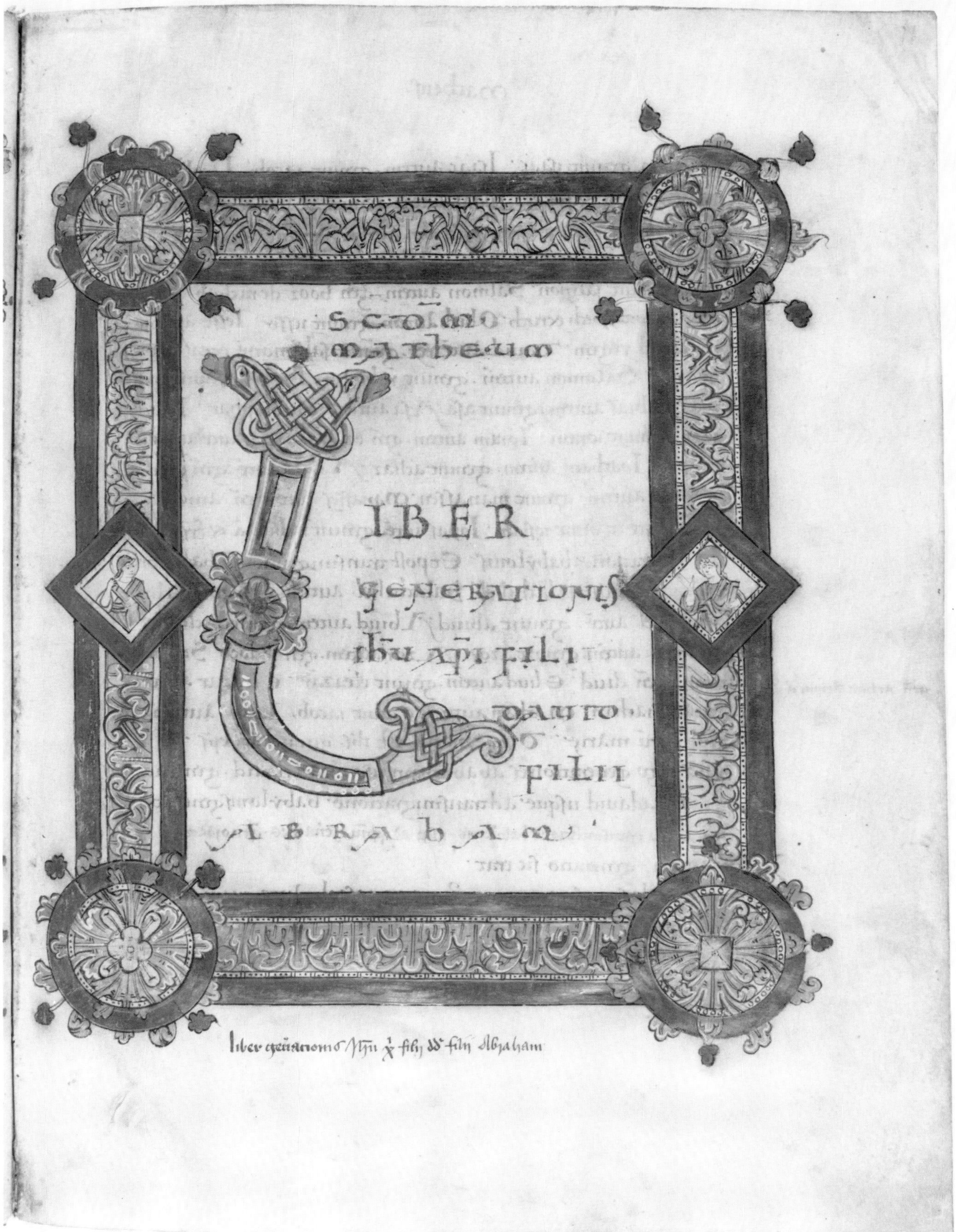

9.17 Cambridge, Pembroke College 301, f. 11r

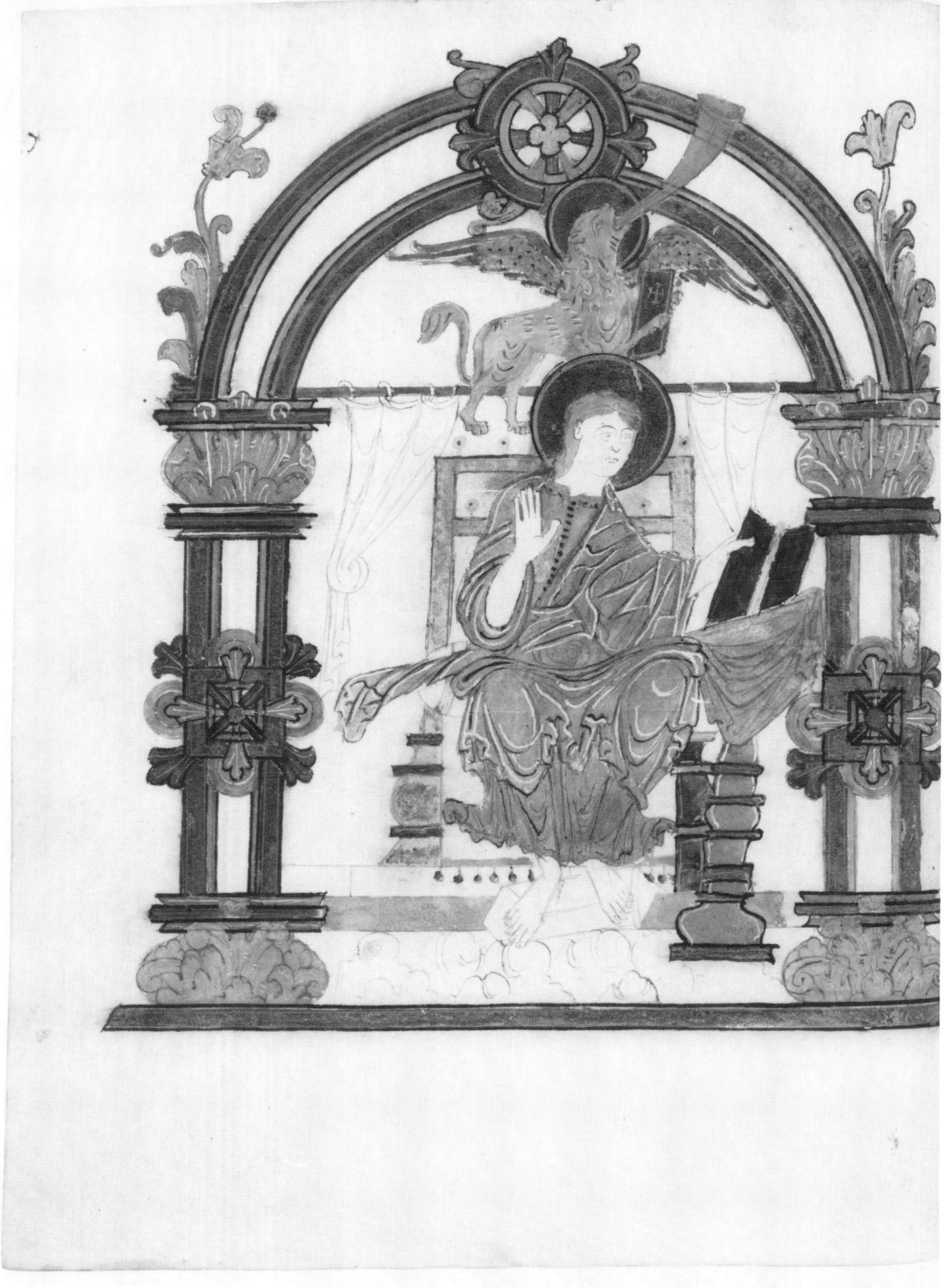

9.18 Cambridge, Pembroke College 301, f. 44v

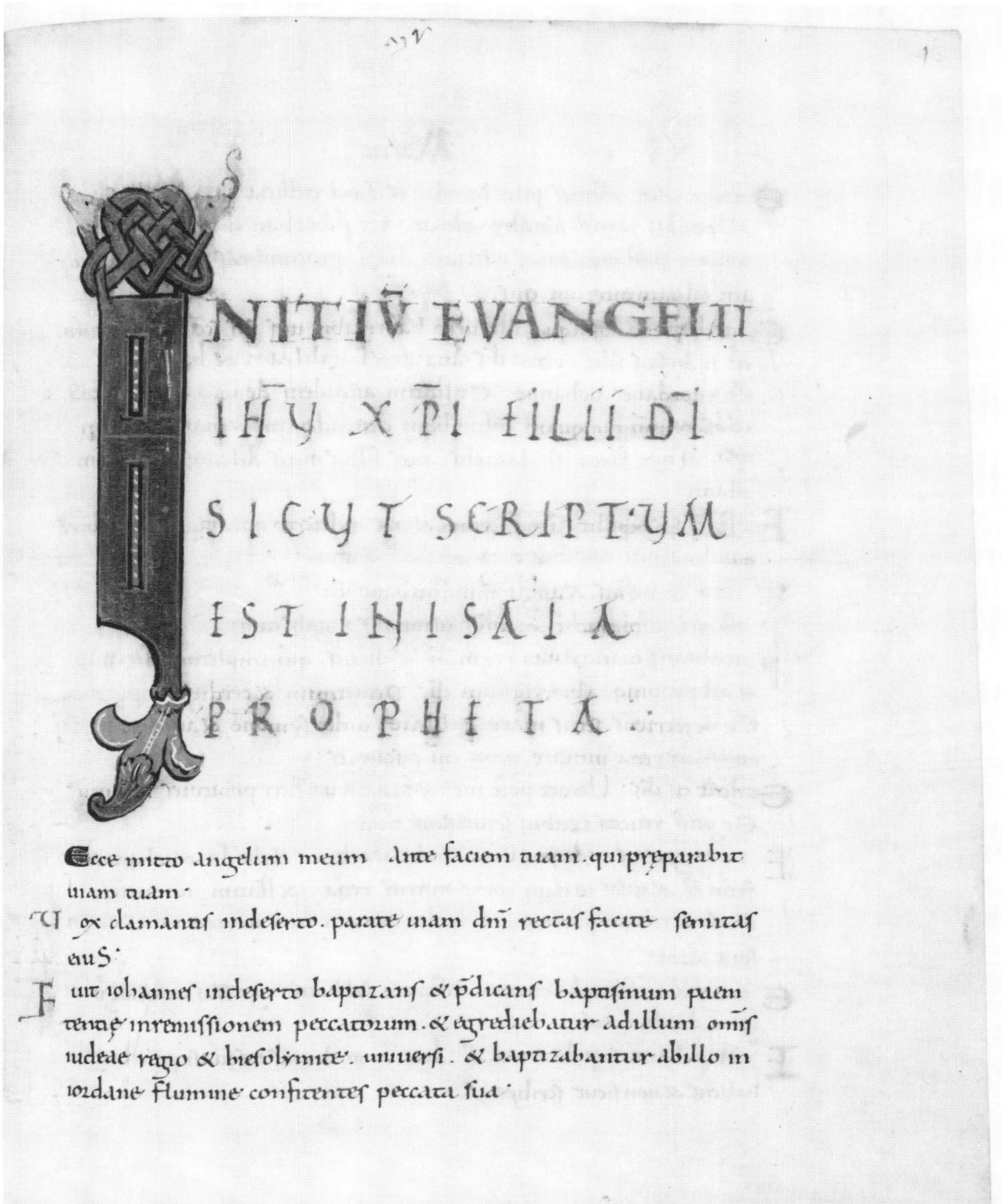

INITIV̄ EVANGELII
IHV XPI FILII DI
SICVT SCRIPTVM
EST IN ISAIA
PROPHETA

Ecce mitto angelum meum ante faciem tuam. qui preparabit uiam tuam.
Uox clamantis indeserto. parate uiam dn̄i rectas facite semitas eius.
Fuit iohannes indeserto baptizans & pdicans baptismum paenitentiae inremissionem peccatorum. & egrediebatur adillum omnis iudeae regio & hiesolimite. uniuersi. & baptizabantur abillo in iordane flumine confitentes peccata sua.

9.19 Cambridge, Pembroke College 301, f. 45r

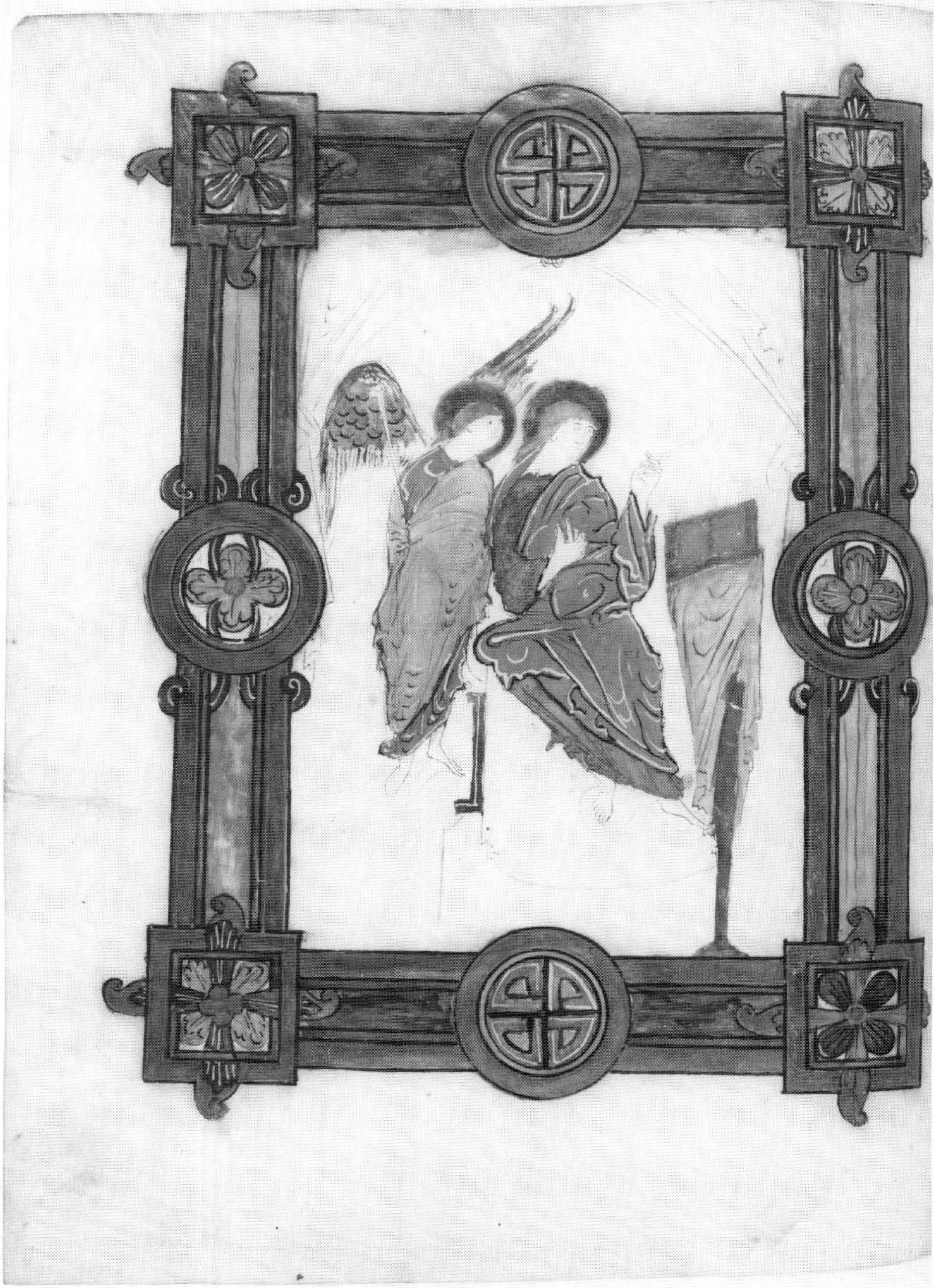

9.20 Cambridge, Pembroke College 301, f. 70v

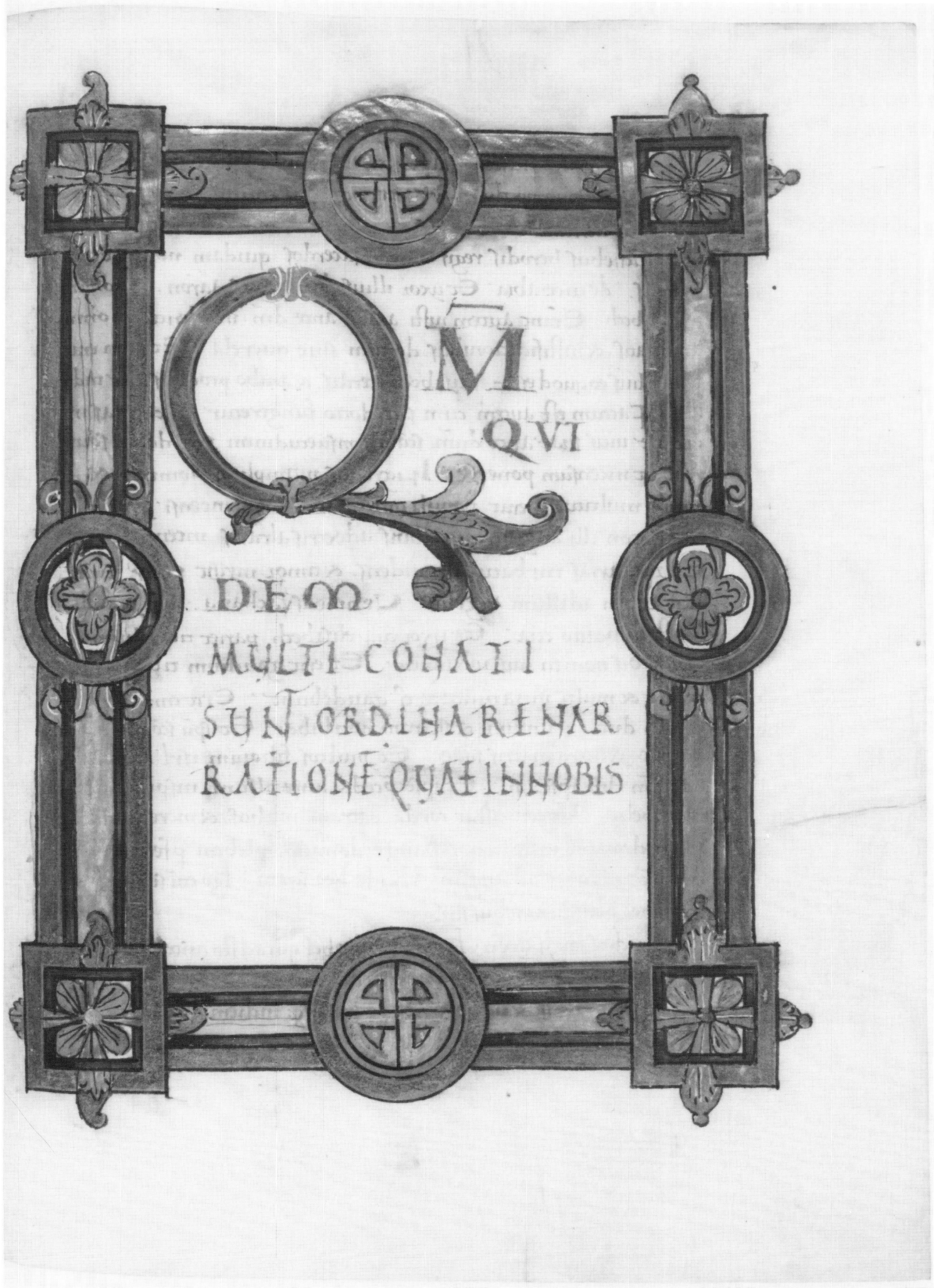

9.21 Cambridge, Pembroke College 301, f. 71r

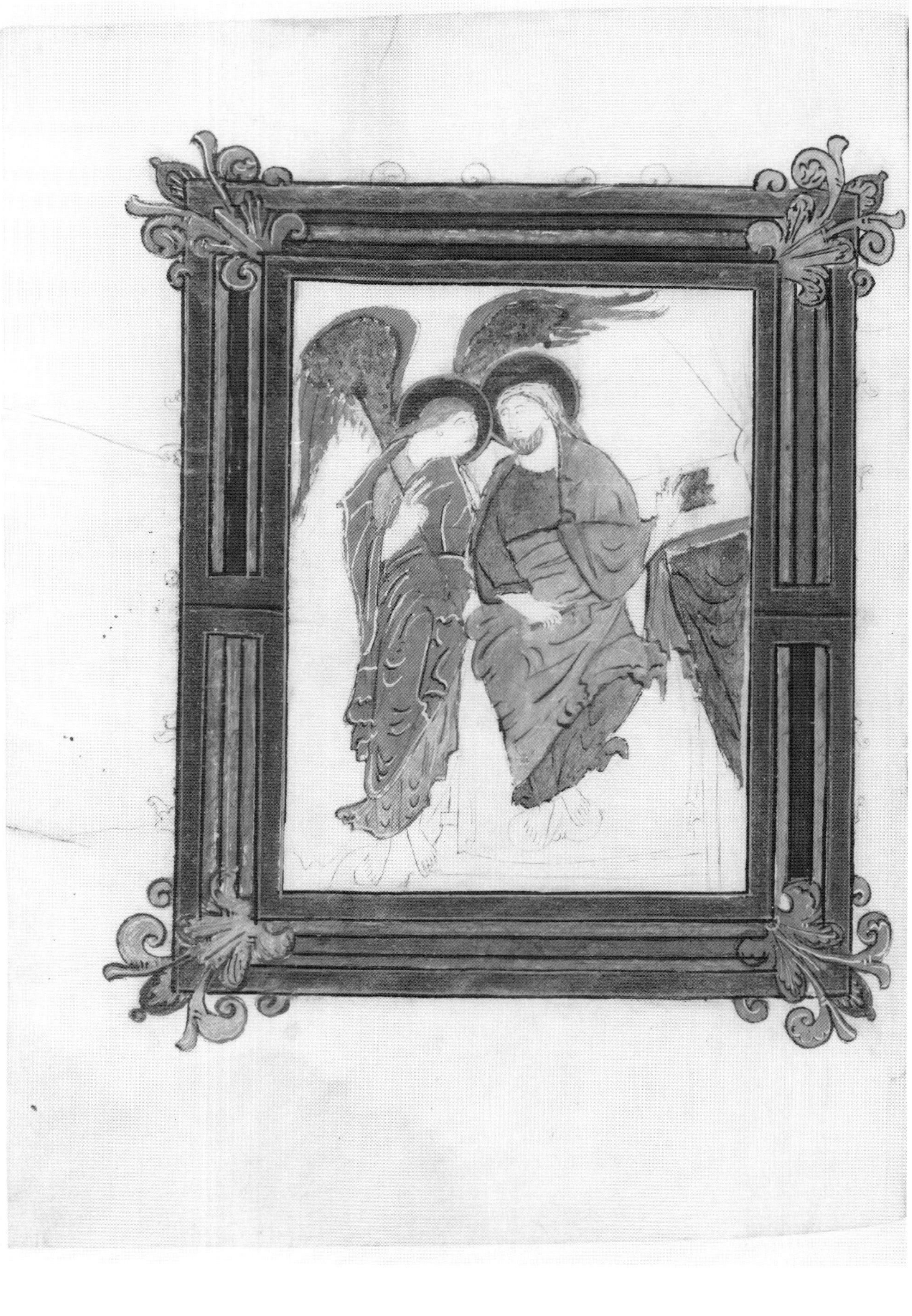

9.22 Cambridge, Pembroke College 301, f. 108v

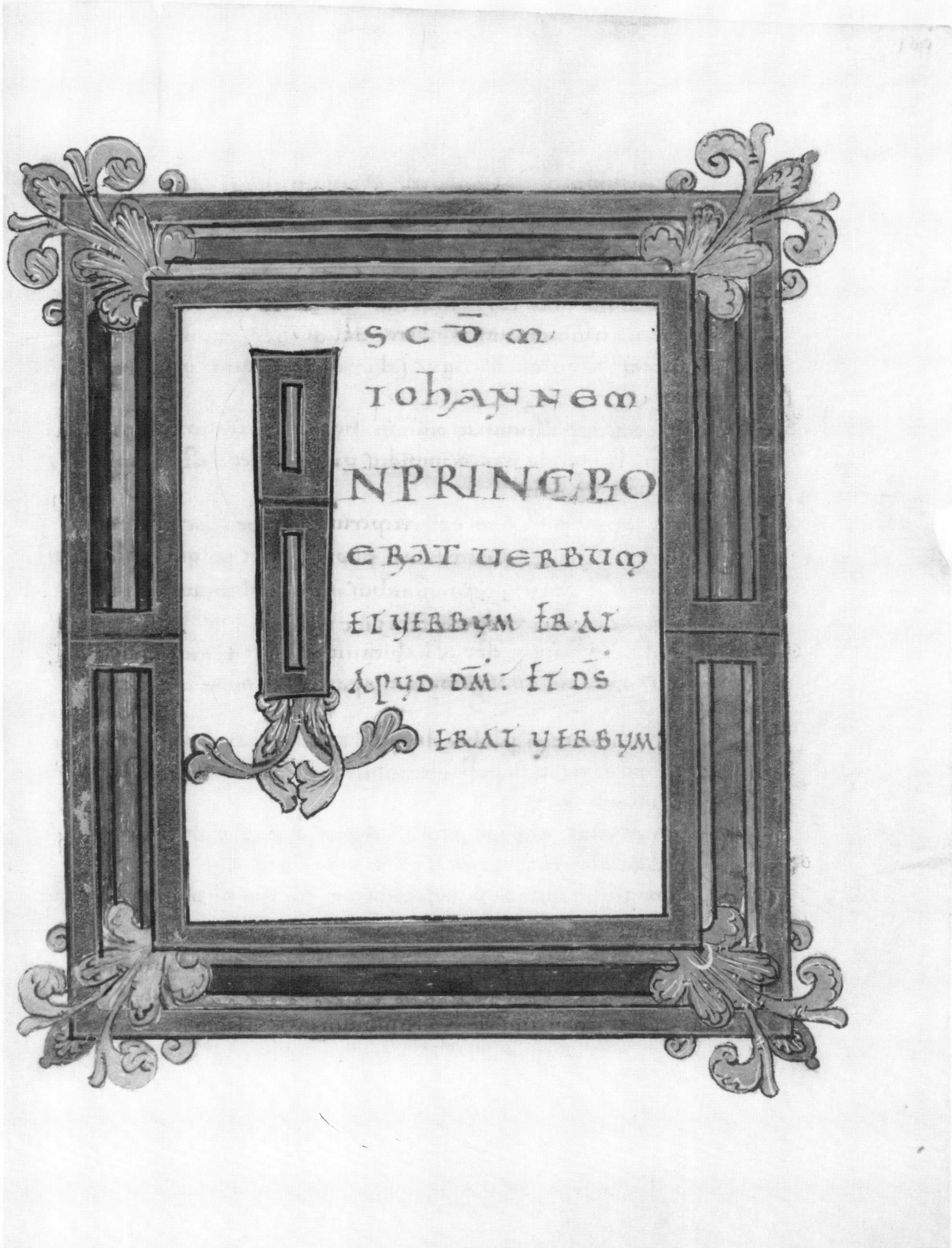

9.23 Cambridge, Pembroke College 301, f. 109r

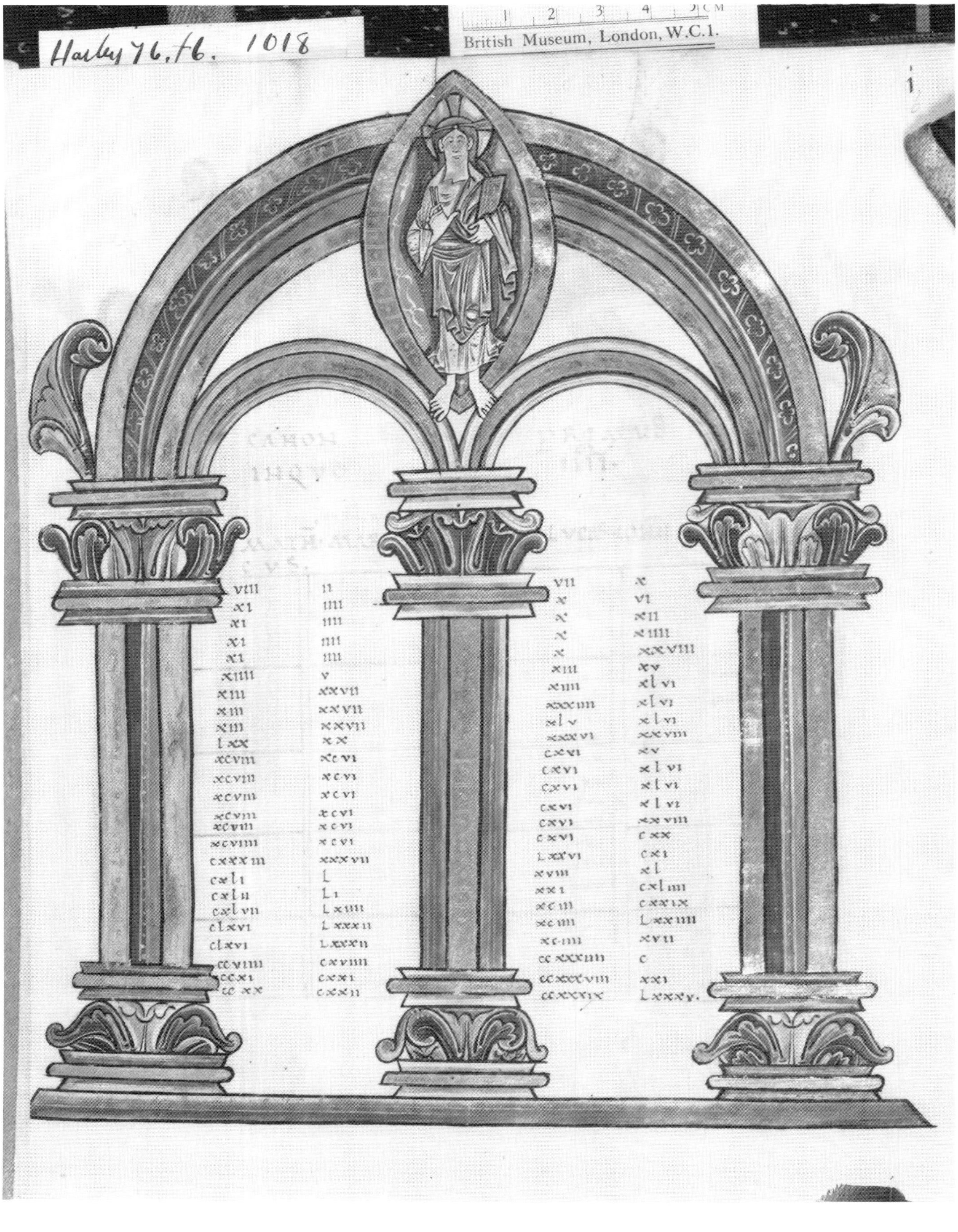

10.1 London, B.L., Harley 76, f. 6r

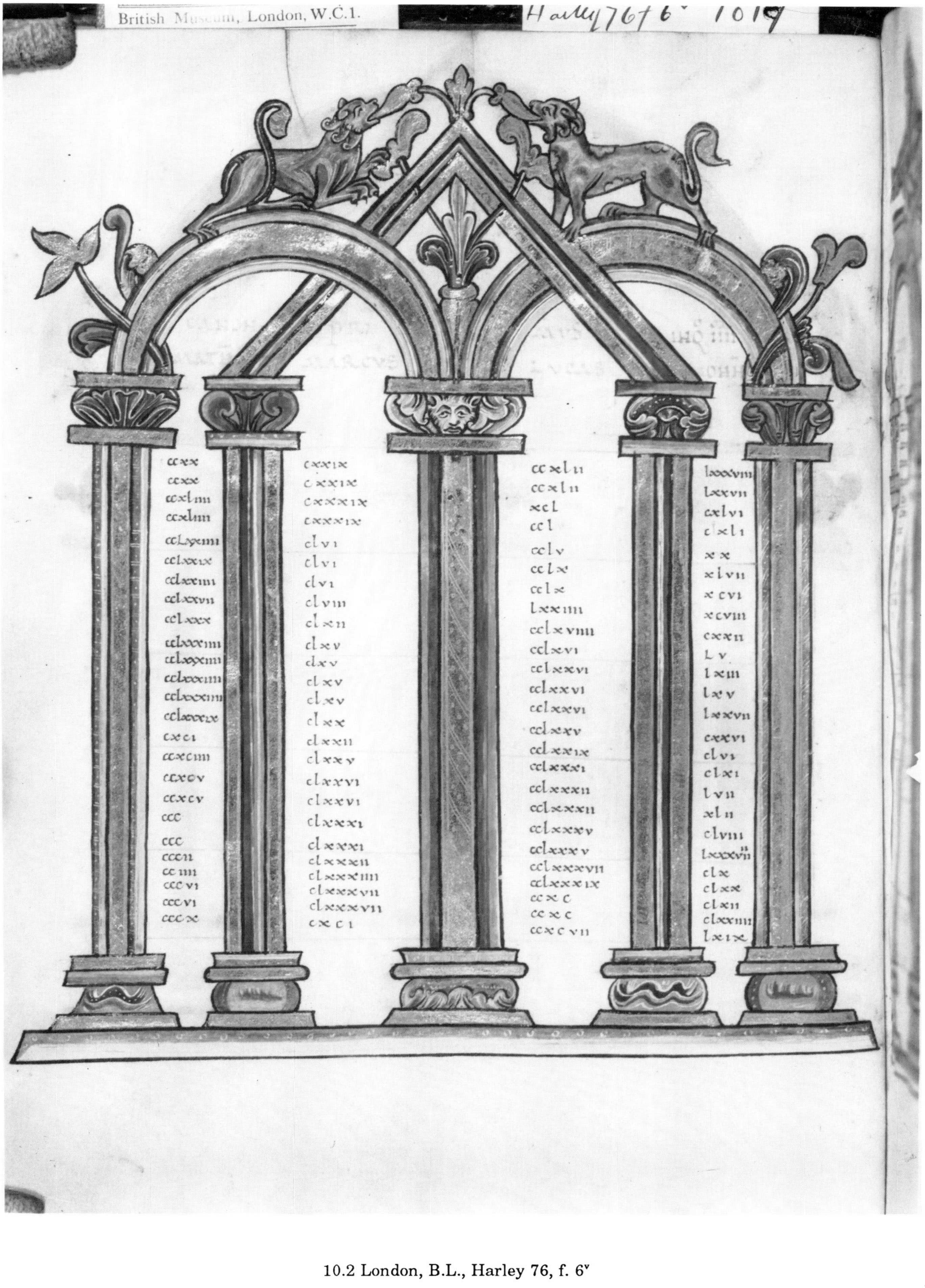

10.2 London, B.L., Harley 76, f. 6v

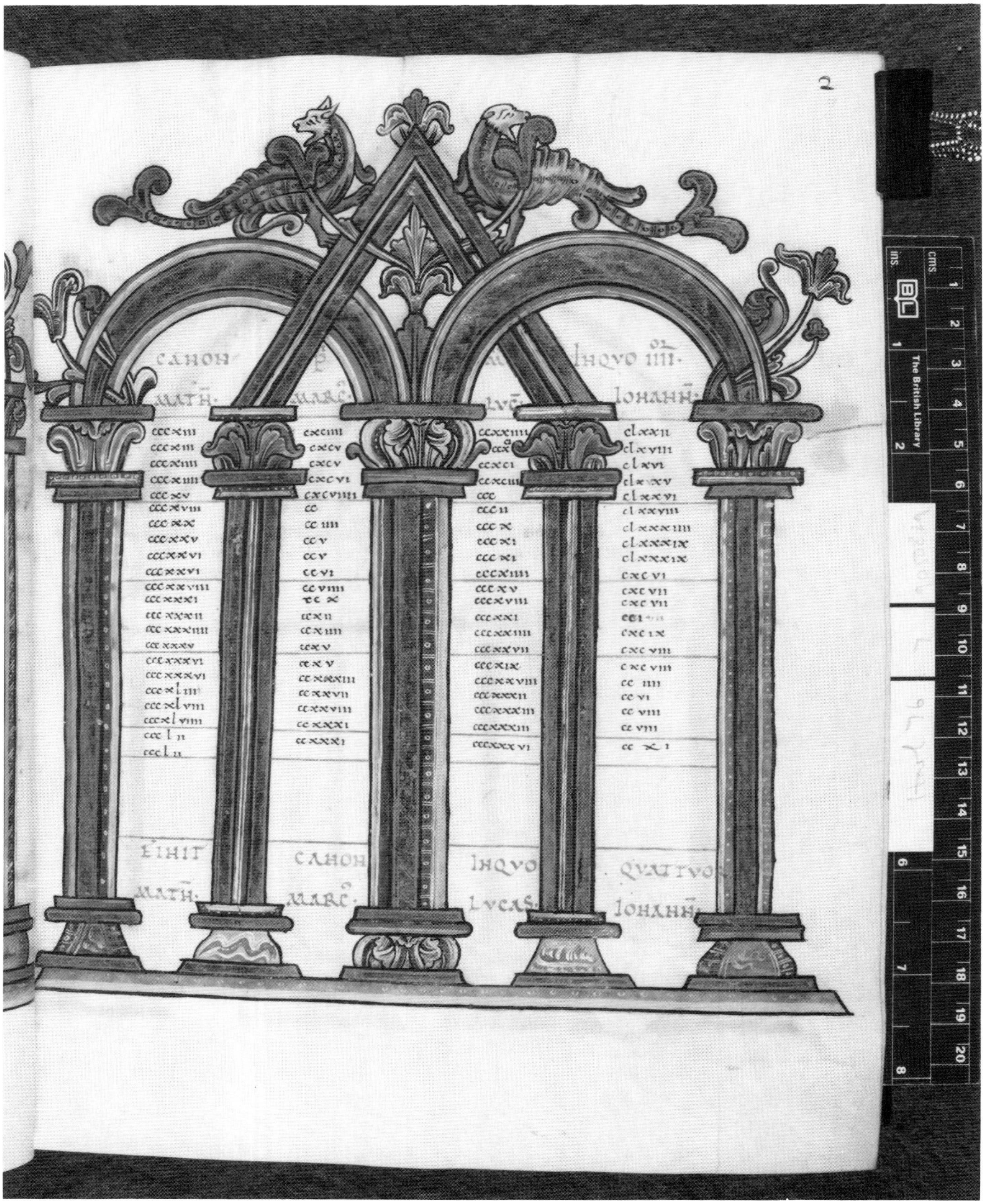

10.3 London, B.L., Harley 76, f. 7r

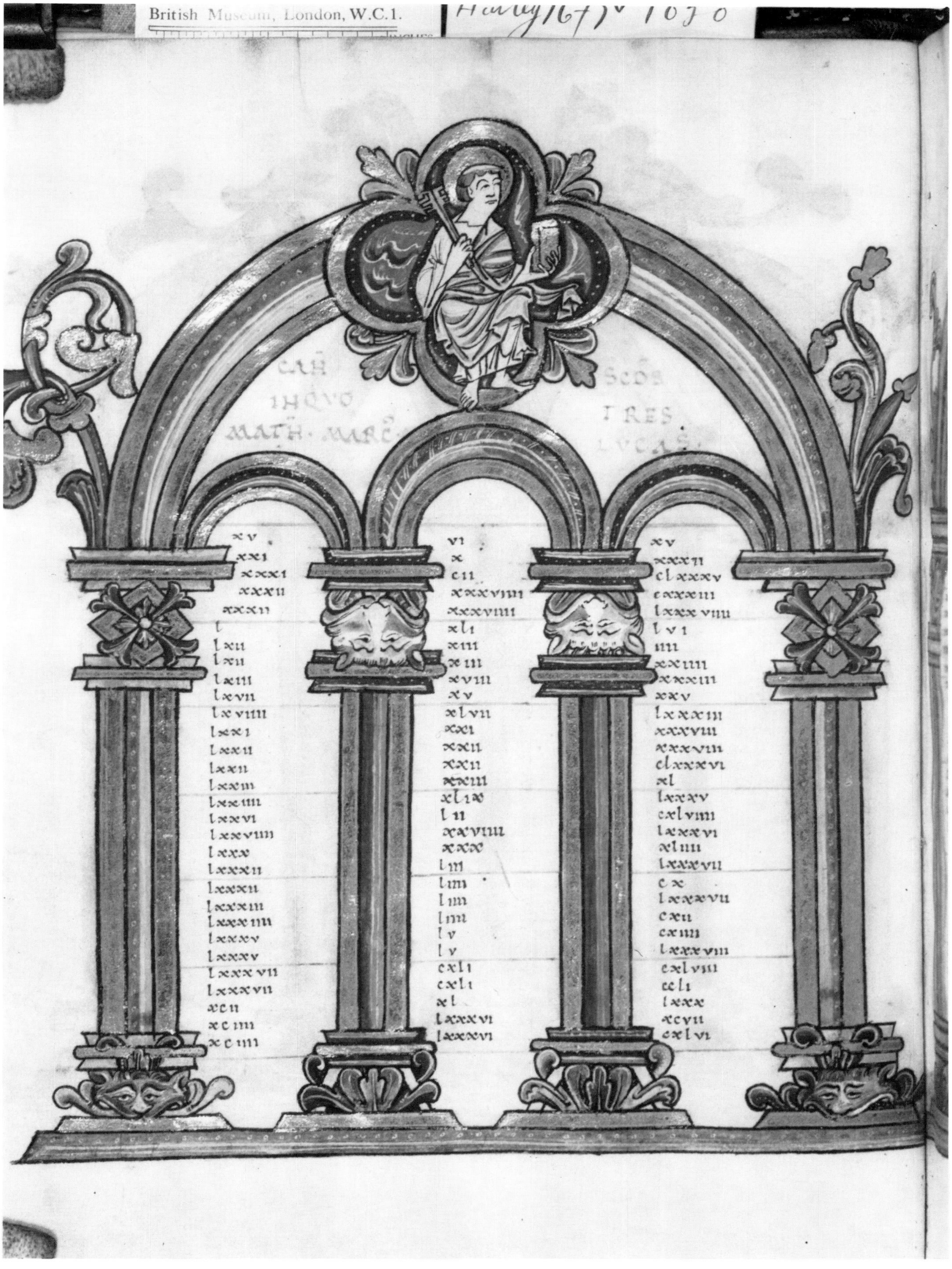

10.4 London, B.L., Harley 76, f. 7v

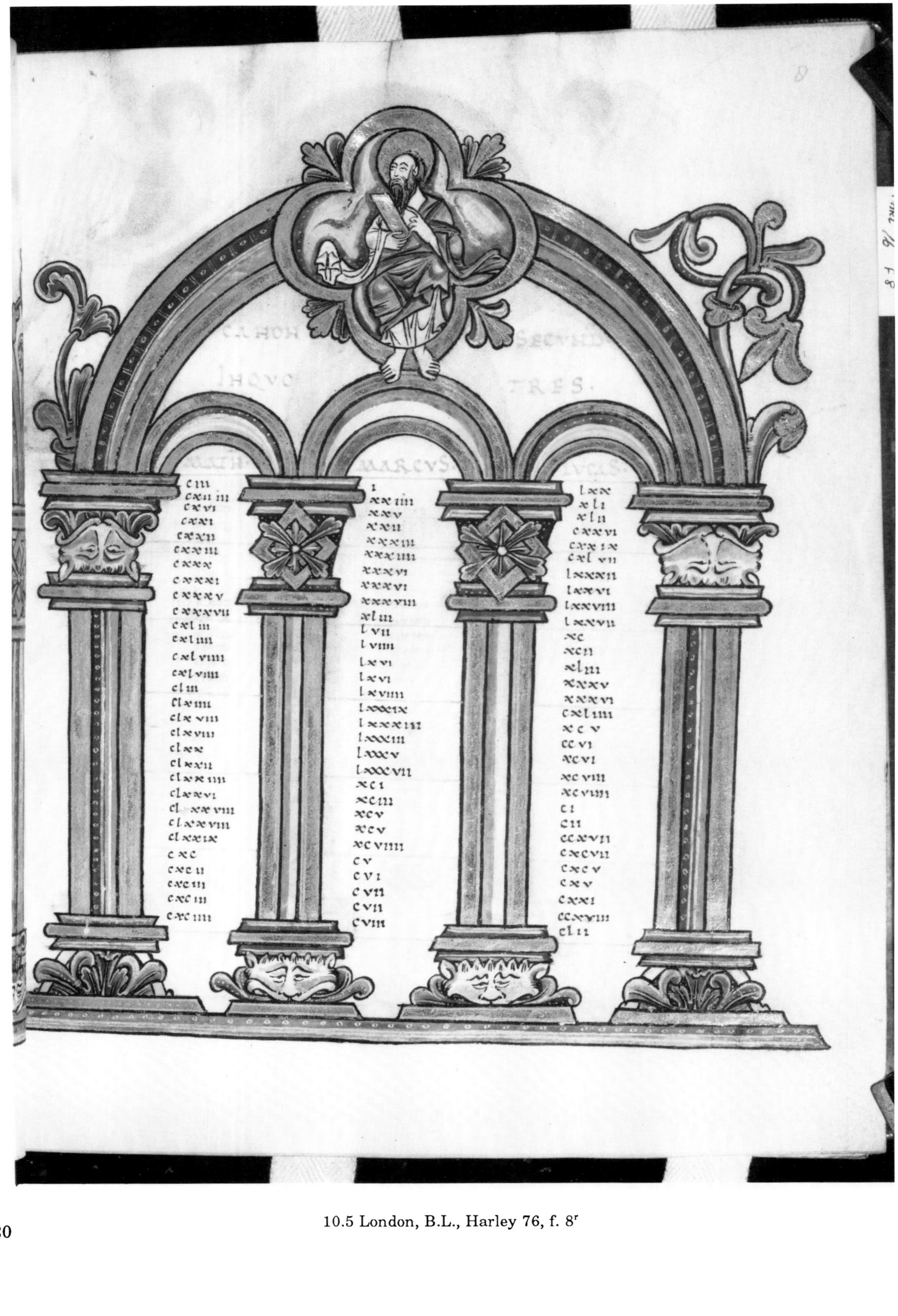

10.5 London, B.L., Harley 76, f. 8r

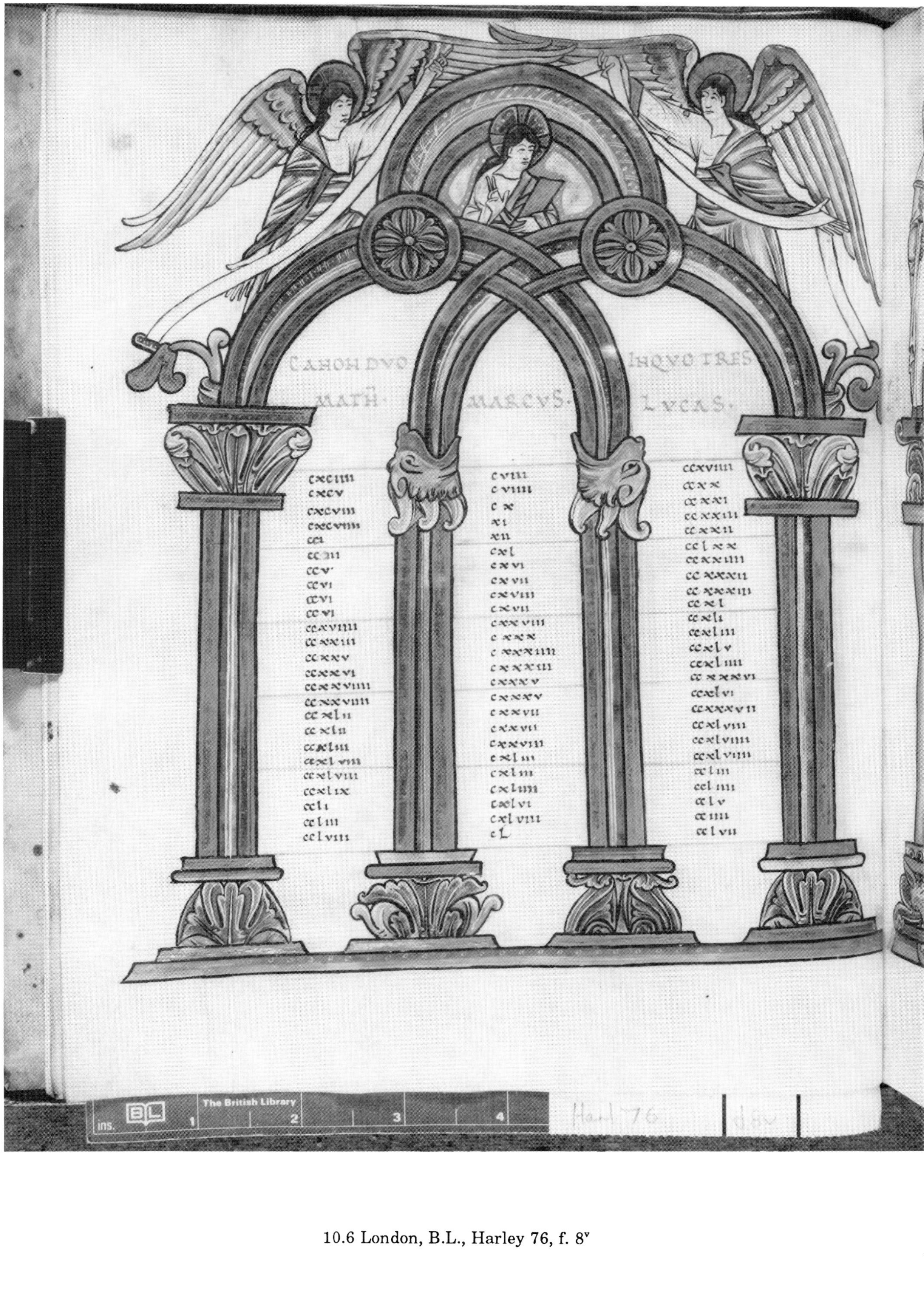

10.6 London, B.L., Harley 76, f. 8v

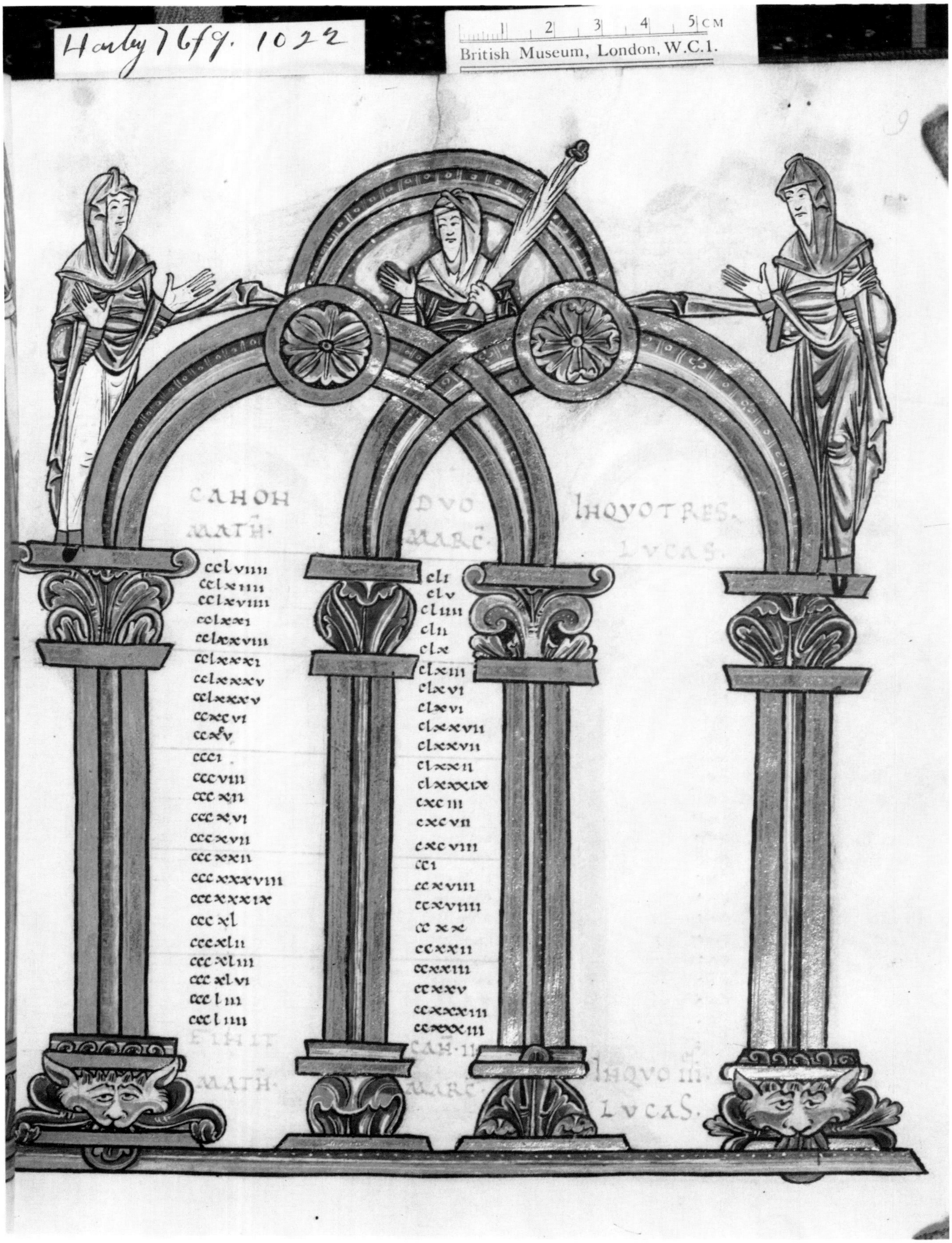

10.7 London, B.L., Harley 76, f. 9r

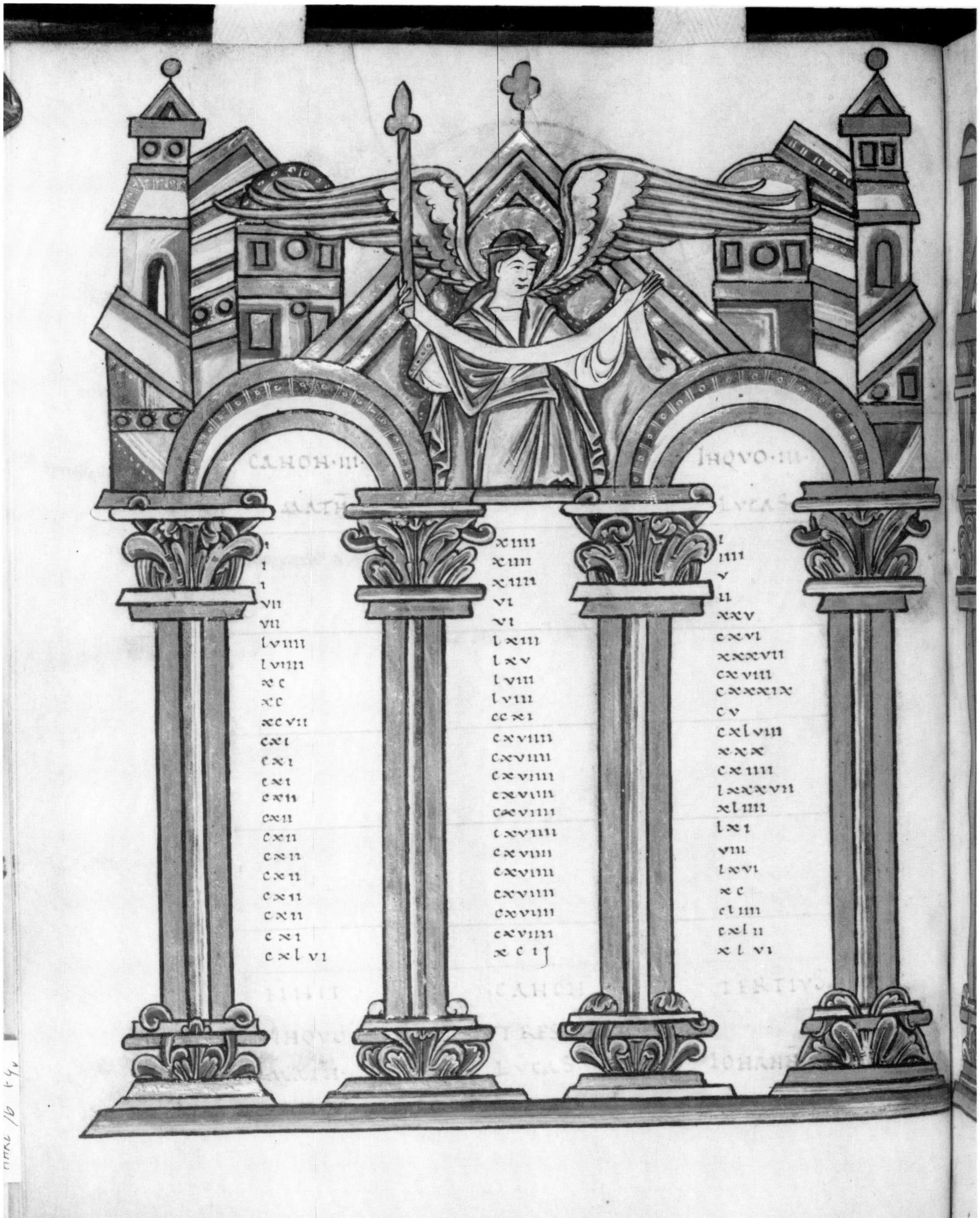

10.8 London, B.L., Harley 76, f. 9v

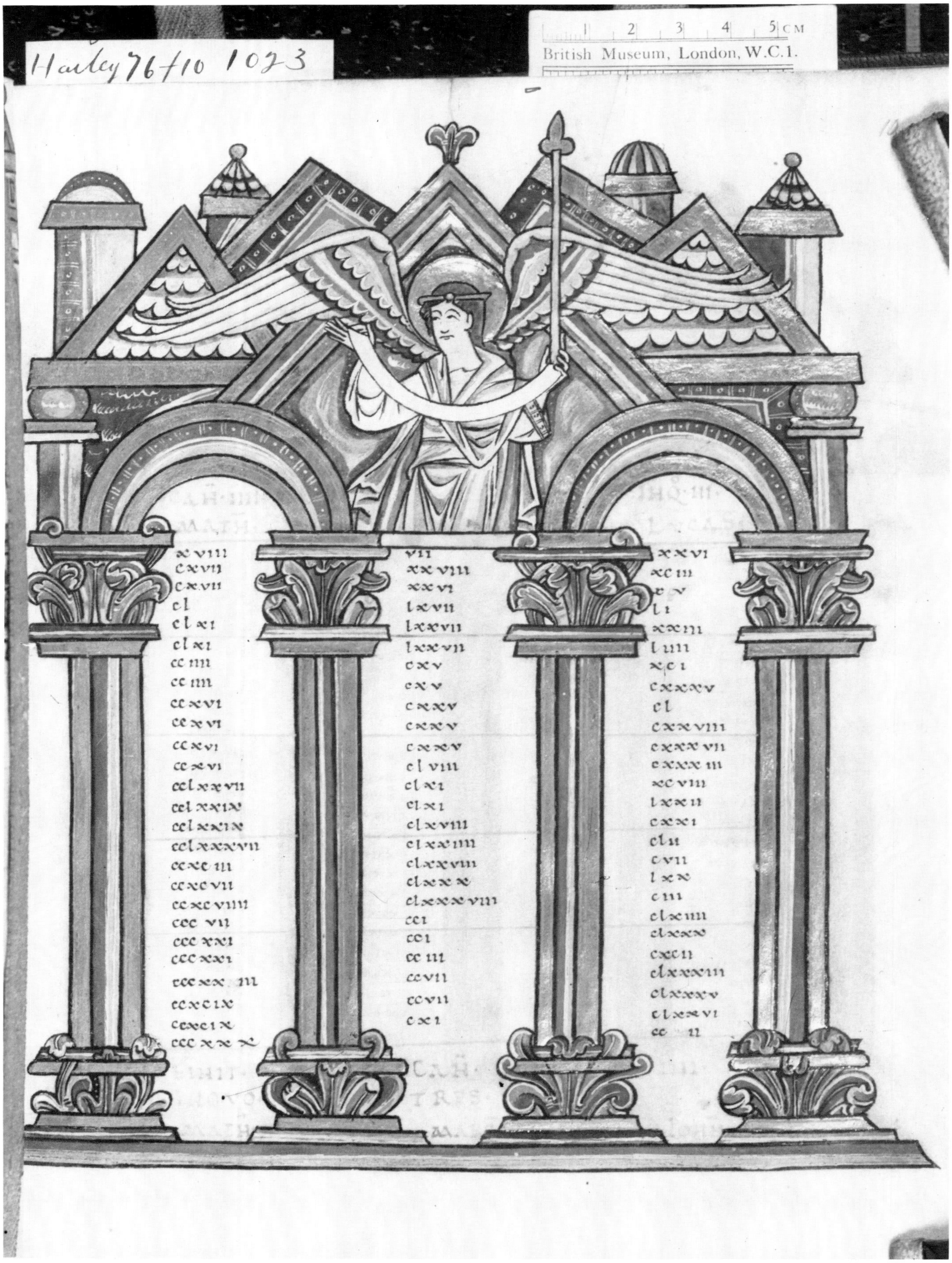

10.9 London, B.L., Harley 76, f. 10r

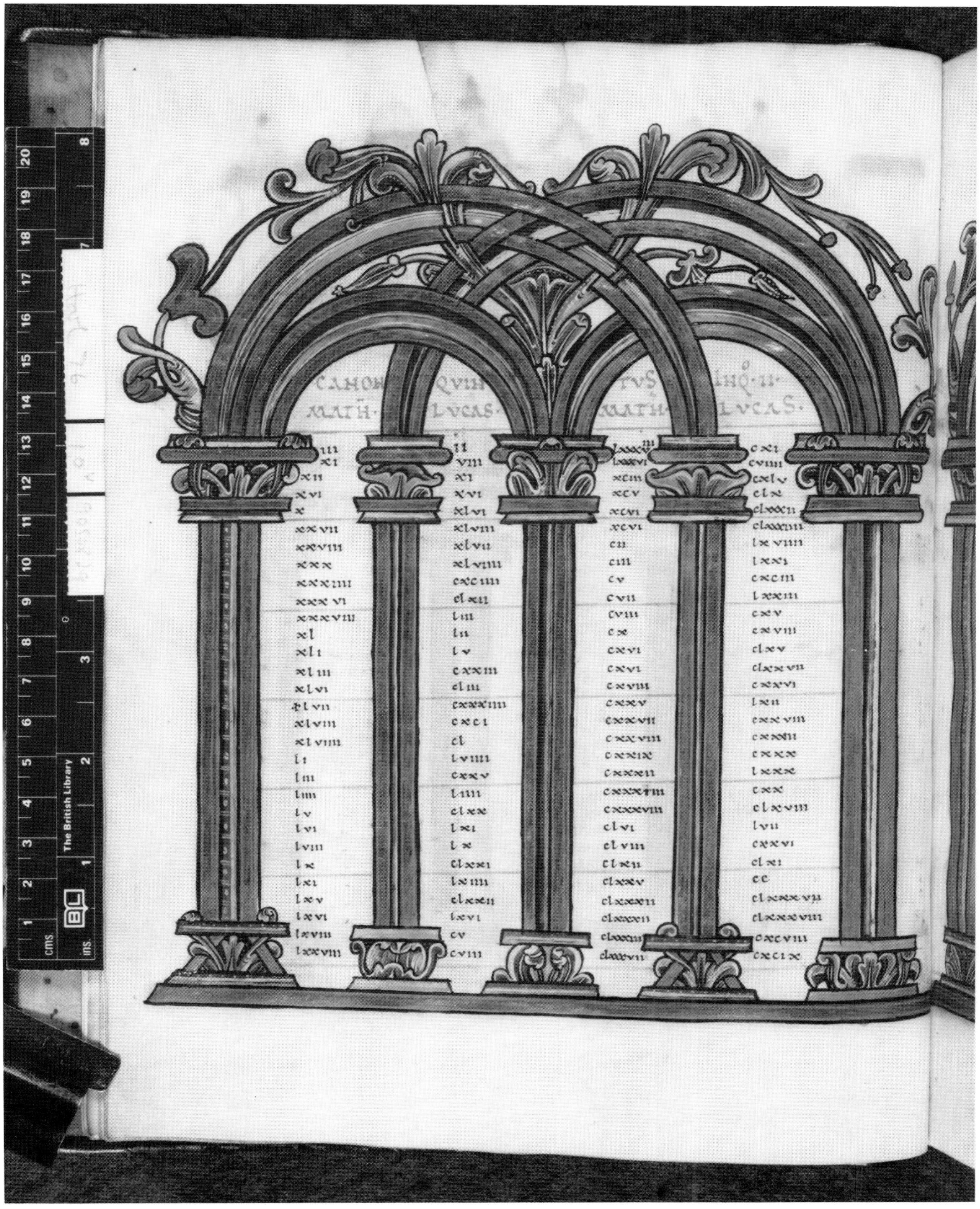

10.10 London, B.L., Harley 76, f. 10v

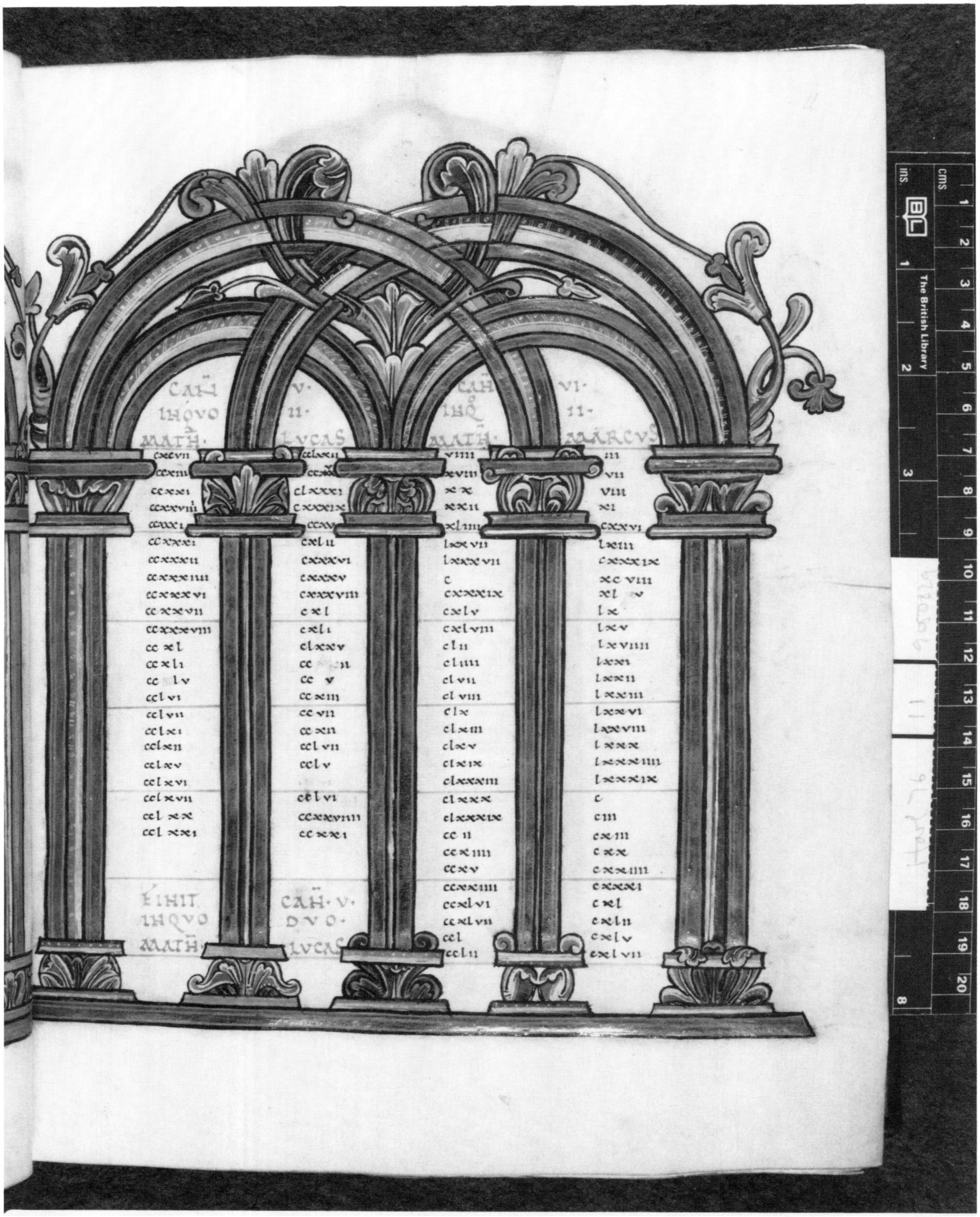

10.11 London, B.L., Harley 76, f. 11r

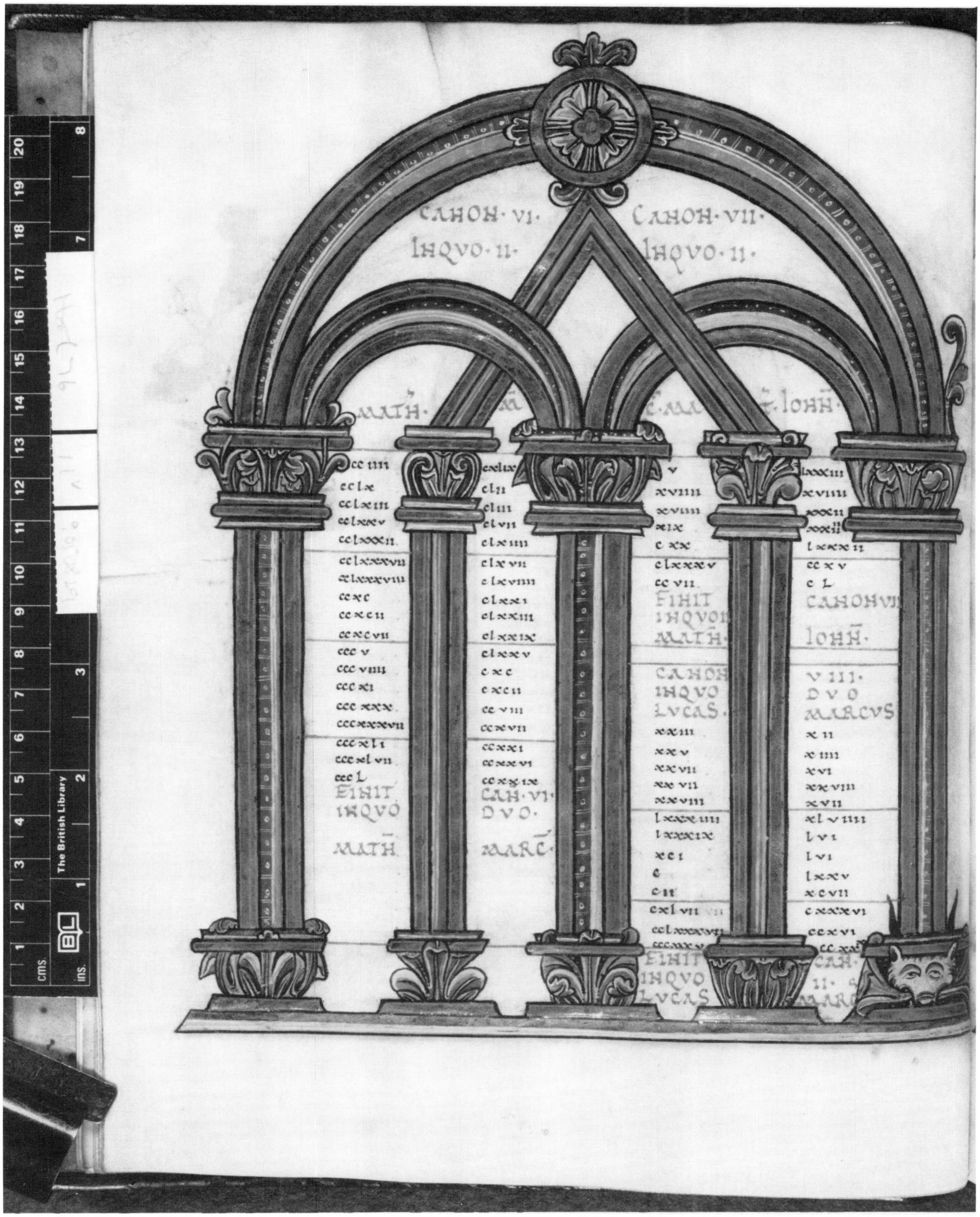

10.12 London, B.L., Harley 76, f. 11v

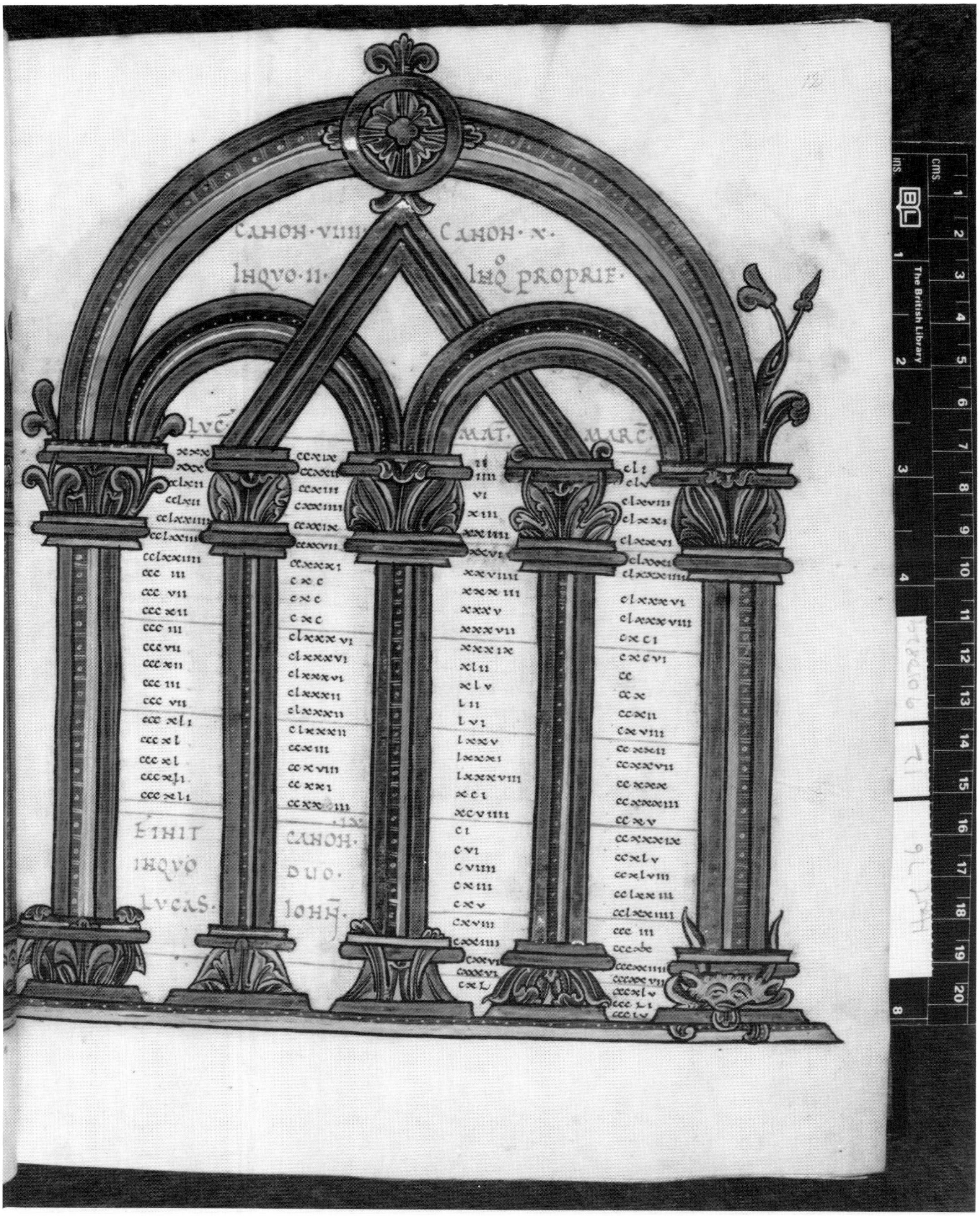

10.13 London, B.L., Harley 76, f. 12r

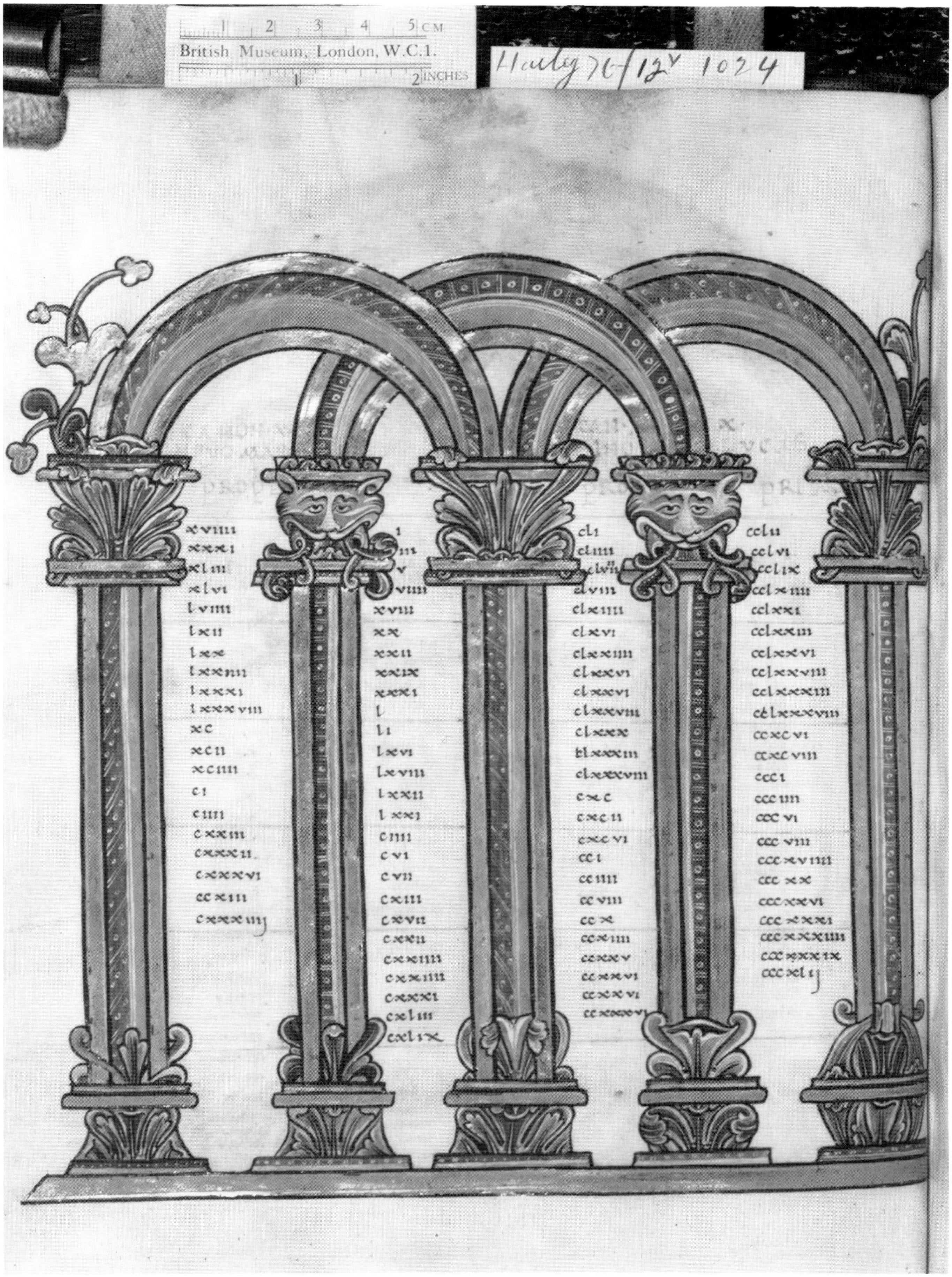

10.14 London, B.L., Harley 76, f. 12ᵛ

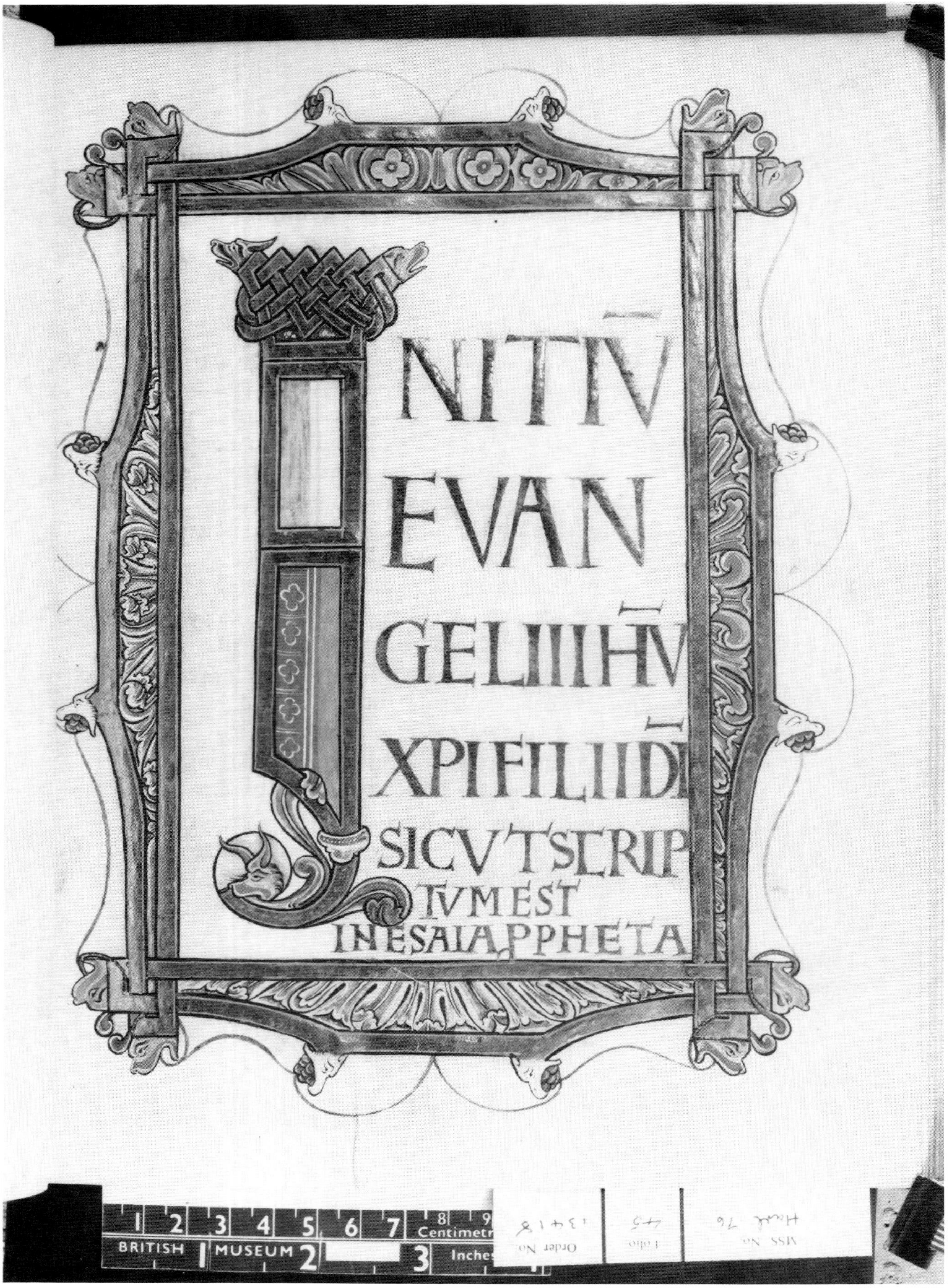

10.15 London, B.L., Harley 76, f. 45r

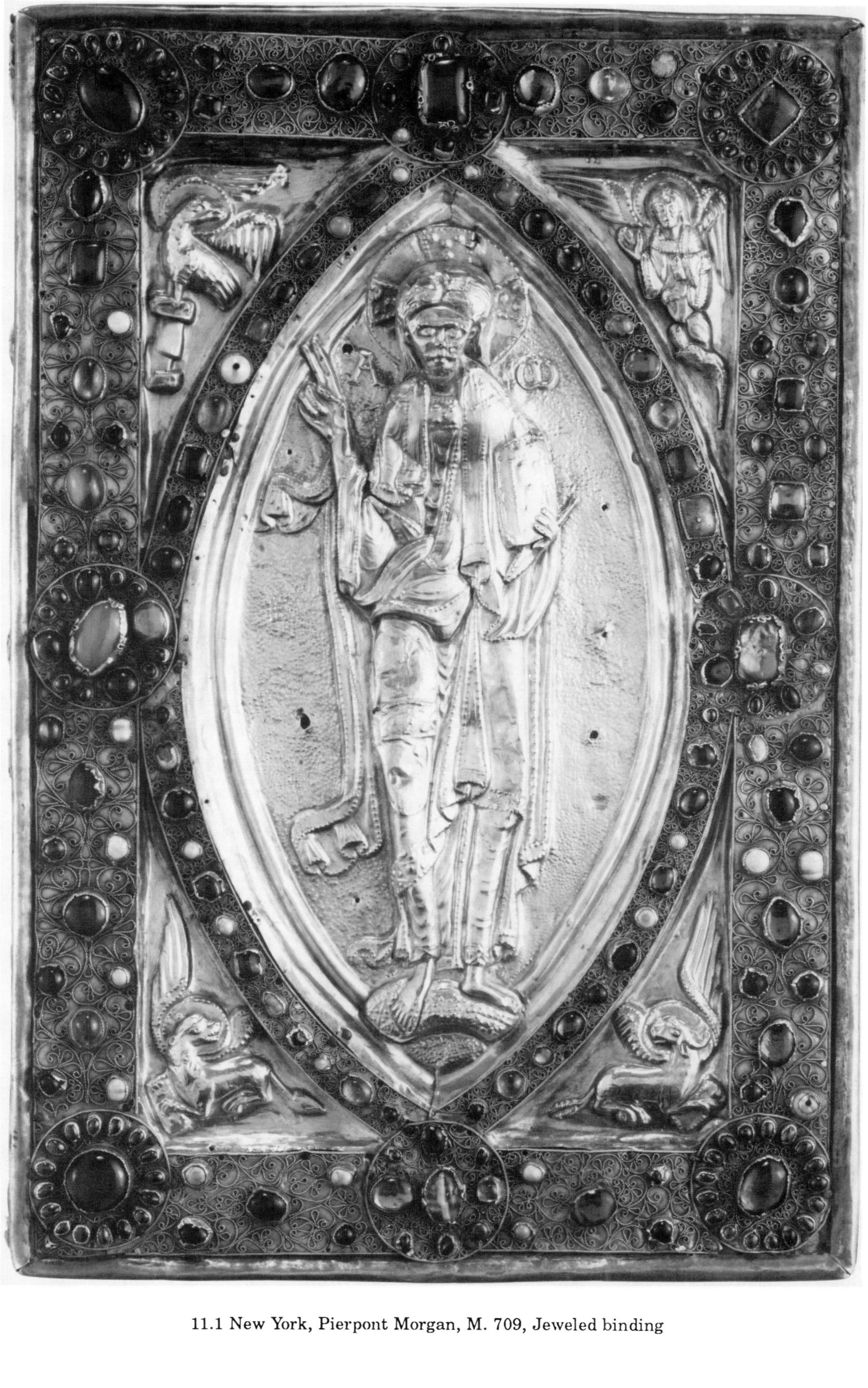

11.1 New York, Pierpont Morgan, M. 709, Jeweled binding

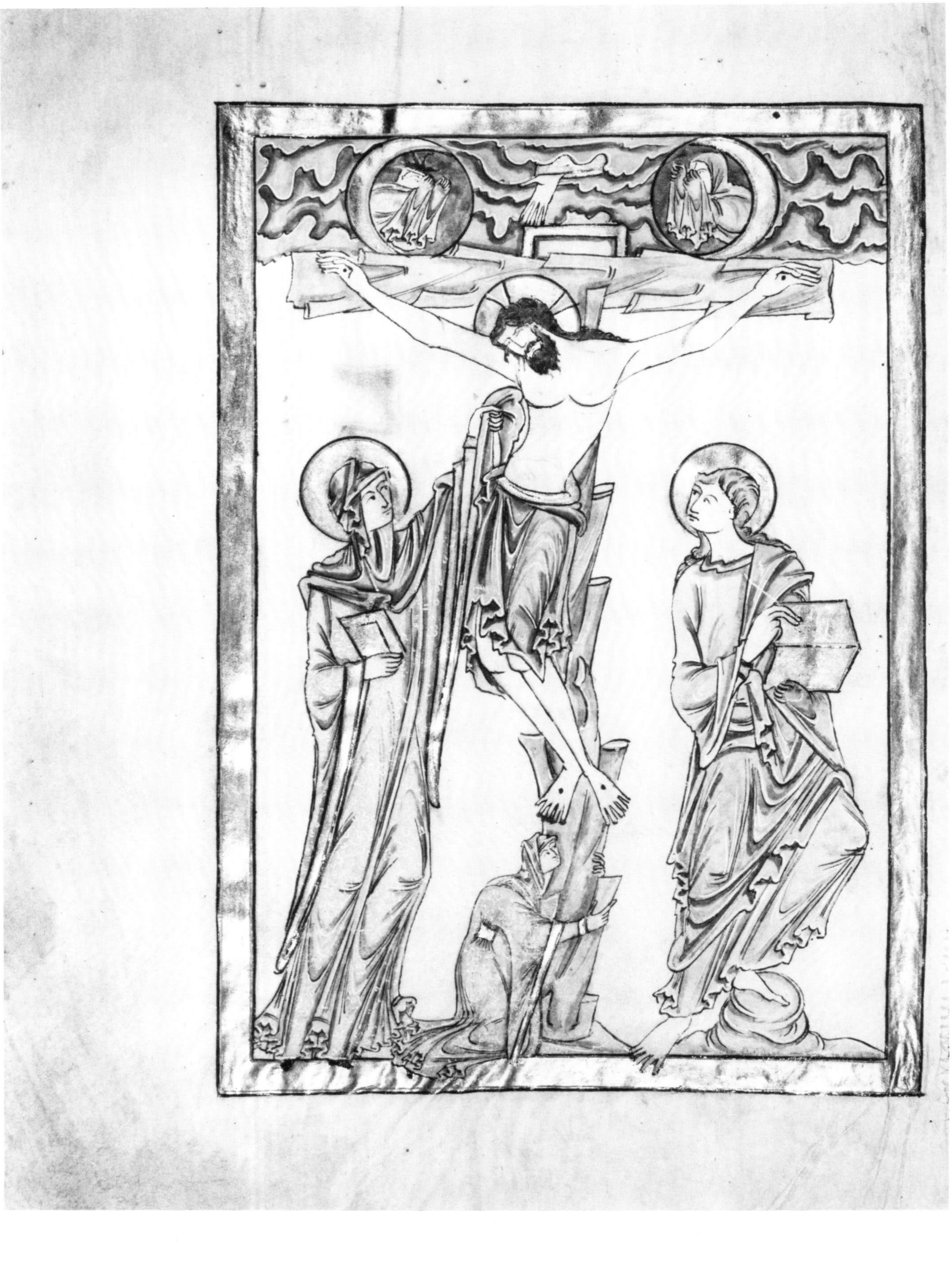

11.2 New York, Pierpont Morgan, M. 709, f. 1v

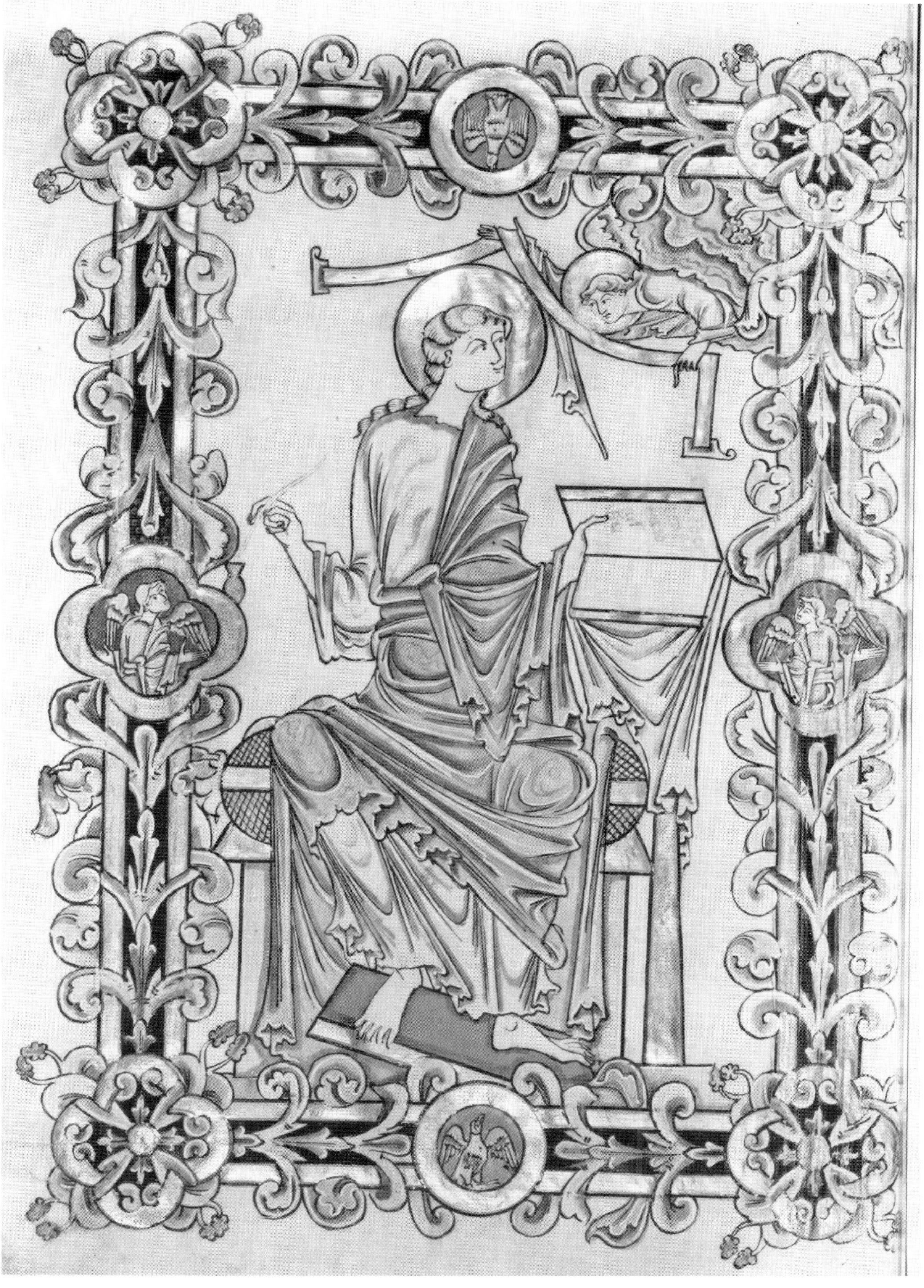

11.3 New York, Pierpont Morgan, M. 709, f. 2v

11.4 New York, Pierpont Morgan, M. 709, f. 3r

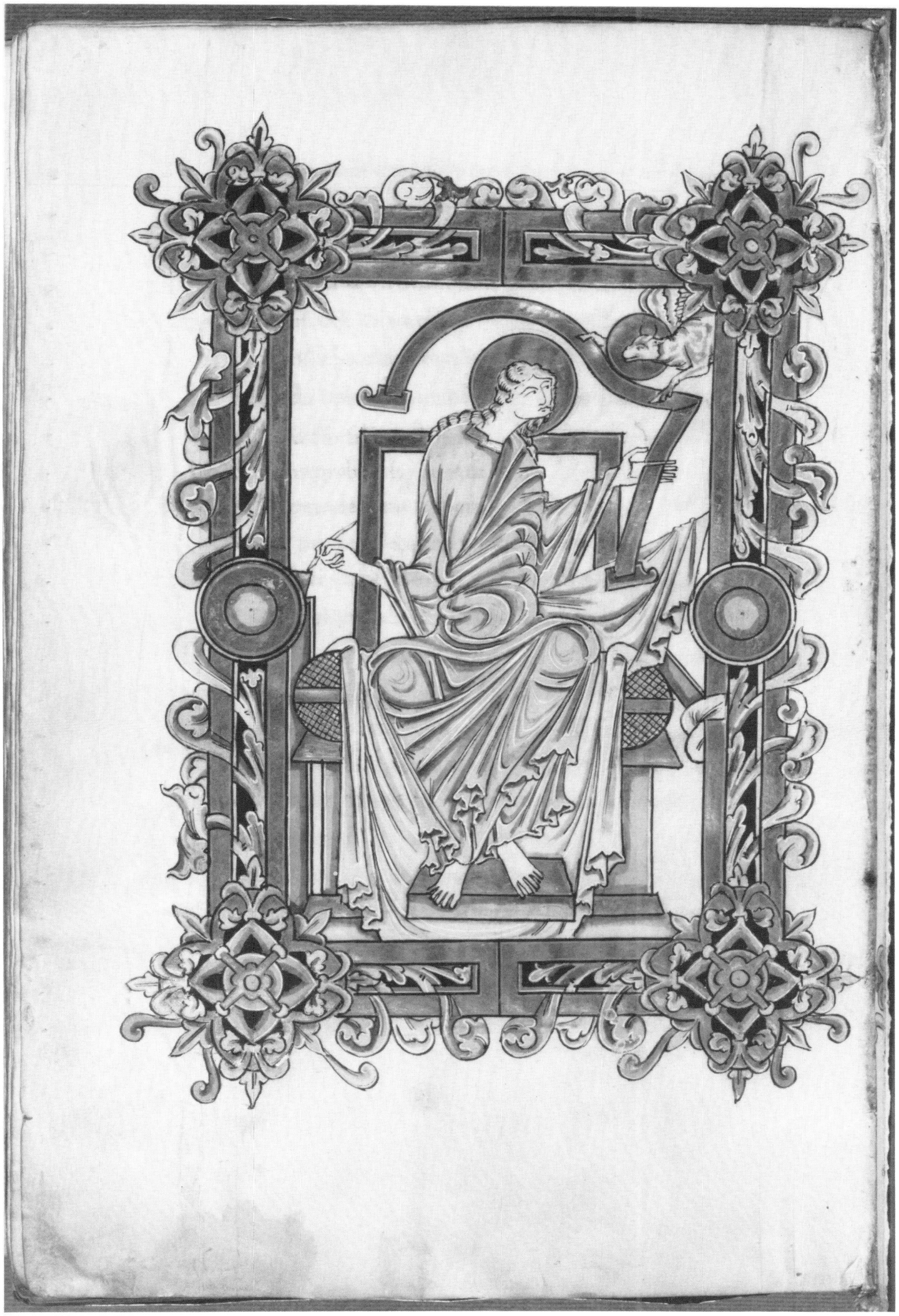

11.5 New York, Pierpont Morgan, M. 709, f. 48v

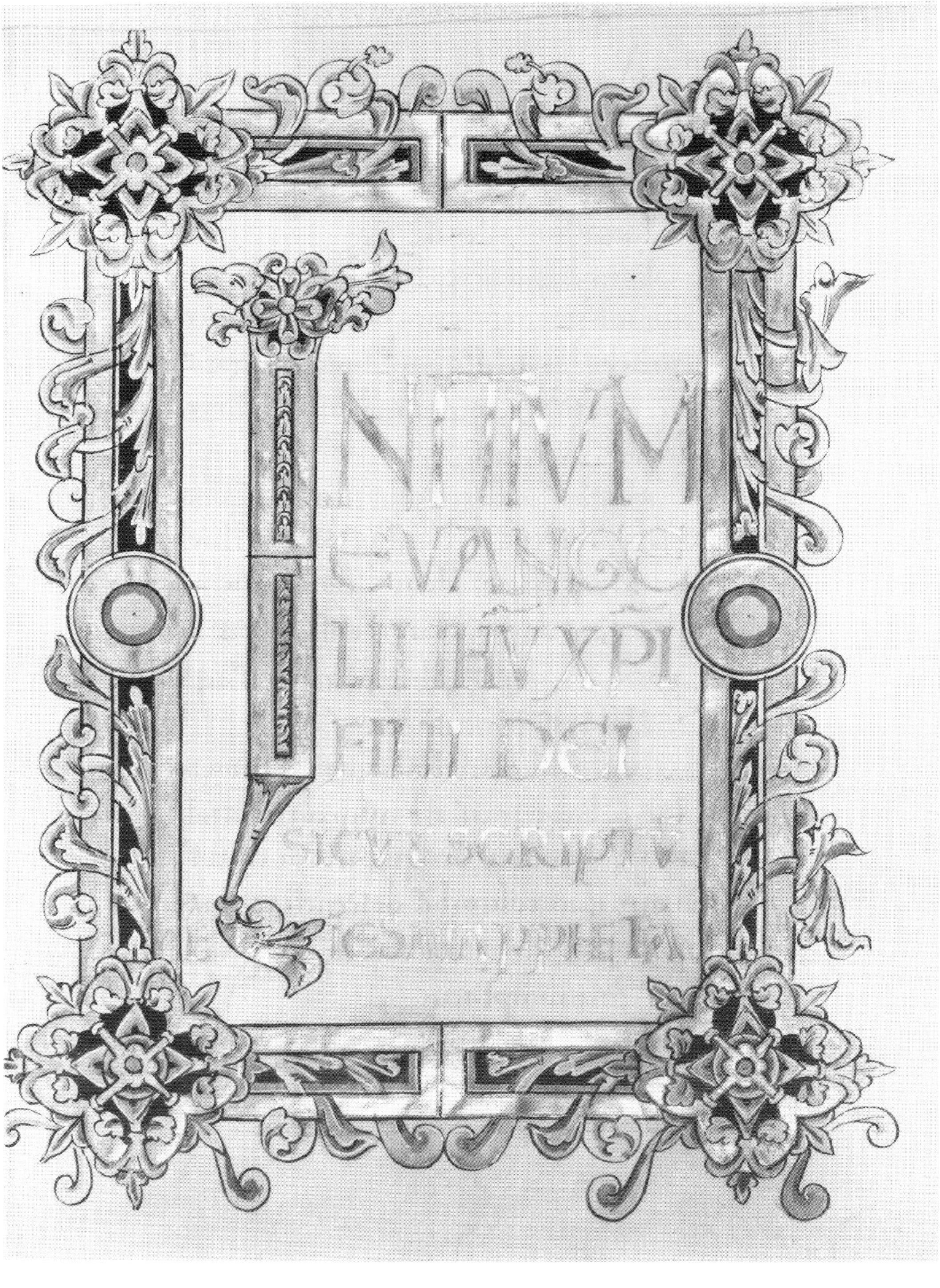

11.6 New York, Pierpont Morgan, M. 709, f. 49r

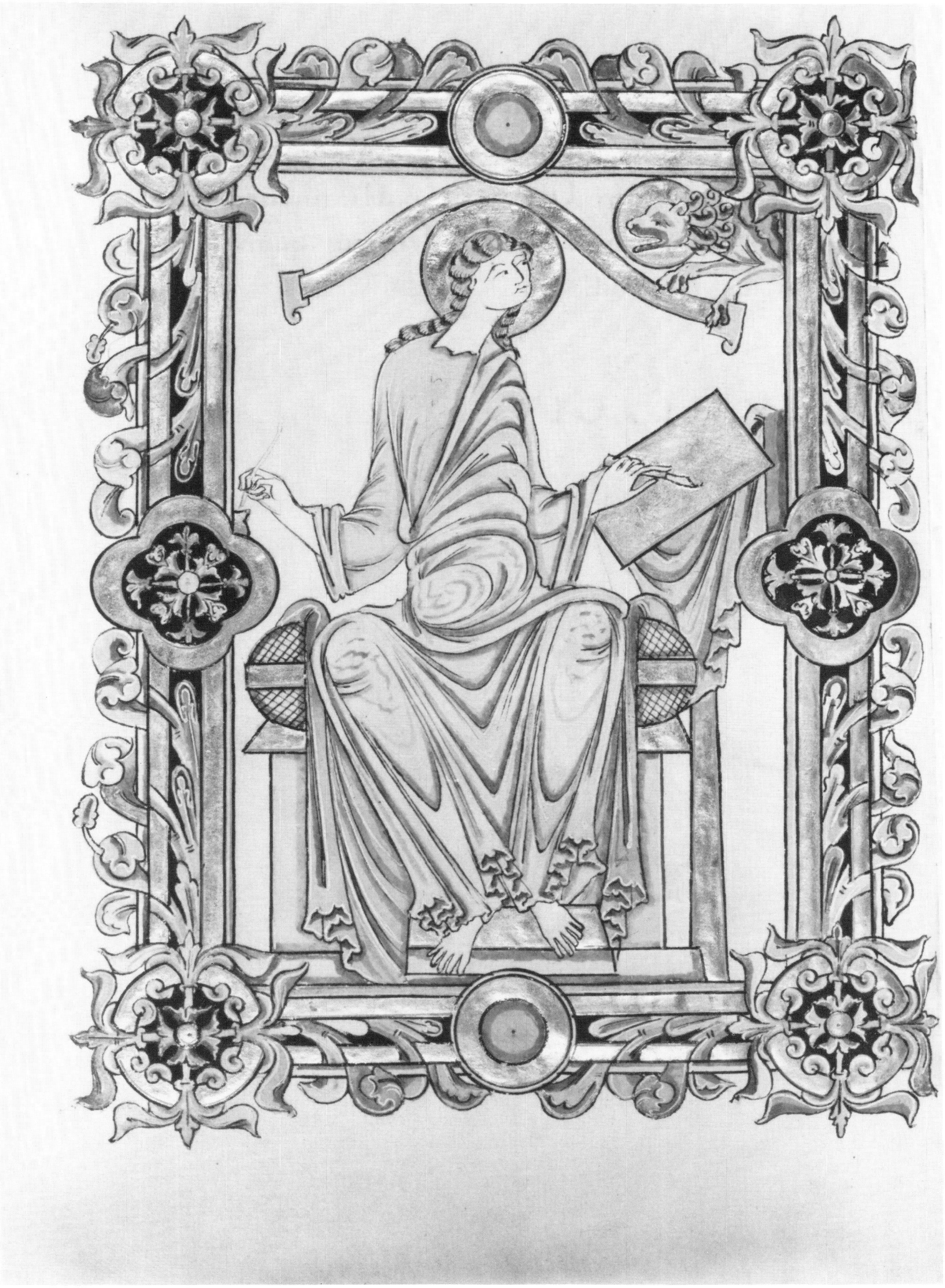

11.7 New York, Pierpont Morgan, M. 709, f. 77v

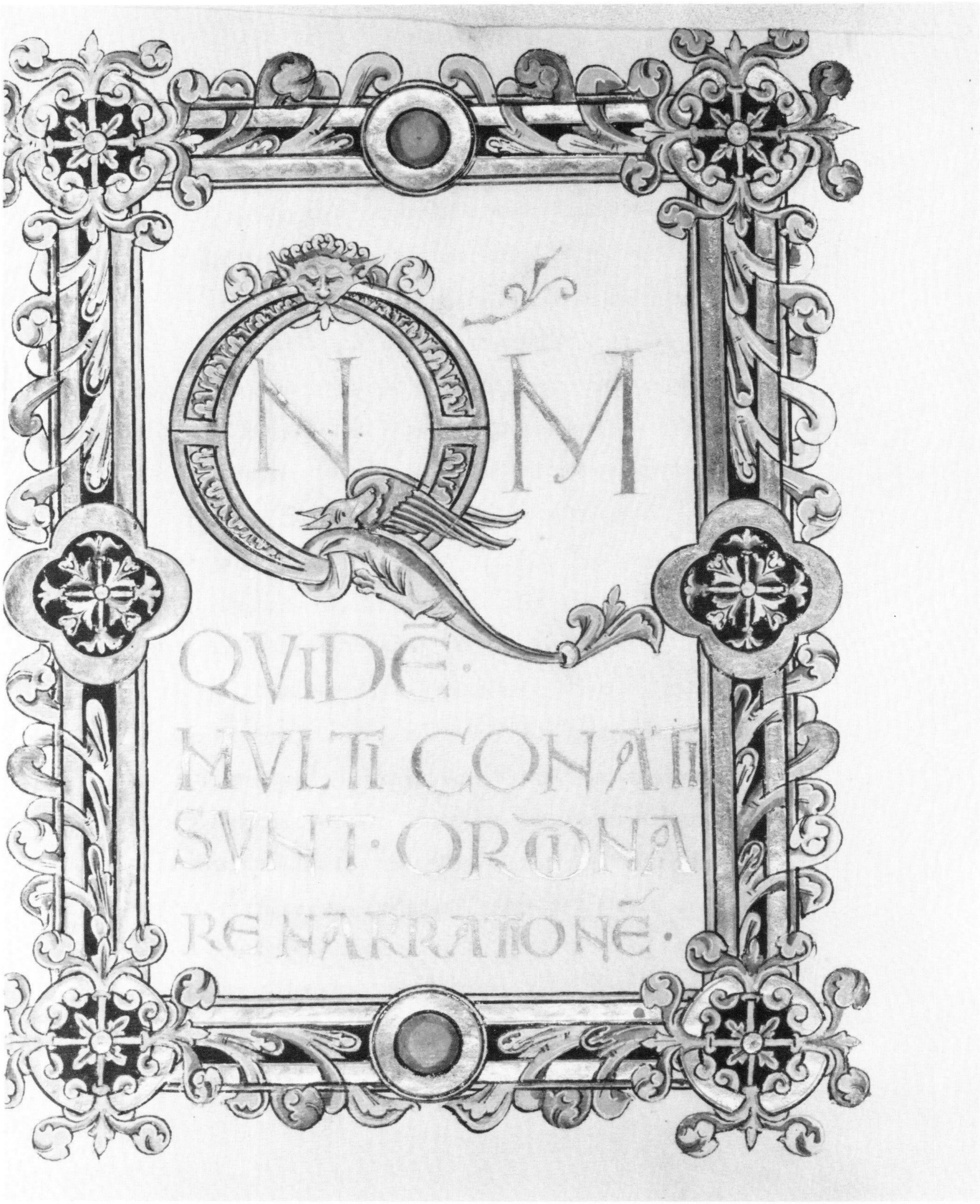

11.8 New York, Pierpont Morgan, M. 709, f. 78r

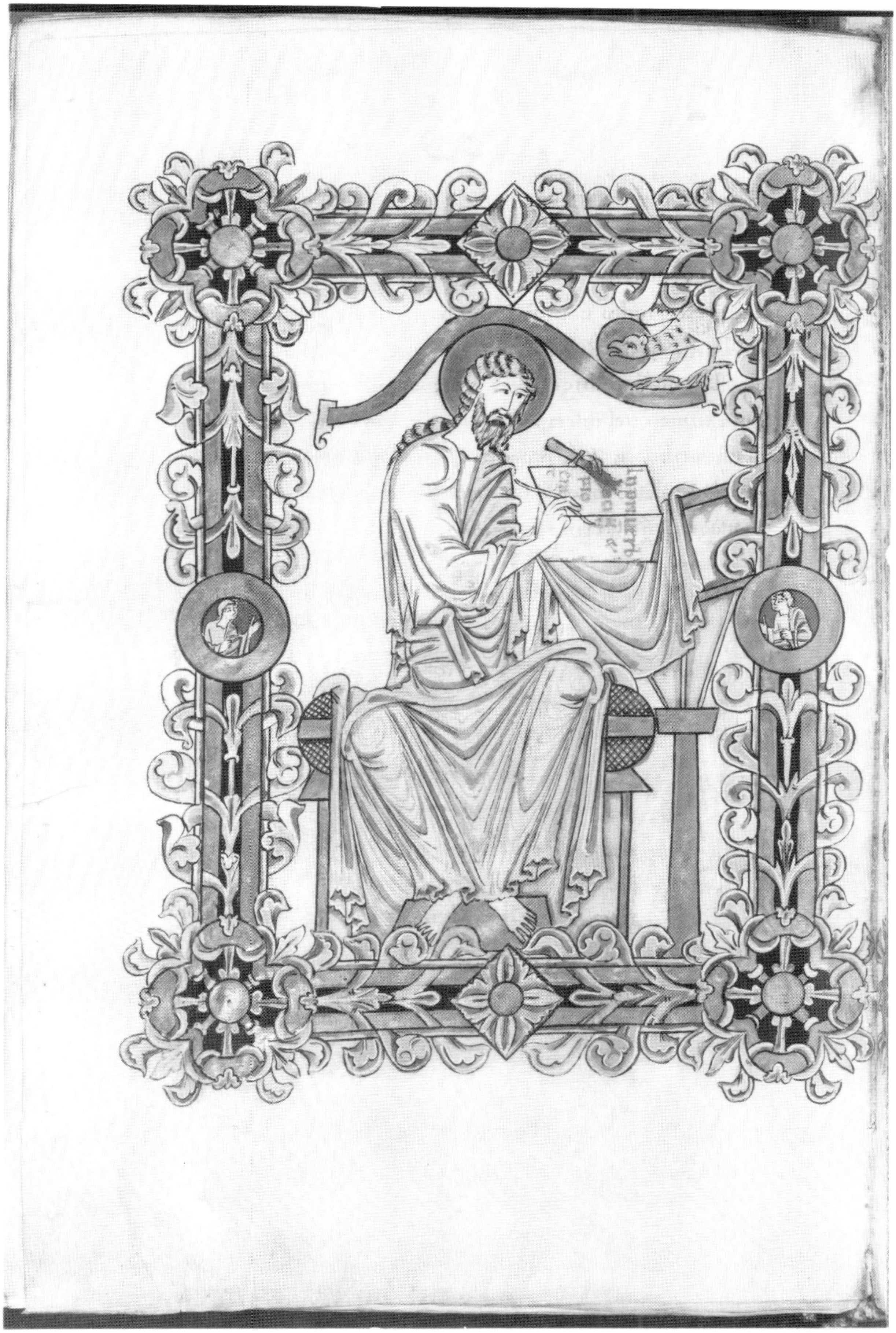

11.9 New York, Pierpont Morgan, M. 709, f. 122v

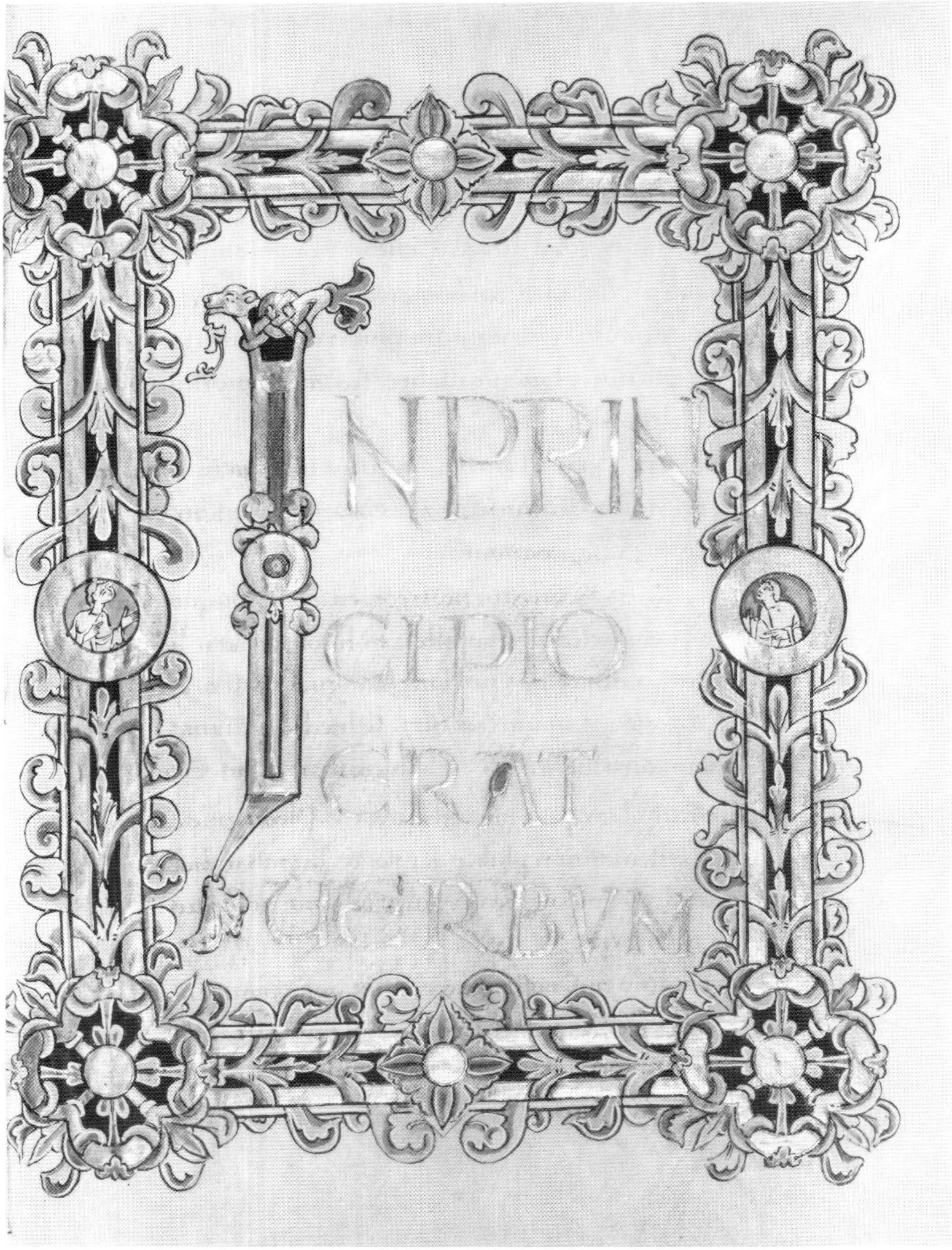

11.10 New York, Pierpont Morgan, M. 709, f. 123r

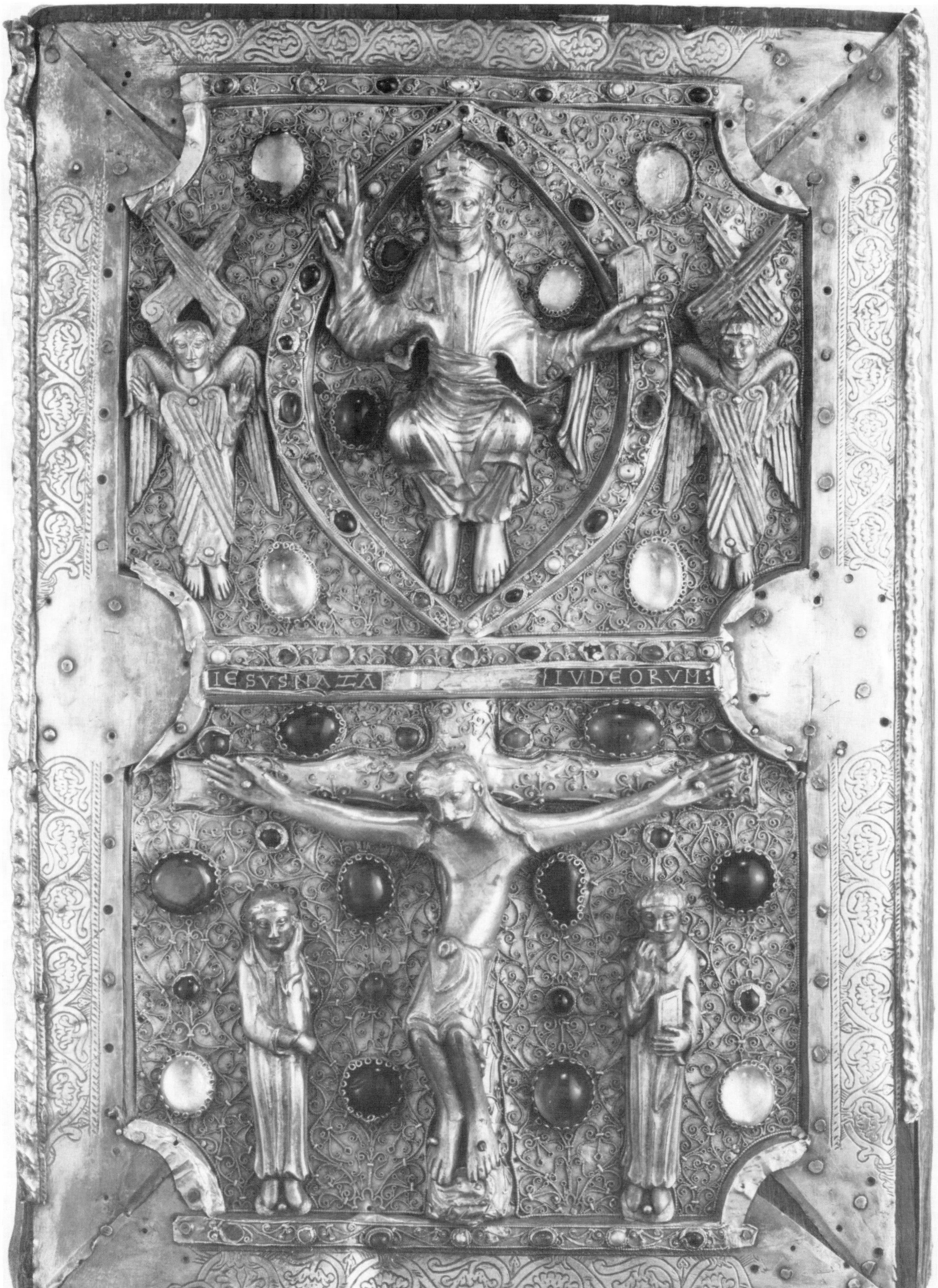

12.1 New York, Pierpont Morgan, M. 708, Jeweled binding

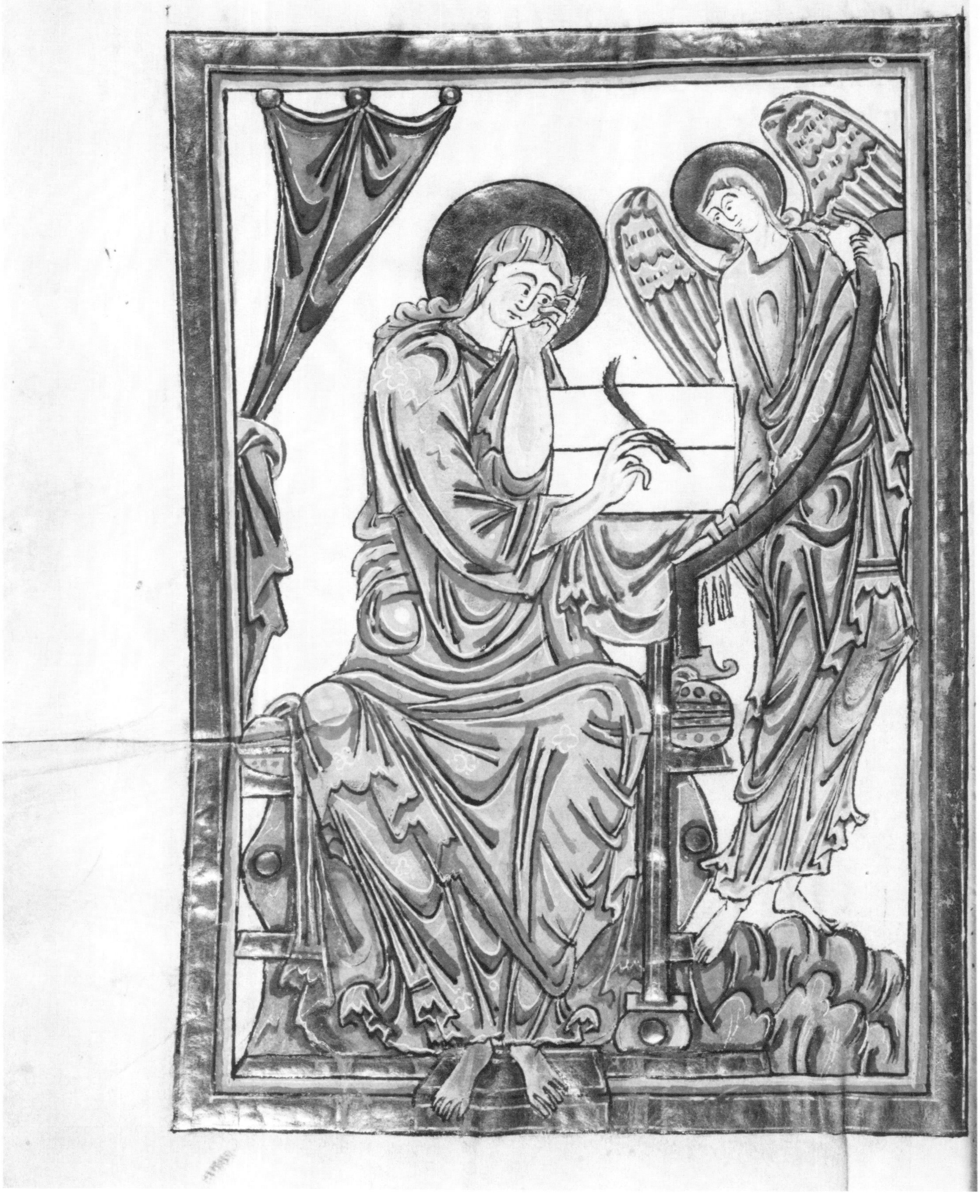

12.2 New York, Pierpont Morgan, M. 708, f. 2v

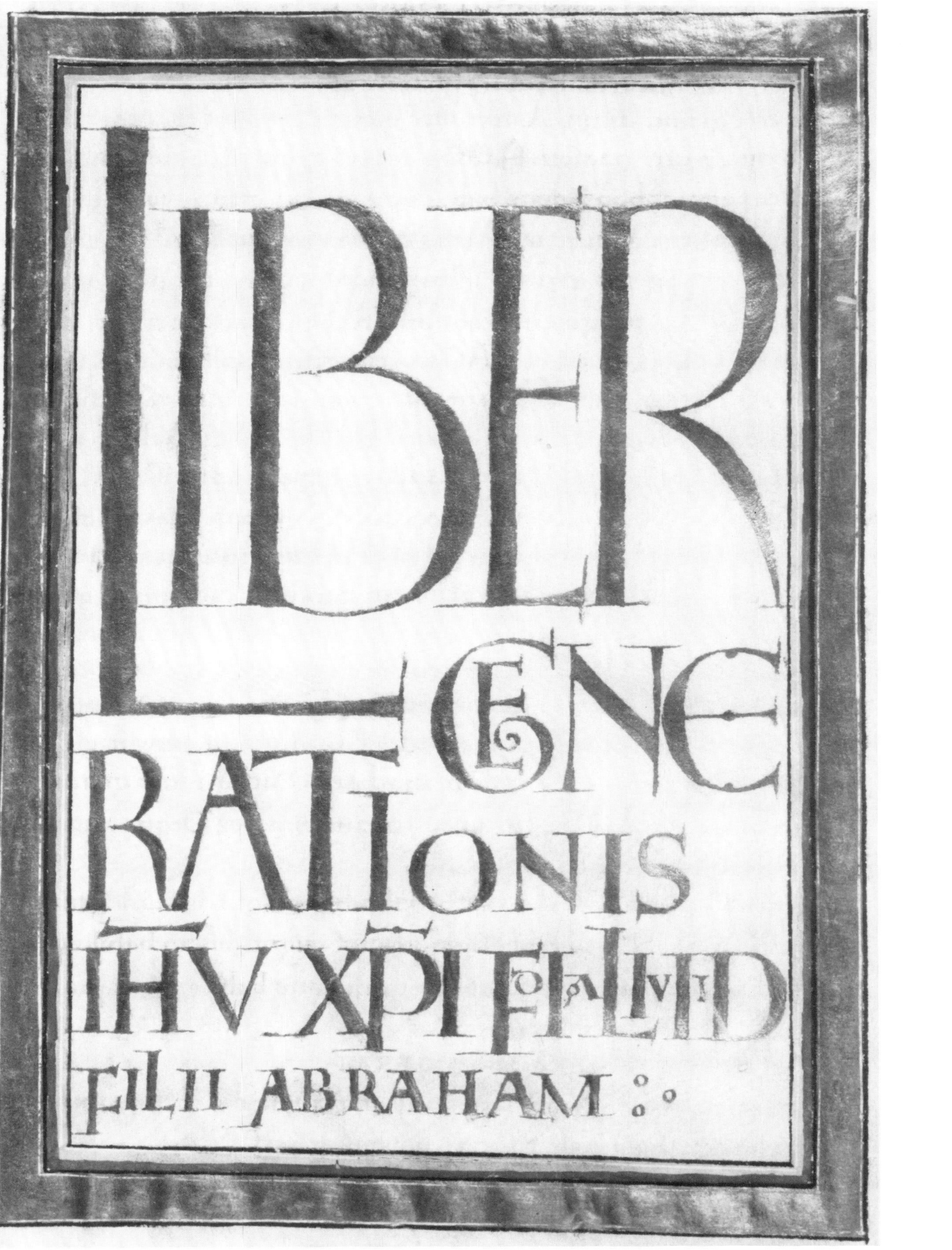

12.3 New York, Pierpont Morgan, M. 708, f. 3r

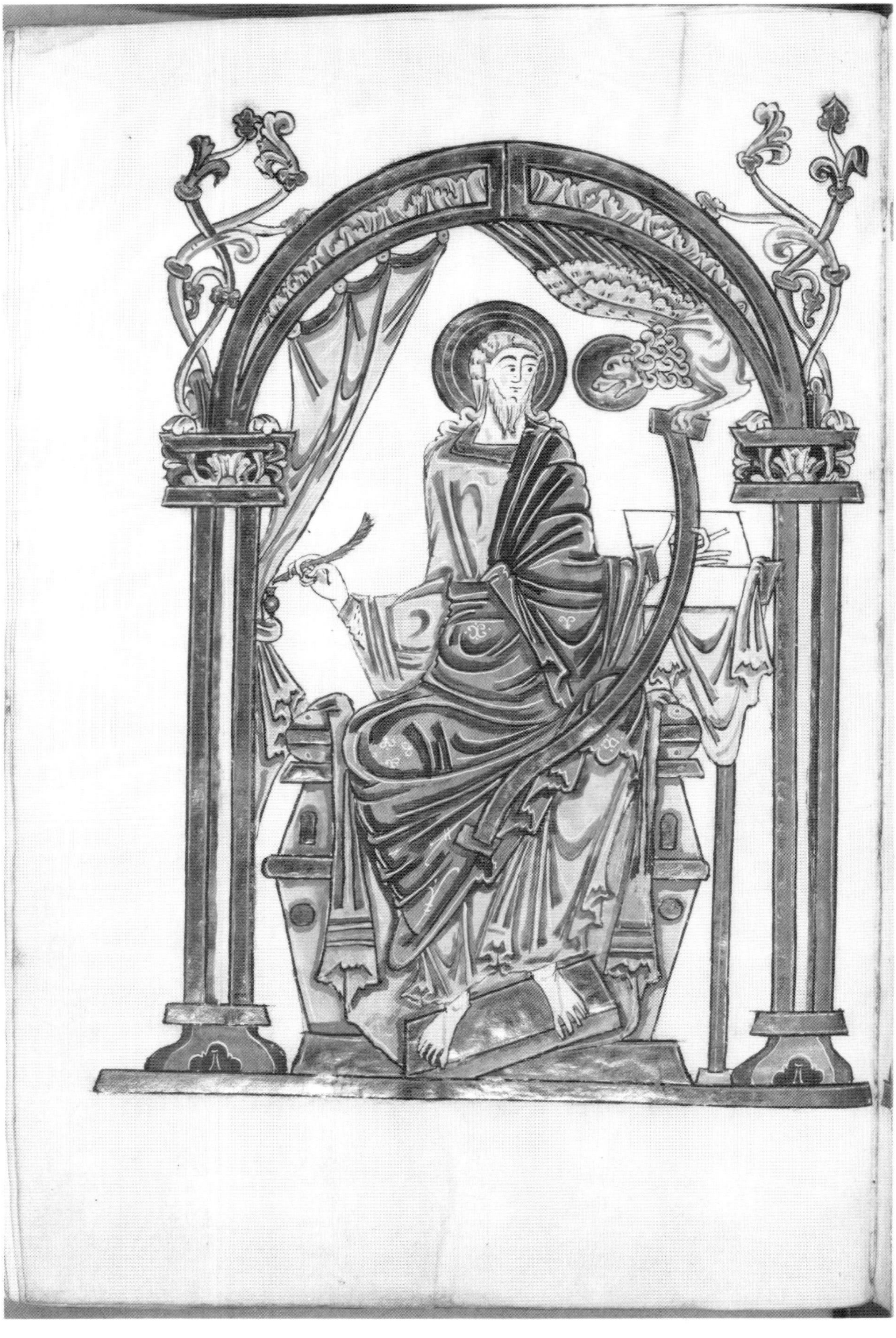

12.4 New York, Pierpont Morgan, M. 708, f. 26ᵛ

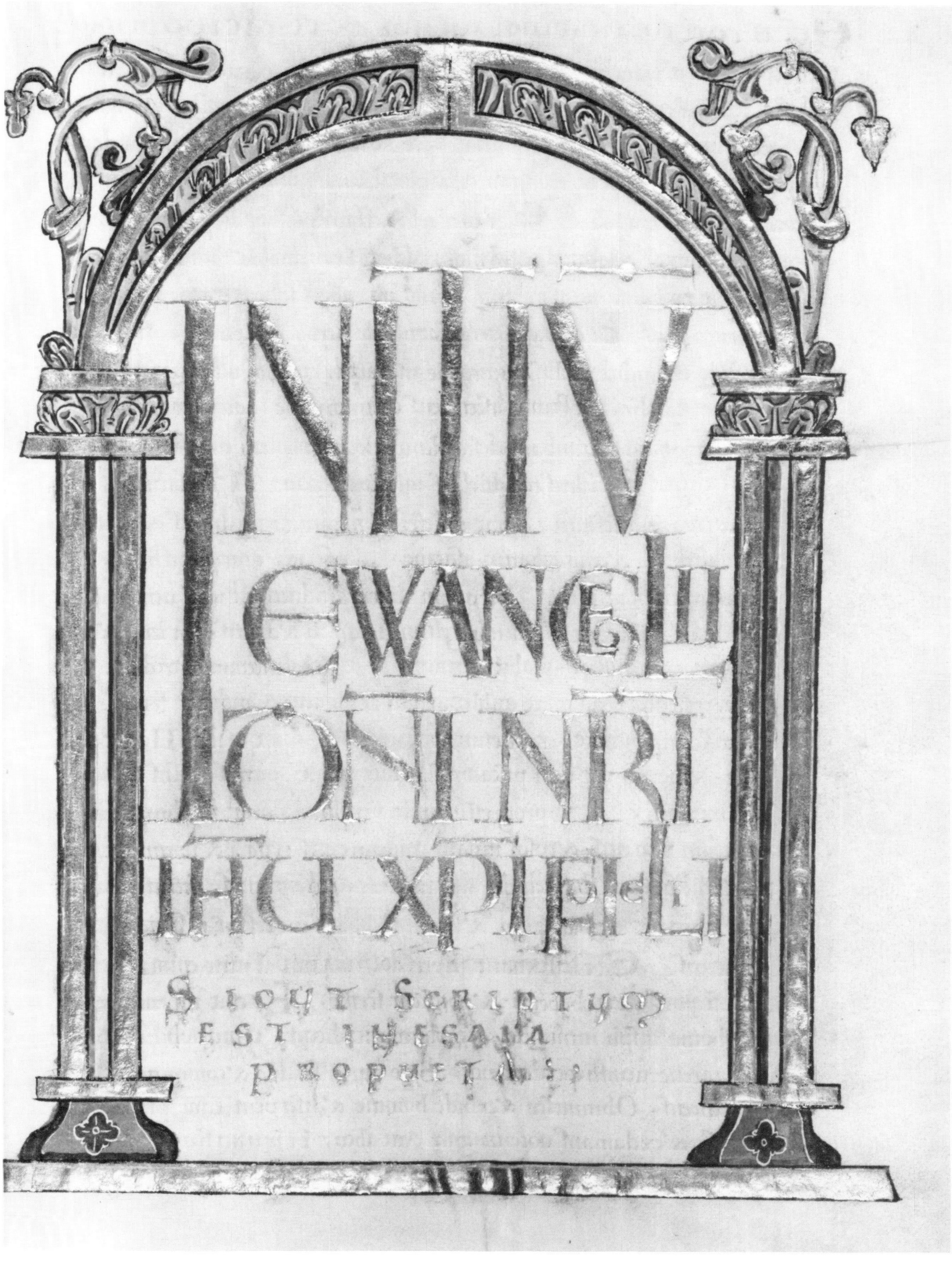

12.5 New York, Pierpont Morgan, M. 708, f. 27r

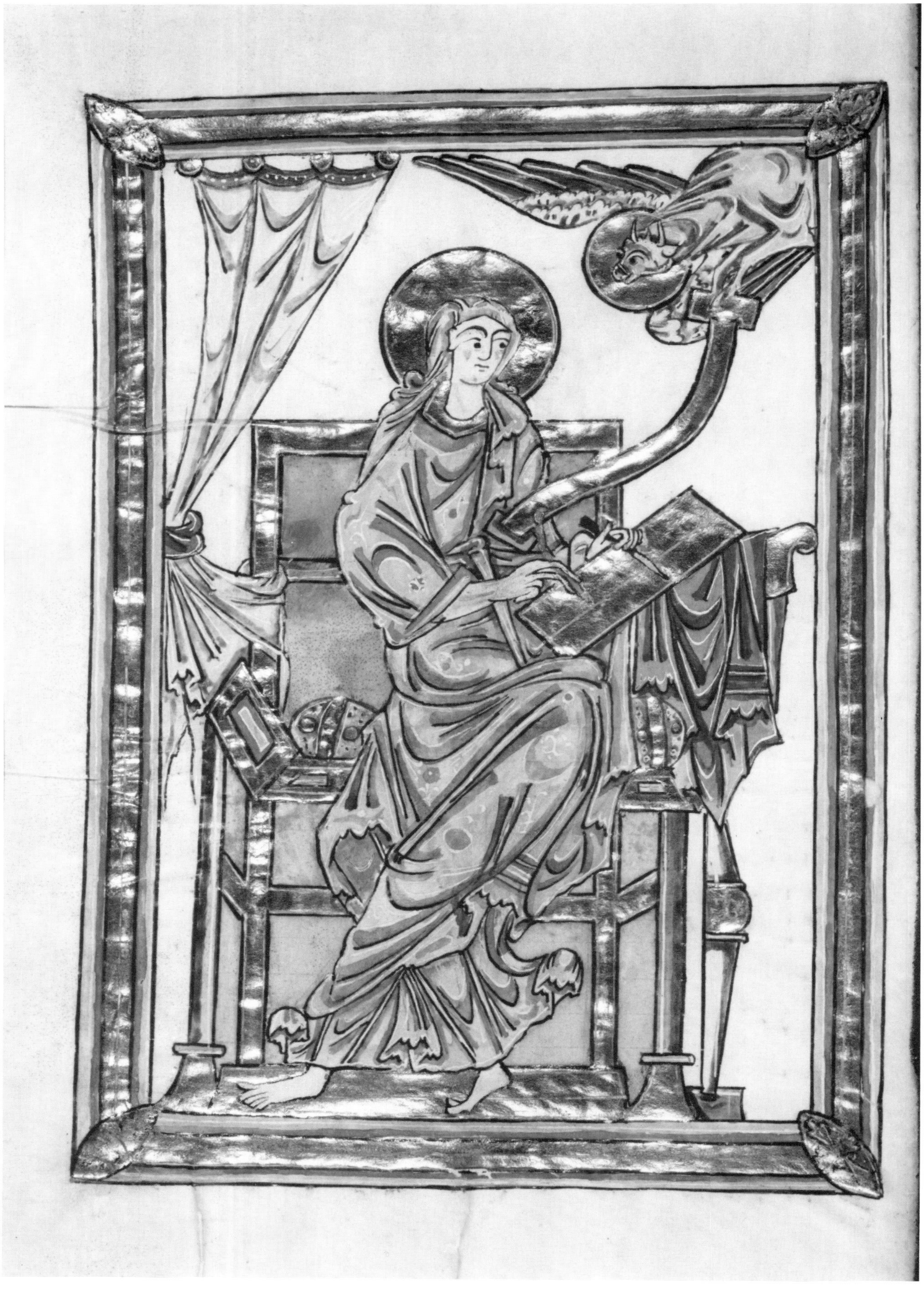

12.6 New York, Pierpont Morgan, M. 708, f. 42v

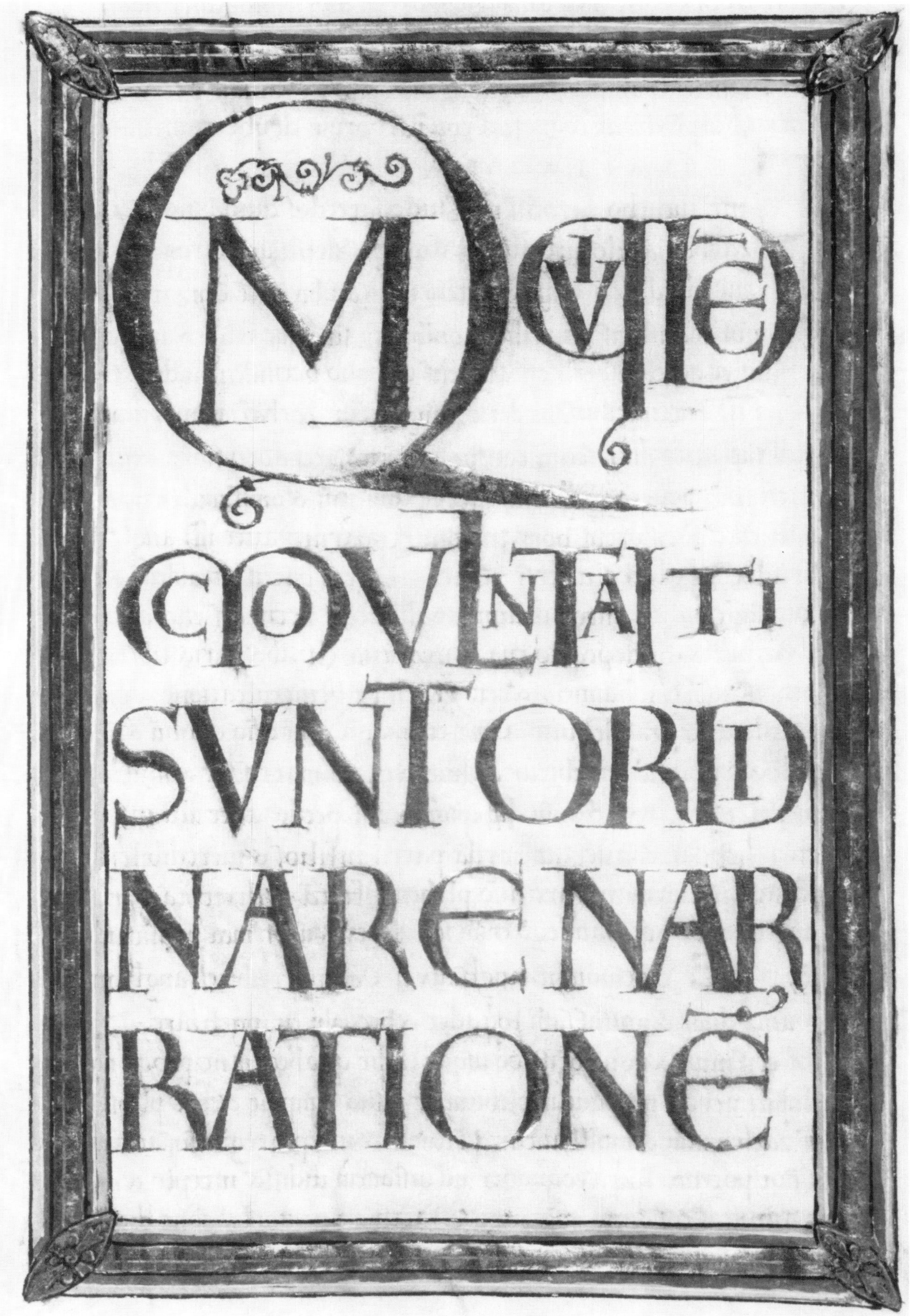

12.7 New York, Pierpont Morgan, M. 708, f. 43r

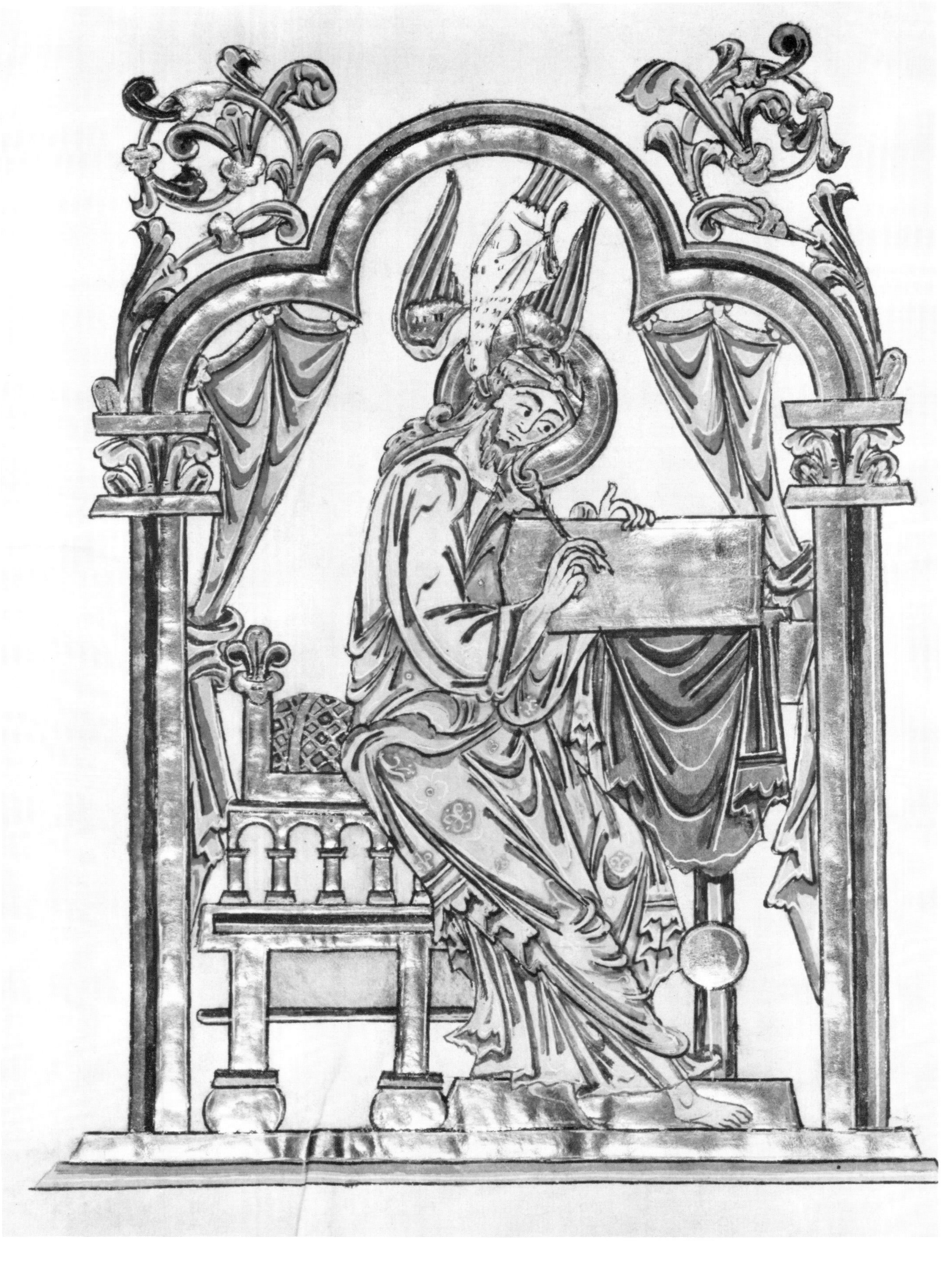

12.8 New York, Pierpont Morgan, M. 708, f. 66v

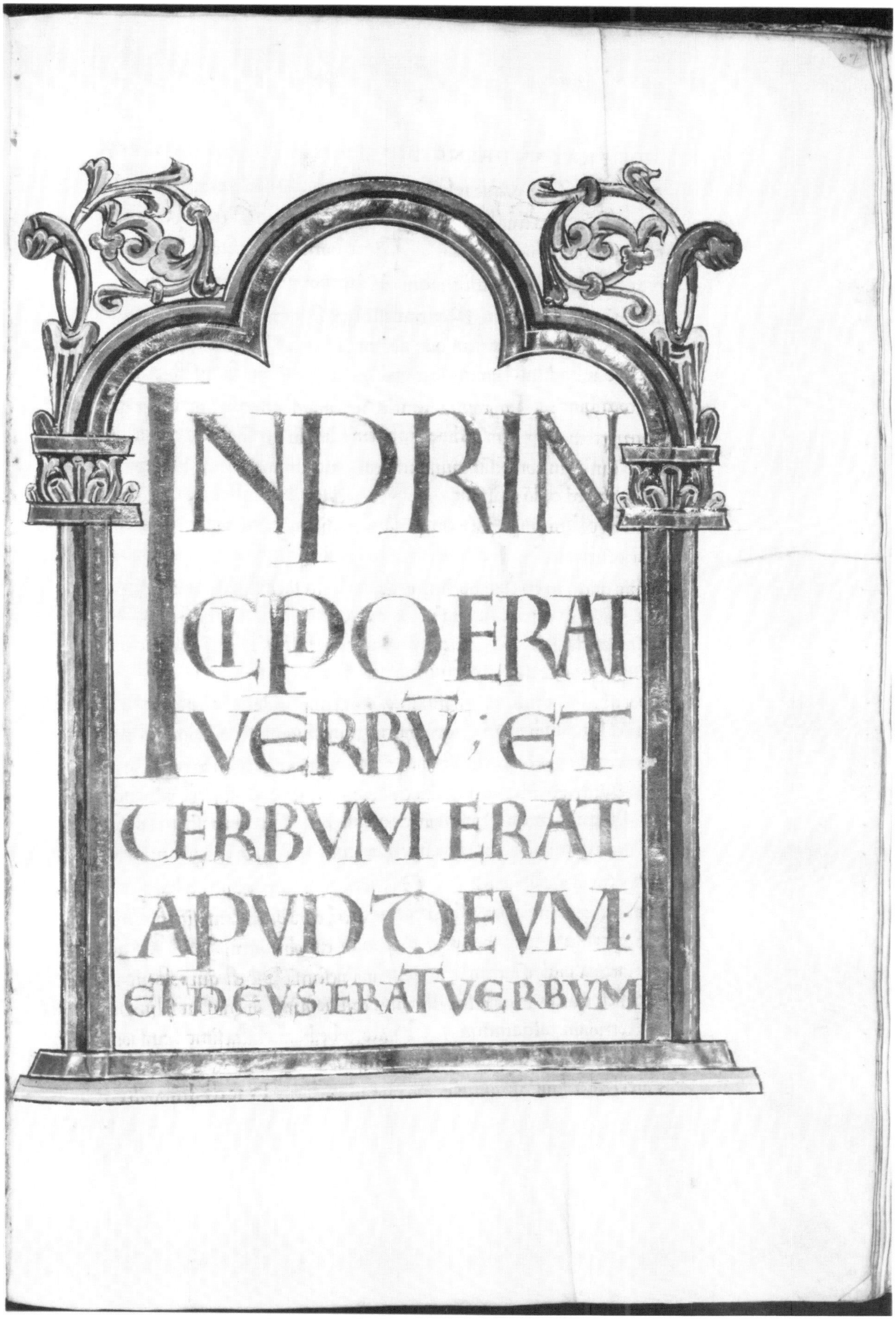

12.9 New York, Pierpont Morgan, M. 708, f. 67r

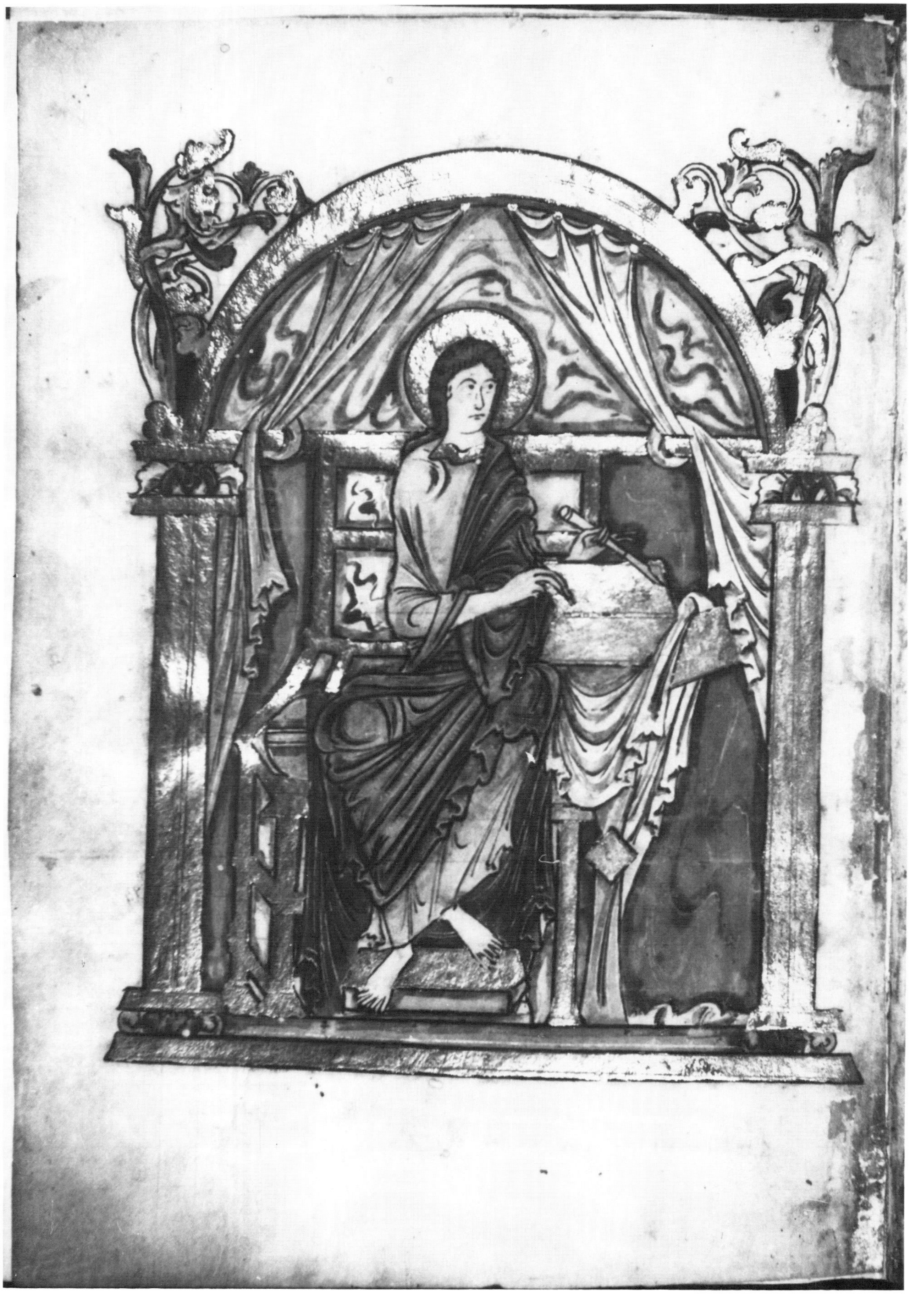

13.1 Monte Cassino, Archivio della Badia, BB. 437, 439, p. 2^{v}

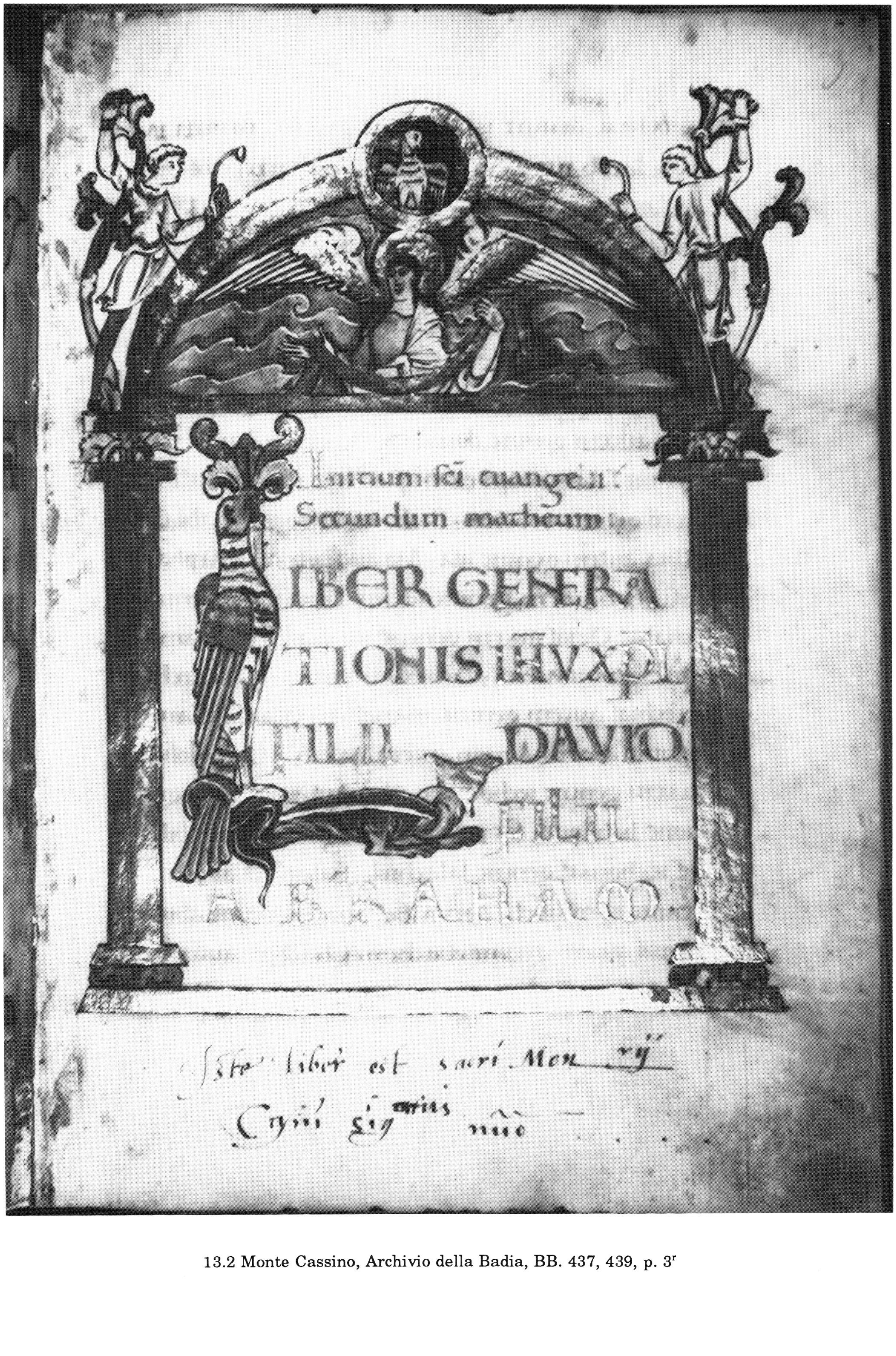

13.2 Monte Cassino, Archivio della Badia, BB. 437, 439, p. 3r

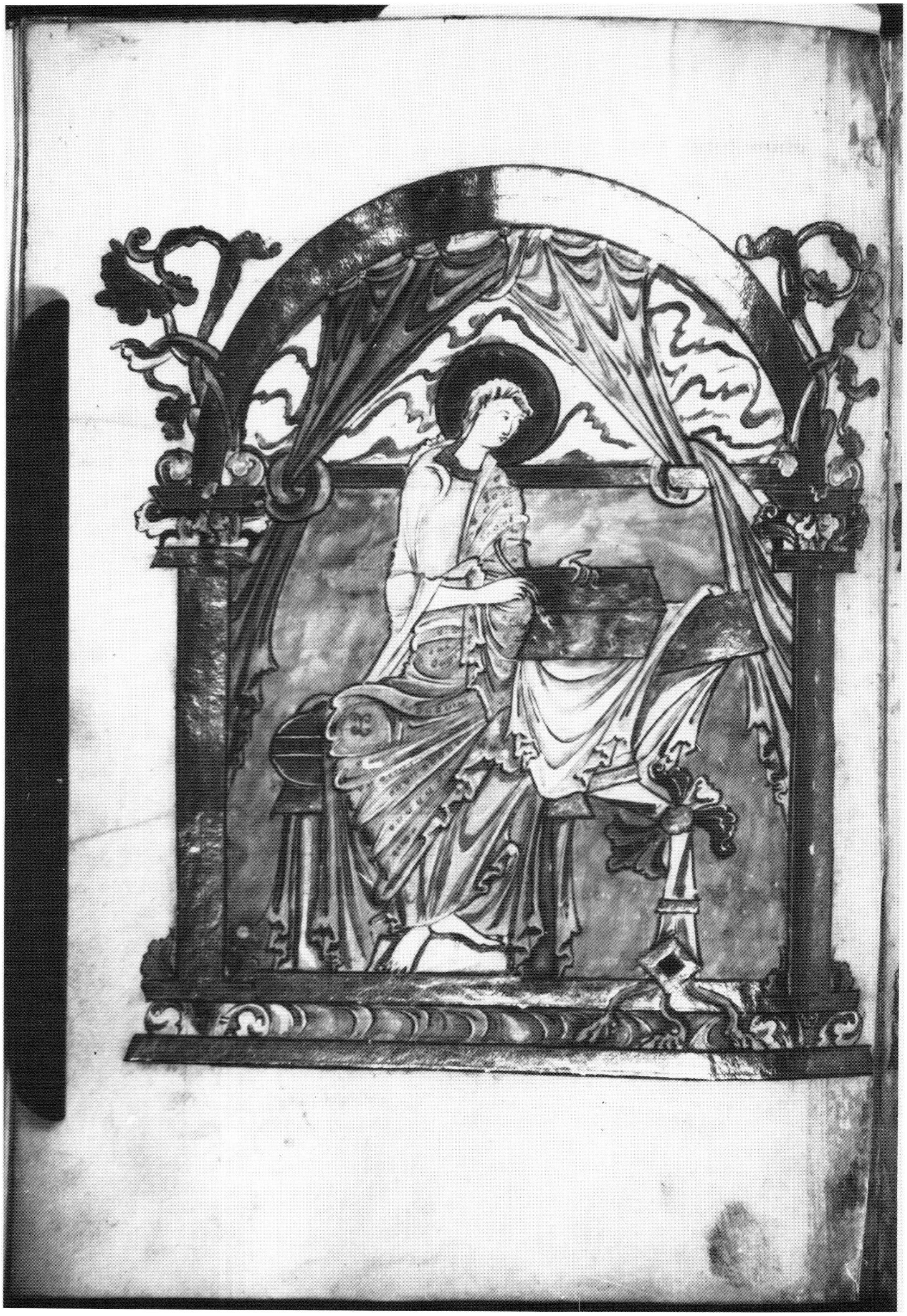

13.3 Monte Cassino, Archivio della Badia, BB. 437, 439, p. 102ᵛ

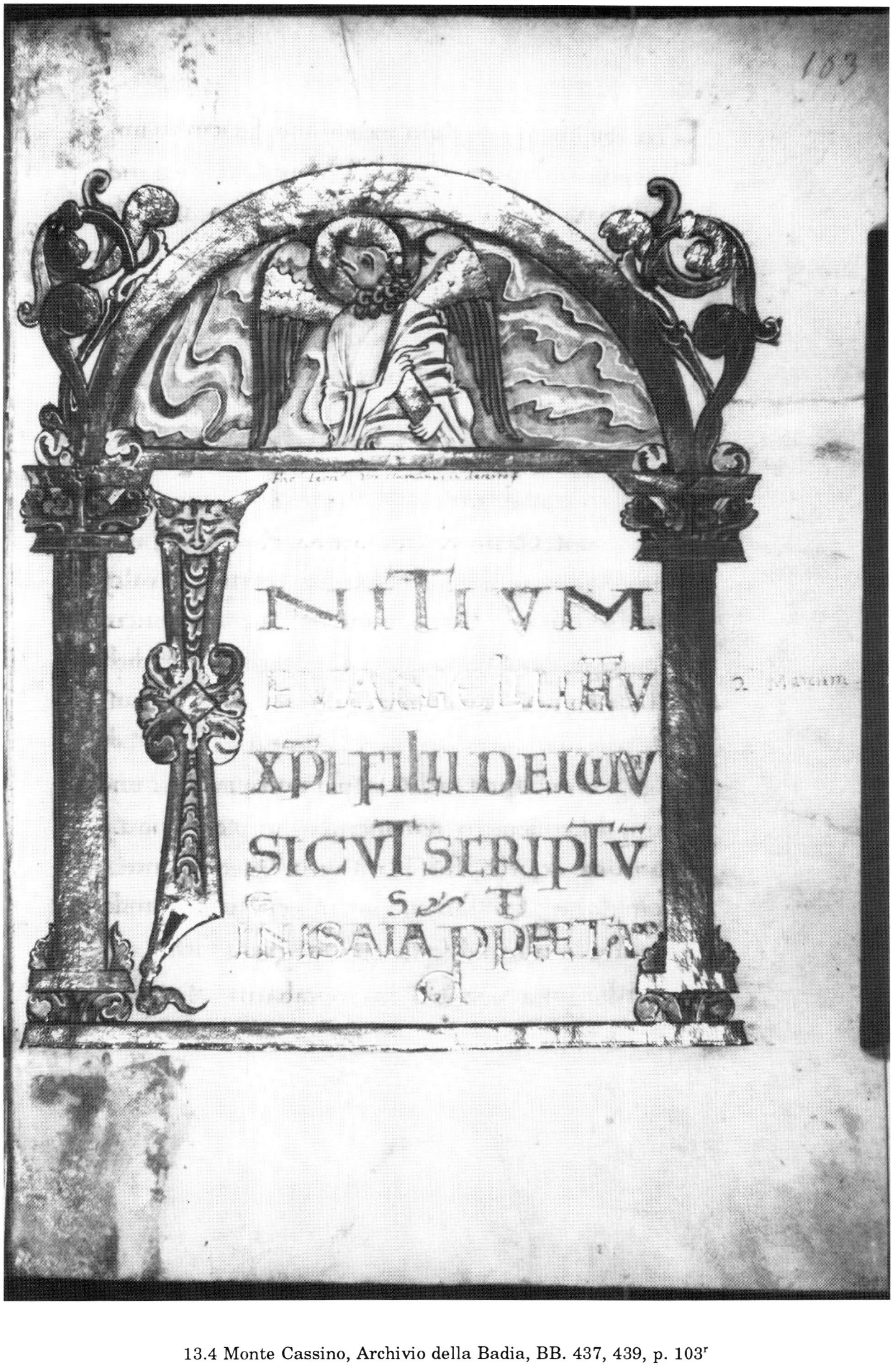

13.4 Monte Cassino, Archivio della Badia, BB. 437, 439, p. 103r

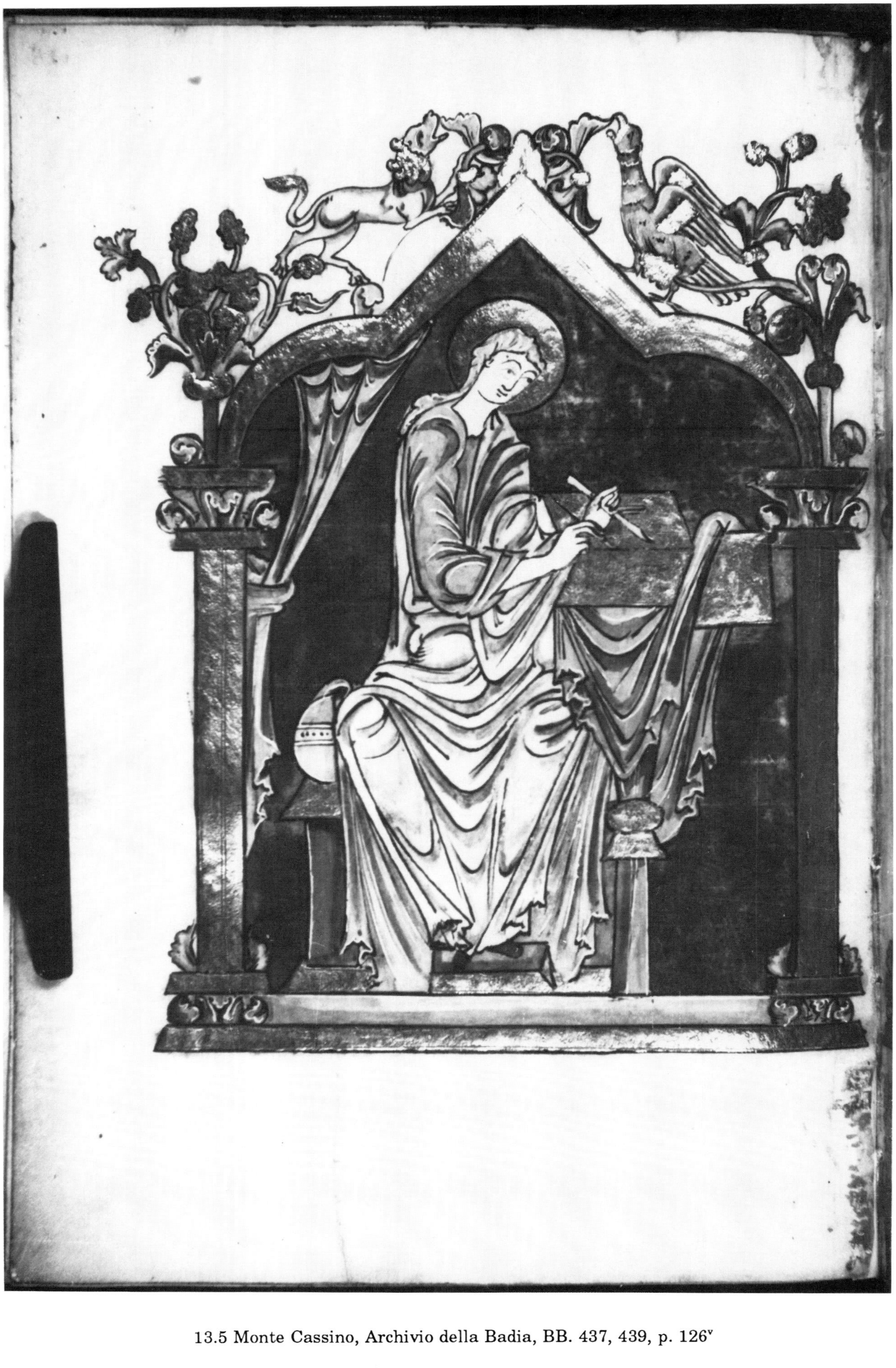

13.5 Monte Cassino, Archivio della Badia, BB. 437, 439, p. 126v

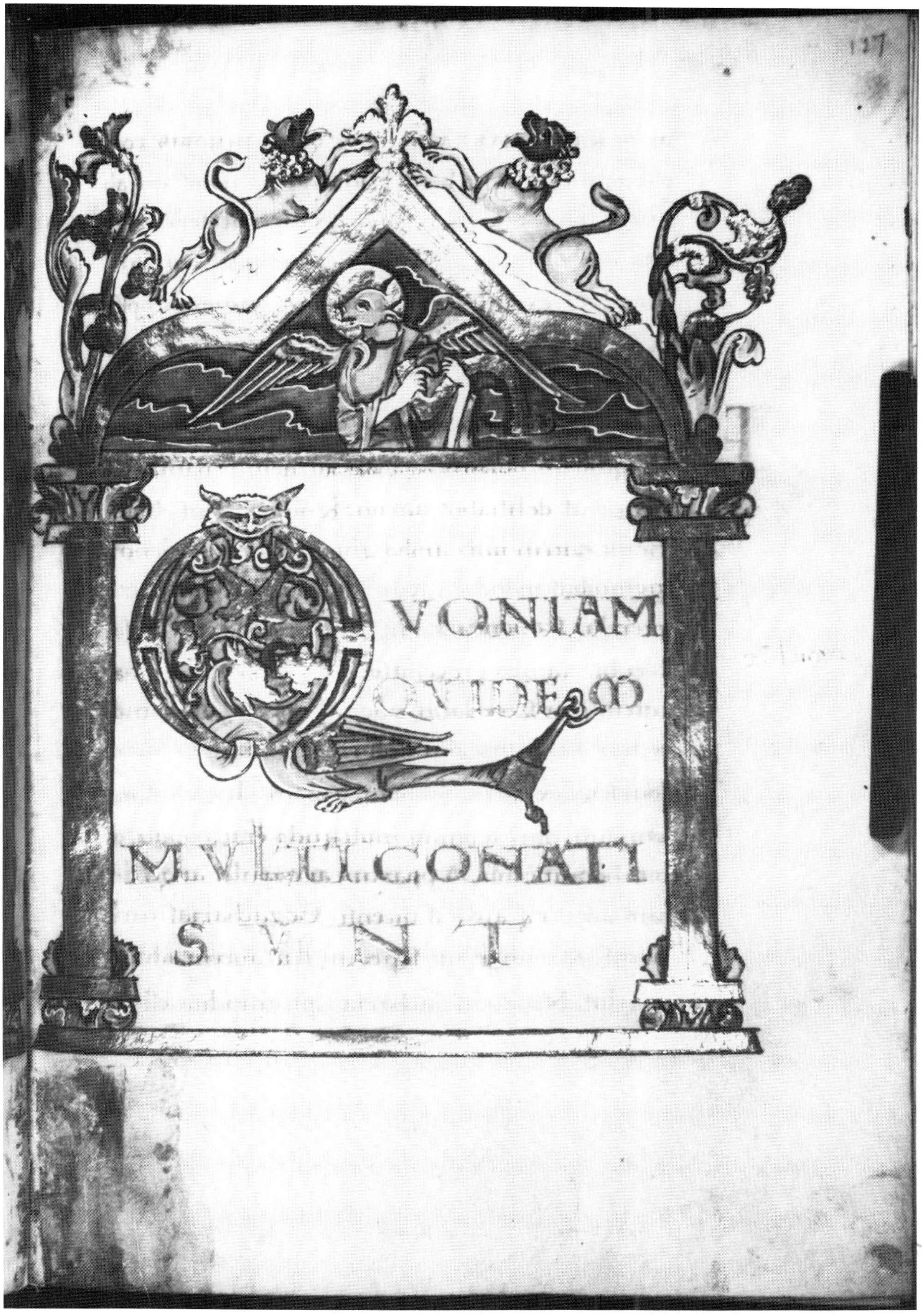

13.6 Monte Cassino, Archivio della Badia, BB. 437, 439, p. 127r

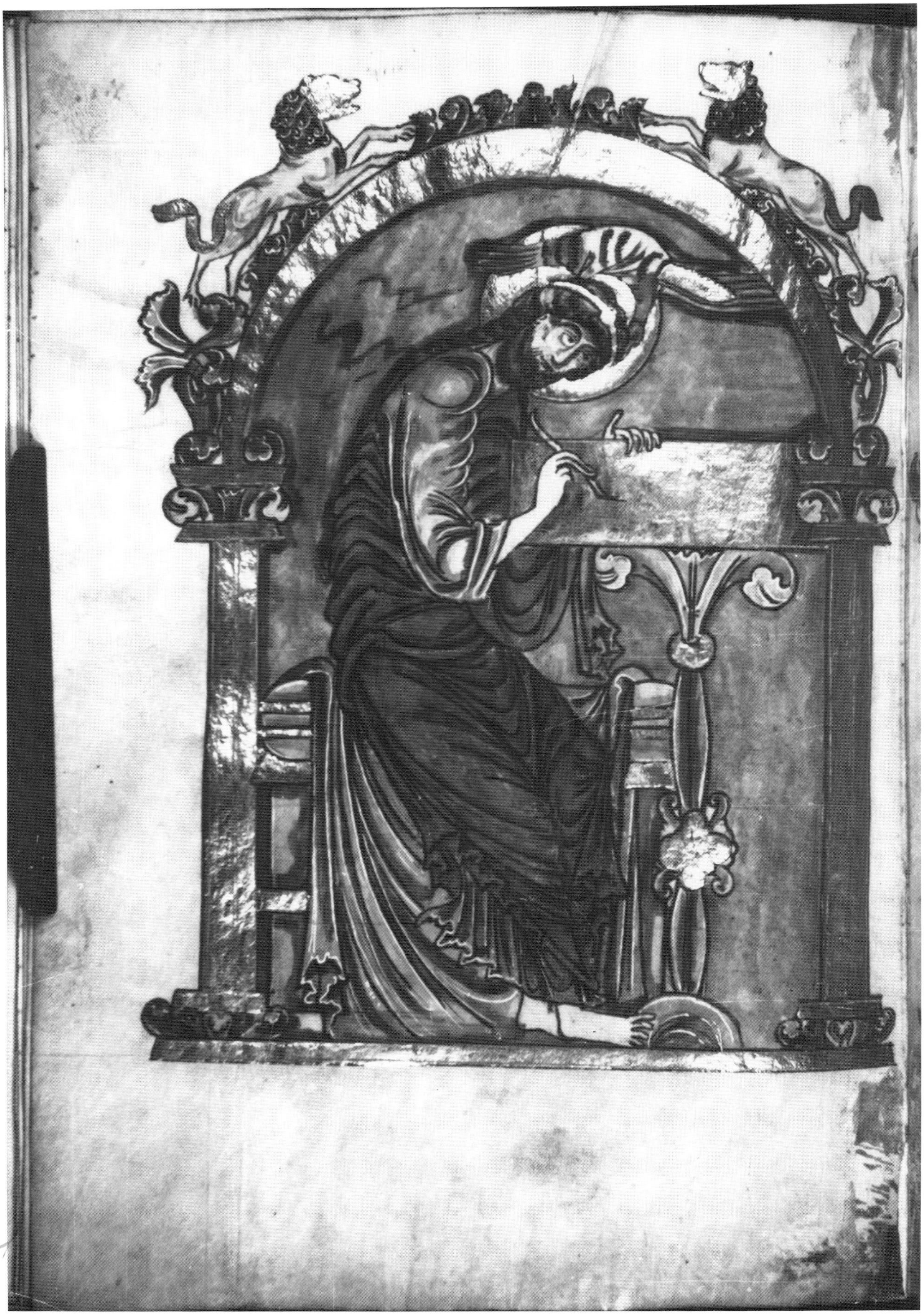

13.7 Monte Cassino, Archivio della Badia, BB. 437, 439, p. 166[v]

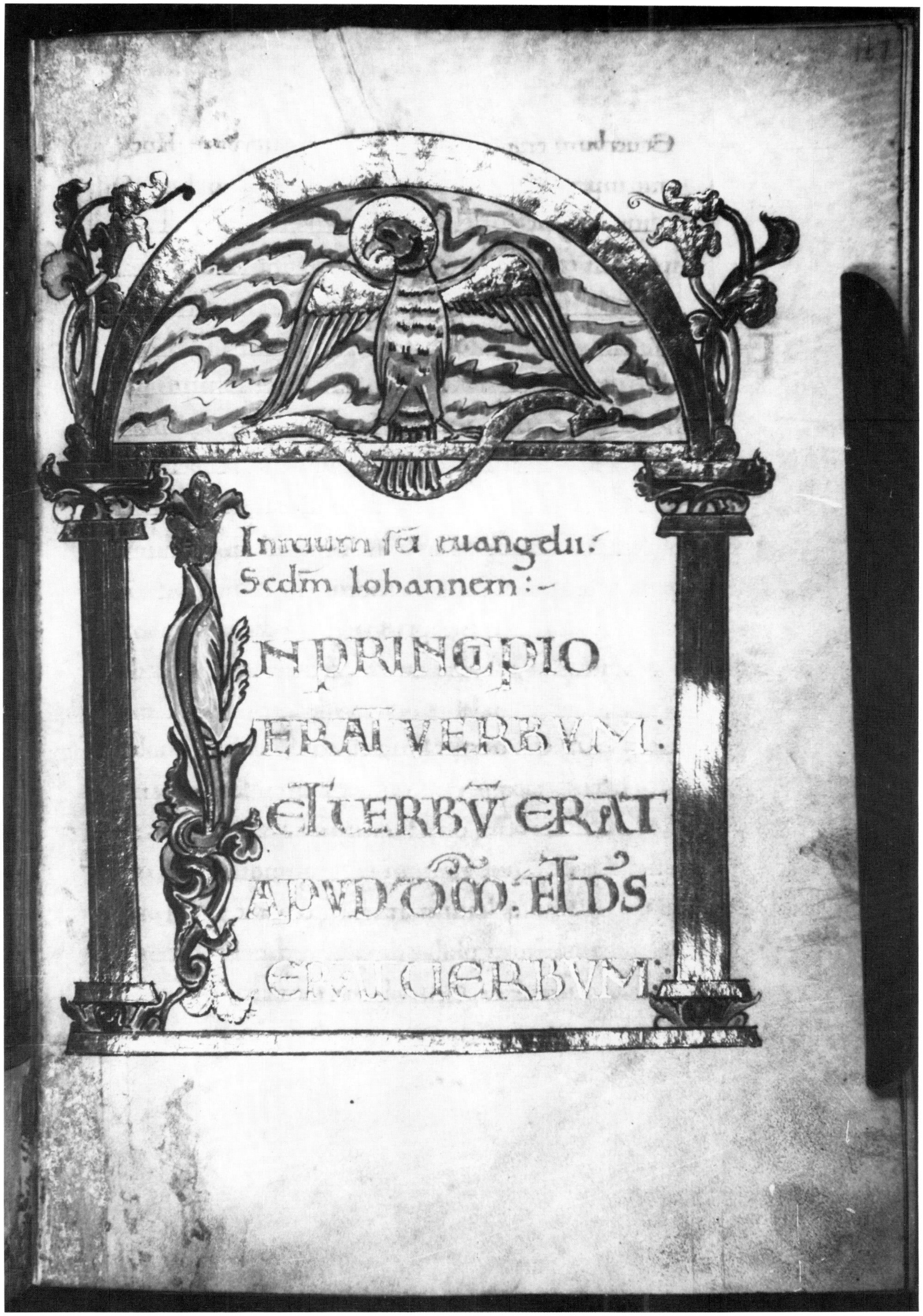

13.8 Monte Cassino, Archivio della Badia, BB. 437, 439, p. 167r

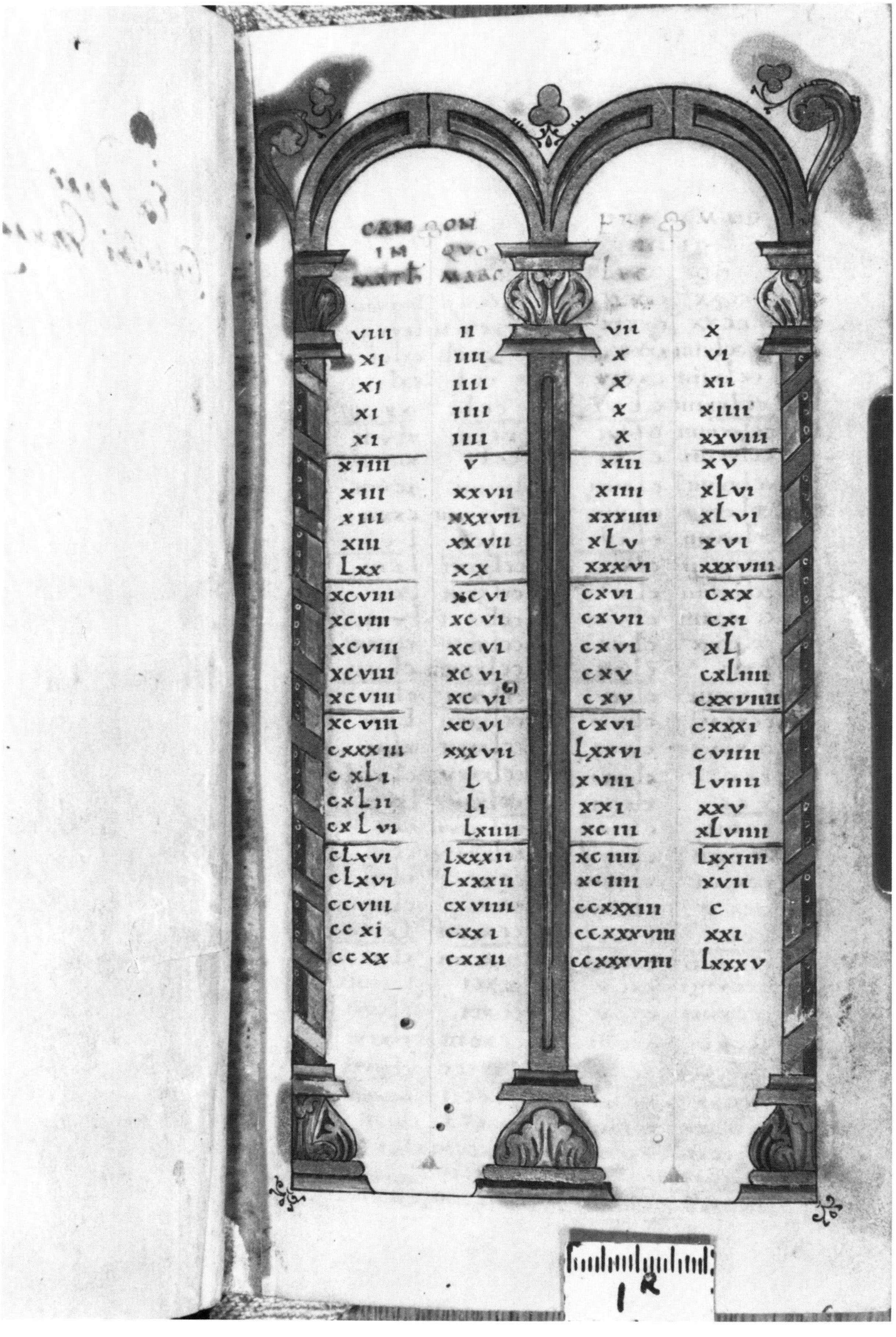

14.1 Cambridge, Pembroke College 302, f. 1r

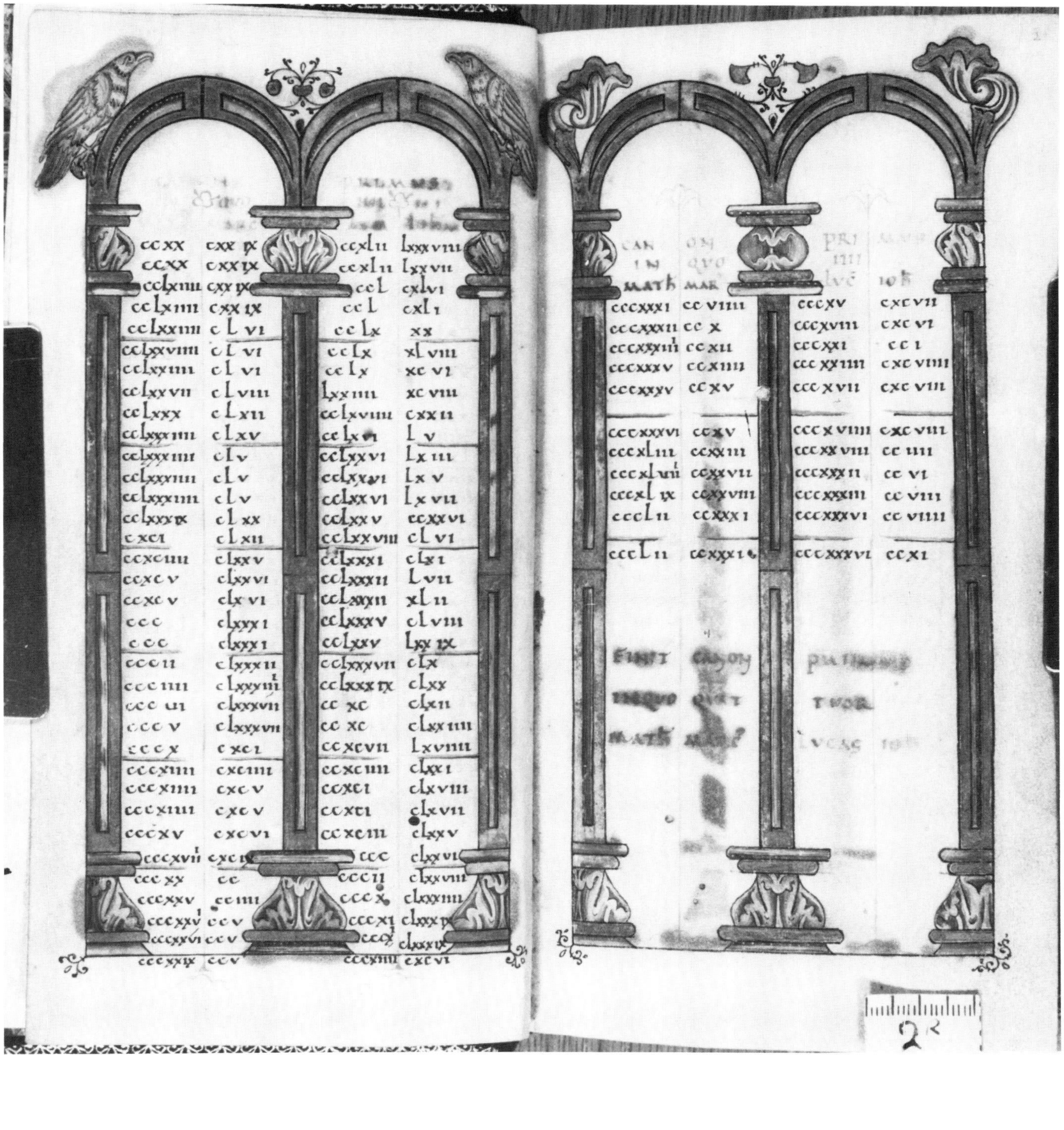

14.2 Cambridge, Pembroke College 302, ff. 1^{v}–2^{r}

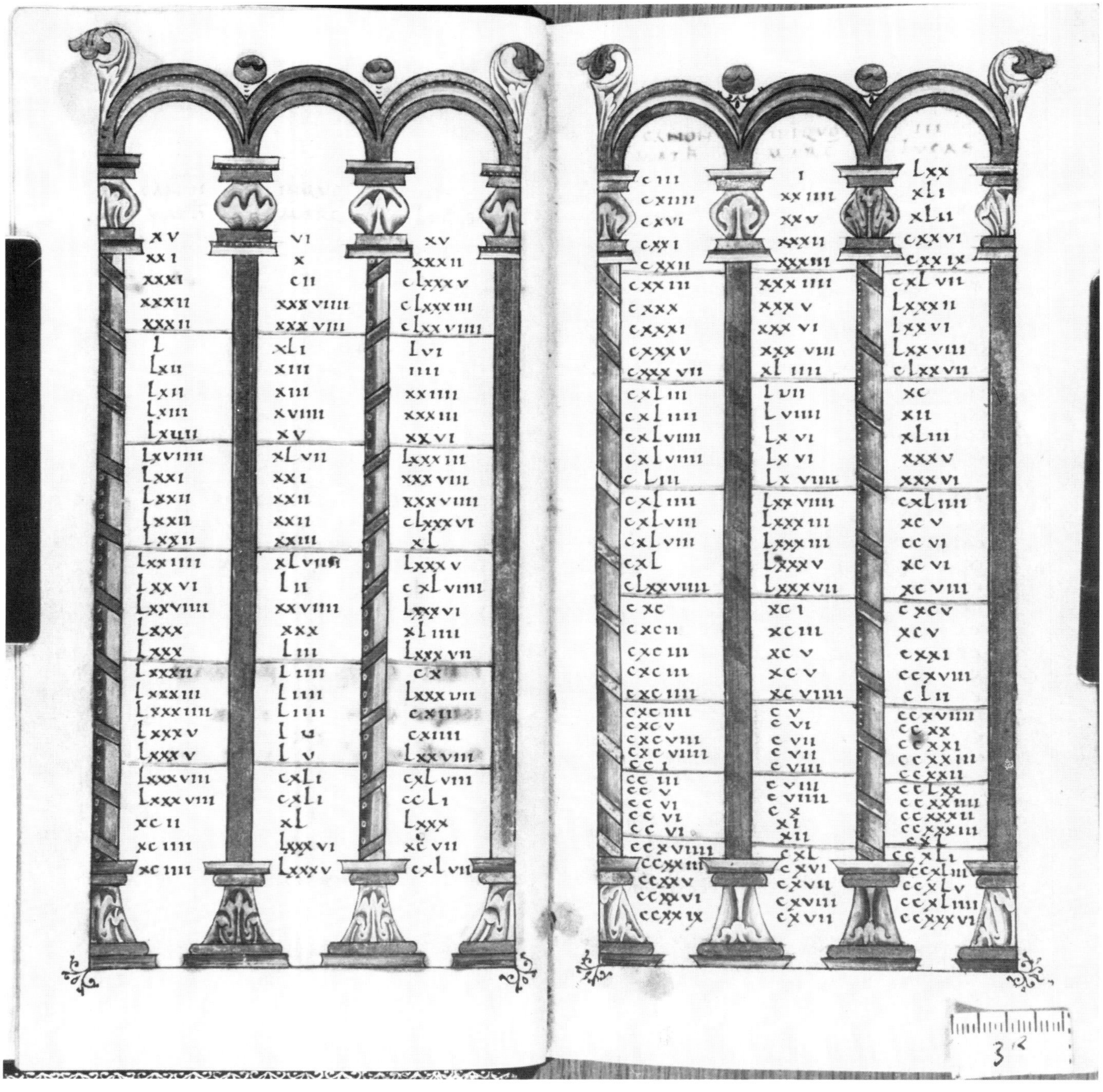

14.3 Cambridge, Pembroke College 302, ff. 2ᵛ–3ʳ

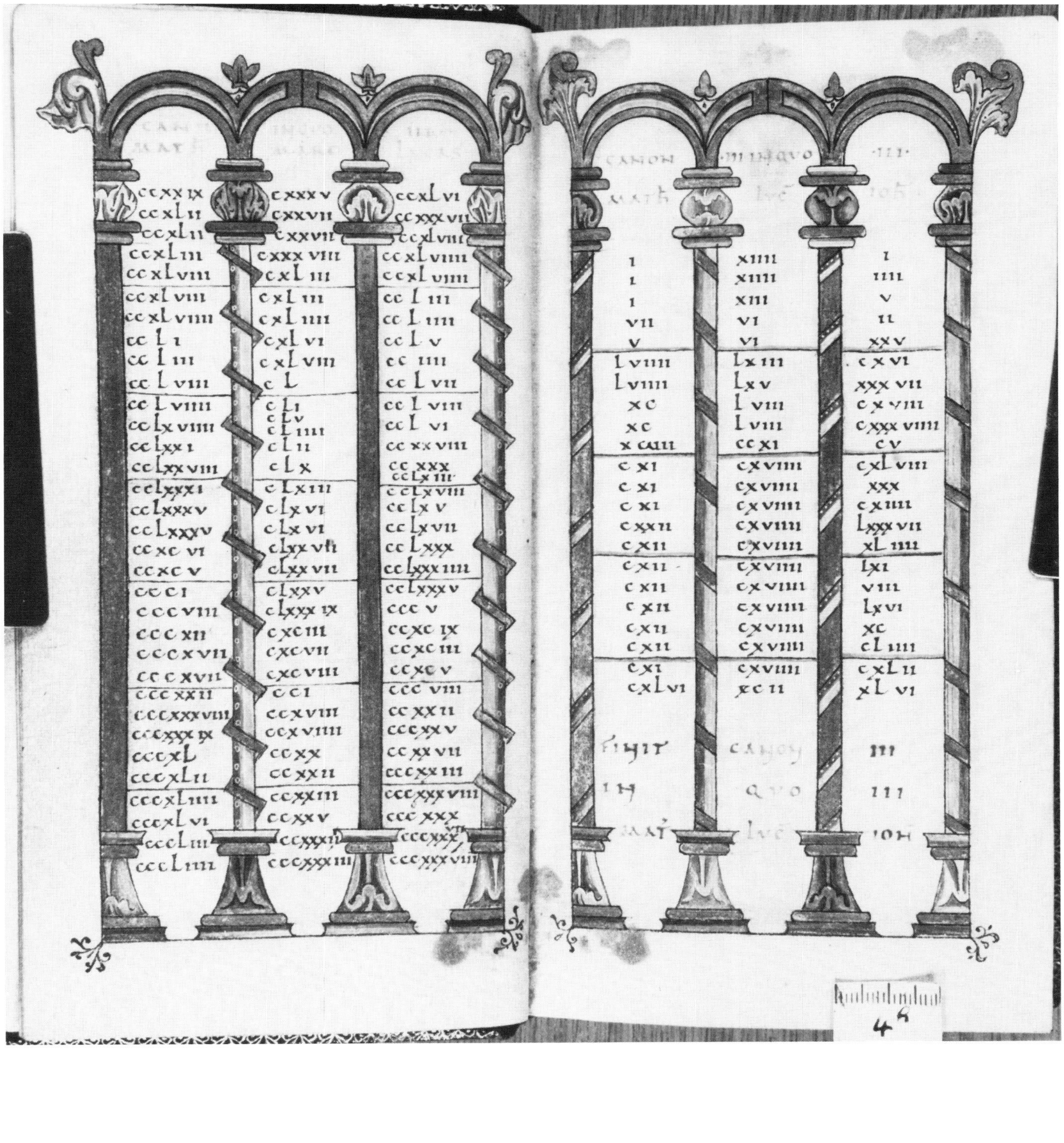

14.4 Cambridge, Pembroke College 302, ff. 3ᵛ–4ʳ

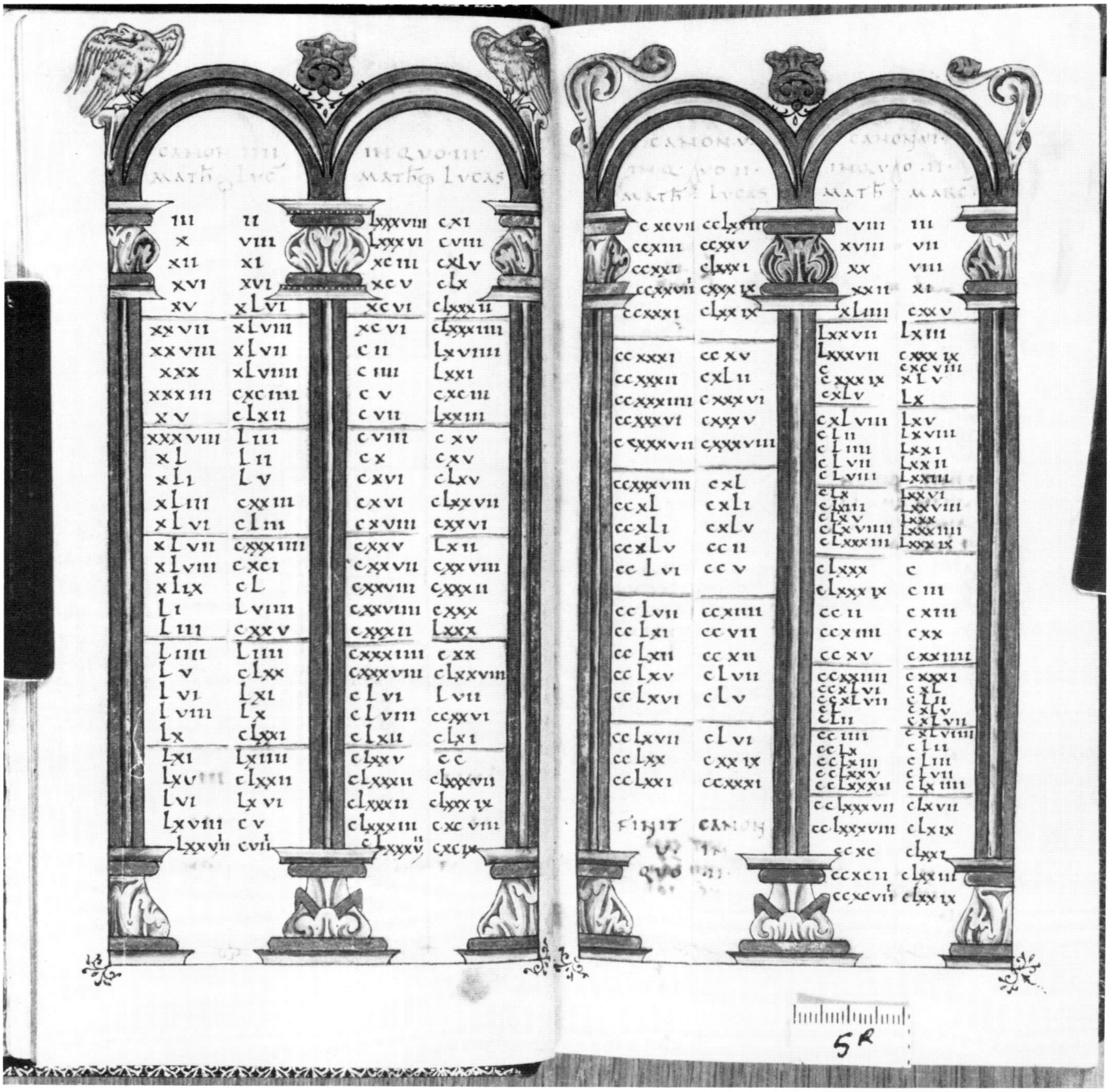

14.5 Cambridge, Pembroke College 302, ff. 4v–5r

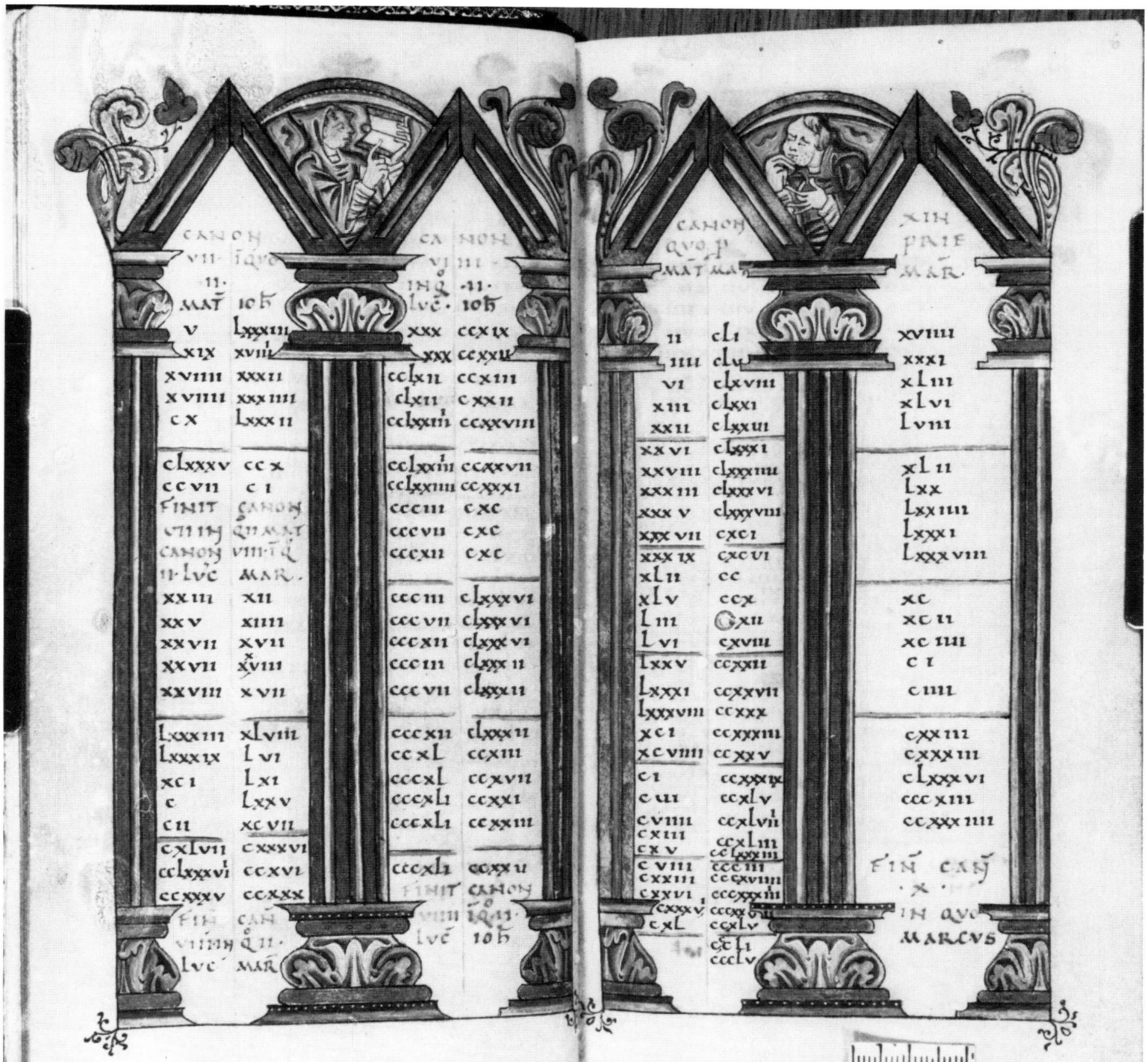

14.6 Cambridge, Pembroke College 302, ff. 5v–6r

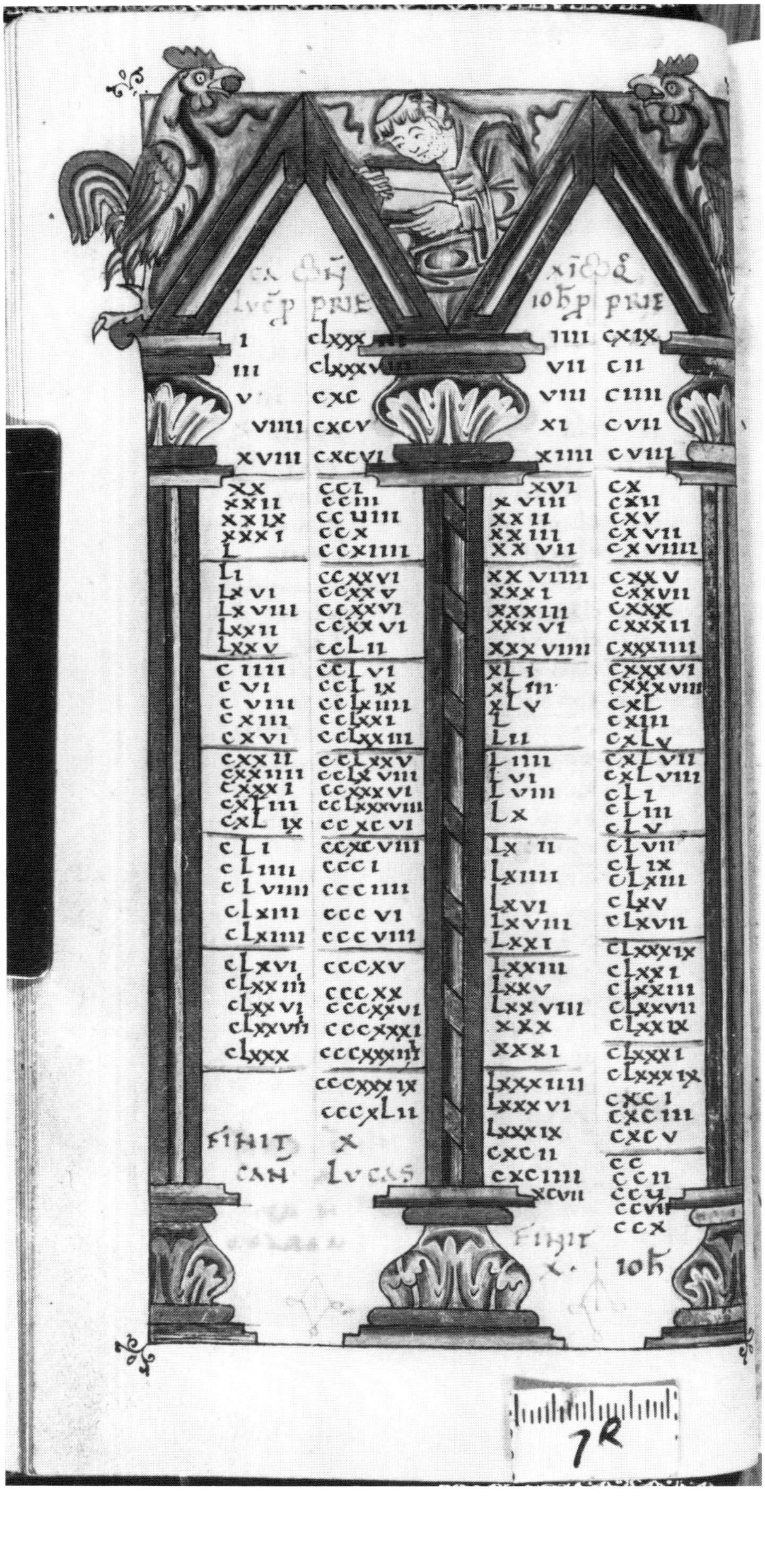

14.7 Cambridge, Pembroke College 302, f. 6v

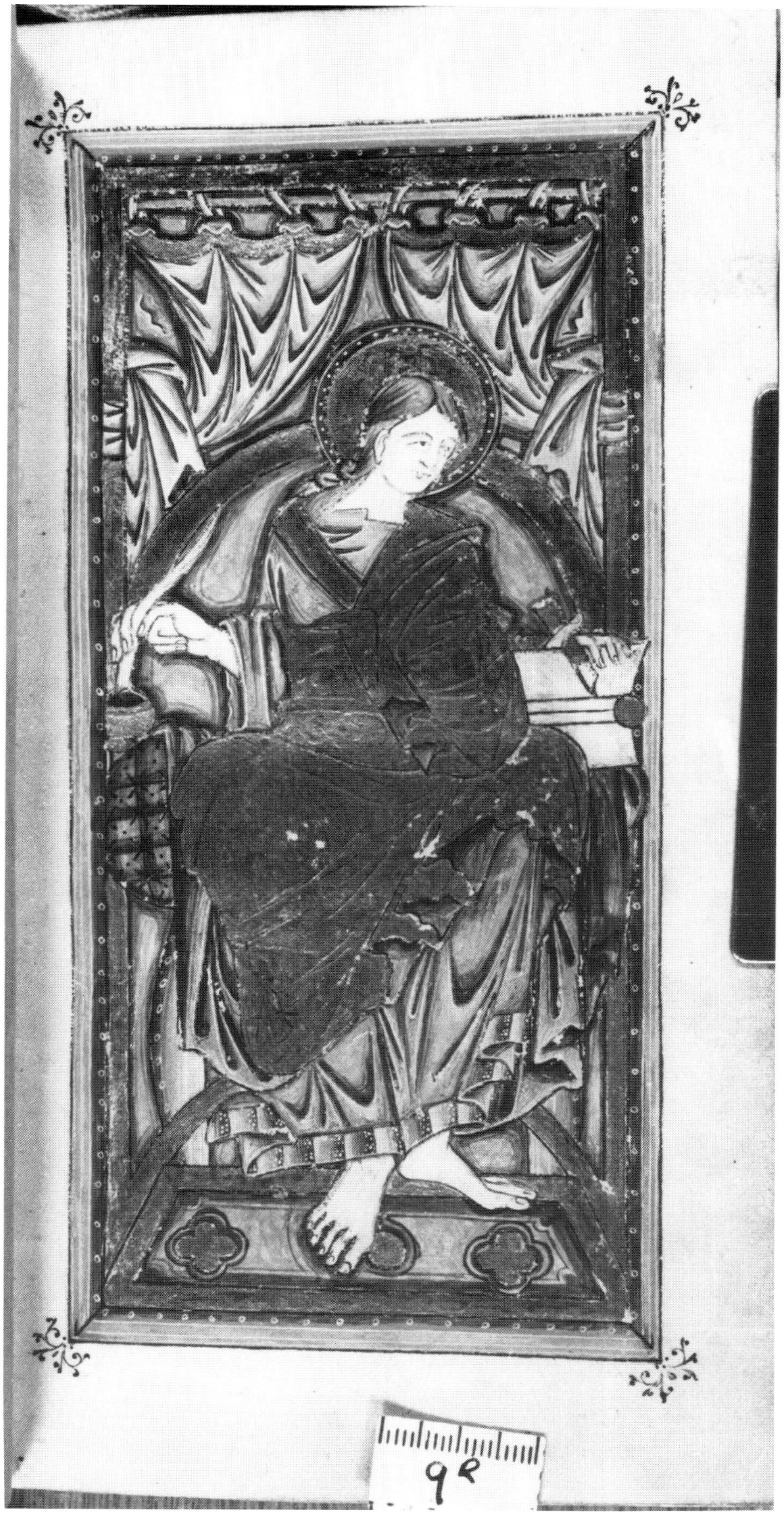

14.8 Cambridge, Pembroke College 302, f. 9r

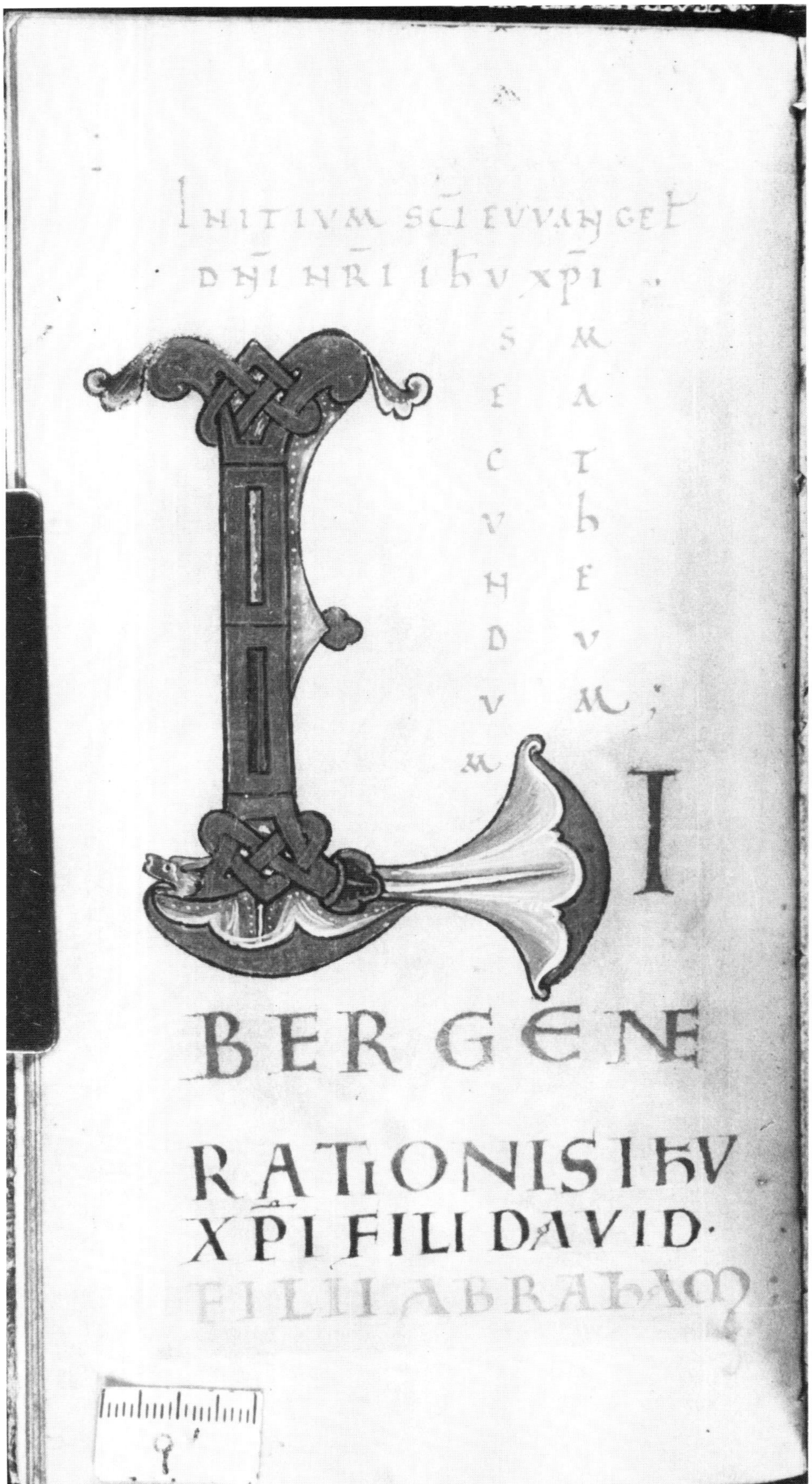

14.9 Cambridge, Pembroke College 302, f. 9v

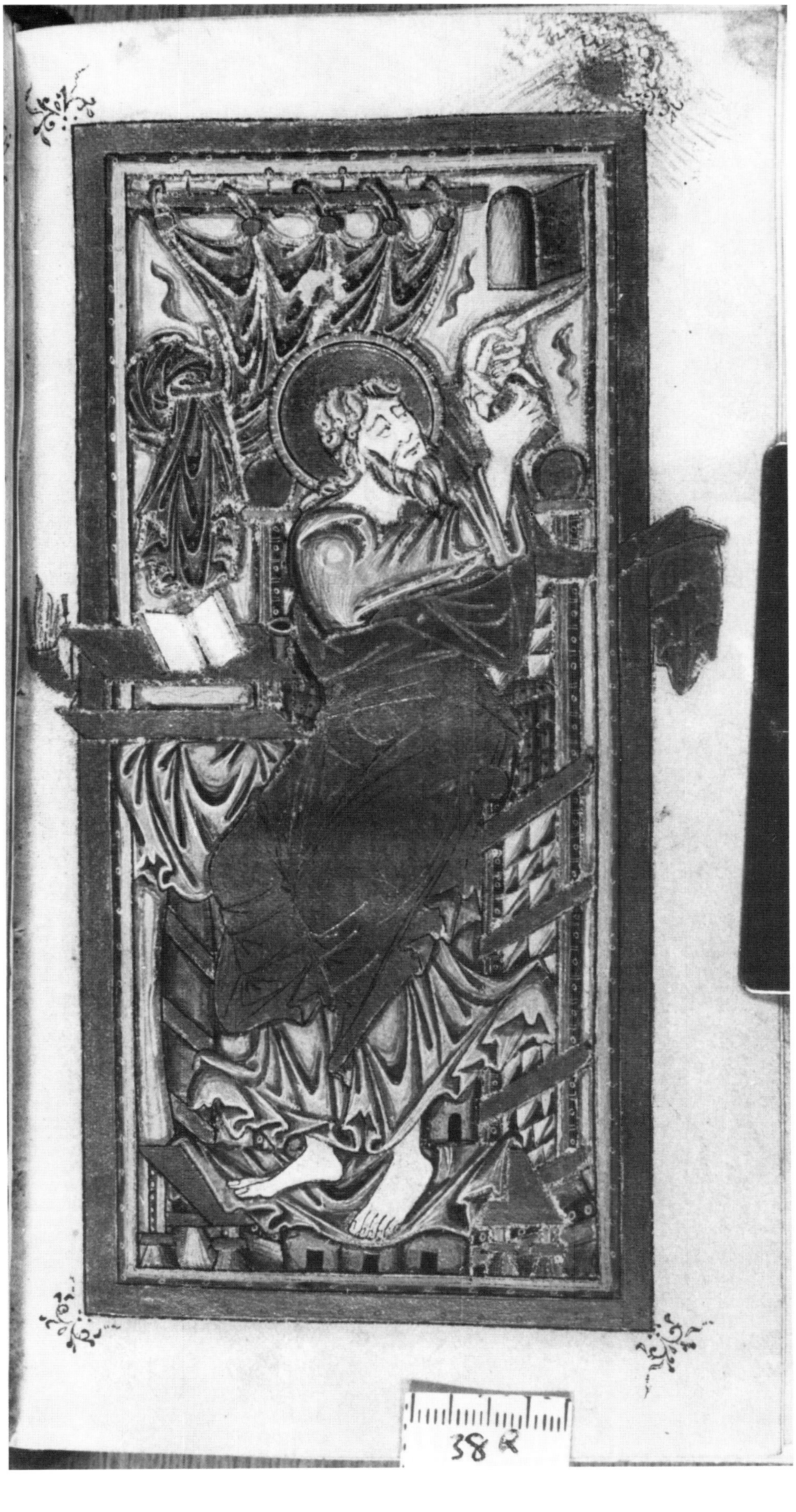

14.10 Cambridge, Pembroke College 302, f. 38r

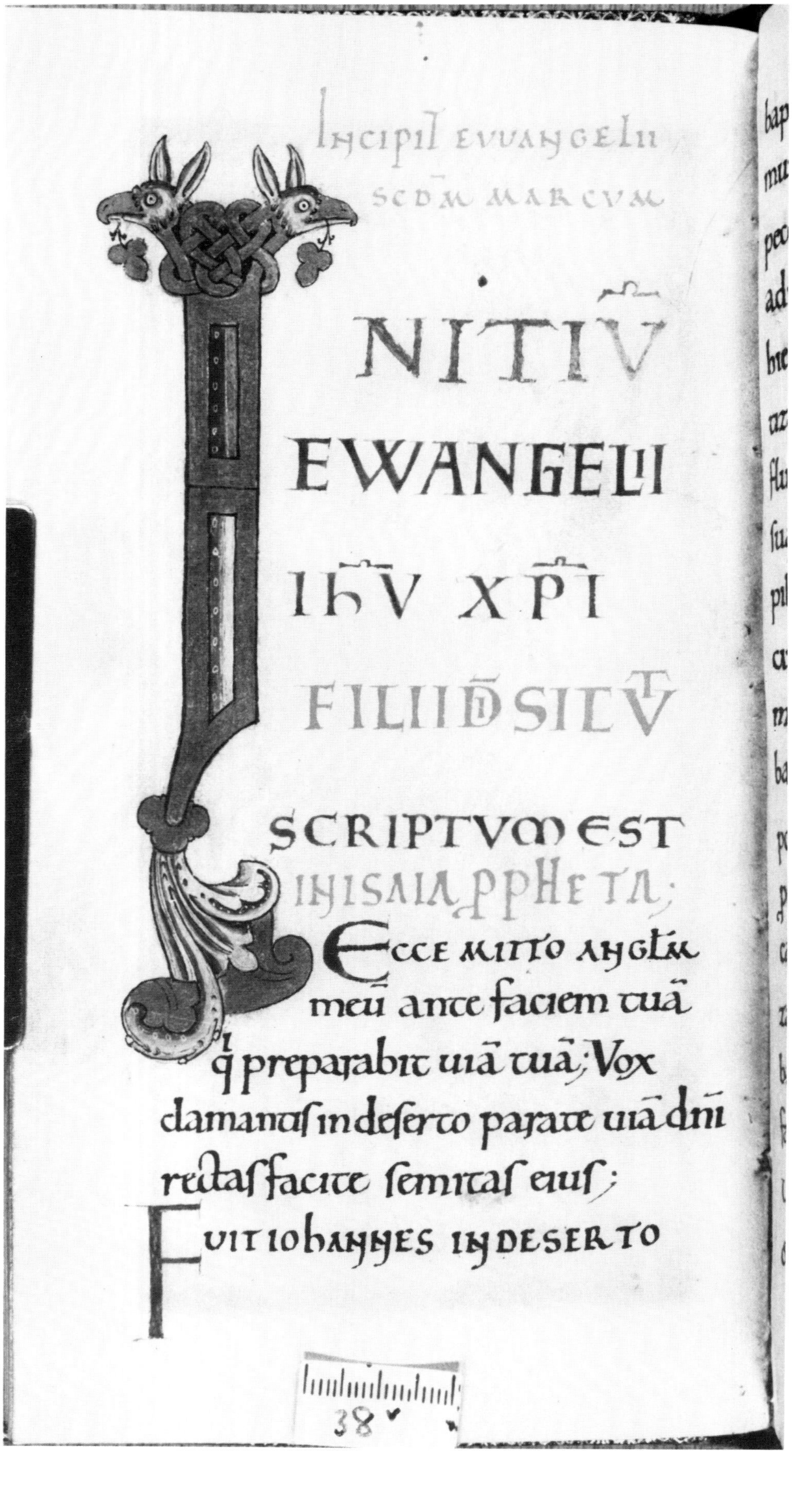

14.11 Cambridge, Pembroke College 302, f. 38v

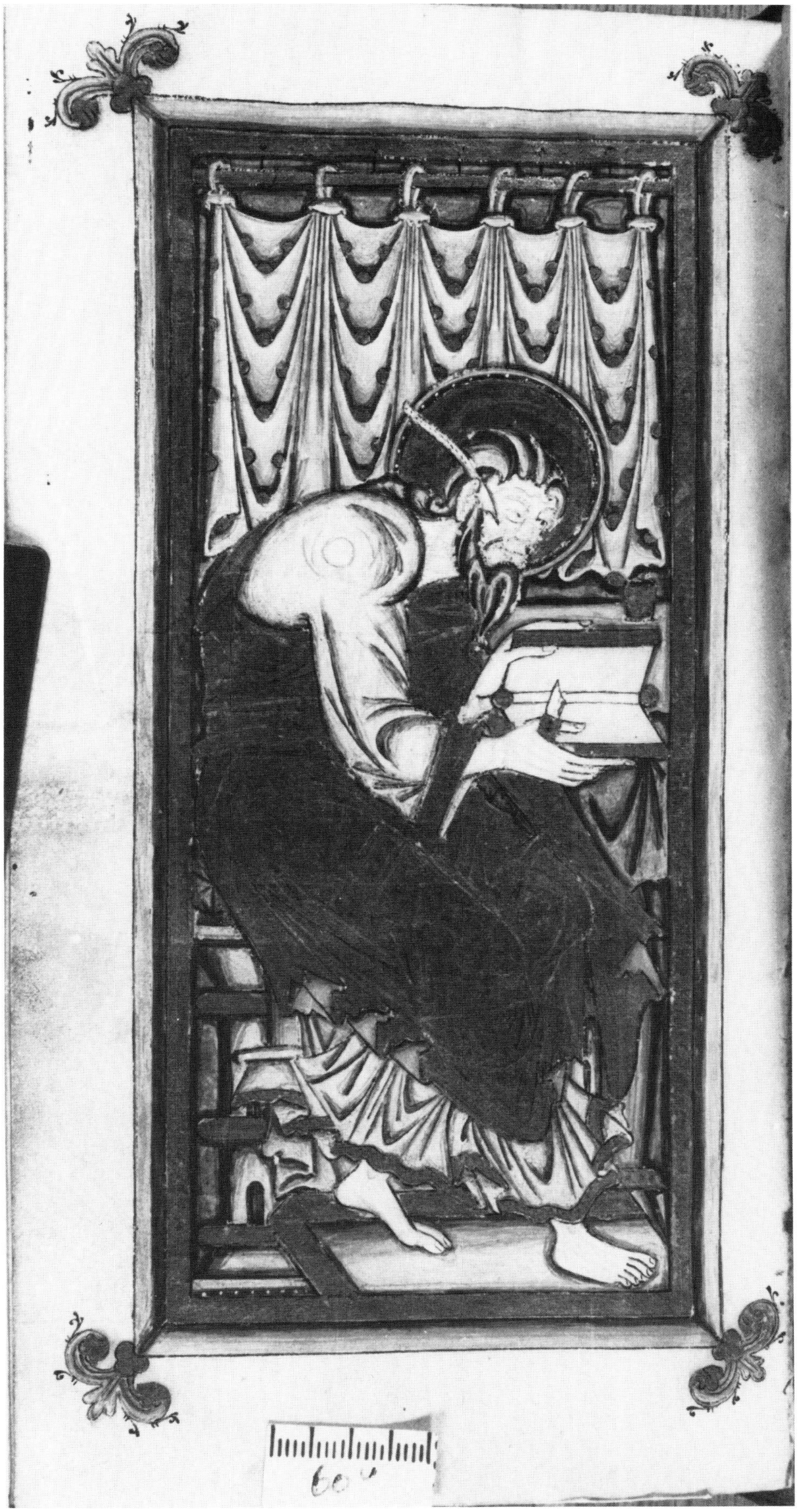

14.12 Cambridge, Pembroke College 302, f. 60v

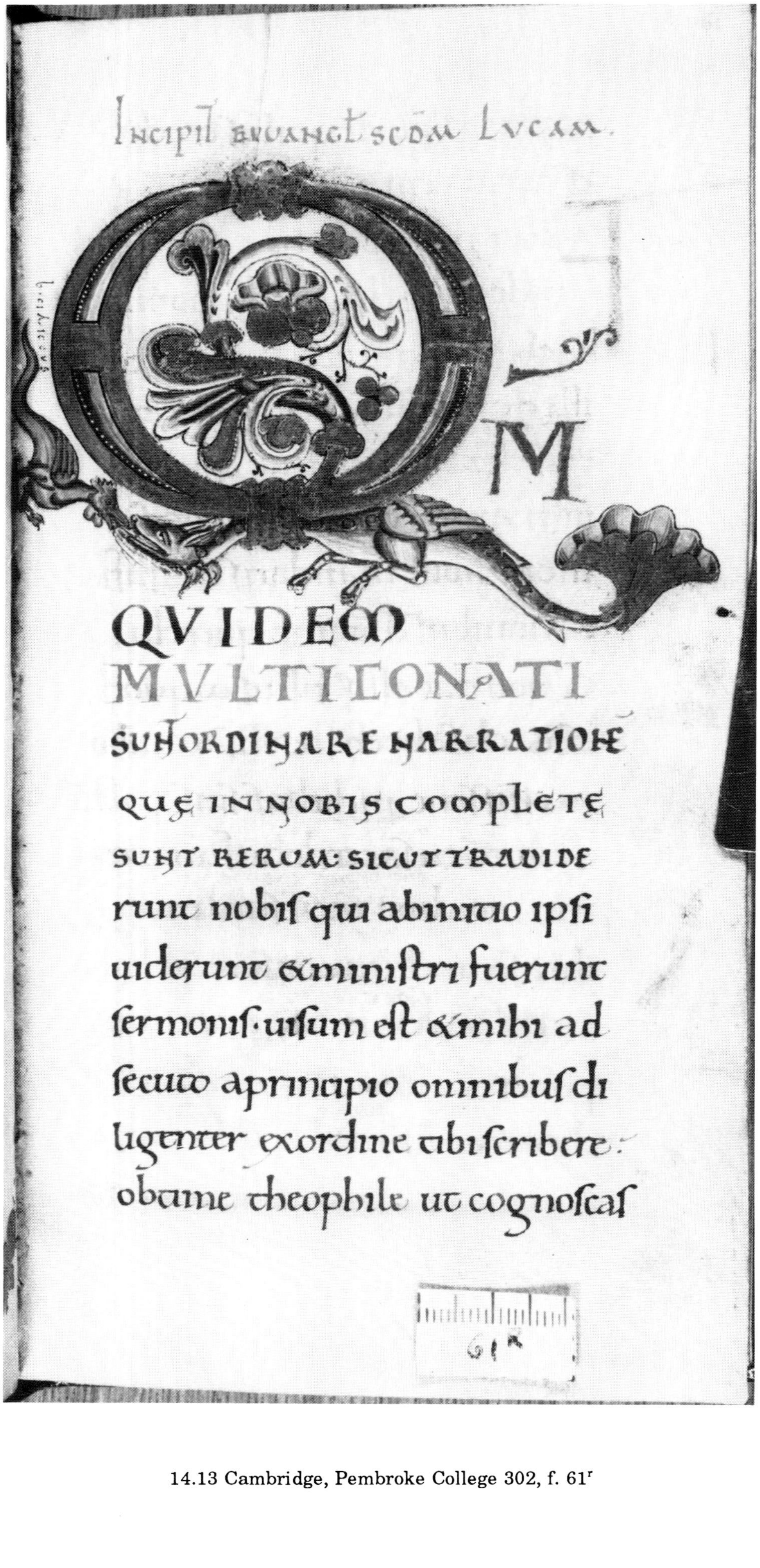

14.13 Cambridge, Pembroke College 302, f. 61r

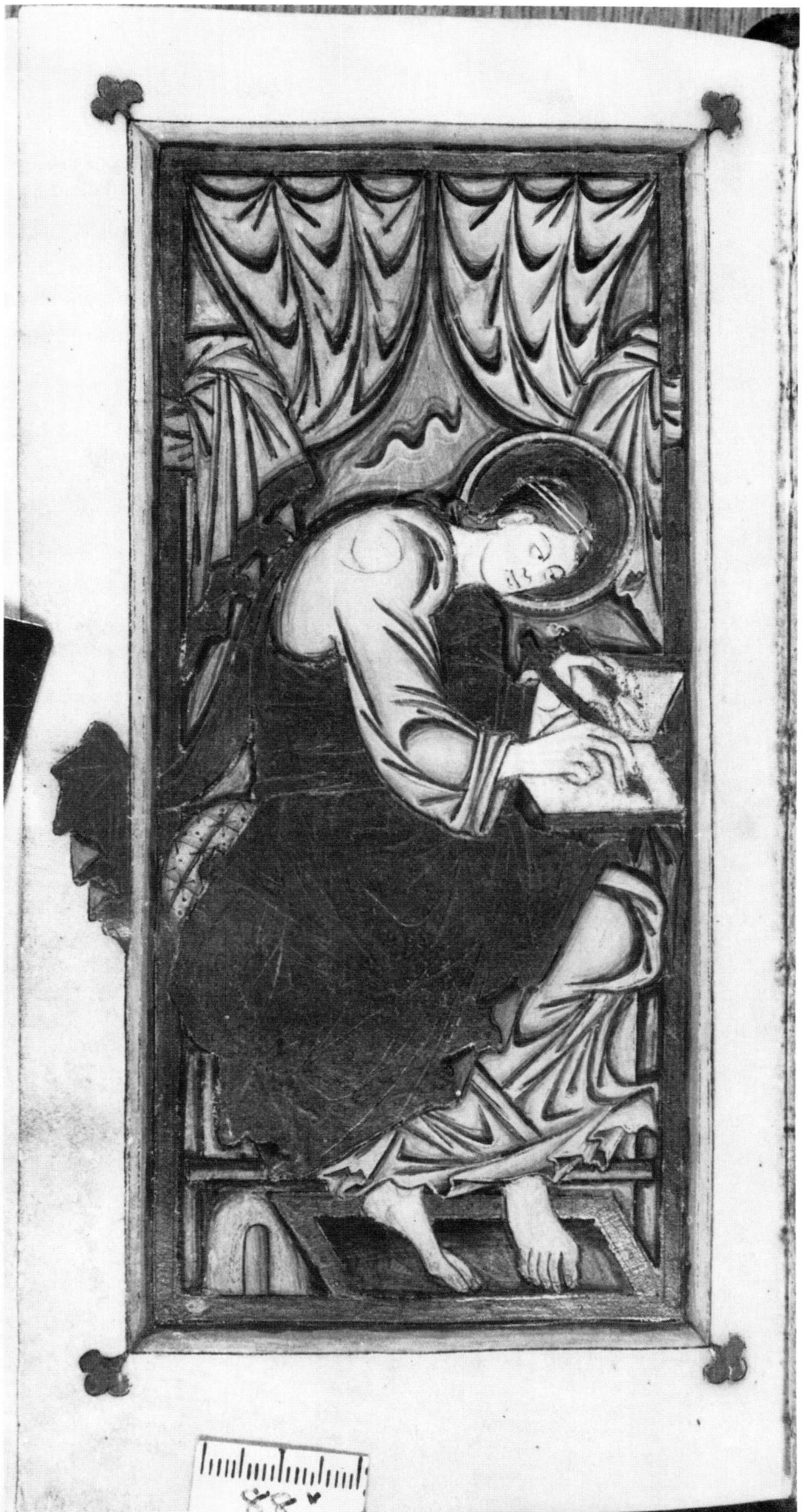

14.14 Cambridge, Pembroke College 302, f. 88v

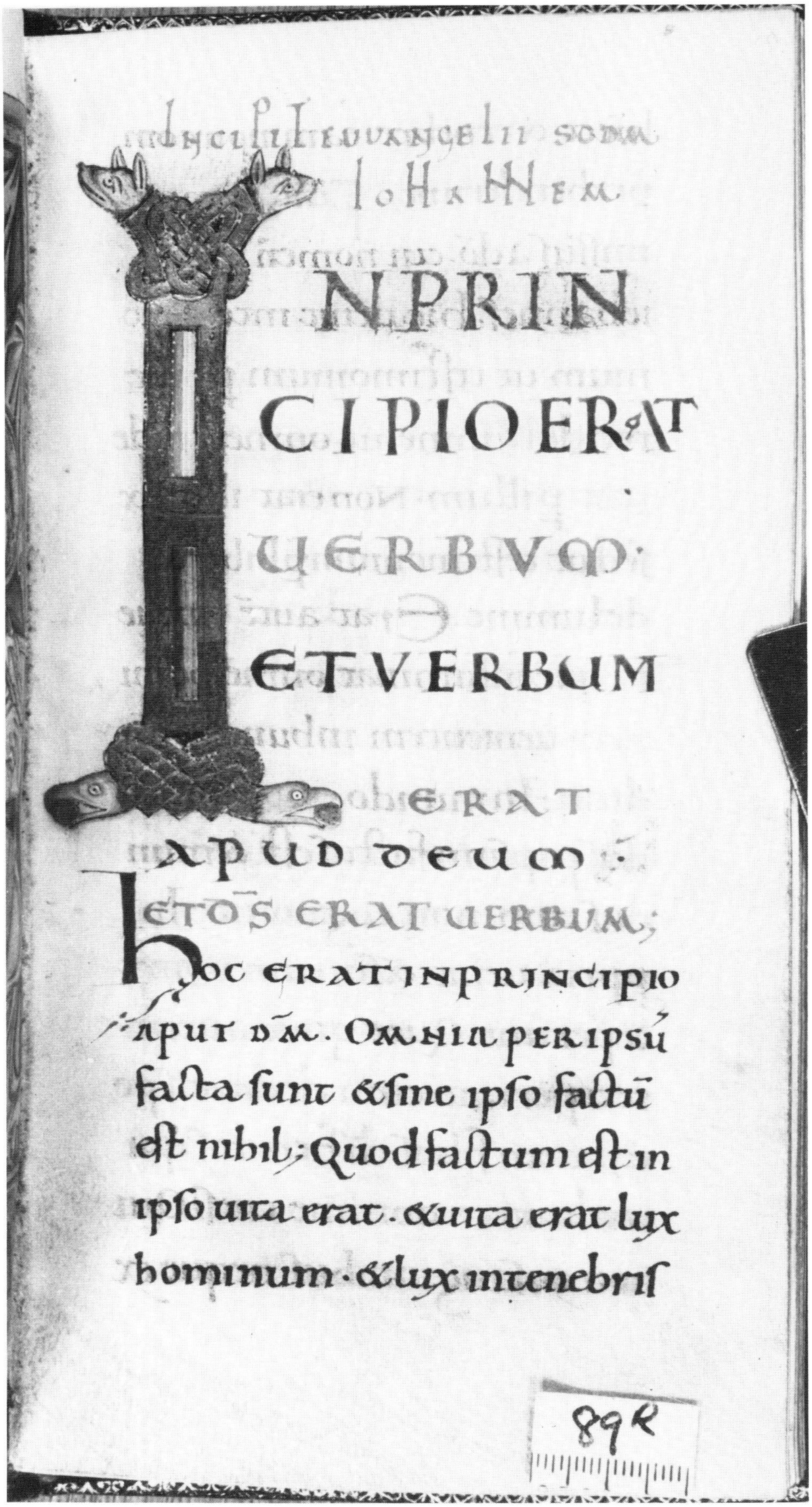

INCIPIT EUUANGELII SCDM
IOHANNEM
IN PRIN
CIPIO ERAT
UERBUM·
ET UERBUM
ERAT
APUD DEUM·
ET DS ERAT UERBUM;
HOC ERAT IN PRINCIPIO
APUT DM· OMNIA PER IPSŪ
facta sunt & sine ipso factū
est nihil; Quod factum est in
ipso uita erat· & uita erat lux
hominum· & lux in tenebris

89R

14.15 Cambridge, Pembroke College 302, f. 89r

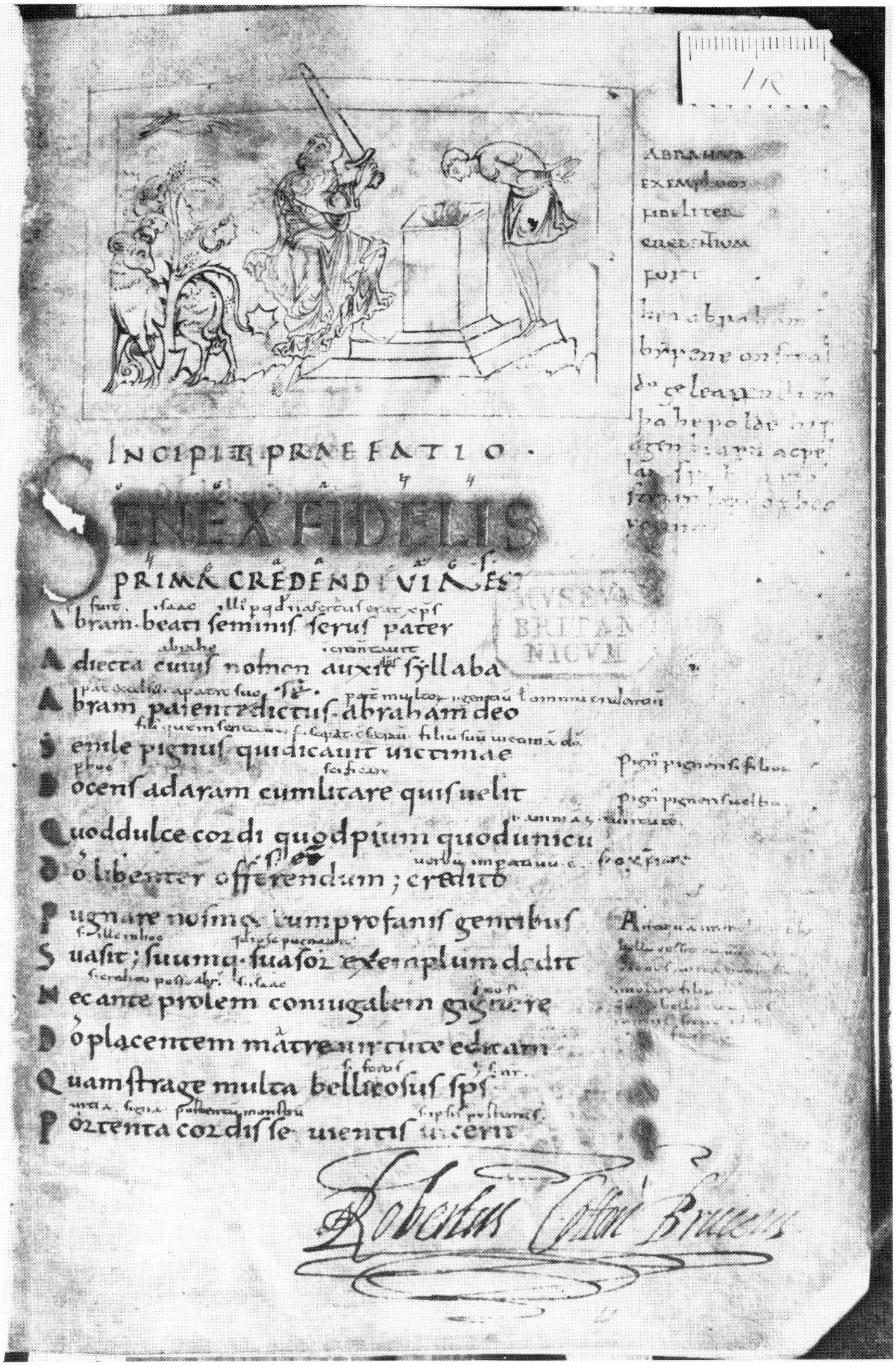
INCIPIT PRAEFATIO

SENEX FIDELIS PRIMA CREDENDI VIA EST

Abram beati seminis seruus pater
Adiecta cuius nomini auxit syllaba
Abram parens dictus abraham deo
Senile pignus qui dicauit uictimae
Docens ad aram cum litare quis uelit
Quod dulce cordi quod pium quod unicu[m]
Deo libenter offerendum credito
Pugnare nosmet cum profanis gentibus
Suasit; suumque suasor exemplum dedit
Nec ante prolem coniugalem gignere
Deo placentem matre uirtute editam
Quam strage multa bellicosus spiritus
Portenta cordis seruientis uicerit

Abraham exemplum fideliter credentium fuit

Robertus Cotton Bruceus

15.1 London, B.L., Cotton Cleo. C. VIII, f. 4r

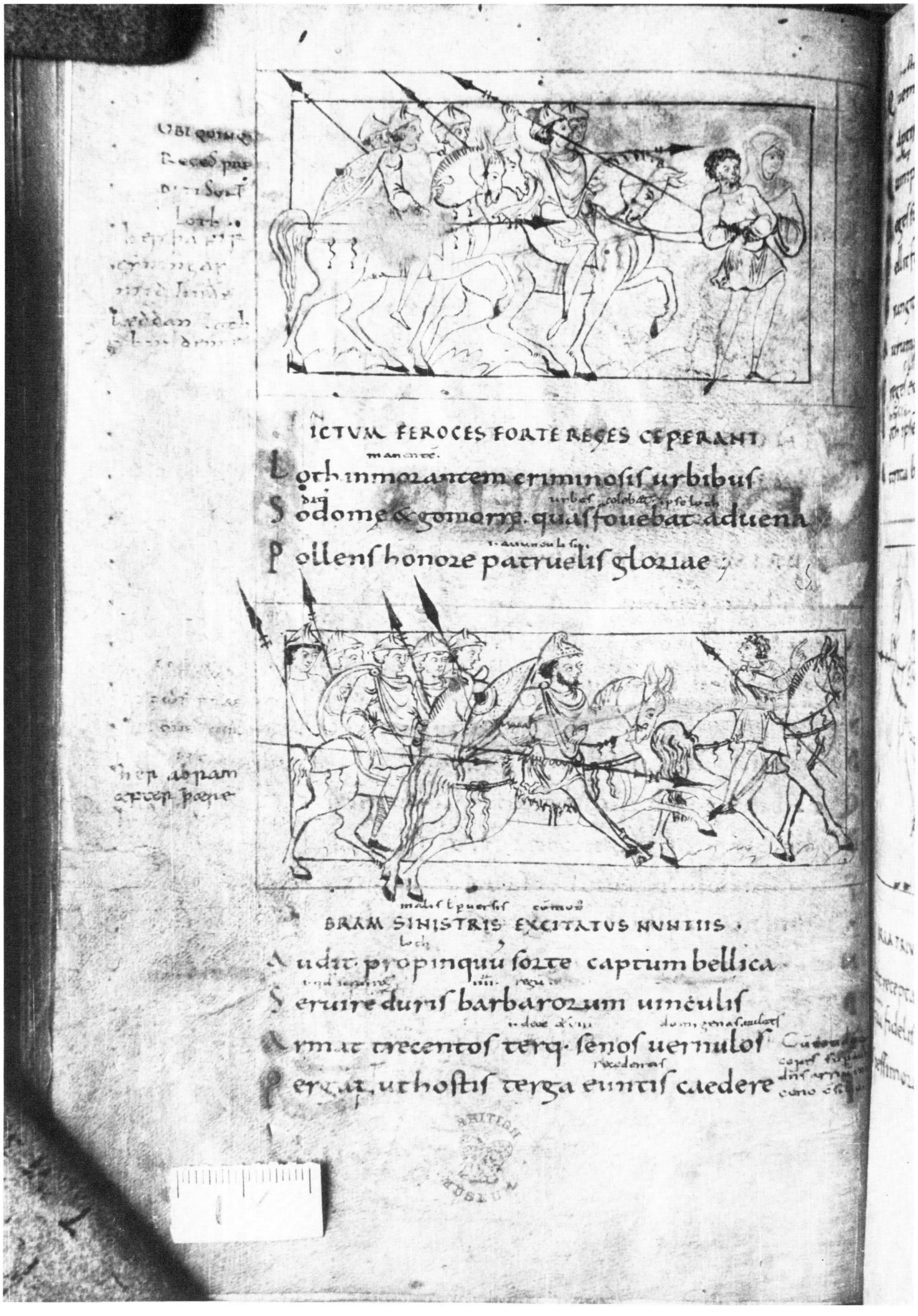

15.2 London, B.L., Cotton Cleo. C. VIII, f. 4ᵛ

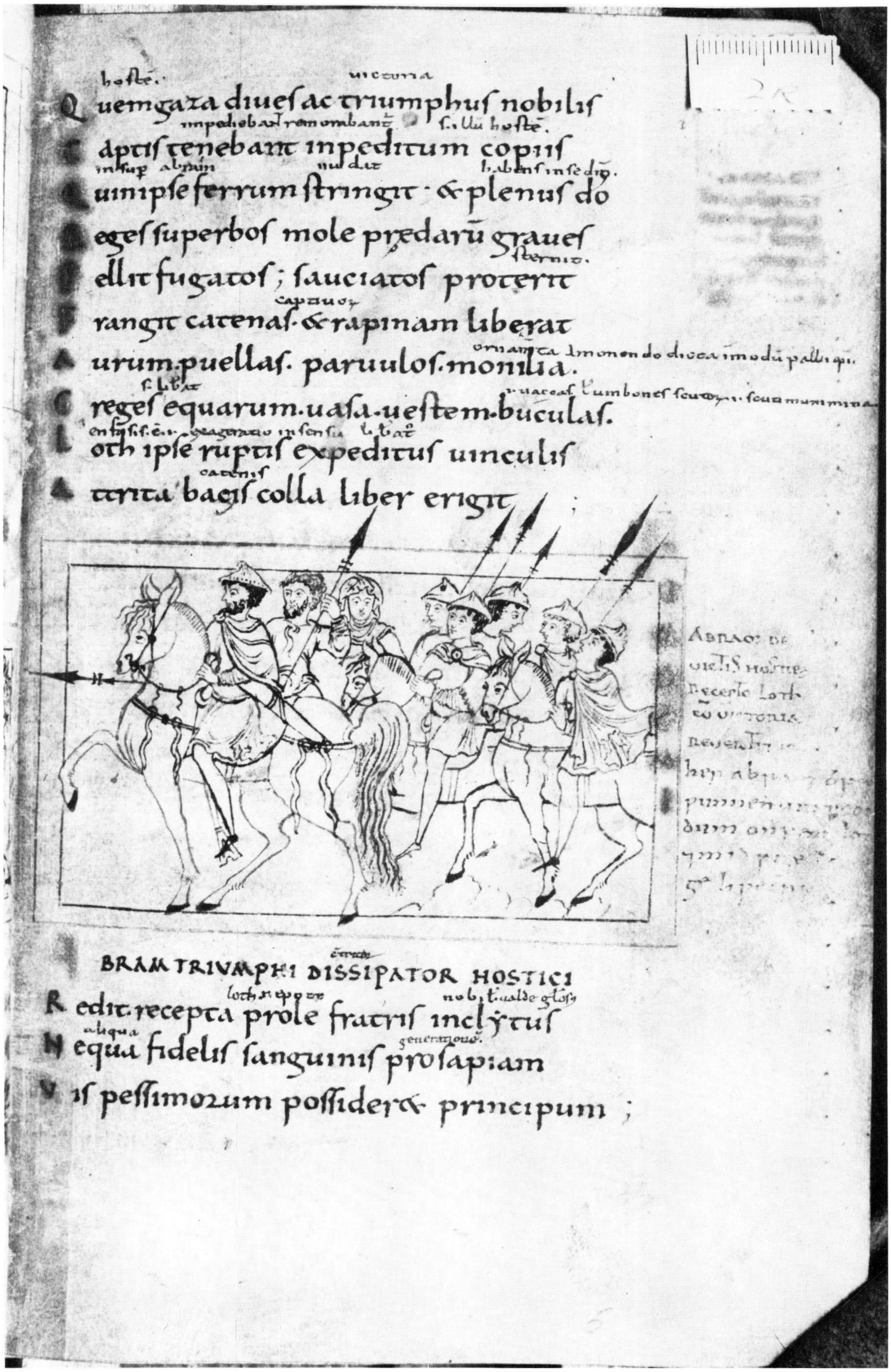
Quem gaza dives ac triumphus nobilis
Captis tenebant impeditum copiis
Quin ipse ferrum stringit & plenus do
Reges superbos mole prędarū graves
Pellit fugatos; sauciatos proterit
Frangit catenas & rapinam liberat
Aurum puellas parvulos monilia
Greges equarum vasa vestem buculas
Loth ipse ruptis expeditus vinculis
Attrita bacis colla liber erigit;

ABRAM TRIVMPHI DISSIPATOR HOSTICI
Redit recepta prole fratris inclytus
Nequa fidelis sanguinis prosapiam
Vis pessimorum possideret principum;

15.3 London, B.L., Cotton Cleo. C. VIII, f. 5r

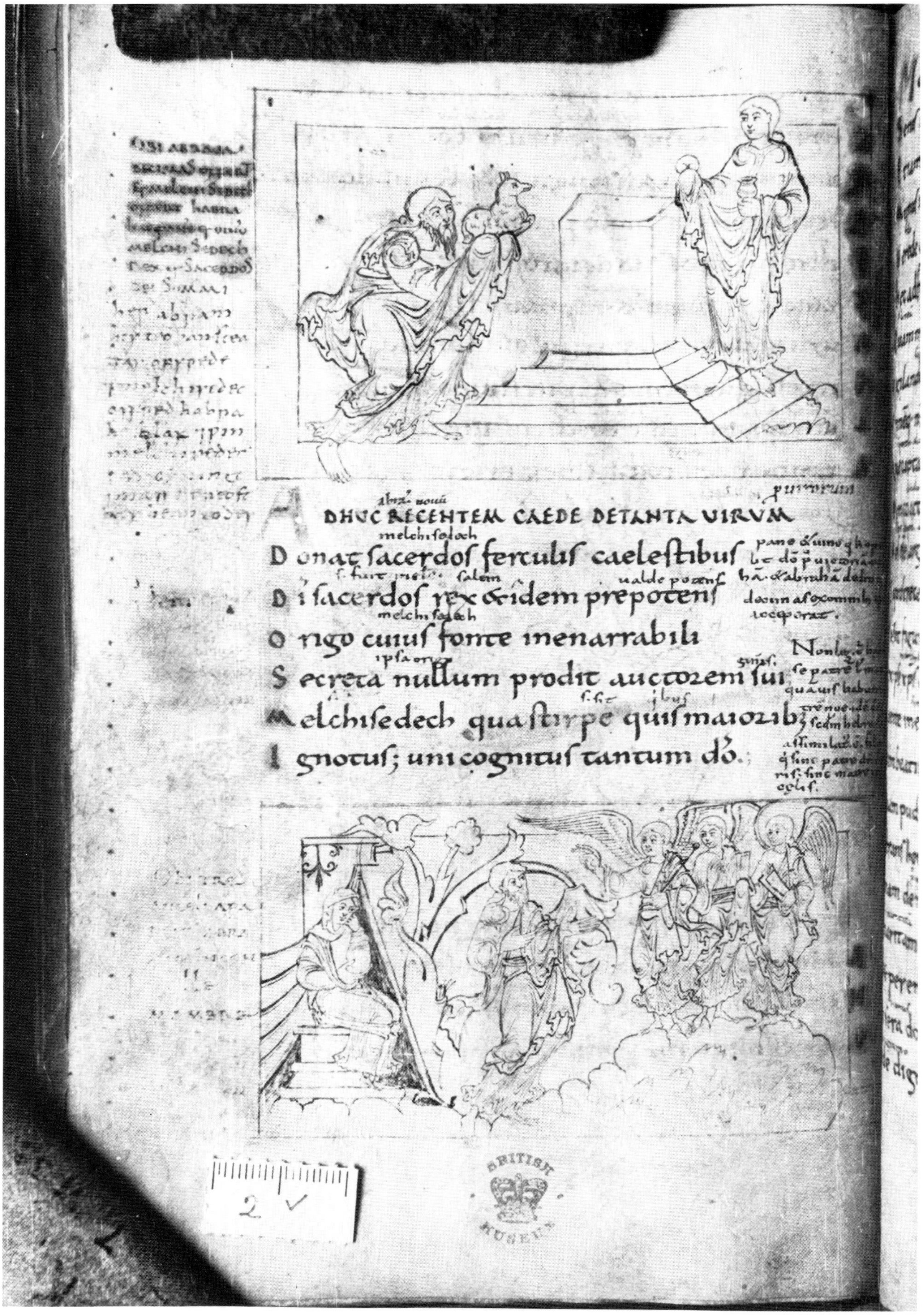

15.4 London, B.L., Cotton Cleo. C. VIII, f. 5v

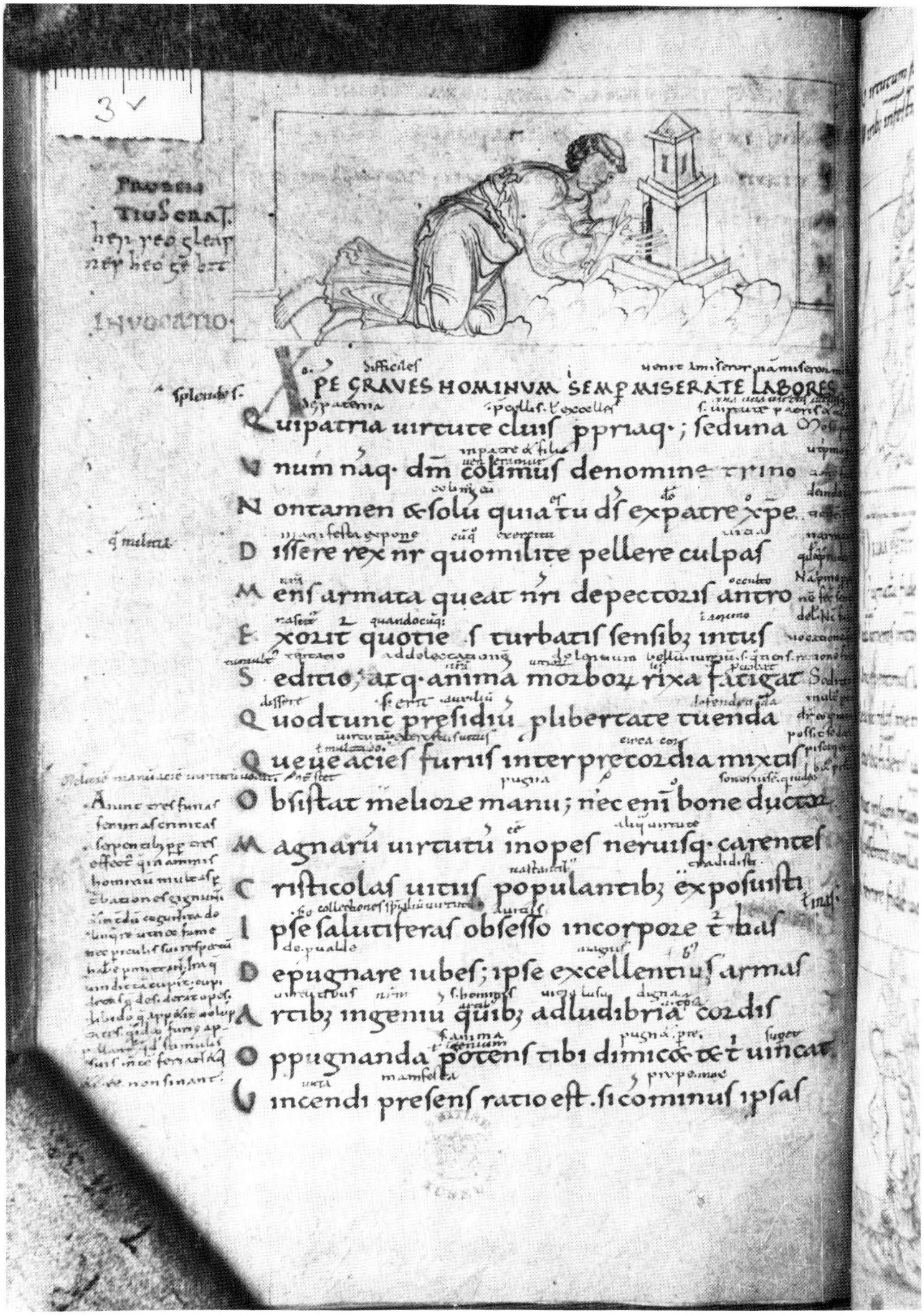

15.5 London, B.L., Cotton Cleo. C. VIII, f. 6v

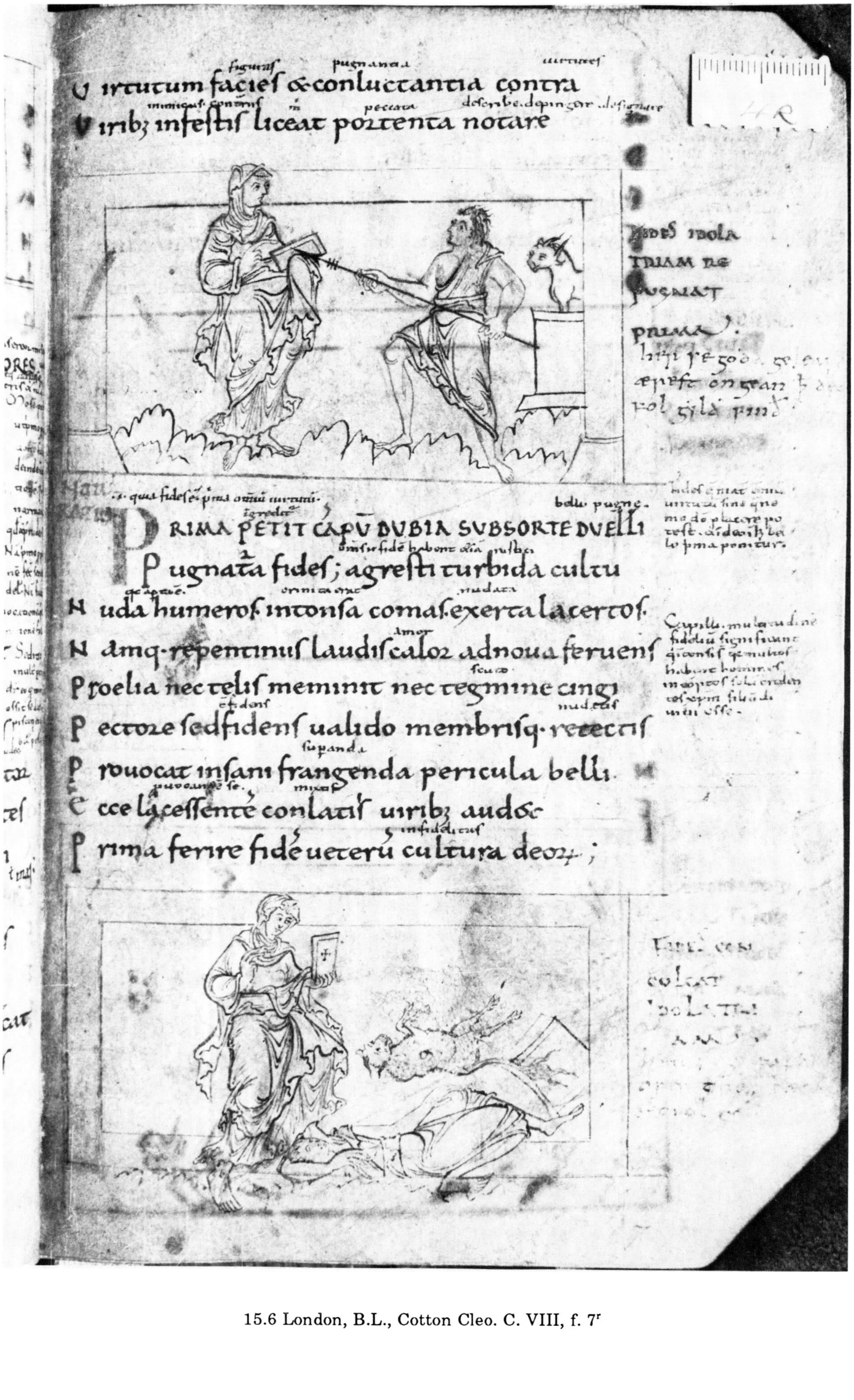
Virtutum facies & conluctantia contra
Virib; infestis liceat portenta notare

Fides idolatriam pugnat prima

Prima petit capū dubia sub sorte duelli
Pugnata fides; agresti turbida cultu
Nuda humeros. intonsa comas. exerta lacertos.
Namq· repentinus laudis calor ad noua feruens
Proelia nec telis meminit nec tegmine cingi
Pectore sed fidens ualido membrisq· retectis
Prouocat insani frangenda pericula belli.
Ecce lacessentē conlatis uirib; audens
Prima ferire fidē ueterū cultura deo;

15.6 London, B.L., Cotton Cleo. C. VIII, f. 7r

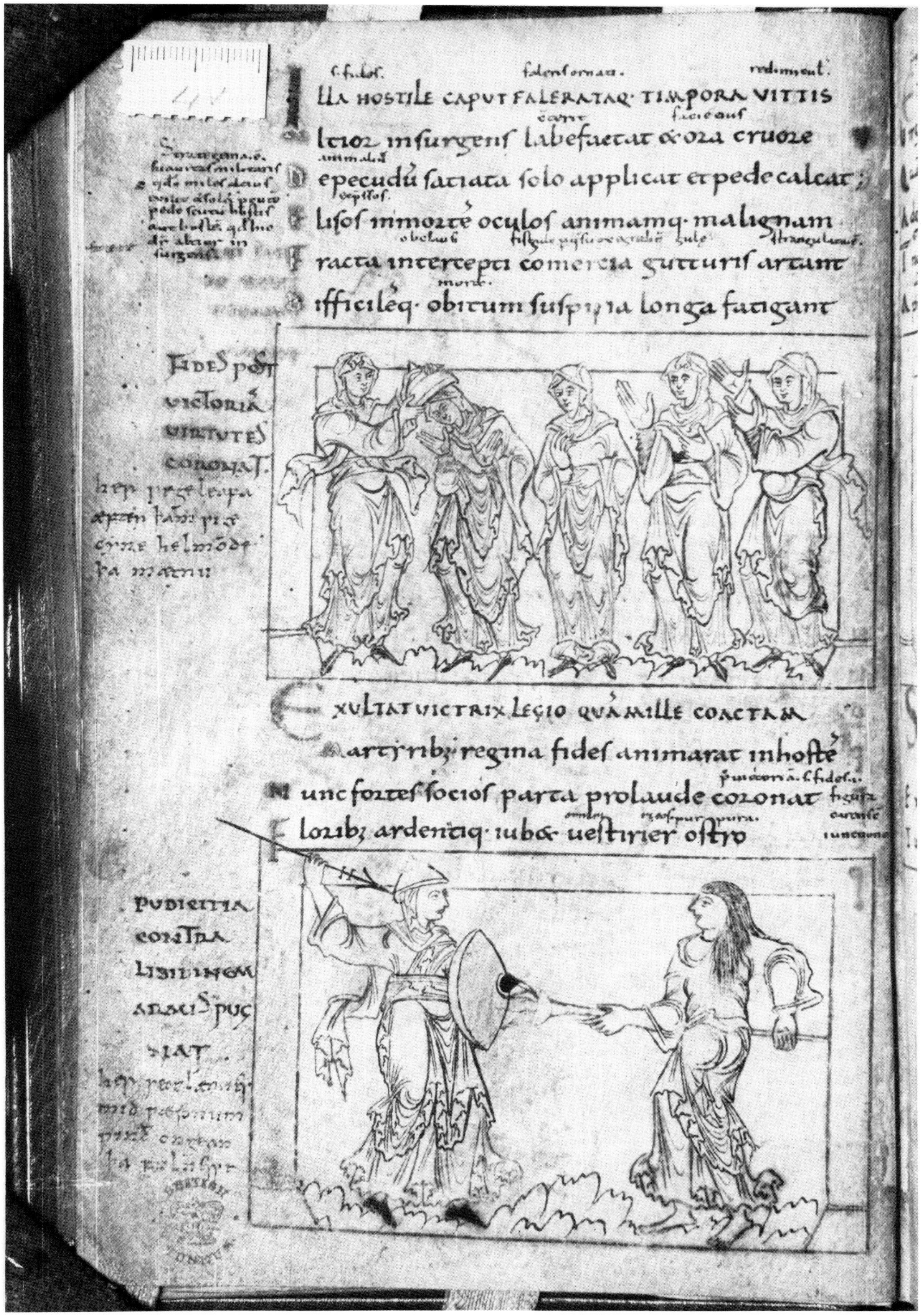

15.7 London, B.L., Cotton Cleo. C. VIII, f. 7v

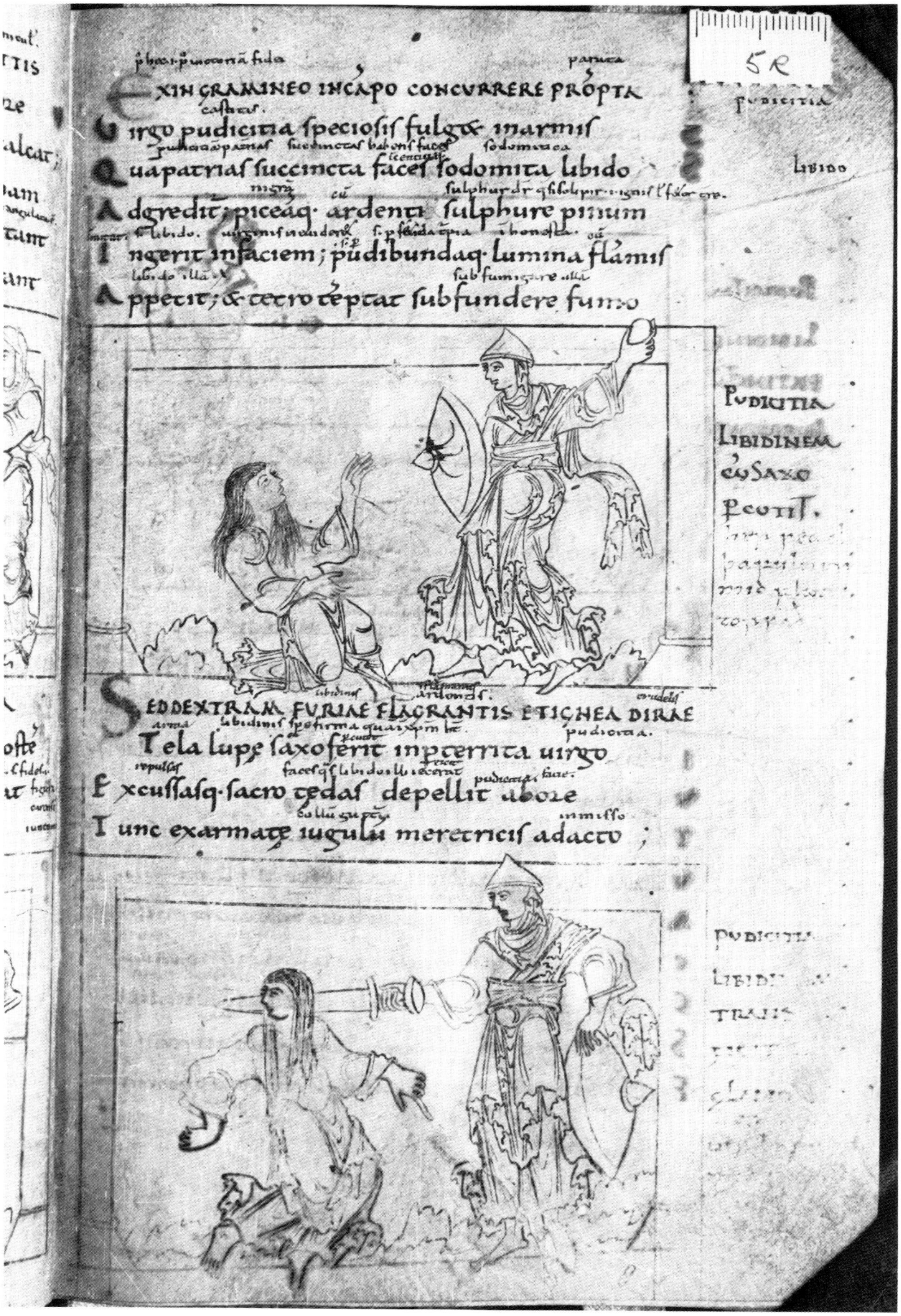

15.8 London, B.L., Cotton Cleo. C. VIII, f. 8r

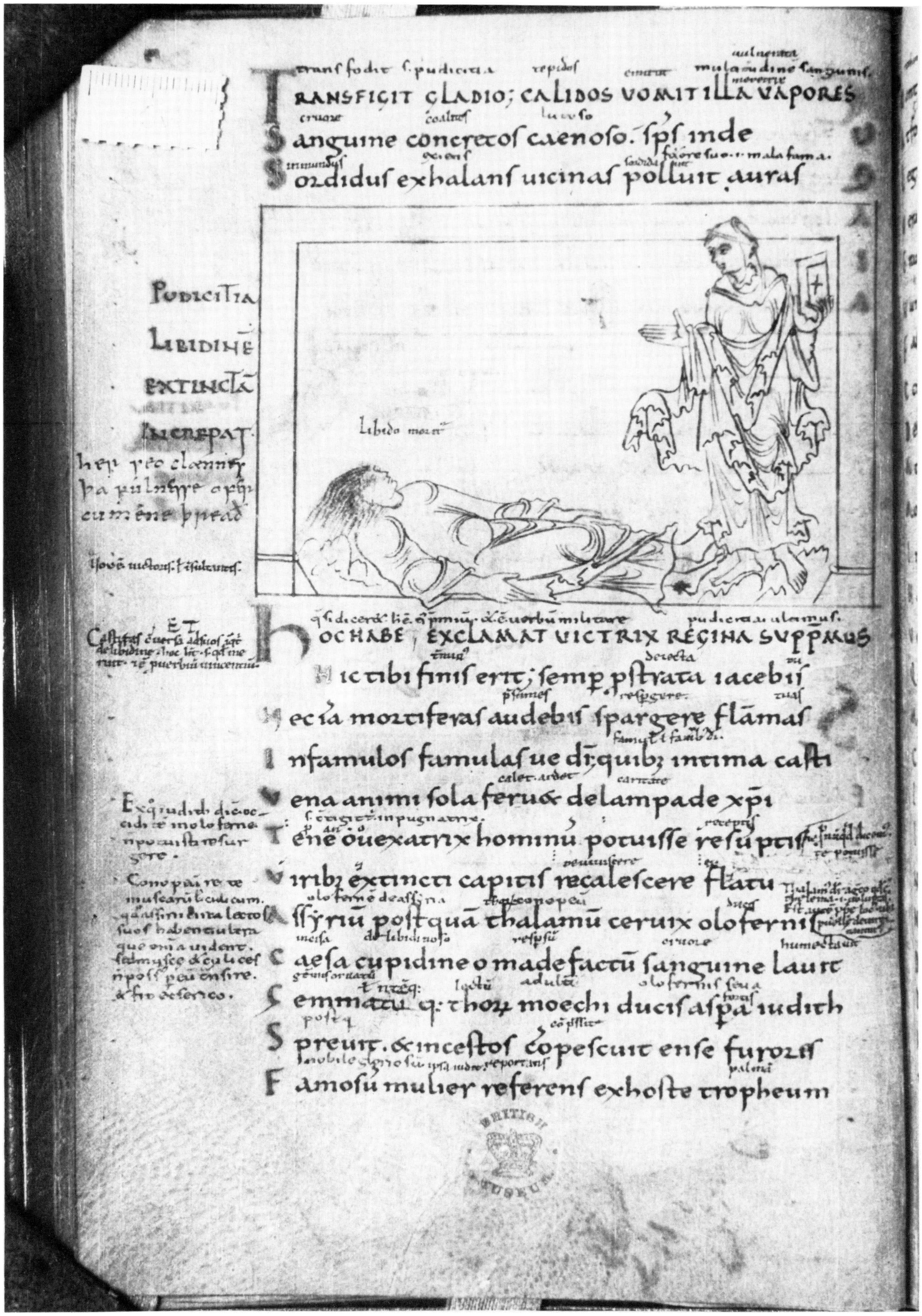

15.9 London, B.L., Cotton Cleo. C. VIII, f. 8v

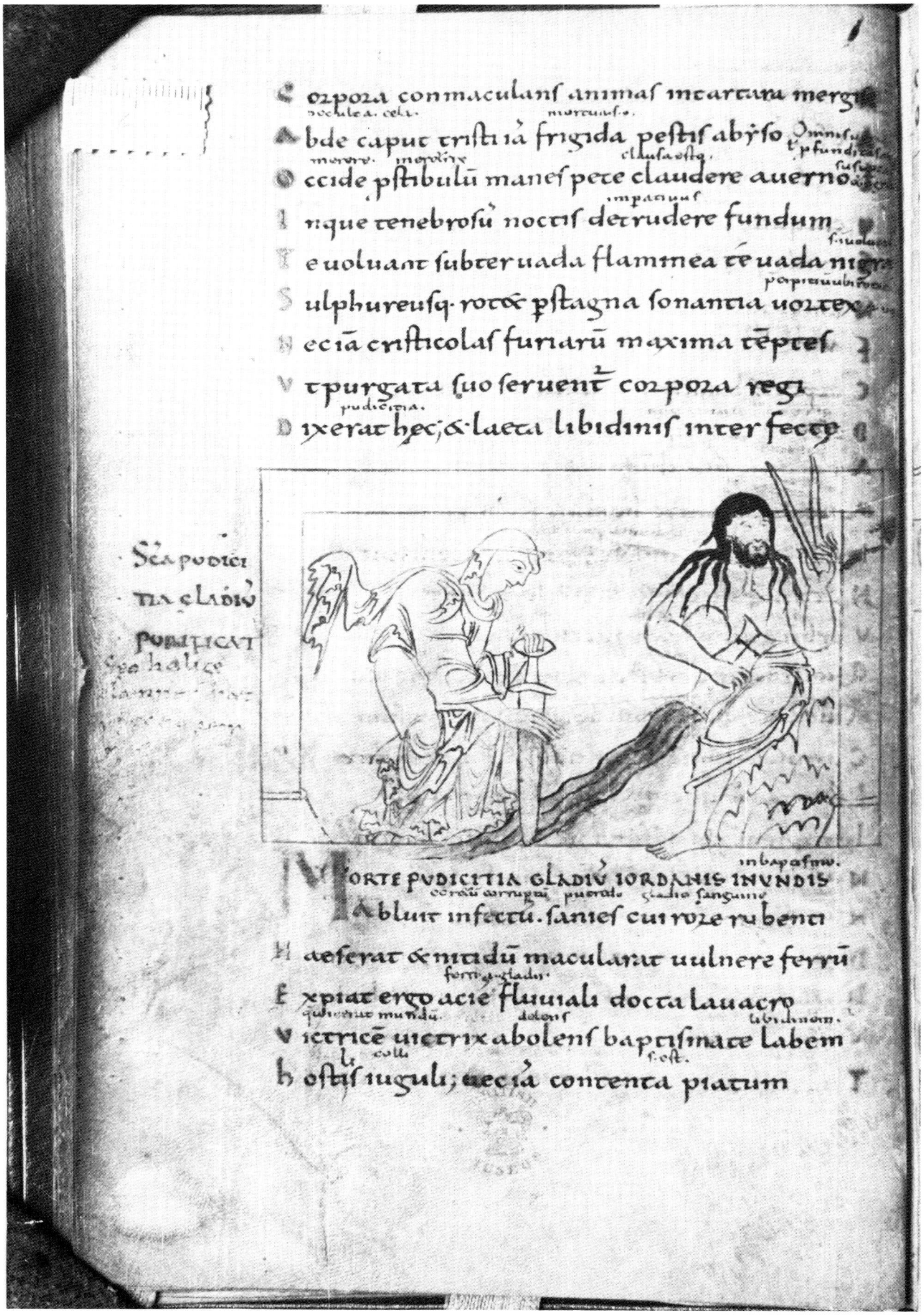
Corpora commaculans animas in tartara mergis
Abde caput tristi iam frigida pestis abysso
Occide prostibulum manes pete claudere auerno
Inque tenebrosum noctis detrudere fundum
Te uoluant subter uada flammea te uada nigra
Sulphureusque rotet per stagna sonantia uertex
Nec iam cristicolas furiarum maxima temptes
Ut purgata suo seruentur corpora regi
Dixerat haec, et laeta libidinis interfectae

Sca pudicitia gladium purificat

Morte pudicitia gladium iordanis in undis
Abluit infectum. sanies cui roze rubenti
Haeserat et nitidum maculat uulnere ferrum
Expiat ergo aciem fluuiali docta lauacro
Uictricem uictrix abolens baptismate labem
Hostis iuguli; nec iam contenta piatum

15.10 London, B.L., Cotton Cleo. C. VIII, f. 9v

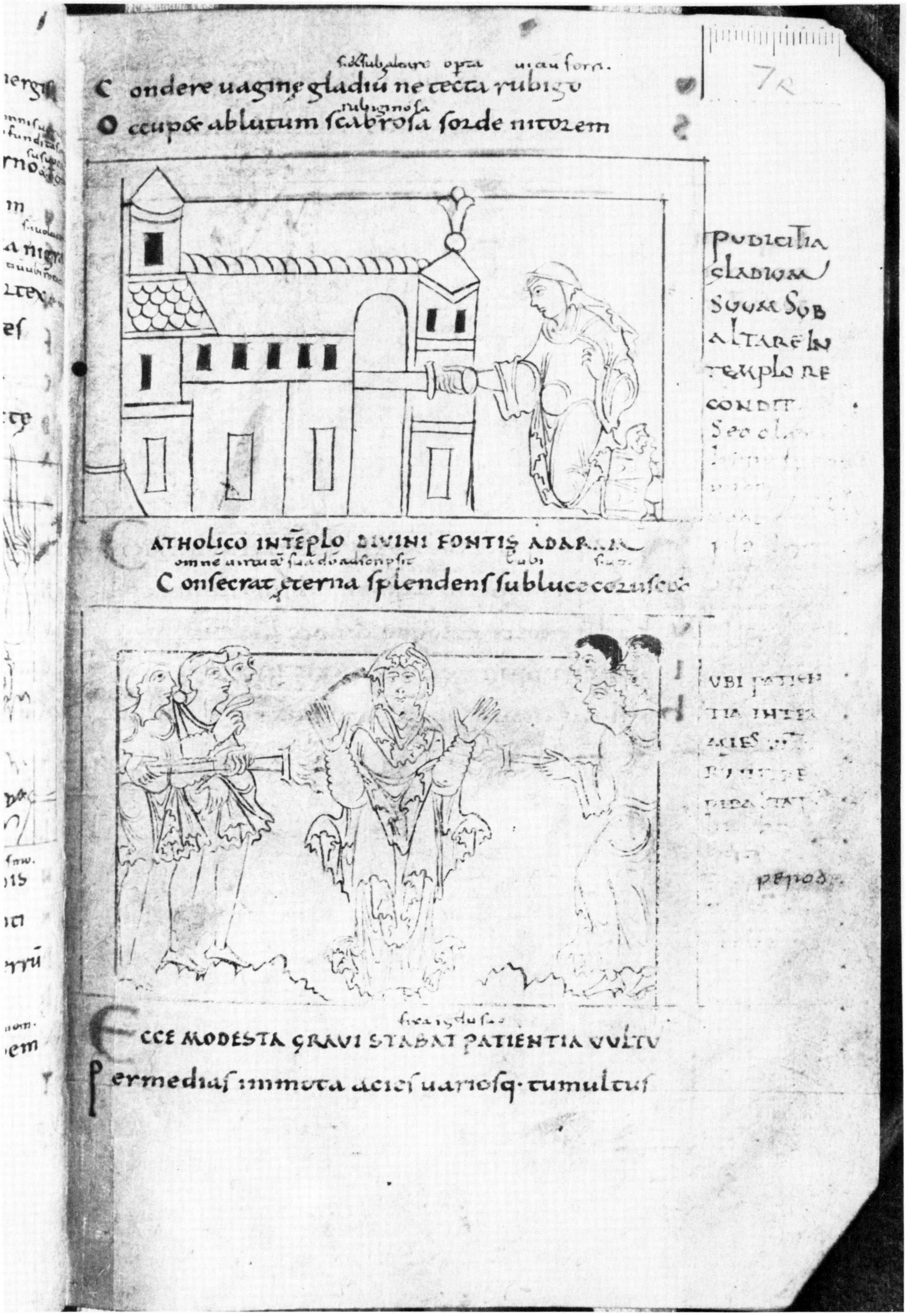

15.11 London, B.L., Cotton Cleo. C. VIII, f. 10r

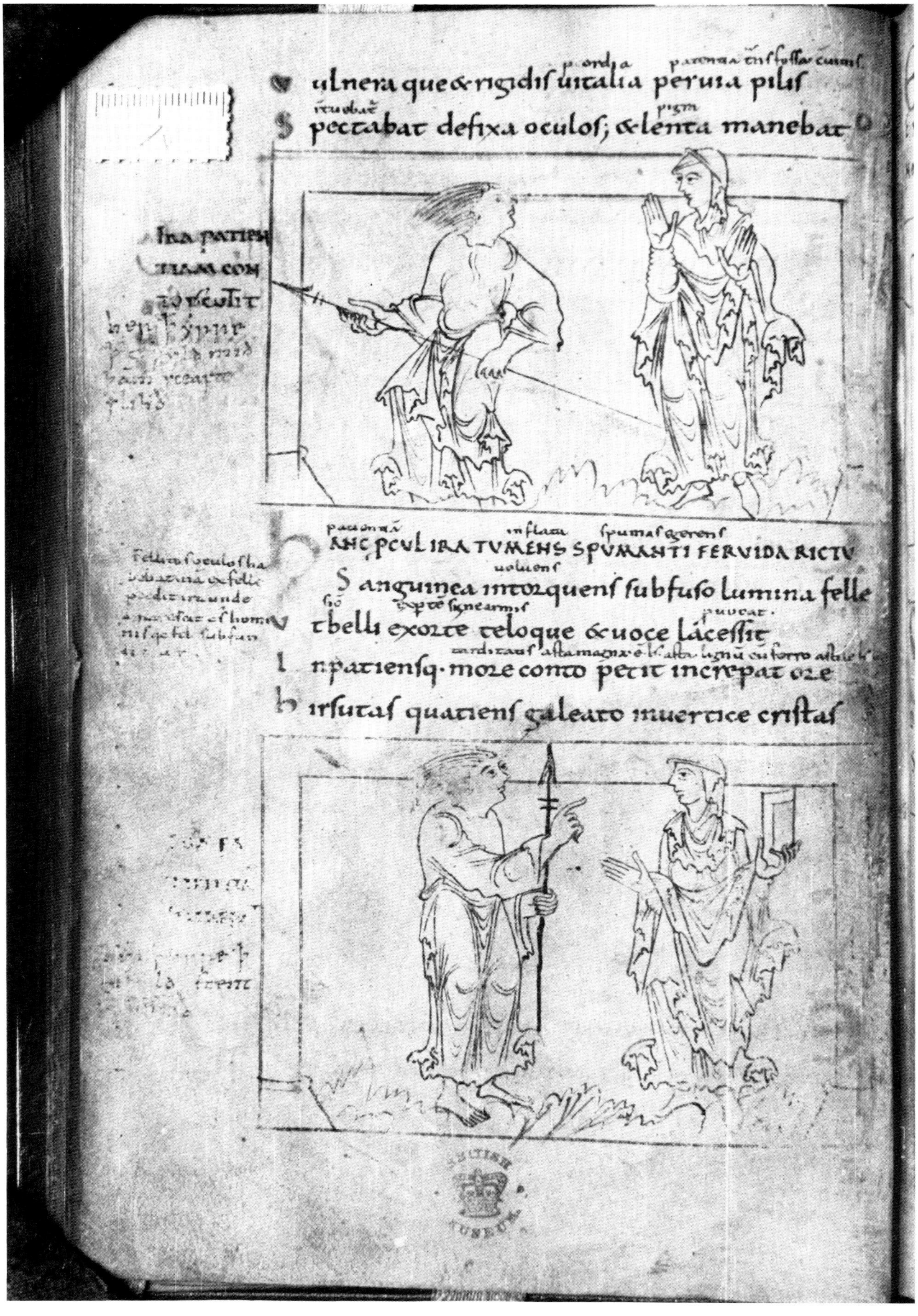

15.12 London, B.L., Cotton Cleo. C. VIII, f. 10v

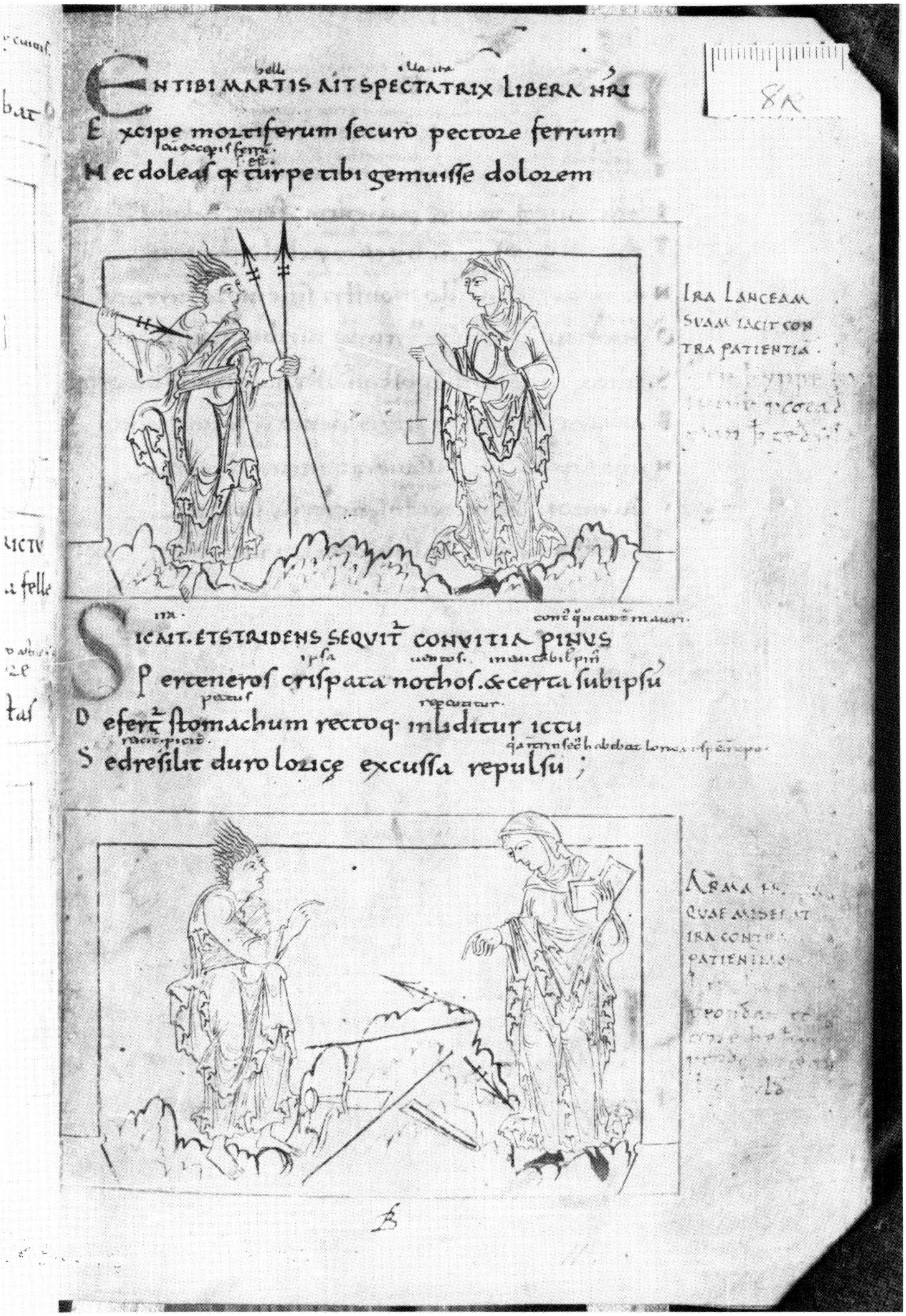
EN TIBI MARTIS AIT SPECTATRIX LIBERA NRI
Excipe mortiferum securo pectore ferrum
Hec doleas q turpe tibi gemuisse dolorem

IRA LANCEAM SUAM IACIT CONTRA PATIENTIA

SIC AIT. ET STRIDENS SEQUIT CONVITIA PINUS
Per teneros crispata nothos. & certa sub ipsu
Defert stomachum rectoq. inliditur ictu
Sed resilit duro lorice excussa repulsu;

15.13 London, B.L., Cotton Cleo. C. VIII, f. 11r

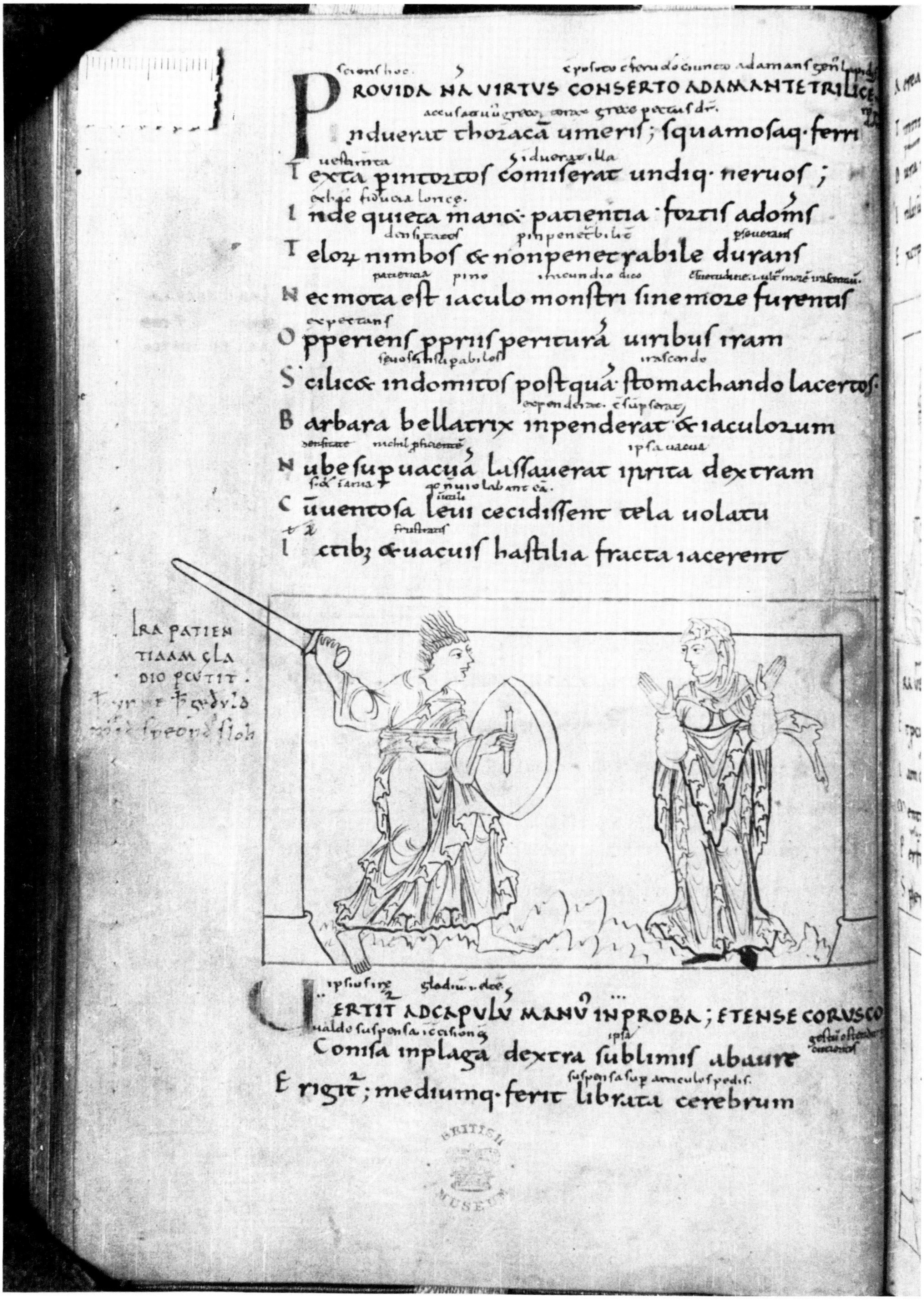

15.14 London, B.L., Cotton Cleo. C. VIII, f. 11v

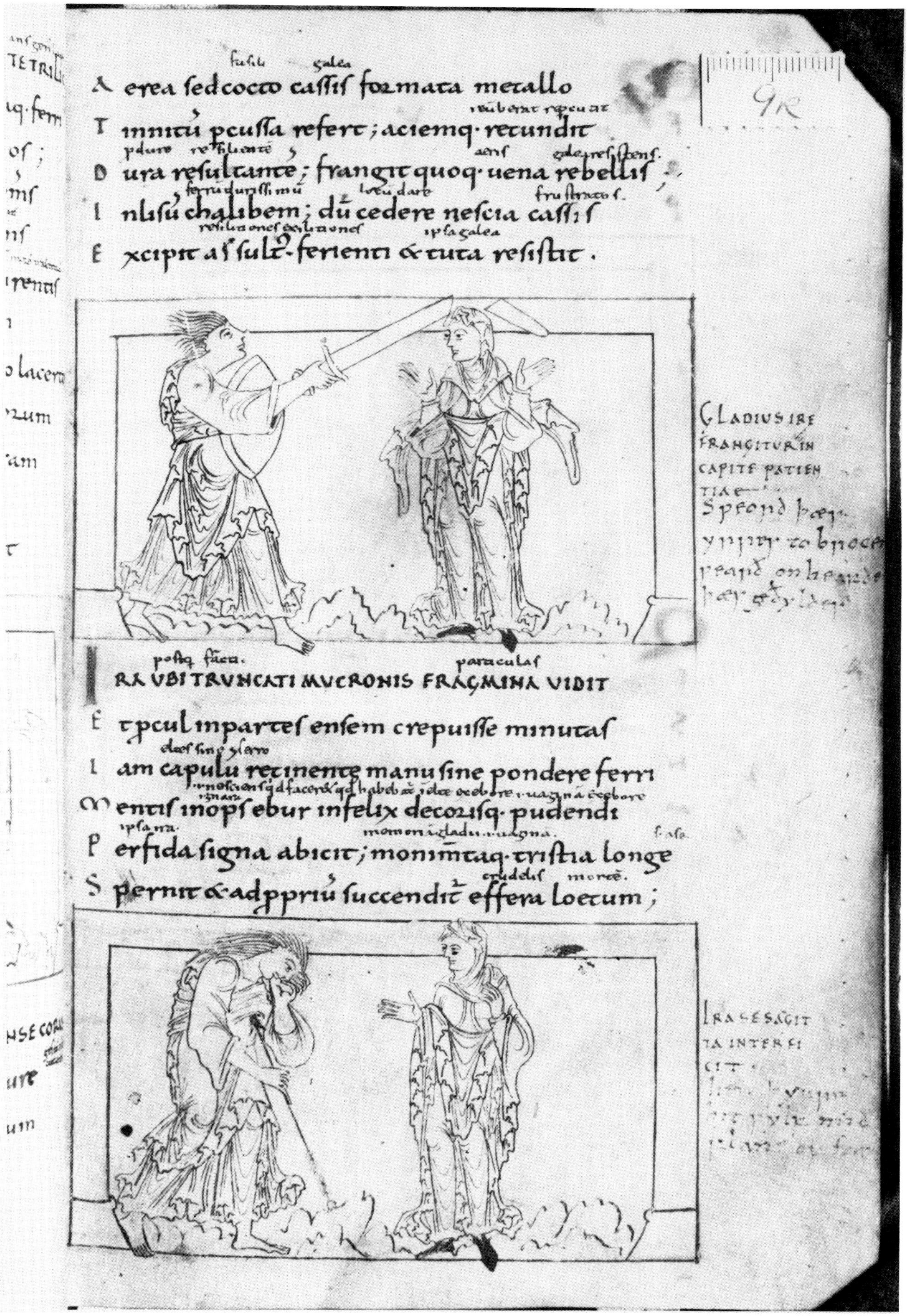

15.15 London, B.L., Cotton Cleo. C. VIII, f. 12r

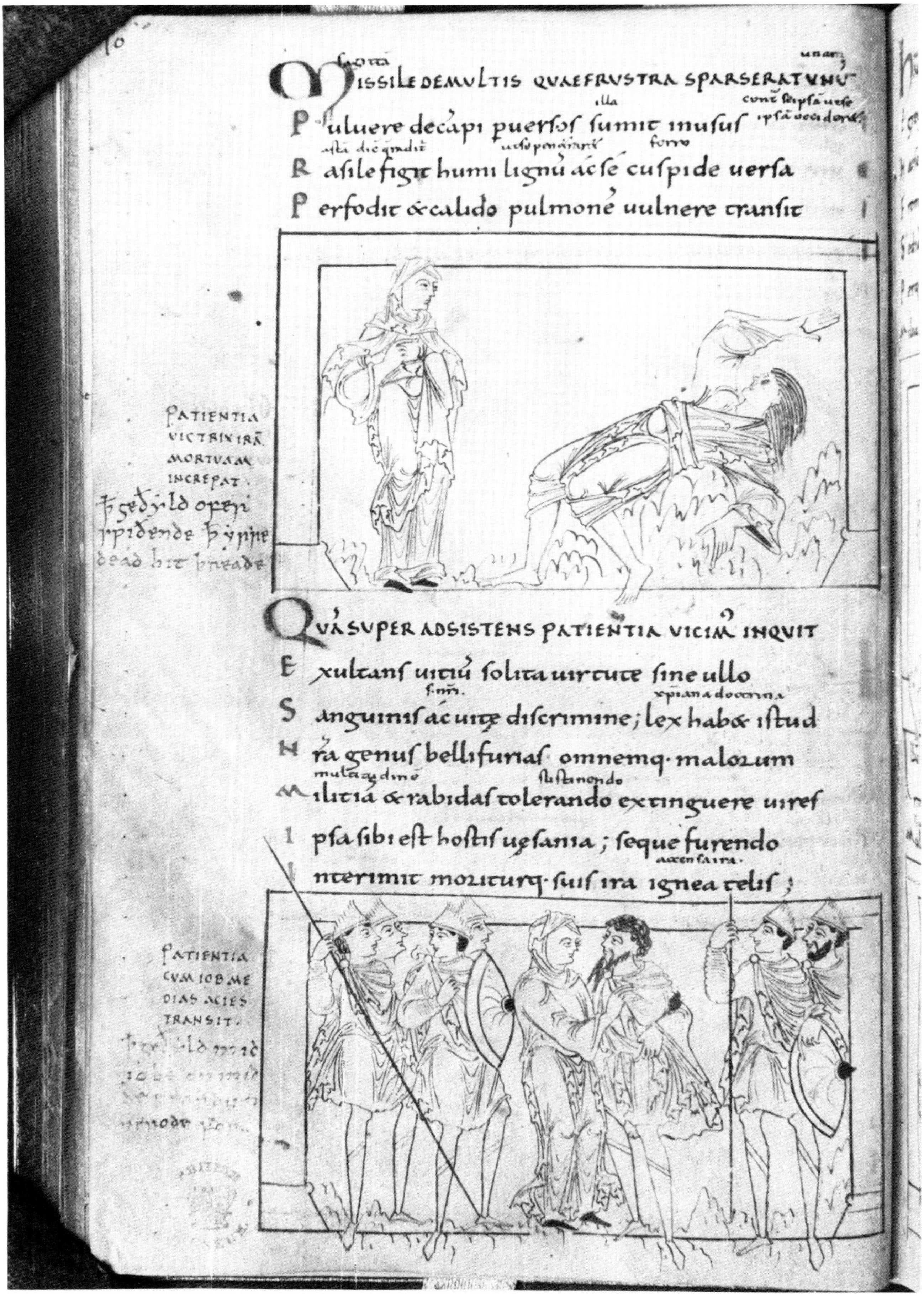

15.16 London, B.L., Cotton Cleo. C. VIII, f. 12v

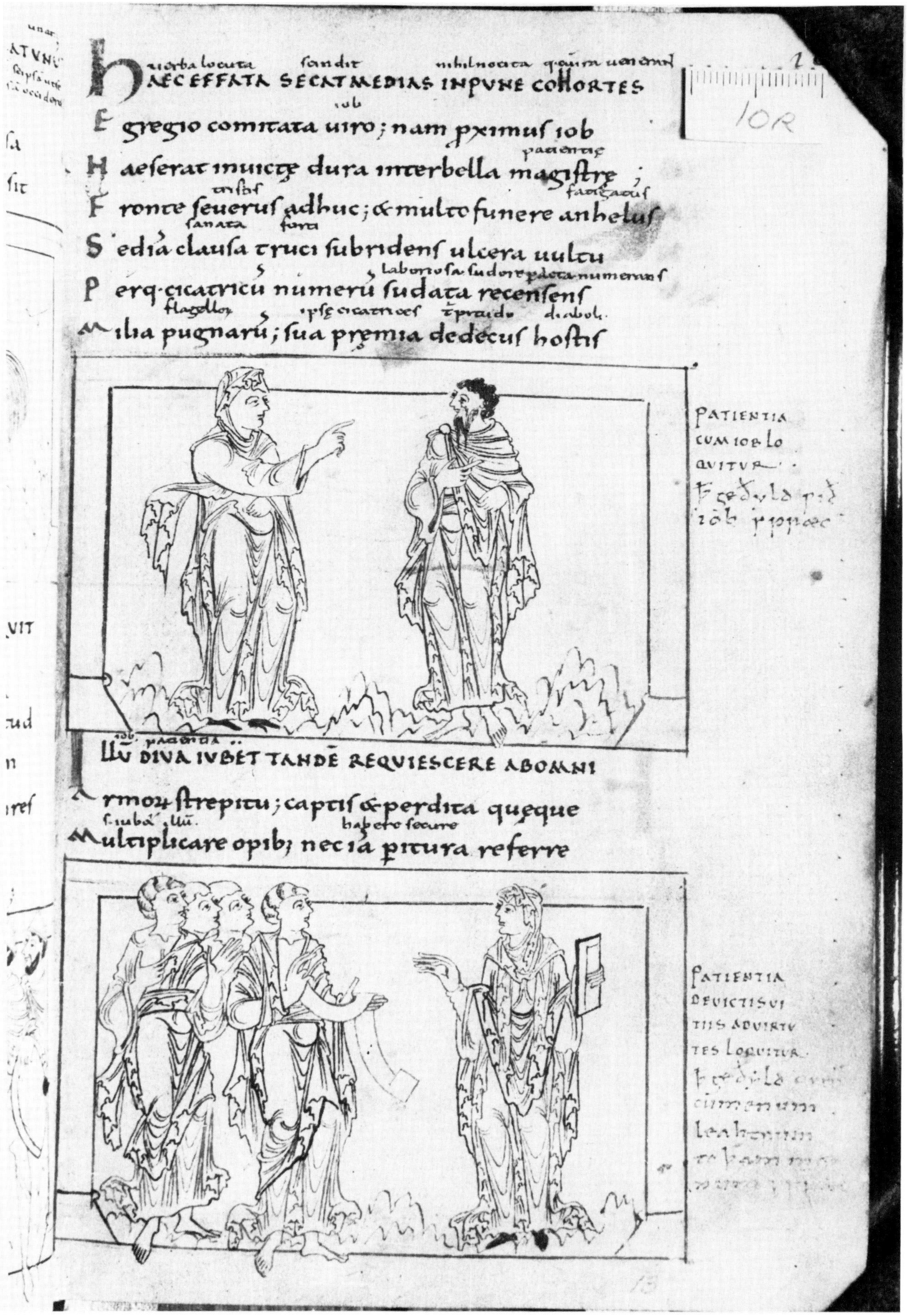

15.17 London, B.L., Cotton Cleo. C. VIII, f. 13r

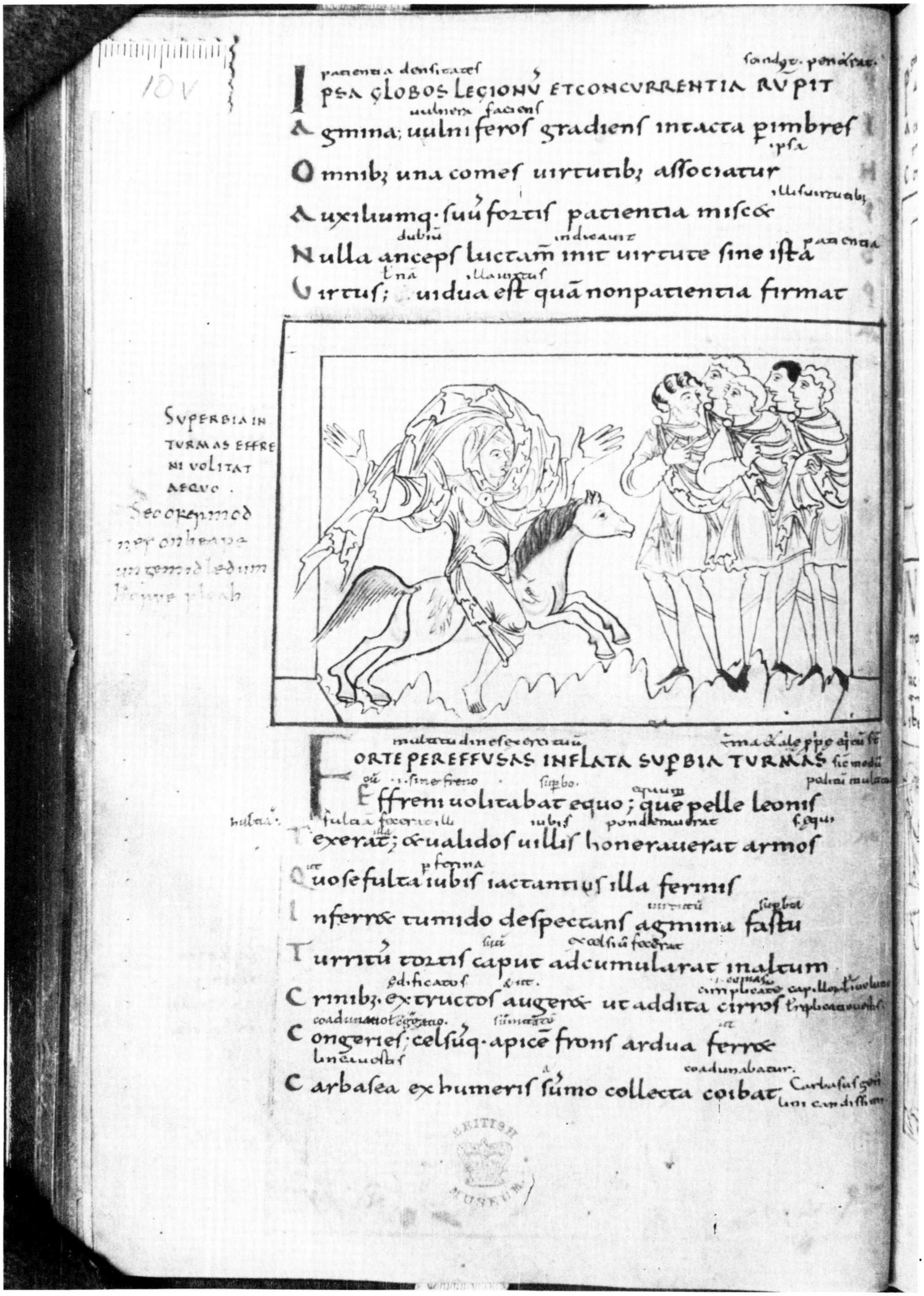
Ipsa globos legionū et concurrentia rupit
Agmina; uulniferos gradiens intacta p imbres
Omnib; una comes uirtutib; associatur
Auxiliumq· suū fortis patientia miscet
Nulla anceps luctam init uirtute sine ista
Virtus; uidua est quā non patientia firmat

Superbia in turmas effreni uolitat aequo.

Forte per effusas inflata supbia turmas
Effreni uolitabat equo; que pelle leonis
Texerat; et ualidos uillis honerauerat armos
Quo se fulta iubis iactantius illa ferinis
Inferret tumido despectans agmina fastu
Turritū tortis caput adcumularat in altum
Crinib; extructos augeret ut addita cirros
Congeries; celsumq· apice frons ardua ferret
Carbasea ex humeris summo collecta coibat

15.18 London, B.L., Cotton Cleo. C. VIII, f. 13v

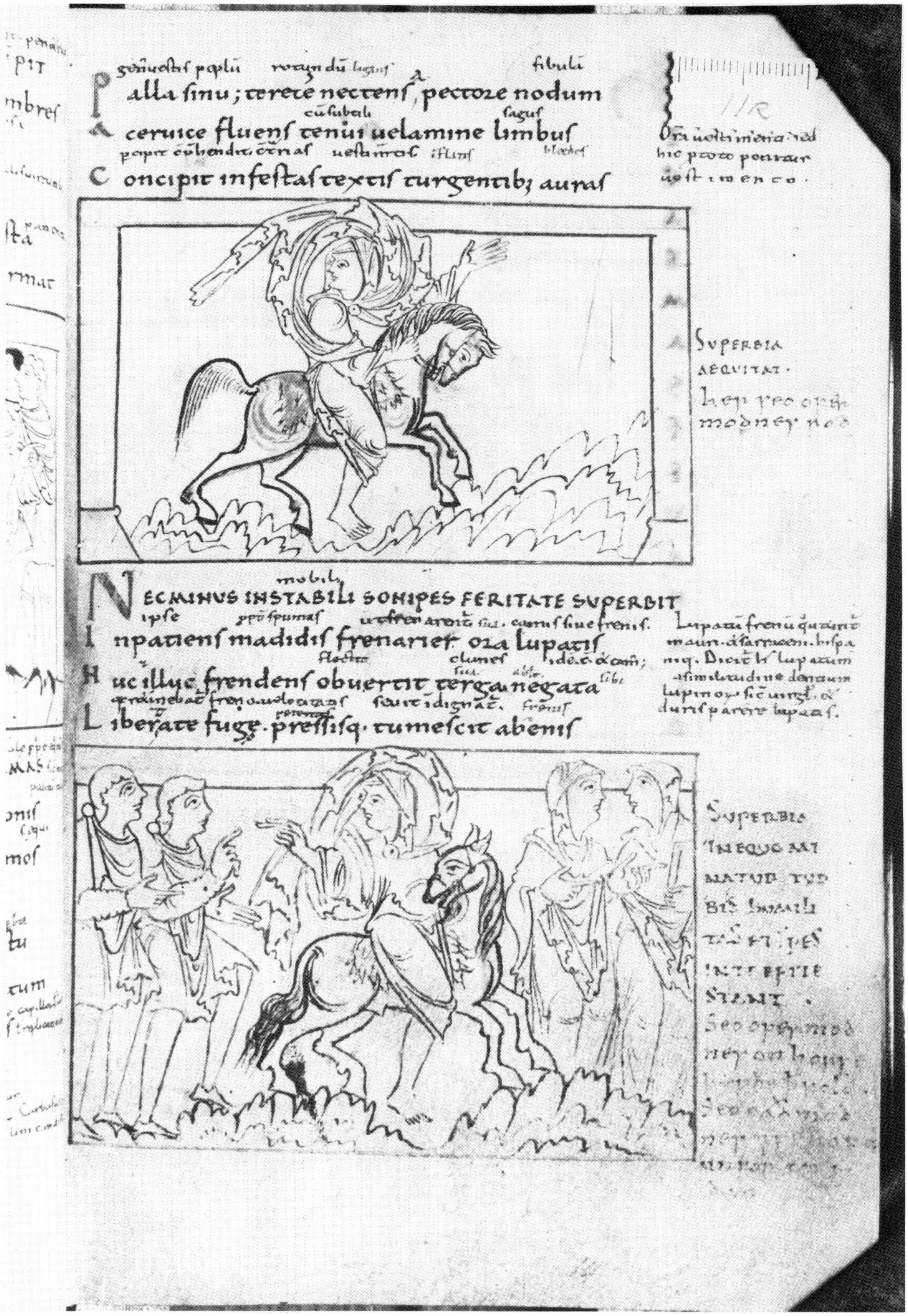

15.19 London, B.L., Cotton Cleo. C. VIII, f. 14r

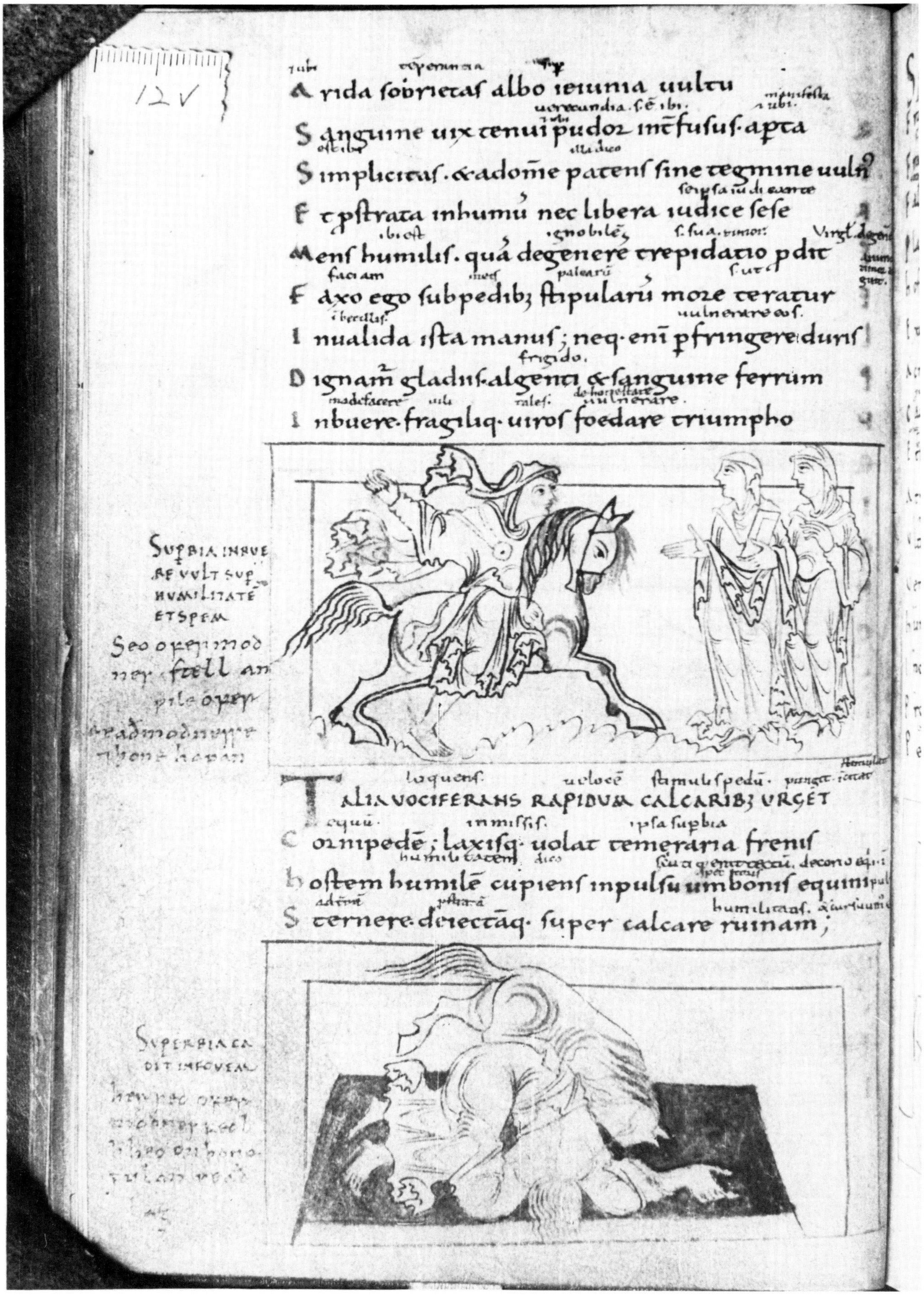

15.20 London, B.L., Cotton Cleo. C. VIII, f. 15v

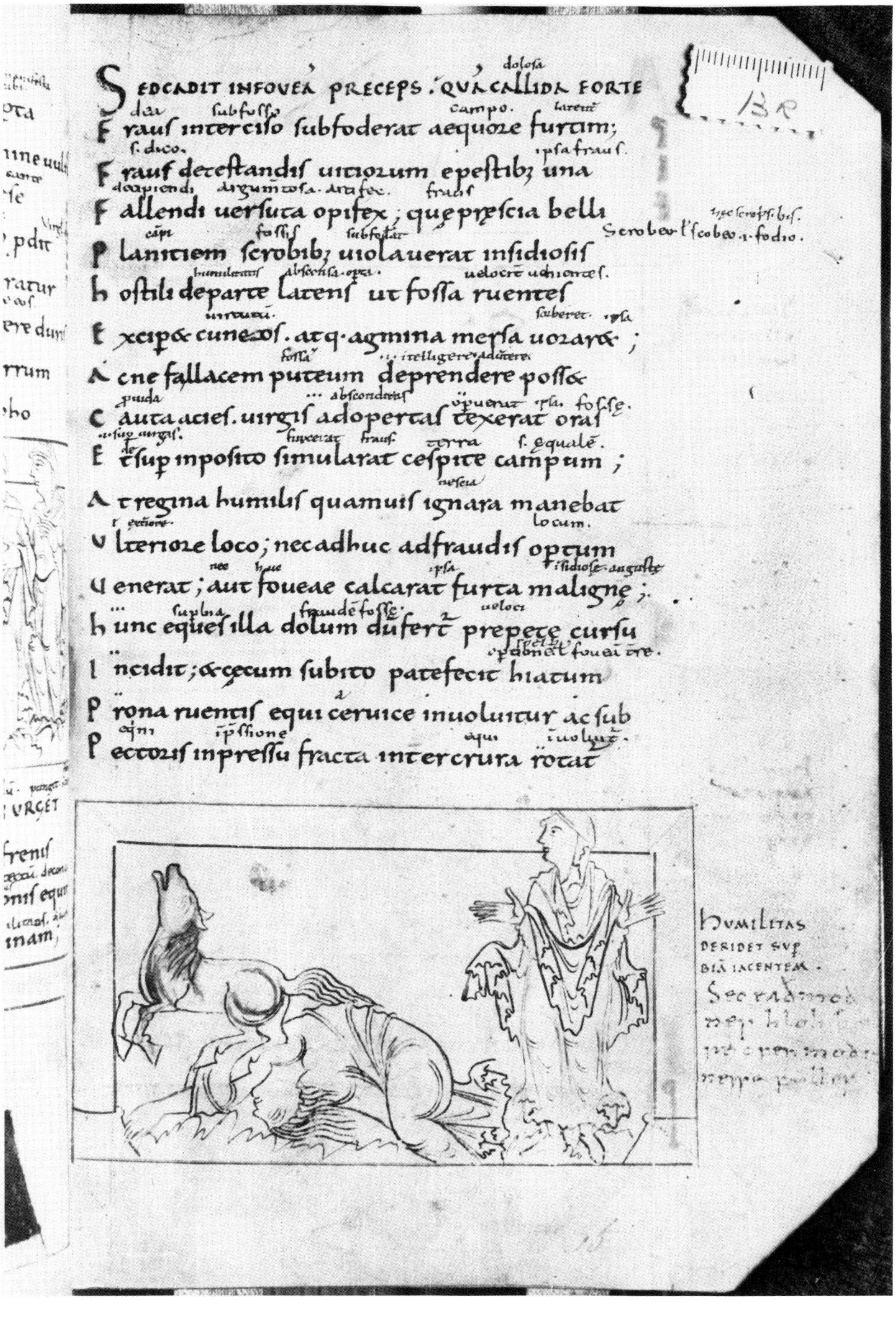
Sed cadit in fovea praeceps. Qua callida forte
Fraus interciso subfoderat aequore furtim;
Fraus detestandis vitiorum e pestibus una
Fallendi versuta opifex; que praescia belli
Planitiem scrobibus violaverat insidiosis
Hostili de parte latens ut fossa ruentes
Exciperet cuneos. atque agmina mersa voraret;
Ac ne fallacem puteum deprendere posset
Cauta acies. virgis adopertas texerat oras
Et superimposito simularat cespite campum;
At regina humilis quamvis ignara manebat
Ulteriore loco; nec adhuc ad fraudis opertum
Venerat; aut foveae calcarat furta maligne;
Hunc eques illa dolum dum fertur praepete cursu
Incidit; et caecum subito patefecit hiatum
Prona ruentis equi cervice involvitur ac sub
Pectoris inpressu fracta inter crura rotat

Humilitas deridet superbiam iacentem.

15.21 London, B.L., Cotton Cleo. C. VIII, f. 16r

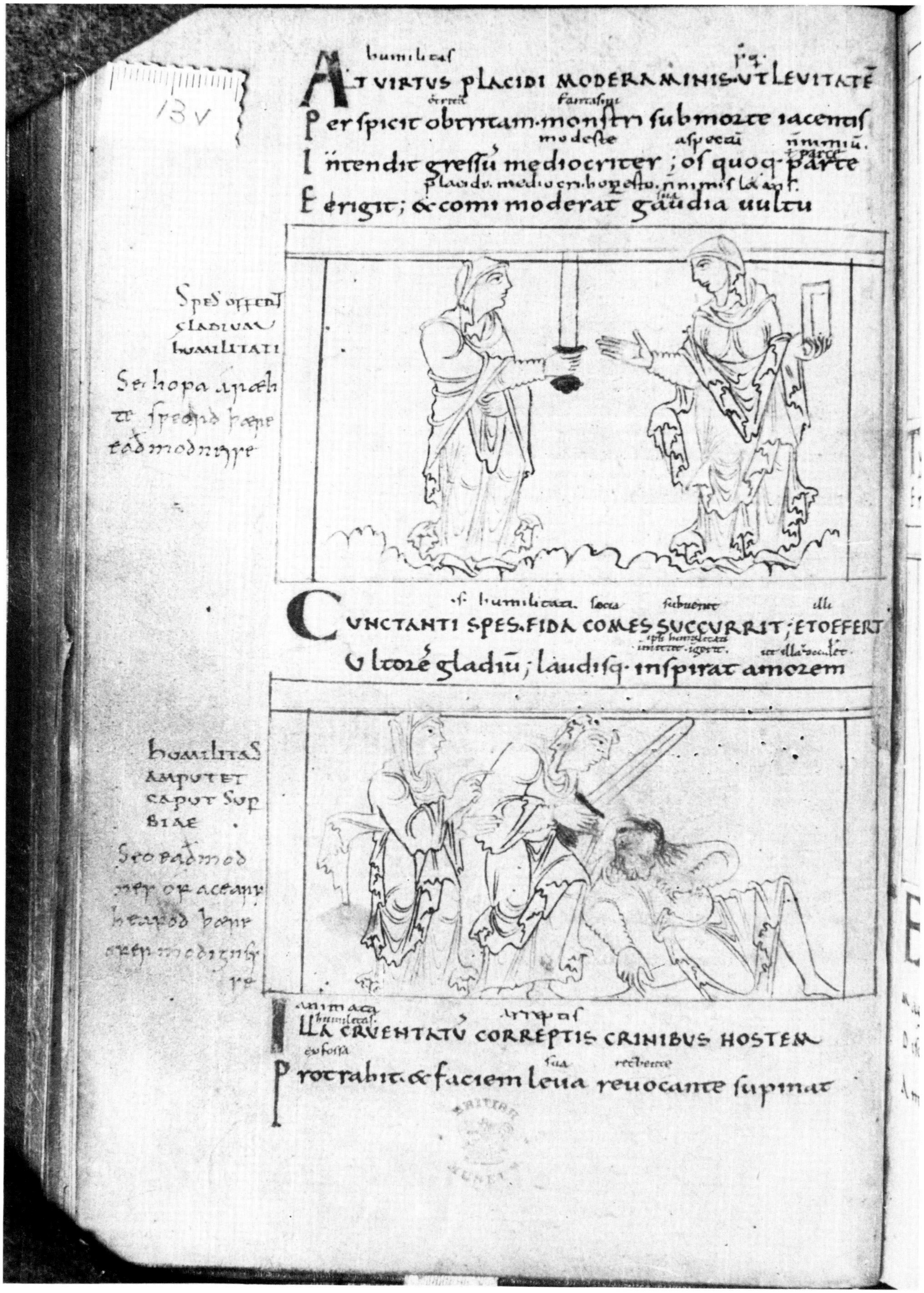

15.22 London, B.L., Cotton Cleo. C. VIII, f. 16v

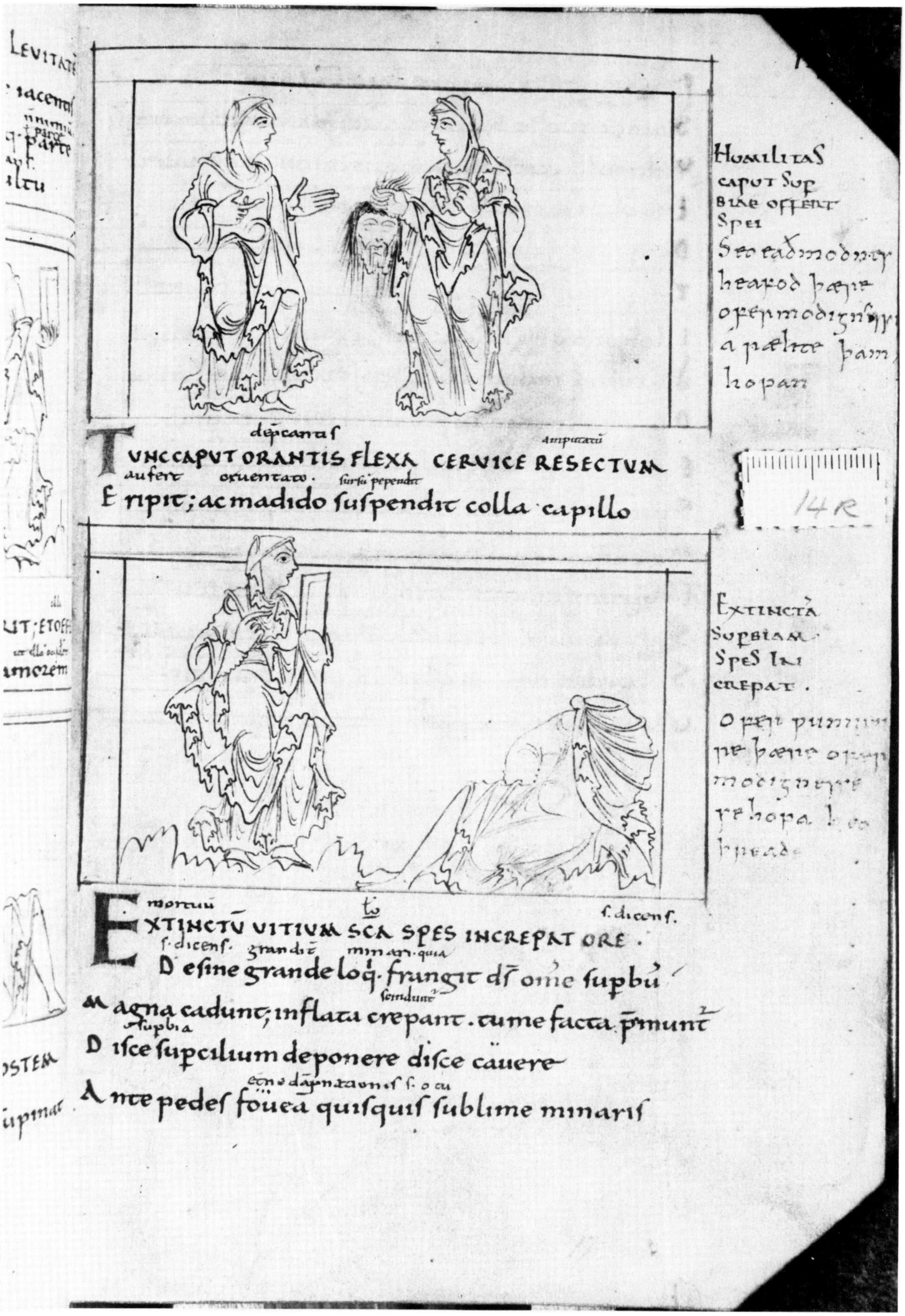

15.23 London, B.L., Cotton Cleo. C. VIII, f. 17r

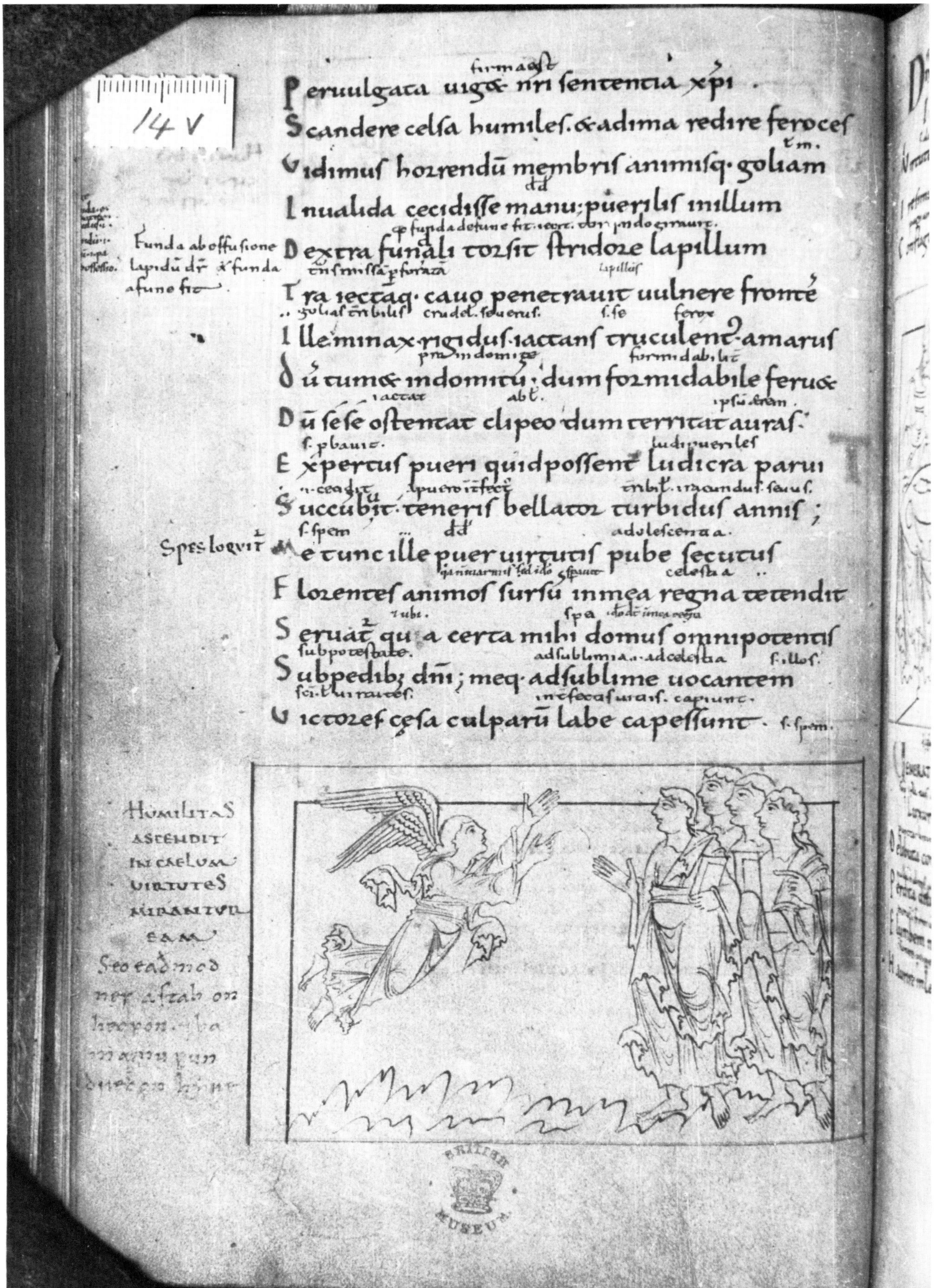

Peruulgata uiget nri sententia xpi .
Scandere celsa humiles. et adima redire feroces
Vidimus horrendū membris animisq· goliam
Inualida cecidisse manu; puerilis inillum
Dextra funali torsit stridore lapillum
Traiectaq· cauo penetrauit uulnere frontē
Ille minax rigidus iactans truculentus amarus
Dū tumet indomitū; dum formidabile feruet
Dū sese ostentat clipeo dum territat auras.
Expertus pueri quid possent ludicra parui
Succubuit teneris bellator turbidus annis ;
Me tunc ille puer uirtutis pube secutus
Florentes animos sursū inmea regna tetendit
Seruatus qui a certa mihi domus omnipotentis
Subpedib; dn̄i ; meq· adsublime uocantem
Victores cesa culparū labe capessunt .

HUMILITAS ASCENDIT IN CAELUM VIRTUTES MIRANTUR EAM

15.24 London, B.L., Cotton Cleo. C. VIII, f. 17v

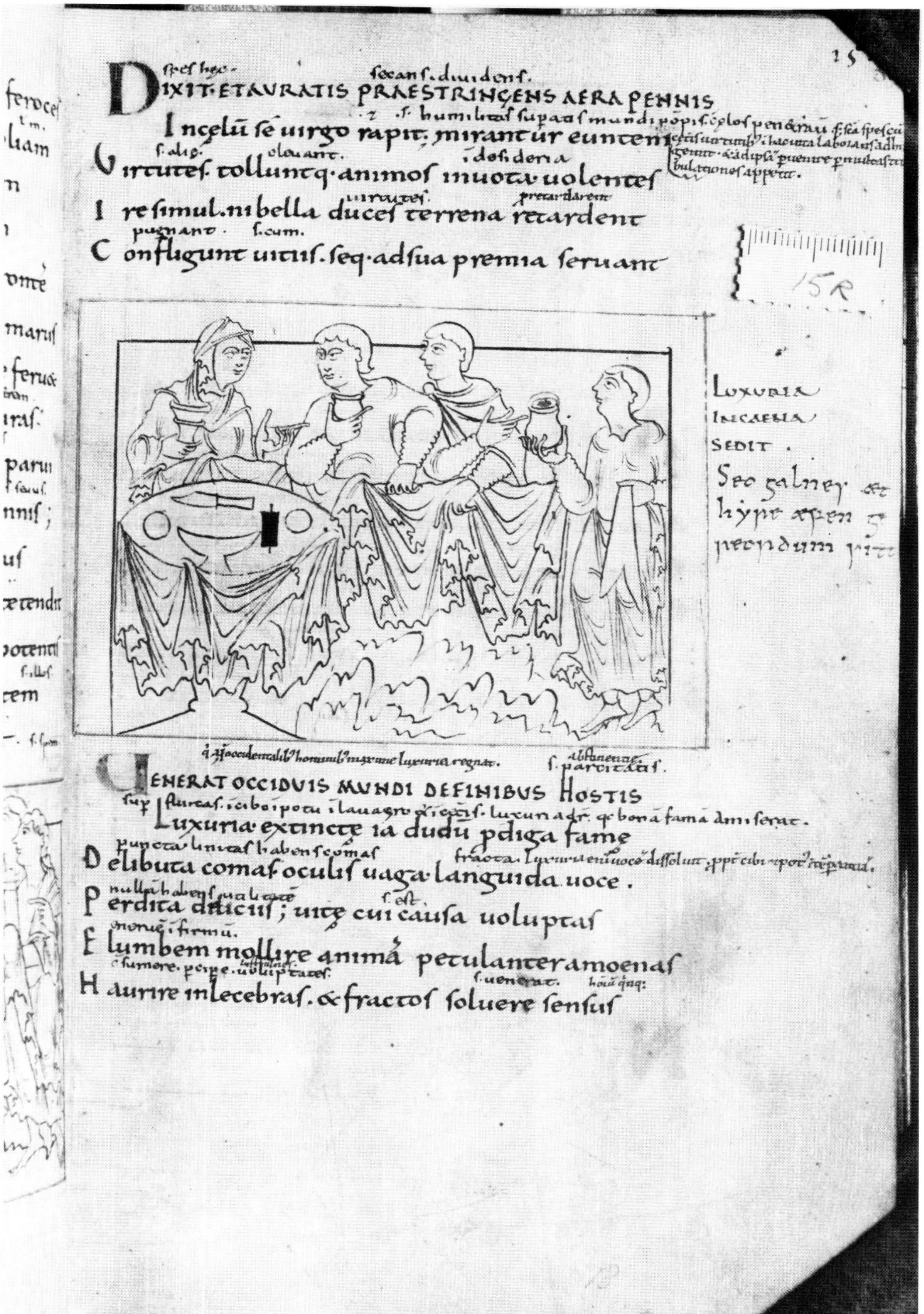

15.25 London, B.L., Cotton Cleo. C. VIII, f. 18r

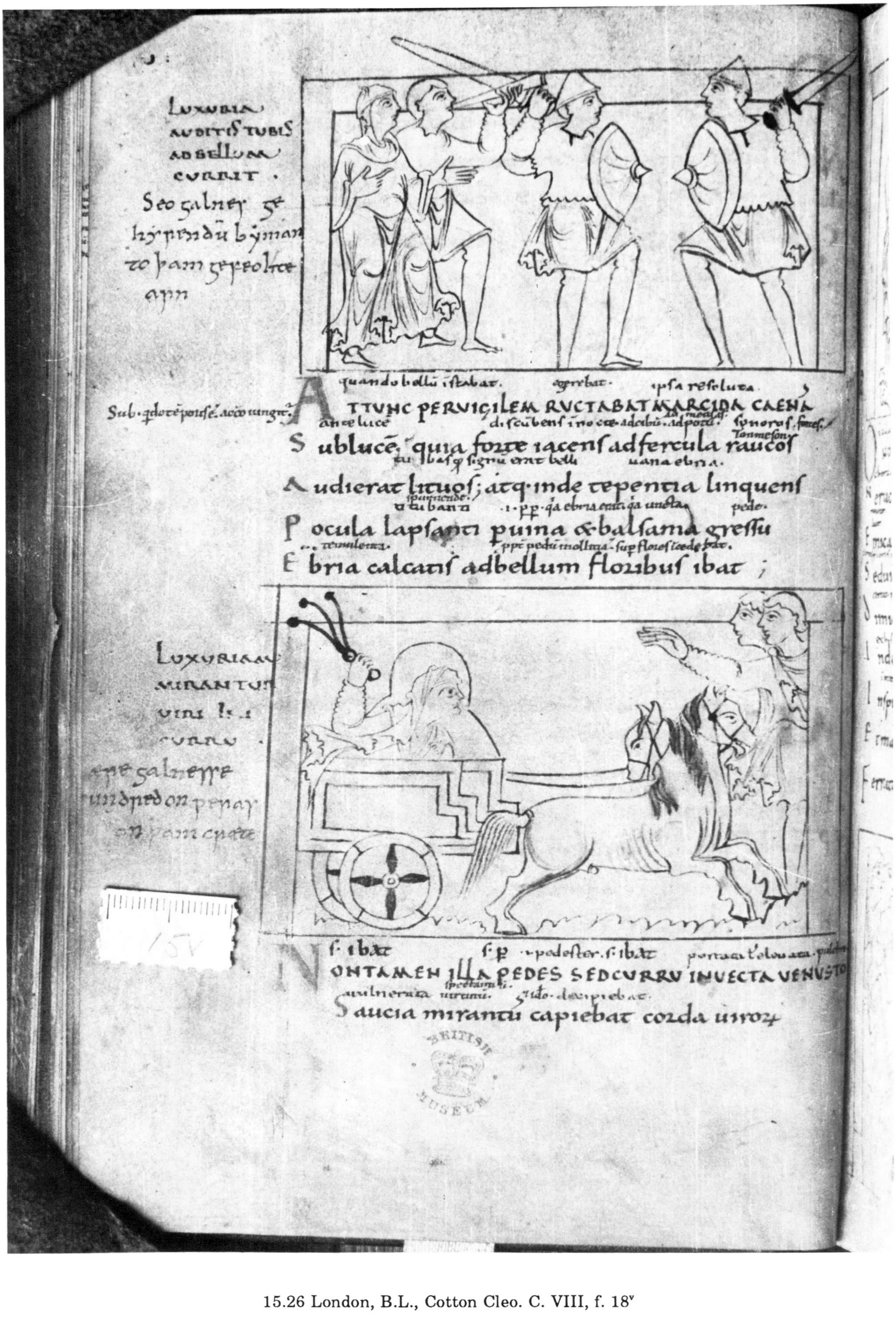

15.26 London, B.L., Cotton Cleo. C. VIII, f. 18ᵛ

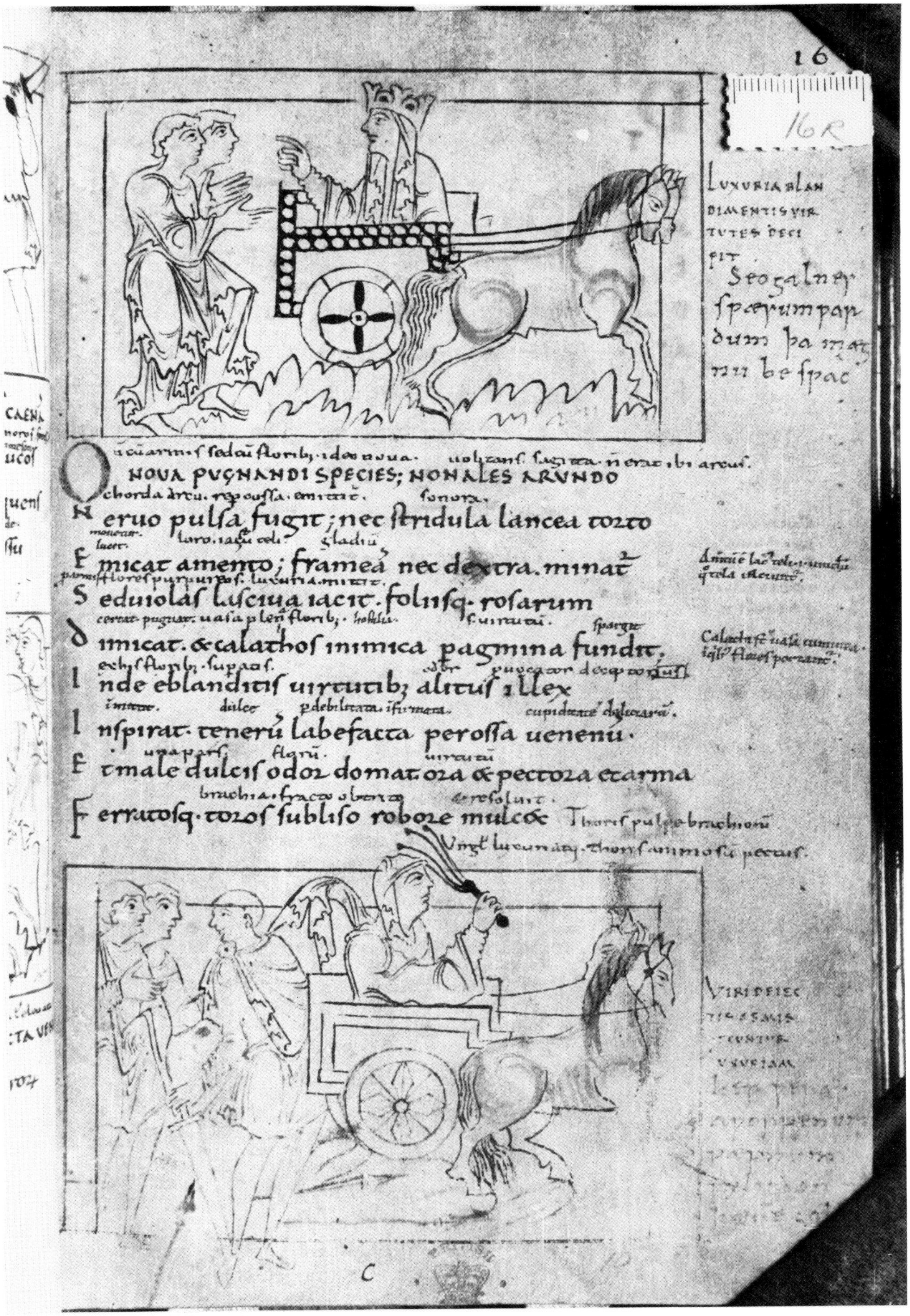

15.27 London, B.L., Cotton Cleo. C. VIII, f. 19r

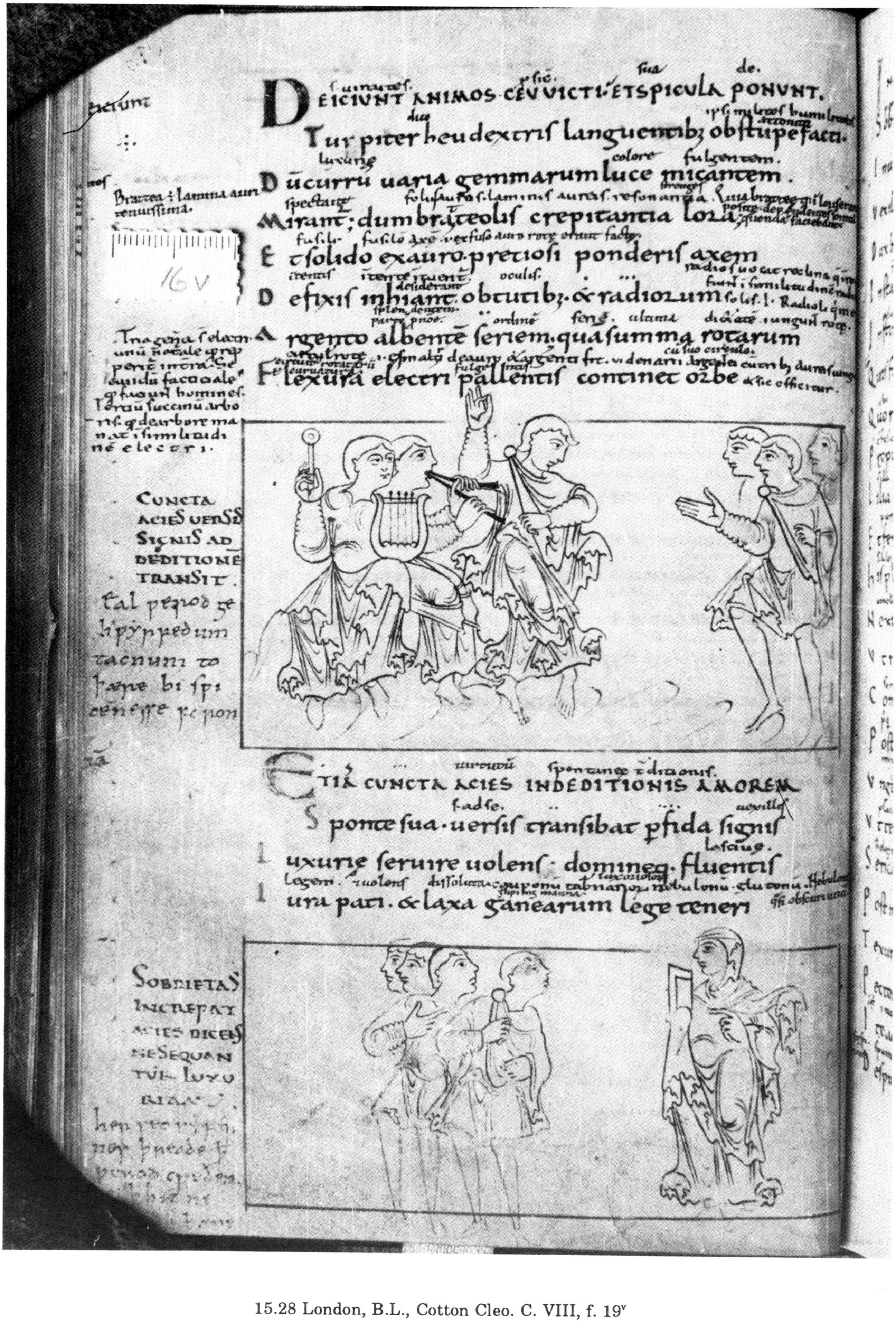

15.28 London, B.L., Cotton Cleo. C. VIII, f. 19v

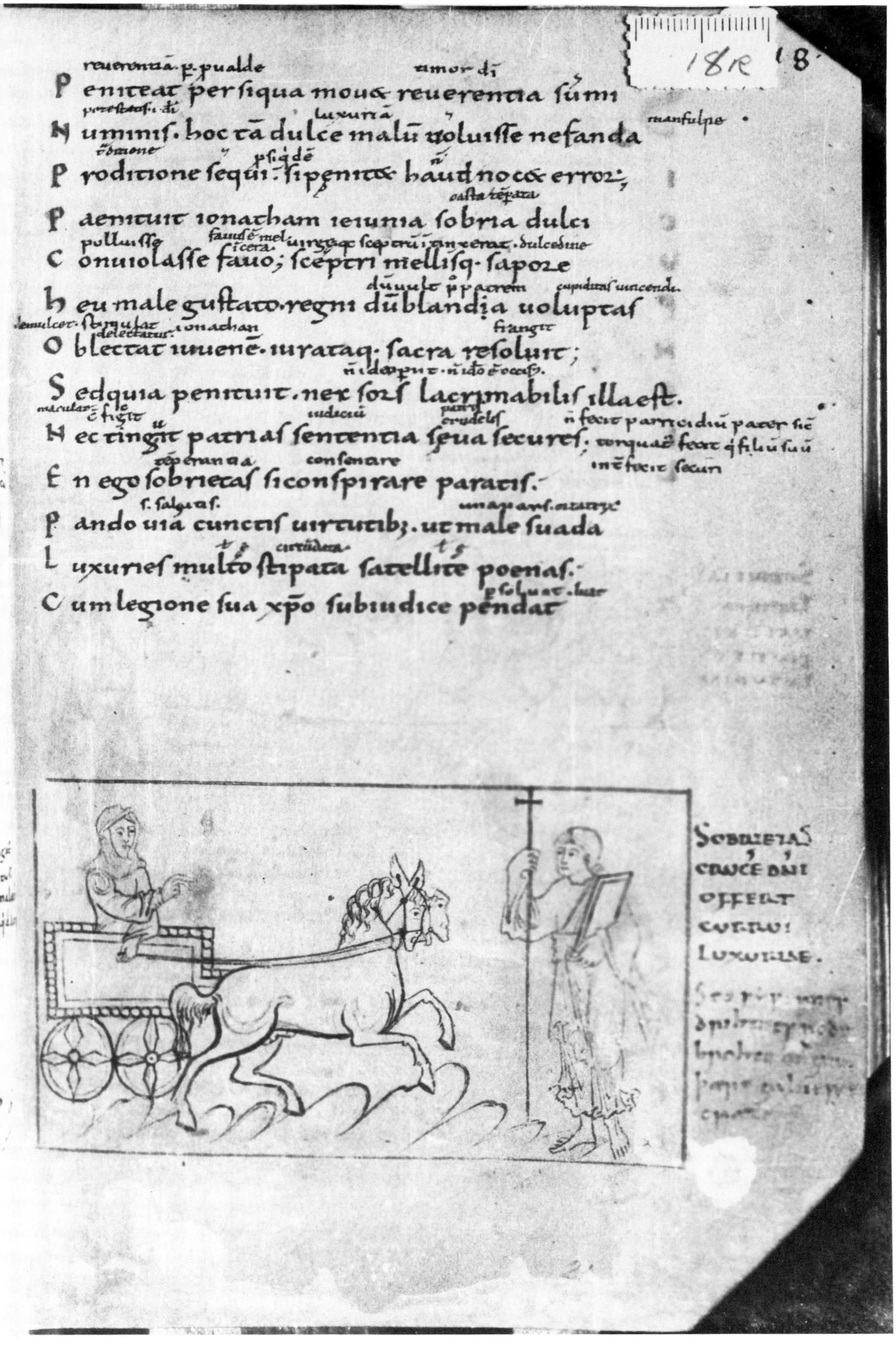
Peniteat per siqua mouet reuerentia summi
Numinis. hoc tam dulce malum uoluisse nefanda
Proditione sequi. si penitet haud nocet error;
Paenituit ionatham ieiunia sobria dulci
Conuiolasse fauo; sceptri mellisque sapore
Heu male gustato regni dum blandia uoluptas
Oblectat iuuenem. iurataque sacra resoluit;
Sed quia penituit. nec sors lacrimabilis illa est.
Nec tingit patrias sententia seua secures;
En ego sobrietas si conspirare paratis.
Pando uiam cunctis uirtutibus. ut male suada
Luxuries multo stipata satellite poenas
Cum legione sua xpo sub iudice pendat

15.29 London, B.L., Cotton Cleo. C. VIII, f. 21r

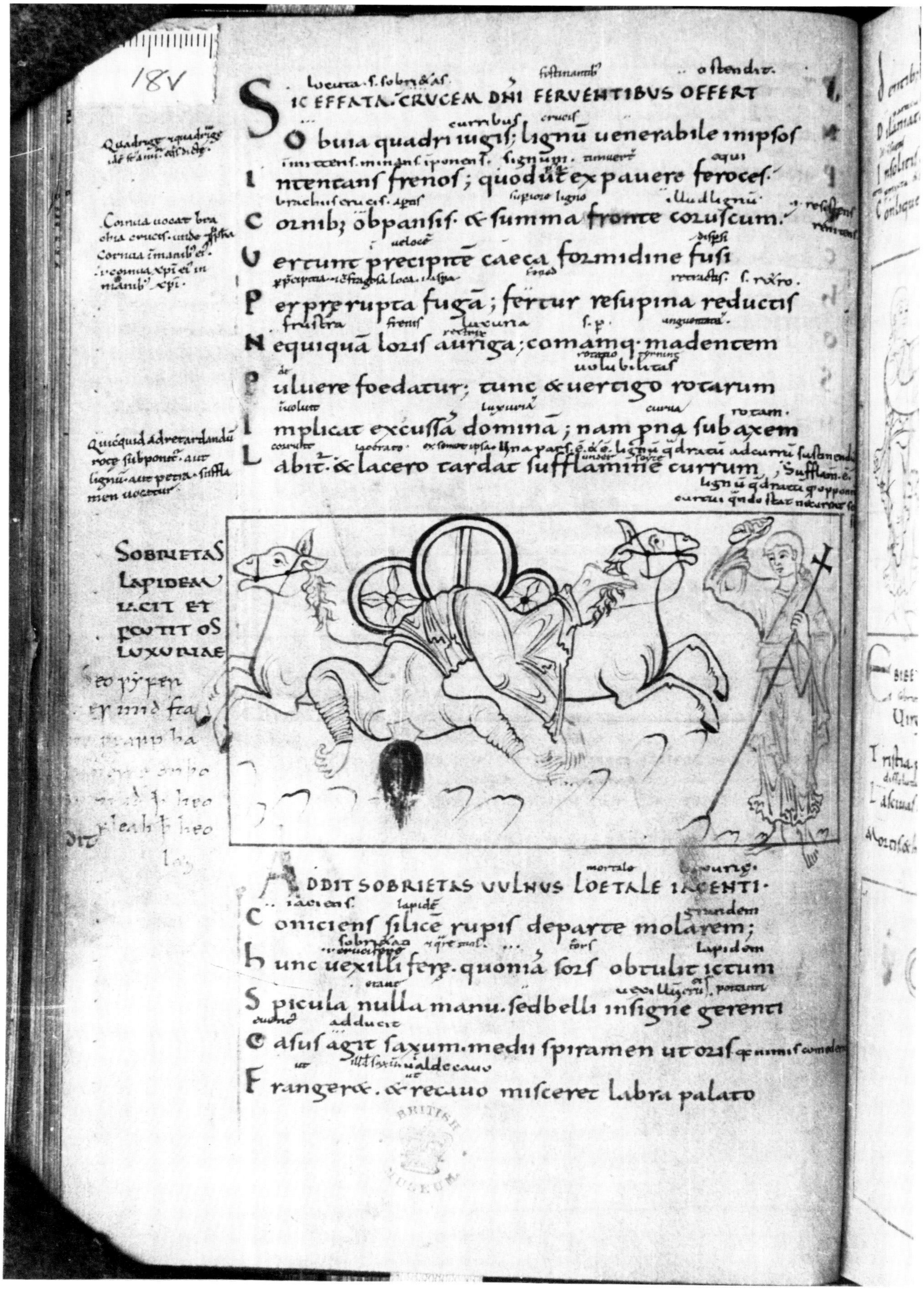
SIC EFFATA CRUCEM DNI FERVENTIBUS OFFERT
Obuia quadriiugis; lignū uenerabile inpsos
Intentans frenos; quod ut expauere feroces
Cornibꝫ obpansis & summa fronte coruscum
Uertunt precipitē caeca formidine fusi
Per prerupta fugā; fertur resupina reductis
Nequiquā loris auriga; comamq; madentem
Puluere foedatur; tunc & uertigo rotarum
Implicat excussā dominā; nam pna sub axem
Labit & lacero tardat sufflamine currum

SOBRIETAS LAPIDEAM IACIT ET PCUTIT OS LUXURIAE

ADDIT SOBRIETAS UULNUS LOETALE IACENTI
Conicienf silice rupis de parte molarem;
Hunc uexilli ferr quoniā sors obtulit ictum
Spicula nulla manu sed belli insigne gerenti
Casus agit saxum medii spiramen ut oris
Frangeret & recauo misceret labra palato

15.30 London, B.L., Cotton Cleo. C. VIII, f. 21v

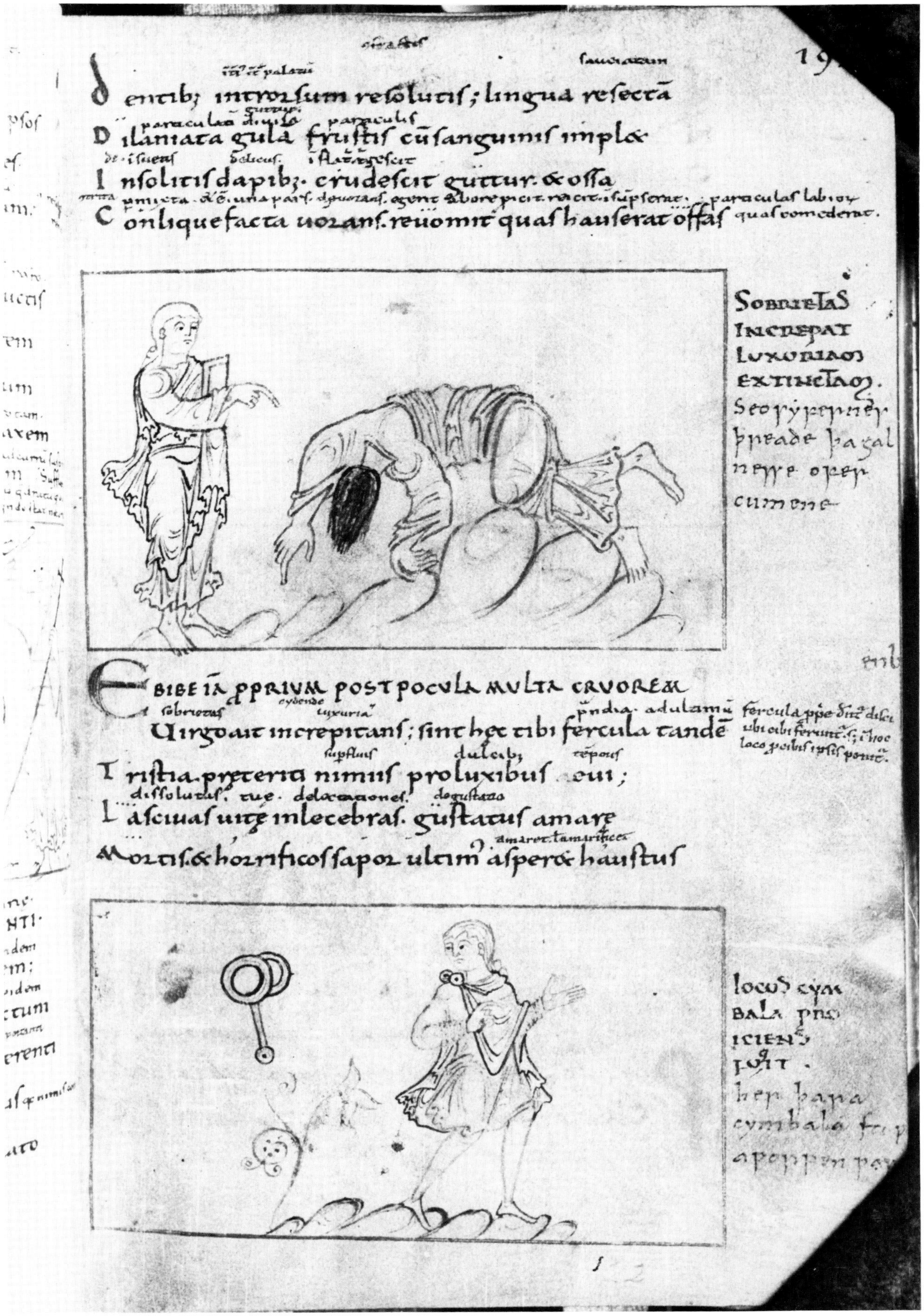

Dentib; introrsum resolutis; lingua resecta
Dilaniata gula frustis cu sanguinis implet
Insolitis dapib; crudescit guttur. & ossa
Conliquefacta uorans. reuomit quas hauserat offas

Sobrietas increpat luxoriam extinctam.

Ebibe iam proprium post pocula multa cruorem
Uirgo ait increpitans; sint hec tibi fercula tande
Tristia preteriti nimius proluxibus eui;
Lasciuas uite inlecebras. gustatus amare
Mortis & horrificos sapor ultim' asperet haustus

Iocus cymbala proiciens fugit.

15.31 London, B.L., Cotton Cleo. C. VIII, f. 22r

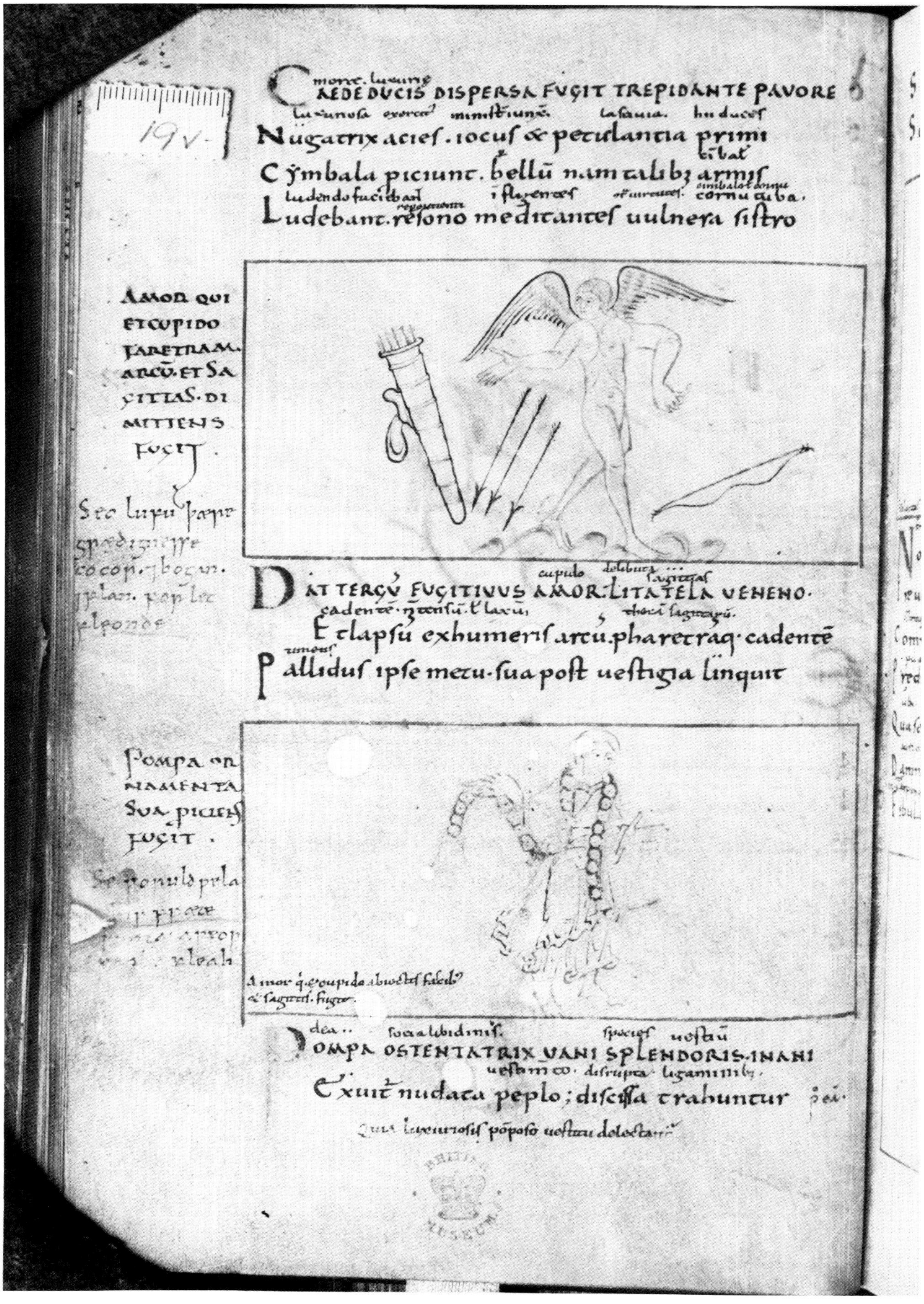

15.32 London, B.L., Cotton Cleo. C. VIII, f. 22v

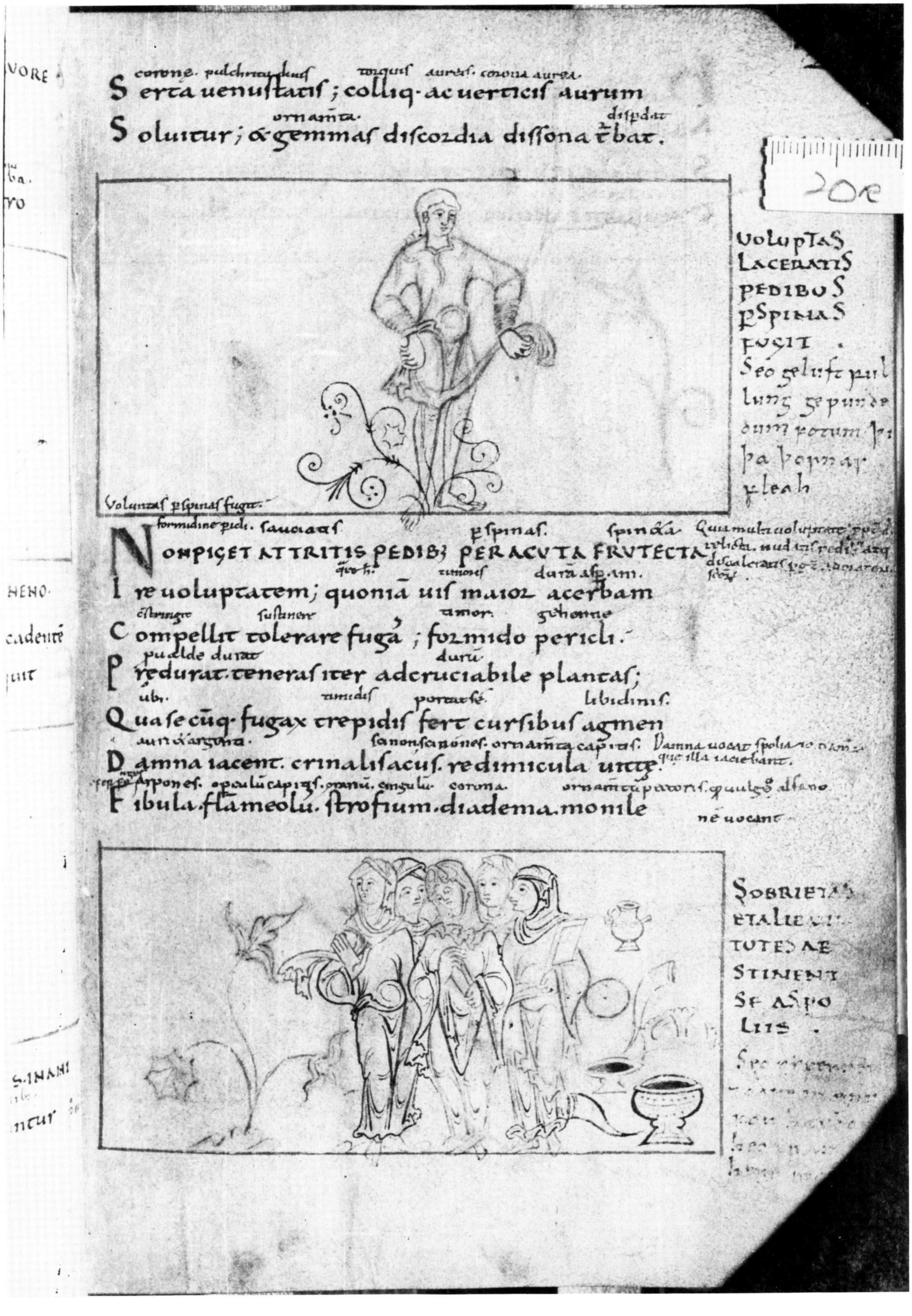

15.33 London, B.L., Cotton Cleo. C. VIII, f. 23r

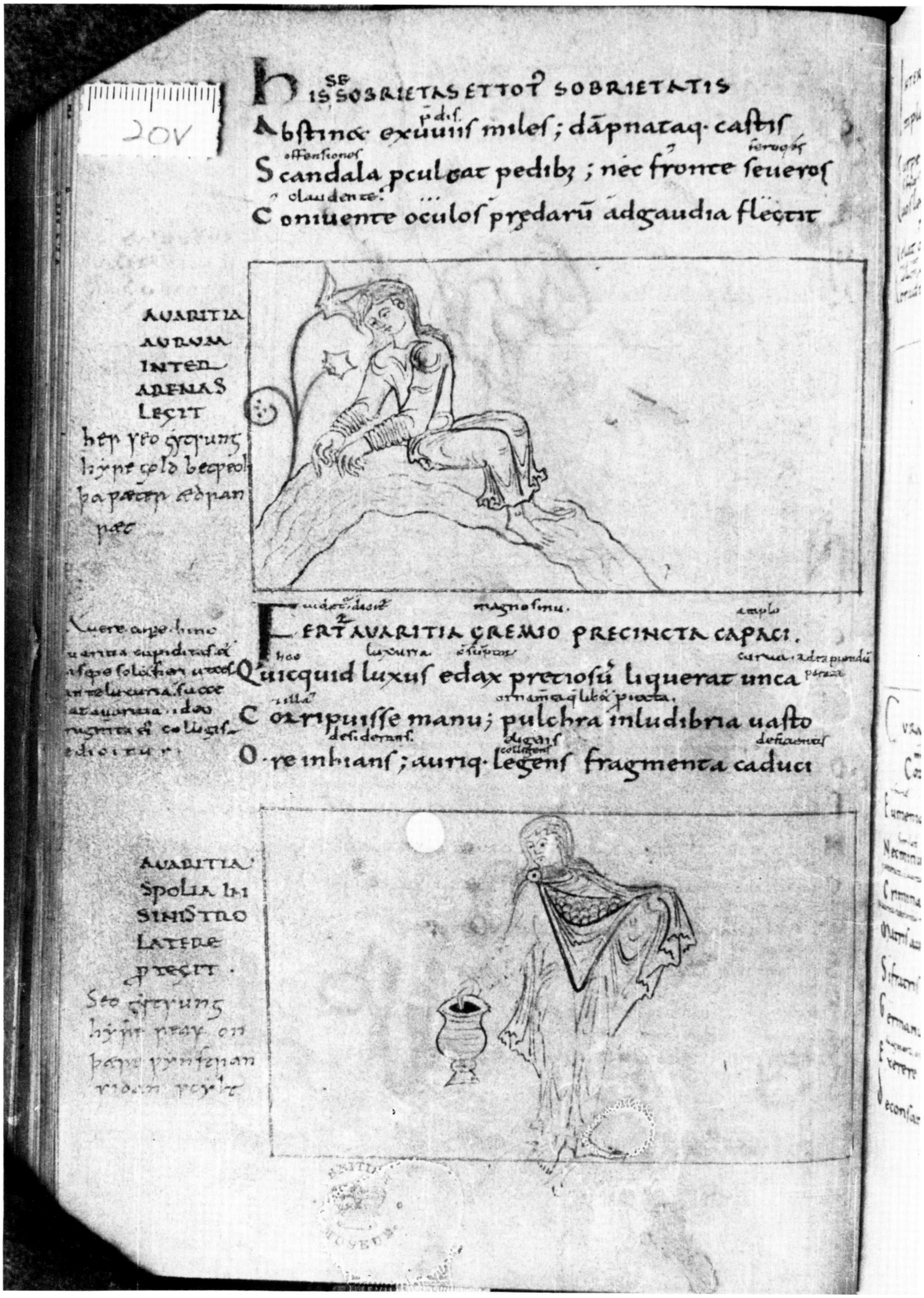

His sobrietas et tot sobrietatis
Abstinet exuuiis miles; dãpnataq· castis
Scandala pculcat pedibz; nec fronte seueros
Coniuente oculos prędarũ adgaudia flectit

AVARITIA AURUM INTER ARENAS LEGIT

FERT AVARITIA GREMIO PRECINCTA CAPACI.
Quicquid luxus edax pretiosũ liquerat unca
Corripuisse manu; pulchra inludibria uasto
Ore inhians; auriq· legens fragmenta caduci

AVARITIA SPOLIA IN SINISTRO LATERE PREGIT ·

15.34 London, B.L., Cotton Cleo. C. VIII, f. 23v

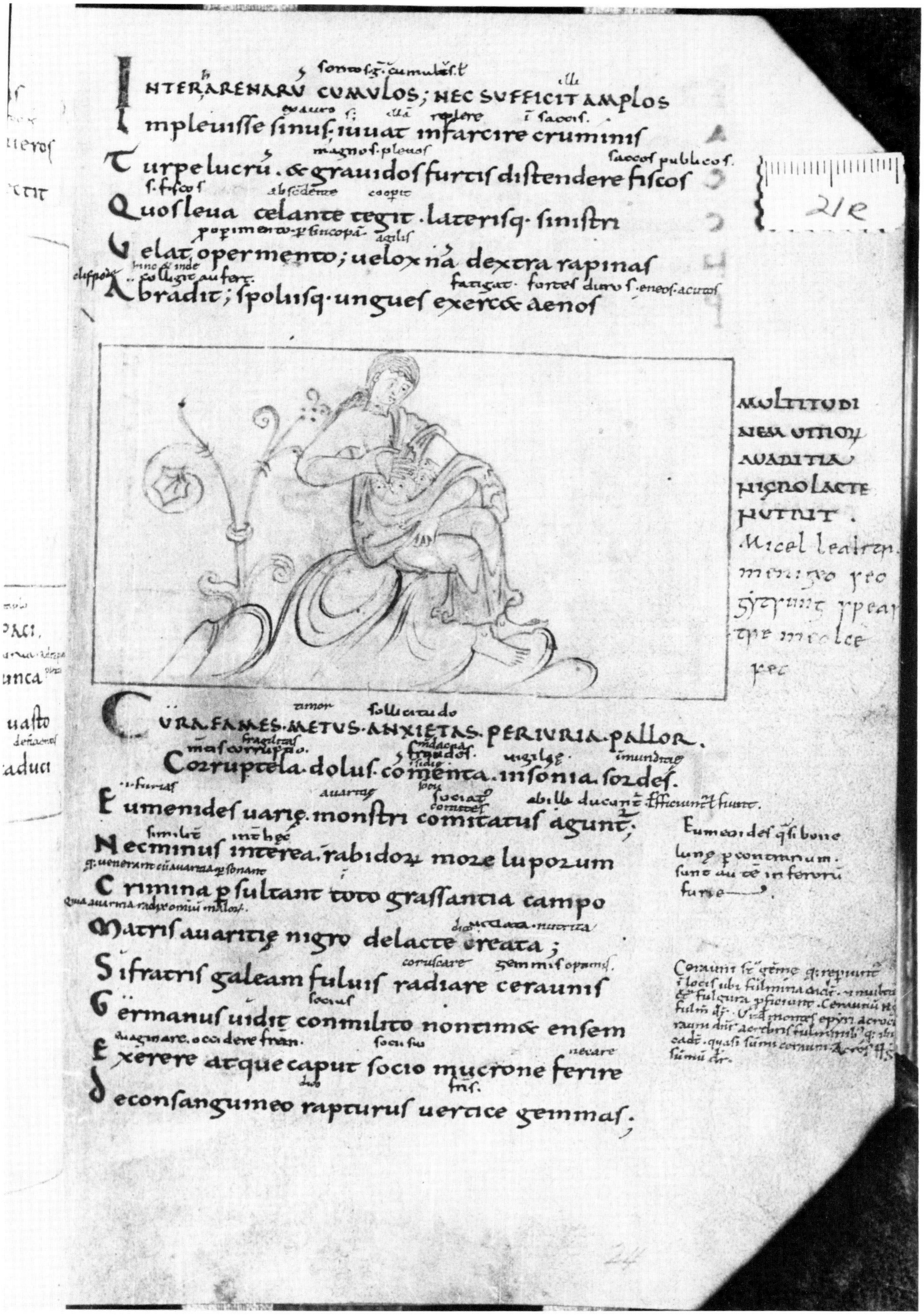
Inter harenarum cumulos; nec sufficit amplos
Impleuisse sinus; iuuat infarcire cruminis
Turpe lucrum. et grauidos furtis distendere fiscos
Quos leua celante tegit. laterisque sinistri
Velat opermento; uelox nam dextra rapinas
Abradit; spoliisque ungues exercet aenos

MULTITUDINEM UITIORUM AUARITIA NIGRO LACTE NUTRIT.

Cura fames metus anxietas periuria pallor
Corruptela dolus commenta insomnia sordes.
Eumenides uariae monstri comitatus agunt;
Nec minus interea rabidorum more luporum
Crimina persultant toto grassantia campo
Matris auaritiae nigro de lacte creata;
Si fratris galeam fului radiare ceraunis
Germanus uidit commilito non timet ensem
Exerere atque caput socio mucrone ferire
De consanguineo rapturus uertice gemmas;

15.35 London, B.L., Cotton Cleo. C. VIII, f. 24r

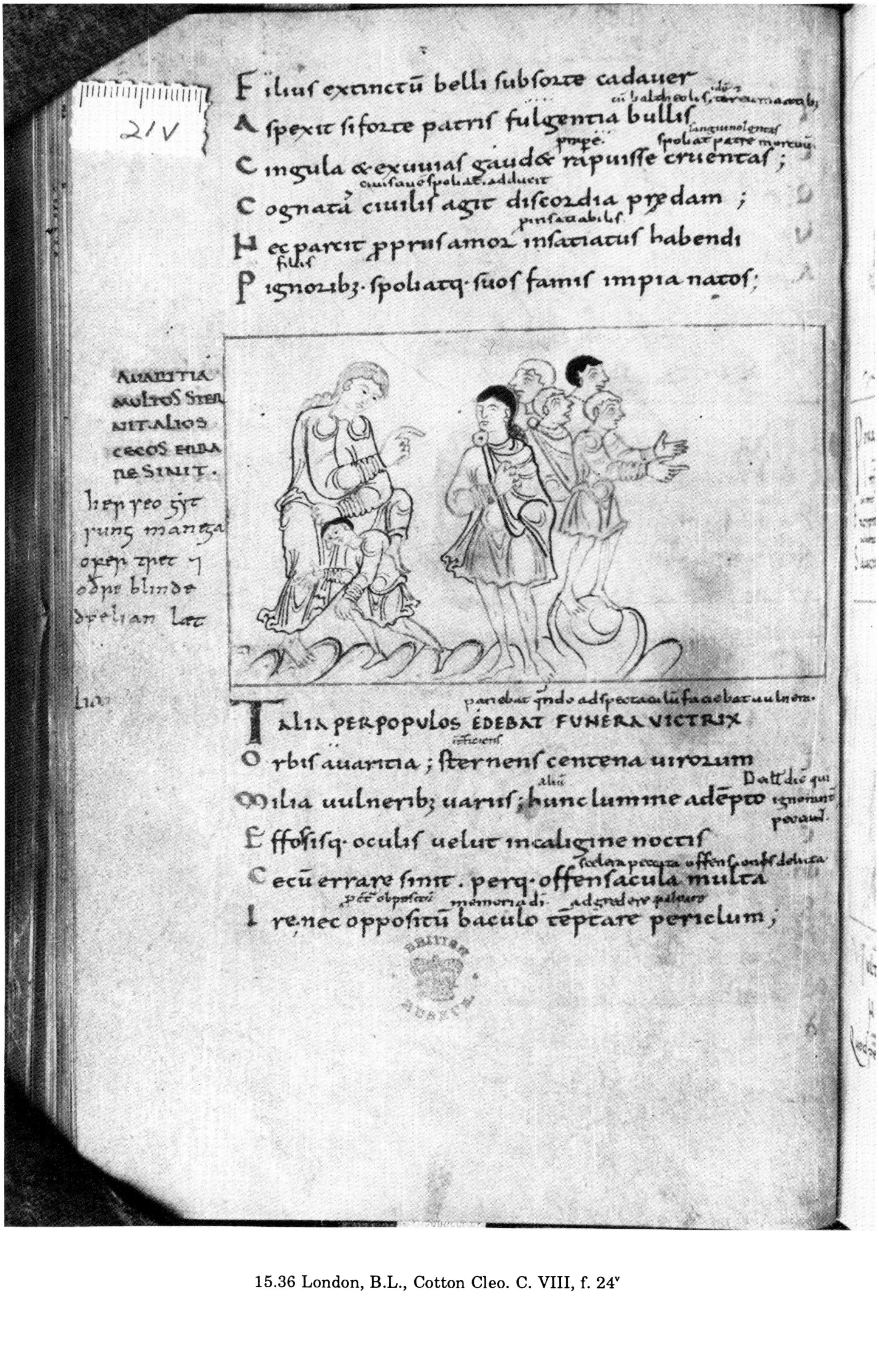
Filius extinctu belli sub sorte cadaver
Aspexit si forte patris fulgentia bullis
Cingula & exuuias gaudet rapuisse cruentas;
Cognata ciuilis agit discordia predam;
Nec parcit p pri s amor insatiatus habendi
Pignoribz. spoliatq. suos famis impia natos;

Auaritia multos sternit. alios cecos fieri ne sinit.

Talia per populos edebat funera victrix
Orbis auaritia; sternens centena uirorum
Milia uulneribz uariis; hunc lumine adepto
Effossisq. oculis uelut in caligine noctis
Cecu errare sinit. perq. offensacula multa
Ire, nec oppositu baculo temptare periclum;

15.36 London, B.L., Cotton Cleo. C. VIII, f. 24v

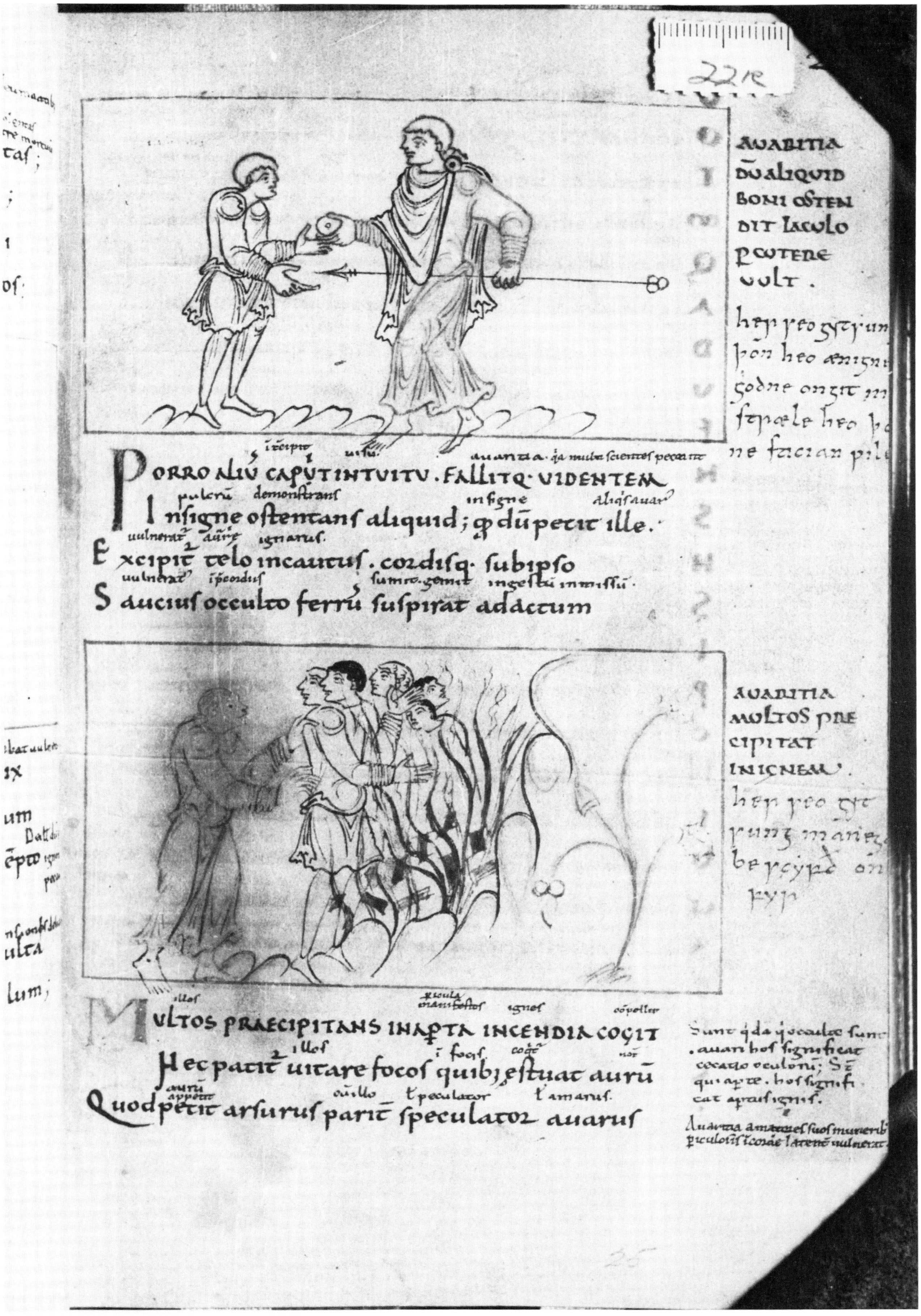

15.37 London, B.L., Cotton Cleo. C. VIII, f. 25r

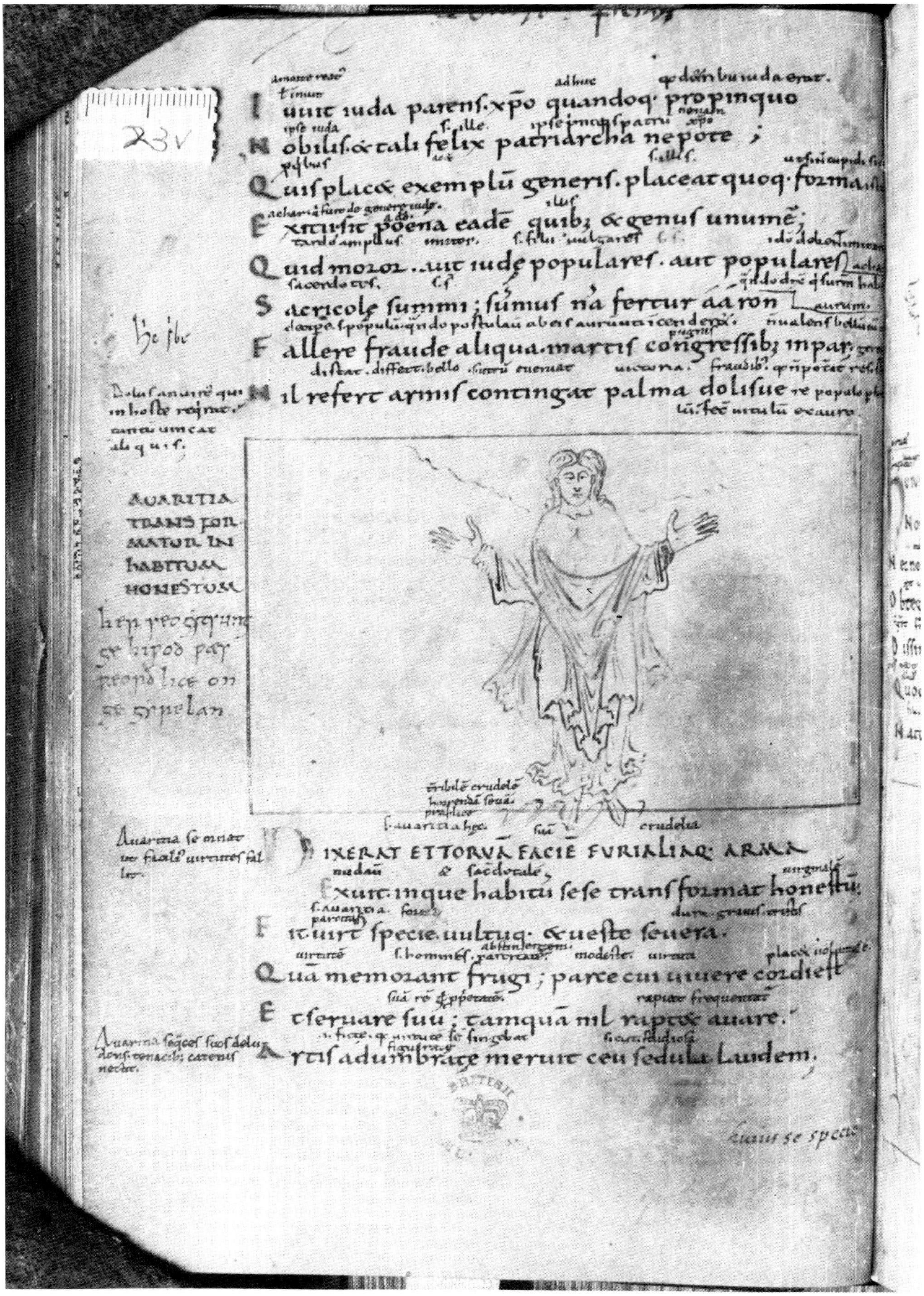

15.38 London, B.L., Cotton Cleo. C. VIII, f. 26v

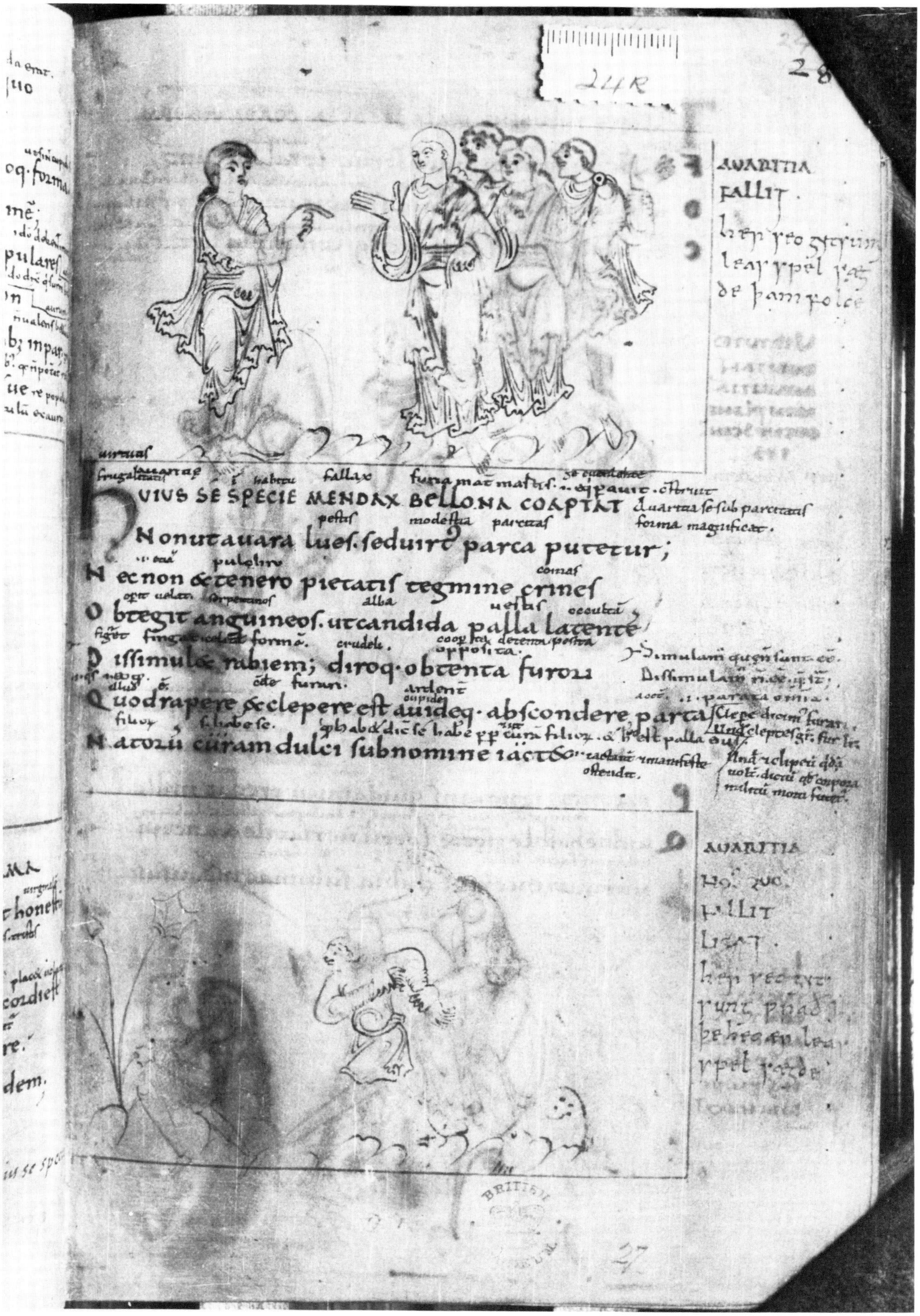
AVARITIA
FALLIT

HUIUS SE SPECIE MENDAX BELLONA COAPTAT
Non ut auara lues, sed uirt parca putetur;
Nec non et tenero pietatis tegmine crines
Obtegit anguineos, ut candida palla latente
Dissimulet rabiem; diroque obtenta furori
Quod rapere et clepere est auideque abscondere parta
Natorum curam dulci sub nomine iactet

15.39 London, B.L., Cotton Cleo. C. VIII, f. 27r

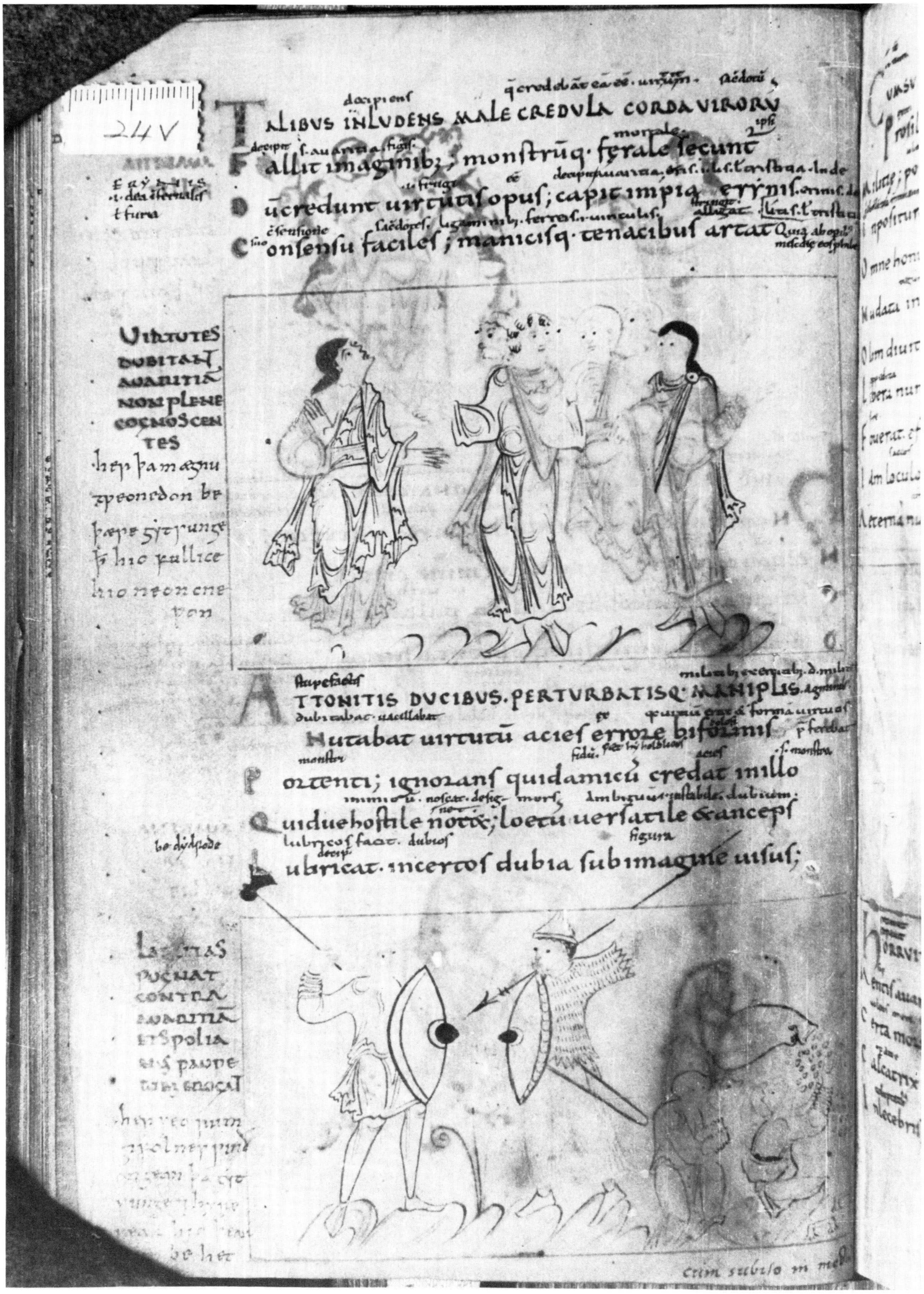
Talibus inludens male credula corda viroru
Fallit imaginib; monstruq· ferale secunt
Ducredunt uirtutis opus; capit impia erynis
Consensu faciles; manicisq· tenacibus artat

Uirtutes dubitant avaritia non plene cognoscentes

Attonitis ducibus· perturbatisq· maniplis
Nutabat uirtutu acies errore biformis
Portenti; ignorans quid amicu credat in illo
Quidue hostile notet; loetu uersatile et anceps
Lubricat· incertos dubia sub imagine uisus;

Largitas pugnat contra avaritia et spolia eius pauperibus erogat

15.40 London, B.L., Cotton Cleo. C. VIII, f. 27v

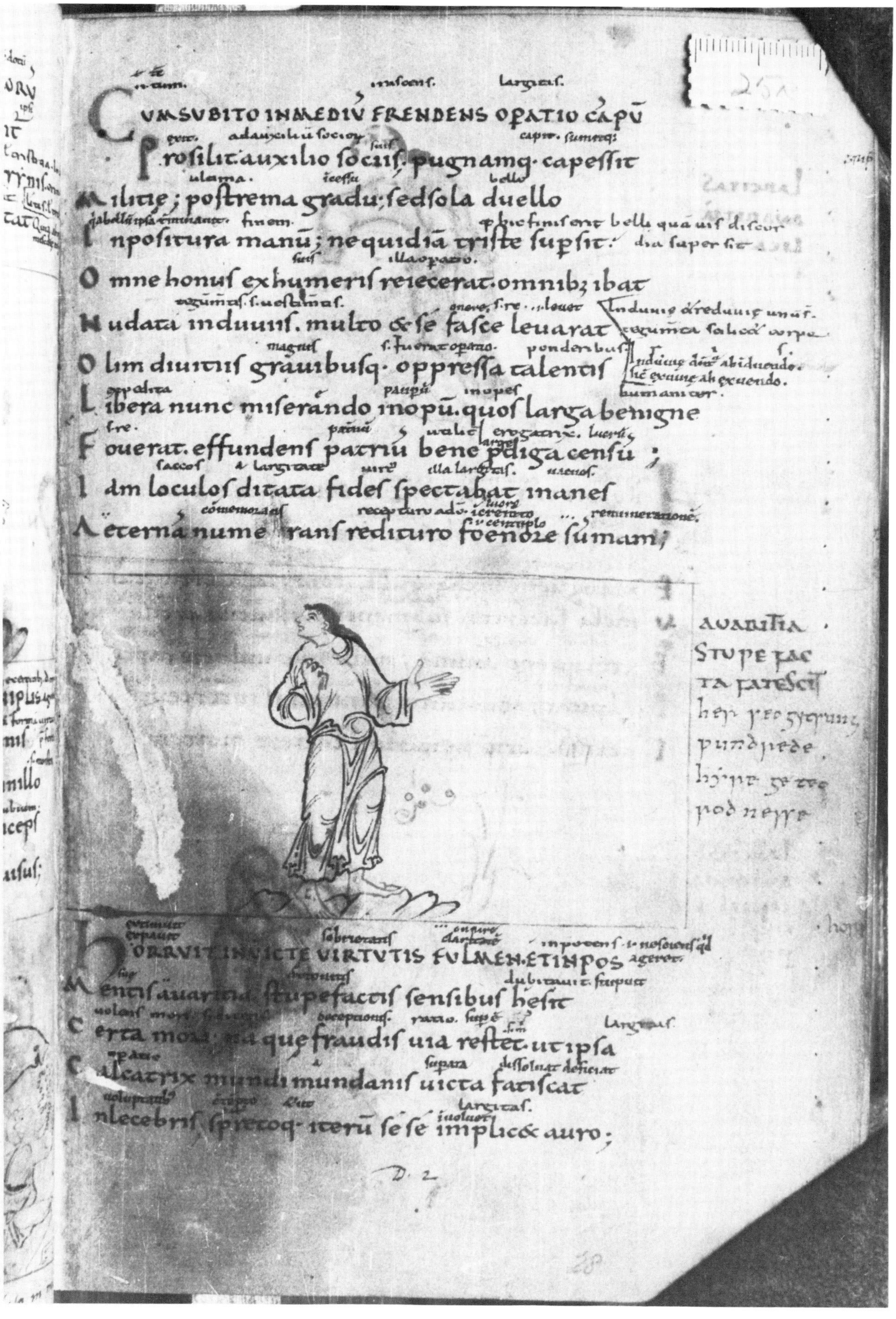

15.41 London, B.L., Cotton Cleo. C. VIII, f. 28r

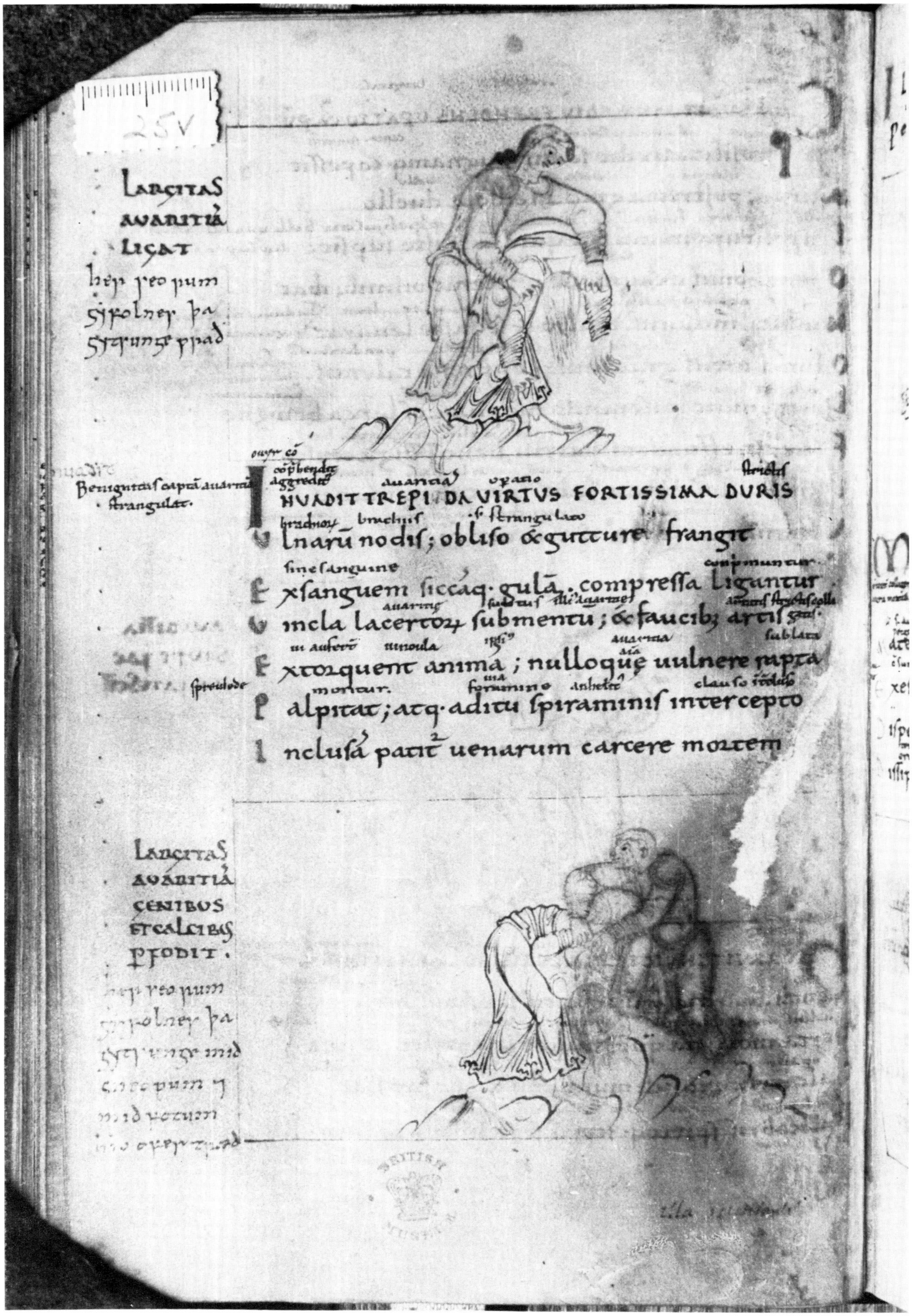

LARGITAS AVARITIĀ LIGAT

INUADIT TREPIDA VIRTUS FORTISSIMA DURIS
Ulnarū nodis; obliso & gutture frangit
Exsanguem siccaq· gulā· compressa ligantur
Vincla lacertorū sub mentu; & faucib; artis
Extorquent anima; nulloque uulnere rupta
Palpitat; atq· aditu spiraminis intercepto
Inclusa patit̄ uenarum carcere mortem

LARGITAS AVARITIĀ GENIBUS ET CALCIBUS PRODIT.

15.42 London, B.L., Cotton Cleo. C. VIII, f. 28ᵛ

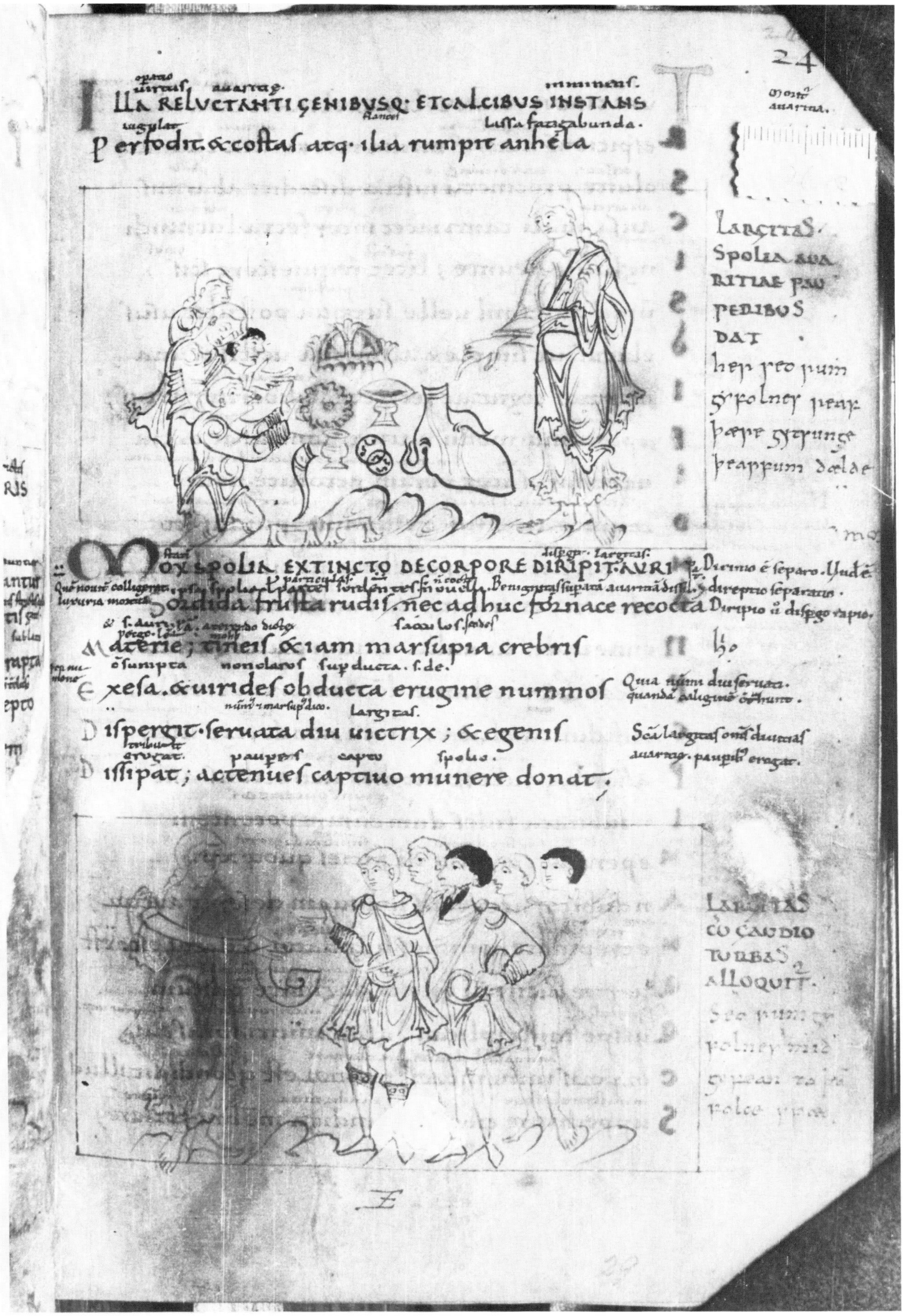

15.43 London, B.L., Cotton Cleo. C. VIII, f. 29r

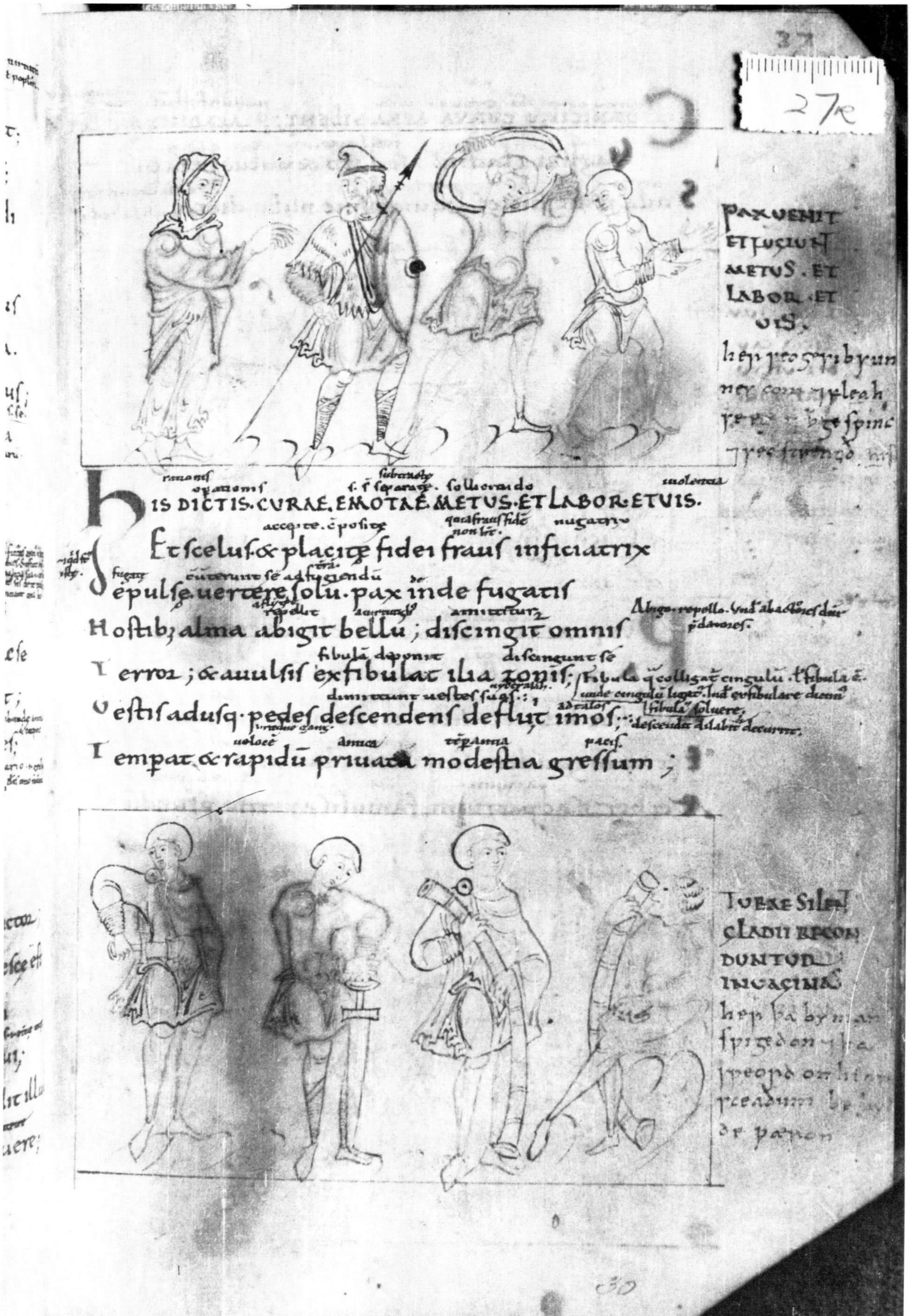

15.44 London, B.L., Cotton Cleo. C. VIII, f. 30r

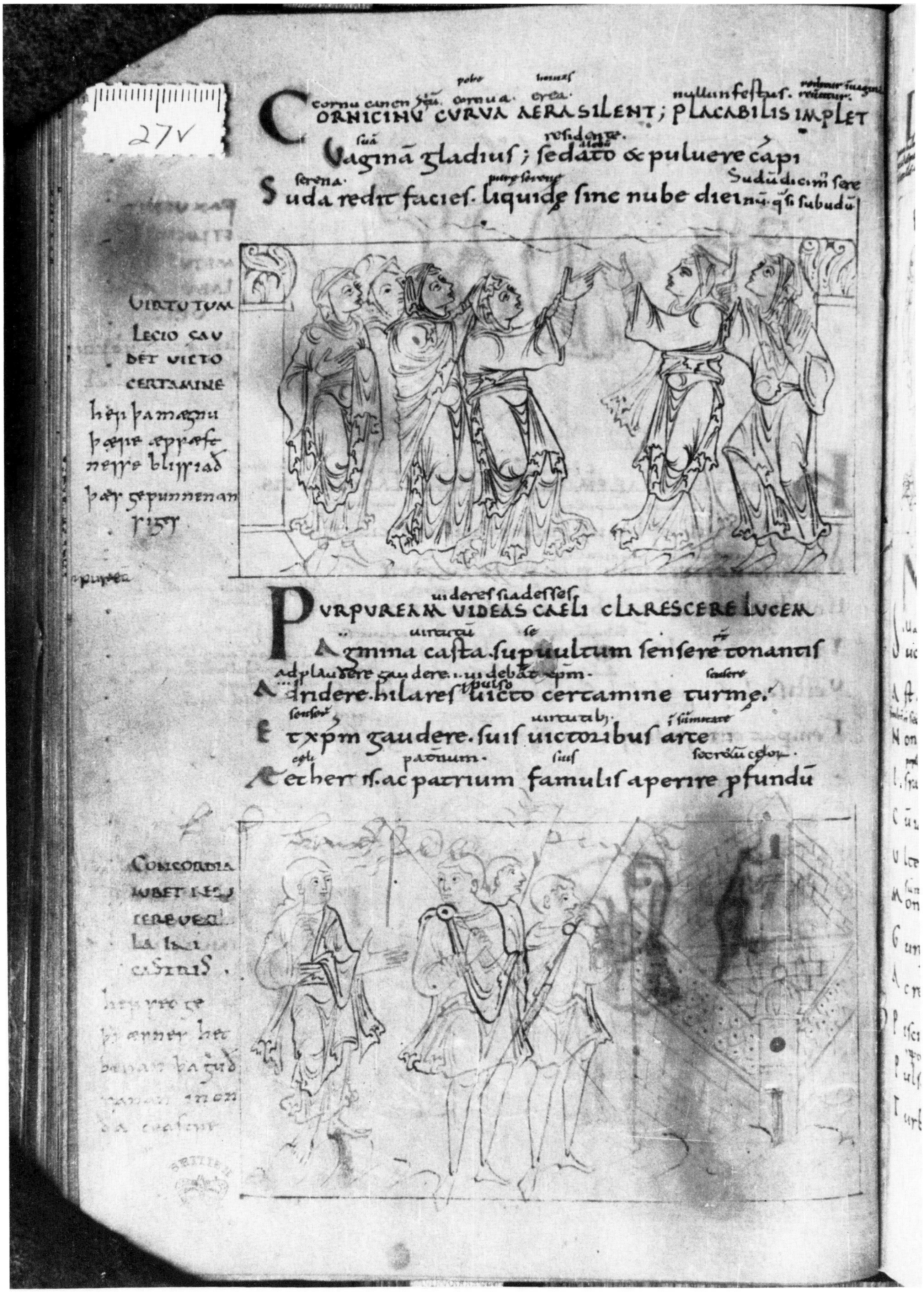

15.45 London, B.L., Cotton Cleo. C. VIII, f. 30v

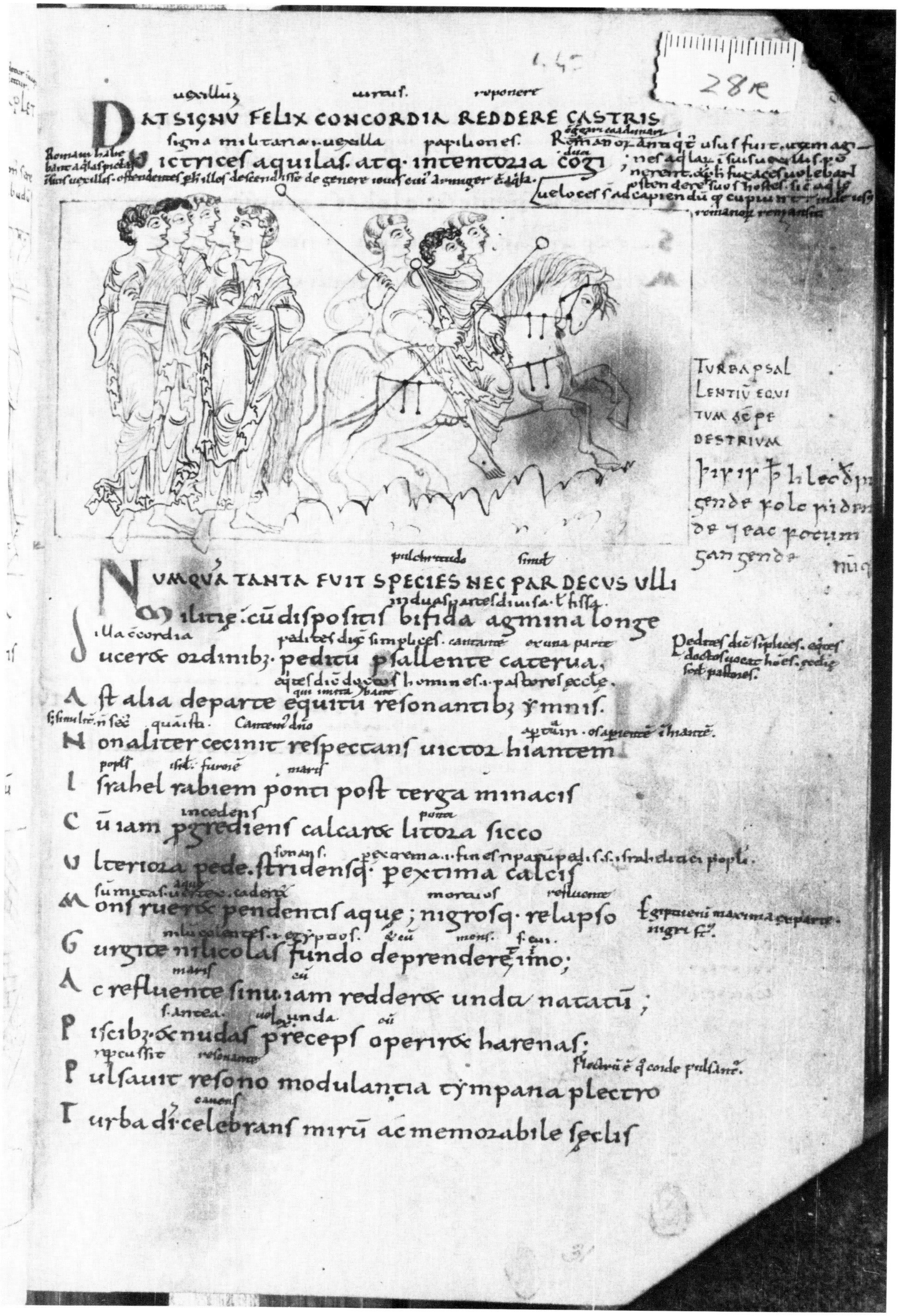

15.46 London, B.L., Cotton Cleo. C. VIII, f. 31r

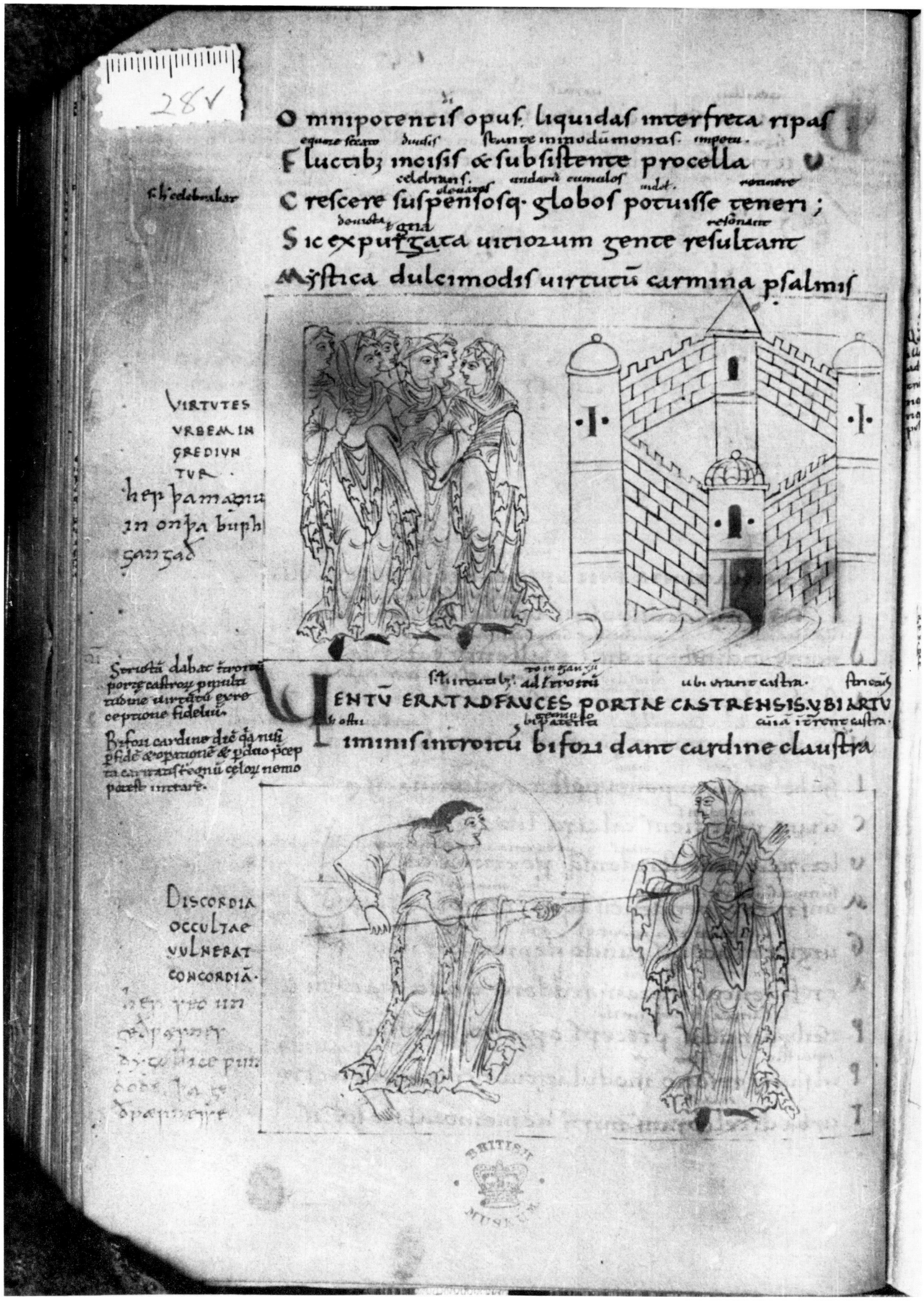

15.47 London, B.L., Cotton Cleo. C. VIII, f. 31v

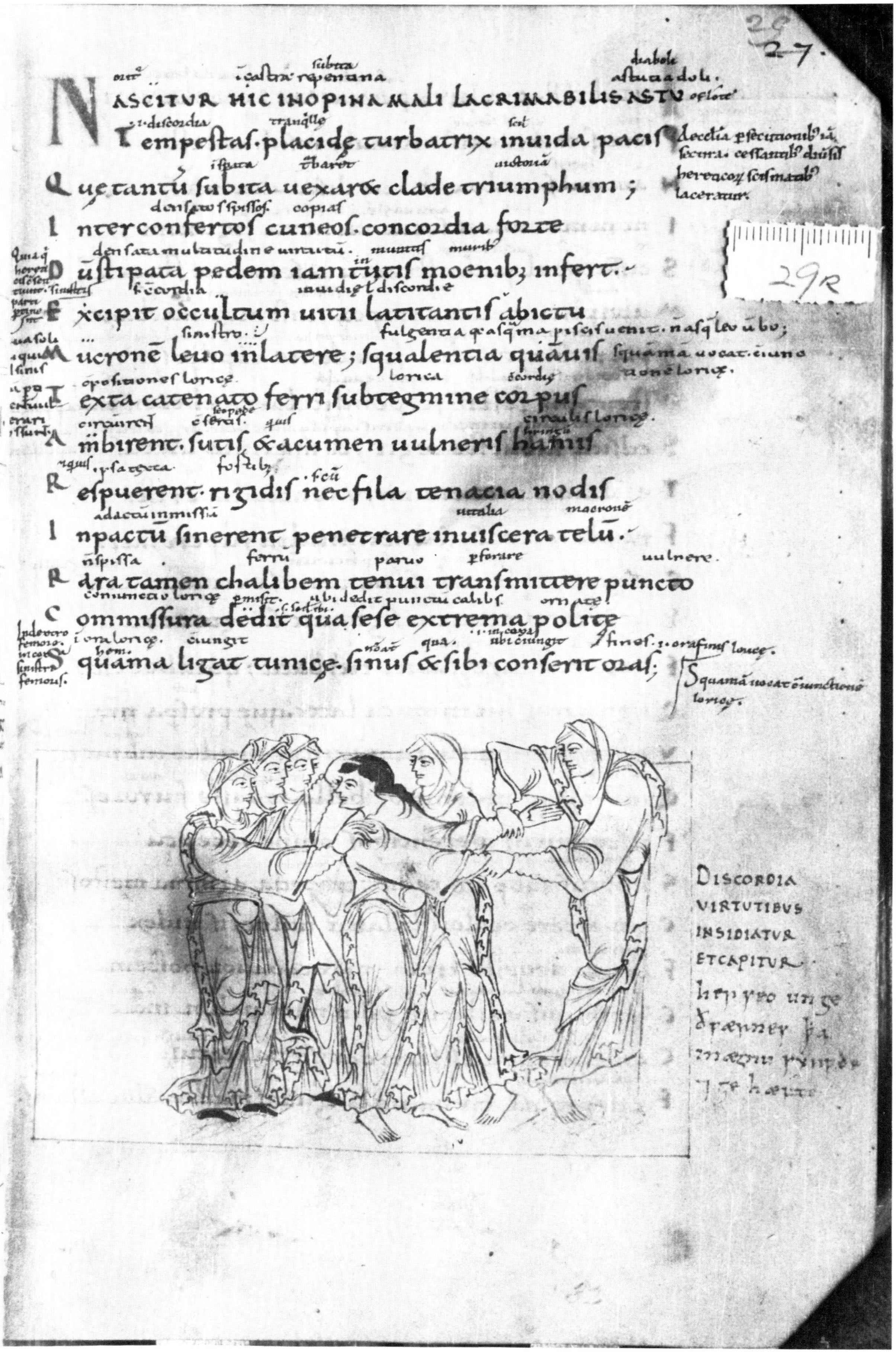

15.48 London, B.L., Cotton Cleo. C. VIII, f. 32r

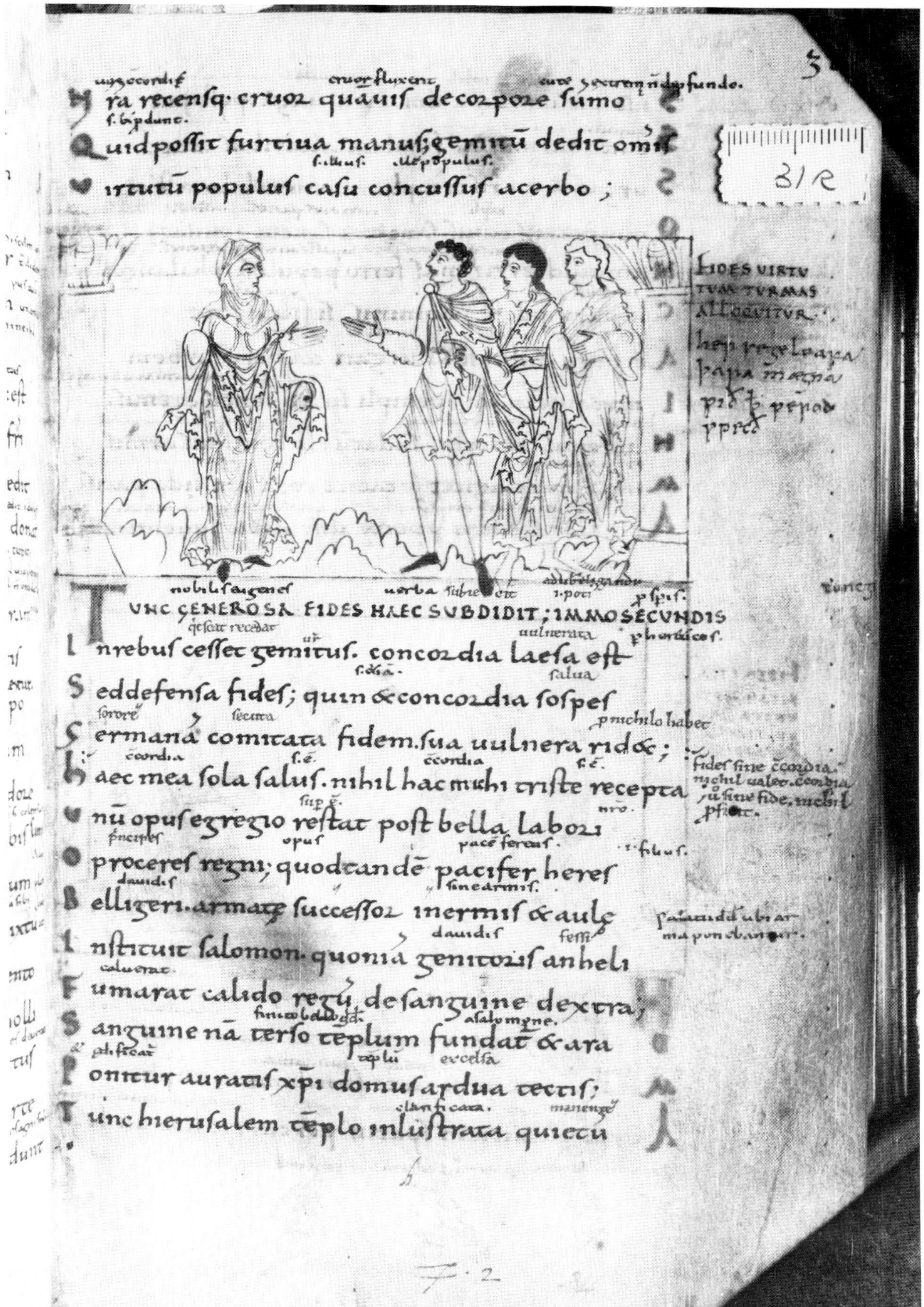

15.49 London, B.L., Cotton Cleo. C. VIII, f. 34r

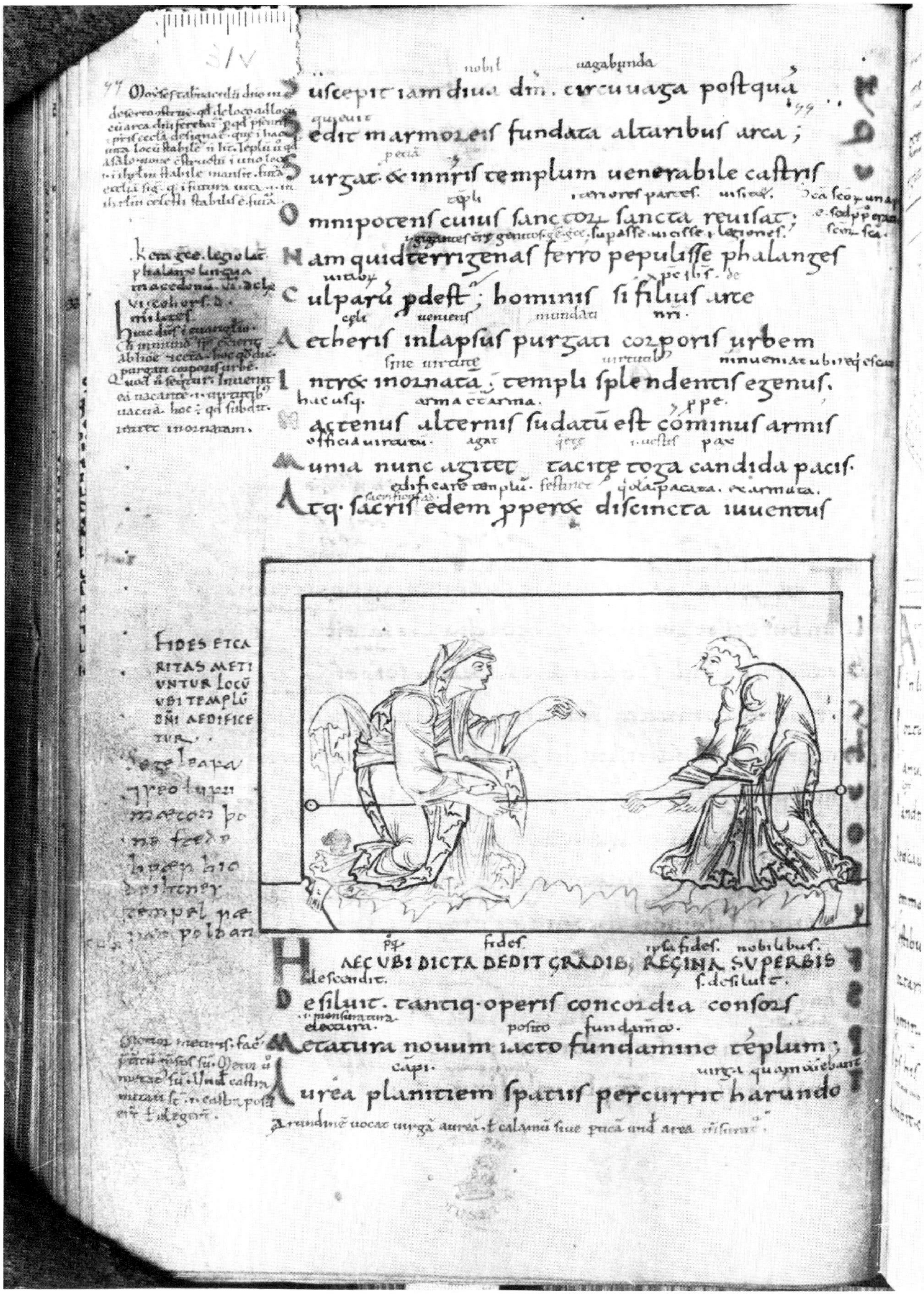

15.50 London, B.L., Cotton Cleo. C. VIII, f. 34v

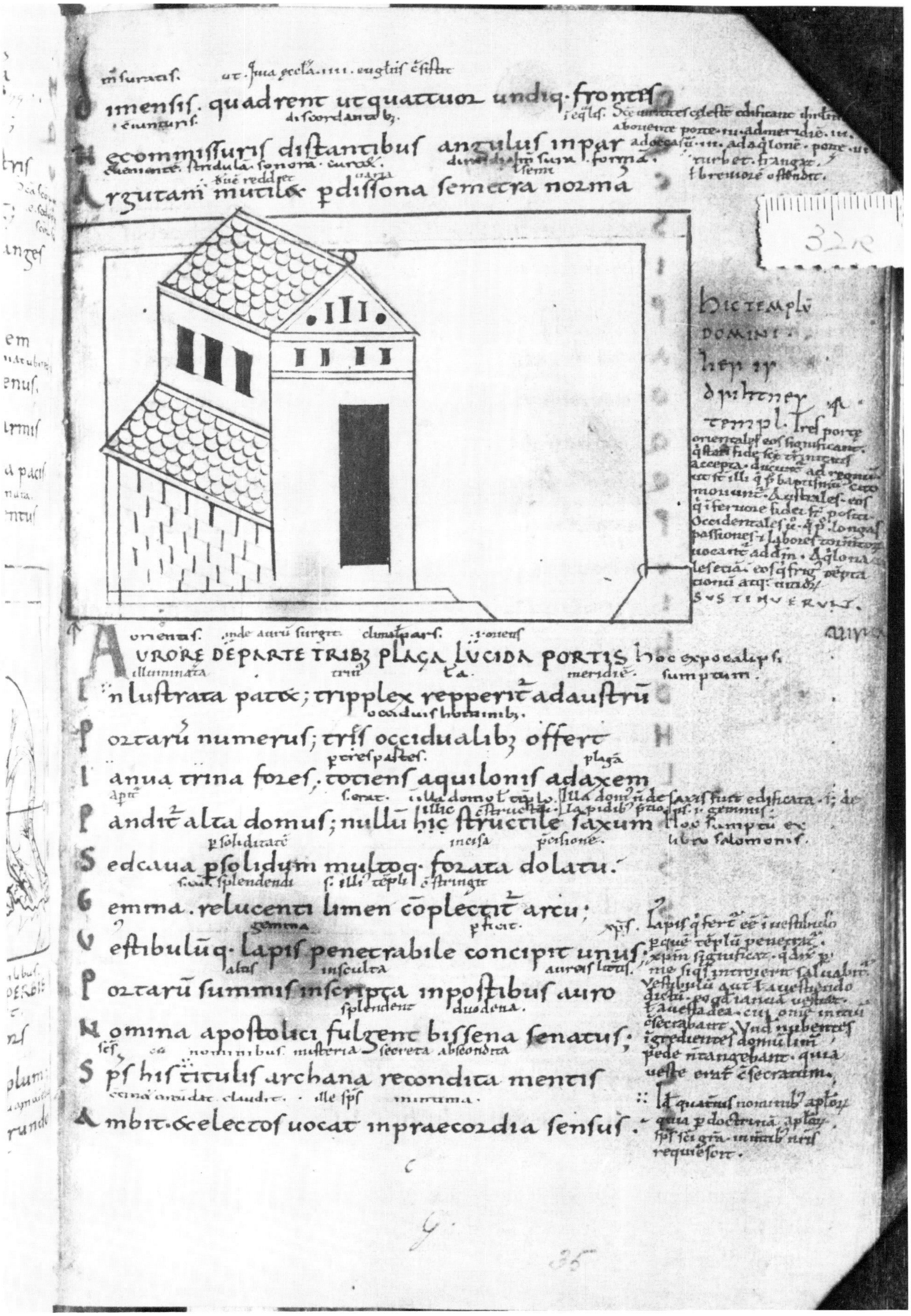
[D]imensis. quadrent ut quattuor undiq. frontis
[H]ecommissuris distantibus angulus inpar
Argutam mutila& pdissona serrectra norma

Hic templū domini

Aurore departe trib; plaga lucida portis
[I]nlustrata patet; tripplex repperit adaustrū
Portarū numerus; tris occidualib; offert
Ianua trina fores; totiens aquilonis adaxem
Pandit alta domus; nullū hic structile saxum
Sedcaua psolidum multoq. forata dolatu.
Gemma. relucenti limen coplectit arcu;
Vestibulūq. lapis penetrabile concipit unus;
Portarū summis inscripta inpostibus auro
Nomina apostolici fulgent bissena senatus;
Sps his titulis archana recondita mentis
Ambit. & electos uocat inpraecordia sensus.

15.51 London, B.L., Cotton Cleo. C. VIII, f. 35r

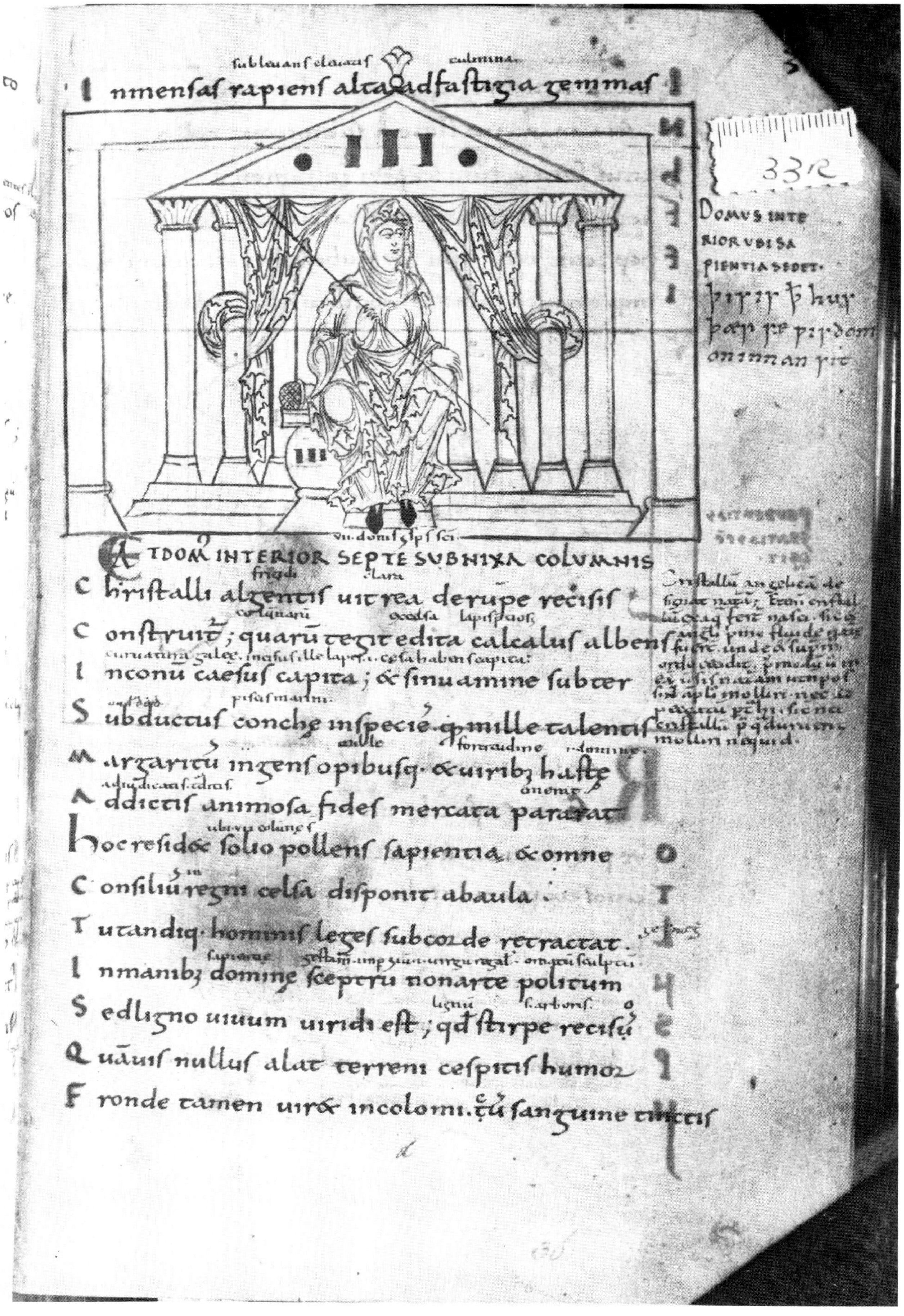
Inmensas rapiens alta ad fastigia gemmas

DOMUS INTERIOR UBI SAPIENTIA SEDET·

Et dom interior septe subnixa columnis
Christalli algentis uitrea de rupe recisis
Construit; quarū tegit edita calcalus albens
Inconū caesus capita; & sinuamine subter
Subductus conche in specie q̄ mille talentis
Margaritū ingens opibusq· & uirib; haste
Addictis animosa fides mercata pararat
Hoc residet solio pollens sapientia & omne
Consiliū regni celsa disponit ab aula·
Tutandiq· hominis leges sub corde retractat·
In manib; domine sceptrū non arte politum
Sed ligno uiuum uiridi est; qd stirpe recisū
Quāuis nullus alat terreni cespitis humor
Fronde tamen uir& incolomi. tū sanguine tinctis

15.52 London, B.L., Cotton Cleo. C. VIII, f. 36r

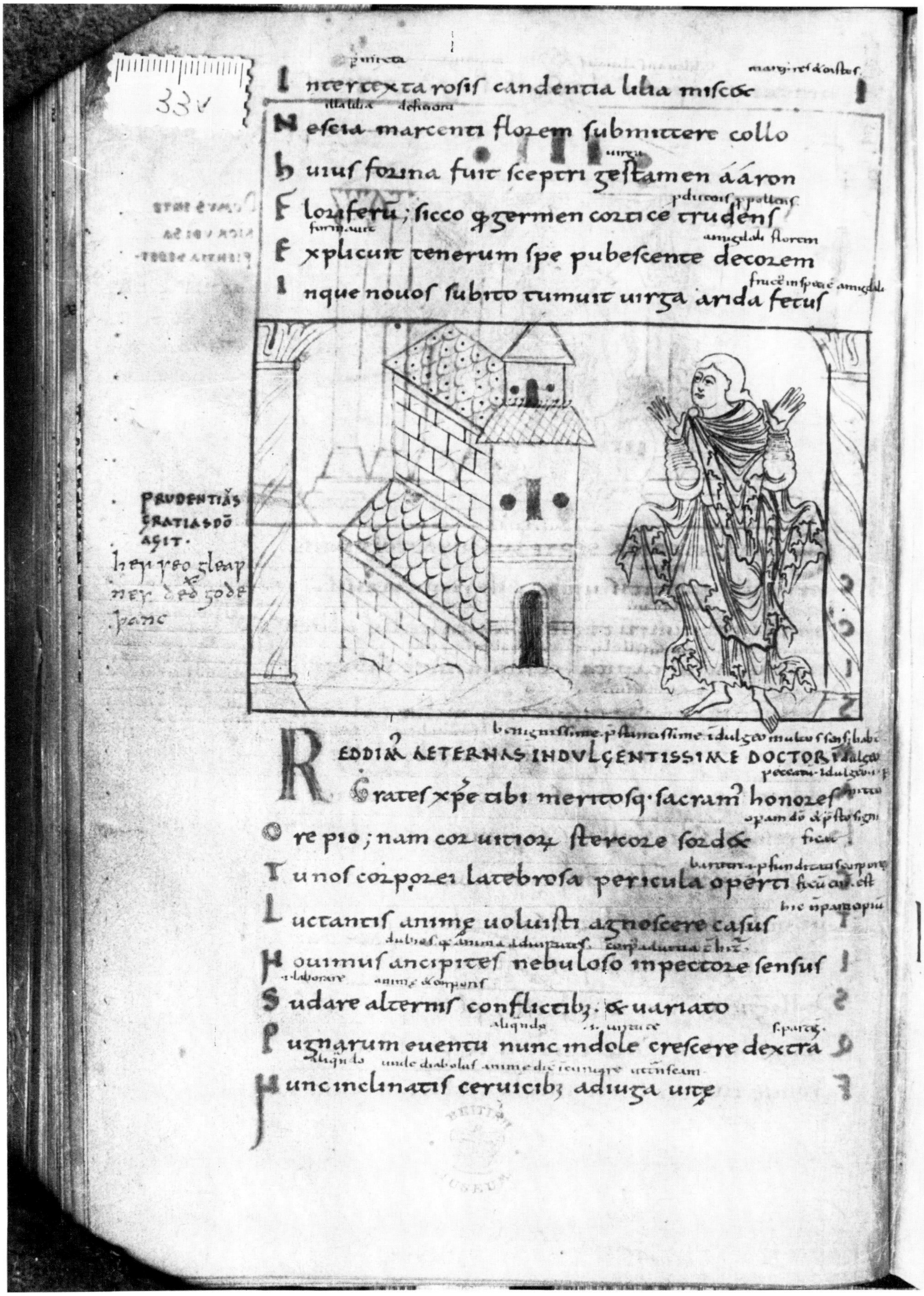
Inter texta rosis candentia lilia miscet
Nescia marcenti florem submittere collo
Huius forma fuit sceptri gestamen aaron
Floriferu; sicco quod germen cortice trudens
Explicuit tenerum spe pubescente decorem
Inque nouos subito tumuit uirga arida fetus

PRUDENTIA GRATIAS DO AGIT.

REDDIM(US) AETERNAS INDULGENTISSIME DOCTOR
Grates xpe tibi meritosq(ue) sacram(us) honores
Ore pio; nam cor uitior(um) stercore sordet
Tu nos corporei latebrosa pericula operti
Luctantis anime uoluisti agnoscere casus
Nouimus ancipites nebuloso in pectore sensus
Sudare alternis conflictib(us) et uariato
Pugnarum euentu nunc indole crescere dextra
Nunc inclinatis ceruicib(us) ad iuga uite

15.53 London, B.L., Cotton Cleo. C. VIII, f. 36v

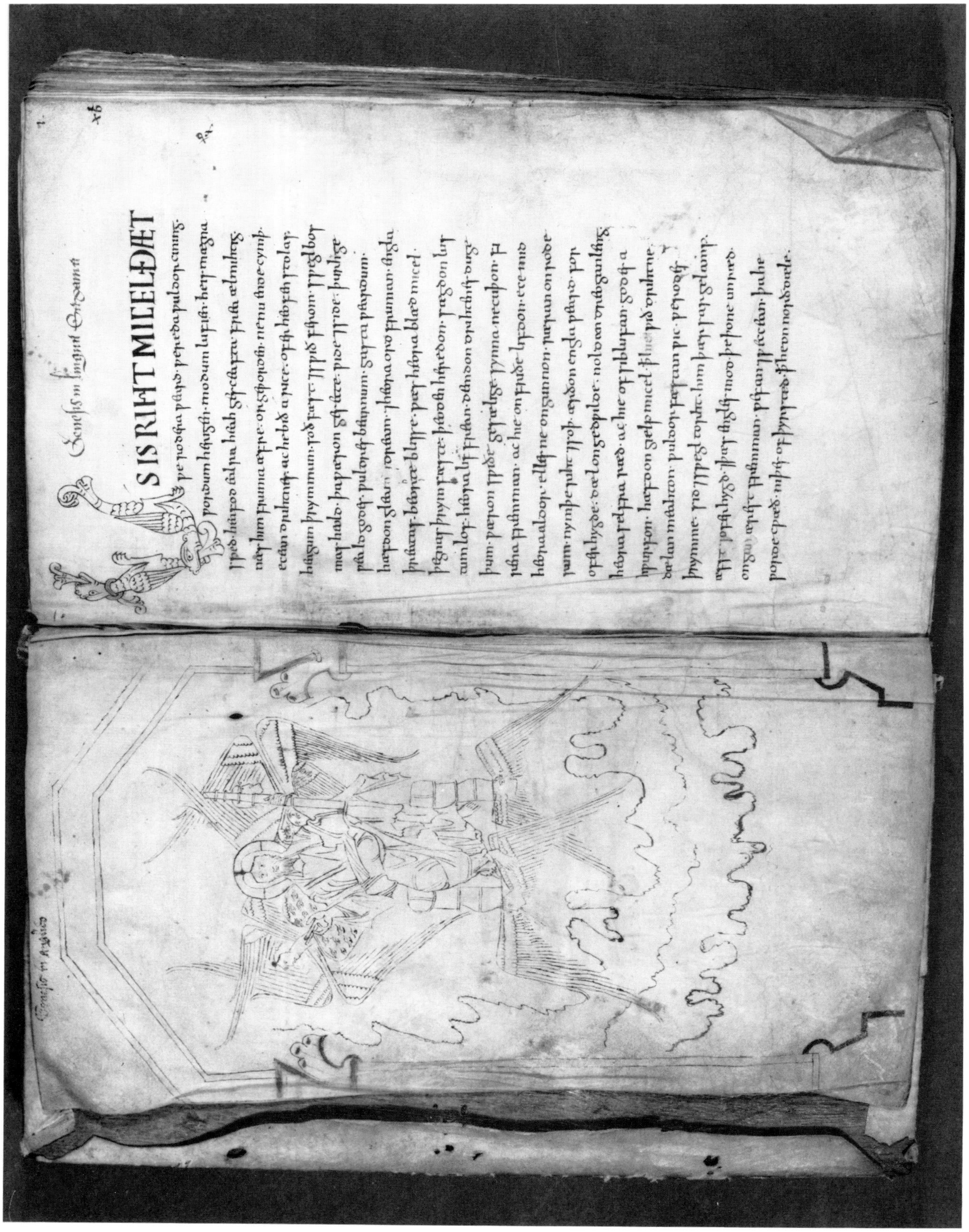

16.1 Oxford, Bodl. Lib., Junius 11, Frontispiece and p. 1

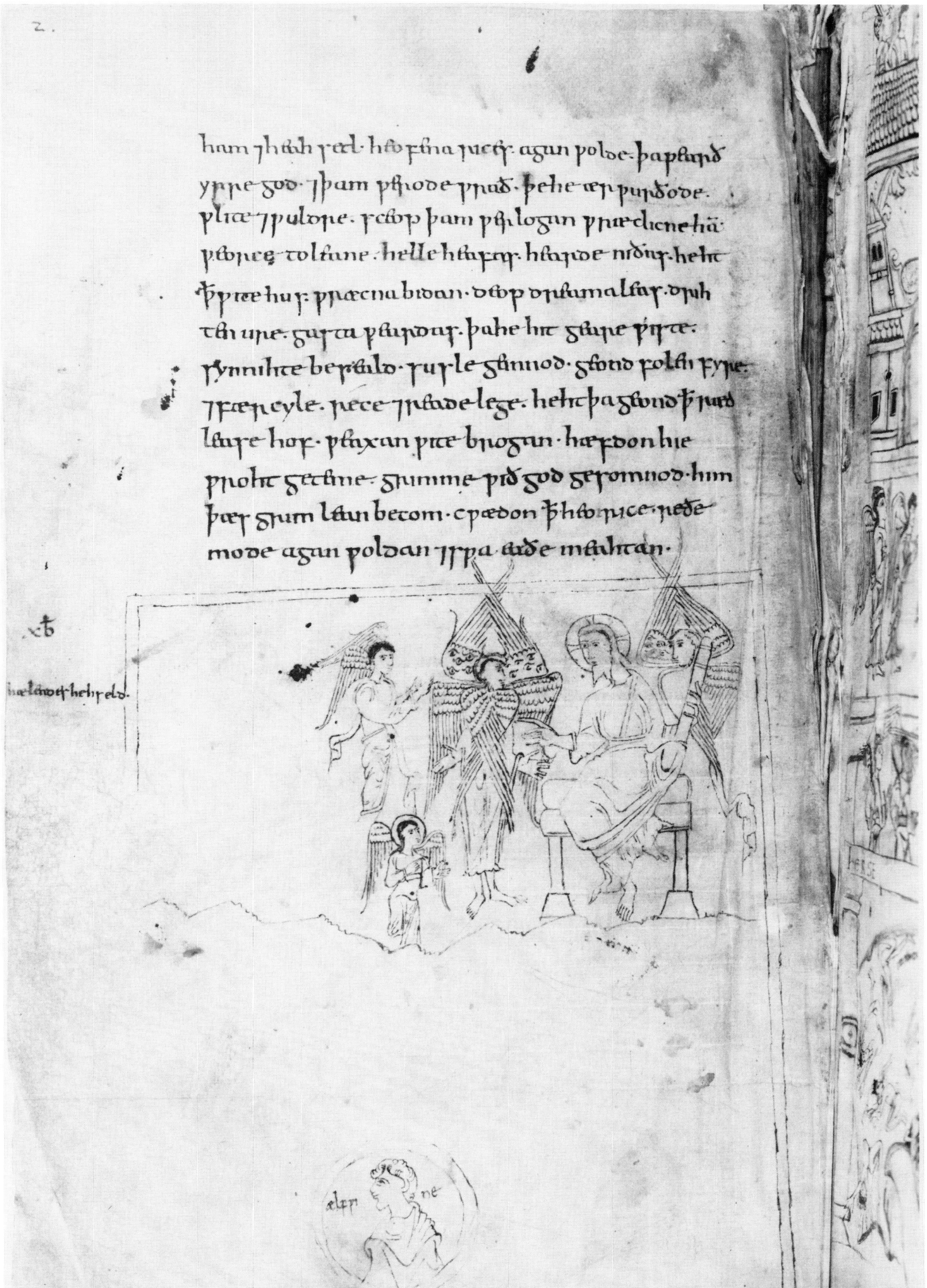

16.2 Oxford, Bodl. Lib., Junius 11, p. 2

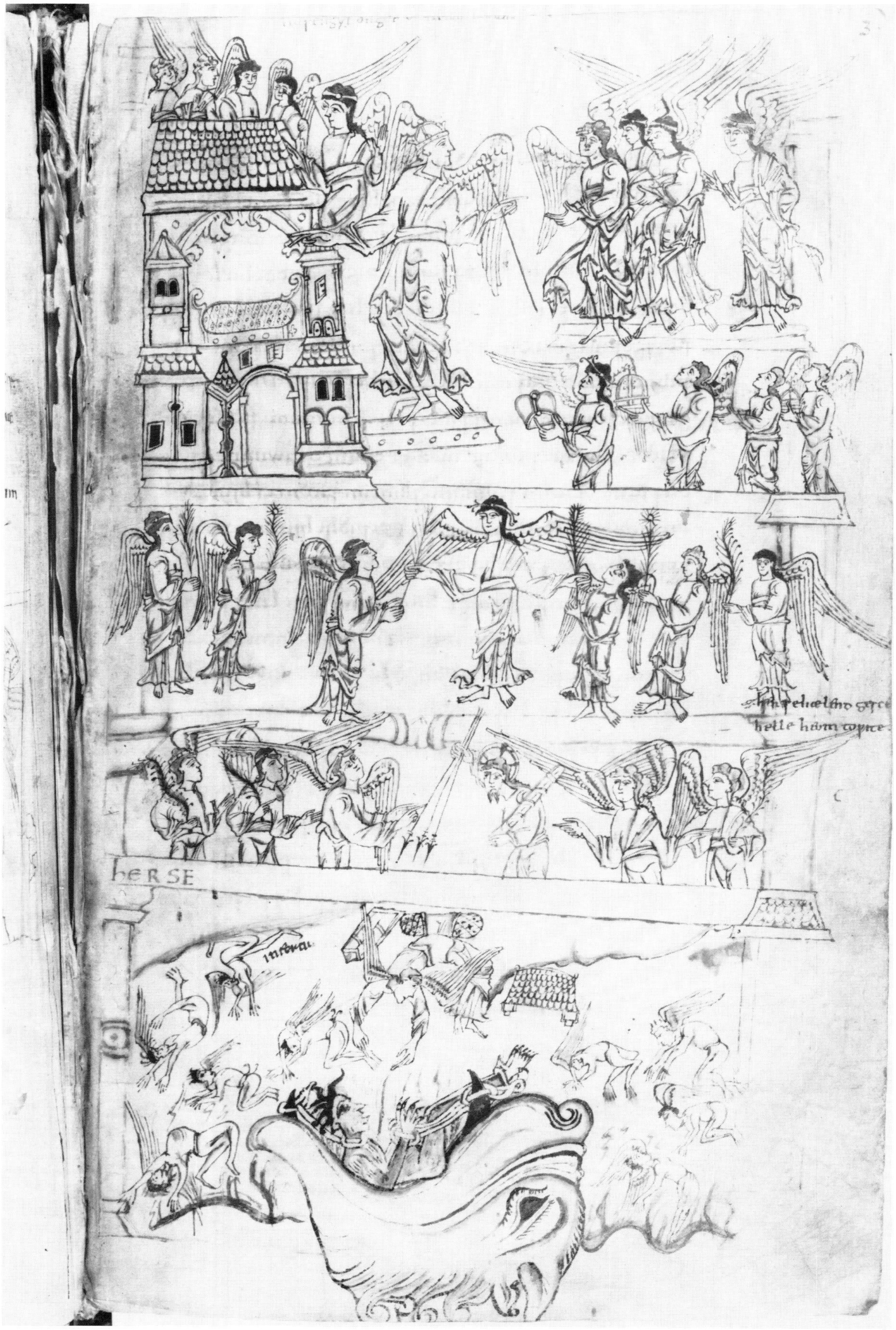

16.3 Oxford, Bodl. Lib., Junius 11, p. 3

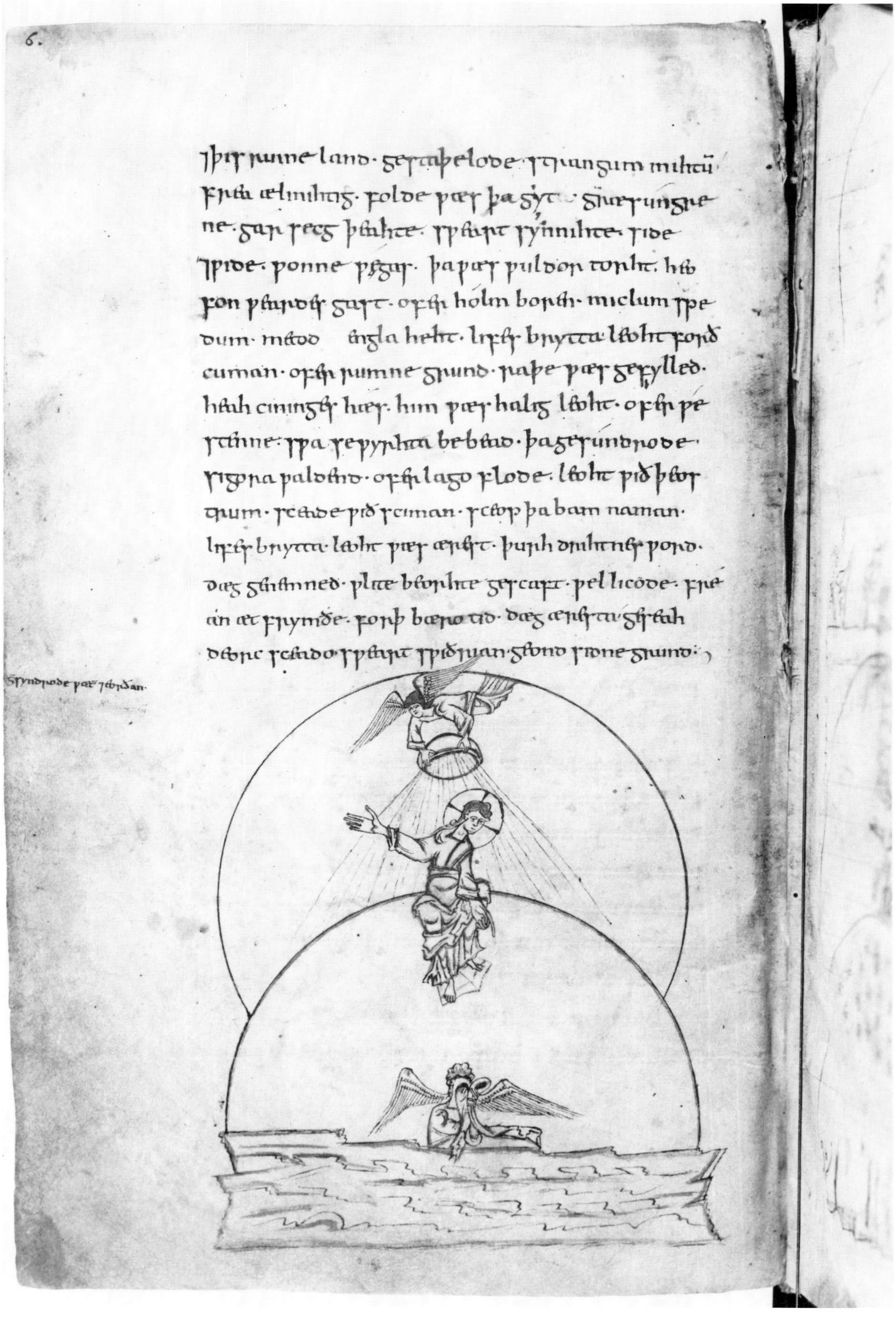

16.4 Oxford, Bodl. Lib., Junius 11, p. 6

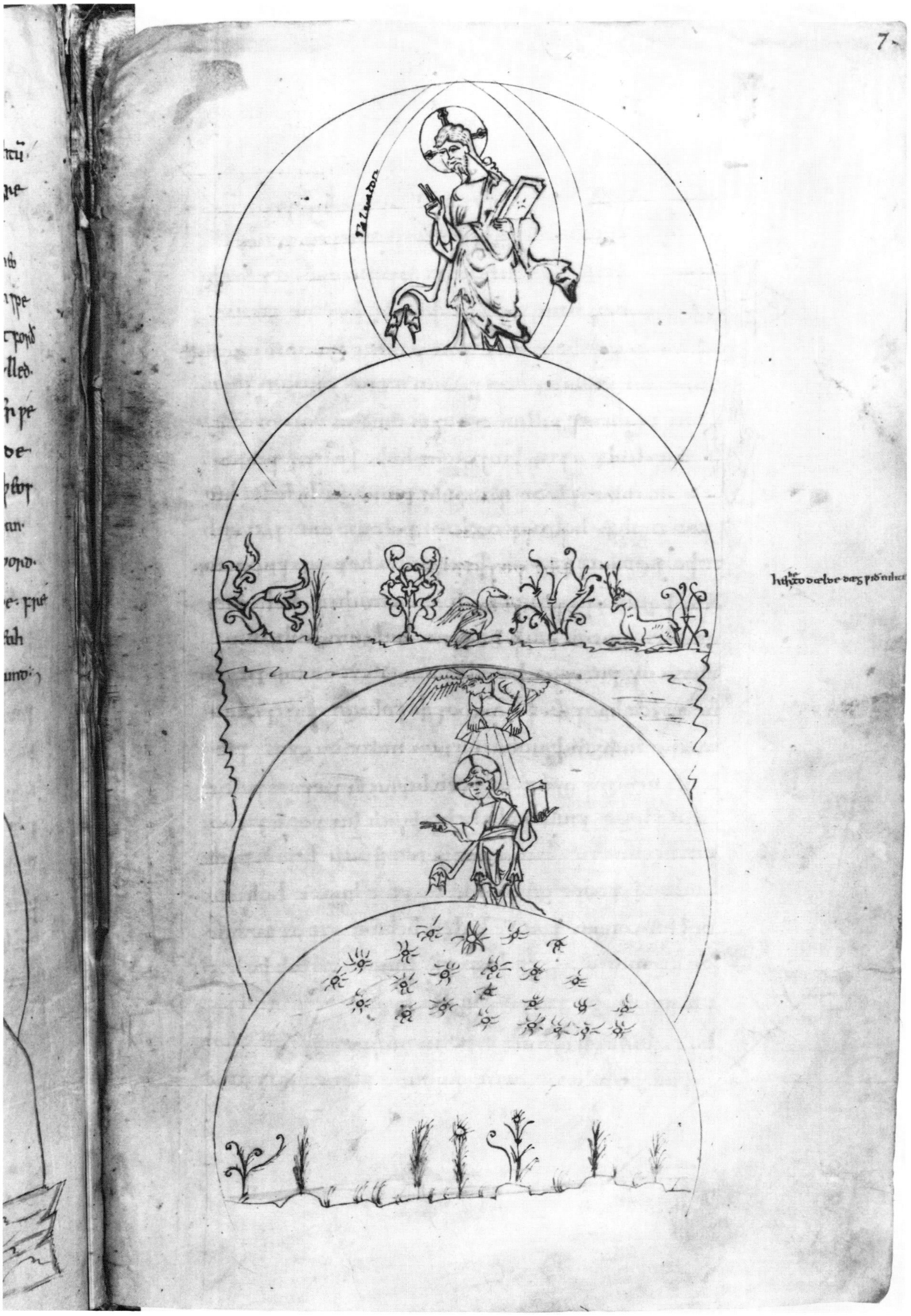

16.5 Oxford, Bodl. Lib., Junius 11, p. 7

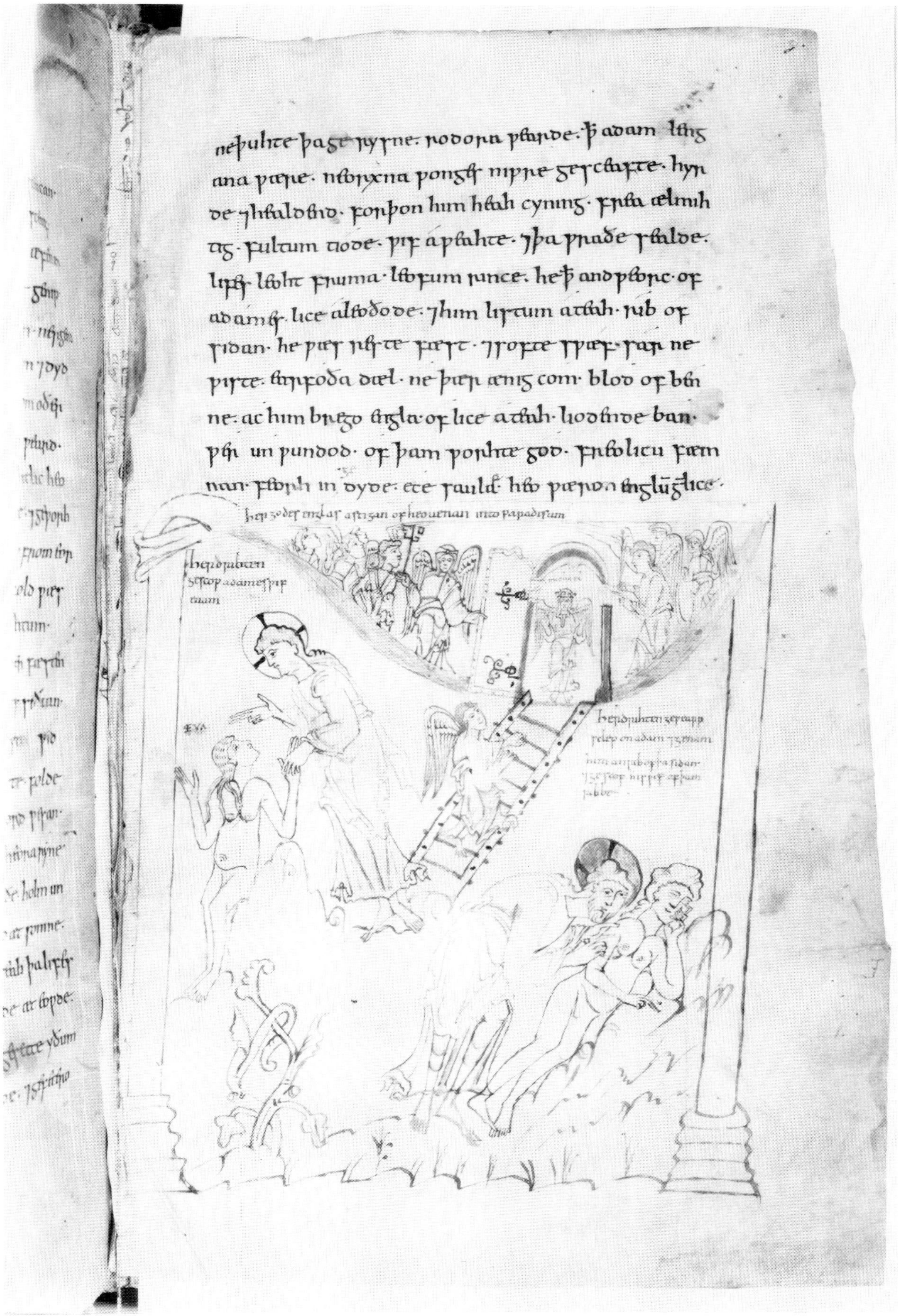

16.6 Oxford, Bodl. Lib., Junius 11, p. 9

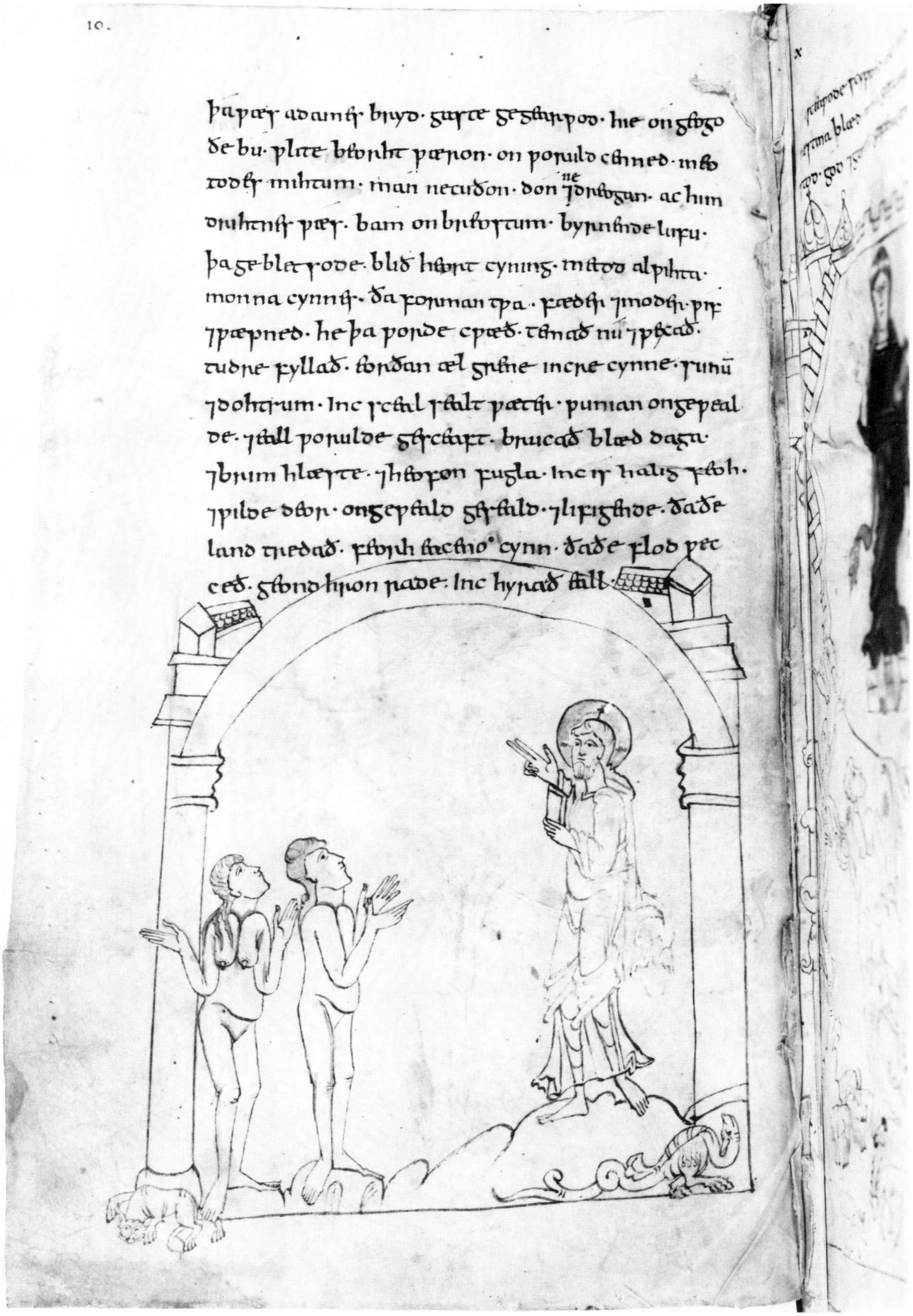

10.

þa wæs adames bryd. gaste gegearwod. hie on geogo
ðe bu. wlite beorhte wæron. on woruld cenned. meo
todes mihtum. man necuðon. don ne dreogan. ac him
drihtnes wæs. bam on breostum. byrnende lufu.
þa gebletsode. bliðheort cyning. metod alwihta.
monna cynnes. ða forman twa. fæder 7 moder. wif
7 wæpned. he þa worde cwæð. temað nu 7 weaxað.
tudre fyllað. eorðan ælgrene. incre cynne. sunu
7 dohtrum. inc sceal sealt wæter. wunian ongeweal
de. 7 eall worulde gesceaft. brucað blæd daga.
7 brimes hlæste. 7 heofon fugla. inc is halig feoh.
7 wilde deor. ongeweald geseald. 7 lifigende. ða ðe
land tredað. feorh berendra cynn. ða ðe flod wec
ceð. geond hron rade. inc hyrað eall.

16.7 Oxford, Bodl. Lib., Junius 11, p. 10

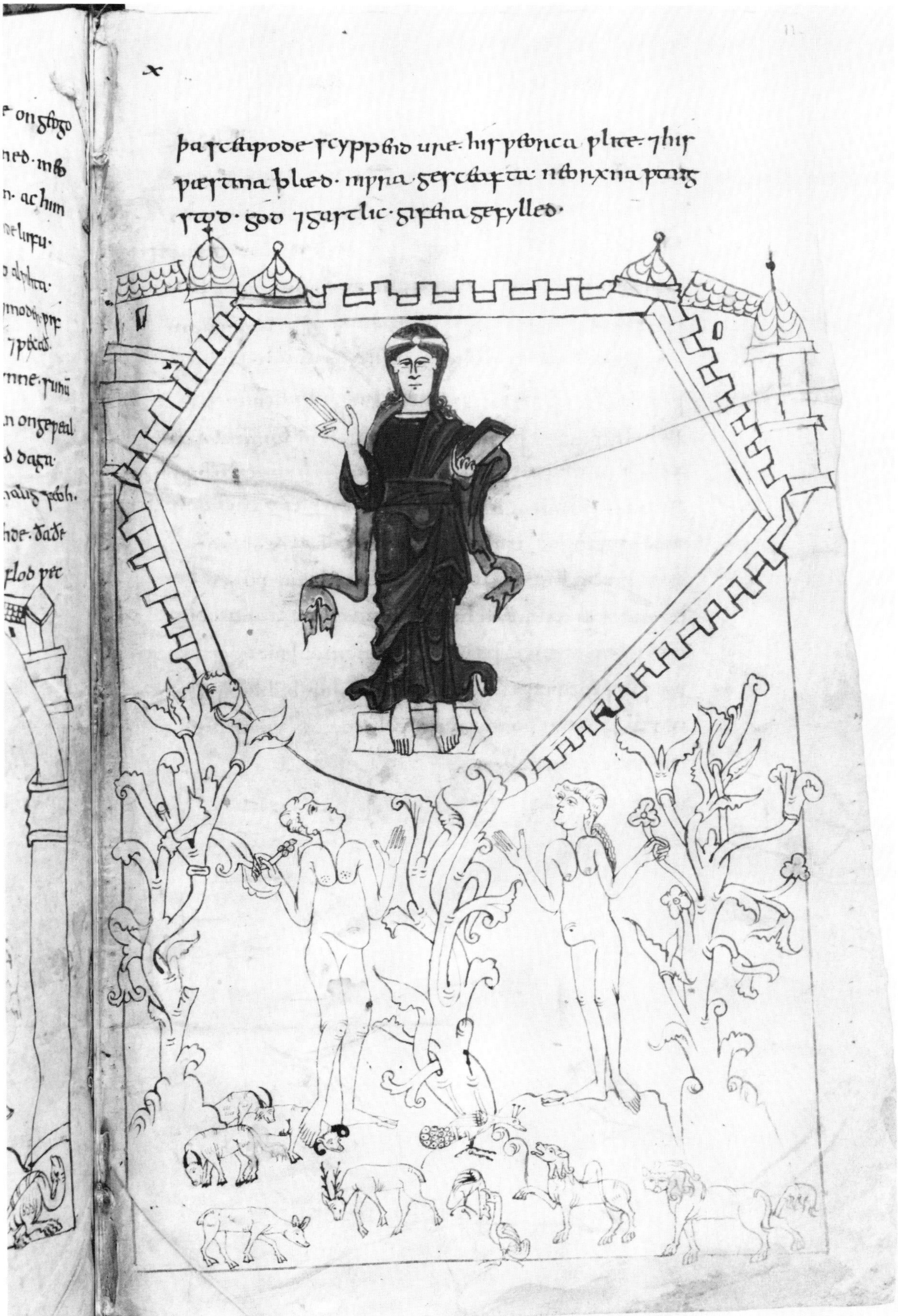

16.8 Oxford, Bodl. Lib., Junius 11, p. 11

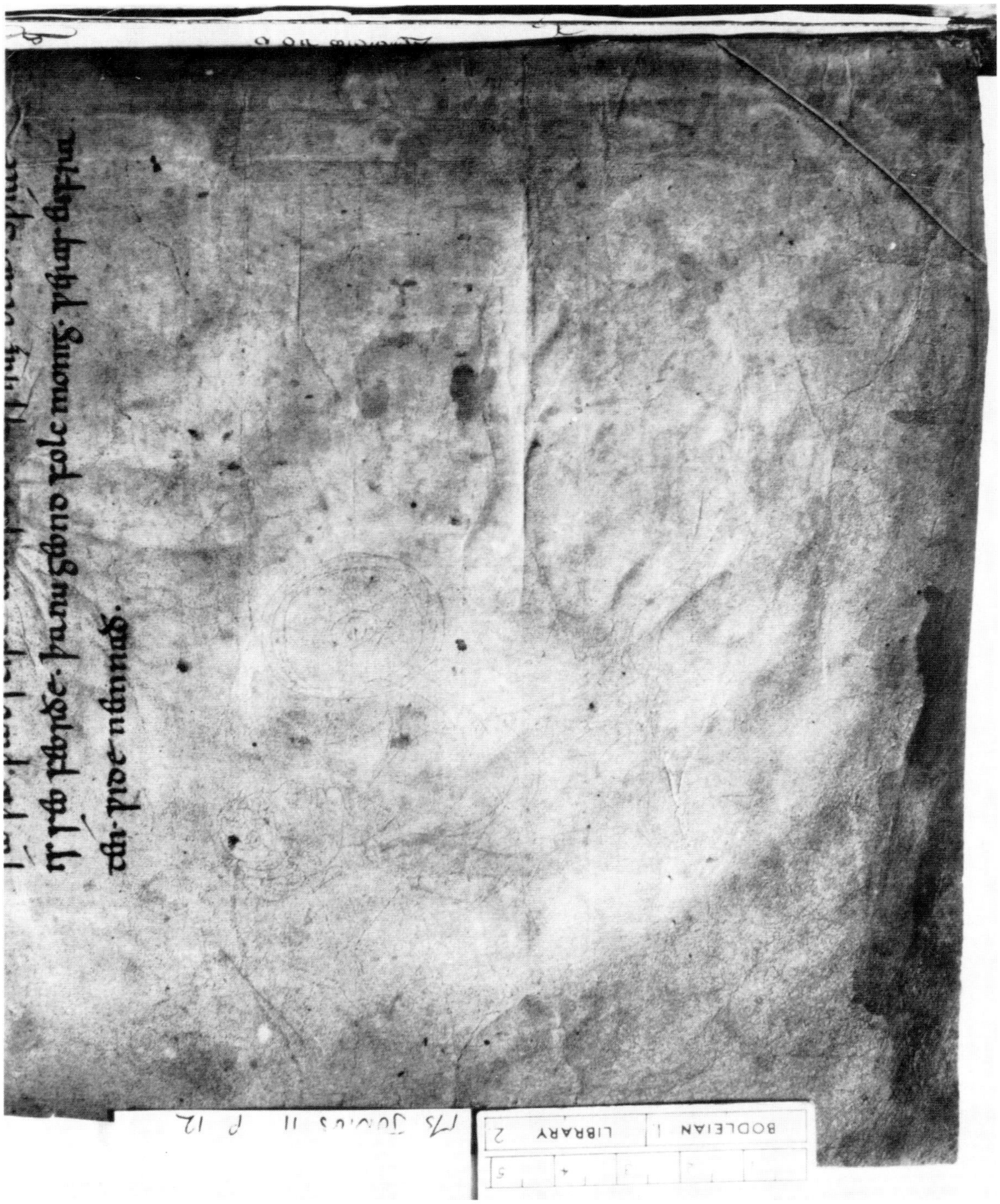

16.9 Oxford, Bodl. Lib., Junius 11, p. 12

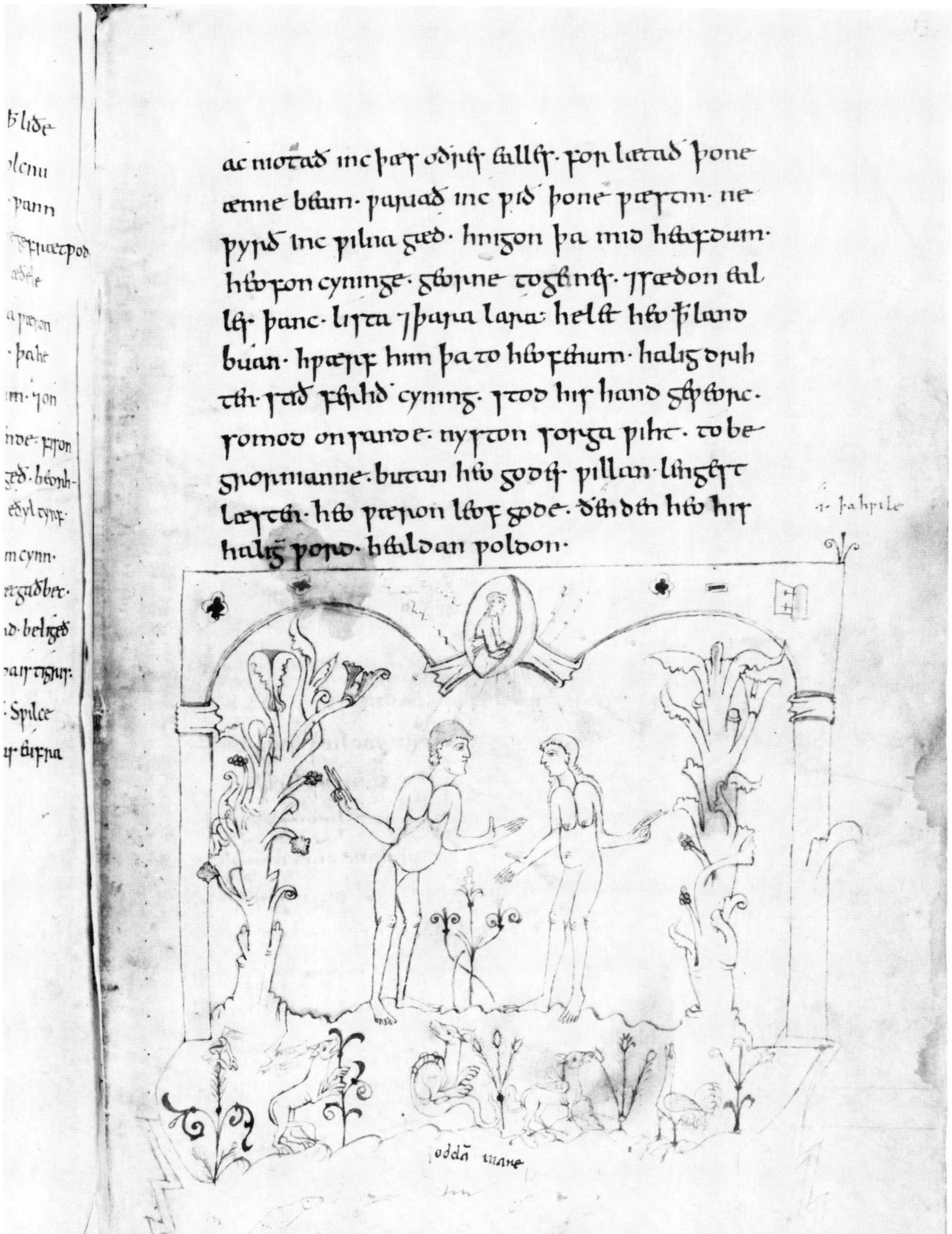

ac motað inc þæs oðres ealles. forlætað þone
ænne beam. warniað inc wið þone wæstm. ne
wyrð inc wilna gæd. hnigon þa mid heafdum.
heofoncyninge. georne togenes. and sædon eal
les þanc. lifes and þara lara. he let heo þæt land
buan. hwearf him þa to heofenum. halig drih
ten. stiðferhð cyning. stod his handgesceaft.
somod on sande. nyston sorga wiht. to be
grornianne. butan heo godes willan lengest
læston. heo wæron leof gode. ðenden heo his
halig word. healdan woldon.

16.10 Oxford, Bodl. Lib., Junius 11, p. 13

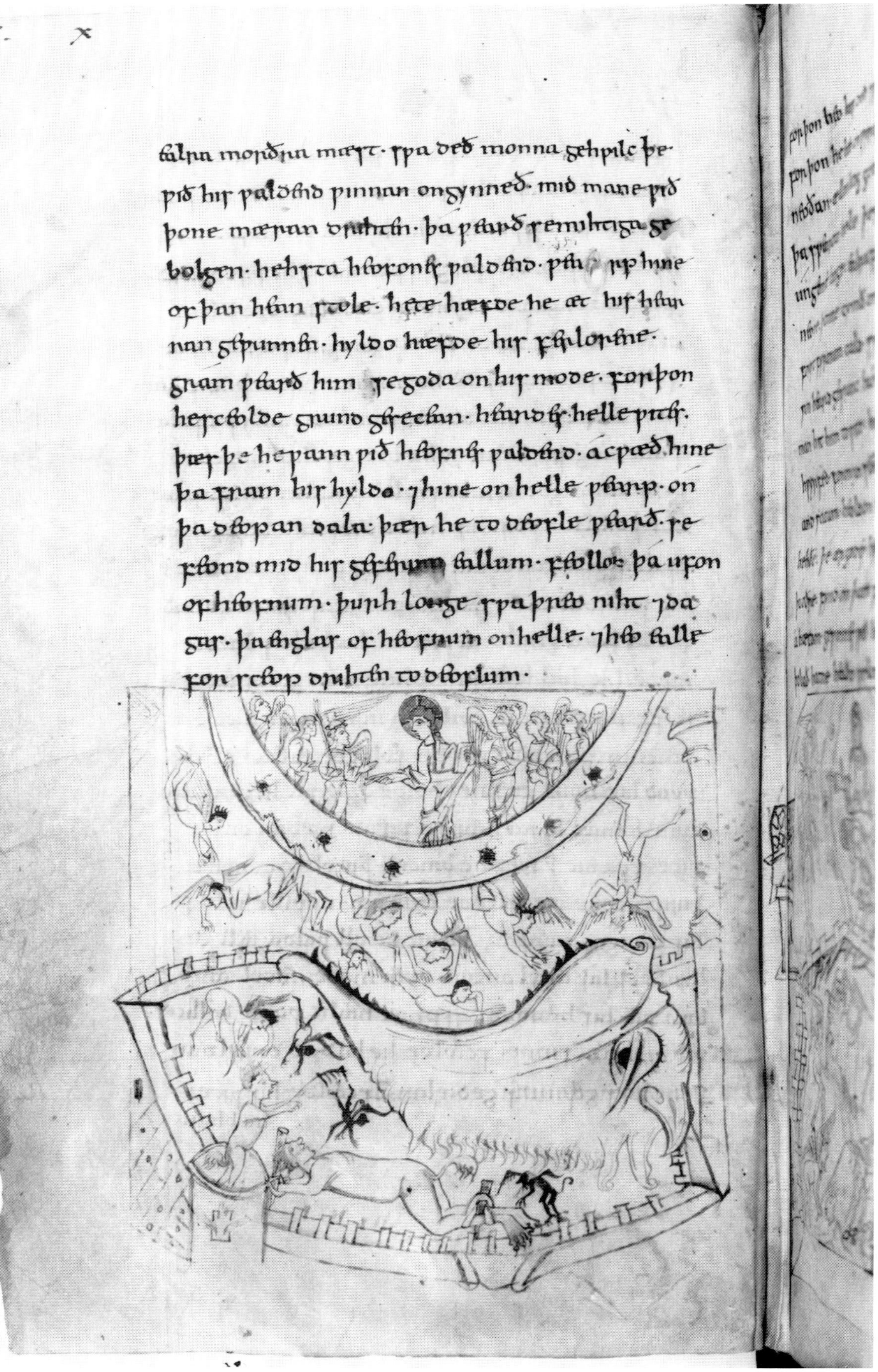

16.

ealra morðra mæst. swa deð monna gehwilc þe
wið his waldend winnan ongynneð. mid mane wið
þone mæran drihten. þa wearð se mihtiga ge
bolgen. hehsta heofones waldend. wearp hine
of þan hean stole. hete hæfde he æt his hear
ran gewunnen. hyldo hæfde his ferlorene.
gram wearð him se goda on his mode. forþon
he sceolde grund gesecean. heardes hellewites.
þæs þe he wann wið heofnes waldend. acwæð hine
þa fram his hyldo. 7 hine on helle wearp. on
þa deopan dala. þær he to deofle wearð. se
feond mid his geferum eallum. feollon þa ufon
of heofnum. þurh longe swa þreo niht 7 da
gas. þa englas of heofnum on helle. 7 heo ealle
forsceop drihten to deoflum.

16.11 Oxford, Bodl. Lib., Junius 11, p. 16

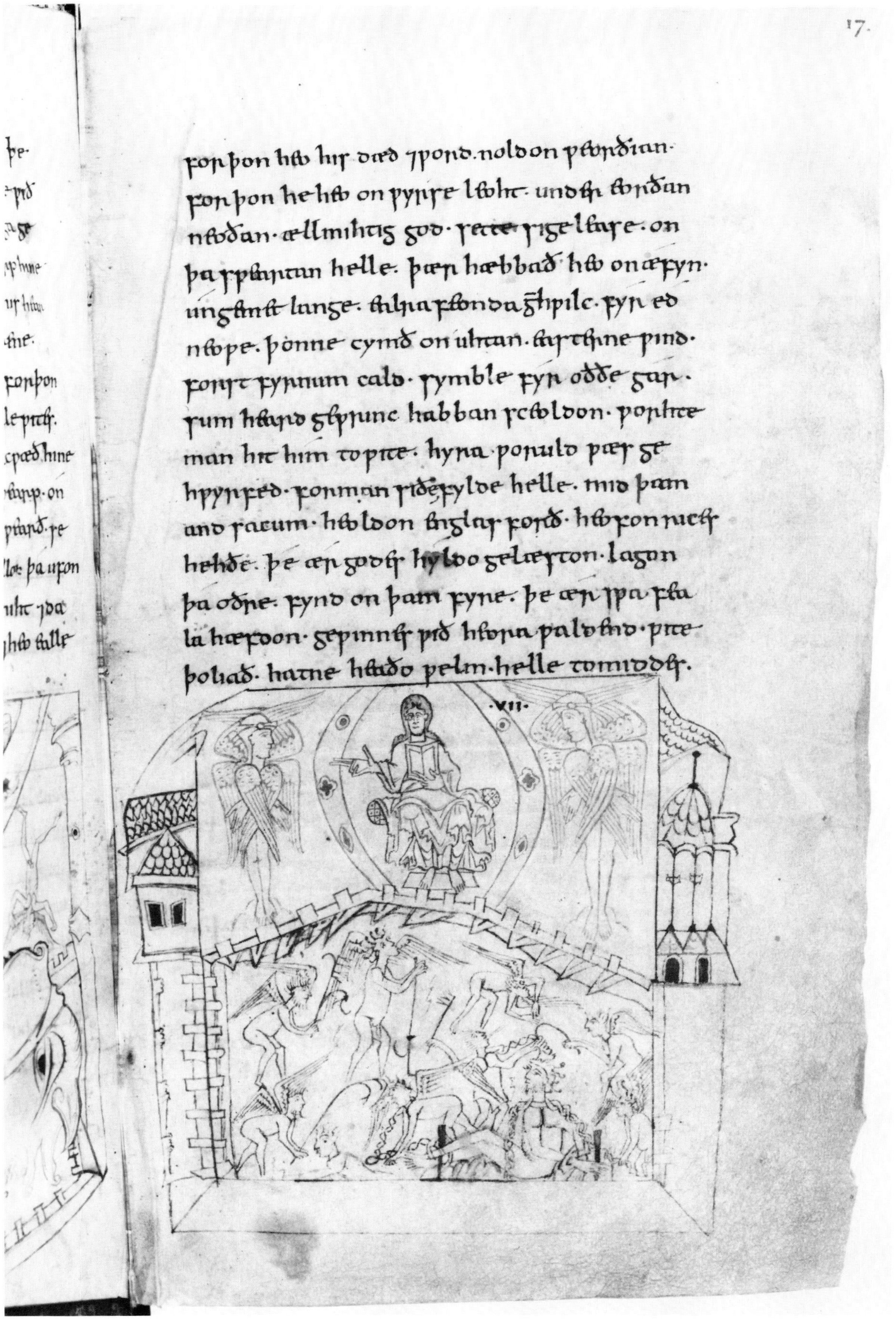
17.

forþon heo his dæd ⁊ word. noldon weorðian.
forþon he heo on wyrse leoht. under eorðan
neoðan. ællmihtig god. sette sigelease. on
þa sweartan helle. þær hæbbað heo on æfyn.
ungemet lange. ealra feonda gehwilc. fyr ed
neowe. þonne cymð on uhtan. easterne wind.
forst fyrnum cald. symble fyr oððe gar.
sum heard geswinc habban sceoldon. worhte
man hit him to wite. hyra woruld wæs ge
hwyrfed. forman siðe fylde helle. mid þam
andsacum. heoldon englas forð. heofonrices
hehðe. þe ær godes hyldo gelæston. lagon
þa oðre. fynd on þam fyre. þe ær swa feala
hæfdon. gewinnes wið heora waldend. wite
þoliað. hatne heaðo welm. helle tomiddes.

16.12 Oxford, Bodl. Lib., Junius 11, p. 17

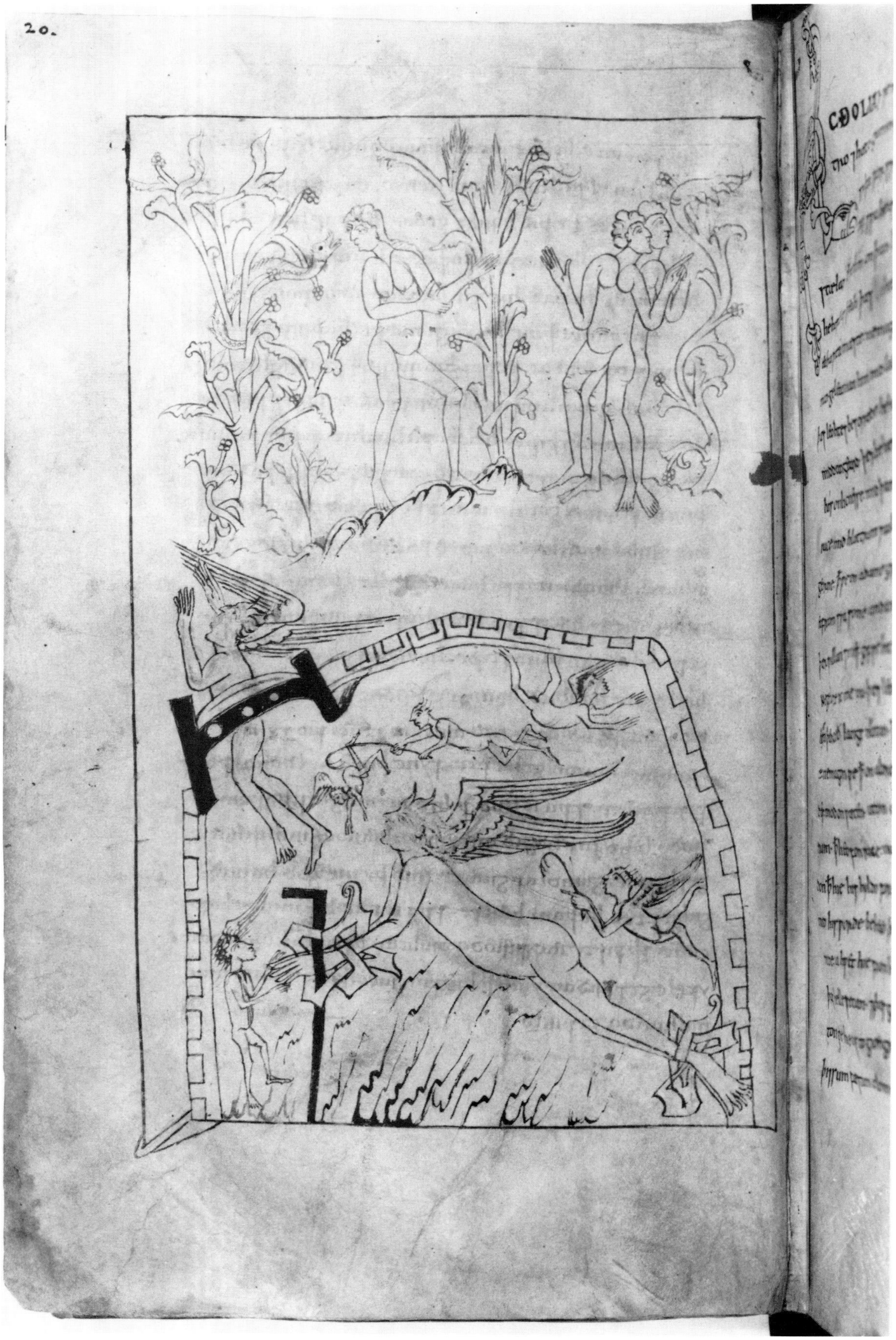

16.13 Oxford, Bodl. Lib., Junius 11, p. 20

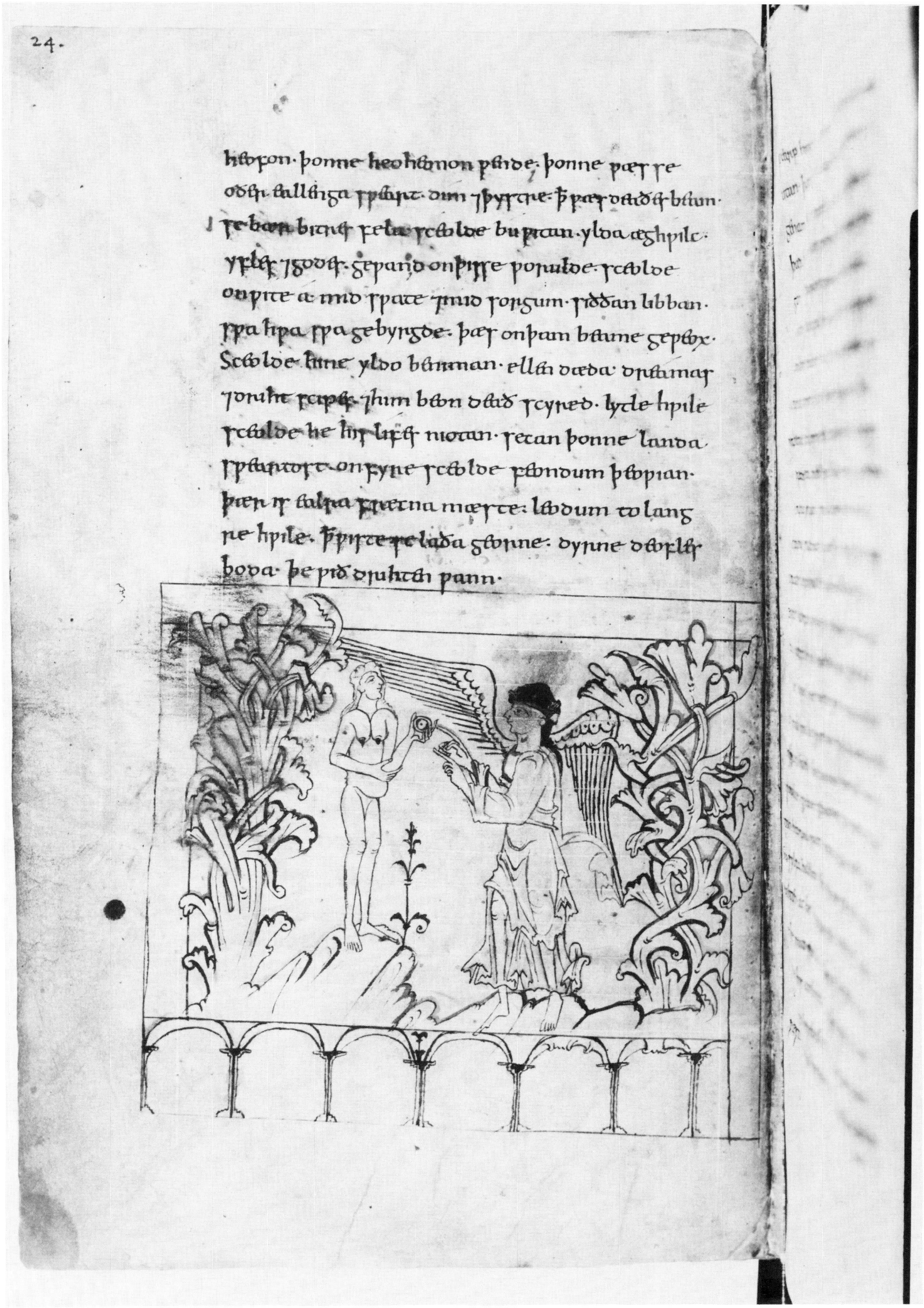

16.14 Oxford, Bodl. Lib., Junius 11, p. 24

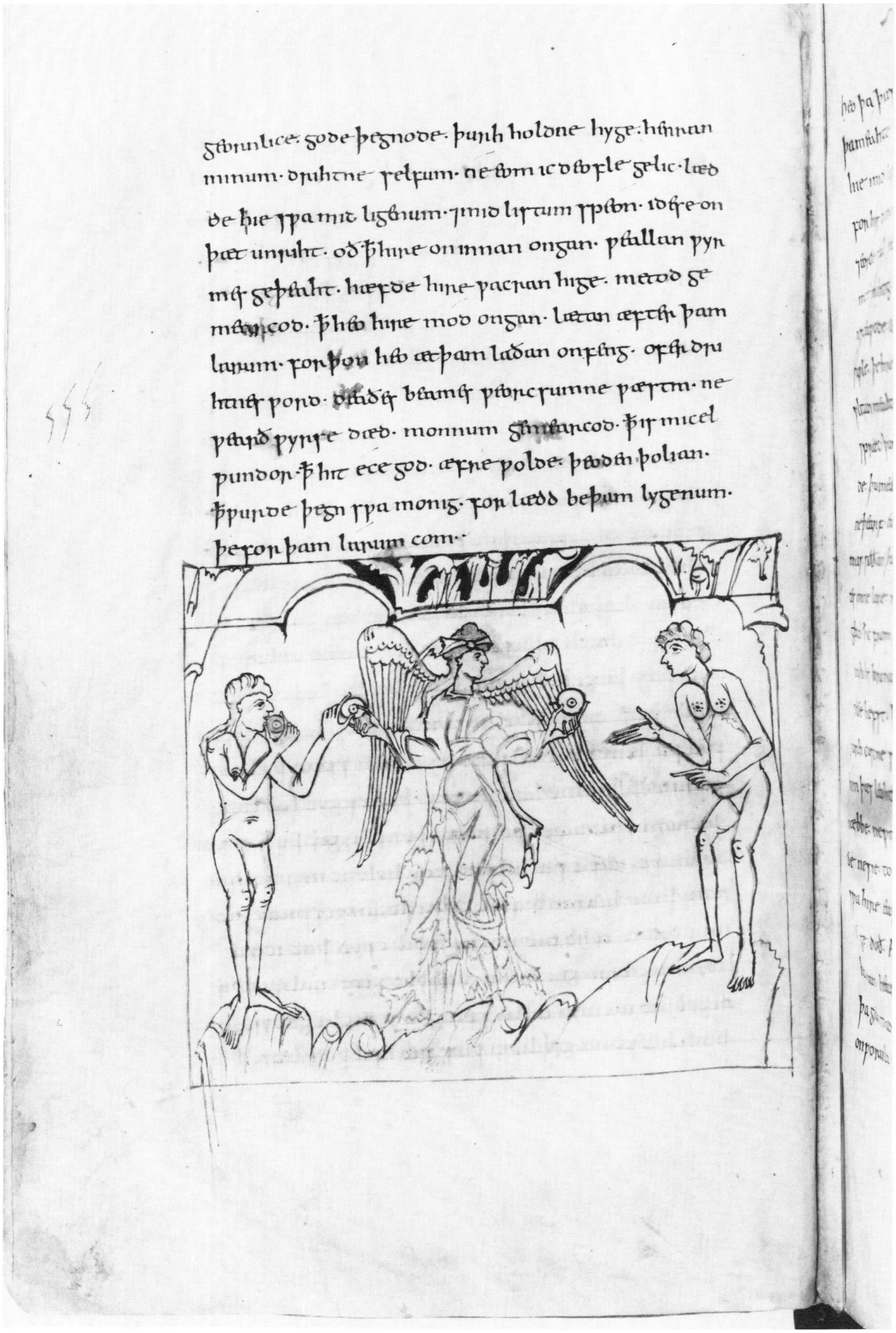

geornlice. gode þegnode. þurh holdne hyge. hirran
minum. drihtne selfum. ne [illegible] deofle gelic. læd
de hie swa mid ligenum. 7 mid listum speon. idese on
þæt unriht. oð þæt hire on innan ongan. weallan wyr
mes geþeaht. hæfde hire wacran hige. metod ge
mearcod. þæt heo hire mod ongan. lætan æfter þam
larum. forþon heo æt þam laðan onfeng. ofer dri
htnes word. deaðes beames. weorcsumne wæstm. ne
wearð wyrse dæd. monnum gemearcod. þæt is micel
wundor þæt hit ece god. æfre wolde. þeoden þolian.
þæt wurde þegn swa monig. forlæd be þam lygenum.
þe for þam larum com.

16.15 Oxford, Bodl. Lib., Junius 11, p. 28

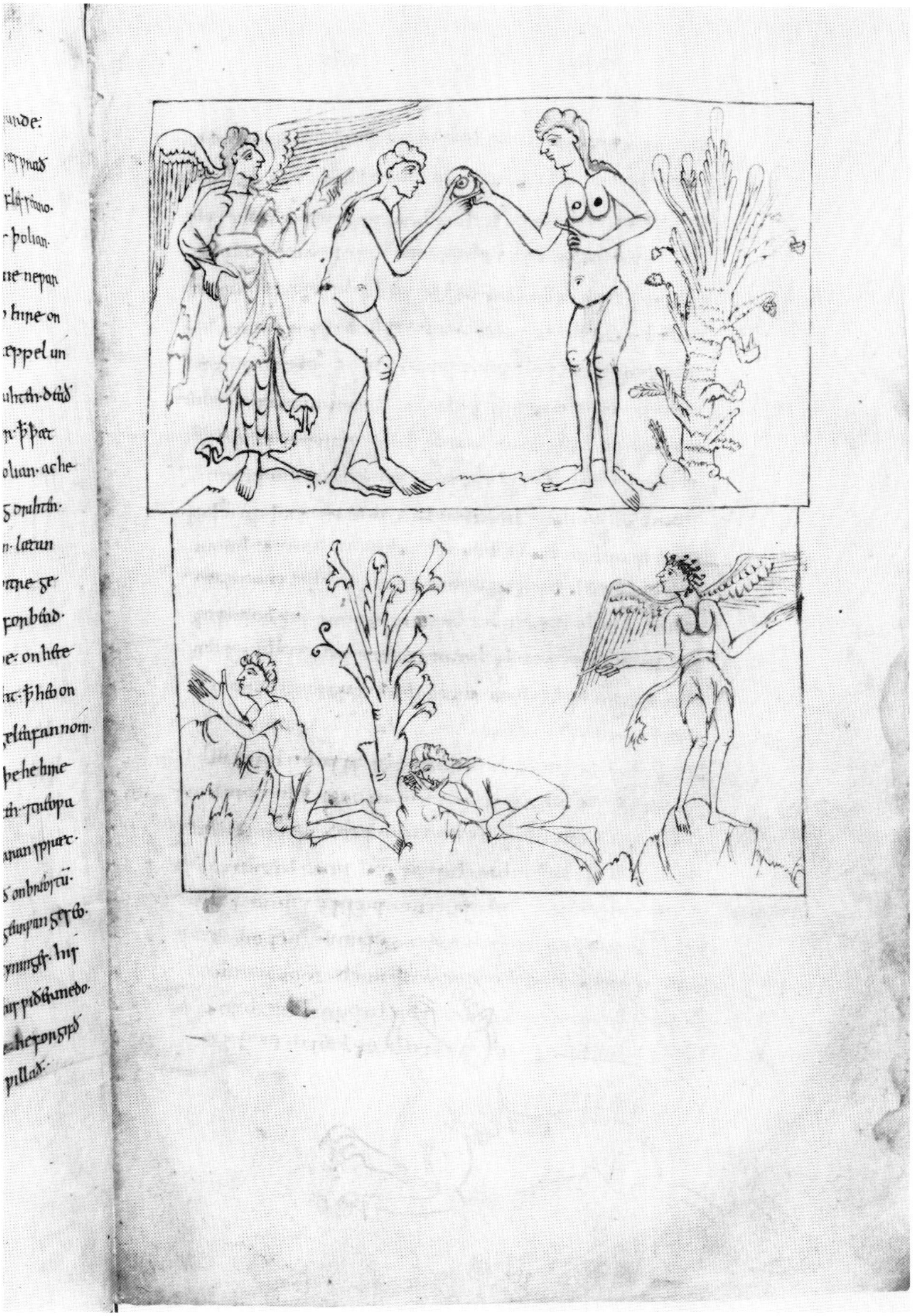

16.16 Oxford, Bodl. Lib., Junius 11, p. 31

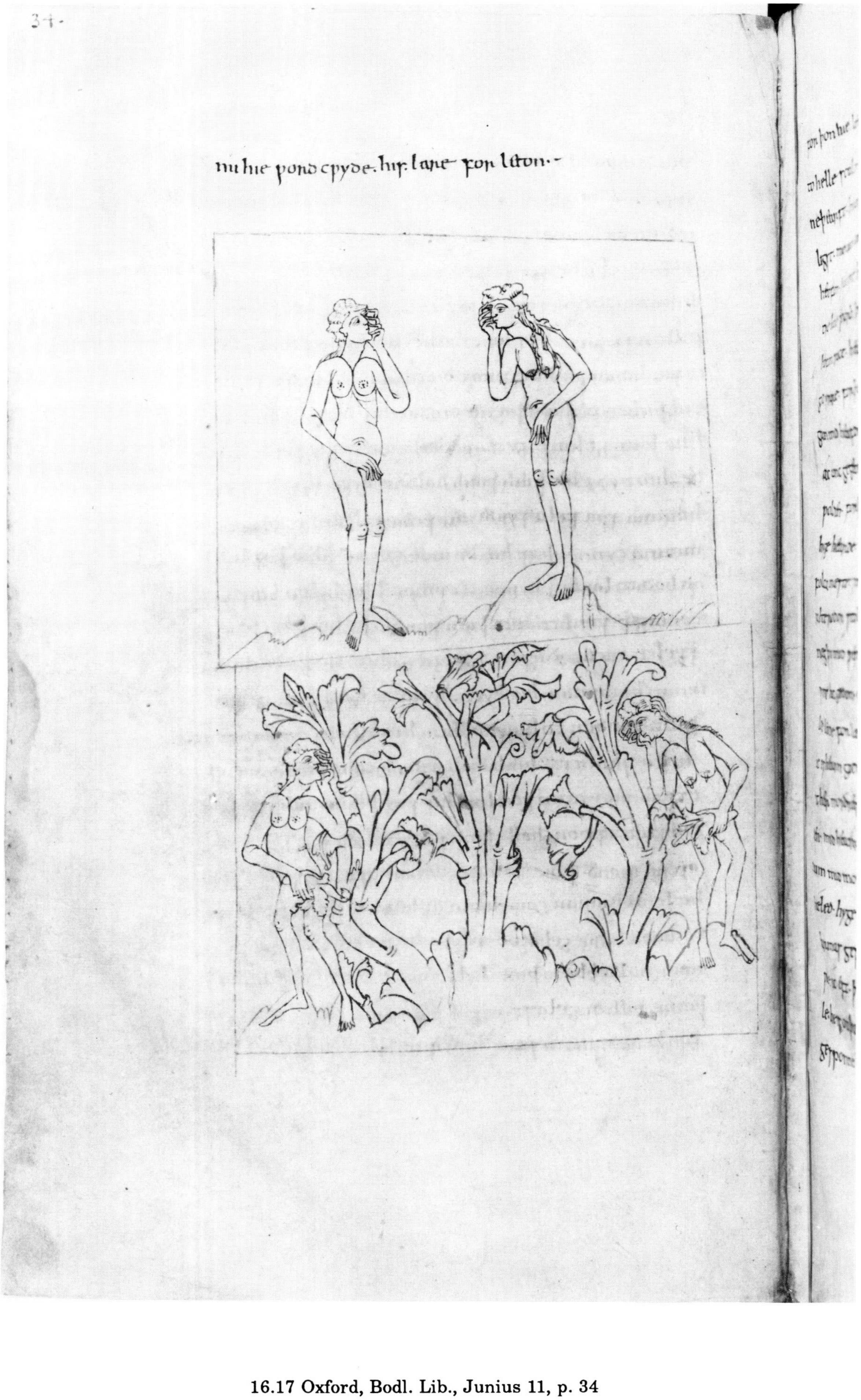

16.17 Oxford, Bodl. Lib., Junius 11, p. 34

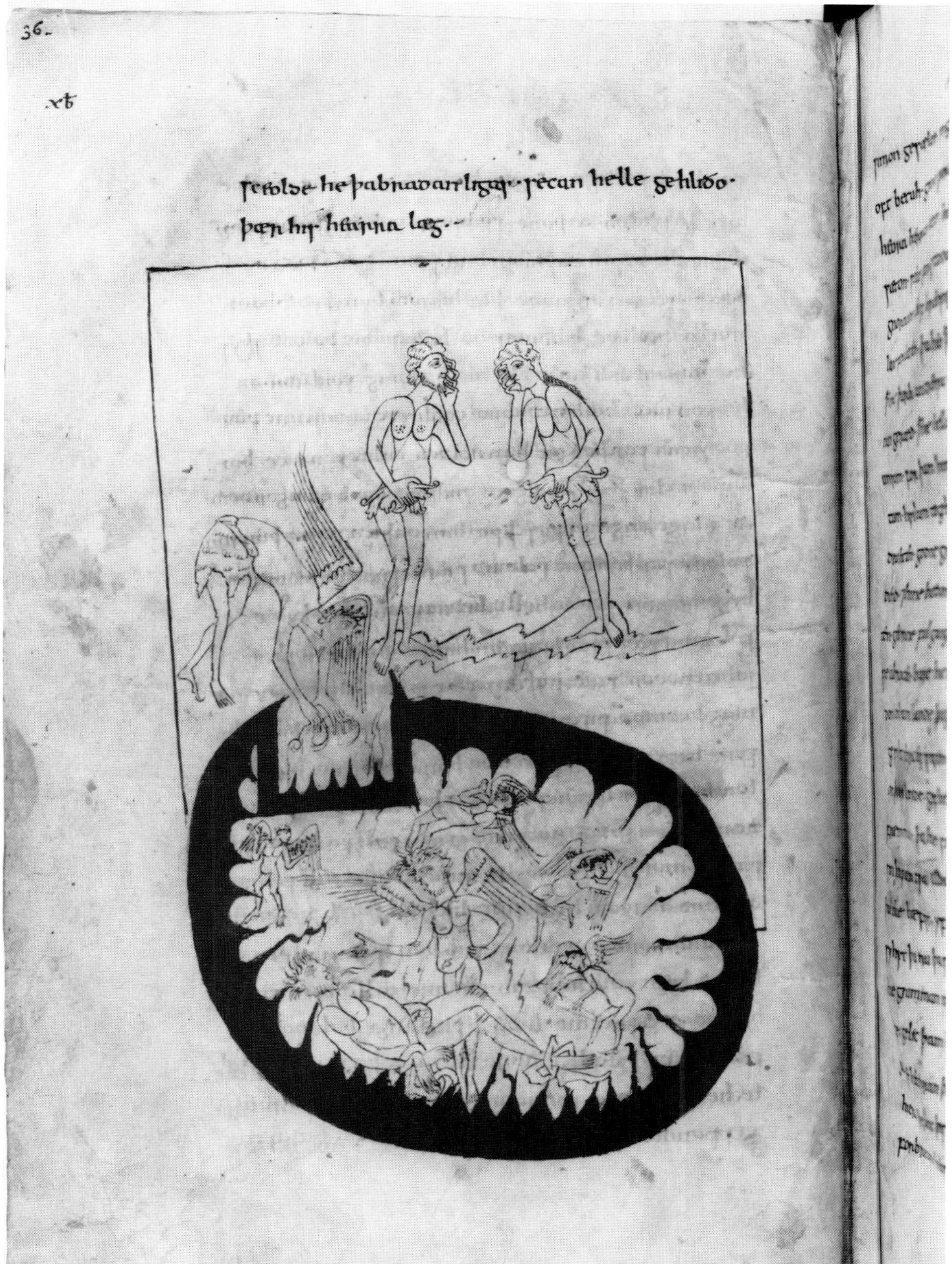

16.18 Oxford, Bodl. Lib., Junius 11, p. 36

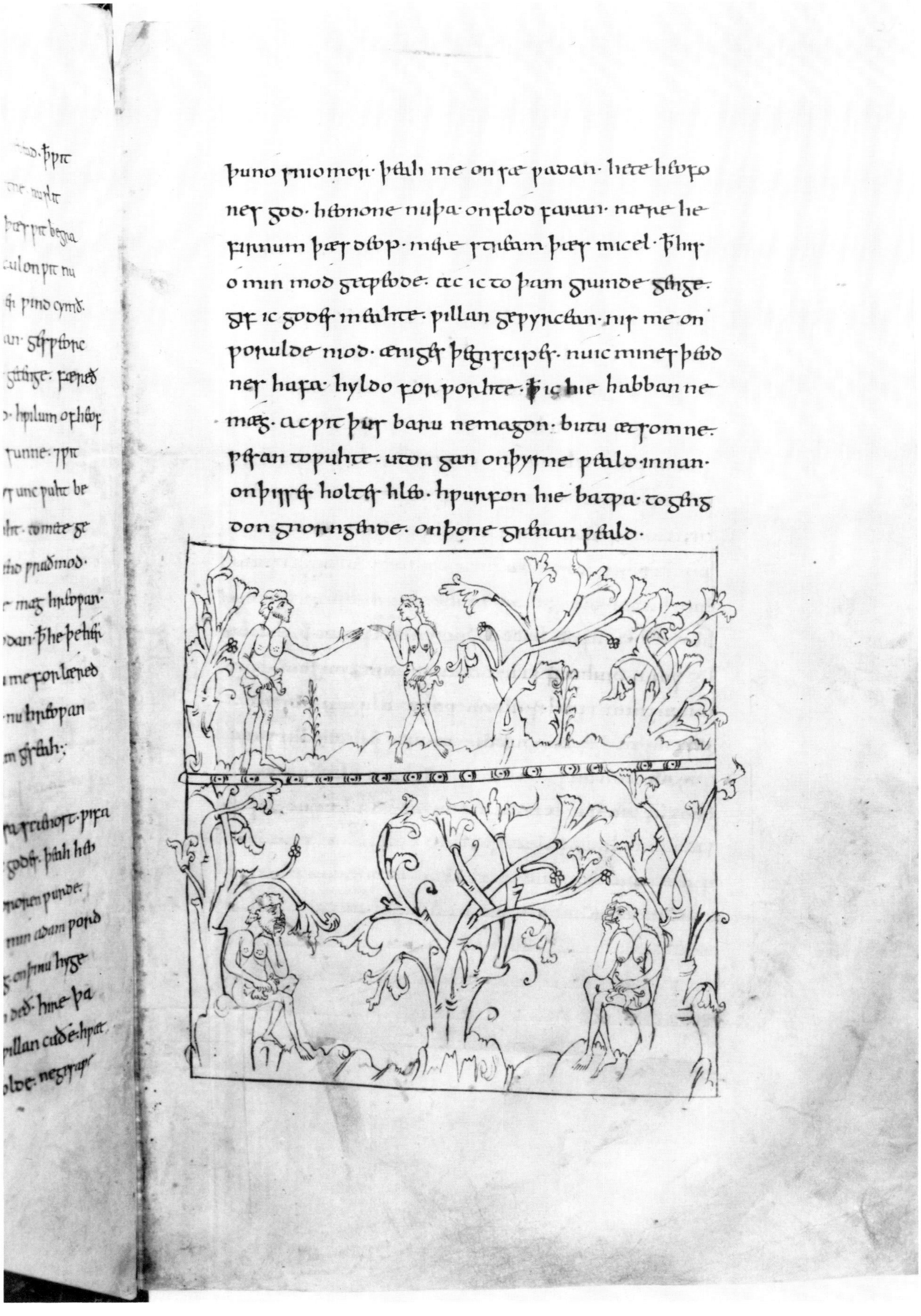

16.19 Oxford, Bodl. Lib., Junius 11, p. 39

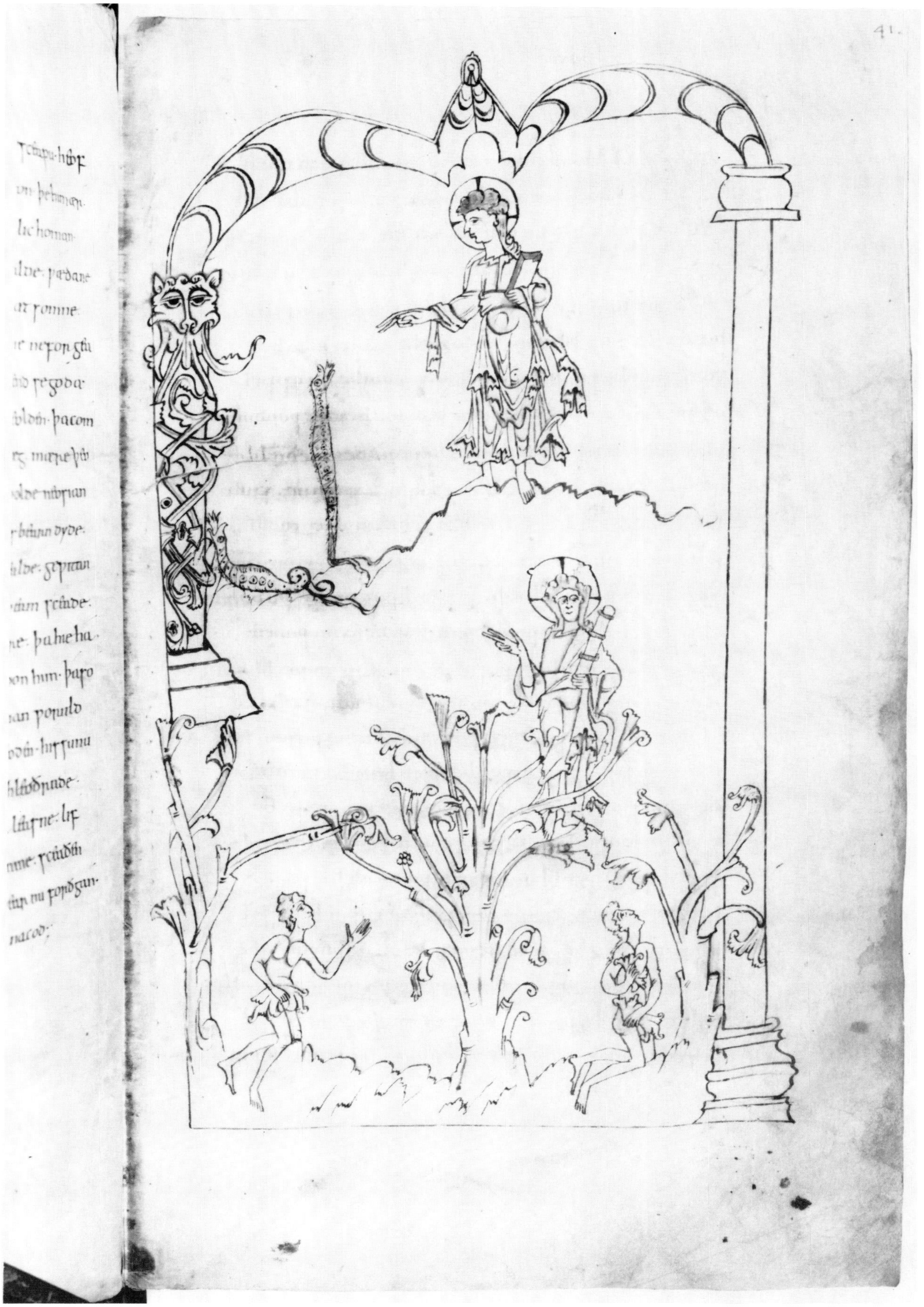

16.20 Oxford, Bodl. Lib., Junius 11, p. 41

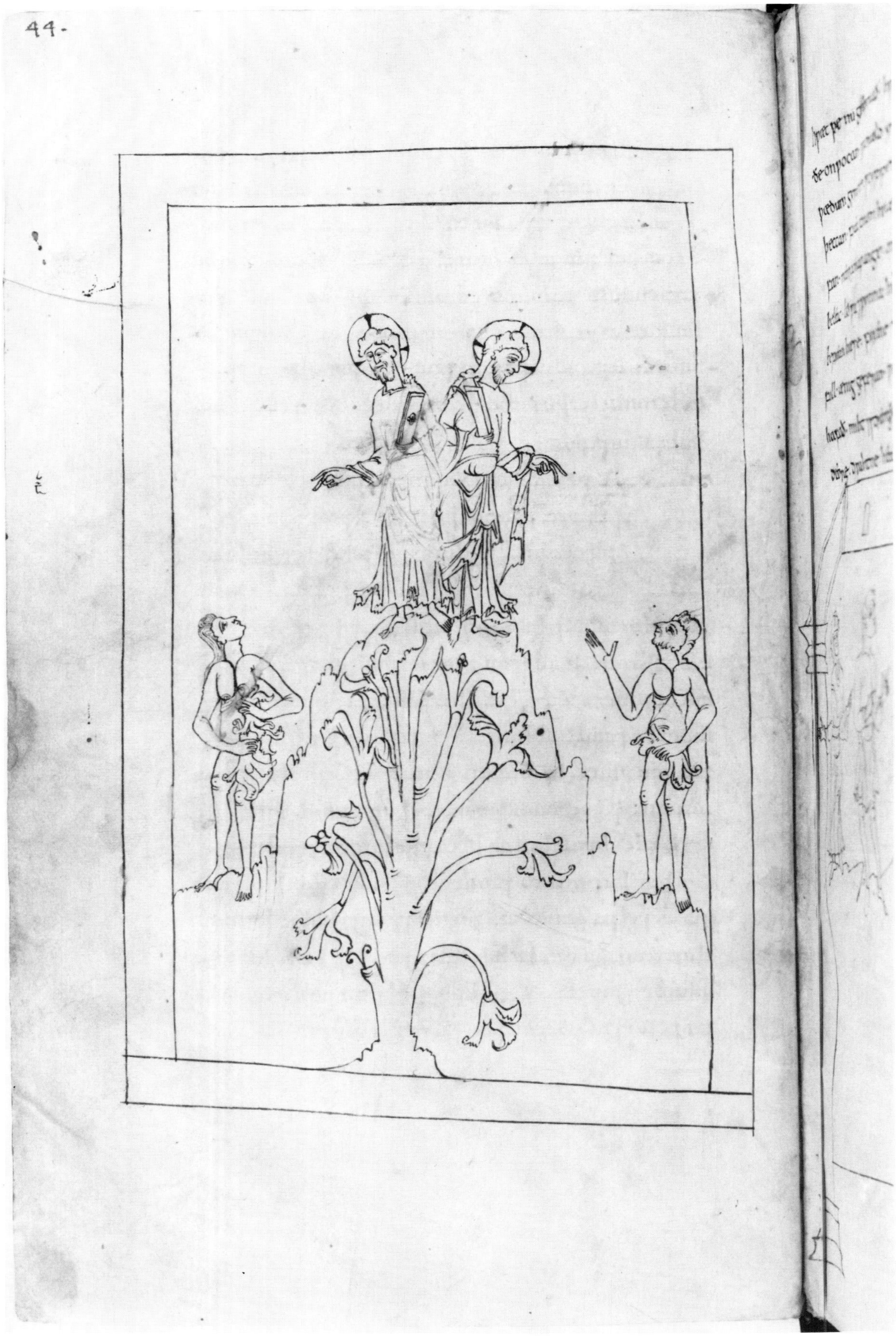

16.21 Oxford, Bodl. Lib., Junius 11, p. 44

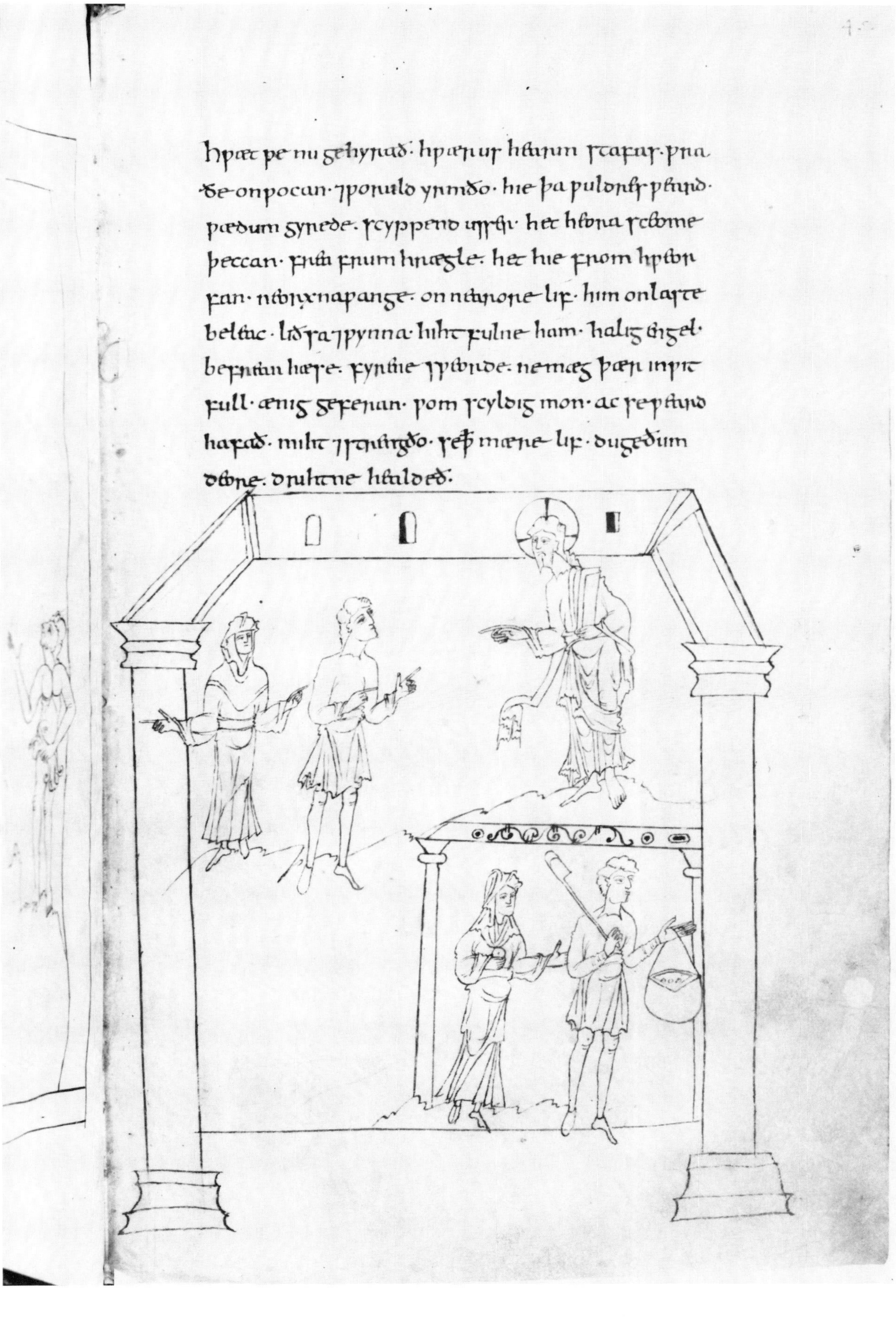

16.22 Oxford, Bodl. Lib., Junius 11, p. 45

No hwæðre ælmihtig. ealra wolde. adame 7 euan.
arna ofteon. fæder æt frymðe. þeah þe he him from
swice. ac he him to frofre. let hwæðere forð wesan.
hyrstedne hrof. halgum tunglum. 7 him grund we
lan ginne sealde. het þam sinhiwum. sæs 7 eorðan.
tuddor teondra. teohha gehwilcre. to woruld nytte.
wæstmas fedan. Gesæton þa æfter synne. sorgful
re land. eard 7 eðyl. unspedigran. fremena gehwilcre.
þonne se frum stol wæs. þe hie æfter dæde. of adri
fen wurdon. Ongunnon hie þa be godes hæse. bearn
astrienan. swa him metod bebead. adames 7 euan.
aforan wæron. freolicu twa frum bearn cenned.
cain 7 abel. us cyðað bec. hu þa dæd fruman. duge
þa stryndon. welan 7 wiste. will gebroðor.

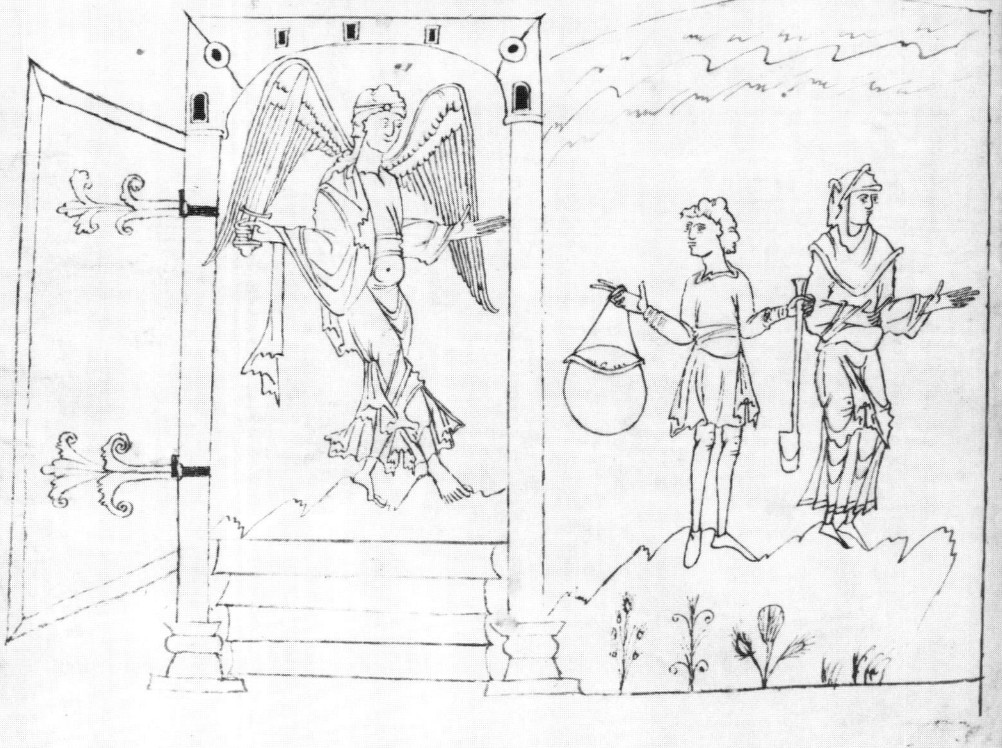

16.23 Oxford, Bodl. Lib., Junius 11, p. 46

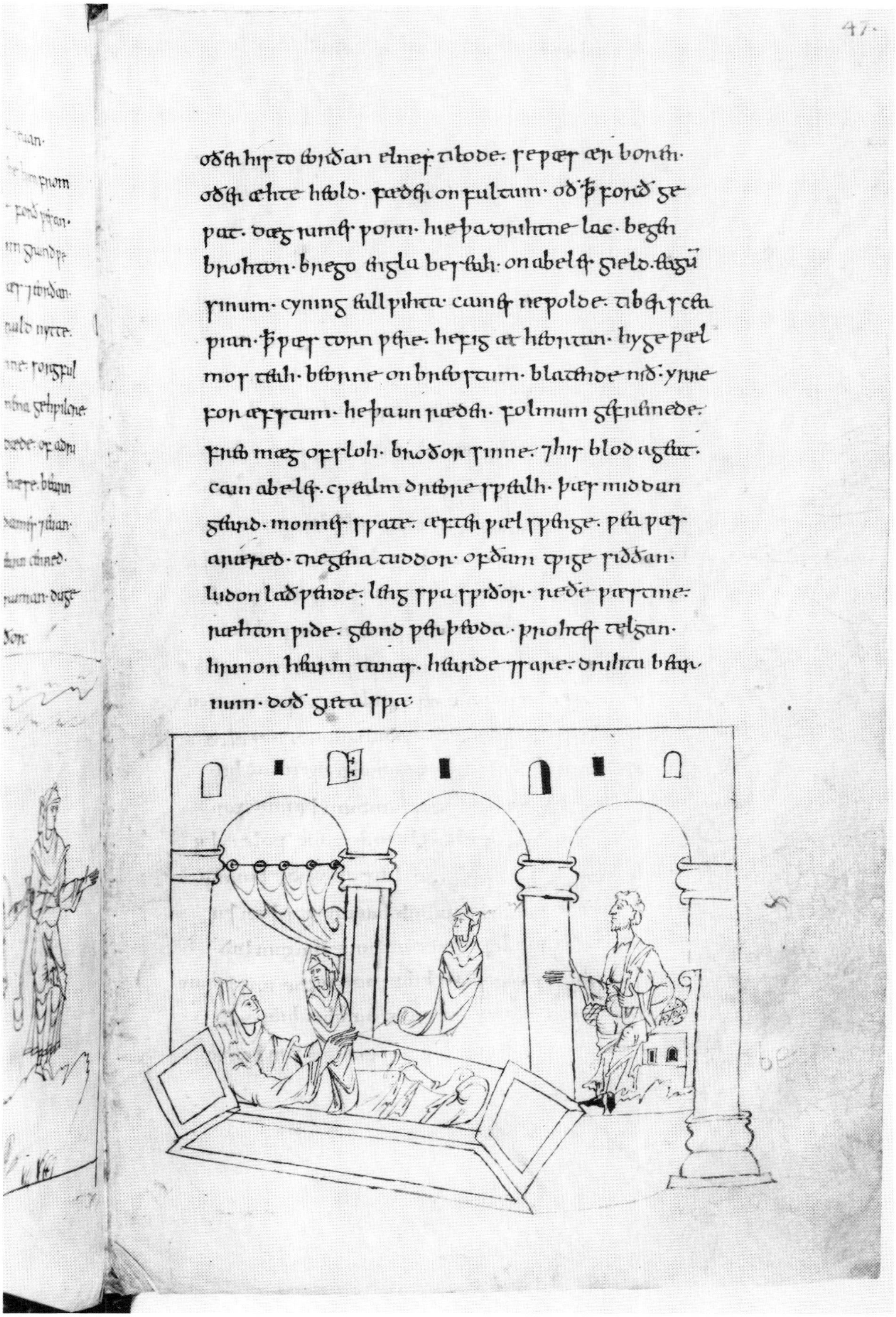

16.24 Oxford, Bodl. Lib., Junius 11, p. 47

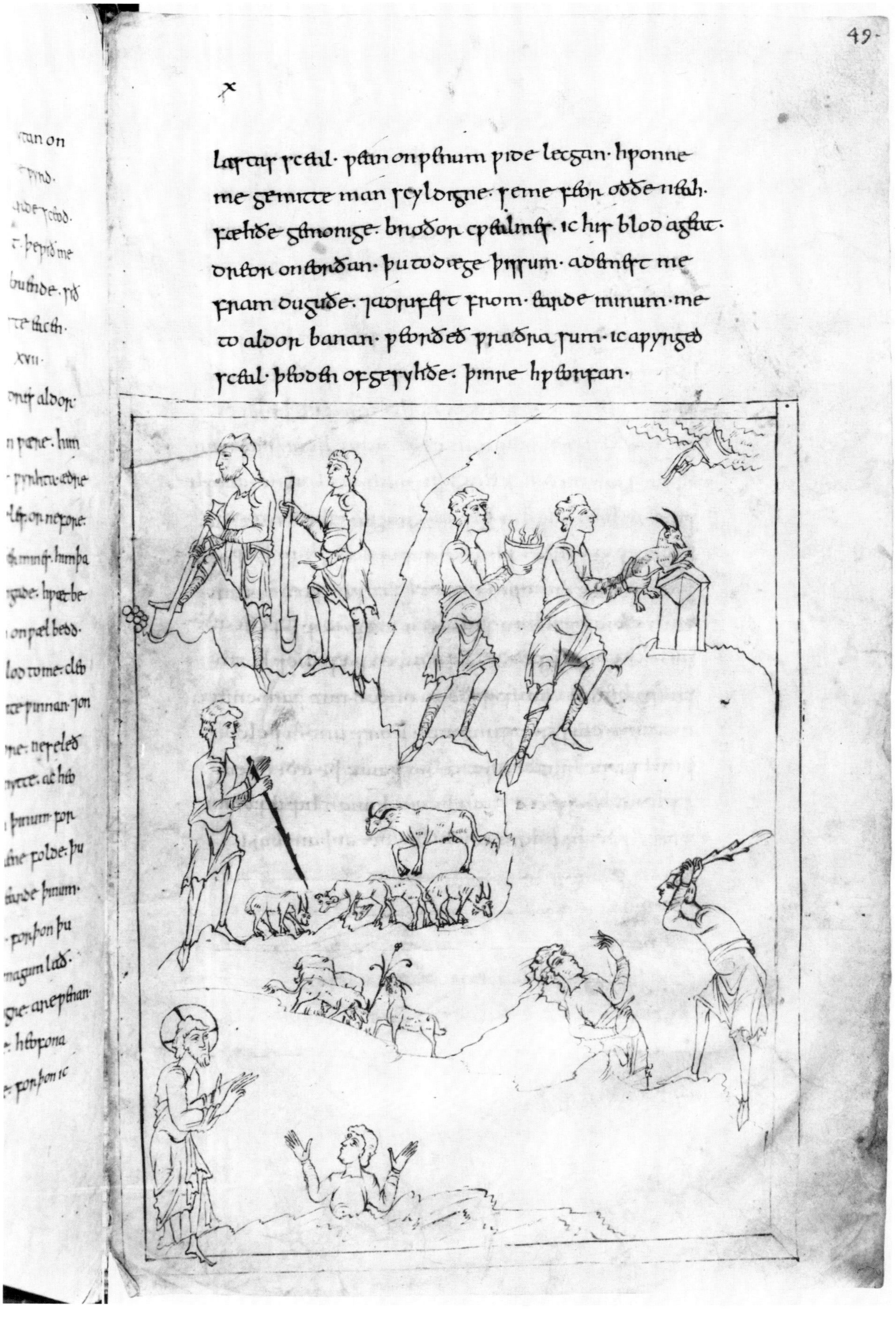

16.25 Oxford, Bodl. Lib., Junius 11, p. 49

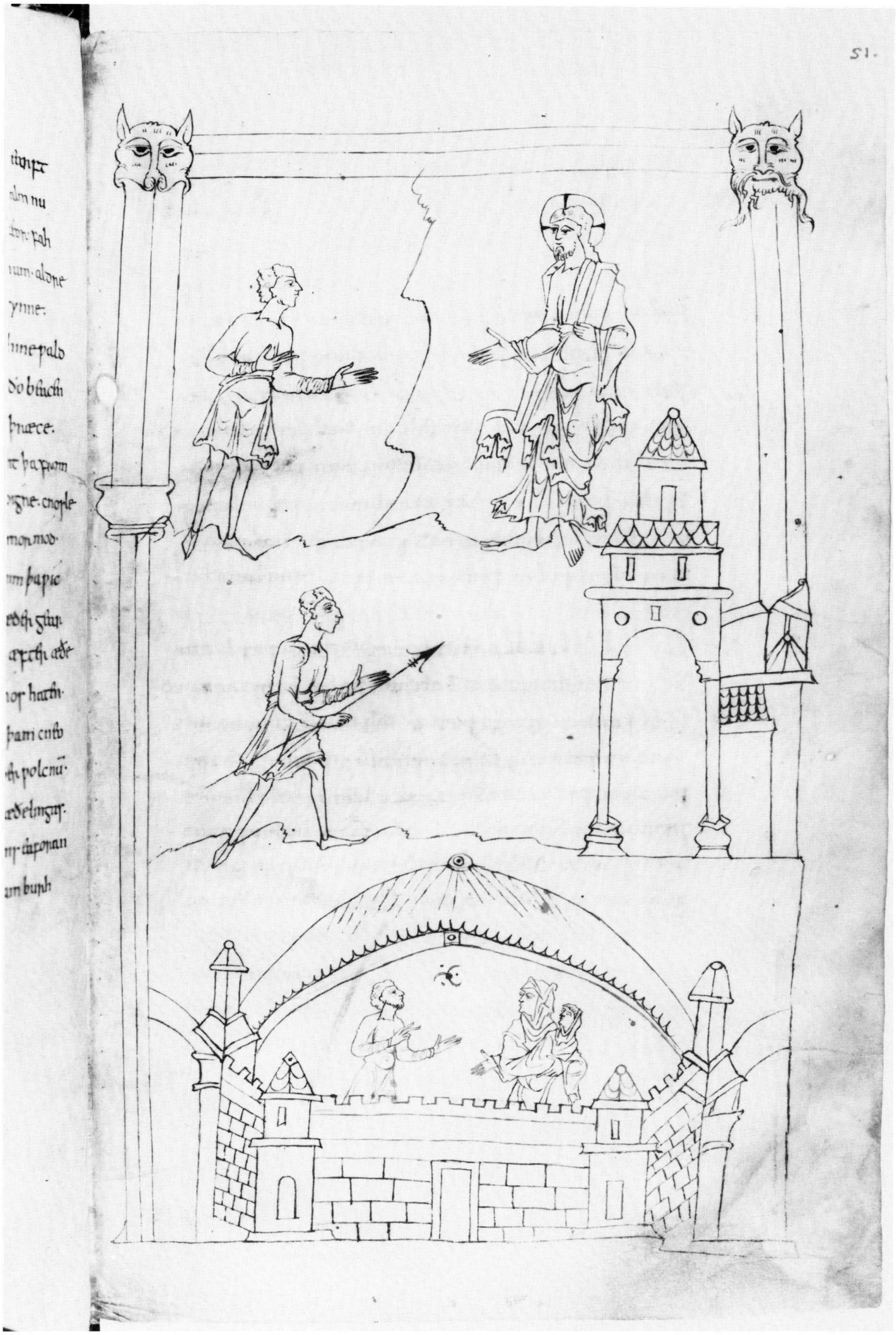

16.26 Oxford, Bodl. Lib., Junius 11, p. 51

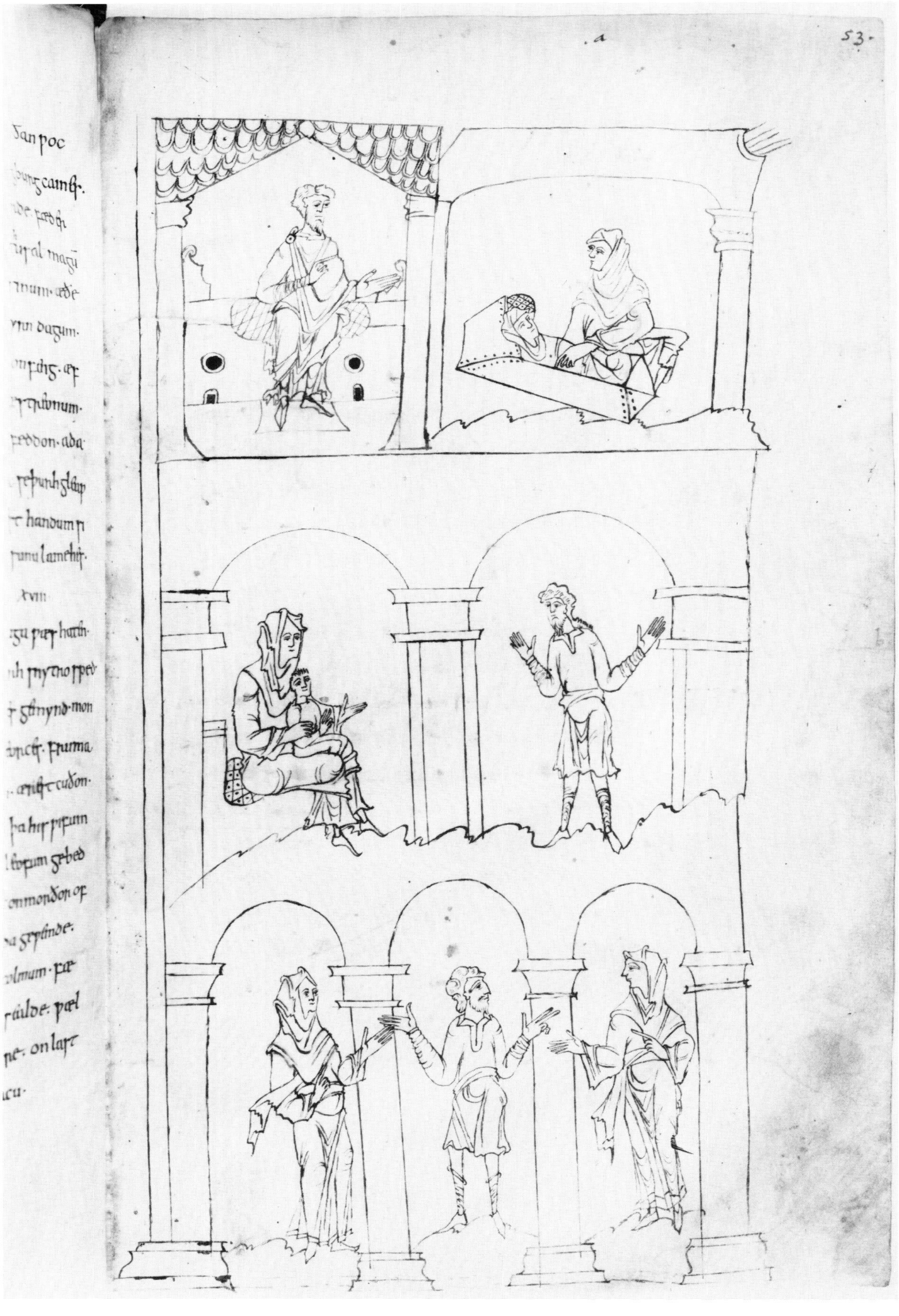

16.27 Oxford, Bodl. Lib., Junius 11, p. 53

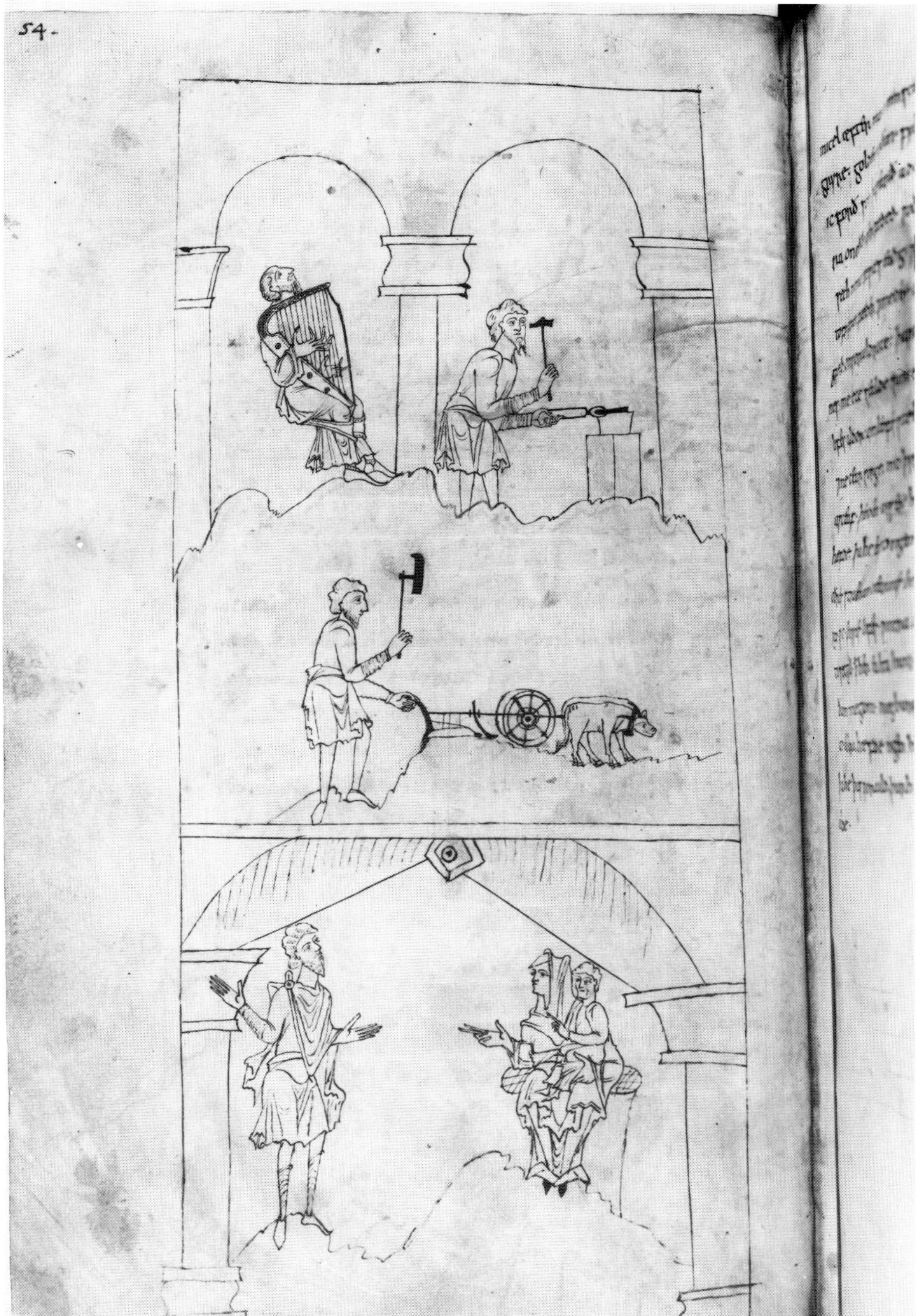

16.28 Oxford, Bodl. Lib., Junius 11, p. 54

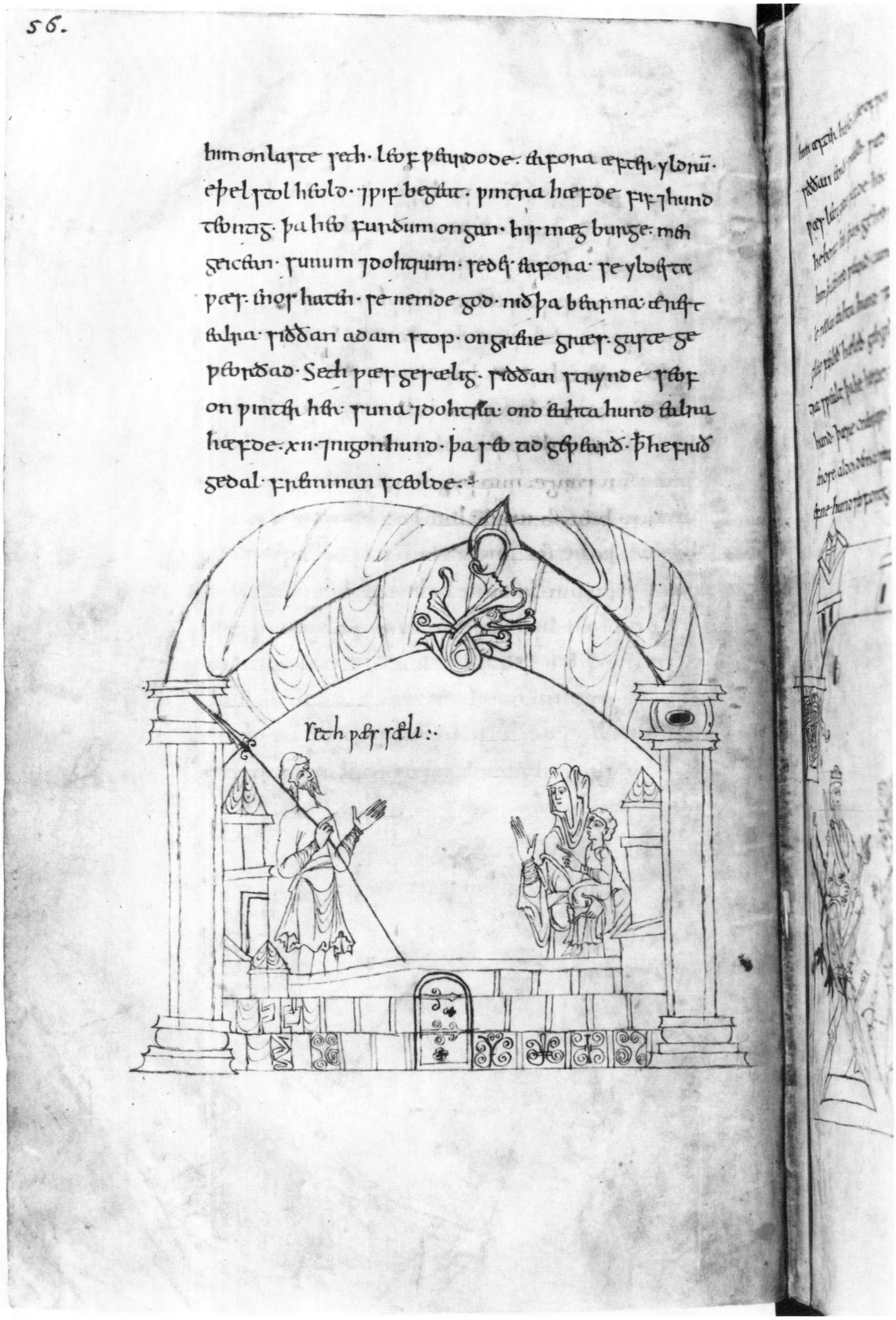

16.29 Oxford, Bodl. Lib., Junius 11, p. 56

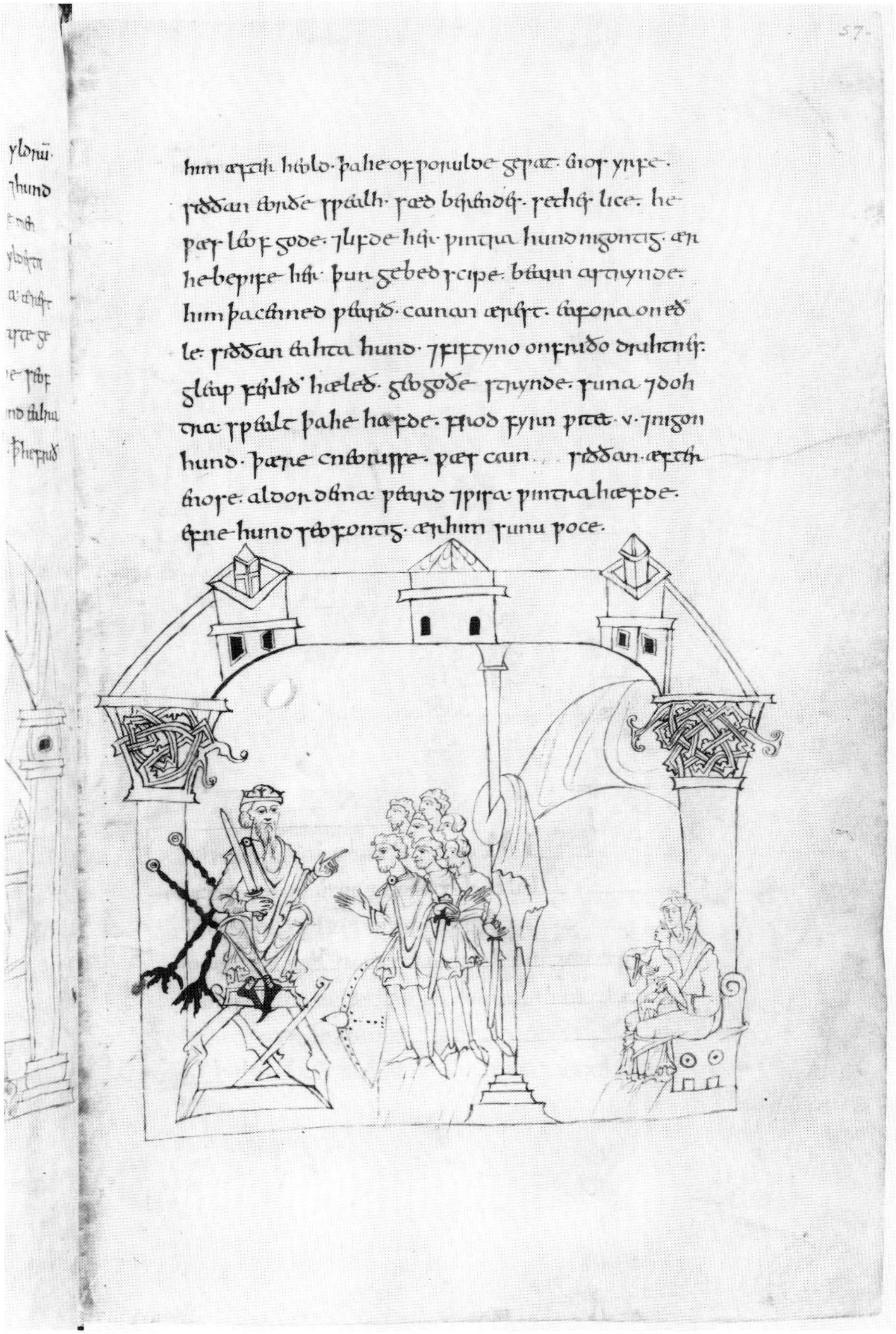

16.30 Oxford, Bodl. Lib., Junius 11, p. 57

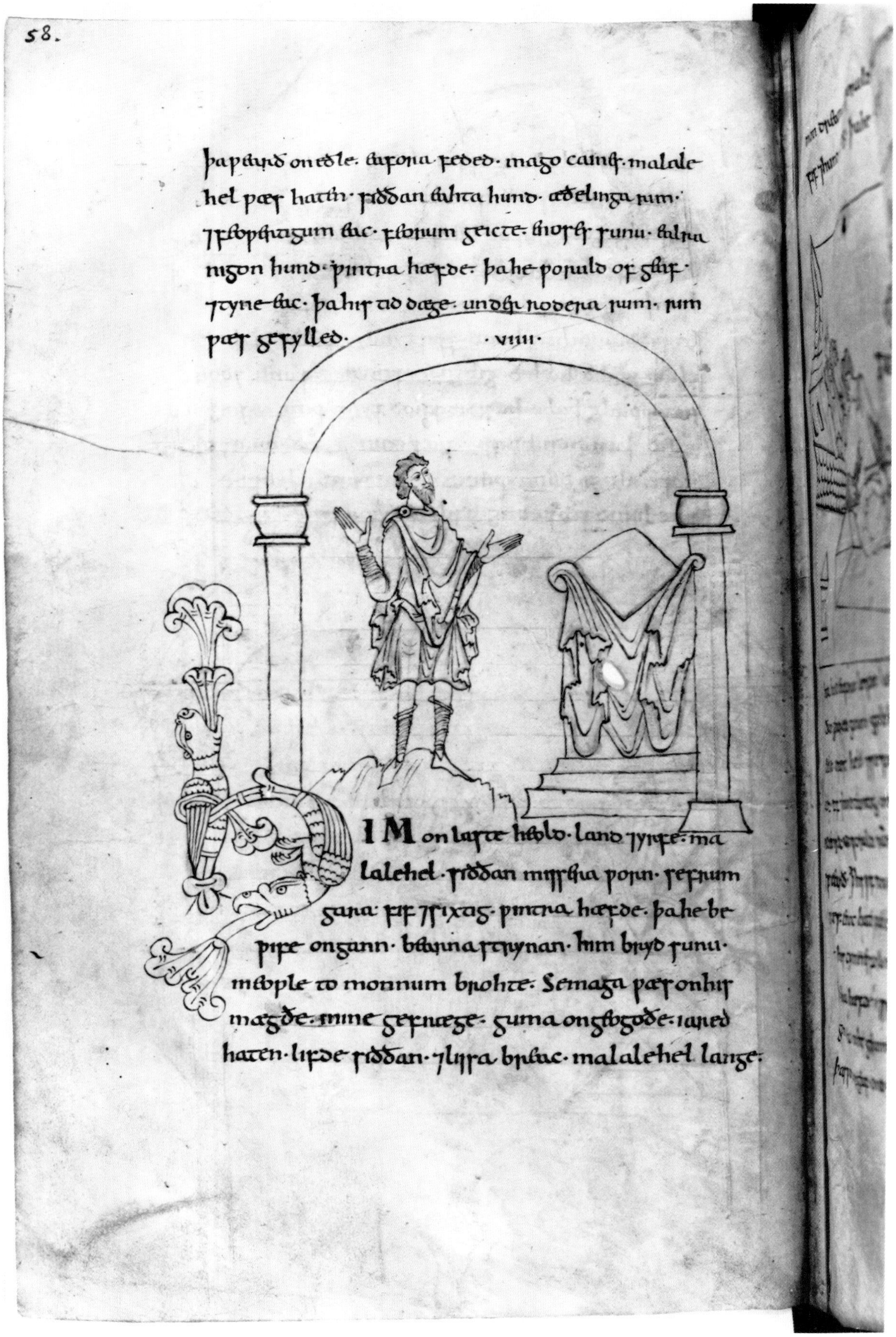

16.31 Oxford, Bodl. Lib., Junius 11, p. 58

mon drihtna his· worulde gestreona· wintra hæfde
fif 7 hund nigontig· þa he forð gewat·

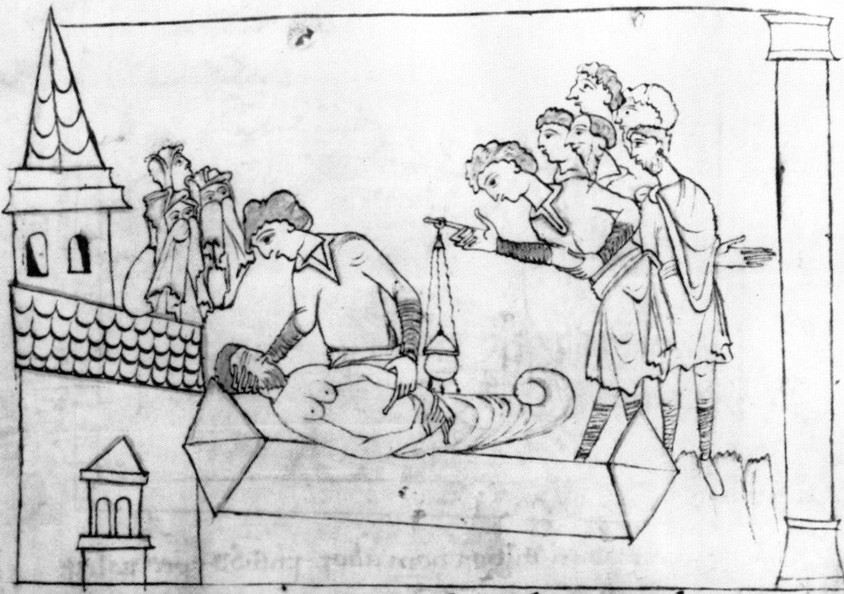

7eahta hund eaforan læfde· land 7 leodweard· longe
siððan· iared gumum· gold bryttade· se eorl wæs
æðele· æfæst hæleð· 7 se frumgar· his freo magū
leof· fif 7 hund teontig· on feore lifde· wintra ge
bidenra· on worulde her· 7 syxtig eac· þa se sæl
gewearð· þ his wif sunu· on worulde brohte· se eafo
ra wæs· enoc haten· freolic frumbearn· fæder hin
þa gyt· his cynnes forð· eaforum icte· eafora eahta
hund· ealra hæfde v· 7 syxtig· þa he forð gewat· 7 ni
gon hund eac· niht gerimes· wine frod wintres· þa he
þas worulde ofgeaf· ond iared þa gelæstum læfde· land

16.32 Oxford, Bodl. Lib., Junius 11, p. 59

60.

7 leod weard. leofum suna:

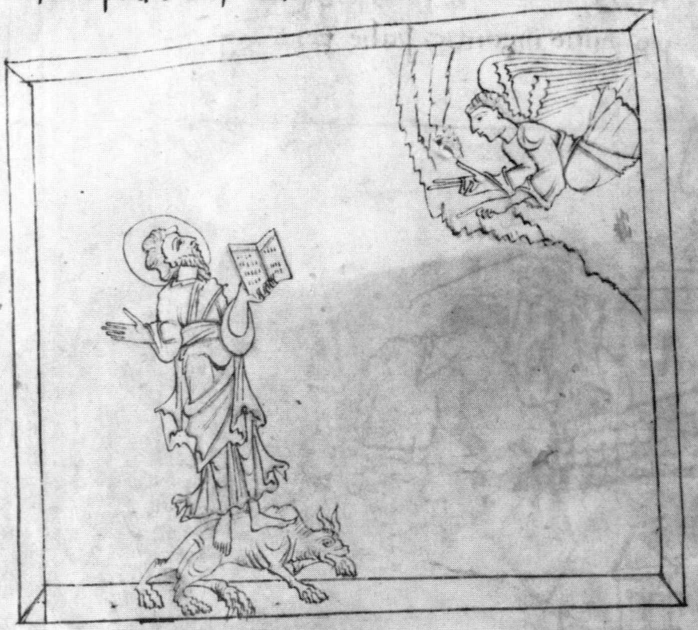

enoch siððan ealdor dom ahof. freoðo sped folces
wisa. nalles feallan let. dom 7 driht scipe. þenden he
hyrde wæs. heafod maga. breac blæd daga. bearna
strynde. þreo hund wintra. him wæs þeoden hold.
rodera waldend. se rinc heonon. on lic homan. lisse
sohte. drihtnes duguðe. nalles deaðe swealt. middan
geardes. swa her men doþ. geonge 7 ealde. þonne him
god heora. æhta 7 æt wist. eorðan gestreona. on genim
eð. 7 heora aldor somed. ac he cwic gewat. mid
cyning engla. of þyssum lænan life feran. on þam
gearwum. þe his gast onfeng. ær hine to moncynne
modor brohte. he þam yldestan. eaferan læfde.

16.33 Oxford, Bodl. Lib., Junius 11, p. 60

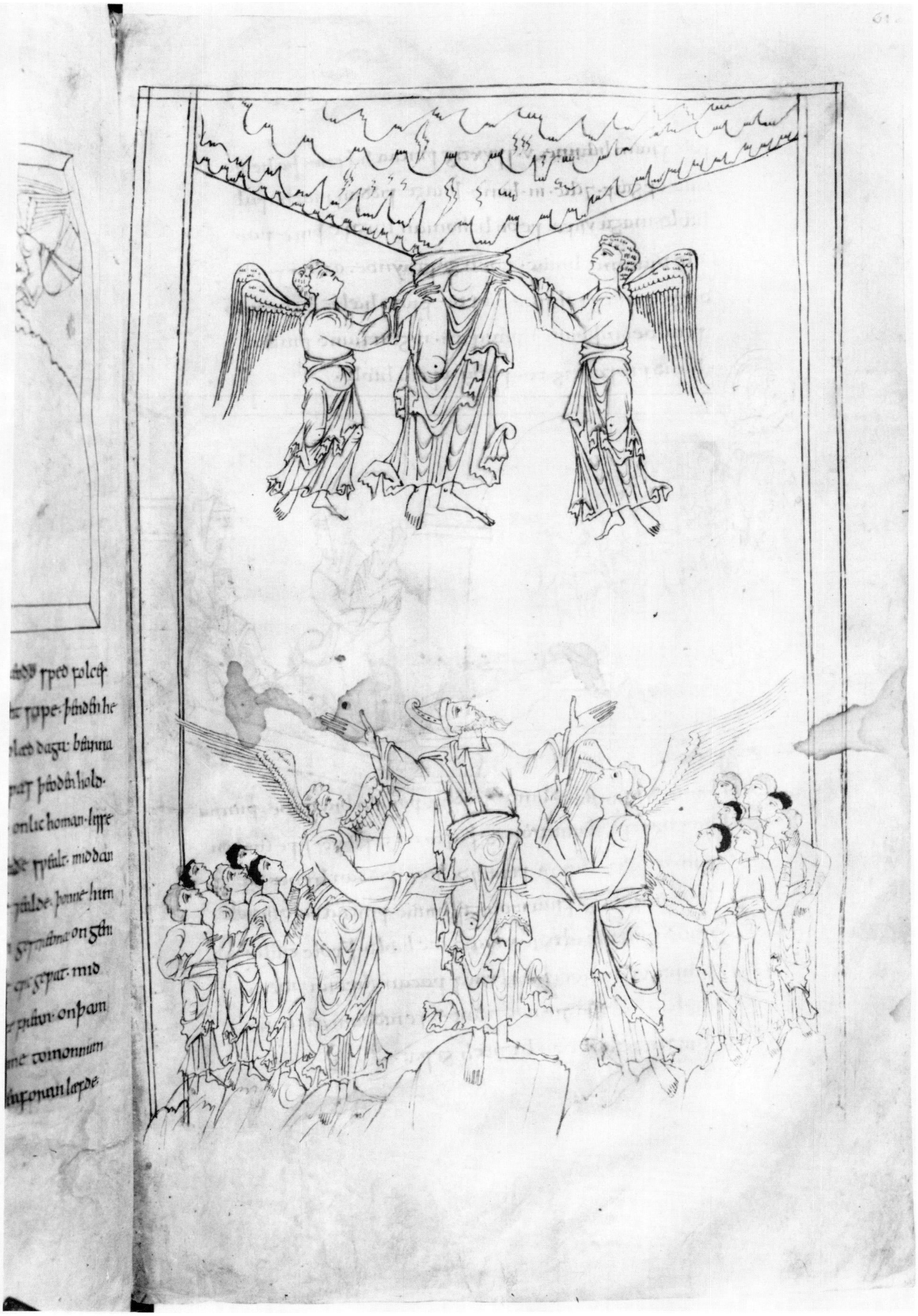

16.34 Oxford, Bodl. Lib., Junius 11, p. 61

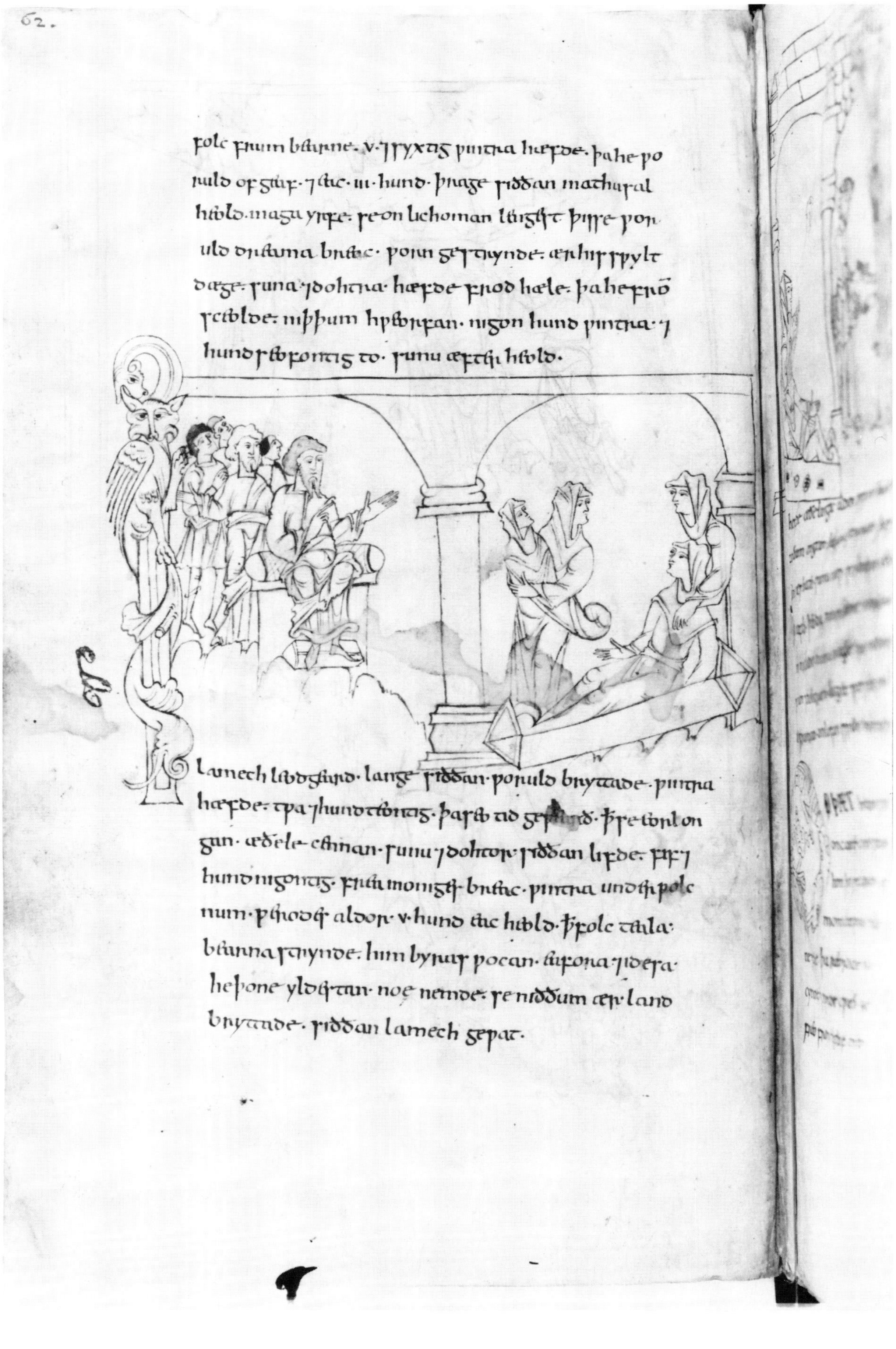

16.35 Oxford, Bodl. Lib., Junius 11, p. 62

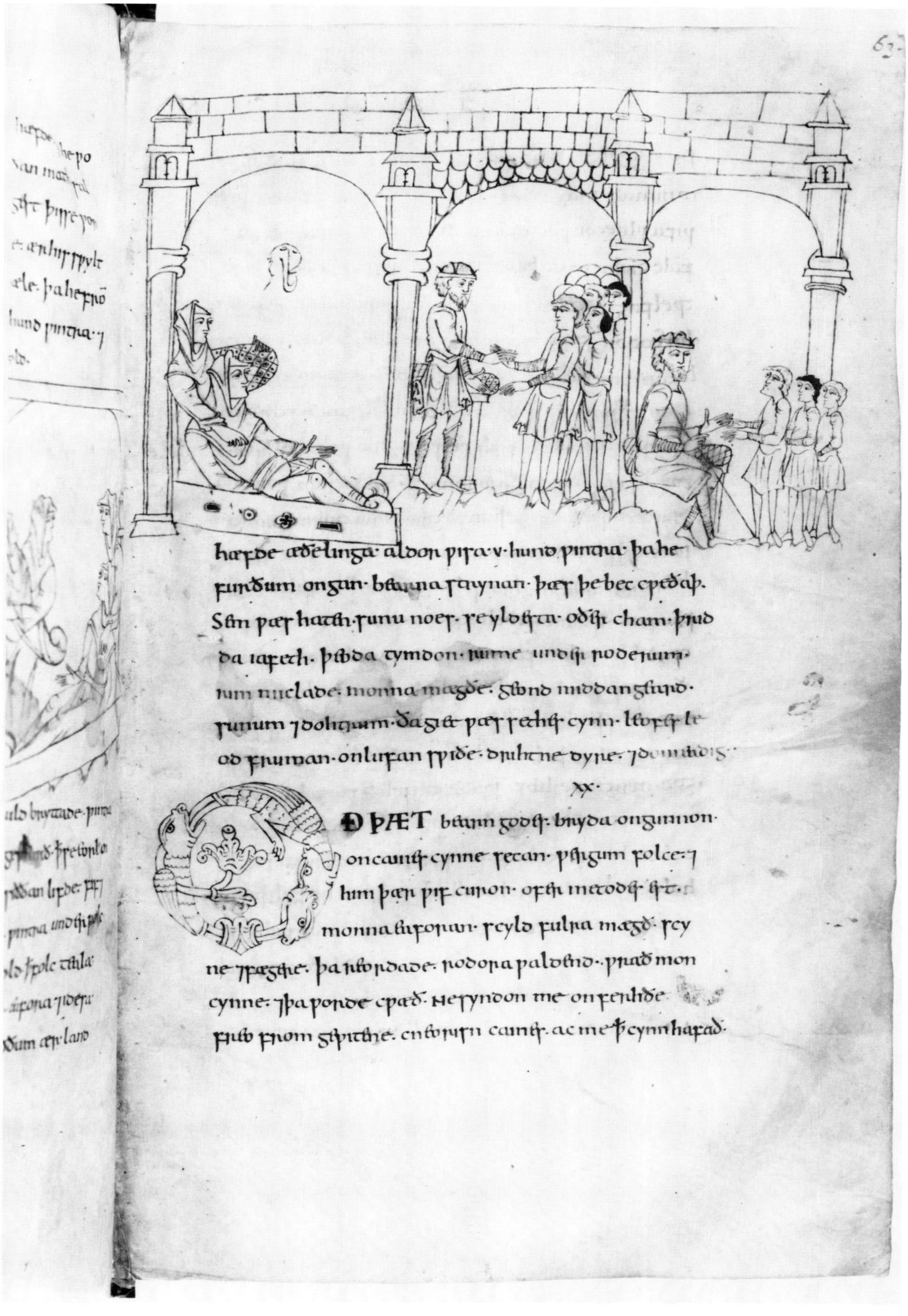

16.36 Oxford, Bodl. Lib., Junius 11, p. 63

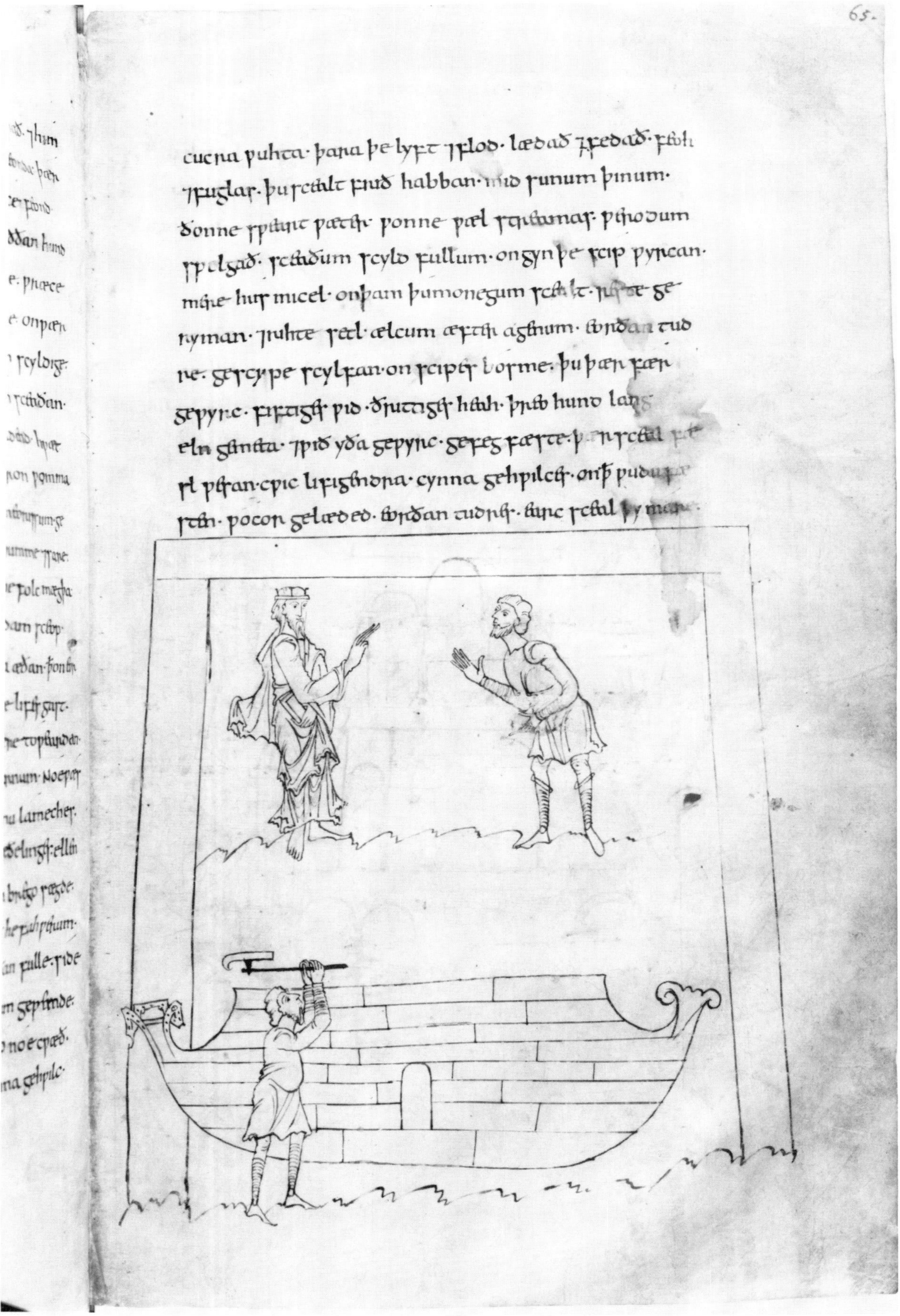
65.

cucra wuhta · þara þe lyft 7 flod · lædað 7 fedað · feoh
7 fuglas · þu scealt frið habban · mid sunum þinum ·
ðonne sweart wæter · wonne wælstreamas · werodum
swelgað · sceaðum scyldfullum · ongyn þe scip wyrcan ·
merehus micel · on þam þu monegum scealt · reste ge
ryman · 7 rihte sete ælcum æfter agenum · eorðan tud
re · gescype scylfan on scipes bosme · þu þæt fær
gewyrc · fiftiges wid · ðrittiges heah · þreohund lang
elngemeta · 7 wið yða gewyrc · gefeg fæste · þær sceal fæ
sl wesan cwiclifigendra · cynna gehwilces · on þæt wudu fæ
sten · wocor gelæded · eorðan tudres · earc sceal þy mare ·

16.37 Oxford, Bodl. Lib., Junius 11, p. 65

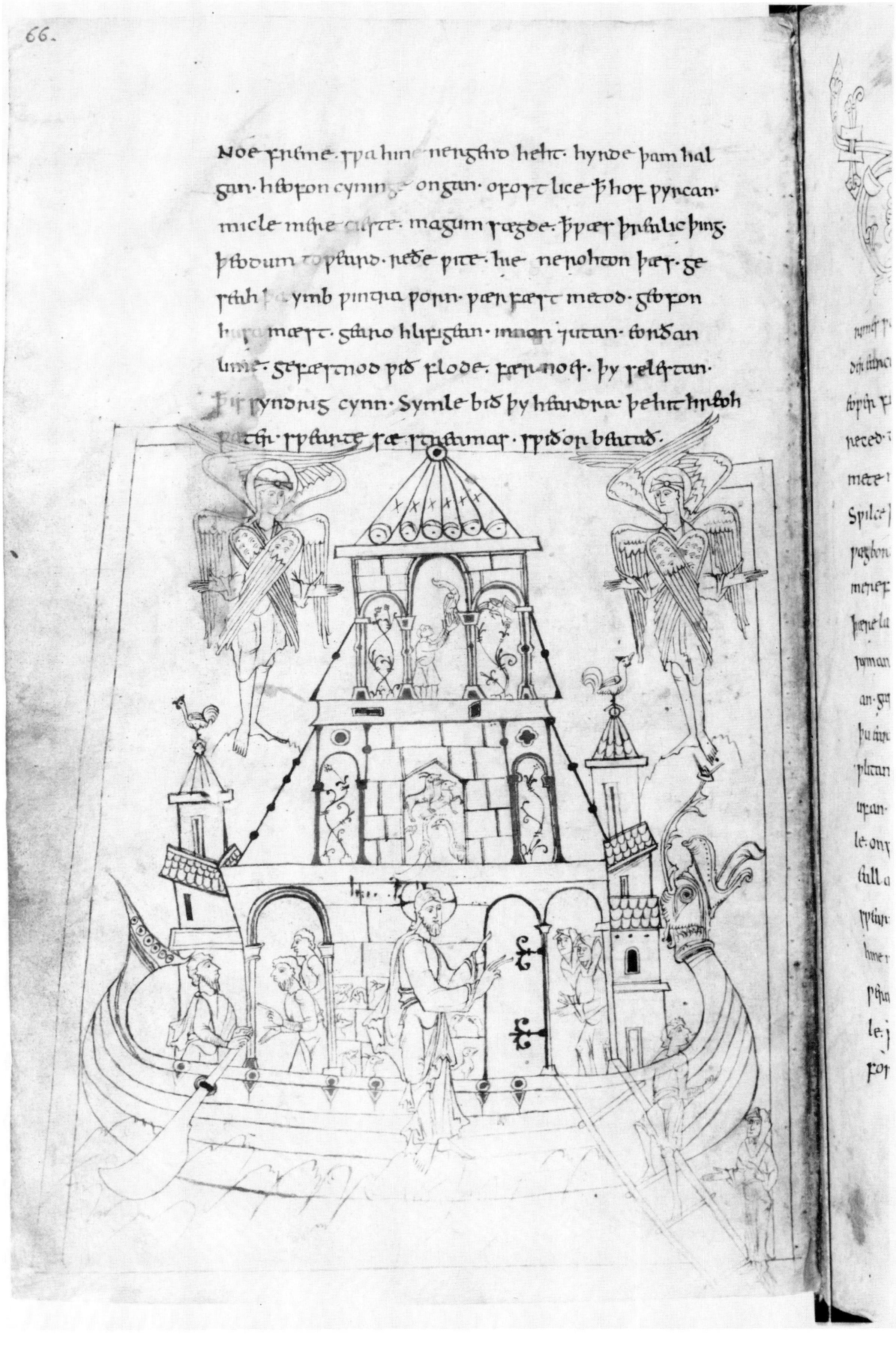

16.38 Oxford, Bodl. Lib., Junius 11, p. 66

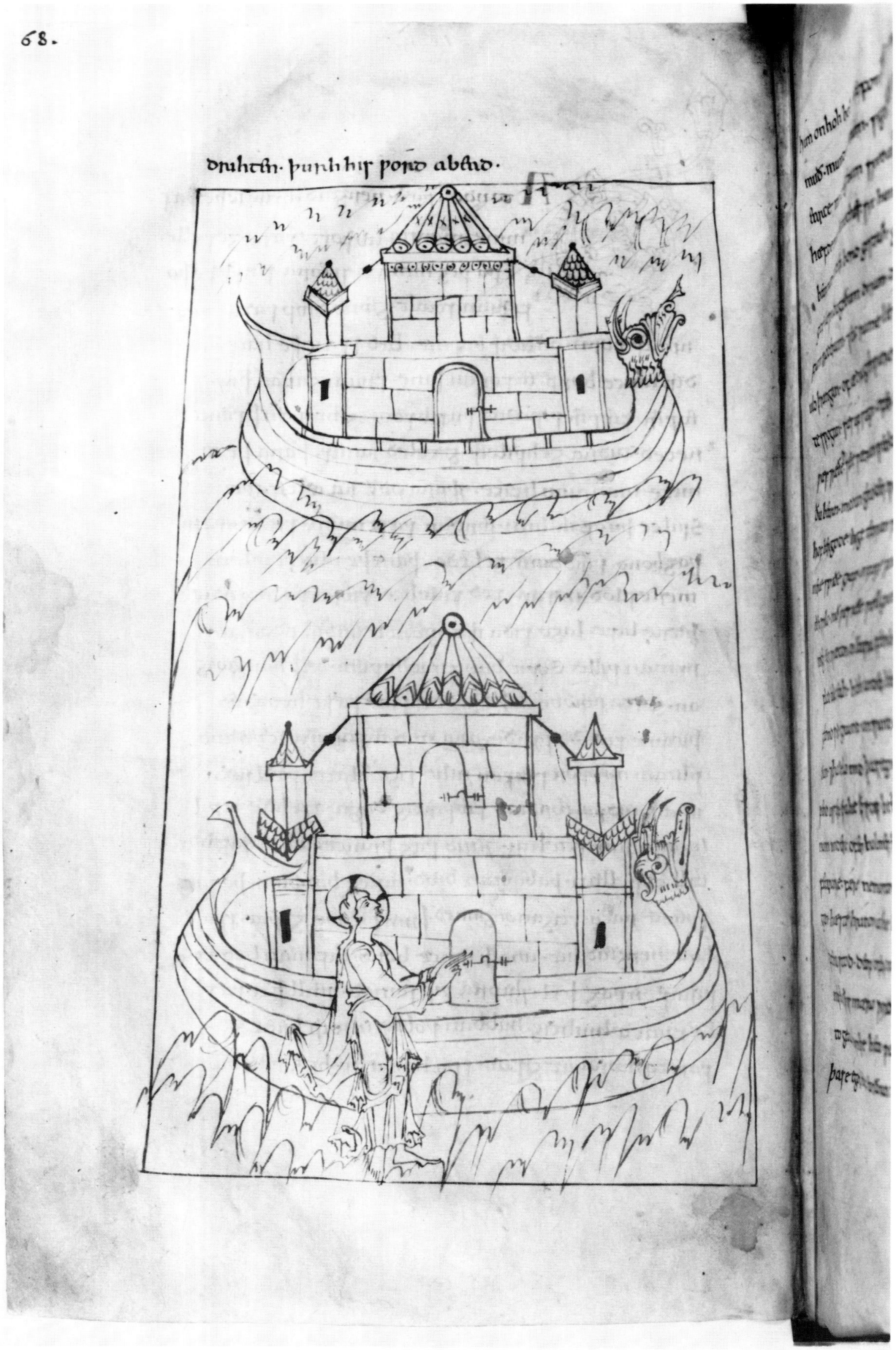

16.39 Oxford, Bodl. Lib., Junius 11, p. 68

16.40 Oxford, Bodl. Lib., Junius 11, p. 70

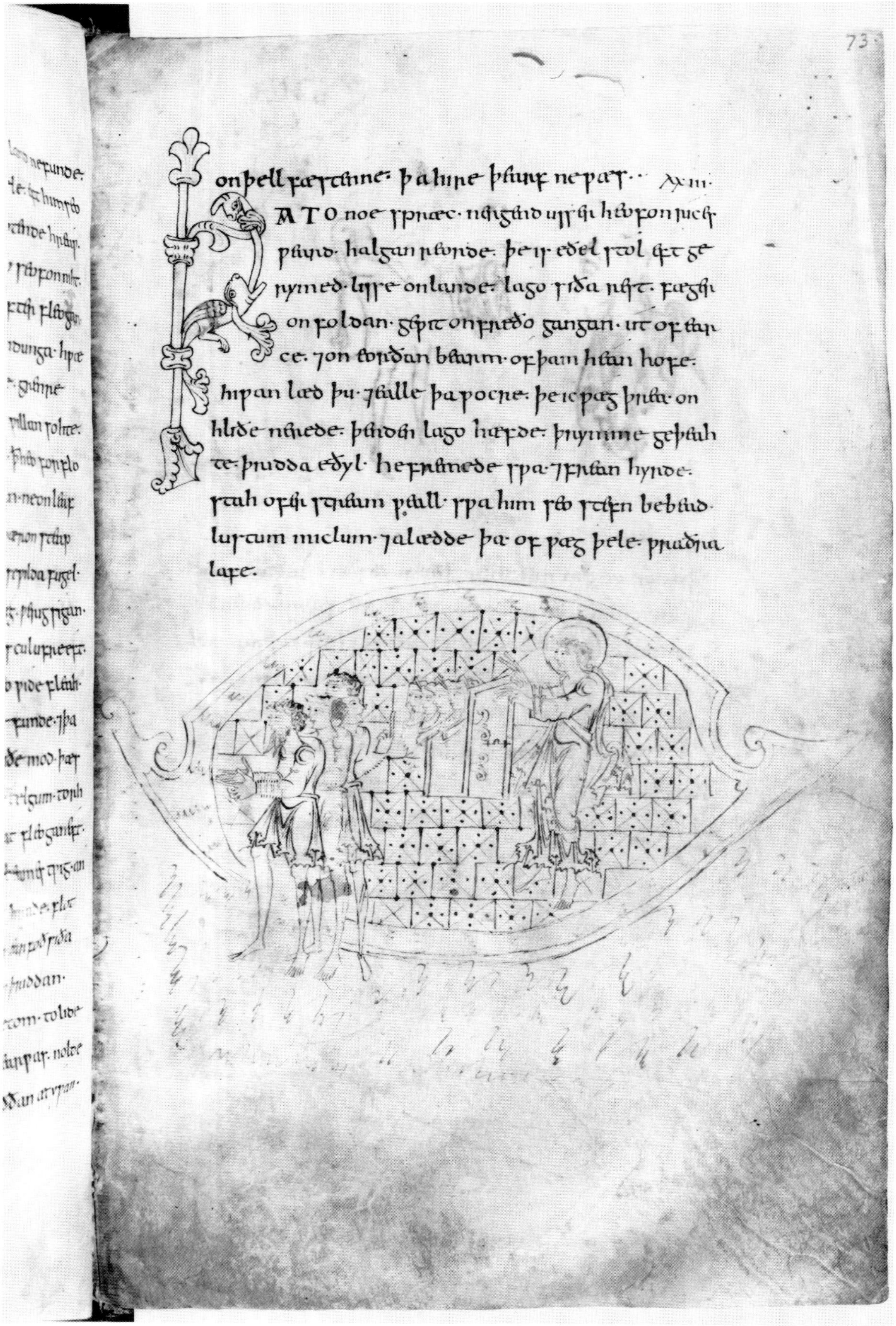

16.41 Oxford, Bodl. Lib., Junius 11, p. 73

74.

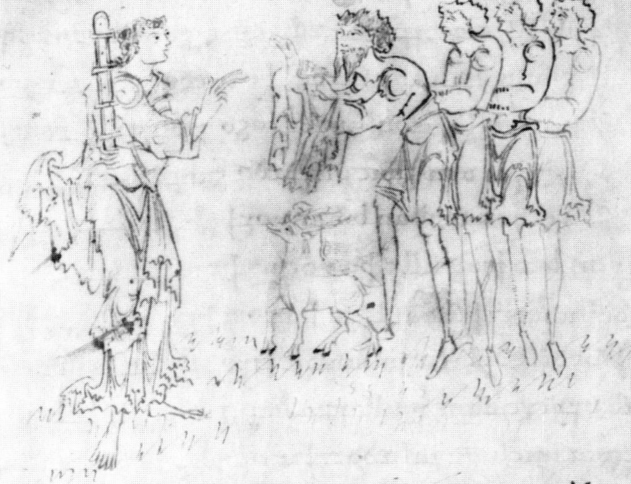

þa noe ongan. nergende lac. rædfæst reðran. 7 ge
genam. on eallum dæl. æhtum sinum. ðam þe
him to dugeðum. drihten sealde. gleaw to þam giel
de. 7 þa gode selfum. torht mod hæle. tiber on
sægde. cyninge engla. huru cuð dyde. nergend usser
þa he noe gebletsade. 7 his bearn somed. þæt he þæt gyld
on þanc. agifen hæfde. 7 on geoguð hade. godum dæ
dum. ær geearnod. þa him ealra wæs. ara este. æl
mihtig god. dom fæst dugeþa. þa gyt drihten cwæð.
wuldres aldor. word to noe. Tymað nu 7 tiedrað. tires
brucað. mid gefean fryðo. fyllað eorðan. eall ge
iceað. eow is eðel stol. holmes hlæst. 7 heofon fugla.
7 wilde deor. on geweald geseald. eorðe ælgrene. 7 eac
en feoh. næfre ge mid blode. beod gereordu. unar
lice. æte þicgeað. besmiten mid synne. sawl dreore.

16.42 Oxford, Bodl. Lib., Junius 11, p. 74

sohte gewinne. þa him wlite beorhte. wæstmas broh
te. geartorhte gife. grene folde. Ða þæt geeode. þæt se
eadega wer. on his wicum wearð. wine druncen. swæf
symbelwerig. ⁊ him selfa sceaf. reaf of lice. swa ge
rysne ne wæs. læg þa limnacod. he lyt ongeat. þæt him
on his inne. swa earme gelamp. þa him on hreðre.
heafodswima. on þæs halgan hofe. heortan clypte.
swiðe on slæpe. sefa nearwode. þæt he ne mihte. onge
mynd drepen. hine handum self mid hrægle wryon.
⁊ sceome þeccan. swa gesceapu wæron. werum ⁊ wifum.
siððan wuldres þegn. ussum fæder ⁊ meder. fyrene
sweorde. on laste beleac. lifes eðel. þa com ærest cam.
in siðian. eafora noes. þær his aldor læg. ferhðe for
stolen. þær he freondlice. on his agenum fæder. are
ne wolde. gescildan. ne þa sceonde huru. hleomagum
helan. ac he hlihhende. broðrum sægde. hu se beorn
hine reste on recede.

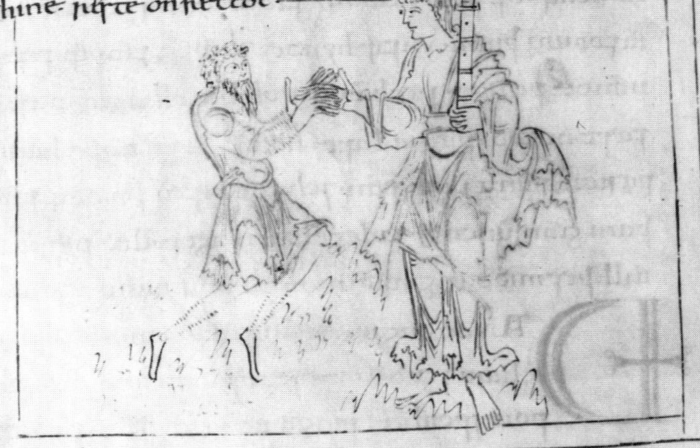

16.43 Oxford, Bodl. Lib., Junius 11, p. 76

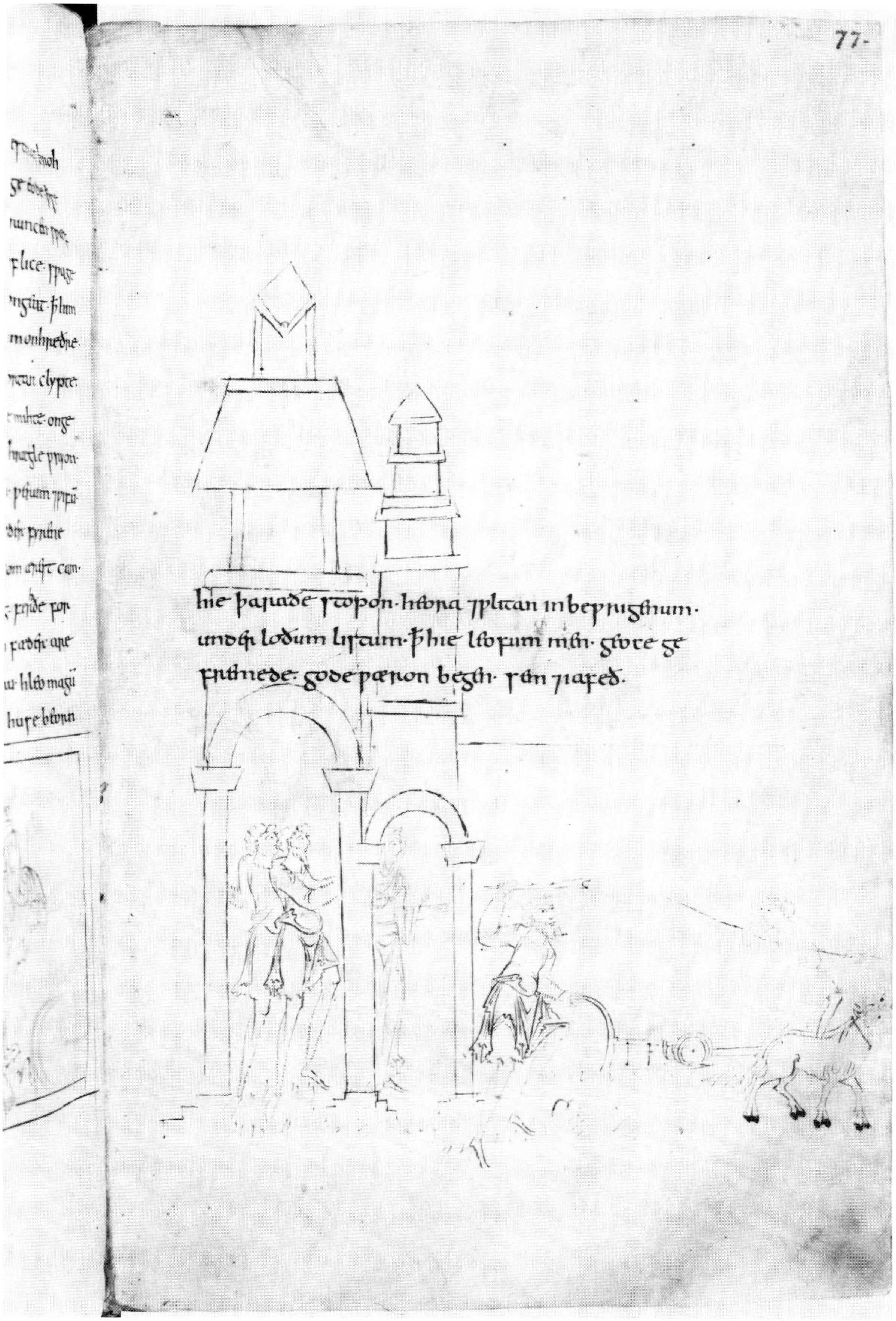

16.44 Oxford, Bodl. Lib., Junius 11, p. 77

78.

Ða of slæpe onbrægd · sunu lameches · ⁊ þa sona
ongeat · þ him cyne godum · cham ne wolde · þa him
wæs are þearf · ænige cyðan · hyldo ⁊ treowa · þæt
þam halgan wæs · sar on mode · ongan þa his sel
fes bearn · wordum wyrgean · cwæð he wesan sceolde ·
hean under heofnum · hleo maga þeow · cham on eor
ðan · him þa cwyde syððan ⁊ his from cynne · swec
ne sceodon · þa nyttade · noe siððan · mid sunum sinu
sidan rices · ðreo hund wintra · þisses lifes · freo men
æfter flode ⁊ fiftig eac · þa he forð gewat ·

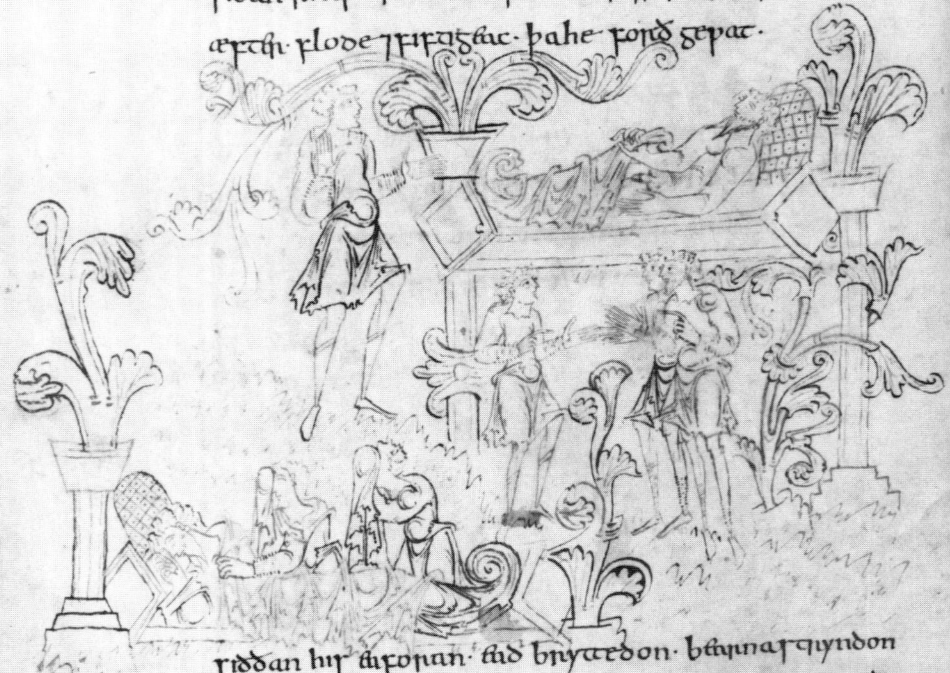

siððan his eaforan · ead bryttedon · bearna stryndon
him wæs beorhtlic wela · þa wearð iafede · geogoð afed
ed · hyhtlic heorð werod · heafod maga · sunu ⁊ dohtra
he wæs selfa til · heold a rice · eðel dreamas · blæd

16.45 Oxford, Bodl. Lib., Junius 11, p. 78

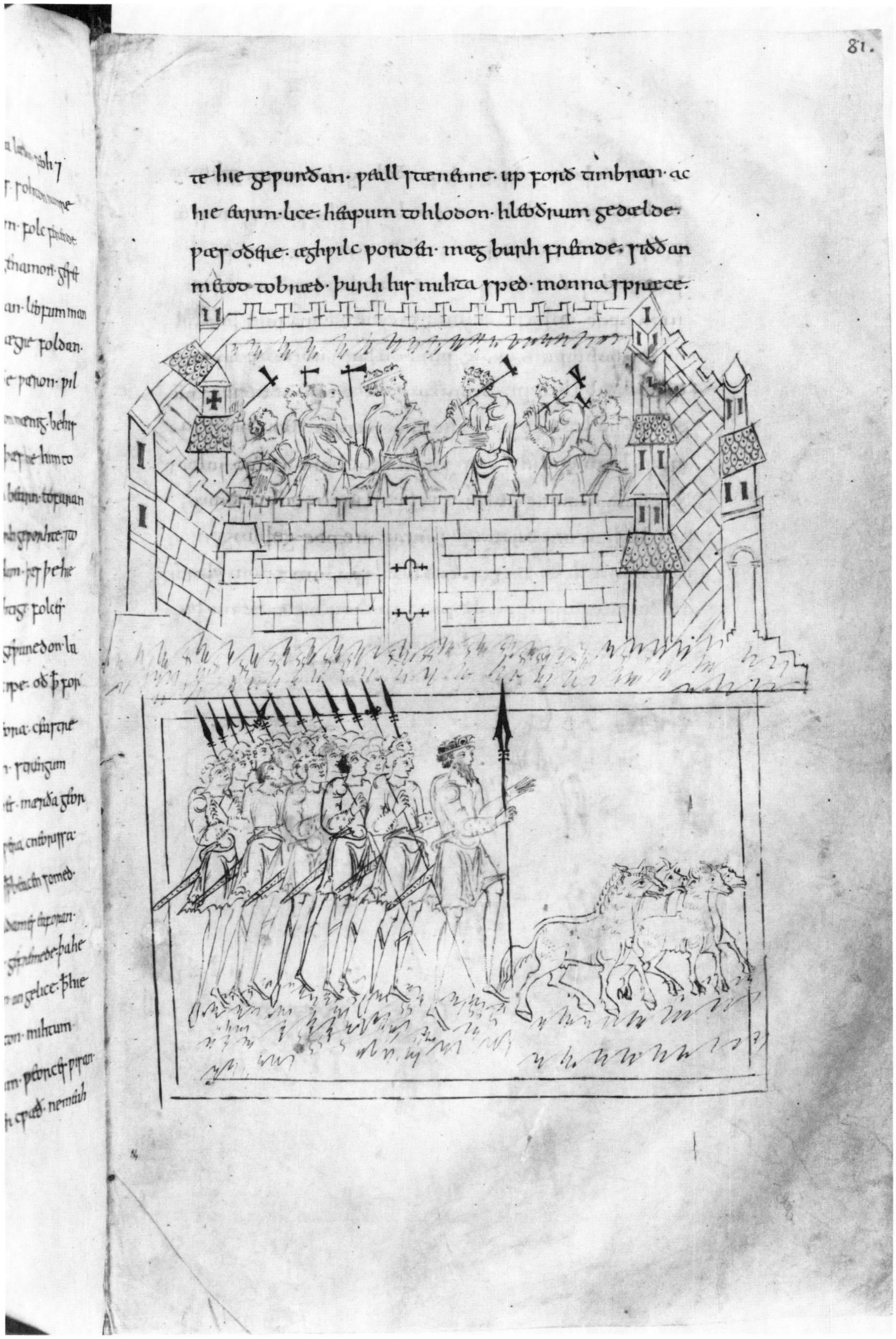

16.46 Oxford, Bodl. Lib., Junius 11, p. 81

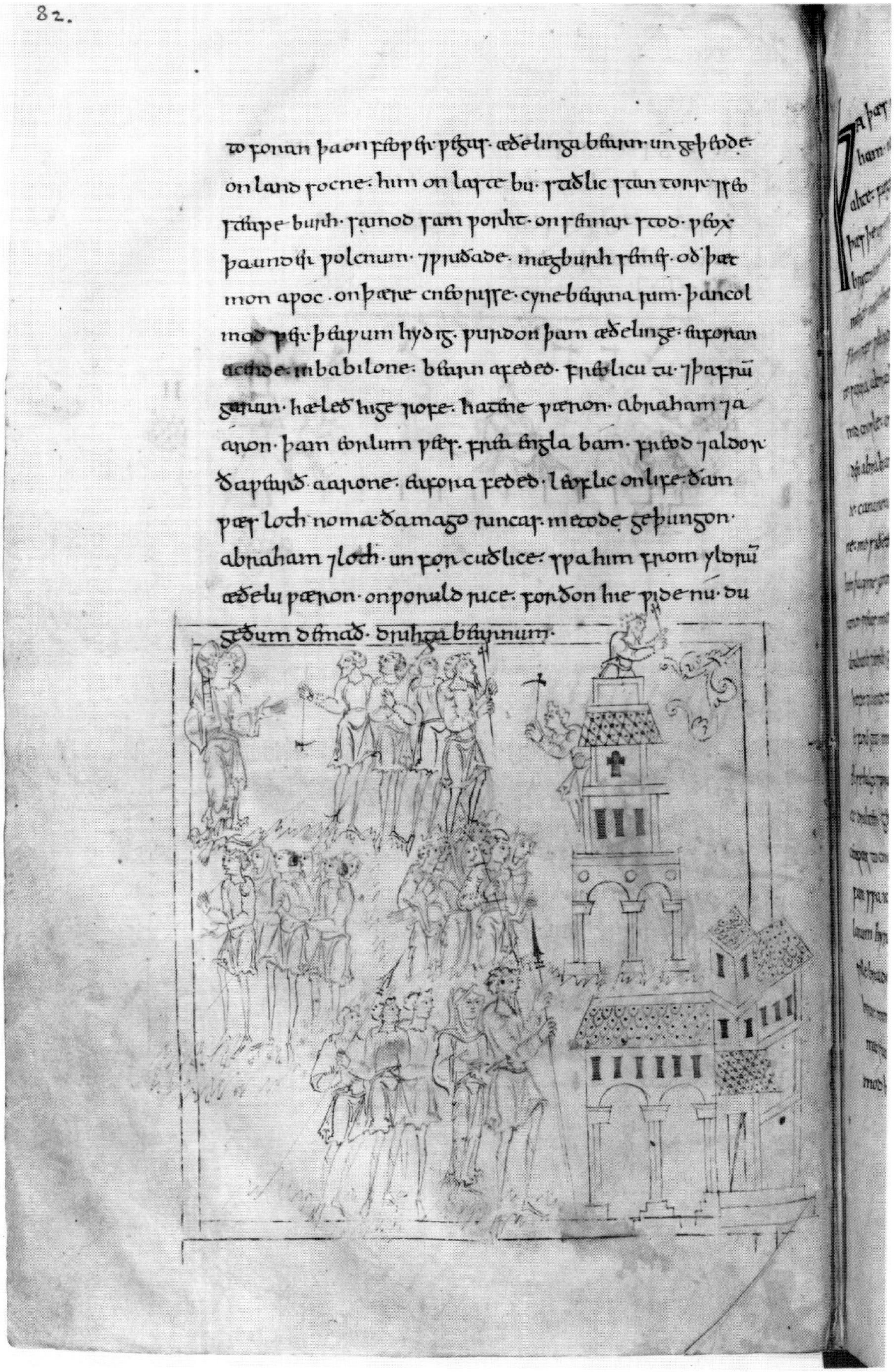

16.47 Oxford, Bodl. Lib., Junius 11, p. 82

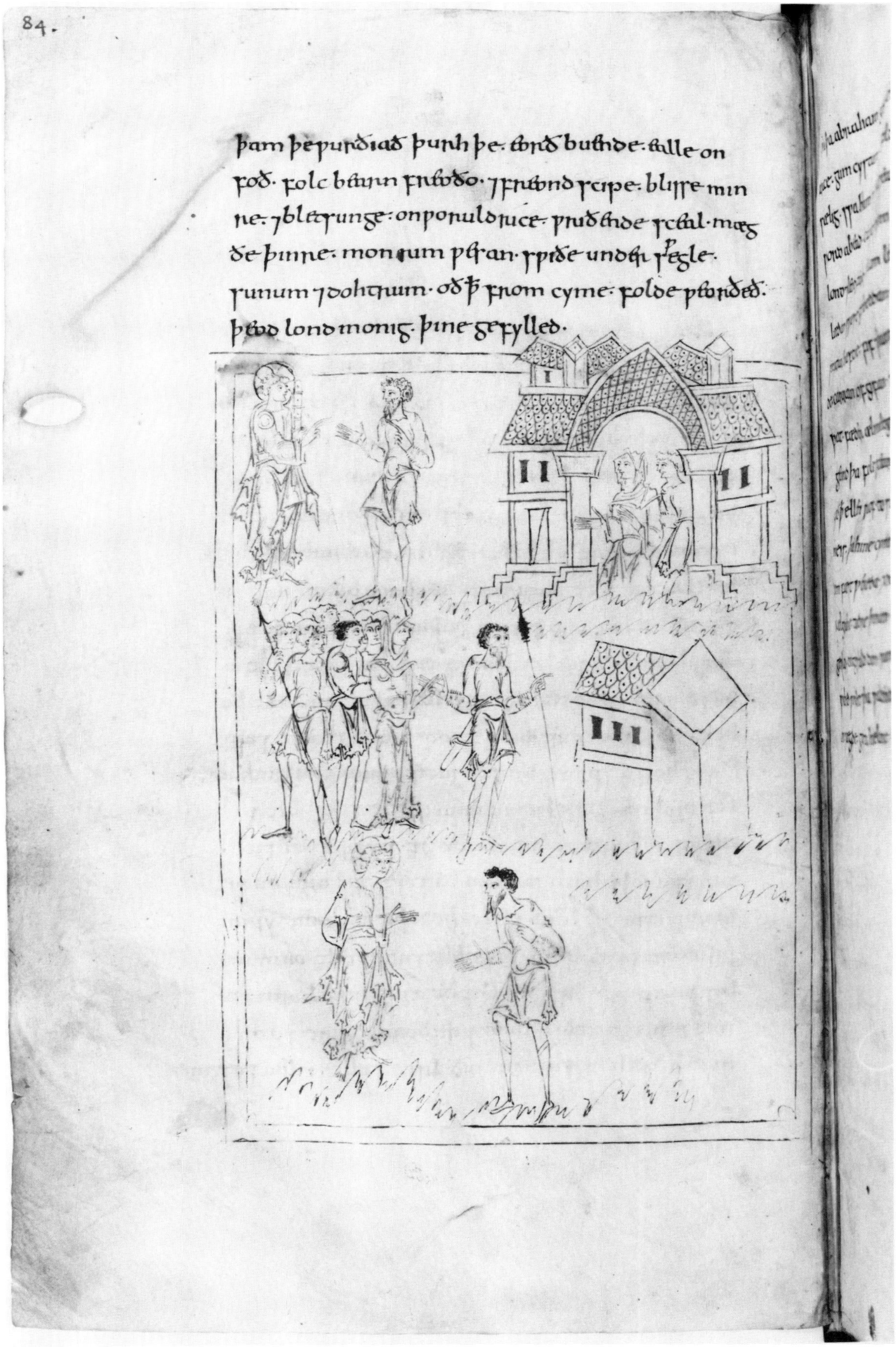

16.48 Oxford, Bodl. Lib., Junius 11, p. 84

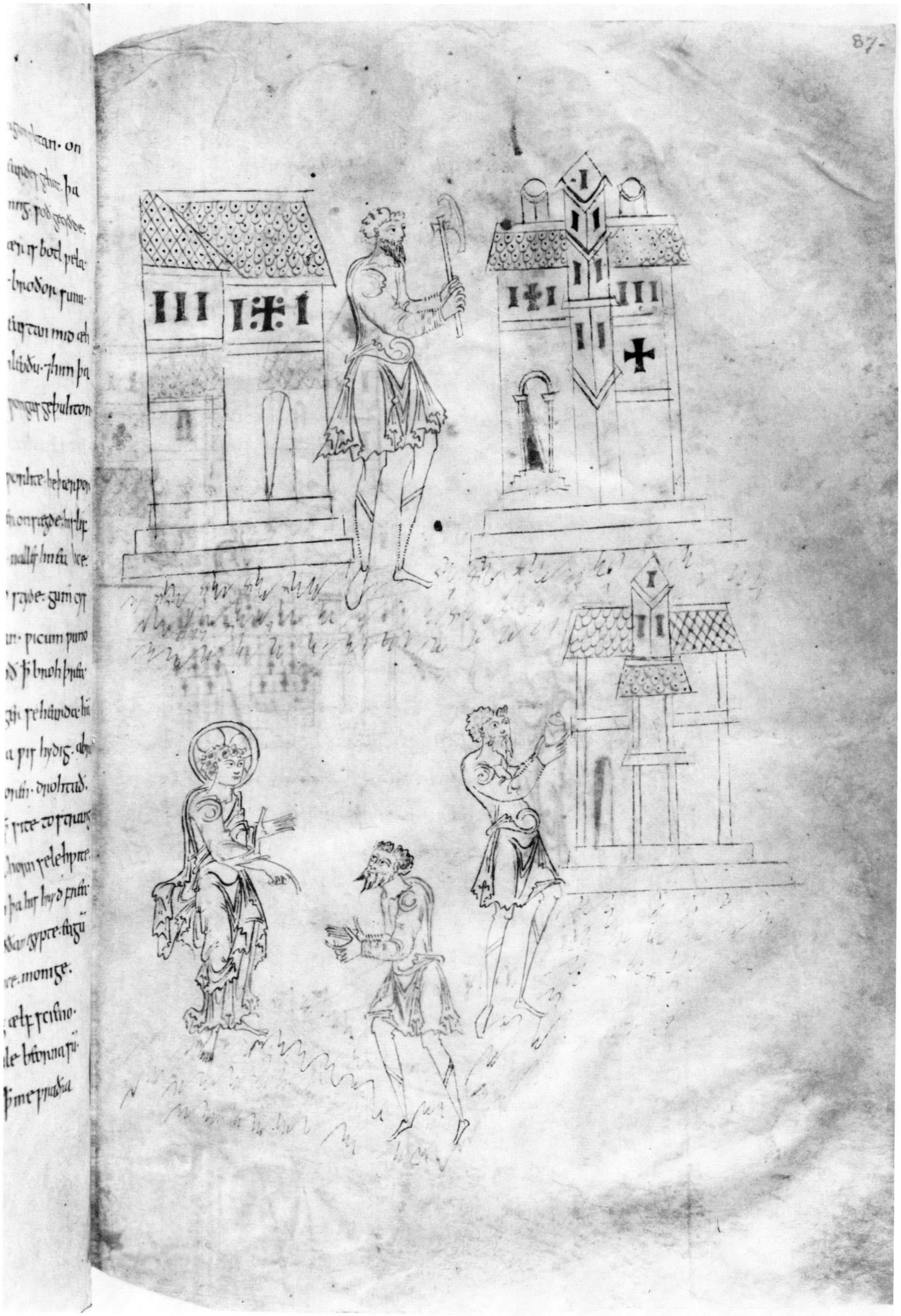

16.49 Oxford, Bodl. Lib., Junius 11, p. 87

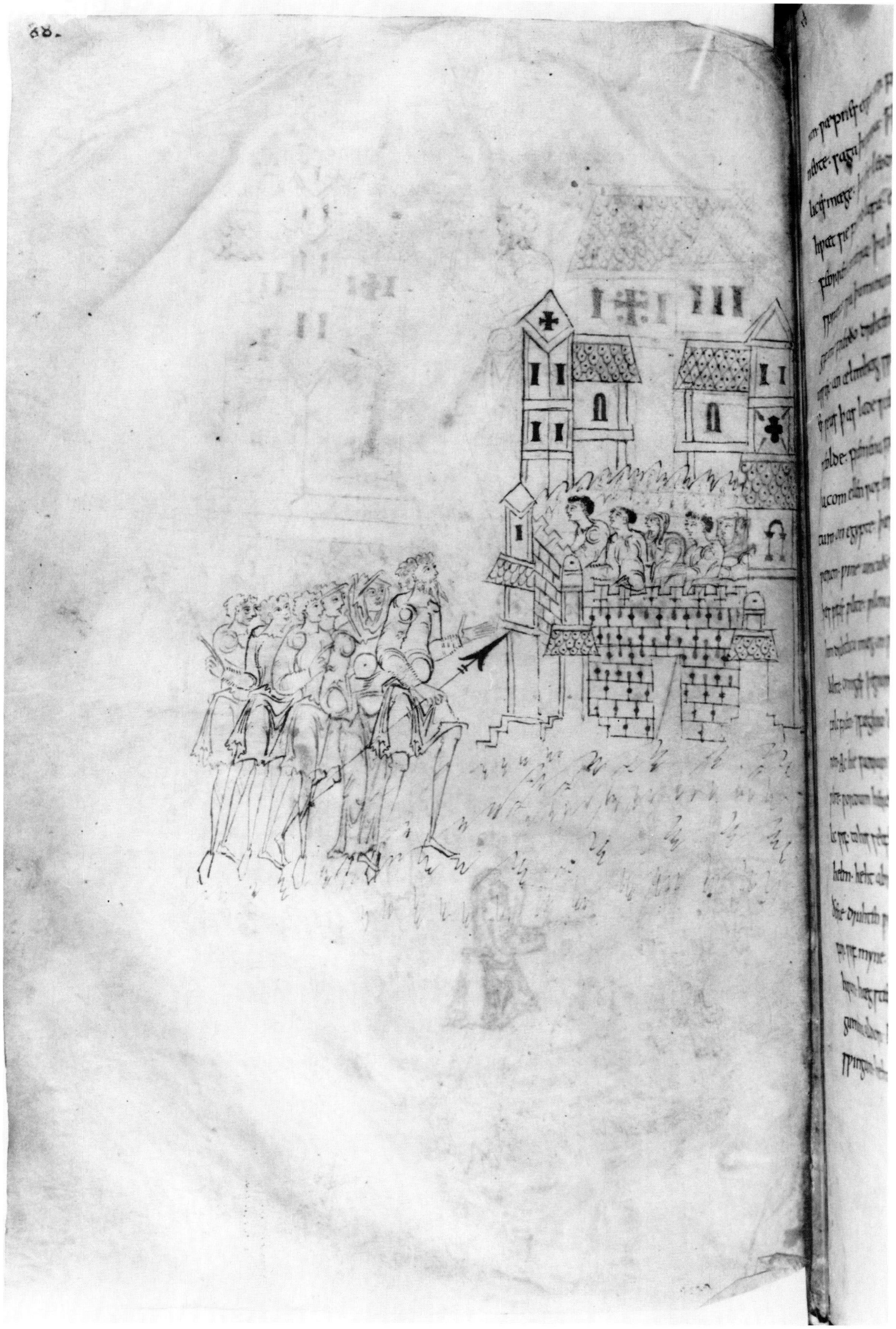

16.50 Oxford, Bodl. Lib., Junius 11, p. 88

96. xt

unfrom wæron. gewat him abraham ða. on þa wig
node. wiðþa ⁊ wod sceon. leodfruma monna. loth wæs a
hreðed. torl mid æhtum. idese ahwurfon. wif on
willan. wide gesawon. freomæga feorh banan. fug
las slitan. on ecg wale. abraham gefrede. sið
monna sæt. sinc ⁊ bryda. æðelinga bearn. oð lærn
on mæged hlefna magum. nefne mon talþa. li
fighðna hæh. lyde wefede. þon wundlicon wigsið
atolah. þara he wið swa miclum. mægne gehwærde.

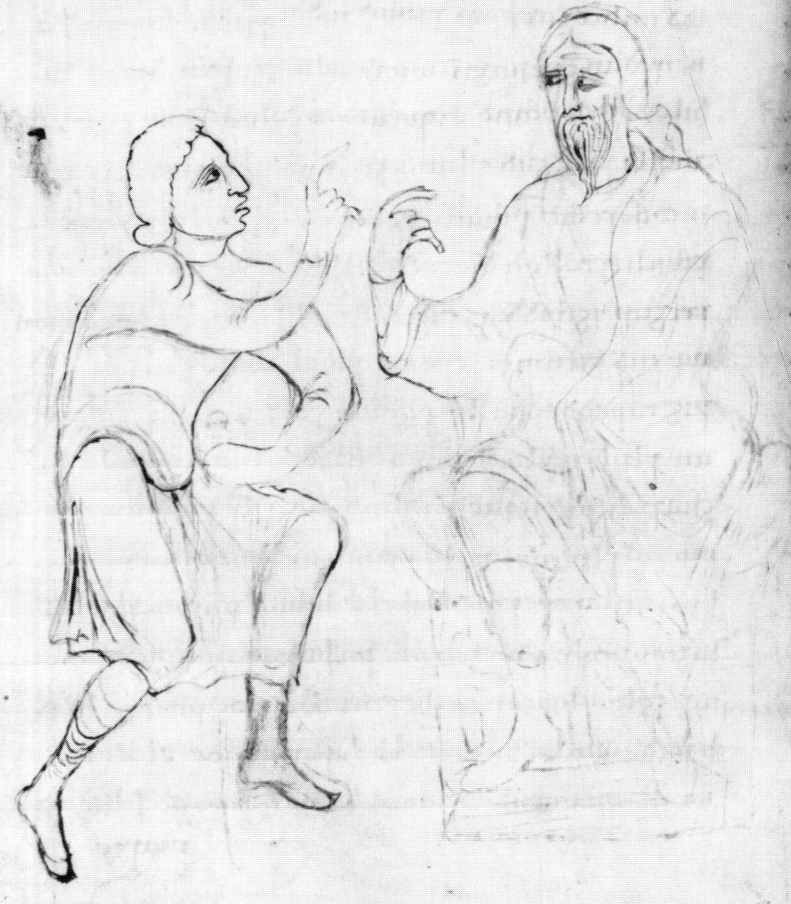

16.51 Oxford, Bodl. Lib., Junius 11, p. 96